Reference Tables

Unemployment Rates for the Civilian Labor Force Over Age 16, 1947–2019 (data displayed graphically in Figure 2.2 on p. 30)

Year	Rate	Year	Rate
1947	3.9	1981	7.6
1948	3.8	1982	9.7
1949	5.9	1983	9.6
1950	5.3	1984	7.5
1951	3.3	1985	7.2
1952	3.0	1986	7.0
1953	2.9	1987	6.2
1954	5.5	1988	5.5
1955	4.4	1989	5.3
1956	4.1	1990	5.6
1957	4.3	1991	6.8
1958	6.8	1992	7.5
1959	5.5	1993	6.9
1960	5.5	1994[†]	6.1
1961	6.7	1995[†]	5.6
1962	5.5	1996[†]	5.4
1963	5.7	1997[†]	4.9
1964	5.2	1998[†]	4.5
1965	4.5	1999[†]	4.2
1966	3.8	2000[†]	4.0
1967	3.8	2001[†]	4.7
1968	3.6	2002[†]	5.8
1969	3.5	2003[†]	6.0
1970	4.9	2004[†]	5.5
1971	5.9	2005[†]	5.1
1972	5.6	2006[†]	4.6

(*Continued*)

(*Continued*)

Year	Rate	Year	Rate
1973	4.9	2007[†]	4.6
1974	5.6	2008[†]	5.8
1975	8.5	2009[†]	9.3
1976	7.7	2010[†]	9.6
1977	7.1	2011[†]	8.9
1978	6.1	2012[†]	8.1
1979	5.8	2013[†]	7.4
1980	7.1	2014[†]	6.2
		2015[†]	5.3
		2016[†]	4.9
		2017[†]	4.4
		2018[†]	3.9
		2019[†]	3.7

Source: 1947–1966: U.S. Bureau of Labor Statistics, *Employment and Earnings 13* (January 1967, Table A-1. 1967–1974: U.S. President, *Economic Report of the President* (Washington, DC: U.S. Government Printing Office, February 2016), Table B-12. 1975–2019: U.S. President, *Economic Report of the President* (Washington, DC: U.S. Government Printing Office, February 2020), Table B.

† In 1994, changes were made in the Current Population Survey, on which estimates of unemployment are based, that increased the reported unemployment rate by 0.5 percent. Increases were especially noticeable among women, teenagers, and elderly people. Definitions did not change, but the new questionnaire apparently led more respondents to report that they were actively engaged in searching for a job or were on layoff status. Thus, data for 1994 and beyond are not directly comparable to those for earlier years.

Employment Distribution by Major Nonfarm Sector, 1954–2019 (data displayed graphically in Figure 2.3 on p. 32)

Year	Goods-producing industries*(%)	Nongovernment services (%)	Government services (%)
1954	37.7	48.3	14.0
1964	33.8	49.6	16.6
1974	29.8	52.0	18.2
1984	24.9	58.1	17.0
1994	19.9	63.2	16.9
2004	16.6	67.0	16.4
2014	13.8	70.6	15.6
2019	13.9	71.2	14.9

Source: U.S. Department of Labor, Bureau of Labor Statistics, "Employment Situation Summary," Table B-1, at www.bls.gov

* These industries include manufacturing, construction, and mining.

Table 2.1 Labor Force Participation Rates by Gender, 1950–2020

Year	Total (%)	Men (%)	Women (%)
1950	59.9	86.8	33.9
1960	60.2	84.0	37.8
1970	61.3	80.6	43.4
1980	64.2	77.9	51.6
1990	66.5	76.4	57.5
2000	67.2	74.7	60.2
2010 (February)	64.8	71.0	58.9
2020 (February)	63.4	69.3	57.8

Sources: 1950–1980: U.S. President, *Employment and Training Report of the President*, (Washington, D.C.: U.S. Government Printing Office), transmitted to the Congress 1981, Table A-1.

1990: U.S. Bureau of Labor Statistics, *Employment and Earnings* 45 (February 1998), Tables A-1 and A-2.

2000: U.S. Bureau of Labor Statistics, *Employment Situation* (News Release, October 2001), Table A-1.

2010 and 2020: U.S. Bureau of Labor Statistics, *Employment Situation*, Table A-1. Data are available online at http://www.bls.gov.

Table 2.2 Nominal and Real Hourly Earnings, U.S. Production and Nonsupervisory Employees in the Private Sector, 1980–2019

	1980	**1990**	**2000**	**2010**	**2019**
Average Hourly Earnings (current dollars)	$6.84	$10.20	$14.02	$19.05	$23.48
Consumer price index (CPI), using 1982–1984 as a base	82.4	130.7	172.2	218.1	255.7
Average hourly earnings, 2019 dollars (using CPI)	$21.22	$19.96	$20.82	$22.33	$23.48
Average hourly earnings, 2019 dollars (using CPI inflation less 0.9 percent per year)	$14.79	$15.33	$17.52	$20.60	$23.48

Source: U.S. President, *Economic Report of the President* (Washington, DC: U.S. Government Printing Office, 2020), Table B30-; and U.S. Department of Labor, Bureau of Labor Statistics, *Archived Consumer Price Index Supplemental Files*, Historical CPI-U (May 2020),at www.bls.gov/cpi /supplemental-files.

Modern Labor Economics

Modern Labor Economics: Theory and Public Policy, now in its fourteenth edition, continues to be the leading text for one-semester courses in labor economics at the undergraduate and graduate levels.

It offers a thorough overview of the modern theory of labor market behavior and reveals how this theory is used to analyze public policy. Designed for students who may not have extensive backgrounds in economics, the text balances theoretical coverage with examples of practical applications that allow students to see concepts in action.

The authors believe that showing students the social implications of the concepts discussed in the course will enhance their motivation to learn. Consequently, this text presents numerous examples of policy decisions that have been affected by the ever-shifting labor market.

This new edition continues to offer the following:

- a balance of relevant, contemporary examples
- coverage of the current economic climate
- an introduction to basic methodological techniques and problems
- tools for review and further study

This fourteenth edition presents updated data throughout and a wealth of new examples, such as the impact of COVID-19 lockdowns, gig work, nudges, monopsony power in the technology industry, and the effect of machine learning on inequality.

Supplementary materials for students and instructors are available on the book's companion website.

Ronald G. Ehrenberg is the Irving M. Ives Professor of Industrial and Labor Relations and Economics at Cornell University. He has been honored for his teaching by receiving Cornell's highest university-wide award: the Stephen H. Weiss Presidential Fellowship "for effective, inspiring, and distinguished teaching of undergraduate students and for outstanding contributions to undergraduate education."

Robert S. Smith is Professor of Economics at Cornell University. He has been honored for his teaching by receiving Cornell's highest university-wide award: the Stephen H. Weiss Presidential Fellowship "for effective, inspiring, and distinguished teaching of undergraduate students and for outstanding contributions to undergraduate education."

Kevin F. Hallock is President and Professor of Economics at the University of Richmond. He previously served as Dean of the Cornell SC Johnson College of Business, Dean of the School of Industrial and Labor Relations, the Joseph R. Rich '80 Professor of Economics and Human Resource Studies, and Director of the Institute for Compensation Studies at Cornell University.

Modern Labor Economics

Theory and Public Policy

INTERNATIONAL STUDENT EDITION

Fourteenth Edition

Ronald G. Ehrenberg, Robert S. Smith, and Kevin F. Hallock

Routledge
Taylor & Francis Group

NEW YORK AND LONDON

Fourteenth edition published 2023
by Routledge
605 Third Avenue, New York, NY 10158

and by Routledge
2 Park Square, Milton Park, Abingdon, Oxon, OX14 4RN

Routledge is an imprint of the Taylor & Francis Group, an informa business

First edition published by Scott Foresman 1982
Thirteenth edition published by Routledge 2018

ISBN: 978-0-367-34698-0 (pbk)

Typeset in Galliard
by Apex CoVantage, LLC

Access the companion website: www.routledge.com/cw/ehrenberg

Not for distribution in North America

Contents

Reference Tables	i
Preface	xx
Acknowledgments	xxiv

1 Introduction 1

The Labor Market   1
Labor Economics: Some Basic Concepts   2
   Positive Economics   3
   The Models and Predictions of Positive Economics   4
   EXAMPLE 1.1 Positive Economics: What Does It Mean to "Understand"
     Behavior?   5
   Normative Economics   7
   EXAMPLE 1.2 Do We Need "Nudges" to Make the Right Decisions for
     Ourselves?   9
   Normative Economics and Government Policy   11
   Efficiency Versus Equity   12
Plan of the Text   13
Review Questions   14
Problems   15
Selected Readings   16
   APPENDIX 1A   17
   Statistical Testing of Labor Market Hypotheses   17
A Univariate Test   17
Multiple Regression Analysis   20
The Problem of Omitted Variables   21
Notes   24

2 Overview of the Labor Market   26

The Labor Market: Definitions, Facts, and Trends   27
   The Labor Force and Unemployment   28
   EXAMPLE 2.1 The Unemployment Consequences of the Sudden
     COVID-19 Lockdown in March 2020   30
   Industries and Occupations: Adapting to Change   31
   The Earnings of Labor   32
   EXAMPLE 2.2 Real Wages Across Countries and Time: Big Macs per
     Hour Worked   35
How the Labor Market Works   37
   The Demand for Labor   38
   The Supply of Labor   42
   The Determination of the Wage   44

EXAMPLE 2.3 The Black Death and the Wages of Labor   47
EXAMPLE 2.4 Prosecuting Workers Who Leave Their Employers   49
Applications of the Theory   50
   Who Is Underpaid and Who Is Overpaid?   50
   Unemployment and Responses to Technological Change Across
      Countries   53
   *EMPIRICAL STUDY 2.1 PAY LEVELS AND THE SUPPLY OF MILITARY
      OFFICERS: OBTAINING SAMPLE VARIATION FROM CROSS-
      SECTION DATA*   54
Review Questions   55
Problems   57
Notes   58
Selected Readings   61

3   **The Demand for Labor**   62

Profit Maximization   62
   Marginal Income From an Additional Unit of Input   64
   *EXAMPLE 3.1 The Marginal Revenue Product of College Football
      Stars*   64
   Marginal Expense of an Added Input   65
The Short-Run Demand for Labor When Both Product and Labor Markets Are
   Competitive   66
   A Critical Assumption: Declining *MP*$_L$ 66
   From Profit Maximization to Labor Demand   67
The Demand for Labor in Competitive Markets When Other Inputs Vary   72
   Labor Demand in the Long Run   72
   EXAMPLE 3.2 Coal Mining Wages and Capital Substitution   74
   More Than Two Inputs   75
Labor Demand When the Product Market Is Not Competitive   76
   Maximizing Monopoly Profits   77
   Do Monopolies Pay Higher Wages?   77
Policy Application: The Labor Market Effects of Employer Payroll Taxes and
   Wage Subsidies   78
   Who Bears the Burden of a Payroll Tax?   78
   Employment Subsidies as a Device to Help Unemployed People   81
   *EMPIRICAL STUDY 3.1 DO WOMEN PAY FOR EMPLOYER-FUNDED
      MATERNITY BENEFITS? USING CROSS-SECTION DATA OVER TIME
      TO ANALYZE "DIFFERENCES IN DIFFERENCES"*   82
Review Questions   83
Problems   85
Notes   87
Selected Readings   88
   *APPENDIX 3A Graphical Derivation of a Firm's
      Labor Demand Curve*   89
The Production Function   89
Demand for Labor in the Short Run   90
Demand for Labor in the Long Run   92
   Conditions for Cost Minimization   92
   The Substitution Effect   94
   The Scale Effect   94
   Notes   96

4   Labor Demand Elasticities   97

The Own-Wage Elasticity of Demand   97
   The Hicks–Marshall Laws of Derived Demand   99
   Estimates of Own-Wage Labor Demand Elasticities   102
   Applying the Laws of Derived Demand: Inferential Analysis   104
   EXAMPLE 4.1 Why Are Union Wages So Different in Two Parts of the
     Trucking Industry?   105
The Cross-Wage Elasticity of Demand   106
   Can the Laws of Derived Demand Be Applied to Cross-Elasticities?   107
   Estimates Relating to Cross-Elasticities   109
Policy Application: Effects of Minimum-Wage Laws   110
   History and Description   110
   Employment Effects: Theoretical Analysis   110
   Employment Effects: Empirical Estimates   115
   EXAMPLE 4.2 The Employment Effects of the First U.S. Federal
     Minimum Wage   115
   Does the Minimum Wage Fight Poverty?   116
   "Living Wage" Laws   117
Applying Concepts of Labor Demand Elasticity to the Issue of Technological
   Change   118
   EXAMPLE 4.3 Do Robots and Online Hiring Platforms Create or Destroy
     Jobs?   120
   EMPIRICAL STUDY 4.1 ESTIMATING THE LABOR DEMAND CURVE:
     TIME SERIES DATA AND COPING WITH "SIMULTANEITY"   124
Review Questions   126
Problems   128
Notes   130
Selected Readings   135

5   Frictions in the Labor Market   136

Frictions on the Employee Side of the Market   137
   The Law of One Price   137
   Monopsonistic Labor Markets: A Definition   139
   Profit Maximization Under Monopsonistic Conditions   140
   EXAMPLE 5.1 Monopsony Power in Labor Markets: The Case of
     Antitrust in the High-Tech Industry   144
   How Do Monopsonistic Firms Respond to Shifts in the Supply Curve?   145
   Monopsonistic Conditions and the Employment Response to Minimum-
     Wage Legislation   148
   Job-Search Costs and Other Labor Market Outcomes   149
   Monopsonistic Conditions and the Relevance of the Competitive
     Model   151
Frictions on the Employer Side of the Market   152
   Categories of Quasi-fixed Costs   152
   EXAMPLE 5.2 Does Employment-Protection Legislation Protect
     Workers?   153
   The Employment/Hours Trade-Off   156
   EXAMPLE 5.3 "Renting" Workers as a Way of Coping With Hiring
     Costs   157
Training Investments   159
   The Training Decision of Employers   159

The Types of Training   160
EXAMPLE 5.4 General Training and Training Contracts   161
Training and Post-Training Wage Increases   162
Employer Training Investments and Recessionary Layoffs   164
Hiring Investments   165
   The Use of Credentials   165
   Internal Labor Markets   165
   How Can the Employer Recoup Its Hiring Investments?   166
   *EMPIRICAL STUDY 5.1 WHAT EXPLAINS WAGE DIFFERENCES FOR
      WORKERS WHO APPEAR SIMILAR? USING PANEL DATA TO DEAL
      WITH UNOBSERVED HETEROGENEITY*   167
Review Questions   168
Problems   170
Notes   173
Selected Readings   178

6   **Supply of Labor to the Economy: The Decision to Work   179**

Trends in Labor Force Participation and Hours of Work   179
   Labor Force Participation Rates   179
   Hours of Work   182
   EXAMPLE 6.1 Gig Work and the Choice of Working Hours   183
A Theory of the Decision to Work   184
   Some Basic Concepts   184
   Analysis of the Labor/Leisure Choice   188
   EXAMPLE 6.2 The Labor Supply of New York City Taxi Drivers   188
   *EXAMPLE 6.3 Do Large Inheritances Induce Labor Force
      Withdrawal?*   195
   Empirical Findings on the Income and Substitution Effects   202
   EXAMPLE 6.4 Daily Labor Supply at the Ballpark   202
   EXAMPLE 6.5 Labor Supply Effects of Income Tax Cuts   204
Policy Applications   205
   Budget Constraints With "Spikes"   205
   *EXAMPLE 6.6 Staying Around One's Kentucky Home: Workers'
      Compensation Benefits and the Return to Work*   207
   Programs With Net Wage Rates of Zero   208
   Subsidy Programs With Positive Net Wage Rates   211
   *EXAMPLE 6.7 Wartime Food Requisitions and Agricultural Work
      Incentives*   214
   *EMPIRICAL STUDY 6.1 ESTIMATING THE INCOME EFFECT AMONG
      LOTTERY WINNERS: THE SEARCH FOR "EXOGENEITY"*   215
Review Questions   217
Problems   219
Notes   220
Selected Readings   226

7   **Labor Supply Household Production, the Family, and the
    Life Cycle   227**

A Labor Supply Model That Incorporates Household Production   227
   The Basic Model for an Individual: Similarities With the
      Labor-Leisure Model   228
   The Basic Model for an Individual: Some New Implications   230

EXAMPLE 7.1 Obesity and the Household Production Model   231
Joint Labor Supply Decisions in the Household   233
  Specialization of Function   234
  Do Both Partners Work for Pay?   235
  The Joint Decision and Interdependent Productivity at Home   236
  Labor Supply in Recessions: The "Discouraged" Versus the "Added"
    Worker   236
  EXAMPLE 7.2 Child Labor in Poor Countries   238
Life Cycle Aspects of Labor Supply   240
  The Substitution Effect and When to Work Over a Lifetime   240
  EXAMPLE 7.3 How Does Labor Supply Respond to Housing
    Subsidies?   241
  The Choice of Retirement Age   242
  EXAMPLE 7.4 Inducing Earlier Retirement in the 1930s   246
Policy Application: Childcare and Labor Supply   247
  Childcare Subsidies   247
  Child Support Assurance   250
  EMPIRICAL STUDY 7.1 THE EFFECTS OF WAGE INCREASES ON
    LABOR SUPPLY (AND SLEEP): TIME-USE DIARY DATA AND SAMPLE
    SELECTION BIAS   252
Review Questions   254
Problems   256
Notes   258
Selected Readings   263

8 Compensating Wage Differentials and Labor Markets   264
Job Matching: The Role of Worker Preferences and Information   264
  Individual Choice and Its Outcomes   265
  Assumptions and Predictions   267
  Empirical Tests for Compensating Wage Differentials   269
  EXAMPLE 8.1 Working on the Railroad: Making a Bad Job Good   270
Hedonic Wage Theory and the Risk of Injury   271
  Employee Considerations   271
  Employer Considerations   273
  The Matching of Employers and Employees   274
  EXAMPLE 8.2 Parenthood, Occupational Choice, and Risk   276
  EXAMPLE 8.3 Indentured Servitude and Compensating
    Differentials   278
  Normative Analysis: Occupational Safety and Health Regulation   279
Hedonic Wage Theory and Employee Benefits   284
  Employee Preferences   284
  Employer Preferences   285
  The Joint Determination of Wages and Benefits   287
  Policy EXAMPLE: Employer-Provided Healthcare Benefits   289
  EMPIRICAL STUDY 8.1 HOW RISKY ARE ESTIMATES OF
    COMPENSATING WAGE DIFFERENTIALS FOR RISK? THE "ERRORS
    IN VARIABLES" PROBLEM   290
Review Questions   292
Problems   293
Notes   295
Selected Readings   300

APPENDIX 8A Compensating Wage Differentials and Layoffs 300
Unconstrained Choice of Work Hours 301
Constrained Hours of Work 302
The Effects of Uncertain Layoffs 302
The Observed Wage–Layoff Relationship 304
Notes 304

9   Investments in Human Capital Education and Training   306
EXAMPLE 9.1 War and Human Capital 306
Human Capital Investments: The Basic Model 308
   The Concept of Present Value 308
   Modeling the Human Capital Investment Decision 310
The Demand for a College Education 311
   Weighing the Costs and Benefits of College 311
   Predictions of the Theory 313
   EXAMPLE 9.2 Can Language Affect Investment Behavior? 315
   *EXAMPLE 9.3 Did the G.I. Bill Increase Educational Attainment for
      Returning World War II Veterans?* 316
   *EXAMPLE 9.4 When Investments in Human Capital Are Less Risky Than
      Investments in Physical Assets* 318
   Market Responses to Changes in College Attendance 319
Education, Earnings, and Post-Schooling Investments in Human Capital 319
   Average Earnings and Educational Level 320
   On-the-Job Training and the Concavity of Age–Earnings Profiles 321
   The Fanning Out of Age–Earnings Profiles 322
   Women and the Acquisition of Human Capital 323
Is Education a Good Investment? 326
   Is Education a Good Investment for Individuals? 326
   *EXAMPLE 9.5 Valuing a Human Asset: The Case of the Divorcing
      Doctor* 327
   Is Education a Good Social Investment? 329
   *EXAMPLE 9.6 The Socially Optimal Level of Educational
      Investment* 334
   Is Public Sector Training a Good Social Investment? 336
   *EMPIRICAL STUDY 9.1 ESTIMATING THE RETURNS TO EDUCATION
      BY USING A SAMPLE OF TWINS: COPING WITH THE PROBLEM OF
      UNOBSERVED DIFFERENCES IN ABILITY* 337
Review Questions 339
Problems 340
Notes 341
Selected Readings 352
   APPENDIX 9A A "Cobweb" Model of Labor Market Adjustment 353
An Example of "Cobweb" Adjustments 353
Adaptive Expectations 355
Rational Expectations 355
Notes 356

10 Worker Mobility: Migration, Immigration, and Turnover   357
The Determinants of Worker Mobility 358
Geographic Mobility 359
   The Direction of Migratory Flows 359

*EXAMPLE 10.1 The Great Migration: U.S. Southern Black People
    Move North* 360
Personal Characteristics of Migrants 360
The Role of Distance 361
The Earnings Distribution in Sending Countries and International
    Migration 362
EXAMPLE 10.2 Migration and One's Time Horizon 362
The Returns to International and Domestic Migration 363
Policy Application: Restricting Immigration 366
    U.S. Immigration History 366
    Naive Views of Immigration 369
    An Analysis of the Gainers and Losers 371
    Do the Overall Gains From Immigration Exceed the Losses? 375
    *EXAMPLE 10.3 Illegal Immigrants, Personal Discount Rates, and
        Crime* 377
    *EXAMPLE 10.4 Immigrants and Labor Mobility in the United
        States* 379
Employee Turnover 380
    Age Effects 380
    Wage Effects 380
    Effects of Employer Size 380
    Cyclical Effects 381
    Employer Location 381
    Is More Mobility Better? 382
    *EMPIRICAL STUDY 10.1 DO POLITICAL REFUGEES INVEST MORE IN
        HUMAN CAPITAL THAN ECONOMIC IMMIGRANTS DO? THE USE OF
        SYNTHETIC COHORTS* 383
Review Questions 384
Problems 386
Notes 387
Selected Readings 394

11 Pay and Productivity Wage Determination Within the Firm 395
    *EXAMPLE 11.1 The Wide Range of Possible Productivities: The Case of
        the Factory that Could Not Cut Output* 395
Motivating Workers: An Overview of the Fundamentals 396
    The Employment Contract 397
    Coping With Information Asymmetries 397
    Motivating Workers 400
    EXAMPLE 11.2 Calorie Consumption and Type of Pay 401
    Motivating the Individual in a Group 402
    *EXAMPLE 11.3 The Effects of Low Relative Pay on Worker
        Satisfaction* 402
    Compensation Plans: Overview and Guide to the Rest of the Chapter 404
Productivity and the Basis of Yearly Pay 404
    Employee Preferences 404
    Employer Considerations 406
    EXAMPLE 11.4 Poor Group Incentives Doom the Shakers 407
Productivity and the Level of Pay 411
    Why Higher Pay Might Increase Worker Productivity 411
    Efficiency Wages 412

EXAMPLE 11.5 Did Henry Ford Pay Efficiency Wages?   412
Productivity and the Sequencing of Pay   413
   Underpayment Followed by Overpayment   414
   Promotion Tournaments   417
   EXAMPLE 11.6 The "Rat Race" in Law Firms   418
   Career Concerns and Productivity   420
Applications of the Theory: Explaining Two Puzzles   421
   Why Do Earnings Increase With Job Tenure?   421
   Why Do Large Firms Pay More?   423
   *EMPIRICAL STUDY 11.1 ARE WORKERS WILLING TO PAY FOR
      FAIRNESS? USING LABORATORY EXPERIMENTS TO STUDY
      ECONOMIC BEHAVIOR*   424
Review Questions   426
Problems   427
Notes   428
Selected Readings   438

12   Gender, Race, and Ethnicity in the Labor Market   439

Measured and Unmeasured Sources of Earnings Differences   440
   Earnings Differences by Gender   441
   *EXAMPLE 12.1 Bias in the Selection of Musicians by Symphony
      Orchestras*   443
   EXAMPLE 12.2 Does Gig Work Eliminate the Gender Pay Gap?   450
   Earnings Differences Between Black Americans and White Americans   450
   *EXAMPLE 12.3 Race Discrimination Might "Strike" When Few Are
      Looking: The Case of Umpires in Major League Baseball*   454
   Earnings Differences by Ethnicity   455
Theories of Market Discrimination   457
   Personal-Prejudice Models: Employer Discrimination   457
   Personal-Prejudice Models: Customer Discrimination   463
   Personal-Prejudice Models: Employee Discrimination   463
   *EXAMPLE 12.4 Fear and Lathing in the Michigan Furniture
      Industry*   464
   Statistical Discrimination   465
   EXAMPLE 12.5 "Ban the Box" and Statistical Discrimination   466
   Noncompetitive Models of Discrimination   467
   A Final Word on the Theories of Discrimination   471
Federal Programs to End Discrimination   471
   Equal Pay Act of 1963   472
   Title VII of the Civil Rights Act   472
   EXAMPLE 12.6 Comparable Worth and the University   474
   The Federal Contract Compliance Program   476
   Effectiveness of Federal Antidiscrimination Programs   477
   *EMPIRICAL STUDY 12.1 CAN WE CATCH DISCRIMINATORS IN THE
      ACT? THE USE OF FIELD EXPERIMENTS IN IDENTIFYING LABOR
      MARKET DISCRIMINATION*   478
Review Questions   480
Problems   482
Notes   484
Selected Readings   495

APPENDIX 12A Estimating Comparable-Worth Earnings Gaps: An Application of Regression Analysis   497
APPENDIX 12B Estimating the Gender Pay Gap in a Large International Company   500
Notes   500

13   Unions and the Labor Market   502

Union Structure and Membership   502
  International Comparisons of Unionism   503
  The Legal Structure of Unions in the United States   505
  Constraints on the Achievement of Union Objectives   508
  EXAMPLE 13.1 A Downward-Sloping Demand Curve for Football Players   509
  The Monopoly-Union Model   510
  The Efficient-Contracts Model   512
The Activities and Tools of Collective Bargaining   516
  Union Membership: An Analysis of Demand and Supply   516
  EXAMPLE 13.2 The Effects of Deregulation on Trucking and Airlines   519
  Union Actions to Alter the Labor Demand Curve   521
  Bargaining and the Threat of Strikes   522
  EXAMPLE 13.3 Permanent Replacement of Strikers   525
  Bargaining in the Public Sector: The Threat of Arbitration   527
The Effects of Unions   530
  The Theory of Union Wage Effects   530
  Evidence of Union Wage Effects   533
  Evidence of Union Total Compensation Effects   535
  The Effects of Unions on Employment   535
  The Effects of Unions on Productivity and Profits   536
  Normative Analyses of Unions   537
  EMPIRICAL STUDY 13.1 WHAT IS THE GAP BETWEEN UNION PAY AND NONUNION PAY? THE IMPORTANCE OF REPLICATION IN PRODUCING CREDIBLE ESTIMATES   539
Review Questions   541
Problems   542
Notes   544
Selected Readings   554
  APPENDIX 13A Arbitration and the Bargaining Contract Zone   555
Notes   558

14   Unemployment   559

A Stock-Flow Model of the Labor Market   561
  Duration of Unemployment   562
  Paths to Unemployment   562
Rates of Flow Affect Unemployment Levels   563
Frictional Unemployment   566
  The Theory of Job Search   567
  EXAMPLE 14.1 How Discerning Should Unemployed People Be in the Search for Work?   569
  Effects of Unemployment Insurance Benefits   571
Structural Unemployment   573

Occupational and Regional Unemployment Rate Differences 574

EXAMPLE 14.2 Structural Unemployment as a Threat to Social Well-Being 575

International Differences in Long-Term Unemployment 576

Whether Efficiency Wages Cause Structural Unemployment 577

Demand-Deficient (Cyclical) Unemployment 579

Downward Wage Rigidity 580

EXAMPLE 14.3 Nominal Wage Cuts for Construction Workers in the Great Recession 581

EXAMPLE 14.4 Recessions and Worker Effort 584

Financing U.S. Unemployment Compensation 584

Seasonal Unemployment 586

EXAMPLE 14.5 Unemployment Insurance and Seasonal Unemployment: A Historical Perspective 587

When Do We Have Full Employment? 588

Defining the Natural Rate of Unemployment 588

Unemployment and Demographic Characteristics 589

What Is the Natural Rate? 590

EMPIRICAL STUDY 14.1 DO RE-EMPLOYMENT BONUSES REDUCE UNEMPLOYMENT? THE RESULTS OF SOCIAL EXPERIMENTS 590

Review Questions 592

Problems 593

Notes 595

Selected Readings 605

15 **Inequality in Earnings** 607

Measuring Inequality 607

Earnings Inequality Since 1980: Some Descriptive Data 610

EXAMPLE 15.1 Differences in Earnings Inequality Across Developed Countries 614

The Increased Returns of Higher Education 615

EXAMPLE 15.2 Changes in the Premium to Education at the Beginning of the Twentieth Century 616

Growth of Earnings Dispersion in Human-Capital Groups 617

The Underlying Causes of Growing Inequality 618

Changes in Supply 618

Changes in Demand: Technological Change 620

EXAMPLE 15.3 Will Machine Learning Increase Earnings Inequality? 621

EXAMPLE 15.4 Are Early Childhood Programs a Vehicle for Reducing Earnings Inequality? 623

Changes in Institutional Forces 626

Is Inequality Inherited? 627

EMPIRICAL STUDY 15.1 DO PARENTS' EARNINGS DETERMINE THE EARNINGS OF THEIR CHILDREN? THE USE OF INTERGENERATIONAL DATA IN STUDYING ECONOMIC MOBILITY 628

Review Questions 630

Problems 631

Notes 633

Selected Readings 638

APPENDIX 15A Lorenz Curves and Gini Coefficients 639

Notes 642

16 **The Labor Market Effects of International Trade and
    Production Sharing**   643

Why Does Trade Take Place? 644

Trade Between Individuals and the Principle of Comparative
Advantage 644

The Incentives for Trade Across Different Countries 646

*EXAMPLE 16.1 The Growth Effects of the Openness to Trade: Japan's
Sudden Move to Openness in 1859* 650

Effects of Trade on the Demand for Labor 651

Product Demand Shifts 651

Shifts in the Supply of Alternative Factors of Production 653

The Net Effect on Labor Demand 655

*EXAMPLE 16.2 Could a Quarter of U.S. Jobs Be Offshored? Might Your
Future Job Be Among Them?* 656

Will Wages Converge Across Countries? 659

Policy Issues 660

Subsidizing Human-Capital Investments 661

Income Support Programs 662

Subsidized Employment 663

How Narrowly Should We Target Compensation? 663

*EMPIRICAL STUDY 16.1 EVALUATING EUROPEAN ACTIVE LABOR
MARKET POLICIES: THE USE OF META-ANALYSIS* 665

Summary 667

Review Questions 667

Problems 668

Notes 669

Selected Readings 673

Answers to Odd-Numbered Review Questions and Problems   675
Index   725

Preface

Modern Labor Economics: Theory and Public Policy has grown out of decades of experience in teaching labor market economics and conducting research aimed at influencing public policy. Our text develops the modern theory of labor market behavior, summarizes empirical evidence that supports or contradicts each hypothesis, and illustrates in detail the usefulness of the theory for public policy analysis. We believe that showing students the social implications of concepts enhances the motivation to learn them and that using the concepts of each chapter in an analytic setting allows students to see the concepts in action. The extensive use of detailed policy applications constitutes a major contribution of this text.

If, as economists believe, passing "the market test" is the ultimate criterion for judging the success of an innovation, launching this fourteenth edition of *Modern Labor Economics* is an endeavor that we have approached with both satisfaction and enthusiasm. We believe that economic analysis has become more widely accepted and valued in the area of policy analysis and evaluation and that labor economics has become an ever-more-vibrant and ever-more-vigorous field in economics. *Modern Labor Economics* was first published about a decade after the neoclassical analysis of the labor market replaced institutional treatment as the dominant paradigm, and in the intervening decades, this paradigm has grown increasingly sophisticated in its treatment of labor market issues and the institutions that affect them. This period has been an exciting and rewarding time to be a labor economist, and our enthusiasm for bringing this field to the student remains unabated.

New to This Edition

Modern Labor Economics, often known as "Ehrenberg and Smith," welcomes a third author to this fourteenth edition: Kevin F. Hallock. Professor Hallock is the president of the University of Richmond, and has served as the dean of the Cornell SC Johnson College of Business at Cornell University, the Kenneth F. Kahn '69 dean of the School of Industrial and Labor Relations at Cornell, and the Joseph R. Rich '80 professor of economics and human resource studies at the School of Industrial and Labor Relations. He has written extensively in the areas of compensation, unemployment, discrimination, and measurement, and he was the founding director of Cornell's Institute of Compensation Studies.

- This fourteenth edition of *Modern Labor Economics* has been thoroughly updated to include the latest descriptive data pertaining to the labor market and the latest references to professional literature. Through these updates, our goal is to make our textbook a comprehensive reference for critical factual information about the labor market *and* to reflect the professional literature in labor economics.

- Boxed examples, which illustrate the applicability of economic concepts to the understanding of both daily life and historical developments, have been key characteristics of *Modern Labor Economics* in its previous 13 editions. In this fourteenth edition, we have added 14 new boxed examples, including three on the effects of unemployment (including that created by the COVID-19 lockdowns) and two on gig work. Other new boxed examples address "nudges," monopsony power in the high-tech sector, "ban-the-box" legislation, the introduction of robots, the effects of machine learning on inequality, and the human-capital topics of early childhood education, general-training contracts that workers sign, and educational investments among populations victimized by forced migration.

- Another feature of *Modern Labor Economics* has long been the presence of several chapter appendices, which allow professors and students to delve more deeply into more-technical topics if they are so inclined. This fourteenth edition contains eight such appendices, including a new one on the empirical issues of analyzing the gender pay gap in a large international company.

Overview of the Text

Modern Labor Economics is designed for one-semester or one-quarter courses in labor economics at the undergraduate or graduate level for students who may not have extensive backgrounds in economics. Since 1974, two of us have taught such courses at the School of Industrial and Labor Relations at Cornell University; the other of us has been teaching about labor markets since 1995. The undergraduate course requires only principles of economics as a prerequisite, and the graduate course (for students in a professional program akin to a master of business administration program) has no prerequisites. We have found that being highly technical in one's presentation is not necessary to convey important concepts and that students with limited backgrounds in economics can comprehend a great deal of material in a single course. However, for students who have taken intermediate microeconomics, we have included eight chapter appendixes that discuss more-advanced material or develop technical concepts in much greater detail than the text discussion permits.

Labor economics has always been an "applied" branch of study, and a thorough grounding in the field requires at least an acquaintance with basic methodological techniques and problems. Appendix 1A in Chapter 1 presents a brief overview of regression analysis. Then, each succeeding chapter ends with an "empirical study"—relevant to that chapter's content—that introduces students to different *methodological* issues faced by economists conducting applied research. We hope that this unique feature of the text-book will both enlighten students about and interest them in the challenges of empirical research.

After the book's introduction to basic economic concepts in Chapter 1, Chapter 2 presents a quick overview of demand and supply in labor markets so that students can see from the outset the interrelationship of the major forces at work shaping labor market behavior. This chapter can be skipped or skimmed by students with strong backgrounds in economics or by students in one-quarter courses. Chapters 3, 4, and 5 are concerned primarily with the demand for labor, and Chapters 6, 7, 8, 9, and 10 focus on labor supply issues.

Beginning with Chapter 11, the concepts of economics are used to analyze several topics of special interest to students of labor markets. The relationship between pay and productivity is analyzed in Chapter 11, and the earnings of women and underrepresented minority groups—encompassing issues of discrimination—are the subjects of Chapter 12. Chapter 13 uses economic concepts to analyze collective bargaining and labor unions in the private and public sectors, and Chapter 14 discusses the issue of unemployment.

Chapters 15 and 16 analyze two issues of major policy importance over the past two or three decades: the growth in earnings inequality (Chapter 15) and the effects of greater international trade and production sharing (Chapter 16). Both chapters serve a dual role: analyzing important policy issues while reviewing and using key concepts presented in earlier chapters.

In addition to the use of public policy examples, the inclusion of technical appendixes, and our end-of-chapter discussions of methodological issues, the text has a number of other important pedagogical features. First, each chapter contains boxed examples that illustrate an application of that chapter's theory in a nontraditional, historical, business, or cross-cultural setting. Second, each chapter contains a number of discussion or review questions that allow students to apply what they have learned to specific policy issues. To enhance student mastery, we provide answers to the odd-numbered questions at the back of the book. Third, lists of selected readings at the end of chapters refer students to more-advanced sources of study. Fourth, the footnotes in the text have been updated to cite the most recent literature on each topic; they are intended as references for students and professors alike who may want to delve more deeply into a given issue.

Accompanying Supplements

The book is supported by a comprehensive companion website, featuring a study guide, quizzes, quantitative and econometric exercises, chapter introductions, review questions and problems, applications, PowerPoint lectures, case studies, web links, and an instructor's manual. These materials have been thoroughly updated for the fourteenth edition and are available at www.routledge.com/cw/ehrenberg.

The publishers thank Elizabeth Wheaton for providing the quantitative and econometric exercises; Leonie Stone for providing the instructor's manual, PowerPoint lectures, and study guide; and Richard Haskell for providing the case studies.

Acknowledgments

Enormous debts are owed to four groups of people. First are those instrumental in teaching us the concepts and social relevance of labor economics when we were students or young professionals: Orley Ashenfelter, Frank Brechling, David Card, George Delehanty, Dale Mortensen, John Pencavel, Orme Phelps, and Mel Reder. Second are the generations of undergraduate and graduate students who sat through the lectures that preceded the publication of each new edition of *Modern Labor Economics* and, by their questions and responses, forced us to make ourselves clear. Third, we are indebted to all the reviewers who, over many years, have provided valuable feedback on the prospect of new editions. Fourth, many of our colleagues in the labor economics group at Cornell, along with Tim Schmidle, and Dara Gocheski have contributed both formally and informally to this fourteenth edition. Finally, we are grateful to Emily Chase and Louisa Heywood for research assistance on this fourteenth edition. They are the kind of students who make working at Cornell and Richmond such a privilege.

Ronald G. Ehrenberg
Robert S. Smith
Kevin F. Hallock

Introduction

Economic theory provides powerful, and surprising, insights into individual and social behavior. These insights help us understand important aspects of our lives. Beyond this, however, government, business, labor, and other groups have increasingly come to understand the usefulness of the concepts and thought processes of economists in formulating social policy.

This book presents an application of economic analysis to the behavior of and relationships between employers and employees. The aggregate compensation received by U.S. employees from their employers was $11.5 trillion in the year 2019, whereas all *other* forms of personal income for that year—from investments, self-employment, pensions, and various government assistance programs—amounted to $7.2 trillion. The *employment* relationship, then, is one of the most fundamental relationships in our lives, so it attracts a good deal of legislative attention. Knowing the fundamentals of labor economics is thus essential to an understanding of a huge array of social problems and programs, both in the United States and elsewhere.

As economists who have been actively involved in the analysis and evaluation of public policies, we obviously believe that labor economics is useful in understanding the effects of these programs. Perhaps more importantly, we also believe that policy analysis can be useful in teaching the fundamentals of labor economics. We have therefore incorporated such analyses into each chapter, with two purposes in mind. First, we believe that seeing the relevance and social implications of concepts studied enhances the student's motivation to learn. Second, using the concepts of each chapter in an analytical setting reinforces understanding by helping the student to see them "in action."

The Labor Market

There is a rumor that a former U.S. secretary of labor attempted to abolish the term *labor market* from departmental publications. He believed that it demeaned workers to regard labor as being bought and sold like so much grain, oil, or steel. True, labor is unique in several ways. Labor services can only be rented; workers themselves cannot be bought and sold. Further, because labor services cannot be separated from workers, the conditions under which such services are rented are often as important as the price. Indeed, *nonpecuniary factors*—such as work environment, the risk of injury, the personalities of managers, the perceptions of fair treatment, and the flexibility of work hours—loom larger in employment transactions than they do in markets for commodities and other goods. Finally, a host of institutions and pieces of legislation that influence the employment relationship do not exist in other markets.

Nevertheless, the circumstances under which employers rent and employees rent out labor services clearly constitute a market, for several reasons. First, institutions such as job boards and employment agencies have been developed to facilitate contacts between buyers and sellers of labor services. Second, once a contact has been arranged, information about price and quality is exchanged in employment applications and interviews. Third, when an agreement has been reached, some kind of *contract*, whether formal or informal, is executed, covering compensation, conditions of work, job security, and even the duration of the job. These contracts typically (but not exclusively—more on that in Chapter 11) call for employers to compensate employees for their *time* and not for what they produce. This form of compensation requires that employers give careful attention to worker motivation and dependability in the selection and employment process.

The end result of employer–employee transactions in the labor market is, of course, the placement of people in jobs at certain rates of pay. This allocation of labor serves not only the personal needs of individuals but the needs of the larger society as well. Through the labor market, our most important national resource—labor—is allocated to firms, industries, occupations, and regions.[1]

Labor Economics: Some Basic Concepts

Labor economics is the study of the workings and outcomes of the market for labor. More specifically, labor economics is concerned primarily with the behavior of employers and employees in response to the general incentives of wages, prices, profits, and nonpecuniary aspects of the employment relationship, such as working conditions. These incentives serve both to motivate and to limit individual choice. The focus in economics is on inducements for behavior that are impersonal and apply to a wide range of people.

In this book, we examine, for example, the relationship between wages and employment opportunities; the interactions between wages, income, and the decision to work; the way that general market incentives affect occupational choice; the relationship between wages and undesirable job characteristics; the incentives for and effects of educational and training investments; and the effects of unions on wages, productivity, and turnover. In the process, we analyze the employment and wage effects of such social policies as the minimum wage, overtime legislation, safety and health regulations, welfare reform, payroll taxes, unemployment insurance, immigration policies, and antidiscrimination laws.

Our study of labor economics is conducted on two levels. Most of the time, we use economic theory to analyze "what is"; that is, we explain people's behavior by using a mode of analysis called *positive economics*. Less commonly, we use *normative economic analysis* to judge "what should be."

Positive Economics

Positive economics is a theory of behavior in which people are typically assumed to respond favorably to benefits and negatively to costs. In this regard, positive economics closely resembles Skinnerian psychology, which views behavior as shaped by rewards and punishments. The rewards in economic theory are pecuniary and nonpecuniary gains (benefits), whereas the punishments are forgone opportunities and the training needed to become certified to do the job (costs). For example, a person motivated to become a surgeon because of the earnings and status that surgeons command must give up the opportunity to become a lawyer and must be available for emergency work around the clock. Both the benefits and the costs must be considered in making this career choice.

Scarcity   The pervasive assumption underlying economic theory is that of resource *scarcity*. According to this assumption, individuals and society alike do not have the resources to meet all of their wants. Thus, any resource devoted to satisfying one set of desires could have been used to satisfy another set, which means that there is a cost (sometimes called an opportunity cost) to any decision or action. The real cost of using labor hired by a government contractor to build a road, for example, is the production lost by not devoting this labor to the production of some other good or service. Thus, in popular terms, "there is no such thing as a free lunch," and we must always make choices and live with the rewards and costs that these choices bring us. Moreover, we are always constrained in our choices by the resources available to us.

Rationality   A second basic assumption of positive economics is that people are *rational*: they have an objective and pursue it in a reasonably consistent fashion. When considering *people*, economists assume that the objective being pursued is *utility maximization*; that is, people are assumed to strive toward the goal of making themselves as happy as they can (given their limited resources). Note that this is not necessarily income maximization. Utility, of course, is generated by both pecuniary dimensions and nonpecuniary dimensions of employment.

When considering the behavior of *firms*, which are inherently nonpersonal entities, economists assume that the goal of behavior is *profit maximization*. Profit maximization is really just a special case of utility maximization in which pecuniary gain is paramount and nonpecuniary factors are ignored.

The assumption of rationality implies a *consistency* of response to general economic incentives and an *adaptability* of behavior when those incentives change. These two characteristics of behavior underlie predictions about how workers and firms will respond to various incentives.[2]

The Models and Predictions of Positive Economics

Behavioral predictions in economics flow more or less directly from the two fundamental assumptions of scarcity and rationality. Workers must continually make choices, such as whether to look for other jobs, accept overtime, move to another area, or acquire more education. Employers must also make choices concerning, for example, the level of output and the mix of machines and labor to use in production. Economists usually assume that when making these choices, employees and employers are guided by their desires to maximize utility or profit, respectively. However, what is more important to the economic theory of behavior is not the *particular* goal of either employees or employers; rather, it is that economic actors weigh the costs and benefits of various alternative transactions in the context of achieving *some* goal or another.

One might object that these assumptions are unrealistic and that people are not nearly as calculating, as well informed about alternatives, or as amply endowed with choices as economists assume. Economists are likely to reply that if people are not calculating, are totally uninformed, or do not have any choices, then most predictions suggested by economic theory will not be supported by real-world evidence. They thus argue that the theory underlying positive economics should be judged on the basis of its *predictions*, not its assumptions.

The reason we need to make assumptions and create a relatively simple theory of behavior is that the actual workings of the labor market are almost inconceivably complex. Millions of workers and employers interact daily, all with their own sets of motivations, preferences, information, and perceptions of self-interest. What we need to discover are general principles that provide useful insights into the labor market. We hope to show in this text that a few forces are so basic to labor market behavior that they alone can predict or explain many of the outcomes and behaviors observed in the labor market.

Any time that we attempt to explain a complex set of behaviors and outcomes by using a few fundamental influences, we have created a *model*. Models are not intended to capture every complexity of behavior; instead, they are created to strip away random and idiosyncratic factors, to focus on general principles. An analogy from the physical sciences may make the nature of models and their relationship to actual behavior clearer.

A Physical Model   Using simple calculations of velocity and gravitational pull, physicists can predict where a ball will land if it is kicked with a certain force at a given angle to the ground. The actual point of landing may vary from the predicted point because of wind currents and any spin that the ball might have—factors ignored in basic calculations. If a hundred balls are kicked, none may ever land exactly on the predicted spot, although they will tend to cluster around it. The accuracy of the model, although not perfect, may be good enough to enable a football coach to decide whether to attempt a field goal. The point is that for policy purposes, we usually just need to know the *average tendencies* of outcomes. To estimate these tendencies, we need to know the important forces at work, but we must confine ourselves to few enough influences so that calculating estimates remains feasible. (A further comparison of physics and positive economics is in Example 1.1.)

EXAMPLE 1.1

Positive Economics: What Does It Mean to "Understand" Behavior?

The purpose of positive economic analysis is to analyze, or understand, the behavior of people as they respond to market incentives. But in a world that is extremely complex, just what does it mean to "understand" behavior? One theoretical physicist put it the following way:

> We can imagine that this complicated array of moving things which constitutes "the world" is something like a great chess game being played by the gods, and we are observers of the game. We do not know what the rules of the game are; all we are allowed to do is to watch the playing. Of course, if we watch long enough, we may eventually catch on to a few of the rules. The rules of the game are what we mean by fundamental physics. Even if we know every rule, however, . . . what we really can explain in terms of those rules is very limited, because almost all situations are so enormously complicated that we cannot follow the plays of the game using the rules, much less tell what is going to happen next. We must, therefore, limit ourselves to the more basic question of the rules of the game. If we know the rules, we consider that we "understand" the world.[a]

If the behavior of nature, which does not have a will, is so difficult to analyze, understanding the behavior of people is even more of a challenge. Since people's behaviors do not mechanistically follow a set of rules, the goal of positive economics is most realistically stated as trying to discover people's behavioral tendencies.

Source: The Feynman Lectures on Physics by Richard P. Feynman, 2011. Reprinted by permission of Basic Books, a member of the Perseus Books Group

---

An Economic Model   To really grasp the assumptions and predictions of economic models, we consider a concrete example. Suppose we begin by asserting that being subject to resource scarcity, workers will prefer high-paying jobs to low-paying ones *if* all other job characteristics are the same in each job. Thus, they will quit lower-paying jobs to take higher-paying ones if they believe sufficient improvement is likely. This principle does not imply that workers care only about wages or that all are equally likely to quit. Workers obviously care about a number of employment characteristics, and improvement in any of these on their current job makes turnover less likely. Likewise, some workers are more receptive to change than other workers are. Nevertheless, if we hold other factors constant and increase only wages, we should clearly observe that the probability of quitting will fall.

On the employer side of the market, we can consider a similar prediction. Firms need to make a profit to survive. If they have high turnover, their costs will be higher than otherwise, because of the need to search for, hire, and train replacements. With high turnover, they will be less able, therefore, to afford to pay higher wages. However, if they could reduce turnover (and the costs of turnover) enough by paying increasing wages, it might well be worth incurring the added wage costs. Thus, both the utility-maximizing behavior of employees and the profit-maximizing behavior of firms lead us to expect lower turnover to be associated with higher wages, and higher turnover with lower wages, other things being equal.

We note three important facets about the foregoing predictions:

1. The predictions emerge directly from the twin assumptions of scarcity and rationality. Employees and employers, both mindful of their scarce resources, are assumed to be on the lookout for chances to improve their well-being. The predictions are also based on the assumptions that employees are aware of, or can learn about, alternative jobs and that these alternatives are open to them.

2. We made the prediction of a negative relationship between wages and voluntary turnover by holding other things equal. The theory does not deny that job characteristics other than wages matter to employees or that employers can lower turnover by varying policies other than the wage rate (for example, by improving working conditions). However, in keeping these other factors constant, our model predicts a negative relationship if the basic assumptions are valid.

3. The *assumptions* of the theory concern the individual behavior of employers and employees, but the *predictions* are about an aggregate relationship between wages and turnover. The prediction is *not* that all employees will remain in their jobs if their wages are increased but that *enough* will remain for turnover to be cut by raising wages. The test of the prediction thus lies in finding out whether the predicted relationship between wages and turnover exists by using aggregate data from firms or industries.

Careful statistical studies support the hypothesis that higher pay reduces voluntary turnover. One study, for example, estimated that a 10 percent increase in wages, holding worker characteristics constant, reduced the quit rate by 1 percent.[3] (The statistical technique commonly used by economists to test hypotheses is introduced in Appendix 1A.)

Normative Economics

Understanding normative economics begins with learning about two kinds of economic transactions. One kind is entered into voluntarily, because all parties to the transaction gain. If Sally is willing to create blueprints for $20 per hour, for example, and Ace Engineering Services is willing to pay someone up to $22 per hour to do the job, both gain by agreeing to Sally's appointment at an hourly wage between $20 and $22; such a transaction is mutually beneficial. The role of the labor market is to facilitate these voluntary, mutually advantageous transactions. If the market is successful in facilitating *all* possible mutually beneficial transactions, it can be said to have produced a condition that economists call *Pareto* (or "economic") *efficiency*.[4] (The word *efficiency* is used by economists in a specialized sense to denote a condition in which all mutually beneficial transactions have been concluded. This definition of the word is more comprehensive than definitions of cost minimization.) If Pareto efficiency were actually attained, no more transactions would be undertaken voluntarily, because they would not be *mutually* advantageous.

The second kind of transaction is one in which one or more parties *lose*. These transactions often involve the redistribution of income, from which some gain at the expense of others. Transactions that are explicitly redistributional, for example, are not entered into voluntarily unless motivated by charity (in which case the donors gain nonpecuniary satisfaction); otherwise, redistributional transactions are mandated by government through tax and expenditure policies. Thus, whereas markets facilitate *voluntary* transactions, the government's job is often to make certain transactions *mandatory*.

Any normative statement—a statement about what *ought* to exist—is based on some underlying value. Government policies affecting the labor market are often based on the widely shared, but not universally agreed on, value that society should try to make the distribution of income more equal. Social welfare programs, minimum-wage laws, and restrictions on immigration are examples of policies based on *distributional* considerations. Other labor market policies are intended either to change or to overrule the choices that workers make in maximizing their utility. The underlying value in these cases is frequently that workers should not be allowed to place themselves or their families at risk of physical or financial harm. The wearing of such personal protective devices as hard hats, earplugs, and face masks, for example, is seen as so *meritorious* in certain settings that it is required of workers even if they would choose otherwise.

Policies seeking to redistribute income or force the consumption of meritorious goods are often controversial because some workers will feel worse off when the policies are adopted. These transactions must be governmentally mandated because they will not be entered into voluntarily.

Markets and Values   Economic theory, however, reminds us that one class of transactions has no losers. Policies or transactions from which all affected parties gain can be said to be *Pareto improving* because they promote Pareto efficiency. These policies or transactions can be justified on the grounds that they unambiguously enhance social welfare; therefore, they can be unanimously supported. Policies with this justification are of special interest to economists because economics is largely the study of market behavior—voluntary transactions in the pursuit of self-interest.

A transaction can be unanimously supported when one of the following three scenarios occurs:

1. All parties who are affected by the transaction gain.

2. Some parties gain, and no one else loses.

3. Some parties gain and some lose from the transaction, but the gainers fully compensate the losers.

When the compensation in *3* takes place, case *3* is converted to case *2*. In practice, economists often judge a transaction by whether the gains of the beneficiaries exceed the costs borne by the losers, thus making *possible* that there would be no losers. However, when the compensation of losers is *possible* but does *not* take place, some individuals are in fact worse off. Many economists, therefore, argue that compensation *must* take place for a government policy to be justified on the grounds that it promotes Pareto efficiency.

As noted earlier, the role of the labor market is to facilitate voluntary, mutually advantageous transactions. Hardly anyone would argue against at least some kind of government intervention in the labor market if the market is failing to promote such transactions. But why do markets fail?

Market Failure: Ignorance   Critical to the accomplishment of mutually beneficial transactions is that the parties to the transaction be well informed of its consequences. A worker who smokes, for example, may take a job in an asbestos-processing plant not knowing that the combination of smoking and inhaling asbestos dust substantially increases the risk of lung disease. Had the worker known this, they probably would have stopped smoking or changed jobs, but both transactions were blocked by ignorance.

Although ignorance is often rooted in the lack of access to information, it can also be caused by human fallibility in the *processing* of available information. People may have prejudices, fears, or instincts that inhibit information processing, leading them to make decisions that do not advance their respective long-run self-interests.[5] Example 1.2 illustrates one such instinct (inertia) and steps that might be taken to deal with it.

Market Failure: Transaction Barriers   Also, some barrier might hinder the completion of a transaction that could be mutually beneficial. Often, such a barrier is created by laws that prohibit certain transactions. For example, as recently as three or four decades ago, many U.S. states prohibited employers from hiring women to work more than 40 hours a week. As a consequence, firms that wanted to hire workers for more than 40 hours a week could not transact with those women who wanted to work overtime—to the detriment of both parties. Society as a whole thus suffers losses when transactions that are mutually beneficial are prohibited by government.

Another barrier to mutually beneficial transactions may be the expense of completing the transactions. Lower-skilled workers facing limited opportunities in one region might desire to move to take better jobs. Alternatively, they might want to enter job-training programs. In either case, they might lack the funds to finance the desired transactions. A further cost of completing a transaction that might serve a worker's long-run self-interest is making the effort to overcome the inertia mentioned in Example 1.2; many of us tend to procrastinate and put off to the last minute doing difficult things we know we should do (such as seeking job retraining or searching for a job if we are unemployed).

EXAMPLE 1.2

Do We Need "Nudges" to Make the Right Decisions for Ourselves?

One cost of completing a transaction is overcoming one's inertia. Alex may want to eat healthily but in a cafeteria line be drawn to take a dessert rather than a salad because desserts are closer and salads are across the room. Casey may want to save for the future but postpones signing up for an employer-sponsored savings plan because of the paperwork required. Can we craft policies to overcome inertia as a transaction barrier?

One creative solution to the problem of inertia is to use that inertia to "nudge" (but not force) people into making better decisions. For example, if salads were made more accessible in a cafeteria line and desserts less accessible, more people might choose salads (but of course could consume desserts if they wanted to take the trouble to do so). Similarly, if fast-food restaurants routinely filled drink orders with medium-size cups and forced customers to *ask* for supersize ones, we might drink less soda.

In the workplace, employers could routinely sign all employees up for their savings plan but allow those who do not want it to fill out the needed paperwork to withdraw from the plan. As with food selection, "nudging" helps people make better decisions by reducing the costs of making a decision that might improve their long-run utility, thus creating a situation in which their inertia must be overcome if they want to make a different choice.

See Richard H. Thaler and Cass R. Sunstein, *Nudge: Improving Decisions about Health, Wealth, and Happiness*, New Haven, CT: Yale University Press, 2008.

Market Failure: Externalities Market failure can also arise when a buyer and a seller agree to a transaction that imposes costs or benefits on people who were *not party to their decision*; in other words, some decisions have costs or benefits that are "external" to the decision makers. Why do these externalities cause market failure?

When buyers and sellers make their decisions, they generally weigh the costs and benefits only to themselves and, of course, decide to complete a transaction when the benefits outweigh the costs. If *all* transaction costs and benefits fall to the decision makers, then society can be assured that the transaction represents a step toward Pareto efficiency. However, if costs or benefits fall to people who were *not* able to influence the decision, then the transaction may not have positive net benefits to society.

For us to have confidence that a particular transaction is a step toward Pareto efficiency, the decision must be *voluntarily* accepted by all who are affected by it. If there are externalities to a transaction, people who are affected by it—but who cannot influence the ultimate decision—are being *forced* into a transaction that they may not have been willing to make. If so, the costs of the transaction might be greater than the benefits, once *all* the costs and benefits (and not just those of the decision makers) have been counted.

Child labor offers a stark example of externalities, because children do not have the competence or the power to make many important decisions affecting their lives. If parents are selfish and ignore the interests of their children in making decisions about sending them to work or to school, then society cannot trust their decisions as advancing economic efficiency (because the costs and benefits to the children have been ignored in making work/school decisions).

Externalities would also exist if, say, workers had no mechanism to transfer *their* costs of being injured at work to their *employers*, who are the ones making the decisions about how much to spend to reduce workplace risk. If such a mechanism does not exist (a question that we explore in Chapter 8), then our workplaces will be less safe than they should be, because employers are ignoring at least some costs (the ones borne by workers) in making their decisions about risk reduction.

Market Failure: Public Goods A special kind of externality is sometimes called the free-rider problem. For example, suppose that a union representing workers in the noisy sawmill industry intends to sponsor research on the effects of excessive noise on workers' hearing loss. This research is expensive, but because it would be useful to unions or individual workers in other noisy industries, the sawmill-workers union considers whether it could defray its expenses by selling its findings to other interested parties. The union would quickly realize, however, that once its findings become known to its members or its first "customers," the results would quickly become available to all—through word-of-mouth, newspaper, or Internet sources—even to those free riders who do not pay.

Such research findings constitute an example of what is called a *public good*—a good that can be consumed by any number of people at the same time, including those who do not pay. Because nonpayers cannot be excluded from consuming the good, no potential customer will have an incentive to pay. Knowing this, the potential provider of the good or service (the sawmill-workers union in our example) will probably decide not to produce it.

In the case of public goods, private decision makers ignore the benefits to others when making their decisions because they have no mechanism to "capture" these benefits. As a result, society will under-invest in such goods unless a government, which can *compel* payments through its tax system, steps in to produce the public goods.

Market Failure: Price Distortion   A special barrier to transaction is caused by taxes, subsidies, and other forces that create "incorrect" prices. Prices powerfully influence the incentives to transact, and the prices asked or received in a transaction should reflect the true preferences of the parties to it. When prices become decoupled from preferences, parties may be led to make transactions that are not socially beneficial or to avoid others that would be advantageous. If plumbers charge \$25 per hour, but their customers must pay an additional tax of \$5 to the government, customers who are willing to pay between \$25 and \$30 per hour and would hire plumbers in the absence of the tax are discouraged from doing so—to the detriment of both parties.

Normative Economics and Government Policy

Solutions to problems that prevent the completion of socially beneficial transactions frequently involve governmental intervention. If the problem is a lack of information about health risks, say, one obvious solution is for the government to take steps to ensure that workers are informed about such risks. If the problem is that some law prevents women, say, from working the hours that they want, an obvious solution is to repeal the law.

For other types of transaction barriers, the needed intervention is for the government to either compel or actively promote transactions different from the ones that would be made by "the market" (i.e., those made by private decision makers). When the government decides to "replace" a market decision made by one of its own, the policy prescription is complicated by the need to guess just what the appropriate transaction is. In the following subsections, we discuss government interventions that deal with two examples of transaction barriers.

Capital Market Imperfections   Workers find obtaining loans that would allow them to obtain job training or finance a cross-country move to obtain a better job difficult, because usually all they can offer to secure the loan is their promise to pay it back. The government, however, might make such loans even if it faced the same risk of default, because enabling workers to acquire new skills or move to where workers are needed would strengthen the overall economy. Of course, if the government did decide to make these loans, it would have to decide on the appropriate circumstances for approving such loans, including how much money to loan.

Externalities   Earlier, we argued that parents may not take the welfare of their children into account when making decisions about whether to send them to work or to school. A solution to this problem that most societies have undertaken is to require children to stay in school until they reach a certain age and to provide at least that level of schooling at public expense. Ideally, of course, deciding on the mandatory school-leaving age would require the government to look carefully at the *lifetime benefits* of various schooling levels (see Chapter 9) and compare them to both the direct costs of education and the opportunity costs of the children's lost production. Performing the cost–benefit analyses needed to intelligently address the problem of externalities requires a solid grasp of economic theory (which we discuss in Chapter 8).

Efficiency Versus Equity

The social goal of a more equitable distribution of income is often of paramount importance to political decision makers, and disputes can arise over whether equity or economic efficiency should be the prime consideration in setting policy. One source of dispute is rooted in the problem that no one unique set of transactions is Pareto efficient. In fact, a *number* of sets of transactions can satisfy our definition of economic efficiency, and questions can arise on which set is the most equitable.

To understand the multiple sets of efficient transactions that are possible, we return to our example of the woman willing to create blueprints for $20 per hour. If Ace Engineering Services is willing to pay up to $22 per hour for blueprints and Sally is willing to work for $20, their agreement on her employment at an hourly wage of, say, $21 would be beneficial to both parties. However, the same can be said for an agreement on wages of either $20.25 or $21.75 per hour. We can objectively judge any of these potential agreements as *efficient* (relative to her not working) because both parties are better off than they would have been if they had not transacted. But which of the potential agreements is more *equitable* remains unclear unless we define a subjective standard for "fairness."

The second source of dispute over equity and efficiency is rooted in the following problem: To achieve more equity, steps *away* from Pareto efficiency must often be taken.[6] Minimum-wage laws, for example, block transactions that parties might be willing to make at a lower wage; thus, some who would have accepted jobs at less than the legislated minimum are not offered any at all, because their services are "priced out of the market." Similarly, social welfare programs have often been structured so that recipients who find paid work receive, in effect, a zero wage—a price distortion of major proportions but one that is neither easily nor cheaply avoided (as we see in Chapter 6).

Normative economics tends to stress efficiency over equity considerations, not because it is more important but because it can be more easily analyzed mathematically. For a transaction to be mutually beneficial, all that is required is for each party to individually feel better off. Thus, studying voluntary transactions (i.e., market behavior) is useful when taking economic efficiency into account. Equity considerations, however, always involve comparing the welfare lost by some against the utility gained by others—which, given the impossibility of measuring happiness, cannot be scientifically done. For policy decisions that are based on considerations of equity, society usually turns to guidance from the political system, not from markets.

Plan of the Text

The study of labor economics is mainly a study of the interplay between employers and employees—or between demand and supply. Chapter 2 presents a quick overview of demand and supply in the labor market, allowing students to see from the outset the interrelationship of the major forces at work shaping labor market behavior. Chapters 3, 4, and 5 are concerned primarily with the demand for labor. Consequently, they are devoted to analyzing employers' incentives and behaviors.

Chapters 6, 7, 8, 9, and 10 contain analyses of various aspects of workers' labor supply behavior. They address issues of whether to work for pay (as opposed to consuming leisure or working around the home without pay), the choice of occupations or jobs with different characteristics, and decisions that workers must make about educational and other investments designed to improve their earning capacities. Like the earlier "demand" chapters, these "supply" chapters necessarily incorporate aspects of behavior on the other (here, employer) side of the labor market.

Chapters 11, 12, 13, 14, 15, and 16 address special topics of interest to labor economists, including the effects of institutional forces on the labor market. Chapter 11 analyzes how the compensation of workers can be structured to create incentives for greater productivity. Chapter 12 analyzes wage differentials associated with race, gender, and ethnicity. Chapter 13 deals with the labor market effects of labor unions. Chapter 14 focuses on an analysis of unemployment. The final two chapters discuss the phenomena of inequality (Chapter 15) and globalization (Chapter 16) while reviewing most of the major concepts introduced earlier in the text.

At the end of each chapter are several features that are designed to improve readers' understanding. First, starting with Chapter 2, readers will find a summary of an empirical study related to concepts introduced in the text. These summaries are designed to convey, in a nontechnical way, how researchers can creatively confront the challenges of testing the predictions of economic theory in the "real world." Because the summaries often assume a basic familiarity with regression analysis (a basic statistical tool in economics), we introduce this technique in Appendix 1A.

The end-of-chapter materials also include a set of review questions that are designed to test understanding of the chapter's concepts and how these concepts can be applied to policy issues. The questions are ordered by level of difficulty (the more difficult ones come later), and answers to the odd-numbered questions are in a separate section at the end of the textbook. Some numerically based problems follow the review questions, and again answers to the odd-numbered problems are at the end of the textbook.

For students who want to go more deeply into the concepts introduced in the text of each chapter, we provide extensive footnotes designed to provide references to seminal works and the most recent literature. At the end of each chapter, we also provide selected readings that go more deeply into the material. Many chapters also have an appendix that delves deeper into a specialized topic that may be of interest to some readers.

Review Questions

1. Using the concepts of normative economics, when would the labor market be judged to be at a point of optimality? What imperfections might prevent the market from achieving this point?

2. Are the following statements positive or normative? Why?

   a. Employers should not be required to offer pensions to their employees.

   b. Employers offering pension benefits will pay lower wages than they would if they did not offer a pension program.

   c. If the further immigration of lower-skilled foreigners is prevented, the wages of lower-skilled immigrants already here will rise.

   d. The military draft compels people to engage in a transaction that they would not voluntarily enter into; it should therefore be avoided as a way of recruiting military personnel.

   e. If the military draft were reinstituted, military salaries would probably fall.

3. Suppose that the federal government needs workers to repair a levee along a flood-prone river. From the perspective of normative economics, what difference does it make whether nondisabled workers are compelled to work (for pay) on the levee or whether a workforce is recruited through the normal process of making job offers to applicants and relying on their voluntary acceptance?

4. What are the functions and limitations of an economic model?

5. In this chapter, a simple model was developed that predicted that workers employed in jobs paying wages less than they could get in comparable jobs elsewhere would tend to quit to seek higher-paying jobs. Suppose that we observe a worker who, after repeated harassment or criticism from her boss, quits an $8-per-hour job to take another job paying $7.50 per hour. Answer the three following questions:

   a. Is this woman's behavior consistent with the economic model of job quitting outlined in the text?

   b. Can we test to see whether this woman's behavior is consistent with the assumption of rationality?

   c. Suppose that the boss in question had harassed other employees, but this woman was the only one who quit. Can we conclude that economic theory applies to the behavior of some people but not to others?

6. A law in one town of a Canadian province limits large supermarkets to just four employees on Sundays. Analyze this law by using the concepts of normative economics.

7. Child labor laws generally prohibit children from working until age 14 and restrict younger teenagers to certain kinds of work that are not considered dangerous. Reconcile the prohibitions of child labor legislation with the principles underlying normative economic analysis.

8. In discussing ways to reduce lung diseases caused by workplace hazards, one commentator said, "Gas masks are uncomfortable to wear, but economists argue that they are the socially preferred method for reducing the inhalation of toxic substances whenever they can be produced for less than it takes to alter a ventilation system." Following the perspective of normative economics, comment on this quotation.

Problems

1. (Appendix 1A) You have collected the following data (see Table 1P.1) on 13 randomly selected teenage workers in the fast-food industry. What is the general relationship between age and wage? Plot the data, and then construct a linear equation for this relationship.

Table 1P.1 Assumed Wages and Ages of Fast Food Workers

Age (years)	Wage (dollars per hour)	Age (years)	Wage (dollars per hour)
16	$7.25	18	$8.00
16	$8.00	18	$8.50
17	$7.50	18	$9.50
17	$8.00	19	$8.50
17	$8.25	19	$8.75
18	$7.25	19	$10.00
18	$7.75		

2. (Appendix) Suppose that a least squares regression yields the following estimate:

$$W_i = -1 + 0.3A_i$$

where W is the hourly wage rate (in dollars) and A is the age (in years).

A second regression from another group of workers yields the following estimate:

$$W_i = 3 + 0.3A_i - 0.01(A_i)^2$$

a. How much is a twenty-year-old predicted to earn according to the first estimate?

b. How much is a twenty-year-old predicted to earn according to the second estimate?

3. (Appendix) Suppose that you estimate the following relationship between wages and age:

$$W_i = -1 + 0.3A_i$$

$$(0.1)$$

(the standard error is in parentheses). Are you confident that wages actually rise with age?

4. (Appendix) Suppose that you have information on which of the 13 randomly selected teenage workers in the fast-food industry worked part time and which worked full time. Variable F_i is equal to 1 if the worker is employed full time, and it is equal to 0 otherwise. With this information, you estimate the following relationship between wages, age, and full-time employment:

$$W_i = -0.5 + 0.25A_i + 0.75F_i$$

$$(0.10) \quad (0.20)$$

(the standard errors are in parentheses).

a. How much is a 20-year-old who works full time predicted to earn according to this estimate?

b. How much is a 20-year-old who works part time predicted to earn according to this estimate?

5. (Appendix) Given the regression estimate in problem 4, evaluate the statistical significance of the estimated coefficients in the regression.

6. (Appendix) Compare the first regression estimate in problem 2 with the regression estimate in problem 4.

a. Is an omitted variable bias present when the full-time variable is not included? Explain.

b. What can be said about the correlation between age and full-time employment? Explain.

Selected Readings

Autor, David. "Work of the Past, Work of the Future." *The American Economic Review* 109 (May 2019): 1–32.

Boyer, George R., and Robert S. Smith. "The Development of the Neoclassical Tradition in Labor Economics." *Industrial and Labor Relations Review* 54 (January 2001): 199–223.

Friedman, Milton. *Essays in Positive Economics.* Chicago: University of Chicago Press, 1953.

Hausman, Daniel M. "Economic Methodology in a Nutshell." *Journal of Economic Perspectives* 3 (Spring 1989): 115–128.

McCloskey, Donald. "The Rhetoric of Economics." *Journal of Economic Literature* 21 (June 1983): 481–517.

APPENDIX 1A

Statistical Testing of Labor Market Hypotheses

This appendix briefly introduces how labor economists test hypotheses. In this chapter, we discuss how one might attempt to test the hypothesis that, other things being equal, one should expect to observe that the higher the wage a firm pays, the lower the voluntary labor turnover among its employees will be. Put another way, if we define a firm's quit rate as the proportion of its workers who voluntarily quit in a given time period (e.g., a year), we expect to observe that the higher a firm's wages are, the lower its quit rate will be, holding *other* factors affecting quit rates constant.

A Univariate Test

An obvious first step is to collect data on the quit rates among a set of firms during a given year and match these data with the firms' wage rates. This type of analysis is called *univariate* because we are analyzing the effects on quit rates of just one other variable (the wage rate). The data are called *cross-sectional* because they provide observations across behavioral units at a point in time.[7] Table 1A.1 contains such information for a hypothetical set of 10 firms in a single labor market in a given year, such as 2019. For example, firm A is assumed to have paid an average hourly wage of $8 and to have experienced a quit rate of 40 percent in 2019.

The data on wages and quit rates are presented graphically in Figure 1A.1. Each dot in this figure represents a quit-rate/hourly wage combination for one of the firms in Table 1A.1. Firm A, for example, is represented in the figure by point *A*, which shows a quit rate of 40 percent and an hourly wage of $8, while point *B* shows comparable data for firm B. According to a visual inspection of all 10 data points in this figure, firms paying higher wages in our hypothetical sample indeed have lower quit rates. Although the data points in Figure 1A.1 obviously do not lie on a single straight line, their

Table 1A.1 Average-Wage and Quit-Rate Data for a Set of 10 Hypothetical Firms in a Single Labor Market in 2019

Firm	Average hourly wage paid ($)	Quit rate (%)	Firm	Average hourly wage paid ($)	Quit rate (%)
A	8	40	F	16	20
B	8	30	G	20	25
C	12	35	H	20	15
D	12	25	I	24	20
E	16	30	J	24	10

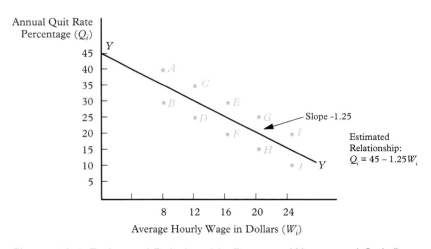

Figure 1A.1 Estimated Relationship Between Wages and Quit Rates by Using Data From Table 1A.1

pattern suggests that on average, a linear (straight-line) relationship between a firm's quit rate and its wage rate.

Any straight line can be represented by the general equation

$$Y = a + bX \tag{1A.1}$$

Variable Y is the *dependent variable*, and it is generally shown on the vertical axis of the graph depicting the line. Variable X is the *independent*, or *explanatory*, variable, which is usually shown on the horizontal axis.[8] The letters a and b are the *parameters* (the fixed coefficients) of the equation, where a represents the intercept and b the slope of the line. Put differently, a is the value of Y when the line intersects the vertical axis ($X = 0$). The slope, b, indicates the vertical distance that the line travels for each one-unit increase in the horizontal distance. If b is a positive number, the line slopes upward (going from left to right); if b is a negative number, the line slopes downward.

If one were to try to draw the straight line that best fits the points in Figure 1A.1, the line would clearly slope downward and would not go through all 10 points. It would lie above some points and below others; thus, it would "fit" the points but only with some error. We could model the relationship between the data points on the graph, then, as follows:

$$Q_i = \alpha_0 + \alpha_1 W_i + \varepsilon_i \tag{1A.2}$$

Here, Q_i represents the quit rate for firm i, and it is the dependent variable. The independent variable is W_i, firm i's wage rate. α_0 and α_1 are the parameters of the line, and α_0 is the intercept and α_1 the slope. The term ε_i is a random *error term*; it is included in the model because we do not expect that the line (given by $Q_i = \alpha_0 + \alpha_1 W_i$) will connect all the data points perfectly. Behaviorally, we are assuming the presence of random factors unrelated to wage rates that also cause the quit rate to vary across firms.

We seek to estimate what the true values of α_0 and α_1 are. Each pair of values of α_0 and α_1 defines a different straight line, and an infinite number of lines can be drawn that "fit" points *A–J*. We look into which of these straight lines fits the data the best. Some precise criterion must be used to decide which line fits the best, and the procedure typically used by statisticians and economists is to choose that line for which the sum (in our example, across all firms) of the squared vertical distances between the line and the individual data points is minimized. The line that is estimated from the data and that uses this method, which is called *least squares regression analysis*, has a number of desirable properties.[9]

Application of this method to the data found in Table 1A.1 yields the following estimated line:

$$Q_i = 45 - 1.25\,W_i \qquad\qquad\qquad\qquad (1A.3)$$
$$(5.3)(0.31)$$

The estimate of a_0 is 45, and the estimate of a_1 is -1.25.[10] Thus, if a firm had a wage rate of \$8/hour in 2019, we would predict that its annual quit rate would have been $45 - 1.25 \times (8)$, or 35 percent. This estimated quit–wage relationship is drawn in Figure 1A.1 as the line *YY*. (The numbers in parentheses after the equation will be discussed later.)

Several things should be noted about this relationship. First, taken at face value, this estimated relationship implies that firms paying their workers *nothing* (a wage of 0) would have been projected to have *only* 45 percent of their workers quit each year $(45 - 1.25 \times (0) = 45)$, whereas firms paying their workers more than \$36 an hour would have had negative quit rates.[11] The former result is nonsensical (why would any workers stay if they are paid nothing?), and the latter result is logically impossible (the quit rate cannot be less than zero). As these extreme examples suggest, using linear models to make predictions that take one outside the range of observations used in the estimation (in the example, wages from \$8 to \$24) is irrational. The relationship between wages and quit rates cannot be assumed to be linear (represented by a straight line) for very low and very high values of wages. Fortunately, the linear regression model used in the example can be easily generalized to allow for nonlinear relationships.

Second, the estimated intercept (45) and slope (−1.25) that we obtained are only estimates of the "true" relationship, and uncertainty is associated with these estimates. The uncertainty arises partly from the fact that we are trying to infer the true values of a_0 and a_1—that is, the values that characterize the wage–quit relationship in the entire population of firms—from a sample of just 10 firms. The uncertainty about each estimated coefficient is measured by its *standard error*, or the estimated standard deviation of the coefficient. These standard errors are reported in parentheses under the estimated coefficients in equation (1A.3); for example, given our data, the estimated standard error of the wage coefficient is 0.31, and that of the intercept term is 5.3. The larger the standard error, the greater the uncertainty about our estimated coefficient's value.

Under suitable assumptions about the distribution of ε_i, the random error term in equation (1A.2), we can use these standard errors to test hypotheses about the estimated coefficients.[12] In our example, we test the hypothesis that α_1 is negative (which implies, as suggested by theory, that higher wages reduce quits) against the *null hypothesis* that α_1 is 0 and that wages and quits have no relationship. One common test involves computing for each coefficient a *t statistic*, which is the ratio of the coefficient to its standard error. A heuristic rule, which can be made precise, is that if the absolute value of the *t* statistic is greater than 2, the hypothesis that the true value of the coefficient equals 0 can be rejected. Put another way, if the absolute value of a coefficient is at least twice the size of its standard error, one can be fairly confident that the true value of the coefficient is a number other than 0; in this case, we say that the estimated coefficient is *statistically significant* (a shorthand way of saying that it is significantly different from 0 in a statistical sense). In our example, the *t* statistic for the wage coefficient is $-1.25/0.31$, or -4.0, which leaves us confident that the true relationship between wage levels and quit rates is negative.

Multiple Regression Analysis

The preceding discussion has assumed that the only variable influencing quit rates, other than random (unexplained) factors, is a firm's wage rate. The discussion of positive economics in this chapter stresses, however, that the prediction of a negative relationship between wages and quit rates is made holding all other factors constant. As we will discuss in Chapter 10, economic theory suggests that many factors besides wages systematically influence quit rates. These include characteristics both of firms (e.g., employee benefits offered, working conditions, and firm size) and of their workers (e.g., age and level of training). If any of these other variables that we have omitted from our analysis tend to vary across firms systematically with the wage rates that the firms offer, the resulting estimated relationship between wage rates and quit rates will be incorrect. In such cases, we must take these other variables into account by using a model with more than one independent variable. We rely on economic theory to indicate which variables should be included in our statistical analysis and to suggest the direction of causation.

To illustrate this procedure, suppose for simplicity that the only variable affecting a firm's quit rate besides its wage rate is the average age of its workforce. With other factors kept constant, older workers are less likely to quit their jobs, for a number of reasons (as workers grow older, ties to friends, neighbors, and coworkers become stronger, and the psychological costs involved in changing jobs—which often requires a geographic move— grow larger). To capture the effects of both wage rates and age, we assume that a firm's quit rate is given by

$$Q_i = \alpha'_0 + \alpha'_1 W_i + \alpha'_2 A_i + \varepsilon_i \qquad (1A.4)$$

A_i is a variable representing the age of firm *i*'s workers. Although A_i could be measured as the average age of the workforce, or as the percentage of the firm's workers older than some age level, for expositional convenience, we have defined it as a *dichotomous variable*. A_i is equal to 1 if the average age of firm i's workforce is greater than 40, and it is equal to 0 otherwise. Theory suggests that α'_2 is negative, which means that whatever values of α'_0, α'_1, and W_i pertain (while keeping all other facts constant), firms with workforces having an average age above 40 years should have lower quit rates than firms with workforces having an average age equal to or below age 40.

The parameters of equation (1A.4)—that is, the values of α'_0, α'_1, and α'_2—can be estimated by using *multiple regression analysis*, a method that is analogous to the one described earlier. This method finds the values of the parameters that define the best straight-line relationship between the dependent variable and the set of independent variables. Each parameter tells us the effect on the dependent variable of a one-unit change in the corresponding independent variable, *holding the other independent variables constant*. Thus, the estimate of α'_1 tells us the estimated effect on the quit rate (Q) of a one-unit change in the wage rate (W), holding the age of a firm's workforce (A) constant.

The Problem of Omitted Variables

If we use a univariate regression model in a situation calling for a multiple regression model—that is, if we leave out an important independent variable—our results may suffer from *omitted variables bias*. We illustrate this bias because it is an important pitfall in hypothesis testing and because it illustrates the need to use economic theory to guide empirical testing.

To simplify our example, we assume that we know the true values of α'_0, α'_1, and α'_2 in equation (1A.4) and that this model has no random error term (each ε_i is 0). Specifically, we assume that

$$Q_i = 50 - 1.25\,W_i - 10A_i \tag{1A.5}$$

Thus, at any level of wages, a firm's quit rate will be 10 percent lower if the average age of its workforce exceeds 40 than it will be if the average age is less than or equal to 40.

Figure 1A.2 graphically illustrates this assumed relationship between quit rates, wage rates, and workforce average age. For all firms that employ workers whose average age is less than or equal to 40, A_i equals 0 and thus their quit rates are given by the line Z_0Z_0. For all firms that employ workers whose average age is greater than 40, A_i equals 1 and thus their quit rates are given by the line Z_1Z_1. The quit-rate schedule for the latter set of firms is 10 percent below the one for the former set. Both schedules indicate, however, that a \$1 increase in a firm's average hourly wage will reduce its annual quit rate by 1.25 percent (i.e., both lines have the same slope).

Now, suppose that a researcher were to estimate the relationship between quit rates and wage rates but ignored the fact that the average age of a firm's workers also affects the quit rate. That is, suppose that they were to omit a measure of age and estimate the following equation:

$$Q_i = a_0 + \alpha_1 W_i + \varepsilon_i \tag{1A.6}$$

How the estimated value of α_1 corresponds to the true slope of the wage–quit schedule, which we have *assumed* to be -1.25, is crucial.

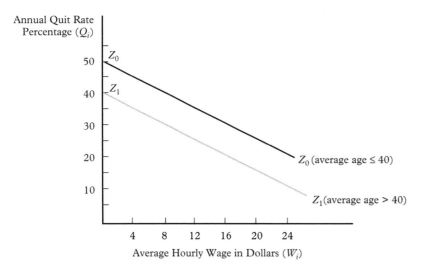

Figure 1A.2 True Relationships Between Wages and Quit Rates (Equation 1A.5)

The answer depends heavily on how average wages and the average age of employees vary across firms. Table 1A.2 lists combinations of quit rates and wages for three hypothetical firms that employed older workers (average age greater than 40) and three hypothetical firms that employed younger workers. Given the wage that each firm paid, the values of its quit rate can be derived directly from equation (1A.5).

The earnings of workers tend to increase as they age.[13] On average, then, firms employing older workers are assumed in the table to have higher wages than firms employing younger workers. The wage–quit combinations for these six firms are indicated by the dots on the lines Z_0Z_0 and Z_1Z_1 in Figure 1A.3,[14] which reproduce the lines in Figure 1A.2.

Table 1A.2 Hypothetical Average-Wage and Quit-Rate Data for Three Firms That Employed Older Workers and Three That Employed Younger Workers

Firm	Employ older workers ($A_i = 1$)		Firm	Employ younger workers ($A_i = 0$)	
	Average hourly wage paid ($)	**Quit rate (%)**		**Average hourly wage paid ($)**	**Quit rate (%)**
k	16	20	p	8	40
l	20	15	q	12	35
m	24	10	r	16	30

When we estimate equation (1A.6) by using these six data points, we obtain the following straight line:

$$Q_i = 57 - 2\,W_i \qquad\qquad\qquad (1A.7)$$
$$ (5.1)\;(0.31)$$

This estimated relationship is denoted by the line XX in Figure 1A.3. The estimate of a_1, which equals -2, implies that every dollar increase in wages reduces the quit rate by 2 percent, yet we know (by assumption) that the actual reduction is 1.25 percent. Our estimated response overstates the sensitivity of the quit rate to wages because the estimated equation ignored the effect that age has on quits.

Put differently, quit rates are lower in high-wage firms *both* because the wages they pay are higher *and* because high-wage firms tend to employ older workers, who are less likely to quit. By ignoring age in the analysis, we mistakenly conclude that quit rates are more sensitive to wage changes than they actually are. Therefore, by omitting from our model an important explanatory variable (age) that both affects quit rates and is associated with wage levels, we have obtained a wrong estimate of the effect of wages on quit rates.

This discussion highlights the "other things held equal" nature of most hypotheses in labor economics. In testing hypotheses, we must control for other factors that are expected to influence the variable of interest. Typically, this is done by specifying that the dependent variable is a function of a *set* of variables. This specification must be guided by economic theory, and one reason for learning economic theory is that it can guide us in testing

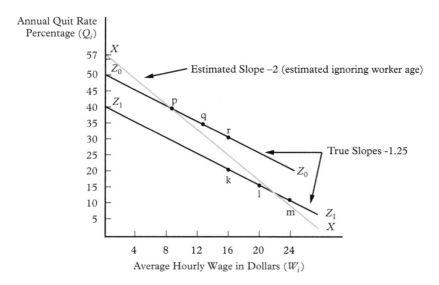

Figure 1A.3 Estimated Relationships Between Wages and Quit Rates by Using Data From Table 1A.2

hypotheses about human behavior. Without a firm grounding in theory, analyses of behavior can easily fall victim to omitted variables bias.

Having said this, we must point out that having data on all variables that could conceivably influence what is being examined is neither possible nor crucial. As emphasized in this chapter, testing economic models involves looking for *average* relationships and ignoring idiosyncratic factors. Two workers at the same age and being paid the same wage rate may exhibit different quit behaviors because, for example, one wants to leave town to get away from a dreadful relative. This idiosyncratic factor is not important for the testing of an economic model of quit rates, because having a relative has neither a predictable effect on quits (some relatives are desirable to be around) nor any correlation with one's wage rate. To repeat, omitted variables bias is a problem only if the omitted variable has an effect on the dependent variable (quit rate) *and* is correlated with an independent variable of interest (wages).

Notes

1. For an article that examines work from a philosophical perspective, see Yoram Weiss, "Work and Leisure: A History of Ideas," *Journal of Labor Economics* 27 (January 2009): 1–20.

2. For articles on rationality and the related issue of preferences, see Gary Becker, "Irrational Behavior and Economic Theory," *Journal of Political Economy* 70 (February 1962): 1–13; Richard H. Thaler, "From Homo Economicus to Homo Sapiens," *Journal of Economic Perspectives* 14 (Winter 2000): 133–141; Stefano DellaVigna, "Psychology and Economics: Evidence from the Field," *Journal of Economic Literature* 47 (June 2009): 315–372; Andrei Schleifer, "Psychologists at the Gate: A Review of Daniel Kahneman's *Thinking Fast and Slow*," *Journal of Economic Literature* 50 (December 2012): 1080–1091.

3. V. Bhaskar, Alan Manning, and Ted To, "Oligopsony and Monopsonistic Competition in Labor Markets," *Journal of Economic Perspectives* 16 (Spring 2002): 158.

4. Pareto efficiency gets its name from the Italian economist Vilfredo Pareto, who, around 1900, insisted that economic science should make normative pronouncements only about unambiguous changes in social welfare. Rejecting the notion that utility can be measured (and therefore compared across individuals), Pareto argued that we can know whether a transaction improves social welfare only on the basis of the testimony or behavior of the affected parties. If they as individuals regard themselves as better off, then the transaction is unambiguously good—even though we are unable to measure how much better off they feel.

5. For a full discussion and analysis of human vulnerabilities in making decisions, see George A. Akerloff and Robert J. Shiller, *Phishing for Phools: The Economics of Manipulation and Deception* (Princeton, NJ:

Princeton University Press, 2015). For an article arguing that Pareto efficiency requires that the parties to a voluntary transaction must properly comprehend the information underlying their choices, see Sandro Ambuehl and Axel Ockenfels, "The Ethics of Incentivizing the Uninformed," *American Economic Review Papers and Proceedings* 107 (May 2017): 91–95.

6. For a lucid discussion of the trade-offs between efficiency and equity, see Arthur Okun, *Equality and Efficiency: The Big Trade-Off* (Washington, DC: Brookings Institution, 1975).

7. Several other types of data are also used frequently by labor economists. One could look, for example, at how a given firm's quit rate and wage rate vary over time. Observations that provide information on a single behavioral unit over a number of time periods are called *time-series* data. Sometimes, labor economists have data on the behavior of a number of observational units (e.g., employers) for a number of time periods; combinations of cross-sectional and time-series data are called *panel* data.

8. An exception occurs in the supply and demand curves that firms face, in which the independent variable, price, is typically shown on the vertical axis.

9. These properties include that on average, the correct answer for a_1 is obtained; the estimates are the most precise possible among a certain class of estimators; and the sum of the positive and negative vertical deviations of the data points from the estimated line will be 0. For a more formal treatment of the method of least squares, see any statistics or econometrics text. A good introduction for a reader with no statistical background is Larry D. Schroeder, David L. Sjoquist, and Paula E. Stephan, *Understanding Regression Analysis: An Introductory Guide* (Beverly Hills, CA: Sage, 1986).

10. Students with access to computer software for estimating regression models can easily verify this result.

11. For example, at a wage of \$40/hour, the estimated quit rate would be 45 - 1.25 × (40), or 10 percent per year.

12. These assumptions are discussed in any econometrics text.

13. Reasons why this occurs are discussed in Chapters 5, 9, and 11.

14. The fact that the dots fall exactly on a straight line is a graphic representation of the assumption that equation (1A.5) has no random error term. If random error is present, the dots would fall around, but not all on, a straight line.

Overview of the Labor Market

Every society—regardless of its wealth, its form of government, or the organization of its economy—must make basic decisions. It must decide what and how much to produce, how to produce it, and how the output shall be distributed. These decisions require finding out what consumers want, what technologies for production are available, and what the skills and preferences of workers are; deciding where to produce; and coordinating all such decisions so that, for example, the millions of people in New York City and the isolated few in an Alaskan fishing village can all buy the milk, bread, meat, vanilla extract, mosquito repellent, and shoe polish that they desire at the grocery store. The process of coordination involves creating incentives so that the right amount of labor and capital will be employed at the right place at the required time.

These decisions can, of course, be made by administrators employed by a centralized bureaucracy. The types of information that this bureaucracy must obtain and process to make the millions of needed decisions wisely, and the number of incentives that it must create to ensure that these decisions are coordinated, are truly extraordinary. It boggles the mind even more to consider the major alternative to centralized decision-making—the decentralized marketplace. Millions of producers striving to make a profit observe the prices that millions of consumers are willing to pay for products and the wages that millions of workers are willing to accept for work. Combining these pieces of information with data on various technologies, they decide where to produce, what to produce, whom to hire, and how much to produce. No one is in charge, and although market imperfections impede progress toward achieving the best allocation of resources, millions of people find jobs that enable them to purchase the items that they desire each year. The production, employment, and consumption decisions are all made and coordinated by price signals arising from the marketplace.

The market that allocates workers to jobs and coordinates employment decisions is the *labor market*. With roughly 160 million workers and almost eight million employers in the United States, thousands of decisions about career choice, hiring, quitting, compensation, and technology must be made and coordinated every day.

Because we believe that students must understand the "big picture" at the outset, this chapter presents an overview of what the labor market does and how it works. After seeing how the buying and selling sides of the labor market are coordinated at an overall (or "market") level, we in subsequent chapters turn to more-detailed analyses of individual behavior on each side.

The Labor Market: Definitions, Facts, and Trends

Every market has buyers and sellers, and the labor market is no exception: The buyers are employers, and the sellers are workers. Some of these participants may not be active at any given moment in the sense of seeking new employees or new jobs, but on any given day, thousands of firms and workers will be "in the market," trying to transact. If, as in the case of doctors or mechanical engineers, buyers and sellers are searching throughout the entire nation for each other, we describe the market as a *national labor market*. If buyers and sellers search only locally, as is often the case for data entry clerks or automobile mechanics, the labor market is a *local* one.

When we speak of a particular "labor market"—for taxi drivers, say— we are using the term *loosely* to refer to the companies trying to hire people to drive their cabs and the people seeking employment as cabdrivers. The efforts of these buyers and sellers of labor to transact and establish an employment relationship constitute the market for cabdrivers. However, neither the employers nor the drivers are confined to this market; both could simultaneously be in other markets as well. An entrepreneur with $100,000 to invest might be thinking of operating either a taxi company or a car wash, depending on the projected revenues and costs of each. A person seeking a cab-driving job might also be trying to find work as an actor. Thus, all the various labor markets that we can define on the basis of industry, occupation, geography, transaction rules, or job characteristics are interrelated to some degree. We speak of these narrowly defined labor markets for the sake of convenience.

Some labor markets, particularly those in which the sellers of labor are represented by a labor union, operate under a formal set of rules that partly govern buyer–seller transactions. In the unionized construction trades, for example, employers must hire from a list of eligible union members. In other unionized markets, the employer has discretion over who gets hired but is constrained by a union–management agreement in such matters as the order in which employees may be laid off, procedures regarding employee complaints, levels of compensation, and promotions. The markets for government jobs and jobs with large nonunion employers also tend to operate under rules that constrain the authority of management and ensure the fair treatment of employees. When a formal set of rules and procedures guides and constrains the employment relationship *within* a firm, an *internal labor market* is said to exist.[1]

The Labor Force and Unemployment

Figure 2.1 highlights some basic definitions concerning labor market status. The term *labor force* refers to all those over 16 years of age who are employed, actively seeking work, or expecting recall from a layoff. Those in the labor force who are not employed for pay are *unemployed* people.[2] People who are not employed and are neither looking for work nor waiting to be recalled from layoff by their employers are not counted as part of the labor force. The total labor force thus consists of employed people and unemployed people.

The number and identities of people in each labor market category are always changing, and as we shall see in Chapter 14, the flows of people from one category to another are sizable. Figure 2.1 suggests four major flows between labor market states:

1. Employed workers become unemployed by *quitting* voluntarily or *being laid off* (being involuntarily separated from the firm, either temporarily or permanently).

2. Unemployed workers obtain employment by *being newly hired* or by *being recalled* to a job from which they were temporarily laid off.

3. Those in the labor force, whether employed or unemployed, can leave the labor force by *retiring* or otherwise deciding against taking or seeking work for pay (*dropping out*).

4. Those who have never worked or looked for a job expand the labor force by *entering* it, while those who have *dropped out* do so by leaving the labor force.

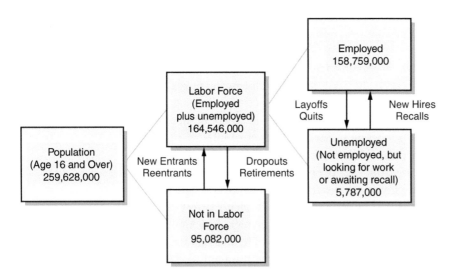

Figure 2.1 Basic Definitions Concerning Labor Market Status

Source: Labor Force Status of the U.S. Adult Civilian Population, February 2020 (seasonally adjusted)

Table 2.1 Labor Force Participation Rates by Gender, 1950–2020

Year	Total (%)	Men (%)	Women (%)
1950	59.9	86.8	33.9
1960	60.2	84.0	37.8
1970	61.3	80.6	43.4
1980	64.2	77.9	51.6
1990	66.5	76.4	57.5
2000	67.2	74.7	60.2
2010 (February)	64.8	71.0	58.9
2020 (February)	63.4	69.3	57.8

Sources: 1950–1980: U.S. President, *Employment and Training Report of the President* (Washington, DC: U.S. Government Printing Office), transmitted to the Congress 1981, Table A-1

1990: U.S. Bureau of Labor Statistics, *Employment and Earnings* 45 (February 1998), Tables A-1 and A-2

2000: U.S. Bureau of Labor Statistics, *Employment Situation* (News Release, October 2001), Table A-1

2010 and 2020: U.S. Bureau of Labor Statistics, *Employment Situation*, Table A-1

Data are available online at www.bls.gov.

In February 2020, over 164 million people were in the labor force, representing 63 percent of the entire population over age 16. An overall *labor force participation rate* (labor force divided by population) of 63 percent is higher than the rates of about 60 percent that prevailed before the 1980s but—as is shown in Table 2.1—lower than the rate in 2000. Underlying changes over time in the overall labor force participation rate are a continued decline in the participation rate for men and a dramatic rise in the participation rate for women before 2000, with a decline since then. These trends and their causes will be discussed in detail in Chapters 6 and 7.

The ratio of those unemployed to those in the labor force is the *unemployment rate*. While this rate is crude and has several imperfections, it is the most widely cited measure of labor market conditions. When the unemployment rate is below 5 percent in the United States, the labor market is considered *tight*, indicating that jobs in general are plentiful and hard for employers to fill, and that most of those who are unemployed will find other work quickly. When the unemployment rate is higher—say, 7 percent or above—the labor market is described as *loose*, in the sense that workers are abundant and jobs are relatively easy for employers to fill. To say that the labor market as a whole is loose, however, does not imply that no shortages can be found anywhere; to say that it is tight can still mean that in some occupations or places, the number of those seeking work exceeds the number of jobs available at the prevailing wage.

Figure 2.2 Unemployment Rates for the Civilian Labor Force, 1947–2019

Figure 2.2 shows the overall unemployment in the seven decades since the end of World War II (data displayed graphically in Figure 2.2 are contained in a table inside the front cover). The data indicate that through the 1960s, the unemployment rate was usually in the range of 3.5 percent to 5.5 percent, twice going up to around 6.8 percent. In the 1970s, 1980s, and early 1990s, the unemployment rate almost never went below 5.5 percent, and it went to over 9.5 percent in the early 1980s. The rate was below 5 percent in 7 of the 11 years from 1997 through 2007, before rising to over 9 percent during the recession starting in 2008. From 2010 until 2019, the unemployment fell every year, from a high of 9.6 percent in 2010 to 3.7 percent in 2019. (As explained in Example 2.1, the unemployment rate jumped dramatically in March and April 2020, when states required most employees to stay at home to stop the spread of the novel coronavirus and the disease that it causes, COVID-19.) In Chapter 14, we discuss various issues related to unemployment and its measurement.

EXAMPLE 2.1

The Unemployment Consequences of the Sudden COVID-19 Lockdown in March 2020

In late 2019, the world began to suffer from the spread of COVID-19, a disease caused by novel coronavirus for which there was no vaccine. By March 2020, cases of COVID-19 were spreading so quickly in the United States that state governments took abrupt actions to limit the spread of the disease by keeping most people (except for "essential workers") at home. Schools and government offices were required to close, and states ordered employers producing "nonessential" goods and services to send their workers home. While the production and sale of food and pharmaceuticals were permitted, restaurants and stores were closed to in-person sales, and most manufacturing and construction activity was halted. People avoided using public transportation (as many of those who remained employed worked from home) and canceled business and vacation travel.

This sudden "lockdown" was designed to slow the spread of the virus, and in its strictest form, it lasted until late May or early June of 2020 in most places in the United States. The overall unemployment rate in the United States increased dramatically, from 3.8 percent in February to 14.4 percent (the highest monthly rate since the Great Depression in the 1930s) in April.

The increases in unemployment, however, were different in that they depended on one's occupation. Office support workers, many of whom can work remotely, went from an unemployment rate of 3.3 percent to 12.7 percent; sales workers, who often deal face to face with customers, experienced a rise from 4.2 to 16.2 percent.

Among those who engage in services, such professionals as lawyers and architects can often work largely from home, and this group of highly-skilled workers had an increase in unemployment from 1.8 to 8.8 percent. On the contrary, low-skilled service providers (those who park cars, tend restaurants, clean hotel rooms, and the like) saw their unemployment rates rise from 4.6 to 23.6 percent.

Source: U.S. Department of Labor, Bureau of Labor Statistics, *Employment Situation*, Data Retrieval: Labor Force Statistics (CPS), Table A-23. Data available online at www.bls.gov

Industries and Occupations: Adapting to Change

As we pointed out earlier, the labor market is the mechanism through which workers and jobs are matched. Over the past half century, the number of some kinds of jobs has expanded and the number of others has contracted. Both workers and employers have had to adapt to these changes in response to signals provided by the labor market. The labor market changes occurring in a dynamic economy are sizable; for example, in the summer of 2019, 7.4 million U.S. jobs with private employers (5.8 percent of all workers in the private sector) ended because establishments either contracted or closed, and another 7.4 million jobs were created in expanding or newly opening establishments.[3]

An examination of the industrial distribution of employment from 1954 to 2019 reveals the kinds of changes that the labor market has had to facilitate. Figure 2.3, which graphs data presented in a table inside the front cover, discloses a major shift: Employment in goods-producing industries (largely manufacturing) has fallen as a share of total nonfarm employment, whereas private sector services have experienced dramatic growth. Thus, whereas a smaller share of the U.S. labor force is working in factories, job opportunities with private employers have expanded in wholesale and retail trade, education and healthcare, professional and business services, leisure

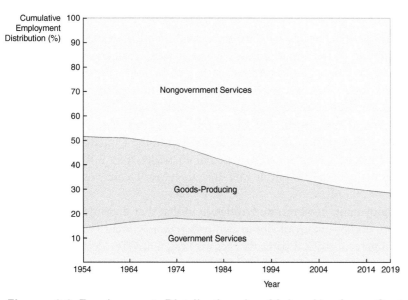

Figure 2.3 Employment Distribution by Major Nonfarm Sector, 1954–2019 (detailed data in table inside front cover)

and hospitality activities, finance, and information services. Government employment as a share of the total has fluctuated in a relatively narrow range over the period.

The combination of shifts in the industrial distribution of jobs and changes in the production technology in each sector has also required that workers acquire new skills and work in new jobs. Since 1983, for example, the share of U.S. workers in managerial and professional jobs rose from 23 percent to 40 percent, the share in lower-level service jobs rose from 14 percent to over 17 percent, and the share in administrative support, sales, and factory jobs fell from 63 percent to 43 percent.[4]

In recent years, researchers have also begun to wonder whether the number of "contingent" workers—that is, workers who in their main job work as independent contractors or supply their labor to "temporary help" firms that then "rent" their services (when needed) to other employers—is growing. Sometimes called members of the gig economy, approximately 10 percent of U.S. workers are in this "contingent" category—in that they do not have a traditional relationship with an employer or a predictable work schedule or set of yearly hours of work. Recent studies do not make clear whether contingent workers are a growing fraction of the workforce.[5]

The Earnings of Labor

The actions of buyers and sellers in the labor market serve both to allocate and to set prices for various kinds of labor. From a social perspective, these prices act as signals or incentives in the allocation process—a process that relies primarily on individual and voluntary decisions. From the workers' point of view, the price of labor is important in determining income—and hence purchasing power.

Nominal and Real Wages   The *wage rate* is the price of labor per working hour.[6] The *nominal wage* is what workers get paid per hour in a given currency; nominal wages are most useful in comparing the pay of various workers at a given time. *Real wages*, nominal wages divided by some measure of prices, suggest how much can be purchased with workers' nominal wages. For example, if a worker earns $64 a day and a pair of shoes cost $32, we could say the worker earns the equivalent of two pairs of shoes a day (real wage = $64 ÷ $32 = 2).

Calculations of real wages are especially useful in comparing the purchasing power of workers' earnings over a period of time when both nominal wages and product prices are changing. For example, suppose that we were interested in trying to determine what happened to the real wages of U.S. production and nonsupervisory workers over the period from 1980 to 2019. We can note from Table 2.2 that the average hourly earnings of these workers in the private sector were $6.84 in 1980, $10.20 in 1990, and $23.48 in 2019; thus, nominal wage rates were clearly rising over this period. However, the prices that such workers had to pay for the items they bought were also rising over this period, so a method of accounting for price inflation must be used in calculating real wages.

The most widely used measure for comparing the prices consumers face over several years is a consumer price index (CPI). Generally speaking, this index is derived by determining what a fixed bundle of consumer goods and services (including food, housing, clothing, transportation, medical care, and entertainment) costs each year for the urban consumer. The cost of this bundle in the base period is then set to equal 100, and the index numbers for all other years are set proportionately to this base period. For example, if the bundle's average cost over the 1982–1984 period is considered the base, then the average value of the index over this period is set to 100, and if the bundle were to cost twice as much in 2006, then the index for 2006 would be set to 200. From the second line in Table 2.2, we can see that with a 1982–1984 base, the CPI was 82.4 in 1980 and 255.7 in 2019—implying that prices had more than tripled (255.7/82.4 = 3.1) over that period. Put differently, a dollar in 2019 appears to have bought about one-third as much as a 1980 dollar.

We can use information from the first two rows of Table 2.2 to put the average hourly earnings for each year into 2019 dollars by multiplying each year's nominal wage rate by the price increase between that year and 2019. Because prices rose 3.103 times between 1980 and 2019, $6.84 in 1980 was equivalent to $21.22 in 2019.

The CPI   Our calculations in Table 2.2 suggest that real wages for U.S. production and nonsupervisory workers were almost the same in 2000 as they were in 1980 (having fallen during the 1980s), but rose by almost 13 percent from 2000 to 2019. A lively debate exists, however, about whether real-wage calculations based on the CPI are accurate indicators of changes in the purchasing power of an hour of work for the ordinary American. The issues are technical and beyond the scope of this text, but they

Table 2.2 Nominal and Real Hourly Earnings, U.S. Nonsupervisory Workers in the Private Sector, 1980–2019 (U.S. dollars)

	1980	1990	2000	2010	2019
Average hourly earnings (current dollars)	$6.84	$10.20	$14.02	$19.05	$23.48
Consumer Price Index CPI, using 1982–1984 as a base	82.4	130.7	172.2	218.1	255.7
Average hourly earnings, 2019 dollars (using CPI)	$21.22	$19.96	$20.82	$22.33	$23.48
Average hourly earnings, 2019 dollars (using CPI inflation less 0.9 percent per year)	$14.79	$15.33	$17.52	$20.60	$23.48

Sources: U.S. President, *Economic Report of the President* (Washington, DC: U.S. Government Printing Office, 2020), Table B30; and U.S. Department of Labor, Bureau of Labor Statistics, *Archived Consumer Price Index Supplemental Files*, Historical CPI-U (May 2020), at www.bls.gov/cpi/supplemental-files

center on two problems associated with using a fixed bundle of goods and services to compare prices from year to year.

One problem is that consumers *change* the bundle of goods and services they actually buy over time, partly in response to changes in prices. If the price of beef rises, for example, consumers may eat more chicken; pricing a fixed bundle may thus understate the purchasing power of current dollars, because it assumes that consumers still purchase the former quantities of beef. For this reason, the bundles used for pricing purposes are updated periodically.

The more difficult issue involves the *quality* of goods and services. Suppose that hospital costs rise by 50 percent over a five-year period, but at the same time, new diagnostic equipment and surgical techniques are perfected. Some of the increased price of hospitalization, then, reflects the availability of new services—or quality improvements in previously provided ones—rather than reductions in the purchasing power of a dollar. The problem is that we have not yet found a satisfactory method for feasibly separating the effects of changes in quality.

After considering these problems, some economists believe that the CPI has overstated inflation by as much as 0.9 percentage points per year.[7] Although not everyone agrees that inflation is overstated by this much, we should recalculate real-wage changes by supposing that it is. Inflation, as measured by the CPI, averaged 1.77 percent per year from 2010 to 2019, and in Table 2.2, we therefore estimated that it would take $22.33 in 2019 to buy what $19.05 could purchase nine years earlier. Comparing $22.33 with what was actually paid in 2019—$23.48—we conclude that real wages had risen by 5.15 percent from 2010 to 2019. If the true decline in purchasing power were instead only 0.87 percent per year during that period, then it would have taken a wage of only $20.60 in 2019 to match the purchasing power of $19.05 in 2010. Because workers were actually paid $23.48 in 2019, if true inflation was 0.9 percentage points below that indicated by the CPI, then real wages rose by 13.98 percent (not just 5.15 percent) over that period. We make similar adjustments in the calculation of real wages for the other decades shown in Table 2.2; doing so suggests, for example, that real wages rose slightly, rather than fell, from 1980 to 1990. Thus, estimated changes in real wage rates are sensitive to the magnitude of adjustments in the CPI that many economists think should be made. (Example 2.2 provides a discussion of related problems in calculating real wages and provides a clever solution to them.)

EXAMPLE 2.2

Real Wages Across Countries and Time: Big Macs per Hour Worked

Real wage rates are calculated by dividing the nominal wage rate by some measure of consumer prices. Because measures of the real wage are intended to indicate how many goods or services can be purchased by working one hour, such measures are relied on to reflect differences in living standards across countries or across time. Three major difficulties, however, hinder generating useful measures of the real wage.

First, we want to measure nominal wages (the numerator) to reflect the wages of workers with comparable skill levels. Comparing real wages of auto mechanics with bicycle repairers is of little use. Second, the prices used in the denominator of our real wage calculation should relate to goods or services of comparable quality. For example, if we try to compare, across countries, how many pairs of shoes an hour of work buys, then we face the problem that shoes in Italy and shoes in Afghanistan could be of different quality.

Third, if we use a price index (such as the CPI) in our denominator, we are confronted with the fact that the basket of goods and services on which the index is measured varies over time and across countries. For example, when the basket of goods (starches, meats, tea, sugar, cloth, and so forth) purchased by the typical Londoner in 1704 was used to compare real wages in London, England, and Canton, China, the real wage was higher in London; however, when the basket of the same goods purchased by the Cantonese person was used, the real wage was higher in Canton.

A clever measure of real wages that avoids the problems noted earlier is the "Big Mac per hour of work" (BMPH) index—or how many Big Macs a staff member at a McDonald's restaurant can purchase with wages from an hour of work. The numerator of BMPH contains the wages for jobs that are completely comparable across time and place; operations at McDonald's restaurants are standardized through a lengthy operating manual that covers all aspects of food preparation and delivery. The denominator of the index contains the price of a product (a Big Mac) that is also standardized across countries and time. Thus, BMPH offers a true comparison of purchasing power (albeit of a limited good) across time and place.

What does the BMPH tell us? In the United States, for example, BMPH was 2.41 in 2007; that is, a McDonald's staff member was able to purchase 2.41 Big Macs with wages from an hour of work. In contrast, BMPH was 3.09 in Japan, 2.23 in Western Europe, 2.19 in Canada, 1.19 in Russia, 0.57 in China, and 0.35 in India. Comparing BMPH over time, however, indicates that from 2000 to 2007, the index fell 7–9 percent in the United States and Canada but rose 50–60 percent in China and India and 150 percent in Russia. From 2007 to 2011, BMPH continued to rise in Russia and China, while it fell in the other places.

Source: Orley Ashenfelter, "Comparing Real Wage Rates," *American Economic Review* 102 (April 2012): 617–642

Wages, Earnings, Compensation, and Income   We often apply the term *wages* to payments received by workers who are paid on a salaried basis (e.g., monthly) rather than on an hourly basis. The term is used this way merely for convenience and is of no consequence for most purposes. However, we schematically distinguish between wages, earnings, and income, as in Figure 2.4. The term *wages* refers to the payment for a *unit* of time, whereas *earnings* refers to wages multiplied by the number of time units (typically hours) worked. Thus, earnings depend on both wages and the length of time that the employee works.

Both wages and earnings are normally defined and measured in terms of direct monetary payments to employees (before taxes for which the employee is liable). *Total compensation*, on the other hand, consists of earnings plus *employee benefits*—benefits that are either payments in kind or deferred. Examples of *payments in kind* are employer-provided healthcare and health insurance, wherein the employee receives a service or an insurance policy

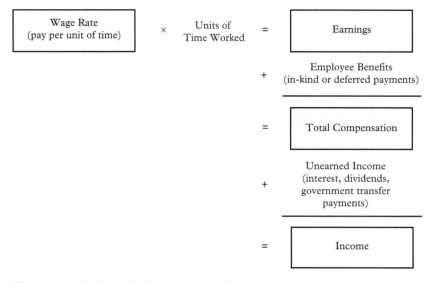

Figure 2.4 Relationships Between Wages, Earnings, Compensation, and Income

rather than money. Paid vacation time is also in this category, since employees are given days off instead of cash:[8]

Deferred payments can take the form of employer-financed retirement benefits, including Social Security taxes, for which employers set aside money now that enables their employees to receive pensions later.

Income—the total command over resources of a person or family during some time period (usually a year)—includes earnings, benefits, and *unearned income*, which includes dividends or interest received on investments and transfer payments received from the government in the form of food stamps, welfare payments, unemployment compensation, and the like.

How the Labor Market Works

As shown diagrammatically in Figure 2.5, the labor market is one of three markets in which firms must successfully operate if they are to survive; the other two are the capital market and the product market. The labor and capital markets are the major ones in which firms' inputs are purchased, and the product market is the one in which output is sold. In reality, of course, a firm may deal in many labor, capital, or product markets simultaneously.

Studying the labor market begins and ends with an analysis of the demand for and supply of labor. On the demand side of the labor market are employers, whose decisions about the hiring of labor are influenced by conditions in all three markets. On the supply side of the labor market are workers and potential workers, whose decisions about where (and whether) to work must consider their other options for how to spend time.

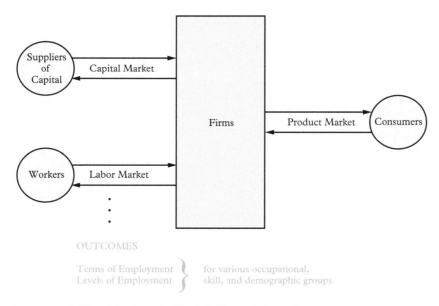

Figure 2.5 **The Markets in Which Firms Must Operate**

Remember that the major labor market outcomes are related to the following:

1. the *terms of employment* (e.g., wages, compensation levels, working conditions)
2. the *levels of employment*

In analyzing both these outcomes, one must usually differentiate among the various occupational, skill, or demographic groups that make up the overall labor market. Any labor market outcome is always affected, to one degree or another, by the forces of both demand and supply. To paraphrase economist Alfred Marshall, it takes both demand and supply to determine economic outcomes, just as it takes both blades of a pair of scissors to cut cloth.

In this chapter, we present the basic outlines and broadest implications of the simplest economic model of the labor market. In later chapters, we add some complexities to this basic model and explain assumptions and implications more fully. However, the simple model of demand and supply presented here offers some insights into labor market behavior that can be useful in the formulation of social policy. Every piece of analysis in this text is an extension or modification of the basic model presented in this chapter.

The Demand for Labor

Firms combine various factors of production—mainly capital and labor—to produce goods or services that are sold in a product market. Their total output and how they combine labor and capital depend on three forces: product demand, the amount of labor and capital that they can acquire at given prices, and the choice of technologies available to them. When we study the demand for labor, we are interested in finding out how the number of workers employed by a firm or set of firms is affected by changes in one or more of these three forces. To simplify the discussion, we study one change at a time while holding other forces constant.

Wage Changes   How does the number of employees (or total labor hours) demanded vary when wages change? Suppose, for example, that we could vary the wages facing a certain industry over a long period of time but keep the technology available, the conditions under which capital is supplied, and the relationship between product price and product demand unchanged. What would happen to the quantity of labor demanded if the wage rate were *increased*?

First, higher wages imply higher costs and, usually, higher product prices. Because consumers respond to higher prices by buying less, employers tend to reduce their levels of output and employment (other things being equal). This decline in employment is called a *scale effect*—the effect on desired employment of a smaller scale of production.

Second, as wages increase (assuming the price of capital does not change, at least initially), employers have incentives to cut costs by adopting a

technology that relies more on capital and less on labor. Desired employment then falls because of a shift toward a more *capital-intensive* mode of
production. This second effect is termed a *substitution effect*, because as
wages rise, capital is *substituted* for labor in the production process.

The effects of various wages on employment levels might be summarized
in a table showing the labor demanded at each wage level. Table 2.3 illustrates such a *demand schedule*. The relationship between wages and employment tabulated in Table 2.3 could be graphed as a *demand curve*. Figure 2.6
shows the demand curve generated by the data in Table 2.3. Note that
the curve has a negative slope, indicating that as wages rise, less labor is
demanded. (Note also that we follow convention in economics by placing
the wage rate on the *vertical* axis despite its being an *independent* variable
in the context of labor demand by a firm.) A demand curve for labor tells
us how the desired level of employment, measured in either labor hours or
number of employees, varies with changes in the price of labor when the
other forces affecting demand are held constant.

Changes in Other Forces Affecting Demand What happens
to labor demand when one of the forces other than the wage rate changes?

First, suppose that *demand for the product* of a particular industry were
to increase, so that at any output price, more of the goods or services in
question could be sold. Suppose in this case that technology and the conditions under which capital and labor are made available to the industry do
not change. Output levels would clearly rise as firms in the industry sought
to maximize profits, and this *scale effect* (or *output effect*) would increase the
demand for labor at any given wage rate. (As long as the relative prices of
capital and labor remain unchanged, no *substitution effect* occurs.)

How would this change in the demand for labor be illustrated by using
a demand curve? Since the technology available and the conditions under
which capital and labor are supplied have remained constant, this change
in product demand would increase the labor desired at any wage level that
might prevail. In other words, the entire labor demand curve *shifts* to the

Table 2.3 Labor Demand Schedule for a Hypothetical Industry

Wage rate ($)	Desired employment level
6.00	250
8.00	190
10.00	160
12.00	130
14.00	100
16.00	70

Note: Employment levels can be measured in number of employees or
number of labor hours demanded. We have chosen here to use number of
employees.

Figure 2.6 Labor Demand Curve (Based on Data in Table 2.3)

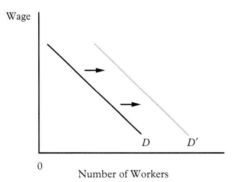

Figure 2.7 Shift in Demand for Labor because of an Increase in Product Demand

right. This rightward shift, shown as a movement from *D* to *D′* in Figure 2.7, indicates that at every possible wage rate, the number of workers demanded has increased.

Second, consider what would happen if the product demand schedule, technology, and labor supply conditions were to remain unchanged but *the supply of capital* changed so that capital prices fell to 50 percent of their prior level. How would this change affect the demand for labor?

Our method of analyzing the effects on labor demand from a change in the price of *another* productive input is familiar: We must consider the scale and substitution effects. First, when capital prices decline, the costs of producing tend to decline. Reduced costs stimulate increases in production, and these increases tend to raise the level of desired employment at any given wage. The scale effect of a fall in capital prices thus tends to increase the demand for labor at each wage level.

The second effect of a fall in capital prices would be a substitution effect, whereby firms adopt more-capital-intensive technologies in response to cheaper capital. Such firms would substitute capital for labor and would use less labor to produce a given amount of output than before. With less labor

Figure 2.8 Possible Shifts in Demand for Labor because of a Fall in Capital Prices

being desired at each wage rate and output level, the labor demand curve tends to shift to the left.

A fall in capital prices, then, generates *two opposing effects* on the demand for labor. The scale effect pushes the labor demand curve rightward, while the substitution effect pushes it to the left. As emphasized by Figure 2.8, either effect could dominate. Thus, economic theory does not yield a clear-cut prediction about how a fall in capital prices would affect the demand for labor. (A *rise* in capital prices would generate the same overall ambiguity of effect on the demand for labor, where the scale effect pushes the labor demand curve leftward and the substitution effect pushes it rightward.)

The hypothesized changes in product demand and capital supply just discussed have tended to *shift* the demand curve for labor. We distinguish between a *shift* in a demand curve and *movement along* a curve. A labor demand curve graphically shows the *labor desired* as a function of the *wage rate*. When the *wage* changes and other forces are held unchanged, one *moves along* the curve. However, when one of the *other forces* changes, the labor demand curve *shifts*. Unlike wages, these forces are not directly shown when the demand curve for labor is drawn. Thus, when *they* change, a different relationship between wages and desired employment prevails, and this shows up as a shift in the demand curve.

Market, Industry, and Firm Demand   The demand for labor can be analyzed on three levels:

1. To analyze the demand for labor *by a particular firm*, we would examine how an increase in the wage of, say, machinists would affect their employment by a particular aircraft manufacturer.

2. To analyze the effects of this wage increase on the employment of machinists *in the entire aircraft industry*, we would use an industry demand curve.

3. Finally, to see how the wage increase would affect the *entire labor market* for machinists in all industries in which they are used, we would use a market demand curve.

We shall see in Chapters 3 and 4 that firm, industry, and market labor demand curves vary in *shape* to some extent because *scale effects* and *substitution effects* have different strengths at each level. However, the scale and substitution effects of a wage change work in the same direction at each level, such that firm, industry, and market demand curves generally *slope downward*.

Long Term Versus Short Term   We can also distinguish between *long-run* and *short-run* labor demand curves. Over short periods of time, employers find difficult substituting capital for labor (or vice versa), and customers may not change their product demand much in response to a price increase. Fully adjusting for consumption and production behavior takes *time*. Over longer periods of time, of course, responses to changes in wages or other forces affecting the demand for labor are larger and completer.

The Supply of Labor

Having examined a simple model of behavior on the buyer (or demand) side of the labor market, we now turn to the seller (or supply) side of the market. For the purposes of this chapter, we assume that workers have already decided to work and that the question facing them is what occupation and what employer to choose.

Market Supply   To first consider the supply of labor to the entire market (as opposed to the supply to a particular firm), suppose that the market that we are considering is the one for legal assistants (or paralegals). How will supply respond to changes in the wages that paralegals might receive?

If the salaries and wages in *other* occupations are held constant and the wages of paralegals rise, we would expect to find more people wanting to become paralegals. For example, suppose that each of 100 people in a high school graduating class has the option of becoming an insurance agent or a paralegal. Some of these 100 people will prefer to be insurance agents even if paralegals are better paid, because they like the challenge and sociability of selling. Some would want to be paralegals even if the pay were comparatively poor, because they hate the pressures of selling. Many, however, could see themselves doing either job; for them, the compensation in each occupation would be a major factor in their decision.

Thus, the supply of labor to a particular market is positively related to the wage rate prevailing in that market, holding other wages constant. That is, if the wages of insurance agents are held constant and the wages of paralegals rise, more people will want to become paralegals because of the relative improvement in compensation (as shown graphically in Figure 2.9).

As with demand curves, each supply curve is drawn with other prices and wages held constant. If one or more of these other prices or wages were to change, it would cause the supply curve to *shift*. As the salaries of insurance agents *rise*, some people will change their minds about becoming paralegals and choose to become insurance agents. In graphical terms (see Figure 2.10), increases in the salaries of insurance agents would cause the supply curve of paralegals to shift to the left.

Figure 2.9 Market Supply Curve for Paralegals

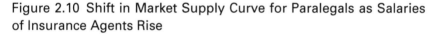

Figure 2.10 Shift in Market Supply Curve for Paralegals as Salaries of Insurance Agents Rise

Supply to Firms Having decided to become a paralegal, an individual would then have to decide which offer of employment to accept. If all employers were offering paralegal jobs that were more or less alike, the choice would be based entirely on compensation. Any firm unwise enough to attempt paying a wage below what others are paying would find it could not attract any employees (or at least none of the caliber that it wanted). Conversely, no firm would be foolish enough to pay more than the going wage, because it would be paying more than it would have to pay to attract a suitable number and quality of employees. Supply curves to a *firm*, then, are *horizontal*, as shown in Figure 2.11, indicating that at the going wage, a firm could get all the paralegals that it needs. If the paralegal wage paid by others in the market is W_0, then the firm's labor supply curve is S_0; if the wage falls to W_1, the firm's labor supply curve becomes S_1.

The difference in slope between the market supply curve and the supply curve to a firm is directly related to the type of choice facing workers. In deciding whether to *enter* the paralegal labor market, workers must weigh both the compensation *and* the job requirements of alternative options (such as being an insurance agent). If wages for paralegals were to fall, not everyone would withdraw from that market, because the jobs of insurance agent and paralegal are not perfect substitutes. Some people would remain paralegals after a wage decline because they dislike the job requirements of insurance agents.

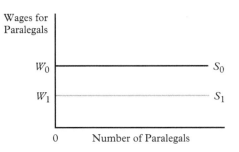

Figure 2.11 Supply of Paralegals to a Firm at Alternative Market Wages

Once the decision to become a paralegal had been made, however, the choice of *which employer* to work for would be a choice among alternatives in which the job requirements were nearly the *same*. Thus, the choice would have to be made on the basis of compensation alone. If a firm were to lower its wage offers below those of other firms, it would lose all its applicants. The horizontal supply curve is, therefore, a reflection of supply decisions made among alternatives that are perfect substitutes for one another.

We have argued that firms wishing to hire paralegals must pay the going wage or lose all applicants. While this may seem unrealistic, it is not a bad proposition with which to start our analysis. If a firm offers jobs *comparable* to those offered by other firms but at a lower level of pay, it might be able to attract a few applicants of the quality it desires because a few people will be unaware of compensation elsewhere. Over time, however, knowledge of the firm's poor pay would become more widespread, and the firm would have to rely solely on less-qualified people to fill its jobs. It could secure quality employees at below-average pay only if it offered *noncomparable* jobs (more pleasant working conditions, longer paid vacations, and so forth). This factor in labor supply is discussed further in Chapter 8. For now, we assume that individual firms, like individual workers, are *wage takers*; that is, the wages that they pay to their workers must be pretty close to the going wage if they face competition in the labor market. Neither individual workers nor firms can set a wage much different from the going wage and still hope to transact. (Exceptions to this elementary proposition are analyzed in Chapter 5.)

The Determination of the Wage

The wage that prevails in a particular labor market is heavily influenced by labor supply and demand, regardless of whether the market involves a labor union or other nonmarket forces. In this section, we analyze how the interplay of supply and demand in the labor market affects wages.

The Market-Clearing Wage   Recall that the market demand curve indicates how many workers employers would want at each wage rate, holding capital prices and the product demand schedule constant. The market supply curve indicates how many workers would enter the market at each wage level, holding the wages in other occupations constant. These curves can be

placed on the same graph to reveal some interesting information, as shown in Figure 2.12.

For example, suppose the market wage were set at W_1. At this low wage, Figure 2.12 indicates that demand *exceeds* supply. Employers would be competing for the few workers in the market, and a shortage of workers would exist. The desire of firms to attract more employees would lead them to increase their wage offers, thus driving up the overall level of wage offers in the market. As wages rose, two things would happen. First, more workers would choose to enter the market and look for jobs (a movement along the supply curve); second, increasing wages would induce employers to seek fewer workers (a movement along the demand curve).

If wages were to rise to W_2, supply would exceed demand. Employers would desire fewer workers than the number available, and not everyone desiring such employment would be able to find jobs, resulting in a surplus of workers. Employers would have long lines of eager applicants for any opening and would find that they could fill their openings with qualified applicants even if they offered lower wages. Furthermore, if they could pay lower wages, they would want to hire more employees. Some employees would be more than happy to accept lower wages if they could just find a job. Others would leave the market and look for work elsewhere as wages fell. Thus, supply and demand would become more equal as wages fell from the level of W_2.

The wage rate at which demand equals supply is the *market-clearing* (equilibrium) wage. At W_e in Figure 2.12, employers can fill the number of openings that they have and all employees who want jobs in this market can find them. At W_e, there is no surplus and no shortage. All parties are satisfied, and no forces would alter the wage. The market is in equilibrium in the sense that the wage will remain at W_e.

The market-clearing wage, W_e, thus becomes the *going wage* that individual employers and employees must face. In other words, wage rates are determined by the market and "announced" to individual market participants. Figure 2.13 graphically depicts *market* supply and demand in panel (a), along with the supply and demand curves for a typical *firm* (firm A) in that market in panel (b). All firms in the market pay a wage of W_e, and the total employment of L equals the sum of employment in each firm.

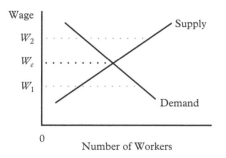

Figure 2.12 Market Demand and Supply

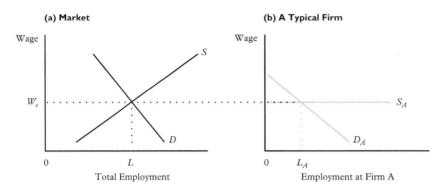

Figure 2.13 Demand and Supply at the Market and Firm Levels

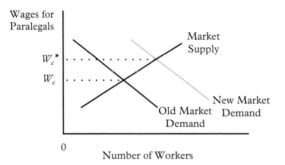

Figure 2.14 New Labor Market Equilibrium After Demand Shifts Right

Disturbing the Equilibrium   What could happen to change the market-clearing wage once it has been reached? Changes could arise from shifts in either the demand curve or the supply curve. Suppose, for example, that the increase in paperwork accompanying the greater government regulation of industry caused firms to demand more paralegal help (at any given wage rate) than before. Graphically, as in Figure 2.14, this greater demand would be represented as a rightward shift of the labor demand curve. If W_e were to persist, there would be a labor shortage in the paralegal market (because demand would exceed supply). This shortage would induce employers to improve their wage offers. Eventually, the paralegal wage would be driven up to W_e^*. Notice that in this case, the equilibrium level of *employment* will also rise.

   The market wage can also increase if the labor supply curve shifts to the left. As shown in Figure 2.15, such a shift creates a labor shortage at the old equilibrium wage of W_e, and as employers scramble to fill their job openings, the market wage is bid up to W_e'. In the case of a leftward-shifting labor supply curve, however, the increased market wage is accompanied by a decrease in the equilibrium level of employment. (See Example 2.3 for an analysis of the labor market effects of the leftward shift in labor supply accompanying the Black Death in 1348–1351.)

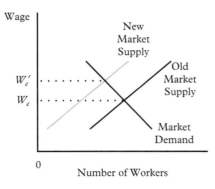

Figure 2.15 New Labor Market Equilibrium After Supply Shifts Left

If a leftward shift in labor supply is accompanied by a rightward shift in labor demand, the market wage can rise dramatically. Such a condition occurred in Egypt during the early 1970s. Lured by wages over six times higher in Saudi Arabia and other oil-rich Arab countries, roughly half of Egypt's construction workers left the country just as a residential building boom in Egypt got under way. The combination of a leftward-shifting labor supply curve and a rightward-shifting labor demand curve drove the real wages of Egyptian construction workers up by over 100 percent in just five years![9] (This notable wage increase was accompanied by a net employment *increase* in Egypt's construction industry. The first review question at the end of this chapter asks you to analyze these events graphically.)

A fall in the market-clearing wage rate would occur if there were increased supply or reduced demand. An increase in supply would be represented by a rightward shift of the supply curve as more people entered the market at each wage (see Figure 2.16). This rightward shift would cause a surplus in the old equilibrium wage (W_e) and lead to behavior that reduced the wage to W_e'' in Figure 2.16. Note that the equilibrium employment level has increased. A decrease (leftward shift) in labor demand would also cause a decrease in the market-clearing wage, although such a shift would be accompanied by a *fall* in employment.

EXAMPLE 2.3

The Black Death and the Wages of Labor

An example of what happens to wages when the supply of labor suddenly shifts occurred when plague—the Black Death—struck England (among other European countries) in 1348–1351. Estimates vary, but historians generally agree that plague killed between 17 percent and 40 percent of the English population in that short period of time. This shocking loss of life had the immediate effect of raising the wages of laborers. As the supply curve shifted to the left, a shortage of workers was created at the old wage levels, and competition among employers for the surviving workers drove the wage level dramatically upward.

Reliable figures are hard to come by, but many believe wages rose by 50–100 percent over the three-year period. A thresher, for example, earning 2½ pence per day in 1348 earned 4½ pence in 1350, and mowers receiving 5 pence per acre in 1348 were receiving 9 pence in 1350. Whether the overall rise in wages was this large or not, clearly a labor shortage and an unprecedented increase in wages occurred. A royal proclamation, commanding lessors to share their scarce workers with neighbors and threatening workers with imprisonment if they refused work at the pre-plague wage, was issued to address this shortage, but it was ignored. The shortage was too severe and market forces were simply too strong for the rise in wages to be thwarted.

The discerning student might wonder at this point about the demand curve for labor. Did it not also shift to the left as the population—and the number of consumers—declined? It did, but this leftward shift was not as pronounced as the leftward shift in supply. While fewer customers were available for labor's output, the customers who remained consumed greater amounts of goods and services per capita than before. The money, gold and silver, and durable goods that had existed before 1348 were divided among many fewer people by 1350, and this rise in per capita wealth was associated with a widespread and dramatic increase in the level of consumption, especially of luxury goods. Thus, the leftward shift in labor demand was dominated by the leftward shift in supply, and the predictable result was a large increase in wages.

Sources: Harry A. Miskimin, *The Economy of Early Renaissance Europe, 1300–1460* (Englewood Cliffs, NJ: Prentice-Hall, 1969); George M. Modlin and Frank T. deVyver, *Development of Economic Society* (Boston: D.C. Heath, 1946); Douglass C. North and Robert Paul Thomas, *The Rise of the Western World* (Cambridge: Cambridge University Press, 1973); Philip Ziegler, *The Black Death* (New York: Harper and Row, 1969)

See Nico Voightländer and Hans-Joachim Voth, "Gifts of Mars: Warfare and Europe's Early Rise to Riches," *Journal of Economic Perspectives* 27 (Fall 2013): 165–186, for a similar analysis of the effects of European wars in the fifteenth to eighteenth centuries

Disequilibrium and Nonmarket Influences That a market-clearing wage exists in theory does not imply that it has been reached—or reached quickly—in practice. Because labor services cannot be separated from the worker, and because labor income is by far the most important source of spending power for most people, the labor market is subject to forces that impede the adjustment of both wages and employment to changes in supply or demand. Some of these barriers to adjustment are themselves the result of economic forces that will be discussed later in the text. For example, changing jobs often requires an employee to invest in new skills (see Chapter 9) or bear costs of moving (Chapter 10). On the employer side of the market, hiring workers can involve an initial investment in searching and training (Chapter 5), while dismissing them or cutting their wages can be perceived as unfair and therefore have consequences for the productivity of those who remain (Chapter 11).

Other barriers to adjustment are rooted in *nonmarket* forces: laws, customs, or institutions constraining the choices of individuals and firms.

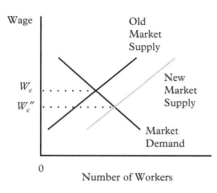

Figure 2.16 New Labor Market Equilibrium After Supply Shifts Right

Although forces keeping wages *below* their market-clearing levels are not unknown (see Example 2.4), nonmarket forces usually serve to keep wages *above* market levels. Minimum-wage laws (discussed in Chapter 4) and unions (Chapter 13) are examples of influences explicitly designed to raise wages beyond those dictated by the market. Likewise, when cutting wages is widely believed to be unfair, laws or customs may arise that prevent wages from falling in markets experiencing leftward shifts in demand or rightward shifts in supply.

People commonly believe that labor markets adjust more quickly when market forces are calling for wages to rise as opposed to pressuring them to fall. If this is so, then those markets observed to be in disequilibrium for long periods will tend to be ones with above-market wages. The existence of above-market wages implies that the supply of labor exceeds the number of jobs being offered (refer to the relative demand and supply at wage W_2 in Figure 2.12); therefore, if enough markets are experiencing above-market wages, the result will be widespread *unemployment*.

EXAMPLE 2.4

Prosecuting Workers Who Leave Their Employers

These days, employees (with the principal exception of those in the military) are generally free to leave their employers for any reason, including the receipt of a superior job offer elsewhere. In nineteenth-century Britain, however, workers would often sign long-term contracts with their employers, and these employers could then prosecute them for breach of contract under the Master and Servant law if they left for better pay or working conditions. These prosecutions served to limit employee choice and mobility, and in periods when the labor demand curve shifted to the right, prosecutions would rise—thus holding down wages. Indeed, when the Master and Servant law was repealed in 1875 and coercion against employee mobility was removed, employers had to respond to rightward shifts in the labor demand curve by raising wages. Wages rose more in counties where prosecutions had been more common.

Source: Suresh Naidu and Noam Yuchtman, "Coercive Contract Enforcement: Law and the Labor Market in Nineteenth Century Industrial Britain," *American Economic Review* 103 (February 2013): 107–144

Applications of the Theory

Although this simple model of how a labor market functions is refined and elaborated on in the following chapters, it can explain many important phenomena, including the issues of when workers are overpaid or underpaid and what explains international differences in unemployment.

Who Is Underpaid and Who Is Overpaid?

We pointed out in Chapter 1 that a fundamental value of normative economics is that, as a society, we should strive to complete all those transactions that are mutually beneficial. Another way of stating this value is to say that we must strive to use our scarce resources as effectively as possible, which implies that output should be produced in the least costly manner so that the most can be obtained from such resources. This goal, combined with the labor market model outlined in this chapter, suggests how we can define what it means to be overpaid.

Above-Market Wages   We claim that workers are *overpaid* if their wages are higher than the market-clearing wage for their job. Because a labor surplus exists for jobs that are overpaid, a wage above market has two implications (see Figure 2.17). First, employers are paying more than necessary to produce their output (they pay W_H instead of W_e); they could cut wages and still find enough qualified workers for their job openings. In fact, if they did cut wages, they could expand output and make their product cheaper and more accessible to consumers. Second, at wage W_H, more workers want jobs than can find them (Y workers want jobs, but only V openings are available). If wages were reduced below W_H a little, more of these disappointed workers could find work. A wage above market thus causes consumer prices to be higher and output to be lower than is possible, and it creates a situation in which not all workers who want the jobs in question can get them.

An interesting example of above-market wages was seen in the labor market of Houston, Texas, in 1988. Bus cleaners working for the Houston Metropolitan Transit Authority received $10.08 per hour, or 70 percent more

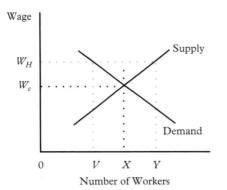

Figure 2.17 Effects of an Above-Market Wage

than the $5.94 received by cleaners working for private bus companies in Houston. One (predictable) result of this overpayment is that the quit rate among Houston's Transit Authority cleaners was only *one-seventh* as great as the average for cleaners nationwide.[10]

To better understand the social losses attendant on overpayment, let us return to the principles of normative economics. Can reducing overpayment create a situation in which the gainers gain more than the losers lose? Suppose in the case of Houston's Transit Authority cleaners that the wage of only *newly hired* cleaners was reduced—to $6.40, say. Current cleaners thus would not lose, but many others who were working elsewhere at $5.94 would jump at the chance to earn a higher wage. Taxpayers, realizing that transit services could now be expanded at lower cost than before, would increase their demand for such services, thus creating jobs for these additional workers. Some workers would gain, while no one lost—and social well-being would clearly be enhanced.[11] The wage reduction, in short, would be *Pareto improving* (see Chapter 1).

Below-Market Wages   We claim that workers are *underpaid* if their wages are below market-clearing levels. At below-market wages, employers have difficulty finding workers to meet the demands of consumers, and a labor shortage thus exists. They also have trouble keeping the workers that they do find. If wages were increased, output would rise and more workers would be attracted to the market. Thus, an increase would benefit the people in society in *both* their consumer and their worker roles. Figure 2.18 shows how a wage increase from W_L to W_e would increase employment from V to X (at the same time wages were rising).

Wages in the U.S. Army illustrate how the market adjusts to below-market wages. Before 1973, when the military draft was eliminated, the government could pursue a policy of paying below-market wages to military recruits, because the resultant gap between supply and demand could be filled by conscription. Not surprisingly, when comparing wages in the late 1970s with those in the past decade of the military draft, we find that the average military cash wages paid to enlisted personnel rose 19 percent more than those of comparable civilian workers.

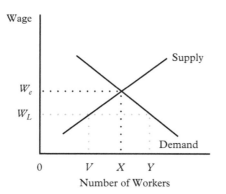

Figure 2.18 Effects of a Below-Equilibrium Wage

Economic Rents   The concepts of underpayment and overpayment involve the *social* issue of producing desired goods and services in the least costly way; therefore, we compared wages paid with the *market-clearing wage*. At the level of *individuals*, however, comparing the wage received in a job with one's *reservation wage*, the wage below which the worker would refuse (or quit) the job in question, is often useful. The amount by which one's wage exceeds one's reservation wage in a particular job is the amount of their *economic rent*.

Consider the labor supply curve to, say, the military. As shown in Figure 2.19, if the military is to hire L_1 people, it must pay W_1 in wages. These relatively low wages will attract to the military those who most enjoy the military culture and are least averse to the risks of combat. If the military is to be somewhat larger and to employ L_2 people, then it must pay a wage of W_2. This higher wage is required to attract those who would have found a military career unattractive at the lower wage. If W_2 turns out to be the wage that equates supply and demand and if the military pays that wage, everyone who would have joined up for less would be receiving an economic rent.

Put differently, the supply curve to an occupation or industry is a schedule of reservation wages that indicates the labor forthcoming at each wage level. The difference between the wage actually paid and workers' reservation wages—the shaded area in Figure 2.19—is the amount of the rent. Because each worker potentially has a different reservation wage, rents may well differ for each worker in the market. In Figure 2.19, the greatest rents are received by those L_0 individuals who would have joined the military even if the wage were only W_0. If W_2 is the market-clearing wage, they collect an economic rent of W_2-W_0.

Why don't employers reduce the wage of each employee down to their reservation level (this is sometimes called perfect price discrimination)? Although capturing employee rents would seem to be lucrative, because by definition it could be done without the workers' quitting, attempting to do so would create resentment, and such a policy would be extremely costly, if

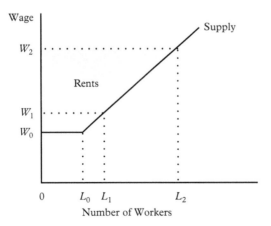

Figure 2.19 Labor Supply to the Military: Different Preferences Imply Different Rents

not impossible, to implement. Employers do not know the true reservation wages of each employee or applicant, and finding it would involve experiments in which the wage offers to each worker either started high and were cut or started low and were raised. This would be costly, and if workers realized that the firm was *experimenting*, they would attempt to disguise their true reservation wages and adopt the strategic behavior associated with bargaining (e.g., bluffing). Therefore, firms usually pay according to the job, one's level of experience or longevity with the employer, and considerations of merit—but not according to preferences.[12]

Unemployment and Responses to Technological Change Across Countries

We noted earlier that labor markets are often influenced by nonmarket forces that keep wages above market-clearing levels. Because these nonmarket forces generally take the form of laws, government programs, customs, or institutions (e.g., labor unions), their strength typically varies across countries. Can we rightly form some conclusions about the countries in which they are most pronounced?

Theory presented in this chapter suggests that if wages are above market-clearing levels, unemployment will result (the number of people seeking work will exceed the number of available jobs). Furthermore, if wages are held above market-clearing levels and the labor demand curve *shifts leftward*, unemployment will rise to even higher levels (you should be able to show this by drawing a graph with an unchanging supply curve, a fixed wage rate, and a leftward-shifting demand curve). Moreover, above-market wages deter the growth of *new* jobs, so wages "stuck" above market-clearing levels can also cause those who suffer a spell of unemployment to remain in that status for a long time. Thus, measures of the incidence and duration of unemployment—which, fortunately, are comparably defined and estimated in several advanced economies—can sometimes be used to infer the relative strength of nonmarket forces across countries. Consider, for example, what happened to unemployment rates in Europe and North America in the 1980s and 1990s.

One phenomenon characterizing the 1980s was an acceleration of technological change, associated primarily with computerization, in the advanced economies of the world. These changes led to a fall in the demand for less-skilled, less-educated, lower-paid workers. In Canada and the United States, the decline in demand for low-skilled workers led to a fall in their real wages throughout the 1980s; despite that, the unemployment rate for less-educated workers rose over that decade—from 7.2 percent to 8.5 percent in the United States and from 6.3 percent to 9.3 percent in Canada.

In the two European countries for which we have data on wages and unemployment by skill level, however, nonmarket forces caused the real wages of low-paid workers to *rise* over the decade, leading to increases in unemployment for less-educated workers that were much more pronounced. In France, real wages among the lowest-paid workers rose 1 percent per year, and its unemployment rate increased from 4.6 percent to 10.7 percent over the decade. In Germany, where the pay of low-wage workers rose an average of 5 percent per year, unemployment rates among these workers went from 4.4 percent to 13.5 percent.[13]

EMPIRICAL STUDY 2.1

PAY LEVELS AND THE SUPPLY OF MILITARY OFFICERS: OBTAINING SAMPLE VARIATION FROM CROSS-SECTION DATA

Economic theory predicts that the supply to a particular occupation is expected to increase when the pay for that occupation increases or when the pay in alternative occupations falls. In the late 1960s, the U.S. government was considering a policy change that eventually resulted in the elimination of the military draft, and it needed to estimate how much military pay would have to rise—relative to civilian pay—to attract the needed number of officers and enlisted personnel without the presence of a draft. Estimating the labor supply curve of, say, officers depends on whether we can obtain an appropriate data set.

Any study of how (independent) variable *X* affects (dependent) variable *Y* requires the researcher's having access to a data set in which both *X* and *Y* show considerable *variation*. Put differently, scientific research into cause and effect requires that we observe how *different* causes produce *different* effects. Researchers who are able to conduct laboratory experiments expose their subjects to different "treatments" and then look for differences in outcomes. Economists are rarely able to conduct experiments, so they must look for data sets in which *X* and *Y* naturally differ across the observations in a sample.[14] If the ratio of military pay to civilian pay is our independent variable (*X*) and if the number of people who decide to join the military as officers is our dependent variable (*Y*), how can we generate a sample in which both variables display enough variation to estimate a relationship?

One way is to use data over a period of 20–30 years ("time series" data), where each year's relative wage and number of new officers represents one observation in the sample. The problem with a time series is that samples are necessarily small (because of the few years for which we have good data). Behavior can also be affected by all kinds of changing conditions or preferences over time (e.g., wars, new occupations both in and out of the military, and changing attitudes of the labor force toward risk), so that with time series data, we also need to control for these time-related changes to be confident that we have isolated the effects of *pay* on labor supply decisions.

Another way to study the effects of relative pay on labor supply is to use cross-section data, which involves collecting observations on pay and labor supply for different people at one point in time. This usually allows for a much larger data set, but it requires that those in the data set be operating in sufficiently different environments that X and Y will actually vary. Within any year, for example, military pay for entry-level officers is the same for everyone, so we can use cross-section data to study military supply decisions only if the *civilian wages* facing sample members can be accurately measured and turn out to vary significantly.

One study done in the late 1960s analyzed enrollment data from 82 reserve officer training corps (ROTC) programs offered by universities in 1963. The supply variable (Y) in this study was measured as the percentage of men at each of the 82 universities enrolled in an army, navy, or air force ROTC program (the military was almost all male at that time). Because military pay facing ROTC graduates at each of the 82 institutions was the same, differences in civilian pay opportunities for recent graduates represented the only pay variable that could be used. It turned out that the average earnings of recent male college graduates from each of the 82 universities were both available and varied enough across the universities to be useful; thus, the variable measuring pay (X) was the average earnings in 1963 of men who graduated from each of the universities in 1958.

Theory leads us to expect that the higher civilian pay was for the graduates of a university, the lower would be its ROTC enrollments. The results indeed estimated a negative and statistically significant relationship between civilian pay and ROTC enrollments.[a] The size of the estimated relationship suggested that where civilian pay was 10 percent higher, ROTC enrollments were 20 percent lower. This finding implies that if military pay were to have risen by 10 percent, holding civilian pay constant, ROTC enrollments would have risen by 20 percent. Clearly, ROTC enrollments were responsive to civilian salaries.

[a] Other independent variables were added to the estimating equation, to account for the fact that the sampled universities offered different mixes of army, navy, and air force ROTC programs. Furthermore, because students in the U.S. South may have had a greater preference for military service at any pay level, the list of independent variables also included a variable indicating whether the university was located in the U.S. South.

Source: Stuart H. Altman and Alan E. Fechter, "The Supply of Military Personnel in the Absence of a Draft," *American Economic Review* 57 (May 1967): 19–31

Review Questions

1. As discussed earlier, in the early 1970s, Egypt experienced a dramatic outflow of construction workers seeking higher wages in Saudi Arabia at

the same time that the demand for their services rose in Egypt. Graphically represent these two shifts of supply and demand, and then use the graph to predict the direction of change in wages and employment in Egypt's construction sector during that period.

2. Analyze the impact of the following changes on wages and employment in a given occupation:

   a. a decrease in the danger of the occupation

   b. an increase in product demand

   c. increased wages in alternative occupations

3. What would happen to the wages and employment levels of engineers if government expenditures on research and development programs were to fall? Show the effect graphically.

4. Suppose that a particular labor market were in market-clearing equilibrium. What could happen to cause the equilibrium wage to fall? Suppose that price levels were rising each year but that money wages were "sticky downward" and never fell. How would real wages in this market adjust?

5. Assume that you have been hired by a company to conduct a salary survey of its arc welders, whom the company suspects are overpaid. Given the company's expressed desire to maximize profits, what definition of *overpaid* would you apply to this situation, and how would you identify whether arc welders are, in fact, overpaid?

6. Ecuador is the world's leading exporter of bananas, which are grown and harvested by a large labor force that includes many children. Assume that Ecuador were to outlaw the use of child labor on banana plantations. Using economic theory in its positive mode, analyze what would happen to employment and wages in the banana farming industry in Ecuador. Use supply and demand curves in your analysis.

7. Unions can raise wages paid to their members in two ways. First, unions can negotiate a wage rate that lies above the market-clearing wage. While management cannot pay below that rate, management does have the right to decide how many workers to hire. Second, construction unions often have agreements that require management to hire only union members, but they also have the power to control entry into the union. Hence, they can raise wages by restricting labor supply.

   a. Graphically depict the first method by using a labor supply and a labor demand curve.

   b. Graphically depict the second method by using a labor supply and a labor demand curve.

8. Assume that the invasion of Iraq increased the desired size of the U.S. military, and assume that potential recruits were reduced by the prospect of facing dangerous, unpleasant wartime conditions. First, analyze how the war affected the supply curve and the demand curve for

military personnel. Second, use your analysis to predict how the war affected the wages and the employment level of military personnel.

9. Suppose that the Occupational Safety and Health Administration were to mandate that all punch presses be fitted with an expensive device to prevent injuries to workers. This device does not improve the efficiency with which punch presses operate. What does this requirement do to the demand curve for labor? Explain.

10. Suppose that we were to observe that employment levels in a certain region suddenly declined as a result of a fall in the region's demand for labor and as a result of wages that are fixed in the short run. If the *new* labor demand curve remains unchanged for a long period and the region's labor supply curve does not shift, will employment in the region likely recover? Explain.

11. In the economic recovery of 2003–2004, job growth in Canada was much faster than job growth in the United States. Please answer the following questions: Generally speaking, how does economic growth affect the demand curve for labor? Assuming that growth does not affect the labor supply curve in either country and assuming that the faster job growth in Canada was accompanied by slower (but positive) wage growth there than in the United States, what would these assumptions tell us about the reasons for the relatively faster job growth in Canada?

12. When COVID-19 initially struck the United States in the spring of 2020, many stores and personal-service establishments shut down almost immediately. Schools went to remote teaching. Consider the occupations of delivery driver for FedEx, schoolteacher, and barber. When the lockdowns began (mandating that all but essential workers stay home), what were the short-term implications for wages and employment of these three occupations, and why?

Problems

1. Suppose that the adult population is 210 million and that 130 million are employed and five million are unemployed. Calculate the unemployment rate and the labor force participation rate.

2. Suppose that the supply curve for schoolteachers is $L_S = 20,000 + 350W$ and that the demand curve for schoolteachers is $L_D = 100,000 - 150W$, where L = the number of teachers and W = the daily wage.

   a. Plot the supply and demand curves.

   b. What are the equilibrium wage and employment levels in this market?

   c. Now suppose that at any given wage, 20,000 more workers are willing to work as schoolteachers. Plot the new supply curve, and find the new wage and employment level. Why doesn't employment grow by 20,000?

3. Have the real average hourly earnings of private sector workers in the United States risen during the past 12 months? Go to the Bureau of

Labor Statistics website (http://bls.gov) to find the numbers needed to answer the question.

4. Suppose that the adult population of a city is 9,823,000 and that 3,340,000 people are not in the labor force and 6,094,000 are employed.

   a. Calculate the number of adults who are in the labor force and the number of adults who are unemployed.

   b. Calculate the labor force participation rate and the unemployment rate.

5. The CPI (with a base of 100 in 1982–1984) rose from 130.7 in 1990 to 201.6 in 2006. The federal minimum wage (nominal hourly wage) in 1990 was $3.80, and it was $5.15 in 2006. Calculate the minimum wage in real (1982–1984) dollars. Did the federal minimum wage increase or decrease in real dollars from 1990 to 2006?

6. Table 2P.6 gives the demand and supply for cashiers in retail stores.

Table 2P.6 Demand and Supply for Cashiers

Wage rate ($)	Number of cashiers demanded	Number of cashiers supplied
6.00	200	70
8.00	180	100
10.00	170	120
12.00	150	150
14.00	130	160
16.00	110	175
18.00	80	190

   a. Plot the supply and demand curves.

   b. What are the equilibrium wage and employment levels in this market?

   c. Suppose that the number of cashiers demanded increases by 30 at every wage rate. Plot the new demand curve. What are the equilibrium wage and employment level now?

7. From the original demand function in problem 6 (see Table 2P.6), how many cashiers would have jobs if the wage paid were $16.00 per hour? Discuss the implications of a $16 wage in the market for cashiers.

Notes

1. An analysis of internal labor markets can be found in Michael L. Wachter and Randall Wright, "The Economics of Internal Labor Markets," *University of Pennsylvania Law Review* 29 (Spring 1990): 240–262.

2. The official definition of *unemployment* for purposes of government statistics includes those who have been laid off by their employers, those who have been fired or have quit and are looking for other work, and those who are just entering or re-entering the labor force but have not found a job yet. The extent of unemployment is estimated from a monthly survey of some 50,000 households called the current population survey (CPS). Interviewers ascertain whether household members are employed, whether they meet one of the aforementioned conditions (in which case they are considered "unemployed"), or whether they are out of the labor force.

3. U.S. Department of Labor, Bureau of Labor Statistics, "Business Employment Dynamics: Third Quarter 2019," News Release USDL 20–0718 (April 29, 2020), www.bls.gov.

4. U.S. Department of Labor, Bureau of Labor Statistics, *Employment and Earnings*: 31 (January 1984), Table 20; *Employment and Earnings Online* (January 2019), Table 10 (at www.bls.gov).

5. Lawrence F. Katz and Alan B. Krueger, "Understanding Trends in Alternative Work Arrangements in the United States" (Working Paper No. 25425, National Bureau of Economic Research, Cambridge, MA, January 2019); Katherine G. Abraham, John Haltiwanger, Kristin Sandusky, and James Spletzer, "The Rise of the Gig Economy: Fact or Fiction?" *AEA Papers and Proceedings* 109 (May 2019): 357–361.

6. In this book, we define *hourly wage* in the way that most workers would if asked to state their "straight-time" wage. It is the money that a worker would lose per hour if they had an unauthorized absence. When wages are defined in this way, a paid holiday becomes an "employee benefit," as we note in the following, because leisure time is granted while pay continues. Thus, a worker paid $200 for 25 hours—20 of which are working hours and five of which are time off—will be said to earn a wage of $8 per hour and receive time off worth $40. An alternative is to define the wage in terms of actual hours worked—or as $10 per hour in this example. We prefer our definition because if the worker seizes an opportunity to work one fewer hour in a particular week, their earnings would fall by $5, not $10 (as long as the reduction in hours does not affect the hours of paid holiday or vacation time for which the worker is eligible).

7. For a review of studies on this topic, see David E. Lebow and Jeremy B. Rudd, "Measurement Error in the Consumer Price Index: Where Do We Stand?" *Journal of Economic Literature* 41 (March 2003): 159–201. These authors place the upward bias in the CPI at between 0.3 percent and 1.4 percent per year, with the most likely bias being 0.9 percent. A recent review of issues with the CPI can be found in Erica L. Groshen, Brian C. Moyer, Ana M. Aizcorbe, Ralph Bradley, and Daniel M. Friedman, "How Government Statistics Adjust for Potential Biases from Quality Change and New Goods in an Age of Digital Technologies:

A View from the Trenches," *Journal of Economic Perspectives* 31 (Spring 2017): 187–210.

8. Measures of total compensation could, of course, also include such job attributes as working conditions, promotion possibilities, the collegiality of coworkers, and even a value of office size.

9. Bent Hansen and Samir Radwan, *Employment Opportunities and Equity in Egypt* (Geneva: International Labour Office, 1982): 74. For a book on labor shortages, see Burt S. Barnow, John Trutko, and Jaclyn Schede Piatak, *Occupational Shortages: Concepts, Causes, Consequences, and Cures* (Kalamazoo, MI: W.E. Upjohn Institute for Employment Research, 2013).

10. William J. Moore and Robert J. Newman, "Government Wage Differentials in a Municipal Labor Market: The Case of Houston Metropolitan Transit Workers," *Industrial and Labor Relations Review* 45 (October 1991): 145–153.

11. If the workers who switched jobs were getting paid approximately what they were worth to their former employers, these employers would lose $5.94 in output but save $5.94 in costs—and their welfare would thus not be affected. The presumption that employees are paid what they are worth to the employer is discussed at length in Chapter 3.

12. We know of at least one example where an employer offered its employees choice over the *type* of pay that they received: Kevin F. Hallock and Craig A. Olson, "Employees Choice over Method of Pay" (Working Paper, Cornell University ILR School, DigitalCommons@ILR, Ithaca, NY, February 2009), https://digitalcommons.ilr.cornell.edu/cgi/viewcontent.cgi?article=1096&context=workingpapers. Employees were told their total compensation level but were then offered some choice over the mix of pay. For example, if an employee was paid $100,000 in total compensation, they could choose to take $100,000 as salary or to take $90,000 of their pay as salary and put $10,000 toward a bonus pool that would pay out (depending on individual and group performance in the year) from between $0 and $25,000.

13. Earnings data for all four countries are for workers in the lowest decile (lowest 10 percent) of their country's earnings distribution. These data are found in Organisation for Economic Co-operation and Development (OECD), *Employment Outlook: July 1993* (Paris: OECD, 1993), Table 5.3. Data on unemployment rates are from Federal Reserve Bank of Kansas City, *Reducing Unemployment: Current Issues and Policy Options* (Kansas City, MO: Federal Reserve Bank of Kansas City, 1994): 25. For analyses of the relative performance of labor markets in Europe and the United States, see Francine D. Blau and Lawrence M. Kahn, *At Home and Abroad: U.S. Labor-Market Performance in International Perspective* (New York: Russell Sage Foundation, 2002); Gilles Saint-Paul, "Why Are European Countries Diverging in Their Unemployment Experience?" *Journal of Economic Perspectives* 18 (Fall 2004):

49–68; Richard Freeman, *America Works: The Exceptional U.S. Labor Market* (New York: Russell Sage Foundation, 2007); Stephen Nickell, "Is the U.S. Labor Market Really that Exceptional? A Review of Richard Freeman's *America Works: The Exceptional U.S. Labor Market*," *Journal of Economic Literature* 46 (June 2008): 384–395. For an article on the employment effects of rigid nominal wages in Indian villages, see Supreet Kaur, "Nominal Wage Rigidity in Village Labor Markets," *American Economic Review* 109 (October 2019): 3585–3616.

Selected Readings

Blau, Francine D., and Lawrence M. Kahn. *At Home and Abroad: U.S. Labor-Market Performance in International Perspective*. New York: Russell Sage Foundation, 2002.

Freeman, Richard. *America Works: The Exceptional U.S. Labor Market*. New York: Russell Sage Foundation, 2007.

Hjort, Jonas, and Jonas Poulsen. "The Arrival of Fast Internet and Employment in Africa." *The American Economic Review*, 109 (March 2019): 1032–1079.

Nickell, Stephen. "Is the U.S. Labor Market Really That Exceptional? A Review of Richard Freeman's *America Works: The Exceptional U.S. Labor Market*." *Journal of Economic Literature* 46 (June 2008): 384–395.

President's Commission on an All-Volunteer Armed Force. *Report of the President's Commission on an All-Volunteer Armed Force*. Chapter 3, "Conscription Is a Tax," 23–33. Washington, DC: U.S. Government Printing Office, February 1970.

Rottenberg, Simon. "On Choice in Labor Markets." *Industrial and Labor Relations Review* 9 (January 1956): 183–199. [Robert J. Lampman. "On Choice in Labor Markets: Comment." *Industrial and Labor Relations Review* 9 (July 1956): 636–641.]

Saint-Paul, Gilles. "Why Are European Countries Diverging in Their Unemployment Experience?" *Journal of Economic Perspectives* 18 (Fall 2004): 49–68.

The Demand for Labor

The demand for labor is a derived demand, in that workers are hired for the contribution they can make toward producing some good or service for sale. However, the wages that workers receive, the employee benefits that they qualify for, and even their working conditions are all influenced, to one degree or another, by the government. There are minimum-wage laws, pension regulations, restrictions on firing workers, safety requirements, immigration controls, and government-provided pension and unemployment benefits that are financed through employer payroll taxes. All these requirements and regulations have one thing in common: They increase employers' costs of hiring workers.[1]

We explained in Chapter 2 that both the scale and the substitution effects accompanying a wage change suggest that the demand curve for labor is a *downward-sloping function of the wage rate.* If this rather simple proposition is true, then policies that mandate increases in the costs of employing workers will have the undesirable side effect of reducing their employment opportunities. If the reduction is large enough, lost job opportunities could actually undo any help provided to workers by the regulations. Understanding the characteristics of labor demand curves, then, is absolutely crucial for anyone interested in public policy. To a great extent, how one feels about many labor market regulatory programs is a function of one's beliefs about labor demand curves.

This chapter identifies *assumptions* underlying the proposition that labor demand is a downward-sloping function of the wage rate. Chapter 4 takes the downward-sloping nature of labor demand curves as given, addressing instead why, in the face of a given wage increase, declines in demand might be large in some cases and barely perceptible in others.

Profit Maximization

The fundamental assumption of labor demand theory is that firms—the employers of labor—seek to maximize profits. In doing so, firms are assumed to continually ask themselves whether they can make changes that will improve profits. Two things should be noted about this constant search for enhanced profits. First, a firm can make changes only to variables that are within its control. Because the price that a firm can charge for its product and the prices that it must pay for its inputs are determined largely by others (the "market"), a firm's profit-maximizing decisions involve mainly the question of *whether, and how, to increase or decrease output.*

Second, because the firm is assumed to constantly search for profit-improving possibilities, our theory must address the *small* ("marginal") changes that must be made almost daily. Major decisions whether to open a new plant or introduce a new product line, for example, are relatively rare; once having made them, the employer must approach profit maximization incrementally, through the trial-and-error process of small changes. We therefore need to understand the basis for these incremental decisions, paying particular attention to when an employer *stops* making changes in output levels or in its mix of inputs.

(With respect to the employment of inputs, analyzing marginal changes implies considering a small change in one input *while holding employment of other inputs constant.* Thus, when analyzing the effects of adjusting the labor input by one unit, for example, we will do so on the assumption that capital is held constant. Likewise, marginal changes in capital will be considered assuming that the labor input is held constant.)

In incrementally deciding on its optimal level of *output*, the profit-maximizing firm will want to expand output by one unit if the added revenue from selling that unit is greater than the added cost of producing it. As long as the marginal revenue from an added unit of output exceeds its marginal cost, the firm will continue to expand output. Likewise, the firm will want to contract output whenever the marginal cost of production exceeds marginal revenue. Profits are maximized (and the firm stops making changes) when output is such that marginal revenue equals marginal cost.

A firm can expand or contract output, of course, only by altering its use of *inputs*. In the most general sense, we will assume that a firm produces its output by combining two types of inputs, or *factors of production: labor* and *capital*. Thus, the rules stated earlier for deciding whether to marginally increase or decrease output have three important corollaries for the employment of labor and capital:

1. If the income generated by employing one more unit of an input exceeds the additional expense, then add a unit of that input.

2. If the income generated by one more unit of input is less than the additional expense, reduce employment of that input.

3. If the income generated by one more unit of input is equal to the additional expense, no further changes in that input are desirable.[2]

Decision rules 1 to 3 state the profit-maximizing criterion in terms of *inputs* rather than outputs; as we will see later, these rules are useful guides to deciding *how*—as well as *whether*—to marginally increase or decrease output. Let us more narrowly define and examine the components of these decision rules.

Marginal Income From an Additional Unit of Input

Employing one more unit of either labor or capital generates additional income for the firm because of the added output that is produced and sold. Similarly, reducing the employment of labor or capital reduces a firm's income flow because the output available for sale is reduced. Thus, the marginal income associated with a unit of input is found by multiplying two quantities: the change in physical output produced (called the input's *marginal product* [MP]) and the marginal revenue (MR) generated per unit of physical output. We will therefore call the marginal income produced by a unit of input the input's *marginal revenue product*. For example, if the presence of a tennis star increases attendance at a tournament by 20,000 spectators and the organizers net $25 from each additional fan, the marginal income produced by this star is equal to their marginal product (20,000 fans) times the marginal revenue of $25 per fan. Thus, their marginal revenue product equals $500,000. (For an actual calculation of marginal revenue product in college football, see Example 3.1.)

EXAMPLE 3.1

The Marginal Revenue Product of College Football Stars

Calculating a worker's marginal revenue product is often complicated because of a lack of data and the difficulty of making sure that everything else is being held constant and that only *additions* to revenue are counted. Perhaps for this reason, economists have been attracted to the sports industry, which generates so many statistics on player productivity and team revenues.

Football is a big-time concern on many campuses, and some star athletes generate huge revenues for their colleges, even though they are not paid—except by receiving a free education.[3] Richard Borghesi collected data from 2003 to 2014 on a host of statistics on college football teams, including revenue, expenses, and recruiting expenses in each of the 13 top football conferences. He also collected information on the number of three-, four-, and five-star athletes (five-star athletes are the most highly recruited out of high school) who had been recruited to each team.

Borghesi found that

if amateurism rules were rescinded and college football players were compensated according to their revenue-generating abilities then five-, four-, three-, and low-star players would be entitled to annual salaries of $799,000, $361,000, $29,000, and $21,000, respectively, in addition to athletic scholarships covering tuition, books, and room and board.

Source: Richard Borghesi, "Pay for Play: The Financial Value of NCAA Football Players," *Applied Economics* 49:46 (February 2017): 4657–4667

Marginal Product Formally, we define the *marginal product of labor*, or MP_L, as the change in physical output (ΔQ) produced by a change in the units of labor (ΔL), holding capital constant:[4]

$$MP_L = \Delta Q / \Delta L \text{ (holding capital constant)} \qquad (3.1)$$

Likewise, the marginal product of capital (MP_K) is defined as the change in output associated with a one-unit change in the stock of capital (ΔK), holding labor constant:

$$MP_K = \Delta Q / \Delta K \text{ (holding labor constant)} \qquad (3.2)$$

Marginal Revenue The definitions in equations (3.1) and (3.2) reflect the fact that a firm can expand or contract its output only by increasing or decreasing its use of either labor or capital. The marginal revenue that is generated by an extra unit of output depends on the characteristics of the product market in which that output is sold. If the firm operates in a purely competitive product market, and therefore has many competitors and no control over product price, the marginal revenue per unit of output sold is equal to product price (P). If the firm has a differentiated product, and thus has some degree of monopoly power in its product market, extra units of output can be sold only if product price is reduced (because the firm faces the *market* demand curve for its particular product); students should recall from introductory economics that in this case, marginal revenue is less than price ($MR < P$).[5]

Marginal Revenue Product Combining the definitions presented in this section, the firm's marginal revenue product of labor, or MRP_L, can be represented as

$$MRP_L = MP_L \cdot M_R \text{ (in the general case)} \qquad (3.3a)$$

or as

$$MRP_L = MP_L \cdot P \text{ (if the product market is competitive)} \qquad (3.3b)$$

Likewise, the firm's marginal revenue product of capital (MRP_K) can be represented as $MP_K \cdot M_R$ in the general case or as $MP_K \cdot P$ if the product market is competitive.

Marginal Expense of an Added Input

Changing the levels of labor or capital employed, of course, will add to or subtract from the firm's total costs. The marginal expense of labor (ME_L) that is incurred by hiring more labor is affected by the nature of competition in the labor market. If the firm operates in a competitive labor market and has no control over the wages that must be paid (it is a "wage taker"), then ME_L is simply equal to the market wage. Put differently, firms in competitive labor markets have labor supply curves that are horizontal at the going wage (refer back to Figure 2.11); if they hire an additional hour of labor, their costs increase by an amount equal to the wage rate, W.

In this chapter, we will maintain the assumption that the labor market is competitive and that the labor supply curve to firms is therefore *horizontal* at the going wage. In Chapter 5, we will relax this assumption and analyze how upward-sloping labor supply curves to individual employers alter the marginal expense of labor.

In the analysis that follows, the marginal expense of adding a unit of capital will be represented as C, which can be thought of as the expense of renting a unit of capital for one time period. The specific calculation of C need not concern us here, but it clearly depends on the purchase price of the capital asset, its expected useful life, the rate of interest on borrowed funds, and even special tax provisions regarding capital.

The Short-Run Demand for Labor When Both Product and Labor Markets Are Competitive

The simplest way to understand how the profit-maximizing behavior of firms generates a labor demand curve is to analyze the firm's behavior over a period of time so short that the firm cannot vary its stock of capital. This period is what we will call the *short run*, and, of course, the time period involved varies from firm to firm (e.g., an accounting service might be able to order and install a new computing system for the preparation of tax returns within three months, whereas an oil refinery may take five years to install a new production process). What is simplifying about the short run is that, with capital fixed, a firm's choice of output level and its choice of employment level are two aspects of the same decision. Put differently, in the short run, the firm needs only to decide *whether* to alter its output level; *how* to increase or decrease output is not an issue, because only the employment of labor can be adjusted.

A Critical Assumption: Declining MP_L

We defined the MP_L as the change in the (physical) output of a firm when it changes its employment of labor by one unit, holding capital constant.

Table 3.1 The Marginal Product of Labor in a Hypothetical Car Dealership (Capital Held Constant)

Number of salespeople	Total cars sold	Marginal product of labor
0	0	0
1	10	10
2	21	11
3	26	5
4	29	3

Because the firm can vary its employment of labor, we must consider how increasing or decreasing labor will affect labor's marginal product. Consider Table 3.1, which illustrates a hypothetical car dealership with salespeople who are all equally hardworking and persuasive. With no sales staff, the dealership is assumed to sell zero cars, but with one salesperson, it will sell 10 cars per month. Thus, the marginal product of the first salesperson hired is 10. If a second person is hired, total output is assumed to rise from 10 to 21, implying that the marginal product of a second salesperson is 11. If a third equally persuasive salesperson is hired, sales rise from 21 to 26 ($MP_L = 5$), and if a fourth is hired, sales rise from 26 to 29 ($MP_L = 3$).

Table 3.1 assumes that adding an extra salesperson increases output (cars sold) in each case. As long as output *increases* as labor is added, labor's marginal product is *positive*. In our example, however, MP_L increased at first (from 10 to 11) but then fell (to five and eventually to three). Why?

The initial rise in marginal product occurs *not* because the second salesperson is better than the first; we ruled out this possibility by our assumption that the salespeople were equally capable. Rather, the rise could be the result of cooperation between the two in generating promotional ideas or helping each other out in some way. Eventually, however, as more salespeople are hired, MP_L must fall. A fixed building (remember that capital is held constant) can contain only so many cars and customers; thus, each additional increment of labor must eventually produce progressively smaller increments of output. This law of *diminishing marginal returns* is an empirical proposition that derives from the fact that as employment expands, each additional worker has a progressively smaller share of the capital stock to work with. For expository convenience, we assume that MP_L is always decreasing.[6]

From Profit Maximization to Labor Demand

From the profit-maximizing decision rules discussed earlier, the firm should, clearly, keep increasing its employment of labor as long as labor's marginal revenue product exceeds its marginal expense. Conversely, it should keep decreasing its employment of labor as long as the expense saved is greater than the income lost. *Profits are maximized, then, only when employment is such that any further one-unit change in labor would have a marginal revenue product equal to marginal expense*:

$$MRP_L = ME_L \tag{3.4}$$

Under our current assumptions of competitive product and labor markets, we can symbolically represent the profit-maximizing level of labor input as that level at which

$$MP_L \cdot P = W \tag{3.5}$$

Clearly, equation (3.5) is stated in terms of some *monetary* unit (e.g., dollars).

Alternatively, however, we can divide both sides of equation (3.5) by product price, *P*, and state the profit-maximizing condition for hiring labor in terms of *physical quantities*:

$$MP_L = W/P \tag{3.6}$$

This is an extraordinarily important identity in the economics of labor markets. We defined MP_L as the change in physical output associated with a one-unit change in labor, so the left-hand side of equation (3.6) is obviously in physical quantities. To understand that the right-hand side is also in physical quantities, note that the numerator, *W*, is the dollars per unit of labor, and the denominator, *P*, is the dollars per unit of output. Thus, the ratio W/P has the dimension of physical units. For example, if a woman is paid $10 per hour and the output that she produces sells for $2 per unit, from the firm's viewpoint, she is paid five units of output per hour (10 ÷ 2). From the perspective of the firm, these five units represent her "real wage."

Labor Demand as Real Wages   The demand for labor can be analyzed in terms of either *real* or *money* wages. Which version of demand analysis is used is a matter of convenience only. In this and the following section, we give examples of both.

Figure 3.1 shows an MP_L schedule for a representative firm. In this figure, the MP_L is tabulated on the vertical axis and the number of units of labor employed on the horizontal axis. The negative slope of the schedule indicates that each additional unit of labor employed produces a progressively smaller (but still positive) increment in output. Because the real wage and MP_L are both measured in the same dimension (units of output), we can also plot the real wage on the vertical axis of Figure 3.1.

Given any real wage (by the market), the firm should thus employ labor to the point at which MP_L just equals the real wage; see equation (3.6). In other words, *the firm's demand for labor in the short run is equivalent to the downward-sloping segment of its MP_L schedule.*[7]

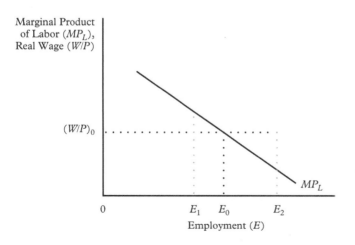

Figure 3.1 Demand for Labor in the Short Run (Real Wage)

To see that this is true, pick any real wage—for example, the real wage denoted by $(W/P)_0$ in Figure 3.1. We have asserted that the firm's demand for labor is equal to its MP_L schedule and, consequently, that the firm would employ E_0 employees. Now, suppose that a firm initially employed E_2 workers, as indicated in Figure 3.1, where E_2 is *any* employment level greater than E_0. At the employment level, E_2, the MP_L is less than the real wage rate; the marginal real cost of the last unit of labor hired is therefore greater than its marginal product. As a result, profit could be increased by decreasing the level of employment. Similarly, suppose instead that a firm initially employed E_1 employees, where E_1 is *any* employment level less than E_0. Given the specified real wage, $(W/P)_0$, the MP_L is greater than the real wage rate at E_1; consequently, the marginal additions to output of an extra unit of labor exceed its marginal real cost. As a result, a firm could increase its profit level by expanding its level of employment.

Hence, to maximize profits, given any real wage rate, a firm should stop employing labor at the point at which any additional labor would cost more than it would produce. This profit-maximization rule implies two things. First, the firm should employ labor up to the point at which its real wage equals MP_L—but not beyond that point. Second, its profit-maximizing level of employment lies in the range where its MP_L is *declining*. If $W/P = MP_L$, but MP_L is *increasing*, then adding another unit of labor will create a situation in which marginal product *exceeds* W/P. As long as adding labor causes MP_L to exceed W/P, the profit-maximizing firm will continue to hire labor. It will stop hiring only when an extra unit of labor would decrease MP_L below W/P, which will happen only when MP_L is declining. Thus, the only employment levels that could possibly be consistent with profit maximization are those in the range where MP_L is decreasing.

Labor Demand as Money Wages

In some circumstances, labor demand curves are more readily conceptualized as downward-sloping functions of *money* wages. To make the analysis as concrete as possible, in this section, we analyze the demand for department store detectives.

At a business conference one day, a department store executive boasted that their store had reduced theft to 1 percent of total sales. A colleague shook their head and said, "I think that's too low. I figure it should be about 2 percent of sales." How can more shoplifting be better than less? The answer is based on the fact that reducing theft is costly in itself. A profit-maximizing firm will not want to take steps to reduce shoplifting if the added costs that it must bear in so doing exceed the value of the savings that such steps will generate.

Table 3.2 shows a hypothetical MRP_L schedule for department store detectives. Hiring one detective would, in this example, save $50 worth of thefts per hour. Two detectives could save $90 worth of thefts each hour, or $40 more than hiring just one. The MRP_L of hiring a second detective is thus $40. A third detective would add $20 more to thefts prevented each hour.

Table 3.2 Hypothetical Schedule of Marginal Revenue Productivity
of Labor for Store Detectives

Number of detectives on duty during each hour store is open	Total value of thefts prevented per hour	Marginal value of thefts prevented per hour (MRP_L)
0	$0	$—
1	$50	$50
2	$90	$40
3	$110	$20
4	$115	$5
5	$117	$2

The MRP_L declines from $40 to $20 *not* because the added detectives are incompetent; in fact, we assume that all are equally alert and well trained. MRP_L declines, in part, because surveillance equipment (capital) is fixed; each added detective decreases the equipment per person. However, the MRP_L also declines because it becomes progressively harder to generate savings. With just a few detectives, the only thieves caught will be the more-obvious, less-experienced shoplifters. As more detectives are hired, preventing theft by the more-expert shoplifters becomes possible, but they are harder to detect and fewer in number. Thus, MRP_L falls because theft prevention becomes more difficult once all those who are easy to catch have been apprehended.

To draw the demand curve for labor, we need to determine how many detectives the store will want to hire at any given wage rate, keeping in mind that employers—through part-time employment—are able to hire fractional workers. For example, at a wage of $50 per hour, how many detectives will the store want? Using the $MRP_L = W$ criterion in equation (3.5), the answer is "up to one." At $40 per hour, the store would want to stop hiring at two, and at $20 per hour, it would stop at three. The labor demand curve that summarizes the store's profit-maximizing employment of detectives is shown in Figure 3.2.

Figure 3.2 illustrates a fundamental point: The labor demand curve in the short run slopes downward because it *is* the MRP_L curve—and the MRP_L curve slopes downward because of labor's diminishing marginal product. The demand curve and the MRP_L curve coincide; this could be demonstrated by graphing the MRP_L schedule in Table 3.2, which would yield the same curve as that in Figure 3.2. When one detective is hired, MRP_L is $50; when two are hired, MRP_L is $40; and so forth. Because MRP_L always equals W for a profit maximizer who takes wages as given,[8] the MRP_L curve and labor demand curve (expressed as a function of the money wage) must be the same.

An implication of our example is that the store finds some level of shoplifting more profitable to tolerate than to eliminate. This level will be higher

Figure 3.2 Demand for Labor in the Short Run (Money Wage)

at high wages for store detectives than at lower wages. To say the theft rate is "too low" thus implies that the marginal costs of crime reduction exceed the marginal savings generated, and the firm is therefore failing to maximize profits.

Finally, we must emphasize that the marginal product of an individual is *not* a function solely of their personal characteristics. As stressed earlier, the marginal product of a worker depends on the number of similar employees that the firm has already hired. An individual's marginal product also depends on the size of the firm's capital stock; increases in the firm's capital stock shift the entire MP_L schedule up. Speaking of an individual's productivity as an immutable factor that is associated only with their characteristics, independent of the characteristics of the other inputs that they have to work with, is therefore incorrect.

Market Demand Curves   The demand curve (or schedule) for an individual firm indicates how much labor that firm will want to employ at each wage level. A *market demand curve* (or schedule) is just the *summation* of the labor demanded by all firms in a particular labor market at each level of the *real* wage.[9] If three firms are in a certain labor market and if at a *given* real wage firm A wants 12 workers, firm B wants 6, and firm C wants 20, then the market demand at that real wage is 38 employees. More important, because market demand curves are so closely derived from firm demand curves, they too will *slope downward* as a function of the real wage. When the real wage falls, the number of workers that existing firms want to employ increases. In addition, the lower real wage may make new firms' entering the market profitable for them. Conversely, when the real wage increases, the number of workers that existing firms want to employ decreases, and some firms may be forced to cease operations completely.

Objections to the Marginal Productivity Theory of Demand Two kinds of objections are sometimes raised to the theory of labor demand introduced in this section. The first is that almost no employer can ever be heard uttering the words "marginal revenue product of labor" and that the theory assumes a degree of sophistication that most employers do not have. Employers, some argue, are unable in many situations to accurately measure the output of individual workers.

These first objections can be answered as follows: Whether employers can verbalize the profit-maximizing conditions or whether they can explicitly measure the MRP_L, they must at least *intuit* them to survive in a competitive environment. Competition "weeds out" employers who are not good at generating profits, just as competition weeds out pool players who do not understand the intricacies of how speed, angles, and spin affect the motion of bodies through space. Yet one could canvass the pool halls of the United States and probably find few who could verbalize Newton's laws of motion. The point is that employers can *know* concepts without being able to verbalize them. Those that are not good at maximizing profits will not last long in competitive markets.

The second objection is that in many cases, adding labor while holding capital constant would seem to not add to output at all. For example, one administrative assistant and one computer can produce output, but adding a second assistant while holding the number of computers constant might seem to produce nothing extra, because that assistant would have no machine on which to work.

The answer to this second objection is that the two assistants could take turns using the computer so that neither became fatigued to the extent that mistakes increased and typing speeds slowed down. The second assistant could also answer the telephone and expedite work in other ways. Thus, even with technologies that seem to require one machine per person, labor will generally have a marginal product greater than zero if capital is held constant.

The Demand for Labor in Competitive Markets When Other Inputs Vary

An implication of this theory of labor demand is that, because labor can be varied in the short run—that is, at any time—the profit-maximizing firm will always operate so that labor's marginal revenue product will equal the wage rate (which is labor's marginal expense in a competitive labor market). What we must now consider is how the firm's ability to adjust *other* inputs affects the demand for labor. We first analyze the implications of being able to adjust capital in the long run, and we then turn our attention to the case of more than two inputs.

Labor Demand in the Long Run

To maximize profits in the long run, the firm must adjust both labor and capital so that the marginal revenue product of each equals its marginal expense. Using the definitions discussed earlier in this chapter, profit maximization requires that the following two equalities be satisfied:

$$MP_L \cdot P = W \text{ (a restatement of equation (3.5))} \qquad (3.7a)$$

$$MP_K \cdot P = C \text{ (the profit-maximizing condition for capital)} \qquad (3.7b)$$

Equations (3.7a) and (3.7b) can be rearranged to isolate *P*, so these two profit-maximizing conditions can also be expressed as

$$P = W/MP_L \text{ (a rearrangement of equation (3.7a))} \qquad (3.8a)$$

$$P = C/MP_K \text{ (a rearrangement of equation (3.7b))} \qquad (3.8b)$$

Furthermore, because the right-hand sides of equations (3.8a) and (3.8b) equal the same quantity, *P*, profit maximization therefore requires that

$$W/MP_L = C/MP_K \qquad (3.8c)$$

The economic meaning of equation (3.8c) is key to understanding how the ability to adjust capital affects the firm's demand for labor. Consider the left-hand side of equation (3.8c): The numerator is the cost of a unit of labor, and the denominator is the extra output produced by an added unit of labor. Therefore, the ratio W/MP_L turns out to be the added cost of producing an added unit of output when using labor to generate the increase in output.[10] Analogously, the right-hand side is the marginal cost of producing an extra unit of output by using capital. Equation (3.8c) suggests that **to maximize profits,** *the firm must adjust its labor and capital inputs so that the marginal cost of producing an added unit of output using labor is equal to the marginal cost of producing an added unit of output using capital.* Why is this condition a requirement for maximizing profits?

To maximize profits, a firm must be producing its chosen level of output in the least costly manner. Logic suggests that as long as the firm can expand output more cheaply by using one input than the other, it cannot be producing in the least costly way. For example, if the marginal cost of expanding output by one unit using labor were $10 and the marginal cost using capital were $12, the firm could keep output constant and lower its costs of production. How? It could reduce its capital by enough to cut output by one unit (saving $12) and then add enough labor to restore the one-unit cut (costing $10). Output would be the same, but costs would have fallen by $2. Thus, for the firm to be maximizing profits, it must be operating such that further marginal changes in both labor and capital would neither lower costs nor add to profits.

Given equations (3.8a) to (3.8c), what would happen to the demand for labor in the long run if the wage rate (*W*) facing a profit-maximizing firm were to rise? First, as we discussed in the section "The Short-Run Demand for Labor When Both Product and Labor Markets Are Competitive," the rise in *W* disturbs the equality in equation (3.8a), and the firm will want to cut back on its use of labor even before it can adjust capital. Because the MP_L is assumed to rise as employment is reduced, any cuts in labor will raise MP_L. Second, because each unit of capital now has less labor working with it, the MP_K falls, disturbing the equality in equation (3.8b). By itself, this latter inequality will cause the firm to want to reduce its stock of capital.

Third, the rise in W will initially end the equality in equation (3.8c), meaning that the marginal cost of production using labor will now exceed the marginal cost using capital. If the earlier cuts in labor are made in the short run, the associated increase in MP_L and decrease in MP_K will work toward restoring equality in equation (3.8c); however, if producing an extra unit of output using labor remains more costly than using capital, the firm will want to substitute capital for labor in the long run. Substituting capital for labor means that the firm will produce its profit-maximizing level of output (which is clearly reduced by the rise in W) in a more capital-intensive way. The act of substituting capital for labor will also serve to increase MP_L and reduce MP_K, thereby reinforcing the return to equality in equation (3.8c).

EXAMPLE 3.2

Coal Mining Wages and Capital Substitution

That wage increases have both a *scale effect* and a *substitution effect*, both of which tend to reduce employment, is widely known—even by many of those pushing for higher wages. John L. Lewis was president of the United Mine Workers from the 1920s through the 1940s, when wages for miners were increased considerably, even though he fully knew that this would induce the substitution of capital for labor. According to Lewis,

> Primarily the United Mine Workers of America insists upon the maintenance of the wage standards guaranteed by the existing contractual relations in the industry, in the interests of its own membership. . . . But in insisting on the maintenance of an American wage standard in the coal fields the United Mine Workers is also doing its part, probably more than its part, to force a reorganization of the basic industry of the country upon scientific and efficient lines. The maintenance of these rates will accelerate the operation of natural economic laws, which will in time eliminate uneconomic mines, obsolete equipment, and incompetent management.
>
> The policy of the United Mine Workers of America will inevitably bring about the utmost employment of machinery of which coal mining is physically capable. . . . Fair wages and American standards of living are inextricably bound up with the progressive substitution of mechanical for human power. It is no accident that fair wages and machinery will walk hand-in-hand.

Source: John L. Lewis, *The Miners' Fight for American Standards* (Indianapolis: Bell, 1925): 40, 41, 108

In the end, the increase in W will cause the firm to reduce its desired employment level, for two reasons. The firm's profit-maximizing level of output will fall, and the associated reduction in required inputs (both capital and labor) is an example of the *scale effect*. The rise in W also causes the firm to substitute capital for labor so that it can again produce in the least costly manner; changing the mix of capital and labor in the production process is an example of the *substitution effect*. The scale and substitution effects of a wage increase will have an ambiguous effect on the firm's desired stock of *capital*, but both effects serve to reduce the demand for *labor*. Thus, as illustrated in Example 3.2, the long-run ability to adjust capital lends further theoretical support to the proposition that the labor demand curve is a downward-sloping function of the wage rate.

More Than Two Inputs

Thus far, we have assumed that only two inputs are involved in the production process: capital and labor. Labor can be subdivided into many categories; for example, labor can be categorized by age, educational level, and occupation. Other inputs that are used in the production process include materials and energy. If a firm is seeking to minimize costs, in the long run, it should employ all inputs up until the point that the marginal cost of producing an added unit of output is the same regardless of which input is increased. This generalization of equation (3.8c) leads to the somewhat-obvious result that the demand for *any* category of labor will be a function of its own wage rate *and* (through the scale and substitution effects) the wage or prices of all other categories of labor, capital, and supplies.

If Inputs Are Substitutes in Production The demand curve for each category of labor will be a downward-sloping function of the wage rate paid to workers in that category, for the reasons discussed earlier. But how is it affected by wage or price changes for *other* inputs? If two inputs are *substitutes in production* (i.e., if the greater use of one in producing output can compensate for reduced use of the other), then increases in the price of the *other* input may shift the entire demand curve for a *given* category of labor either to the right or to the left, depending on the relative strength of the substitution and scale effects. If an increase in the price of one input shifts the demand for *another* input to the left, as in panel (a) of Figure 3.3, the scale effect has dominated the substitution effect, and the two inputs are

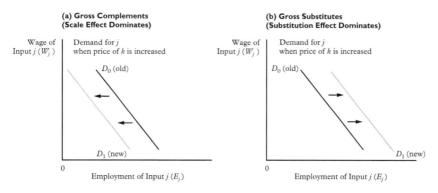

Figure 3.3 Effect of an Increase in the Price of One Input (*k*) on Demand for Another Input (*j*), Where Inputs Are Substitutes in Production

said to be *gross complements*; if the increase shifts the demand for the other input to the right, as in panel (b) of Figure 3.3, the substitution effect has dominated, and the two inputs are *gross substitutes*.

If Inputs Are Complements in Production   If, instead, the two inputs must be used together—in which case they are called *perfect complements* or *complements in production*—then the reduced use of one implies the reduced use of the other. In this case, no substitution effect, only a scale effect, occurs, and the two inputs must be gross complements.

Examples   Consider an example of a snow-removal firm in which higher-skilled and lower-skilled workers are substitutes in production— snow can be removed using either lower-skilled workers (with shovels) or higher-skilled workers (driving snowplows). Let us focus on demand for the higher-skilled workers. Other things being equal, an increase in the wage of higher-skilled workers would cause the firm to employ fewer of them; their demand curve would be a downward-sloping function of their wage. If only the wage of *lower-skilled* workers increased, however, the employer would want fewer lower-skilled workers than before and more of the now relatively less-expensive higher-skilled workers, to remove any *given amount of snow*. To the extent that this substitution effect dominated over the scale effect, the demand for higher-skilled workers would shift to the right. In this case, higher-skilled and lower-skilled workers would be gross substitutes. In contrast, if the reduction in the scale of output caused employment of higher-skilled workers to be reduced, even though higher-skilled workers were being substituted for lower-skilled workers in the production process, higher-skilled and lower-skilled workers would be considered gross complements.

In this firm, snowplows and higher-skilled workers are complements in production. If the price of snowplows were to go up, the employer would want to cut back on their use, which would result in a reduced demand at each wage for the higher-skilled workers who drove the snowplows. As noted earlier, inputs that are complements in production are always gross complements.

Labor Demand When the Product Market Is Not Competitive

Our analysis of the demand for labor, in both the short run and the long run, has so far taken place under the assumption that the firm operates in competitive product and labor markets. This is equivalent to assuming that the firm is both a price taker and a wage taker; that is, it takes both *P* and *W* as given and makes decisions only about the levels of outputs and inputs. We next explore the effects of noncompetitive (monopolistic) *product* markets on the demand for labor, and we continue to assume that the labor market is competitive (the effects of noncompetitive *labor* markets are analyzed in Chapter 5).

Maximizing Monopoly Profits

As explained earlier in endnote 4 and the surrounding text, product-market monopolies are subject to the *market* demand curve for their output, and they therefore do not take output price as given. They can expand their sales only by reducing product price, which means that their MR from an extra unit of output is less than product price (P). Using the general definition of marginal revenue product in equation (3.3a) and applying the usual profit-maximizing criteria outlined in equation (3.4) to a monopoly that searches for workers in a competitive *labor* market (so that $ME_L = W$), the monopolist would hire workers until its MRP_L equals the wage rate:

$$MRP_L = MR \cdot MP_L = W \qquad (3.9)$$

Now we can express the demand for labor in the short run in terms of the real wage by dividing equation (3.9) by the firm's product price, P, to obtain

$$\frac{MR}{P} \cdot MP_L = \frac{W}{P} \qquad (3.10)$$

Since marginal revenue is always less than a monopoly's product price, the ratio MR/P in equation (3.10) is less than 1. Therefore, the labor demand curve for a firm that has monopoly power in the output market will lie below and to the left of the labor demand curve for an *otherwise-identical* firm that takes product price as given. Put another way, just as the level of profit-maximizing output is lower under monopoly than it is under competition, other things being equal, so is the level of employment.

The *wage* rates that monopolies pay, however, are not necessarily different from competitive levels even though *employment* levels are. An employer with a product-market monopoly may still be a small part of the market for a particular kind of employee and thus be a *price taker* in the labor market. For example, a local utility company might have a product-market monopoly, but it would have to compete with all other firms to hire clerks and thus would have to pay the going wage.

Do Monopolies Pay Higher Wages?

Economists have long suspected that product-market monopolies pay wages that are *higher* than what competitive firms would pay.[11] Monopolies are often regulated by the government to prevent them from exploiting their status and earning monopoly profits, but they are allowed to pass along to consumers their costs of production. Thus, although the managers of a monopoly are unable to maximize profits, they can enhance their *utility* by paying high wages and passing the costs along to consumers in the form of higher prices. The ability to pay high wages makes a manager's life more pleasant by making it possible to hire people who might be more personable or have other characteristics that managers find desirable.

The evidence on monopoly wages, however, is less clear. Some studies suggest that firms in industries with relatively few sellers *do* pay higher wages than competitive firms for workers with the same education and experience. Other studies of regulated monopolies, however, have obtained mixed results on whether wages tend to be higher for comparable workers in these industries.[12]

Policy Application: The Labor Market Effects of Employer Payroll Taxes and Wage Subsidies

We now apply labor demand theory to the phenomena of employer payroll taxes and wage subsidies. Governments widely finance certain social programs through taxes that require *employers* to remit payments on the basis of their total payroll costs. As we see next, new or increased payroll taxes levied on the employer raise the cost of hiring labor, and they might therefore be expected to reduce the demand for labor. Conversely, if the government were to subsidize the wages paid by employers, then arguably the demand for labor would increase; indeed, wage subsidies for particular disadvantaged groups in society are sometimes proposed as a way to increase their employment. In the next section, we analyze the effects of payroll taxes and subsidies.

Who Bears the Burden of a Payroll Tax?

Payroll taxes levied on employers typically require them to pay the government a certain percentage of their employees' earnings, often up to some maximum amount. Unemployment insurance and Social Security retirement, disability, and Medicare programs are prominent examples in the United States. Does taxing employers to generate revenues for these programs relieve *employees* of a financial burden that would otherwise fall on them?

Let us begin to analyze the effects of employer payroll taxes on *employees* by considering the labor demand curve in a particular labor market in the absence of an employer payroll tax. Before the imposition of a payroll tax, let us assume that the only labor cost to firms was the wage that they paid to their workers. Let us further assume that the pretax labor demand curve for this particular labor market is D_0, in Figure 3.4. Demand curve D_0 indicates that at a labor cost (wage) of $20 per hour, firms would have wanted to hire E_1 workers; at $19, E_2 workers; at $12, E_3 workers; and at $11, E_4 workers.

Now suppose that the government imposes a payroll tax on employers equal to the fixed amount of $1 per labor hour. This tax means that employers' labor costs are now equal to the wage that the workers receive *plus* the $1 per hour tax. Thus, if employee wages happened to be $11 per hour, employer costs would be $12 per hour—and instead of wanting E_4 workers, they would want only E_3 (the number they want when labor costs are $12 per hour). Likewise, if wages paid to employees were $19 per hour, employer costs would now be $20, and employers would now want to hire E_1 workers instead of E_2. As we expect, then, because the payroll tax takes the hourly

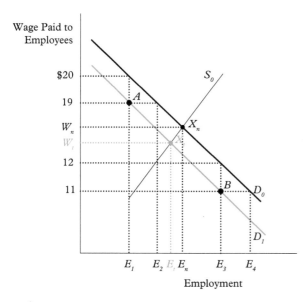

Figure 3.4 The Market Demand Curve and Effects of an Employer-Financed Payroll Tax

cost of labor above the wage rate paid to workers, employers want to hire fewer workers *at any given wage rate received by their employees.*

Shifting the Labor Demand Curve

If, as in Figure 3.4, we keep the *wages received by workers* on the vertical axis, we must draw a new demand curve (D_1) to reflect the demand for labor with the $1 per hour payroll tax. If the wage to employees were $19 per hour, employers' labor costs would be $20 per hour—so at a wage of $19, firms would now demand only E_1 workers (at point A in Figure 3.4). If the wage paid to workers happened to be $11, then firms would want to hire the workers that they desire when hourly labor costs are $12 ($E_3$, at point B). Points A and B are points on a *shifted* labor demand curve; this new demand curve must be drawn to reflect the labor-demand effects of the payroll tax. (Students are advised to draw their own labor demand curves before and after a fixed hourly payroll tax and to prove to themselves that the *vertical* distance between the original and the shifted curves is equal to the hourly payroll tax.)

What are the effects on the market wage and employment outcomes of this shift in the labor demand curve caused by the payroll tax on employers? To see these effects in Figure 3.4, we assume that the labor supply curve to this market is S_0. Before the payroll tax was imposed, the equilibrium wage and employment outcomes with no taxes were found at intersection X_n, with wage W_n and employment level E_n as market outcomes. Once the labor demand curve shifts to D_1 to reflect the $1-per-hour payroll tax, the intersection of the demand and supply curve moves to X_t; the market wage falls to W_t and employment falls to E_t.

We can see from Figure 3.4, then, that the payroll tax levied on *employers* puts downward pressure both on the wages that employees receive and on their employment levels. Put differently, even though the payroll tax is paid to the government by employers, *employees* bear a burden in the form of potentially lower wage rates and lower employment levels. Employees are thus not exempted from bearing costs when the government chooses to generate revenues through a payroll tax on employers.

Effects of Labor Supply Curves   How the payroll-tax costs ultimately borne by employees are distributed between lower wages and lower employment depends on the shape of their market labor supply curve. Figure 3.5 illustrates an extreme case in which a labor supply curve is completely vertical—meaning that labor supply is not at all responsive to wage changes. In Figure 3.5, we can see that if the labor supply curve were vertical, the imposition of an employer payroll tax would cause employee wages to fall—from W_0 to W_0-X—and employment would stay constant. The costs borne by workers in this case are felt in their wages but not in their employment levels.[13]

In the example shown in Figure 3.5, employers are willing to employ the same number of employees as before the tax *because the wages that they pay to employees have fallen by $1—the amount of the tax* (remember that the vertical distance between the pretax labor demand curve and the post-tax labor demand curve is equal to the amount of the payroll tax). When employee wages fall by the amount of the tax, the hourly labor costs of employers stay the same, so they will want to employ the same number of workers.

Figure 3.6 illustrates the effects of an employer payroll tax when the labor supply curve is at the other extreme and is completely horizontal. Labor supply curves are more horizontal if the number of workers who want work in the market is more responsive to changes in wages, and a horizontal labor supply curve implies that firms can get any quantity of labor that they want at the going wage (as might be the case if the labor market is "loose," with a high level of unemployment). If the labor supply curve is horizontal, we can see from Figure 3.6 that employee wages do not change at all, but the drop in employment from E_n to E_t is large. More generally, then, an employer

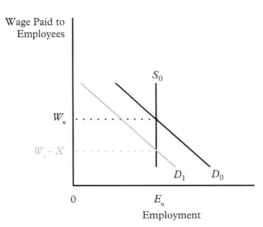

Figure 3.5 Employer Payroll-Tax Effects With a Vertical Labor Supply Curve

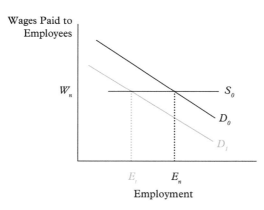

Figure 3.6 Employer Payroll-Tax Effects With a Horizontal Labor Supply Curve

payroll tax imposed on a market with a more horizontal labor supply curve will cause the effects on employees to be felt mostly on their employment levels and not much on their wages.

Employment Subsidies as a Device to Help Unemployed People

The opposite of a payroll tax on employers is a government subsidy of employers' payrolls. This subsidy could take the form of government *payments* to employers that are based on the size of their payrolls, or they could take the form of a *reduction in existing payroll taxes*. What are the likely effects on employee wages and employment levels of payroll subsidies to employers?

We can analyze the effects of payroll subsidies by assuming that the payroll tax of $1 per labor hour shown in Figures 3.4 to 3.6 is removed. With the payroll tax, the labor demand curve in these figures is D_1, and when the payroll tax is rescinded, the labor demand curve moves to D_0. Shifting from D_1 to D_0 puts upward pressures on employee wages and employment levels—and the mix of these effects depends on the shape of the labor supply curve. As can be seen in Figures 3.5 and 3.6, the more vertical is the labor supply curve (Figure 3.5), the more the effects will be felt as wage increases; the more horizontal is the supply curve (Figure 3.6), the more the effects will be evident in employment gains.

As suggested in our discussion of Figure 3.6, the labor supply curve is likely to be relatively horizontal in labor markets characterized by high unemployment; in these markets, more workers are available at the prevailing wage than jobs are available for them. The existence of an unemployment-related horizontal labor supply curve suggests that employer payroll subsidies might be an effective tool to increase employment opportunities. Indeed, a recent study of a cut in payroll taxes that Swedish employers had to pay for workers in their early 20s suggests that such tax cuts have the promise of expanding employment for workers facing high unemployment rates.[14]

EMPIRICAL STUDY 3.1

Do Women Pay for Employer-Funded Maternity Benefits? Using Cross-Section Data Over Time to Analyze "Differences in Differences"

During the last half of 1976, Illinois, New Jersey, and New York passed laws requiring that employer-provided health-insurance plans treat pregnancy the same as illness (i.e., coverage for doctor's bills and hospital costs had to be the same for pregnancy as for illnesses or injuries). These mandates increased the cost of health insurance for women of childbearing age by an amount that was equal to about 4 percent of their earnings. Were these increases in employer costs borne by employers, or did they reduce the wages of women by an equivalent amount?

A problem confronting researchers on this topic is that the adopting states are all states with high incomes and that are likely to have state legislation encouraging the expansion of employment opportunities for women. Thus, comparing wage *levels* across states would require that we statistically control for all the factors, besides the maternity-benefit mandate, that affect wages. Because we can never be sure that we have adequate controls for the economic, social, and legal factors that affect wage levels by state, we need to find another way to perform the analysis.

Fortunately, answering the research question is facilitated by several factors:

1. Some states adopted these laws and some did not.
2. Even in states that adopted these laws, the insurance cost increases applied only to people of childbearing age who chose to have children (and to their spouses) and not to single people who opted not to have children or to older workers.
3. The adopting states passed these laws during the same time period, so variables affecting women's wages that change over time (such as recessions or the rising presence of women in the labor force) do not cloud the analysis.

Factors 1 and 3 allow the conduct of what economists call a differences-in-differences analysis. Specifically, these factors allow us to compare wage *changes*, from the pre-adoption years to the post-adoption ones, among people of childbearing age who chose to have children in adopting states (the experimental group) to wage changes over the same period for people of the same age in states that did not adopt (a comparison group). By comparing in-state *changes* in wages, we avoid the need to find measures that would control for the economic, social, and public policy forces that make the initial wage *level* in one state differ from that in another; whatever the factors are that raise wage levels in New Jersey, for example, they were there both before and after the adoption of mandated maternity benefits.

One might argue, of course, that the adopting and nonadopting states were subject to *other* forces (unrelated to maternity benefits) that led to different degrees of wage change over this period. For example, the economy of New Jersey might have been booming during the period when maternity benefits were adopted, whereas economies elsewhere might not have been. However, if an adopting state is experiencing unique wage pressures in addition to those imposed by maternity benefits, the effects of these other pressures should show up in the wage changes experienced by single men or older women—groups in the adopting states that were not affected by the mandate. Thus, we can exploit factor 2 by also comparing the wage changes for people of childbearing age who chose to have children in adopting states to those for single people who opted not to have children or for older women in the same states.

These three factors enabled one researcher to measure how the wages of married women aged 20–40 changed from 1974–1975 to 1977–1978 in the three adopting states. These changes were then compared to changes in wages for married women of the same age in nonadopting (but economically similar) states. To account for forces *other than changing maternity benefits* that could affect wage changes across states during this period, the researcher also measured changes in wages for unmarried men and workers over age 40. This study concluded that in the states adopting mandated maternity benefits, the post-adoption wages of women in the 20–40 age group were about 4 percent lower than they would have been without adoption. This finding suggests that the entire cost of maternity benefits was quickly shifted to women of childbearing age.

Source: Jonathan Gruber, "The Incidence of Mandated Maternity Benefits," *American Economic Review* 84 (June 1994): 622–641. For a study that did not find measurable effects of mandated health benefits on *wages* but did find that mandates were accompanied by increased reliance on part-time workers (for whom the provision of health insurance was not required), see Thomas C. Buchmueller, John DiNardo, and Robert G. Valletta, "The Effect of an Employer Health Insurance Mandate on Health Insurance Coverage and the Demand for Labor: Evidence from Hawaii," *American Economic Journal: Economic Policy* 3 (November 2011): 25–51.

Review Questions

1. In a statement during the 1992 presidential campaign, one organization attempting to influence the political parties argued that the wages paid by U.S. firms in their Mexican plants were so low that they "have no relationship with worker productivity." Comment on this statement by using the principles of profit maximization.

2. Assume that wages for keyboarders (data entry clerks) are lower in India than in the United States. Does this mean that keyboarding jobs in the United States will be lost to India? Explain.

3. The Occupational Safety and Health Administration promulgates safety and health standards. These standards typically apply to machinery (capital), which is required to be equipped with guards, shields, and the like. An alternative to these standards is to require the employer to furnish personal protective devices to employees (labor)—such as earplugs, hard hats, and safety shoes. *Disregarding* the issue of which alternative approach offers greater protection from injury, what aspects of each alternative must be taken into account when analyzing the possible *employment* effects of the two approaches to safety?

4. Suppose that prisons historically have required inmates to perform, *without pay*, various cleaning and food preparation jobs in the prison. Now, suppose that prisoners are offered paid work in factory jobs in the prison and that the cleaning and food preparation tasks are now performed by nonprisoners hired to do them. Would you expect to see any differences in the *technologies* used to perform these tasks? Explain.

5. Years ago, the United Kingdom adopted a program that placed a tax—to be collected from employers—on wages in *service* industries. Wages in manufacturing industries were not taxed. Discuss the wage and employment effects of this tax policy.

6. Suppose that the government were to subsidize the wages of all women in the population by paying their *employers* 50 cents for every hour they work. What would be the effect on the wage rate that women received? What would be the effect on the net wage that employers paid? (The net wage would be the wage at which women received less 50 cents.)

7. The United States has been subject to flows of undocumented immigrants—mostly with low skill levels—across the U.S.–Mexico border. The government has considered ways to reduce the flow, and one potential policy is to impose larger financial penalties on employers who hire undocumented workers. What effect would this policy have on the employment of lower-skilled undocumented immigrants? What effect would it have on the demand for higher-skilled "native" labor?

8. If anti-sweatshop movements are successful in raising pay and improving working conditions for apparel workers in foreign countries, how will these changes abroad affect labor market outcomes for workers in the apparel and retailing industries in the United States? Explain.

9. The unemployment rate in country X is currently over 10 percent, and the youth (under age 25) unemployment rate is about 22 percent. Over the next few years, one million people on the unemployment rolls will be offered subsidized jobs (the government subsidy will go to employers who create new jobs, and the subsidy will be X euros per hour per employee hired). Use the theory studied in this course to analyze how wage subsidies to employers are likely to affect employment levels in country X.

10. Suppose that all employers in the Internet industry currently allow their programmers and web designers to work from home, which appeals to

those with childcare or other responsibilities that can be accomplished at a reduced cost than if they had to leave home and commute to work. Now suppose that these employers become convinced that they can increase the productivity of their programmers and designers by requiring them to work together in company offices. Use concepts covered in Chapters 2 and 3 to analyze the likely labor market effects of this new policy on the Internet industry.

Problems

1. An experiment conducted in Tennessee found that the scores of second-graders and third-graders on standardized tests for reading, math, listening, and word study skills were the same in small classrooms (13 to 17 students) as in regular classrooms (22 to 25 students). Suppose that there is a school that had 90 third-graders taught by four teachers that added two additional teachers to reduce class sizes. If the Tennessee study can be generalized, what is the marginal product of labor (MP_L) of these two additional teachers?

2. The marginal revenue product of labor at the local sawmill is $MRP_L = 20 - 0.5L$, where $L =$ the number of workers. If the wage of sawmill workers is $10 per hour, then how many workers will the mill hire?

3. Suppose that the supply curve for lifeguards is $L_S = 20$ and that the demand curve for lifeguards is $L_D = 100 - 20W$, where $L =$ the number of lifeguards and $W =$ the hourly wage. Graph both the demand and supply curves. Now, suppose that the government imposes a tax of $1 per hour per worker on companies that hire lifeguards. Draw the new (after-tax) demand curve in terms of the employee wage. How will this tax affect the wage of lifeguards and the number employed as lifeguards?

4. The output of workers at a factory depends on the number of supervisors hired (see Table 3P.4). The factory sells its output for $0.50 each, it hires 50 production workers at a wage of $100 per day, and it needs to decide how many supervisors to hire. The daily wage of supervisors is $500, but output rises as more supervisors are hired, as shown in Table 3P.4. How many supervisors should it hire?

Table 3P.4 Supervisors and Output

Supervisors	Output (units per day)
0	11,000
1	14,800
2	18,000
3	19,500
4	20,200
5	20,600

5. (Appendix 3A) The Hormsbury Corporation produces yo-yos at its factory. Both its labor and capital markets are competitive. Wages are \$12 per hour, and yo-yo-making equipment (a computer-controlled plastic extruding machine) rents for \$4 per hour. The production function is $q = 40K^{0.25}L^{0.75}$, where q = boxes of yo-yos per week, K = hours of yo-yo equipment used, and L = hours of labor. Therefore, $MP_L = 30K^{0.25}L^{-0.25}$ and $MP_K = 10K^{-0.75}L^{0.75}.$ Determine the cost-minimizing capital–labor ratio at this firm.

6. Table 3P.6 shows the number of cakes that could be baked daily at a local bakery, depending on the number of bakers.

Table 3P.6 Bakers and Cake Production

Number of bakers	Number of cakes
0	0
1	10
2	18
3	23
4	27

a. Calculate the MP_L.

b. Do you observe the law of diminishing marginal returns? Explain.

c. Suppose each cake sells for \$10. Calculate the MRP_L.

d. Draw the MRP_L curve, which is the demand curve for bakers.

e. If each baker is paid \$80 per day, how many bakers will the bakery owner hire, given that the goal is to maximize profits? How many cakes will be baked and sold each day?

7. (Appendix 3A) Creative Dangles is an earring design and manufacturing company. The production function for earrings is $Q = 25KL$, where Q = pairs of earrings per week, K = hours of equipment used, and L = hours of labor. Workers are paid \$8 per hour, and the equipment rents for \$8 per hour.

a. Determine the cost-minimizing capital–labor ratio at this firm.

b. How much does producing 10,000 pairs of earrings cost?

c. Suppose that the rental cost of equipment decreases to \$6 per hour. What is the new cost-minimizing capital–labor ratio?

8. (Appendix 3A) The demand curve for gardeners is $G_D = 19 - W$, where G = the number of gardeners, and W = the hourly wage. The supply curve is $G_S = 4 + 2W$.

a. Graph the demand curve and the supply curve. What is the equilibrium wage and equilibrium number of gardeners hired?

b. Suppose that the town government imposes a $2 per hour tax on all gardeners. Indicate the effect of the tax on the market for gardeners. What is the effect on the equilibrium wage and the equilibrium number of gardeners hired? How much does the gardener receive? How much does the customer pay? How much does the government receive as tax revenue?

Notes

1. In fact, in the United States, wages and salaries make up only about 69 percent of the total cost to the company for the average employee; the rest includes paid time off, insurance, retirement, Social Security, Medicare, unemployment insurance, and workers' compensation. See www.bls.gov/news.release/pdf/ecec.pdf, Table 1 [March 2020].

2. Readers who are comfortable with calculus may recognize that the "one-unit" changes described here could be any infinitesimally small change.

3. In the spring of 2020, the governing body of the National Collegiate Athletic Association agreed that players could profit from their "name, image and likeness," so long as their own university did not pay them (Brakkton Booker, "College Athletes Are Now Closer to Getting Paid After NCAA Board OKs Plan," *NPR*, April 29, 2020).

4. The symbol Δ (the uppercase Greek letter delta) is used to signify "a change in."

5. A competitive firm can sell added units of output at the market price because it is so small relative to the entire market that its output does not affect the price. A monopolist, however, *is* the supply side of the product market, so to sell extra output, it must lower the price. Because it must lower the price on *all* units of output and not just on the extra units to be sold, the MR associated with an additional unit is below the price.

6. We lose nothing by this assumption, because we show later in this section that a firm will never be operated at a point where its MP_L is increasing. We also note that when we state that the MP_L is always decreasing, we technically mean always decreasing after the first person is hired.

7. We should add here "provided that the firm's revenue exceeds its labor costs." Above some real wage level, this may fail to occur, and the firm will go out of business (employment will drop to zero).

8. Again, we assume that wages are "given," because we have assumed a perfectly competitive labor market and any one firm can have no material influence on the market wage for an occupation.

9. If firms' demand curves are drawn as a function of the money wage, they represent the downward-sloping portion of the firms' MRP_L curves. In a competitive industry, the price of the product is given to the firm by the market; thus, at the firm level, the MRP_L has imbedded a given product price. When aggregating labor demand to the *market* level, product price can no longer be taken as given, and the aggregation is no longer a simple summation.

10. Because $MP_L = \Delta Q/\Delta L$, the expression W/MP_L can be rewritten as $W \cdot \Delta L/\Delta Q$. Because $W\Delta L$ represents the added cost from employing one more unit of labor, the expression $W\Delta L/\Delta Q$ equals the cost of an added unit of output when that unit is produced by adding labor.

11. For a full statement of this argument, see Armen Alchian and Reuben Kessel, "Competition, Monopoly, and the Pursuit of Money," in *Aspects of Labor Economics*, ed. H.G. Lewis (Princeton, NJ: Princeton University Press, 1962).

12. Ronald G. Ehrenberg, *The Regulatory Process and Labor Earnings* (New York: Academic Press, 1979); Barry T. Hirsch, "Trucking Regulation, Unionization, and Labor Earnings," *Journal of Human Resources* 23 (Summer 1988): 296–319; S. Nickell, J. Vainiomaki, and S. Wadhwani, "Wages and Product Market Power," *Economica* 61 (November 1994): 457–473; Marianne Bertrand and Sendhil Mullainathan, "Is There Discretion in Wage Setting? A Test Using Takeover Legislation," *RAND Journal of Economics* 30 (Autumn 1999): 535–554.

13. For a study finding that employer payroll taxes resulted in lower employee wages, see Patricia M. Anderson and Bruce D. Meyer, "The Effects of the Unemployment Insurance Payroll Tax on Wages, Employment, Claims and Denials," *Journal of Public Economics* 78 (October 2000): 81–106.

14. Emmanuel Saez, Benjamin Schoefer, and David Seim, "Payroll Taxes, Firm Behavior, and Rent Sharing: Evidence from a Young Workers' Tax Cut in Sweden," *American Economic Review* 109 (May 2019): 1717–1763; see also David Neumark, "Spurring Job Creation in Response to Severe Recessions: Reconsidering Hiring Credits," *Journal of Policy Analysis and Management* 32 (Winter 2013): 142–171.

Selected Readings

Blank, Rebecca M., ed. *Social Protection Versus Economic Flexibility: Is There a Trade-Off?* Chicago: University of Chicago Press, 1994.

Hamermesh, Daniel S. *Labor Demand*. Princeton, NJ: Princeton University Press, 1993.

Neumark, David. "Spurring Job Creation in Response to Severe Recessions: Reconsidering Hiring Credits." *Journal of Policy Analysis and Management* 32 (Winter 2013): 142–171.

APPENDIX 3A

Graphical Derivation of a Firm's Labor Demand Curve

This chapter describes the derivation of a firm's labor demand curve. This appendix will present the *same* derivation graphically. This graphical representation permits a more rigorous derivation, but our conclusion that demand curves slope downward in both the short run and the long run will remain unchanged.

The Production Function

Output can generally be viewed as being produced by combining capital and labor. Figure 3A.1 illustrates this production function graphically and depicts several aspects of the production process.

Consider the convex curve labeled $Q = 100$. Along this line, every combination of labor (L) and capital (K) produces 100 units of output (Q). That is, the combination of labor and capital at point A (L_a, K_a) generates the same 100 units of output as the combinations at points B and C. Because each point along the $Q = 100$ curve generates the same output, that curve is called an *isoquant* (*iso* = "equal," *quant* = "quantity").

Two other isoquants are shown in Figure 3A.1 ($Q = 150$, $Q = 200$). These isoquants represent higher levels of output than the $Q = 100$ curve does. The fact that these isoquants indicate higher output levels can be seen by holding labor constant at L_b (say) and then observing the different levels of capital. If L_b is combined with K_b in capital, 100 units of Q are produced. If L_b is combined with K'_b, 150 units are produced (K'_b is greater than K_b).

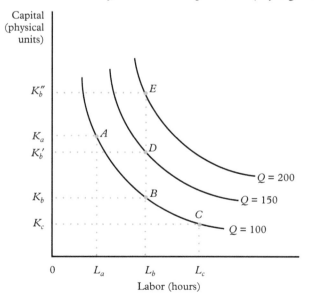

Figure 3A.1 A Production Function

If L_b is combined with even more capital (K_b'', say), 200 units of Q could be produced.

Note that the isoquants in Figure 3A.1 have *negative* slopes, reflecting an assumption that labor and capital are substitutes. If, for example, we cut capital from K_a to K_b, we could keep output constant (at 100) by increasing labor from L_a to L_b. Labor, in other words, could be substituted for capital to maintain a given production level.

Finally, note the *convexity* of the isoquants. At point A, the $Q = 100$ isoquant has a steep slope, suggesting that to keep Q constant at 100, a given decrease in capital could be accompanied by a *modest* increase in labor. At point C, however, the slope of the isoquant is relatively flat. This flatter slope means that the same given decrease in capital would require a much *larger* increase in labor for output to be held constant. The decrease in capital permitted by a given increase in labor while output is being held constant is called the *marginal rate of technical substitution* (*MRTS*) between capital and labor. Symbolically, the *MRTS* can be written as

$$MRTS = \frac{\Delta K}{\Delta L}\Big|\bar{Q} \tag{3.A1}$$

where Δ means "change in" and $\bar{Q}$ means "holding output constant." The *MRTS* is negative because if L is increased, K must be reduced to keep Q constant.

Why does the absolute value of the *MRTS* diminish as labor increases? When labor is highly used in the production process and capital is not prevalent (point C in Figure 3A.1), capital can do many jobs. Labor is easy to replace; if capital is increased, it will be used as a substitute for labor in parts of the production process where it will have the highest payoff. As capital becomes progressively more used and labor less so, the few remaining workers will be doing jobs that are hardest for a machine to do, at which point a lot of capital will be required to substitute for a worker.[1]

Demand for Labor in the Short Run

This chapter argues that firms will maximize profits in the short run (K fixed) by hiring labor until labor's marginal product (MP_L) is equal to the real wage (W/P). The reason for this decision rule is that the real wage represents the *cost* of an added unit of labor (in terms of output), whereas the marginal product is the *output* added by the extra unit of labor. As long as the firm, by increasing labor (K fixed), gains more in output than it loses in costs, it will continue to hire employees. The firm will stop hiring when the marginal cost of added labor exceeds MP_L.

The requirement that $MP_L = W/P$ in order for profits to be maximized means that the firm's labor demand curve in the short run (in terms of the *real* wage) is identical to its MP_L schedule (refer to Figure 3.1). The MP_L is the extra output produced by one-unit increases in the amount of labor employed, holding capital constant; as such, consider the production function displayed in Figure 3A.2. Holding capital constant at K_a, the firm can

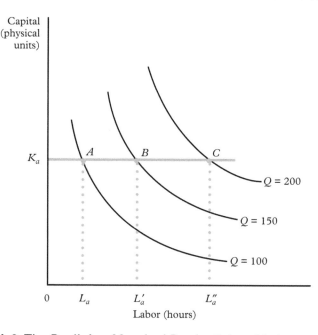

Figure 3A.2 The Declining Marginal Productivity of Labor

produce 100 units of Q if it employs labor equal to L_a. If labor is increased to L_a', the firm can produce 50 more units of Q; if labor is increased from L_a' to L_a'', the firm can produce an additional 50 units. Notice, however, that the required increase in labor to get the latter 50 units of added output, $L_a'' - L_a'$, is larger than the extra labor required to produce the first 50-unit increment $(L_a' - L_a)$. This difference can only mean that as labor is increased when K is held constant, each successive labor hour hired generates progressively smaller increments in output. Put differently, Figure 3A.2 graphically illustrates the diminishing marginal productivity of labor.

Why does labor's marginal productivity decline? This chapter explains that labor's marginal productivity declines because, with K fixed, each added worker has less capital (per capita) with which to work. Is this explanation proven in Figure 3A.2? The answer is, regrettably, no. Figure 3A.2 is drawn *assuming* diminishing marginal productivity. Renumbering the isoquants could produce a different set of marginal productivities. (To see this, change $Q = 150$ to $Q = 200$, and change $Q = 200$ to $Q = 500$. Labor's marginal productivity would then rise.) However, the logic that labor's marginal product must eventually fall as labor is increased—holding buildings, machines, and tools constant—is compelling. Further, as this chapter points out, even if MP_L rises initially, the firm will stop hiring labor only in the range where MP_L is declining; as long as MP_L is above W/P and *rising*, it will pay to continue hiring.

The assumptions that MP_L declines eventually and that firms hire until $MP_L = W/P$ are the bases for the assertion that a firm's short-run demand curve for labor slopes downward. The graphical, more-rigorous derivation of the demand curve in this appendix confirms the analysis in the chapter.

However, it also emphasizes more clearly than the chapter analysis did that the downward-sloping nature of the short-run labor demand curve is based on an *assumption*—however reasonable—that MP_L declines as employment is increased.

Demand for Labor in the Long Run

Recall that a firm maximizes its profits by producing at a level of output (Q^*) where marginal cost equals MR. That is, the firm will keep increasing output until the addition to its revenues generated by an extra unit of output equals the marginal cost of producing that extra unit of output. Because MR, which is equal to output *price* for a competitive firm, is not shown in our graph of the production function, the profit-maximizing level of output cannot be determined. However, continuing our analysis of the production function can illustrate some important aspects of the demand for labor in the long run.

Conditions for Cost Minimization

In Figure 3A.3, profit-maximizing output is assumed to be Q^*. How will the firm combine labor and capital to produce Q^*? It can maximize profits only if it produces Q^* in the least expensive way; that is, it must minimize the costs of producing Q^*. To better understand the characteristics of cost minimization, refer to the three *isoexpenditure* lines—AA', BB', and DD'—in Figure 3A.3. Along any one of these lines, the costs of employing labor and capital are equal.

For example, line AA' represents total costs of $1,000. Given an hourly wage (W) of $10 per hour, the firm could hire 100 hours of labor and incur total costs of $1,000 if it used no capital (point A'). In contrast, if the price

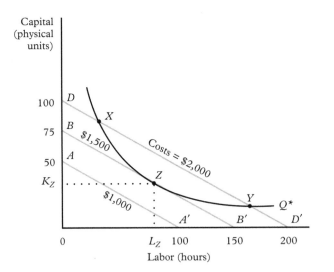

Figure 3A.3 Cost Minimization in the Production of Q^* (Wage = $10 per Hour; Price of a Unit of Capital = $20)

of a unit of capital (C) is $20, the firm could produce at a total cost of $1,000 by using 50 units of capital and no labor (point A). All the points between A and A' represent combinations of L and K that at $W = $10 and $C = $20 cost $1,000 as well.

The problem with the isoexpenditure line of AA' is that it does not intersect the isoquant Q^*, implying that Q^* cannot be produced for $1,000. At prices of $W = $10 and $C = $20, the firm cannot buy enough resources to produce output level Q^* and hold total costs to $1,000. The firm can, however, produce Q^* for a total cost of $2,000. Line DD', representing expenditures of $2,000, intersects the Q^* isoquant at points X and Y. The problem with these points, however, is that they do not minimize costs; Q^* can be produced for less than $2,000.

Since isoquant Q^* is convex, the cost-minimizing combination of L and K in producing Q^* will come at a point where an isoexpenditure line is *tangent* to the isoquant (i.e., just barely touches isoquant Q^* at only one place). Point Z, where labor equals L_Z and capital equals K_Z, is where Q^* can be produced at minimal cost, *given* that $W = $10 and $C = $20. No lower isoexpenditure curve touches the isoquant, meaning that Q^* cannot be produced for less than $1,500.

An important characteristic of point Z is that the slope of the isoquant at point Z and the slope of the isoexpenditure line are the same (the slope of a curve at a given point is the slope of a line tangent to the curve at that point). The slope of the isoquant at any given point is the *MRTS*, as defined in equation (3A.1).

Another way of expressing equation (3A.1) is

$$MRTS = \frac{-\Delta K / \Delta Q}{\Delta L / \Delta Q} \qquad (3A.2)$$

Equation (3A.2) directly indicates that the *MRTS* is a ratio reflecting the reduction of capital required to decrease output by one unit if enough extra labor is hired so that output is tending to increase by one unit. (The ΔQs in equation (3A.2) cancel each other and keep output constant.) If equation (3A.2) is pursued one step further, the numerator and denominator can be rearranged to obtain the following:[2]

$$MRTS = \frac{-\Delta K / \Delta Q}{\Delta L / \Delta Q} = \frac{-\Delta Q / \Delta L}{\Delta Q / \Delta K} = -\frac{MP_L}{MP_K} \qquad (3A.3)$$

where MP_L and MP_K are the marginal productivities of labor and capital, respectively.

The slope of the *isoexpenditure line* is equal to the negative of the ratio W/C (in Figure 3A.3, W/C equals $10 \div 20$, or 0.5).[3] Thus, at point Z, where Q^* is produced in the minimum-cost fashion, the following equality holds:

$$MRTS = -\frac{MP_L}{MP_K} = -\frac{W}{C} \qquad (3A.4)$$

Equation (3A.4) is simply a rearranged version of equation (3.8c).[4]

The economic meaning, or logic, behind the characteristics of cost minimization can most easily be seen by stating the $MRTS$ as $-\dfrac{\Delta K / \Delta Q}{\Delta L / \Delta Q}$ (see equation 3A.2 and equating this version of the $MRTS$ to $-\dfrac{W}{C}$:

$$\frac{\Delta K / \Delta Q}{\Delta L / \Delta Q} = -\frac{W}{C} \tag{3A.5}$$

or

$$\frac{\Delta K}{\Delta Q} \cdot C = \frac{\Delta L}{\Delta Q} \cdot W \tag{3A.6}$$

Equation (3A.6) makes plain that to be minimizing costs, the cost of producing an extra unit of output by adding only labor must equal the cost of producing that extra unit by employing only additional capital. If these costs differed, the company could reduce total costs by expanding its use of the factor with which output can be increased more cheaply and cutting back on its use of the other factor. Any point where costs can still be reduced while Q is held constant is obviously not a point of cost minimization.

The Substitution Effect

If the wage rate, which was assumed to be $10 per hour in Figure 3A.3, goes up to $20 per hour (holding C constant), what will happen to the cost-minimizing way of producing output of Q^*? Figure 3A.4 illustrates the answer that common sense would suggest: Total costs rise, and more capital and less labor are used to produce Q^*. At $W = 20, 150 units of labor can no longer be purchased if total costs are to be held to $1,500; in fact, if costs are to equal $1,500, only 75 units of labor can be hired. Thus, the isoexpenditure curve for $1,500 in costs shifts from BB' to BB'' and is no longer tangent to isoquant Q^*. Q^* can no longer be produced for $1,500, and the cost of producing Q^* will rise. In Figure 3A.4, we assume the least costly expenditure rises to $2,250 (isoexpenditure line EE' is the one tangent to isoquant Q^*).

Moreover, the increase in the cost of labor relative to capital induces the firm to use more capital and less labor. Graphically, the old tangency point of Z is replaced by a new one (Z'), where the marginal productivity of labor is higher relative to MP_K, as our discussions of equations (3.8c) and equation (3A.4) explained. Point Z' is reached (from Z) by adding more capital and reducing the employment of labor. The movement from L_z to L'_z is the *substitution effect* generated by the wage increase.

The Scale Effect

When Q^* can no longer be produced for $1,500, but instead involves at least $2,250 in costs, this generally means that it is no longer the

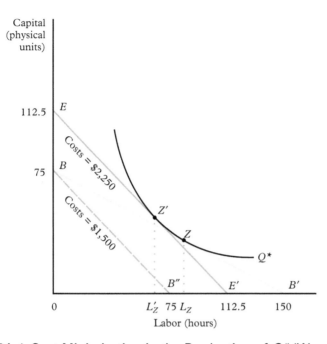

Figure 3A.4 Cost Minimization in the Production of Q^* (Wage = $20 per Hour; Price of a Unit of Capital = $20)

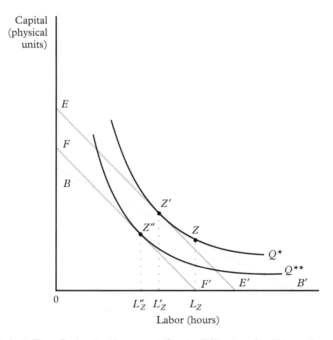

Figure 3A.5 The Substitution and Scale Effects of a Wage Increase

profit-maximizing level of production. The new profit-maximizing level of production will be less than Q^* (how much less cannot be determined unless we know something about the product demand curve; nevertheless, we make the following assumptions to show an example of the size of the effect).

Suppose that the profit-maximizing level of output falls from Q^* to Q^{**}, as shown in Figure 3A.5. Because all isoexpenditure lines have the new slope of -1 when $W = \$20$ and $C = \$20$, the cost-minimizing way to produce Q^{**} lies on an isoexpenditure line parallel to EE'. We find this cost-minimizing way to produce Q^{**} at point Z', where an isoexpenditure line (FF') is tangent to the Q^{**} isoquant.

The *overall* response in the employment of labor to an increase in the wage rate has been a fall in labor usage from L_z to L''_z. The decline from L_z to L''_z is called the substitution effect, as we have noted. It results because the *proportions* of K and L used in production change when the ratio of wages to capital prices (W/C) changes. The *scale effect* can be seen as the reduction in employment from L'_z to L''_z, wherein the usage of K and the usage of L are cut back solely because of the reduced *scale* of production. Both effects are simultaneously present when wages increase and capital prices remain constant, but as Figure 3A.5 emphasizes, the effects are conceptually distinct and occur for different reasons.

Together, these effects lead us to assert that the long-run labor demand curve slopes downward. Note that the entirety of Appendix 3A has plotted just two points on the long-run demand curve. The first point is at a wage of $10 per hour and a quantity of labor of L_z, and the second point is at a wage of $20 per hour and a quantity of labor of L''_z where $L_z > L''_z$.

Notes

1. Here is one example. Over time, telephone operators (who used to place long-distance calls) were replaced by a capital-intensive direct-dialing system. Those operators who remain employed, however, perform tasks that are the most difficult for a machine to perform—handling collect calls, dispensing directory assistance, and acting as troubleshooters when problems arise.

2. This is done by making use of the fact that dividing one number by a second one is equivalent to *multiplying* the first by the *inverse* of the second.

3. Note that $10/20 = 75/150$, or $0B/0B'$.

4. The negative signs on each side of equation (3A.4) cancel each other out and can therefore be ignored.

Labor Demand Elasticities

The focus of this chapter is on the *degree* to which employment responds to changes in wages. In 1995, a heated debate broke out among economists and policymakers about the employment effects of minimum-wage laws. Clearly, the standard theory developed in Chapter 3 predicts that if wages are raised above their market equilibrium level by a minimum-wage law, employment opportunities will be reduced as firms move up (and to the left) along their labor demand curves. Two prominent labor economists, however, after reviewing previous work on the subject and doing new studies of their own, published a 1995 book in which they concluded that the predicted job losses associated with increases in the minimum wage simply could not be observed to occur, at least with any regularity.[1]

The book triggered a highly charged discussion of a long-standing question: How responsive is employment demand to given changes in wages?[2] Good reasons, analyzed in Chapter 3, undergird expectations that as wages rise along a given labor demand curve, employment opportunities will diminish; the topic of Chapter 4 is to analyze what makes these job losses larger or smaller.

The responsiveness of labor demand to a change in wage rates is normally measured as an *elasticity*, which in the case of labor demand is the percentage change in employment brought about by a 1 percent change in wages. We begin our analysis by defining, analyzing, and measuring *own-wage* and *cross-wage* elasticities. We then apply these concepts to analyses of minimum-wage laws and the employment effects of technological innovations.

The Own-Wage Elasticity of Demand

The *own-wage elasticity of demand* for a category of labor is defined as the percentage change in its employment (E) induced by a 1 percent increase in its wage rate (W):

$$\eta_{ii} = \frac{\%\Delta E_i}{\%\Delta W_i} \tag{4.1}$$

In equation (4.1), we use the subscript i to denote category of labor i, the Greek letter η (eta) to represent elasticity, and the notation %Δ to represent "percentage change in." Because, as the previous chapter showed, labor demand curves slope downward, an increase in the wage rate will cause employment to decrease; the own-wage elasticity of demand is therefore a negative number. What is at issue is its magnitude. The larger its *absolute value* (its magnitude, ignoring its sign), the larger the percentage decline in employment associated with any given percentage increase in wages.

Labor economists often focus on whether the absolute value of the elasticity of demand for labor is greater than or less than 1. If it is greater than 1, a 1 percent increase in wages will lead to an employment decline of greater than 1 percent; this situation is referred to as an *elastic* demand curve. In contrast, if the absolute value is less than 1, the demand curve is said to be *inelastic*: A 1 percent increase in wages will lead to a proportionately smaller decline in employment. If demand is elastic, aggregate earnings (defined here as the wage rate times the employment level) of individuals in the category will decline when the wage rate increases, because employment falls at a faster rate than wages rise. Conversely, if demand is inelastic, aggregate earnings will increase when the wage rate is increased. If the elasticity equals 1, the demand curve is said to be *unitary elastic*, and aggregate earnings will remain unchanged if wages increase.

Figure 4.1 shows that the flatter of the two demand curves graphed (D_1) has greater elasticity than the steeper (D_2). Beginning with any wage (e.g., W), a given wage change (e.g., to W') will yield greater responses in employment with demand curve D_1 than with D_2. To judge the different elasticities of response brought about by the same percentage wage increase, compare $(E_1 - E'_1)/E_1$ with $(E_2 - E'_2)/E_2$. Clearly, the more elastic response occurs along D_1.

To speak of a demand curve as having "an" elasticity, however, is technically incorrect. Given demand curves generally have elastic and inelastic ranges, and although we are usually interested only in the elasticity of demand in the range around the current equilibrium wage rate in any market, we cannot fully understand elasticity without comprehending that it can vary along a given demand curve.

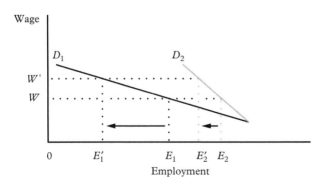

Figure 4.1 Relative Demand Elasticities

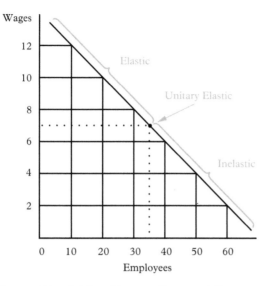

Figure 4.2 Different Elasticities Along a Demand Curve

To illustrate, suppose that we examine the typical straight-line demand curve that we have used so often in Chapters 2 and 3 (see Figure 4.2). One feature of a linear (straight-line) demand curve is that at *each* point along the curve, a unit change in wages induces the *same* response in units of employment. For example, at any point along the demand curve shown in Figure 4.2, a $2 decrease in wages will increase the demand for employment by 10 workers.

However, the same responses in *unit* changes along the demand curve do *not* imply equal *percentage* changes. To see this point, look first at the upper end of the demand curve in Figure 4.2 (the end where wages are high and demand for employment is low). A $2 decrease in wages when the base is $12 represents a 16.67 percent reduction in wages, while an addition of 10 workers when the starting point is also 10 represents a 100 percent increase in demand. Demand at this point is clearly *elastic*. However, if we look at the same unit changes in the lower region of the demand curve (low wages, high demand for employment), demand there is inelastic. A $2 reduction in wages from a $4 base is a 50 percent reduction, while an increase of 10 workers from a base of 50 is only a 20 percent increase. Because the percentage increase in employment is smaller than the percentage decrease in wages, demand is seen to be inelastic at this end of the curve. Thus, the upper end of a straight-line demand curve will exhibit greater elasticity than the lower end will. Moreover, a straight-line demand curve will actually be elastic in some ranges and inelastic in others (as shown in Figure 4.2).

The Hicks–Marshall Laws of Derived Demand

The factors that influence own-wage elasticity can be summarized by the Hicks–Marshall laws of derived demand—four laws named after two distinguished U.K. economists, John Hicks and Alfred Marshall, who are closely associated with their development.[3] These laws assert that other things being equal, the own-wage elasticity of demand for a category of labor is generally higher under the following conditions:

1. when the price elasticity of demand for the product being produced is higher
2. when other factors of production can be more easily substituted for the category of labor
3. when the supply of other factors of production is more highly elastic (i.e., usage of other factors of production can be increased without substantially increasing their prices)
4. when the cost of employing the category of labor is a larger share of the total costs of production

In seeking to explain why these laws generally hold, pretend that we can divide the process by which an increase in the wage rate affects the demand for labor into two steps. First, an increase in the wage rate increases the relative cost of the category of labor in question and induces employers to use less of it and more of other inputs (the *substitution effect*). Second, when the wage increase causes the marginal costs of production to rise, pressures to increase product prices and reduce output ensue, causing a fall in employment (the *scale effect*). The four laws of derived demand each deal with substitution or scale effects.

Demand for the Final Product   We noted earlier that wage increases cause production costs to rise and tend to result in product price increases. The greater the price elasticity of demand for the final product, the larger the percentage decline in output associated with a given percentage increase in price and the greater the percentage decrease in output, the greater the percentage loss in employment (other things being equal). Thus, *the greater the elasticity of demand for the product, the greater the elasticity of demand for labor*.

One implication of this first law is that other things being equal, the demand for labor at the *firm* level will be more elastic than the demand for labor at the *industry*, or market, level. For example, the product demand curves facing *individual* carpet-manufacturing companies are highly elastic because the carpet of company X is a close substitute for the carpet of company Y. Compared with price increases at the *firm* level, however, price increases at the *industry* level will not have as large an effect on demand, because the closest substitutes for carpeting are hardwood, ceramic, or some kind of vinyl floor covering—none a close substitute for carpeting. (For the same reasons, the labor demand curve for a monopolist is less elastic than for an individual *firm* in a competitive industry. Monopolists, after all, face *market* demand curves for their product, because they are the only seller in the particular market.)

Another implication of this first law is that *wage elasticities will be higher in the long run than in the short run*. The reason for this is that price elasticities of demand in product markets are higher in the long run. In the short run, a product may not have any good substitutes, or consumers may be locked into their current stock of consumer durables. After a period of time, however, new products that are substitutes may be introduced, and consumers will begin to replace durables that have worn out.

Substitutability of Other Factors   As the wage rate of a category of labor increases, firms have an incentive to try to substitute other, now relatively cheaper, inputs for the category. Suppose, however, that there were no substitution possibilities; a given number of units of the type of labor *must* be used to produce one unit of output. In this case, no reduction in employment occurs because of the substitution effect. In contrast, when substitution possibilities do present themselves, a reduction in employment owing to the substitution effect will accompany whatever reductions are caused by the scale effect. Hence, other things being equal, *the easier it is to substitute other factors of production, the greater the wage elasticity of labor demand will be.*[4]

Limitations on substitution possibilities need not be solely technical ones. For example, as we shall see in Chapter 13, labor unions often try to limit substitution possibilities by including specific work rules in their contracts (e.g., minimum crew size for railroad locomotives). Alternatively, the government may legislate limitations by specifying minimum employment levels for safety reasons (e.g., each public swimming pool in New York state must always have a lifeguard present). Such restrictions make the demand for labor less elastic, but substitution possibilities that are not feasible in the short run may well become feasible over longer periods of time. For example, if the wages of railroad workers went up, companies could buy more powerful locomotives and operate with larger trains and fewer locomotives. Likewise, if the wages of lifeguards rose, cities might build larger, but fewer, swimming pools. Both adjustments would occur only in the long run, which is another reason why the demand for labor is more elastic in the long run than in the short run.

The Supply of Other Factors   Suppose that, as the wage rate increased and employers attempted to substitute other factors of production for labor, the prices of these other factors were bid up. This situation might occur, for example, if we were trying to substitute capital equipment for labor. If producers of capital equipment were already operating their plants at near capacity, so that taking on new orders would cause them substantial increases in costs because they would have to work their employees at overtime and pay them a wage premium, they would accept new orders only if they could charge a higher price for their equipment. Such a price increase would dampen firms' "appetites" for capital and thus limit the substitution of capital for labor.

For another example, suppose that an increase in the wages of lower-skilled workers caused employers to attempt to substitute higher-skilled employees for lower-skilled employees. If only a fixed number of higher-skilled workers were available in an area, their wages would be bid up by employers. As in the previous example, the incentive to substitute alternative factors would be reduced, and the reduction in lower-skilled employment because of the substitution effect would be smaller. In contrast, if the prices of other inputs did not increase when employers attempted to increase their use, other things being equal, the substitution effect—and thus the wage elasticity of labor demand—would be larger.

Note again that prices of other inputs are less likely to be bid up in the long run than in the short run. In the long run, existing producers of capital equipment can expand their capacity and new producers can enter the market. Similarly, in the long run, more high-skilled workers can be trained. This observation is an additional reason why the demand for labor will be more elastic in the long run.

The Share of Labor in Total Costs   Finally, the share of the category of labor in total costs is crucial to the size of the elasticity of labor demand. If the category's initial share were 20 percent, a 10 percent increase in the wage rate, other things being equal, would raise total costs by 2 percent. In contrast, if its initial share were 80 percent, a 10 percent increase in the wage rate would increase total costs by 8 percent. Since employers would have to increase their product prices by more in the latter case, output and employment would fall more in that case. *Thus, the greater the category's share in total costs, the greater the wage elasticity of demand.*[5]

Estimates of Own-Wage Labor Demand Elasticities

We now turn to the results of studies that estimate own-wage demand elasticities for labor as a generic input (i.e., labor undifferentiated by skill level). The estimates we discuss are based on studies that use wage, output, and employment data from firms or narrowly defined industries. Thus, the employment responses being estimated approximate those that would be expected to occur in a firm that had to raise wages to remain competitive in the labor market. These estimates suggest what might be a "typical" response but, of course, are not indicative of what would happen with any particular firm.

As our analysis has indicated, employers' labor demand responses to a wage change can be broken down into two components: a scale effect and a substitution effect. These two effects can themselves be expressed as elasticities, and their sum is the own-wage labor demand elasticity. In Table 4.1, we display the results of estimates of the following:

1. the short-run scale effect

2. the substitution effect

3. the overall elasticity of demand for labor in the long run

The scale effect (expressed as an elasticity) is defined as the percentage change in employment associated with a given percentage change in the

Table 4.1 Components of the Own-Wage Elasticity of Demand for Labor: Empirical Estimates Using Plant-Level Data

Estimated elasticity	
Short-run scale effect	
British manufacturing firms, 1974–1982	–0.53
Substitution effect	
32 studies using plant or narrowly defined industry data	Average: –0.45 (typical range: –0.15 to –0.75)
Overall labor demand elasticity	
British plants, 1984	–0.93
British coal mines, 1950–1980	–1.0 to –1.4

Source: Daniel S. Hamermesh, *Labor Demand* (Princeton, NJ: Princeton University Press, 1993): 94–104

wage, *holding production technology constant*; that is, it is the employment response that occurs without a substitution effect. By definition, the *short-run* labor demand elasticity includes *only* the scale effect, although we noted earlier that the scale effect is likely to be greater in the long run than it is in the short run (owing to greater possibilities for *product market* substitutions in the long run). Therefore, estimates of short-run labor demand elasticities will be synonymous with the short-run scale effect, which may approximate the long-run scale effect if product market substitutions are relatively swift. A study using data from U.K. manufacturing plants estimated the short-run, own-wage labor demand elasticity to be –0.53 (see Table 4.1). The short-run labor demand curve for a typical firm or narrowly defined sector, therefore, would appear to be inelastic.

The substitution effect, when expressed as an elasticity, is the percentage change in employment associated with a given percentage change in the wage rate, *holding output constant.* That is, it is a measure of how employers change their production techniques in response to wage changes, even if output does not change (i.e., even if the scale effect is absent). Many more studies of substitution effects have been done because they are easier to credibly estimate. One careful summary of 32 studies estimating substitution-effect elasticities placed the average estimated elasticity at –0.45 (displayed in Table 4.1), with most estimates falling into the range of –0.15 to –0.75.[6]

With the short-run scale elasticity and the substitution elasticity each close to –0.5, estimates of the long-run overall elasticity of demand for labor are, unsurprisingly, close to unitary in magnitude. Table 4.1 indicates that a study of plants across several U.K. industries estimated an own-wage elasticity of –0.93, whereas another of U.K. coal mines placed the elasticity of demand for labor in the range of –1.0 to –1.4. Thus, these estimates suggest that if the market wages a firm must pay rise by 10 percent, the firm's employment will shrink by close to 10 percent in the long run, other things being equal (i.e., unless something else occurs that also affects the demand for labor). More-recent studies of the elasticity of demand for labor estimate elasticities in the same general range.[7]

Applying the Laws of Derived Demand: Inferential Analysis

Because empirical estimates of demand elasticities that may be required for making particular decisions are often lacking, guessing what these elasticities are likely to be is frequently necessary. In making these guesses, we can apply the laws of derived demand to predict at least relative magnitudes for various types of labor. Consider first the demand for unionized New York City garment workers. As we discuss in Chapter 13, because labor unions are complex organizations, they cannot always specify their goals. Nevertheless, most unions clearly value both wage *and* employment opportunities for their members. This observation leads to the simple prediction that other things being equal, the more elastic the demand for labor, the smaller the wage gain that a union will succeed in winning for its members. The reason for this prediction is that the more elastic the demand curve, the greater the percentage of employment decline associated with any given percentage increase in wages. As a result, we can expect the following:

1. Unions would win larger wage gains for their members in markets with more inelastic labor demand curves.

2. Unions would strive to take actions that reduce the wage elasticity of demand for their members' services.

3. Unions might first seek to organize workers in markets in which labor demand curves are more inelastic (because the potential gains to unionization are higher in these markets).

Because of foreign and domestic competition, the price elasticity of demand for the clothing produced by New York City garment workers is extremely high. Employers can easily find other inputs to substitute for these workers—that is, lower-paid nonunion garment workers in the U.S. South or in other countries. These facts lead one to predict that the wage elasticity of demand for New York City unionized garment workers is high. Consequently, union wage demands in this industry have historically been moderate. The union has also sought to reduce the elasticity of product demand by supporting policies that reduce foreign competition, and it has pushed for higher federal minimum wages to reduce employers' incentives to move their plants to the U.S. South. (For another illustration of how an elastic *product* demand inhibits union wage increases, see Example 4.1.)

Next, consider the wage elasticity of demand for unionized airplane pilots in the United States. Only a small share of the costs of operating large airplanes goes to pay pilots' salaries; such salaries are dwarfed by fuel and capital costs. Furthermore, substitution possibilities are limited; airlines have little room to substitute lower-skilled labor for higher-skilled pilots (although airlines can substitute capital for labor by reducing the number of flights they offer while increasing the size of airplanes). In addition, before the deregulation of the airline industry in 1978, many airlines faced no competition on many of their routes or were prohibited from reducing their prices to compete with other airlines that flew the same routes. These factors all suggest that the wage elasticity of demand for airline pilots was quite low (inelastic). As one might expect, pilots' wages were also quite high because their union could push for large wage increases without fear that these increases would substantially reduce pilots' employment levels. However, after airline deregulation, competition among airline carriers increased substantially, leading to a more elastic labor demand for pilots. As a result, many airlines "requested," and won, reduced wages from their pilots.

EXAMPLE 4.1

Why Are Union Wages So Different in Two Parts of the Trucking Industry?

The trucking industry's "general freight" sector, made up of motor carriers that handle nonspecialized freight requiring no special handling or equipment, is split into two segments. One type of general freight carrier exclusively handles full truckloads (TLs), taking them directly from a shipper to a destination. The other type of carrier handles less-than-truckload (LTL) shipments, which involve multiple shipments on each truck and an intricate coordination of pickups and deliveries. These two segments of the general freight industry have different *elasticities of product demand*; thus, the union that represents truck drivers has a different ability to raise wages (without suffering unacceptable losses of employment) in each segment.

The TL part of the industry has a competitive product market, because firms or individuals can relatively easily enter the market; one needs only a truck, the proper driver's license, and access to a cell phone (to call a freight broker, who matches available drivers with shipments needing delivery). Because this part of the industry has many competing firms, with the threat of even more if prices rise, each firm faces a relatively elastic product demand curve.

Firms specializing in LTL shipments must have a complex system of coordinated routes running between and within cities, and they must therefore be large enough to support their own terminals for storing and transferring shipments from one route to another. The LTL segment of the industry is not easily entered and thus is partially monopolized. From 1980 to 1995—a time period over which the number of TL carriers tripled—generally the only new entrants into the LTL market were regional subsidiaries of pre-existing national carriers. Thus, in 1987 for example, the four largest LTL carriers accounted for 37 percent of total LTL revenues, while the four largest TL carriers accounted for only 11 percent of TL revenues.

The greater extent of competition in the TL part of the industry implies that at the firm level, *product* demand is more elastic there than in the LTL sector; other things being equal, then, we would expect the *labor* demand curve to also be more elastic in the TL sector. Because unions worry about potential job losses when negotiating with carriers about wages, we would expect to find that union wages are lower in the TL than in the LTL part of the industry. In fact, a 1991 survey revealed that the union mileage rates (drivers are typically compensated on a cents-per-mile basis) were dramatically different in the two sectors:

TL sector

Average union rate: 28.4 cents per mile ratio, union to nonunion rate: 1.23

LTL sector

Average union rate: 35.8 cents per mile ratio, union to nonunion rate: 1.34

These data are consistent with the theoretical implication that a union's power to raise wages is greater when product (and therefore labor) demand is relatively inelastic. In the less-competitive LTL segment of the trucking industry, union drivers' wages are higher, both absolutely and relative to nonunion wages, than they are in the more competitive TL sector.

Sources: Michael H. Belzer, "Collective Bargaining After Deregulation: Do the Teamsters Still Count?" *Industrial and Labor Relations Review* 48 (July 1995): 636–655; Michael H. Belzer, *Paying the Toll: Economic Deregulation of the Trucking Industry* (Washington, DC: Economic Policy Institute, 1994)

The Cross-Wage Elasticity of Demand

Because firms may employ several categories of labor and capital, the demand for any one category can be affected by price changes in the others. For example, if the wages of carpenters rose, more people might build brick homes and the demand for *masons* might increase. An increase in carpenters' wages might decrease the overall level of home building in the economy, however, which would decrease the demand for *plumbers*. Finally, changes in the price of *capital* could increase or decrease the demand for workers in all three trades.

The direction and magnitude of these effects can be summarized by examining the elasticities of demand for inputs with respect to the prices of *other* inputs. The *elasticity of demand for input j with respect to the price of input k* is the percentage change in the demand for input *j* induced by a 1 percent change in the price of input *k*. If the two inputs are both categories of labor, these *cross-wage elasticities of demand* are given by

$$\eta_{jk} = \frac{\% \Delta E_j}{\% \Delta W_k} \tag{4.2}$$

and

$$\eta_{kj} = \frac{\% \Delta E_k}{\% \Delta W_j} \tag{4.3}$$

where, again, the Greek letter η is used to represent elasticity. If the cross-elasticities are positive (with an increase in the price of one "category" increasing the demand for the other), the two are said to be *gross substitutes*. If these cross-elasticities are negative (and an increase in the price of one "category" reduces the demand for the other), the two are said to be *gross complements* (refer back to Figure 3.3).

Whether two inputs are gross substitutes or gross complements depends on the relative sizes of the scale and substitution effects. To see this, suppose that we assume that adults and teenagers are substitutes in production. A decrease in the teenage wage will thus have opposing effects on adult employment. On the one hand, a substitution effect occurs: For a given level of output, employers will now have an incentive to substitute teens for adults in the production process and reduce adult employment. On the other hand, a scale effect occurs: A lower teenage wage reduces costs and provides employers with an incentive to increase employment of all inputs, including adults.

If the scale effect proves to be smaller than the substitution effect, adult employment will move in the same direction as teenage wages, and the two groups will be gross substitutes. In contrast, if the scale effect is larger than the substitution effect, adult employment and teenage wages will move in opposite directions, and the two groups will be gross complements. Knowing that two groups are substitutes in production, then, is not sufficient to tell us whether they are gross substitutes or gross complements.[8]

Because economic theory cannot indicate in advance whether two given inputs will be gross substitutes or gross complements, the major policy questions about cross-wage elasticities of demand relate to the issue of their *sign*; that is, we often most want to know whether a particular cross-elasticity is positive or negative. Before turning to a review of actual findings, we analyze underlying forces that determine the signs of cross-elasticities.

Can the Laws of Derived Demand Be Applied to Cross-Elasticities?

The Hicks–Marshall laws of derived demand are based on four technological or market conditions that determine the size of *own-wage* elasticities. Each of the four conditions influences the substitution or the scale effect, and as noted earlier, the relative strengths of these two effects are also what determine the sign of *cross-elasticities*. The laws that apply to own-wage elasticities cannot be applied directly to cross-elasticities, because with cross-elasticities, the substitution effect (if one occurs) and the scale effect work in opposite directions. The same underlying considerations, however, are basic to an analysis of cross-elasticities.

We discuss these four considerations in the context of cross-elasticities with the following example in mind. Let us return, then, to the question of what might happen to the demand for adult workers if the wages of teenage workers were to fall. As noted earlier, the answer depends on the relative strengths of the scale and substitution effects. What determines the strength of each?

The Scale Effect   The most immediate effect of a fall in the wages of teenagers would be reduced production costs for those firms that employ them. Competition in the product market would ensure that lower costs are followed by price reductions, which should stimulate increases in both product demand and the level of output. Increased levels of output tend to cause increases in employment of all kinds of workers, including adults. This chain of events obviously describes behavior underlying the scale effect, and we now investigate what conditions are likely to make for a strong (or weak) scale effect.

The initial cost (and price) reductions would be greater among those employers for whom teenage wages constituted a higher proportion of total costs. Other things being equal, greater price reductions would result in greater increases in both product demand and overall employment. Thus, *the share of total costs devoted to the productive factor whose price is changing* influences the size of the scale effect. The larger this share, other things being equal, the greater the scale effect (and the more likely gross complementarity will exist). This tendency is analogous to the fourth Hicks–Marshall law discussed earlier; the difference is that with cross-elasticities, the factor whose *price* is changing is not the same as the one for which *employment* changes are being analyzed.

The other condition that greatly influences the size of the scale effect is product demand elasticity. In the earlier case, of teenage wage reductions, the greater the increase in product demand when firms reduce their prices, the greater the tendency for employment of all workers, including adults, to increase. More generally, *the greater the price elasticity of product demand, other things being equal, the greater the scale effect (and thus the greater the likelihood of gross complementarity)*. The effects of product demand elasticity are thus similar for both own-wage and cross-wage elasticities.

The Substitution Effect   After teenage wages fall, firms will also have incentives to alter their production techniques so that teenagers are more heavily used. Whether the greater use of teenagers causes an increase or some loss of adult jobs partially depends on a technological question: Are teenagers and adults substitutes or complements in production? If they are complements in production, the effect on adults of changing productive techniques will reinforce the scale effect and serve to unambiguously increase adult employment (meaning, of course, that adults and teenagers would be gross complements). If they are substitutes in production, however, then changing productive techniques involves increasing the ratio of teenagers to adults, and the question then becomes whether this substitution effect is large or small relative to the scale effect.

A technological condition affecting the size of the substitution effect is a direct carryover from the second Hicks–Marshall law discussed earlier: *The substitution effect will be greater when the category of labor whose price has changed is easily substituted for other factors of production*. During an analysis of the effects on adult employment of a decline in the teenage wage, when teenagers are more easily substituted for adults, the substitution effect (and therefore the chances of gross substitutability between the two categories of labor) will clearly be greater.

Another condition influencing the size of the substitution effect associated with a reduction in the teenage wage relates to the labor supply curve of adults. If the adult labor supply curve were upward sloping and rather steep, then adult wages would tend to fall as teenagers were substituted for adults and the demand curve for adults shifted left. This fall would blunt the substitution effect because adults would also become cheaper to hire. Conversely, if the adult labor supply curve were relatively flat, adult wages would be less affected by reduced demand and the substitution effect would be less blunted. As in the case of own-wage elasticities, *more-elastic supply curves of substitute inputs also lead to a greater substitution effect, other things being equal, in the case of cross-wage elasticities.*[9]

Estimates Relating to Cross-Elasticities

Estimating at least the *sign* of cross-wage labor demand elasticities is useful for answering many public policy questions. For example, if we were to reduce the *teenage* minimum wage, how would this affect the demand for *adult* labor? If *capital* were to be subsidized, how would this affect the demand for *labor*? Or, to take a hotly debated issue in recent years (and one that we return to in Chapter 10), when *immigrant* labor becomes more available, what are the likely effects on the demand for various types of *native* labor? These questions, of course, are really asking whether the pairs of inputs italicized in each sentence are gross complements or gross substitutes.

Although the major policy interest is whether two inputs are *gross* complements or *gross* substitutes, obtaining credible estimates is challenging (because estimating scale effects is difficult). Therefore, most of the cross-wage empirical studies to date focus on whether two factors are substitutes or complements *in production*. These studies estimate the employment response for one category of labor to a wage or price change elsewhere, *holding output constant* (which in effect allows us to focus just on changes in the *mix* of factors used in production). The factors of production paired together for analysis in these studies are numerous, and the results are not always clear-cut; nevertheless, the findings taken as a whole support at least a few generalizations:[10]

1. Labor and energy are clearly substitutes in production, although their degree of substitutability is small. Labor and materials are probably substitutes in production, where the degree of substitutability is again small.

2. Higher-skilled labor and lower-skilled labor are substitutes in production.[11]

3. We are not certain whether either higher-skilled or lower-skilled labor is a substitute for or a complement with capital in the production process. What does appear to be true is that higher-skilled (or well-educated) labor is more likely to be complementary with capital than is lower-skilled

labor—and that if they are both substitutes for capital, the degree of substitutability is smaller for higher-skilled labor.[12]

4. The finding summarized in 3 suggests that, generally speaking, higher-skilled labor is more likely than lower-skilled labor to be a *gross* complement with capital. This finding is important to our understanding of recent trends in the earnings of higher-skilled and lower-skilled workers (see Chapter 15), because the prices of computers and other high-tech capital goods have fallen dramatically in recent decades. As we discuss later in this chapter, computer and information technologies appear to be substitutes in production for workers who perform routine or repetitive tasks, and appear to be complements in production for those high-skilled workers for whom access to better information technologies increases their productivity.[13]

Policy Application: Effects of Minimum-Wage Laws

History and Description

The Fair Labor Standards Act of 1938 was the first major piece of protective labor legislation adopted at the national level in the United States. Among its provisions were a minimum wage rate, below which hourly wages could not be reduced, an overtime-pay premium for workers who worked long workweeks, and restrictions on the use of child labor. When initially adopted, the federal minimum wage was set at $0.25 an hour and covered roughly 43 percent of all nonsupervisory wage and salary workers—primarily those employed in larger firms involved in interstate commerce (manufacturing, mining, and construction). Both the basic minimum wage and coverage under the minimum wage have expanded over time. Indeed, as of 2009 (and continuing into 2019), the federal[14] minimum wage was set at $7.25 an hour, and roughly 90 percent of all nonsupervisory workers were covered by its provisions.

The minimum wage rate is specified in *nominal* terms and not in terms *relative* to some other wage or price index. As illustrated in Figure 4.3, the nominal wage rate has usually been raised only once every few years. Until the early 1980s, newly legislated federal minimum wage rates were typically around 45 percent of the average hourly wage of production and nonsupervisory employees. During the years between legislation, productivity growth and inflation caused average wages to rise, which caused the minimum wage to often fall by 10 or more percentage points relative to the average wage before being raised again. In the years after 2000, even the newly legislated federal minimums were below 40 percent of the average wage for production and nonsupervisory workers.

Employment Effects: Theoretical Analysis

Since the minimum wage was first legislated, a concern has been that it will reduce employment, especially among the groups that it is intended

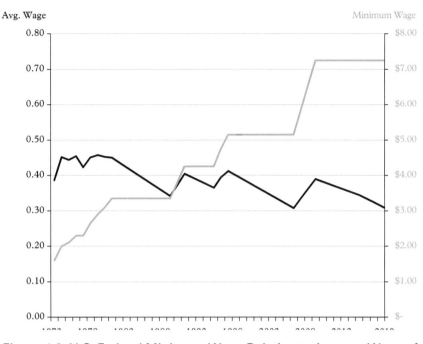

Figure 4.3 U.S. Federal Minimum Wage Relative to Average Wage of Production and Nonsupervisory Employees, 1973–2019

to benefit. In the face of downward-sloping labor demand curves, a policy that compels firms to raise the wages paid to all low-wage workers can be expected to *reduce employment opportunities* for the least skilled or least experienced. Furthermore, if the percentage loss of employment among low-wage workers is greater than the percentage increase in their wages—that is, if the demand curve for low-wage workers is *elastic*—then the *aggregate* earnings of low-wage workers could be made smaller by an increase in the minimum wage.

In evaluating the findings of research on the employment effects of minimum wages, we must keep in mind that good research must be guided by good theory. Theory provides us with a road map that directs our explorations into the real world, and it suggests several issues that must be addressed by any research study of the minimum wage.

Nominal Versus Real Wages   Federal minimum-wage levels in the United States have been set in nominal terms and adjusted by Congress only sporadically. The result is that general price inflation gradually lowers the real minimum wage during the years between congressional action, so what appears to be a fixed minimum wage turns out to have constantly changing incentives for employment.[15]

Also, the federal minimum wage in the United States is uniformly applied to a large country characterized by regional differences in prices. Taking account of regional differences in prices or wages, we find that the federal real minimum wage in Mississippi is higher than it is in Pennsylvania, where wages and prices are generally higher. Recognizing such regional differences in the real minimum wage leads to the prediction that employment effects of a uniformly applied minimum-wage law generally will be most adverse in regions with the lowest costs of living. (Researchers must also take into account the fact that many states have their own minimum-wage laws, many having minimums that exceed the federal minimum.)

Holding Other Things Constant   Predictions of job loss associated with higher minimum wages are made *holding other things constant.* In particular, the prediction grows out of what is expected to happen to employment as one moves up and to the left along a *fixed* labor demand curve. If the labor demand curve were to shift at the same time as a new minimum becomes effective, the employment effects of the shift could be confounded with those of the new minimum.

Consider, for example, Figure 4.4, in which, for simplicity, we have omitted the labor supply curve and focused on only the demand side of the market. Suppose that D_0 is the demand curve for low-skilled labor in year 0, in which year the real wage is W_0/P_0 and the employment level is E_0. Further assume that in the absence of any change in the minimum wage, the money wage and the price level would both increase by the same percentage over the next year, so that the real wage in year 1 (W_1/P_1) would be the same as that in year 0.

Now, suppose that in year 1, two things happen. First, the minimum wage rate is raised to W_2, which is greater than W_1, so that the real wage increases to W_2/P_1. Second, because the economy is expanding, the demand for low-skilled labor shifts out to D_1. The result of these two changes is that employment increases from E_0 to E_1.

Comparisons of observed employment levels at two points of time have led some investigators to conclude that minimum wage increases had no adverse employment effects. However, this simple before/after comparison is not the correct one *if* labor demand has shifted, as in Figure 4.4. Rather, we should ask, how did the actual employment level in period 1 compare with the level that *would have prevailed* in the absence of the increase in the

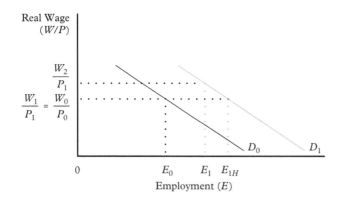

Figure 4.4 Minimum-Wage Effects: Growing Demand Obscures Job Loss

minimum wage? Since demand grew between the two periods, this hypothetical employment level would have been E_{1H}. Note that E_{1H} is greater than E_1, the actual level of employment in period 1. In a growing economy (the shift of labor demand curve D_0 to labor demand curve D_1), then, the expected effect of a one-time increase in the minimum wage (from W_1 to W_2) is to *reduce the rate of growth of employment* (going from E_0 to only E_1 and not all the way to E_{1H}). Controlling for all the "other things" besides wages that affect labor demand turns out to be the major difficulty in measuring employment changes caused by the minimum wage.

Effects of Uncovered Sectors   The federal minimum-wage law, like many government regulations, has an *uncovered* sector. Coverage has increased over the years, but the law still does not apply to some non-supervisory workers (mainly those in small firms in the retail trade and service industries). Also, with millions of employers and limited resources for governmental enforcement, *noncompliance* with the law may be widespread, creating another kind of noncoverage.[16] The existence of uncovered sectors significantly affects how the overall employment of low-wage workers will respond to increases in the minimum wage.

Consider the labor market for lower-skilled, low-wage workers that is depicted in Figure 4.5. The market has two sectors. In one, employers must pay wages equal to at least the minimum wage of W_1; wages in the uncovered sector are free to vary with market conditions and can, therefore, be less than the minimum wage. While the total labor supply to both markets taken as a whole is fixed at E_T (i.e., the total labor supply curve is vertical), workers can freely move from one sector to the other in seeking better job offers. Free movement between sectors suggests that in the absence of minimum-wage regulations, the wage in each sector will be the same. Referring to Figure 4.5, let us assume that this "pre-minimum" wage is W_0 and that total employment of E_T is broken down into E_0^c in the covered sector plus E_0^u in the uncovered sector: $E_T = E_0^c + E_0^u$

If a minimum wage of W_1 is imposed on the covered sector, all lower-skilled workers will prefer to work there because $W_1 > W_0$ (and we assume

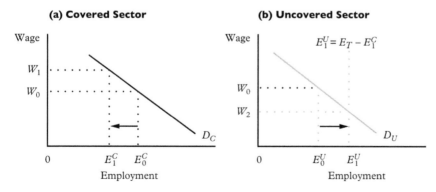

Figure 4.5 Minimum-Wage Effects: Incomplete Coverage Causes Employment Shifts

that all other attributes of the jobs are the same across sectors). However, the increase in wages in that sector, from W_0 to W_1, decreases demand, and covered sector employment will therefore fall from E_0^c to E_1^c. Some workers who previously had, or would have found, jobs in the covered sector must now seek work in the uncovered sector. Thus, to the E_0^u workers formerly working in the uncovered sector are added E_0^c- other workers seeking jobs there. Hence, all lower-skilled workers in the market who are not lucky enough to find "covered jobs" at W_1 must now look for work in the uncovered sector,[17] and the (vertical) supply curve to that sector becomes $E_1^u = E_0^u + (E_0^c - E_1^c) = E_T - E_1^c$. The increased supply of workers to that sector drives down the wage there from W_0 to W_2.

The presence of an uncovered sector thus suggests the possibility that employment among lower-skilled workers will be rearranged, but not decreased, by an increase in the minimum wage. In the foregoing example, all E_T workers remained employed after the minimum was imposed. Rather than reducing the overall employment of lower-skilled workers, then, a partially covering minimum-wage law might serve to shift employment out of the covered sector to the uncovered sector, which would further lead wages in the uncovered sector to be driven down.

The magnitude of any employment shift from the covered sector to the uncovered sector, of course, depends on the size of the latter; the smaller it is, the lower are the chances that job losers from the covered sector will find employment there. Whatever the size of the uncovered sector, however, its presence means that the *overall* loss of employment is likely to be less than the loss of employment in the covered sector.

Intersectoral Shifts in Product Demand   The employment effects of a wage change are the result of scale and substitution effects. Substitution effects stem from changes in how firms choose to produce, and scale effects are rooted in consumer adjustments to changes in product prices. Recall that faced with a given increase (say) in the minimum wage, firms' increases in costs will generally be greater when the share of low-wage labor in total costs is greater; thus, the same increase in the minimum wage can lead to rather different effects on product prices among different parts of the covered sector. Furthermore, if these subsectors compete with each other for customers, scale effects of the increased wage might serve to *increase* employment among some firms in the covered sector.

Suppose, for example, that convenience stores sell items that supermarkets also carry and that a minimum-wage law raises the wages paid to low-skilled workers in both kinds of stores. If low-skilled labor costs are a higher fraction of total costs in convenience stores than they are in supermarkets, then, other things being equal, the minimum-wage law would raise costs in convenience stores by a greater percentage. With prices of items increasing more in convenience stores than in supermarkets, consumers would tend to shift some of their convenience store purchases to supermarkets. Thus, the minimum wage increase could have an ambiguous effect on employment in supermarkets. On the one hand, increased costs of low-skilled workers in supermarkets would create scale and substitution effects that cause employment to decline. On the other hand, because supermarkets may pick up business formerly going to convenience stores, these supermarkets may experience a scale effect that could work to increase their demand for labor.

Employment Effects: Empirical Estimates

Although the initial employment effects of adopting a minimum wage in the United States were readily observed (see Example 4.2), the effects of more-recent increases are not as obvious and must therefore be studied by using sophisticated statistical techniques. The demographic group for which the effects of minimum wages are expected to be most visible is composed of teenagers—a notoriously low-paid group—but studies of how mandated wage increases have affected their employment have produced no consensus.

EXAMPLE 4.2

The Employment Effects of the First U.S. Federal Minimum Wage

When the federal minimum wage first went into effect, on October 24, 1938, its impact was expected to be substantial on the economy of the U.S. South, where wages were much lower than in the rest of the country. An examination of one of the largest manufacturing industries in the U.S. South, seamless hosiery, verifies these predictions.

By 1940, nearly one-third of the labor force in the seamless hosiery industry earned within 2.5 cents per hour of the minimum wage (which was then 32.5 cents per hour). A longitudinal survey of 87 firms shows that employment, which had been rising, reversed course and started to fall, even though overall demand for the product and production levels were rising. Employment fell by 5.5 percent in southern mills but rose by 4.9 percent in northern mills. Even more strikingly, employment fell by 17 percent in mills that had previously paid less than the new minimum wage, while it stayed almost the same at higher-wage mills.

Before the passage of the minimum wage, only a slow movement from the use of hand-transfer to converted-transfer knitting machines took place. (A converted-transfer machine had an attachment to enable automated production for certain types of work.) The minimum wage seems to have accelerated this trend. In the first two years of the law's existence, a 23 percent decrease in the number of hand-transfer machines, a 69 percent increase in converted-transfer machines, and a 10 percent increase in fully automatic machines occurred. In addition, the machines were used more intensively than before. A night shift was added at many mills, and these workers did not receive extra pay for working this undesirable (to most workers) shift. Finally, total imports of seamless hosiery surged by about 27 percent within two years of the minimum wage's enactment.

Source: Andrew J. Seltzer, "The Effects of the Fair Labor Standards Act of 1938 on the Southern Seamless Hosiery and Lumber Industries," *Journal of Economic History* 57 (June 1997): 396–415

Widely reviewed and replicated studies of employment changes in the fast-food industry, for example, disagree on whether employment was affected at all by minimum wage increases in the early 1990s.[18] Studies that have reviewed and updated earlier estimates of how *overall* teenage employment has responded to increases in the minimum wage, however, have found negative effects on employment. Once account is taken of the extent to which minimum wage increases raised the average wage of teenagers, the implications of these studies are that the elasticity of demand for teenagers is in the range of –0.4 to –1.9.[19]

Estimates of how increases in the minimum wage affect employment for *all* low-wage workers, not just teenagers, suggests an own-wage labor demand elasticity that is considerably lower. One study examined the employment status of those who were at or near the minimum wage right before it increased and then looked at their employment status a year later. The estimated decline in the probability of employment implied that the labor demand curve facing these workers has an own-wage elasticity of roughly –0.15.[20] Another study found that employment reductions associated with minimum-wage increases were roughly twice as large two years after the increase than they were immediately afterwards, mostly because job growth declines in expanding establishments; however, yet another study found no effect on low-wage employment in most industries in both the short run and the long run.[21]

Given that some studies estimated no effect on employment, and that many of those that do show an effect estimate an own-wage labor demand elasticity well below unity (the average we saw in Table 4.1), we remain notably uncertain about how employment among low-wage workers responds to increases in the minimum wage. We return to this issue in Chapter 5 and offer a possible reason why *mandated* wage increases might have a smaller and more uncertain effect on labor demand than wage increases generated by market forces.

Does the Minimum Wage Fight Poverty?

Aside from the potentially adverse effects on employment opportunities for low-wage workers, two other reasons suggest that the minimum wage is a relatively ineffective instrument to reduce poverty.[22] First, many who live in poverty are not affected by the minimum wage, either because they are not employed or because their wages, while low, are already above the minimum. For example, one study of the minimum wage increases in 1990–1991 divided the distribution of family incomes into 10 equally sized groups (deciles). Among adults in the lowest decile, 80 percent were below the poverty line (given the size of their families), yet only about one-quarter of them worked; of those who did work, less than one-third earned wages that were less than the new minimum.[23] Thus, even without any loss of employment opportunities, fewer than 10 percent of those in the lowest income decile stood to benefit from the 1990–1991 increases in the minimum wage.

Second, many of those most affected by the minimum wage are teenagers, who may not reside in poor families. The study cited earlier found that only 19 percent of the estimated earnings increases generated by the higher minimum wage went to families with incomes below the poverty line, while over 50 percent of the increases went to families whose incomes were at least twice the poverty level.

Despite these limitations of minimum-wage laws as a means for fighting poverty, in the 2020 presidential campaign and in many state and local governmental discussions, raising the federal minimum wage from $7.25 to $15 per hour was discussed. We use the theory more in depth in Chapter 5 to analyze the potential effects of such a large increase, but two comments on it are in order here. First, the employment effects of increasing the minimum wage have been studied in the context of increases (over two to three years) that have never exceeded 40 percent. A *doubling* of the minimum wage is far outside the bounds of what we have observed in the past, so whether the employment effects found in the past would help us predict such a large increase is unclear. Second, doubling the minimum wage would expand the number of workers affected beyond teenagers and the very low paid, and so could—if employment effects were not too large—serve to reduce the number in poverty more effectively than a lower minimum wage.

"Living Wage" Laws

Perhaps because the federal minimum wage is relatively low and has not been changed often, roughly 100 cities, counties, and school districts in the United States have adopted "living wage" ordinances. These ordinances apply to a subset of employers within their jurisdictions and impose wage floors that are higher than either federal or state minimum wages (or both) on these employers. The affected employers are generally those performing contracts with the local government, although in some cases, the ordinances also apply to employers receiving business assistance from the city or county. Living wage levels usually relate to the federal poverty guidelines, which in 2016 were $20,160 for a family of three and $24,300 for a family of four in the continental United States (it takes wages of $10 to $12 per hour working full time for a year to reach these poverty lines). In 2016, typical wage levels specified by living wage laws were in the range of $10 to $15 per hour.

The potentially beneficial effects of living wage ordinances for low-wage workers are obviously limited by the rather narrow group of employers to which they apply. The benefits are also reduced, of course, if these laws cause the affected employers to either reduce their employment levels or move their operations to cities that do not have living wage regulations.

Estimating the employment effects of adopting living wage laws, however, requires more than merely comparing employment changes in cities with and without such regulations, because the two groups of cities may have fundamentally different employment or wage trends. Cities with rapidly expanding employment opportunities, for example, may decide differently about adopting a living wage law than cities with stagnant or declining opportunities. Because these laws are relatively new and because the best way to evaluate their employment effects is subject to debate, currently no consensus has been reached on how living wage ordinances affect employment.[24]

Applying Concepts of Labor Demand Elasticity to the Issue of Technological Change

We are living in an era of extraordinary technological innovation. The computing power that can be purchased per dollar of expenditure has doubled *each year or two* for the past 50 years.[25] Further, the ability to digitize (convert to the computer language of ones and zeroes) text, sounds, photos, videos, and data from instruments or sensors—like a global positioning system (GPS)—has revolutionized both consumption and production possibilities.[26] Taken together, the expansion of computing power and digitization have created entirely new ways to shop, make travel plans, obtain the news, fill out tax returns, read books, communicate with each other, take photographs, listen to music, and find our way around areas new to us. Those who view these stunning innovations positively point to the improvements that they have made to our standard of living: Comparing and then ordering a myriad of goods, services, or music is far easier to do online than visiting stores; navigating and filling out tax returns by using tax preparation programs is usually cheaper than taking them to a tax preparation expert; using audio and visual devices, we can hold meetings with those far away from us without our having to travel; and using a GPS is easier than using a map.

Those who lament these technological advancements point out the stresses that these innovations have created for many workers. We have seen the closure or shrinkage of department stores, bookstores, and newspapers. Tax preparers and travel agents have had to find new jobs, and those who made a living from selling musical recordings have seen their revenues and employment opportunities decline. Are the concepts underlying the elasticity of demand for labor useful in making judgments about the effects of technological change on workers?

Product Demand Shifts   Two aspects of technological change affect the demand for labor. One is product demand. *Shifts* in product demand curves tend to shift labor demand curves in the same direction, and changes in the *elasticity* of product demand with respect to product price tend to cause qualitatively similar changes in the own-wage elasticity of labor demand. The invention of new products (e.g., personal computers, electronic books, and digital music players) that serve as substitutes for old ones (e.g., typewriters, printed books, and DVD players) tend to shift the labor demand curve in the older sector to the left, causing loss of employment in that sector. If greater product substitution possibilities are also created by these new inventions, the introduction of new products can increase the *elasticity* of product—and labor—demand. Greater labor demand elasticity increases the amount of job loss associated with collectively bargained wage increases of any given magnitude, thus reducing the power of unions to secure wage increases without much job loss. While benefiting consumers and providing jobs in the new sectors, the introduction of new products does necessitate some painful changes in established industries, as workers, unions, and employers must all adjust to a new environment.

Substitutes or Complements in Production? The second aspect of technological change that affects the demand for labor relates to how goods or services are *produced*. Is a given category of labor a substitute or complement *in production* with the now-less-expensive technology? Computers and robots are excellent at following well-specified rules—and thus they can perform routine operations quickly and accurately. They are (at least so far) not suited to creating new ideas or "thinking outside of the box." Thus, the new technologies have tended to be *substitutes in production* with occupations that perform repetitive shop-floor functions or routine office tasks, such as making computations or searching data sets for answers to questions.

The new technologies, however, are *complements in production* with occupations that either create or program the technologies or use them to become more productive. Engineers or technicians, for example, are required to reprogram robots when factory conditions change, even slightly; data analysts can pose more creative questions that have become answerable with the huge data sets now available; high-skilled managers can make use of new networking technologies to manage more people in more places; architects can use computer applications to visualize their plans faster and more accurately; and radiologists can improve the speed and accuracy of their diagnoses by using artificial intelligence to highlight areas of scans predicted to indicate health problems.[27]

Gross Substitutes or Gross Complements? If a category of labor is a complement in production with the new technology, then no substitution effect occurs and *gross complementarity* exists. However, if the two factors are substitutes in production, they may be either *gross substitutes* (if the substitution effect dominates the scale effect) or *gross complements* (if the scale effect dominates). Workers in jobs for which the new technology is highly substitutable tend to be replaced by capital; those in jobs for which the new technology is not easily substituted, or in new jobs created by the technological innovation, might find that they are gross complements with capital (see Example 4.3).

Clearly, whether capital and a given type of labor are gross substitutes or gross complements depends on several factors, all of which are highly specific to particular industries and production processes. Perhaps the most that can be said generally is that substitution effects associated with recent technological innovations have reduced the demand for routine-task jobs both on the shop floor and in the office. On the contrary, gross complementarity with computer and information technologies is more likely for those performing nonroutine managerial or analytical jobs—for which the new technologies are complements in production. Gross complementarity is also more likely for those in nonroutine low-skilled jobs, such as landscaping, childcare, or home care; these service workers may experience an increase in demand (via a dominant scale effect) as the high-skilled workers who benefit from technological advances experience higher incomes and seek help with yard maintenance, childcare, or house cleaning.

Thus, technological change has increased the demand for workers at both the high end and the low end of the wage spectrum while reducing demand for factory and office jobs in the middle of the wage spectrum. In Chapter 15, we return to an analysis of this "polarization."[28]

Economists have also tried to understand how automation in recent decades has affected the *overall* demand for labor. On the one hand, automation can replace labor by taking over tasks (typically the routine tasks mentioned earlier) previously performed by labor; this displacement effect tends to shift the labor demand curve to the left. On the other hand, automation can create new jobs (in app development or computer security, for example) or enhance productivity in existing occupations—such as with managers, architects, or radiologists, as discussed earlier; the development of new or enhanced tasks tends to shift the labor demand curve to the right. Technological change is less favorable to labor if the latter effect is weaker than the former—which might have been the case in the past two decades.[29]

EXAMPLE 4.3

Do Robots and Online Hiring Platforms Create or Destroy Jobs?

Whether technological change ultimately decreases the demand for labor (as it would if labor and capital are gross substitutes) or increases it through gross complementarity is an open question. As we see next from two high-tech innovations—robots and online labor markets—we do not have any clear answers.

Industrial robots, machines that can be programmed to perform several manual tasks (such as welding, painting, assembling, and packaging) and do not require a human operator, number around two for every thousand workers in the United States. The number of robots per thousand workers has quadrupled from the early 1990s, and roughly half of industrial robots in the United States are in two industries: automotive and electronics manufacturing.

One study estimated that when industrial robots are introduced into a local labor market, about 6 jobs are lost locally for every robot introduced. Put differently, the substitution effect of robots for workers dominates any scale effect in the local labor market, shifting the labor demand curve in that market area to the left. However, areas that buy (but do not make) the robot-produced goods experience a scale effect from the lower-priced goods, and the increases in their real income serve to shift the labor demand curve in those areas to the right. This rightward shift reduces, but does not fully offset, the job losses in the producing areas—and the overall effect on employment is estimated to be 3.3 jobs lost for every robot introduced.

The development of online labor market platforms offers a more hopeful analysis for workers. The spread of the Internet and the digitization of texts, sounds, photos, videos, and all kinds of data have allowed online labor markets to develop and flourish. Online hiring platforms have made it easier for freelancers who live far away from the employing organization to work on accounting, marketing, web development, and other tasks. Workers willing to work as freelancers, often in their spare time or around household duties, can register and apply for the jobs with employers from around the world. One such platform reports having 14 million users in 180 countries. Has the spread of these platforms caused local jobs to be lost to remote workers?

One study found that most of the freelancers employed (often women) are in low-income countries, and they are hired by small startups that find hiring labor locally to be impractical or too costly. Some 60 percent of the small businesspeople surveyed for this study said that in the absence of the online platform, they would have done the job themselves, whereas only 15 percent said they would have hired a worker locally. Thus, the falling cost—created by digitization—of hiring workers remotely has led to some substitution of freelancers (often in low-wage countries) for local employees. The larger (scale) effect, however, appears to be in the creation of new jobs, as small business owners find hiring remotely cheaper than doing the tasks themselves. These benefits to startups increase their chances of survival and expansion, thus creating a potential rightward shift in the labor demand curve in the local labor market.

Sources: Daron Acemoglu and Pascual Restrepo, "Robots and Jobs: Evidence from US Labor Markets," *Journal of Political Economy* 128 (June 2020): 2188–2244; Arjay Agrawal, John Horton, Nicola Lacetera, and Elizabeth Lyons, "Digitization and the Contract Labor Market: A Research Agenda," in *Economic Analysis of the Digital Economy*, eds. Avi Goldfarb, Shane M. Greenstein, and Catherine E. Tucker (Chicago: University of Chicago Press, 2015): 219–250

Overall Effects of Technological Change   According to the preceding analysis, technological innovations clearly affect the demand for labor through both the scale effect and the substitution effect. In many public discussions of technological change, however, scale effects are overlooked, and the focus is on the substitution effect—sometimes in frightening words. For example, in a book titled *The Collapse of Work*, published in 1979, the authors referred to technological change as creating a "jobs holocaust" and called for policies designed to cope with "ever-increasing unemployment."[30] Because of the fears created by technological change, we need to pause and use economic analysis to consider whether technological change creates, *for an entire society*, more harm than good.

Fortunately, the fear that technological change creates a "jobs holocaust" has proven groundless. When *The Collapse of Work* was published, for example, 60 percent of adults in the United States were working, and among all those who wanted to work, 5.8 percent were unemployed. In early 2020, after four decades of rapid technological innovation, the percentage of adults working was roughly 60 percent and the unemployment rate was hovering around 3.5 percent.

Technological change, however, does impose costs on *some* workers—those who face decreased demand for their services and must therefore bear the costs of changing jobs. These costs may involve wage loss, temporary unemployment, or the need to invest in learning new skills. But because technological innovation also enhances the demand for *other* workers and results in lower costs or greater product variety for *consumers,* we naturally look for a way to analyze whether the *overall net effects* of technological change are positive or negative. Put differently (and in the context of the normative principles outlined in Chapter 1), can economic theory be used to tell us whether, in a society, the gainers gain more from technological change than the losers lose?

To begin our analysis, let us consider a society that has a fixed amount of labor and capital resources, and for the sake of simplicity, let us assume that these resources can be used to produce two goods, food and clothing. Figure 4.6 summarizes the production possibilities that we assume for this simple society. If all labor and capital inputs were devoted to the production of food, 200 million units of food (and no clothing) could be produced (see point *Y*). Similarly, if all resources were devoted to the production of clothing, 100 million units of clothing (and no food) could be produced (point *X*). If, say, 50 percent of the resources were devoted to food and 50 percent to clothing, the society could produce 100 million units of food and 50 million units of clothing (point *A*). Limits on the combinations of food and clothing that this society could produce are displayed in Figure 4.6 along line *XY*, which is called a production possibilities curve.[31] All combinations along or below (southwest of) *XY* are possible; combinations above *XY* (to the northeast of it) cannot be produced.

In complex, modern societies, the *actual* mix of food and clothing produced can be decided by the government, by the market, or by some combination of the two. At one extreme, a centralized governmental bureaucracy could mandate how much food and clothing are to be produced; at the other, the decision could arise from the market interactions between consumers

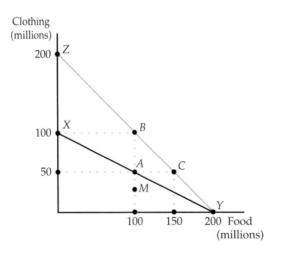

Figure 4.6 The Production Possibilities for a Hypothetical Society

(demand) and producers (supply). Of course, even in a market setting, government could influence the mix of food and clothing produced—through taxes, subsidies, or regulations that alter the cost or methods of producing food and clothing.

Whatever the decision-making process, we normally assume that a society would want to choose a mix of food and clothing that lies *on* the production possibilities curve rather than a mix that lies *below* the curve. If, for example, a society were to choose the combination of food and clothing represented by point *M* in Figure 4.6, it would not be producing as much food or clothing as it could, given its technology and resources. In short, its resources would be under-used, and its consumers would not have available to them all the goods that these resources would allow. Let us start our analysis, then, by supposing that the society depicted in Figure 4.6 chooses point *A* along *XY* and produces 100 million units of food and 50 million of clothing.

Now, imagine that someone invents a device that doubles the speed of the sewing process, making it possible to produce twice as much clothing with any level of inputs. Thus, if all resources were devoted to the production of clothing, this new device would permit the production of 200 million units of clothing (point *Z*)—a large increase over the old maximum level of 100 million units. However, the new device does nothing to enhance the production of food, so if all resources were devoted to the production of food, this society could still produce only 200 million units of food. The new set of production possibilities is depicted by the blue line (*ZY*) in Figure 4.6.

According to Figure 4.6, clearly the new technological invention expands the consumption possibilities for those in this society. They might choose to keep half of their resources allocated to food production and half to clothing production; if so, they could consume the same 100 million units of food but increase their clothing consumption from 50 million to 100 million units (see point *B* in Figure 4.6). Alternatively, they could choose to keep clothing consumption at 50 million units, which with the new device now would require only 25 percent of society's resources to produce, and devote 75 percent of their inputs to food; food production would then increase from 100 million to 150 million units (see point *C* in Figure 4.6). Finally, instead of keeping the production of one good constant and increasing the other, they could choose to allocate inputs so that *more of both goods are produced* (see all the points between *B* and *C*).

Obviously, choosing any point other than *B* involves a reallocation of labor and capital for the food and clothing industries. Even if society were to continue allocating half of its resources to each industry, however, the new sewing technology might change the occupational requirements in the clothing industry—requiring that workers in that industry learn new skills or accept different employment conditions. The faster and more smoothly these inter- and intra-industry changes occur, the faster the move from the initial point on *XY* to a new point on *ZY*. For a society to *actually* obtain the increased production made possible by technological change, then, it must have policies or institutions that promote (or at least permit) the mobility of capital and labor.

To this point, our analysis of the effects of technological change has demonstrated that such change makes possible for society to obtain more goods and services from its limited resources, thus potentially increasing average consumption per capita.[32] But would greater *average* consumption levels be enough to guarantee that society *as a whole* gains from technological change? To answer this question, we must return to some principles of both positive and normative analysis, introduced in Chapter 1.

Economic theory assumes that individuals, as both workers and consumers, are attempting to maximize their utility. Furthermore, we usually assume that utility is enhanced when individuals are able to consume more goods or services (including leisure; see endnote 32). Thus, one might think that when technological change increases the *average* consumption per capita, economic theory leads us to say that society has been made better off—but that is not completely correct.

EMPIRICAL STUDY 4.1

ESTIMATING THE LABOR DEMAND CURVE: TIME SERIES DATA AND COPING WITH "SIMULTANEITY"

When a proposed labor market policy increases the cost of labor, we frequently want economists to tell us more than "it will reduce employment." We want to know *how much* employment will be affected. Thus, for practical purposes, estimates of the elasticity of demand for labor are helpful.

Estimating the elasticity of demand for labor is actually difficult, which helps account for how few studies of demand elasticity were cited in Table 4.1. First, we can obtain credible estimates only if we have data on wages and employment for groups of workers who are reasonably homogeneous in terms of their job requirements, their substitutability with capital, and the characteristics of product demand facing their employers. Given the diversity of firms that hire workers in a given occupation (e.g., security guards are hired by retailers, schools, and movie stars), homogeneity often requires analyzing groups so narrow that data are difficult to obtain.

A second problem in estimating labor demand curves is that wages and employment

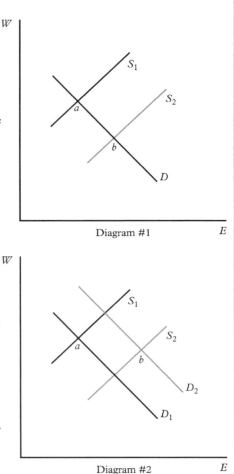

Diagram #1

Diagram #2

are determined *simultaneously* by the interaction of supply and demand curves, and both curves show a (different) relationship between wages and employment. If we gather data just on wage and employment levels, we will not be able to tell whether we are estimating a demand curve, a supply curve, or neither. Consider diagrams 1 and 2, which show wage (*W*) and employment (*E*) outcomes in the market for an occupation.

What we hope to do is illustrated in diagram 1. There the labor demand curve remains unchanged, but the supply curve shifts for some reason. All that is observed by the researcher are points *a* and *b*, but connecting them traces out the demand curve (of course, credible estimates would require many more than two observations).

Thus, if the demand curve is not shifting, we can "identify" it if we can observe a shifting supply curve. In reality, however, both supply curves and demand curves can shift over time (see diagram 2). When both shift, drawing a line between points *a* and *b* traces out neither a supply curve nor a demand curve. How can we identify the demand curve when both are likely to be shifting? First, we must have access to variables that cause the demand curve to shift; if we can *control* for factors that shift the demand curve over time, we—in a statistical sense—can shift it back to its original position and create a situation like that in diagram 1. Second, for the condition in diagram 1 to be met, we must also find at least one variable that *shifts the supply curve but does not affect demand*. (Some variables, like real income levels, can theoretically affect both labor demand curves *and* labor supply curves. If all our "shift" variables are expected to affect both curves, we are back in the situation depicted by diagram 2, where we cannot distinguish between the two curves.)

A study of the demand for coal miners in the United Kingdom (cited at the bottom of Table 4.1) illustrates how to estimate a labor demand curve for a specific occupation. The occupation is found in one industry, which is homogeneous in terms of product demand and employer technology, and time-series data on wages and employment were available for several years (the study used data from 1950 to 1980). The researchers were able to gather data on factors that were expected to shift the labor demand curve (e.g., the price of oil, which is a substitute for coal in generating electricity). They also had access to data on variables that were expected to shift the supply curve—including those (such as wages in alternative jobs miners might choose) that were expected to shift *only* the supply curve. The researchers were thus able to identify the labor demand function, and their use of regression analyses suggested that the labor demand elasticity (of employment changes with respect to wage changes) in British coal mining was −1.0 to −1.4.

Source: Alan A. Carruth and Andrew J. Oswald, "Miners' Wages in Post-War Britain: An Application of a Model of Trade Union Behaviour," *Economic Journal* 95 (December 1985): 1003–1020

Consider an (admittedly extreme) case in which the sole beneficiary of technological change is society's richest person, who makes $100 billion per year, and the costs fall on one million low-wage workers, who each make $16,000 per year. If the rich person gains $5 billion from technological change, while costs of $4,000 fall on each of the one million low-wage workers (for a total of $4 billion in costs), society as a whole gains $1 billion in overall consumption. However, as explained later on, this $1 billion gain could be associated with *a loss in overall utility* in society.[33]

The gain to the rich person in our example represents 5 percent of their annual income, and with such a huge income to begin with, the addition of $5 billion may not add much to this person's utility. The loss of $4,000 per worker for each of one million workers is equal to 25 percent of their annual income, and the associated loss of utility may—in the aggregate—be larger than the relatively small gains to the rich person. The only way to ensure that society as a whole gains (in terms of *utility*) in this case is to require the gainer to compensate all of those who lose income. If the person who gained were required to distribute $4 billion of the gains to those who bore the costs of change, the workers would end up being no worse off, and the gainer would still be ahead because of the $1 billion that they get to keep. Thus, after the compensation of those who lose income takes place, a normative condition put forth in Chapter 1 would hold: Some would gain from technological change, and no one would lose.

To restate the normative principle outlined in Chapter 1, *we can be sure that society gains from any economic transaction—technological change in this case—only when all those who lose from it are fully compensated* and at least one person is better off. Because most technological change occurs through decisions made by the millions of firms in the marketplace, what is needed to compensate those who lose jobs as a result of these decisions is a broad set of social insurance policies that can assist displaced workers. Unemployment insurance, for example, can support workers during their search for new jobs, and wage supplements of one form or another can minimize their loss of income if they have to take a lower-wage job; training programs can assist with the acquisition of new skills; government employment centers or online "job banks" can help the workers locate job openings; public wage subsidies can be paid to firms that add new workers; and in some countries, the government operates as the "employer of last resort"—putting to work those who cannot find new jobs. In Chapter 3, we analyzed wage subsidies to employers, and later on, we analyze the effects of many of these other programs.

Review Questions

1. Suppose that the government raises the minimum wage by 20 percent. Given the four Hicks–Marshall laws of derived demand as they apply to a particular industry, analyze the conditions under which job loss among teenage workers in that industry would be smallest.

2. California employers of more than 50 workers are now required to offer paid family leave for workers with newborn children. Under this law,

businesses with more than 50 workers are required to hold a job for a worker who goes on paid leave for up to six weeks. When on leave, workers receive 55 percent of their normal pay. What are the likely responses on the demand (employer) side of the labor market? Include in your analysis a consideration of factors that would affect the *size* of these responses.

3. The federal government, in an effort to stimulate job growth, passes a law that gives a tax credit to employers who invest in new machinery and other capital goods. Applying the concepts underlying cross-elasticities, discuss the conditions under which employment gains in a particular industry will be largest.

4. The public utilities commission in a state lifts price controls on the sale of natural gas to manufacturing plants and allows utilities to charge market prices (which are 30 percent higher). What conditions would minimize the extent of manufacturing job loss associated with this price increase?

5. Many employers provide health insurance for their employees, but others—primarily small employers—do not. Suppose that the government wants to ensure that all employees are provided with health-insurance coverage that meets or exceeds some standard. Suppose also that the government wants employers to pay for this coverage and is considering two options.

Option A: An employer not voluntarily offering its employees acceptable coverage would be required to pay a tax of *X* cents per hour for each labor hour employed. The funds collected would support government-provided health coverage.

Option B: This is the same as option A, except that the government-provided coverage would be financed by a tax collected as a fraction of the employer's total revenues.

Compare and contrast the labor market effects of each of the two options.

6. In 1942, the government promulgated regulations that prohibited the manufacture of many types of garments by workers who did the sewing, stitching, and knitting in their homes. If these prohibitions are repealed so that clothing items may now be made either by workers in factories or by independent contractors doing work in their homes, what effect will this have on the labor demand curve for *factory workers* in the garment industry?

7. Briefly explain how the following programs would affect the elasticity of demand for labor in the steel industry:

   a. an increased tariff on steel imports

   b. a law illegalizing the laying off of workers for economic reasons

   c. a boom in the machinery industry (which uses steel as an input)—causing production in that industry to rise

   d. a decision by the owners of steel mills to operate each mill longer than has been the practice in the past

e. an increase in the wages paid by employers in the steel industry

f. a tax on each ton of steel produced

8. In 2012, a group in Germany proposed a "wealth tax"—on buildings, machinery, and equipment—that would be levied on all employers having at least $1.4 million invested in such assets. Use theory learned in this chapter to analyze the labor market effects on employees in large German firms, and explain under what conditions German workers would be *worse* off.

Problems

1. Suppose that the demand for dental hygienists is $L_D = 5,000 - 20W$, where L = the number of dental hygienists and W = the daily wage. What is the own-wage elasticity of demand for dental hygienists when $W = \$100$ per day? Is the demand curve elastic or inelastic at this point? What is the own-wage elasticity of demand when $W = \$200$ per day? Is the demand curve elastic or inelastic at this point?

2. Professor Pessimist argues before Congress that reducing the size of the military will have grave consequences for the typical U.S. worker. He argues that if a million individuals were released from the military and were instead employed in the civilian labor market, average wages in the civilian labor market would fall dramatically. Assume that the demand curve for civilian labor does not shift when workers are released from the military. *First*, draw a simple diagram depicting the effect of this influx of workers from the military. *Next*, using your knowledge of the definition of the own-wage elasticity of labor demand, the magnitude of this elasticity for the economy as a whole, and the size of civilian employment in comparison with this flood from the military, graph these events and estimate the magnitude of the reduction in wages for civilian workers as a whole. Do you concur with Professor Pessimist?

3. Suppose that the demand for burger flippers at fast-food restaurants in a small city is $L_D = 300 - 20W$, where L = the number of burger flippers and W = the wage in dollars per hour. The equilibrium wage is $4 per hour, but the government puts in place a minimum wage of $5 per hour.

   a. How does the minimum wage affect employment in these fast-food restaurants? Draw a graph to show what has happened, and estimate the effects on employment in the fast-food sector.

   b. Suppose that the city just mentioned has an uncovered sector where $L_S = 100 + 80W$ and $L_D = 300 - 20W$, before the minimum wage is put in place. Suppose that all the workers who lose their jobs as burger flippers because of the introduction of the minimum wage seek work in the uncovered sector. What happens to wages and employment in that sector? Draw a graph to show what happens, and analyze the effects on both wages and employment in the uncovered sector.

4. Table 4P.4 gives the demand for labor at Homer's Hideaway, a motel in a small town.

Table 4P.4 Labor Demand for Homer's Hideaway

Wage ($)	Number of hours
40	2
32	3
24	4
16	5
8	6

a. Draw the demand for labor curve.

b. Calculate the wage elasticity of demand at points along the demand curve. Indicate whether the elasticity is elastic, inelastic, or unitary elastic.

c. As you slide down along the demand curve, does the demand curve become more or less elastic?

5. Union A faces a demand curve in which a wage of $20 per hour leads to demand for 20,000 person-hours and a wage of $25 per hour leads to demand for 10,000 person-hours. Union B faces a demand curve in which a wage of $30 per hour leads to demand for 30,000 person-hours, whereas a wage of $25 per hour leads to demand for 33,000 person-hours.

a. Which union faces the *more* elastic demand curve?

b. Which union will be more successful in increasing the total income (wages times person-hours) of its membership?

6. Calculate the own-wage elasticity of demand for the following occupations: a, b, and c. E_D and W are the original employment and wage. E'_D and W' are the new employment and wage. State whether the demand is elastic, inelastic, or unitary elastic.

a. $\%\Delta E_D = 5$, $\%\Delta W = -10$

b. $E_D = 50$, $W = 7$

   $E'_D = 40$, $W' = 8$

c. $E_D = 80$, $W = 8$

   $E'_D = 100$, $W' = 6$

7. When the cost of dough-making machines fell by 10 percent, the demand for assistant bakers fell by 15 percent. What is the cross-wage elasticity of demand for assistant bakers in this case? Are assistant bakers and dough-making machines gross substitutes or gross complements?

Notes

1. David Card and Alan B. Krueger, *Myth and Measurement: The New Economics of the Minimum Wage* (Princeton, NJ: Princeton University Press, 1995).

2. Six reviews of Card and Krueger, *Myth and Measurement*, appear in the book review section of the July 1995 issue of *Industrial and Labor Relations Review* 48, no. 4. More-recent reviews of findings can be found in Jonathan Meer and Jeremy West, "Effects of the Minimum Wage on Employment Dynamics," *Journal of Human Resources* 51 (Spring 2016): 500–522; David Neumark, "The Econometrics and Economics of the Employment Effects of Minimum Wages: Getting from Known Unknowns to Known Knowns," *German Economic Review* 20 (August 2019): 293–329.

3. John R. Hicks, *The Theory of Wages*, 2nd ed. (New York: St. Martin's Press, 1966): 241–247; Alfred Marshall, *Principles of Economics*, 8th ed. (London: Macmillan, 1923): 518–538.

4. Under certain conditions, greater substitutability may not lead to a more elastic labor demand; see Robert S. Chirinko and Debdulal Mallick, "The Elasticity of Derived Demand, Factor Substitution, and Product Demand: Corrections to Hicks' Formula and Marshall's Four Rules," *Labour Economics* 18 (2011): 708–711.

5. An exception to the law occurs when employers can more easily substitute other factors of production for the category of labor than customers can substitute other products for the product being produced; in this case, the law is reversed. Suppose, for example, that the elasticity of product demand among a firm's customers were zero; in this case, a rising wage rate would create only a substitution effect. With a larger labor share and thus a higher ratio of labor to capital, the *percentage* fall in labor usage as wages rise will tend to be smaller, thus causing the elasticity of demand for labor to be smaller. For more on the effects of labor's share on the elasticity of demand, see Saul D. Hoffman, "Revisiting Marshall's Third Law: Why Does Labor's Share Interact with the Elasticity of Substitution to Decrease the Elasticity of Labor Demand?" *Journal of Economic Education* 40 (Fall 2009): 437–445. Hoffman also argues that the third law holds only when the elasticity of final product demand is greater than the elasticity of substitution.

6. Daniel S. Hamermesh, *Labor Demand* (Princeton, NJ: Princeton University Press, 1993): 103.

7. An analysis of the wages and employment of U.S. women in the period following World War II estimates that the overall elasticity of demand for their labor was similar—in the range of –1.0 to –1.5. See Daron Acemoglu, David H. Autor, and David Lyle, "Women, War and Wages: The Effect of Female Labor Supply on the Wage Structure at Midcentury," *Journal of Political Economy* 112 (June 2004): 497–551. Estimates of the own-wage elasticity of demand for higher-skilled

and lower-skilled manufacturing labor in Germany are somewhat lower (–0.6 to –1.3); see John T. Addison, Lutz Bellmann, Thorsten Schank, and Paulino Teixeira, "The Demand for Labor: An Analysis Using Matched Employer–Employee Data from the German LIAB. Will the High Unskilled Worker Own-Wage Elasticity Please Stand Up?" *Journal of Labor Research* 29 (June 2008): 114–137. A recent study of labor demand elasticities across U.S. cities and industries estimated elasticities, respectively, in the –0.3 to –1.0 range; see Paul Beaudry, David A. Green, and Benjamin Sand, "In Search of Labor Demand," *American Economic Review* 108 (September 2018): 2714–2757.

8. As noted in Chapter 3, if two groups are complements in production, a decrease in the price of one should lead to increased employment of the other. Complements in production are always gross complements (no substitution effect occurs if the two factors are not substitutes in production).

9. The share of the teenage wage bill in total costs influences the substitution effect as well as the scale effect in the example that we are analyzing. For example, if teenage labor costs were a large fraction of total costs, the possibilities for further substitution of teenagers for adults would be rather limited (this can be easily seen by considering an example in which teenagers constituted 100 percent of all production costs). Thus, while a larger share of teenagers in total cost would make for a relatively large-scale effect, it also could reflect a situation in which the possibilities of substituting teenagers for adults are smaller than they would be otherwise.

10. Hamermesh, *Labor Demand*, 105–127.

11. James D. Adams, "The Structure of Firm R&D, the Factor Intensity of Production, and Skill Bias," *Review of Economics and Statistics* 81 (August 1999): 499–510; Antonio Ciccone and Giovanni Peri, "Long-Run Substitutability between More and Less Educated Workers: Evidence from U.S. States, 1950–1990," *Review of Economics and Statistics* 87 (November 2005): 652–663.

12. See Claudia Goldin and Lawrence Katz, "The Origins of Technology-Skill Complementarity," *Quarterly Journal of Economics* 113 (May 1998): 693–732; Anders Akerman, Ingvil Gaarder, and Magne Mogstad, "The Skill Complementarity of Broadband Internet," *Quarterly Journal of Economics* 130 (November 2015): 1781–1824, for citations to the literature.

13. See Paul Gaggl and Greg C. Wright, "A Short-Run View of What Computers Do: Evidence from a UK Tax Incentive," *American Economic Journal: Applied Economics* 9 (July 2017): 262–294 for recent evidence and citations to the literature.

14. States are free to set higher minima. For example, although in July 2020 the federal minimum wage was $7.25 per hour, it was $8.56 in Florida, $12 in California, and $13.50 in Washington.

15. See Peter Brummund and Michael R. Strain, "Does Employment Respond Differently to Minimum Wage Increases in the Presence of Inflation Indexing?" *Journal of Human Resources* 55 (Summer 2020): 999–1024, for an example of a study that shows the minimum wage increases lead to different employment outcomes in states where minimum wages are indexed to inflation.

16. Orley Ashenfelter and Robert S. Smith, "Compliance with the Minimum Wage Law," *Journal of Political Economy* 87 (April 1979): 335–350. A more recent study of noncompliance (among apparel contractors) can be found in David Weil, "Public Enforcement/Private Monitoring: Evaluating a New Approach to Regulating the Minimum Wage," *Industrial and Labor Relations Review* 58 (January 2005): 238–257 and an example from Canada can be found in Dionne Pohler and Chris Riddell, "Multinationals' Compliance with Employment Law: An Empirical Assessment Using Administrative Data from Ontario, 2004 to 2015," *Industrial and Labor Relations Review* 72 (May 2019): 606–635.

17. Under some circumstances, remaining unemployed for a while and searching for jobs in the higher-paying covered sector might be rational for these unemployed workers. In Chapter 13, we explore this possibility of "wait unemployment"—which is discussed by Jacob Mincer, "Unemployment Effects of Minimum Wage Changes," *Journal of Political Economy* 84 (August 1976): S87–S104. At this point, we simply note that if it occurs, unemployment will result.

18. See David Neumark and William Wascher, "Minimum Wages and Employment: A Case Study of the Fast-Food Industry in New Jersey and Pennsylvania: Comment," *American Economic Review* 90 (December 2000): 1362–1396; David Card and Alan B. Krueger, "Minimum Wages and Employment: A Case Study of the Fast-Food Industry in New Jersey and Pennsylvania: Reply," *American Economic Review* 90 (December 2000): 1362–1420. A more recent study is by Arindrajit Dube, T. William Lester, and Michael Reich, "Minimum Wage Effects Across State Borders: Estimates Using Contiguous Counties," *Review of Economics and Statistics* 92 (November 2010): 945–964. These studies contain references to earlier studies and reviews on this topic.

19. David Neumark, J.M. Ian Salas, and William Wascher, "Revisiting the Minimum Wage-Employment Debate: Throwing Out the Baby with the Bathwater?" *Industrial and Labor Relations Review* 67 (May 2014): 608–648, and the studies that they cite suggest that the elasticity of teenage employment to changes in the minimum wage generally falls into the range of –0.2 to –0.6. Dividing these elasticities by the estimated elasticity of response in the average teen wage to changes in the minimum wage (the percentage change in the average teen wage divided by the percentage change in the minimum wage was in the range of 0.32 to 0.48) yields estimates of the elasticity of the labor demand curve for teenagers. One study suggests that most of the effects

of minimum wages on teenage employment are observed in temporary jobs or new hires; see Jeffrey P. Thompson, "Using Local Labor Market Data to Re-Examine the Employment Effects of the Minimum Wage," *Industrial and Labor Relations Review* 62 (April 2009): 343–366.

20. David Neumark, Mark Schweitzer, and William Wascher, "The Effects of Minimum Wages Throughout the Wage Distribution," *Journal of Human Resources* 39 (Spring 2004): 425–450. This study finds that the elasticity of employment to changes in the minimum wage for those at the minimum is −0.12, whereas the elasticity of their wages to changes in the minimum is 0.8; dividing −0.12 by 0.8 equals the estimated demand elasticity of −0.15. More elastic responses of employment to minimum-wage changes are found by Joseph J. Sabia, Richard V. Burkhauser, and Benjamin Hansen, "Are the Effects of Minimum Wage Increases Always Small? New Evidence from a Case Study of New York State," *Industrial and Labor Relations Review* 65 (April 2012): 350–376. However, even these results are contested: see Saul D. Hoffman, "Are the Effects of Minimum Wage Increases Always Small? A Reanalysis of Sabia, Burkhauser, and Hansen," *Industrial and Labor Relations Review* 69 (March 2016), along with Joseph J. Sabia, Richard V. Burkhauser, and Benjamin Hansen, "When Good Measurement Goes Wrong: New Evidence that New York State's Minimum Wage Reduced Employment," *Industrial and Labor Relations Review* 69 (March 2016): 295–319. A summary of the employment effects found by studies of the minimum wage can be found in Katharine G. Abraham and Melissa S. Kearney, "Explaining the Decline in the US Employment-to-Population Ratio: A Review of the Evidence," *Journal of Economic Literature* 58 (September 2020): 585–643.

21. Meer and West, "Effects of the Minimum Wage on Employment Dynamics"; Doruk Cengiz, Arindrajit Dube, Attila Lindner, and Ben Zipperer, "The Effect of Minimum Wages on Low-Wage Jobs," *Quarterly Journal of Economics* 134 (August 2019): 1405–1454.

22. See Thomas MaCurdy, "How Effective Is the Minimum Wage at Supporting the Poor?" *Journal of Political Economy* 123:2 (April 2015): 497–545, for a discussion of the effects of the minimum wage on poverty.

23. Richard V. Burkhauser, Kenneth A. Couch, and David C. Wittenburg, " 'Who Gets What' from Minimum Wage Hikes: A Re-Estimation of Card and Krueger's Distributional Analysis in *Myth and Measurement: The New Economics of the Minimum Wage*," *Industrial and Labor Relations Review* 49 (April 1996): 547–552. For a summary of studies on how minimum-wage laws (and other social policies) affect poverty, see David Neumark, "Alternative Labor Market Policies to Increase Economic Self-Sufficiency: Mandating Higher Wages, Subsidizing Employment, and Increasing Productivity" (Working Paper No. 14807, National Bureau of Economic Research, Cambridge, MA, March 2009); see also Joseph J. Sabia and Richard V. Burkhauser,

"Minimum Wages and Poverty: Will a $9.50 Federal Minimum Wage Really Help the Working Poor?" *Southern Economic Journal* 76 (January 2010): 592–623. For a different view of minimum-wage laws, see Bruce E. Kaufman, "Institutional Economics and the Minimum Wage: Broadening the Theoretical and Policy Debate," *Industrial and Labor Relations Review* 63 (April 2010): 427–453. For evidence that minimum-wage laws help poor people enough to reduce recidivism among ex-offenders, see Amanda Y. Agan and Michael D. Makowsky, "The Minimum Wage, EITC, and Criminal Recidivism" (Working Paper No. 25116, National Bureau of Economic Research, Cambridge, MA, September 2018).

24. One promising way to estimate the employment effects is to compare employment changes in cities that implemented living wage laws with those in cities that passed such laws but saw them derailed by some outside force (the state legislature or a court decision). This approach is included in Scott Adams and David Neumark, "The Effects of Living Wage Laws: Evidence from Failed and Derailed Living Wage Campaigns," *Journal of Urban Economics* 58 (September 2005): 177–202. For estimated employment effects of *city* minimum wages, see Arindrajit Dube, Suresh Naidu, and Michael Reich, "The Economic Effects of a Citywide Minimum Wage," *Industrial and Labor Relations Review* 60 (July 2007): 522–543; Ekaterina Jardim, Mark C. Long, Robert Plotnick, Emma van Inwegen, Jacob Vigdor, and Hilary Wething, "Minimum Wage Increases, Wages, and Low-Wage Employment: Evidence from Seattle" (Working Paper No. 23532, National Bureau of Economic Research, Cambridge, MA, May 2018).

25. Erik Brynjolfsson and Andrew McAfee, *The Second Machine Age: Work, Progress, and Prosperity in a Time of Brilliant Technologies* (New York: W.W. Norton, 2014): 41.

26. Brynjolfsson and McAfee, *The Second Machine Age*, 63.

27. Ajay Agrawal, Joshua S. Gans, and Avi Goldfarb, "Artificial Intelligence: The Ambiguous Labor Market Impact of Automating Prediction," *Journal of Economic Perspectives* 33 (Spring 2019): 31–50; Gaggl and Wright, "A Short-Run View of What Computers Do: Evidence from a UK Tax Incentive."

28. See David Autor, David Dorn, and Gordon H. Hanson, "Untangling Trade and Technology: Evidence from Local Labour Markets," *The Economic Journal* 125 (May 2015): 621–646, for a recent article and citations to earlier studies. For an analysis of the growth of low-skill "service" jobs, see David H. Autor and David Dorn, "The Growth of Low-Skill Service Jobs and the Polarization of the US Labor Market," *American Economic Review* 103 (August 2015): 1553–1597.

29. Daron Acemoglu and Pascual Restrepo, "Automation and New Tasks: How Technology Displaces and Reinstates Labor," *Journal of Economic Perspectives* 33 (Spring 2019): 3–30.

30. Clive Jenkins and Barrie Sherman, *The Collapse of Work* (Fakenham, England: Eyre Methuen, 1979): chapter 20.

31. The production possibilities "curve" in Figure 4.6 is a straight line, which reflects the simplifying assumption that the ratio at which food can be "transformed" into clothing, and vice versa, never changes. This assumption is not necessary to the argument but does make it a bit easier to grasp initially. This is also sometimes called a production possibilities frontier.

32. For ease of illustration, we have confined our analysis to the two goods of food and clothing—but the analysis and its conclusions are unaffected if we consider a society in which people can consume many goods or services, including leisure (see Chapter 6).

33. See Richard Layard, "Happiness and Public Policy: A Challenge to the Profession," *The Economic Journal* 116 (March 2006): C24–C33, for a discussion of psychologically based findings that people in wealthy economies are *loss averse*; that is, their gains in utility from increases in income are smaller than their losses in utility from reduced income.

Selected Readings

Beaudry, Paul, David A. Green, and Benjamin Sand. "In Search of Labor Demand." *American Economic Review* 108 (September 2018): 2714–2757.

Brynjolfsson, Erik, and Andrew McAfee. *The Second Machine Age: Work, Progress, and Prosperity in a Time of Brilliant Technologies.* New York: W.W. Norton & Company, 2014.

Card, David, and Alan B. Krueger. *Myth and Measurement: The New Economics of the Minimum Wage.* Princeton, NJ: Princeton University Press, 1995.

Card, David, and Alan B. Krueger. "Review Symposium: *Myth and Measurement: The New Economics of the Minimum Wage.*" *Industrial and Labor Relations Review* 48 (July 1995).

Cunningham, Wendy. *Minimum Wages and Social Policy: Lessons from Developing Countries.* Washington, DC: World Bank, 2007.

Hamermesh, Daniel S. *Labor Demand.* Princeton, NJ: Princeton University Press, 1993.

Kennan, John. "The Elusive Effects of Minimum Wages." *Journal of Economic Literature* 33 (December 1995): 1950–1965.

MaCurdy, Thomas. "How Effective Is the Minimum Wage at Supporting the Poor?" *Journal of Political Economy* 123:2 (April 2015): 497–545.

Neumark, David, and William L. Wascher. *Minimum Wages.* Cambridge, MA: MIT Press, 2010.

Frictions in the Labor Market

Up to this point in our analysis of the labor market, we have treated the cost of labor to employers as having two characteristics. First, we have assumed that the wage rate that employers must pay is *given* to them by the market; that is, the supply of labor curve *to a firm* has been assumed to be horizontal (at the market wage).[1] An employer cannot pay less than the going wage, because if it did so, *its workers would instantly quit and go to firms paying the going wage*. Likewise, it can acquire all the labor it wants at the market wage, so paying more would only raise its costs and reduce its ability to compete in the product market (as noted in Chapter 3, only firms with product-market monopolies could pay more than they have to and still survive). Individual employers in competitive product markets, then, have been seen as wage takers (not wage makers), and their labor market decisions have involved only *how much* labor and capital to employ.

Second, we have treated all labor costs as *variable*—that is, as being strictly proportional to the length of time that the employee works. Variable labor costs, such as the hourly wage rate, recur every period and, of course, can be reduced if the hours of work are reduced. By assuming that all labor costs are variable, we have in effect assumed that firms can instantaneously adjust their labor input and associated costs as market conditions change.

The purpose of this chapter is to consider how the demand for labor is affected when we assume that both workers and firms find *making changes costly* when demand or supply conditions are altered. Because higher costs of change, generally speaking, cause workers and firms to display more resistance to change, economists borrow (loosely) a concept from physics and talk about these costs as causing labor market "frictions." In this chapter, we analyze the implications of frictions in the labor market. That is, we explore the implications of assuming that workers find changing employers costly and that firms find hiring and firing workers costly. These assumptions are, of course, closer to reality for most firms and workers, so this is a sensible step beyond the more basic model that we have already introduced.

In the first section, we consider frictions on the *employee* side of the market, analyzing the labor market effects of costs employees face when moving among employers. As the costs to workers of changing employers rise, the hiring decisions *firms* make differ from predictions of the competitive model—especially in the presence of government-mandated wages. We also briefly investigate the implications of workers' mobility costs for the observed correlations between wages and labor market experience, tenure with one's employer, and unemployment.

In the final three sections of this chapter, we turn to an analysis of costs that *employers* bear when changing the level of employment. We distinguish between variable labor costs, which are hourly in nature, and "quasi-fixed" costs that are associated only with the *number* of workers hired (including investments that firms make in hiring and training workers). The presence of quasi-fixed costs on the employer side of the market raises interesting questions that we address concerning firms' use of overtime, their decisions to train some workers but not others, who is laid off during business downturns, the relationship between pay and productivity, and the effects on job growth of employment-protection laws.

Frictions on the Employee Side of the Market

In this section, we first analyze a major implication of assuming that employees can move among employers in a costless way and the evidence *against* this assumption. We then build a model of wage and employment decisions on the basis of the assumption that employee mobility is costly, and we explore the labor market predictions of this model, which is more realistic for many firms and workers.

The Law of One Price

The simple model of the labor market, which is based on the assumption of costless employee mobility among employers, has a powerful and testable prediction: *Workers who are of equal skills in occupations receive the same wage.*[2] This implication is known as the "law of one price," and it rests squarely on the assumption that workers can move from employer to employer without delay and without cost. If a firm currently paying the market wage were to attempt to pay even a penny less per hour, this model implies that it would instantly lose all its workers to firms paying the going wage. Furthermore, because an employer can obtain all the labor that it wants at the going wage, none would get any advantage from paying more than the market. Thus, the market assures that all workers with the same skill set receive the same wages.

The problem with this prediction is that it does not seem to be supported by the facts. For example, how are we to explain that the average wage for paralegals in Santa Fe, New Mexico, was 17 percent lower in 2019 than the average pay for paralegals in Carson City, Nevada, despite the fact that both cities are state capitals of similar size and have comparable costs of living?[3] We may also question how the market could permit the wages of shipping and inventory clerks in natural gas distribution facilities to average (at $27.50 per hour) 17 percent more than similar clerks in electric power generation and distribution plants.[4]

If workers were completely mobile across employers, these geographic, inter-firm, or cross-industry wage differentials in occupations could not be maintained (unless, as we note in footnote 2, the working conditions at high-paying and low-paying firms were different or the workers themselves had different skill sets). Workers in these occupations who found themselves in low-wage firms would quit and move to the higher-wage firms, even if it meant changing the area in which they live or the industry in which they work. The fact that these wage differences are observed suggests that *worker mobility is costly* and, therefore, limited in some way.

And this makes perfect sense. It takes time and effort for paralegals in Santa Fe, for example, to find out that wages are higher in Carson City—and once having found out, they will find it costly to apply, interview, move across states, and leave their friends and relatives in Santa Fe. Similar costs will be borne by workers who may be candidates to move from the area in which they live to firms or industries paying higher wages; they must first go to the trouble of acquiring information and then bear the costs of applying and moving to a new employer. These costs inhibit worker mobility such that workers are less responsive to wage changes than the simple model assumes. That is, as mobility costs rise, workers become more "locked in" to their current employers.

Some of these mobility costs are monetary in nature (printing résumés, buying clothes for interviewing, hiring movers), but all employment changes also involve nonmonetary costs: the expenditure of time for completing applications and interviews, giving up valued nonwage benefits on one's current job (flexible scheduling, specific job duties, employer location, opportunities to socialize with colleagues, etc.),[5] and the stress of leaving the "known" for a new place of employment. Workers are likely to differ in how they evaluate these nonmonetary costs, so some find moving more aggravating (costly) than others do.

Assuming that worker mobility is costly has profound theoretical implications rooted in the shape of the labor supply curve to individual employers. Instead of being horizontal, as assumed earlier, *the supply of labor curve to firms becomes upward sloping when employee mobility is assumed to be costly.* Consider the relationship shown by the solid line in Figure 5.1. If firm A is paying, say, $9.25 per hour and decides to raise its wage to $9.50, it could increase the number of workers willing to work for it from E_0 to E_H. The higher wage would attract workers from other firms whose costs of moving are relatively low, and it would reduce the chances that any of its current employees will leave; however, this wage increase is unlikely to attract *all* the other workers in the market, because some would find it too costly to change employers for this modest pay increase. Likewise, if firm A were to reduce its wage to $9.00, the number of workers it can attract might go down to E_L, as it would likely lose some of its current workers but (because of mobility costs) would not likely lose them all. The supply curve traced out by these responses to firm A's wage changes would look like the solid line in Figure 5.1.

Figure 5.1 The Supply of Labor to Firm A: Worker-Mobility Costs Increase the Slope of the Labor Supply Curve Facing Individual Employers

How would *increased* costs of mobility affect the labor supply curve facing firm A? With higher mobility costs, wage increases would yield *smaller* increases in labor supply, and wage decreases would result in *smaller* reductions in labor supply. To fix ideas, let us return to Figure 5.1. Suppose that a wage increase to $9.50 had increased supply to the firm only to E_M and that a decrease to $9.00 would reduce labor supply only to E_N. The labor supply curve that these responses would generate is shown by the dashed-line curve in Figure 5.1, which is steeper—or less elastic—than the solid one (recall that the elasticity at a point on a labor supply curve is defined as the percentage change in supplied labor divided by the percentage change in the wage offered).

Thus, the higher workers' mobility costs, the steeper the labor supply curve facing a firm. Conversely, as mobility costs fall, other things being equal, the labor supply curve to firms flattens and becomes more elastic. In the special case of zero mobility costs, the labor supply curve to individual firms becomes horizontal—and thus infinitely elastic—at the market wage. Several recent studies of how the wage paid by a firm affects its employees' likelihood of quitting, as well as its ability to recruit new applicants, suggest that labor supply elasticities to individual employers are far from infinite in magnitude.[6]

Monopsonistic Labor Markets: A Definition

Economists describe the presence of upward-sloping labor supply curves to *individual employers* as creating *monopsonistic* conditions in the labor market. Explaining why we use this terminology takes us back to Chapter 2 and the distinction between supply of labor curves to a *market* as opposed to individual firms in the market.

A labor market monopsonist is, strictly speaking, a firm that is the only buyer of labor in its labor market: a coal mine in an isolated small town[7] in

West Virginia, for example, or a pineapple plantation on a tiny Hawaiian island. In both cases, the employer faces (as the only employer in the market) the *market* supply of labor curve, which we noted in Chapter 2 slopes upward. For example, if a coal mine operator in an isolated town wants to expand its labor supply, it cannot simply get workers at the going wage from competing mines in the local area (there are no other firms). Instead, it will have to increase wages to attract miners who must move in from out of town; attract workers from other occupations whose preferences were such that, at the old, lower mining wage, they preferred to work at a job that was less dangerous or dusty; or induce people currently out of the labor force to seek paid employment.

In Chapter 3, we first developed the labor demand curve under the twin assumptions that both product markets and labor markets were competitive. Toward the end of the chapter, we briefly analyzed how *product-market* monopolies (only one *seller* of a product) affect the demand for labor, but we deferred the analysis of conditions under which the *labor market* is not competitive. We now return to our analysis of labor demand and consider the implications when the labor market is not completely competitive—that is, when mobility costs impede workers' entry to, and exit from, various places of employment. We call such labor markets *monopsonistic*.

Before proceeding, however, we must emphasize that when we describe a labor market as monopsonistic, we are not thinking exclusively of the rather rare case of pure monopsony (single employers in isolated places). Indeed, our analysis of monopsonistic labor markets rests *only* on the assumption that *the labor supply curves facing individual employers slope upward* (and are not horizontal). In this analysis, it does not matter *why* these curves slope upward. Being the only employer in town is clearly one potential cause, and one can easily generalize that when workers have *just a few employers* to choose from in a labor market, they are more "locked in" to their current jobs.[8] However, in the previous section, we argued that these curves can slope upward because employees find *changing jobs costly*—even when there are several potential employers for them in their labor market. Thus, despite the term *monopsonistic*, the analysis that follows applies to labor markets that might have many employers in them.

Profit Maximization Under Monopsonistic Conditions

Recall from Chapter 3 that profit-maximizing firms will hire labor as long as an added worker's marginal revenue product is greater than their marginal expense. Hiring will stop when marginal revenue product equals marginal expense. When a firm assumes that extra workers can be attracted to the firm at the going wage rate (i.e., when labor supply curves to firms are horizontal), then the marginal expense is simply equal to the wage rate. When firms face upward-sloping labor supply curves, however, the marginal expense of hiring labor *exceeds* the wage. We now analyze how both wages

Table 5.1 Labor Supply Schedule for a Hypothetical Firm Operating in a Monopsonistic Market

Offered wage ($)	Supply of labor	Total hourly labor cost ($)	Marginal expense of labor ($)
8	10	80	
9	11	99	19
10	12	120	21
11	13	143	23

and employment are affected when the marginal expense of labor exceeds the wage rate.

Why the Marginal Expense of Labor Exceeds the Wage Rate

We start by considering why an upward-sloping labor supply curve causes the marginal expense of labor to exceed the wage rate. To see this, take the hypothetical example of a start-up firm that must attract employees from other employers. Its potential employees find changing jobs costly, and for some, the costs are higher than for others. Therefore, the start-up firm faces an upward-sloping labor supply schedule like that represented in Table 5.1. If the firm wants to operate with 10 employees, it must pay $8 per hour; if it wants to attract 11 employees, it must pay $9 per hour; and if it wants 12 workers, it must pay $10 per hour.

Simple multiplication indicates that its hourly labor costs with 10 employees would be $80, but with 11 employees, it would be $99; thus, the *marginal* expense of adding the eleventh worker is $19. If the firm were to operate with 12 workers instead of 11, its hourly costs would rise from $99 to $120, for a marginal expense equal to $21. One can immediately see that the marginal expenses of $19 and $21 are far greater than the wages paid (of $10 and $11).

Why is the marginal expense in this case so much greater than the wage? In moving from 10 to 11 workers, for example, the firm would have to pay one dollar more per hour to each of the 10 it originally planned to hire and then pay $9 to the added worker—for a total of $19 in extra costs. The marginal expense, then, includes the wages paid to the extra worker (as was the case in Chapter 3), plus the additional cost of raising the wage for all other workers.[9]

The hypothetical data in Table 5.1 are graphed in Figure 5.2. The (solid) supply curve in Figure 5.2 indicates, of course, the number of employees attracted to the firm at each wage level. In short, it represents, for the firm in question, the *wage it must pay* to get to each of the employment levels that it is considering. The dashed line represents the *marginal expense*—the added cost of increasing the employment level by one worker. The marginal expense curve both *lies above* the supply curve and is *steeper in slope* (i.e., goes up at a faster rate).[10]

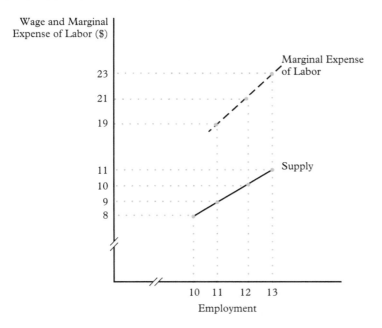

Figure 5.2 A Graph of the Firm-Level Data in Table 5.1

The Firm's Choice of Wage and Employment Levels

What are the labor market effects caused by having the marginal expense of labor lie above the wage rate? To maximize profits, we know that any firm—including those in monopsonistic markets—should hire labor until the point at which the marginal revenue product of labor (MRP_L) equals labor's marginal expense (ME_L):

$$MRP_L = ME_L \tag{5.1}$$

To illustrate the effects of having ME_L exceed the wage (W), we turn to Figure 5.3, which displays, for a given employer, its labor supply curve, the associated marginal expense of labor curve, and the downward-sloping curve depicting the firm's MRP_L.

Any firm in a monopsonistic labor market must make two decisions about hiring. First, like firms in competitive labor markets, it must decide *how much labor to hire*. This decision, consistent with the profit-maximizing criterion in equation (5.1), is made by finding the employment level at which $MRP_L = ME_L$. In Figure 5.3, the profit-maximizing level of employment for the firm shown is E^* because at E^*, $MRP_L = ME_L$ (note the intersection of the relevant curves at point X).

Second, the firm must find the *wage rate necessary* to generate E^* employees. In Figure 5.3, the wage rate that will attract E^* workers is W^* (note point Y on the labor supply curve). The firm's labor supply curve represents the relationship between its potential wage rates and the number of workers interested in working there. Thus, this second decision (about wages) is shown graphically by reading from the labor supply curve the wage needed to attract the profit-maximizing number of workers.

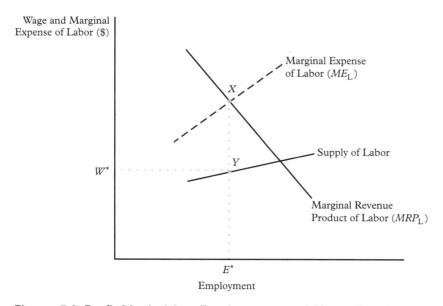

Figure 5.3 Profit-Maximizing Employment and Wage Levels in a Firm Facing a Monopsonistic Labor Market

Monopsonistic Conditions and Firms' Wage Policies

A difference between competitive and monopsonistic labor markets that immediately stands out concerns the wage policies of employers. In a competitive labor market, where individual firms are wage takers and can hire all the labor they want at the going wage, employers decide only on the number of workers they want to hire; the wage they pay is given to them by the market. We have seen, however, that firms facing monopsonistic conditions have a second decision to make: They must decide on the wage to pay as well. Further, whereas firms in competitive labor markets hire until the MRP_L equals the (given) wage, firms in monopsonized markets pay workers a wage less than their marginal revenue product.[11]

The implication that firms in monopsonistic labor markets must have their own wage policies does not suggest, of course, that they set wages without constraints. We saw in the model depicted in Figure 5.3 that the wages they pay are determined both by their MRP_L curve and by the labor supply curve that they face; both curves were given to the firm and thus were outside its control. Furthermore (and not illustrated in Figure 5.3), firms must make labor market decisions that allow them to remain competitive in their product markets. Thus, monopsonistic conditions do not give firms a completely free hand in deciding on their wages; they must still face constraints imposed by both labor markets and product markets. (These constraints are reduced, of course, if so few employers are in a labor market that they can agree not to compete for labor; in Example 5.1, we give an example of this type of agreement.)

Within the product markets and labor market constraints facing firms, however, different firms in monopsonistic labor markets may well offer different wages to equivalent workers. The labor supply and MRP_L curves would not likely be the same for different firms in the same labor market; thus, we should not be surprised if exactly comparable workers were to have different marginal productivities and receive different wages at different firms. Thus, a firm that employs older equipment and has a lower MRP_L could coexist with one that has new equipment and a higher MRP_L, by paying a lower wage to the same kind of worker. Indeed, a careful summary of studies on wage differences and the law of one price found strong evidence suggesting that the same worker would receive different pay if they worked for different employers.[12]

EXAMPLE 5.1

Monopsony Power in Labor Markets: The Case of Antitrust in the High-Tech Industry

In 2011, a large class-action lawsuit was brought by plaintiffs representing a class of 64,000 "high-tech" employees against their employers (the defendants in the case): Adobe, Apple, Google, Intel, Intuit, Lucasfilm, and Pixar. The plaintiffs alleged that "without the knowledge or consent of their employees, defendants' senior executives entered into an interconnected web of express agreements to eliminate competition among them for skilled labor." (We note that this case is also related to recent discussions and disputes about noncompete agreements, where employees agree in advance to not work for a competitor firm for some time. But in this lawsuit, the employees were not party to the allegedly secret agreements among the firms.)

Among the allegations of the plaintiffs was that the defendants engaged in a conspiracy that included the following:

1. agreements not to actively recruit each other's employees
2. agreements to notify each other when making an offer to another's employee
3. agreements that, when offering a position to another company's employee, neither company would counteroffer above the initial offer

In 2009 and 2010, the Antitrust Division of the United States Department of Justice (DOJ) investigated these firms, before they were defendants in this case, and the DOJ found that defendants' agreements "disrupted the normal price-setting mechanisms that apply to a labor setting."

One question that came from the case was the following: Could agreements to not recruit each other's employees lead to suppressive effects on the wages of the employees? That is, were the wages of the employees lower than they would have been if not for the alleged agreements among the defendants? Plaintiffs argued the answer to this question was clearly yes, for a variety of reasons, and sued the defendant companies for lost earnings.

After a long legal battle, the plaintiffs and defendants settled their dispute just before a trial. Judge Lucy Koh approved two separate settlements; the first was between the plaintiffs and defendants Intuit, Disney, and Pixar for $20 million, and the second was between the plaintiffs and defendants Adobe, Apple, Google, and Intel for $415 million. This is the largest employment class-action case ever. This case is important for the work in this chapter, for a variety of reasons, including that it is clear evidence that employers can exhibit monopsony power in labor markets and that we have to be careful about the assumptions that we use in our basic economic models.

Sources: United States District Judge Lucy Koh, 2015, "Order Granting Plaintiffs' Motion for Final Approval of Class Action Settlement with Defendants Adobe Systems Incorporated, Apple Inc., Google Inc., and Intel Corporation In Re: High-Tech Employee Antitrust Litigation," Case No. 11-CV-02509-LHK; and Joseph R. Saveri et al., 2011, "Consolidated Amended Complaint in Re: High-Tech Employee Antitrust Litigation," Master Docket No. 11-CV-2509-lHK. A great deal of filings for the case can be found at www.hightechemployeelawsuit.com/

How Do Monopsonistic Firms Respond to Shifts in the Supply Curve?

In a monopsonistic labor market, the firm does not really have a labor demand curve. Labor demand curves for a firm are essentially derived from sequentially asking, "If the market wage were at some level (say, $10), what would be the firm's profit-maximizing level of employment? If, instead, the wage were $12, what would be the firm's desired level of employment?" Under monopsonistic conditions, the firm is not a wage taker, so asking hypothetical questions about the level of wages facing the firm is meaningless. Given the firm's labor supply curve and its schedule of marginal revenue product (MRP_L at various levels of employment), this scenario has only one profit-maximizing level of employment and only one associated wage rate, both of which are chosen by the firm.

Shifts in Labor Supply That Increase ME_L Consider the short-run and long-run effects on a monopsonistic firm's desired level of employment if the supply curve facing the firm shifts (but remains upward sloping). Suppose, for example, that the labor supply curve were to shift to the left, reflecting a situation in which fewer people were willing to work at any given wage level. With the competitive model of labor demand, a leftward shift of a market supply curve would cause the market wage to increase and the level of employment to fall, as employers moved to the left along their labor demand curves. Will these changes in wages and employment occur under monopsonistic conditions?

In Figure 5.4, the MRP_L curve is fixed (we are in the short run), and the leftward shift of the labor supply curve is represented by a movement to curve S' from the original curve S. With a supply curve of S, the firm's marginal expense of labor curve was ME_L, and it chose to hire E workers and pay them a wage of W. When the supply curve shifts to S', the firm's marginal labor expenses shift to a higher curve ME_L'. Therefore, its new profit-maximizing level of employment falls to E', and its new wage rate increases to W'. Thus, in a monopsonistic model (just as with the competitive model), a leftward shift in labor supply increases ME_L, raises wages, and reduces firms' desired levels of employment in the short run.

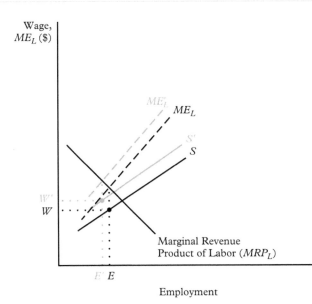

Figure 5.4 The Monopsonistic Firm's Short-Run Response to a Leftward Shift in Labor Supply: Employment Decreases and Wage Increases

In the long run, labor's increased marginal expense induces the substitution of capital for labor as firms seek to find the cost-minimizing mix of capital and labor. Recall that the cost-minimizing conditions for capital and labor under *competitive* conditions were given in equation $(3.8c)$—$W/MP_L = C/MP_K$—in which the wage rate was treated as the marginal expense of labor. In a monopsonistic labor market, ME_L exceeds W, so the left-hand side of equation (3.8c) must be written in its general form:

$$ME_L/MP_L = C/MP_K \qquad\qquad (5.2)$$

Clearly, if a monopsonist is minimizing its costs of production and its ME_L is increased, it will want to restore equality to equation (5.2) by substituting capital for labor. Thus, employment decreases even more in the long run than in the short run.[13]

Effects of a Mandated Wage

Let us next consider what would happen if some nonmarket force (e.g., a minimum-wage law) were to compel the firm to pay a particular wage rate that was higher than the one that it was paying. Would the firm's desired level of employment decline? For a monopsonistic firm's short-run response, refer to Figure 5.5, where the firm initially equates MRP_L and ME_L at point A and chooses to hire E_0 workers, which requires it to pay a wage of W_0.

Suppose now that a mandated wage of W_m is set in Figure 5.5. This mandate prevents the firm from paying a wage less than W_m and effectively creates a horizontal portion (BD) in the labor supply curve facing the firm (which is now BDS). The firm's marginal expense of labor curve is now

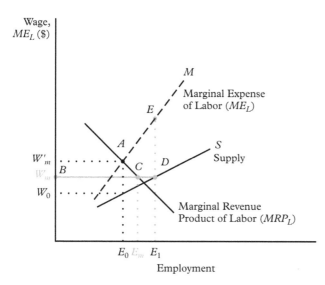

Figure 5.5 Minimum-Wage Effects Under Monopsonistic Conditions: Both Wages and Employment Can Increase in the Short Run

BDEM, because up to employment level E_1, the marginal expense of labor is equal to W_m. The firm, which maximizes profits by equating marginal revenue with marginal expense (this equality is now at point C), will hire E_m workers. Even though wages have risen from W_0 to W_m, desired employment rises from E_0 to E_m. This is striking and important, so we emphasize it: In a labor market with monopsonistic conditions, imposing a minimum wage can lead to an increase in the wage and an *increase* in employment.

For a monopsonistic firm, then, a mandated wage can simultaneously increase the *average* cost of labor (i.e., the wages paid to workers) and reduce ME_L. The decrease in *marginal* expense induces the firm to expand output and employment in the short run. Thus, because an upward-sloping supply curve is converted to one that is horizontal, at least for employment near the current level, both wages and employment might be able to increase with the imposition of a mandated wage on a monopsonistic firm.

This possibility is subject to two qualifications, however. First, in the context of Figure 5.5, employment will increase only if the mandated wage is set between W_0 and W'_m. A mandated wage above W'_m would increase ME_L above its current level (W'_m) and cause the profit-maximizing level of employment to fall below E_0. (The reader can verify this by drawing a horizontal line from any point above W'_m on the vertical axis and noting that it will intersect the MRP_L curve to the left of E_0.)

Second, Figure 5.5, with its fixed MRP_L curve, depicts only the short-run response to a mandated wage. In the long run, two (opposing) effects on employment are possible. With a mandated wage that is *not too high*, a monopsonistic firm's ME_L is reduced, causing a *substitution* of labor for capital in the long run. Although the monopsonistic firm's *marginal* expense of labor may have fallen, labor's *average* cost (the wage) has increased. Producing the same level of output is now more expensive than it was before; thus, profits will decline. If a firm is in a competitive product market, its initial profit level will be normal for that market, so the decline will push its profits below normal. Some owners will get out of the market, putting downward pressure on employment. If this latter (*scale*) effect is large enough, employment in monopsonistic sectors could fall in the long run if a mandated wage were imposed.

In summary, then, the presence of monopsonistic conditions in the labor market introduces uncertainty into how employment will respond to the imposition of a mandated wage *if* the new wage reduces the firm's marginal expense of labor. Any shift in the supply of labor curve that *increases* the marginal expense of labor, of course, will unambiguously reduce employment.

Monopsonistic Conditions and the Employment Response to Minimum-Wage Legislation

In discussing labor-demand elasticities in Chapter 4, we cited studies suggesting that the overall demand for labor might have an elasticity close to -1 (see the discussion around Table 4.1)—yet toward the end of Chapter 4, we found that employment losses associated with minimum-wage increases are far less elastic and are sometimes zero. Our analysis of monopsonistic conditions in the labor market can help explain this paradox. On the one hand, as we saw in Figure 5.5, if the labor market is monopsonistic, increases in the minimum wage *raise* wages but—if modest enough in size (i.e., if they remain below W'_m)—can *reduce* the marginal expense of labor. Thus, our expectations about the direction of employment changes caused by a higher minimum wage are ambiguous when monopsonistic conditions prevail: Some firms might experience increases in employment (because ME_L falls), but others might be forced to close because higher total labor costs render their operations unprofitable. (Note that Figure 5.5 depicts the employment responses only of employers that remain in business.) On the other hand, the elasticities presented in Table 4.1 were estimated from wage and employment outcomes that were generated by *market* forces. Graphically, these estimates were derived from analyses like the one presented in Figure 5.4, where a leftward shift in the supply curve unambiguously caused wages to rise and employment to fall. If monopsonistic conditions exist, then theory leads us to expect that employment responses to wage changes generated by legislated wage increases might be different from (i.e., smaller than) employment responses generated by *market* forces. The presence of monopsonistic conditions in labor markets can thus help explain why the expected negative employment effects of minimum-wage laws have not materialized.[14]

What does our analysis here imply for the discussions in recent years about *doubling* the minimum wage? The analysis of mandated wage increases in the previous section suggests that *large* increases in the minimum wage—increases that take the minimum wage above W'_m in Figure 5.5—will raise both wages *and* the ME_L; thus, if the minimum wage is raised above W'_m, it can be expected to unambiguously reduce employment. Indeed, raising the minimum wage above W'_m would have an effect similar to the shift of the labor-supply curve shown in Figure 5.4, and—unlike the case of modest minimum-wage hikes—the resulting losses in employment would not be mitigated by reductions in ME_L. Thus, the relatively small employment losses associated with minimum-wage hikes to date might not predict large increases in the minimum wage now being discussed in public dialogues in the United States.

Can we credibly assert that monopsonistic conditions underlie the small or uncertain direction of employment changes that have been found in minimum-wage studies to date? Most of these studies focus on teenagers, and one might think that teenagers could move almost without cost from one part-time job to another. If mobility were almost costless for teenagers, they would freely move among employers in response to small wage differentials, the teenage labor market would correspond closely to the competitive model, and we would have to look elsewhere for an explanation of the uncertain estimated effects of minimum wages on teenage employment.

We have argued that mobility is hindered (made more costly) by imperfect information about alternative wage offers and job requirements, by the time and aggravation of applying and being evaluated, and by the necessity of giving up valued nonwage job characteristics that might be difficult to replace in the new job. Teenagers, as well as adults, face these categories of cost. Moreover, teenagers often take jobs with the intent of staying only a short time, and they might perceive the total gains from going to a higher-paying employer as too small to justify the investment of time and effort needed to change employers. Thus, the labor supply curves to firms that typically employ teenagers (e.g., fast-food outlets) are likely to be upward sloping, and monopsonistic conditions prevail even in these places.

Job-Search Costs and Other Labor Market Outcomes

The presence of job mobility costs for workers means that they must make decisions about when to search for a new employer (and incur the costs of search) and when to stay put. These decisions about search have some interesting implications that can help explain why wages rise with both labor market experience and the length of time (tenure) with a particular employer. Other reasons why wages rise with experience and tenure are discussed later in the text; however, our current discussion of job-search costs warrants paying attention to these implications here. We also discuss how job-search costs affect decisions by those who are unemployed.

Wage Levels, Luck, and Search We have seen that employee mobility costs can create monopsonistic conditions that result in pay differences among workers who have equal productive capabilities. Monopsonistic conditions, however, are not the sole cause of wage differences for workers who appear to be similar. Indeed, we spend much time later in this text analyzing wage differences associated with job or worker characteristics that are often not easily measured or observed: different working conditions (Chapter 8), different on-the-job training requirements or opportunities (Chapter 9), and different ways to use pay in creating incentives for productivity (Chapter 11). In addition, we analyze wage differences associated with racial, ethnic, and gender differences that may be unrelated to productive characteristics—including discrimination (Chapter 12).

What the theory of monopsonistic labor markets offers to the analysis of wage differences, however, is the implication that to some extent, a worker's wage depends on luck.[15] Some workers will be fortunate enough to obtain a job offer from a high-paying employer, and some will not. Furthermore, given the costs of changing employers, the mobility from low-wage to high-wage firms may never be great or rapid enough to bring wages into equality.

When workers who might think they can get improved job offers face costs in searching for employers, we are naturally drawn to thinking about an employee–employer "matching" process that occurs over a period that might be lengthy. Workers can be viewed as wanting to obtain the best match possible but find that there is a cost to getting better matches. Those who see their jobs as a poor match (perhaps because of low pay) have more incentives to search for other offers than do workers who are lucky enough to already have good matches (high wages). Over time, as the unlucky workers have more opportunity to acquire offers, matches for them should improve—but, of course, at some wage levels, likely wage increases from a search are so small (or, given the worker's expected stay on the job, so short-lived) that further search is not worth the cost.

Labor market studies have observed that workers' wages tend to increase both with overall labor market experience and, holding labor market experience constant, with the length of time that they stay with their respective employers ("job tenure").[16] Job-search considerations might play a role in producing these patterns, and we briefly discuss them here.

Wages and Labor Market Experience One of the things that make job searches costly is that it takes time and effort to obtain job offers. Furthermore, job openings occur more or less randomly over time such that during any one period in which a worker is "in the market," not all potentially attractive openings even exist. As time passes, however, jobs open up, and workers have a chance to decide whether to apply. Those who have spent more time in the labor market have had more chances to acquire better offers and thus improve on their initial job matches. Although other explanations are explored in Chapter 9, the costs of job searches figure as one explanation for why we observe that, in general, *workers' wages improve the longer they are active in the labor market.*

Wages and Job Tenure With costly job searches, workers who are fortunate enough to find jobs with high-paying employers will have little incentive to continue searching, whereas those who are less fortunate will want to search again. This means that the workers who have been with their firms the longest will tend to be the ones who got higher wages to begin with, and we should therefore observe a positive correlation between tenure and earnings. Indeed, as noted earlier, empirical studies also find that among workers with the same skills and labor market experience, *those who have longer job tenure with their employers also tend to have higher wages.* Although there are other potential explanations for this relationship as well (see Chapters 9 and 11), the problem of costly job searches suggests that while longer job tenures can cause higher wages, higher wages can also cause longer job tenures.

Job-Search Costs and Unemployment Job-search costs can also help to explain the existence (and level) of unemployment. Although we analyze unemployment in more depth in Chapter 14, the relationship between search costs and the phenomenon of unemployment is important to introduce at this point. Briefly put, searching for job offers is something that unemployed people must do, and the search process takes time and effort. The longer a worker must wait to receive an acceptable offer, the longer the unemployed worker will remain unemployed. Thus, higher job-search costs will tend to lengthen the spells of unemployment and hence increase the unemployment rate.[17]

Monopsonistic Conditions and the Relevance of the Competitive Model

If employee mobility costs mean that monopsonistic conditions exist in the typical labor market, does this imply that the competitive model is irrelevant or misleading? Although we have seen that the competitive model indeed offers predictions that are at least partially contradicted by the evidence, the model likely remains relevant, especially in the long run.

The major difference between the competitive and monopsonistic models, of course, is the assumption about employee mobility costs. When we consider workers as a group, however, mobility costs are likely to be higher in the near term than over the long haul. For example, for a paralegal with a family established in Santa Fe to move their family to Carson City would be costly. Likewise, an established shipping clerk working with an electric utility might find it aggravating or time-consuming searching for, and then moving to, a similar job at a natural gas facility. However, "moving among" job offers is less costly for a recent graduate or immigrant who is trying to decide where in the country to locate or in which industry to work. Recent graduates or immigrants have to search and make a decision anyway (established workers often do not), and when choosing among offers, they have much less to give up, in terms of established relationships, by taking one offer over the other. As time passes, those established in jobs retire and are replaced by new workers who see the advantages of locating in certain areas or accepting work in certain industries; thus, over time, we expect wage differences owing to luck to dissipate—even if mobility costs are present in the short run. One study, for example, found that new immigrants to the

United States are more likely to be clustered in states offering the highest wages for their skill groups and that their presence has helped to narrow regional wage differences.[18]

Also, monopsonistic conditions notwithstanding, employers cannot deviate too far from the market when setting wages, because if they do, they will encounter problems in attracting, retaining, and motivating their workers (a topic to which we return in Chapter 11). Nobel laureate Paul Samuelson put the issue the following way in his bestselling economics textbook:

> Just because competition is not 100 per cent perfect does not mean that it must be zero. The world is a blend of (1) competition and (2) some degree of monopoly power over the wage to be paid. A firm that tries to set its wage too low will soon learn this. At first, nothing much need happen; but eventually, it will find its workers quitting a little more rapidly than would otherwise be the case. Recruitment of new people of the same quality will get harder and harder, and slackening off in the performance and productivity of those who remain on the job will become noticeable.[19]

Frictions on the Employer Side of the Market

Employers also face frictions in searching for and hiring employees. These frictions cause firms to bear costs that are associated with the number of workers hired rather than the hours they work, and they are called "quasi-fixed" costs because they are either difficult or impossible to cut in the short run—unlike variable costs (such as hourly wages), which can be readily cut by reducing the hours of work. The presence of quasi-fixed costs slows the adjustment of employment levels to changing market conditions faced by firms. The types of quasi-fixed costs are first discussed in this section, and we then move to an analysis of their implications for the labor market behavior of firms.

Categories of Quasi-fixed Costs

Employers often incur substantial quasi-fixed costs in hiring and compensating their employees. In general, these costs fall into two categories: *investments* in their workforce and certain *employee benefits*. We discuss each type of quasi-fixed costs next.

Labor Investments　When an employer has a job vacancy, it must incur certain costs in finding a suitable employee to hire. It has to advertise the position, screen applications, interview potential candidates, and (in the case of highly sought-after applicants) "wine and dine" the selected worker. A survey of employers in 2016, for example, found that the average employer spent $4,129 on hiring a worker and that the process took over 40 days.[20] Once hired, they incur the additional costs of orienting the new worker and getting them on the payroll.

EXAMPLE 5.2

Does Employment-Protection Legislation Protect Workers?

Many European countries have adopted employment-protection policies that make dismissing employees more costly for employers. These policies contain provisions for determining when dismissal is "unjustified" or "unfair," and some (as in Greece) go so far as saying that neither lack of business nor lack of competence is a justifiable reason for dismissal. Although many countries have policies that do not go that far—requiring only that firms attempt to transfer or retrain candidates for dismissal—the severance pay required when dismissals are considered "unjust" is frequently in the range of eight to 12 months of pay.

Procedural inconveniences to employers, such as the need to notify or obtain the approval of third parties (e.g., labor unions) and the rights of employees to challenge dismissal in a legal setting, are also part of these laws; additional procedures and delays are imposed on employers that want to make collective layoffs. Finally, these policies also regulate and restrict the use of temporary employees or employees on fixed-length contracts, because the use of these employees is seen as a way around the goal of employment protection.

A study that rated the strictness of each country's employment-protection laws found that those with the strictest laws indeed had lower movements of workers from employment into unemployment. That is, stronger employment-protection policies do reduce layoffs. However, the stronger these policies are, the slower the flow out of unemployment, because the costs of these policies also inhibit employers from creating new jobs, in part because they might fear that they cannot reduce employment in the future. Although the reduced flows both into and out of unemployment tend to have offsetting effects on the overall unemployment rate, the study found that stricter employment protection is associated with more *long-term* unemployment and *lower employment levels for women and youth.*

Sources: OECD Employment Outlook: 2004 (Paris: Organisation for Economic Co-operation and Development, 2004), chapter 2; Lawrence M. Kahn, "The Impact of Employment Protection Mandates on Demographic Temporary Employment Patterns: International Microeconomic Evidence," *Economic Journal* 117 (June 2007): F333–F356

For a study finding productive benefits to laws that protect workers' jobs, see Viral Acharya, Ramin Baghai, and Krishnamurthy Subramanian, "Wrongful Discharge Laws and Innovation," *Review of Financial Studies* 27 (January 2014): 301–346.

A hiring cost not to be overlooked—especially because it has been the subject of public policy debates—is the cost of *terminating* the worker. Every employee that a firm hires might also have to be let go because of economic circumstances or their job performance. As we discuss in Example 5.2, policies that require severance pay or otherwise increase the costs of *ending* the employment relationship, thus add to the quasi-fixed costs of *hiring* workers.

Table 5.2 Hours Spent on Training in Employee's First Three Months on the Job

Activity	Average hours
Hours of formal instruction by training personnel	19
Hours spent by management in orientation, informal training, extra supervision	59
Hours spent by coworkers in informal training	34
Hours spent by new worker watching others do work	41
Total	153

Source: John Bishop, "The Incidence of and Payoff to Employer Training" (Working Paper No. 94–17, Cornell University Center for Advanced Human Resource Studies, July 1994): 11

In addition to the hiring costs, firms typically provide formal or informal training to both their new and continuing workers. The costs of this training generally fall into three classes:

1. the *explicit* monetary costs of formally employing trainers and providing training materials

2. the *implicit*, or opportunity, costs of lost production incurred when experienced employees take time to demonstrate procedures to trainees in less-formal settings

3. the *implicit*, or opportunity, costs of the trainee's time

A survey in the early 1990s found that in the first three months (or 520 hours of work) that an employee is with a firm, about 30 percent (153 hours) of their time is spent in training. The data from this study, summarized in Table 5.2, also suggest that little of this training was formal classroom-type instruction; most took place informally at the workstation.[21]

Hiring and training costs can be categorized as *investments* because they are incurred in the present and have benefits (in the form of increased productivity) only in the future. Investments are inherently risky because, once made, the costs are "sunk," and there are no guarantees about future returns. Later in this chapter, we analyze the effects of these investments on employer behavior.

Employee Benefits   Besides their direct wage and salary earnings, workers also typically receive nonwage compensation in the form of employer-provided medical and life insurance, retirement plans, vacation days, Social Security payments, and other *employee benefits*. Table 5.3 details the employee benefits received by workers in 2020, and many of these benefits represent quasi-fixed costs to the employer. That is, many employee benefits are associated with the number of employees but not with the hours that they work.

Table 5.3 Employee Benefits as a Percentage of Total Compensation, 2020 (Average Hourly Cost in Parentheses)

Legally required payments	**7.2**	**($2.72)**
Social Security	5.6	($2.11)
Workers' compensation	1.2	($0.46)
[a] Unemployment insurance and other	0.4	($0.15)
Retirement	**5.2**	**($1.97)**
[a] Employment costs based on benefit formulas (defined benefit plans)	3.2	($1.20)
Employer costs proportional to earnings (defined contribution plans)	2.0	($0.76)
[a] Insurance (medical, life)	8.7	($3.27)
[a] Paid vacations, holidays, sick leave	7.3	($2.76)
Other	**2.9**	**($1.10)**
Total	**31.3**	**($11.82)**

[a] Category of costs believed by authors to be largely quasi-fixed (see discussion in the text).

Source: U.S. Labor Department, Bureau of Labor Statistics, "Employer Costs for Employee Compensation—March 2020," Table 1, news release USDL: 20–1232 (June 18, 2020)

Most life and medical insurance policies have premiums to the employer that are charged on a per-worker basis and are not proportional to the hours worked. Pay for time not worked (vacation, holidays, and sick leave) also tends to be quasi-fixed.[22] Some pension costs are proportional to hours worked because many employers offer *defined contribution* plans and make payments to a retirement fund for each worker that are proportional to wage or salary earnings. However, some employers have *defined benefit* pension plans that promise pension payments to retirees that are a function of years of service, not hours of work; the costs of these plans are thus quasi-fixed.

In the category of legally required benefits, workers' compensation insurance costs are strictly proportional to hours worked, because they are levied on employers as a percentage of payroll; likewise, the Social Security taxes that employers must pay are proportional for most of their employees.[23] However, the unemployment insurance payroll-tax liability is specified to be a percentage (the tax rate) of each employee's yearly earnings up to a maximum level (the taxable wage base), which in 2019 was between $7,000 and $16,500 in about half of all U.S. states.[24] Since most full-time employees earn more than $16,500 per year, having an employee work an additional hour per week will *not* cause any increase in the typical employer's payroll-tax liability. Therefore, unemployment insurance costs are a quasi-fixed cost to most employers.

In Table 5.3, we have indicated (by a superscript *a*) which nonwage costs are usually of a quasi-fixed nature. The data suggest that almost 20 percent of total compensation costs—or $7.38 per hour for the average worker (over $14,000 per year if the worker is full time)—are quasi-fixed. The quasi-fixed nature of many nonwage labor costs has important effects on employer hiring and overtime decisions. These effects are discussed in the following section.

The Employment/Hours Trade-Off

The simple model of the demand for labor presented in the preceding chapters spoke to the quantity of labor demanded, making no distinction between the number of individuals employed by a firm and the average length of its employees' workweek. Holding all other inputs constant, however, a firm can produce a given level of output with various combinations of the number of employees hired and the number of hours worked per week. Presumably, increases in the number of employees hired will allow for shorter workweeks, whereas longer workweeks will allow for fewer employees, other things being equal.

In Chapter 3, we defined the marginal product of labor (MP_L) as the change in output generated by an added unit of labor, holding capital constant. Once we have distinguished between the *number* of workers hired (which we will denote by M) and the *hours* that each works on average (H), we must think of two marginal products of labor. MP_M is the added output associated with an added worker, holding both capital and average hours per worker constant. MP_H is the added output generated by increasing average hours per worker, holding capital and the number of employees constant. As with MP_L, we assume that both MP_M and MP_H are positive but that they decline as M and H (respectively) increase.[25]

How does a firm determine its optimal employment/hours combination? Is a firm ever rational to work its existing employees at overtime on a regularly scheduled basis, even though it must pay them a wage premium, rather than hiring additional employees?

Determining the Mix of Workers and Hours   The fact that certain labor costs are not related to hours, whereas others are, leads employers to think of "workers" and "hours per worker" as two substitutable labor inputs. Thus, the profit-maximizing employer weighs the cost of producing an added unit of output by hiring more workers against the cost of producing an added unit of output by employing its current workers for more hours. According to our discussion of equation (3.8c), profit maximization can be achieved only when these two costs are equal. Thus, if the marginal expense of hiring an added worker is ME_M and the marginal expense of hiring current workers for an extra hour is ME_H, then for profits to be maximized, the following condition must hold:

$$\frac{ME_M}{MP_M} = \frac{ME_H}{MP_H} \qquad\qquad (5.3)$$

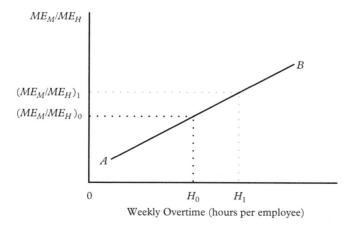

Figure 5.6 The Predicted Relationship Between ME_M/ME_H and Overtime Hours

The left-hand side of equation (5.3) is the cost of an added unit of output produced by hiring more workers, and the right-hand side is the cost of an added unit of output produced by hiring workers for more hours.

One implication of equation (5.3) is that if for some reason ME_M rises relative to ME_H, firms will want to substitute hours for workers by hiring fewer employees but having each work more hours. (An alternative to hiring more workers or increasing hours is to "rent" workers; see Example 5.3.) Conversely, if ME_H rises relative to ME_M, the employer will want to produce its profit-maximizing level of output at a higher ratio of workers to average hours per worker. The relationship between ME_M/ME_H and hours of work is graphed in Figure 5.6, which indicates that as ME_M rises relative to ME_H, other things being equal, hours of work per employee tend to rise.

Policy Analysis: The Overtime Pay Premium   In the United States, the Fair Labor Standards Act of 1938 requires that employees covered by the act (generally nonsupervisory workers paid hourly) receive an overtime pay premium of at least 50 percent of their regular hourly wage for each hour worked in excess of 40 per week. Many overtime hours are worked because of unusual circumstances that are difficult or impossible to meet by hiring more workers: rush orders, absent workers, and mechanical failures. However, some overtime is regularly scheduled; for example, over 20 percent of men who are skilled craft workers or technicians usually work more than 44 hours per week.[26]

EXAMPLE 5.3

"Renting" Workers as a Way of Coping With Hiring Costs

One indication that the quasi-fixed costs of hiring are substantial can be seen in the existence of temporary-help agencies. Temporary-help agencies specialize in recruiting workers who are then put to work in client firms that need temporary workers. The temporary-help agency bills its clients, and its hourly charges are generally above the wage that the client would pay if it hired workers directly—a premium that the client is willing to pay because it is spared the investment costs associated with hiring or firing workers. Because obtaining jobs through the temporary-help agency also saves employees repeated investment costs associated with searching and applying for available temporary openings, its employees are willing to take a wage less than they otherwise would receive. The difference between what its clients are charged and what its employees are paid permits the successful temporary-help agency to cover its recruiting and assignment costs.

Because employers do not have to bear the quasi-fixed costs of hiring workers— or of firing them if it turns out that product demand is insufficient to support their employment—temporary-help agencies are often used during periods of heightened uncertainty. For example, during the Great Recession of 2008 and 2009, the temporary-help industry—which employs about 2 percent of all workers in the U.S.—accounted for 11 percent of all job losses. Correspondingly, during the recovery period after 2009, temporary-help agencies accounted for over 13 percent of all employment gains.

Source: Susan N. Houseman and Carolyn J. Heinrich, "Temporary Help Employment in Recession and Recovery" (Working Paper No. 15–227, W.E. Upjohn Institute for Employment Research, Kalamazoo, MI, 2015); Lewis M. Segal and Daniel G. Sullivan, "The Growth of Temporary Services Work," *Journal of Economic Perspectives* 11 (Spring 1997): 117–136

Given the 50% premium that must be paid for overtime work, we can conclude that employers who regularly schedule overtime do so because it is cheaper than incurring the quasi-fixed costs of employing more workers. Indeed, the production workers most likely to work long hours on a regular basis are those for which hiring and training costs are higher. For example, while over 20 percent of male craft workers are scheduled for more than 44 hours each week, only 12 percent of lower-skilled men usually work more than 44 hours.[27]

In 2019, the U.S. Department of Labor updated earlier revisions to federal overtime regulations that redefined which jobs are exempt from coverage. Generally speaking, for a job to be exempt from the requirements of overtime pay, the employee must be paid on a salaried basis (not by the hour) and perform specified administrative, professional, or executive duties. The 2019 revisions disallowed exemptions for lower-paying salaried jobs (paying less than $684 per week), regardless of duties. Also exempt are jobs in which total pay exceeds $107,432 per year.[28]

Overtime and Spreading the Work   Some argue that the 50% premium requirement for overtime protects workers by "spreading the work" (creating more job openings) through reduced usage of overtime. One reason to be cautious in our expectations that increased coverage (covering more occupations and types of job) will create more jobs is that applying the overtime premium increases the average cost of labor even if a firm *eliminates* its prior use of overtime. Firms using overtime before *could* have increased their workforce and reduced the use of overtime earlier; the fact that they did not suggests that the quasi-fixed costs of hiring made that a more costly option. If they now eliminate overtime and hire more workers at the same base wage rate, their labor costs will clearly rise. Increased labor costs will tend to both decrease the scale of output and increase firms' incentives to substitute capital for labor, thereby reducing the total labor hours demanded by affected firms. Thus, even if base wages are not changed, all the reduced overtime hours are unlikely to be replaced by hiring more workers.

Overtime and Total Pay   Will newly covered salaried workers experience an increase in earnings? They might not, because their base pay may change in response to changes in overtime coverage. We have seen that many overtime hours are regularly scheduled, and in these cases, employers and employees might mutually agree (informally, at least) on a "package" of weekly hours and total compensation. If so, firms that regularly schedule overtime hours might respond to a legislated increase in coverage by reducing the basic salary in a way that, after taking the newly required overtime payments into account, would leave the total compensation per worker unchanged. Indeed, one study of wages in the United States found that when mandated overtime premiums rose, base pay tended to fall, most notably in firms that regularly scheduled the most overtime.[29] Another study on the effects of overtime premiums in the United States also found evidence that base wages adjust to mandated changes in these premiums in a way that suggests that employers and employees regard hours and pay as a package; this study found that legislated expansions in overtime coverage have had no measurable effect on overtime hours worked.[30]

Training Investments

We have identified employer-provided training as an important investment that can increase the quasi-fixed costs of hiring workers. The costs of training, even if provided by the employer, are often at least partly paid by workers themselves in one way or another, so training investments represent a rather unique friction in the labor market. This section explores the implications of this friction for both employer behavior and employee behavior.

The Training Decision of Employers

Consider an employer who has just hired a new employee. If the employer decides to bear the cost of training this worker, it will incur the explicit and implicit training costs discussed earlier—including, of course, the forgone output of the worker during training. Thus, in the training period, the employer is likely to bear costs on behalf of this new worker that are greater than the worker's marginal revenue product. Under what conditions would an employer be willing to undertake this kind of investment?

As with any investment, an employer that bears net costs during the training period would only do so if it believes that it can collect returns on that investment *after training*. The prospect of increased employee productivity motivates an employer to offer training, but the only way that the employer can make a return on its investment is to "keep" some of that added post-training revenue by not giving all of it to the worker in the form of a wage increase.

Put succinctly, for a firm to invest in training, two conditions must be met. First, the training that employees receive must increase their marginal revenue productivity more than it increases their wage. Second, the employees must stay with the employer long enough for the employer to receive the required returns (obviously, the longer the employees stay with the firm, other things being equal, the more profitable the investment will be).[31]

The Types of Training

At the extremes are two types of training that employers can provide. *General training* teaches workers skills that can be used to enhance their productivity with many employers; learning how to speak English, use a word-processing program, drive a truck, or create websites are examples of general training. At the other end of the spectrum is *specific training*, which teaches workers skills that increase their productivity only with the employer providing the training. Examples of specific training include teaching workers how to use a machine unique to their workplace or orienting them to particular procedures and people whom they will need to deal with in various circumstances that they will encounter at work.

General Training   Paying for general training can be a rather risky investment for an employer, because if the employer tries to keep post-training wage increases below increases in marginal revenue productivity, trained workers might leave because their increased skills are valuable to any employer. Because general training can raise productivity with other employers too, trained workers may have incentives to look for higher wage offers from employers that have no training costs to recoup.

Thus, theory suggests that if employee mobility costs are not high, employers will be deterred from investing in general training. The likelihood of making back their required returns is low, because the gap between marginal revenue product and the post-training wage might not be sufficiently great, or the expected tenure of the trained workers with the firms sufficiently long, to recoup their investment costs. When worker-mobility costs are low, firms either will not provide the training or will require the employees to pay for it by offering a low—or, in the case of some interns, a zero—wage rate during the training period. Research finds, however, that firms often *do* invest in general training, a fact that suggests worker mobility among firms is costly and that the labor market is therefore characterized by monopsonistic conditions. A related possibility is that while the skills taught to employees are general in nature, the *combinations* of general skills required by particular employers vary markedly, and this variability reduces the transferability of skills among employers.[32] For another reason why firms might provide general training to their employees, see Example 5.4.

EXAMPLE 5.4

General Training and Training Contracts

Theory predicts that employers have weak incentives to provide general training, because trained workers might capitalize on their enhanced skills to obtain work elsewhere—before the employer who invested in their training has a chance to recoup its investment costs. Yet firms often do invest in general training of their employees, which implies that worker mobility must be constrained in some way. One constraint might be the mobility costs discussed in the first part of this chapter, but another is created by the presence of "training contracts," which impose a financial penalty on the trained worker if they leave the firm within a certain period after training. For example, some master's of business administration (MBA) students receive tuition assistance from their employers, and a subset of those have a resulting obligation to work for their firm for at least a year after receiving their degree.

Trucking offers another example of firm-provided general training where training contracts are common. Over 1.8 million drivers of heavy trucks are employed in the United States, and they all need to have a commercial driver's license (CDL) to operate their respective trucks. In long-haul (full truckload) trucking, the drivers are paid by the mile, not by salary, and they must drive long distances from home. Working conditions are such that yearly turnover rate among truckers is high—frequently around 100 percent in many long-haul firms.

The major requirement to be a heavy truck driver is to take and pass a formal CDL training course. These courses can be given by private truck-driving schools or even by community colleges, but over half of the 30 largest long-haul trucking firms report providing CDL training to their drivers. Such training is costly, involving hours of classroom work, simulated driving exercises, and behind-the-wheel experience. Courses last two to three weeks, and costs can run into the thousands of dollars.

CDL training is a classic example of *general* training, because a CDL license can qualify the driver to drive for any trucking firm. With such high turnover rates, firms would have no incentives to offer such training unless they can induce drivers to stay with them long enough to recoup the training expenses. A study was done of one large trucking firm that had been giving training to thousands of drivers each year without a training contract. Facing high turnover, it adopted (in 2000) a requirement that its trainees sign a contract obligating them to pay a fine of $3,500–$4,000 if they left the firm before working there for 12 months. It later adopted an 18-month contract, with a fine of $5,000 if the worker left before 18 months—although the fine was reduced $65 per week for every week the driver worked for the firm. While the firm was able to collect only about 30 percent of the fines owed to it, it found that turnover was reduced by 15 percent after imposing the contract.

Source: Mitchell Hoffman and Stephen V. Burks, "Training Contracts, Employee Turnover, and the Returns from Firm-Sponsored General Training" (Working Paper No. 23247, National Bureau of Economic Research, Cambridge, MA, March 2017)

Specific Training   Employers have stronger incentives to invest in *specific* training, because such training does not raise the worker's productivity with other firms, and it therefore does not make the worker more attractive to competing employers. While the training itself does not increase the outside offers that an employee might be able to receive, a firm undertaking investments in specific training must nevertheless take precautions to prevent the trained employee from quitting, because once the employee has quit, the employer's investment has been destroyed (i.e., returns on the investment cannot be realized). Thus, concerns about the possibility that trained employees will quit before the employer can receive its required investment returns exist relative both to specific training and to general training. These concerns lead us to a discussion of who bears the costs of training and of the size of post-training wage increases.

Training and Post-Training Wage Increases

Consider a situation in which worker-mobility costs are relatively low, and the *employer* is considering bearing all the costs of training. With investment costs to recoup, the employer would be unable to raise wages very much after training and still have incentives to invest. We know that higher wages reduce the probability of a worker's quitting, so by failing to increase the wage much after training, the employer would put its investment at risk. Trained workers might decide to quit at even a small provocation (the boss is in a bad mood one day, for example, or they are asked to work overtime for a while), and without some assurance that trained employees will stay, the firm would be reluctant to make a training investment for which it bore all the costs, even if the training is specific.

Conversely, if a firm's *employees* paid for their own training by taking a lower wage than they could get elsewhere during the training period, they would require the benefits of a much higher post-training wage to make employment at the firm attractive. If they were to get all of their improved marginal revenue product in the form of a wage increase, however, an employer that finds it relatively inexpensive to hire and fire workers would have little to lose by firing *them* at the smallest provocation—and if they get fired, *their* investment has been destroyed.

Thus, if labor market frictions are otherwise small, the best way to provide incentives for on-the-job training is for employers and employees to *share* the costs and returns of the investment.[33] If *employees* pay part of these costs, the post-training wage can be increased more than if employers bear all the training costs—and the increased post-training wage protects *firms'* investments by reducing the chances that trained workers will quit. The training costs borne by *employers* must be recouped by not raising the post-training wage very much, but this condition helps protect *workers'* investments by making retaining them attractive for firms unless the provocation is major (a bit later in this chapter, we discuss the issue of layoffs in more detail). Put differently, if both employers and employees share in the costs of training, and thus share in the returns, they both have something to lose if the employment relationship is ended in the post-training period.

Empirical studies measuring the wage profiles associated with on-the-job training in the United States, however, suggest that *employers bear much of the costs and reap most of the returns associated with training.* Wages apparently are not depressed enough during the training period to offset the employer's direct costs of training, so subsequent wage increases are much smaller than productivity increases.[34] A survey of employers, summarized in Figure 5.7, estimated that productivity increases, which generally rose with the hours of initial on-the-job training, were far larger than wage increases over a worker's first two years with an employer. Other studies that directly link the wage profiles of U.S. workers with the amount of training that they have received find that post-training wage increases are relatively modest.[35]

The evidence that employers bear much of the training costs and reap much of the returns suggests that these employers believe that their workers face relatively high worker-mobility costs. These firms are willing to bear the investment costs because they do not feel the need to raise the post-training wage much in order to retain their trained employees.

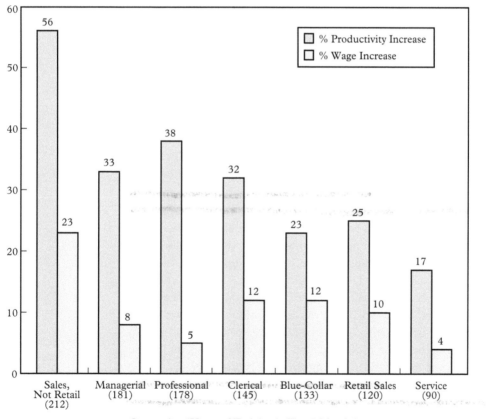

Figure 5.7 Productivity and Wage Growth, First Two Years on Job, by Occupation and Initial Hours of Employer Training

Source: John Bishop, "The Incidence of and Payoff to Employer Training" (Working Paper No. 94–17, Cornell University Center for Advanced Human Resource Studies, July 1994), Table 1

Employer Training Investments and Recessionary Layoffs

We have seen that employers have incentives to invest in worker training only when the post-training marginal revenue productivity is expected to be sufficiently above the wage so that the investment returns are attractive. Suppose that a firm has made the investment but that at some point thereafter it finds that its workers' marginal revenue productivity falls below what it expected because of a business downturn (a "recession"). If it cannot lower wages for one reason or another (in Chapter 14, we discuss why wages might be inflexible in a downward direction), will the firm want to lay off its trained workers?

In general, firms will not want to lay off their workers as long as the workers are bringing in revenues that are in excess of their wages. Even if the gap between marginal revenue productivity and wage is not sufficient to yield an attractive return on the firm's training investment, those training costs—once incurred—are "sunk." Although the firm might wish it had not invested in training, the best that it can do after training is get what returns it can. Laid-off workers clearly bring in no returns to the employer, so its incentives are to retain any worker whose marginal revenue productivity exceeds their wage. Of course, if the downturn causes marginal revenue productivity to fall *below* the wage rate, firms do have incentives to lay off trained workers (unless they believe that the downturn will be short and do not want to take the risk that the laid-off workers will search for other employment).

The presence of employer training investments, then, offers an explanation for two phenomena that we observe in the labor market. *First, as a general rule, we observe that workers who are least susceptible to being laid off during recessions are the most skilled and those with the longest job tenures.*[36] Older and more-skilled workers are those most likely to have been the objects of past employer training investments, and they therefore tend to enter recessions with larger gaps between marginal revenue product and wage.[37] These gaps cushion any fall in marginal revenue product and provide their employers with stronger incentives to keep on employing them during the downturn. Workers who enter the recession with wages closer to marginal revenue productivity are more likely to find that the downturn causes their marginal revenue product to fall below their wage, and when this occurs, employers may find that laying them off is profitable.

Second, we observe that average labor productivity—output per labor hour—falls in the early stages of a recession and rises during the early stages of recovery. As demand and output start to fall, firms that have invested in worker training respond by keeping their trained workers on the payroll even though their marginal productivity falls. Such "labor hoarding" causes output per worker to fall. Of course, when demand picks up again, firms can increase output without proportionately increasing their employment because, in effect, they have maintained an inventory of trained labor. In the latter situation, output per worker rises.

Hiring Investments

In addition to training employees, firms must also evaluate them when making hiring, placement, and promotion decisions. They may therefore find that training programs—even ones with a "general" component—can be used to help them discover the learning abilities, work habits, and motivation levels of new employees.[38] Thus, some of what appears to be general training may actually represent an investment in firm-specific information about employees that will be useful later on in making assignments and deciding on promotions. We conclude this chapter with a section that in greater detail analyzes hiring and screening investments.

The Use of Credentials

Since firms often bear the costs of hiring and training workers, they have an interest in making these costs as low as possible. Other things being equal, firms should prefer to obtain a workforce of a given quality at the least possible cost. Similarly, they should prefer to hire workers who are fast learners, because such workers could be trained at less cost. Unfortunately, extensively investigating the background of every individual who applies for a job may prove expensive for firms trying to ascertain applicants' skill levels and abilities to undertake training.

One way to reduce these costs is to rely on *credentials*, or *signals*, in the hiring process rather than intensively investigating the qualities of individual applicants.[39] For example, if, *on average*, college graduates are more productive than high school graduates, an employer might specify that a college degree is a requirement for the job. Rather than interviewing and testing all applicants to try to ascertain the productivity of each, the firm may simply select its new employees from the pool of applicants who meet this educational standard.

Such forms of *statistical discrimination*, judging individuals by *group* characteristics, have obvious costs. On the one hand, for example, some high school graduates may be fully qualified to work for a firm that insists on college graduates. Excluding them from the pool of potential applicants imposes costs on them (they do not get the job); however, it also imposes costs on the employer *if* other qualified applicants cannot be readily found. On the other hand, some unproductive workers may be among the group of college graduates, and an employer who hires them may well suffer losses while these workers are employed. However, if the reduction in hiring costs that arises when *signals* (such as educational credentials, marital status, or age) are used is large, an employer's using them may prove profitable even if an occasional unsatisfactory worker sneaks through.[40]

Internal Labor Markets

One of the difficulties in hiring employees is that such personal attributes as dependability, motivation, honesty, and flexibility are difficult to judge from interviews, employment tests, and even the recommendations of former employers. This difficulty has led many larger firms to create an *internal labor market*, in which workers are hired into relatively low-level jobs and higher-level jobs are filled only from within the firm. This policy gives employers a chance to observe *actual* productive characteristics of the employees hired, and this information is then used to determine who stays with the firm and how fast and how high employees are promoted.

The *benefits* of using an internal labor market to fill vacancies are that the firm knows a lot about the people working for it. Hiring decisions for upper-level jobs in either the blue-collar workforce or the white-collar workforce will thus offer few surprises to the firm. The *costs* of using the internal labor market are associated with the restriction of competition for the upper-level jobs to those in the firm. Those in the firm may not be the best employees available, but they are the only ones whom the firm considers for these jobs. Firms most likely to decide that the benefits of using an internal labor market outweigh the costs are those whose upper-level workers must have a lot of firm-specific knowledge and training that can best be attained by on-the-job learning over the years.[41]

As noted earlier, firms that pay for *training* want to ensure that they obtain employees who can learn quickly and will remain with them long enough for the training costs to be recouped through the post-training surplus. For these firms, the internal labor market offers two attractions. First, it allows the firm to observe workers on the job and thus make better decisions about which workers will be the recipients of later, perhaps expensive, training. Second, the internal labor market tends to foster an attachment to the firm by its employees. They know that they have an inside track on upper-level vacancies because outsiders will not be considered. If they quit the firm, they would lose this privileged position. They are thus motivated to become long-term employees of the firm. Additional implications of internal labor markets for wage policies within the firm are discussed in Chapter 11.

How Can the Employer Recoup Its Hiring Investments?

Whether a firm invests in training its workers or in selecting them, it will do so only if it believes that it can generate an acceptable rate of return on its investment. For a labor investment to be worthwhile, an employer must be able to benefit from a situation in which workers are paid less than their marginal value to the firm in the post-investment period. How can employers generate a post-investment surplus from their *hiring* investments?

Suppose that applicants for a job vacancy have average, below-average, or above-average productivity but that the employer cannot tell which without making some kind of investment in acquiring that information. If the firm does not make this investment, it must assume that any particular applicant is of average ability and pay accordingly. If the firm makes an investment in acquiring information about its applicants, however, it could then hire *only* those whose productivity is above average. The surplus required to pay back its investment costs would then be created by paying these above-average workers a wage less than their true productivity.

Would the firm pay its new workers the average wage even though they are above average in productivity, thereby obtaining the full surplus? As with the case of training, the firm would probably decide to pay a wage greater than the average (to increase the likelihood that the workers in whom it has invested will remain) but still below workers' actual productivity. If its workers quit, the firm would have to invest in acquiring information about their replacements.

While the self-interest of employers would drive them to pay an above-average wage to above-average workers, two things could allow the screening firm to pay a wage that is still lower than workers' full productivity. One is the presence of mobility costs among employees. The other is that the information that one employer finds out through a costly screening process may not be observable by other employers unless they too make an investment of their own. Either of these conditions would inhibit employees from obtaining wage offers from competing firms that could afford to pay full-productivity wages because they had no screening expenses to recoup.[42]

EMPIRICAL STUDY 5.1

WHAT EXPLAINS WAGE DIFFERENCES FOR WORKERS WHO APPEAR SIMILAR? USING PANEL DATA TO DEAL WITH UNOBSERVED HETEROGENEITY

To test whether the law of one price holds in the labor market, we must test to determine whether workers who are productively equivalent receive different wages. If we try to use cross-sectional data at one point in time to perform our test, however, we will run up against a huge problem: Researchers cannot observe all the characteristics that affect worker productivity. For example, we cannot measure how willing a worker is to work overtime with little notice, how pleasant the worker is to customers or coworkers, how organized or driven the employee is, whether they are a "team player," or whether they have a sunny personality. Without some way to account for worker differences in these characteristics that are important but not directly observed (what economists have come to call "unmeasured worker heterogeneity"), we cannot credibly test to determine whether the law of one price holds.

To better understand the problem, suppose that we estimate the average relationship between wages that employees receive and their measured characteristics by using a sample of cross-sectional data. We can then use this relationship to derive an expected wage for a particular woman, say, given her age, education, occupation, and other observed qualities. If her actual wage exceeds her expected wage, we do not know whether she is merely lucky (and the law of one price does not hold) or whether she has unobserved qualities that employers value (and is therefore more productive than average, given her measured characteristics).

Fortunately, we have a way to confront the problem of unobserved heterogeneity, but it requires undertaking the expense of gathering "panel data"—data that allow for observations on the same individual over two or more years. If we can follow individuals over time, we can analyze how their wages *change* as they move from job to job, from employer to employer, or from one educational level to another. If the woman in our example who received a higher-than-expected wage with her first employer now changes jobs and receives an above-expected wage with the next, the likelihood is that she is an above-average producer and did not merely get lucky twice.

Thus, if we can follow individual workers through time, we can control for their unobserved personal productive characteristics ("person effects") by focusing on how the same person's wage varies when some measurable condition (e.g., education, occupation, or employer) changes. To understand how the ability to control for person effects influences conclusions about how closely labor market outcomes correspond to predictions concerning the law of one price, consider findings from a 1999 study that used panel data from France.

When the relationships between wages and measured worker productive characteristics were analyzed in a cross-section of several million French workers, the researchers found that these measured characteristics could explain only approximately 30 percent of the variation in wages across the population. This finding seems to suggest that the predictions of the law of one price are badly off. Once person effects (in addition to the measured characteristics) had been accounted for by using panel data, however, the researchers were able to account for 77 percent of the variation in French wages. Although variation in wages still apparently cannot be completely explained by employee characteristics (observed and unobserved), the use of panel data permits a more valid test of the law of one price. The findings from using panel data suggest that the level of variation due to luck might be less than meets the eye.

Source: John M. Abowd, Francis Kramarz, and David N. Margolis, "High Wage Workers and High Wage Firms," *Econometrica* 67 (March 1999): 251–333

Review Questions

1. How do worker-mobility costs affect the slope of labor supply curves to individual firms?

2. Why do upward-sloping labor supply curves to firms cause the marginal expense of labor to exceed the wage rate?

3. Suppose that an author argues that output per worker usually grows during the first year of an expansion because firms are slow to hire new labor. Is this argument supported by the theory learned in this chapter?

4. "Minimum-wage laws help low-wage workers because they simultaneously increase wages and decrease the marginal expense of labor." Analyze this statement.

5. An author recently asserted that low-wage jobs provide fewer hours of work than high-wage jobs do. According to economic theory, is this statement likely to be correct? Why?

6. Workers in a certain job are trained by the company, and the company calculates that to recoup its investment costs, the workers' wages must be $5 per hour below their marginal productivity. Suppose that after training, wages are set at $5 below marginal productivity but that developments in the product market quickly (and permanently) reduce marginal productivity by $2 per hour. If the company does not believe that it can lower wages or employee benefits, how will its employment level be affected in the short run? How will its employment level be affected in the long run? Explain why, and when you do so, be sure to define what you mean by the short run and the long run.

7. For decades, most large employers bought group health insurance from insurers who charged them premiums on a *per-worker* basis. In 1993, a proposal for a national health insurance plan contained a provision requiring group health insurers to charge premiums based on *payroll* (in effect, financing health insurance by a payroll "tax"). Assuming the *total* premiums paid by employers remain the same, what are the labor market implications of this proposed change on how health insurance is financed?

8. The manager of a major league baseball team argues, "Even if I thought player X was washed up, I couldn't get rid of him. He's in the third year of a four-year, $40-million deal. Our team is in no position financially to eat the rest of his contract." Analyze the manager's reasoning by using economic theory.

9. The president of France has announced that his government is considering abandoning its 2002 law that placed a cap on the hours that French employees could work each week (French workers were not allowed to work more than 35 hours per week). The reasons for eliminating the cap on weekly hours were listed as "unanticipated adverse consequences" in the areas of skill formation and employment levels. Use economic theory learned in this course to analyze the effects of the hours cap on skill formation and employment levels.

10. The state of North Carolina created a program for state-subsidized training for disadvantaged workers at its community colleges. Employers adding at least 12 jobs can arrange for a community college to

provide a program tailored to the individual firm. The college places ads for new hires and screens the applicants, the firms choose whom they want trained from the list supplied by the college, and the college provides the training (using equipment supplied by the firm). Finally, the firm selects employees from among those who successfully complete the training. Trainees are not paid during the training period. Analyze the likely effects on wages, employment, and hours of work associated with adopting this program.

Problems

1. Suppose that a firm's labor supply curve is $E = 5W$, where W is the hourly wage.

   a. Solve for the hourly wage that must be paid to attract a given number of workers (E) to the firm.

   b. Express the total hourly labor cost associated with any given level of employment.

   c. Express the marginal expense of labor (ME_L) incurred when an employer hires an additional worker.

2. Assume that the labor supply curve to a firm is the one given in problem 1. If the firm's marginal revenue product (MRP_L) = $240 - 2E$, what is the profit-maximizing level of employment (E^*), and what is the wage level (W^*) that the firm would have to pay to obtain E^* workers?

3. A firm is considering hiring a worker and providing the worker with general training. The training costs $1,000, and the worker's MRP_L during the training period is $3,000. If the worker can costlessly move to another employer in the post-training period and that employer will pay a wage equaling the new MRP_L, how much will the training firm pay the worker in the training period?

4. As with the own-wage elasticity of demand for labor, the elasticity of the supply of labor can be similarly classified. The elasticity of the supply of labor is *elastic* if elasticity is greater than 1. It is *inelastic* if the elasticity is less than 1, and it is *unitary elastic* if the elasticity of supply equals 1. For each of the following occupations, calculate the elasticity of supply, and state whether the supply of labor is elastic, inelastic, or unitary elastic. E_S and W are the original supply of workers and wage. E'_S and W' are the new supply of workers and wage, respectively.

   a. $\%\Delta E_S = 7$, $\%\Delta W = 3$

   b. $E_S = 120$, $W = \$8$
      $E'_S = 90$, $W' = \$6$

   c. $E_S = 100$, $W = \$5$
      $E'_S = 120$, $W' = \$7$

5. The supply of labor is given in Table 5P.5 for Teddy's Treats, a dog biscuit company, which is a profit-maximizing monopsonist.

Table 5P.5 Supply of Labor to Teddy's Treats

Offered wage ($)	Supply of labor (number of hours)
4	18
5	19
6	20
7	21
8	22

a. Calculate the total labor cost and the marginal expense of labor for each level of employment.

b. Draw the supply of labor curve and the marginal expense of labor curve.

6. Table 5P.6 features the MRP_L of Teddy's Treats, the dog biscuit company in problem 5.

Table 5P.6 Marginal Revenue Product of Labor, Teddy's Treats

Number of hours	MRP_L
18	29
19	27
20	25
21	23
22	21

a. Add the marginal revenue product curve to the drawing in problem 5.

b. If Teddy's Treats is maximizing profits, how many hours of labor will be hired? What wage will be offered?

7. Suppose that the workers at Teddy's Treats increase the number of hours that they are willing to work at each wage rate. The new supply is in Table 5P.7:

Table 5P.7 New Supply of Labor to Teddy's Treats

Offered wage ($)	Supply of labor (number of hours)
4	19
5	20
6	21
7	22
8	23

a. Calculate the total labor cost and the marginal expense of labor associated with each employment level.

b. Draw the new supply and marginal expense curves.

c. Compare the supply of labor and marginal expense of labor curves with the corresponding curves in problem 5. What changes occurred?

d. Assuming that MRP_L is unchanged, how many hours of labor will now be hired? What wage will now be offered?

8. Suppose that the marginal expense of hiring another worker is $150 and that the marginal expense of hiring current workers for an extra hour is $10. The added output associated with an added worker, holding both capital and average hours per worker constant, is 120. The added output generated by increasing average hours per worker, holding capital and the number of employees constant, is 7. If the firm is interested in maximizing profits, what should it do?

9. Table 5P.9 gives the quantity of labor, the offered wage, and the MRP_L at Toasty Tasties, a restaurant that specializes in breakfast and lunch.

Table 5P.9 Supply of Labor and Marginal Revenue Product of Labor, Toasty Tasties

Quantity of labor (number of hours)	Offered wage ($)	MRP_L ($)
5	6	—
6	8	50
7	10	38
8	12	26
9	14	14
10	16	2
11	18	1

a. Calculate the marginal expense of labor.

b. Draw the supply of labor, the marginal expense of labor, and the MRP_L curves at Toasty Tasties.

c. To maximize profits, how many hours of labor should be hired? What wage will the employer offer?

d. What would happen if some nonmarket force were to compel the firm to pay its employees $14 per hour?

e. What would happen if some nonmarket force were to compel the firm to pay its employees $26 per hour?

f. What would happen if some nonmarket force were to compel the firm to pay its employees an hourly wage that is larger than $26 per hour?

Notes

1. We have also assumed here that no other job attributes (such as benefits and working conditions) vary across employers.

2. This prediction should be qualified by adding "if they are working in similar environments." As we discuss in Chapter 8, we do expect that similar workers will be paid differently if they are working in cities with different costs of living, say, or if some of them work in more dangerous or unpleasant settings than others.

3. U.S. Department of Labor, Bureau of Labor Statistics, "Occupational Employment Statistics," www.bls.gov/oes/current/oessrcma.htm#N.

4. U.S. Department of Labor, Bureau of Labor Statistics, "Occupational Employment Statistics," http://www.bls.gov/oes/current/oes435071. htm. For more-careful studies of intra-occupational wage differences and the law of one price, see Stephen Machin and Alan Manning, "A Test of Competitive Labor Market Theory: The Wage Structure among Care Assistants in the South of England," *Industrial and Labor Relations Review* 57 (April 2004): 371–385; V. Bhaskar, Alan Manning, and Ted To, "Oligopsony and Monopsonistic Competition in Labor Markets," *Journal of Economic Perspectives* 16 (Spring 2002): 155–174; Dale T. Mortensen, *Wage Dispersion: Why Are Similar Workers Paid Differently?* (Cambridge, MA: Massachusetts Institute of Technology, 2003); Samuel Berlinski, "Wages and Contracting Out: Does the Law of One Price Hold?" *British Journal of Industrial Relations* 46 (March 2008): 59–75.

5. For a theory of monopsonistic competition that is based on different preferences among employees for nonwage benefits, see V. Bhaskar and Ted To, "Minimum Wages for Ronald McDonald Monopsonies: A Theory of Monopsonistic Competition," *Economic Journal* 109 (April 1999): 190–203; Arindrajit Dube, Jeff Jacobs, Suresh Naidu, and Siddharth Suri, "Monopsony in Online Labor Markets," *American Economic Review: Insights* 2 (March 2020): 33–46; David Card, Ana Rute Cardoso, Joerg Heining, and Patrick Kline, "Firms and Labor Market Inequality: Evidence and Some Theory," *Journal of Labor Economics* 36 (January 2018): S13–S70; Thibaut Lamadon, Magne Mogstad, and Bradley Setzler, "Imperfect Competition, Compensating Differentials and Rent Sharing in the U.S. Labor Market" (Working Paper No. 25954, National Bureau of Economic Research, Cambridge, MA, June 2019).

6. An entire issue of the Orley C. Ashenfelter, Henry S. Farber, and Michael R. Ransom, "Modern Models of Monopsony in Labor Markets: A Brief Survey," *Journal of Labor Economics* 28 (April 2010) was devoted to articles on monopsonistic conditions in labor markets. Especially relevant to estimates of the labor supply curve facing employers are the articles by Douglas O. Staiger, Joanne Spetz, and Ciaran S. Phibbs, "Is There Monopsony in the Labor Market? Evidence from a Natural Experiment," *Journal of Labor Economics* 28 (2010): 211–236; Torberg

Falch, "The Elasticity of Labor Supply at the Establishment Level," *Journal of Labor Economics* 28 (April 2010): 237–266; Michael R. Ransom and David P. Sims, "Estimating the Firm's Labor Supply Curve in a 'New Monopsony' Framework: Schoolteachers in Missouri," *Journal of Labor Economics* 28 (April 2010): 331–356. The introduction to the issue by Ashenfelter, Farber, and Ransom, "Modern Models of Monopsony in Labor Markets: A Brief Survey," 203–210, provides an excellent synopsis of the papers. For more-recent tests and evidence of monopsonistic conditions in particular labor markets, see Jordan Matsudaira, "Monopsony in the Low-Wage Labor Market? Evidence from Minimum Nurse Staffing Regulations," *Review of Economics and Statistics* 96 (March 2014): 92–102; Dube, Jacobs, Naidu, and Suri, "Monopsony in Online Labor Markets"; Arindrajit Dube, Laura Giuliano, and Jonathan Leonard, "Fairness and Frictions: The Impact of Unequal Raises on Quit Behavior," *American Economic Review* 109 (February 2018): 620–663.

7. For an interesting examination of spatial issues with respect to monopsony, see Matthew E. Kahn and Joseph Tracy, "Monopsony in Spatial Equilibrium" (Working Paper No. 26295, National Bureau of Economic Research, Cambridge, MA, June 2020).

8. See José Azar, Ioana Marinescu, and Marshall Steinbaum, "Measuring Labor Market Power in Two Ways," *American Economic Review Papers and Proceedings* 109 (May 2019): 317–321.

9. We are assuming here that the firm plans to offer its prospective workers the same wage and does not have the ability to find out which of its applicants would work for less. For a fuller discussion of this issue, one that includes some empirical results that support this assumption, see Alan Manning, *Monopsony in Motion: Imperfect Competition in Labor Markets* (Princeton, NJ: Princeton University Press, 2003): chapter 5.

10. In the hypothetical example outlined in Table 5.1 and Figure 5.2, the slope of the supply curve is 1; to obtain one more worker, the firm must raise its wage by $1. The slope of the marginal expense curve, however, is 2 (in going from 11 to 12 workers, for example, the marginal expense rises from $19 to $21). In general, employing a bit of calculus makes it easier to show that if the supply curve to a firm is a straight line, the marginal expense curve associated with that supply curve will have a slope that is *twice as steep*.

11. The stronger the monopsonistic conditions are in a labor market, the steeper will be the labor supply curve facing each firm in the market and the more wages will be below marginal revenue product. For papers on this topic, see José Azar, Ioana Marinescu, and Marshall Steinbaum, "Labor Market Concentration," *Journal of Human Resources* 55 (2020); Efraim Benmelech, Nittai Bergman, and Hyunseob Kim, "Strong Employers and Weak Employees: How Does Employer Concentration Affect Wages?" (Working Paper No. 24307, National Bureau of Economic Research, Cambridge, MA, February 2018).

12. See Mortensen, *Wage Dispersion*, chapter 1.

13. This is because we showed in Figure 5.4 that employment falls in the short run, and now equation (5.2) implies that employment will also fall in the long run.

14. R. Kaj Gittings and Ian M. Schmutte, "Getting Handcuffs on an Octopus: Minimum Wages, Employment, and Turnover," *Industrial and Labor Relations Review* 69 (October 2016): 1133–1170; José Azar, Emiliano Huet-Vaughn, Ioana Marinescu, Bledi Taska, and Till von Wachter, "Minimum Wage Employment Effects and Labor Market Concentration" (Working Paper No. 26101, National Bureau of Economic Research, Cambridge, MA, July 2019).

15. For an interesting analysis of the role of luck in generating income, see Robert H. Frank, *Success and Luck: Good Fortune and the Myth of Meritocracy* (Princeton, NJ: Princeton University Press, 2016).

16. Manning, *Monopsony in Motion*, chapter 6.

17. See Manning, *Monopsony in Motion*, chapter 9, for a discussion of job search and unemployment.

18. George Borjas, "Does Immigration Grease the Wheels of the Labor Market?" *Brookings Papers on Economic Activity* (2001): 69–119; also see Sari Pekkala Kerr, William R. Kerr, and Wiiliam F. Lincoln, "Skilled Immigration and the Employment Structure of US Firms," *Journal of Labor Economics* 33 (July 2015), S147–S186.

19. Paul A. Samuelson, *Economics: An Introductory Analysis* (New York: McGraw-Hill, 1951): 554.

20. Society for Human Resource Management, "2016 Human Capital Benchmarking Report," November 2016, www.shrm.org/hr-today/trends-and-forecasting/research-and-surveys/Documents/2016-Human-Capital-Report.pdf. For research on the importance and difficulties of screening applicants for managerial positions, see Achyuta Adhvaryu, Anant Nyshadham, and Jorge A. Tamayo, "Managerial Quality and Productivity Dynamics" (Working Paper No. 25852, National Bureau of Economic Research, Cambridge, MA, May 2019).

21. For other studies and related references, see Harley Frazis, Maury Gittleman, and Mary Joyce, "Correlates of Training: An Analysis Using Both Employer and Employee Characteristics," *Industrial and Labor Relations Review* 53 (April 2000): 443–462.

22. Also note that these types of benefits that cost the employer the same for all workers end up, therefore, being a much larger fraction of the total compensation for employees with low wages than for employees with high wages.

23. The Social Security payroll-tax liability of employers is specified as a percentage of each employee's earnings up to a maximum taxable wage base. In 2020, this tax was 6.20 percent of earnings up to $137,700 for retirement and disability insurance and 1.45 percent on *all* earnings

for Medicare. Because the maximum earnings base exceeded the annual earnings of most workers, the employer's payroll tax liability is increased when a typical employee works an additional hour per week.

24. U.S. Department of Labor, Employment and Training Administration, "Comparison of State Unemployment Laws 2019," (oui.doleta.gov/unemploy/comparison/2010–2019/comparison2019.asp).

25. When the number of employees is increased, the decline in MP_M may be a result of the reduced quantity of capital now available to each individual employee. When the hours that each employee works per week are increased, the decline in MP_H may occur because after some point, fatigue sets in.

26. Daniel Hecker, "How Hours of Work Affect Occupational Earnings," *Monthly Labor Review* 121 (October 1998): 8–18.

27. Dora L. Costa, "Hours of Work and the Fair Labor Standards Act: A Study of Retail and Wholesale Trade, 1938–1950," *Industrial and Labor Relations Review* 53 (July 2000): 648–664, references empirical work on the use of overtime. Also see Hecker, "How Hours of Work Affect Occupational Earnings," 10.

28. U.S. Department of Labor, Wage and Hour Division, "News Release: U.S. Department of Labor Issues Final Overtime Rule," September 24, 2019 (at dol.gov/newroom/releases/whd/whd20190924).

29. Anthony Barkume, "The Structure of Labor Costs with Overtime Work in U.S. Jobs," *Industrial and Labor Relations Review* 64 (October 2010): 128–142.

30. Stephen J. Trejo, "Does the Statutory Overtime Premium Discourage Long Workweeks?" *Industrial and Labor Relations Review* 56 (April 2003): 530–551.

31. In Chapter 9, we expand on these ideas when we explore human capital, education, and training.

32. Edward P. Lazear, "Firm-Specific Human Capital: A Skill-Weights Approach," *Journal of Political Economy* 117 (October 2009): 914–940; Daron Acemoglu and Jörn-Steffen Pischke, "Beyond Becker: Training in Imperfect Labour Markets," *Economic Journal* 109 (February 1999): F112–F142; Mark A. Loewenstein and James R. Spletzer, "General and Specific Training: Evidence and Implications," *Journal of Human Resources* 34 (Fall 1999): 710–733; Laurie J. Bassi and Jens Ludwig, "School-to-Work Programs in the United States: A Multi-Firm Case Study of Training, Benefits, and Costs," *Industrial and Labor Relations Review* 53 (January 2000): 219–239; Edwin Leuven, Hessel Oosterbeek, Randolph Sloof, and Chris van Klaveren, "Worker Reciprocity and Employer Investment in Training," *Economica* 72 (February 2005): 137–149; Colleen Flaherty Manchester, "General Human Capital and Employee Mobility: How Tuition Reimbursement Increases Retention through Sorting and Participation," *Industrial and Labor Relations Review* 65 (October 2012): 951–974.

33. For an examination of market power and the earnings distribution, and evidence that employers don't fully exert market power, see Douglas A. Webber, "Firm Market Power and the Earnings Distribution," *Labour Economics* 35 (August 2015): 123–134; see Azar, Marcinescu, and Steinbaum, "Labor Market Concentration," for an example of research that estimates the amount of concentration in local labor markets.

34. John Bishop, "The Incidence of and Payoff to Employer Training" (Working Paper No. 94–17, Cornell University Center for Advanced Human Resource Studies, July 1994); Margaret Stevens, "An Investment Model for the Supply of General Training by Employers," *Economic Journal* 104 (May 1994): 556–570.

35. David Blanchflower and Lisa Lynch, "Training at Work: A Comparison of U.S. and British Youths," in *Training and the Private Sector: International Comparisons*, ed. Lisa Lynch (Chicago: University of Chicago Press for the National Bureau of Economic Research, 1994): 233–260; Jonathan R. Veum, "Sources of Training and Their Impact on Wages," *Industrial and Labor Relations Review* 48 (July 1995): 812–826; Alan Krueger and Cecilia Rouse, "The Effect of Workplace Education on Earnings, Turnover, and Job Performance," *Journal of Labor Economics* 16 (January 1998): 61–94; Judith K. Hellerstein and David Neumark, "Are Earnings Profiles Steeper than Productivity Profiles? Evidence from Israeli Firm-Level Data," *Journal of Human Resources* 30 (Winter 1995): 89–112.

36. See Hilary Hoynes, Douglas L. Miller, and Jessamyn Schaller, "Who Suffers During Recessions?" *Journal of Economic Perspectives* 26 (Summer 2012): 27–48.

37. In unionized settings, seniority rules often influence the order in which employees are laid off in a recession. In Chapter 13, we discuss labor unions in more detail.

38. Margaret Stevens, "An Investment Model for the Supply of General Training by Employers." Also see W. R. Bowman and Stephen L. Mehay, "Graduate Education and Employee Performance: Evidence from Military Personnel," *Economics of Education Review* 18 (October 1999): 453–463.

39. See Michael Spence, "Job Market Signaling," *Quarterly Journal of Economics* 87 (August 1973): 355–374. Refer to Chapter 9 for a more detailed discussion of signaling.

40. In Chapter 12, statistical discrimination is discussed in much more detail.

41. For a detailed discussion of internal labor markets, see Paul Osterman, ed., *Internal Labor Markets* (Cambridge, MA: MIT Press, 1984); George Baker and Bengt Holmstrom, "Internal Labor Markets: Too Many Theories, Too Few Facts," *American Economic Review* 85 (May 1995): 255–259; Jed DeVaro, Antti Kauhanen, and Nelli Valmari,

"Internal and External Hiring," *Industrial and Labor Relations Review* 72 (August 2019): 981–1008.

42. Firms that hire inexperienced workers (those without a job history that indicates their dependability, motivation, ability to learn, and other personal characteristics) are making a risky investment, in that some workers may not prove to be satisfactory performers. If these firms cannot recoup their investment costs by minimizing wage increases for workers whom they retain, those firms may be averse to hiring inexperienced workers—and this aversion may help explain why youth unemployment rates are typically higher than average. For a more detailed analysis of hiring inexperienced workers, see Amanda Pallais, "Inefficient Hiring in Entry-Level Labor Markets," *American Economic Review* 104 (November 2014): 3565–3599.

Selected Readings

Ashenfelter, Orley C., Henry S. Farber, and Michael R. Ransom. "Modern Models of Monopsony in Labor Markets." *Journal of Labor Economics* 28 (April 2010): 203–210.

Becker, Gary. *Human Capital.* 2nd ed. New York: National Bureau of Economic Research, 1975.

Card, David, and Alan B. Krueger, *Myth and Measurement: The New Economics of the Minimum Wage, 20th Anniversary Edition.* Princeton, NJ: Princeton University Press, 2016.

Hart, Robert. *Working Time and Employment.* London: Allen and Unwin, 1986.

Lynch, Lisa, ed. *Training and the Private Sector: International Comparisons.* Chicago: University of Chicago Press, 1994.

Manning, Alan. *Monopsony in Motion: Imperfect Competition in Labor Markets.* Princeton, NJ: Princeton University Press, 2003.

Manning, Alan, ed. "Modern Models of Monopsony in Labor Markets: Tests and Papers from a Conference Held in Sundance, Utah, November 2008, Organized by Orley Ashenfelter, Henry Farber, and Michael Ransom." *Journal of Labor Economics* 28 (April 2010): 203–472.

Osterman, Paul, ed. *Internal Labor Markets.* Cambridge, MA: MIT Press, 1984.

Parsons, Donald. "The Firm's Decision to Train." In *Research in Labor Economics 11*, eds. Lauri J. Bassi and David L. Crawford, 53–75. Greenwich, CT: JAI Press, 1990.

Williamson, Oliver, et al. "Understanding the Employment Relation: The Analysis of Idiosyncratic Exchange." *Bell Journal of Economics* 16 (Spring 1975): 250–280.

Supply of Labor to the Economy: The Decision to Work

This chapter and the next four focus on issues of *worker* behavior. More specifically, Chapters 6, 7, 8, 9, and 10 discuss and analyze various aspects of *labor supply*. Labor supply decisions can be roughly divided into two categories. The first, which is addressed in this chapter and the next, includes decisions about whether to work at all and, if so, how long to work—including how many hours in a day and years in a lifetime. Questions that must be answered include whether to participate in the labor force, whether to seek part-time work or full-time work, and how long to work both at home and for pay. The second category of decisions, which is addressed in Chapters 8, 9, and 10, deals with the questions that must be faced by a person who has decided to seek work for pay: the occupation or general class of occupations in which to seek offers (Chapters 8 and 9) and the geographical area in which offers should be sought (Chapter 10).

This chapter begins with some basic facts concerning labor force participation rates and hours of work. We then develop a theoretical framework that can be used in the analysis of decisions to work for pay. This framework is also useful for analyzing the structure of various government-funded income maintenance programs.

Trends in Labor Force Participation and Hours of Work

When a person is working or actively seeks work, they are, by definition, in the *labor force*. As pointed out in Chapter 2, the *labor force participation rate* is the percentage of a given population that either has a job or is looking for one. Thus, one clear-cut statistic important in measuring people's willingness to seek employment is the labor force participation rate.

Labor Force Participation Rates

One of the most dramatic changes in the labor market over the past six decades has been the increased labor force participation of women, especially

Table 6.1 Labor Force Participation Rates of Women Over 16 Years of Age in the United States, by Marital Status, 1900–2018 (Percentage)

Year	All women	Single never married	Widowed, divorced, or separated	Married spouse present
1900	20.6	45.9	32.5	5.6
1910	25.5	54.0	34.1	10.7
1920	24.0			9.0
1930	25.3	55.2	34.4	11.7
1940	26.7	53.1	33.7	13.8
1950	29.7	53.6	35.5	21.6
1960	37.7	58.6	41.6	31.9
1970	43.3	56.8	40.3	40.5
1980	51.5	64.4	43.6	49.8
1990	57.5	66.7	47.2	58.4
2000	59.9	68.9	49.0	61.1
2010	58.6	63.3	48.8	61.0
2018	57.1	64.5	45.9	58.2

Sources: 1900–1950: Clarence D. Long, *The Labor Force Under Changing Income and Employment* (Princeton, NJ: Princeton University Press, 1958), Table A—6

1960–2018: U.S. Department of Labor, Bureau of Labor Statistics, *Handbook of Labor Statistics*, Bulletin 2340 (Washington, DC: U.S. Government Printing Office, 1989), Table 6; U.S. Census Bureau, *2010 Statistical Abstract*, Section 12 (Table 598), www.census.gov/compendia/statab/2012/tables//12s0597.pdf; and U.S. Department of Labor, Bureau of Labor Statistics, *Women in the Labor Force: A Databook*, Report 1040 (December 2011) and Report 1084 (December 2019), Table 4

married women. Table 6.1 shows the dimensions of this change. As recently as 1950, less than 25 percent of married women were in the labor force, but by 1980, this percentage had doubled—and by 2000, it had reached 61 percent. Since 2000, however, the labor force participation rates for women in all marital groups have fallen.[1] One interest of this chapter is in understanding the forces underlying these changes.

As can be seen in Table 6.2, a second set of changes in labor force participation is the decrease in the participation rates of men, especially among the young and the more senior. The most substantial decreases in the United States have been among those 65 and older, from about 42 percent in 1950 to about half that currently—although since 1990 rates have been climbing. Participation rates for men in the 20–24 and 25–44 age groups fluctuated a

Table 6.2 Labor Force Participation Rates for Men in the United States, by Age, 1900–2018 (Percentage)

Year	14–19	16–19	20–24	25–44	45–64	Over 65
1900	61.1		91.7	96.3	93.3	68.3
1910	56.2		91.1	96.6	93.6	58.1
1920	52.6		90.9	97.1	93.8	60.1
1930	41.1		89.9	97.5	94.1	58.3
1940	34.4		88.0	95.0	88.7	41.5
1950	39.9	63.2	82.8	92.8	87.9	41.6
1960	38.1	56.1	86.1	95.2	89.0	30.6
1970	35.8	56.1	80.9	94.4	87.3	25.0
1980		60.5	85.9	95.4	82.2	19.0
1990		55.7	84.4	94.8	80.5	16.3
2000		52.8	82.6	93.0	80.4	17.7
2010		34.9	74.5	90.6	79.4	22.1
2018		34.2	73.2	90.0	79.1	24.0

Sources: 1900–1950: Clarence D. Long, *The Labor Force Under Changing Income and Employment* (Princeton, NJ: Princeton University Press, 1958), Table A—2

1960: U.S. Department of Commerce, Bureau of the Census, Census of Population, 1960: Employment Status, Subject Reports PC(2)—6A, Table 1

1970: U.S. Department of Commerce, Bureau of the Census, Census of Population, 1970: Employment Status and Work Experience, Subject Reports PC(2)—6A, Table 1

1980–2018: U.S. Census Bureau, 2010 Statistical Abstract, Section 12 (Table 575), www.census.gov/compendia/statab/2010edition.html; and U.S. Department of Labor, Bureau of Labor Statistics, *Women in the Labor Force: A Databook*, Report 1034 (December 2011), and Report 1084 (December 2019), Table 1

bit from 1950 to 2000 but remained quite stable during that period; since 2000, however, participation rates in both groups have fallen, especially in the younger group, and they have fallen even more dramatically among teenagers. The labor force participation rates of men in the 45–64 age group have fallen in every decade since 1960.[2]

The trends in U.S. labor force participation rates have also been reflected in other industrialized countries. In Table 6.3, for countries with comparable data, we display the trends in participation rates for women in the 25–54 age group and for men near the age of early retirement (55 to 64 years old). Typically, the fraction of women in the labor force rose from half or less in 1965 to three-quarters or more roughly 50 years later. Among men between the ages of 55 and 64, participation fell markedly in each country through the early 2000s but has risen since—especially in Europe. Thus, while we see some differences in trends across the countries, common forces are likely influencing labor supply trends in the industrialized world.

Table 6.3 Labor Force Participation Rates of Women and Older Men, Selected Countries, 1965–2019 (Percentage)

Country	1965	1973	1983	2003	2019
Women, Ages 25 to 54					
Canada	33.9	44.0	65.1	81.1	83.6
France	42.8	54.1	67.0	79.6	83.1
Germany	46.1	50.5	58.3	78.9	83.3
Japan	—	53.0[a]	59.5	67.7	80.0
Sweden	56.0	68.9	87.1	85.4	88.7
United States	45.1	52.0	67.1	75.6	76.0
Men, Ages 55 to 64					
Canada	86.4	81.3	72.3	65.4	72.6
France	76.0	72.1	53.6	42.9	59.4
Germany	84.6	73.4	63.1	52.0	79.4
Japan	—	86.3[a]	84.7	83.0	88.8
Sweden	88.3	82.7	77.0	75.4	84.2
United States	82.9	76.9	69.4	68.7	71.5

[a] Data are for 1974 (earlier data not comparable).

Source: Organisation for Economic Co-operation and Development, *Labour Force Statistics* (Paris: OECD, various dates), https://stats.oecd.org/Index. aspx?QueryId=64197

Hours of Work

Because data on labor force participation include both employed people and those who want a job but do not have one, they constitute a relatively pure measure of labor supply. In contrast, the weekly or yearly hours of work put in by the typical employee are often thought to be determined only by the demand side of the market. After all, don't employers, in responding to the factors discussed in Chapter 5, set the hours of work expected of their employees? They do, of course, but hours worked are also influenced by *employee* preferences on the supply side of the market, especially in the long run.

Even though employers set work schedules, employees can exercise their preferences regarding hours of work through their choice of part-time work or full-time work, their decisions to work at more than one job (see Example 6.1 for one way to do this), or their selection of occupations and employers.[3] For example, female managers who work full-time average more hours of work per week than full-time clerical workers, and male sales workers work more hours per week than their full-time counterparts in skilled craft jobs. Moreover, different employers offer different mixes of full-time work and part-time work, require different weekly work schedules, and have different policies regarding vacations and paid holidays.

EXAMPLE 6.1
Gig Work and the Choice of Working Hours

One way for workers to adjust their hours of work to suit their preferences is to become self-employed. About 10 percent of U.S. workers have self-employment income, and most of those (7.5 percent of all workers) work alone—that is, they are "solo" self-employed, in that they hire no one to work for or with them. These workers include artists, writers, consultants of various kinds, repair or construction workers, house cleaners, childcare providers, and drivers. Of those who work solo, about one in seven (or about 1 percent of all workers in the United States) are gig workers (e.g., Lyft or Uber drivers), who are paid by the job and connect with clients through an app. Most gig workers (around 84 percent) have other, more traditional, jobs and are not dependent on gig work for their only income. They appear to use their gig earnings to "top up" their earnings from their other job or to replace a sudden reduction in earnings from that job.

Are those with solo self-employment earnings happy with their hours of work? About half are, but one-third would like to work more hours and about one-fifth would like to work fewer. Thus, self-employment helps at least some to work the hours they want, but it is not a perfect mechanism to do so.

Source: Tito Boeri, Giulia Giupponi, Alan B. Krueger, and Stephen Machin, "Solo Self-Employment and Alternative Work Arrangements: A Cross-Country Perspective on the Changing Composition of Jobs," *Journal of Economic Perspectives* 34 (Winter 2020): 170–195

Employer offers regarding both hours and pay are intended to enhance their profits, but they must also satisfy the preferences of current and prospective employees. For example, if employees who receive an hourly wage of $X for 40 hours per week really wanted to work only 30 hours at $X per hour, some enterprising employer (presumably one with relatively lower quasi-fixed costs) will eventually seize on their dissatisfaction and offer jobs with a 30-hour workweek, ending up with a more satisfied, productive workforce in the process.

Although the labor supply preferences of employees must be satisfied in the long run, most of the short-run changes in hours of work seem to emanate from the *demand* side of the market.[4] Workweeks typically vary over the course of a business cycle, for example, where longer hours are worked in periods of robust demand. In analyzing trends in hours of work, then, we must carefully distinguish between the forces of supply and those of demand.

In the first part of the twentieth century, workers in U.S. manufacturing plants typically worked 55 hours per week in years of strong economic activity; in the past two decades, U.S. manufacturing workers have worked, on average, fewer than 40 hours per week during similar periods. For example, in the years 1988, 1995, and 2004—when the unemployment rate was roughly 5.5 percent and falling—manufacturing production workers averaged 38.4, 39.3, and 38.6 hours per week, respectively. In general, the decline in weekly hours of manufacturing work in the United States occurred before 1950, and since then, hours of work have shown little tendency to decline.[5]

A Theory of the Decision to Work

Can labor supply theory help us to understand the long-run trends in labor force participation and hours of work noted earlier? Because labor is the most abundant factor of production, we can say that any country's well-being in the long run depends heavily on the willingness of its people to work. Leisure and other ways of spending time that do not involve work for pay are also important in generating well-being; however, any economy relies heavily on goods and services produced for market transactions. Therefore, understanding the *work-incentive* effects of higher wages and incomes, different kinds of taxes, and various forms of income maintenance programs is important.

The decision to work is ultimately a decision about how to spend time. One way to use our available time is to spend it in pleasurable leisure activities. The other major way that people use time is to work. We can work around the home, performing such *household production* as raising children, building, sewing, or even growing food. Alternatively, we can work for pay and use our earnings to purchase food, shelter, clothing, childcare, and other goods and services.

Because working for pay and engaging in household production are two ways of getting the same jobs done, we shall initially ignore the distinction between them and treat work activities as working for pay. We shall therefore be characterizing the decision to work as a choice between leisure and working for pay. Most of the crucial factors affecting work incentives can be understood in this context, but insight into labor supply behavior can also be enriched by a consideration of household production; we do this in Chapter 7.

If we regard the time spent eating, sleeping, and otherwise maintaining ourselves as more or less fixed by natural laws, then the discretionary time that we have (e.g., 16 hours a day) can be allocated to either work or leisure. We begin our analysis of the work/leisure choice by analyzing the *demand for leisure hours.*

Some Basic Concepts

Basically, the demand for a good is a function of three factors:

1. the *opportunity cost* of the good (which is often equal to *market price*)

2. one's level of *wealth*

3. one's set of *preferences*

For example, the consumption of heating oil varies with the *cost* of such oil; as that cost rises, consumption tends to fall unless one of the other two factors intervenes. As *wealth* rises, people generally want larger and warmer houses that obviously require more oil to heat.[6] Even if the price of energy and the level of personal wealth were to remain constant, the demand for energy could rise if a falling birthrate and lengthened life span resulted in a higher proportion of the population's being older and therefore wanting warmer houses. This change in the composition of the population amounts to a shift in the overall *preferences* for warmer houses and thus leads to a change in the demand for heating oil. (Economists usually assume that preferences are given and not subject to immediate change. For policy purposes, changes in prices and wealth are crucial in explaining changes in demand because these variables are more susceptible to change by government or market forces.)

Opportunity Cost of Leisure   To apply this general analysis of demand to the demand for leisure, we must first ask, what is the opportunity cost of leisure? The cost of spending an hour watching television is basically what one could earn if one had spent that hour working. Thus, the opportunity cost of an hour of leisure is equal to one's *wage rate*—the *extra earnings* that a worker can take home from an *extra hour of work*.[7]

Wealth and Income   Next, we must understand and be able to measure wealth. Naturally, wealth includes a family's holdings of bank accounts, financial investments, and physical property. Workers' skills can also be considered assets, since these skills can be, in effect, rented out to employers for a price. The more one can get in wages, the larger the value of one's human assets. Unfortunately, we usually cannot directly measure people's wealth. Measuring the *returns* from that wealth is easier because data on total *income* are readily available from government surveys. Economists often use total income as an indicator of total wealth because the two are conceptually so closely related.[8]

Defining the Income Effect   Theory suggests that if income increases while wages and preferences are held constant, the number of leisure hours demanded will rise. Put differently, *if income increases, holding wages constant, the desired hours of work will go down*. (Conversely, if income is reduced while the wage rate is held constant, the desired hours of work will go up.) Economists call the response of desired hours of leisure to changes in income, with wages held constant, the *income effect*. The income effect is based on the simple notion that as incomes rise, holding leisure's opportunity cost constant, people will want to consume more leisure (which means working less).

Because we have assumed that time is spent either in leisure or in working for pay, the income effect can be expressed in terms of the *supply of working hours* and the demand for leisure hours. Because the ultimate focus of this chapter is labor supply, we choose to express this effect in the context of labor supply.

Using algebraic notation, we define the income effect as the change in desired hours of work (ΔH) produced by a change in income (ΔY), holding wages constant ($\bar{W}$):

$$\text{Income Effect} = \frac{\Delta H}{\Delta Y}\bigg|\bar{W} < 0 \qquad (6.1)$$

We say the income effect is *negative* because the *sign* of the *fraction* in equation (6.1) is *negative*. If income goes up (while wages are held constant), hours of work fall. If income goes down, hours of work increase. The numerator (ΔH) and denominator (ΔY) in equation (6.1) move in opposite directions, giving a negative sign to the income effect.

Defining the Substitution Effect　Theory also suggests that *if income is held constant, an increase in the wage rate will raise the price and reduce the demand for leisure, thereby increasing work incentives.* (Likewise, a decrease in the wage rate will reduce leisure's opportunity cost and the incentives to work, holding income constant.) This *substitution effect* occurs because as the cost of leisure changes, income held constant, leisure and work hours are substituted for each other.

In contrast to the income effect, the substitution effect is *positive*. Because this effect is the change in desired hours of work (ΔH) induced by a change in the wage (ΔW), holding income constant ($\bar{Y}$), the substitution effect can be written as follows:

$$\text{Substitution Effect} = \frac{\Delta H}{\Delta W}\bigg|\bar{Y} > 0 \qquad (6.2)$$

Because the numerator (ΔH) and denominator (ΔW) always move in the same direction, at least in theory, the substitution effect has a positive sign.

Observing Income and Substitution Effects Separately　When wages rise or fall, both income and substitution effects are simultaneously present, often working against each other. At times, however, we can observe situations or programs that create only one effect or the other.

Receiving an inheritance offers an example of the income effect by itself. The bequest enhances wealth (income) *independent* of the hours of work. Thus, income is increased *without* a change in the compensation received from an hour of work. In this case, the income effect induces the person to consume more leisure, thereby reducing the willingness to work. (Some support for this theoretical prediction can be seen later, in Example 6.2.)

Observing the substitution effect by itself is rare, but one example comes from the 1980 presidential campaign, when candidate John Anderson proposed a program aimed at conserving gasoline. His plan consisted of raising the gasoline tax but offsetting this increase by a reduced Social Security tax payable by individuals on their earnings. The idea was to raise the price of gasoline without reducing people's overall spendable income.

For our purposes, this plan is interesting because, for the typical worker, it would have created only a substitution effect on labor supply. Social Security revenues are collected by a tax on earnings, so reductions in the tax are, in effect, increases in the wage rate for most workers. For the average person, however, the increased wealth associated with this wage increase would have been exactly offset by increases in the gasoline tax.[9] Hence, wages would have been increased while income was held more or less constant. This program would have created a substitution effect that induced people to work more hours.

Both Effects Occur When Wages Rise While the foregoing examples illustrate situations in which the income or the substitution effect is present by itself, *normally both effects are present, often working in opposite directions*. The presence of both effects' working in opposite directions creates ambiguity in predicting the overall labor supply response in many cases.

Consider the case of a person who receives a wage increase. The labor supply response to a simple wage increase will involve *both* an income effect and a substitution effect. The *income effect* is the result of the worker's enhanced wealth (or potential income) after the increase. For a given level of work effort, they now have a greater command over resources than before (because more income is received for any given number of hours of work). The *substitution effect* results from the fact that the wage increase raises the opportunity costs of leisure. Because the actual labor supply response is the *sum* of the income and substitution effects, we cannot predict the response in advance; theory simply does not tell us which effect is stronger.

If the *income* effect is stronger, the person will respond to a wage increase by decreasing their labor supply. This decrease will be *smaller* than if the same change in wealth were due to an increase in *nonlabor* wealth, because the substitution effect is present and acts as a moderating influence. However, as seen in Example 6.2, when the *income* effect dominates, the substitution effect is not large enough to prevent labor supply from *declining*. Of course, when wages rise, it is possible the *substitution* effect could very well dominate. If so, the actual response to wage increases will be to *increase* labor supply.

Should the substitution effect dominate, the person's individual labor supply curve—relating, say, their desired hours of work to wages—will be *positively sloped*. That is, labor supplied will increase with the wage rate. If, on the other hand, the income effect dominates, the person's individual labor supply curve will be *negatively sloped*. Economic theory cannot say which effect will dominate, and in fact, individual labor supply curves could be positively sloped in some ranges of the wage and negatively sloped in others. In Figure 6.1, for example, the person's desired hours of work increase (substitution effect dominates) when wages go up as long as wages are low (below W^*). At higher wages, however, further increases result in reduced hours of work (the income effect dominates); economists refer to such a curve as *backward bending*.

Analysis of the Labor/Leisure Choice

This section introduces indifference curves and budget constraints—visual aids that make the theory of labor supply easier to understand and to apply to complex policy issues. These graphical aids visually depict the basic factors underlying the supply of labor discussed earlier.

EXAMPLE 6.2

The Labor Supply of New York City Taxi Drivers

Testing the theory of labor supply is made difficult by the fact that most workers cannot change their hours of work very much without changing jobs. Taxi drivers in New York City, however, do choose their own hours of work, so we look into how their hours of work—reflected in miles driven—responded to fare increases approved by the city's Taxi and Limousine Commission. Between 1996 and 2004, these fare increases raised the hourly pay of taxi drivers by an average of 19 percent, and a careful study of how drivers responded found that they *reduced* their miles driven by about 4 percent. Clearly, then, the income effect of their wage increases was stronger than the substitution effect.

Source: Orley Ashenfelter, Kirk Doran, and Bruce Schaller, "A Shred of Credible Evidence on the Long-Run Elasticity of Labor Supply," *Economica* 77 (October 2010): 637–650

For more analysis on this topic, see Henry S. Farber, "Why You Can't Find a Taxi in the Rain and Other Labor Supply Lessons from Cab Drivers," *Quarterly Journal of Economics* 130 (November 2015): 1975–2026.

Preferences   Let us assume that two major categories of goods make people happy—leisure time and the goods that people can buy with money. If we take the prices of goods as fixed, then they can be compressed into one index that is measured by money income (with prices fixed, more money income means that consuming more goods is possible). Using two categories, leisure and money income, allows our graphs to be drawn in two-dimensional space.

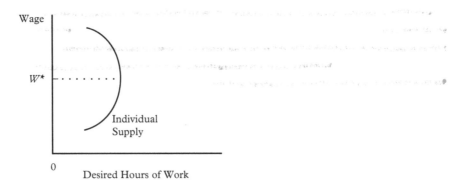

Figure 6.1 An Individual Labor Supply Curve Can Bend Backward

Since both leisure and money can be used to generate satisfaction (or *utility*), these two goods are to some extent substitutes for each other. If forced to give up some money income, some increase in leisure time could be substituted for this lost income to keep a person as happy as before.

To understand how preferences can be graphed, suppose that a thoughtful consumer/worker were asked to decide how happy they would be with a daily income of $64 combined with eight hours of leisure (point *a* in Figure 6.2). This level of happiness could be called utility level *A*. Our consumer/worker could name *other combinations* of money income and leisure hours that would *also* yield utility level *A*; assume that our respondent named five other such combinations. All six combinations of money income and leisure hours that yield utility level *A* are represented by heavy dots in Figure 6.2. The curve connecting these dots is called an *indifference curve*, which connects the various combinations of money income and leisure that yield equal utility. (The term *indifference curve* is derived from the fact that because each point on the curve yields equal utility, a person is truly indifferent about where on the curve they will be.)

Our worker/consumer could no doubt achieve a higher level of happiness if they could combine the eight hours of leisure with an income of $100 per day instead of just $64 a day. This higher satisfaction level could be called utility level *B*. The consumer could name other combinations of money income and leisure that would also yield *this* higher level of utility. These combinations are denoted by the Xs in Figure 6.2, which are connected by a second indifference curve.

Indifference curves have certain specific characteristics that are reflected in the way they are drawn:

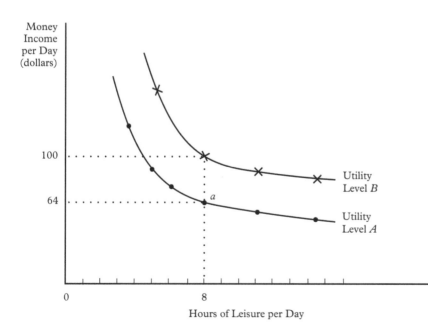

Figure 6.2 Two Indifference Curves for the Same Person

1. Utility level *B* represents more happiness than level *A* does. Every level of leisure consumption is combined with a higher income on *B* than on *A*. Hence, our respondent prefers all points on indifference curve *B* to any point on curve *A*. A whole set of indifference curves could be drawn for this one person, each representing a different utility level. Any such curve that lies to the northeast of another one is preferred to any curve to the southwest because the northeastern curve represents a higher level of utility.

2. Indifference curves *do not intersect.* If they did, the point of intersection would represent one combination of money income and leisure that yielded two levels of satisfaction. We assume that our worker/consumer is not so inconsistent in stating their preferences that this could happen.

3. Indifference curves are *negatively sloped* because if either income is increased or leisure hours are increased, the other is reduced in order to preserve the same level of utility. If the slope is steep, as at segment *LK* in Figure 6.3, a given loss of income need not be accompanied by a large increase in leisure hours to keep utility constant.[10] When the curve is relatively flat, however, as at segment *MN* in Figure 6.3, a given decrease in income must be accompanied by a large increase in the consumption of leisure to hold utility constant. Thus, when indifference curves are relatively steep, people do not value money income as highly as when such curves are relatively flat; when they are flat, a loss of income can be compensated for only by a large increase in leisure if utility is to be kept constant.

4. Indifference curves are *convex*—steeper at the left than at the right. This shape reflects the assumption that when money income is relatively high and leisure hours are relatively few, leisure is more highly valued (and

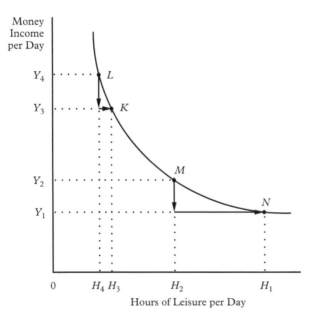

Figure 6.3 An Indifference Curve

income less valued) than when leisure is abundant and income relatively scarce. At segment *LK* in Figure 6.3, a great loss of income (e.g., from Υ_4 to Υ_3) can be compensated for by just a little increase in leisure, whereas a little loss of leisure time (e.g., from H_3 to H_4) would require a relatively large increase in income to maintain equal utility. What is relatively scarce is more highly valued.

5. Conversely, when income is low and leisure is abundant (segment *MN* in Figure 6.3), income is more highly valued. For utility to remain constant, losing income (e.g., by moving from Υ_2 to Υ_1) would require a huge increase in leisure. Again, what is relatively scarce is assumed to be more highly valued.

6. Finally, different people have different sets of indifference curves. The curves drawn in Figures 6.2 and 6.3 were for *one person*. Another person would have a completely different set of curves. People who value leisure more highly, for example, would have had indifference curves that were generally steeper (see Figure 6.4a). People who do not value leisure highly would have relatively flat curves (see Figure 6.4b). Thus, individual preferences can be portrayed graphically.

Income and Wage Constraints   Everyone would like to maximize their utility, which would be ideally done by consuming every available hour of leisure combined with the highest conceivable income.[11] Unfortunately, the resources that anyone can command are limited. Thus, all that is possible is to do the best one can, given limited resources. To see these resource limitations graphically requires superimposing constraints on one's set of indifference curves to see which combinations of income and leisure are available and which are not.

Suppose that the person whose indifference curves are graphed in Figure 6.2 had no source of income other than labor earnings. Suppose, further, that they could earn $8 per hour. Figure 6.5 includes the two indifference curves shown in Figure 6.2 as well as a straight line (*ED*) connecting combinations of leisure and income that are possible for a person with an $8 wage and no outside income. If 16 hours per day are available for work and leisure,[12] and if this person consumes all 16 in leisure, then money income will be zero (point *D* in Figure 6.5). If five hours a day are devoted to work, income will be $40 per day (point *M*), and if 16 hours a day are worked, income will be $128 per day (point *E*). Other points on this line—for example, the point of 15 hours of leisure (one hour of work) and $8 of income— are also possible. This line, which reflects the combinations of leisure and income that are possible for the individual, is called the *budget constraint.* Any combination to the right of the budget constraint is not achievable; the person's command over resources is simply not sufficient to attain these combinations of leisure and money income.

The *slope* of the budget constraint is a graphical representation of the wage rate. One's wage rate is properly defined as the increment in income ($\Delta\Upsilon$) derived from an increment in hours of work (ΔH):

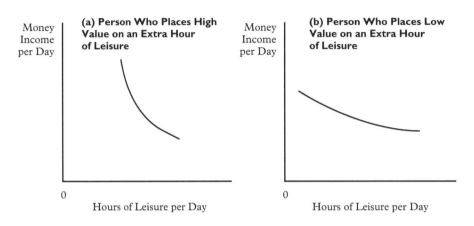

Figure 6.4 Indifference Curves for Two People

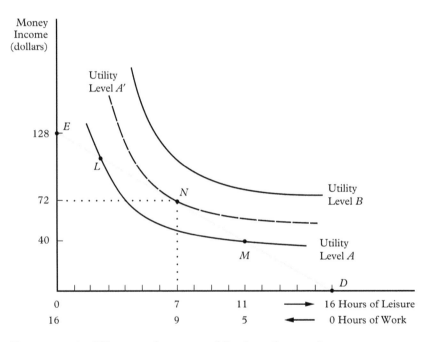

Figure 6.5 Indifference Curves and Budget Constraint

$$\text{Wage Rate} = \frac{\Delta Y}{\Delta H} \qquad\qquad (6.3)$$

Now $\Delta Y/\Delta H$ is exactly the slope of the budget constraint (in absolute value).[13] Figure 6.5 shows how the constraint rises $8 for every one-hour increase in work: If the person works zero hours, income per day is zero; if the person works one hour, they earn $8 in income; if they work five hours, they earn $40 in income. The constraint rises by $8 because the wage rate is $8 per hour. If the person could earn $16 per hour, the constraint would rise twice as fast and therefore be twice as steep.

According to Figure 6.5, our consumer/worker cannot achieve utility level *B*. They can achieve *some* points on the indifference curve representing utility level *A*—specifically, those points between *L* and *M* in Figure 6.5. However, if our consumer/worker is a utility maximizer, they will realize that a utility level *above A* is possible. Given that an infinite number of indifference curves can be drawn between curves *A* and *B* in Figure 6.5, one representing each possible level of satisfaction between *A* and *B*, we can draw a curve (*A´*) that is northeast of curve *A* and just *tangent* to the budget constraint at point *N*. Any movement along the budget constraint *away* from the tangency point places the person on an indifference curve lying *below A´*. Point *N* is the point at which this person maximizes utility, given their budget constraint. Put differently, given their earning power and indifference curves, point *N* is the one and only point yielding the highest utility.

Workers who face the same budget constraint, but who have different preferences for leisure, make different choices about hours of work. If the person whose preferences were depicted in Figure 6.5 had placed lower values on leisure time—and therefore had indifference curves that were comparatively flatter, such as the one shown in Figure 6.4b—then the point of tangency with constraint *ED* would have been to the left of point *N* (indicating more hours of work). Conversely, if they had steeper indifference curves, signifying that leisure time was more valuable (see Figure 6.4a), then the point of tangency in Figure 6.5 would have been to the right of point *N*, and fewer hours of work would have been desired. Indeed, some people have indifference curves so steep (i.e., preferences for leisure so strong) that there is no point of tangency with *ED*. For these people, as is illustrated by Figure 6.6, utility is maximized at the "corner" (point *D*); they desire no work at all and therefore are not in the labor force.

The Income Effect   Suppose now that the person depicted in Figure 6.5 receives a source of income independent of work. Suppose further that this *nonlabor* income amounts to about $36 per day. Thus, even if this person worked zero hours per day, their daily income would be $36. Naturally, if the person worked more than zero hours, their daily income would be equal to $36 plus earnings (the wage multiplied by the hours of work).

Our person's command over resources has clearly increased, as can be shown by drawing a new budget constraint to reflect the nonlabor income. As shown by the darker blue line in Figure 6.7, the end points of the new constraint are point *d* (zero hours of work and $36 of money income) and point *e* (16 hours of work and $164 of income—$36 in nonlabor income plus $128 in earnings). Note that the new constraint is *parallel* to the old one. Parallel lines have the same slope; because the slope of each constraint reflects the wage rate, we can infer that the increase in nonlabor income has not changed the person's wage rate.

We have just described a situation in which a pure *income effect* should be observed. Income (wealth) has been increased, but the wage rate has remained unchanged. The previous section noted that if wealth *increased* and the opportunity cost of leisure (here the wage) remained constant, the

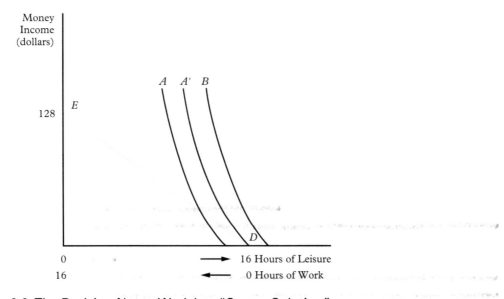

Figure 6.6 The Decision Not to Work Is a "Corner Solution"

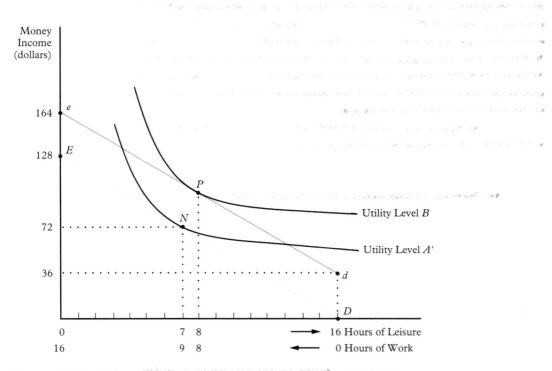

Figure 6.7 Indifference Curves and Budget Constraint (With an Increase in Nonlabor Income)

person would consume more leisure and work *less.* We thus concluded that the income effect was negative, and this negative relationship is illustrated graphically in Figure 6.7.

When the old budget constraint (*ED*) was in effect, the person's highest level of utility was reached at point *N*, working nine hours a day. With the new constraint (*ed*), the optimum hours of work are eight per day (point *P*). The new source of income, because it does not alter the wage, has caused an income effect that results in one fewer hour of work per day. Statistical analyses of people who received large inheritances (Example 6.3) or who won large lottery prizes[14] support the prediction that labor supply is reduced when unearned income rises.

The theory also predicts that if, keeping wages constant, income were to *fall* (owing, say, to a disaster that reduces the value of an asset), desired work hours would increase. A recent study, for example, found that graduates leaving college with student debt (the opposite of an asset) had the same wage rate but worked about 6 percent more hours than comparable graduates leaving college with no student debt.[15]

EXAMPLE 6.3
Do Large Inheritances Induce Labor Force Withdrawal?

Do large bequests of unearned income reduce people's incentives to work? One study divided people who received inheritances in 1982–1983 into two groups: those who received small bequests (averaging $7,700) and those who received larger ones, averaging $346,200. The study then analyzed changes in the labor force participation behavior of the two groups between 1982 and 1985. Not surprisingly, those who received the larger inheritances were more likely to drop out of the labor force. Specifically, in an environment in which other forces were causing the labor force participation rate among the small-bequest group to rise from 76 percent to 81 percent, the rate in the large-bequest group fell from 70 percent to 65 percent. Somewhat more surprising was the fact that, perhaps in anticipation of their bequests, those ultimately receiving large bequests had lower labor force participation rates to begin with.

Source: Douglas Holtz-Eakin, David Joulfaian, and Harvey S. Rosen, "The Carnegie Conjecture: Some Empirical Evidence," *Quarterly Journal of Economics* 108:2 (1993): 413–435

Income and Substitution Effects With a Wage Increase   Suppose that instead of increasing one's command over resources by receiving a source of nonlabor income, the wage rate were to be increased from $8 to $12 per hour. This increase, as noted earlier, would cause *both* an income effect and a substitution effect; workers would be wealthier *and* face a higher opportunity cost of leisure (wage). Theory tells us in this case that the substitution effect pushes them toward more hours of work and the income effect toward fewer, but it cannot tell us which effect will dominate.

Figures 6.8 and 6.9 illustrate the possible effects of the foregoing wage change on a person's labor supply, which we now assume is initially eight hours per day. Figure 6.8 illustrates the case in which the observed response by a worker is to increase the hours of work; in this case, the substitution effect is stronger than the income effect. Figure 6.9 illustrates the case in

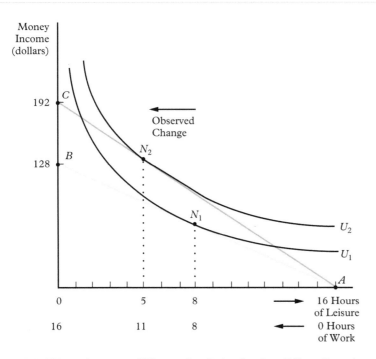

Figure 6.8 Wage Increase Where the Substitution Effect Dominates

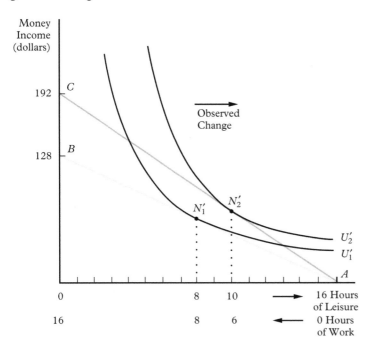

Figure 6.9 Wage Increase Where the Income Effect Dominates

which the income effect is stronger and the response to a wage increase is to reduce the hours of work. The difference between the two figures lies *solely* in the shape of the indifference curves that might describe a person's preferences; the budget constraints, which reflect wealth and the wage rate, are the same.

Figures 6.8 and 6.9 both show the old constraint, *AB*, the slope of which reflects the wage of $8 per hour. They also show the new one, *AC*, which reflects the $12 wage. Because we assume that workers have no source of nonlabor income, both constraints are anchored at point *A*, where income is zero if a person does not work. Point *C* on the new constraint is now at $192 (16 hours of work times $12 per hour).

For the worker whose preferences are depicted in Figure 6.8, the wage increase makes utility level U_2 the highest that can be reached. The tangency point at N_2 suggests that 11 hours of work is optimum. When the old constraint was in effect, the utility-maximizing hours of work were eight per day (point N_1). Thus, the wage increase would cause this person's desired hours of work to increase by three per day.

For the worker whose preferences are depicted in Figure 6.9, the wage increase would make utility level U'_2 the highest one possible (the prime emphasizes that workers' preferences differ and that utility *levels* in Figures 6.8 and 6.9 cannot be compared). Utility is maximized at N'_2, at 6 hours of work per day. Thus, for preferences like those in Figure 6.9, working hours fall from eight to six as the wage rate increases.

Isolating Income and Substitution Effects
We have graphically depicted the income effect by itself (Figure 6.7) and the two possible outcomes of an increase in wages (Figures 6.8 and 6.9), which combine the income and substitution effects.

Can we graphically isolate the substitution effect? The answer is yes, and the most meaningful way to do this is to return to the context of a wage change, such as the one depicted in Figures 6.8 and 6.9. We arbitrarily choose to analyze the response shown in Figure 6.8.

Figure 6.10 has three panels. Panel (a) repeats Figure 6.8; it shows the final, overall effect of a wage increase on the labor supply of the person whose preferences are depicted. As we saw earlier, the effect of the wage increase in this case is to raise the person's utility from U_1 to U_2 and to induce this worker to increase desired hours of work from eight to 11 per day. Embedded in this overall effect of the wage increase, however, is an income effect pushing toward less work and a substitution effect pushing toward more. These effects are graphically separated in panels (b) and (c).

Panel (b) of Figure 6.10 shows the income effect of the overall response to the wage change. By definition, the income effect is the change in desired hours of work brought on by increased wealth, holding the wage rate constant. To reveal this embedded effect, we ask a hypothetical question: What would have been the change in labor supply if the person depicted in panel (a) had reached the new indifference curve (U_2) with a change in *nonlabor* income instead of a change in their wage rate? We choose U_2 because we know that the individual ends up on U_2 after the wage change—depicted in panel (a).

We begin to answer this question graphically by moving the old constraint (*AB*) to the northeast, which depicts the greater command over leisure time

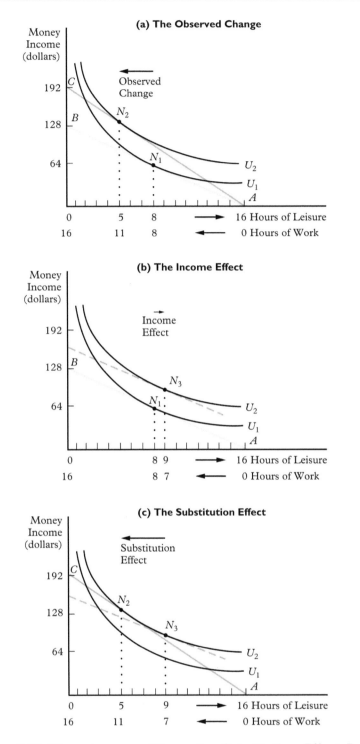

Figure 6.10 Wage Increase Where the Substitution Effect Dominates: Isolating Income and Substitution Effects

and goods—and hence the higher level of utility—associated with greater wealth. The constraint is shifted outward while maintaining its original slope (reflecting the old $8 wage), which holds the wage constant and is moved to the northeast just enough to be tangent with U_2. The dashed line in panel (b), which is parallel to AB, depicts this hypothetical movement of the old constraint, and it results in a tangency point at N_3. This tangency suggests that had the person received nonlabor income, with no change in the wage, sufficient to reach the new level of utility, they would have *reduced* work hours from 8 (N_1) to 7 (N_3) per day. This shift is graphical verification that the income effect is negative, assuming that leisure is a normal good.

The substitution effect is the effect on labor supply of a change in the wage rate, holding wealth constant. It can be seen in panel (c) of Figure 6.10 as the difference between where the person actually ended up on indifference curve U_2 (tangency at N_2) and where they would have ended up with a pure income effect (tangency at N_3). Comparing tangency points on the *same* indifference curve is a graphical approximation to holding wealth constant. Thus, *with* the wage change, the person represented in Figure 6.10 ended up at point N_2, working 11 hours a day. *Without* the wage change, the person would have chosen to work seven hours a day (point N_3). The wage change *by itself*, holding utility (or real wealth) constant, caused work hours to increase by four per day.[16] This increase demonstrates that the substitution effect is positive.

To summarize, the observed effect of raising wages from $8 to $12 per hour increased the hours of work in Figure 6.10 from eight to 11 per day. This observed effect, however, is the *sum* of two component effects. The income effect, which operates because a higher wage increases one's real wealth, tended to *reduce* the hours of work from eight to seven per day. The substitution effect, which captures the pure effect of the change in leisure's opportunity cost, tended to push the person toward four more hours of work per day. The end result was an increase of three in the hours worked each day. So, as we showed earlier, the substitution effect dominates in this case.

Which Effect Is Stronger?   Suppose that a wage increase changes the budget constraint facing a worker, from CD to CE in Figure 6.11. If the worker had a relatively flat set of indifference curves, the initial tangency along CD might be at point A, implying a relatively heavy work schedule. If the person had more steeply sloped indifference curves, the initial tangency might be at point B, where hours at work are fewer.

One important influence on the size of the income effect is the extent of the northeast movement of the new constraint: The more the constraint shifts outward, the greater the income effect will tend to be. For a person with an initial tangency at point A, for example, the northeast movement is larger than that for a person whose initial tangency is at point B. Put another way, the increased command over resources made possible by a wage increase is attainable only if one works, and the more work oriented the person is, the greater will be their increase in resources. Other things

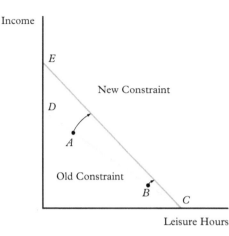

Figure 6.11 The Initial Hours of Work Affect the Size of the Income Effect

being equal, people who work longer hours exhibit greater income effects when wage rates change.

To take this reasoning to the extreme, suppose that a person's indifference curves were so steep that the person was initially out of the labor force (i.e., when the budget constraint was *CD* in Figure 6.11, their utility was maximized at point *C*). The wage increase and the resultant new constraint, *CE*, can induce only one of two outcomes: The person will either begin to work for pay or remain out of the labor force. *Reducing* the hours of paid employment is not possible. For those who are out of the labor force, then, a decision to participate as wage offers rise would indicate a dominant substitution effect. Conversely, if someone currently working decides to change their participation decision by dropping out of the labor force when wages fall, the substitution effect has again dominated. Thus, the *labor force participation decisions brought about by wage changes exhibit a dominant substitution effect*. We turn now to a more detailed analysis of the decision whether to join the labor force.

The Reservation Wage   An implication of our labor supply theory is that if people who are not in the labor force place a value of $X on the marginal hour of leisure, then they would be unwilling to take a job unless the offered wages were greater than $X. Because they will "reserve" their labor unless the wage is $X or more (see Example 6.4), economists say that they have a *reservation wage* of $X. The reservation wage, then, is the wage below which a person will not work, and in the labor/leisure context, it represents the value placed on an hour of lost leisure time.[17]

Refer back to Figure 6.6, which graphically depicts a person's choosing not to work. The reason why there was no tangency between an indifference curve and the budget constraint—and the reason why the person remained out of the labor force—was that the wage was everywhere lower than their marginal value of leisure time.

Often, people are thought to behave as if they have both a reservation wage *and a certain number of work hours* that must be offered before they will consider taking a job. The reasons are not difficult to understand and are illustrated in Figure 6.12. Suppose that taking a job entails two hours of commuting time (round trip) per day. These hours, of course, are unpaid, so the worker's budget constraint must reflect that if a job is accepted, two hours of leisure are given up before they earn any increase in income. These fixed costs of working are reflected in Figure 6.12 by segment *AB*. Segment *BC*, of course, reflects the earnings that are possible (once at work), and the slope of *BC* represents the person's wage rate.

Is the wage underlying *BC* great enough to induce the person to work? Consider indifference curve U_1, which represents the highest level of utility that this person can achieve given budget constraint *ABC*. Utility is maximized at point *A*, and the person chooses not to work. This choice clearly shows that the offered wage (given the 2-hour commute) is below the person's reservation wage, but can we show the latter wage graphically? To take work with a two-hour commute, the person depicted in Figure 6.12 must find a job able to generate a combination of earnings and leisure time that yields a utility level equal to, or greater than, U_1. This is possible only if the person's budget constraint is equal to (or to the right of) *ABD*, which is tangent to U_1 at point *X*. The person's reservation wage, then, is equal to the slope of *BD*, and you can readily note that in this case, the slope of *BD* exceeds the slope of *BC*, which represents the currently offered wage. Moreover, to bring utility up to the level of U_1 (the utility associated with not working), the person shown in Figure 6.12 must be able to find a job at the reservation wage that offers four hours of work per day. Put differently, at this person's reservation wage, they would want to consume 10 hours

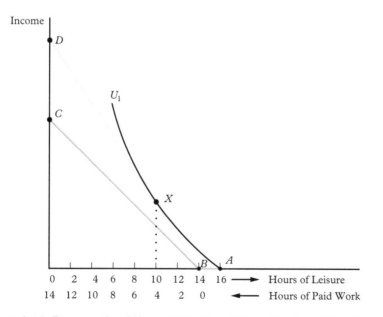

Figure 6.12 Reservation Wage With Fixed Time Costs of Working

of leisure daily, and with a two-hour commute, this implies four hours of work.

Empirical Findings on the Income and Substitution Effects

Labor supply theory suggests that the choices that workers make concerning their desired hours of work depend on their wealth and the wage rate that they can command, in addition to their preferences. In particular, this theory suggests the existence of a negative income effect and a positive substitution effect. Empirical tests of labor supply theory generally attempt to determine whether these two effects can be observed, if they operate in the expected directions, and what their relative magnitudes are.

Most recent studies of labor supply have taken large samples of individuals in order to analyze how labor force participation and hours of work are affected by changes in wage rates and income—often induced by changes in taxes—holding other influences (e.g., age) constant. Historically, studies of male labor force behavior and female labor force behavior have been done separately because of the different roles that men and women have typically played in performing household work and child-rearing—activities that clearly affect labor supply decisions but about which information is usually limited.

EXAMPLE 6.4

Daily Labor Supply at the Ballpark

The theory of labor supply rests in part on the assumption that once workers' offered wages climb above their reservation wages, they will decide to participate in the labor market. An implication of this theory is that in jobs for which hiring is done on a daily basis and for which wages fluctuate widely from day to day, we should observe daily fluctuations in participation. These expectations are supported by the daily labor supply decisions of vendors at Major League Baseball games.

One such study examined the individual labor supply behavior of vendors in one ballpark over the course of the 1996 major league baseball season. Vendors walk through the stands selling food and drinks, and their earnings are completely determined by the sales that they are able to make each day. The vendors studied could freely choose whether to work any given game, and the data collected by this study clearly suggest they made their decisions by weighing their opportunity cost of working against their expected earnings during the course of the game. (Expected earnings, of course, are related to a number of factors, including how many fans were likely to attend the game.)

The study was able to compare the actual amount earned by each vendor at each game with the number of vendors who had decided to work. The average amount earned by vendors was $43.81, with a low of $26.55 for one game and a high of $73.15 for another—and about 45 vendors worked the typical game at this ballpark. The study found that an increase in average earnings of $10 (which represents about a one standard deviation increase from the mean of $43.81) lured about six extra vendors to the stadium.

Clearly, then, vendors behaved as if they had reservation wages that they compared with expected earnings when they decided whether to work particular games.

Source: Gerald Oettinger, "An Empirical Analysis of the Daily Labor Supply of Stadium Vendors," *Journal of Political Economy* 107 (April 1999): 360–392

For another example of flexible work see M. Keith Chen, Judith A. Chevalier, Peter E. Rossi, and Emily Oehlsen, "The Value of Flexible Work: Evidence from Uber Drivers," *Journal of Political Economy* 127:6 (2019): 2735–2794.

A comprehensive review of numerous studies of the labor supply behavior of men finds that the sizes of the estimated effects vary with both the data and the statistical methodology used. Taken as a whole, however, the studies find strong evidence that, as theory suggests, observed substitution effects are positive and observed income effects are negative. What is less clear is which effect dominates when wages change; indeed, studies have typically found the two effects to be roughly similar in magnitude, but a comprehensive study has suggested that the substitution effect may be dominant.[18] Studies of the retirement behavior of older men (a topic that we address in Chapter 7) find, also as theory suggests, that the substitution effect dominates the decision to withdraw from the labor force.[19]

Substitution and income effects are also critical to the analysis of the falling labor force participation rates of men, noted in our discussion of Table 6.2. Of particular concern is the decline—since the year 2000—in labor force participation among native-born men in their prime working years (ages 25–54) with a high school degree or less. High school graduates in this group have seen their participation rates drop from bit more than 90 percent to around 85 percent, while the labor force participation rates of high school dropouts in this group have fallen from 75 percent to 65 percent. Fewer job opportunities have reduced wages for these men and increased the effort needed to find work—thus creating substitution effects pushing this group toward lower participation rates. Moreover, greater access to income from nonwork sources (living with parents for the younger men in this group and access to government disability payments for older men) have created income effects that also push them toward reductions in labor supply.[20]

Studies of the labor supply behavior of women generally have found a greater responsiveness to wage changes than is found among men. As noted earlier, labor supply can be measured both by labor force participation rates and by hours of work. Historically, women's labor force participation rates have been more responsive than men's to wage changes. (As seen in Example 6.5, the labor force participation rate for married women has also been more responsive to wage changes than have been their hours of work.) However, the past two decades have provided evidence that the labor supply behavior of women has become much more similar to that for men—meaning that the labor supply of women is *becoming less responsive to wage changes* than it used to be. The reduced responsiveness has been especially noticeable in women's labor force participation decisions, where the differences between men and women have been greatest.[21] This growing similarity in labor supply behavior may well reflect a growing similarity in the expectations held by women and men concerning work and careers.

EXAMPLE 6.5
Labor Supply Effects of Income Tax Cuts

In 1986, Congress changed the personal income tax system in the United States by drastically reducing tax rates on upper levels of income. Before this change, for example, families paid a 50 percent tax rate on taxable incomes over $170,000; after the change, this tax rate was reduced to 28 percent. The tax rate on taxable incomes over $50,000 was also set at 28 percent, down from about 40 percent. Lower income tax rates have the effect of increasing take-home earnings, and they therefore act as an increase in (after-tax) wage rates. Because lower rates generate an income and a substitution effect that work in opposite directions, they have an ambiguous anticipated effect on labor supply. Can we find out which effect is stronger in practice?

The 1986 changes served as a *natural experiment* (abrupt changes in only one variable, the sizes of which vary by group). The changes were sudden, large, and different for families of different incomes. For married women in families that, without their earnings, had incomes at the 99th percentile of the income distribution (i.e., the upper 1 percent), the tax rate cuts meant a 22 percent increase in their take-home wage rates. For women in families with incomes at the 90th percentile, the smaller tax rate cuts meant a 12 percent increase in take-home wages. It turns out that married women at the 99th and 90th percentiles of family income were similar in age, education, and occupation—and increases in their labor supply had been similar before 1986. Therefore, comparing their responses to different changes in their after-tax wage rates should yield insights into how the labor supply of married women responded to tax rate changes.

One study compared labor supply increases, from 1984 to 1990, for married women in the 99th and 90th percentiles. It found that the labor force participation rate for women in the 99th percentile rose by 19.4 percent and that, if working, their hours of work rose by 12.7 percent during that period. In contrast, both labor force participation and hours of work for women at the 90th percentile rose only by about 6.5 percent. The data from this natural experiment, then, suggest that women who experienced larger increases in their take-home wages desired greater increases in their labor supply—which implies that the substitution effect dominated the income effect for these women. Also, consistent with both theory and the results from other studies (discussed in this text), the dominance of the substitution effect was more pronounced for labor force participation decisions than it was for hours-of-work decisions.

Source: Nada Eissa, "Taxation and Labor Supply of Married Women: The Tax Reform Act of 1986 as a Natural Experiment" (Working Paper No. 5023, National Bureau of Economic Research, Cambridge, MA, February 1995)

A study by Alexander Bick and Nicola Fuchs-Schúndeln, "Quantifying the Disincentive Effects of Joint Taxation on Married Women's Labor Supply," *American Economic Review Papers and Proceedings* 107 (May 2017): 100–105, also estimates that female labor supply increases as income tax rates fall.

Policy Applications

Many income maintenance programs create budget constraints that increase income while reducing the take-home wage rate (thus causing the income and substitution effects to work in the same direction). Therefore, using labor supply theory to analyze the work-incentive effects of various social programs is both instructive and important. We characterize these programs by the budget constraints that they create for their recipients.

Budget Constraints With "Spikes"

Some social insurance programs compensate workers who are unable to work because of a temporary work injury, a permanent disability, or a layoff. Workers' compensation insurance replaces most of the earnings lost when workers are hurt on the job, and private or public disability programs do the same for workers who become physically or emotionally unable to work for other reasons. Unemployment compensation is paid to those who have lost a job and have not been able to find another. Although exceptions can be found in the occasional jurisdiction,[22] these *income replacement* programs generally share a common characteristic: They pay benefits only to those who are not working.

To understand the consequences of paying benefits only to those who are not working, let us suppose that a workers' compensation program is structured so that, after injury, workers receive their pre-injury earnings for as long as they are off work. Once they work even one hour, however, they are no longer considered disabled and cannot receive further benefits. The effects of this program on work incentives are analyzed in Figure 6.13,

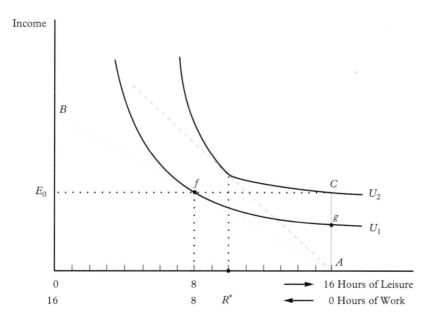

Figure 6.13 Budget Constraint With a Spike

which assumes that the pre-injury budget constraint was AB and pre-injury earnings were E_0 (= AC). Furthermore, we assume that the worker's "market" budget constraint (i.e., the constraint in the absence of a workers' compensation program) is unchanged, so that after recovery, the pre-injury wage can again be earned. Under these conditions, the post-injury budget constraint is BAC, and the person maximizes utility at point C—a point of no work.

Note that constraint BAC contains the segment AC, which looks like a spike. This spike creates severe work-incentive issues, for two reasons. First, the returns associated with the first hour of work are *negative*. That is, a person at point C who returns to work for one hour would find their income to be considerably reduced by working. Earnings from this hour of work would be more than offset by the reduction in benefits, which creates a negative *net wage*. The substitution effect associated with this program characteristic clearly discourages work.[23]

Second, our assumed no-work benefit of AC is equal to E_0, the pre-injury level of earnings. If the worker values leisure at all (as is assumed by the standard downward slope of indifference curves), being able to receive the old level of earnings while also enjoying more leisure clearly enhances utility. The worker is better off at point C than at point f, the pre-injury combination of earnings and leisure hours, because they are on indifference curve U_2 rather than U_1 (put another way, the individual has the same earnings, E_0, at points f and C but works eight hours at point f and zero at point C). Allowing workers to reach a higher utility level without working generates an income effect that discourages, or at least slows, the return to work.

Indeed, the program that we have assumed raises a worker's reservation wage above their pre-injury wage, meaning that a return to work is possible only if the worker qualifies for a higher-paying job. To see this graphically, observe the dashed blue line in Figure 6.13 that begins at point A and is tangent to indifference curve U_2 (the level of utility made possible by the social insurance program). The slope of this line is equal to the person's reservation wage, because if the person can obtain the desired hours of work at this or a greater wage, utility will be at least equal to that associated with point C. Note also that for labor force participation to be induced, the reservation wage must be received for at least R^* hours of work.

Given that the work-incentive aspects of income replacement programs often quite justifiably take a backseat to the goal of making unfortunate workers "whole" in some economic sense, creating programs that avoid work disincentives is not easy. For the preferences of the worker depicted in Figure 6.13, a benefit of slightly less than Ag would ensure minimal loss of utility while still providing incentives to return to work as soon as physically possible (work would allow indifference curve U_1 to be attained—see point f—whereas not working and receiving a benefit of less than Ag would not). Unfortunately, workers differ in their preferences, so the optimal benefit—one that would provide work incentives yet ensure only minimal loss of utility—differs for each individual.

For programs that create spikes, the best that policymakers can do—unless they want to set the no-work benefit so low (below Ag in Figure 6.13) that recipients will prefer to work—is to use administrative means to encourage them to return to work. Unemployment insurance (UI), for example, replaces something like half of lost earnings for the typical worker, but the program puts an upper limit on the weeks that each unemployed worker can receive benefits.[24] Workers' compensation replaces two-thirds of lost earnings for the average worker but must rely on doctors—and sometimes judicial hearings—to determine whether a worker continues to be eligible for benefits. (For evidence that higher workers' compensation benefits indeed induce longer absences from work, see Example 6.6.[25])

EXAMPLE 6.6

Staying Around One's Kentucky Home: Workers' Compensation Benefits and the Return to Work

Workers injured on the job receive workers' compensation insurance benefits while away from work. In the United States, these benefits vary by state, but they are calculated for most workers as some fraction (normally two-thirds) of weekly, pretax earnings. For high-wage workers, however, weekly benefits are typically capped at a maximum, which again varies by state.

On July 15, 1980, Kentucky raised its maximum weekly benefit by 66 percent. It did not alter benefits in any other way, so this change effectively granted large benefit increases to high-wage workers but without awarding them to anyone else. Because those injured before July 15 were ineligible for the increased benefits, even if they remained off work after July 15, this policy change created a nice natural experiment: One group of injured workers was able to obtain higher benefits, whereas another group was not. Did the group receiving higher benefits show evidence of reduced labor supply, as suggested by theory?

The effects of increased benefits on labor supply were unmistakable. High-wage workers ineligible for the new benefits typically stayed off the job for four weeks, but those injured after July 15 stayed away for five weeks—25 percent longer. No increases in the typical time away from work were recorded among lower-paid injured workers, who were unaffected by the changes in benefits.

Source: Bruce D. Meyer, W. Kip Viscusi, and David L. Durbin, "Workers' Compensation and Injury Duration: Evidence from a Natural Experiment," *American Economic Review* 85 (June 1995): 322–340

Workers who receive more-generous unemployment benefits stay out of work longer: See David Card, Andrew Johnston, Pauline Leung, Alexander Mas, and Zhuan Pei, "The Effect of Unemployment Benefits on the Duration of Unemployment Insurance Receipt: New Evidence from a Regression Kink Design in Missouri, 2003–2013," *American Economic Review Papers and Proceedings* 105 (May 2015): 126–130.

Programs With Net Wage Rates of Zero

The programs just discussed were intended to confer benefits on those who are unable to work, and the budget-constraint spike was created by the eligibility requirement that to receive benefits, one must not be working. Other social programs, such as Temporary Assistance for Needy Families (TANF, previously referred to as welfare), have different eligibility criteria and calculate benefits differently. These programs factor income needs into their eligibility criteria and then pay benefits on the basis of the difference between one's actual earnings and one's needs. Paying people the difference between their earnings and their needs creates a net wage rate of zero; thus, the work-incentive problems associated with these public assistance programs result from the fact that they increase the income of program recipients while also drastically reducing the price of leisure.

Nature of Income Subsidies   Originally, income maintenance (or "welfare") programs tended to take the form of a guaranteed annual income, under which the relevant government agency determined the income needed by an eligible person (Y_n in Figure 6.14) on the basis of family size, area living costs, and local program regulations. Actual earnings were then subtracted from this needed level, and a payment was issued to the person each month for the difference. If the person did not work, they received a subsidy of Y_n. If the person worked and if earnings caused dollar-for-dollar reductions in welfare benefits, then a budget constraint like

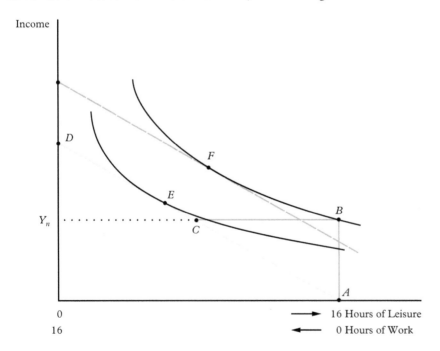

Figure 6.14 Income and Substitution Effects for the Basic Welfare System

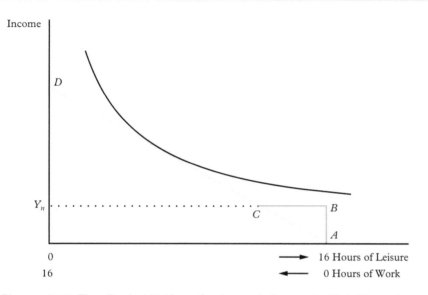

Figure 6.15 The Basic Welfare System: A Person's Not Choosing Welfare

ABCD in Figure 6.14 was created (their budget constraint in the absence of the subsidy program would be *AD*). The person's income remained at Y_n as long as they were subsidized. If receiving the subsidy, then, an extra hour of work yielded *no* net increase in income, because the extra earnings resulted in an equal reduction in the subsidy. The net wage of a person on the program—and therefore their price of leisure—was zero, which is graphically shown by the segment of the constraint having a slope of zero (*BC*).[26]

Thus, a welfare program like the one summarized in Figure 6.14 increases the income of poor people by moving the lower end of the budget constraint out from *AC* to *ABC*; as indicated by the dashed hypothetical constraint in Figure 6.14, this shift creates an *income effect* tending to reduce labor supply from the hours associated with point *E* to those associated with point *F*. However, it *also* causes the wage to effectively drop to zero; every dollar earned is matched by a dollar reduction in welfare benefits. This dollar-for-dollar reduction in benefits induces a huge *substitution effect*, causing those accepting the subsidy to reduce their hours of work to zero (point *B*). Of course, if a person's indifference curves were sufficiently flat so that the curve tangent to segment *CD* passed *above* point *B* (see Figure 6.15), then that person's utility would be maximized by choosing work instead of welfare.[27]

Welfare Reform   In light of the disincentives for work built into traditional welfare programs, the United States in the 1990s adopted major changes to its income-subsidy programs. The Personal Responsibility and Work Opportunity Reconciliation Act (PRWORA) of 1996 gave states more authority over how they could design their own welfare programs, intending to lead to more experimentation in program characteristics aimed at encouraging work, reducing poverty, and moving people off welfare.[28]

PRWORA also placed a five-year (lifetime) time limit on the receipt of welfare benefits and required that after two years on welfare, recipients must
work at least 30 hours per week. These changes appear to have had the effect
of increasing the labor force participation rates of single mothers (the primary beneficiaries of the old welfare system); the participation rate for single
mothers jumped from 68 percent in 1994 to roughly 78 percent in 2000—a
much larger increase than was observed for other groups of women.[29]

Lifetime Limits   Both lifetime limits and work requirements can be
analyzed by using the graphical tools developed in this chapter. Lifetime
limits on the receipt of welfare have the effect of ending eligibility for transfer payments, either by forcing recipients off welfare or by inducing them to
leave so that they can "save" their eligibility in case they need welfare later
in life. Thus, in terms of Figure 6.14, the lifetime limit ultimately removes
ABC from the potential recipient's budget constraint, which then reverts to
the market constraint of *AD*.

Clearly, the lifetime limit increases work incentives by ultimately eliminating the income subsidy. However, within the limits of their eligible years,
potential welfare recipients must choose when to receive the subsidy and
when to "save" their eligibility in the event of a future need. Federal law
provides for welfare subsidies only to families with children under the age
of 18; consequently, the closer one's youngest child is to 18 (when welfare
eligibility ends anyway), the smaller are the incentives of the parent to forgo
the welfare subsidy and save eligibility for the future.[30]

Work Requirements   As noted earlier, PRWORA introduced a
work requirement into the welfare system, although in some cases, unpaid
work or enrolling in education or training programs counts toward that
requirement. States differ in how the earnings affect welfare benefits, and
many have rules that allow welfare recipients to keep most of what they earn
(by not reducing, at least by much, their welfare benefits); we analyze such
programs in the next section. For now, we can understand the *basic* effects
of a work requirement by maintaining our assumption that earnings reduce
welfare benefits dollar for dollar.

Figure 6.16 illustrates the budget constraint associated with a minimum
work requirement of six hours a day (30 hours per week). If the person fails
to work the required six hours a day, no welfare benefits are received, and
they will be along segment *AB* of the constraint. If the work requirement is
met but earnings are less than Y_n, welfare benefits are received (see segment
BCD). If the work requirement is exceeded, income (earnings plus benefits)
remains at Y_n—the person is along *CD*—until earnings rise above needed
income and the person is along segment *DE* of the constraint and no longer
eligible for welfare benefits.

The work-incentive effects of this *work requirement* can be seen from analyzing Figure 6.16 in the context of people whose skills are such that they
are potential welfare recipients. At one extreme, some potential recipients
may have such steeply sloped indifference curves (reflecting a strong preference, or a need, to stay at home) that utility is maximized along segment

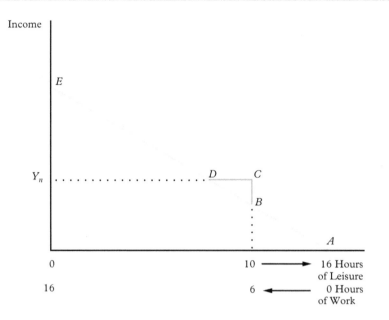

Figure 6.16 The Welfare System With a Work Requirement

AB, where so little market work is performed that they do not qualify for welfare. At the opposite extreme, others may have such flat indifference curves (reflecting a strong preference for income and a weak preference for leisure) that their utility is maximized along segment *DE*; that is, they work so many hours that their earnings disqualify them for welfare benefits.

In the middle of these extremes are those whose preferences lead them to work enough to qualify for welfare benefits. Clearly, if their earnings reduce their benefits dollar for dollar—as shown by the horizontal segment *DC* in Figure 6.16—they will want to work just the *minimum hours* needed to qualify for welfare, because their utility will be maximized at point *C* and not along *DC*. (For labor supply responses to different forms of a work requirement—requisitions of food from farmers during wartime—see Example 6.7)

Subsidy Programs With Positive Net Wage Rates

So far, we have analyzed the work-incentive effects of income maintenance programs that create net wage rates for program recipients that are either negative or zero (i.e., they create constraints that have either a spike or a horizontal segment). Most current programs, however, including those adopted by states under PRWORA, create positive net wages for recipients. Do these programs offer a solution to the problem of work incentives? We answer this question by analyzing a relatively recent and rapidly growing program: the Earned Income Tax Credit (EITC).

The EITC program makes income tax credits available to low-income families that have at least one worker. A tax credit of $1 reduces a person's income taxes by $1, and in the case of the EITC, if the tax credit for which workers qualify exceeds their total income tax liability, the government will mail them a check for the difference. Thus, the EITC functions as an earnings subsidy, and because the subsidy goes only to those who work, the EITC is seen by many as an income maintenance program that preserves work incentives. This view led Congress to vastly expand the EITC under President Bill Clinton and it is now the largest cash subsidy program directed at low-income households who have children.

The tax credits offered by the EITC program vary with one's earnings and the number of dependent children. For the purposes of our analysis, which is intended to illustrate the work-incentive effects of the EITC, we focus on the credits in the year 2019 offered to unmarried workers who have two children. Figure 6.17 graphs the relevant program characteristics for a worker who could earn a market (unsubsidized) wage reflected by the slope of AC and who has two children. As we will see later, for such a worker, the EITC created a budget constraint of $ABDEC$.

For workers who have earnings of $14,570 or less, the tax credit was calculated at 40 percent of earnings. That is, for every dollar earned, a tax credit of 40 cents was also earned; thus, for those who had earnings of under $14,570, net wages ($W_n$) were 40 percent higher than market wages (W). Note that this tax credit is represented by segment AB on the EITC constraint in Figure 6.17 and that the slope of AB *exceeds the slope of the market constraint AC.*

The maximum tax credit allowed for a single parent who has two children was $5,828 in 2019. Workers who earned between $14,570 and $19,040 per year qualified for this maximum tax credit. Because these workers experienced no increases or reductions in tax credits per added dollar of earnings, their net wage is equal to their market wage. The constraint facing

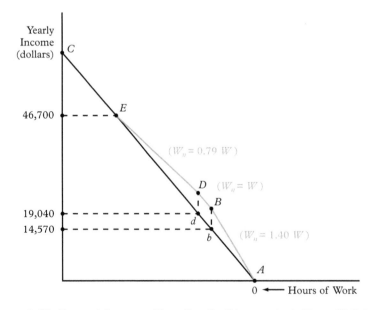

Figure 6.17 Earned Income Tax Credit (Unmarried, Two Children), 2019

workers who have earnings in this range is represented by segment *BD* in Figure 6.17, which has a slope equal to that of segment *AC*.

For earnings above $19,040, the tax credit was gradually phased out, such that when earnings reached $46,700, the tax credit was zero. Because after $19,040 each dollar earned reduced the tax credit by 21 cents, the net wage of EITC recipients was only 79 percent of their market wage (note that the slope of segment *DE* in Figure 6.17 is flatter than the slope of *AC*).

Looking closely at Figure 6.17, we can see that EITC recipients fall into one of three "zones": along *AB*, along *BD*, or along *DE*. The incomes of workers in all three zones are enhanced, which means that all EITC recipients experience an income effect that pushes them in the direction of less work. However, the program creates quite different net wage rates in the zones, and therefore, the substitution effect differs across zones.

For workers who have earnings below $14,570, the net wage is greater than the market wage (by 40 percent), so along segment *AB*, workers experience an increase in the price of leisure. Workers with earnings below $14,570, then, experience a substitution effect that pushes them in the direction of more work. With an income effect and a substitution effect that push in opposite directions, which effect will dominate is uncertain. What we can predict, though, is that some of those who would have been out of the labor force in the absence of the EITC program will now decide to seek work (earlier, we discussed the fact that for nonparticipants in the labor force, the substitution effect dominates).

Segments *BD* and *DE* represent two other zones, in which theory predicts that labor supply will *fall*. Along *BD*, the net wage is equal to the market wage, so the price of leisure in this zone is unchanged while income is enhanced. Workers in this zone experience a pure income effect. Along segment *DE*, the net wage is actually below the market wage, so in this zone, *both* the income effect and the substitution effect push in the direction of reduced labor supply.

Using economic theory to analyze labor supply responses induced by the constraint in Figure 6.17, we can come up with two predictions. First, if an EITC program is started or expanded, we expect to observe that the labor force participation rate of low-wage workers will increase. Second, a new or expanded EITC program should lead to a reduction in working hours among those along *BD* and *DE* (the effect on hours along *AB* is ambiguous).

As suggested by Figure 6.17, the earnings-related EITC benefits are complex to calculate, such that knowledge about the program is likely to vary across individuals. Among eligible individuals who have the most knowledge of the program, hours of work appear to increase along segment *AB* in Figure 6.17—meaning that the substitution effect along this segment is dominant. Along segment *DE*, where both the income effect and the substitution effect are predicted to cause hours of work to decrease, the predicted reduction in hours worked among knowledgeable workers seems to occur. Whether the labor force participation rate increases, as predicted by theory, among those eligible for the program is less clear.[31]

EXAMPLE 6.7

Wartime Food Requisitions and Agricultural Work Incentives

Countries at war often adopt "work requirement" policies to obtain needed food supplies involuntarily from their farming populations. Not surprisingly, how these requisitions are carried out can have enormous effects on the work incentives of farmers. Two alternative methods are contrasted in this example: One was used by the Bolshevik government during the civil war that followed the Russian Revolution and the other by Japan during World War II.

From 1917 to 1921, the Bolsheviks requisitioned from farmers all food in excess of the amounts needed for the farmers' own subsistence; in effect, the surplus was confiscated and given to soldiers and urban dwellers. Graphically, this policy created a budget constraint for farmers like ACY_s in the following diagram (a). Because farmers could keep their output until they reached the subsistence level of income (Y_s), the market wage prevailed until the income of Y_s was reached. After that, their net wage was zero (on segment CY_s), because any extra output went to the government. Thus, a prewar market constraint of AB was converted to ACY_s, which led to most farmers' maximizing utility near point C. Acreage planted dropped by 27 percent from 1917 to 1921, while harvested output fell by 50 percent.

(a) Farmers' Budget Constraint during Russian Civil War

Japan during World War II handled its food requisitioning policy completely differently. It required a quota to be delivered by each farmer to the government at very low prices, paying farmers the lump sum of EF in diagram (b). Japan, however, allowed farmers to sell any produce above the quota at higher (market) prices. This policy converted the prewar constraint of AB to one much like EFG in diagram (b). In effect, farmers had to work AE hours for the government, for which they were paid EF, but they were then allowed to earn the market wage after that. This policy preserved farmers' work incentives and apparently created an income effect that increased the total hours of work by Japanese farmers; despite war-induced shortages of capital and labor, rice production was greater in 1944 than in 1941.

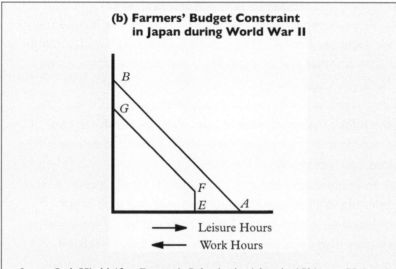

Source: Jack Hirshleifer, *Economic Behavior in Adversity* (Chicago: University of Chicago Press, 1987): 16–21, 39–41

EMPIRICAL STUDY 6.1

ESTIMATING THE INCOME EFFECT AMONG LOTTERY WINNERS: THE SEARCH FOR "EXOGENEITY"

Regression analysis, described in Appendix 1A, allows us to analyze the effects of one or more *independent* variables on a *dependent* variable. This statistical procedure is based on an important assumption: Each independent variable is *exogenous* (determined by some outside force and not itself influenced by the dependent variable). That is, we assume that the chain of causation runs from the independent variables to the dependent variable, where no feedback from the dependent variable affects those that we assume are independent.

   The issue of exogeneity arises when estimating the effects on hours of work caused by a change in income (wages held constant). Theory leads us to predict that desired hours of work are a function of wages, wealth, and preferences. Wealth is not usually observed in most data sets, so *nonlabor* income, such as the returns from financial investments, is used as a proxy for it. Measuring the effect that nonlabor income (an independent variable, if our assumptions are right) has on desired hours of work (our dependent variable), holding the wage constant, is intended to capture the income effect predicted by labor supply theory.

   The problem is that those who have strong preferences for income and weak preferences for leisure, for example, may tend to accumulate financial assets over time and end up with relatively high levels of nonlabor income later on. Put differently, high levels of work hours (supposedly our dependent variable) may create high levels of nonlabor income (what we hoped would be our independent variable); thus, when we estimate a correlation between work hours and nonlabor income, we cannot be sure whether we are estimating the income effect, some relationship between hard work and savings, or a mix of both (a problem analogous to the one discussed in the Empirical Study at the end of Chapter 4). In estimating the income effect, therefore, researchers must be careful to use measures of nonlabor income that are truly exogenous and not themselves influenced by the desired hours of work.

Are lottery winnings an exogenous source of nonlabor income? Once a person has entered a lottery, winning is a completely random event and thus is not affected by work hours; however, entering the lottery may not be so independent. If those who enter the lottery also have the strongest preferences for leisure, for example, then correlating work hours and lottery winnings across different individuals would not necessarily isolate the income effect. Rather, it might just reflect that those with stronger preferences for leisure (and thus lower work hours) were more likely to enter (and thus win) the lottery.

Therefore, if we want to measure the income effect associated with winning the lottery, we need to find a way to hold both wages *and* preferences for leisure constant. One study of how winning the lottery affected labor supply took account of the preferences of lottery players by performing a before-and-after analysis using panel data on winners and nonwinners. That is, for winners—defined as receiving prizes over $20,000, with a median prize of $635,000—the authors compared hours of work for six years before winning to hours of work during the six years after winning. By focusing on each individual's *changes* in hours and lottery winnings over the two periods, the effects of preferences (which are assumed to be unchanging) drop out of the analysis.

"Nonwinners" in the study were defined as lottery players who won only small prizes, ranging from $100 to $5,000. Labor supply changes for them before and after their small winnings were then calculated and compared to the changes observed among the winners. The study found that for every $100,000 in prizes, winners reduced their hours of work such that their earnings went down by roughly $11,000 (i.e., winners spent about 11 percent of their prize on "buying" leisure). These findings, of course, are consistent with the predictions concerning the income effect of nonlabor income on labor supply.

Source: Guido W. Imbens, Donald B. Rubin, and Bruce I. Sacerdote, "Estimating the Effect of Unearned Income on Labor Earnings, Savings, and Consumption: Evidence from a Survey of Lottery Players," *American Economic Review* 91 (September 2001): 778–794

Matteo Picchio, Sigrid Suetens, and Jan C. van Ours, "Labour Supply Effects of Winning a Lottery," *Economic Journal* 128 (June 2018): 1700–1729, find that labor-supply effects

—fewer hours worked, but not withdrawal from the labor force—persist for many years among those winning large prizes. Also see an example using data from Sweden in David Cesarini, Erik Lindqvist, Matthew Notowidigdo, and Robert Ostling, "The Effect of Wealth on Individual and Household Labor Supply: Evidence from Swedish Lotteries," *American Economic Review* 107 (December 2017): 3917–3946.

Review Questions

1. Given the definitions in footnote 6, is the following statement true, false, or uncertain? "Leisure must be an inferior good for an individual's labor supply curve to be backward bending." Explain your answer.

2. Evaluate the following quote: "Higher take-home wages for any group should increase the labor force participation rate for that group."

3. Suppose that a government is considering several options to ensure that legal services are provided to poor people.

   Option A: All lawyers would be required to devote 5 percent of their work time to poor people, free of charge.

   Option B: Lawyers would be required to provide 100 hours of work, free of charge, to poor people.

   Option C: Lawyers who earn over $50,000 in a given year would have to donate $5,000 to a fund that the government would use to help poor people.

   Discuss the likely effects of each option on the hours of work among lawyers. (*Drawing* the constraints created by each option will help you.)

4. The way the workers' compensation system works now, employees permanently injured on the job receive a payment of $X each year, whether they work or not. Suppose the government were to implement a new program in which those who did not work at all got $0.5X, but those who did work got $0.5X plus workers' compensation of 50 cents *for every hour worked* (of course, this subsidy would be in addition to the wages paid by their employers). What would be the change in work incentives associated with this change in the way workers' compensation payments were calculated?

5. A firm wants to offer paid sick leave to its workers, but it wants to encourage them not to abuse it by being unnecessarily absent. The firm is considering two options:

   a. Workers are entitled to 10 days of paid sick leave per year, and any unused leave days at the end of the year are converted to cash at the worker's daily wage rate.

   b. Workers are entitled to 10 days of paid sick leave per year, and if no sick days are used for two consecutive years, the company agrees to buy the worker a $100,000 life insurance policy.

Compare the work-incentive effects of the two options, both immediately and in the long run.

6. In 2002, a French law went into effect that cut the standard workweek from 39 to 35 hours (workers got paid for 39 hours even though they worked 35) while prohibiting overtime hours from being worked. (Overtime in France is paid at 25 percent above the normal wage rate.)

    a. Draw the old budget constraint, showing the overtime premium after 39 hours of work.

    b. Draw the new budget constraint.

    c. Analyze which workers in France are better off under the 2002 law. Are any worse off? Explain.

7. Suppose that a proposal provides poor people with housing subsidies that are tied to their income levels. These subsidies take the form of vouchers that poor people can turn over to their lessors in full or partial payment of their housing expenses. The yearly subsidy will equal $2,400 as long as earnings do not exceed $8,000 per year. The subsidy is to be reduced by 60 cents for every dollar earned in excess of $8,000; that is, when earnings reach $12,000, the person is no longer eligible for rent subsidies.

Draw an arbitrary budget constraint for a person, assuming that they receive no government subsidies. Then draw in the budget constraint that arises from this housing subsidy proposal. After drawing in the budget constraint associated with the proposal, analyze the effects of this proposed housing subsidy program on the labor supply behavior of various groups in the population.

8. The Tax Reform Act of 1986 was designed to reduce the marginal tax rate (the tax rate on the last dollar earned) while eliminating enough deductions and loopholes so that total revenues collected by the government could remain constant. Analyze the work-incentive effects of tax reforms that lower marginal tax rates while keeping total tax revenues constant.

9. The current UI program in the United States gives workers $X per day if they are unemployed but zero if they take a job for even one hour per day. Suppose that the law is changed so that UI beneficiaries can keep getting benefits of $X per day if they work two or fewer hours per day, but if they work more than two hours per day, their UI benefits end. Draw the old and new budget constraints (clearly labeled) associated with the UI program, and analyze the work incentives of this proposed change.

10. Assume that the current disability insurance (DI) benefit for those who are unable to work is $X per day and that DI benefits go to *zero* if a worker accepts a job for even one hour per week. Suppose that the benefit rules are changed so those disabled workers who take jobs that pay less than $X per day receive a benefit that brings *their total daily income*

(earnings plus the DI benefit) up to $X. As soon as their labor market earnings rise above $X per day, their disability benefits end. Draw the old and new budget constraints (clearly labeled) associated with the DI program, and analyze the work-incentive effects of the change in benefits.

Problems

1. When the Fair Labor Standards Act began to mandate paying 50 percent more for overtime work, many employers tried to avoid it by cutting hourly pay so that total pay and hours remained the same.

   a. Assuming that this 50 percent overtime pay premium is newly required for all work beyond eight hours per day, draw a budget constraint that pictures a strategy of cutting hourly pay so that at the original hours of work, total earnings remain the same.

   b. Suppose that an employer initially paid $11 per hour and had a 10-hour workday. What hourly base wage will the employer offer so that the total pay for a 10-hour workday will stay the same?

   c. Will employees who used to work 10 hours per day want to work more or fewer than 10 hours in the new environment (which includes the new wage rate and the mandated overtime premium)?

2. Nina is able to select her weekly work hours. When a new bridge opens up, it cuts one hour off Nina's total daily commute to work. If both leisure and income are normal goods, what is the effect of the shorter commute on Nina's work time?

3. Suppose that you win a lottery, and your after-tax gain is $50,000 per year until you retire. As a result, you decide to work part time at 30 hours per week in your old job instead of the usual 40 hours per week.

   a. Calculate the annual income effect from this lottery gain on the basis of a 50-week year. Interpret the results in light of the theory presented in this chapter.

   b. What is the substitution effect associated with this lottery win? Explain.

4. The federal minimum wage was increased on July 24, 2009, to $7.25 from $6.55. If 16 hours per day are available for work and leisure, draw the daily budget constraint for a worker who was earning the minimum wage rate of $6.55 and the new budget constraint after the increase.

5. Suppose that Michael receives $50 per day as interest on an inheritance. His wage rate is $20 per hour, and he can work a maximum of 16 hours per day at his job. Draw his daily budget constraint.

6. Stella can work up to 16 hours per day at her job. Her wage rate is $8.00 per hour for the first eight hours. If she works more than eight hours, her employer pays a 50 percent premium. Draw Stella's daily budget constraint.

7. Teddy's daily budget constraint is shown in the following chart. Teddy's employer pays him a base wage rate plus overtime if he works more than the standard hours. What is Teddy's daily nonlabor income? What is Teddy's base wage rate? What is Teddy's overtime wage rate? How many hours does Teddy need to work to receive overtime?

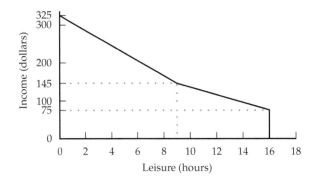

Notes

1. For articles on changes in female labor force participation over time, see Francine D. Blau and Lawrence M. Kahn, "Female Labor Supply: Why is the United States Falling Behind?" *American Economic Review: Papers & Proceedings* 103 (May 2013): 251–256; Claudia Goldin and Claudia Olivetti, "Shocking Labor Supply: A Reassessment of the Role of World War II on Women's Labor Supply," *American Economic Review: Papers & Proceedings* 103 (May 2013): 257–262; Chinhui Juhn and Simon Potter, "Changes in Labor Force Participation in the United States," *Journal of Economic Perspectives* 20 (Summer 2006): 27–46; Claudia Goldin and Joshua Mitchell, The New Life Cycle of Women's Employment: Disappearing Humps, Sagging Middles, Expanding Tops," *Journal of Economic Perspectives* 31 (Winter 2017): 161–182.

2. For a discussion of these trends, see Stephanie Aaronson, Tomaz Cajner, Bruce Fallick, Felix Galbis-Reig, Christopher Smith, and William Wascher, "Labor Force Participation: Recent Developments and Future Prospects," *Brookings Papers on Economic Activity* (Fall 2014): 197–275. For the related topic of explaining changes in the employment–population ratio, see Katharine G. Abraham and Melissa S. Kearney, "Explaining the Decline in the U.S. Employment-to-Population Ratio: A Review of the Evidence," *Journal of Economic Literature* 58 (September 2020): 585–643.

3. At any time, roughly 5 percent of U.S. workers hold more than one job. See Etienne Lalé, "Multiple Jobholding Over the Past Two Decades," *Monthly Labor Review* (April 2015), www.bls.gov/opub/mlr/2015/article/multiple-jobholding-over-the-past-two-decades.htm; Christina H. Paxson and Nachum Sicherman, "The Dynamics of Dual Job Holding and Job Mobility," *Journal of Labor Economics* 14 (July 1996):

357–393. For a study that tests (and finds support for) the assumption that workers are *not* restricted in their choice of work hours, see John C. Ham and Kevin T. Reilly, "Testing Intertemporal Substitution, Implicit Contracts, and Hours Restriction Models of the Labor Market Using Micro Data," *American Economic Review* 92 (September 2002): 905–927; for an opposing view regarding the ability to choose hours or work schedules, see John Ameriks, Joseph Briggs, Andrew Caplin, Minjoon Lee, Matthew D. Shapiro, and Christopher Tonetti, "Older Americans Would Work Longer if Jobs Were Flexible," *American Economic Journal: Macroeconomics* 12 (January 2020): 174–209. For a related discussion on multiple jobholders, see M. Keith Chen, Judith A. Chevalier, Peter Rossi, and Emily Oehlsen, "The Value of Flexible Work: Evidence from Uber Drivers," *Journal of Political Economy* 127:6 (December 2019): 2735–2794.

4. See, for example, Joseph G. Altonji and Christina H. Paxson, "Job Characteristics and Hours of Work," in *Research in Labor Economics*, vol. 8, ed. Ronald G. Ehrenberg (Greenwich, CT: JAI Press, 1986); Orley Ashenfelter, "Macroeconomic Analyses and Microeconomic Analyses of Labor Supply," *Carnegie-Rochester Conference Series on Public Policy* 21 (1984): 117–156. A different study has shown that workers' desired labor supply adjustments come more from changing jobs than from changing hours with the same employer; see Richard Blundell, Mike Brewer, and Marco Francesconi, "Job Changes and Hours Changes: Understanding the Path of Labor Supply Adjustment," *Journal of Labor Economics* 26 (July 2008): 421–454; also see Richard Blundell, Monica Costa Dias, Costas Meghir, and Jonathan Shaw, "Female Labor Supply, Human Capital, and Welfare Reform," *Econometrica* 84:5 (September 2016): 1705–1753.

5. The averages cited in this paragraph refer to *actual* hours of work (obtained from the *Census of Manufactures*), not the more commonly available "hours paid for," which include paid time off for illness and vacations. An additional study found an unexpected *expansion* of work hours among highly educated men during the past two decades of the twentieth century; see Peter Kuhn and Fernando Lozano, "The Expanding Workweek? Understanding Trends in Long Work Hours among U.S. Men, 1979–2006," *Journal of Labor Economics* 26 (April 2008): 311–343. For a recent study of wages and hours, see Alexander Bick, Adam Blandin, and Richard Rogerson, "Hours and Wages" (Working Paper No. 26722, National Bureau of Economic Research, Cambridge, MA, January 2020).

6. When the demand for a good rises with wealth, economists say the good is a *normal good*. If demand falls as wealth rises, the good is said to be an *inferior good* (traveling or commuting by bus is sometimes cited as an example of an inferior good).

7. This assumes that individuals can work as many hours as they want at a fixed wage rate. While this assumption may seem overly simplistic, it

will not lead to wrong conclusions with respect to the issues analyzed in this chapter. More rigorously, leisure's marginal opportunity cost is the marginal wage rate (the wage that one could receive for an extra hour of work).

8. The best indicator of wealth is permanent, or long-run potential, income. Current income may differ from permanent income, for a variety of reasons (unemployment, illness, unusually large amounts of overtime work, etc.). For our purposes here, however, the distinction between current income and permanent income is not too important.

9. An increase in the price of gasoline will reduce the income that people have left for expenditures on nongasoline consumption only if the demand for gasoline is inelastic. In this case, the percentage reduction in gasoline consumption is smaller than the percentage increase in price; total expenditures on gasoline would thus rise. Our analysis assumes this to be the case. For a study of how gasoline taxes affect labor supply, see Sarah West and Roberton Williams, "Empirical Estimates for Environmental Policy Making in a Second-Best Setting" (Working Paper No. 10330, National Bureau of Economic Research, March 2004).

10. Economists call the change in money income needed to hold utility constant when leisure hours are changed by one unit the *marginal rate of substitution* between leisure and money income. This marginal rate of substitution can be graphically understood as the slope of the indifference curve at any point. At point *L*, for example, the slope is relatively steep, so economists would say that the marginal rate of substitution at point *L* is relatively high.

11. Our assumption in this model is that we can consider only income and time.

12. Our assumption that eight hours per day are required for sleeping and other "maintenance" activities is purely for ease of exposition. These activities themselves are a matter of economic choice, at least to some extent; see, for example, Jeff E. Biddle and Daniel S. Hamermesh, "Sleep and the Allocation of Time," *Journal of Political Economy* 98:5, pt. 1 (October 1990): 922–943. Modeling a three-way choice between work, leisure, and maintenance activities would complicate our analysis but would not change the essential insights that theory can offer about the labor/leisure choice that workers must make.

13. The vertical change for a one-unit change in horizontal distance is the definition of *slope*. *Absolute value* refers to the magnitude of the slope, disregarding whether it is positive or negative. The budget constraint drawn in Figure 6.5 is a straight line (and thus has a constant slope). In economic terms, a straight-line budget constraint reflects the assumption that the wage rate at which one can work is fixed and that it does not change with the hours of work. However, the major theoretical implications derived from using a straight-line constraint would be unchanged by employing a convex one, so for ease of exposition, we

are using the fixed-wage assumption. One could easily also account for bonuses after a certain number of hours in a day, for example, but we ignore that here.

14. Guido W. Imbens, Donald B. Rubin, and Bruce I. Sacerdote, "Estimating the Effects of Unearned Income on Labor Earnings, Savings, and Consumption: Evidence from a Survey of Lottery Players," *American Economic Review* 91 (September 2001): 778–794. Similar behavior was found among recent mothers when Spain adopted a universal child benefit in 2007; see Libertad González, "The Effect of a Universal Child Benefit on Conceptions, Abortions, and Early Maternal Labor Supply," *American Economic Journal: Economic Policy* 5 (August 2013): 160–188. Studies of an income effect produced by eligibility for government-provided health insurance include Katherine Baicker, Amy Finkelstein, Jae Song, and Sarah Taubman, "The Impact of Medicaid on Labor Market Activity and Program Participation: Evidence from the Oregon Health Insurance Experiment," *American Economic Review Papers and Proceedings* 104 (May 2014): 322–328; Craig Garthwaite, Tal Gross, and Matthew J. Notowidigdo, "Public Health Insurance, Labor Supply, and Employment Lock," *Quarterly Journal of Economics* 129 (May 2014): 653–696.

15. Gerald Eric Daniels Jr. and Andria Smythe, "Student Debt and Labor Market Outcomes," *AEA Papers and Proceedings* 109 (May 2019): 171–175.

16. In our initial definition of the substitution effect, we held *money income* constant, whereas in the graphical analysis, we held *utility* constant. These slightly different approaches were followed for explanatory convenience, and they represent (respectively) the theoretical analyses suggested by Evgeny Slutsky and John Hicks.

17. See Alan B. Krueger and Andreas I. Mueller, "A Contribution to the Empirics of Reservation Wages," *American Economic Journal: Economic Policy* 8 (February 2016): 142–179; Alexandre Mas and Amanda Pallais, "Labor Supply and the Value of Non-work Time: Experimental Estimates from the Field," *American Economic Review: Insights* 1 (June 2019): 111–126 for studies of reservation wages.

18. Michael P. Keane, "Labor Supply and Taxes: A Survey," *Journal of Economic Literature* 49 (December 2011): 961–1075; Alexander Bick, Nicola Fuchs-Schündeln, and David Lagakos, "How Do Hours Worked Vary with Income? Cross-Country Evidence and Implications," *American Economic Review* 108 (January 2018): 170–199.

19. Franco Peracchi and Finis Welch, "Trends in the Labor Force Transitions of Older Men and Women," *Journal of Labor Economics* 12 (April 1994): 210–242.

20. Ariel J. Binder and John Bound, "The Declining Labor Market Prospects of Less-Educated Men," *Journal of Economic Perspectives* 33 (Spring 2019): 163–190.

21. Keane, "Labor Supply and Taxes: A Survey"; Francine D. Blau and Lawrence M. Kahn, "Changes in the Labor Supply Behavior of Married Women: 1980–2000," *Journal of Labor Economics* 25 (July 2007): 393–438; Bradley T. Heim, "Structural Estimation of Family Labor Supply with Taxes: Estimating a Continuous Hours Model Using a Direct Utility Specification," *Journal of Human Resources* 44 (Spring 2009): 350–385; Kelly Bishop, Bradley Heim, and Kata Mihaly, "Single Women's Labor Supply Elasticities: Trends and Policy Implications," *Industrial and Labor Relations Review* 63 (October 2009): 146–168.

22. UI and workers' compensation programs in the United States are run at the state level and thus to some extent vary in their characteristics.

23. In graphical terms, the budget constraint contains a vertical spike, and the slope of this vertical segment is infinitely negative. In economic terms, the implied infinitely negative (net) wage arises from the fact that even one minute of work causes a person to lose their entire benefit. For empirical evidence, see Susan Chen and Wilbert van der Klaauw, "The Work Disincentive Effects of the Disability Insurance Program in the 1990s," *Journal of Econometrics* 142 (February 2008): 757–784; David H. Autor, Mark Duggan, Kyle Greenberg, and David S. Lyle, "The Impact of Disability Benefits on Labor Supply: Evidence from the VA's Disability Compensation Program," *American Economic Journal: Applied Economics* 8 (July 2016): 31–68. For an analysis of disability insurance usage, see David H. Autor and Mark G. Duggan, "The Growth in the Social Security Disability Rolls: A Fiscal Crisis Unfolding," *Journal of Economic Perspectives* 20 (Summer 2006): 71–96.

24. During the spring of 2020 as the world was facing the COVID-19 pandemic, the US federal government added $600 per week to state unemployment payments for workers who lost their jobs. This resulted in situations where many individuals received more in UI benefits when not working than they earned when working.

25. For a summary of evidence on the labor supply effects of UI and workers' compensation, see Alan B. Krueger and Bruce D. Meyer, "Labor Supply Effects of Social Insurance," in *Handbook of Public Economics*, vol. 4, eds. Alan Auerbach and Martin Feldstein (Amsterdam: North Holland, 2002); Peter Kuhn and Chris Riddell, "The Long-Term Effects of Unemployment Insurance: Evidence from New Brunswick and Maine, 1940–1991," *Industrial and Labor Relations Review* 63 (January 2010): 183–204. Disability insurance programs also create spikes; for evidence on how the labor supply of workers who qualify for disability payments respond to more-generous disability benefits, see Lex Borghans, Anne C. Gielen, and Erzo F.P. Luttmer, "Social Support Substitution and the Earnings Rebound: Evidence from a Regression Discontinuity in Disability Insurance Reform," *American*

Economic Journal: Economic Policy 6 (November 2014): 34–70; David Autor, Mark Duggan, and Jonathan Gruber, "Moral Hazard and Claims Deterrence in Private Disability Insurance," *American Economic Journal: Applied Economics* 6 (October 2014): 110–141; Nicole Maestas, Kathleen J. Mullen, and Alexander Strand, "Does Disability Insurance Receipt Discourage Work? Using Examiner Assignment to Estimate Causal Effects of SSDI Receipt," *American Economic Review* 103 (August 2013): 1797–1829; Alexander Gelber, Timothy J. Moore, and Alexander Strand, "The Effect of Disability Insurance Payments on Beneficiaries' Earnings," *American Economic Journal: Economic Policy* 9 (August 2017): 229–261.

26. Gary Burtless, "The Economist's Lament: Public Assistance in America," *Journal of Economic Perspectives* 4 (Winter 1990): 57–78, summarizes a variety of public assistance programs in the United States before 1990. This article suggests that in actual practice, benefits were usually reduced by something less than dollar for dollar (perhaps by 80 or 90 cents per dollar of earnings).

27. See Robert Moffitt, "Incentive Effects of the U.S. Welfare System: A Review," *Journal of Economic Literature* 30 (March 1992): 1–61, for a summary of the literature on labor supply effects of the welfare system.

28. For a comprehensive summary of the reforms and various analyses of them, see Jeffrey Grogger and Lynn A. Karoly, *Welfare Reform: Effects of a Decade of Change* (Cambridge, MA: Harvard University Press, 2005).

29. Rebecca M. Blank, "Evaluating Welfare Reform in the United States," *Journal of Economic Literature* 40 (December 2002): 1105–1166.

30. Jeffrey Grogger, "Time Limits and Welfare Use," *Journal of Human Resources* 39 (Spring 2004): 405–424; also see Marc K. Chan, "Measuring the Effects of Welfare Time Limits," *Journal of Human Resources* 53 (Winter 2018): 232–271.

31. See Raj Chetty, John N. Friedman, and Emmanuel Saez, "Using Differences in Knowledge Across Neighborhoods to Uncover the Impacts of the EITC on Earnings," *American Economic Review* 103 (December 2013): 2683–2721; Jacob Bastian, "The Rise of Working Mothers and the 1975 Earned Income Tax Credit," *American Economic Journal: Economic Policy* 12 (August 2020): 44–75; Henrik Kleven, "The EITC and the Extensive Margin: A Reappraisal" (Working Paper No. 26405, National Bureau of Economic Research, Cambridge, MA, February 2020), for citations to studies on the labor supply responses to the EITC. For similar findings with respect to labor force participation and hours of work in a different program, see Patrick Kline and Melissa Tartari, "Bounding the Labor Supply Responses to a Randomized Welfare Experiment: A Revealed Preference Approach," *American Economic Review* 106 (April 2016): 972–1014.

Selected Readings

Abraham, Katharine G., and Melissa S. Kearney. "Explaining the Decline in the US Employment-to-Population Ratio: A Review of the Evidence." *Journal of Economic Literature* 58 (September 2020): 585–643.

Blank, Rebecca M. "Evaluating Welfare Reform in the United States." *Journal of Economic Literature* 40 (December 2002): 1105–1166.

Card, David E., and Rebecca M. Blank, eds. *Finding Jobs: Work and Welfare Reform.* New York: Russell Sage Foundation, 2000.

Hoffman, Saul D., and Laurence S. Seidman. *Helping Working Families: The Earned Income Tax Credit.* Kalamazoo, MI: W.E. Upjohn Institute for Employment Research, 2002.

Killingsworth, Mark R. *Labor Supply.* Cambridge, England: Cambridge University Press, 1983.

Krause, Eleanor, and Isabel Sawhill. "What We Know and Don't Know About Declining Labor Force Participation: A Review" (Center for Children and Families at Brookings, The Brookings Institution, Washington, DC, May 2017), www.brookings.edu/wp-content/uploads/2017/05/ccf_20170517_declining_labor_force_participation_sawhill1.pdf.

Linder, Staffan B. *The Harried Leisure Class.* New York: Columbia University Press, 1970.

Moffitt, Robert. "Incentive Effects of the U.S. Welfare System: A Review." *Journal of Economic Literature* 30 (March 1992): 1–62.

Labor Supply
Household Production, the
Family, and the Life Cycle

In Chapter 6, the theory of labor supply focused on the simple case in which individuals decide how to allocate their time between labor and leisure. This chapter elaborates on this simple labor supply model by taking account of three issues. First, much of the time spent at home is given to work activities (e.g., cooking and childcare), not leisure. Second, for those who live with partners, decisions about work for pay, household work, and leisure are usually made in a way that takes account of the activities and income of other household members. Third, just as time at paid work is substitutable with time at home, time spent working for pay in one part of the life cycle is substitutable with time at other points in life. These refinements of our simple model do not alter the fundamental considerations or predictions of labor supply theory, but they do add useful richness to it.

A Labor Supply Model That Incorporates Household Production

In Chapter 6, we built a model of labor supply on the simple assumption that people have only two ways to spend time: working for pay or consuming leisure. In reality, of course, the choices are more complex—and much of the time spent at home is in activities (cooking, cleaning, washing dishes, cleaning laundry, childcare, etc.) that are closer to work than to leisure. Can we build a model of labor supply that takes account of these other uses of household time?

To get a sense for how employed people actually allocate their time, consider the data in Table 7.1, which breaks down activities into four categories (paid work, household work, leisure, and personal care) for three household groupings based on the presence and ages of children. The averages in the table suggest that women who have very young children and who are employed outside the home spend more time in household work activities and less time performing paid (or "market") work than women who have older children. Employed women in all three categories of households spend more time in household work and less time in paid work than men

Table 7.1 Weekly Hours Spent in Household Work, Paid Work, and Leisure Activities by Employed Men and Women Over Age 18, 2019

	Households with children < 6		Households with children 6–17		Households with no children < 18	
	Women	Men	Women	Men	Women	Men
Paid Work[a]	33	42	34	46	37	43
Household Work[b]	37	24	27	17	19	14
Leisure[c]	26	29	31	32	34	37
Personal Care[d]	71	71	74	71	76	73

[a] Includes commuting time

[b] Includes time spent purchasing goods/services and caring for others

[c] Includes time spent in volunteer and educational activities

[d] Includes time spent sleeping and eating

Source: U.S. Department of Labor, Bureau of Labor Statistics, "American Time Use Survey—2019 Results," Table 8B at www.bls.gov/news.release/pdf/atus.pdf

do—but the disparities in household work hours shrink as children grow older. Time spent in leisure, which is somewhat greater for men than for women, increases for both women and men as children age.[1] Personal care time varies little across groupings.

The Basic Model for an Individual: Similarities With the Labor-Leisure Model

Incorporating household activities other than leisure into our model of labor supply does not require significant changes in the model developed in Chapter 6, but it does require us to replace the category of leisure time with one we will call household production time (or household time, for short). Time spent in household production includes doing chores or relaxing at home, but it also includes time spent on chores or relaxation that take one out of the household, such as shopping or going to a movie.

To illustrate the major effects of including household activities other than leisure into our model, let us consider a hypothetical household with one decision maker, Sally, who is the unmarried mother of small children. As we assumed in Chapter 6, we here suppose that Sally needs eight hours a day for personal care, so she therefore has 16 hours per day available for paid work, leisure, or household work. In Figure 7.1, we put Sally's available time on the horizontal axis—where household time runs from left to right and market work (paid work) time runs from right to left.

As before, we assume that Sally is trying to maximize her utility. She can acquire the commodities that enhance her utility—a clean house, good meals, happy children, relaxation activities—either by spending household time to *make* these commodities herself or by earning income that allows

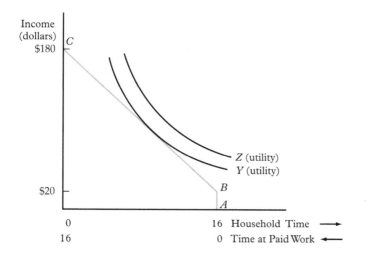

Figure 7.1 Household Time and Income Are Substitutes in the Production of Commodities That Sally Consumes

her to *buy* goods or services from others. Taken together, the two axes in Figure 7.1 reflect the two sources of inputs that can be used to produce utility for Sally: Household time is on the horizontal axis, and income is on the vertical axis.[2]

Sally's choices about how to use her time, as we discussed in Chapter 6, are affected by her preferences, her income, and her wage rate. These influences are discussed in the following sections.

Preferences As in Chapter 6, we continue to use downward-sloping indifference curves to graphically represent Sally's preferences. Nutritional meals, for example, generate utility for her, and one option she has is to grow her own food and fully prepare her meals at home. Other options, which could yield meals of equal utility, would involve mixing more purchased goods or services with less household preparation time—for example, buying packaged foods to be heated at home or eating meals in a restaurant. Relaxation also produces utility, and relaxation that generates *equal utility* could involve time but not much in the way of purchased goods (a day hiking in a local park) or more purchased goods and less time (an evening at a nightclub).

Because purchased goods and time are substitutes for each other in producing commodities that generate utility, Sally's indifference curves slope downward (as explained in Chapter 6). We also continue to draw these curves as convex, for reasons similar to those given in Chapter 6; that is, we assume that if Sally were trying to substitute more and more purchased goods for her time in the production of childcare, say, she would find doing so and keeping her utility constant increasingly difficult. Finally, our graphical presentation of Sally's preferences assumes that if her ability to command resources were to increase—so that she could move from indifference curve *Y* in Figure 7.1 to indifference curve *Z*—her utility would increase. These assumptions lead to indifference curves for Sally that are identical to those presented in Chapter 6.

Budget Constraint   Of course, Sally must make her choices about spending time in the context of her income and wage rate, and the budget constraint that she faces limits those choices. The constraint *ABC* in Figure 7.1 is drawn on the assumption that Sally can earn $10 per hour and that if she does not work for pay, she would have unearned income of $20 per day.

The constraint *ABC*, as with those we drew in Chapter 6, runs between the two axes. At the lower right, the constraint tells us how much income she can spend if she performs no market work and spends all available time in household production ($20); at the upper left, it tells us how much income she could spend if she allocates all 16 hours to working for pay ($160 + $20 = $180). As before, the slope of the constraint reflects her wage rate, which is also the opportunity cost of household time (i.e., if the wage she can earn is $10 per hour, an hour spent in doing household chores or in leisure requires her to forgo $10 of potential earnings). Thus, we draw her budget constraint, *ABC* in Figure 7.1, just as we drew constraints in Chapter 6.

Income and Substitution Effects   With budget constraints and indifference curves shaped in the same way, the labor-leisure model of Chapter 6 and the household production model analyzed here unsurprisingly have the same underlying labor supply implications. Specifically, if we assume that Sally's income rises and her wage rate—the opportunity cost of household time—is held constant, the household model predicts that she will spend more time in household production (consuming more commodities that bring her utility) and less time at paid work. Likewise, if her wage rate were to rise, holding her income constant, she would increase her hours of paid work, because the cost of staying at home would have risen while her wealth would not have. In short, *the income and substitution effects introduced in* Chapter 6 *work in the same way* if we place our labor supply model in the context of household production rather than leisure.

The Basic Model for an Individual: Some New Implications

While changing the focus from leisure time to the broader category of household production time does not fundamentally alter our labor supply model, it does lead to additional topics of analysis that will be addressed in this and succeeding sections. One immediate insight is obvious but crucial: Decisions about labor supply and decisions about how to produce the commodities we consume are jointly made. Thus, the choices made about market work, how many children a family has, how children are raised, how meals are prepared (see Example 7.1), and so forth are affected by the same set of forces. This insight has spawned an entire subfield in economics: economic analyses of the family, which go beyond the labor supply issues introduced here to deal with issues of marriage, divorce, fertility, child-rearing practices, and other activities that families undertake and decisions that they make.[3]

EXAMPLE 7.1
Obesity and the Household Production Model

Obesity is a major health problem in the United States. During the period from the late 1970s to 2012, the percentage of adult Americans considered obese rose from 14 percent to 35 percent. Obesity is now the second leading cause of early death; 300,000 premature deaths each year are associated with complications from obesity (heart disease, stroke, and diabetes, among others). One estimate indicates the annual costs of obesity (medical treatment plus lost productivity) is $190 billion. Obesity, of course, is related to both genetic and other family influences, but the abrupt increase suggests that other factors may also have come into play. Can economic theory give us insights into this problem?

The model of household production presented in this chapter suggests that time spent in household work, such as meal preparation, will be responsive to changes in *preferences* and to both the *income and substitution effects*. As income grows, holding wages constant, we expect more time to be devoted to producing the goods that we consume at home. However, as wages increase, holding income constant, the increase in the opportunity cost of time causes people to allocate *less* time to the household and more time to working for pay. If opportunity costs or changes in preferences have induced more people (women in particular) to seek market work and to spend less time in household work (including food preparation), we would expect the demand for convenience foods to grow.

Indeed, between 1972 and 1997—when the percentage of U.S. women who were employed rose from 44 percent to 60 percent—the number of fast-food restaurants per capita doubled, and the number of full-service restaurants per capita rose by one-third. Fast-food restaurants, in particular, serve foods that are high in caloric content, and one recent study found that the increase in the availability of these restaurants is strongly associated with increased obesity. That is, holding personal characteristics constant, the study found that the incidence of obesity increased more in areas with greater growth in restaurants per capita.

Moreover, the study also found evidence that both the income effect and the substitution effect influenced obesity in the predicted direction. Within given geographic areas and various demographic groups defined by gender, race, marital status, and education, the study found that individuals with higher family incomes—holding wages for their demographic group constant—were *less* likely to be obese. This finding is consistent with the prediction that the *income effect* induces people to spend more time at home and become less dependent on fattening convenience foods.

However, individuals in areas and groups with higher hourly wages (and hours of market work)—holding income constant—had *increased* probabilities of being obese. The latter finding suggests that as the opportunity costs of time rise, the *substitution effect* may induce people to spend less time at home and rely more on convenience foods. Indeed, a recent study finds that as workers' wages (and the cost of time) rise, they spend less time eating meals and more time "grazing" while they work, which also leads to weight gain.

Sources: Shin-Yi Chou, Michael Grossman, and Henry Saffer, "An Economic Analysis of Adult Obesity: Results from the Behavioral Risk Factor Surveillance System," *Journal of Health Economics*

23 (May 2004): 565–587; Charles J. Courtemanche, Joshua C. Pinkston, Christopher J. Ruhm, and George L. Wehby, "Can Changing Economic Factors Explain the Rise in Obesity?" *Southern Economic Journal* 82 (April 2016): 1266–1310; Hunt Allcott, Rebecca Diamond, Jean-Pierre Dubé, Jessie Handbury, Ilya Rahkovsky, and Molly Schnell, "Food Deserts and the Causes of Nutritional Inequality," *The Quarterly Journal of Economics* 134 (November 2019): 1793–1844

We must also more carefully consider the indifference curves in Figure 7.1. The slopes of these curves reflect the difficulty that Sally faces in replacing her household time with purchased goods or services. If she is performing work that is difficult to replace by purchasing goods or services, or if she derives a lot of pleasure from household production, her indifference curves will be steeply drawn—meaning that if she were to reduce her time at home, *she would have to be compensated by a large increase in income* to keep her utility constant. Steeper indifference curves, of course, create tangency points with the budget constraint that are farther to the right in Figure 7.1; thus, the steeper Sally's indifference curves, the more hours she will spend at home and the fewer hours she will supply to the labor market. If her indifference curves are steep enough, she will not even seek market work and therefore not participate in the labor force.

As Sally's children grow older, she might find that it becomes easier to substitute purchased goods or services for her household time; suitable childcare might become easier to find, for example, or daycare needs might fall when children enter school. If her indifference curves were to flatten, she would be more likely to join the labor force—and, if working for pay, more likely to work full time.

The household model, then, predicts that as time at home becomes less necessary or easier to replace with purchased goods and services, labor force participation rates and hours of paid work will rise. Historically, women have borne the primary responsibility for household production, and with inventions such as washing machines and dryers, automatic dishwashers, microwave ovens, online shopping, and electronic banking, substituting purchased goods for household time has become easier. The predictable rise in the labor force participation rates of women was seen in Table 6.1.

The ages of children also likely affect the trade-offs that parents are willing to make between household time and income. Table 7.2 provides evidence consistent with the assertion that as children grow older, the labor force participation rates of their mothers rise. Married women have a labor force participation rate of about 60 percent when an infant is in the home, but their participation rate rises to 63 percent, on average, when the child is age two. For single mothers, the increase in labor force participation is much more dramatic: The average participation rate increases from 58 percent to 75 percent as children grow from infancy to age two. The percentage of employed mothers who work full time stays relatively constant, however, when very young children are at home, although this increases slightly for single mothers.

Table 7.2 Labor Force Participation Rates and Full-Time Employment, Mothers of Young Children, by Age of Child, 2019

Age of youngest child	Labor force participation rate		Percent working full time*	
	Married (%)	Single (%)	Married (%)	Single (%)
Under 1 year	60.5	58.3	74.8	71.8
1 year	63.2	66.5	75.8	73.2
2 years	62.9	75.4	74.6	74.2

* Percentage of *employed* mothers working full time

Source: U.S. Department of Labor, Bureau of Labor Statistics, "Employment Status of Mothers with Own Children Under 3 Years Old by Single Year of Age of Youngest Child and Marital Status, 2018–2019," table 6, at www.bls.gov/news.release/famee.t06.htm

Beyond the implications for one household decision maker in a given year, the household production model produces insights about the decisions that must be made by households that have more than one decision maker. The household production model also has insights for decisions about how to allocate time over an entire lifetime, not just one year. These implications are analyzed in the following sections.

Joint Labor Supply Decisions in the Household

The models depicted in Chapter 6 and so far in this chapter have been for one decision maker, who was assumed to be trying to maximize their utility. For those who live with partners, however, some kind of *joint* decision-making process must be used to allocate the time of each and to agree on who does what in the household. This process is complicated by emotional relationships between the partners, and their decisions about market and household work can be influenced by custom.[4] Nevertheless, economic theory might help provide insights into at least some of the forces that shape the decisions that all households must make.

Just how to model the different decision-making processes that can be used by households is a question of great interest to economists. The formal models of decision-making among couples that have been developed, all of which are based on principles of utility maximization, fall into two general categories.[5] The simplest models extend the assumption of one decision maker to marriage partners, either by assuming that they both have the same preferences or by assuming that one makes all the decisions. These "unitary" models imply that couples should have the same expenditure pattern regardless of which partner receives the income. Not surprisingly, empirical work tends to reject this simple view of how household decisions are made.[6]

A second way to model a household's decision-making process is to assume a "collective" model in which the partners have their own utility functions and *bargain* over the allocation of each other's time. In these models, the power that each has in the bargaining process is seen as related to how well each person would do if the partners were unable to resolve conflict and their relationship was dissolved. These models imply that partners with greater access to resources carry more influence in family decision-making. Evidence in support of the bargaining model is growing, including the alarming fact that women with fewer economic resources of their own are more likely to be victims of domestic violence when disputes arise.[7]

Whatever process partners use to decide on the allocation of their time—and it may be different in different households—nearly all households must face certain issues. We turn now to a brief analysis of some joint decisions that affect labor supply.

Specialization of Function

Partners often find it beneficial to specialize to some extent in the work that needs to be done, both in the market and in the household. Often, one or the other partner bears primary responsibilities for meal planning, shopping, home maintenance, or child-rearing. When both work for pay, one or the other of the partners might be more available for overtime, for job-related travel, or for cutting short a workday if an emergency arises at home. What factors are weighed in deciding who specializes in what?

Theory   Consider a couple who is trying to decide which partner, if either, will take primary responsibility for child-rearing by staying at home or by taking a job that has a less-demanding schedule or a shorter commute. Because the person with primary childcare duties will probably end up spending more hours in the household, the couple needs to answer two questions: Who is *relatively* more productive at home?[8] Who is *relatively* more productive in market work?

For example, a married couple (assume, in this example, a husband and a wife) deciding whether one partner should stay home more and perform most of the child-rearing would want to consider what gains and losses are attendant on either the wife or the husband assuming this responsibility. The losses from staying home are related to the market wage of each, whereas the gains depend on their enjoyment of, and skill at, child-rearing. (Since enjoyment of the parenting process increases utility, we can designate both higher levels of enjoyment *and* higher levels of skill as indicative of greater "productivity" in child-rearing.) Wage rates for women, for reasons discussed in later chapters, typically have been below those for men. Because of socialization, wives have likely been historically more productive than husbands in child-rearing. If a given woman's wage rate is lower than her husband's and the wife is more productive in child-rearing, the family gives up less in market goods and gains more in child-rearing if she takes primary responsibility in this area.

Implications for the Future   Modeling the choice of who handles most of some household duty as influenced by relative household and market productivities is not meant to imply that customs are unimportant in shaping preferences or limiting choices concerning household production; clearly, they are. What the theory of household production emphasizes is that the distribution of household work might well change as wages, incomes, and home productivities change. One study has found that when both spouses work outside the home, the weekly hours that each spends in household work are affected by their relative wage rates. That is, as wives' wages and labor market opportunities rise, the household work done by husbands increases and the share of household work done by wives decreases.[9]

Do Both Partners Work for Pay?

Of course, one partner's specializing in household production by staying home full time is clearly not necessary. Many household chores, from lawn care to childcare, can be hired out or done with more purchased goods or services and less household time.[10] Moreover, evidence indicates that greater hours of household work actually reduce one's future wage offers, so long-term costs are associated with specializing in household work.[11]

Generally speaking, as long as an extra hour of market work by both partners creates the ability to buy more goods or services than are required to compensate for the lost hour of household time, both can enhance their resources if they work for pay during that extra hour. Put in the context of Figure 7.2, if both partners are at a point like A, increasing time in paid work by decreasing time at home from H_0 to H_1 will add more in resources (BD) than is required to compensate for the lost home time (BC).

Clearly, a steeper budget constraint (holding income constant) will tend to increase—through the substitution effect—the desirability of increased hours of market work. However, flatter indifference curves will also have this same effect, because they represent an increased willingness to trade away household hours for income (less income is required to compensate for a

Figure 7.2 Home Versus Market Productivity for a Partner

lost hour at home). We have already mentioned some forces that could lead to flatter indifference curves: inventions that allow for the easier substitution of purchased goods for household time, the reduced value of time spent at home as children age, or greater future wage penalties associated with staying at home.

Another force that could flatten the indifference curves of household partners has received some attention recently. Some assert that couples in the United States are placing a growing value on purchased goods that are *easily observed by others*, such as luxury automobiles or large homes, and less value on the commodities produced in obscurity at home (e.g., playing board games or reading with children).[12] If a growing emphasis is being placed on an individual's or a family's *relative standing* in society, and if status depends on publicly observed consumption, then the increased desire for income would flatten indifference curves and lead to more hours at paid work and fewer hours at home.[13]

The Joint Decision and Interdependent Productivity at Home

We have seen that family labor supply decisions are enhanced by considering the household and market productivities of each partner. However, one partner's productivity at home is affected by the *other* partner's labor supply to the market, making modeling the joint decision quite complex. On the one hand, if a married woman decides to increase her hours worked outside the home, her spouse's marginal productivity at home may *rise* as they take over chores that their wife once performed. Thus, in terms we have discussed earlier, a wife's increased hours of paid work could serve to make the indifference curves of her spouse's *steeper*, causing the wife's spouse to reduce their hours of paid work and increase their hours at home.

On the other hand, if the two spouses enjoy each other's company, the value that the spouse places on their time at home could be *reduced* if their wife is home less often, *flattening* the wife's spouse's indifference curves and pushing toward an increase in their hours of paid work. Theory cannot predict whether one spouse will have steeper or flatter indifference curves if the other spouse reduces time at home, and empirical work on this topic has produced no consensus.[14]

Labor Supply in Recessions: The "Discouraged" Versus the "Added" Worker

Changes in one partner's productivity, either at home or in market work, can alter the family's basic labor supply decision. Consider, for example, a "traditional" family in which market work is performed by a husband and in which his wife is employed full time in the home. What will happen if a recession causes the husband to become unemployed?

Added-Worker Effect The husband's market productivity declines, at least temporarily. The drop in his market productivity relative to his household productivity (which is unaffected by the recession) makes it more likely that the family will find his engaging in household production beneficial. If the wage that his wife can earn in paid work is not affected, the family *might* decide that to try to maintain the family's heretofore level of utility (which might be affected by both consumption and *savings* levels), *she* should seek market work and *he* should substitute for her in home production for as long as the recession lasts. He might remain a member of the labor force as an unemployed worker awaiting recall, and as she begins to look for work, she becomes an added member of the labor force. Thus, in the face of falling family income, the number of family members seeking market work might increase. This potential response is akin to the income effect, in that as family income falls, fewer commodities are consumed—and the less time spent in consumption is matched by more desired hours of work for pay.[15]

Discouraged-Worker Effect At the same time, however, we must look at the *wage rate* someone without a job can *expect* to receive if they look for work. This expected wage, denoted by $E(W)$, can actually be written as a precise statistical concept:

$$E(W) = \pi W \tag{7.1}$$

where W is the wage rate of people who have the job and π is the probability of obtaining the job if out of work. For someone without a job, the opportunity cost of staying home is $E(W)$. The reduced availability of jobs that occurs when the unemployment rate rises causes the *expected wage of those without jobs to fall* sharply, for two reasons. First, an excess of labor supply over demand tends to push down real wages (for those with jobs) during recessionary periods. Second, the chances of getting a job fall in a recession. Thus, both W and π fall in a recession, causing $E(W)$ to decline.

Noting the *substitution effect* that accompanies a falling expected wage, some have argued that people who would otherwise have been looking for work become discouraged in a recession and tend to drop out of the labor market. Looking for work has such a low expected payoff for them that they decide that spending time at home is more productive than spending time in job search. The reduction of the labor force associated with discouraged workers in a recession is a force working against the added-worker effect— just as the substitution effect works against the income effect. (As illustrated in Example 7.2, income and substitution effects can also help analyze the issue of child labor.)

Which Effect Dominates? Of course, both the added-worker and the discouraged-worker effects might coexist, because "added" workers and "discouraged" workers will be different groups of people. Which group predominates, however, is an important question. If the labor force is swollen by added workers during a recession, the published unemployment rate will likewise become swollen (the added workers will increase the number of people looking for work). If workers become discouraged and drop out of the labor market after having been unemployed, the decline in people seeking jobs will depress the unemployment rate. Knowledge of which effect predominates is needed in order to make accurate inferences about the actual state of the labor market from the published unemployment rate.

We know that the added-worker effect does exist, although it tends to be rather small. The added-worker effect is confined to the relatively few families whose sole breadwinner loses a job, and some evidence shows that it may be reduced by the presence of unemployment insurance benefits; furthermore, as more and more women become regularly employed for pay, the added-worker effect will tend to both decline and become increasingly confined to teenagers. In contrast, the fall in expected real wages occurs in nearly *every* household, and since the substitution effect is relatively strong for married women, studies have consistently found the discouraged-worker effect to be dominant.[16] Other things being equal, *the labor force tends to shrink during recessions and grow during periods of economic recovery.*

EXAMPLE 7.2
Child Labor in Poor Countries

The International Labour Organization (ILO) estimated that in 2004, 126 million children worldwide—roughly 8 percent of all children—performed work that was hazardous to their physical or educational development. Many fear that child labor is on the rise, driven by an increase in the use of low-wage labor from poor countries in the production of manufactured products sold in rich countries. What are the predictions of economic theory concerning child labor?

Household production theory views choices about household and labor market activities as functions of market wages, household productivity, and family income. One of the labor supply decisions the household must make is whether, and when, to send children into the labor force—and theory suggests that two conflicting forces have been created by the recent globalization of production.

On the one hand, the creation of manufacturing jobs in poor countries increases the earnings opportunities for their residents. If such residents choose to leave what they are currently doing and take a manufacturing job, we must assume (if their decision is voluntarily made) that they believe that they will be better off. Thus, the new job opportunities represent a wage increase, and the related *substitution effect* would tend to draw them, and possibly their children, into these jobs. While many children in these new jobs will have previously worked at either a lower-paying job or in the household (performing agricultural or craft work), others may have parents who interpret the higher wages their children can earn as an inducement to send them to work rather than to school. The decisions of this latter group of parents would *increase* the use of child labor.

On the other hand, an increase in parental earnings opportunities would create an *income effect* that could reduce the use of child labor in families. Many families are too poor to forgo the income that children can provide (the World Bank estimates that in 2001, 1.1 billion people in the world had consumption levels below $1 a day and that 2.7 billion lived on less than $2 a day). If child and adult labor are seen by parents as alternative means of providing family income, when adult earnings rise, an *income effect* is generated that could induce parents to *withdraw* their children from the labor force.

To date, two pieces of data suggest that the income effect dominates the substitution effect and that as earnings opportunities increase, parents want more leisure (or schooling) for their children. First, child labor is greatest in the poorest parts of the world—highest in Africa and Asia and lowest in Europe and North America. Second, the number of children performing hazardous work fell by 26 percent from 2002 to 2006, with the decline being largest (33 percent) for children under the age of 15. One can thus hope that as incomes grow and schooling becomes more available in poor countries, child labor will one day become a thing of the past.

Sources: Kaushik Basu, "Child Labor: Cause, Consequence, and Cure, with Remarks on International Labor Standards," *Journal of Economic Literature* 37:3 (September 1999): 1083–1119; International Labour Office, Office of the Director-General, "The End of Child Labour: Within Reach" (Report I (B), International Labour Conference, 95th Session, International Labour Office, Geneva, 2006); Shanina Amin, Shakil Quayes, and Janet M. Rives, "Are Children and Parents Substitutes or Complements in the Family Labor Supply Decision in Bangladesh?" *Journal of Developing Areas* 40 (Fall 2006): 15–37. Also see Eric V. Edmonds and Norbert Schady, "Poverty Alleviation and Child Labor," *American Economic Journal: Economic Policy* 4 (November 2012): 100–124

Hidden Unemployment The dominance of the discouraged-worker effect creates what some call the *hidden* unemployed—people who would like to work but believe that jobs are so scarce that looking for work is of no use. Because they are not looking for work, they are not counted as unemployed in government statistics. Focusing on the period from 2007 to 2009, when the overall official unemployment rate rose from 4.6 percent to 9.3 percent, can give some indication of the size of hidden unemployment.

In 2007, an average of 7.1 million people (4.6 percent of the labor force) were counted as unemployed. In addition, 369,000 people indicated that they wanted work but were not seeking it (and were, therefore, not in the labor force) because they believed that jobs were unavailable to them; this group constituted 0.5 percent of those adults not in the labor force. By 2009, some 14.3 million people (9.3 percent of the labor force) were officially counted as unemployed, but 778,000 others were among the group not seeking work, because they believed jobs were unavailable. Coinciding with reduced job opportunities, the number of "discouraged workers" had grown to 1 percent of those adults not in the labor force. If discouraged workers were counted as unemployed members of the labor force, the unemployment rate would have been 4.9 percent in 2007 and 9.7 percent by 2009; thus, while the official unemployment rate went up 4.7 percentage points, a rate that included discouraged workers would have gone up by 4.8 percentage points.[17]

Life Cycle Aspects of Labor Supply

Because market productivity (wages) and household productivity vary over the life cycle, people vary the hours that they supply to the labor market over their lives. In the early adult years, relatively fewer hours are devoted to paid work than in later years and more time is devoted to schooling. In the very late years, people fully or partially retire, although at varying ages. In the middle years (e.g., 25 to 50), we have seen that the presence of children is associated with varying hours of paid work. Although the issue of schooling is examined in depth in Chapter 9, expanding on the model of household production discussed in this chapter to include life-cycle considerations can enrich our understanding of labor supply behavior in several areas, two of which are discussed in the following sections.

The Substitution Effect and When to Work Over a Lifetime

Just as joint decisions about market and household work involve comparing market and home productivities of the two partners, deciding *when* to work over the course of one's life involves comparing market and home productivities *over time*. The basic idea here is that people tend to perform the most market work when their earning capacity is high relative to home productivity. Conversely, they engage in household production when their earning capacity is relatively low.

Suppose that a sales representative working on a commission basis knows that her potential income is around $90,000 in a certain year but that July's income potential will be twice that of November's. Would her scheduling her vacation (a time-intensive activity) in November be rational? The answer depends on her market productivity relative to her household productivity for the two months. Her market productivity (her wage rate) is higher in July than in November, which means that the opportunity costs of a vacation are greater in July. However, if she has children who are free to vacation in July but not in November, she may decide that her household productivity (in terms of utility) is so much greater in July than in November that the benefits of vacationing in July outweigh the costs. If she does not have children of school age, the utility generated by a November vacation may be sufficiently close to that of a July vacation that the smaller opportunity costs make a November vacation preferable.

Similar decisions can be made over longer periods of time, even one's entire life. As Chapter 9 shows, market productivity (reflected in the wage) starts low in the young adult years, rises rapidly with age, then levels off and even falls in the later years, as shown in panel (a) of Figure 7.3. This general pattern occurs in each of the broad educational groupings of workers, although the details of the wage trajectories differ. With an *expected* path of wages over their lives, workers can generate rough predictions of two variables critical to labor supply decisions: lifetime wealth and the costs of leisure or household time that they will face at various ages. Thus, if home

Figure 7.3 Life-Cycle Allocation of Time

productivity is more or less constant as they age, workers who make labor supply decisions by taking expected lifetime wealth into account will react to *expected* (life cycle) wage increases by unambiguously increasing their labor supply. Such wage increases raise the cost of leisure and household time but do not increase expected lifetime wealth; these wage increases, then, are accompanied only by a substitution effect.

Introducing life-cycle considerations into labor supply theory yields a prediction that the profiles of time spent at, and away from, market work will resemble those shown in panel (b) of Figure 7.3; that is, workers spend more time at paid work activities in their (relatively high-wage) middle years. Similarly, life-cycle considerations suggest that the consumption of time-intensive leisure activities occurs primarily in one's early and late years. (That travelers abroad are predominantly young adults and elderly people is clearly related to the fact that for these groups, opportunity costs of time are lower.)

If workers make labor supply decisions with the life cycle in mind, they will react differently to expected and unexpected wage changes. Expected wage changes will generate only a substitution effect, because estimates of lifetime wealth will remain unchanged (see Example 7.3). *Unexpected* wage changes, however, will cause them to revise their estimates of lifetime wealth, and these changes will be accompanied by both substitution and income effects. Empirical tests of the life-cycle model of labor supply have, as yet, provided no consensus on the importance of life-cycle considerations in the labor supply decisions of most workers.[18]

EXAMPLE 7.3

How Does Labor Supply Respond to Housing Subsidies?

As we saw in Chapter 6, Figure 6.17 (on the Earned Income Tax Credit), subsidies to families that become less generous as family income rises create two incentives to reduce work hours. First, the subsidy enhances the consumption possibilities of affected families, and it is thus accompanied by an *income effect* that reduces desired work hours. Second, if the earnings of family members rise, the subsidy is reduced; this reduction acts like a tax that reduces the wage rate, creating a *substitution effect* that also reduces desired hours of work.

In the United States, one of the largest federal subsidies to poor people comes in the form of housing vouchers, which support about two million households each year. Eligible families can present vouchers to their lessors to help pay for their rent (the lessors then turn in the vouchers to the government for reimbursement). The value of the vouchers depends on family income, where families with lower incomes receive vouchers of higher values.

Owing to budgetary limits, many more families typically apply for vouchers than can receive them. Chicago, for example, opened its housing-voucher waitlist in 1997 for the first time in 12 years, and over 82,000 income-eligible families applied for vouchers. The city randomly assigned the applicants to a waiting list and told the top 35,000 that they could expect to receive a voucher in the near future; the other 47,000 were told they would not receive one.

A study of how these Chicago housing subsidies affected labor supply found two results of interest to us in the context of this chapter. One finding was that, consistent with our analysis of both the income and substitution effects, the hours of work of able-bodied, working-age voucher recipients decreased by 6 percent after they started receiving the vouchers.

The other finding was noted among the fortunate 35,000 applicants who were told that they would receive vouchers in the future. The study found that work hours increased in the years *after* families were told that they could expect to receive a voucher but *before* they actually received one. This increase is consistent with the predictions of the life-cycle model of labor supply; that is, given their expected lifetime wealth (which was enhanced by the prospect of a housing voucher), families appear to have wanted to move their labor supply from periods when their take-home wages would be relatively low—after they received vouchers (the value of which was smaller if they earned more)—to a period when take-home wages were higher. Note that eligible families were randomly assigned to whether they received vouchers, so that the employment effects can be interpreted as causal effects of the program.

Source: Brian A. Jacob and Jens Ludwig, "The Effects of Housing Assistance on Labor Supply: Evidence from a Voucher Lottery," *American Economic Review* 102 (February 2012): 272–304

The Choice of Retirement Age

A multiyear perspective is also required to more fully model workers' retirement decisions, because *yearly* retirement benefits, expected *lifetime* benefits, and lifetime *earnings* are all influenced by the date of retirement. Yearly retirement benefits are received by retirees in the form of pension payments, usually in monthly installments; the size of these benefits is directly or indirectly related to a retiree's past earnings per year and the number of years that they worked. The total value of these promised yearly benefits over the expected remaining lifetime of the retiree is what we mean by "expected lifetime benefits." This value is obviously affected by the size of the yearly benefits and the age (and remaining life expectancy) of the retiree, but finding the value involves more than simply adding up the yearly benefits.

Summing yearly benefits over several future years must take account of the fact that over time, current sums of money can grow "automatically" with interest. For example, if the interest rate is 10 percent per year, an employer who promises to pay a worker $1,000 *this* year has undertaken a greater expense (and is thus offering something of greater value) than one who promises to pay a worker $2,000 *in 10 years.* In the former case, the employer needs to have $1,000 on hand right now, whereas in the latter case, the employer needs to set aside only $772 now (at 10 percent interest, $772 will grow into $2,000 in 10 years). Economists therefore say that $772 is the "present value" of the promised $2,000 in 10 years (at a 10 percent interest rate).[19]

In Chapter 9, we discuss how to calculate present values; for now, all you need to know is that the present value of a stream of future income is the fund that one must possess *today* to guarantee this stream in the future, given an assumed rate of interest at which the money left in the fund can be invested. For example, if a pension system promises to make payments of $10,000 per year for 17 years to a retiree, one might think that it must have funds of $170,000 now to guarantee the promised flow of payments. However, if it can invest its funds at a 2 percent yearly rate of interest, we can use a standard formula to calculate that it must have roughly $143,000 on hand *now* to guarantee the payments. It will draw down the fund by $10,000 per year, but funds that remain can be invested and generate interest of 2 percent per year, which, of course, can be used to help fund future payments. Thus, we can say that the *present* value of a stream of $10,000 payments for 17 years is $143,000 if the interest rate is 2 percent.

The purpose of this section is to explore some of the economic factors that affect the age of retirement. For the sake of illustration, we discuss the retirement incentives facing a 62-year-old man who earns, and can continue to earn, $40,000 per year, as shown in Table 7.3. To further simplify our discussion, we assume this man has no pension other than that provided by Social Security and that, for him, retirement means the cessation of all paid work.

The retirement incentives facing this worker are related to three basic factors:

1. the present value of income available to him over his remaining life expectancy if he retires now, at age 62
2. the *change* in this sum if retirement is delayed
3. preferences regarding household time and the goods one can buy with money

As we show later on, in terms of the labor supply analyses in this chapter and Chapter 6, factor 1 is analogous to nonlabor income, and factor 2 is analogous to the wage rate.

Graphing the Budget Constraint   Table 7.3 summarizes the present value now (at age 62) of pension and earned income available to our hypothetical worker at each possible retirement age, up to age 70. If the man retires at age 62, the present value of income over his remaining

Table 7.3 Assumed Social Security Benefits and Earnings for a Hypothetical Man, Age 62 (Yearly Wage = $40,000; Interest Rate = 2%; Life Expectancy = 17 Years)

Age of retirement[b]	*Present Value[a] of Remaining Lifetime:*			
	Yearly Soc. Sec. benefit ($)	**Earnings ($)**	**Soc. Sec. benefits ($)**	**Total ($)**
62	10,752	0	153,666	153,666
63	11,568	39,216	157,067	196,283
64	12,684	77,662	162,980	240,642
65	13,836	115,355	167,502	282,857
66	15,012	152,309	170,362	322,671
67	16,404	188,538	173,478	362,016
68	17,820	224,057	174,402	398,459
69	19,248	258,880	172,897	431,777
70	20,712	293,019	169,056	462,075

[a] Present values calculated as of age 62. All dollar values are as of the current year.

[b] Yearly Social Security benefits are estimated assuming that such benefits begin *in the year retirement starts*. Thus, the table ignores the fact that after a worker reaches normal retirement age (age 67 for those born after 1959), they can receive Social Security benefits before retiring; however, delaying receipt of benefits does increase their yearly levels.

life expectancy is $153,666. If he delays retirement until age 63, the present value of his remaining lifetime income rises by $42,617, to $196,283; most of this increase comes from added earnings (shown in the third column), but note that the present value of his lifetime pension benefits also rises slightly if he delays retirement (see the fourth column). Delaying retirement until age 64 would add an even greater amount to the present value of his future lifetime income—which would rise from $196,283 to $240,642. Because a later retirement age implies fewer years over which benefits will be received, whether lifetime pension benefits rise or fall with retirement age depends on how yearly pension benefits are changed with the age of retirement. In Table 7.3, the lifetime benefits shown in the fourth column increase slightly if retirement is delayed to age 68, but they fall at later ages of retirement.

    The data in the last column of Table 7.3 are presented graphically in Figure 7.4 as budget constraint *ABJ*. Segment *AB* represents the present value of lifetime income if our worker retires at age 62 and, as such, represents nonlabor income. The slope of segment *BC* represents the $42,617 increase in lifetime income (to $196,283) if retirement is delayed to age 63, and the slopes of the other segments running from points *B* to *J* similarly reflect the increases in discounted lifetime income associated with delaying retirement by a year. These slopes, therefore, represent the yearly *net wage*.

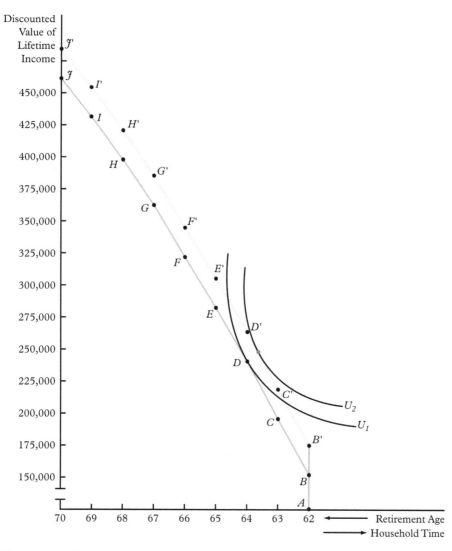

Figure 7.4 Choice of Optimum Retirement Age for Hypothetical Worker (Based on Data in Table 7.3)

Changes in the Constraint

Given preferences summarized by curve U_1, the optimum age of retirement for our hypothetical worker is age 64. How would his optimum age of retirement change if Social Security benefits were increased?[20] The answer depends on how the increases are structured. If the benefit increases were such that the same fixed amount was unexpectedly added to lifetime benefits at each retirement age, the constraint facing our 62-year-old man would shift up (and out) to ABJ'. The slopes along the segments between B' and J' would remain parallel to those along BJ; thus, an income effect with no substitution effect would occur (i.e., no change in the yearly net wage). The optimum age of retirement would be reduced, as shown in Figure 7.4.

Alternatively, if Social Security benefits were adjusted in a way that produced larger increases in the present value of lifetime benefits when retirement is deferred past age 62, point *B* would be unaffected, but the segments between *B* and the vertical axis would become more steeply sloped. The increased slope of the constraint would induce the behavior associated with a wage increase; a substitution effect would move our hypothetical worker in the direction of later retirement, but the income effect associated with greater lifetime wealth would push in the direction of earlier retirement. We do not know which effect would dominate.

Incentives to retire are also affected by economic conditions. For example, the Great Recession of 2008–2009 affected retirement-age workers along two dimensions. First, the decline in stock prices reduced the value of investment funds that workers had accumulated to finance their retirement; this reduction in the value of pension assets created an income effect that pushed these workers to delay retirement. Second, however, many older workers lost their jobs and faced lower pay if they continued working— creating a substitution effect that pushed them toward earlier retirement. Both effects have been documented in studies of how retirement ages were affected by the Great Recession.[21]

Example 7.4 describes a government pension plan during the Great Depression of the 1930s, in which both the income effect and the substitution effect also pushed workers toward earlier retirement.

EXAMPLE 7.4

Inducing Earlier Retirement in the 1930s

Well before what we in the United States know today as Social Security retirement benefits became fully phased in during the 1940s, the federal government of the United States provided funds to help states set up Old Age Assistance (OAA) programs—and by 1939, all states had an OAA program. OAA programs differed in amount by state, but all programs shared two characteristics: First, they were designed to provide retirement benefits to people over the age of 65 who had low incomes, and second, benefits were reduced by a dollar for every dollar of earnings that the recipient might make. When the program was established, therefore, the basic benefit provided to someone who qualified acted as an income effect that pushed the worker toward earlier retirement. Further, the fact that benefits were reduced by a dollar for each dollar of recipients' earnings served to reduce their effective wage rate to zero—which also pushed recipients toward earlier retirement. In effect, then, the OAA programs adopted by states created a budget constraint similar to the welfare constraint shown earlier in Figure 6.14.

Given our theory of how income and substitution effects act on the age at which workers choose to retire, a study of the effects of the OAA programs in the 1930s, unsurprisingly, found that these programs induced many 65- to 74-year-old men to retire—and the largest effects occurred in the states with more-generous retirement benefits. Indeed, the study found that the OAA programs accounted for over half of the decline in the labor force participation rate of older men in the 1930s.

Source: Daniel K. Fetter and Lee M. Lockwood, "Government Old-Age Support and Labor Supply: Evidence from the Old Age Assistance Program," *American Economic Review* 108 (August 2018): 2174–2211

Perhaps in part because firms might now want experienced workers to stay longer, many private sector pension plans have been changed so that benefits for early retirement have been reduced and the additions to the value of lifetime pension benefits if retirement is delayed have grown larger. In terms of Figure 7.4, reducing the benefits associated with early retirement cuts the height of AB' to below AB, which tends to move the entire constraint down and to the left; workers' lifetime wealth tends to fall, and an income effect pushes them toward later retirement. Increases in the present value of lifetime pension benefits that are associated with later retirement increases the slope of BJ', creating a substitution effect (by increasing the opportunity cost of retiring a year earlier) that also works in the direction of later retirement.[22]

A complete analysis of the retirement decision, of course, must also take account of preferences for household production. Research has found, for example, that those who work for pay engage in more household work activities and have fewer hours of leisure than people who do not work for pay. Furthermore, it found that older people engage in both household work and leisure at different times of the day than they did when younger. Taken together, the study suggests that retirement decisions are affected if the demand for leisure rises with age and suggests that allowing older workers to have phased retirement (part-time work for a few years) or flexible scheduling might be a better way to increase retirement ages than changing pension formulas.[23]

Policy Application: Childcare and Labor Supply

For many families, a critical element of what we have called household production is the supervision and nurturing of children. Most parents are concerned about providing their children with quality care, whether this care is produced mostly in the household or is purchased to a great extent outside the home. Society at large also has a stake in the quality of care that parents provide for their children. Such programs take many forms, from tax credits for childcare services purchased by working parents to governmental subsidies for daycare, school lunches, and healthcare. The purpose of this section is to consider the labor market implications of programs to support the care of children.

Childcare Subsidies

Roughly half of U.S. children under age five are cared for by paid providers of childcare, and on average, childcare costs represent 10 percent of family income—although that percentage increases as family earnings fall.[24] Childcare costs obviously rise with the hours of care, but part of these costs appear to be fixed: One study found that childcare costs per hour of work were three times greater for women who worked fewer than 10 hours per week than for those who worked more.[25] Over the past two decades, however,

federal spending on childcare subsidies has more than doubled, and the purpose of this section is to analyze the effects of these greater subsidies on the
labor supply of parents.

Reducing the Fixed Costs of Care   Suppose for a moment
that childcare costs are purely fixed, so that without a subsidy, working parents must pay a certain amount per day no matter how many hours their
children are in care. Figures 7.5 and 7.6 illustrate how a subsidy that covers
the entire cost of childcare affects the labor supply incentives of a mother
who has daily unearned income equal to *ab*.[26]

Consider first the case of a mother who is not now working (Figure 7.5). If she decides to work, she must choose from points along the
line *cd*, where the distance *bc* represents the fixed costs of childcare. The
slope of *cd*, of course, represents her wage rate. Given her preferences and
the constraint depicted in Figure 7.5, this woman receives more utility
from not working (at point *b*) than she would from working (point *X*). If
the fixed cost were reduced to zero by a childcare subsidy, such that her
constraint were now *abe*, her utility would be maximized at point *Y* on
curve U_3 and she would now find it beneficial to work. *Thus, childcare subsidies that reduce or remove the fixed cost of childcare encourage work among
those previously out of the labor force.* (Such subsidies do not guarantee that
all those out of the labor force would now join it, because some people
would have such steep indifference curves that work would still not maximize utility.)

Now, consider the case represented in Figure 7.6 of a woman who is
already working when the subsidy is adopted. Before the subsidy, her utility
was maximized at point X' on indifference curve U'_1, a point at which H'_1
hours are worked. When the subsidy generates the constraint *abe*, her utility

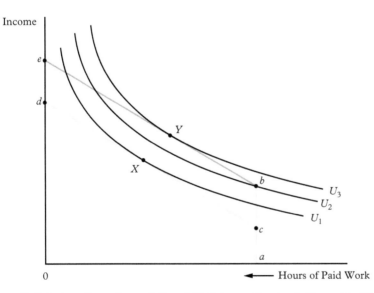

**Figure 7.5 Labor Supply and Fixed Childcare Costs: A Parent Initially
out of the Labor Force**

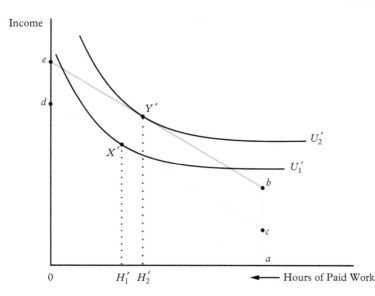

Figure 7.6 Labor Supply and Fixed Childcare Costs: A Parent Initially Working for Pay

is then maximized at point Y' (on U_2'), and she will reduce her hours of work to H_2'. *Thus, for those already working, removing the fixed cost of childcare has a pure income effect that pushes them toward fewer hours of work.* (Note, however, that the woman depicted in Figure 7.6 remains in the labor force.)

Reducing the Hourly Costs of Care Now, let us take a case in which the costs of childcare are purely hourly and have no fixed component. If such costs, say, are $5 per hour, they simply reduce the hourly take-home wage rate of a working parent by $5. If a government subsidy were to reduce the childcare costs to zero, the parent would experience an increase in the take-home wage, and the labor supply effects would be those of a wage increase. For those already working, the subsidy would create an income effect and a substitution effect that work in opposite directions on the desired hours of work. For those not in the labor force, the increased take-home wage would make their joining the labor force more likely (the substitution effect dominates in participation decisions).

Observed Responses to Childcare Subsidies Our analysis here suggests that childcare subsidies, which in actuality reduce *both* the fixed and the hourly cost of care, would have a theoretically ambiguous effect on the hours of work among those already in the labor force. The effect on labor force participation, however, is theoretically clear: Childcare subsidies should increase the labor force participation rates among parents, especially mothers. Empirical studies of the relationship between childcare costs and labor force participation are consistent with this latter prediction: When costs go down, labor force participation goes up. Furthermore, the greatest increases appear to be among those with the lowest incomes.[27]

Child Support Assurance

The vast majority of children who live in poor households have an absent parent. The federal government has taken several steps to ensure, for families receiving public assistance, that absent parents contribute adequately to their children's upbringing. Greater efforts to collect child support payments are restricted in their effectiveness by the lack of resources among some absent parents, deliberate noncompliance by others, and the lack of court-awarded child support obligations in many more cases of divorce. To enhance the resources of single-parent families, some have proposed the creation of child support assurance programs. The essential feature of these programs is a guaranteed child support benefit that would be paid by the government to the custodial parent in the event that the absent parent does not make payments. If the absent parent makes only a portion of the required support payment, the government would make up the remainder.

A critical question to ask about such a program is how it would affect the labor supply of custodial parents. The answer provided by economic theory is not completely straightforward. Consider a single mother who has two options for supporting herself and her children. One option is to work outside the home with no support from the absent father or from the government system. In Figure 7.7, we assume that the budget constraint provided by this option can be graphed as *AB*, which has a slope that represents her wage rate. The mother's other option is to apply for assistance benefits, which we assume would guarantee her an income of *AC*. Recall from Chapter 6 that these payments are typically calculated by subtracting from a family's "needed" level of income (*AC*) its actual income from other sources,

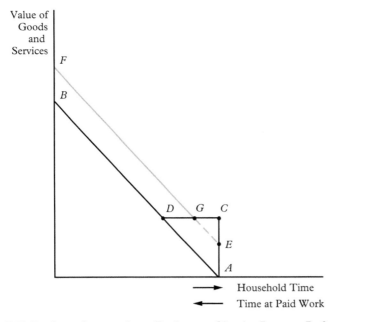

Figure 7.7 Budget Constraints Facing a Single Parent Before and After a Child Support Assurance Program Is Adopted

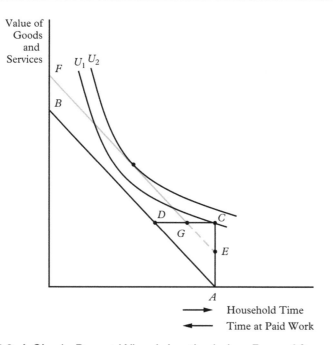

Figure 7.8 A Single Parent Who Joins the Labor Force After a Child Support Assurance Program Is Adopted

including earnings. Thus, the budget constraint is *ACDB*, and segment *CD* reflects a take-home wage rate equal to zero.

If the mother's indifference curves are steeply sloped (meaning, of course, that she is less able or less willing to substitute for her time at home), her utility is maximized at point *C*; she applies for government benefits and does not work for pay. If her utility curves are relatively flat, her utility is maximized along segment *DB*, and in this case, she works for pay and does not rely on government benefits to supplement her income.

Suppose that a child support assurance program is adopted that guarantees support payments of *AE* to the mother, regardless of her income. If she works, the effect of the new program would be to add the amount *AE* (= *BF*) to her earnings. If she does not work and remains on government assistance, her *welfare* benefits are reduced by *AE*; thus, her child support benefits *plus* her welfare benefits continue to equal *AC*. After the child support assurance program is implemented, her budget constraint is *ACGF*.[28]

How will the new child support programs affect the mother's time in the household and her hours of paid work? This scenario has three possibilities. First, some mothers will have utility functions so steeply sloped that they will remain out of the labor force and spend all their time in the household (they will remain at point *C* in Figure 7.7). These mothers would receive child support payments of *AE* and welfare benefits equal to *EC*.

Second, for those who worked for pay before and were therefore along segment *DB*, the new program produces a pure income effect. These mothers will continue to work for pay, but their utility is now maximized along *GF*, and they can be expected to reduce their desired hours of work outside the home.

Third, some women, like the one whose isoquants (U_1 and U_2) are shown in Figure 7.8, will move from being on welfare to seeking paid work; for these women, the supply of labor to market work increases. These women formerly maximized utility at point *C*, but the new possibility of working *and* still being able to receive an income subsidy now places their utility-maximizing hours of paid work along segment *GF*.

On balance, then, the hypothetical child support assurance program discussed earlier can be expected to *increase the labor force participation rate* among single mothers (and thus reduce the number on welfare) while *reducing the desired hours of paid work* among those who take jobs. Studies that analyze the labor market effects of child support payments (from absent fathers) have found that the labor supply responses among single mothers are consistent with theoretical expectations.[29]

EMPIRICAL STUDY 7.1

THE EFFECTS OF WAGE INCREASES ON LABOR SUPPLY (AND SLEEP): TIME-USE DIARY DATA AND SAMPLE SELECTION BIAS

We have seen that the expected effects of a wage increase on labor supply are theoretically ambiguous; if the substitution effect dominates, the effect will be to increase desired hours of work, but if the income effect dominates, desired hours will decrease. How labor supply would be affected by wage increases associated with, say, income-tax rate reductions is therefore a question that must be answered empirically—and the research in this area must contend with problems of measuring both hours of work and the wage rate.

Hours of work in studies of labor supply are typically measured through household surveys, which ask workers how many hours they worked "last week." The answers given by workers to this question are somewhat suspect. Whereas those who are paid by the hour have reason to keep careful track of their weekly work hours, salaried workers do not, and many are therefore inclined to give the easy answer of "40." Indeed, when work hours derived from these household surveys are compared to work hours derived from *diary* studies (which are more expensive to collect, because they ask workers in detail about how they used time in the past 24 hours), we find substantial differences. For example, whereas data from household surveys imply that, for men, weekly hours at work fell by 2.7 percent from 1965 to 1981, diary studies suggest the decline was in fact 13.5 percent.[a]

Measuring wage rates is problematic, for two reasons. First, the hourly "wage" for salaried workers is conventionally calculated by dividing their "earnings last week" by their own estimate of how many hours they worked. If they overstate their hours of work, their calculated wage is then understated—and the lower calculated wage is thus associated negatively (and spuriously) with the overstated hours of work. Understating their work hours creates the opposite bias.

Second, those who are not working do not have an observable wage rate. Should we just drop them from the sample and focus our analysis on those for whom a wage is observed? We cannot simply exclude those not in the labor force from our study of labor supply. Theory suggests that potential workers compare their wage offers to their reservation wages, and if offers lie below the reservation wage, they decide not to work. The statistical methods that we use to analyze data rely on their being randomly generated, and dropping those who are not working (either because they have unusually high reservation wages or unusually low wage rates) would make the sample nonrandom, by introducing the element of what economists call sample selection bias.

If those not in the labor force must be in our analysis, what is the appropriate wage to use for them? Surely, they could earn *something* if they worked, so their potential wage is not zero—it simply is not observed. Because we do not directly observe reservation wages or wage offers, we must use statistical methods to *impute* a wage for those not in the labor force. Fortunately, techniques for dealing with this imputation problem have been developed, and one is illustrated in the study to be described.

An interesting use of diary-derived data can be seen in a study that analyzed how wages affect sleep, nonmarket (leisure plus household work) time, and labor supply. The diary data address the accuracy problems noted earlier in estimating hours of work (the dependent variable when analyzing labor supply). *Wages* for employed people were conventionally measured and statistically related to their personal characteristics, such as education, union status, and place of residence; this statistical relationship was then used to *predict* wages for everyone in the sample, including those not in the labor force.

When the researchers used regression techniques to relate hours of work to predicted wages, they found that increased wages *reduced* the labor supply of men—but so slightly that the effect was essentially zero. Thus, for men, the results imply that the income effect and substitution effect are essentially of equal strength and cancel each other out. For women, the substitution effect dominated, where a 10 percent increase in wages was associated with a 2 percent *increase* in hours of work. (Interestingly, higher wages were associated with men's spending *more* time in nonmarket activities—presumably leisure—while they led to women's spending less time in such activities. Higher wages led to less sleep for both men and women, but these effects were small.)

[a] F. Thomas Juster and Frank P. Stafford, "The Allocation of Time: Empirical Findings, Behavioral Models, and Problems of Measurement," *Journal of Economic Literature* 29 (June 1991): 494.

Source: Jeff E. Biddle and Daniel S. Hamermesh, "Sleep and the Allocation of Time," *Journal of Political Economy* 98:5, pt. 1 (October 1990): 922–943

Review Questions

1. Suppose that 5 percent unemployment is defined as "full employment" but that current unemployment is 7 percent. Suppose further that we use the information in Table 7R.1.

Table 7R.1 Assumed Labor Force, Employment and Unemployment

Unemployment Rate (%)	Labor Force	Unemployment	Employment
5	6,000	300	5,700
7	5,600	392	5,208

   a. What is the amount of "hidden" unemployment when the unemployment rate is 7 percent?

   b. If the population is 10,000, what change occurs in the participation rate as a result of the marginal change in the unemployment rate?

   c. What is the economic significance of hidden unemployment? Should measured and hidden unemployment be added to obtain a "total unemployment" figure?

2. A study of the labor force participation rates of women in the post–World War II period noted the following:

   > Over the long run, women have joined the paid labor force because of a series of changes affecting the nature of work. Primary among these was the rise of the clerical and professional sectors, the increased education of women, laborsaving advances in households, declining fertility rates, and increased urbanization.

   Relate each of these factors to the household production model of labor supply outlined in this chapter.

3. In a debate in the 1976 U.S. presidential campaign, candidate Jimmy Carter argued,

   > While it is true that much of the recent rise in employment is due to the entrance of married women and teenagers into the labor force, this influx of people into the labor force is itself a sign of economic decay. The reason these people are now seeking work is because the primary breadwinner in the family is out of work and extra workers are needed to maintain the family income.

   Comment on this quote.

4. Is the following statement true, false, or uncertain? Why? "If a married woman's husband gets a raise, she tends to work less, but if *she* gets a raise, she tends to work more."

5. Suppose daycare centers charge working parents for each hour their children spend at the centers (no fixed costs of care). Suppose, too,

that the federal government passes subsidy legislation so that the hourly cost per child now borne by the parents is cut in half. Would this policy cause an increase in the labor supply of parents with small children?

6. Assume that a state government currently provides no childcare subsidies to working single parents, but it now wants to adopt a plan that will encourage labor force participation among single parents. Suppose that childcare costs are hourly, and suppose that the government adopts a childcare subsidy that pays $3 per hour for each hour the parent works, up to eight hours per day. Draw a current budget constraint (net of childcare costs) for an assumed single mother and then draw in the new constraint. Discuss the likely effects on labor force participation and hours of work.

7. Suppose that as the ratio of the working population to the retired population continues to fall, the voters approve a change in the way Social Security benefits are calculated—a way that effectively cuts every retired person's benefits in half. This change affects all those in the population, no matter what their age or current retirement status, and it is accompanied by a 50 percent reduction in payroll taxes. What would be the labor supply effects on those workers who are close to the typical age of retirement (62 to 65)? What would be the labor supply effects on those workers just beginning their careers (e.g., workers in their 20s)?

8. A state government wants to provide incentives for single parents to enter the labor market and become employed. It is considering a policy of paying single parents of children under age 18 $20 per day if the parent works at least six hours a day, five days a week. Draw an assumed current daily budget constraint for a single parent, and then draw in the constraint that would be created by the $20 subsidy. Discuss the likely effects on labor force participation and hours of work.

9. Teenagers under age 18 in New York state are prohibited from working more than eight hours a day, except if they work as golf caddies, babysitters, or farmworkers. Consider a 16-year-old whose primary household work in the summer is studying for college entrance exams and practicing a musical instrument but who also has two options for paid work. She can work for $6 per hour with a catering service (limited to eight hours per day) or work for $5 per hour as a babysitter (with no limitations on hours worked).

    a. First, draw the daily budget constraints for each of her paid-work options (assume that she can work either for the catering service or as a babysitter but cannot do both).

    b. Next, analyze the possible labor supply decisions that this 16-year-old can make, including the effects of the state law restricting most paid work to eight hours a day.

10. Assume that a state government currently provides no childcare subsidies to working single parents, but it now wants to adopt a plan that will

encourage labor force participation among single parents. Suppose that childcare costs are hourly and that the government adopts a childcare subsidy of $4 per hour if the single parent works four or more hours per day. Draw the current daily budget constraint (assume a wage that is net of the hourly childcare costs) for a single mother, and then draw in the new constraint. Discuss the likely effects on labor force participation and hours of work.

11. Company X has for some time hired skilled technicians on one-year contracts to work at a remote location. It offers a $10,000 signing bonus and an hourly wage rate of $20 per hour. Company Y now enters the market and offers no signing bonus but offers an hourly wage of $25. Both companies want to attract workers who will work longer than 2,000 hours during the year (all hours are paid at the straight-time wage rate given earlier).

   a. First, suppose that workers receive offers from both companies; on the same graph, draw the income-household time ("budget") constraints for the coming year under both offers. (Clearly label which is company X and which is company Y.)

   b. Second, consider a worker for company X who chose to work 2,500 hours last year. Suppose that her contract is up and that she now has offers from both company X and company Y. Can we tell which offer she will choose, assuming that her preferences for income and household time have not changed? Explain (or demonstrate). If she changes companies, will she continue to work 2,500 hours, or will she increase hours or reduce them? Explain fully.

Problems

1. Table 7P.1 gives information for 2018 and 2019 on the thousands of people who are in the labor force, the thousands of people who are defined as unemployed, and the thousands of people not in the labor force because they believe that no job is available. The latter group consists of "discouraged" workers, and some regard them as the *hidden* unemployed (they have searched for work in the past and are available to work, but they believe jobs are so scarce that looking for work is of no use).

Table 7P.1 Labor Force, Unemployment, and Discouraged Workers 2018 and 2019 (in thousands)

Date	Number in labor force	Number unemployed	Number discouraged
2018	155,761	6,314	423
2019	157,538	6,001	392

Source: Bureau of Labor Statistics, U.S. Department of Labor, Current Population Survey (CPS), Tables A-1 and A-13

    a. Calculate the officially defined unemployment rates for 2018 and 2019. What is the change in the unemployment rate from 2018 to 2019?

    b. Calculate unofficial unemployment rates that include the hidden unemployed for both dates. What is the change in this unemployment rate from 2018 to 2019?

    c. If the officially defined unemployment rate is falling, what effect would you expect this to have on the number of discouraged workers? How has the change in the number of discouraged workers affected the change in the officially defined unemployment rate from 2018 to 2019?

2. Suppose that a single parent can work up to 16 hours per day at a wage rate of $10 per hour. Various income maintenance programs have been developed to assure a minimum level of income for low-income families. Aid to Families with Dependent Children (AFDC) was established with the Social Security Act of 1935. The family was given an income subsidy depending on family size. Under this program, the family's benefit was reduced by $1 for every dollar earned. Suppose that the maximum daily subsidy for the single parent described in this problem is $40.

    a. Draw the daily budget constraint without program participation for the single parent described in this problem.

    b. On the same graph, draw the daily budget constraint under AFDC for the single parent described in this problem.

    c. What effect does this program have on the incentive to work? Explain.

3. The following figure gives two daily budget constraints for a low-income individual. One budget line is the one in which the individual, who can work up to 16 hours per day, receives no subsidy from the government.

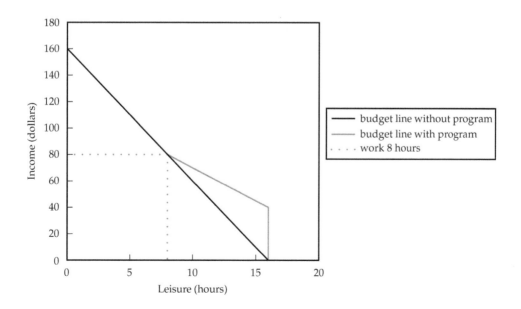

The other budget line represents participation in an income maintenance program that offers a no-work benefit and phases out this subsidy as earnings increase.

a. What is the individual's wage rate if they don't participate in the program?

b. What is the program's no-work benefit? What is the effective wage rate when participating in the program?

c. If, absent the subsidy program, the individual had chosen to work fewer than eight hours per day, would she be better off participating in the program or not participating? If the individual had chosen to work more than eight hours per day, would she be better off participating in the program or not participating?

d. What will be the labor supply response for an individual who had chosen to work eight hours before the program is implemented and now qualifies for the program?

4. Suppose that a single parent can work up to 16 hours per day at a wage rate of $10 per hour. Various income maintenance programs have been developed to assure a minimum level of income for low-income families, such as AFDC (see problem 2). One of the problems with AFDC is that benefits were reduced by $1 for every dollar earned. An alternative income maintenance program is Temporary Assistance for Needy Families (TANF), which also offers a no-work benefit but has a smaller reduction in wages for every dollar earned. A simplified version of this type of program is one that would give this single parent a $40 (no-work) grant, accompanied by a benefit reduction of 75 cents for every dollar earned.

a. Draw the daily budget constraint without any program participation for the single parent described in this problem.

b. On the same graph, draw the daily budget constraint under TANF for the single parent described in this problem. At what level of income does the subsidy end? How many hours of work would this be? Discuss the effect of program participation on work incentives.

c. On the same graph, draw the daily budget constraint under AFDC for the single parent described in problem 2.

d. Compare the effect of the TANF program on work incentives against the effect of the AFDC program on work incentives.

Notes

1. A study of those who lost their jobs during the Great Recession of 2008–2010 found that both household work hours and (especially) leisure hours increased; see Mark Aguiar, Erik Hurst and Loukas Karabarbounis, "Time Use During the Great Recession," *American Economic Review* 103 (August 2013): 1664–1696. Another study suggests that

high-earning workers with low leisure hours are moving closer to their jobs in an attempt to reduce commuting times; see Lena Edlund, Cecilia Machado, and Maria Micaela Sviatschi, "Bright Minds, Big Rent: Gentrification and the Rising Returns to Skill" (Working Paper No. 21729, National Bureau of Economic Research, Cambridge, MA, November 2015).

2. As mentioned in Chapter 6, income represents the goods or services that Sally is able to purchase, given the fixed level of prices for these goods or services.

3. See Francine D. Blau, Marianne A. Ferber, and Anne E. Winkler, *The Economics of Women, Men, and Work*, 7th ed. (Boston: Pearson Education, Inc., 2014); Shelly Lundberg and Robert A. Pollak, "The American Family and Family Economics," *Journal of Economic Perspectives* 21 (Spring 2007): 3–26, for works that summarize economic analyses of fertility, child-rearing, and other important decisions made by households. For studies that analyze the trade-offs between market work and household work, see Alexander M. Gelber and Joshua W. Mitchell, "Taxes and Time Allocation: Evidence from Single Women and Men," *Review of Economic Studies* 79 (July 2012): 863–897; Richard Rogerson, "Structural Transformation and the Deterioration of European Labor Market Outcomes," *Journal of Political Economy* 116 (April 2008): 235–259; Alexander Bick and Nicola Fuchs-Schündeln, "Taxation and Labour Supply of Married Couples Across Countries: A Macroeconomic Analysis," *Review of Economic Studies* 85:3 (July 2018): 1543–1576.

4. See Julie A. Nelson, "I, Thou, and Them: Capabilities, Altruism, and Norms in the Economics of Marriage," *American Economic Review* 84 (May 1994): 126–131; Claire Brown, "An Institutional Model of Wives' Work Decisions," *Industrial Relations* 24 (Spring 1985): 182–204.

5. See Shelly Lundberg and Robert A. Pollak, "Bargaining and Distribution in Marriage," *Journal of Economic Perspectives* 10 (Fall 1996): 139–158; Marianne Bertrand, Emir Kamenica, and Jessica Pan, "Gender Identity and Relative Income Within Households," *Quarterly Journal of Economics* 130 (May 2015): 571–614.

6. Francine D. Blau, Marianne A. Ferber, and Anne E. Winkler, *The Economics of Women, Men, and Work*, 49.

7. Richard Blundell, Pierre-Andre Chiappori, and Costas Meghir, "Collective Labor Supply with Children," *Journal of Political Economy* 113 (December 2005): 1277–1306; Lauren Cherchye, Bram De Rock, and Frederic Vermeulen, "Married with Children: A Collective Labor Supply Model with Detailed Time Use and Intrahousehold Expenditure Information," *American Economic Review* 102 (December 2012): 3377–3405; Anna Aizer, "The Gender Wage Gap and Domestic Violence," *American Economic Review* 100 (September 2010): 1847–1859; Shalini Roy, Melissa Hidrobo, John Hoddinott, and Akhter Ahmed, "Transfers, Behavior Change, Communication, and Intimate Partner

Violence: Postprogram Evidence from Rural Bangladesh," *The Review of Economics and Statistics* 101 (December 2019): 865–877.

8. The point here is relative advantage and not absolute advantage. One partner might actually be more productive in the market *and* at home than the other partner, but what matters is relative advantage.

9. Joni Hersch and Leslie S. Stratton, "Housework, Wages, and the Division of Household Time for Employed Spouses," *American Economic Review* 84 (May 1994): 120–125; Marianne Bertrand, Claudia Goldin, and Lawrence F. Katz, "Dynamics of the Gender Gap for Young Professionals in the Financial and Corporate Sectors," *American Economic Journal: Applied Economics* 2 (July 2010): 228–255; James Feyrer, Bruce Sacerdote, and Ariel Dora Stern, "Will the Stork Return to Europe and Japan? Understanding Fertility within Developed Nations," *Journal of Economic Perspectives* 22 (Summer 2008): 3–22. For an international view see Christina Boll and Elisabeth Bublitz, "A Cross-Country Comparison of Gender Differences in Job-Related Training: The Role of Working Hours and the Household Context," *British Journal of Industrial Relations* 56 (September 2018): 503–555.

10. Evidence shows, for example, that the influx of low-skilled immigrants— who can perform such household chores as cleaning and childcare— increases the hours of market work performed by high-skilled women; see Patricia Cortés and José Tessada, "Low-Skilled Immigration and the Labor Supply of Highly Skilled Women," *American Economic Journal: Applied Economics* 3 (July 2011): 88–123.

11. Joni Hersch and Leslie S. Stratton, "Housework and Wages," *Journal of Human Resources* 37 (Winter 2002): 217–229; Elizabeth Ty Wilde, Lily Batchelder, and David T. Ellwood, "The Mommy Track Divides: The Impact of Childbearing on Wages of Women of Differing Skill Levels" (Working Paper No. 16582, National Bureau of Economic Research, Cambridge, MA, December 2010).

12. Robert H. Frank, *Luxury Fever: Why Money Fails to Satisfy in an Era of Excess* (New York: The Free Press, 1999).

13. David Neumark and Andrew Postlewaite, "Relative Income Concerns and the Rise in Married Women's Employment," *Journal of Public Economics* 70 (October 1998): 157–183, offers an example of an attempt to analyze whether *status* concerns drive women to increased work for pay.

14. For papers on this topic, see Dominique Goux, Eric Maurin, and Barbara Petrongolo, "Worktime Regulations and Spousal Labor Supply," *American Economic Review* 104 (January 2014): 252–276; Melissa A. Boyle and Joanna N. Lahey, "Spousal Labor Market Effects from Government Health Insurance: Evidence from a Veterans Affairs Expansion," *Journal of Health Economics* 45 (2016): 63–76; David Autor, Andreas Kostøl, Magne Mogstad, and Bradley Setzler, "Disability Benefits, Consumption Insurance, and Household Labor Supply," *American Economic Review* 109 (July 2019): 2613–2654.

15. For a recent study on the "added-worker effect," see Richard Blundell, Luigi Pistaferri, and Itay Saporta-Eksten, "Consumption Inequality and Family Labor Supply," *American Economic Review* 106 (February 2016): 387–435.

16. T. Aldrich Finegan, Roberto V. Peñaloza, and Mototsugu Shintani, "Reassessing Cyclical Changes in Workers' Labor Market Status: Gross Flows and the Types of Workers Who Determine Them," *Industrial and Labor Relations Review* 61 (January 2008): 244–257; Catalina Amuedo-Dorantes and Jean Kimmel, "Moonlighting Over the Business Cycle," *Economic Inquiry* 47 (October 2009): 754–765; Michael Elsby, Bart Hobijn, Fatih Karahan, Gizem Koşar Ayşegül Şahin, "Flow Origins of Labor Force Participation Fluctuations," *American Economic Association Papers and Proceedings* 109 (May 2019): 461–464; also see Melvin Stephens Jr., "Worker Displacement and the Added Worker Effect," *Journal of Labor Economics* 20 (July 2002): 504–537; Paul Bingley and Ian Walker, "Household Unemployment and the Labour Supply of Married Women," *Economica* 68 (May 2001): 157–185; Hans G. Bloemen, "Job Search, Search Intensity, and Labor Market Transitions: An Empirical Analysis," *Journal of Human Resources* 40 (Winter 2005): 231–269; see Alan B. Krueger, Judd Cramer, and David Cho, "Are the Long-Term Unemployed on the Margins of the Labor Market?" *Brookings Papers on Economic Activity* (Spring 2014): 229–280, for a study of recession-related labor-force withdrawal and the re-entry of unemployed people.

17. To say that including discouraged workers would change the published unemployment rate does not imply that it *should* be done. For a summary of the arguments for and against counting discouraged workers as unemployed, see the final report of the National Commission on Employment and Unemployment Statistics, *Counting the Labor Force* (Washington, DC: NCEUS, 1979): 44–49.

18. See Michael Keane and Richard Rogerson, "Micro and Macro Labor Supply Elasticities: A Reassessment of Conventional Wisdom," *Journal of Economic Literature* 50 (June 2012): 464–476; Richard Rogerson and Johanna Wallenius, "Nonconvexities, Retirement, and the Elasticity of Labor Supply," *American Economic Review* 103 (June 2013): 1445–1462; Blundell, Pistaferri, and Saporta-Eksten, "Consumption Inequality and Family Labor Supply"; John C. Ham and Kevin T. Reilly, "Testing Intertemporal Substitution, Implicit Contracts, and Hours Restriction Models of the Labor Market Using Micro Data," *American Economic Review* 92 (September 2002): 905–927.

19. This is easily calculated as $2,000 \div (1.1)^{10} = 772$.

20. The analysis in this section borrows heavily from Olivia S. Mitchell and Gary S. Fields, "The Effects of Pensions and Earnings on Retirement: A Review Essay," in *Research in Labor Economics*, vol. 5, ed. Ronald G. Ehrenberg (Greenwich, CT: JAI Press, 1982): 115–155.

21. Courtney C. Coile and Phillip B. Levine, "Recessions, Retirement, and Social Security," *American Economic Review* 101 (2011); Gopi Shah Godi, John B. Shoven, and Sita Nataraj Slavov, "What Explains Changes in Retirement Plans during the Great Recession?" *American Economic Review: Papers and Proceedings* 101 (May 2011): 23–34.

22. Leora Friedberg and Anthony Webb, "Retirement and the Evolution of Pension Structure," *Journal of Human Resources* 40 (Spring 2005): 281–308. The income and substitution effects of the described changes to private sector pensions clearly work in the same direction for earlier ages of retirement; however, if the increased slope of $B'J'$ is steep enough, the new constraint might cross the old one at later ages of retirement and create a zone in the new constraint that lies to the northeast of the original one. In this new zone, the substitution effect associated with the increased slope of $B'J'$ would be at least partially offset by an income effect that pushes toward earlier retirement—so the ultimate effect on retirement age in this zone is ambiguous. For other economic analyses of retirement, see Richard Disney and Sarah Smith, "The Labour Supply Effect of the Abolition of the Earnings Rule for Older Workers in the United Kingdom," *Economic Journal* 112 (March 2002): 136–152; Jonathan Gruber and David A. Wise, eds., *Social Security Programs and Retirement Around the World: Micro-estimation*, NBER Conference Report Series (Chicago: University of Chicago Press, 2004); Jeffrey B. Liebman, Erzo F.P. Luttmer, and David G. Seif, "Labor Supply Responses to Marginal Social Security Benefits: Evidence from Discontinuities," *Journal of Public Economics* 93 (December 2009): 1208–1223.

23. Daniel S. Hamermesh and Stephen Donald, "The Time and Timing Costs of Market Work" (Working Paper No. 13127, National Bureau of Economic Research, May 2007).

24. U.S. Census Bureau, "Who's Minding the Kids? Child Care Arrangements: Spring 2011," Table 6, www.census.gov/prod/2013pubs/p70-135.pdf; also see Patricia M. Anderson and Phillip B. Levine, "Child Care and Mothers' Employment Decisions," in *Finding Jobs: Work and Welfare Reform*, eds. David E. Card and Rebecca M. Blank (New York: Russell Sage Foundation, 2000): 426.

25. David C. Ribar, "A Structural Model of Child Care and the Labor Supply of Married Women," *Journal of Labor Economics* 13 (July 1995): 558–597.

26. Note that an important assumption in this example is that she has non-labor income. This income could come, for example, from a partner who is working or from a government subsidy.

27. See Anderson and Levine, "Child Care and Mothers' Employment Decisions," for a summary of empirical work on how the cost of child care affects mothers' decisions to work. For a more recent publication, see Erdal Tekin, "Child-Care Subsidies, Wages, and Employment of Single Mothers," *Journal of Human Resources* 42 (Spring 2007): 453–487;

Pierre Lefebvre and Philip Merrigan, "Child-Care Policy and the Labor Supply of Mothers with Young Children: A Natural Experiment from Canada," *Journal of Labor Economics* 26 (July 2008): 519–548. Francine Blau and Lawrence Kahn, "Female Labor Supply: Why is the U.S. Falling Behind?" *American Economic Review Papers and Proceedings* 103 (May 2013): 251–256, finds that women's labor force participation rates are rising faster in Europe than in the United States because "family-friendly" policies are expanding faster in Europe.

28. Irwin Garfinkel, Philip K. Robins, Pat Wong, and Daniel R. Meyer, "The Wisconsin Child Support Assurance System: Estimated Effects on Poverty, Labor Supply, Caseloads, and Costs," *Journal of Human Resources* 25 (Winter 1990): 1–31.

29. John W. Graham and Andrea H. Beller, "The Effect of Child Support Payments on the Labor Supply of Female Family Heads," *Journal of Human Resources* 24 (Fall 1989): 664–688; Wei-Yin Hu, "Child Support, Welfare Dependency, and Women's Labor Supply," *Journal of Human Resources* 34 (Winter 1999): 71–103.

Selected Readings

Becker, Gary S. "A Theory of the Allocation of Time." *Economic Journal* 75 (September 1965): 493–517.

Becker, Gary S. *A Treatise on the Family*. Cambridge, MA: Harvard University Press, 1991.

Blau, David M., and V. Joseph Hotz, eds. "Special Issue on Child Care." *Journal of Human Resources* 27 (Winter 1992).

Blau, Francine D., and Anne E. Winkler. *Economics of Women, Men and Work*. 8th ed. New York: Oxford University Press, 2018.

Fields, Gary S., and Olivia S. Mitchell. *Retirement, Pensions, and Social Security*. Cambridge, MA: MIT Press, 1984.

Ghez, Gilbert R., and Gary S. Becker. *The Allocation of Time and Goods Over the Life Cycle*, chapter 3. New York: Columbia University Press, 1975.

Gronau, Reuben. "The Measurement of Output of the Nonmarket Sector: The Evaluation of Housewives' Time." In *The Measurement of Economic and Social Performance*, ed. Milton Moss, 163–189. New York: National Bureau of Economic Research, 1973.

Hamermesh, Daniel. *Spending Time: The Most Valuable Resource*. New York: Oxford University Press, 2019.

Layard, Richard, and Jacob Mincer, eds. "Trends in Women's Work, Education, and Family Building." *Journal of Labor Economics* 3:1, pt. 2 (January 1985).

Compensating Wage Differentials and Labor Markets

Chapters 6 and 7 analyzed workers' decisions about *whether to seek employment* and *how long to work*. Chapters 8 and 9 analyze workers' decisions about the industry, occupation, or firm in which they will work. This chapter emphasizes the influence on job choice of such daily, *recurring* job characteristics as the work environment, the risk of injury, and the generosity of employee benefits and other forms of pay. Chapter 9 analyzes the effects of required educational *investments* on occupational choice.

Job Matching: The Role of Worker Preferences and Information

One of the major functions of the labor market is to provide the signals and the mechanisms by which workers who are seeking to maximize their utility can be matched to employers who are trying to maximize profits. Matching is a formidable task because workers have varying skills and preferences and because employers offer jobs that differ in requirements and working environment. The process of finding the worker–employer pairings that are best for each is truly one of trial and error, and whether the process is woefully deficient or reasonably satisfactory is an important policy issue that can be analyzed by using economic theory in its normative mode.

The assumption that workers are attempting to maximize utility implies that they are interested in both the pecuniary aspects and the nonpecuniary aspects of their jobs. On the one hand, we expect that higher compensation levels in a job (holding job tasks constant) would attract more workers to it. On the other hand, pay is, clearly, not all that matters: Occupational tasks; other job attributes, such as working conditions; and how workers' preferences mesh with those tasks are critical elements in the matching process. The focus of this chapter is on how the labor market accommodates worker preferences.

If all jobs in a labor market were *exactly alike* and located in the *same place*, an individual's decision about where to seek work would be a simple matter of choosing the job with the highest compensation. Any differences in the pay offered by employers would cause movement by workers from low-paying to high-paying firms. If they did not encounter any barriers inhibiting this movement, as discussed in Chapter 5, the market would force wage and job-characteristic offers of all employers to be the same.

All jobs are not alike, however. Some jobs are in clean, modern spaces, and others are in noisy, dusty, or dangerous environments. Some permit employee discretion in regard to the hours or the pace of work, while others impose less flexibility. Some employers offer more-generous employee-benefit packages than others, and different *places* of employment involve different commuting distances and neighborhood characteristics. In this chapter, we discuss the ways that differences in job characteristics influence individual choice and observable market outcomes.

Individual Choice and Its Outcomes

Suppose that several lower-skilled workers have received offers from two employers. Employer X pays $15 per hour and offers clean, safe working conditions. Employer Y also pays $15 per hour but offers employment in a dirty, noisy factory. Which employer would the workers choose? Most would undoubtedly choose employer X because the pay is the same while the job is performed under more agreeable conditions.

Clearly, however, $15 is not an equilibrium wage in both firms.[1] Because firm X finds attracting applicants at $15 easy, it will hold the line on any future wage increases. Firm Y, however, must clean up the plant, pay higher wages, or do both if it wants to fill its vacancies. Assuming that it decides not to alter working conditions, it must pay a wage *above* $15 to be competitive in the labor market. The *extra* wage that it must pay to attract workers is called a *compensating wage differential*, because the higher wage is paid to compensate workers for the undesirable working conditions. If such a differential did not exist, firm Y could not attract the high-skilled workers that firm X can obtain.[2]

An Equilibrium Differential Suppose that firm Y raises its wage offer to $15.50, while the offer from X remains at $15. Will this 50-cent-per-hour differential—an extra $1,000 per year—attract *all* the workers in our group to firm Y? If it did attract them all, firm X would have an incentive to raise its wages, and firm Y might want to lower its offers a bit; the 50-cent differential in this case would *not* be an equilibrium differential.

More than likely, however, the higher wage in firm Y would attract only *some* of the group to firm Y. Some people are not bothered much by dirt and noise, and they might decide to take the extra pay and put up with the poorer working conditions. Those who are sensitive to noise or dust might decide that they would rather be paid less than expose themselves to such working conditions. If both firms could obtain the quantity and quality of workers that they wanted, the 50-cent differential *would* be an equilibrium differential, in the sense that there would be no forces causing the differential to change.

The desire of workers to avoid unpleasantness or risk, then, should force employers offering unpleasant or risky jobs to pay higher wages than they would otherwise have to pay. This wage differential serves two related, socially desirable ends. First, it serves a *social* need by giving people an incentive to voluntarily do dirty, dangerous, or unpleasant work. Second, at an *individual* level, it serves as a reward to workers who accept unpleasant jobs by paying them more than comparable workers in more pleasant jobs.

The Allocation of Labor   A number of jobs are unavoidably nasty or would be very costly to make safe and pleasant (coal mining, deep-sea diving, and police work are examples). Employers essentially have two ways to recruit the necessary labor for such jobs. One is to compel people to do these jobs (the military draft is the most obvious contemporary example of forced labor). The second way is to induce people to do the jobs voluntarily.

Most modern societies rely mainly on incentives, compensating wage differentials, to recruit people to voluntarily take unpleasant jobs. Workers will mine coal, bolt steel beams together 50 stories off the ground, or agree to work at night because, compared to alternative jobs for which they could qualify, these jobs pay well. Night work, for example, can be stressful because it disrupts normal patterns of sleep and family interactions; however, employers often find keeping their plants and machines in operation around the clock to be efficient. The result is that employees who are working night shifts are paid higher wages than they would receive if they worked during the day.[3]

Compensation for Workers   Compensating wage differentials also serve as *individual* rewards by paying those who accept bad or arduous working conditions more than they would otherwise receive. In a parallel fashion, those who opt for more-pleasant conditions have to "buy" them by accepting lower pay. For example, if a person takes the $15-per-hour job with firm X, they are giving up the $15.50-per-hour job with less pleasant conditions in firm Y. The better conditions are being bought, in a real sense, for 50 cents per hour.

Thus, compensating wage differentials become the prices at which good working conditions can be purchased by, or bad ones sold by, workers. Contrary to what is commonly asserted, a monetary value *can* often be attached to events or conditions whose effects are primarily psychological in nature. Compensating wage differentials provide the key to the valuation of these nonpecuniary aspects of employment.

For example, how much do workers value a work schedule that permits them to enjoy leisure activities and sleep at the usual times? If nightshift workers, for example, earn $1,000 per year more than they otherwise would earn, the reasoning needed to answer this question is straightforward. Those who have difficulty sleeping during the day, or whose favorite leisure activities require the companionship of family or friends, are not likely to be attracted to night work for only $1,000 extra per year; they are quite willing to forgo a $1,000 earnings premium to obtain a normal work schedule. Others, however, are less bothered by the unusual sleep and leisure patterns, and they are willing to work at night for the $1,000 premium. While some of these latter workers would be willing to give up a normal work schedule for *less* than $1,000, others find the decision to work at night a close call at the going wage differential. If the differential were to marginally fall, a few working at night would change their minds and refuse to continue, while if the differential rose a bit above $1,000, a few more could be recruited to night work. Thus, the $1,000 yearly premium represents what those *at the margin* (the ones closest to changing their minds) are willing to pay for a normal work schedule.[4]

Assumptions and Predictions

We have seen how a simple theory of job choice by individuals leads to the *prediction* that compensating wage differentials will be associated with various job characteristics. Positive differentials (higher wages) will accompany "bad" characteristics, while negative differentials (lower wages) will be associated with "good" ones. However, this prediction can be made *only* by *holding other things equal*.[5]

Our prediction about the existence of compensating wage differentials grows out of the reasonable assumption that if an informed worker has a choice between a job with "good" working conditions and a job of equal pay with "bad" working conditions, they will choose the "good" job. If the employee is a low-skilled laborer, they may be choosing between an unpleasant job spreading hot asphalt or a more comfortable job in an air-conditioned warehouse. In either case, they are going to receive something close to the wage rate that low-skilled workers typically receive. However, our theory would predict that this worker would receive *more* from the asphalt-spreading job than from the warehouse job.

Thus, the predicted outcome of our theory of job choice is *not* simply that employees working under "bad" conditions receive more than those working under "good" conditions. The prediction is that, *holding worker characteristics constant*, employees in bad working conditions receive higher wages than those working under more-pleasant conditions. The characteristics that must be held constant include all the other things that influence wages: skill level, age, experience, race, gender, union status, region, and so forth. Three assumptions have been used to arrive at this prediction.

Assumption 1: Utility Maximization   Our first assumption is that workers seek to maximize their *utility*, not their income. Compensating wage differentials will arise only if some people do *not* choose the highest-paying job offered, preferring instead a lower-paying but more pleasant job. This behavior allows those employers offering lower-paying, pleasant jobs to be competitive. Thus, utility-maximizing workers will consider both

the pay *and* how much they think they will enjoy the duties and conditions of the job when deciding among job offers.

Assumption 2: Worker Information

The second assumption implicit in our analysis is that workers are aware of the job characteristics of potential importance to them. Whether they know about them before they take the job or find out about them soon after taking it is not too important. In either case, a company offering a "bad" job with no compensating wage differential would have trouble recruiting or retaining workers—trouble that would eventually force it to raise its wage.

Of course, workers would likely quickly learn about danger, noise, rigid work discipline, job insecurity, and other obvious bad working conditions. They would equally likely *not* know the *precise* probability of being laid off, say, or of being injured on the job. However, even with respect to these probabilities, their own direct observations or word-of-mouth reports from other employees could give them enough information to evaluate the situation with some accuracy. For example, the proportions of employees who consider their work dangerous have been shown to be closely related to the actual injury rates published by the government for the industries in which they work.[6] This finding illustrates that although workers probably cannot state the precise probability of being injured, they do form accurate judgments about the relative risks of several jobs.

Predictions might disappoint us, however, with respect to *obscure* characteristics. For example, although we now know that asbestos dust is highly damaging to worker health, this fact was not widely known 50 years ago. One reason why information on asbestos dangers in plants was so long in being generated is that it takes more than 20 years for asbestos-related disease to develop. Cause and effect were thus obscured from workers and researchers alike, creating a situation in which job choices were made in ignorance of this risk. Compensating wage differentials for this danger could thus not possibly have arisen at that time. Our predictions about compensating wage differentials, then, hold only for job characteristics that workers know about.

Assumption 3: Worker Mobility

The final assumption implicit in our theory is that workers have a range of job offers from which to choose. Without a range of offers, workers would not be able to select the combination of job characteristics that they desire or avoid the ones to which they do not wish to be exposed. A compensating wage differential for risk of injury, for example, simply could not arise if workers were able to obtain only dangerous jobs. The act of choosing safe jobs over dangerous ones forces employers offering dangerous work to raise wages.

One manner in which this choice can occur is for each job applicant to receive several job offers from which to choose. However, another way in which choice could be exercised is for workers to be (at least potentially) highly mobile. In other words, workers with few concurrent offers could take jobs and continue their search for work if they thought an improvement could be made. Thus, even with few offers at any *one* time, workers could conceivably have relatively wide choice over a *period* of time, which would eventually allow them to select jobs that maximized their utility.

How mobile are workers? As of January 2018, about one-fifth of all U.S. workers who were 20 years of age or older had been with their employers for a year or less, and over 3.5 percent started with a new employer each month. For some, finding a new employer was necessary because they were fired or laid off by their previous employer, but roughly 2 percent of workers in the United States *voluntarily* quit their jobs in any given *month*— and roughly 40 percent of those go to jobs paying lower wages (possibly because of more-attractive working conditions or benefits).[7] Thus, a substantial number of workers in the United States move among employers every year.

Empirical Tests for Compensating Wage Differentials

The prediction that there are compensating wage differentials for undesirable job characteristics is over 200 years old. Adam Smith, in his *Wealth of Nations*, published in 1776, proposed five "principal circumstances which . . . make up for a small pecuniary gain in some employments, and counterbalance a great one in others." Among the circumstances that Smith listed were the constancy of employment, the difficulty of learning the job, the probability of success, and the degree of trust placed in the worker. While our discussion in this chapter could focus on any one of these, most of the work to date has focused on his assertion that "the wages of labour vary with the ease or hardship, the cleanliness or dirtiness, the honourableness or dishonourableness of the employment."[8]

We encounter two difficulties in actually estimating compensating wage differentials. First, we must be able to create data sets that allow us to match, at the level of individual workers, their relevant job characteristics with their personal characteristics (age, education, union status, and so forth) that also influence wages. Second, we must be able to specify in advance those job characteristics that are generally regarded as disagreeable (e.g., not everyone may regard outdoor work or repetitive tasks as undesirable).[9]

The most extensive testing for the existence of compensating wage differentials has been done with respect to the risks of injury or death on the job, primarily because higher levels of such risks are unambiguously "bad." These studies generally, but not always, support the prediction that wages will be higher whenever risks on the job are higher. Estimates of such compensating differentials for the United States suggest that wages tend to be around 2 percent higher for workers facing three times the average risk of a job-related fatality than for those who face the average yearly level of risk (which is about one in 30,000).[10] We will come back to these estimates later in this chapter.

Many other studies of compensating wage differentials have been done, but because they are spread thinly across a variety of job characteristics, judging the strength of their support for the theory is problematic. Nonetheless, positive wage premiums have been related, holding other influences constant, to such disagreeable characteristics as night work, an inflexible work schedule, a work schedule set on short notice, having to stand a lot, working in a noisy or polluted environment, and having an unsteady job (see Example 8.1 for less-formal data on another "bad" working condition: working away from home).[11] We also have evidence of compensating wage differentials for working internationally[12] and for long hours of work[13] (we will return to the topic of long hours in Chapter 12, because men, typically with fewer household duties, tend to work longer hours—thus raising their wages relative to those for equally qualified women).

EXAMPLE 8.1

Working on the Railroad: Making a Bad Job Good

While compensating wage differentials are difficult to precisely measure, the theory in this chapter can often find general support in everyday discussions of job choice. This example is based on a newspaper article about the exclusive use of members of the Navajo Nation by the Santa Fe Railway to repair and replace its 9,000 miles of track between Los Angeles and Chicago.

The 220 members of the Navajo Nation were organized into two "steel gangs." Workers did what machines cannot: pull and sort old spikes, weld the rails together, and check the safety of the new rails. The grueling work was intrinsically unappealing: Jobs lasted for only five to eight months per year; much of the work was done in sweltering desert heat; workers had to live away from their families and were housed in bunk cars with up to 16 other workers; and the remote locations rendered the off-hours boring and lonely.

Two hypotheses about jobs such as these can be derived from the theory in this chapter. These hypotheses are listed next, along with supporting quotations or facts from the newspaper article.

Hypothesis 1: Companies that offer unappealing jobs find recruiting and retaining employees difficult. Workers who take these jobs are the ones for whom the conditions are least disagreeable.

They had tried everyone. The Navajos were the only ones willing to be away from home, to do the work, and to do a good job.

[A Santa Fe recruiter]

Lonely? No, I never get lonely. There is nothing but Navajo here. . . . We speak the same language and understand one another. . . . It's a good job.

[A steel gang worker with 16 years' experience]

Hypothesis 2: The jobs are made appealing to the target group of workers by raising wages well above those of their alternatives.

I wish I could stay home all the time and be with my family. It's just not possible. Where am I going to find a job that pays $900 every two weeks?

[A steel gang veteran of 11 years]

(Steel gang wages in the early 1990s ranged between $12 and $17 per hour, well above the national average of about $10 per hour for "handlers and laborers.")

Source: Paula Moñarez, "Navajos Keep Rail Lines Safe," *Long Beach Independent Press-Telegram*, May 14, 1992, D1

Hedonic Wage Theory and the Risk of Injury

We now turn to a graphical presentation of the theory of compensating wage differentials, which has become known as *hedonic* wage theory.[14] The graphic tools used permit additional insights into the theory and greatly clarify the normative analysis of important regulatory issues. In this section, we analyze the theory of compensating wage differentials for a *negative* job characteristic, the risk of injury, and apply the concepts to a normative analysis of governmental safety regulations.

Job injuries are an unfortunate characteristic of the workplace, and injury rates vary considerably across occupations and industries. For example, we noted that whereas the average yearly rate of fatal injury in the U.S. workplace is about one in 30,000, the rates for truck drivers and roofers are seven to 14 times higher. Roughly 2 percent of U.S. workers are injured seriously enough each year that they cannot perform their normal duties for at least a day, but even in the manufacturing sector, these rates vary from 1 percent in petroleum manufacturing to 3.8 percent in wood manufacturing.[15] The fatality rate for workers in 2018 was 0.4 per 100,000 employees in office and administrative support occupations, but was 22.8 in farming, fishing, and forestry occupations.[16]

To simplify our analysis of compensating wage differentials for the risk of injury, we assume that compensating differentials for every *other* job characteristic have already been established. This assumption allows us to see more clearly the outcomes of the job selection process, and because the same analysis could be repeated for every other characteristic, our conclusions are not obscured by it. To obtain a complete understanding of the job selection process and the outcomes of that process, we must, as always, consider both the employer side and the employee side of the market.

Employee Considerations

We assume, safely, that employees dislike the risk of being injured on the job. A worker who is offered a job for $12 per hour in a firm in which 3 percent of the workforce is injured each year would achieve a certain level of utility from that job. If the risk of injury were increased to 4 percent, holding other job characteristics constant, the job would have to pay a higher wage to produce the same level of utility (except in the unlikely event that

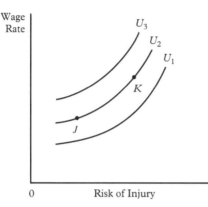

Figure 8.1 A Family of Indifference Curves Between Wages and Risk of Injury

the costs of wage loss, medical treatment, and suffering caused by the added injuries were *completely* covered by the firm or its insurance company after the fact).[17]

Other combinations of wage rates and risk levels could be devised that would yield the same utility as the $12 per hour and 3 percent risk offer. These combinations can be connected on a graph to form an indifference curve (e.g., the curve U_2 in Figure 8.1). Unlike the indifference curves drawn in Chapters 6 and 7, those in Figure 8.1 slope upward because risk of injury is a "bad" job characteristic, not a "good" one (such as leisure). In other words, if risk increases, wages must rise if utility is to be held constant.

As in the previous chapters, each possible level of utility has a corresponding indifference curve. Because a higher wage at a given risk level will generate more utility, indifference curves lying to the northwest represent higher utility. Thus, all points on curve U_3 in Figure 8.1 are preferred to all of those on U_2, and those on U_2 are preferred to the ones on U_1.[18] The fact that each indifference curve is convex (when viewed from below) reflects the normal assumption of diminishing marginal rates of substitution. At point K of curve U_2, the person receives a relatively high wage and faces a high level of risk. They will be willing to give up a lot in wages to achieve a given reduction in risk because risk levels are high enough to place them in imminent danger, and the consumption level of the goods that are bought with wages is already high. However, as risk levels and wage rates fall (e.g., to point J), the person becomes less willing to give up wages in return for the given reduction in risk; the danger is no longer imminent, and consumption of other goods is not as high.

People differ, of course, in their aversion to the risk of being injured. Those who are more sensitive to this risk require large wage increases for any increase in risk, while those who are less sensitive require smaller wage increases to hold utility constant. The more sensitive workers will have indifference curves that are steeper at any level of risk, as illustrated in Figure 8.2. At risk level R_1, the slope at point C is steeper than at point D. Point C lies on the indifference curve of worker A, who is highly sensitive to risk, while point D lies on an indifference curve of worker B, who is less sensitive. Of

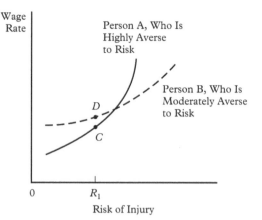

Figure 8.2 Representative Indifference Curves for Two Workers Who Differ in Their Aversion to Risk of Injury

course, each person has a whole family of indifference curves that are not shown in Figure 8.2, and each will attempt to achieve the highest level of utility possible.

Employer Considerations

Employers are faced with a wage vs. risk trade-off of their own that derives from three assumptions. First, reducing the risk of injury facing employees is presumably costly. Safety equipment must be placed on machines, production time must be sacrificed for safety training sessions, protective clothing must be furnished to workers, and so forth. Second, competitive pressures presumably force many firms to operate at *zero profit* (i.e., at a point at which all costs are covered and the rate of return on capital is about what it is for similar investments).[19] Third, all *other* job characteristics are presumably given or already determined. The consequence of these three assumptions is that if a firm undertakes a program to reduce the risk of injury, it must reduce wages to remain competitive.

Thus, forces on the employer side of the market tend to cause low risk to be associated with low wages and high risk to be associated with high wages, *holding other things constant*. These "other things" may be employee benefits or other job characteristics; assuming that they are given does not affect the validity of our analysis (even though it may seem at first unrealistic). The major point is that if a firm spends *more on safety*, it must spend *less on other things* if it is to remain competitive. In our theoretical analyses, the term *wages* can thus be thought of as shorthand for "terms of employment."

The employer trade-offs between wages and levels of injury risk can be graphed through the use of *isoprofit curves*, which show the various combinations of risk and wage levels that yield a given level of profits (*iso* means "equal"). Thus, all the points along a given curve, such as those depicted in Figure 8.3, are wage–risk combinations that yield the *same* level of profits. Curves to the southeast represent higher profit levels because with all other

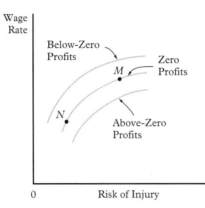

Figure 8.3　A Family of Isoprofit Curves for an Employer

items in the employment contract given, each risk level is associated with a *lower* wage level. Curves to the northwest, conversely, represent lower profit levels.

Note that the isoprofit curves in Figure 8.3 are concave (from below). This concavity is a graphic representation of our assumption that there are diminishing marginal returns to safety expenditures. Suppose, for example, that the firm is operating at point M in Figure 8.3—a point where the risk of injury is high. The first expenditures by the firm to reduce risk will have a relatively high return because the firm will clearly choose to attack the safety problem by eliminating the most obvious and cheaply eliminated hazards. Because the risk reductions are relatively inexpensive to obtain, the firm need not reduce wages much to keep profits constant. Thus, the isoprofit curve at point M is relatively flat. At point N, however, the curve is steeply sloped, indicating that wages will have to be reduced by quite a bit if the firm is to maintain its profits in the presence of a program to reduce risk. This large wage reduction is required because at this point, further increases in safety are costly.

We also assume that employers differ in the ease with which (cost at which) they can eliminate hazards. We have just indicated that the cost of reducing risk levels is reflected in the *slope* of the isoprofit curve. In firms where injuries are costly to reduce, large wage reductions will be required to keep profits constant in the face of a safety program; the isoprofit curve in this case will be steeply sloped. The isoprofit curve of one such firm is shown as the dashed curve YY' in Figure 8.4. The isoprofit curves of firms where injuries are easier to eliminate are flatter. Note that the solid curve XX' in Figure 8.4 is flatter at each level of risk than YY'; this is most easily seen at point R' and indicates that firm X can reduce risk more cheaply than firm Y can.

The Matching of Employers and Employees

The aim of employees is to achieve the highest possible utility from their choice of a job. If they receive two offers at the same wage rate, they will

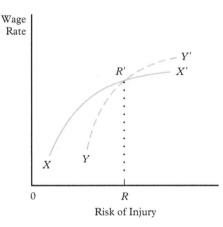

Figure 8.4 The Zero-Profit Curves of Two Firms

choose the lower-risk job. If they receive two offers in which the risk levels are equal, they will accept the offer with the higher wage rate. More generally, they will choose the offer that falls on the highest, or most northwest, indifference curve.

In obtaining jobs, employees are constrained by the offers that they receive from employers. Employers, for their part, are constrained by two forces. On the one hand, they cannot make outrageously lucrative offers, because they will be driven out of business by firms whose costs are lower. On the other hand, if their offered terms of employment are low, they will be unable to attract employees (who will choose to work for other firms). These two forces compel firms in competitive markets to operate on their zero-profit isoprofit curves.

To better understand the offers that firms make, refer to Figure 8.4, where two firms are depicted. Left of point R', firm X, the firm that can more cheaply reduce injuries, can make higher wage offers at low levels of risk than can firm Y. Because it can produce safety more cheaply, it can pay higher wages at low levels of risk and still remain competitive. Any offers along segment XR' will be preferred by employees to those along YR' because, for given levels of risk, higher wages are paid.

At higher levels of risk (those to the right of point R'), however, firm Y can outbid firm X for employees. Firm X does not save much money if it permits the risk level to rise above R, because risk reduction is so cheap. Because firm Y *does* save itself a lot by operating at levels of risk beyond R, it is willing to pay relatively high wages at high risk levels. For employees, offers along $R'Y'$ will be preferable to those along $R'X'$, so those employees working at high-risk jobs will work for Y.

Graphing worker indifference curves and employer isoprofit curves together can show which workers choose which offers. Figure 8.5 contains the zero-profit curves of two employers (X and Y) and the indifference curves of two employees (A and B). Employee A maximizes utility (along A_2) by working for employer X at wage W_{AX} and risk level R_{AX}, while employee B maximizes utility on utility curve B_2 by working for employer Y at wage W_{BY} and risk level R_{BY}.

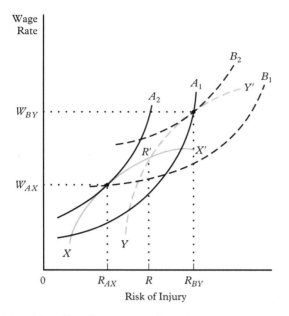

Figure 8.5 Matching Employers and Employees

Looking at A's choice more closely, we see that if they took the offer that B accepted—W_{BY} and R_{BY}—the level of utility achieved would be A_1, which is less than A_2. Person A values safety highly, and wage W_{BY} is just not high enough to compensate for the high level of risk. Person B, whose indifference curves are flatter (signifying that they are less averse to risk), finds the offer of W_{BY} and R_{BY} on curve B_2 superior to the offer that A accepts. Person B is simply not willing to take a cut in pay to W_{AX} in order to reduce risk from R_{BY} to R_{AX}, because that would place them on curve B_1.

EXAMPLE 8.2

Parenthood, Occupational Choice, and Risk

The theory of compensating wage differentials is built on the assumption that among workers in a given labor market, those with the stronger aversions to risk will select safer (but lower-paying) jobs. Testing the implications of this assumption is difficult because measuring risk aversion is not generally possible and because holding "all else equal" is notoriously difficult. However, one study analyzed workers' choices when the relative strength of aversion to injury risk could be logically inferred.

We know that women are usually found in safer jobs than men are. In the mid 1990s, for example, men made up 54 percent of all workers but constituted 92 percent of workers killed on the job. What is not so well known is that among each gender group is an equally striking pattern—*men and women who are single parents choose to work in safer jobs.*

This study argues that workers who are raising children feel a greater need to avoid risk on the job because they have loved ones who depend on them, and of course, this should be especially true for single parents. Indeed, the study found that married women without children worked in jobs with a greater risk of death than married women with children, but that single mothers chose to work in even safer jobs.

> The study found that among men, those who were single parents worked in safer jobs than married men did, but married men with children apparently did not behave much differently than those without. The study argues that because married men are typically not in the role of caregiver to their children, they seem to believe that they can take higher-paying, riskier jobs but adequately protect their children through buying life insurance. Married women, in contrast, do not find life insurance as effective in protecting children, because it provides only money, which cannot replace care and nurturing.
>
> *Source*: Thomas DeLeire and Helen Levy, "Worker Sorting and the Risk of Death on the Job," *Journal of Labor Economics* 22 (October 2004): 925–953

The matching of worker A with firm X and worker B with firm Y is not accidental or random.[20] Since X can "produce" safety more cheaply than Y can, logically X will be a low-risk producer who attracts employees, such as A, who value safety highly. Likewise, employer Y generates a lot of cost savings by operating at high risk levels and can thus afford to pay high wages and still be competitive. Y attracts people such as B, who have a relatively strong preference for money wages and a relatively weak preference for safety. (For a study of how aversion to risk affects job choice, see Example 8.2.)

The Offer Curve   The job-matching process, of course, can be generalized beyond the case of two employees and two employers. To do this, note that in Figure 8.5, the only offers of jobs to workers with a chance of being accepted lie along $XR\Upsilon'$. The curve $XR\Upsilon'$ can be called an *offer curve* because only along $XR\Upsilon'$ are offers that employers can afford to make potentially acceptable to employees. The concept of an offer curve is useful in generalizing our discussion beyond two firms, because a single offer curve can summarize the potentially acceptable offers that any number of firms in a particular labor market can make.

Consider, for example, Figure 8.6, which contains the zero-profit isoprofit curves of firms L through Q. We know from our discussions of Figures 8.4 and 8.5 that employees accept offers along only the most northwest segments of this set of curves; to do otherwise would be to accept a lower wage at each level of risk. Thus, the potentially acceptable offers are found along the darkened curve of Figure 8.6, which we call the offer curve. The more types of firms present in a market, the smoother this offer curve will be; however, it will always slope upward because of our twin assumptions that risk is costly to reduce and that employees must be paid higher wages to keep their utility constant if risk is increased. In some of the examples that follow, the offer curve is used to summarize the feasible, potentially acceptable offers that employers are making in a labor market, because using an offer curve saves our diagrams from becoming cluttered with the isoprofit curves of many employers.

Major Behavioral Insights   From the perspective of "positive economics," our hedonic model generates two major insights. The first is

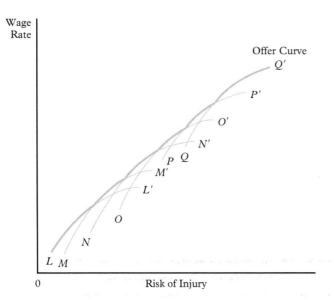

Figure 8.6 An Offer Curve

that wages rise with risk, other things being equal. According to this prediction, compensating wage differentials will arise for job characteristics that are viewed as undesirable by workers whom employers must attract (see Example 8.3). Second, workers with strong preferences for safety will tend to take jobs in firms where safety can be generated most cheaply. Workers who are not as averse to accepting risk will seek out and accept the higher-paying, higher-risk jobs offered by firms that find safety costly to "produce."[21] The second insight, then, is that the job-matching process—if it takes place under the conditions of knowledge and choice—is one in which firms and workers offer and accept jobs in a fashion that makes the most of their strengths and preferences.

EXAMPLE 8.3

Indentured Servitude and Compensating Differentials

In colonial days, indentured servitude offered a way for poor immigrants to obtain passage to the New World. Immigrants who did not have the funds to buy ship passage from their countries of origin could sign a contract (an indenture) with a merchant or sea captain in their country of origin, under which the immigrant would be provided passage and in return would promise to work as a servant in the country of destination for a specified number of years. The merchant or sea captain was then responsible for feeding, clothing, and transporting the servants to their destinations. Upon arrival, the merchant or sea captain would sell the indenture to a local farmer or planter, for whom the servant would work during the duration of the indenture.

From the servants' viewpoint, the major characteristics of an indenture were its length and the destination, some of which provided less harsh working conditions or better post-indenture work opportunities. The market for indentures in Britain was apparently competitive, in that enough British agents were selling these indentures—and the potential servants were well enough informed about destination characteristics—that a compensating differential arose. For example, indentures of adults to be sold in the West Indies, where sugar-plantation workers toiled in unpleasant conditions and had few post-servitude job opportunities, were about nine months (or 16 percent) shorter than indentures sold in Maryland.

Source: David Galenson, "Immigration and the Colonial Labor System: An Analysis of the Length of Indenture," *Explorations in Economic History* 14 (November 1977): 360–377

Normative Analysis: Occupational Safety and Health Regulation

The hedonic analysis of wages in the context of job safety can be normatively applied to government regulations on workplace safety. In particular, we now have the conceptual tools to analyze such questions as the *need* for regulation and, if needed, what the *goals* of the regulation should be.

Do Workers Benefit from the Reduction of Risk?
In 1970, Congress passed the Occupational Safety and Health Act, which directed the U.S. Department of Labor to issue and enforce safety and health standards for all private employers. Safety standards are intended to reduce the risk of traumatic injury, while health standards address worker exposure to substances thought to cause disease. The stated goal of the act was to ensure the highest degree of health and safety protection for the employee.

Despite the *ideal* that employees should face the minimum possible risk in the workplace, implementing this ideal as social *policy* is not necessarily in the best interests of workers. Our hedonic model can show that reducing risk in some circumstances will lower the workers' utility levels. Consider Figure 8.7.

Suppose that a labor market is functioning in line with our textbook models, in that workers are well informed about dangers inherent in any job and are mobile enough to avoid risks that they do not wish to take. In these circumstances, wages will be positively related to risk (other things being equal), and workers will sort themselves into jobs according to their preferences. This market can be modeled graphically in Figure 8.7, where, for simplicity's sake, we have assumed that the market has two kinds of workers and two kinds of firms. Person A, who is averse to the risk of injury, works at wage W_{AX} and risk R_{AX} for employer X. Person B works for employer Y at wage W_{BY} and risk R_{BY}.

Now, suppose the Occupational Safety and Health Administration (OSHA), the Department of Labor agency responsible for implementing the federal safety and health program, promulgates a standard that makes risk levels above R_{AX} illegal. The effects, although unintended and perhaps not immediately obvious, would be detrimental to employees such as B. Reducing risk is costly, and the best wage offer that a worker can obtain at risk R_{AX} is W_{AX}. For B, however, wage W_{AX} and risk R_{AX} generate *less utility* than did Y's offer of W_{BY} and R_{BY}.

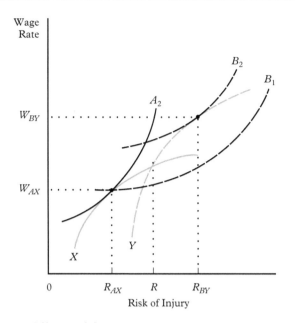

Figure 8.7 The Effects of Government Regulation in a Perfectly Functioning Labor Market

When the government mandates the reduction of risk in a market where workers are compensated for the risks that they take, it penalizes workers such as B, who are not terribly sensitive to risk and appreciate the higher wages associated with higher risk. The critical issue, of course, is whether workers have the knowledge and choice necessary to generate compensating wage differentials. Many people believe that workers are uninformed and unable to comprehend different risk levels, or that they are immobile and thus do not choose risky jobs voluntarily.[22] If this belief were true, government regulation *could* make workers better off. Indeed, while the evidence of a positive relationship between wages and risk of fatal injury should challenge the notion that information and mobility are *generally* insufficient to create compensating differentials, problems obviously persist in specific areas. For example, the introduction each year of new workplace chemicals whose health effects on humans might be unknown for two or more decades (owing to the long gestation periods for most cancers and lung diseases) clearly presents substantial informational problems to affected labor market participants.

To say that worker utility *can* be reduced by government regulation does not, then, imply that it *will* be reduced. The outcome depends on how well the unregulated market functions and how careful the government is in setting its standards for risk reduction. The following section analyzes a government program implemented in a market that has *not* generated enough information about risk for employees to make informed job choices.

How Strict Should OSHA Standards Be? Consider a labor market, like that mentioned previously for asbestos workers, in which ignorance or worker immobility hinders labor market operation. Let us also suppose that the government becomes aware of the health hazard involved and wishes to set a standard regulating worker exposure to this hazard. How stringent should this standard be?

The crux of the problem in setting standards is that reducing hazards is costly; the greater the reduction, the more it costs. Although initially businesses bear these costs, they ultimately respond to them by cutting costs elsewhere and raising prices (to the extent that cutting costs is not possible). Because labor costs constitute a large cost category for most firms, it is natural for businesses facing government-mandated hazard reductions to hold the line on wage increases or adopt policies that are the equivalent of reducing wages: speeding up production, being less lenient with absenteeism, reducing employee benefits, and so forth. Also, particularly in view of any price increases (which, of course, tend to reduce product demand), employment will likely be cut back. Some of the job loss will be in the form of permanent layoffs that force workers to find other jobs—jobs that they presumably could have had before the layoff but chose not to accept. Some of the loss will be in the form of cutting down on hiring new employees who would have regarded the jobs as their best employment option.

Thus, whether in the form of smaller wage increases, more-difficult working conditions, or an inability to obtain or retain one's first choice in a job, the costs of compliance with health standards regularly fall on employees. A graphic example can be used to make an educated guess about whether worker utility will be enhanced or not as a result of the increased protection from risk mandated by an OSHA health standard.

Figure 8.8 depicts the situation that a worker faces when they believe that they have taken a low-risk job when in fact they are exposing themselves to a hazard that has a relatively high probability of damaging their health in 20 years. They receive a wage of W_1 and *believe* that they are at point J, where the risk level is R_1 and the utility level is U_1. Instead, they are in fact at point K, receiving W_1 for accepting (unknowingly) risk level R_2; they would thus experience lower utility (indifference curve U_0 rather than U_1) if they knew the extent of the risk that they were taking.

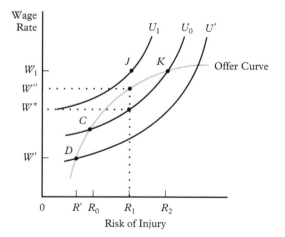

Figure 8.8 A Worker Accepting Unknown Risk

Suppose now that the government discovers that their job is highly hazardous. The government could simply inform the affected workers and let them move to other work. However, if it has little confidence in the ability of workers to understand the information or to find other work, the government could pass a standard that limits employee exposure to this hazard. But what level of protection should this standard offer?

If OSHA forced the risk level down to R', the best wage offer[23] that the worker in our example could obtain is W' (at point D on the offer curve). Point D, however, lies on indifference curve U', which represents a lower level of utility than the worker is in fact getting now (U_0). They would be worse off because of the standard. On the other hand, if the government forced risk levels down to a level less than R_2 but greater than R_0, the worker would be better off because they would be able to reach an indifference curve above U_0 (within the shaded area of Figure 8.8). The worker, therefore, has a set of levels of risk where they are better off than the case without government regulation. To better understand this last point, we briefly explain the concepts underlying *cost–benefit analysis*, the technique that economists recommend for estimating which government mandates will improve social welfare.

Cost–Benefit Analysis The purpose of a cost–benefit analysis in the labor market is to weigh the likely costs of a government regulation against the value that workers place on its expected benefits (as measured by what workers would be willing to pay for these benefits). In the terms of Figure 8.8, the per-worker *costs* of achieving reduced risk under the OSHA standard are reflected along the offer curve, which indicates the wage cuts that firms would have to make to keep profits constant. For example, if OSHA mandated that risk levels fall from R_2 to R_1, employer costs would require that wage offers fall from W_1 to W''. The per-worker *cost* of this standard would therefore be ($W_1 - W''$).

Conceptually, the *benefits* of the OSHA standard can be measured by the wage reductions that workers would be willing to take if they could get the reduced risk. In Figure 8.8, the worker depicted would be willing to take a wage as low as W^* if risk is cut to R_1, because at that wage and risk level, their utility is the same as it is now (recall that they are *actually* at point K on curve U_0). Thus, the *most* that they would be willing to pay for this risk reduction is ($W_1 - W^*$). If wages were forced below W^*, they would be worse off (on a lower indifference curve), and if wages were above W^*, they would be better off than they are now.

In the example graphed by Figure 8.8, a mandated risk level of R_1 would produce benefits that outweigh costs. That is, the amount that workers would be willing to pay ($W_1 - W^*$) would exceed the costs ($W_1 - W''$). If employers could get the wage down to W^*, they would be more profitable than they are now and workers would have unchanged utility. If the wage were W'', workers would be better off and employers would have unchanged profits; a wage between W^* and W'' would make both parties better off. All these possible options would be Pareto improving (at least one party would be better off and neither would be worse off).

In Figure 8.8, mandated risk levels between R_0 and R_2 would produce benefits greater than costs. These risk levels could be accompanied by wage rates that place the parties in the shaded zone, which illustrates all the Pareto-improving possibilities. Risk levels below R_0 would impose costs on society that would be greater than the benefits.[24]

Instead of using textbook graphs, how can we estimate, in a practical way, the wage reductions workers would be willing to bear in exchange for a reduction in risk? The answer lies in estimating compensating wage differentials in markets that appear to work. Suppose that workers are estimated to accept wage cuts of $1,100 per year for reductions in the yearly death rate of one person in 10,000—which is an amount consistent with the most recent analyses of compensating wage differentials.[25] If so, workers apparently believe that, other things being equal, they receive about $1,100 in benefits when the risk of death is reduced by this amount. While estimated values of this willingness to pay are no doubt imprecise, analyzing compensating wage differentials is probably the best way to make an educated guess about what values workers attach to risk reduction.

Even if the estimates of what workers are willing to pay for reduced risk are crude and subject to a degree of error, they can still be used to assess the wisdom of government regulations. If we believe that workers are willing to pay in the neighborhood of $1,100 per year to obtain a one-in-10,000 reduction in the yearly risk of being killed on the job, then safety or health standards imposed by the government that cost far more than that should be reconsidered. For example, in the 1980s, OSHA adopted three regulations whose per-worker costs for a one-in-10,000 reduction in fatal risk ranged between $8,000 and $78,000,000.[26] Even if we think that our willingness-to-pay estimate of $1,100 is half (or a quarter) of the true willingness to pay for risk reduction, these safety and health standards appear to have mandated a level of risk reduction that reduced workers' utility, not enhanced it.

Estimates of the compensating wage differentials for reduced risk of being killed at work are thus useful in judging the *benefits* of government mandates or programs designed to save lives. A compensating wage differential of $1,100 associated with a one in 10,000 *increase* in the yearly risk of a fatal work injury implies that each person would be willing to *pay* (in the form of lower compensation) $1,100 if some program *reduced* the risk of death by one in 10,000. If this program covered 10,000 people, one life would be spared over the next year (of course, we do not know whose life would be spared). Because each person in the group gets the reduced risk of one in 10,000, the total willingness to pay for this hypothetical program that spares one life can be calculated as 10,000 × $1,100 = $11,000,000. Put differently, policymakers could conclude that because the beneficiaries would be willing to pay an aggregate of $11,000,000, the benefits of this program that spares one life per year would be equal to $11,000,000.[27]

Hedonic Wage Theory and Employee Benefits

In Table 5.3, we saw that employee benefits are over 30 percent of the total compensation costs to the firm for the typical worker. Over two-thirds of such benefits relate to pensions and medical insurance, both of which have grown in importance over the past 30 years and have attracted the attention of policymakers. In this section, we use hedonic theory to analyze the labor market effects of employee benefits.

Employee Preferences

The distinguishing feature of most employee benefits is that they compensate workers in a form *other* than currently spendable cash. In general, such benefits fall into two broad categories. The first category consists of *payments in kind*—that is, compensation in the form of such commodities as employer-provided insurance or paid vacation time.[28] The second general type of employee benefit consists of *deferred compensation*, which is compensation that is earned now but will be paid in the form of money later on. Employer contributions to employee pension plans make up the largest proportion of these latter benefits.

Payments in Kind　A well-established tenet of economic theory holds that, *other things being equal*, people would rather receive $X in cash than a commodity that costs $X. The reason is simple. With $X in cash, the person can choose to buy the particular commodity or choose instead to buy a variety of other things. Cash is thus the form of payment that gives the recipient the most discretion and the most options in maximizing utility.[29]

As might be suspected, however, "other things" are not equal. Specifically, such in-kind payments as employer-provided health insurance offer employees a sizable tax advantage because, for the most part, they are not taxable to the employee under current income tax regulations. The absence of a tax on important in-kind payments is a factor that tends to offset their restrictive nature. A worker might prefer $1,000 in cash to $1,000 in some in-kind payment, but if their income tax and payroll tax rates total 25 percent, the comparison is really between $750 in cash and $1,000 in the in-kind benefit.[30]

Deferred Compensation　Like payments in kind, deferred-compensation schemes are restrictive but enjoy a tax advantage over current cash payments. In the case of pensions, for example, employers currently contribute to a pension fund, but employees do not obtain access to this fund until they retire. However, neither the pension fund *contributions* made on behalf of employees by employers nor the *interest* that compounds when these funds are invested is subject to the personal income tax. Only when the retirement benefits are received does the ex-worker pay taxes.

Indifference Curves   Two opposing forces are therefore at work in shaping workers' preferences for employee benefits.[31] On the one hand, these benefits are accorded special tax treatment, a feature of no small significance when one considers that income and Social Security taxes come to well over 20 percent for most workers. On the other hand, benefits involve a loss of discretionary control over one's total compensation. The result is that if we graph worker preferences regarding cash compensation (the wage rate) and employee benefits, we would come up with indifference curves generally shaped like the one shown in Figure 8.9. When cash earnings are relatively large and employee benefits are small (point *J*), workers are willing to give up a lot in terms of cash earnings to obtain the tax advantages of employee benefits. However, once compensation is heavily weighted toward such benefits (point *K*), further increases in benefits reduce discretionary earnings so much that the tax advantages seem small; at point *K*, then, the indifference curve is flatter. Hence, indifference curves depicting preferences between cash earnings and employee benefits are shaped like those in Chapters 6 and 7.[32]

Employer Preferences

Employers also have choices to make in the mix of cash compensation and employee benefits offered to their workers.[33] Their preferences about this mix can be graphically summarized through the use of isoprofit curves.

Isoprofit Curves With a Unitary Slope   The best place to start our analysis of the trade-offs that employers are willing to offer workers between cash compensation and employee benefits is to assume they are totally indifferent about whether to spend $X on wages or $X on benefits. Both options cost the same, so why would they prefer one option to the other?

   If firms were indifferent about the mix of cash and benefits paid to workers, their only concern would be with the *level* of compensation. If the market

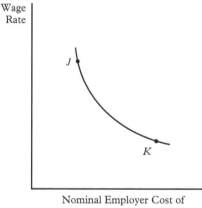

Figure 8.9 An Indifference Curve Between Wages and Employee Benefits

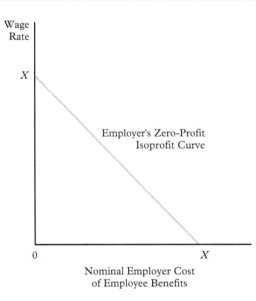

Figure 8.10 An Isoprofit Curve Showing the Wage/Benefit Offers That a Firm Might Be Willing to Make to Its Employees: A Unitary Trade-Off

requires $X in total compensation to attract workers to a particular job, firms would be willing to pay $X in wages, $X in benefits, or adopt a mix of the two that totals $X in cost. These equally attractive options are summarized along the zero-profit isoprofit curve shown in Figure 8.10. Note that this curve is drawn with a slope of −1, indicating that to keep profits constant, every extra dollar that the firm puts into the direct cost of employee benefits must be matched by payroll reductions of a dollar.

Isoprofit Curves With a Flatter Slope

The trade-offs that employers are willing to make between wages and employee benefits are not always one for one. Some benefits produce tax savings to employers when compared to paying workers in cash. For example, Social Security taxes that employers must pay are levied on their cash payroll, not on their employee benefits, so compensating workers with in-kind or deferred benefits instead of an equal amount of cash reduces their tax liabilities.

Moreover, offering benefits that are more valued by one group of prospective workers than another can be a clever way to save on the costs of screening applicants.[34] The key here is to offer benefits that will attract applicants with certain characteristics that the firm is searching for and will discourage applications from others. For example, deferred compensation will generally be more attractive to workers who are more future oriented, and offering tuition assistance will be attractive only to those who place a value on continued education. Applicants who are present oriented or do not expect to continue their schooling will be discouraged from even applying, thus saving employers who offer these two benefits (instead of paying higher wages) the costs of screening applicants whom they would not hire anyway.

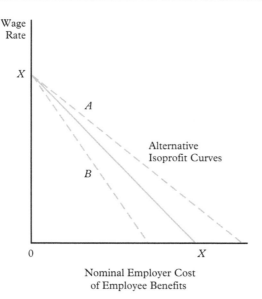

Figure 8.11 Alternative Isoprofit Curves Showing the Wage/Benefit Offers That a Firm Might Be Willing to Make to Its Employees: Non-unitary Trade-Offs

When employee benefits have tax or other advantages to the firm, the isoprofit curve (drawn as we do with benefits on the horizontal axis) is flattened (see curve *A* in Figure 8.11). This flatter curve indicates that benefits nominally costing $300, say, might save enough in other ways that only a $280 decrease in wages would be needed to keep profits constant.

Isoprofit Curves With a Steeper Slope   Employee benefits can also increase employer costs in other areas and thus end up being more expensive than paying in cash. The value of life and health insurance provided by employers, for example, is typically unaffected by the hours of work (as long as employees are considered "full time"). Increasing insurance benefits rather than wage rates, then, will produce an *income effect* without a corresponding increase in the price of leisure. Increasing compensation in this way will push workers in the direction of reduced work hours, possibly through greater levels of absenteeism.[35] If employee benefits increase costs in other areas, the isoprofit curve will steepen (see curve *B* in Figure 8.11)—indicating that to keep profits constant, wages would have to drop by more than $300 if benefits nominally costing $300 are offered.

The Joint Determination of Wages and Benefits

The offer curve in a particular labor market can be obtained by connecting the relevant portions of each firm's zero-profit isoprofit curve. When all firms have isoprofit curves with a slope of −1, the offer curve is a straight line with a negative and unitary slope. One such offer curve is illustrated in Figure 8.12, and the only difference between this curve and the zero-profit

Figure 8.12 Market Determination of the Mix of Wages and Benefits

isoprofit curve in Figure 8.10 is that the latter traced out *hypothetical* offers that *one* firm could make, whereas this one traces out the *actual* offers made by *all* firms in this labor market. Of course, if firms have isoprofit curves whose slopes are different from -1, the offer curve will not look exactly like that depicted in Figure 8.12. Whatever its shape or the absolute value of its slope at any point, it will slope downward.

Employees, then, face a set of wage and employee-benefit offers that imply the necessity for making trade-offs. Those employees (like worker Y in Figure 8.12) who attach relatively great importance to the availability of currently spendable cash will choose to accept offers in which total compensation is largely in the form of wages. Employees who may be less worried about current cash income but more interested in the tax advantages of benefits will accept offers in which employee benefits form a higher proportion of total compensation (see the curve for worker Z in Figure 8.12). Thus, employers will tailor their compensation packages to suit the preferences of the workers whom they are trying to attract. If their employees tend to be young or poor, for example, their compensation packages may be heavily weighted toward wages and include relatively little in the way of pensions and insurance. Alternatively, if they are trying to attract people in an area where family incomes are high and hence employee benefits offer relatively large tax savings, firms may offer packages in which benefits constitute a large proportion of the total.

Figure 8.12 shows that workers who receive more-generous benefits pay for them by receiving lower wages, other things being equal. Furthermore, if employer isoprofit curves have a unitary slope, a benefit that costs the employer $1 to provide will cost workers $1 in wages. In other words, economic theory suggests that workers pay for their own benefits.

Actually observing the trade-off between wages and employee benefits is not easy. Because firms that pay high wages usually also offer good benefit packages, the casual observer often thinks that wages and employee benefits are *positively* related. Casual observation in this case is misleading, however, because it does not allow for the influences of *other factors*—such as the demands of the job and the quality, ability, and training of workers involved—that influence total compensation. The other factors are most conveniently controlled for statistically, and the few statistical studies on this subject tend to support the prediction of a negative relationship between wages and benefits.[36] The policy consequences of a negative wage vs. benefits trade-off are crucial, because government legislation designed to impose or improve employee benefits might well be paid for by workers in the form of lower future wage increases.

Policy Example: Employer-Provided Healthcare Benefits

Health insurance for workers in the United States is provided primarily through employers, where 72 percent of workers had access to employer health insurance policies in 2015. Access rates are greater for full-time workers (88 percent) than part-timer workers (22 percent)—and these rates rise with establishment size, from 58 percent in establishments that have under 100 workers to 90 percent for establishments that have over 500 workers.[37] The average employer paid $2.85 per hour (or $5,700 per year for a full-time worker) for health insurance premiums in 2015,[38] and employees directly paid, on average, another 71 cents per hour ($1,420 per year). Thus, employers directly pay for about 80 percent of the health insurance premiums for their employees.[39]

The Affordable Care Act (ACA, aka "Obamacare") passed in 2010 did not require employers to offer health insurance to their employees, but employers with more than 50 employees who do not offer health insurance may be subject to a fine of up to $2,000 per employee. The ACA, however, did require that all health insurance plans contain certain provisions:[40]

- Young adults must be allowed to remain on their parents' health insurance up to age 26.

- Insurers must not deny coverage to anyone for any reason, including current health status.

- Policies cannot impose lifetime limits on coverage.

- New plans are required to cover certain preventive services where no payment is required by the recipient.

- A minimum set of services must be covered.

The requirements imposed by the ACA tend to increase the health-insurance costs borne by employers in two ways: First, some employers who did not offer health insurance before the ACA now have incentives to offer it, and second, many of those with policies before the ACA now must expand coverage (most notably by covering the young adult children of their workers).

Because employers directly pay, on average, 80 percent of the costs of medical insurance for their employees, the theory of compensating wage differentials suggests that an increase in employer health insurance costs will be accompanied a fall in employee wages. On the *employer* side of the market, the added cost pressures cause firms to seek ways to cut labor costs elsewhere; because *workers* are being offered something of value, they might be willing to take a wage cut to obtain it. Indeed, one study estimated that a 10 percent rise in health insurance premiums was accompanied by a 2.3 percent fall in wages, and an analysis of the ACA requirement that young adult children be covered by their parents' health insurance found that yearly wages went down by about $1,200 in firms that had to newly cover these children.[41] Thus, at least some of the cost of improved healthcare coverage will seemingly be borne by workers in the form of downward pressures on wages.

EMPIRICAL STUDY 8.1

How Risky Are Estimates of Compensating Wage Differentials for Risk? The "Errors in Variables" Problem

Estimating the compensating wage differentials associated with the risk of fatal injury in the workplace requires the researcher to collect data, for a sample of individuals, on individuals' wages and a variety of nonrisk factors that affect these wages (including an indication of their occupation and industry). Measures of the risk of being killed at work are usually obtained from government reports, which tabulate this risk by occupation or industry; risks are then matched to each individual according to the occupation or industry indicated. The objective, of course, is to estimate (using multivariate regression techniques) the effect of risk on wages, after controlling for all other variables that affect wages. How confident can we be in the results obtained?

The two major sources of workplace-death statistics in the United States are the Bureau of Labor Statistics (BLS) and the National Institute for Occupational Safety and Health (NIOSH), but neither source is problem-free. BLS surveys employers about workplace injuries (including fatal injuries), while NIOSH collects its fatality data from an examination of death certificates. However, to judge how a fatality should be recorded is often difficult. For example, roughly 25 percent of U.S. fatalities at work occur in highway accidents, and another 12 percent result from homicides. Thus, the two sources, unsurprisingly, do not agree exactly on whether a fatality was work related; in 1995, for example, BLS data placed the number of workplace fatalities at 6,275, while NIOSH counted 5,314.

A second problem in calculating risk faced by individual workers arises from the happy fact that being killed at work is a relatively rare event (roughly four per 100,000 workers each year). Suppose, for example, we wanted to calculate risks for the 500 detailed occupational categories used by the U.S. Census within each of 200 narrowly defined industries. This would require 100,000 occupation-by-industry cells, and of the roughly 5,500 deaths each year, most cells would show up as having zero risk. For this reason, fatal injury risk is reported at rather aggregated levels—either by industry *or* by occupation, but *not by both together*.

BLS reports risks at the *national* level for industries or occupations, but only for cells that have at least five deaths. Thus, industries or occupations with relatively small numbers of workers or low levels of risk are not represented in their data. NIOSH reports risk measures by *state*, but only for highly aggregated industries and occupations (about 20 of each). Matching risk levels to workers at aggregated levels forces us to assume that all workers in the relevant occupation or industry face the same risk. For example, using NIOSH data for occupations assumes that within each state, police officers and dental assistants face the same risk (both are lumped together in the NIOSH sample as service workers). Alternatively, using BLS industry data forces us to assume that bookkeepers and lumberjacks in the logging industry (a narrowly defined industry in the BLS data) face identical risk.

Clearly, then, there are errors in attributing occupational or industry risk levels to individuals. Regression techniques assume that the *dependent* variable (in this case, the wage rate) is measured with error, but it assumes that the *independent* variables, such as risk of death, are not. When an "errors in variables" problem occurs with a particular independent variable, the estimated effect of that variable on the dependent variable is biased toward zero—which, of course, reduces our confidence in the results.

One study, for example, compared the different compensating wage differentials estimated by using four alternative risk measures: BLS risk by industry, BLS risk reported by occupation, NIOSH data by industry, and NIOSH data by occupation. In three of the four estimates, compensating differentials for added risk were significantly positive (as expected), although they varied in size—where the largest was over twice the size of the smallest. The fourth estimated wage differential was negative and therefore contrary to the predictions of theory.

Another study compared estimates of compensating wage differentials by using injury-risk data at the *industry* level (as done in the studies discussed previously) with estimates using risk data at the *employer* level. While one might expect that data at the employer level would be a more accurate characterization of risk facing an individual worker, injuries—especially with smaller firms—might be so relatively rare that firm-level data for any given year are not an accurate depiction of long-run risk facing the employee. Indeed, this study found that the estimated compensating wage differentials for added risk were *smaller* (but still positive) using firm-level data.

Sources: Dan A. Black and Thomas J. Kniesner, "On the Measurement of Job Risk in Hedonic Wage Models," *Journal of Risk and Uncertainty* 27 (December 2003): 205–220, 2003 Kluwer Academic Publishers; Rafael Lalive, "Did We Overestimate the Value of Health?" *Journal of Risk and Uncertainty* 27 (October 2003): 171–193

Review Questions

1. Building the oil pipeline across Alaska required the use of many construction workers recruited from the continental United States who lived in dormitories and worked in an inhospitable climate. Discuss the creation of a compensating wage differential for these jobs, by using ordinary supply and demand concepts.

2. Statement 1: "Business executives are profit maximizers." Statement 2: "Workers doing filthy, dangerous work receive higher wages, other things being equal." Can both of these statements be generally true? Why?

3. "Three methods are used to allocate labor across a spectrum of jobs that may differ substantially in working conditions: One is the use of force, one is the use of trickery, and one is the use of compensating wage differentials." Comment.

4. Suppose that someone claims that low-wage jobs lack the healthcare and pension benefits enjoyed by higher-wage employees. Assuming this claim to be true, does this fact contradict the theory of compensating wage differentials? Explain.

5. Is the following true, false, or uncertain? "Certain occupations, such as coal mining, are inherently dangerous to workers' health and safety. Therefore, unambiguously, the most appropriate government policy is the establishment and enforcement of rigid safety and health standards." Explain your answer.

6. Suppose that Congress were to mandate that all employers had to offer their employees a life insurance policy worth at least $50,000 in the event of death. Use economic theory, both positively and normatively, to analyze the effects of this mandate on employee well-being.

7. The U.S. government passed a law in 1942 that prohibited garment makers from employing independent contractors working out of their homes. The reason was that those working at home made less money, and policymakers believed that they were being exploited. Comment on the assertion that the difference in pay between factory workers and home workers doing the same tasks constitutes a measure of exploitation.

8. "The concept of compensating wage premiums for dangerous work does not apply to industries like the coal industry, where the union has forced all wages and other compensation items to be the same. Because

all mines must pay the same wage, compensating differentials cannot exist." Is this statement correct? (Assume that wages and other forms of pay must be equal for dangerous and nondangerous mines, and consider the implications for individual labor supply behavior.)

9. In 1991, Germany proposed that the European Union member states collectively agree that no one be allowed to work on Sundays (exceptions could be made for religious groups celebrating the Sabbath on a day other than Sunday). Use economic theory both *positively* and *normatively* to assess, as completely as you can, the effects of prohibiting work on Sundays.

10. In 2005, a federal court authorized United Airlines (UAL) to terminate its pension plan. The government would take over pension payments to retired UAL employees, but this action meant that pension benefits would be less than promised by UAL to both its current retirees and its current workers. What *future* labor market effects would you expect to occur from this sudden and unexpected reduction of pension benefits?

Problems

1. A researcher estimates the following wage equation for underwater construction workers: $W = 10 + 0.5D$, where W = the wage in dollars per hour and D = the depth underwater at which workers work, in meters. On the basis of this information, draw the offer curve and possible indifference curves for workers A and B: A works at a depth of 3 meters, and B works at 5 meters. At their current wages and depths, what is the trade-off (keeping utility constant) between hourly wages and a 1-meter change in depth that each worker is willing to make? Which worker has a greater willingness to pay for reduced depth at 3 meters of depth?

2. Consider the conditions of work in perfume factories. Assume that in New York perfume factories, workers dislike the smell of perfume, while in California plants, workers appreciate the smell of perfume, provided that the level does not climb above S^*. (If it rises above S^*, they will start to dislike it.) Suppose that firms incur no cost to reduce or eliminate the smell of perfume in perfume factories, and assume that the workers have an alternative wage, W^*. Draw a diagram using isoprofit and indifference curves that depicts the situation. (The New York and California isoprofit curves are the same, but their indifference curves differ.) What level of perfume smell is in the New York factories? What level is in the California factories? Is there a wage differential between the California workers and New York workers?

3. (Appendix 8A). Thomas's utility function is $U = \sqrt{Y}$, where Y = annual income. He has two job offers. One is in an industry that has no layoffs and where the annual pay is $40,000. The other industry has uncertainty about layoffs. Half the years are bad years, and layoffs push Thomas's

annual pay down to $22,500. The other years are good years. How much must Thomas earn in the good years in this job to compensate him for the high risk of layoffs?

4. The following two figures represent the labor market for two industries that require workers with the same skills and experience; however, industry B is characterized by much noisier working conditions than industry A is. What is the compensating wage differential between the two industries?

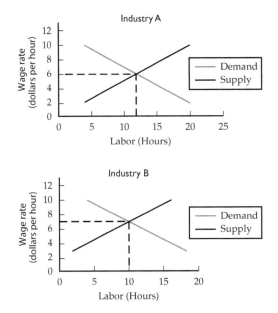

5. Sheldon is indifferent between a combination of 2 percent risk of injury and a wage rate of $15 per hour and a combination of 3 percent risk of injury and a wage rate of $18 per hour. Shelby is indifferent between a combination of 2 percent risk of injury and a wage rate of $16 per hour and a combination of 3 percent risk of injury and a wage rate of $18 per hour.

   a. Who has a stronger aversion toward risk?

   b. Consider a concave market "offer curve." Where along this curve is Sheldon's utility likely to be maximized? Compare this to where Shelby is likely to maximize utility. Explain.

6. The demand for labor in occupation A is $L_D = 20 - W$, where L_D = number of workers demanded for that occupation, in thousands. The supply of labor for occupation A is $L_A = -1.25 + 0.5W$. For occupation B, the demand for labor is similar, but the supply of labor is $L_B = -0.5 + 0.6W$, which is indicative of a more pleasant environment associated with that occupation in comparison with occupation A. What is the compensating wage differential between the two occupations?

7. The zero-profit isoprofit curve for company ABC is $W = 4 + 0.5R$, where W = the wage rate that the firm will offer at particular risk levels, R,

keeping profits at zero. The zero-profit isoprofit curve for company XY is $W = 3 + 0.75R$.

a. Draw the zero-profit isoprofit curves for each firm. What assumption about marginal returns to safety expenditures underlies a linear isoprofit curve?

b. At what risk level will the firms offer the same wage?

c. At low-risk levels, which firm will be preferred by workers? At high-risk levels, which firm will be preferred by workers? Explain.

Notes

1. A few people may be indifferent to noise and dirt in the workplace. We assume here that these people are so rare, or firm Y's demand for workers is so large, that Y cannot fill all its vacancies with just those who are totally insensitive to dirt and noise.

2. This idea is actually as old as the United States. In 1776, in chapter 10 of the *Wealth of Nations*, Adam Smith discussed that wages would vary depending on the "honourableness or dishonorableness" of the job.

3. Peter F. Kostiuk, "Compensating Differentials for Shift Work," *Journal of Political Economy* 98:5, pt. 1 (October 1990): 1054–1075. Shift-work differentials are even larger in France; see Joseph Lanfranchi, Henry Ohlsson, and Ali Skalli, "Compensating Wage Differentials and Shift Work Preferences," *Economics Letters* 74 (February 2002): 393–398. The compensating wage differentials of almost 12 percent have been estimated for registered nurses who work at night; see Edward J. Schumacher and Barry T. Hirsch, "Compensating Differentials and Unmeasured Ability in the Labor Market for Nurses: Why Do Hospitals Pay More?" *Industrial and Labor Relations Review* 50 (July 1997): 557–579; Alexandre Mas and Amanda Pallais, "Valuing Alternative Work Arrangements," *The American Economic Review* 107:12 (December 2017): 3722–3759, who consider, among other issues, the tradeoff between wages and work schedule flexibility.

4. Daniel S. Hamermesh, "The Timing of Work Over Time," *Economic Journal* 109 (January 1999): 37–66, finds evidence that as people become wealthier, they increasingly want to avoid working at night.

5. The point about holding all else constant is crucial. Without it, we might wonder why some jobs that many find extremely disagreeable, for example, are not among the most highly paid in the labor market. The relevant comparison is not all jobs but rather all jobs available to those with a certain level of education or set of skills.

6. W. Kip Viscusi, "Labor Market Valuations of Life and Limb: Empirical Evidence and Policy Implications," *Public Policy* 26 (Summer 1978): 359–386; W. Kip Viscusi and Michael J. Moore, "Worker Learning and

Compensating Differentials," *Industrial and Labor Relations Review* 45 (October 1991): 80–96, suggest that the accuracy of risk perceptions rises with job tenure. For an analysis of how well people estimate their risk of traffic fatality and their overall risk of death, see Henrik Andersson and Petter Lundborg, "Perception of Own Death Risk: An Analysis of Road-Traffic and Overall Mortality Risks," *Journal of Risk and Uncertainty* 34 (February 2007): 67–84. Another study has shown that people do adjust their behavior to even low probabilities of risk; see Daniel Sutter and Marc Poitras, "Do People Respond to Low Probability Risks? Evidence from Tornado Risk and Manufactured Homes," *Journal of Risk and Uncertainty* 40 (April 2010): 181–196. For a discussion of international estimates, see W. Kip Viscusi and Clayton Masterman, "Anchoring Biases in International Estimates of the Value of a Statistical Life," *Journal of Risk and Uncertainty* 54 (April 2017): 103–128.

7. U.S. Department of Labor, Bureau of Labor Statistics, "Employee Tenure Summary," news release USDL 18–1500, www.bls.gov/news.release/tenure.nr0.htm, September 20, 2018, Table 3; U.S. Department of Labor, Bureau of Labor Statistics, "Job Openings and Labor Turnover Survey," www.bls.gov/news.release/archives/jolts_03162018.htm; Peter Rupert, "Wage and Employer Changes Over the Life Cycle," in *Economic Commentary* (Federal Reserve Bank of Cleveland, Cleveland, April 15, 2004).

8. See Adam Smith, *Wealth of Nations* (New York: Modern Library, 1937): book 1, chapter 10.

9. In fact, those workers who prefer some job characteristics that many find disagreeable (e.g., working at night) might benefit greatly because they would not find working at night unpleasant and they would enjoy the wage premium from *most others'* not liking working at night.

10. Thomas J. Kniesner, W. Kip Viscusi, Christopher Woock, and James P. Ziliak, "The Value of a Statistical Life: Evidence from Panel Data," *Review of Economics and Statistics* 94 (February 2012): 74–87.

11. Christophe Daniel and Catherine Sofer, "Bargaining, Compensating Wage Differentials, and Dualism of the Labor Market: Theory and Evidence for France," *Journal of Labor Economics* 16 (July 1998): 546–575; Matthew A. Cole, Robert J.R. Elliott, and Joanne K. Lindley, "Dirty Money: Is There a Wage Premium for Working in a Pollution Intensive Industry?" *Journal of Risk and Uncertainty* 39 (October 2009): 161–180; Emilia Del Bono and Andrea Weber, "Do Wages Compensate for Anticipated Working Time Restrictions? Evidence from Seasonal Employment in Austria," *Journal of Labor Economics* 26 (January 2008): 181–221; Mas and Pallais, "Valuing Alternative Work Arrangements."

12. See Barry Gerhardt and Jerry M. Newman, *Compensation*, 13th ed. (New York: McGraw-Hill, 2020), for a discussion of allowances in expatriate pay packages.

13. See Claudia Goldin, "A Grand Convergence: Its Last Chapter," *American Economic Review* 104 (April 2014): 1091–1119; Youngjoo Cha and Kim A. Weeden, "Overwork and the Slow Convergence in the Gender Gap in Wages," *American Sociological Review* 79 (June 2014): 457–484.

14. The *philosophy* of hedonism (from the Greek word *hèdonè*, meaning "pleasure") is usually associated with Jeremy Bentham, a philosopher of the late eighteenth century who believed that people always behave in ways that they think would maximize their happiness. The analysis that follows is adapted primarily from Sherwin Rosen, "Hedonic Prices and Implicit Markets," *Journal of Political Economy* 82 (January/February 1974): 34–55.

15. U.S. Bureau of Labor Statistics, "2014 Census of Fatal Occupational Injuries (revised data)," www.bls.gov/iif/oshwc/cfoi/cfch0013.pdf; U.S. Bureau of Labor Statistics, "Employer-Reported Workplace Injuries and Illnesses—2014," USDL-15–2086, October 29, 2015.

16. U.S. Department of Labor, Bureau of Labor Statistics, www.bls.gov/charts/census-of-fatal-occupational-injuries/number-and-rate-of-fatal-work-injuries-by-occupation.htm.

17. Compensating wage differentials provide for *ex ante*—"before the fact"—compensation related to injury risk. Workers can also be compensated (to keep utility constant) by *ex post*—"after the fact," or after-injury—payments for damages. Workers' compensation insurance provides for ex post payments, but these payments typically offer incomplete compensation for all the costs of an injury.

18. When a "bad" is on the horizontal axis (as in Figure 8.1) and a "good" on the vertical axis, people with more of the "good" and less of the "bad" are unambiguously better off, and this combination is achieved by moving in a northwest direction on the graph.

19. If returns are permanently below normal, the owners will benefit from closing down the plant and investing their funds elsewhere. If returns are above normal, other investors will be attracted to the industry and profits will eventually be driven down by increased competition.

20. The theoretical implication that workers sort themselves into jobs on the basis of their preferences is directly tested in Alan B. Krueger and David Schkade, "Sorting in the Labor Market: Do Gregarious Workers Flock to Interactive Jobs?" *Journal of Human Resources* 43 (Fall 2008): 859–883.

21. Evidence shows that workers with fewer concerns about off-the-job risk (e.g., smokers) also choose higher-risk jobs; for an analysis of this issue, see W. Kip Viscusi and Joni Hersch, "Cigarette Smokers as Job Risk Takers," *Review of Economics and Statistics* 83 (May 2001): 269–280.

22. Note also that, in reality, employees surely don't face the infinite set of possible wage vs. risk tradeoffs implied by Figures 8.6 and 8.7.

23. Recall the set of wage offers depicted in Figure 8.6.

24. An important question, which we don't answer here, is, where do firms and workers end up in the shaded region—that is, how do they bargain over who gains more?

25. Kniesner, Viscusi, Woock, and Ziliak, "The Value of a Statistical Life: Evidence from Panel Data." For other articles on the value people place on reducing risk, see Jonathan M. Lee and Laura O. Taylor, "Randomized Safety Inspections and Risk Exposure on the Job: Quasi-Experimental Estimates of the Value of a Statistical Life," *American Economic Journal* 11 (November 2019): 350–374; Chris Rohlfs, Ryan Sullivan, and Thomas Kniesner, "New Estimates of the Value of a Statistical Life Using Air Bag Regulations as a Quasi-Experiment," *American Economic Journal: Economic Policy* 7 (February 2015): 331–359.

26. John Morrall III, "Saving Lives: A Review of the Record," *Journal of Risk and Uncertainty* 27 (December 2003): 221–237. The estimated "willingness to pay" of $1,100 for a one-in-10,000 reduction in the risk of death is about what is used by the U.S. Environmental Protection Agency when it performs cost–benefit analyses of proposed federal pollution standards.

27. Economists tend to call this aggregate willingness to pay for a program that is predicted to save one life the "value of a statistical life". This phrase does not imply what a worker would pay to avoid certain death. Rather, it is a shorthand way of saying what workers *in the aggregate* are willing to pay for a program that reduces each person's risk of death (already a low number in the typical case) enough to save one life in the larger population to which the workers belong.

28. A worker earning $15,000 per year for 2,000 hours of work can have their hourly wage increased from $7.50 to $8 through either a straightforward increase in current money payments or a reduction in their working hours to 1,875, with no reduction in yearly earnings. If they receive their raise in the form of paid vacation time, they are in fact being paid in the form of a commodity—leisure time.

29. A famous example of this concept, with respect to giving gifts versus cash, is Joel Waldfogel, "The Deadweight Loss of Christmas," *The American Economic Review* 83:5 (December 1993): 1328–1336.

30. For more detail on how employees consider the relative merits of different forms of compensation, see Kevin F. Hallock, *Pay* (Cambridge: Cambridge University Press, 2012).

31. Nicole Maestas, Kathleen J. Mullen, David Powell, Till von Wachter, and Jeffrey B. Wenger, "The Value of Working Conditions in the United States and the Structure of Wages" (Working Paper No. 25204,

National Bureau of Economic Research, Cambridge, MA, October 2018), examines employee willingness to pay for a host of working conditions.

32. As noted in footnote 12 of Chapter 8, the indifference curves in the previous section sloped *upward* because a "bad" (risk of injury), not a "good" (benefits), was on the horizontal axis.

33. Evidence that employers are sensitive to employee preferences when offering employee benefits can be found in Itzik Fadlon, Jessica Laird, and Torben Heien Nielsen, "Do Employer Pension Contributions Reflect Employee Preferences? Evidence from a Retirement Savings Reform in Denmark," *American Economic Journal: Applied Economics* 8 (July 2016): 196–216.

34. Consider also that firms may offer different forms of cash (salary versus incentives or bonus) that may attract different sorts of workers. This is discussed more in Chapter 11.

35. See Steven G. Allen, "Compensation, Safety, and Absenteeism: Evidence from the Paper Industry," *Industrial and Labor Relations Review* 34 (January 1981): 207–218; Steven G. Allen, "An Empirical Model of Work Attendance," *Review of Economics and Statistics* 63 (February 1981): 77–87.

36. See Edward Montgomery and Kathryn Shaw, "Pensions and Wage Premia," *Economic Inquiry* 35 (July 1997): 510–522, for a paper that references earlier work on compensating wage differentials for pensions.

37. U.S. Department of Labor, Bureau of Labor Statistics, "Employee Benefits in the United States—March 2015," USDL-15-1432 (July 24, 2015), Table 2.

38. U.S. Department of Labor, Bureau of Labor Statistics, "Employer Costs per Hour Worked for Employee Compensation and Costs as a Percent of Total Compensation: Civilian Workers," Economic News Release (June 9, 2016), Table 1.

39. U.S. Department of Labor, Bureau of Labor Statistics, "Employee Benefits in the United States—March 2015," Table 3.

40. The Henry J. Kaiser Foundation, "Summary of Coverage Provisions in the Patient Protection and Affordable Care Act" (July 17, 2012), http://kff.org/health-costs/issue-brief/summary-of-coverage-provisions-in-the-patient/.

41. Katherine Baicker and Amitabh Chandra, "The Labor Market Effects of Rising Health Insurance Premiums," *Journal of Labor Economics* 24 (July 2006): 609–634; Gopi Shah Goda, Monica Farid, and Jay Bhattacharya, "The Incidence of Mandated Health Insurance: Evidence from the Affordable Care Act Dependent Care Mandate" (Working Paper No. 21846, National Bureau of Economic Research, Cambridge, MA, January 2016). Similar results can be seen in Jeffrey Clemens and

David M. Cutler, "Who Pays for Public Employee Health Costs?" *Journal of Health Economics* (December 2014): 65–76; Jay Bhattacharya and M. Kate Bundorf, "The Incidence of Healthcare Costs of Obesity," *Journal of Health Economics* 28 (May 2009): 649–658; Matthew S. Dey and Christopher J. Flinn, "An Equilibrium Model of Health Insurance Provision and Wage Determination," *Econometrica* 73 (March 2005): 571–627.

Selected Readings

Duncan, Greg, and Bertil Holmlund. "Was Adam Smith Right After All? Another Test of the Theory of Compensating Wage Differentials." *Journal of Labor Economics* 1 (October 1983): 366–379.

Fishback, Price V. "Operations of 'Unfettered' Labor Markets: Exit and Voice in American Labor Markets at the Turn of the Century." *Journal of Economic Literature* 36 (June 1998): 722–765.

Greenstone, Michael. "The Continuing Impact of Sherwin Rosen's 'Hedonic Prices and Implicit Markets: Product Differentiation in Pure Competition'." *Journal of Political Economy* 125 (December 2017): 1891–1902.

Rosen, Sherwin. "Hedonic Prices and Implicit Markets: Product Differentiation in Pure Competition." *Journal of Political Economy* 82 (January–February 1974): 34–55.

Rosen, Sherwin. "The Theory of Equalizing Differences." In *Handbook of Labor Economics*, eds. Orley Ashenfelter and Richard Layard, 641–692. New York: North-Holland, 1986.

Viscusi, W. Kip. *Pricing Lives: Guideposts for a Safer Society*. Cambridge, MA: The MIT Press, 2018.

Viscusi, W. Kip, and Joseph E. Aldy. "The Value of a Statistical Life: A Critical Review of Market Estimates Throughout the World." *Journal of Risk and Uncertainty* 27 (August 2003): 5–76.

Appendix 8A

Compensating Wage Differentials and Layoffs

As mentioned in Chapter 8's text, one of the circumstances identified by Adam Smith under which compensating wage differentials would arise involves the "constancy or inconstancy of employment." While evidence, as we shall see, supports this prediction, the relationship between wages and layoff probabilities is by no means as simple as Smith thought. In particular, three issues are relevant to the analysis, all of which we briefly discuss here.[1]

Unconstrained Choice of Work Hours

Suppose that in the spirit of Chapters 6 and 7, employees are free to choose their hours of work in a labor market that offers an infinite choice of work hours. Given the wage that a particular worker can command and their nonwage income, the utility-maximizing choice of working hours would be selected. For the person depicted in Figure 8A.1, the utility-maximizing choice of work hours is H^*, given their offered wage rate (W^*) and level of nonwage income (assumed here to be zero).

If H^* is thought of in terms of yearly work hours, we can easily understand why a worker might *prefer* a job involving a layoff. Suppose H^* is 1,500 hours per year, or essentially three-quarters of the typical "full-time" job of 2,000 hours. One could work six hours a day, five days a week, for 50 weeks a year, or one could work eight hours a day, five days a week, for nine months and agree to be laid off for three months. Which alternative holds more appeal to any given individual depends on their preferences with respect to large blocks of leisure or household time, but clearly, many people value such large blocks. Teachers in the United States, for example, typically work full time during a nine-month school year, and then some of them vacation during the summer. Many other jobs, from the construction trades to work in canning factories, involve predictable seasonal layoffs, and workers in these jobs may have chosen them because they value the leisure or household production time accompanying the layoffs.

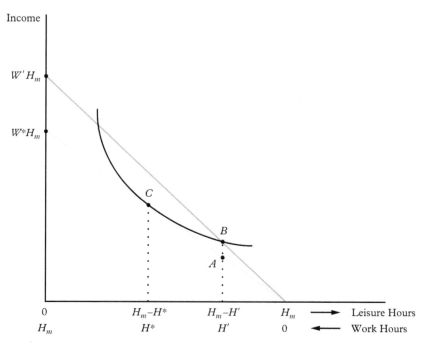

Figure 8A.1 Choice of Hours of Work

In other words, the theory of compensating wage differentials suggests they will be positive only when a job characteristic is regarded as bad by the marginal worker. Predictable blocks of leisure or household time accompanying seasonal layoffs might not be regarded as bad by the marginal worker. In fact, workers in some markets might see layoffs as a mechanism through which they can best achieve their desired yearly hours of work.

Constrained Hours of Work

Suppose that the worker depicted in Figure 8A.1 is offered a choice between a job offering wage W^* and hours H^* and one offering fewer hours than desired because of a predictable layoff each year that reduces the hours of work to H'. Clearly, if the wage for the latter job remains at W^*, the worker's utility will be reduced by taking the job offering H' hours because they will be on an indifference curve passing through point A. The job that offers W^* and H^* is thus clearly preferred.

However, suppose that H' is offered at a wage of W', where W' exceeds W^* by enough such that point B can be reached. Point B, where the wage is W' and hours of work are H', is on the *same* indifference curve as point C (the utility-maximizing point when W^* is the offered wage). Point B is not a point of utility maximization at a wage offer of W', but if the worker is offered an unconstrained choice of hours at wage rate W^*, or a wage of W' where working hours are *constrained* to equal H', they would be indifferent between the two job offers.[2]

In the previous example, $(W' - W^*)$ is the compensating wage differential that would have to arise for the worker to consider a job where hours of work were constrained to lie below those otherwise desired. Many people view a layoff as an event that prevents workers from working the number of hours that they would otherwise desire to work. If this is the case, and if these layoffs are predictable and known with certainty, such as layoffs accompanying model changeovers in the auto industry, then compensating wage differentials associated with the predictable, certain layoff rate would arise in a well-functioning labor market (i.e., one where workers are informed and mobile).[3]

The Effects of Uncertain Layoffs

In the previous section, we assumed that layoffs were predictable and certain. In most cases, however, they are not. Although we might expect layoff rates to be higher in some industries than in others, they are in fact often subject to considerable random fluctuation *within* industries over the years. This *uncertainty* of layoffs is itself another aspect of affected jobs that is usually thought to be a negative feature and for which a compensating wage differential might arise.

Suppose that utility is measurable and is a function only of income, so that it can be graphed against income (Y), as in Figure 8A.2.[4] Suppose also that the person depicted is offered a job for which a wage of W' and yearly hours of H' are known *with certainty*. The utility associated with these H' hours, $U(H')$, is a function of their income at H' hours of work: $W'H'$ (again assuming no nonwage income).

Now, suppose that another job is paying W' in which the *average* hours of work per year are H', but half of the time H_h is worked, and half of the time H_l is worked. Although we have assumed that $0.5H_h + 0.5H_l = H'$, so that over the years the person averages H' hours of work, with the concave utility function that we have drawn, the person's average utility is in the end *below* $U(H')$. To understand this, we must look closely at Figure 8A.2.

When the person's working hours are H_h, which is half the time, they earn $W'H_h$, and this income yields a utility of $U(H_h)$. Thus, half the time, the worker will be at point C enjoying utility level $U(H_h)$. The other half of the time, however, the person will be working H_l hours, be earning $W'H_l$ in income, and be at point A enjoying utility of $U(H_l)$. Their average utility is thus $\bar{U}$, which is $\bar{U} = 0.5\ U(H_h) + 0.5\ U(H_l)$. Note that $\bar{U}$, which is midway between $U(H_h)$ and $U(H_l)$ in our example, lies *below* $U(H')$—the utility derived from a job paying W' and employing the person for H' hours *with certainty* every year.

Why is $\bar{U} < U(H')$ even though H' hours are worked on *average* in both cases? The answer lies in the concavity of the utility function, which economists define as exhibiting *risk aversion*. Moving from $Y(H')$ to $Y(H_h)$ covers the same absolute distance on the horizontal axis as moving from $Y(H')$ to $Y(H_l)$, but the changes in *utility* are not the same in magnitude. In particular, moving from $Y(H')$ to $Y(H_h)$ (points B to C) in the good years adds *less* to utility than moving from $Y(H')$ to $Y(H_l)$ (points B to A) in the bad years takes away. Put differently, the concavity of the total utility curve in Figure 8A.2 implies diminishing marginal utility of income. Thus, in the

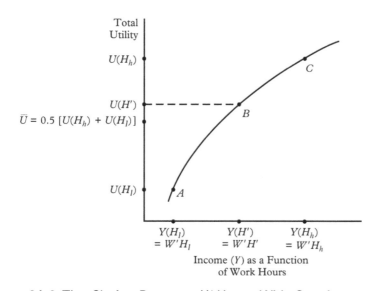

Figure 8A.2 The Choice Between H' Hours With Certainty and H' Hours on Average

unlucky years, when hours are below H', a relatively big drop in utility (as compared to the utility associated with H' hours) occurs, whereas in the lucky years, the added income increases utility by a relatively small amount.

The upshot of this discussion is that when workers are averse to risk—that is, when their utility functions are concave such that they in essence place a larger value on negative changes from a given level of income than they do on positive changes of equal dollar magnitude—they would prefer a job paying W' and offering H' hours with certainty to one paying W' and offering H' hours only on average. Thus, to compensate them for the loss in utility associated with *risk aversion*, they would require a wage above W' for the job offering H' hours only on average.

The Observed Wage–Layoff Relationship

The previous discussion centered on worker preferences regarding layoffs. For compensating wage differentials to arise, of course, employers must be willing to pay them. That is, employers must profit from being able to lay off workers, and if we are to observe firms' pursuing a high-wage, high-layoff strategy, their gains from layoff must exceed their costs of higher wages.

The previous discussion also neglected unemployment insurance (UI) payments to laid-off workers. This topic is discussed in some detail in Chapter 14. Here, we need note only that if UI payments fully compensate laid-off workers for their lost utility, compensating wage differentials will not arise. Compensating wage differentials will arise only if UI payments do not fully compensate laid-off workers.[5]

One study that carefully examined the relationship between wages and layoffs suggests that the compensating wage differential for an average probability of layoff is around 4 percent of wages, where over 80 percent of this differential was related to the aversion to risk associated with the variability (uncertainty) in layoff rates facing workers over time. Workers in the high-layoff industries of automobile manufacturing and construction received estimated compensating wage differentials ranging over the early 1970s from 6 percent to 14 percent and 6 percent to 11 percent, respectively.[6] A study of farm workers around 1990 found that those who risked unemployment by working seasonally were paid from 9 percent to 12 percent more per hour than those who held permanent jobs in farming.[7]

Notes

1. The analysis in this appendix draws heavily on John M. Abowd and Orley Ashenfelter, "Anticipated Unemployment, Temporary Layoffs, and Compensating Wage Differentials," in *Studies in Labor Markets*, ed. Sherwin Rosen (Chicago: University of Chicago Press, 1981): 141–170.

2. Point *B* is not a point of tangency; that is, at a wage of *W'*, the worker depicted in Figure 8A.1 would prefer to work more than *H'* hours if

they were free to choose work hours. We have assumed in the discussion that the choice is constrained such that hours cannot exceed H'.

3. A similar argument can be used to predict that workers will receive compensating wage differentials if they are forced to work longer hours than they would otherwise prefer. For the argument and evidence in support of it, see Ronald G. Ehrenberg and Paul L. Schumann, "Compensating Wage Differentials for Mandatory Overtime," *Economic Inquiry* 22 (December 1984).

4. Although economists typically work with *ordinal* utility functions, which specify the relative ranking of alternatives but do not assign each alternative a numerical value of utility, the analysis of choice under uncertainty requires the use of *cardinal* utility functions (ones in which each alternative is assigned a specific numerical value of utility).

5. We note that in some cases, UI payments pay *more* than workers earned before layoff. This was the case during the first half of 2020, when workers, in addition to their normal state unemployment payments, were paid an additional $600 per week from the federal government amid the COVID-19 crisis.

6. These estimates are from the Abowd and Ashenfelter article in footnote 1 of Appendix 8A here. Similar evidence can be found in Elisabeth Magnani, "Product Market Volatility and the Adjustment of Earnings to Risk," *Industrial Relations* 41 (April 2002): 304–328. For those interested in how UI benefits affect wages, see David A. Anderson, "Compensating Wage Differentials and the Optimal Provision of Unemployment Insurance," *Southern Economic Journal* 60 (January 1994): 644–656.

7. Enrico Moretti, "Do Wages Compensate for Risk of Unemployment? Parametric and Semiparametric Evidence from Seasonal Jobs," *Journal of Risk and Uncertainty* 20 (January 2000): 45–66.

Investments in Human Capital: Education and Training

Many labor supply choices require a substantial initial *investment* on the part of the worker. Recall that investments, by definition, entail an initial cost that one hopes to recoup over some period of time. Thus, for many labor supply decisions, *current* wages and working conditions are not the only deciding factors. Modeling these decisions requires developing a framework that incorporates investment behavior and a *lifetime* perspective.

Workers undertake three major kinds of labor market investments: education and training, migration, and searching for new jobs. All three investments involve an initial cost, and all three are made in the hope and expectation that the investment will pay off well into the future. To emphasize the essential similarity of these investments to other kinds of investments, economists refer to them as investments in *human capital*, a term that conceptualizes workers as embodying a set of skills that can be "rented out" to employers. The knowledge and skills that a worker has—which come from education and training, including the learning that experience yields—generate a certain *stock* of productive capital. The *value* of this productive capital is derived from how much these skills can earn in the labor market. Job search and migration are also activities that increase the value of one's human capital by increasing the price (wage) received for a given stock of skills.

EXAMPLE 9.1

War and Human Capital

We can illustrate the relative importance of physical and human capital by noting some interesting facts about severely war-damaged cities. The atomic attack on Hiroshima in 1945 destroyed 70 percent of the city's buildings and killed about 30 percent of the population. Survivors fled the city in the aftermath of the bombing, but within three months, two-thirds of the city's surviving population had returned. Because the air-burst bomb left the city's underground utility networks intact, power was restored to surviving areas in one day. Through railway service began again in two days, and telephone service was restarted in a week. Production plants responsible for three-quarters of the city's industrial production (many were located on the outskirts of the city and were undamaged) could have begun normal operations within 30 days.

In Hamburg, Germany, a city of around 1.5 million in the summer of 1943, Allied bombing raids over a ten-day period in July and August destroyed about half of the buildings in the city and killed about 3 percent of the city's population. Although considerable damage was dealt to the water supply system, electricity and gas service became adequate within a few days after the last attack, and within four days, the telegraph system was again operating. The central bank was reopened, and its business had begun to function normally after one week. Postal service was resumed within 12 days of the attack. The Strategic Bombing Survey reported that within five months, Hamburg had recovered up to 80 percent of its former productivity.

The speed and success of recovery from these disasters prompted one economist to offer the following two observations:

1. The fraction of the community's real wealth represented by visible material capital is small relative to the fraction represented by the accumulated knowledge and talent of the population.
2. There are enormous reserves of energy and effort in the population not drawn upon in ordinary times but which can be utilized under special circumstances such as those prevailing in the aftermath of disaster.

Source: Jack Hirshleifer, *Economic Behavior in Adversity* (Chicago: University of Chicago Press, 1987): 12–14, 78–79

Society's total wealth is a combination of human capital and nonhuman capital. Human capital includes accumulated investments in such activities as education, job training, and migration, whereas nonhuman capital includes society's stock of natural resources, buildings, and machinery. Total per capita wealth in the United States, for example, was estimated to be roughly $517,000 in 2010, about 70 percent of which was in the form of human capital.[1] (Example 9.1 illustrates the overall importance of human capital in another way.)

Investment in the knowledge and skills of workers takes place in three stages. First, in early childhood, the acquisition of human capital is determined largely by the decisions of others. Parental resources and guidance, plus our cultural environment and early schooling experiences, help to influence basic language and mathematical skills, attitudes toward learning, and general health and life expectancy (which themselves affect the ability to work). Second, teenagers and young adults go through a stage in which they acquire knowledge and skills as full-time students in a high school, college, university, or vocational training program. Finally, after entering the labor market, workers' additions to their human capital generally take place on a part-time basis, through on-the-job training, online education, or participation in relatively short, formal training programs. In this chapter, we focus on the latter two stages.

One of the challenges of any behavioral theory is to explain why people faced with what appears to be the same environment make different choices. We see in this chapter that individuals' decisions about investing in human capital are affected by the ease and speed with which they learn, their aspirations and expectations about the future, and their access to financial resources.

Human Capital Investments: The Basic Model

Like any other investment, an investment in human capital entails costs that are borne in the near term with the expectation that benefits will accrue in the future. Generally speaking, we can divide the *costs* of adding to human capital into three categories:

1. *Out-of-pocket* or *direct* expenses, including tuition costs and expenditures on books and other supplies.

2. *Forgone earnings* that arise because during the investment period, people usually cannot work, at least not full time.

3. *Psychological losses* that occur because learning is often difficult and tedious.

In the case of educational and training investments by workers, the expected *returns* are in the form of higher future earnings, increased job satisfaction over their lifetime, and a greater appreciation of nonmarket activities and interests. Even if we could quantify all the future benefits, adding them up over the relevant years is not a straightforward procedure, because of the *delay* involved in receiving these investment returns.

The Concept of Present Value

When an investment decision is made, the investor commits to a *current* outlay of expenses in return for a stream of expected *future* benefits. Investment returns are clearly subject to an element of risk (because no one can predict the future with certainty), but they are also *delayed* in the sense that they typically flow in over what may be a long period. The investor needs to compare the value of the current investment outlays with the current value of expected returns, but in so doing must take into account effects of the delay in returns. We explain how this is done.

Suppose that a woman is offered $100 now or $100 in a year. Would she be equally attracted to these two alternatives? No, because if she received the money now, she could either spend (and enjoy) it now or invest the $100 and earn interest over the next year. If the interest rate were, say, 5 percent, $100 now could grow into $105 in a year's time. Thus, $100 received *now* is worth more than $100 to be received in a year.

With an interest rate of 5 percent, an offer of $105 would need to be received in a year to match the value of getting $100 now. Because $100 now could be grown into \$105 at the end of a year, these two offers have equivalent value. Another way of putting this equivalence is to say that with a 5 percent interest rate, the future value in a year (B_1) of \$100 now is \$105. This calculation can be shown algebraically by recognizing that after a year, the woman could have her principal (B_0) of \$100 plus interest ($r = 0.05$) on that principal:

$$B_1 = B_0 + B_0(r) = B_0(1 + r) = 100(1.05) = 105 \tag{9.1}$$

We can also say that the present value (B_0) of \$105 to be received *in a year* is (at a 5 percent interest rate) \$100. Because $B_1 = B_0(1 + r)$, the following is also true:

$$B_0 = \frac{B_1}{(1 + r)} = \frac{105}{1.05} = 100 \tag{9.2}$$

Thus, receiving \$105 in one year is equivalent to receiving \$100 in the present and investing it at 5 percent for one year. The procedure for taking a future value and transforming it into its present-value equivalent is called *discounting*. If the future return is only a year away, we discount (divide) it by the factor $(1 + r)$ to calculate its present-value equivalent.

What if the return is two years away? If we were to take a present sum of B_0 and invest it, then after one year, it would equal $B_1 = B_0(1 + r)$. At the end of that first year, we could take our new asset (B_1) and invest it for another year at interest rate r. At the end of two years, then, we would have the sum B_2:

$$B_2 = B_1 + B_1(r) = B_1(1 + r) \tag{9.3}$$

Substituting equation (9.1) into equation (9.3) yields the following:

$$B_2 = B_0(1 + r) + B_0(1 + r)(r) = B_0(1 + r)(1 + r) = B_0(1 + r)^2 \tag{9.4}$$

(Equation (9.4) illustrates the law of compound interest because in the second period, interest is earned on both the original principal and the interest earned in the first period.)

Now, if $B_2 = B_0(1 + r)^2$, the following is also true:

$$B_0 = \frac{B_2}{(1 + r)^2} \tag{9.5}$$

To find the present value of a benefit to be received in two years, then, requires that we discount the future benefit by $(1 + r)^2$. If the benefit were to be received in three years, we can use the logic underlying equations (9.3) and (9.4) to calculate that the discount factor would be $(1 + r)^3$, benefits in four years would be discounted to their present values by dividing by $(1 + r)^4$, and other benefits over given years could be discounted similarly. Clearly, the discount factors rise exponentially, reflecting that current funds can earn compound interest if left invested at interest rate r.

If a human capital investment yields returns of B_1 in the first year, B_2 in the second, and so forth for T years, the sum of these benefits has a present value that is calculated as follows:

$$\text{Present Value} = \frac{B_1}{1+r} + \frac{B_2}{(1+r)^2} + \frac{B_3}{(1+r)^3} + \cdots + \frac{B_T}{(1+r)^T} \qquad (9.6)$$

where the interest rate (or discount rate) is r. As long as r is positive, benefits in the future will be progressively discounted. For example, if $r = 0.06$, benefits payable in 30 years would receive a weight that is only 17 percent of the weight placed on benefits payable immediately ($1.06^{30} = 5.74$; $1/5.74 = 0.17$). The smaller r is, the greater the weight placed on future benefits; for example, if $r = 0.02$, a benefit payable in 30 years would receive a weight that is 55 percent of the weight given to an immediate benefit.

Modeling the Human Capital Investment Decision

Our model of human capital investment assumes that people are utility maximizers and take a lifetime perspective when making choices about education and training. They are therefore assumed to compare the near-term investment costs (C) with the present value of expected future benefits when they make a decision, say, about additional schooling. Investment in additional schooling is attractive if the present value of future benefits exceeds costs:

$$\frac{B_1}{1+r} + \frac{B_2}{(1+r)^2} + \cdots + \frac{B_T}{(1+r)^T} > C \qquad (9.7)$$

Utility maximization, of course, requires that people continue to make additional human capital investments as long as condition (9.7) is met and that they stop only when the benefits of additional investment are equal to or less than the additional costs.

We can use two ways to measure whether the criterion in (9.7) has been met. Using the *present-value method*, we can specify a value for the discount rate, r, and then determine how the present value of benefits compares with costs. Alternatively, we can adopt the *internal rate of return method*, which asks, how large could the discount rate be and still render the investment profitable? Clearly, if the benefits are so large that even a high discount rate would render investment profitable, then the project is worthwhile. In practice, we calculate this internal rate of return by setting the present value of benefits equal to costs, solving for r, and then comparing r to the rate of return on other investments.[2]

Some basic implications of the model embedded in expression (9.7) are illustrated graphically in Figure 9.1, which depicts human capital decisions in terms of marginal costs and marginal benefits (focus for now on the black lines in the figure). The marginal costs (MC) of each additional unit of human capital (e.g., the tuition, supplies, forgone earnings, and psychological costs of an additional year of schooling) are assumed to be constant. The present

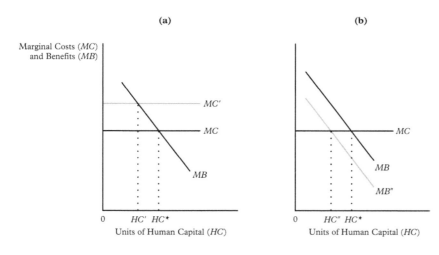

Figure 9.1 The Optimum Acquisition of Human Capital

value of the marginal benefits (*MB*) is shown as declining, because each added year of schooling means fewer years over which benefits can be collected. The utility-maximizing amount of human capital (*HC**) for any individual is shown as that amount for which *MC* = *MB*.

Those who find learning to be especially arduous implicitly attach a higher marginal psychological cost to acquiring human capital. As shown by the blue line, *MC′*, in Figure 9.1a, individuals with higher *MC* acquire lower levels of human capital (compare *HC′* with *HC**). Similarly, those who expect smaller future benefits from additional human capital investments (the blue line, *MB″*, in Figure 9.1b) acquire less human capital.

This straightforward theory yields some interesting insights about the behavior and earnings of workers. Many of these insights can be discovered by analyzing the decision confronting young adults about whether to invest full time in college after leaving high school.

The Demand for a College Education

The demand for a college education, as measured by the percentage of graduating high school seniors who enroll in college, is surprisingly variable. For men, enrollment rates went from 55.2 percent in 1970, down to 46.7 percent in 1980, back up to 58 percent in 1990, and even higher to 66.9 percent by 2018. The comparable enrollment rates for women started lower, at 48.5 percent in 1970, rose slowly during the 1970s, and have since risen quickly thereafter, reaching 71.4 percent by 2018. Why have enrollment rates followed these patterns?

Weighing the Costs and Benefits of College

Clearly, people attend college when they believe that they will be better off by so doing. For some, at least part of the benefits may be short term—they

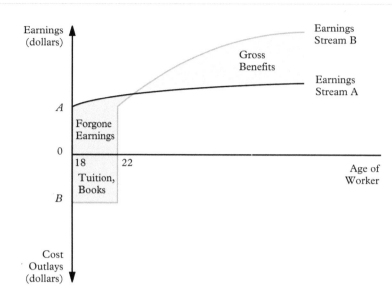

Figure 9.2 Alternative Earnings Streams

like the courses or the lifestyle of a student—and to this extent, college is at least partially a *consumption* good. The consumption benefits of college, however, are unlikely to change much over the course of a decade, so changes in college attendance rates over relatively short periods of time probably reflect changes in *MC* or benefits associated with the *investment* aspects of college attendance.

A person considering college has, in some broad sense, a choice between two streams of earnings over their lifetime. Stream A begins immediately but does not rise very high; it is the earnings stream of a high school graduate. Stream B (the college graduate) has a negative income for the first four years (owing to college tuition costs and the fact that students earn either zero or certainly less than they would have earned during these four years in the absence of attending college), followed by a period when the salary may be less than what the high school graduate makes, but then it takes off and rises above stream A. Both streams are illustrated in Figure 9.2. (Why these streams are differentially *curved* is discussed later in this chapter.) The streams shown in Figure 9.2 are stylized so that we can emphasize some basic points. Actual earnings streams are shown in Figures 9.3 and 9.4.

Generally, the earnings of the college graduate would have to rise above those of the high school graduate to induce someone to invest in a college education (unless, of course, the consumption-related returns were large). The gross benefits—the difference in earnings between the two streams—must total much more than the costs, because such returns are in the future and are therefore discounted. For example, suppose that obtaining a four-year college education costs $50,000 per year and that the real interest rate (the nominal rate less the rate of inflation) is 3 percent. The after-college returns—if the same each year—must be $8,653 in constant-dollar terms (i.e., after taking away the effects of inflation) each year for 40 years in order to justify the investment on purely monetary grounds. These returns must be $8,653 because $200,000 invested at a 3 percent interest rate can provide a payment (of interest and principal) totaling $8,653 a year for 40 years, starting in year 5.[3]

Predictions of the Theory

In deciding whether to attend college, no doubt few students make the precise calculations suggested in expression (9.7). Nevertheless, if they make less-formal estimates that take into account the same factors, we can make—and will explain—four predictions concerning the demand for college education:

1. "Present-oriented" people are less likely to go to college than forward-looking people (other things being equal).

2. The benefits of a college education rise with the length of time (T in equation (9.7)) over which they can be obtained; thus, most college students will be young, because they will have more time to recover the costs of the investment.

3. College attendance will decrease if the costs of college rise (other things being equal).

4. College attendance will increase if the gap between the earnings of college graduates and high school graduates widens (again, other things being equal).

Present-Oriented Perspective   Although we all discount the future somewhat with respect to the present, psychologists use the term *present oriented* to describe people who do not weight future events or outcomes heavily. In terms of expressions (9.6) and (9.7), a present-oriented person is one who uses a high discount rate (r).

Suppose that we were to calculate investment returns by using the *present-value method*. If r is large, the present value of benefits associated with college will be lower than if r is smaller. Thus, a present-oriented person would impute smaller benefits to college attendance than one who is less present oriented, and those who are present oriented would be less likely to attend college. Using the *internal rate of return method* for evaluating the soundness of a college education, we would arrive at the same result. If a college education earns an 8 percent rate of return but the individuals in question are so present oriented that they would insist on a 25 percent rate of return before investing, they would likewise decide not to attend.

The prediction that present-oriented people are less likely to attend college than forward-looking ones is difficult to substantiate because the rates of discount that people use in making investment decisions can rarely be quantified.[4] However, the model does suggest that people who have a high propensity to invest in education will also engage in other forward-looking behavior. Certain medical statistics tend to support this prediction.

In the United States, a strong statistical correlation exists between education and health status.[5] People with more years of schooling have lower mortality rates, fewer symptoms of disease (such as high blood pressure, high cholesterol levels, abnormal X-rays), and a greater tendency to report themselves to be in good health. This effect of education on health is independent of income, which appears to have no effect of its own on health status except at the lowest poverty levels. Is this correlation between education and health a result of better use of medical resources by better-educated people? Seemingly, no. Better-educated people undergoing surgery choose the same doctors, enter the hospital at the same stage of disease, and have the same length of stay as less-educated people of equal income.

What *might* cause this correlation is a more forward-looking attitude among those who have obtained more education. People with lower discount rates are more likely to attend college, and they are *also* more likely to adopt forward-looking habits of health. They might choose healthier diets, be more aware of health risks, and make more use of preventive medicine. This explanation for the correlation between education and health is not the only plausible one, but it receives some direct support from U.S. data on cigarette smoking.[6] From 1966 to 1987, the proportion of male college graduates who smoked fell by 50 percent, whereas it was unchanged among male high school dropouts. The less-educated group was likely as informed of smoking dangers, but they were probably less willing to give up a present source of pleasure for a distant benefit. Thus, we have at least some evidence that people who invest in education also engage in *other* forward-looking behavior. (See Example 9.2 for evidence that the way languages *grammatically* treat future events affects the investment behaviors of their native speakers.)

Age   Given similar *yearly* benefits of going to college, young people have a larger present value of *total* benefits than do older workers simply because they have a longer remaining work life ahead of them.[7] In terms of expression (9.7), T is greater for younger people than for older ones. We would therefore expect younger people to have a greater propensity than older people to obtain a college education or engage in other forms of training activity. This prediction is parallel to the predictions in Chapter 5 about which workers employers will decide to invest in when they make decisions about hiring or specific training.

Costs   A third prediction of our model is that human capital investments are more likely when costs are lower. The major monetary costs of college attendance are forgone earnings and the direct costs of tuition, books, and fees. (Food and lodging are not always opportunity costs of going to college, because some of these costs would have to be incurred in any event.) Thus, when forgone earnings or tuition costs fall, other things being equal, we expect a rise in college enrollment; conversely, when either of these costs rise, theory predicts a fall in college enrollment.[8]

EXAMPLE 9.2

Can Language Affect Investment Behavior?

Languages differ in how future events are framed. In talking about today's weather, English speakers would say, "It is cold today," but in discussing tomorrow's weather, the language requires them to say, "It will be cold tomorrow." In German, however, the equivalent statements would be "It is cold today" and "It is cold tomorrow." Might the fact that German does not require a strong separation of the present from the future cause its speakers to feel the future is less distant, thereby causing them to be more forward-looking in making decisions? Put differently, do those who speak languages that do not grammatically distinguish the future from the present have lower discount rates than those raised to speak languages that require a strong distinction?

 As stated in the text, quantifying people's discount rates is difficult. However, if those speaking languages that do not grammatically separate the present and future have lower discount rates, then we should observe that they are more likely to make investments of one kind or another than those who speak languages, like English, that require a strong separation of future and present. Interestingly, one study did find that in cultures where the present and future are not grammatically separated, people were more likely to engage in such future-oriented behaviors as saving for retirement and investing in their health (exercising, quitting smoking, and dieting).

Source: M. Keith Chen, "The Effect of Language on Economic Behavior: Evidence from Savings Rates, Health Behaviors, and Retirement Assets," *American Economic Review* 103 (April 2013): 690–731

Potential college students, however, vary in their access to the funds required to pay for tuition, books, and fees—and high school students' access to SAT tests also varies.[9] Some cover all or part of these costs from the generosity of others (public funding, their families, or college scholarships), while others must bear the costs of taking out loans or generating their own funds through working. Put differently, *the costs of accessing a college education* widely vary, and those who find it costly or impossible to obtain such access are said by economists to be "credit constrained." Subsidized, low-interest government loans to college students and publicly funded universities are two major ways in which society has tried to deal with credit constraints facing potential college students. Most studies find that relaxing these constraints (making borrowing easier or cheaper) increases college attendance and that the public policies undertaken in the United States to relax the constraints have been largely successful.[10]

The costs of college attendance are an additional reason why older people are less likely to attend than younger ones. As workers age, their greater experience and maturity result in higher wages and therefore greater opportunity costs of college attendance. Interestingly, as suggested by Example 9.3, college attendance by military veterans (who are older than the typical college student) has been responsive to the educational subsidies for which they are eligible.[11]

In addition to the financial costs of a college investment are the *psychological* costs that we mentioned earlier. Our theory predicts that students who have greater aptitudes for the kind of learning that college demands are more likely to attend—and more likely to complete their degrees—than those for whom learning is more difficult or unpleasant.[12]

Mounting evidence shows that the acquisition of human capital is powerfully influenced by family background—that is, by the parental investments and family environments that affect both the *cognitive* skills and the *behavioral* skills (such as attentiveness, motivation, and coping strategies) needed to succeed in high school and beyond. Evidence shows, for example, that children from single-parent or low-income households enter kindergarten with fewer of the cognitive *and* social-emotional skills required for success in school; this fact has led to a growing interest among economists in whether, and how, *early childhood* programs improve both of these skills and thus permanently lower the psychological cost of schooling for the students whom they target.[13]

EXAMPLE 9.3

Did the G.I. Bill Increase Educational Attainment for Returning World War II Veterans?

Veterans returning from service in World War II were eligible to receive unprecedented federal support through the G.I. Bill if they chose to attend college. Benefits under the G.I. Bill substantially subsidized the costs of a college education, covering the tuition charged by almost all private universities and all public universities and providing monthly stipends ranging from roughly 50 to 70 percent of the median income in the United States at the time. After the war, many veterans enrolled in college—and total college enrollments jumped by more than 50 percent from their prewar levels. Over 2.2 million veterans attended college under the bill, accounting for about 70 percent of the male student body at the peak of the bill's usage. Because of these effects, Senator Ralph Yarborough called the World War II G.I. Bill "one of the most beneficial, far-reaching programs ever instituted in American life."

Did the G.I. Bill really have a big effect, or did it merely subsidize returning veterans who would have gone to college anyway? A recent article helps to answer this question by comparing the college attendance of male veterans with otherwise-similar individuals. It finds that among high school graduates, World War II veterans completed an average of about 4 more months of college than did nonveterans, and that they had a 6 percent greater college completion rate. Similar estimates were obtained when comparing those eligible for war service and G.I. Bill subsidies with those born too late to serve in the war.

The conclusions of this study are that the responses of veterans to the G.I. Bill's subsidies were quite similar to the contemporary responses of students to changes in tuition costs. In both cases, a 10 percent reduction in the cost to students of attending college resulted in a 4 or 5 percent increase in college attendance and completion.

Sources: John Bound and Sarah Turner, "Going to War and Going to College: Did the G.I. Bill Increase Educational Attainment for Returning Veterans?" *Journal of Labor Economics* 20 (October 2002): 784–815; Keith W. Olson, *The G.I. Bill, the Veterans, and the Colleges* (Lexington: University Press of Kentucky, 1974)

Economists have also begun to recognize that beyond the effects of parenting, "peer effects" can alter the psychological costs of attending school. If status with one's peers is enhanced by studying hard and getting good grades, the costs of studying are reduced—while the opposite occurs if status is reduced by academic achievement.[14]

In sum, several factors cause the costs of college attendance to vary across individuals, and these factors help to explain why individuals facing the same general environment make different decisions about investing in human capital. We now turn to another set of forces that affect human capital decisions: the expected benefits associated with a human capital investment.

Earnings Differentials   The fourth prediction of human capital theory is that the demand for education is positively related to the increases in *expected* lifetime earnings from a college education; however, the expected benefits for any individual are rather uncertain.[15] As a first approximation, however, we reasonably conjecture that the *average* returns received by recent college graduates have an important influence on students' decisions.

Dramatic changes in the average monetary returns to a college education over the past four decades are at least partially, if not largely, responsible for the changes in college enrollment rates noted earlier. The first and third columns of Table 9.1, for example, show that the decline in male enrollment rates during the 1970s was correlated with a decline in the college/high school earnings differential, while the higher enrollment rates after 1980 were associated with larger earnings differentials.[16]

Table 9.1 Changes in College Enrollments and the College/High School Earnings Differential, by Gender, 1970–2018

Year	College enrollment rates of new high school graduates		Ratios of mean earnings of college to high school graduates, ages 25–34, previous year[a]	
	Male (%)	*Female (%)*	*Male*	*Female*
1970	55.2	48.5	1.38	1.42
1980	46.7	51.8	1.19	1.29
1990	58.0	62.2	1.48	1.59
2000	59.9	66.2	1.60	1.74
2010	62.8	74.0	1.59	1.66
2018	66.9	71.4	1.72	1.66

[a] This covers year-round, full-time workers. Data for the first two years are for personal income, not earnings; however, in the years for which both income and earnings are available, the ratios are essentially equal.

Sources: U.S. Department of Education, *Digest of Education Statistics 2018* (December 2019), Table 302.10, at https://nces.ed.gov/programs/digest/d19/tables/dt19_302.10.asp?current=yes; U.S. Bureau of the Census, *Money Income of Families and Persons in the United States*, Current Population Reports P-60, no. 66 (Table 41), no. 129 (Table 53); U.S. Bureau of the Census, Current Population Survey Tables for Personal Income, PINC-04, at www.census.gov/data/tables/time-series/demo/income-poverty/cps-pinc-04.html

The second and fourth columns of Table 9.1 document changes in enrollment rates and earnings differentials for women. Unlike enrollment rates for men, those for women generally rose throughout the five decades; however, notably, they rose most after 1980, when the college/high school earnings differential rose most sharply. Why did enrollment rates among women increase in the 1970s, when the earnings differential fell? Despite the reduced earnings differential, the expected returns to education for women quite plausibly rose because of increases in their intended labor force attachment and hours of work outside the home (both of which increase the period over which the earnings differential will be received).[17]

Human capital investments, like other investments, entail uncertainty.[18] (See Example 9.4 for how the perceived risk of losing one's physical possessions affects the willingness to invest in human capital.) While individuals find knowing the *average* earnings differentials between college and high school graduates helpful, they must also assess their *own* probabilities of success in specific fields requiring a college degree.[19] If, for example, the average returns to college are rising but the spread between the earnings of the most successful college graduates and the least successful ones is growing, individuals who believe that they are likely to be in the latter group may be deterred from making an investment in college. Recent studies have pointed to the importance of friends, demographic characteristics, and neighborhoods in the human capital decisions of individuals, even after controlling for the effects of parental income or education. Although these peer effects can affect educational decisions by affecting costs, as discussed earlier, the presence of role models also likely helps to reduce the uncertainty that inevitably surrounds estimates of future success in specific areas.[20]

EXAMPLE 9.4

When Investments in Human Capital Are Less Risky Than Investments in Physical Assets

We can view the decision whether to invest in human capital as one that is made in the context of deciding *where* to invest one's resources. Should one invest in physical assets (homes or automobiles, say) or invest in one's education? One's preferences for physical assets might be reduced if one has a family history of losing those assets by forced migration—leading to the prediction that groups of people with a family history of being uprooted from their homes might show a greater preference for investments in human capital than they would otherwise show.

At the end of World War II, 2.1 million Polish residents in the Eastern territories (Kresy) were expelled from the area, which became part of the Soviet Union, and forced to move to the Western territories; in the process, they lost most of their possessions. A recent study compared the educational outcomes of the descendants of the Kresy migrants to those of other groups whose prewar educational levels were similar. The study found that, indeed, descendants of Kresy migrants have significantly higher levels of education, on average,

> than other Poles—a finding the authors attribute to a greater preference among the Kresy descendants for the possession of human capital than for physical assets.
>
> *Source*: Sacha O. Becker, Irena Grosfeld, Pauline Grosjean, Nico Voitländer, and Ekaterina Zhursavskaya, "Forced Migration and Human Capital: Evidence from Post-WWII Population Transfers," *American Economic Review* 110 (May 2020): 1430–1463

Market Responses to Changes in College Attendance

Like other market prices, the returns to college attendance are determined by the forces of both employer demand and employee supply. If more high school students decide to attend college when presented with higher returns to such an investment, market forces are put into play that will tend to lower these returns in the future. Increased numbers of college graduates put downward pressure on the wages observed in labor markets for these graduates, other things being equal, whereas a fall in the number of high school graduates tends to raise wages in markets for less-educated workers.

Thus, adding to uncertainties about expected payoffs to an investment in college is the fact that current returns might be an unreliable estimate of future returns. A high return now might motivate an individual to opt for college, but it will also cause many *others* to do likewise. An influx of college graduates in four years could put downward pressure on returns at that time, which reminds us that all investments—even human capital ones—involve outlays now and uncertain returns in the future. (For an analysis of how the labor market might respond when workers behave as if the returns observed currently will persist into the future, see Appendix 9A.)

Education, Earnings, and Post-Schooling Investments in Human Capital

The preceding section used human capital theory to analyze the decision to undertake a formal educational program (college) on a full-time basis. We now turn to an analysis of workers' decisions to acquire training at work. The presence of on-the-job training is difficult for the economist to directly observe; much of it is informal and not publicly recorded. We can, however, use human capital theory and certain patterns in workers' lifetime earnings to draw inferences about their demand for this type of training.

Figures 9.3 and 9.4 graph the 2018 earnings of men and women of various ages who have different levels of education. These figures reveal four notable characteristics:

1. Average earnings of full-time workers rise with the level of education.

2. The most rapid increase in earnings occurs early, thus giving a concave shape to the age–earnings profiles of both men and women.

3. Age–earnings profiles tend to fan out, so that education-related earnings differences later in workers' lives are greater than those early on.

4. The age–earnings profiles of men tend to be more concave and to fan out more than those for women.

Can human capital theory help explain these empirical regularities?

Average Earnings and Educational Level

Our *investment* model of educational choice implies that earnings rise with the level of education, because if they did not, the incentives for students to invest in more education would disappear. The average earnings of more-educated workers in Figures 9.3 and 9.4 thus unsurprisingly exceed those of less-educated workers.

Remember, however, that *earnings* are influenced by both wage rates and hours of work. Data on *wage rates* are probably most relevant when

Figure 9.3 Money Earnings (Mean) for Full-Time, Year-Round Male Workers, 2018

Source: See endnote 21

Figure 9.4 Money Earnings (Mean) for Full-Time, Year-Round Female Workers, 2018

Source: See endnote 21

we look at the returns to an educational investment, because they indicate pay per unit of time at work. Wage data, however, are less widely available than earnings data. A crude, but readily available, way to control for working hours when using earnings data is to focus on full-time, year-round workers—which we do in Figures 9.3 and 9.4. More-careful statistical analyses, however, which control for hours of work and factors other than education that can increase wage rates, come to the same conclusion suggested by Figures 9.3 and 9.4: More education is associated with higher pay.

On-the-Job Training and the Concavity of Age–Earnings Profiles

The age–earnings profiles in Figures 9.3 and 9.4 typically rise steeply early on, and then tend to flatten.[21] Human capital theory explains the concavity of these profiles in terms of *on-the-job training*, and in Chapters 10 and 11, we encounter other potential explanations for why earnings rise in this way with age.[22]

Training Declines With Age   Training on the job can occur through learning by doing (skills improving with practice), through formal training programs at or away from the workplace, or by informally working under the tutelage of a more experienced worker. All forms entail reduced productivity among trainees during the learning process, and both formal and informal training also involve a commitment of time by those who serve as trainers or mentors. Training costs are either shared by workers and the employer, as with specific training, or are borne mostly by the employee (in the case of general training).

From the perspective of workers, training depresses wages during the learning period but allows them to rise with enhanced productivity afterward. Thus, workers who opt for jobs that require a training investment are willing to accept lower wages in the short run to get higher pay later on. As with other human capital investments, returns are generally larger when the post-investment period is longer, so we would expect workers' investments in on-the-job training to be greatest at younger ages and to fall gradually as they grow older.

Figure 9.5 graphically depicts the life cycle implications of human capital theory as it applies to on-the-job training. The individual depicted has completed full-time schooling and is able to earn E_s at age A_0. Without further training, if the knowledge and the skills that the worker possess do not depreciate over time, earnings would remain at E_s over the life cycle. If the worker chooses to invest in on-the-job training, their future earnings potential can be enhanced, as shown by the (dashed) curve E_p in the figure. Investment in on-the-job training, however, has the near-term consequence that actual earnings are below potential; thus, in terms of Figure 9.5, actual earnings (E_a) lie below E_p as long as the worker is investing. In fact, the gap between E_p and E_a equals the worker's investment costs.

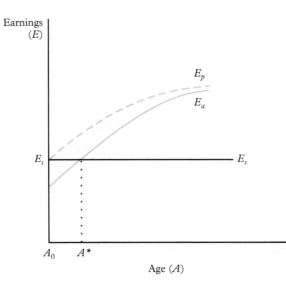

Figure 9.5 Investment in on-the-Job Training Over the Life Cycle

Figure 9.5 is drawn to reflect the theoretical implication, noted earlier, that human capital investments decline with age. With each succeeding year, actual earnings become closer to potential earnings; furthermore, because workers become less willing to invest in human capital as they age, the yearly *increases* in potential earnings become smaller and smaller. Thus, curve E_p takes on a concave shape, quickly rising above E_s but flattening later in the life cycle. Curve E_a (which is what we observe in Figures 9.3 and 9.4) takes on its concave shape for the same reasons.[23]

The Fanning Out of Age–Earnings Profiles

Earnings differences across workers with different educational backgrounds tend to become more pronounced as they age. This phenomenon is also consistent with what human capital theory would predict.

Investments in human capital tend to be more likely when the expected earnings differentials are greater, when the initial investment costs are lower, and when the investor has either a longer time to recoup the returns or a lower discount rate. The same can be said of people who have the ability to learn more quickly. The ability to learn rapidly shortens the training period, and fast learners probably also experience lower psychic costs (lower levels of frustration) during training.

Thus, people who have the ability to learn quickly are those most likely to seek out—and be presented by employers with—training opportunities. But who are these fast learners? They are most likely the people who, because of their abilities to learn, were best able to reap benefits from formal schooling. Thus, human capital theory leads us to expect that workers who invested more in schooling will also invest more in post-schooling job training.[24]

The tendency of the better-educated workers to invest more in job training is an explanation for why their age–earnings profiles start low, rise quickly, and keep rising after the profiles of their less-educated counterparts have leveled off. Their earnings rise more quickly because they are investing more heavily in job training, and they rise for a longer time for the same reason. The idea is that people with the ability to learn quickly select the ultimately high-paying jobs where much learning is required and thus put their abilities to greatest advantage.

Women and the Acquisition of Human Capital

A comparison of Figures 9.3 and 9.4 immediately reveals that the earnings of women who work full time year-round are lower than those of men of equivalent age and education and that women's earnings in each educational group rise less steeply with age. The purpose of this section is to analyze these differences in the context of human capital theory (a completer analysis of male/female wage differentials is presented in Chapter 12).

A major difference in the incentives of men and women to make human capital investments has historically been in the length of work life (in terms of both hours and years of paid work) over which the costs of a human capital investment can be recouped. Chapters 6 and 7 clearly showed how rapidly working for pay has increased among women in recent decades, and this fact obviously should have made human capital investments more lucrative for women. Nevertheless, Table 9.2 shows that, on average, women are still less likely than men to be in the labor force and, if employed, are less likely to work full time. Furthermore, women employed full time average fewer hours of work per week than men in each of the occupations shown.

That women have shorter expected work lives than men have is caused primarily by the role that women have historically played in child-rearing and household production. This traditional role, while undergoing significant change, has caused many women to drop out of the labor market for a

Table 9.2 Labor Force Participation Rates, Part-Time Employment Status, and Hours of Work in the United States, by Gender (2019)

	Women	Men
Labor force participation rate, age 16 and over	57.4%	69.2%
Percent of employed who worked full time	71.6%	83.5%
Average weekly hours of full-time workers, by occupation:		
Management, business, and financial	42.6	45.7
Professional specialty	41.1	43.3
Office/administrative support	40.2	41.8
Sales	41.1	44.2
Installation and repair	42.3	43.0

Sources: U.S. Bureau of Labor Statistics website—Labor Force Statistics from the Current Population Survey, available at www.bls.gov/cps/tables.htm, Tables 2, 22, 23

period of time in their childbearing years. Thus, female workers often have not had the continuity of experience that their male counterparts accumulate. If this historical experience causes younger women who are making important human capital decisions to expect a discontinuity in their own labor force participation, they might understandably avoid occupations or fields of study in which their skills depreciate during the period out of the labor market.[25] Moreover, historical experience could cause employers to avoid hiring women for jobs that require much on-the-job training—a practice that itself would reduce the returns that women can expect from a human capital investment. Human capital theory, however, *also* predicts that recent changes in the labor force participation of women, especially married women of childbearing age, are causing dramatic changes in the acquisition of both job training and formal schooling by women. We turn now to a discussion of recent changes in these two areas.

Women and Job Training   Women appear to receive less on-the-job training than men do, although the gap is probably narrowing. One survey of employer-provided training found that during a six-month period in 1995, women reported receiving 41.5 hours of both formal and informal training, whereas men received 47.6 hours; differences were mainly in the area of informal training.[26] To the extent that on-the-job training causes age–earnings profiles to be concave, an explanation for the flatter age–earnings profiles of women may be rooted in their lower levels of such training.

This human capital explanation for the flatter age–earnings profiles among women does not directly address whether the lower levels of job training emanate from the employer side or the employee side of the market, but both possibilities are theoretically plausible. If employers expect female workers to have shorter work lives, they might be less likely to provide training to them.[27] Alternatively, if women expect themselves to have shorter work lives, they might be less inclined to seek out jobs requiring high levels of training. Finally, if women expect employers to bar them from occupations that require a lot of training or experience, incentives to enter these occupations will be diminished.[28]

While human capital theory predicts that the traditional role of women in child-rearing will lead to reduced incentives for training investments, it also suggests that as this role changes, the incentives for women to acquire training will change. We should thus expect to observe a growing concavity in women's age–earnings profiles over the past decades, and Figure 9.6 indicates that this expectation is generally supported.

The blue lines in Figure 9.6 are the 2018 profiles for female college and high school graduates, and the black lines indicate the comparable profiles for 1990 (adjusted to 2018 dollars).[29] A visual comparison reveals that the earnings profile for high school graduates are remarkably similar but that the profile for college graduates has become much steeper, particularly for women in their 30s. This faster earnings growth among college-educated women at the early stages of their careers suggests that they might be receiving more on-the-job training than they did roughly three decades ago.

Figure 9.6 The Increased Concavity of Women's Age–Earnings Profiles

Women and Formal Schooling As Table 9.1 suggested, dramatic changes have occurred in recent years in the level of formal education that women receive. Their fields of study have also changed markedly. These changes undoubtedly reflect the increased returns of human capital investments arising from women's increased attachment to the labor force and longer expected work lives. Table 9.3 outlines some of the magnitudes of these changes.

Women, who traditionally were less likely than men to graduate from college, now represent almost 60 percent of both bachelor's and master's graduates. There have also been dramatic shifts in the fields in which women major, most notably in the areas of business (graduate and undergraduate)—a field in which women have gone from under 10 percent of all majors to almost half by 2017. While still underrepresented in computer science and engineering, women have posted dramatic gains in these areas as well.[30] The data in Table 9.3 suggest that women's expected work lives have grown so fast that investing in bachelor's and master's degrees has become more attractive over the past five decades.

Table 9.3 Percentages of Women among College and University Graduates, by Degree and Field of Study, 1971 and 2017

Percentage of Women among:	Bachelor's Degree		Master's Degree	
	1971	**2017**	**1971**	**2017**
Total	43.4%	57.3%	40.1%	59.4%
Business majors	9.1	47.0	3.9	47.3
Computer science majors	13.6	19.1	10.3	30.9
Education majors	74.5	81.1	56.2	77.2
Engineering majors	0.8	20.4	1.1	24.9
English majors	66.7	70.4	61.0	66.8
Health majors	77.1	84.1	55.9	81.6

Sources: U.S. National Center for Education Statistics, *Digest of Education Statistics 1993* (1993), Tables 235, 269, 271–273, 275, 278; *Digest of Education Statistics 2018* at nces.ed.gov/programs/digest/d18/, Table 318.30

According to the data in Table 9.3, in the United States at least, women are now *more* likely than men to invest in a college degree. The growth in the percentage of women investing in a college degree can be clearly related to their lengthening attachment to the labor force (analyzed in Chapter 6). Yet this attachment, on average, is still lower for women than for men, and so attachment by itself cannot explain why women are so much more likely than men to attend college.

One potential explanation for why women invest more in schooling may have to do with gender differences in the earnings premium associated with college; Table 9.1 also shows that—except for the most recent year—the earnings ratios of college to high school graduates have been higher for women than for men. Another potential explanation, however, is that the *psychic costs* of schooling are lower for women than for men. Some have argued, for example, that the secondary-school performance of girls has exceeded that of boys for the past century, partly because they exhibit fewer behavioral problems in elementary and secondary schools and partly because they spend more time doing homework than boys do.[31]

Is Education a Good Investment?

The question of whether more education would be a good investment is one that concerns both individuals and government policymakers. Individuals ask, will I increase my monetary and psychological income enough to justify the costs of additional education? Governments must decide whether the expected social benefits of enhanced productivity outweigh the opportunity costs of investing more social resources in the educational sector. We pointed out earlier that these questions can be answered by using either the *present-value* method (an illustration of which is in Example 9.5) or the *internal-rate-of-return* method. The latter is used primarily in the sections that follow.

Is Education a Good Investment for Individuals?

Individuals in the United States about to make an investment in a college education are typically committing themselves to total monetary costs of at least $25,000 per year, and some pay as much as $75,000 per year. Does evidence show that this investment pays off for the typical student? Several studies have tried to answer this question by calculating the internal rates of return to educational investments. Although the methods and data used vary, these studies normally estimate benefits by calculating earnings differentials at each age from age–earnings profiles such as those in Figures 9.3 and 9.4. *Earnings* are usually used to measure benefits, because higher wages and stabler jobs are both payoffs of more education. (Although the estimated rates of return discussed later relate only to the monetary returns to education, we should note that many [but not all] recent studies have found substantial nonmonetary benefits—such as better health and more life satisfaction—to investments in more schooling.[32] Consequently, we should consider the more easily measured monetary benefits to be a lower bound on the true benefits of investments in schooling.)

Estimating the monetary returns to an educational investment involves comparing the earnings of similar people who have different levels of education. Estimates using conventional data sets statistically analyze the earnings increases associated with increases in schooling, after controlling for the effects on earnings of *other* factors that can be measured, such as age, race, gender, health status, union status, and residential location. These studies, of which there have been hundreds, typically estimate rates of return that fall into the range of 5–12 percent.[33]

Ability Bias   One problem with these conventional estimates is that they might overstate the gain that an individual could obtain by investing in education, because they do not distinguish between the contribution that *ability* makes to higher earnings and the contribution made by *schooling*.[34] The problem is that, first, people who are smarter, harder working, and more dynamic are likely to obtain more schooling and, second, since such characteristics may also be useful at work, such people might be more productive and hence earn higher-than-average wages, even if they did not complete more years of schooling than others did. When measures of true ability are not observed or accounted for, the studies attribute *all* the earnings differentials associated with college to college itself and none to ability, even though *some* of the added earnings college graduates typically receive might have been received by an equally able high school graduate who did not attend college.

EXAMPLE 9.5

Valuing a Human Asset: The Case of the Divorcing Doctor

State divorce laws typically provide for the assets acquired during marriage to be divided in some equitable fashion. Among the assets to be divided is often the value of human capital investments made by either spouse during marriage. How these acquired human capital values are estimated can be illustrated by the following example.

Dr. Doe married right after he had acquired a license to practice as a general practitioner. Instead of opening a general (family) practice, however, Dr. Doe undertook specialized training to become a surgeon. During his training (residency) period, the income of Dr. Doe and his wife was much lower than it would have been had he been working as a general practitioner. Thus, both spouses were investing in Dr. Doe's human capital.

Shortly after his residency was completed and he had acquired board certification as a general surgeon, Dr. Doe and his wife decided to divorce. She sued him for an equitable division of the asset value of his certification as a general surgeon. How can this asset value be estimated? The asset value of Dr. Doe's certificate as a general surgeon is the present value of his estimated *increase in lifetime earnings* that this certificate made possible. The most reasonable estimate of his increase in yearly earnings is calculated by subtracting the average earnings of general practitioners (which is an estimate of what Dr. Doe could have earned in the absence of his training as a surgeon) from what the typical general surgeon earns.

In 2019, the mean earnings of general surgeons were roughly $252,040 and those of general practitioners were $201,440. Thus, assuming Dr. Doe is an "average" doctor, obtaining his certificate as a surgeon increased his earnings capacity by $50,600 per year in 2019 dollars.[a] Assuming a remaining work life of 25 years and a real interest rate (which takes account of what inflation will do to the earnings differential) of 2 percent, the present value of the asset Dr. Doe acquired as the result of his surgical training comes to $987,500. (It would then be up to the court to divide this asset equitably between the two divorcing spouses.)

[a] Earnings data are from the U.S. Department of Labor, Bureau of Labor Statistics website under "May 2015 National Occupational Employment and Wage Estimates, United States": www.bls.gov/oes/current/oes_nat.htm#29-0000

The formula used to calculate present value is the one given in endnote 3, where $X = $50,600$, $r = 0.02$, and $n = 25$.

Some studies have attempted to control for ability by using measures of intelligence quotient (IQ) or scores on aptitude tests, but disputes continue over how much these tests reveal about innate abilities. One clever way to control for ability without relying on these tests is to analyze earnings differences among sets of identical twins (see Empirical Study 9.1 at the end of this chapter). Identical twins have the same genes, so they will have the same innate abilities. Most are raised together, so they have likely experienced similar environmental factors, and one would think that measuring earnings differences that are associated with differences in schooling *within pairs of twins* would yield an unbiased estimate of the returns to education. The most recent studies of twins estimate rates of return that are not too different from the conventional estimates noted earlier; these studies, then, suggest that ability bias in the conventional estimates might not be very large.[35]

Returns for Whom?   As discussed earlier in this chapter, people who make educational investments are likely to differ from people who do not; for example, people who seek more schooling may have lower psychic costs of learning, or lower discount rates, than those who do not make the investment. Thus, the returns to schooling for those who *do* invest may be different from the returns facing those who chose *not* to invest. For policies that attempt to encourage the noninvestors to seek more schooling, what we really want to know is the rate of return that they would experience if their choices about schooling were to change.

Economists have recently tried, therefore, to find contexts in which people have different levels of education, not because of choices they have made but because of factors beyond their control.[36] Compulsory schooling laws—laws that require children to start school at a certain age and remain in school until they reach the legal school-leaving age—have provided one such context. Comparing the years of education and earnings of high school dropouts, some of whom, by the accident of their birthday, will have been forced into more schooling than others, represents one approach that has been taken to estimate the returns facing those not currently investing in schooling. To date, a consensus estimate of these returns has not been reached.[37]

Is Education a Good Social Investment?

The issue of education as a social investment has been of heightened interest in the United States in recent years, especially because of three related developments. First, product markets have become more global, increasing the elasticity of both product demand and labor demand. As a result, U.S. workers are now facing more competition from workers in other countries. Second, the growing availability of high-tech capital has created new products and production systems that might require workers to have greater cognitive skills and to be more adaptable, efficient learners.[38] Third, U.S. elementary and secondary school students have scored relatively poorly, as can be seen from data in Table 9.4, on achievement tests in mathematics and science.

The combination of these three developments has caused concern about the productivity of the United States' future workforce, relative to workers elsewhere, and has led to a series of questions about the U.S. educational system. Are we devoting enough resources to educating our current and future workforce? Should the resources that we devote to education be reallocated in some way? Should we demand more of students in elementary and secondary schools?

Table 9.4 International Comparisons of Schooling, 2015

Country	2015 expenditures per pupil, elementary and secondary level (USD)	2015 math test scores, 15-year-olds	2015 science test scores, 15-year-olds
France	9,897	493	495
Germany	10,863	506	509
Japan	10,167	532	538
United Kingdom	11,078	492	509
United States	12,424	470	496

Source: U.S. National Center for Education Statistics, *Digest of Education Statistics, 2018*, Tables 605.10, 602.40 at the National Center for Education Statistics website—http://nces.ed.gov/programs/digest/d18/tables/dt18_605.10   and   http://nces.ed.gov/programs/digest/d18/tables/dt18_602.40

The Social Cost   As can be seen from Table 9.4, the United States devotes relatively more resources to schooling than do some other developed countries—having spent over $12,000 per student in elementary and secondary schools in 2015. The relatively poor performance of U.S. students on achievement tests, however, has led to questions about whether the United States is devoting too many or too few resources to education—or whether it is not using its educational resources wisely enough. To answer these questions, we must try to understand how education and productivity are related.

The Social Benefit   The view that increased educational investments increase worker productivity is a natural outgrowth of the observation that such investments enhance the earnings of individuals who undertake them. If individual A's productivity is increased because of more schooling, then *society's* stock of human capital has increased as a result. Some argue, however, that the additional education received by individual A also creates benefits for individual B, who must work with A. If more schooling causes A to communicate more clearly or solve problems more creatively, then B's productivity will also increase. The benefits of an educational investment may also extend beyond labor market productivity, by lowering crime, improving health, and increasing democratic participation. In terms of concepts that we introduced in Chapter 1, education might create positive externalities so that the social benefits are *larger* than the private benefits.[39]

Others argue that the returns to society are *smaller* than the returns to individuals. They believe that the educational system is used by society as a screening device that sorts people by their (predetermined) ability. As discussed later, this alternative view, in its extreme form, sees the educational system as a means of *finding out* who is productive, not of enhancing worker productivity.

The Signaling Model   An employer seeking to hire workers is never completely sure of the actual productivity of any applicant, and in many cases, the employer may remain unsure long after an employee has been hired. What an employer *can* observe are certain indicators that firms believe to be correlated with productivity: age, experience, education, and other personal characteristics. Some indicators, such as age, are immutable. Others, such as formal education, can be *acquired* by workers. Indicators that can be acquired by individuals can be called *signals*; our analysis here focuses on the signaling aspect of formal education.

Let us suppose that firms wanting to hire new employees for particular jobs know that two groups of applicants are in roughly equal proportions. One group has a productivity of 2, let us say, and the other has a productivity of 1. Furthermore, suppose that these productivity levels cannot be changed by education and that employers cannot readily distinguish which applicants are from which group. If they were unable to make such distinctions, firms would be forced to assume that all applicants are "average"; that is, they would have to assume that each had a productivity of 1.5 (and would offer them wages of up to 1.5).

Although workers in this simple example would be receiving what they were worth on *average*, any firm that could devise a way to distinguish between the two groups (at little or no cost) could enhance its profits. When wages equal 1.5, workers with productivities equal to 1 are receiving more than they are worth. If these applicants could be discovered and either rejected or placed into lower-paying jobs, the firm could obviously increase its profits. In the end, using educational attainment as a hiring standard can increase profits even if education does not enhance productivity. We can illustrate this by using a simple example.

An Illustration of Signaling

To illustrate the use of educational signaling, suppose that employers come to believe that applicants with at least e^* years of education beyond high school are the ones with productivity 2 and that those with less than e^* are in the lower-productivity group. With this belief, workers with fewer than e^* years would be rejected for any job paying a wage above 1, whereas those with at least e^* would find that competition among employers drives their wages up to 2. This simple wage structure is illustrated in Figure 9.7.[40] If additional schooling does not enhance productivity, can requiring the signal of e^* really distinguish between the two groups of applicants? The answer is yes *if the costs to the worker of acquiring the added schooling are negatively related to their on-the-job productivity.*

If workers with at least e^* years of education beyond high school can obtain a wage of 2, whereas those with fewer can earn a wage of only 1, all workers would want to acquire the signal of e^* if it were costless for them to do so. As we argued earlier, however, schooling costs are both large and different for different individuals. In particular, the psychic costs of education are probably inversely related to ability: Those who learn easily can acquire the educational signal (of e^* in this case) more cheaply than others. If—and this is critical—those who have *lower* costs of acquiring education are *also*

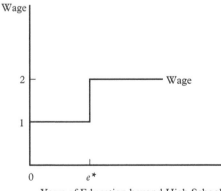

Years of Education beyond High School

Figure 9.7 The Benefits to Workers of Educational Signaling

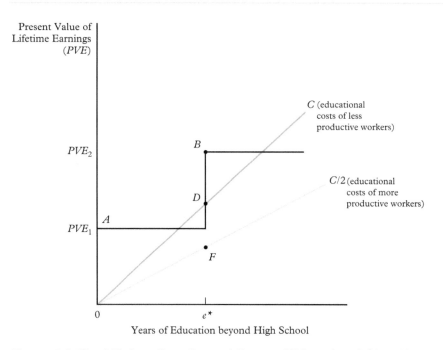

Figure 9.8 The Lifetime Benefits and Costs of Educational Signaling

more productive on the job, then requiring educational signals can be useful for employers.

To understand the role of educational costs in signaling, refer to Figure 9.8, in which the reward structure from Figure 9.7 is expressed in terms of the present value of lifetime earnings (at a wage of 1, their discounted lifetime earnings total PVE_1, whereas at a wage of 2, they total PVE_2). Now assume that each year of education costs C for those with less productivity and $C/2$ for those with greater productivity.

Workers will choose the level of schooling at which the difference between their discounted lifetime earnings and their total educational costs is maximized. For those with yearly educational costs of C, the difference between lifetime earnings and total educational costs is maximized at zero years of education beyond high school. For these workers, the net benefit of an additional e^* years (distance BD) is less than the net benefit of zero additional years (distance $A0$). For them, the benefits of acquiring the signal of e^* years is not worth the added costs.

For those whose costs are $C/2$, the net benefits of investing in e^* (distance BF) can be seen to exceed the net benefits of other schooling choices. Therefore, only those with costs of $C/2$—the workers with higher productivities—find acquiring e^* years of schooling advantageous. In this example, then, schooling attainment signals productivity.[41]

Some Cautions About Signaling   Our simple example demonstrated how education could have value even if it did not directly enhance worker productivity. However, for education to have signaling value in this case, on-the-job productivity and the costs of education must

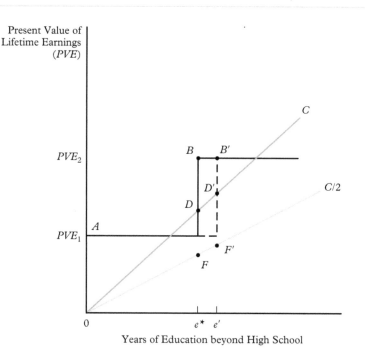

Figure 9.9 Requiring a Greater Signal May Have Costs but Not Benefits

be *negatively* related. If the higher costs reflected along line *C* were associated with lower cognitive ability or a distaste for learning, then conceivably, these costs could be indicative of lower productivity. If, however, those with costs along *C* have higher costs only because of lower family wealth (and therefore smaller contributions from others toward their schooling costs), then they may be no less productive on the job than those along line *C/2*. In this latter case, signaling would fail, because it would indicate only those with low family wealth, not those with lower productivity.

Even when educational signaling is a useful way to predict future productivity, an *optimum* signal exists beyond which society would not find it desirable to go. Suppose, for example, that employers now requiring *e** years for entry into jobs paying a wage of 2 were to raise their hiring standards to *e′* years, as shown in Figure 9.9. Those with educational costs along *C* would still find remaining at zero years of schooling beyond high school in their best interests, and those with costs along *C/2* would find investing in the required signal of *e′* profitable (because distance *B′F′* is greater than *A0*). Requiring more schooling (*e′*) of those who are selected for high-wage jobs, however, is more costly for those workers (and thus for society as a whole). Although the new required signal would distinguish between the two groups of workers, it would do so at increased (and unnecessary) costs to individuals, which cannot be socially optimal.[42]

Investing in educational signals can clearly be beneficial for individuals, but if schooling has *only* signaling value, is it a worthy investment for society to make? If the only purpose of schools is to provide signals, why encourage investments in the expansion or qualitative upgrading of schooling? If 50 years ago being a high school graduate signaled above-average intelligence and work discipline, why incur the enormous costs of expanding college attendance only to find out that now these qualities are signaled by having a bachelor's degree? The issue is of even more importance in less-developed countries, where mistakes in allocating extremely scarce capital resources could be disastrous (see Example 9.6). Before attempting to decide whether schooling has social value when all it produces are signals, let us first turn to the more basic question of whether we can figure out if schooling enhances, or merely signals, human capital.

Signaling or Human Capital   Direct evidence on the role that schooling plays in society is difficult to obtain. Advocates of the signaling viewpoint, for example, might point to the higher rates of return for college graduates than for college dropouts as evidence that schooling is a signaling device.[43] They argue that what is learned in school is proportional to the time spent there and that an added bonus (rate of return) just for a diploma is proof of the signaling hypothesis. Advocates of the view that schooling enhances human capital would counter that those who graduate after four years have learned more than four times what the first-year dropout has learned. They argue that dropouts are more likely to be poorer students—the ones who overestimated their returns to schooling and quit when they discovered their mistake. Thus, their relatively low rate of return is associated not with their dropping out but with their *reason* for dropping out.

To take another example, proponents of the human capital view could argue that the fact that earnings differentials between college graduates and high school graduates grow with age supports their view. If schooling were just a signaling device, employers would rely on it *initially*, but as they accumulated direct information from experience with their employees, schooling would play a smaller role in determining earnings. Signaling advocates could counter that continued growth in earnings differentials is evidence that educational attainment is a *successful* signaling device.[44]

EXAMPLE 9.6

The Socially Optimal Level of Educational Investment

In addition to asking whether schooling is a good social investment, we could also ask, what is the socially optimal *level* of schooling? The general principle guiding our answer to this question is that society should increase or reduce its educational investments until the marginal rate of return (to society) equals the marginal rate of return on other forms of capital investment (e.g., investment in physical capital).

The rationale for this principle is that if society has some funds that it wants to invest, it will desire to invest them in projects yielding the highest rates of return. If an investment in physical capital yields a 20 percent rate of return and the same funds invested in schooling yield (holding the riskiness of the investment constant) only a 10 percent return, society will clearly prefer to invest in physical capital. As long as the two rates of return differ, society could be made better off by reducing its investments in low-yield projects and increasing them in those with higher rates of return.

The text has discussed many of the difficulties and biases inherent in estimating rates of return to schooling. However, the general principle of equating the rates of social return on all forms of investments is still a useful one to consider. It suggests, for example, that capital-poor countries should invest in additional schooling only if the returns are very high—higher, in all probability, than the rates of return required for optimality in more-capital-rich countries.

Indeed, the rates of return to both secondary schooling and higher education appear to be generally higher in less-developed countries than in more-developed countries. One review estimated that the social rate of return on secondary schooling investments averaged 10.3 percent in high-income countries, 12.8 percent in middle-income countries, and 18.1 percent in low-income countries. Comparable social rates of return on investments in higher education were 9.7 percent in high-income countries, 11.4 percent in middle-income countries, and 13.2 percent in low-income countries.

Source: George Psacharopoulos and Harry Anthony Patrinos, "Returns to Investment in Education: A Decennial Review of the Global Literature" (Policy Research Working Paper No. 8402, Education Global Practice, World Bank Ground, Washington, DC, April 2018), Table 4

School Quality Given the difficulty of generating predictions of labor market outcomes that can directly distinguish the signaling from the human capital hypothesis, you may wonder if other ways can resolve the debate. A research strategy with some potential grows out of issues related to school quality.

As mentioned earlier, concerns have been raised about the cognitive achievement of U.S. students. If schooling primarily performs a signaling function, by helping to *discover* people's cognitive abilities, we would not necessarily look to the educational system to remedy the problem of low cognitive achievement. However, if schooling can enhance the kinds of skills that pay off in the labor market, then increased investment in the quality of the nation's schools could be warranted.

Proponents of the signaling and human capital views of education can agree that people of higher cognitive ability are likely to be more productive; where they disagree is whether better schools can enhance worker productivity by improving cognitive skills. Advocates of the signaling viewpoint cite a substantial literature suggesting that demonstrating a relationship between schooling expenditures and student performance on *tests of cognitive skill* is difficult, although the evidence on this question is mixed.[45] Advocates of the human capital view, however, find support in studies of *earnings* and school quality. These studies generally indicate that students attending higher-quality schools (i.e., ones with greater resources per student) have higher subsequent earnings, other things being equal.[46]

Clearly, assessments of the social returns to schooling that examine the role of school quality have so far yielded somewhat-ambiguous results. Better schools may enhance labor market earnings, but evidence that they enhance measured cognitive abilities is mixed. One possibility, of course, is that better schools enhance productivity by enhancing creativity, better work habits, or other "soft" skills that may be valued in the labor market but are not captured especially well by standardized tests of cognitive achievement. Indeed, more and more evidence is showing that social skills, such as the ability to work well with others, are increasingly valued by employers.[47] Another possibility, however, is that better schools give students better information about their own interests and abilities, thus helping them to make more-successful career choices.

Does the Debate Matter?   In the end, perhaps the debate between advocates of the signaling and human capital views of schooling is not terribly important. The fact is that schooling investments offer *individuals* monetary rates of return that are comparable to those received from other forms of investment. For individuals to recoup their human capital investment costs requires willingness on the part of employers to pay higher wages to people with more schooling; for employers to be willing to do this, schools must be providing a service that they could not perform more cheaply themselves.

For example, we argued earlier that to profit from an investment of $200,000 in a college education, college graduates must be paid (assuming a real interest rate of 3 percent) at least $8,653 more per year than they would have received otherwise. Naturally, this requires that they find employers who are willing to pay them the higher yearly wage. If college merely helps *reveal* who is more productive, employers who believe that they could find this out for less than a yearly cost of $8,653 per worker would clearly have incentives to adopt their own methods of screening workers.

The fact that employers continue to emphasize (and pay for) educational requirements in the establishment of hiring standards suggests one of two things. Either more education *does* enhance worker productivity or it is a *less expensive* screening tool than any other that firms could use. In either case, the fact that employers are willing to pay a high price for an educated workforce seems to suggest that education produces social benefits.[48]

Is Public Sector Training a Good Social Investment?

Policymakers should also ask whether government job training programs can be justified on the basis of their returns. During the past four decades, the federal government has funded a variety of these programs that primarily targeted disadvantaged adults and youths. Some programs have served trainees who applied voluntarily, and others have been mandatory programs for public assistance recipients (who stood to lose benefits if they did not enroll). Some of these programs have provided relatively inexpensive help in searching for work, while others have directly provided work experience or (in the case of the Job Corps) comprehensive services associated with living away from home. Over these decades, however, roughly half of those enrolled received classroom training at vocational schools or community colleges, and another 15 percent received in-plant training. The per-student costs of these latter two types of programs have been in the range of $4,900 to $10,000 (in 2019 dollars).[49]

EMPIRICAL STUDY 9.1

ESTIMATING THE RETURNS TO EDUCATION BY USING A SAMPLE OF TWINS: COPING WITH THE PROBLEM OF UNOBSERVED DIFFERENCES IN ABILITY

Researchers doing empirical studies must always be aware of how their results are affected by the problem of *omitted variables*. We only rarely have access to data on all relevant independent variables, and the regression techniques described in Appendix 1A contain an error term that explicitly assumes that the variables we have do not fully explain all the variation in a given dependent variable. If an omitted variable is not correlated with any observed independent variable, then no bias is imparted to the estimates of how the independent variables affect the dependent variable.

However, if an omitted independent variable is correlated with a particular observed one, the estimated effect of the observed variable will be biased. The *omitted variables bias*, and one solution to it, can be illustrated by the problem of estimating the returns to schooling when researchers do not have data on innate learning ability (which is difficult to observe).

The returns to education are conventionally estimated by using multivariate regression techniques to analyze, for a cross-section of workers, by how much earnings are increased with an additional year of schooling—after controlling for other observed factors that influence earnings. However, if people with higher innate capacities for learning and earning (higher *ability*) are the ones who pursue more education, then estimates of the returns to schooling will also include any labor market rewards for *ability* unless researchers are able to measure innate learning ability. Put differently, if education and ability levels are positively correlated, but we do not observe data on innate ability, our estimates of the effects of schooling will be biased upward (we discussed this earlier as *ability bias*). Lacking a way to control for learning ability, then, makes problematic estimating how much more a typical person (with a given ability level) would earn if they invested in another year of schooling. Can we find a way to correct for ability bias, and if so, can we estimate how large that bias is?

A clever way to avoid the problems of ability bias is to use a sample of identical twins, because such twins have precisely the same genetic material, are presumably raised together, and thus have similar abilities. With the same ability and family background, identical twins should have similar incentives for educational investments; however, random factors (marriage, divorce, career interests, accidents) can intervene and cause twins to have different schooling levels. By statistically analyzing, for several sets of twins, how the earnings differences between each twin in a pair are affected by differences in their years of schooling, we can estimate the returns to schooling in a way that decreases ability bias.

One careful study analyzed 340 pairs of identical twins who attended the annual Twinsburg Twins Festival in Twinsburg, Ohio, during the summers of 1991, 1992, and 1993. By looking at differences in earnings and education within each of the 340 pairs, the authors estimated that the returns to schooling were about 9 percent. In contrast, when they estimated the returns to schooling in the conventional way (not controlling for ability), the estimated rate of return was 10 percent. They thus conclude that failure to control for ability imparts only a small upward bias to the conventional estimates of the rate of return to schooling.

Source: Orley Ashenfelter and Cecilia Rouse, "Income, Schooling, and Ability: Evidence from a New Sample of Identical Twins," *Quarterly Journal of Economics* 113 (February 1998): 253–284

Evaluating these programs requires comparing their costs with an estimate of the present value of their benefits, which are measured by calculating the increase in wages made possible by the training program. Calculating the benefits involves estimating what trainees would have earned in the absence of training, and the researcher must successfully confront several thorny issues. Nevertheless, summaries of credible studies of U.S. training programs have concluded that adult women constitute the one group among disadvantaged peoples who clearly benefits from these training programs; adult men and youth show no consistent earnings increases across studies. The average increase in earnings for women in training programs is roughly $2,200 per year (2019 dollars).[50] Were these increases large enough to justify program costs?

The programs had direct costs of $4,900 to $10,000 per trainee, but they also had opportunity costs in the form of forgone output. The typical female trainee was in her program for 16 weeks, and while many of the trainees had been on public assistance before training, the opportunity costs of their time surely were not zero. Recall from Chapter 7 that a person can be productive both at home and in the workplace. If we place an hourly value on trainee time equal to the federal minimum wage ($7.25 per hour in 2019), spending 16 weeks in training had opportunity costs of roughly $4,600; thus, the total costs of training were probably in the range of $9,500 to $14,600 per participant.

If benefits of $2,200 per year were received annually for 20 years after training, and if the appropriate discount rate is 2 percent, the present value of benefits comes to roughly $36,000. Benefits of this magnitude are clearly in excess of costs. Indeed, the present value of benefits for voluntary training would still be in excess of $12,050 (the approximate midpoint of the cost range) if the yearly earnings increases lasted for just seven years.[51]

Review Questions

1. Women receive lower wages, on average, than men of equal age. What concepts of human capital help to explain this phenomenon? Explain. Why does the discrepancy between earnings for men and those for women grow with age?

2. "The vigorous pursuit by a society of tax policies that tend to equalize wages across skill groups will frustrate the goal of optimum resource allocation." Comment.

3. A few years ago, a prominent medical college inadvertently accepted more applicants than it could accommodate in its first-year class. Not wanting to arbitrarily delay the entrance date of the students admitted, it offered them one year of free tuition if they would delay their medical studies by one year. Discuss the factors entering into a student's assessment of whether they should take this offer.

4. When plant X closed, employer Y (which offers no training to its workers) hired many of X's employees after they had completed a lengthy, full-time retraining program offered by a local agency. The city's Equal Opportunity Commission noticed that the workers who employer Y hired from X were predominantly young, and it launched an age-discrimination investigation. During this investigation, employer Y claimed that it hired *all* the applicants from X who had successfully completed the retraining program, without regard to age. From what you know of human capital theory, does Y's claim sound credible? Explain.

5. Why do those who argue that more education "signals" greater ability believe that the most able people will obtain the most education?

6. A study shows that for U.S. high school dropouts, obtaining general educational development (GED) certification by part-time study after high school has little payoff. It also shows, however, that for immigrants who did not complete high school in their native countries, obtaining GED certification has a relatively large payoff. Can signaling theory be used to explain these results?

7. In many countries, higher education is heavily subsidized by the government (i.e., university students do not bear the full cost of their college education). Although they may have good reasons for heavily subsidizing university education, doing so also comes with some dangers. Using human capital theory, explain what these dangers are.

8. Many crimes against property (e.g., burglary) can be thought of as acts that have immediate gains but run the risk of long-run costs. If imprisoned, the criminal loses income from both criminal and noncriminal

activities. Using the framework for occupational choice in the long run and what you know about human capital theory, analyze what kinds of people are most likely to engage in criminal activities. What can society do to reduce crime?

9. A recent study in the United Kingdom found that female doctors are much more likely than male doctors to be in the field of all-purpose family medicine, choosing not to pursue additional training in one of the specialties (e.g., surgery). It also found that half of the female doctors in family medicine worked part time, whereas only 10 percent of the male doctors in family medicine did so. Use human capital theory to analyze whether these two facts are likely to be related. Explain fully.

10. The following statement was overheard at a party: "It is just not right that Joe, who never went to college, makes more than Ken, who has a master's degree. People with higher degrees deserve to earn more." Use human capital theory to comment on this quotation.

Problems

1. Becky works in sales but is considering quitting work for two years to earn a master's of business administration. Her current job pays $90,000 per year (after taxes), but she could earn $130,000 per year (after taxes) if she had an MBA. Tuition is $70,000 per year, and the cost of an apartment near campus is equal to the $20,000 per year that she is currently paying. Becky's discount rate is 6 percent per year. She just turned 48 and plans to retire when she turns 60, whether or not she gets her MBA. Given this information, should she go to school to earn her MBA? Explain carefully.

2. (Appendix 9A). Suppose that the supply curve for optometrists is given by $L_s = -6 + 0.6W$ and that the demand curve is given by $L_D = 50 - W$, where W = annual earnings in thousands of dollars per year and L = thousands of optometrists.

   a. Find the equilibrium wage and employment levels.

   b. Now, suppose that the demand for optometrists increases and that the new demand curve is $L'_D = 66 - W$. Assume that this market is subject to the "cobweb" phenomenon explained in Appendix 9A, in that it takes about three years to produce people who specialize in optometry. While this adjustment is taking place, the short-run supply of optometrists is fixed. Calculate the wage and employment levels in each of the first three rounds, and find the new long-run equilibrium. Draw a graph to show these events.

3. Suppose that you are offered $100 now or $125 in five years. Let the interest rate be 4 percent. Calculate the present value of the $125 option. Which option should you take if your goal is to choose the option with the larger present value?

4. Prepaid college tuition plans, also known as prepaid education arrangements (PEAs), allow you to prepay college tuition at present-day prices. The value of the investment is guaranteed by the state to cover public college tuition, regardless of its future cost. You are considering the purchase of an education certificate for $25,000, which will cover the future tuition costs of your eight-year-old daughter. You expect the tuition costs of your daughter's bachelor's degree to total $50,000 in 10 years. What would your personal discount rate need to be in order for it to be worthwhile for you to make the investment and purchase the certificate?

5. Theodore is considering a one-year training program, which charges $20,000 in tuition, to learn how to install airport-screening equipment. If he enrolls in the program, his opportunity cost in forgone income is the $100,000 per year that he can now earn. After completing the program, he is promised a job for five years that has a yearly salary of $130,000. (After five years, the equipment is expected to be obsolete, but Theodore plans to retire at that time anyway.) Assume that Theodore's personal discount rate is 5 percent. Should Theodore enroll in the program? Why? (Show your calculations.)

Notes

1. United Nations (UNU-IHDP and UNEP), *Inclusive Wealth Report 2014: Measuring Progress Toward Sustainability* (Cambridge: Cambridge University Press, 2014), Data Annex.

2. We note that estimating *r* several years into the future—and estimating future benefits by year—is not easy, but we assume that we know these variables for the purposes of these calculations.

3. This calculation is made using the annuity formula:

$$Y = X \frac{1 - [1/(1 + r)^n]}{r},$$

where Y = the total investment ($200,000 in our example), X = the yearly payment ($8,653), r = the rate of interest (0.03), and n = the number of years (40). These returns are assumed to start in the year after college ends—that is, in year 5.

4. A study that inferred personal discount rates from the choices of separation-pay options made by military retirees found that those officers with graduate degrees had lower discount rates than officers without graduate degrees, and that college-educated officers had lower discount rates than enlisted personnel (who generally do not have college educations). See John T. Warner and Saul Pleeter, "The Personal Discount Rate: Evidence from Military Downsizing Programs," *American Economic Review* 91 (March 2001): 33–53. For a paper on the role of impatience in the formation of human capital, see Brian C. Cadena and Benjamin J. Keys, "Human Capital and the Lifetime Costs of Impatience," *American*

Economic Journal: Economic Policy 7 (August 2013): 126–153. For more on time preferences, see the review by Jonathan Cohen, Keith Marzilli Ericson, David Laibson, and John Myles White, "Measuring Time Preferences," *Journal of Economic Literature* 58 (June 2020): 299–347.

5. The analysis of the correlation between education and health status is taken from Victor Fuchs, "The Economics of Health in a Post-Industrial Society," *Public Interest* (Summer 1979): 3–20. For additional studies see Damon Clark and Heather Royer, "The Effect of Education on Adult Mortality and Health: Evidence from Britain," *American Economic Review* 103 (October 2013): 2087–2120; Titus J. Galama, Adrina Lleras-Muney, and Hans van Kippersluis, "The Effect of Education on Health and Mortality: A Review of Experimental and Quasi-Experimental Evidence" (Working Paper No. 24225, National Bureau of Economic Research, Cambridge, MA, January 2018).

6. For example, perhaps healthy people, who have longer life spans, are more likely to invest in human capital because they expect to experience a longer payback period. Alternatively, we could argue that the higher incomes of college graduates later in life mean that they have more to lose from illness than do noncollege graduates. Data on smoking come from U.S. Department of Health and Human Services, Public Health Service, "Smoking Tobacco and Health" (DHHS publication no. (CDC) 87–8397, October 1989): 5. For a study of smoking and wages, see Irina B. Grafova and Frank P. Stafford, "The Wage Effects of Personal Smoking History," *Industrial and Labor Relations Review* 62 (April 2009): 381–393. For studies of the effects of wages on smoking, see George Wehby, Dhaval Dave, and Robert Kaestner, "Effects of the Minimum Wage on Infant Health," *Journal of Policy Analysis and Management* 39 (Spring 2020): 411–443; Hilary Hoynes, Doug Miller, and David Simon, "Income, the Earned Income Tax Credit, and Infant Health," *American Economic Journal: Economic Policy* 7 (February 2015): 172–211.

7. For other evidence that expected work life affects human capital decisions, see Emily Oster, Ira Shoulson, and E. Ray Dorsey, "Limited Life Expectancy, Human Capital and Health Investments," *American Economic Review* 103 (August 2013): 1977–2002; Victoria Baranov and Hans-Peter Kohler, "The Impact of AIDS Treatment on Savings and Human Capital Investment in Malawi," *American Economic Journal: Applied Economics* 10 (January 2018): 266–306.

8. For example, evidence shows that the increased employment opportunities in the construction industry during a housing boom in the early 2000s reduced college attendance by both young men and young women; see Kerwin Kofi Charles, Erik Hurst, and Matthew J. Notowidigdo, "Housing Booms and Busts, Labor Market Opportunities, and College Attendance," *American Economic Review* 108 (October 2018): 2947–2994. Similarly, high school dropout rates among men rose when jobs in hydraulic fracturing and drilling for natural gas sharply increased; see Elizabeth U. Cascio and Ayushi Narayan, "Who Needs a Fracking

Education? The Educational Response to Low-Skill Biased Technological Change" (Working Paper No. 21359, National Bureau of Economic
Research, Cambridge, MA, February 2019).

9. George Bulman, "The Effect of Access to College Assessments on
    Enrollment and Attainment," *American Economic Journal: Applied
    Economics* 7 (October 2015): 1–36; also see Timothy N. Bond, George
    Bulman, Xiaoxiao Li, and Jonathan Smith, "Updating Human Capital
    Decisions: Evidence from SAT Score Shocks and College Applications,"
    Journal of Labor Economics 36 (July 2018): 807–839.

10. For recent studies that refer to previous literature, see Jeffrey T. Den-
    ning, Benjamin M. Marx, and Lesley J. Turner, "ProPelled: The Effects
    of Grants on Graduation, Earnings, and Welfare," *American Economic
    Journal: Applied Economics* 11 (July 2019): 193–224; Stephen Teng
    Sun and Constantine Yannelis, "Credit Constraints and Demand for
    Higher Education: Evidence from Financial Deregulation," *The Review
    of Economics and Statistics* 98 (March 20–16): 12–24; also see Katharine
    G. Abraham and Melissa A. Clark, "Financial Aid and Students' College
    Decisions: Evidence from the District of Columbia's Tuition Assistance
    Grant Program," *Journal of Human Resources* 41 (Summer 2006):
    578–610; Pedro Carneiro and James J. Heckman, "The Evidence on
    Credit Constraints in Post-Secondary Schooling," *Economic Journal*
    112 (October 2002): 705–734. The latter article analyzes reasons why
    family income and college attendance rates are positively correlated; it
    concludes that financial credit constraints are much less important in
    explaining this relationship than are the attitudes and skills that children
    acquire from their parents.

11. Also see Joshua D. Angrist, "The Effect of Veterans' Benefits on
    Education and Earnings," *Industrial and Labor Relations Review* 46
    (July 1993): 637–652.

12. John Bound, Michael F. Lovenheim, and Sarah Turner, "Why Have
    College Completion Rates Declined? An Analysis of Changing Student
    Preparation and Collegiate Resources," *American Economic Journal:
    Applied Economics* 2 (July 2010): 129–157. One of the other conditions
    that render learning more difficult is heat: Hot classrooms that are not air
    conditioned reduce learning; on this, see R. Jisung Park, Joshua Good-
    man, Michael Hurwitz, and Jonathan Smith, "Heat and Learning,"
    American Economic Journal: Economic Policy 12 (May 2020): 306–339.

13. For articles that contain citations to the extensive literature on this
    topic, see Greg J. Duncan and Katherine Magnuson, "Investing in
    Preschool Programs," *Journal of Economic Perspectives* 27 (Spring
    2013): 109–132; Richard J. Murnane, "U.S. High School Graduation
    Rates: Patterns and Explanations," *Journal of Economic Literature* 51
    (June 2013): 370–422; Jorge Luis Garcia, James J. Heckman, Dun-
    can Ermini Leaf, and María José Prados, "Quantifying the Life-Cycle
    Benefits of an Influential Early-Childhood Program," *Journal of Polit-
    ical Economy* 128 (July 2020): 2502–2541; Thomas Cornelissen and

Christian Dustmann, "Early School Exposure, Test Scores, and Non-cognitive Outcomes," *American Economic Journal: Economic Policy* 11 (May 2019): 35–63; James J. Heckman and Ganesh Karapakula, "Intergenerational and Intragenerational Externalities of the Perry Preschool Project" (Working Paper No. 25889, National Bureau of Economic Research, Cambridge, MA, May 2019); Nicholas W. Papageorge and Kevin Thom, "Genes, Education and Labor Market Outcomes: Evidence from the Health and Retirement Study" (Working Paper No. 25114, National Bureau of Economic Research, Cambridge, MA, September 2018). For papers on the effects of mentoring later in the educational process, see Scott Carrell and Bruce Sacerdote, "Why Do College-Going Interventions Work?" *American Economic Journal: Applied Economics* 9 (July 2017): 124–151; Adam M. Lavecchia, Philip Oreopoulos, and Robert S. Brown, "Long-Run Effects from Comprehensive Student Support: Evidence from Pathways to Education," *American Economic Review: Insights* 2 (June 2020): 209–224.

14. Scott E. Carrell, Mark Hoekstra, and Elira Kuka, "The Long-Run Effects of Disruptive Peers," *American Economic Review* 108 (November 2018): 3377–3415; Joseph G. Altonji and Richard K. Mansfield, "Estimating Group Effects Using Averages of Observables to Control for Sorting on Unobservables: School and Neighborhood Effects," *American Economic Review* 108 (October 2018); Eric Chyn, "Moved to Opportunity: The Long-Run Effects of Public Housing Demolition on Children," *American Economic Review* 108 (October 2018): 3028–3056; Raj Chetty, John N. Friedman, Nathaniel Hendren, Maggie R. Jones, and Sonya R. Porter, "The Opportunity Atlas: Mapping the Childhood Roots of Social Mobility" (Working Paper No. 25147, National Bureau of Economic Research, Cambridge, MA, February 2020). For a review of what is known about the effects of prenatal and early childhood events on human capital acquisition, see Douglas Almond, Janet Currie, and Valentina Duque, "Childhood Circumstances and Adult Outcomes: Act II," *Journal of Economic Literature* 56 (December 2018): 1360–1446.

15. For an historical analysis of earnings differentials and educational decisions, see Claudia Goldin and Lawrence F. Katz, *The Race Between Education and Technology* (Cambridge, MA: Belknap Press, 2008). For a study that incorporates uncertainty into the projection of future earnings, see Joseph G. Altonji, "The Demand for and Return to Education When Education Outcomes Are Uncertain," *Journal of Labor Economics* 10 (January 1993): 48–83. For studies on the accuracy of students' knowledge about salaries, see Julian R. Betts, "What Do Students Know About Wages? Evidence from a Survey of Undergraduates," *Journal of Human Resources* 31 (Winter 1996); Jeff Dominitz and Charles F. Manski, "Eliciting Student Expectations of the Returns to Schooling," *Journal of Human Resources* 31 (Winter 1996): 1–56. For an article on locational variations in the returns on schooling, see Dan Black, Natalia

Kolesnikova, and Lowell Taylor, "Earnings Functions When Wages and Prices Vary by Location," *Journal of Labor Economics* 27 (January 2009): 21–48.

16. The earnings differentials shown may overstate the "real" earnings differences between college graduates and high school graduates, given that college graduates have increasingly chosen to live in cities that have higher living costs; see Enrico Moretti, "Real Wage Inequality," *American Economic Journal: Applied Economics* 5 (January 2013): 65–103.

17. For evidence that women who have "traditional" views of their economic roles receive lower rates of return on, and invest less in, human capital, see Francis Vella, "Gender Roles and Human Capital Investment: The Relationship Between Traditional Attitudes and Female Labour Market Performance," *Economica* 61 (May 1994): 191–211. For an interesting analysis of historical trends in women's college attendance, see Claudia Goldin, Lawrence Katz, and Ilyana Kuziemko, "The Homecoming of American College Women: The Reversal of the College Gender Gap," *Journal of Economic Perspectives* 20 (Fall 2006): 133–156.

18. For a paper on the effects of both graduating during a recession and the role of luck in obtaining one's first job after college, see Hannes Schwandt and Till von Wachter, "Unlucky Cohorts: Estimating the Long-Term Effects of Entering the Labor Market in a Recession in Large Cross-Sectional Data Sets," *Journal of Labor Economics* 37 (January 2019): S161–S198; also see Lisa B. Kahn, "The Long-Term Labor Market Consequences of Graduating From College in a Bad Economy," *Labour Economics* 17:2 (April 2010): 303–316.

19. Students attending college also learn about their own abilities and interests, and each year they have the option to continue or drop out; see Kevin M. Stange, "An Empirical Investigation of the Option Value of College Enrollment," *American Economic Journal: Applied Economics* 4 (January 2012): 49–84.

20. For papers on the issues discussed in this paragraph, see Kerwin Kofi Charles and Ming-Ching Luoh, "Gender Differences in Completed Schooling," *Review of Economics and Statistics* 85 (August 2003): 559–577; Ira N. Gang and Klaus F. Zimmermann, "Is Child Like Parent? Educational Attainment and Ethnic Origin," *Journal of Human Resources* 35 (Summer 2000): 550–569; Eric Maurin and Sandra McNally, "Vive la Révolution! Long-Term Educational Returns of 1968 to the Angry Students," *Journal of Labor Economics* (January 2008): 1–33; also see Carolyn Sloane, Erik Hurst, and Dan Black, "A Cross-Cohort Analysis of Human Capital Specialization and the College Gender Wage Gap" (Working Paper No. 26348, National Bureau of Economic Research, February 2020).

21. Data in these figures come from the U.S. Bureau of the Census website: www.census.gov/data/tables/time-series/demo/income-poverty/cps-pinc/pinc-04.html. These data match average earnings with age

and education in a given year and do not follow individuals through time. For a paper that uses longitudinal data on *individuals*, see Richard W. Johnson and David Neumark, "Wage Declines and Older Men," *Review of Economics and Statistics* 78 (November 1996): 740–748; for a paper that follows *cohorts* of individuals through time, see David Card and Thomas Lemieux, "Can Falling Supply Explain the Rising Return to College for Younger Men? A Cohort-Based Approach," *Quarterly Journal of Economics* 116 (May 2001): 705–746.

22. For discussions of the relative importance of the human capital explanation for rising age–earnings profiles, see Ann P. Bartel, "Training, Wage Growth, and Job Performance: Evidence from a Company Database," *Journal of Labor Economics* 13 (July 1995): 401–425; Charles Brown, "Empirical Evidence on Private Training," in *Research in Labor Economics*, vol. 11, eds. Lauri J. Bassi and David L. Crawford (Greenwich, CT: JAI Press, 1990): 97–114; Jacob Mincer, "The Production of Human Capital and the Life Cycle of Earnings: Variations on a Theme," *Journal of Labor Economics* 15:1, pt. 2 (January 1997): S26–S47; Thierry Magnac, Nicolas Pistolesi, and Sébastien Roux, "Post-Schooling Human Capital Investments and the Life Cycle of Earnings," *Journal of Political Economy* 126 (June 2018): 1219–1250.

23. For those who invest in on-the-job training, actual earnings start below E_s, approach it near age A^*, and continue to rise above it afterward. Age A^* is called the *overtaking age*, and it is the age at which workers with the same level of schooling have equivalent earnings regardless of whether they have invested in on-the-job training. The concept of an overtaking age has an interesting empirical implication.

We can observe the educational levels that workers possess, but we cannot observe workers' E_p or the time that they have spent in on-the-job training. Thus, when we use statistical methods to analyze earnings differences across individuals, the correlation between earnings and education will be strongest at A^*, where $E_a = E_s$. This is because correlation between schooling and earnings is weakened both before A^* and after A^* by the presence of on-the-job training, which we cannot measure and for which we therefore cannot statistically control. Interestingly, we find that educational and earnings levels correlate most strongly at about 10 years after labor market entry. This finding offers support for the human capital explanation of age–earnings profiles that are based on job training. For the seminal work on estimating the effects of earnings on wages, see Jacob Mincer, *Schooling, Experience, and Earnings* (New York: Columbia University Press for National Bureau of Economic Research, 1974).

24. For studies showing that on-the-job training is positively correlated with both educational level and ability, see Joseph G. Altonji and James R. Spletzer, "Worker Characteristics, Job Characteristics, and the Receipt of On-the-Job Training," *Industrial and Labor Relations Review* 45 (October 1991): 58–79; Joseph Hight, "Younger Worker Participation

in Post-School Education and Training," *Monthly Labor Review* 121 (June 1998): 14–21. For a study suggesting that investments in formal school and investments in vocational training are complementary investments, see Adriana Kugler, Maurice Kugler, Juan Saavedra, and Luis Omar Herrera Prada, "Long-Term Direct and Spillover Effects of Job Training: Experimental Evidence from Colombia" (Working Paper No. 21607, National Bureau of Economic Research, Cambridge, MA, October 2015).

25. For a discussion of the wage losses facing women who interrupt their labor force attachment at childbirth, see Nikolay Angelov, Per Johansson, and Erica Lindahl, "Parenthood and the Gender Gap in Pay," *Journal of Labor Economics* 34 (July 2016): 545–579; Elizabeth Ty Wilde, Lily Batchelder, and David T. Ellwood, "The Mommy Track Divides: The Impact of Childbearing on Wages of Women of Differing Skill Levels" (Working Paper No. 16582, National Bureau of Economic Research, December 2010). Losses were also suffered by U.S. men who involuntarily withdrew from their careers by being drafted into military service during the Vietnam War; see Joshua D. Angrist, Stacy H. Chen, and Jae Song, "Long-term Consequences of Vietnam-Era Conscription: New Estimates Using Social Security Data," *American Economic Review: Papers and Proceedings* 101 (May 2011): 334–338. A study comparing the wage effects of interruptions for both genders is Christy Spivey, "Time Off at What Price? The Effects of Career Interruptions on Earnings," *Industrial and Labor Relations Review* 59 (October 2005): 119–140. For a discussion of women's employment over time, see Claudia Goldin and Joshua Mitchell, "The New Life Cycle of Women's Employment: Disappearing Humps, Sagging Middles, Expanding Tops," *Journal of Economic Perspectives* 31 (Winter 2017): 161–182.

26. H. Frazis, M. Gittleman, M. Horrigan, and M. Joyce, "Results from the 1995 Survey of Employer-Provided Training," *Monthly Labor Review* 121 (June 1998): 3–13.

27. See Chapter 12 for a discussion of statistical discrimination.

28. For an article on women's pay expectations and resulting outcomes, see Peter F. Orazem, James D. Werbel, and James C. McElroy, "Market Expectations, Job Search, and Gender Differences in Starting Pay," *Journal of Labor Research* 24 (Spring 2003): 307–321.

29. Data come from the U.S. Bureau of the Census, "Historical Income Tables: People," Table P-33, www.census.gov/data/tables/time-series/demo/income-poverty/historical-income-people.html.

30. A study that differently measures gender changes in undergraduate majors, however, concludes that aside from business majors, changes since the 1970s have not been dramatic. See Sarah E. Turner and William G. Bowen, "Choice of Major: The Changing (Unchanging) Gender Gap," *Industrial and Labor Relations Review* 52 (January 1999): 289–313.

31. Goldin, Katz, and Kuziemko, "The Homecoming of American College Women: The Reversal of the College Gender Gap."

32. Philip Oreopoulos and Kjell G. Salvanes, "Priceless: The Nonpecuniary Benefits of Schooling," *Journal of Economic Perspectives* 25 (Winter 2011): 159–184; James J. Heckman, John Eric Humphries, and Gregory Veramendi, "Returns to Education: The Causal Effects of Education on Earnings, Health and Smoking," *Journal of Political Economy* 126 (October 2018): S197–S246; Clark and Royerr, "The Effect of Education on Adult Mortality and Health: Evidence from Britain."

33. See David Card, "Estimating the Return to Schooling: Progress on Some Persistent Econometric Problems," *Econometrica* 69 (September 2001): 1127–1160; David Card, "The Causal Effect of Education on Earnings," in *Handbook of Labor Economics*, eds. Orley Ashenfelter and David Card (New York: Elsevier, 1999): 1802–1863, for comprehensive reviews. For a recent study, see Manudeep Bhuller, Magne Mogstad, and Kjell G. Salvanes, "Life Cycle Earnings, Education Premiums and Internal Rates of Return," *Journal of Labor Economics* 35 (October 2017): 993–1030.

34. An investment in education should also raise wages more than *overall* wealth—which (recalling Chapters 6 and 7) should cause hours of work to rise. Thus, some of the increased earnings from more education could be associated with reduced leisure, which would constitute another source of upward bias. This point is made by C.M. Lindsay, "Measuring Human Capital Returns," *Journal of Political Economy* 79 (November/December 1971): 1195–1215. A recent study found that female graduates of highly selective colleges earn more than women from less selective colleges, primarily because their labor force participation rates are higher; see Suqin Ge, Elliott Isaac, and Amalia Miller, "Elite Schools and Opting In: Effects of College Selectivity on Career and Family Outcomes" (Working Paper No. 25315, National Bureau of Economic Research, Cambridge, MA, November 2018).

35. See Orley Ashenfelter and Cecilia Rouse, "Income, Schooling, and Ability: Evidence from a New Sample of Identical Twins," *Quarterly Journal of Economics* 113 (February 1998): 253–284; Andrew Leigh and Chris Ryan, "Estimating Returns to Education Using Different Natural Experiment Techniques," *Economics of Education Review* 27 (April 2008): 149–160; Vikesh Amin, "Returns to Education: Evidence from UK Twins: Comment," *American Economic Review* 101 (June 2011): 1629–1635.

36. One such study is Ben Ost, Weixiang Pan, and Douglas Webber, "The Returns to College Persistence for Marginal Students: Regression Discontinuity Evidence from University Dismissal Policies," *Journal of Labor Economics* 35 (July 2018): 779–805.

37. For a paper that refers to similar studies, see Melvin Stephens Jr. and Dou-Yan Yang, "Compulsory Education and the Benefits of Schooling,"

American Economic Review 104 (June 2014): 1777–1792. For a different approach to estimating the returns facing those who have *not* chosen to invest, see Pedro Carneiro, James J. Heckman, and Edward J. Vytlacil, "Estimating Marginal Returns to Education," *American Economic Review* 101 (October 2011): 2754–2781; Andrew J. Hussey and Omari H. Swinton, "Estimating the *ex ante* Expected Returns To College," *American Economic Review; Papers and Proceedings* 101 (May 2011): 598–602.

38. For a discussion of cognitive skills and earnings and for a review of previous studies, see Eric A. Hanushek and Ludger Woessmann, "The Role of Cognitive Skills in Economic Development," *Journal of Economic Literature* 46 (September 2008): 607–668. For a study of the importance of noncognitive skills, see James J. Heckman, John Eric Humphries, and Tim Kautz, *The Myth of Achievement Tests: The GED and the Role of Character in American Life* (Chicago: University of Chicago Press, 2014).

39. For an example of a study (with references to others) on the external effects of education on productivity, see Enrico Moretti, "Workers' Education, Spillovers, and Productivity: Evidence from Plant-Level Data," *American Economic Review* 94 (June 2004): 656–690; Susana Iranzo and Giovanni Peri, "Schooling Externalities, Technology and Productivity: Theory and Evidence from U.S. States," *The Review of Economics and Statistics* 91 (November 2009): 420–443. For a review of evidence on the nonproduction social benefits of education, see Lance Lochner, "Non-Production Benefits of Education: Crime, Health, and Good Citizenship" (Working Paper No. 16722, National Bureau of Economic Research, Cambridge, MA, January 2011). A recent study of peer effects is Thomas Cornelissen, Christian Dustmann, and Uta Schönberg, "Peer Effects in the Workplace," *American Economic Review* 107 (February 2017): 425–456.

40. This analysis is based on Michael Spence, "Job Market Signaling," *Quarterly Journal of Economics* 87 (August 1973): 205–221.

41. Those with costs $C/2$ don't get more schooling, because they have already signaled themselves as "high-quality" types at e^* and will therefore earn the higher wage; they need not get additional schooling, because it leads to no additional benefit and is costly. Those with costs $C/2$ would not get less schooling than e^*, because any less would drop them to the lower wage—and with a lower wage, they would be better off with no schooling, because obtaining schooling is costly.

42. We stress here that, for this to always hold, we must assume that education does not increase productivity.

43. Dropouts naturally have lower earnings than graduates do, but because they have also invested less, whether their *rates of return* should be lower is unclear. For further discussion and evidence, see David A. Jaeger and Marianne E. Page, "Degrees Matter: New Evidence on Sheepskin Effects in the Returns to Education," *Review of Economics and Statistics* 78

(November 1996): 733–740; Thomas J. Kane and Cecilia Elena Rouse, "Comment on W. Norton Grubb: 'The Varied Economic Returns to Postsecondary Education: New Evidence from the Class of 1972,'" *Journal of Human Resources* 30 (Winter 1995): 205–221, calls into question the benefits of graduation independent of the number of *credits* taken.

44. Attempts to distinguish between the two views include W. Bentley MacLeod, Evan Riehl, Juan E. Saavedra, and Miguel Urquiola, "The Big Sort: College Reputation and Labor Market Outcomes," *American Economic Journal: Applied Economics* 9 (July 2017): 223–261; Niklas Engbom and Christian Moser, "Returns to Education through Access to Higher-Paying Firms: Evidence from US Matched Employer-Employee Data," *American Economic Review: Papers and Proceedings* 107 (May 2017): 374–378; Damon Clark and Paco Martorell, "The Signaling Value of a High School Diploma," *Journal of Political Economy* 122 (April 2014): 282–318; Joseph Altonji, "The Effects of High School Curriculum on Education and Labor Market Outcomes," *Journal of Human Resources* 30 (Summer 1995): 409–438; Andrew Weiss, "Human Capital vs. Signaling Explanations of Wages," *Journal of Economic Perspectives* 9 (Fall 1995): 133–154; Wim Groot and Hessel Oosterbeek, "Earnings Effects of Different Components of Schooling: Human Capital versus Screening," *Review of Economics and Statistics* 76 (May 1994): 317–321; Kelly Bedard, "Human Capital versus Signaling Models: University Access and High School Dropouts," *Journal of Political Economy* 109 (August 2001): 749–775; Harley Frazis, "Human Capital, Signaling, and the Pattern of Returns to Education," *Oxford Economic Papers* 54 (April 2002): 298–320.

45. See, for example, Joshua Hyman, "Does Money Matter in the Long Run? Effects of School Spending on Educational Attainment," *American Economic Journal: Economic Policy* 9 (November 2017): 256–280; Eric A. Hanushek, John F. Kain, Daniel M. O'Brien, and Steven G. Rivkin, "The Market for Teacher Quality" (Working Paper No. 11154, National Bureau of Economic Research, February 2005); Charles T. Clotfelter, Helen F. Ladd, and Jacob L. Vigdor, "How and Why Do Teacher Credentials Matter for Student Achievement?" (Working Paper No. 12828, National Bureau of Economic Research, January 2007); Thomas J. Kane, Jonah E. Rockoff, and Douglas Staigner, "What Does Certification Tell Us About Teacher Effectiveness? Evidence from New York City" (Working Paper No. 12155, National Bureau of Economic Research, July 2006); Eric A. Hanushek and Dennis D. Kimko, "Schooling, Labor Force Quality, and the Growth of Nations," *American Economic Review* 90 (December 2000): 1184–1208; Alan B. Krueger and Diane M. Whitmore, "The Effect of Attending a Small Class in the Early Grades on College-Test Taking and Middle School Test Results: Evidence from Project STAR," *Economic Journal* 111 (January 2001): 1–28; David Autor, David Figlio, Krzysztof Karbownik, Jeffrey Roth, and Melanie Wasserman, "School Quality and the

Gender Gap in Educational Achievement," *American Economic Review Papers and Proceedings* 106 (May 2016): 289–295. For evidence on charter schools, see Will Dobbie and Roland G. Fryer, "Charter Schools and Labor Market Outcomes" (Working Paper No. 22502, National Bureau of Economic Research, Cambridge, MA, August 2016); Dennis Epple, Richard Romano and Ron Zimmer, "Charter Schools: A Survey of Research on their Characteristics and Effectiveness" (Working Paper No. 21256, National Bureau of Economic Research, Cambridge, MA, June 2015). For a study of for-profit colleges, see Stephanie Riegg Cellini and Nicholas Turner, "Gainfully Employed? Assessing the Employment and Earnings of For-Profit College Students Using Administrative Data," *Journal of Human Resources* 54 (Spring 2019): 342–370.

46. For citations to the literature analyzing links between school resources and labor market outcomes, see C. Kirabo Jackson, Rucker C. Johnson, and Claudia Persico, "The Effects of School Spending on Educational and Economic Outcomes: Evidence from School Finance Reforms," *Quarterly Journal of Economics* 131 (February 2016): 157–218; Rucker C. Johnson and C. Kirabo Jackson, "Reducing Inequality through Dynamic Complementarity: Evidence from Head Start and Public School Spending," *American Economic Journal: Economic Policy* 11 (November 2019): 310–349.

47. David J. Deming, "The Growing Importance of Social Skills in the Labor Market," *Quarterly Journal of Economics* 132 (November 2017): 1593–1640.

48. Kevin Lang, "Does the Human Capital/Educational Sorting Debate Matter for Development Policy?" *American Economic Review* 84 (March 1994): 353–358, comes to a similar conclusion through a more formal argument.

49. Robert J. LaLonde, "The Promise of Public Sector–Sponsored Training Programs," *Journal of Economic Perspectives* 9 (Spring 1995): 149–168, gives a brief history of federally sponsored training programs and summarizes several issues relevant to evaluating their efficacy.

50. David H. Greenberg, Charles Michalopoulos, and Philip K. Robins, "A Meta-Analysis of Government-Sponsored Training Programs," *Industrial and Labor Relations Review* 57 (October 2003): 31–53. Several studies find that the Job Corps training program for youth and young adults had a positive rate of return; see German Blanco, Carlos A. Flores, and Alfonso Flores-Lagunes, "The Effects of Job Corps Training on Wages of Adolescents and Young Adults," *American Economic Review: Papers and Proceedings* 103 (May 2013): 418–422.

51. Paul Lengermann, "How Long Do the Benefits of Training Last? Evidence of Long Term Effects Across Current and Previous Employers," *Research in Labor Economics* 18 (1999): 439–461, found that the gains from formal and company training last at least nine years. For an analysis of the returns to Job Corps training, see Peter Z. Schochet, John

Burghardt, and Sheena McConnell, "Does Job Corps Work? Impact Findings from the National Job Corps Study," *American Economic Review* 98 (December 2008): 1864–1886. For reference to studies of vocational education, see Paul Ryan, "The School-to-Work Transition: A Cross-National Perspective," *Journal of Economic Literature* 29 (March 2001): 34–92. For an evaluation of a program in Germany that combines training, job practice, and income support, see Simen Markussen and Knut Røed, "Leaving Poverty Behind: The Effects of Generous Income Support Paired with Activation," *American Economic Journal: Economic Policy* 8 (February 2016): 180–211. Conscripted service in the military also seems to increase the human capital of disadvantaged men, at least in peacetime; see David Card and Ana Rute Cardoso, "Can Compulsory Military Service Raise Civilian Wages? Evidence from the Peacetime Draft in Portugal," *American Economic Journal: Applied Economics* 4 (October 2014): 57–93.

Selected Readings

Becker, Gary. *Human Capital.* New York: National Bureau of Economic Research, 1975.

Borjas, George J. "Earnings Determination: A Survey of the Neoclassical Approach." In *Three Worlds of Labor Economics*, eds. Garth Mangum and Peter Philips. Armonk, NY: M.E. Sharpe, 1988.

Card, David. "The Causal Effect of Education on Earnings." In *Handbook of Labor Economics*, eds. Orley Ashenfelter and David Card. New York: Elsevier, 1999.

Clotfelter, Charles T., Ronald G. Ehrenberg, Malcolm Getz, and John Siegfried. *Economic Challenges in Higher Education.* Chicago: University of Chicago Press, 1991.

Friendlander, Daniel, David H. Greenberg, and Philip K. Robins. "Evaluating Government Training Programs for the Economically Disadvantaged." *Journal of Economic Literature* 35 (December 1997): 1809–1855.

Goldin, Claudia, and Lawrence F. Katz. *The Race Between Education and Technology.* Cambridge, MA: Belknap Press, 2008.

Hanushek, Eric A., and Ludger Woessmann. *The Knowledge Capital of Nations: Education and the Economics of Growth.* Cambridge, MA: MIT Press, 2015.

Heckman, James J., John Eric Humphries, and Tim Kautz. *The Myth of Achievement Tests: The GED and the Role of Character in American Life.* Chicago: University of Chicago Press: 2014.

Krueger, Alan B., and Mikael Lindahl. "Education for Growth: Why and for Whom?" *Journal of Economic Literature* 39 (December 2001): 1101–1136.

Mincer, Jacob. *Schooling, Experience, and Earnings.* New York: National Bureau of Economic Research, 1974.

Schultz, Theodore. *The Economic Value of Education.* New York: Columbia University Press, 1963.

Spence, Michael. "Job Market Signaling." *Quarterly Journal of Economics* 87 (August 1973): 355–374.

APPENDIX 9A

A "Cobweb" Model of Labor Market Adjustment

The adjustment of college enrollments to changes in the returns to education is not always smooth or rapid, particularly in special fields, such as engineering and law, that are highly technical. The problem is that if engineering wages (say) were to go up suddenly in a given year, the supply of graduate engineers would not be affected until three or four years later (owing to the time it takes to learn the field). Likewise, if engineering wages were to fall, those students enrolled in an engineering curriculum would understandably be reluctant to immediately leave the field. They have already invested a lot of time and effort and may prefer to take their chances in engineering rather than devote more time and money to learning a new field.[1]

The failure of supply to respond immediately to changed market conditions can cause *boom-and-bust cycles* in the market for highly technical workers. If educational planners in government or the private sector are unaware of these cycles, they may seek to stimulate or reduce enrollments at times when they should be doing exactly the opposite, as illustrated next.

An Example of "Cobweb" Adjustments

Suppose that the market for engineers is in equilibrium, where the wage is W_0 and the number of engineers is N_0 (see Figure 9A.1). Let us now assume that the demand curve for engineers shifts from D_0 to D_1. Initially, this increase in the demand for engineers does *not* induce the supply of engineers to increase beyond N_0, because it takes a long time to become an engineer once one has decided to do so. Thus, although the increased demand for engineers causes more people to decide to enter the field, the number available for employment *at the moment* is N_0. These N_0 engineers, therefore, can *currently* obtain a wage of W_1 (in effect, this leads to a vertical supply curve at N_0 for a few years until the supply of engineering graduates increases).

The *current* engineering wage, W_1, is now above W^*, the new *long-run* equilibrium wage caused by the intersection of D_1 and S. The market, however, is unaware of W^*, observing only W_1. If people are myopic and assume that W_1 is the new equilibrium wage, N_1 people will enter the engineering field (see Figure 9A.2). When these N_1 all graduate, a *surplus* of engineers will ensue (remember that W_1 is *above* long-run equilibrium).

With the supply of engineers now temporarily fixed at N_1, the wage will fall to W_2. This fall will cause students and workers to shift *out* of engineering, but that effect will not be fully felt for a few years. In the meantime, note that W_2 is below long-run equilibrium (still at W^*). Thus, when supply *does* adjust, it will adjust too much—all the way to N_2. Now another shortage of engineers will ensue, because after supply adjusts to N_2, demand

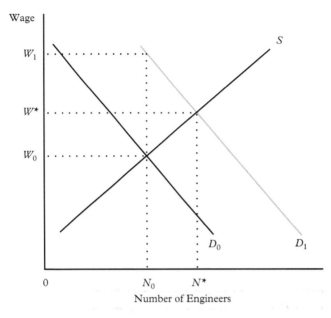

Figure 9.A1 The Labor Market for Engineers

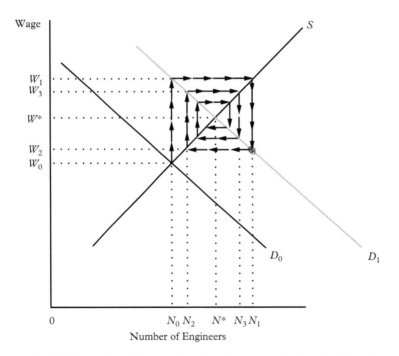

Figure 9.A2 The Labor Market for Engineers: A Cobweb Model

exceeds supply at a wage rate of W_2. This causes wages to rise to W_3, and the cycle repeats itself. Over time, the swings become smaller, and equilibrium is eventually reached. Because the adjustment path in Figure 9A.2 looks somewhat like a cobweb, the adjustment process described earlier is sometimes called a *cobweb model*.

Critical to cobweb models is the assumption that workers form myopic expectations about the future behavior of wages.[2] In our example, these workers first assume that W_1 will prevail in the future and ignore the possibility that the occupational decisions of others will, in four years, drive the wage below W_1. How workers (and other economic actors, such as investors and taxpayers) form expectations about future wage (price) levels is crucial to the understanding of many key issues affecting the labor market.[3]

Adaptive Expectations

The simplest and most naive way to predict future wage levels is to assume that what is observed today is what will be observed in the future; this naive assumption, as noted earlier, underlies the cobweb model. A more sophisticated way to form predictions about the future is to take an *adaptive expectations* approach. Adaptive expectations are formed by setting future expected wages equal to a weighted average of current and past wages. While more weight may be given to current wages than to past wages in forecasting future wage levels, changes in those levels before the current period are not ignored; thus, wage expectations formed adaptively likely do not alternatively overshoot and undershoot the equilibrium wage *by as much as* those formed by using the naive approach. If, however, adaptive expectations also lead workers to first overpredict and then underpredict the equilibrium wage, the cobweb-like behavior of wages and labor supply will still be observed (although the fluctuations will be of a smaller magnitude if the predictions are closer to the mark than those made naively).

Rational Expectations

The most sophisticated way to predict future market outcomes is to use a full-blown model of the labor market. Those who believe in the *rational expectations* method of forming predictions about future wages assume that workers do have such a model in their heads, at least implicitly.[4] Thus, they will realize that a marked increase in the earnings of engineers (say) is likely to be temporary, because supply will expand and eventually bring the returns to an investment in engineering skills in line with those for other occupations. Put differently, the rational expectations model assumes that workers behave as if they have taken (and mastered) a good course in labor economics (including the appendixes of the text) and that they will not be fooled into overpredicting or underpredicting future wage levels.

Clearly, how people form expectations is an important empirical issue. In the case of engineers, lawyers, and dentists, periodic fluctuations in supply that characterize the cobweb model have been found, although the precise mix of naive and rational expectations is not clear.[5] Whether these fluctuations are the result of naive expectations or not, the lesson to be learned from cobweb models should not be lost on government policymakers. If the government chooses to take an active role in dealing with labor shortages and surpluses, it must be aware that because supply adjustments are slow in highly technical markets, wages in those markets tend to *over*-adjust. In other words, to the extent possible, governmental predictions and market interventions should be based on rational expectations. For example, at the initial stages of a shortage, when wages are rising toward W_1 (in our example), the government should be pointing out that W_1 is likely to be *above* the long-run equilibrium. If instead it attempts to meet the current shortage by *subsidizing* study in that field, it will be encouraging an even greater *surplus* later on. The moral of the story is that a complete knowledge of how markets adjust to changes in supply and demand is necessary before we can be sure that government intervention will do more good than harm.

Notes

1. See Lars J. Kirkeboen, Edwin Leuven, and Magne Mogstad, "Field of Study, Earnings, and Self-Selection," *The Quarterly Journal of Economics* 131 (August 2016): 1057–1111, for a study of selection and field of study.

2. Also critical are the assumptions that at the start, demand immediately shifts from D_0 to D_1 and supply doesn't change because of any other reasons.

3. Also critical to cobweb models is that the demand curve be flatter than the supply curve; if it is not, the cobweb *explodes* when demand shifts, and an equilibrium wage is never reached. An exploding cobweb model is an example from economics of the phenomenon of *chaos*. For a general introduction to this fascinating topic, see James Gleick, *Chaos* (New York: Penguin Books, 1987). For an article on chaos theory in the economic literature, see William J. Baumol and Jess Benhabib, "Chaos: Significance, Mechanism, and Economic Applications," *Journal of Economic Perspectives* 3 (Winter 1989): 77–106.

4. Two important early studies in this area are Robert E. Lucas Jr. and Leonard A. Rapping, "Real Wages, Employment and Inflation," *Journal of Political Economy* 77 (September–October 1969): 721–754; Robert E. Lucas Jr. and Leonard A. Rapping, "Price Expectations and the Philips Curve," *The American Economic Review* 59 (June 1969): 342–350.

5. See Jaewoo Ryoo and Sherwin Rosen, "The Engineering Labor Market," *Journal of Political Economy* 112 (February 2004): S110–S140, for an analysis of both the cobweb model and the rational expectations model.

CHAPTER 10

Worker Mobility: Migration, Immigration, and Turnover

While the flow of workers across national borders is not a new phenomenon—after all, it was responsible for the settlement of Australia, Canada, and the United States—immigration over the past two or three decades has significantly raised the share of the foreign-born in Europe and North America. For example, the share of the foreign-born in the European population rose from 7 percent in 1990 to 11 percent in 2019; in North America, the share of foreign-born rose from 10 percent to 16 percent over this period.[1] The dramatic increase in the presence of immigrants, who frequently speak a different language and are often from poorer countries, has stimulated some calls for stricter limits or tighter "border-security" measures—notably in the United States, which shares a long border with a much poorer country (Mexico) and attracts many workers who have not been able to secure an official immigration visa into the United States. Proposals to impose stricter limits on immigration, including those to expel immigrants without work visas, are frequently explained with arguments that immigrants lower the wages of natives or otherwise impose a financial burden on the "host" country. We investigate these arguments in this chapter.

In this chapter, we use economic theory to analyze the decision to emigrate and the labor market effects of immigration. In the process, we examine how immigrants are likely to differ from others in personal characteristics (e.g., age and future orientation), and what factors influence whether immigration raises the per capita real income of native-born people in the host country. We begin the chapter, however, with an analysis of the causes and consequences of *worker mobility*—the larger category of which immigration is an important subset. Worker mobility plays a critical role in market economies. Because the purpose of any market is to promote voluntary exchange, society relies on the free movement of workers among employers to allocate labor in a way that achieves optimal satisfaction (subject to constraints) for both workers and consumers. The flow (either actual or threatened) of workers from lower-paying to higher-paying jobs, for example, is what forces firms that are paying below-equilibrium wages to increase their wage offers. The existence of compensating wage differentials, to take another example, also depends on the ability of informed workers to exercise choice among employment opportunities in the search for enhanced utility.

Mobility, however, is costly. Workers must take time to seek out information on other jobs, and for at least some workers, job search is most efficient if they quit their current job first (to look for work in a new geographic area, for example). Severing ties with the current employer means leaving friends and familiar surroundings, and it may mean giving up valuable employee benefits or the inside track on future promotions.[2] Once a new job has been found, workers may well face the *monetary*, and will almost certainly face the *psychic*, costs of moving to new surroundings—and in the case of immigration, the possible need to learn a new language and adapt to a new culture makes these costs particularly burdensome. In short, workers who move to new employers bear costs in the near term so that utility can be enhanced later on. Therefore, the human-capital model introduced in Chapter 9 can be used to analyze mobility investments by workers.

The Determinants of Worker Mobility

The human-capital model views mobility as an investment in which costs are borne in some early period in order to obtain returns over a longer period of time. If the present value of the benefits associated with mobility exceeds the costs, both monetary and psychological, we assume that people will decide to change jobs, move, or both. If the discounted stream of benefits is not as large as the costs, then people will decide against such a change.

What determines the present value of the net benefits of mobility—that is, the benefits minus the costs—determines the mobility decision. These factors can be better identified by writing out the following formula, which precisely calculates these net benefits:

$$\text{Present Value of Net Benefits} = \sum_{t=1}^{T} \frac{B_t}{(1+r)^t} - C \qquad (10.1)$$

B_t = the increased utility in year t derived from changing jobs
T = the length of time (in years) one expects to work at the new job
r = the rate of discount
C = the utility lost in the move itself (direct and psychic costs)
Σ = a summation—in this case, the summation of the yearly discounted net benefits over a period running from year 1 to year T

Clearly, the present value of the net benefits of mobility will be larger the greater the utility derived from the new job, the less happy one is in the job of origin, the smaller the immediate costs associated with the change, and the longer that one expects to be in the new job or live in the new area (i.e., the greater T is). These observations lead to some clear-cut predictions about which groups in society will be most mobile and about the *patterns* of mobility that we would expect to observe.

Geographic Mobility

The mobility of workers among countries, and among regions within a country, is an important fact of economic life. We have seen that foreign-born people comprise 11 percent to 16 percent of the population of Europe and North America. Moreover, migration *within* the United States is such that roughly 2 percent of the population moves to a different state of residence every year, and one-fourth of those moves involve a change of employers.[3] This importance of job changes suggests that human-capital theory can help us understand which workers are most likely to undertake investments in geographic mobility and the directions in which mobility flows will take place.

The Direction of Migratory Flows

Human-capital theory predicts that migration will flow from areas of relatively poor earnings possibilities to places where opportunities are better. Studies of migratory flows support this prediction. In general, the results of such studies suggest that the *pull* of good opportunities in the areas of destination is stronger than the *push* of poor opportunities in the areas of origin. In other words, while people are more attracted to places where earnings are expected to be better, they do not necessarily come from areas where opportunities are poorest.

The most consistent finding in these detailed studies is that people are attracted to areas where the real earnings of full-time workers are highest. Studies find no consistent relationship, however, between unemployment in a local region and in-migration, perhaps because the number of people moving with a job already in hand is three times as large as the number moving *to look* for work. If one already has a job in a particular field, the area's unemployment rate is irrelevant.[4]

Most studies have found that, contrary to what we might expect, the characteristics of the place of origin do not appear to have much net influence on migration. While those in the poorest places have the greatest *incentives* to move, the very poorest areas also tend to have people with lower levels of wealth, education, and skills—the very people who seem least *willing* (or able) to move.[5] To understand this phenomenon, we must turn from the issue of *where* people go to a discussion of *who* is most likely to move. (In addition, we have the issue of *when* people move. See Example 10.1, which pulls together the issues of who, where, and when in analyzing one of the most momentous internal migrations in the history of the United States— the Great Migration of Black people from the U.S. South to the U.S. North in the first half of the twentieth century.)

EXAMPLE 10.1

The Great Migration: U.S. Southern Black People Move North

Our model predicts that workers will move whenever the present value of the net benefits of migration is positive. After the U.S. Civil War and emancipation, a huge wage gap opened up between the U.S. South and the U.S. North, where northern wages were often twice as high as southern wages. Yet, the migration of Black people out of the U.S. South was very low—only 68,000 during the 1870s.

During World War I, however, the Great Migration began, and over half a million Black people moved out of the U.S. South in the 1910s. The migration of this demographic during the 1920s was almost twice that number, and it exceeded 1.5 million during the 1940s, such that by 1950, over 20 percent of southern-born Black people had left the region.

Why did this migration take so long to get going? One important factor was low education levels, which made obtaining information about outside opportunities difficult. In 1880, more than 75 percent of Black people over age 10 were illiterate, but this figure fell to about 20 percent by 1930. One study finds that in 1900, literate adult Black men were three times more likely to have migrated than those who were illiterate. In 1940, Black people who had attended high school were twice as likely to have migrated than those with zero to four years of schooling. However, rising literacy alone cannot explain the sudden burst of migration.

The outbreak of World War I seems to have triggered the migration in two ways. First, it caused labor demand in northern industry to soar. Second, it brought the collapse of immigration inflows from abroad. Before World War I, growing northern industries had relied heavily on immigrants from Europe as sources of labor. With the immigration flood slowing to a trickle, employers began to hire Black workers—even sending agents to recruit in the U.S. South. Job opportunities for Black people in the U.S. North finally opened up, and many Black people responded by moving.

A study using census data from 1870 to 1950 finds that, as expected, northern states in which wages were highest attracted more Black migrants, as did those in which manufacturing growth was more rapid. Reduced European immigration seems to have spurred Black migration, implying that if European immigration had been completely restricted at the turn of the century, the Great Migration would have started much sooner.

Source: William J. Collins, "When the Tide Turned: Immigration and the Delay of the Great Black Migration," *Journal of Economic History* 57 (September 1997): 607–632; Robert A. Margo, *Race and Schooling in the South, 1880–1950* (Chicago, IL: University of Chicago Press, 1990); also see William J. Collins and Marianne H. Wanamaker, "Selection and Economic Gains in the Great Migration of African Americans: New Evidence from Linked Census Data," *American Economic Journal: Applied Economics* 6 (January 2014): 220–252

Personal Characteristics of Migrants

Migration is highly selective in the sense that it is not an activity in which all people are equally likely to be engaged. To be specific, mobility is much higher among young people and better-educated people, as human-capital theory would suggest.

Age   Age is one important factor in determining who migrates. Among Americans in their late 20s, 9 percent moved to another region within the United States, or to another country, between 2005 and 2010; for those in their late 30s and late 40s, the corresponding percentages were 6 and 3 percent, respectively.[6]

We have two explanations for the fact that migration is an activity primarily for young people. First, the younger one is, the longer the period over which benefits from an investment can be obtained and the larger the present value of these benefits.

Second, a large part of the costs of migration is psychological—the losses associated with giving up friends, community ties, and the benefits of knowing one's way around. As we grow older, our ties to the community become stronger and the losses associated with leaving loom larger.

Education   Educational attainment is a second important predictor of who will move. For example, Americans with college degrees were twice as likely as those without to have moved out of their region between 2005 and 2010.[7]

One cost of migration is that of applying and interviewing for job offers. If one's occupation has a national (or international) labor market, as is the case for many college graduates, recruiters visit college campuses, and arrangements for interviews requiring fly-ins are commonplace—and often at the expense of the employer. However, if the relevant labor market for one's job is localized, the mechanisms for recruiting workers residing in distant areas are less likely to exist, and workers looking for a job far from home will find interviewing relatively costly too (and employers are much less likely to pay for travel to such interviews).

The Role of Distance

Human-capital theory clearly predicts that as migration costs rise, the flow of migrants will fall. The costs of moving increase with distance, for two reasons. First, acquiring trustworthy *information* (often from friends or colleagues) on opportunities elsewhere is easier—especially for workers whose jobs are in "local" labor markets—when employment prospects are closer to home. Second, the time and money cost of a move and for trips back to see friends and relatives, and hence the *psychic* costs of the move, rise with distance. Indeed, we find that among those U.S. workers who moved to a different labor market during 2005–2010, roughly 60 percent moved fewer than 500 miles—and most of those (35 percent of the total) moved fewer than 200 miles away from their original residence.[8]

Interestingly, lack of education appears to be a bigger deterrent to long-distance migration than does age (other influences held constant), a fact that can shed some light on whether information costs or psychic costs are the primary deterrent. As suggested by our arguments in the previous section, the age deterrent is closely related to psychic costs, while educational level and ease of access to information are closely linked. The apparently larger deterrent of educational level suggests that information costs may have more influence than psychic costs on the relationship between migration and distance.[9]

The Earnings Distribution in Sending Countries and International Migration

Up to this point, our examples of factors that influence geographic mobility have related to domestic migration, but the influences of age, access to information, the potential gains in earnings, and distance are all relevant to international migration as well. Additionally, because immigrants are self-selected and the costs of immigration are so high, personal discount rates (or orientation toward the future) are critical and likely to be different for immigrants and nonmigrants. That is, as illustrated in Example 10.2, *immigrants—like others who make significant investments in human capital—are more likely to have lower-than-average personal discount rates.*

EXAMPLE 10.2

Migration and One's Time Horizon

Economic theory suggests that those who have longer time horizons are more likely to make human-capital investments. Can we see evidence of this theoretical implication in the horizons of people who are most likely to migrate? A paper explores the possibility that people who give greater weight to the welfare of their children and grandchildren have a higher propensity to bear the considerable costs of immigration.

Before 1989, the Soviet Union made emigration for Jews difficult, though not impossible. Applying for emigration involved heavy fees; moreover, the applicant's property was often confiscated and their right to work was often suspended. However, after the collapse of the Soviet Union in 1989, these barriers were eliminated. The monetary benefits of migrating were approximately the same before and after 1989, but the costs fell considerably.

How did migrants from the earlier period—who were willing to bear the high costs— differ from those who emigrated only when the costs were reduced? The study finds evidence that Jewish women who migrated to Israel during the earlier period brought with them larger families (on average, 0.4 to 0.8 more children) than otherwise-similar migrants in the later period. This suggests that the benefits of migration to children may have been a decisive factor in the decision to migrate during the pre-1989 period.

Likewise, a survey of women aged 51 to 61 shows that grandmothers who have immigrated to the United States spend over 200 more hours per year with their grandchildren than U.S.-born grandmothers. They are also more likely to report that they consider leaving an inheritance important (rather than spending all their wealth on themselves). Thus, this evidence is consistent with the theoretical implication that those who invest in immigration have longer time horizons (in the sense of putting greater weight on the welfare of their children and grandchildren) than those who do not.

Source: Eli Berman and Zaur Rzakhanov, "Fertility, Migration and Altruism" (Working Paper No. 7545, National Bureau of Economic Research, February 2000)

One aspect of the potential gains from migration that is uniquely important when analyzing international flows of labor is the distribution of earnings in the sending as compared with the receiving country. The relative distribution of earnings can help us predict which skill groups within a sending country are most likely to emigrate.[10]

Some countries have a more compressed (equal) earnings distribution than is found in the United States. In these countries, the average earnings differential between higher-skilled and lower-skilled workers is smaller, implying that the returns to human-capital investments are lower than those in the United States. High-skilled and professional workers from these countries (northern European countries are most notable in this regard) have the most to gain from emigration to the United States. Lower-skilled workers in countries with more equality of earnings are well paid compared with lower-skilled workers in the United States and thus have less incentive to move. Immigrants to the United States from these countries, therefore, tend to be more skilled than the average worker who does not emigrate.

In countries with a less equal distribution of earnings than is found in the United States, higher-skilled workers do relatively well, but lower-skilled workers could reap large gains from emigrating to the United States. These lower-skilled workers may be blocked from making human-capital investments in their own countries (and thus from taking advantage of the high returns to such investments that are implied by the large earnings differentials). Instead, their human-capital investment may take the form of emigrating and seeking work in the United States. Less-developed countries tend to have relatively unequal earnings distributions, so one expects that immigrants from these countries (and especially Mexico, which is closest) will be disproportionately lower skilled.

The Returns to International and Domestic Migration

We have seen that migrants generally move to places that allow them greater earnings opportunities. How great these earnings increases are for individual migrants depends on the reasons and preparation for the move.

Internal Migration for Economic Reasons   The largest earnings increase from migration can be expected among those whose move is motivated by a better job offer and who have obtained this offer through a job-search process undertaken before quitting their previous jobs. A study of adults in their 20s who were in this category found that for moves in the 1979–1985 period, earnings increased 14 percent to 18 percent more than earnings of nonmigrants. Even those who quit voluntarily and migrated for economic reasons *without* a previous job search earned 6 percent to 9 percent more than if they had stayed put.[11] The returns were similar for both men and women who migrated for economic reasons.

Family Migration   Most of us live in families, and if a family has more than one employed person, the decision to migrate is likely to have different earnings effects on the members. You might recall from Chapter 7 that more than one plausible model explains how those who live together actually make joint labor supply decisions, but with migration, a decision to move might well be made if the *family as a whole* experiences a net increase in total earnings. Total family earnings, of course, could be increased even if one partner's earnings were to fall as a result of the move, as long as the other partner experienced relatively large gains. Considering family migration decisions raises the issue of tied movers—those who agree to move for family reasons, not necessarily because the move improves their own earnings.

Among those in their 20s who migrated in the 1979–1985 period, quitting jobs and moving for *family* reasons caused earnings to decrease by an average of 10 percent to 15 percent—although searching for a new job before moving apparently held wage losses to zero.[12] Clearly, migrating as a tied mover can be costly to an individual. Women move more often for family reasons than men do, but as more women complete college or graduate school and enter careers, their willingness to move for family reasons might fall. The growing preference among college-educated couples for living in large urban areas, where both people have access to many alternative job opportunities without moving, reflects the costs of migrating as a tied mover.[13]

Returns to Immigration   Comparing the earnings of *international* immigrants with what they would have earned had they not emigrated is generally not feasible, owing to a lack of data on earnings in the home country—although a comparison of the wages received by Mexican immigrants in the United States with those paid to comparable workers in Mexico suggests that the gain from crossing the border was in the range of $9,000 to $16,000 per year in 2000 (an enormous percentage gain, given that the average per capita income in Mexico was $9,700 in that year).[14]

Most studies of the returns to immigration have focused on comparisons of immigrants' earnings with those of native-born workers in the host country. Figure 10.1 displays, for men who had immigrated to the United States decades ago, the path of their earnings relative to those of native-born U.S. workers with similar amounts of labor market experience. Although not reflecting the experience of recent immigrants, Figure 10.1 illustrates three generalizations about the relative earnings of immigrants over time. First, immigrants earn substantially less than their native-born counterparts when they first arrive in the United States. Second, each succeeding cohort of immigrants has done less well upon entry than its predecessor. Third, the *relative* earnings of immigrants rise over time, which means that their earnings rise faster than those of native-born workers, especially in the first 10 years after immigration.[15]

Immigrants' Initial Earnings   That immigrants initially earn substantially less than native-born workers is hardly surprising. Even after

Figure 10.1 Male Immigrant Workers' Earnings Relative to Those of Native-Born Workers with Similar Labor-Market Experience, by Immigrant Cohort

Source: Adapted from Darren Lubotsky, "Chutes or Ladders? A Longitudinal Analysis of Immigrant Earnings" (Working Paper No. 445, Industrial Relations Section, Princeton University, August 2000), Figure 6

controlling for the effects of education (the typical immigrant is less educated than the typical native-born worker), immigrants earn less because of their difficulties with English (if English is not their native language), their unfamiliarity with U.S. employment opportunities, and their lack of a U.S. work history (and employers' consequent uncertainties about their productivity).

The fall in the initial earnings of successive immigrant groups relative to native-born U.S. workers has been widely studied in recent years. It appears to reflect the fact that immigrants to the United States are coming increasingly from countries with relatively low levels of educational attainment, and they are therefore arriving in the United States with less human capital.[16]

Immigrants' Earnings Growth Earnings of immigrants rise relatively quickly, which could reflect their high rates of investment in human capital after arrival. After entry, immigrants typically invest in themselves by acquiring work experience and improved proficiency in English, and these investments raise the wages that they can attain. For example, one study found that English fluency raises immigrant earnings by an average of 17 percent in the United States, 12 percent in Canada, and 9 percent in Australia. Of course, not all immigrants have the same incentives to become proficient in English, and some are fluent upon arrival. Those who live in enclaves where business is conducted in their native language may have reduced incentives to learn English, whereas those who are not able to return to their native countries have greater incentives to invest time and money in mastering English (political refugees are in the latter group; for an analysis, see the Empirical Study 10.1 at the end of this chapter).[17]

Return Migration   The data underlying Figure 10.1 are from immigrants who remained working in the United States for at least 15 years after first entry. They are the ones for whom the investment in immigration was successful enough that they remained. Many of those for whom immigration does not yield the expected returns decide to return to their country of origin; those who are most likely to return are the ones who were *closest to the margin* (expected the least net gains) when they first decided to come.[18] Return migration highlights another important fact: immigration, like other human-capital investments, entails risk—and not all such investments work out as hoped.

Policy Application: Restricting Immigration

Analytical tools of the economist are incredibly important in the area of immigration policy. Immigration has both economic and cultural consequences, and some evidence shows that people's views on the desirability of immigration might be based largely on their attitudes toward cultural diversity.[19] However, public debate about immigration most often focuses on claims about its economic consequences, so using economic theory is important in guiding our analysis of these outcomes. After a brief outline of the history of U.S. immigration policy, this section analyzes in detail the economic effects of a phenomenon that is currently attracting much discussion in the United States: the immigration of workers whose immigration status is considered "unauthorized" because they do not have the documentation necessary to legally reside in the country.

U.S. Immigration History

The United States is a rich country whose wealth and high standard of living make it an attractive place for immigrants from nearly all parts of the world.[20] For the first 140 years of its history as an independent country, the United States followed a policy of essentially unrestricted immigration (during this time period, the only major immigration restrictions were placed on Asians and on convicts). The flow of immigrants was especially large after 1840, when U.S. industrialization and political and economic upheavals in Europe made immigration an attractive investment for millions.[21] Officially recorded immigration peaked (as a fraction of the population) in the first decade of the twentieth century, when the *yearly* flow of immigrants was more than 1 percent of the population (see Table 10.1).

Restrictions   In 1921, Congress adopted the Quota Law, which set annual quotas on immigration on the basis of nationality. These quotas had the effect of reducing immigration from Eastern and Southern Europe. This act was followed by other laws in 1924 and 1929 that further restricted immigration from Eastern Southern Europe. These various revisions in

Table 10.1 Officially Recorded Immigration: 1901 to 2018

Period	Number (in thousands)	Annual Rate (per thousand of U.S. population)	Year	Number (in thousands)	Annual Rate (per thousand of U.S. population)
1901–1910	8,795	10.4	2011	1,062	3.4
1911–1920	5,736	5.7	2012	1,031	3.3
1921–1930	4,107	3.5	2013	991	3.1
1931–1940	528	0.4	2014	1,017	3.2
1941–1950	1,035	0.7	2015	1,051	3.3
1951–1960	2,515	1.5	2016	1,184	3.7
1961–1970	3,322	1.7	2017	1,127	3.5
1971–1980	4,389	2.0	2018	1,097	3.4
1981–1990[22]	7,338	3.1			
1991–2000[a]	9,082	3.4			
2001–2010	10,501	3.5			

Source: U.S. Department of Homeland Security, *Yearbook of Immigration Statistics: 2018*, Table 1, at www.dhs.gov/immigration-statistics/yearbook/2018/table1

immigration policy were motivated, in part, by widespread concerns over the alleged adverse effect on native employment of the arrival of lower-skilled immigrants from Eastern and Southern Europe.

In 1965, the passage of the Immigration and Nationality Act abolished the quota system that was based on national origin that so heavily favored Northern and Western Europeans. Under this law, as amended in 1990, overall immigration is formally restricted, with most spots reserved for family-reunification purposes and relatively few—roughly 20 percent—reserved for immigrants with special skills who are admitted for employment purposes. (Political refugees, who must meet certain criteria relating to persecution in their home countries, are another category of documented immigrants.) The fact that immigration to the United States is a worthwhile investment for many more people than can legally come, however, has created incentives for people to live in the country without official approval.

Unauthorized Immigration Unauthorized immigration can be divided into two categories of roughly equal size: immigrants who enter legally but overstay or violate the provisions of their visas, and those who enter the country illegally. On an average day in 2018, roughly 222,000 people entered the United States under nonimmigrant visas, usually as visitors for pleasure or business or as students.[23] Once here, the foreigner can look for work, although working at a job under a student or visitor visa is not authorized. If the student or visitor is offered a job, they can apply for an "adjustment of status" to legally become a permanent resident, although the chances for approval as an employment-based immigrant are slim for the ordinary worker.

Many immigrants, however, enter the country without a visa. Immigrants from the Caribbean often enter through Puerto Rico, whose residents are U.S. citizens and thus are allowed free entry to the mainland. Others walk across the Mexican border. Still others are smuggled into the United States, use false documents to get through entry stations, or overstay their nonimmigrant visa.

Between 1990 and 2007, the *yearly increase* in the number of unauthorized immigrants residing in the United States was estimated to be over to 500,000. From 2007 to 2014, however, with an improving job market in Mexico, fewer opportunities in the wake of the Great Recession in the United States, increased border security, and more deportations, the population of unauthorized immigrants declined by about 160,000 per year. With deportations of immigrants *away* from the border annually averaging almost 400,000 during the 2007–2014 period, net declines of about 160,000 imply that inflows of new unauthorized immigrants were roughly 240,000 per year—about half the flows in the earlier period. Almost three-quarters of all unauthorized immigrants are estimated to be from Mexico (59 percent) and Central America (14 percent).[24]

As of 2020, the U.S. population was split over what to do about unauthorized immigration. There were calls for the enhancement of border security, especially along the Mexican border, accompanied by assertions that such immigration is harmful to the U.S. population as a whole—by increasing the population of lower-skilled workers, reducing the wages of native-born workers, and putting greater demands on government spending than the unauthorized immigrants pay in taxes. On the other side were assertions that undocumented immigrants are fulfilling a useful economic function by performing tasks that U.S. workers are increasingly less willing to do and that they should be given a path to achieve legal residency. Before we turn to an economic analysis of the effects of immigration on the receiving country, we briefly describe immigrants from Mexico, who are the focus of much of the current debate.

Immigrants From Mexico   Immigration to the United States from Mexico—both authorized and unauthorized—is large, for two reasons: the huge differential in income per capita between the two countries and the fact that the countries share a long border. In 2007, when almost 12 million Mexican immigrants were living in the United States, they constituted roughly one-third of the entire foreign-born population.[25] Of the 12 million, about half were undocumented.

Earlier, we reviewed theory suggesting that for a country with a *wider* distribution of earnings than is found in the United States, we would expect emigration to the United States to come largely from the lower end of its skill distribution. While the typical Mexican immigrant is less educated than the average American, because educational levels are generally lower in Mexico, the most recent immigrants from Mexico come from the *middle* of Mexico's skill distribution, not the bottom. For example, let us focus on Mexican men between the ages of 28 and 37. In Mexico, 23 percent of this group has between 10 and 15 years of schooling; however, among recent immigrants to the United States, 40 percent were in this educational group. In contrast, whereas in Mexico about two-thirds of this age group have fewer than 10 years of schooling, only about half of those who emigrate from Mexico have fewer than 10 years of education. Why is the *middle* of the Mexican educational distribution overrepresented in the immigrant group, not the lower level?

The cost of crossing the border is high, and it has become higher since the United States increased border surveillance in 2002 and beyond. Surveys done in areas of Mexico that are the source of much migration to the United States suggest that between 80 and 95 percent of undocumented entrants use the services of a smuggler ("coyote"), whom they pay—in advance—to facilitate their crossing. The average fee charged by coyotes is around 2,000 dollars—a substantial fraction of the yearly per capita income in Mexico. Furthermore, the chances are probably around 50 percent that one will spend this money and still get caught (and returned to Mexico). While estimates suggest that this investment can be recouped in 8–11 weeks of work, the fee represents a significant credit constraint that the poorest Mexicans probably cannot overcome.

The policies that people in the United States advocate for are based on their beliefs about the consequences of immigration for employers, consumers, taxpayers, and workers of various skill levels and ethnicities. Nearly everyone with an opinion on this subject has an economic model implicitly or explicitly in mind when addressing these consequences; the purpose of the following sections is to make these economic models explicit and to evaluate them.

Naive Views of Immigration

Two opposing views of unauthorized immigration can be considered naive. One view is that every employed undocumented immigrant deprives a citizen or legal resident of a job. For example, a Department of Labor official told a U.S. House committee studying immigration, "I think it is logical to conclude that if they are actually employed, they are taking a job away from one of our American citizens." According to this view, if x undocumented immigrants are deported and others kept out, the number of unemployed Americans would decline by x.

At the opposite end of the policy spectrum is the equally naive argument that undocumented workers perform jobs no U.S. citizen would do: "You couldn't conduct a hotel in New York, you couldn't conduct a restaurant in New York . . . if you didn't have rough laborers. We haven't got the rough laborers anymore. . . . Where are we going to get the people to do that rough work"[26]

Both arguments are simplistic because they ignore the slopes of the demand and supply curves. Consider, for example, the labor market for the job of "rough laborer"[27]—any job most U.S. citizens find distasteful.

Without lower-skilled immigrants, the restricted supply of U.S. workers to this market would imply a relatively high wage (W_1 in Figure 10.2). N_1 citizens would be employed. If immigrants entered the market, the supply curve would shift outward and perhaps flatten (implying that immigrants were more responsive to wage increases for rough laborers than citizens were). The influx of undocumented immigrants would drive the wage down to W_2, but employment would increase to N_2.

Are U.S. workers unwilling to do the work of rough laborers? In the market depicted in Figure 10.2, many more undocumented immigrants are willing to work at the market wage of W_2 than are U.S. citizens. Only N_3 U.S. citizens would want these jobs at this low wage, and the remaining supply ($N_2 - N_3$) is made up entirely of immigrants. If the United States had no undocumented immigrants, however, N_1 U.S. workers would be employed at wage W_1 as rough laborers. Wages would be higher, as would the prices of the goods or services produced with this labor, but the job would get done. The only shortage of U.S. citizens is at the low wage of W_2; at W_1, no shortage occurs (review Chapter 2 for a discussion of labor shortages).

Would deporting those undocumented immigrants working as rough laborers create the same number of jobs for U.S. citizens? The answer is clearly no. If the N_2–N_3 undocumented immigrants working as laborers at wage W_2 were deported and all other undocumented immigrants were kept from the market, the number of U.S. workers employed as laborers would rise from N_3 to N_1, and their wages would rise from W_2 to W_1 (Figure 10.2). N_2–N_1 jobs would be destroyed by the rising wage rate associated with deportation. Thus, although deportation would increase the employment and wage levels of U.S. workers in the market for laborers, it would certainly not increase employment on a one-for-one basis.[28]

However, deportation *would* create jobs for U.S. citizens on a one-for-one basis in one scenario: when the federal minimum-wage law creates a

Figure 10.2 Demand and Supply of Rough Laborers

surplus of labor. Suppose, for example, that the supply of native-born laborers is represented by ABS_1 in Figure 10.3 and the total supply is represented by ACS_2. Because an artificially high (federal minimum) wage has created a surplus, only N of the N' workers willing to work at the minimum wage can actually find employment. If some of them are undocumented immigrants, deporting them—coupled with successful efforts to deny other immigrants access to these jobs—would create jobs for a comparable number of U.S. workers. However, to prevent the wage level from rising (and thus destroying jobs) after deportation, the demand curve would have to intersect the domestic supply curve (ABS_1) at or to the left of point B.

The foregoing analyses ignore the possibility that if low-wage undocumented immigrant labor is prevented from coming to the jobs, employers might transfer the jobs to countries with abundant supplies of low-wage labor. Thus, perhaps lower-skilled U.S. workers are in competition with foreign lower-skilled workers whether those workers are employed in the United States or elsewhere. However, not all lower-skilled jobs can be moved abroad, because not all outputs can be imported (most lower-skilled services, for example, must be performed at the place of consumption); therefore, our analyses continue to focus on situations in which the "export" of lower-skilled jobs is infeasible or costly.

An Analysis of the Gainers and Losers

The claim that immigration is harmful to U.S. workers is often based on a single-market analysis like that contained in Figure 10.2. Some argue that when immigration increases the supply of rough laborers, both the wages and the employment levels of U.S. citizens working as laborers are reduced. The total wage bill paid to U.S. laborers falls from $W_1 0 N_1 B$ in Figure 10.2

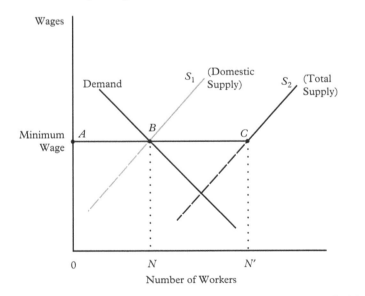

Figure 10.3 Demand and Supply of Rough Laborers Paid a Minimum Wage

to $W_2 0 N_3 D$. Some U.S. workers leave the market in response to the reduced wage, and those who stay earn less.

Even if the immigration of lower-skilled labor were to adversely affect domestic laborers, however, concluding that immigration is necessarily harmful to the U.S. population as a *whole* would be a mistake. Let us look a bit more closely at the gains and losses that we might expect to see from an influx of foreign laborers.

Consumers   The immigration of "cheap labor" clearly benefits consumers who use the output of this labor. If wages are reduced and employment increases, the goods and services produced by this labor are increased in quantity and reduced in price. Indeed, some evidence shows that the influx of low-skilled immigrants (who presumably provide household and childcare services) has facilitated U.S. college-educated women's pursuing careers while rearing children.[29]

Employers   Employers of rough labor (in our ongoing example) obviously benefit, at least in the short run. In Figure 10.2, profits increased from $W_1 AB$ to $W_2 AC$. This rise in profitability will have two major effects. By raising the returns to capital, it will serve as a signal for investors to increase investments in plant and equipment. Increased profits will also induce more people to become employers. The increases in capital and the number of employers will eventually drive profits down to their normal level, but in the end, the country's stock of capital is increased and opportunities are created for some workers to become owners.

Employees in the "Rough Labor" Market   You might recall from Chapters 3 and 4 that the demand curve for labor is affected by both the substitution effect and the scale effect. A consideration of these two effects is critical to understanding how immigration affects native-born workers.

To begin our analysis of how immigration affects native-born workers, let us assume (as we implicitly did in drawing Figure 10.2) that immigrant and native-born laborers have the same skills and are thus completely substitutable; put differently, we begin our analysis by assuming that low-skilled immigrants and low-skilled natives are in the same labor market. If supply to that market increases owing to immigration, the effects on wages and employment depend very much on the *elasticity* of the labor demand curve in that market. If, for example, the labor demand curve in Figure 10.2 were flatter (more elastic) than the one drawn, the decline in laborers' wages would be smaller, and the increase in their employment would be larger, than the changes shown.

What would make for a more elastic labor demand curve? Our analyses in Chapters 3 and 4 suggest that the labor demand curve is more elastic when both the substitution effect and the scale effect are larger. That is, when wages of laborers start to fall owing to increased labor supply, the increase in labor demanded by employers will be larger if the lower cost of production spurs a larger increase in consumer demand (the scale effect) and if the use of laborers in producing any given level of output is greater (the substitution effect). In the presence of an influx of immigrant laborers, then, larger scale and substitution effects will moderate the decline in native laborers' wages (and thus the extent to which they withdraw from work in that market).

Our analysis of the market for laborers has assumed so far that the influx of immigrants does not *shift* the demand curve for laborers (which was held fixed in Figure 10.2). Immigration, however, increases the population of consumers in the United States, thereby increasing the demand for mechanics, bus drivers, retail clerks, teachers, construction workers, truck drivers, and so forth. Some of this population increase may directly call for more rough laborers (such as roofers and meat packers), but the increased demand for other low-wage jobs (landscape workers, parking lot attendants, child-care workers) may arise because the availability of immigrant labor allows more natives to work, or to work longer hours, outside the home.[30] If the labor demand curve in Figure 10.2 were to shift to the right, the downward effects on wages in the market for rough labor would be further moderated (if the shift in demand were large enough, wages for laborers might even rise).

Employees in Other Labor Markets   Let us now consider how the influx of rough laborers affects natives in *other* labor markets. For ease of exposition, we call these other labor markets *skilled*, although all we really mean by this term is that jobs in this market require characteristics (such as the ability to communicate clearly in English) that make the substitution of immigrants for natives difficult.[31]

For workers in skilled markets, a wage change in the market for rough labor will have scale and substitution effects that work in opposite directions. If wages for rough laborers fall, and if higher-skilled and lower-skilled workers are substitutes in production, the substitution effect will tend to *reduce* the demand for higher-skilled workers. The falling cost of lower-skilled labor, however, may also trigger a scale effect that *increases* the demand for higher-skilled labor—and the size of this scale effect would be enhanced by the overall growth in population we noted earlier. Which effect will dominate?

Theoretical analysis cannot *prove* that the scale effect dominates and that the demand for higher-skilled workers is therefore increased by the immigration of lower-skilled labor if the two types of labor are substitutes in the production process; however, an increase in demand for higher-skilled workers remains a distinct possibility. If the scale effect does dominate, the rightward shift in the demand for higher-skilled workers will, as shown in Figure 10.4, tend to increase wages and employment in higher-skilled markets. (Of course, any type of labor that is *complementary* with lower-skilled labor in the production process—supervisory workers, for example—can expect to gain from an influx of lower-skilled immigrants, because no substitution effect would occur.[32])

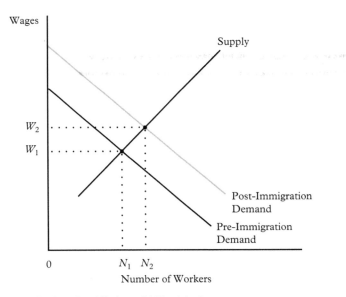

Figure 10.4 Market for Higher-Skilled Labor

Empirical Estimates of the Effects on Native Work-ers

Because of the intense concern about the effects of undocumented immigration on U.S. workers, much of the empirical work has focused on the effects of an influx of lower-skilled immigrants on those in the United States, especially in lower-skilled sectors. Broadly speaking, two general approaches are taken in these studies.

One approach is to examine how the proportion of lower-skilled immigrants in geographical areas affects the wages of natives, especially lower-skilled native workers, in those areas. In these studies, care must be taken to account for the likelihood that immigrants will go to cities with the best opportunities. Once account has been taken of this likelihood, most studies taking this approach find that the influx of lower-skilled immigrants over the past two decades has had rather small (or even negligible) effects on the wages of workers with a high school education or less.[33]

Some economists argue, however, that estimating the effects of immigration using cities as units of observation biases the estimated wage effects on low-skilled natives toward zero. They argue that many low-skilled native workers respond to an influx of immigrants (who compete with them for jobs) by leaving the city, and that these studies thus fail to measure the ultimate effects on native wages. Whether native workers respond to immigration in this way, and—if so—how quickly, is an issue that has not been settled.[34]

The possibility that area-based studies produce biased results because natives migrate in response to immigration has led to a second approach to estimating the effects of immigration on native workers' wages—a method that analyzes, at the national level, how the wages in specific human-capital groups (defined by education and experience) are affected *over time* by changes in the immigrant composition of those groups. This approach requires making assumptions about, first, the degree of substitutability between immigrants and natives *within* human-capital groups and, second, the response of capital investments over time to changes in labor supplies. The results from using this second method are highly affected by these assumptions, and estimates of the effects on native workers vary.[35] Some find that low-skilled immigration lowers the wages of native workers with skills similar to those of immigrants, while others find that the wages of both lower-skilled and higher-skilled native workers are increased—but the magnitudes of wage changes in both sets of studies tend to be small.[36] Researchers do agree, however, that the group of workers most likely to experience any negative wage effects from increased immigration of lower-skilled workers are native-born high school dropouts and *already-residing* lower-skilled immigrants (who are the closest substitutes for new immigrants).[37]

Therefore, how immigration of lower-skilled workers to the United States has affected the wages, on average, of native workers remains unclear. Researchers generally agree, though, that if negative effects on the wages of native workers are occurring, they will be felt mostly in the market for the lower-skilled (those with high school educations or less)—that is, among those with whom immigrants are most substitutable. *The larger question about immigration, however, is whether the losses of low-skilled native workers occur in the context of an overall gain to the U.S. population as a whole.* If so, as with the case of technological change analyzed earlier (see the end of Chapter 4), an important focus of immigration policy should be on shifting some of the overall gains from immigration to those who suffer economic losses because of it. We turn next to an analysis of the economic effects of immigration—especially unauthorized immigration—on U.S. society as a whole.

Do the Overall Gains From Immigration Exceed the Losses?

So far, we have used economic theory to analyze the likely effects of immigration on various groups of natives, including consumers, owners, and both higher-skilled workers and lower-skilled workers. Theory suggests that some of these groups should be clear-cut gainers; among these are owners, consumers, and workers who are complements in production with immigrant workers. Workers whose labor is highly substitutable in production with immigrant labor are the most likely losers from immigration, while the gains or losses for other groups of native workers are theoretically unpredictable, owing to potentially offsetting influences of the substitution and scale effects.

In this section, we use economic theory to analyze a slightly different question: What does economic theory say about the *overall* effects of immigration—particularly undocumented immigration—on the host country? Put in the context of the *normative* criteria presented in Chapter 1, this section asks, if both gainers and losers ensue from immigration among native workers in the host country, would the gainers likely be able to compensate the losers and still feel better off? The answer to this question will be yes if immigration increases the aggregate disposable income of native workers.

What Do Immigrants Add?   Immigrants, whether authorized or undocumented, are both consumers and producers, so whether their influx makes those already residing in the host country richer or poorer, in the aggregate, depends on how much the immigrants *add* to overall production as compared with how much they *consume*. Let us take a simple example of elderly immigrants allowed into the country to reunite with their adult children. If these immigrants do not work and if they are dependent on their children or on U.S. taxpayers for their consumption, then clearly the overall per capita disposable income among natives must fall. (This decline, of course, could well be offset by the increased utility of the reunited families, in which case it would be a price that the host country might be willing to pay.)

If immigrants *work* after their arrival, our profit-maximizing models of employer behavior suggest that they will be paid no more than the value of their marginal revenue product. Thus, if they rely only on their own earnings to finance their consumption, immigrants who work do not reduce the per capita disposable income of natives in the host country. Moreover, if immigrant earnings are not equal to the *full* value of the output that they add to the host country, then the total disposable income of natives will increase.[38]

Immigrants, Taxes, and Public Subsidies   Most host countries (including the United States) have government programs that may distribute benefits to immigrants. If the taxes paid by immigrants are sufficient to cover the benefits that they receive from such programs, then the presence of these immigrants does not threaten the per capita disposable income of natives. Indeed, some government programs, such as national defense, are true "public goods" (whose costs are not increased by immigration), and any taxes paid by immigrants help natives defray the expenses of these programs. However, if immigrants are relatively high users of government support services and if the taxes that they pay do not cover the value of their benefits, then the "fiscal burden" of immigration could be large enough to reduce the aggregate income of natives.

Estimating the fiscal effects of immigrants turns out to be quite complex, because it involves analyzing tax revenues and expenditures at the federal, state, and local levels and involves examining effects over the lifetime of immigrants and their children and grandchildren (the second and third generations). The most comprehensive study to date concludes that immigrants as a whole (authorized and unauthorized) are a net benefit to the country as a whole, but that negative fiscal benefits are more likely to be found at the state and local level among those who immigrated, whereas positive fiscal benefits are more likely to be seen among the second and third generation at the federal level.[39]

Overall Effects of Unauthorized Immigration   Undocumented immigration has been the major focus in recent years of the immigration policy debate in the United States. Many assert that these generally low-skilled workers are the beneficiaries of many government services and that their undocumented status both allows them to escape taxation and is probably associated with a relatively high propensity to commit crimes. We have good reasons to doubt all three assertions; in fact, *unauthorized immigration may be more likely to increase native worker incomes than officially sanctioned immigration.*

First, undocumented immigrants come mainly to work.[40] Therefore, they clearly add to the production of domestic goods and services. Second, although undocumented immigrants do receive emergency room treatment and their children do get schooling, they are ineligible for most government programs (e.g., public assistance, food stamps, Social Security, and unemployment insurance) that transfer resources to low-income citizens. Moreover, as Example 10.3 discusses, poorly educated immigrants—most of whom are undocumented— are *much* less likely to be incarcerated than are similarly educated natives.

EXAMPLE 10.3
Undocumented Immigrants, Personal Discount Rates, and Crime

Immigrants to the United States, including those here illegally, are far less likely than U.S. natives to commit the kinds of violent or property crimes for which incarceration is the punishment. In 2000, for example, 3.4 percent of U.S. natives were institutionalized, and most of those were in prison (the rest were in psychiatric hospitals, drug treatment centers, or long-term-care facilities). In contrast, among immigrants, the rate of institutionalization was roughly *one-fifth* as high (at 0.7 percent). Among those with less than a high school education, a group in which crime rates are higher than average, the gap in the percentage institutionalized between U.S. natives and immigrants was even larger: 11 percent for U.S. natives, compared to 1 percent for immigrants.

Although several factors could be affecting the differential rates of incarceration, one reason for the difference may be rooted in a characteristic that human-capital theory implies that immigrants will possess: a lower-than-average personal discount rate. Immigrants, whether legal or illegal, are self-selected individuals who are willing to bear considerable costs to enter and adapt to a new country with the expectation of benefits that may lie well into the future. Among a group of people facing the same current costs and future benefits, then, those most willing to leave their country of origin and emigrate to a new one are those with relatively low discount rates (i.e., they are the most future oriented).

People who commit crimes tend to be present oriented; in economic terms, they have relatively high discount rates. For criminals, the perceived gains from their criminal act are in the present, whereas the costs—if caught—are in the future. With high discount rates, these future costs look relatively small compared to the current gains. Therefore, economic theory suggests that immigrants and criminals are likely to have different orientations toward the future.

Within the general populace of any country will be a wide distribution of discount rates, and some of those who have high discount rates may turn to crime. However, immigrants are self-selected individuals who tend to have relatively low personal rates of discount, and therefore, criminality among immigrants is unsurprisingly low.

For data on immigrants and incarceration, see Kristin F. Butcher and Anne Morrison Piehl, "Why Are Immigrants' Incarceration Rates So Low? Evidence on Selective Immigration, Deterrence, and Deportation" (Working Paper No. 13229, National Bureau of Economic Research, July 2007). For another study with similar findings, see Aaron Chalfin, "The Long-Run Effect of Mexican Immigration on Crime in US Cities: Evidence from Variation in Mexican Fertility Rates," *American Economic Review Papers and Proceedings* 105 (May 2015): 220–225. Also see Matthew Freedman, Emily Owens, and Sarah Bohn, "Immigration, Employment Opportunities and Criminal Behavior," *American Economic Journal: Economic Policy* 10 (May 2018): 117–151.

Third, despite their wish to hide from the government, because of current immigration policy, unauthorized immigrants cannot avoid paying most taxes (especially payroll, sales, and property taxes); indeed, one study indicated that 75 percent of undocumented immigrants had income taxes withheld but that relatively few filed for a refund.[41] Additionally, since immigration reform legislation was passed in 1986, the typical way that undocumented immigrants qualify for jobs in the United States is to purchase a fake Social Security card. Employers then deduct payroll taxes and remit them to the government, and starting in the mid 1980s, the revenues that cannot be matched to a valid Social Security number (and therefore will not result in a future retirement payment) have risen dramatically—probably because of unauthorized immigration.[42]

Thus, we cannot rule out the possibility that despite governmental efforts to prohibit it, the "transaction" of unauthorized immigration is—to use the normative terminology of Chapter 1—Pareto improving. (Another Pareto-improving benefit of immigration is explained in Example 10.4.) The immigrants themselves clearly gain (otherwise they would go back home), and the size of the gains experienced by Mexican immigrants relative to their incomes in Mexico suggest that these gains are large. Some natives clearly gain, whereas others may lose, but we have just seen that the aggregate gain to natives is quite likely positive.[43] Thus, economic theory suggests that with an overall gain to society, a critical part of the policy debate on unauthorized immigration should focus on programs or policies *that would tax the likely gainers in order to compensate those most likely to lose from such immigration.* In Chapter 16, we return to the issue of how best to compensate those who lose from policies that benefit society in general.

EXAMPLE 10.4

Immigrants and Labor Mobility in the United States

The decision to migrate involves a consideration of the costs and benefits, and our theoretical discussion highlighted the critical role of both one's personal discount rate and the psychic costs of leaving one's current location in making this decision. People who choose to undertake the costly investment of changing the country in which they live generally can be assumed to have a low personal discount rate, low psychic costs of moving, or both.

As we saw in Chapters 2 and 5, mobility among workers is essential for eliminating wage differentials in comparable jobs across employers and geographical areas (the law of one price). As we saw in Chapters 8 and 9, mobility is also crucial for creating wage differentials across jobs that are *not* comparable in duties or requirements. Thus, worker mobility is central to the allocation of workers to employers in a way that produces the greatest social benefit (Pareto efficiency).

The Great Recession of 2007–2009 caused labor demand to shift left almost everywhere in the United States, but this leftward demand shift was greater in some areas than others. In areas where the labor demand contraction is greatest, the percent of the population able to find work tends to fall the most—unless, of course, unemployed workers leave the area and seek work in areas where labor demand is relatively stronger. Immigrants, for reasons noted earlier, may be more likely than natives to move to areas of greater opportunity; thus, the presence of more immigrants may tend to enhance labor mobility and reduce geographical differences in wages and employment.

For example, a recent study found that lower-skilled Mexican-born immigrants to the United States are much more likely to move *within the United States* in response to changes in labor demand than are lower-skilled native workers (who are relatively immobile).[44] Thus, when the Great Recession hit, cities with a higher proportion of Mexican-born workers experienced a greater outflow of workers (a greater shift left in their labor supply curves)— which tended to reduce the fraction of the remaining population that was unemployed. For example, the study found that from 2006 to 2010, the city of Orlando, Florida (which had fewer Mexican-born workers than did Phoenix, Arizona), experienced a decline in the percentage of its adult population with jobs from 78.6 percent to 66 percent. If Orlando had had the same proportion of Mexican-born residents as did Phoenix, and thus had experienced a greater outflow of workers, its employment–population ratio would have fallen only to 68.7 percent.

Source: Brian C. Cadena and Brian K. Kovak, "Immigrants Equilibrate Local Labor Markets: Evidence from the Great Recession," *American Economic Journal: Applied Economics* 8 (January 2016): 257–290

Similar findings are reported in Gaetano Bosso and Giovanni Peri, "Internal Mobility: The Greater Responsiveness of Foreign-Born to Economic Conditions," *Journal of Economic Perspectives* 34 (Summer 2020): 77–98; Ran Abramitzky, Leah Platt Boustan, Elisa Jácome, and Santiago Pérez, "Intergenerational Mobility of Immigrants in the US over Two Centuries" (Working Paper No. 26408, National Bureau of Economic Research, Cambridge, MA, October 2019).

Employee Turnover

This chapter has focused so far on the underlying causes and consequences of geographic mobility, but the mobility of employees among employers (also known as turnover or separations) can take place *without* a change of residence. We noted in Chapter 5 that employees generally find searching for alternative job offers costly, and in this section, we use the principles of our human-capital model to highlight certain *patterns* in employee turnover.

Growing from our discussions in Chapters 8 and 9, we would expect that individuals differ in their personal discount rates and in the psychic costs that they attach to quitting one employer to find another. These differences imply that some workers are much more likely than others to move among employers, even if those in both groups face the same set of wage offers. Indeed, one study found that almost half of all turnover over a three-year period involved the 13 percent of workers who had three or more separations during the period.[45] Despite individual idiosyncrasies, however, *systematic* factors clearly influence the patterns of job mobility.

Age Effects

The theory in this chapter clearly predicts that investments in human capital fall with age. When workers are young, mobility among employers—which may or may not involve geographic mobility—is relatively attractive. As we argued earlier in this chapter, the psychic costs of moving to another employer may be low, and the period over which potential benefits can be gained is relatively long. Further, on-the-job experiences provide workers with valuable insights into their occupational strengths and preferences, so for many workers, the first 10 or so years of work can be characterized as a "job-shopping" phase of working life.[46]

Wage Effects

Human-capital theory predicts that, *other things being equal*, a given worker will have a greater probability of quitting a low-wage job than a higher-paying one. That is, workers employed at lower wages than they could obtain elsewhere are the most likely to quit. Indeed, a strong and consistent finding in studies of worker quit behavior is that, holding worker characteristics constant, employees in industries that have lower wages have higher quit rates. At the level of individual workers, research indicates that those who change employers have more to gain from a job change than those who stay and that, indeed, their wage growth after changing is faster than it would have been had they stayed.[47]

Effects of Employer Size

According to the data in Table 10.2, *quit rates tend to decline as firm size increases*. One explanation for this phenomenon is that large firms offer more

Table 10.2 Monthly Quit Rates per 100 Workers by Firm Size, Selected Industries (1977–1981 Averages)

Industry	Number of employees			
	250	**250–499**	**500–999**	**1,000 and over**
All manufacturing	3.28	3.12	2.40	1.50
Food and kindred products	3.46	4.11	3.95	2.28
Fabricated metal products	3.33	2.64	2.12	1.20
Electrical machinery	3.81	3.12	2.47	1.60
Transportation equipment	3.90	2.78	2.21	1.41

Source: Walter Oi, "The Durability of Worker-Firm Attachments" (Report to the U.S. Department of Labor, Office of the Assistant Secretary for Policy, Evaluation, and Research, March 25, 1983), Table 1

possibilities for transfers and promotions. Another, however, builds on the fact that large firms generally pay higher wages.[48] This explanation asserts that large firms tend to have highly mechanized production processes, where the output of one work team highly depends on that of production groups preceding it in the production chain. Larger firms, some argue, have greater needs for dependable and steady workers, because employees who shirk their duties can impose great costs on a highly interdependent production process. Large firms, then, establish "internal labor markets" for the reasons suggested in Chapter 5; that is, they hire workers at entry-level jobs and carefully observe such hard-to-screen attributes as reliability, motivation, and attention to detail. Once having invested time and effort in selecting the best workers for its operation, a large firm finds such workers' quitting to be costly. Thus, large firms pay high wages to reduce the probability of quitting because they have substantial firm-specific screening investments in their workers.[49]

Cyclical Effects

Another implication of human-capital theory is that workers will have a higher probability of quitting when quickly obtaining a better job is relatively easy for them. Thus, when labor markets are *tight* (jobs are more plentiful relative to job seekers), one would expect the quit rate to be higher than when labor markets are *loose* (few jobs are available and many workers are being laid off). This prediction is confirmed in studies of time-series data. Quit rates tend to rise when the labor market is tight and fall when it is loose. One measure of tightness is the unemployment rate; the negative relationship between the quit rate and unemployment can be readily seen in Figure 10.5.[50]

Employer Location

Economic theory predicts that when the costs of quitting a job are relatively low, mobility is more likely. Industries with high concentrations of

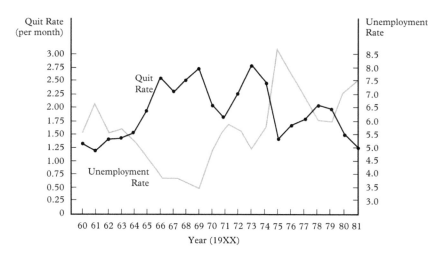

Figure 10.5 The Quit Rate and Labor Market Tightness

employment in urban areas, where a worker's change of employer does not necessarily require investing in a change of residence, appear to have higher rates of turnover (holding wage rates and employee age constant) than industries concentrated in nonmetropolitan areas.[51]

Is More Mobility Better?

On the one hand, mobility is socially useful because it promotes both individual well-being and the quality of job matches. In Chapter 8, we pointed out, for example, that mobility (or at least the *threat* of mobility) was essential to the creation of compensating wage differentials.

Moreover, the greater the number of workers and employers in the market at any given time, the more flexibility an economy has in making job matches that best adapt to a changing environment. Indeed, when focusing on this aspect of job mobility, economists have long worried whether economies have *enough* mobility. A case in point is the concern whether employers have created "job lock" by adopting pension plans and health insurance policies that are not portable if the employee leaves the firm.[52] As we saw in Chapter 5, mobility costs introduce monopsonistic conditions into the labor market, which tend to lower wages relative to marginal revenue product.

On the other hand, however, lower mobility costs (and thus greater mobility) among workers also weaken the incentives of both employers and employees to invest in specific training or information particular to a job match. Failure to make these investments arguably reduces the productive potential of employees.

EMPIRICAL STUDY 10.1

DO POLITICAL REFUGEES INVEST MORE IN HUMAN CAPITAL THAN ECONOMIC IMMIGRANTS DO? THE USE OF SYNTHETIC COHORTS

Individuals who immigrate presumably do so because they believe that they will improve their well-being. For some, the decision is motivated primarily by economic considerations, and the timing of the move is both voluntary and planned; this group can be labeled "economic immigrants." Others may be forced to flee their country of origin for political reasons (often on short notice), and these individuals can often qualify for "refugee" status in the country of destination.

Because refugees have done less advance planning, we might expect that they earn less than comparably-skilled economic immigrants immediately upon arrival in their new country. However, unlike economic immigrants, who can return to their country of origin if the move does not work out, refugees cannot safely return. We might thus suppose that after arrival, refugees also have a greater incentive to invest in human capital (including the mastery of their new country's language if that language is not their native language) and in becoming citizens. Thus, we would expect that their earnings would rise faster than those of economic immigrants.

Ideally, in testing to see whether refugees invest more in human capital and have more rapid earnings growth than economic immigrants, we would like to have data that follow individual immigrants through time. Panel data are expensive to collect, however, because individuals must be located and interviewed at multiple times. Though not a perfect substitute, an alternative to panel data is the use of *synthetic cohorts*.

For example, one U.S. study sampled the earnings, educational level, and proficiency in English—as reported in the 1980 Census of Population—among the cohort of immigrants who came to the United States between 1975 and 1980. The study then sampled, again for those who immigrated in 1975–1980, data on the same variables from the 1990 Census. Because the workers in the 1980 sample are not necessarily the same as those in the 1990 sample (owing to randomized sampling and the possibility that some of those sampled in 1980 had died or had left the United States by 1990), we are not actually obtaining 1990 data on the same group whom we observed in 1980; for this reason, the 1990 cohort can be called "synthetic" (an artificial representation of the earlier cohort).

If the sampling from both census years is random and if all departures from the sample between 1980 and 1990 were randomly determined, the results from this comparison should produce the same results, on average, as we would obtain if we were following the same individuals from 1980 to 1990. *The problem with this use of synthetic cohorts is that the economic immigrants who leave are likely to be those who were least successful in the United States*; thus, the measured earnings gain for the group of economic immigrants from 1980 to 1990 will be biased upward (only those who are relatively successful stay on long enough to be counted in the 1990 data). If economic immigrants who have the smallest earnings growth can leave, whereas refugees cannot, comparisons of the 1980–1990 earnings growth will be biased against finding evidence that supports the hypothesis that refugees will exhibit *greater* earnings growth.

Despite the bias discussed earlier, the study found that although the earnings of refugees were 6 percent lower than those of economic immigrants in 1980, they were 20 percent greater by 1990. Moreover, refugees were more likely to be enrolled in school programs in 1980, a higher proportion of them achieved proficiency in English during the 1980s, and more had attained citizenship between 1980 and 1990. These data appear to be consistent with the hypothesis that refugees have greater incentives to invest in human capital than economic immigrants do, presumably because they cannot return to their respective countries of origin.

Source: Kalena E. Cortes, "Are Refugees Different from Economic Immigrants? Some Empirical Evidence on the Heterogeneity of Immigrant Groups in the United States," *Review of Economics and Statistics* 86 (May 2004): 465–480

Review Questions

1. The licensing of such occupations as nurses and doctors in the United States requires people in those occupations to pass a test administered by the state in which they seek to work. Given that every time a health-care worker moves, some bureaucrat tells them that they can't work, a national newspaper argued that United States could reduce healthcare costs if it removed state-to-state licensing barriers.

   a. From the perspective of positive economics, what are the labor market effects of having states, rather than the federal government, license professionals?

   b. Who would gain and who would lose from the federalization of occupational licensing?

2. One way for the government to facilitate economic growth is for it to pay workers in depressed areas to move to regions where jobs are more plentiful. What would be the labor market effects of such a policy?

3. A television program examining the issue of Mexican immigration stated that most economists believe immigration is a benefit to the United States.

   a. State the chain of reasoning underlying this view.

   b. From a normative perspective, explain whether the key issue is the wage effects on native workers or the subsidies for immigrants that are given by the host country.

4. Suppose the United States increases the penalties for undocumented immigration to include long jail sentences for undocumented *workers.* Analyze the effects of this increased penalty on the wages and employment levels of *all* affected groups of workers.

5. Other things being equal, firms usually prefer their workers to have low quit rates. However, from a social perspective, quit rates can be too low. Why do businesses prefer low quit rates, and what are the social disadvantages of having such rates be "too low"?

6. The past three decades in the United States have been characterized by a wide gap between the wages of those with more education and those with less. Suppose that workers eventually adjust to this gap by investing more in education, leading the wages of lower-skilled workers to rise faster than those of higher-skilled workers (such that the wage gap between the two falls). How would a decline in the wage gap between higher-skilled workers and lower-skilled workers affect immigration to the United States?

7. "The fact that quit rates in Japan are lower than those in the United States suggests that Japanese workers are inherently more loyal to their employers than are U.S. workers." Evaluate this assertion that where quit rates are lower, workers have stronger preferences for loyalty.

8. Two oil-rich Middle East countries compete with each other for the services of immigrants from India and Pakistan who perform menial jobs that local workers are unwilling to perform. Country A does not allow women to work, drive, or go out of the house without a chaperone. Country B has no such restrictions. Would you expect the wages that these two countries pay for otherwise comparable *male* immigrants to be roughly equal? Explain your answer.

9. If one were to build an economic model of crimes such as theft, it would contain the same elements as the human-capital model of investments. The difference is that with theft, unlike with human-capital investments, the gains from the activity are *immediate* and the costs (if caught) are distributed across *future* years. With this distinction in mind, use the elements of human-capital theory to analyze whether immigrants are more or less likely than are citizens of similar income to commit the crime of theft.

10. A recent study by a noted economist has found evidence that a 10 percent increase in immigration within a given skill group reduces the

wages of "natives" in that skill group by 3.5 percent. One social commentator has said, "These findings suggest only one conclusion: Immigration is bad for American workers and therefore bad for American society." Using economic theory, comment on this quote.

Problems

1. Rose lives in a poor country where she earns $5,000 per year. She has the opportunity to move to a rich country as a temporary worker for five years. Doing the same work, she'll earn $35,000 per year in the rich country. The cost of moving is $2,000, and it would cost her $10,000 more per year to live in the rich country. Rose's discount rate is 10 percent. Rose decides not to move because she will be separated from her friends and family. Estimate the psychic costs of Rose's move.

2. Suppose that the demand for rough laborers is $L_D = 100 - 10W$, where W = the wage in dollars per hour and L = the number of workers. If immigration increases the number of rough laborers hired from 50 to 60, by how much will the short-run profits of employers in this market change?

3. Clare lives in France and earns $30,000 per year at her job. She is considering a job offer in the United States, which would give her a salary of $32,000 per year for the next four years, after which she will return to France and start her university education. Moving costs (to the United States and back) would be $6,000, living expenses are similar in both places, and her personal discount rate is 6 percent. If she moved to the United States for this four-year experience, what is the present value of her net gain or loss?

4. Table 10P.4 summarizes the market for labor in an occupation. "Demand" is the number (in thousands) of employees that firms would be interested in hiring at particular wages. "Domestic supply" is the number (in thousands) of native workers who are interested in working in the occupation at particular wages, and "immigrant supply" is the number (in thousands) of immigrants who are interested in working at particular wages.

Table 10P.4 Labor Demand and Supply with Immigration

Wage ($)	Demand	Domestic supply	Immigrant supply
6	30	22	4
8	29	23	4
10	28	24	4
12	27	25	4
14	26	26	4
16	25	27	4
18	24	28	4
20	23	29	4

   a. Graph the following curves for this labor market: demand for labor, domestic supply, and total supply of workers.

   b. What is the equilibrium wage rate before immigration? How many workers would be hired?

   c. What is the equilibrium wage rate after immigration? How many workers would be hired? How many domestic workers would be hired? How many immigrant workers would be hired?

   d. Comparing your answers in parts b and c, has immigration caused a change in the number of domestic workers hired? What was the change, if any? Why did the change, if any, occur?

5. The demand for labor in a domestic industry is $D = 36 - 2W$, where W = the wage rate and D = the number (in thousands) of employees whom the firms would be interested in hiring at particular wage rates. $S_{domestic} = 9 + W$, where $S_{domestic}$ = the number (in thousands) of native workers who are interested in working in the industry at particular wages. $S_{total} = 10 + 2W$, where S_{total} is the *total* number (including immigrants) of workers who are interested in working in the industry at particular wages.

   a. Graph the following curves for this labor market: demand for labor, domestic supply, supply of immigrant workers, and total supply of workers.

   b. What is the equilibrium wage rate before immigration? How many workers would be hired?

   c. What is the equilibrium wage rate after immigration? How many workers would be hired? How many domestic workers would be hired? How many immigrant workers would be hired?

Notes

1. United Nations, Population Division, Department of Economic and Social Affairs, International Migration, "International Immigrant Stock: 2019" (New York: United Nations), www.un.org/en/development/desa/population/migration/data/estimates2/estimatesgraphs.asp?1g1.

2. For occupations that require a state-issued license, differential licensing requirements across states create another mobility cost; see Janna E. Johnson and Morris M. Kleiner, "Is Occupational Licensing a Barrier to Interstate Migration?" *American Economic Journal: Economic Policy* 12 (August 2020): 347–373.

3. U.S. Census Bureau, "State-to-State Migration Flows," www.census.gov/data/tables/time-series/demo/geographic-mobility/state-to-state-migration.html; Henry Hyatt, Erika McEntarfer, Ken Ueda, and Alexandria Zhang, "Interstate Migration and Employer-to-Employer Transitions in the U.S.: New Evidence from Administrative Records Data" (Working Paper CES44-R, U.S. Bureau of the Census, Center for Economic Studies, Washington, DC, May 2018).

4. The level of *new hires* in an area appears to explain migration flows much better than the unemployment rate; see Gary Fields, "Place to Place Migration: Some New Evidence," *Review of Economics and Statistics* 61 (February 1979): 21–32; Robert H. Topel, "Local Labor Markets," *Journal of Political Economy* 94:3, pt. 2 (June 1986): S111–S143, contains an analysis of how permanent and transitory shifts in an area's demand affect migration and wages.

5. For a paper with empirical findings on this topic, see Samuel Bazzi, "Wealth Heterogeneity and the Income Elasticity of Migration," *American Economic Journal: Applied Economics* 9 (April 2017): 219–255.

6. U.S. Census Bureau, "Geographical Mobility: 2005–2010: Detailed Tables," Table 1, www.census.gov/hhes/migration/data/cps/cps2010–5yr.html. For an analysis of internal migration in the United States, with a review of recent trends, see Raven Molloy, Christopher L. Smith, and Abigail Wozniak, "Internal Migration in the United States," *Journal of Economic Perspectives* 25 (Summer 2011): 173–196.

7. U.S. Census Bureau, "Geographical Mobility: 2005–2010: Detailed Tables," Table 1, www.census.gov/hhes/migration/data/cps/cps2010–5yr.html.

8. U.S. Census Bureau, "Geographical Mobility: 2005–2010: Detailed Tables," Table 24, www.census.gov/hhes/migration/data/cps/cps2010–5yr.html.

9. Aba Schwartz, "Interpreting the Effect of Distance on Migration," *Journal of Political Economy* 81 (September/October 1973): 1153–1167.

10. The theory in this section is adapted from Andrew D. Roy, "Some Thoughts on the Distribution of Earnings," *Oxford Economic Papers* 3 (June 1951): 75–106; for a more thorough discussion of this issue, see George J. Borjas, *Friends or Strangers* (New York: Basic Books, 1990), especially chapters 1 and 7.

11. Kristen Keith and Abagail McWilliams, "The Returns to Mobility and Job Search by Gender," *Industrial and Labor Relations Review* 52 (April 1999): 460–477. For a recent study of the returns from rural-to-urban migration in developing countries, see David Lagakos, Ahmed Mushfiq Mobarak, and Michael E. Waugh, "Migration Costs and Observational Returns to Migration in the Developing World" (Working Paper No. 26868, National Bureau of Economic Research, Cambridge, MA, March 2020).

12. Keith and McWilliams, "The Returns to Mobility and Job Search by Gender."

13. Dora L. Costa and Matthew E. Kahn, "Power Couples: Changes in the Locational Choice of the College Educated, 1940–1990," *Quarterly Journal of Economics* 115 (November 2000): 1287–1315.

14. The wage comparisons are expressed in year 2000 dollars and represent U.S.–Mexico wage differences for workers of the same age and with the same education; see Gordon H. Hanson, "The Economic

Consequences of the International Migration of Labor," *American Review of Economics* 1 (September 2009): 179–208. For a study that analyses the problems of estimating the monetary returns to those who immigrate, see Ran Abramitzky, Leah Boustan, and Katherine Eriksson, "Europe's Tired, Poor, Huddled Masses: Self-Selection and Economic Outcomes in the Age of Mass Migration," *American Economic Review* 102 (August 2012): 1832–1856.

15. A recent study that follows individual immigrants through time finds that the earnings of those who remain in the U.S. and do not return (a topic that we discuss a bit later) catch up to the earnings of similar natives within 10 years; see Randall Akee and Maggie R. Jones, "Immigrants' Earnings Growth and Return Migration from the U.S.: Examining their Determinants Using Linked Survey and Administrative Data" (Working Paper No. 25639, National Bureau of Economic Research, Cambridge, MA, March 2019). Differences in earnings using panel data are analyzed in Deborah Rho and Seth Sanders, "Immigrant Earnings Assimilation in the United States: A Panel Analysis," *Journal of Labor Economics* 39 (January 2021): 37–78.

16. George J. Borjas, "The Economics of Immigration," *Journal of Economic Literature* 32 (December 1994): 1667–1717; George J. Borjas, "The Slowdown in the Economic Assimilation of Immigrants: Aging and Cohort Effects Revisited Again," *Journal of Human Capital* 9 (Winter 2015): 483–517.

17. Barry R. Chiswick and Paul W. Miller, "The Endogeneity Between Language and Earnings: International Analyses," *Journal of Labor Economics* 13 (April 1995): 246–288; Barry R. Chiswick and Paul W. Miller, "Language Skills and Earnings among Legalized Aliens," *Journal of Population Economics* 12 (February 1999): 63–91; Heather Antecol, Peter Kuhn, and Stephen J. Trejo, "Assimilation via Prices or Quantities? Sources of Immigrant Earnings Growth in Australia, Canada, and the United States," *Journal of Human Resources* 41 (Fall 2006): 821–840; Eli Berman, Kevin Lang, and Erez Siniver, "Language-Skill Complementarity: Returns to Immigrant Language Acquisition," *Labour Economics* 10 (June 2003): 265–290.

18. Akee and Jones, "Immigrants' Earnings Growth and Return Migration from the U.S.: Examining their Determinants Using Linked Survey and Administrative Data," find that by 10 years after first emigrating some 40 percent have returned—and that the ones who returned suffered earnings losses before their return.

19. David Card, Christian Dustmann, and Ian Preston, "Immigration, Wages, and Compositional Amenities," *Journal of the European Economic Association* 10 (February 2012): 78–119.

20. See Ran Abramitzky and Leah Boustan, "Immigration in American Economic History," *Journal of Economic Literature* 55 (December 2017): 1311–1345, for a historical view of immigration in the United States.

21. In a recent paper, the authors use "linked census records [to] show that immigrants experienced substantial 'catching up' relative to natives' occupational status from 1850 to 1880, but not from 1900 to 1930"; see William J. Collins and Ariell Zimran, "Working Their Way Up? US Immigrants' Changing Labor Market Assimilation in the Age of Mass Migration" (Working Paper No. 26414, National Bureau of Economic Research, Cambridge, MA, October 2019).

22. *This includes illegal immigrants granted amnesty under the Immigration Reform and Control Act of 1986.

23. Waleed Navarro, "Nonimmigrant Admissions to the United States: 2018" (Annual Flow Report, October 2018, U.S. Department of Homeland Security, Office of Immigration Statistics, Washington, DC, October 2019), www.dhs.gov/sites/default/files/publications/immigration-statistics/yearbook/2018/nonimmigrant_admissions_2018.pdf.

24. Gordon Hanson, Chen Liu, and Craig McIntosh, "The Rise and Fall of U.S. Low-Skilled Immigration," *Brookings Papers on Economic Activity* (Spring 2017): 83 151; Bryan Baker and Nancy Rytina, *Estimates of the Unauthorized Immigrant Population Residing in the United States: January 2012* (Washington, DC: U.S. Department of Homeland Security, Office of Immigration Statistics, March 2013); also see Gordon H. Hanson, "Illegal Migration from Mexico to the United States," *Journal of Economic Literature* 44 (December 2006): 869–924; Benjamin Feigenberg, "Fenced Out: The Impact of Border Construction on US-Mexican Migration," *American Economic Journal: Applied Economics* 12 (July 2020): 106–139.

25. U.S. Census Bureau, *Race and Hispanic Origin of the Foreign-Born Population in the United States: 2007* (Washington, DC: American Community Survey Reports, January 2010). Data in the remainder of this section are from Hanson, "Illegal Migration from Mexico to the United States."

26. Both quotes in this section are from Elliott Abrams and Franklin S. Abrams, "Immigration Policy—Who Gets in and Why?" *Public Interest* 38 (Winter 1975): 25–26.

27. We define *rough labor* as low-skilled work that is considered demanding and distasteful to many workers.

28. For a study suggesting that for every five Vietnamese manicurists who immigrated to California, a net of three new jobs were created, see Maya N. Federman, David E. Harrington, and Kathy J. Krynski, "Vietnamese Manicurists: Are Immigrants Displacing Natives or Finding New Nails to Polish?" *Industrial and Labor Relations Review* 59 (January 2006): 302–318. On tradability, see Ariel Burstein, Gordon Hanson, Lin Tian, and Jonathan Vogel, "Tradability and the Labor-Market Impact of Immigration: Theory and Evidence from the United States," *Econometrica* 88 (May 2020): 1071–1112, which includes an analysis of how immigration affects native employment in face-to-face service jobs compared to jobs that produce goods that can be traded to those outside the

local labor market. The authors find, by using data from 1980 to 2012 on U.S. commuting zones, "that a local influx of immigrants crowds out employment of native-born workers more relative to less immigrant-intensive nontradable jobs, but has no such effect across tradable occupations."

29. See Delia Furtado and Henrich Hock, "Low Skilled Immigration and Work-Fertility Tradeoffs among High Skilled US Natives," *American Economic Review: Papers and Proceedings* 100 (May 2010): 224–228; Patricia Cortes and Jose Tessada, "Low-Skilled Immigration and the Labor Supply of Highly Skilled Women," *American Economic Journal: Applied Economics* 3 (July 2011): 88–123, which finds that "low-skilled immigration increases average hours of market work and the probability of working long hours of women at the top quartile of the wage distribution."

30. Furtado and Hock, "Low Skilled Immigration and Work-Fertility Tradeoffs among High Skilled US Natives"; Cortes and Tessada, "Low-Skilled Immigration and the Labor Supply of Highly Skilled Women."

31. Giovanni Peri and Chad Sparber, "Task Specialization, Immigration, and Wages," *American Economic Journal: Applied Economics* 1 (July 2009): 135–169.

32. Studies suggest that the presence of low-skilled immigrants induces low-skilled natives to move into jobs with more-complex tasks, so immigrants and natives are more complements than substitutes. See Gianmarco I.P. Ottaviano, Giovanni Peri, and Greg C. Wright, "Immigration, Offshoring, and American Jobs," *American Economic Review* 103 (August 2013): 1925–1959; Mette Foged and Giovanni Peri, "Immigrants' Effect on Native Workers: New Analysis on Longitudinal Data," *American Economic Journal: Applied Economics* 8 (April 2016): 1–34.

33. For a comprehensive review of studies on how immigration affects the wages of natives, see Francine D. Blau and Lawrence M. Kahn, "Immigration and the Distribution of Incomes," in *Handbook of the Economics of International Migration*, eds. Barry R. Chiswick and Paul W. Miller (Amsterdam: Elsevier, 2015): 793–843.

34. See Blau and Kahn, "Immigration and the Distribution of Incomes"; see Joan Monras, "Immigration and Wage Dynamics: Evidence from the Mexican Peso Crisis," *Journal of Political Economy* 128 (August 2020): 3017–3089, for evidence that the initial negative wage effects on lower-skilled native workers are dissipated by migration to other areas and that the major long-run negative wage effects are on natives who entered lower-skilled occupations during high-immigration years.

35. Methodological reviews can be found in Christian Dustmann, Uta Schönberg, and Jan Stuhler, "The Impact of Immigration: Why Do Studies Reach Such Different Results?" *Journal of Economic Perspectives* 30 (Fall 2016): 131–156; David Card and Giovanni Peri, "*Immigration*

Economics by George J. Borjas: A Review Essay," *Journal of Economic Literature* 54 (December 2016): 1333–1349.

36. Blau and Kahn, "Immigration and the Distribution of Incomes."

37. Francine D. Blau and Christopher Mackie, eds., *The Economic and Fiscal Consequences of Immigration,* The National Academies of Sciences, Engineering, and Medicine (Washington, DC: National Academies Press, 2017). Another group that may be affected disproportionately is youth; see Christopher L. Smith, "The Impact of Low-Skilled Immigration on the Youth Labor Market," *Journal of Labor Economics* 30 (January 2012): 55–89.

38. One study, for example, finds that an influx of immigrants from country *X* to country *Y* serves to increase the exports from *Y* to *X*; see Giovanni Peri and Francisco Requena, "The Trade Creation Effect of Immigrants: Evidence from the Remarkable Case of Spain," *Canadian Journal of Economics* 43 (August 2010): 1433–1459. Other studies have found that immigrants are disproportionately represented among U.S. *inventors*; see William R. Kerr and William F. Lincoln, "The Supply Side of Innovation: H-1B Visa Reforms and U.S. Ethnic Invention," *Journal of Labor Economics* 28 (July 2010): 473–508; Jennifer Hunt and Marjolaine Gauthier-Loiselle, "How Much Does Immigration Boost Innovation?" *American Economic Journal: Macroeconomics* 2 (April 2010): 31–56; Stephen G. Dimmock, Jiekun Huang, and Scott J. Weisbenner, "Give Me Your Tired, Your Poor, Your High-Skilled Labor: H-1B Lottery Outcomes and Entrepreneurial Success" (Working Paper No. 26392, National Bureau of Economic Research, Cambridge, MA, October 2019).

39. Blau and Mackie, *The Economic and Fiscal Consequences of Immigration*; also see Una Okonkwo Osili and Jia Xie, "Do Immigrants and Their Children Free Ride More Than Natives?" *American Economic Review: Papers and Proceedings* 99 (May 2009): 28–34; William N. Evans and Daniel Fitzgerald, "The Economic and Social Outcomes of Refugees in the United States: Evidence from the ACS" (Working Paper No. 23498, National Bureau of Economic Research, Cambridge, MA, June 2017).

40. George J. Borjas, "The Labor Supply of Undocumented Immigrants" (Working Paper No. 22102, National Bureau of Economic Research, Cambridge, MA, March 2016); George J. Borjas, "The Earnings of Undocumented Immigrants" (Working Paper No. 23236, National Bureau of Economic Research, Cambridge, MA, March 2017). Attempted undocumented immigration from Mexico is estimated to be extremely sensitive to changes in Mexico's real wage rate; see Gordon Hanson and Antonio Spilimbergo, "Illegal Immigration, Border Enforcement, and Relative Wages: Evidence from Apprehensions at the U.S.–Mexico Border," *American Economic Review* 89 (December 1999): 1337–1357.

41. Gregory DeFreitas, *Inequality at Work: Hispanics in the U.S. Labor Force* (New York: Oxford University Press, 1991): 228. The same study showed that illegal immigrants rarely use public services.

42. See Office of the Inspector General, Social Security Administration, "Status of the Social Security Administration's Earnings Suspense File," A-03–15–50058, September 2015, https://oig.ssa.gov/sites/default/files/audit/full/pdf/A-03-15-50058.pdf. One report estimates that in 2010, the Social Security program received $13 billion in payroll taxes from unauthorized immigrants; see Social Security Administration, Office of the Chief Actuary, "Effects of Unauthorized Immigration on the Actual Status of the Social Security Trust Funds" (Actuarial Note no. 151, Baltimore, MD, April 2013).

43. For a study of the effects of immigration, including authorized immigration, in several countries, see Michele Battisti, Gabriel Felbermayr, Giovanni Peri, and Panu Poutvaara, "Immigration, Search, and Redistribution: A Quantitative Assessment of Native Welfare" (Working Paper No. 20131, National Bureau of Economic Research, Cambridge, MA, May 2014).

44. For an application that discusses immobility, see Matthew J. Notowidigdo, "The Incidence of Local Labor Demand Shocks," *Journal of Labor Economics* 38 (July 2020): 687–725.

45. Patricia M. Anderson and Bruce D. Meyer, "The Extent and Consequences of Job Turnover," *Brookings Papers on Economic Activity: Microeconomics* (1994): 177–248. For an examination of job mobility within and across companies, see Anders Frederiksen, Timothy Halliday, and Alexander K. Koch, "Within- and Cross-Firm Mobility and Earnings Growth," *Industrial and Labor Relations Review* 69 (March 2016): 320–353; also see Edward P. Lazear and Kristin McCue, "What Causes Labor Turnover to Vary?" (Working Paper No. 24873, National Bureau of Economic Research, Cambridge, MA, December 2018).

46. Jesper Bagger, François Fontaine, Fabien Postel-Vinay, and Jean-Marc Robin, "Tenure, Experience, Human Capital, and Wages: A Tractable Equilibrium Search Model of Wage Dynamics," *American Economic Review* 104 (June 2014): 1551–1596.

47. Edward P. Lazear and Kristin McCue, "What Causes Labor Turnover to Vary?" (Working Paper No. 24873, National Bureau of Economic Research, Cambridge, MA, December 2018).

48. Walter Oi, "The Fixed Employment Costs of Specialized Labor," in *The Measurement of Labor Cost*, ed. Jack E. Triplett (Chicago, IL: University of Chicago Press, 1983).

49. This argument is developed more fully and elegantly in Walter Oi, "Low Wages and Small Firms," in *Research in Labor Economics*, vol. 12, ed. Ronald G. Ehrenberg (Greenwich, CT: JAI Press, 1991).

50. For a related study, see Lisa B. Kahn and Erika McEntarfer, "Employment Cyclicality and Firm Quality" (Working Paper No. 20698, National Bureau of Economic Research, Cambridge, MA, November 2014).

51. Donald O. Parsons, "Models of Labor Market Turnover," *Research in Labor Economics* 1 (1977): 185–223; Farrell E. Bloch, "Labor Turnover

in U.S. Manufacturing Industries," *Journal of Human Resources* 14 (Spring 1979): 236–246.

52. See Stuart Dorsey, "Pension Portability and Labor Market Efficiency: A Survey of the Literature," *Industrial and Labor Relations Review* 48 (January 1995): 276–292; Kevin T. Stroupe, Eleanor D. Kinney, and Thomas J. Kniesner, "Chronic Illness and Health Insurance-Related Job Lock," *Journal of Policy Analysis and Management* 20 (Summer 2001): 525–544; Donna B. Gilleskie and Byron F. Lutz, "The Impact of Employer-Provided Health Insurance on Dynamic Employment Transitions," *Journal of Human Resources* 37 (Winter 2002): 129–162; Mark C. Berger, Dan A. Black, and Frank A. Scott, "Is There Job Lock? Evidence from the Pre-HIPAA Era," *Southern Economic Journal* 70 (April 2004): 953–976; Robert W. Fairlie, Kanika Kapur, and Susan Gates, "Job Lock: Evidence from a Regression Discontinuity Design," *Industrial Relations* 55 (January 2016): 92–121.

Selected Readings

Abowd, John M., and Richard B. Freeman, eds. *Immigration, Trade, and the Labor Market*. Chicago, IL: University of Chicago Press, 1991.

Blau, Francine D., and Lawrence M. Kahn. "Immigration and the Distribution of Incomes." In *Handbook of the Economics of International Migration*, eds. Barry R. Chiswick and Paul W. Miller, 793–843. Amsterdam: Elsevier, 2015.

Blau, Francine D., and Christopher Mackie, eds. *The Economic and Fiscal Consequences of Immigration*. Washington, DC: The National Academies of Sciences, Engineering, and Medicine, 2017.

Borjas, George. *International Differences in the Labor Market Performance of Immigrants*. Kalamazoo, MI: W.E. Upjohn Institute for Employment Research, 1988.

Borjas, George. "The Economics of Immigration." *Journal of Economic Literature* 32 (December 1994): 1667–1717.

Borjas, George J., ed. *Issues in the Economics of Immigration*. Chicago, IL: University of Chicago Press, 2000.

Borjas, George J., and Richard B. Freeman, eds. *Immigrants and the Work Force*. Chicago, IL: University of Chicago Press, 1992.

Chiswick, Barry. "Illegal Immigration and Immigration Control." *Journal of Economic Perspectives* 2 (Summer 1988): 101–115.

Hamermesh, Daniel S., and Frank D. Bean, eds. *Help or Hindrance? The Economic Implications of Immigration for African Americans*. New York: Russell Sage Foundation, 1998.

Hanson, Gordon H. "Illegal Migration from Mexico to the United States." *Journal of Economic Literature* 44 (December 2006): 869–924.

Pay and Productivity: Wage Determination Within the Firm

In the simplest model of the demand for labor (presented in Chapters 3 and 4), employers had few managerial decisions to make; they simply *found* the marginal productivity schedules and market wages of various kinds of labor and hired the profit-maximizing amount of each kind. In a model like this, employers did not need to design a compensation policy.

Many employers, however, give considerable attention to their compensation policies, and some of the reasons have already been explored. For example, employers offering specific training (see Chapter 5) have a zone into which the wage can feasibly fall, and they must balance the costs of raising the wages of their specifically trained workers against the savings generated from a higher probability of retaining these workers. Likewise, when the compensation package is expanded to include such items as employee benefits or job safety (see Chapter 8), employers must decide on the mix of wages and other valued items in the compensation package.[1] We have also seen (in Chapter 5) that under certain conditions, employers will behave monopsonistically, in which case they set their wages rather than take them as given.

EXAMPLE 11.1

The Wide Range of Possible Productivities: The Case of the Factory that Could Not Cut Output

In 1987, a manufacturer of air guns ("BB guns") in New York state found that its sales were lagging behind production. Wanting to cut production by about 20 percent without engaging in widespread layoffs, the company decided to temporarily cut back from a five-day workweek to a four-day workweek. To its amazement, the company found that despite this 20 percent reduction in working hours, production levels were not reduced—its workers produced as many air guns in four days as they previously had in five.

Central to the problem of achieving its desired output reduction was that the company paid its workers on the basis of the number of items that they produced. Faced with the prospect of a temporary cut in their earnings, its workers reduced time on breaks and increased their pace of work sufficiently to maintain their previous levels of output (and earnings). The company was therefore forced to institute artificial caps on employee production; when these individual output quotas had been met, the worker was not allowed to produce more.

The inability to cut output, despite cutting back on hours of work, suggests how wide the range of possible worker productivity can be in some operations. Clearly, then, careful attention by management to the motivation and morale of employees can have important consequences, both privately and socially.

This chapter explores in more detail the complex relationship between compensation and productivity. Briefly put, employers must make managerial decisions rooted in the following practical realities:

1. Workers differ from each other in work habits that greatly affect productivity but are often difficult (costly) to observe before, and sometimes even after, hiring takes place.[2]

2. The productivity of a given worker with a given level of human capital can vary considerably over time or in different environments, depending on their level of motivation (see Example 11.1).

3. Worker productivity over a given period of time is a function of innate ability, the level of effort, and the environment (the weather, general business conditions, tools and surroundings in the workplace, or the actions of other employees).[3]

4. Being highly productive is usually not just a matter of slavishly following orders but rather of *taking the initiative* to help advance the employer's objectives.[4]

Employers, then, must choose management strategies and compensation policies to obtain the right (i.e., profit-maximizing) kind of employees and offer them the optimum incentives for production. In doing so, they must weigh the costs of various policies against the benefits. The focus of this chapter is on the role of firms' compensation policies in optimizing worker productivity.

Motivating Workers: An Overview of the Fundamentals

Employers and employees each have their own objectives and concerns, and the incentives embedded in the employment relationship are critical to aligning these separate interests. We first present an overview of the key features of this relationship before we move on in later sections to analyses of various compensation schemes that employers can adopt to induce high productivity in their employees.

The Employment Contract

The employment relationship can be thought of as a contract between the employer (the "principal") and the employee (the "agent").[5] The employee is hired to help advance the employer's objectives in return for receiving wages and other benefits. Often, there are understandings or implied promises that if employees work hard and perform well, they will be promoted to higher-paying jobs as their careers progress.

Formal Contracts   The agreement by an employee to perform tasks for an employer in return for current and future pay can be thought of as a contract. A *formal* contract, such as one signed by a bank and a homeowner for the repayment of a loan, lays out quite explicitly all that each party promises to do and what will happen if either party fails to perform as promised. Once signed, a formal contract cannot be abrogated by either party, without penalty. Disputes over performance can be referred to courts of law or other third parties for resolution.

Implicit Contracts   Unlike formal contracts, most employment contracts are *incomplete* and *implicit*. They are usually incomplete in the sense that rarely are all the specific tasks that may be required of employees spelled out in advance. Doing so would limit the flexibility of employers in responding to changing conditions, and doing so would also require that employers and employees renegotiate their employment contract when each new situation arises—which would be costly to both parties. In addition, considering all possible outcomes for output facing the worker is difficult or impossible (e.g. consider the difficulties in paying a computer programmer to produce a new video game but not knowing precisely what the game might be).

Employment contracts are also implicit in the sense that they are normally a set of informal understandings that are too vague to be legally enforceable. For example, just what has an employee promised to do when they have agreed to "work hard," and how can their failure to do so be proven? Likewise, what has a firm promised to do when it has promised to "promote deserving employees as opportunities arise"? Furthermore, employees can almost always quit a job at will, and employers in the United States often have great latitude in firing employees; hence, the employment contract is one that can usually be abrogated by one party or the other, without legal penalty.[6]

The severe limits on legal enforceability make it essential that implicit contracts be *self-enforcing*. We turn now to a discussion of the difficulties that must be surmounted in making employment contracts self-enforcing.

Coping With Information Asymmetries

It is often advantageous for one or both parties to an agreement to cheat by reneging on their promises. Opportunities for cheating are enhanced when information is *asymmetric*—that is, when one party knows more than the other about its intentions or performance under the contract. For example, suppose that an insurance company promises a newly hired insurance adjuster that they will receive a big raise in four years if they "do a good job." The company might later try to refuse them the raise that they deserve, by falsely claiming that their work was not good enough. Alternatively, the adjuster, who works out of the office and away from supervisory oversight most of the time, might have incentives to "take it easy," by doing cursory or overly generous estimates of client losses. How can these forms of cheating be avoided?

Of course, sanctions against cheating are embedded in the formal agreements between employers and employees. Employers who break the provisions of agreements that they have signed with their unions can be sued or legally subjected to a strike, for example, but this requires that cheating actually be *proven*. How can we reduce the chances of being cheated when contracts are informal and the threat of formal punishment is absent?

Discouraging Cheating: Signaling One way to avoid being cheated is to transact with a particular "type" of person, and to do this, we must find a way to induce the other party to reveal—or *signal*—the truth about its actual characteristics or intentions. Suppose, for example, that an employer wants to hire employees who are willing to defer current gratification for long-term gain (i.e., it wants employees who do not highly discount the future). Simply asking applicants if they are willing to delay gratification might not evoke honest answers. Employers have ways, however, to cause applicants to signal their preferences indirectly.

As pointed out in Chapter 8, the employer could offer its applicants relatively low current wages and a large pension benefit upon retirement. Potential applicants who have relatively high discount rates would find this pay package less attractive than would applicants who have low discount rates, and they would be discouraged from either applying for the job or accepting an offer if it were tendered.

Another way that this firm could induce applicants to signal something about their true discount rate is to require a college degree or some other training investment as a hiring standard. As noted in Chapter 9, people with high discount rates are less likely to make investments of any kind, so the firm's hiring standard should discourage those with high discount rates from seeking offers.

The essence of signaling, then, is the voluntary revelation of truth in *behavior*, not just statements. Many of the compensation policies discussed in the remainder of this chapter are at least partially aimed at eliciting truthful signals from job applicants or employees.[7]

Discouraging Cheating: Self-Enforcement Even people of the right "type" often have incentives to underperform on their promises. Economists have come to term this type of cheating *opportunistic behavior*, and it occurs not because people intend from the outset to be dishonest but because they generally try to advance their own interests by adjusting their behavior to unfolding opportunities (and because, we assume, they maximize utility and find effort costly). Thus, the challenge is to adopt compensation policies that more or less automatically induce both parties to adhere to their promises.[8]

The key to a self-enforcing agreement is that losses are imposed on the cheater that do not depend on proving that a contract violation has occurred. In the labor market, the usual punishment for cheating on agreements is that the victim severs the employment relationship; consequently, self-enforcement requires that *both employer and employee derive more gains from honest continuation of the existing employment relationship than from severing it.* If workers are receiving more from the existing relationship than they expect to receive elsewhere, they will automatically lose if they shirk their duties and are fired. If employers profit more from keeping their existing workers than from investing in replacements, they will suffer by reneging on promises and having workers quit.

Creating a Surplus   Incentives for both parties to honor an implicit agreement are strongest when workers are getting paid more than they could get in alternative employment, yet less than the value of their marginal product to the firm. The gap between their marginal revenue product to the firm and their alternative wage represents a *surplus* that can be divided between employer and employee. This surplus must be *shared* if the implicit contract is to be self-enforcing, because if one party receives the entire surplus, the other party has nothing to lose by terminating the employment relationship. A graphic representation of the division of a surplus is given in Figure 11.1, where we see that attempts by one party to increase its share of

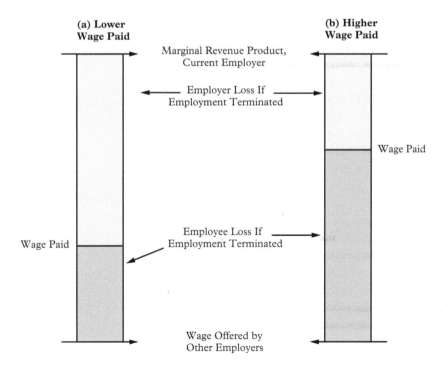

Figure 11.1 Two Alternative Divisions of the Surplus

the surplus will reduce the other party's losses from terminating the employment relationship.

Surpluses are usually associated with some earlier investment by the employer. In Chapter 5, we saw that investments by the firm in specific training or in the hiring/evaluation process enabled workers' productivity and wages to exceed their alternatives. Firms can also create a surplus by investing in their *reputations*. For example, an employer that is well known for keeping its promises about future promotions or pay raises can attract workers of higher productivity at lower cost than can employers that have poor reputations. (A firm that has a poor reputation for performing on its promises must pay a compensating wage differential to attract workers of given quality away from employers with good reputations.) Because the good reputation increases productivity relative to the wage paid, a surplus is created that can be divided between the firm and its workers.

Motivating Workers

Beyond the issue of enforceability, employment contracts address the employer's need to motivate workers. Workers can be viewed as utility maximizers, and "putting forth their best efforts" might entail working hard when they are sick or distracted by personal problems, or it might involve a work pace that they find taxing. Employees can be assumed to do what they feel is in their own interests unless induced to do otherwise by the employer's system of rewards. How can we create rewards that give employees incentives to work toward the goals of their employers?

Pay for Performance   The most obvious way to motivate workers is to pay them according to their individual output. Linking pay to output creates the presumption of strong incentives for productivity, but incentive pay schemes must confront two general problems.[9] One problem is that using output-based pay has both benefits and costs to an employer, and both are affected by the extent to which a worker's output is influenced by forces outside their control. Jane, for example, might be willing to put forth 10 percent more effort if she can be sure that her output (and pay) will rise by 10 percent. If machine breakdowns are so common, however, that she can count on only a 5 percent increase, she may decide that the extra 10 percent of effort is not worth it. From the employer's perspective, then, output-based pay might provide only weak incentives if Jane's effort and the resulting output are not closely linked. From Jane's perspective, a weak link between output and her own effort also puts her earnings at risk of variations that she cannot control—and she may be unwilling to take a job with such a pay scheme unless it pays a compensating wage differential. Thus, unless a worker's output and effort are closely associated, output-based pay might have small benefits to the employer and yet come at added cost.[10]

The second general problem facing pay-for-performance plans is the need to pick an output measure that coincides with the employer's ultimate objective. Quantitative aspects of output (such as the number of complaints handled by a clerk in the customer service department) are easier to measure than the qualitative aspects of friendliness or helpfulness—and yet the qualitative aspects are critical to building a loyal customer base. Moreover, employees in modern plants are often asked to work in teams, and they thus produce several "outputs," including team planning, decision-making, and problem-solving. The quantity and quality of some of these outputs are difficult to measure. Imperfectly designed performance measures can backfire, by inducing employees to allocate their effort toward what is being measured and away from other important aspects of their jobs.[11] Because in many employment situations, measuring performance is extremely difficult, most people are paid for their time.[12]

Time-Based Pay With Supervision	An alternative pay scheme is to compensate workers for the time they work. This reduces the risk of having Jane's pay—to continue our example—vary on a weekly basis, but guaranteeing her a wage without reference to her actual output creates a problem of *moral hazard*: Why should she work hard if that effort is not rewarded? (See Example 11.2 for a comparison of actual work effort under output-based pay and time-based pay.) The danger that workers might only "put in their time" means that employers must closely monitor their behavior.

EXAMPLE 11.2
Calorie Consumption and Type of Pay

We noted in the text that time-based pay raises the question of *moral hazard*; that is, because workers are paid regardless of their output, they might not put forth their best efforts. An interesting examination of this question comes from Bukidon in the Philippines, where workers commonly hold several farming jobs during a year. In some of these jobs, they are paid by the hour, and in some, they are paid directly for their output. Therefore, we are able to observe how hard the same individual works under the two types of pay systems.

A clever study discovered clear-cut evidence that the workers put forth much less effort in these physically demanding jobs when paid by the hour rather than for their output. Measuring effort expended by both weight change and calorie consumption, the study found that workers consumed *23 percent fewer calories* and *gained more weight per calorie consumed* when they were paid by the hour. Both facts suggest that less physical effort was put forth when workers were paid by the hour than when they were paid for their output.

Source: Andrew D. Foster and Mark R. Rosenzweig, "A Test for Moral Hazard in the Labor Market: Contractual Arrangements, Effort, and Health," *Review of Economics and Statistics* 76 (May 1994): 213–227

See Thomas Dohmen and Armin Falk, "Performance Pay and Multidimensional Sorting: Productivity, Preferences, and Gender," *American Economic Review* 101 (April 2011): 556–590, for additional evidence that workers paid for their performance work harder and experience greater levels of stress and exhaustion.

The problem with close supervision is that it is costly. Tasks in almost any workplace are divided so that the economies afforded by specialization are possible, and workers must continually adjust to changing situations within their areas of responsibility. Extremely close supervision would require supervisors to have the same information, at the same time, on the situations facing all their subordinates, in which case they might as well make all the decisions themselves. In short, detailed supervision can destroy the advantages of specialization. As noted earlier, in some instances where output is based on creativity, even knowing what output to be looking for is difficult for the supervisor.

Motivating the Individual in a Group

If workers seek to maximize utility by increasing their *own* consumption of valued goods, then focusing on the link between each individual's pay and performance is sufficient in developing company policy. However, the concern for one's standing in a group is often a factor that also affects a worker's utility. The importance of the *group* in motivating *individuals* presents both problems and opportunities for the employer.

Issues of Fairness   People's concern about their treatment *relative to others* in their reference group means that issues of *status* and *fairness* pervade the employment relationship. A worker who obtains a 7 percent wage increase during a year in which both price and wage increases average 4 percent might be quite happy until they find out that a colleague working in the same job for the same employer received a 10 percent increase (Example 11.3 offers an illustration). Workers who feel unfairly treated might quit, reduce their effort level, steal from the employer, or even sabotage output in order to "settle the score."[13] Unfortunately for employers, however, the fairness of identical policy decisions can often be perceived differently depending on their context.

EXAMPLE 11.3

The Effects of Low Relative Pay on Worker Satisfaction

In March, 2008, a major newspaper in California posted a database containing the salaries of all California public employees, including all nonstudent workers at the University of California. Later that spring, four economists performed a study in which *some* faculty and staff members of the University of California system were sent an email informing them of this website and asking them only whether they were aware of this database. Later, the researchers sent an email to *all* University of California employees, asking them whether they knew about, and had used, the salary database; they were also asked about their level of job and pay satisfaction.

The study found that workers who went to the website and found their pay was *below the median pay* for their department reported *lower levels of satisfaction* with their job than workers with similar pay who did not use the website (and presumably were less likely to know the salaries of their peers). Workers who discovered that their pay was above the median, however, were not more likely to report higher levels of job satisfaction. The results suggest, therefore, that workers are typically concerned about their pay *relative* to that of their peers, but that this concern is primarily about whether they are paid *less* than average.

Source: David Card, Alexandre Mas, Enrico Moretti, and Emmanual Saez, "Inequality at Work: The Effect of Peer Salaries on Job Satisfaction," *American Economic Review* 102 (October 2012): 2981–3003; also see Arindrajit Dube, Laura Giuliano, and Jonathan Leonard, "Fairness and Frictions: The Impact of Unequal Raises on Quit Behavior," *American Economic Review* 109 (February 2019): 620–663

For example, a sample of people was asked to consider the case of two small companies that were not growing as planned and therefore needed to cut costs. Each paid workers $10 per hour, but employer A paid that in salary and employer B paid $9 in salary and $1 in the form of a bonus. Most respondents said it would be unfair for A to cut wages by 10 percent, but they thought it fair if B were to eliminate its bonus. Apparently, pay framed as "salary" connotes a greater entitlement than pay framed as "bonus."[14]

Consider a second example from the same survey. A majority of respondents thought for a successful house painter to cut wages from $9 per hour to $7 per hour would be unfair if they discovered that reliable help could be hired for less. However, they felt that if the painter quit painting and went into landscaping (where wages were lower), paying a $7 wage would be justified. Clearly, the employer is included among the reference groups used by workers in judging fairness, and the *context* of an employer's decision matters as much as its content.

Group Loyalty   Besides concern for their own levels of consumption and their relative treatment within the group, employees are also typically concerned with the status or well-being of the entire group. Although people in a group are always tempted to "free-ride" by taking it easy and enjoying the benefits of others' hard work, most people are willing to make at least some sacrifices for their team, school, work group, community, or country.[15] Because the essence of "doing a good job" so frequently means taking the initiative in many small ways to advance the organization's interests, employers with highly productive workers almost universally pay attention to policies that foster organizational loyalty. Although many of the steps that employers can take to nurture this loyalty go beyond the boundaries of economics, some compensation schemes that we analyze here relate pay to *group* performance quite directly.

Compensation Plans: Overview and Guide to the Rest of the Chapter

Along with the employer's hiring standards, supervisory policies, and general managerial philosophy, its compensation plan greatly affects the incentives of employees to put forth effort. Although a detailed discussion of many managerial policies is outside the scope of this text, the incentives created by compensation schemes fall squarely within the purview of modern labor economics. In what follows, therefore, we use economic concepts to analyze the major characteristics of compensation plans.

Three elements broadly characterize an employer's compensation scheme: the *basis* on which pay is calculated, the *level* of pay in relation to pay for comparable workers elsewhere, and—for employers that have internal labor markets—the *sequencing* of pay over workers' careers. The remainder of the chapter is devoted to analyses of these elements.

Productivity and the Basis of Yearly Pay

Workers can be paid for their time, their output, or some hybrid of the two. Most people in the United States are paid for their time, and we must ask why output-based pay is not more widely used. Because compensation plans must satisfy both the employer and the employee, we organize our analysis around the considerations relevant to each side of the labor market.

Employee Preferences

Piece-rate pay, under which workers earn a certain amount for each item produced, is the most common form of individually based incentive pay for production workers. Another system linking earnings to individuals' output is payment by *commission*, under which workers (usually salespeople) receive a fraction of the value of the items they sell. *Gainsharing* plans are *group*-incentive plans that at least partially tie earnings to gains in group productivity, reductions in cost, increases in product quality, or other measures of group success. *Profit-sharing* and *bonus* plans attempt to relate workers' pay to the profits of their firm or subdivision; this form of pay also rewards work groups rather than individuals.[16] Under all these systems, workers are paid at least somewhat proportionately to their output or to the degree that their employer prospers.

Variability of Pay   If employees were told that their average earnings over the years under a time-based payment system would be equal to their earnings under an output-based pay plan, they would probably prefer to be paid on a *time* basis. Why? Earnings under output-based pay plans clearly vary with whatever measure of output serves as the basis for pay. As mentioned earlier, many things that affect individual or group output depend on the external environment, not just on the level of energy

or commitment the individual worker brings to the job. The number of items that an individual produces in a given day is affected by the age and condition of machinery, interrupted flows of supplies owing to strikes or snowstorms, and the worker's own illness or injury. Commissions earned by salespeople are clearly affected by the overall demand for the product being sold, and this demand can fluctuate for a number of reasons well beyond the control of the individual salesperson. Earnings that depend on some measure of *group* output also vary with the level of effort expended by others in the group.

The possible variations in earnings under output-based pay are thought to be unappealing to workers because of their presumed *risk aversion* (i.e., workers' preference for earnings certainty, even if it means somewhat lower pay). Most workers have monthly financial obligations for housing, food, insurance, utilities, and so forth. If several low-income pay periods are strung together, they might have difficulty in meeting these obligations, even if several high-income pay periods were to follow. All else equal, a worker would prefer the same pay each month to a situation that has the same average but that changes from month to month.

Employees thus prefer the certainty of time-based pay, other things (including the *average* level of earnings) equal, because of their anxiety about periods of lower-than-usual output. To induce risk-averse employees to accept output-based pay, employers would have to pay a compensating wage differential.[17]

Worker Sorting   Setting worker risk aversion aside, we next consider *which* workers will be attracted to piece-rate or commission pay schemes. Because time-based plans pay the same, at least in the short run, to high and low producers alike, workers who gain most from piece rates or commissions are those whose levels of motivation or ability are above average. Thus, employees who choose to work under compensation plans that reward individual productivity signal that they believe themselves to be above-average producers. For example, when a U.S. company that installs glass in automobiles went from time-based pay to piece rates in the mid 1990s, the individual output of *incumbent employees who stayed with the firm* rose by 22 percent; thus, we can conclude that the same employees worked harder under the piece-rate pay system. However, because changing to piece rates made the company attractive to a *different* set of workers—with slower workers leaving and faster ones joining the firm—the *overall* increase in worker productivity was in the neighborhood of 44 percent.[18]

Pay Comparisons   We thus expect that workers paid for their output might earn more than those paid for their time, for three reasons: Incentive pay motivates employees to work harder, it attracts the most productive workers, and it involves risk that may call forth a compensating wage differential. One study of pay in some apparel industries found that workers paid a piece rate earned about 14 percent more than workers paid by the hour. The study estimated that about one-third of this disparity was a compensating differential, and the remainder was related to the incentive and sorting effects.[19]

Employer Considerations

The willingness of employers to pay a premium to induce employees to accept piece rates depends on the costs and benefits to employers of incentive pay schemes. If workers are paid with piece rates or commissions, they bear the consequences of low productivity, as noted earlier; thus, employers can afford to spend less time screening and supervising workers. If workers are paid on a *time* basis, the *employer* accepts the risk of variations in their productivity; when workers are exceptionally productive, profits increase, and when they are less productive, profits decline. Employers, however, may be less anxious about these variations than employees are. They typically have more assets and can thus weather the lean periods more comfortably than individual workers can. Employers also usually have several employees, and the chances are that not all will suffer the same swings in productivity at the same time (unless an external shock to the demand for the firm's product or a morale problem in the firm occurs). Thus, employers might not be as willing to pay for income certainty as workers are.

The other major employer consideration in deciding on the basis for pay concerns the incentives for employee effort. The considerations related to three major types of incentive plans in use are discussed next.

Pay for Output: Individual Incentives   From the employer's perspective, the big advantage of individually based output pay is that it induces employees to adopt a set of work goals that are directly related to output. Indeed, as with the increased output of incumbent workers at the automobile glass installer mentioned earlier, the estimated increases in an individual's productivity associated with switching from time-based pay to piece rates in the forestry industry have been in the range of 20 percent.[20] It has disadvantages too, however.

First, the need to link output-based pay to some measure that can be objectively observed means that workers might be induced to allocate their efforts away from aspects of their performance that are not being measured. If they get paid only for the quantity of items that they individually produce or sell, they may have minimal regard for quality, safety procedures, or the performance or professional development of others on their work team.[21] These problems can create a need for costly quality-control supervision unless workers can be induced to monitor quality themselves. Self-monitoring for quality is only easily induced when a particular item or service can be traced to the worker responsible. For example, the auto glass installer mentioned earlier requires workers who have installed a windshield improperly (which usually results in its breaking) to pay for the replacement glass and then to reinstall it on their own time.

A second problem is that workers might be induced to work so quickly that machines and tools are damaged through lack of proper maintenance or use. Although this problem is mitigated to the extent that production downtime can cause the worker's earnings to drop, it is of enough concern to employers that they frequently require piece-rate workers to provide their *own* machines or tools.

How can firms create pay schemes with the proper incentives when the overall value of individual output is difficult to measure? In the remainder of this section, we explore two options. One is payment based on some measure of *group* output, and the other bases pay at least partly on the *subjective* judgments of supervisors.

Pay for Output: Group Incentives When individual output is difficult to monitor, when individual incentive plans are detrimental to output quality, or when output is generated by teams of interdependent workers, firms sometimes adopt group-incentive pay schemes to more closely align the interests of employer and employee.[22] These plans might tie at least a portion of pay to some component of profits (e.g., group productivity, product quality, or cost reductions), or they might directly link pay with the firm's overall profit level. In still other cases, workers might *own* the firm and split the profits among themselves.[23]

One drawback to group incentives is that groups are composed of individuals, and decisions about shirking are ultimately made at the individual level. A person who works hard to increase group output or the firm's profits winds up splitting the fruits of their labor with all the others, who may not have put out extra effort. Thus, *free-rider* opportunities give workers incentives to cheat on their fellow employees by shirking.[24] (Another downside of group incentives occurs when they attract the wrong sort of workers, and then the good workers leave. One extreme case is discussed in Example 11.4.)

EXAMPLE 11.4

Poor Group Incentives Doom the Shakers

The Shakers were a religious group who practiced celibacy and the communal ownership of property, where all members shared the group's income equally—receiving the average product. They arrived in the United States in 1774 and numbered around 4,000 by 1850, but their membership dwindled thereafter. Their decline is generally attributed to their failure to reproduce and to their declining religious fervor, but economic historian John Murray argues that their group compensation plan was another important reason for their demise.

Those members with a higher-than-average marginal productivity would receive less than the value of their output—and usually less than they could make elsewhere. Thus, high-productivity members had an incentive to quit. Conversely, outsiders with a low marginal productivity had an incentive to join, receiving more than the value of their output and more than they could elsewhere.

Murray uses literacy as a proxy for marginal productivity. When the Shaker communes were established in Ohio and Kentucky, their members were full of religious zeal, which may have initially overcome the incentive problems. These members had a literacy rate of almost 100 percent, far above that of the surrounding population. By the time of the Civil War, however, illiterates were joining the group in significant numbers, and the sect's literacy rates fell below the rates in the surrounding areas. Likewise, Murray finds that literate members were 30 to 40 percent more likely to quit the community (becoming "apostates") than were illiterate members.

Contemporaries began to question the sincerity of the new entrants: They were "bread and butter Shakers," who were intent on free-riding on their more-productive cohorts. Many had been unable or unwilling to provide for themselves in the world outside the commune. Eventually, the changing composition of the Shaker communities caused a crisis in the communes: The average product of the group fell, and the group was wracked by diminishing enthusiasm, internal stress, and declining membership.

Source: John E. Murray, "Human Capital in Religious Communes: Literacy and Selection of Nineteenth Century Shakers," *Explorations in Economic History* 32 (April 1995): 217–235

In small groups, cheating may be easy to detect, and peer pressure can be effectively used to eliminate it. When the group of workers receiving incentive pay is large, however, employers might have to devote managerial resources to building organizational loyalties if shirking is to be discouraged. Interestingly, despite free-rider problems, studies have found that tying pay to group productivity often has positive "peer effects."[25]

Group Incentives and Executive Pay Compensation for top executives provides an interesting example of the potential and the problems of basing pay on group results. Executives run a company but often do not own it, and like other employees, they want to advance their own interests.[26] How can companies align the interests of these key players with those of the owners (shareholders)?

Because firms are trying to maximize profits, we might consider basing executive pay on the firm's profits. But over what time period should profits be measured? Basing this year's pay on current-year profits might create the same adverse incentives discussed earlier with piece rates. A focus on current-year profits could induce executives to pursue only short-run strategies (no investment in research and development for the future, or accounting tricks), which run counter to the firm's long-run interests, in the hopes that they can "take the money and run" to another corporation before the long-run consequences of their decisions are fully observed.

One might think that the strongest way to align the interests of corporate executives and company owners might be to pay them with company stock or the options to buy it. This seemingly rewards top executives for efforts that increase shareholder wealth and punishes them for actions that they initiate that reduce it. Paying high-ranking corporate decision makers with company stock, however, has three drawbacks. First, a company's stock price is affected by more than company performance; it is also influenced by overall investor "bullishness." Moreover, even to the extent that a stock's price reflects the company profitability, that profitability—as in the case of an oil company benefiting from a rise in the price of oil—may have nothing to do with the quality of decisions or the effort of a company's management team. Thus, executives paid with stock are rewarded for luck as well as effort—a fact that might reduce the efforts that they devote to advancing the interests of their firms.[27]

Second, beyond reducing incentives, economy-wide fluctuations in stock prices also cause executives' pay to vary because of things beyond their control, which might force firms to pay them a compensating differential for the added riskiness of their pay. Third, the incentives that stocks provide are related mainly to the *long-term* perspective that they induce corporate executives to take when making decisions that affect a company's strength; once an executive has sold their stock in the company, these incentives are lost. Thus, policymakers interested in executive pay have frequently proposed limits on the ability of executives to sell their company's stock or on the timing of when they can do it.[28]

In practice, the compensation of chief executive officers (CEOs) in the United States has become increasingly responsive to shareholder value. In 1984, 17 percent of CEO pay was in the form of stock or stock options; around 2000, the comparable figure was close to 30 percent; and in 2010, the fraction was more than half for the largest 200 or so companies in the United States.[29] (The remainder of CEO pay was in the form of salary, benefits, pension contributions, and bonuses based on short-term profits.) Companies in industries that feature higher volatility in sales—and thus for whom pay based on profits or share values exposes CEO incomes to greater variations beyond their control—rely more on salary payments, and less on company performance, to attract top executives.[30]

An enormous rise in the fraction of pay in the form of equity (stock and stock options) has taken place for CEOs in the past three decades. Generally speaking, those firms with executive compensation plans more heavily weighted toward stock or stock options have tended to enjoy greater increases in corporate wealth. Some evidence, however, shows that tying pay to stock market values might make CEOs excessively worried about fluctuations in their own income, causing them to shy away from risky projects even when the projects appear profitable.[31]

Recent scandals involving CEOs have raised another concern about aligning their incentives with those of stockholders. The issue is whether CEOs use their close relationship with members of their board of directors (many of whom have been with the company a long time) to negotiate excessive compensation packages. More precisely, do they use their "insider" relationship with those who set their pay to receive compensation that is greater than what is consistent with maximizing shareholder value? Although researchers differ in their answers to this question, most agree that comfort between CEOs and directors is a potential problem and that greater use of "outside" directors or the presence of well-informed stockholders (e.g., institutional investors) could be a critical ingredient in aligning incentives.[32]

Severance and CEOs

CEO pay gets outsized attention from scholars and the media, especially given that each company generally has only one CEO. Many have been critical of the pay of executives, especially when they are given large severance payments after they are fired. Critics ask why they get such payments in the face of failure. The reason is almost always that they negotiated for such payments *at the time they were hired*. CEOs are rare employees who do have explicit employment contracts, and they are often in a strong negotiating position at the time of hire (because they presumably have some other great job at another company) to ask for special arrangements in the event that they are—at some point—fired.[33]

Pay for Time, With Merit Increases

Given employee risk aversion and the problem of devising appropriate measurable outcomes for individual- and group-incentive plans, most employers opt for some form of time based pay. While satisfying employees' desires for pay stability, time pay creates an incentive problem because compensation and output are not directly linked. Employers often try to cope with this problem through the use of *merit-pay* plans, which award larger pay increases to workers whose supervisors rate them as the better performers.

On the one hand, basing pay on supervisory ratings has the potential to create better incentives for workers, because these ratings can take account of the more subjective aspects of performance (friendliness, being a team player) that may be critical to the welfare of the employer.[34] On the other hand, merit-based pay still faces two incentive problems similar to those of output-based pay.

If supervisors are told to base their ratings on worker contributions toward *actual* output, merit pay runs up against the (by-now-familiar) problem that individual effort and output may not correlate well, owing to forces beyond the control of workers. For this reason, supervisors are often asked to rate their subordinates *relative* to each other, on the theory that all face the same external forces of snowstorms, machine breakdowns, and so forth.

The problem of relative rankings for merit-pay purposes is that the *effort* induced among employees might not be consistent with the employer's interests. For example, one way to enhance one's *relative* status is to sabotage the work of others. Finding pages torn out of library books on reserve shortly before major examinations is not unknown at colleges or universities, where grading is often based on relative performance (this is a great reason to have such materials online). Somewhat less sinister than sabotage, but equally inconsistent with employer interests, is noncooperation; one study has shown that the stronger the rewards based on relative performance, the less likely employees are to share their equipment and tools with fellow workers.[35]

Because relative performance ratings usually have a subjective component, another kind of counterproductive effort may take place: *politicking*.[36]

Workers may spend valuable work time "marketing" their services or otherwise ingratiating themselves with their supervisors. Thus, efforts are directed away from productivity itself to generate what is, at best, the *appearance* of productivity.[37]

Productivity and the Level of Pay

Given the difficulties created for both employers and employees by pay-for-performance plans (including merit pay), employers are often driven to search for other monetary incentives that can be used to motivate their workers. In this section, we discuss motivational issues related to the *level* of pay.

Why Higher Pay Might Increase Worker Productivity

Paying higher wages is thought to increase worker productivity, for several reasons. One involves the *type* of worker that the firm can attract; the others are related to the productivity that can be elicited from *given* workers.

Attracting Better Workers   Higher wages can attract better employees by enlarging the firm's applicant pool. A larger pool means that the firm can be more selective, skimming the cream off the top to employ only the most experienced, dependable, or highly motivated applicants.[38]

Building Employee Commitment   The reasons why higher wages are thought to generate greater productivity from workers all relate to the commitment to the firm they build. The higher the wages are relative to what workers could receive elsewhere, the less likely the workers will quit; knowing this, employers are more likely to offer training and more likely to demand longer hours and a faster pace of work from their workers. Employees, on their part, realize that even though supervision may not be detailed enough to detect shirking with certainty, if they are caught cheating on their promises to work hard and are fired as a result, the loss of a job paying above-market wages is costly both now and over their remaining work life.

Perceptions of Equity   A related reason why higher wages might generate more productivity from employees arises from their concern about being treated fairly. Workers who believe that they are being treated fairly are likely to put forth effort, whereas those who think that their treatment is unfair may "get even" by withholding effort or even engaging in sabotage.[39]

One comparison that workers make in judging their treatment is the extent to which they see the employer as profiting from their services. If a highly profitable employer is ungenerous in sharing its good fortune with its workers, even if the wages that it pays already are relatively high, the behavior is often considered unfair. Likewise, workers who are asked to sacrifice leisure and put forth extraordinary effort on the job are likely to expect the firm to make an extraordinary financial sacrifice (i.e., the offer of high pay) to them in return.[40]

Employees also judge the fairness of their pay by comparing it with what they could obtain elsewhere. Raising compensation above the level that workers can earn elsewhere, of course, has both benefits and costs to the employer, as we discuss in the following section.

Efficiency Wages

Although initial increases in pay may well serve to increase productivity and therefore the profits of the firm, after a point the costs to the employer of further increases will exceed the benefits. The above-market pay level at which the marginal revenues to the employer from a further pay increase equal the marginal costs is the level that will maximize profits; this has become known as the *efficiency wage* (see Example 11.5).[41]

EXAMPLE 11.5

Did Henry Ford Pay Efficiency Wages?

The 1908–1914 period saw the introduction of "scientific management" and assembly-line production processes at the Ford Motor Company. The change in production methods led to a change in the occupational composition of Ford's workforce, and by 1914, most of its workers were lower skilled and foreign born. Although these changes proved extremely profitable, worker dissatisfaction was high. In 1913, turnover rates reached 370 percent (370 workers had to be hired each year to keep every 100 positions filled), which was high even by the standards of the Detroit automobile industry at the time. Similarly, absenteeism typically averaged 10 percent a day. Although Henry Ford was obviously having difficulty retaining and eliciting effort from workers, he had little difficulty finding replacements: long lines of applicants always appeared at the factory gates. Hence, Ford's daily wage in 1913 of about $2.50 was at least at the competitive level.

In January 1914, Ford instituted a $5-a-day wage; this doubling of pay was granted only to workers who had been employed at the company for at least six months. At roughly the same time, residency in the Detroit area for at least six months was made a hiring standard for new job applicants. Because the company was limiting the potential applicant flow and was apparently not screening job applicants any more carefully after the pay increase, it appears the motivation for this extraordinary increase in wages was not to increase the quality of new hires.

However, the increase clearly *did* affect the behavior of existing employees. Between March 1913 and March 1914, the quit rate of Ford employees fell by 87 percent, and discharges fell by 90 percent. Similarly, the absentee rate fell by 75 percent during the October 1913 to October 1914 period. Morale and productivity increased, and the company continued to be profitable.

Some evidence shows that at least initially, however, Ford's productivity gains were less than the wage increase. Historians have pointed to the noneconomic factors that influenced Ford's decision, including his paternalistic desire to teach his workers good living habits.

(For workers to receive these increases, investigators from Ford first had to certify that they did not pursue lifestyles that included behavior like excessive gambling or drinking.) Although the wage increase thus probably did not lead to a wage level that maximized the company's profits (a smaller increase probably would have done that), the policy did have a substantial positive effect on worker turnover, effort, morale, and productivity.

Source: Daniel Raff and Lawrence Summers, "Did Henry Ford Pay Efficiency Wages?" *Journal of Labor Economics* 5 (October 1987): S57–S86

The payment of efficiency wages has a wide set of implications that, in recent years, have begun to be explored by economists. For example, the persistence of unemployment is thought by some to result from the widespread payment of above-market wages (see Chapter 14).[42] Furthermore, persistently different wage rates paid to qualitatively similar workers in different industries are the hypothesized result of efficiency-wage considerations.[43]

For our purposes here, however, the most important implications of efficiency wages relate to their effects on productivity, and two types of empirical studies are of interest. One set of studies *infers* the effects of efficiency wages on productivity from the types of firms that pay these wages. That is, if some firms raise wages above the market level for profit-maximizing purposes, we ought to observe that those who do are the ones that, first, stand to gain the most from enhancing worker reliability (perhaps because they have a lot invested in expensive equipment) or, second, find properly motivating their workers through output-based pay or supervision the most difficult.[44] The other kind of study directly relates the effects of efficiency wages to measures of productivity, rates of disciplinary dismissals, or changes in the employer's product market share.[45] The studies so far are limited in number, but they are generally supportive of efficiency-wage theory.

Note that the payment of wages above what workers could earn elsewhere makes sense only because workers expect to have long-term employment relationships with firms. If workers switched jobs every period, they would face no incentive to reduce shirking when a firm paid above-market wages, because firing someone who is going to quit anyway is not an effective penalty; as a result, firms would have no incentive to pursue an efficiency-wage policy. Thus, efficiency wages are likely to arise only in situations where structured internal labor markets exist. The existence of internal labor markets, however, raises *other* possibilities for using pay to motivate workers, and it is to these possibilities that we now turn.

Productivity and the Sequencing of Pay

Employers with internal labor markets have options for motivating workers that grow out of their employees' expected *careers* with the organization. Applicants to and employees of employers with internal labor markets are concerned with the present value of *career* compensation. This "lifetime" perspective increases employers' options for developing compensation policies, because both the pay levels at each step in one's career and the swiftness of promotion to given steps can be varied by the firm while still living within the constraints of having to offer an attractive present value of career compensation. In this section, we analyze several possibilities for sequencing pay over workers' careers that are thought to provide incentives for greater productivity.

Underpayment Followed by Overpayment

Arranging workers' pay over time so that employees are "underpaid" early in their careers and "overpaid" later on may be beneficial to both employer and employee.[46] This sequencing of pay will arguably increase worker productivity and enable firms to pay *higher* present values of compensation than otherwise, for reasons related both to worker sorting and to work incentives. An understanding of these reasons takes us back to the problem of avoiding cheating on an implicit contract in the presence of asymmetric information.

Worker Sorting   Pay plans that delay at least a part of employees' compensation to a time later in their careers have an important signaling component. They will appeal most (and perhaps only) to those workers who intend to stay with the employer a long time and work hard enough to avoid being fired before collecting their delayed pay. In the absence of being able to predict which workers intend to stick around and work diligently, an employer might find an underpay-now, overpay-later compensation plan attractive because of the type of workers likely to sort themselves into their applicant pool.[47]

Work Incentives   A company that pays poorly to begin with but well later on increases the incentives of its employees to work industriously. Once in the job, an employee has incentives to work diligently in order to qualify for the later overpayment. The employer need not devote as many resources to supervision each year as would otherwise be the case, because the firm has several years in which to identify shirkers and withhold from them the delayed reward (if the penalty for shirking is high, then the employer can spend less effort on monitoring). Because all employees work harder than they otherwise would, compensation within the firm tends to be higher also.

Constraints   One feasible compensation-sequencing scheme would pay workers *less* than their marginal product early in their careers and *more* than their marginal product later on. This scheme, however, must satisfy two constraints. First, the present value of the earnings streams offered to employees must be at least equal to alternative streams offered to workers in the labor market; if not, the firm cannot attract the workers that it wants.

Second, the scheme must also satisfy the equilibrium conditions that the firm maximizes profits and does not earn supernormal profits. If profits are not maximized, the firm's existence is threatened; if firms make supernormal profits, new firms will be induced to enter the market. Thus, in neither case would equilibrium exist.

These two conditions will be met if hiring is done until the present value of one's career-long marginal revenue product equals the present value of one's career earnings stream. (This career-long condition is the multi-year analog of the single-year profit-maximization conditions discussed in Chapter 3.) Thus, for firms choosing the underpayment-now, overpayment-later compensation scheme to be competitive in both the labor market and the product market, the present value of the yearly amounts by which marginal revenue product (*MRP*) *exceeds* compensation early on must equal the present value of the later amounts by which *MRP falls short* of pay.

Graphical Analysis   This compensation plan is diagrammed in Figure 11.2. We assume that *MRP* rises over a worker's career but that in the first *t** years of employment, compensation remains below *MRP*. At some point in the worker's career with the firm—year *t** in the diagram—compensation begins to exceed *MRP*. From *t** until retirement in year *r* is the period during which diligent employees are rewarded by receiving compensation in excess of what they could receive elsewhere (i.e., their *MRP*). For the firm to be competitive in both the labor market and the product market, the *present value* of area *A* in the diagram must equal the *present value* of area *B*. (Area *B* is larger than area *A* in Figure 11.2 because sums received further in the future are subjected to heavier discounting when present values are calculated.)

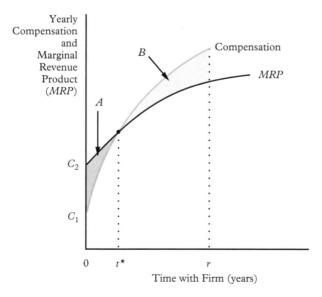

Figure 11.2 A Compensation-Sequencing Scheme to Increase Worker Motivation

Risks   To be sure, making this kind of agreement comes with risks for both parties. On the one hand, employees agreeing to this compensation scheme take a chance that they may be fired without cause or that their employer may go bankrupt before they have collected their reward in the years beyond t^*. Employers will have some incentives to renege, because older workers are being paid a wage that exceeds their immediate value (at the margin) to the firm.

On the other hand, employers who do not wish to fire older people face the risk that these "overpaid" employees will stay on the job longer than is necessary to collect their reward—that is, stay on longer than time r in Figure 11.2. Knowing that their current wage is greater than the wage that they can get elsewhere, because it reflects payment for more than current output, older employees will have incentives to keep working longer than is profitable for the firm.[48]

Employee Safeguards   Some safeguards for employees can be built into the employment contract when this type of pay sequencing is used. Employers can guarantee seniority rights for older workers, under which workers with the shortest durations of employment with the firm are laid off first if the firm cuts back its workforce. Without these seniority rights, firms might be tempted to lay off older workers, whose wages are greater than *MRP*, and keep the younger ones, who are paid less than *MRP* at this point in their careers.[49]

Employees can also be protected later in their careers by obtaining part of their overpayment in the form of vested pension rights. Once vested (within five years of service, under federal law), employees covered by pension plans have rights to a benefit upon retirement even if they are separated from their employer before retirement age.

Ultimately, however, the best protection that older workers have may be the employer's need to recruit *younger* workers. If a certain employer gains a reputation for firing older workers despite an implicit agreement not to do so, that employer will have trouble recruiting new employees. However, if the company is in permanent decline, if it faces an unusually adverse market, or if information on its employment policies is not easily available, incentives to renege on its promises could be strong.

Employer Safeguards   Before 1978, many employers had mandatory retirement ages for their employees, so that they could enforce retirement at point r, for example. However, amendments to the Age Discrimination in Employment Act in 1978 and 1986 precluded mandatory retirement for most workers. Age-discrimination legislation also makes reducing the wages of workers who stay past point r difficult for employers. Thus, employers with underpay-now, overpay-later plans are now faced with greater difficulties in inducing employees to retire.

One action that employers with these plans have taken is to offer large inducements for workers to retire at a certain age. For example, a study of pension plans in 190 of the largest companies in the United States (employing about one-quarter of all workers) found that the present value of pension benefits, summed over the expected lifetime of the retirees, commonly declines as retirement is postponed. This study discovered that for workers with typical earnings and years of service, the present value of pension benefits was over 25 percent greater if retirement occurred five years before, rather than at, normal retirement age.[50]

Who Adopts Delayed Compensation?   One implication of the underpay-now, overpay-later compensation scheme is that it is more likely to exist for jobs in which the close supervision of workers is not feasible. Indeed, one study separated jobs into those that were conducive to close supervision and those that were not; the study found that jobs in which workers could not be closely supervised, older workers were more likely to have relatively higher wages and (in the past at least) be subject to mandatory retirement rules.[51]

Promotion Tournaments

Another form of worker motivation in the context of internal labor markets might best be termed a ***promotion tournament***. Tournaments have three central features: Who will win is uncertain, the winner is selected on the basis of *relative* performance (i.e., performance compared with that of the other "contestants"), and the rewards will be concentrated in the hands of the winner, so there is a big difference between winning and losing. Not all promotions within firms satisfy this definition of a tournament, largely because the rewards are relatively small and the winners are easy to predict. For example, one study found that promotions were typically associated with increased wage growth of 2 percent to 3 percent, and those who received their first promotion most quickly tended to be promoted most quickly later on as well.[52]

   Promotions to very senior leadership positions, however, often take place through a process that fits the description of a tournament.[53] The fortunate vice presidents who are promoted above their rivals to CEO in the United States' largest corporations, for example, can expect to receive an addition to lifetime income that is in excess of $4 million.[54] The magnitude of this payoff suggests that it is a prize offered at the end of a tournament; after all, if one vice president were actually that much more productive than all the others, they would have been promoted (or the others fired) long ago. What determines a tournament's strength of incentives, and what are the problems that promotion tournaments must address?

Incentives for Effort   In any tournament, athletic or otherwise, the contestants must decide how much effort to devote to winning. In tennis, for example, a player must decide how much to risk injury by diving or straining for a ball that is difficult to reach. In the corporate world, parents need to consider whether working another week of nights at the office (on a project, say) is worth sacrificing the time with their children. We can hypothesize that contestants will decide to expend the extra effort if the marginal benefits that they expect to gain exceed the added risk, inconvenience, or disutility.

The marginal benefit that the extra effort produces is a function of two things: the *increased probability of winning* and the value (including prestige) of the *winner's prize*. The extent to which one's chances of winning are improved depends on the now familiar issue of how closely effort is linked to output. If winning is largely a matter of luck, for example, spending extra effort may have little effect on the outcome.[55]

The value of the winner's prize, of course, depends on the disparity between what the winner receives and what the losers receive. Tournaments designed to elicit effort that entails great personal sacrifice or that have so many contestants that extra effort improves one's chances only to a small degree require a large prize to create incentives.

Tournaments also enhance output because of their sorting value. People who have confidence in their own abilities and a willingness to sacrifice now for a shot at the prize are much more likely to enter a tournament than others are. Thus, employees self-select into (or out of) promotion tournaments, and by so doing, they signal things about themselves that employers might otherwise find difficult to judge.[56] (See Example 11.6 for a discussion of the selection issue in law firms.)

EXAMPLE 11.6
The "Rat Race" in Law Firms

Within law firms, partners—who share with each other in the firm's profits—need to be careful about selecting which associates (lawyers who are not partners) to promote into their ranks. In particular, they will want to promote only those associates who are the most capable and most hardworking—that is, those who will contribute more than their share to profits. They thus tend to rely on "billable hours" as an indicator of an associate's productivity.

All applicants out of law school will claim to be hard workers, of course, and even those who have strong preferences for relatively short (or even "normal") hours can pretend to be "long-hours workers" for a time after hire. Employers therefore need to elicit a signal from their applicants or employees about their *long-run* work orientation, and one way to do this is to announce to all applicants that long hours are expected for a long time. These expectations obviously must be reasonable enough that the firms can recruit applicants, but in terms of our signaling discussion in Chapter 9, the announced work requirements must be demanding enough to discourage pretenders from applying. Discouraging pretenders, however, may require hours of work that are in excess of what even those who choose to work for the firm would prefer.

For example, one study of two large law firms in the northeastern United States found that over half of their associates worked more than 50 hours a week—and 70 percent normally worked at least half a day on the weekends. The study also found evidence that if offered a 5 percent wage increase, fully 65 percent of associates would prefer to cut their hours by 5 percent rather than to keep their hours constant and to have their incomes rise. Among those whose *spouses had full-time jobs*—and who therefore had to share household duties—those wanting to work fewer hours exceeded 75 percent.

Source: Renée M. Landers, James B. Rebitzer, and Lowell J. Taylor, "Rat Race Redux: Adverse Selection in the Determination of Work Hours in Law Firms," *American Economic Review* 86 (June 1996): 329–348

Problems   Although a firm that adopts promotion tournaments may reap self-selection benefits, it may also encounter self-selection problems. Promotion tournaments tend to attract "entrants" who are overconfident about their abilities and may harm the interests of their employer by making too many risky decisions—and they tend to discourage entry by those who are averse to risk or who do not work well in a highly competitive environment. More and more evidence, for example, shows that women are less attracted to tournaments than equally productive men and that their performance may be less enhanced by the competition that tournaments induce.[57]

Another problem with tournaments is that, as with merit pay based on relative performance, contestants may allocate effort away from increasing their own output and toward reducing the output of their rivals. Indeed, where sabotage is possible, promotion tournaments can actually reduce an organization's total output.[58]

Yet another problem is that performance during the tournament may not indicate who will do best in the job to which the "winner" is promoted. For example, if a firm is considering who among its sales force should be the next sales *manager*, it may not be the person who makes the most sales. Indeed, one study found that companies that based promotions to sales managers on individual sales volume, rather than managerial potential, incurred a cost in reduced sales by its sales force. However, this same study found that basing promotions on criteria other than individual sales volume weakens the incentive effects of the tournament and leads to the exit of higher-performing sales workers passed over for promotion.[59] Thus, organizations running promotion tournaments must carefully balance the promotion criteria against the performance incentives.

As implied earlier, organizations running promotion tournaments have to be concerned about how to treat the losers. A large disparity in earnings produces large incentives during tournament play, but it also means that the losers do relatively badly. If a firm is perceived as treating losers callously, it will have problems attracting contestants in the first place (after all, most contestants lose). Thus, the firm has to specify a disparity that is large enough to provide incentives but small enough to provide contestants.

Promotion-related incentive plans face additional problems, however, when employees find seeking careers outside their current organization feasible and are able to send at least some signals of their productivity to other potential employers. We turn now to an analysis of situations in which the career concerns of employees might orient their efforts toward seeking employment elsewhere.

Career Concerns and Productivity

Employees often define themselves more as members of a profession or field than as members of a particular organization. Consequently, they may be as motivated to impress *other* employers (in the hopes of receiving future offers) as they are their own. What are the implications of these "career concerns"?

The Distortion of Effort

Other employers can observe objective measures of performance more easily than they can observe subjective measures (e.g., "quality"). As a result, employees who have career concerns have an incentive to allocate their efforts toward measurable areas of performance and to de-emphasize areas that other employers cannot observe. As discussed earlier, executives looking for opportunities elsewhere have incentives to pursue strategies that yield short-run profits (which are highly visible) even if doing so harms the long-term interests of their current employer.[60]

Piece Rates and Effort

Although job possibilities with other employers can distort workers' allocations of their effort, they can also solve yet another problem with piece-rate pay. In a world in which products and technologies are constantly changing, piece rates must be continually reset. In establishing a piece rate, the employer makes a guess about how long completing the task takes and calibrates the piece rate so that the average hourly earnings of its workers are attractive enough to recruit and retain a workforce.

Management, however, can never know for sure just how long completing a task takes, given a reasonably high level of effort by production workers. Moreover, as noted earlier, workers have incentives to "go slow" in trial runs so that management will overestimate task completion time and set a relatively high piece rate. If workers know that the estimated time for task completion is too high, they may deliberately work slowly out of fear that the firm will later reduce the piece rate if it finds out the truth.

Employees who are mobile across firms, however, will be less concerned about their *current* employer's future actions. They are more likely to decide to work at top speed so that other employers are sufficiently impressed to hire them in the future. Where workers' pay is at least partially based on a piece rate, then, career concerns can be helpful in eliciting maximum effort from one's employees.

The Sequencing of Effort

Employees who are concerned about future promotions, whether with their current employer or elsewhere, usually require two general incentives to induce high productivity: one's current pay and the chances of future promotion. When career (i.e., promotion) concerns are strong, employers may not need much in the way of current pay-for-performance incentives to motivate their employees. As career concerns weaken, firms may need to adopt more-current incentives to maintain worker effort.[61]

Workers are more likely to be motivated by career concerns and less by pay for current performance when they are inexperienced. Paying them for current performance runs into the problem that output is a function of ability, effort, and luck—and when workers are young, their abilities are unknown to themselves and their employers. Relating pay to the performance of inexperienced workers may not increase their incentives much, because with ability unknown, the connection between effort and output is unclear. The incentive to work hard is strong for those with career concerns, however, because they realize that employers are observing them to estimate their abilities and their willingness to put in effort.

Moreover, the inability of employers (especially outside employers) to closely monitor workers' efforts can, in the presence of career concerns, lead to *more* effort. Employees realize that future promotions depend in part on employers' beliefs about their *ability*. Because some of their efforts can be hidden, inexperienced workers have incentives to put in extra, hidden effort in an attempt to mislead employers about their ability. For example, an employee expected to work 50 hours a week may put in an extra 20 hours at home to boost performance in an attempt to raise employers' perceptions of their ability.

As one's career progresses, however, ability becomes known with more certainty and the career-based incentives for extraordinary effort decline. Fortunately, as noted earlier, the case for performance-based current pay also becomes stronger. Indeed, one study finds that older CEOs are paid more on the basis of current performance than are younger CEOs.[62]

Applications of the Theory: Explaining Two Puzzles

The conceptual issues outlined in this chapter can help to shed light on two compensation questions that puzzle labor economists: why pay increases with seniority and why larger employers pay higher wages. In both cases, multiple theoretical or data-related reasons can be called upon to explain the empirical phenomenon; some of these were presented in this chapter and some were introduced earlier. This section briefly summarizes these reasons and, where relevant, reviews the results of empirical studies to evaluate which ones seem most relevant.

Why Do Earnings Increase With Job Tenure?

Earnings rise with age and general labor market experience, as we saw in Chapter 9; however, *within* age groups, wages additionally rise as *tenure* with one's employer increases. Why does the length of time with one's

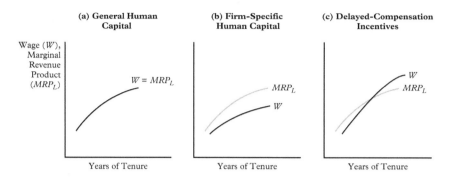

Figure 11.3 Alternative Explanations for the Effect of Job Tenure on Wages

employer matter? Three sets of explanations detail why wage increases should be associated with job tenure, holding age (or general labor market experience) constant.[63]

The simplest assumption is that workers are paid wages equal to their *MRP* at all times—see panel (a) in Figure 11.3—so that wages and productivity rise together as the length of time with an employer increases. Clearly, if general training, which is useful to a number of potential employers, is taking place, wages will rise with *age*—but our question is why they *additionally* rise as tenure with an employer rises. A reason explored in Chapter 5 is related to the *matches* between the job and the worker. With many potential employers for any given worker, and with the costs entailed in any job search, it is unlikely that all workers will quickly find the job that puts their skills to the highest-value (and therefore best-paying) use. Some will get lucky early on, of course, and the lucky ones will tend to stay with their employers and cease further searching. Those who are not so lucky will continue searching for better jobs (and pay) and will therefore have shorter job tenures. Thus, longer tenure and higher wages arguably both reflect the same phenomenon: better (more productive) matches between the job and the worker.

The second explanation asserts that *firm-specific* investments are jointly undertaken by workers and their employers (see Chapter 5). The joint investment creates a surplus that is *shared* by the worker and the firm; therefore, workers generally receive wage increases that are *less* than the increase in their productivity. As illustrated in panel (b) of Figure 11.3, with firm-specific investments, wages are below—and rise more slowly than—marginal revenue productivity.

Finally, this chapter has offered yet a third explanation for rising wage profiles: They may be part of a delayed-compensation incentive system designed to attract and motivate workers who have long-term attachments to their employers. Under this third explanation, which is depicted in panel (c) of Figure 11.3, wages rise *faster* than marginal revenue productivity and ultimately rise above it.[64]

Economists have been interested in devising empirical analyses that distinguish between these competing theories, but directly measuring *productivity* is generally not feasible.[65] Therefore, most studies have identified workers for whom theory suggests that one or another of the earlier explanations is likely (or unlikely) and then compared their wage profiles with those of other workers. Support for an explanation can be inferred if the relative wage profiles display their predicted patterns. For example, delayed-compensation plans are unnecessary if the output of a worker is easily monitored or if the worker is self-employed or paid a piece rate. If we can find evidence that wages for these workers rise *more slowly than average*, it would lend support against the existence of delayed-payment schemes.[66] Likewise, if tenure profiles are steepest during periods when workers are most likely to be receiving training, support for the human-capital explanations could be inferred.[67] To date, the best of the explanations for rising tenure profiles has by no means been discovered—and, of course, each might correctly provide a *partial* explanation for the increase of earnings with job tenure.

Why Do Large Firms Pay More?

Roughly 20 percent of all U.S. private sector employees work in firms with fewer than 20 workers, while about 45 percent work in firms with more than 500. Workers in the latter group, however, are much better paid than workers in the former group with the same education and experience. Especially for supervisory workers, wages rise faster with experience in larger firms.[68]

The explanations that have been offered for why larger firms pay higher wages are rooted in claims that they *need better workers* and/or that they have better *opportunities* to make their workers more productive.[69] One potential explanation, for example, is that economies of scale exist in job training; larger firms are therefore more likely to offer it and, of course, have a greater need to attract workers willing to undertake it.[70]

A second possible explanation is that large firms more often use highly interdependent production processes, which require that workers be exceptionally dependable and disciplined (one shirking worker can reduce the output of an entire team). Workers in highly interdependent production environments are more regimented and have less ability to act independently, and their higher wages can be seen as a compensating wage differential for the unattractiveness of a job requiring rigid discipline.

A third hypothesis is that larger firms find job vacancies more costly. They tend to be more capital intensive and, as noted earlier, have more interdependent production processes. Therefore, an unfilled job or an unexpected quit could more severely disrupt production in larger firms and, by idling much of its labor and capital, impose huge costs on the firm. In an effort to reduce quits and ensure that vacancies can be filled quickly, larger firms thus decide to pay higher wages—even when the work environment is not unattractive and efficiency wages are otherwise unnecessary (because other work incentives exist).[71]

A fourth hypothesis suggests that workers in larger firms are more productive because larger firms have more options for efficiently allocating workers to various tasks and machines. They have enough capital, labor, and customers, so the argument goes, that their workers experience less idleness and the most productive workers can be paired with the newest and most productive machines.[72]

The remaining hypotheses are rooted in concepts discussed in this chapter. One is that large firms make available to workers many steps in a career ladder so that long-term attachments between worker and employer are more attractive than in smaller firms. As has been noted in this chapter, employers whose workers are seeking long-term attachments have more options for using pay to motivate productivity. Efficiency wages are a more effective motivator when a long-term attachment is expected, because workers' losses from being terminated rise with both their wage level *and* the length of their future expected tenure. Deferred-compensation schemes and promotion tournaments can be used *only* in the context of long-term attachment.

EMPIRICAL STUDY 11.1

ARE WORKERS WILLING TO PAY FOR FAIRNESS? USING LABORATORY EXPERIMENTS TO STUDY ECONOMIC BEHAVIOR

When discussing the problems of motivating individuals in a group, we noted that opinion surveys of both workers and human-resource managers suggest that perceptions of *fairness* affect the productivity of employees. Can we obtain independent evidence on whether workers derive utility just from their *own* earnings and the consumption that such earnings permit or whether their *earnings relative to those of others* also affect their utility? In other words, do workers care only about their absolute level of earnings, or does their concern for fairness cause them also to care about how their earnings level compares with the respective earnings levels of others?

If fairness is something that workers value, economic theory predicts that they should be willing to pay a price to obtain it. Finding natural experiments that test this prediction is difficult, so some economists have turned to laboratory experiments as a way to gain insights into what motivates people.

Consider the following game conducted with 112 economics and business students at the University of Wisconsin, Madison. The students were anonymously paired through computers (they never found out with whom they were paired). One was designated the "proposer" and the other the "responder." The objective of the game was to divide up to $12. The proposer indicated how each dollar was to be divided, and the responder then chose how many dollars (zero to 12) were to be divided.

If the proposers indicated, for example, that they would keep 75 percent of all dollars divided, the responders could walk away with at most $3—by proposing to split the whole $12. In this case, the proposers would receive $9. If responders cared only about their own gains and not about rewards to others, they would not choose to shrink the pool. However, if responders cared so much about their relative payoffs that they were willing to give up some gains to retaliate against what they considered unfair treatment by the proposer, they could do so by shrinking the pool. For example, if a responder thought that the 75/25 split was unfair, they might shrink the pool to $8, in which case the responder would walk away with $2 and the proposer would receive only $6. In this case, we would observe responders giving up $1 for the utility gained by inflicting $3 of loss on the proposer.

The results of this laboratory experiment indicated that about half of the responders accepted whatever split was proposed and did not choose to shrink the pool. That is, roughly half were concerned only about their own, absolute payments.

Among the roughly half who were concerned enough about fairness to pay something to retaliate, how much were they willing to pay? The average proposal was for the responder to receive about 40 cents of each dollar split, and with proposals of a 60/40 split, those who were willing to retaliate shrunk the pool by about $3. With a pool now shrunk by $3, these responders indicated that they were willing to give up $1.20 (0.4 × $3) to inflict a loss of $1.80 (0.6 × $3) on the proposer.

Although we might question whether the players chosen for the game and the small amounts of money at risk accurately portray preferences of real workers in real jobs, laboratory experiments such as this one do offer a major advantage over opinion surveys. The players are not merely responding hypothetically to questions; rather, they are engaging in *actual behavior that has a consequential (monetary) outcome*. In recent years, laboratory experiments have become an accepted tool for gaining insight into economic behavior when generating behavioral data from real markets is difficult or infeasible.

Sources: James Andreoni, Marco Castillo, and Ragan Petrie, "What Do Bargainers' Preferences Look Like? Experiments with a Convex Ultimatum Game," *American Economic Review* 93 (June 2003): 672–685; also see Morris Altman, "The Nobel Prize in Behavioral and Experimental Economics: A Contextual and Critical Appraisal of the Contributions of Daniel Kahneman and Vernon Smith," *Journal of Political Economy* 16 (January 2004): 3–41

Although large firms have more opportunities for adopting efficiency wages, deferred-compensation plans, or promotion tournaments, they might also have a greater need to adopt one or more of these schemes. Owing to sheer size, the argument goes, they find monitoring their employees more difficult and thus must turn to other methods to encourage high levels of effort. One study concluded that the firm-size effect is more related to the presence of efficiency wages than to compensating wage differentials for a demanding work environment.[73]

Review Questions

1. Explain the underlying principle and the necessary conditions for implicit contracts in the labor market to be self-enforcing.

2. The earnings of piece-rate workers usually exceed those of hourly paid workers performing the same tasks. Theory suggests three reasons why. What are they?

3. Suppose that as employment shifts out of manufacturing to the service sector, a higher proportion of workers are employed in small firms. What effect would this growth of employment in small firms have on the types of compensation schemes used to stimulate productivity?

4. Suppose that two pizza restaurants employ drivers whose job is to deliver pizzas to those who order over the phone. One company pays its drivers an hourly wage, and the other pays them by the number of pizzas delivered each day (which can be affected by efforts of drivers to deliver and hurry back for the next order). Which company is more likely to experience higher rates of traffic accidents among its drivers? Why?

5. "The way to get power over workers is to underpay them." Comment.

6. Some real estate brokers split the commission revenues generated by each sale with the responsible agent. Others, however, require their agents to pay *them* (the brokers) money up front and then allow the agents to keep the *entire* commission from each sale they make. Which agents would you predict to have the larger volume of sales—those who split all commissions with their employer or those who pay an up-front fee to their employer and then keep the entire commission? Explain.

7. In recent years, many plants have closed, forcing thousands of workers out of their jobs and into new ones. Studies of wage loss suffered by these displaced workers find that *among groups of workers with the same skills and types of training*, workers who had been with the firm for many years and were in the 55–64 age range had greater wage losses than those in the 25–34 age range. How might a compensation scheme designed to enhance worker motivation lead to this result?

8. Suppose that, in commenting on Japan's system of offering some workers lifetime jobs, an analyst claims that Japanese employers are paying their senior workers more than they are worth. Is this comment consistent with economic theory? Explain.

9. A recent magazine article argued that CEO pay has been moving away from stock options, which are often not closely related to a CEO's performance, and toward bonuses that are more discretionary in nature. Use economic theory to analyze the dual claim that stock options are not closely related to CEO performance and that moving away from them and toward discretionary bonuses will strengthen incentives for CEOs to perform well.

Problems

1. Suppose that the market wage is $10 per hour but that Charlie will work harder if his employer pays him a higher wage. The relationship between Charlie's wage and MRP_L is given in Table 11P.1. What is the efficient wage for Charlie?

Table 11P.1 Charlie's Wage Rate and Marginal Revenue Productivity

Wage ($/hour)	MRP_L ($/hour)
8	12.00
10	16.00
12	19.00
14	20.50
16	22.00
18	23.00
20	24.00
22	24.50
24	25.00
26	25.75

2. A firm is considering adopting a plan in which the company pays employees less than their MRP_L early in their careers and more than their MRP_L late in their careers. For a typical worker at the firm, $MRP_L = 10 + 0.1\ T$, where T = the number of years that the worker has been employed at the firm and MRP_L is measured in dollars per hour. The worker's wage per hour is $W = 8 + 0.2\ T$. Assume that this wage is high enough to attract workers from alternative jobs, that the discount rate for the firm is zero, and that the expected tenure of a typical worker is 35 years. If workers retire after 35 years, will this plan be profitable for the firm? Explain. For how many years will the firm underpay its workers?

3. a. The MRP of labor is given by the following equation: $MRP_0 = 20 - L$, where L = number of workers. If the market wage is $5 per hour, how many workers will the employer want to hire?

   b. The employer now finds that employees will work harder if they are paid a higher wage. If the wage rate paid to the workers is at least $6 per hour, the higher productivity of labor is represented by the new marginal product of labor curve: $MRP_1 = 22 - L$. How many workers would the employer want to hire at $6 per hour?

   c. Use economic theory to explain the change in employment levels associated with paying $6 instead of $5.

4. Suppose that the wage rate paid at a particular firm is $W = 5 + 0.5\ T$, where T = the number of years that the worker has been employed at the firm. The marginal revenue product, which is measured in dollars per hour, is $MRP_L = 6 + 3\ T$. Assume that the wage is high enough to attract workers from alternative jobs.

    a. Ignoring the discounting of future values to the present, graph the wages and MRP_L over a period of 12 years.

    b. Would this pay scheme be more attractive to first, a worker who is looking for stable employment with the same firm for the next 12 years or, second, a worker who plans to move to another geographic area in six years, which would necessitate leaving their job? Explain.

Notes

1. See Kevin F. Hallock, *Pay: Why People Earn What They Earn and What You Can Do Now to Make More* (New York: Cambridge University Press, 2012), for a discussion of how large firms set pay policies and for a discussion of the mix of pay.

2. The productivity of supervisors also varies considerably across individuals; see Edward Lazear, Kathryn L. Shaw, and Christopher Stanton, "The Value of Bosses," *Journal of Labor Economics* 33 (October 2015): 823–861.

3. Evidence shows that employees work harder during recessions; see Edward P. Lazear, Kathryn L. Shaw, and Christopher P. Stanton, "Making Do with Less: Working Harder During Recessions," *Journal of Labor Economics* 34, pt. 2 (January 2016): S333–S360.

4. For a stimulating article from which much of the ensuing discussion draws, see Herbert A. Simon, "Organizations and Markets," *Journal of Economic Perspectives* 5 (Spring 1991): 24–44. For more formal treatment of contracts and incentives, refer to James M. Malcomson, "Contracts, Hold-Up and Labor Markets," *Journal of Economic Literature* 35 (December 1997): 1916–1957; Canice Prendergast, "The Provision of Incentives in Firms," *Journal of Economic Literature* 37 (March 1999): 7–63.

5. This is the most common work relationship, but others, such as the case of gig workers, which brings up interesting additional issues discussed later, also exist. See Lawrence F. Katz and Alan B. Krueger, "The Rise and Nature of Alternative Work Arrangements in the United States, 1995–2015" *Industrial and Labor Relations Review* 72 (March 2019): 382–416.

6. The doctrine of *employment at will*, under which employers (and employees) have the right to terminate an employment relationship at any time, has historically prevailed in the United States. Those not subject to this doctrine in the United States have included unionized

workers with contract provisions governing discharges, tenured teachers, and workers under some civil service systems. A number of state courts also have adopted public policy or implicit contract exceptions to the doctrine. For a discussion of these issues, see Ronald G. Ehrenberg, "Workers' Rights: Rethinking Protective Labor Legislation," in *Rethinking Employment Policy*, eds. Lee Bawden and Felicity Skidmore (Washington, DC: Urban Institute Press, 1989). Some evidence also shows that making the firing of workers less costly for employers increases workers' effort; see Pedro S. Martins, "Dismissals for Cause: The Difference that Just Eight Paragraphs Can Make," *Journal of Labor Economics* 27 (April 2009): 257–279.

7. A famous example of this idea is in Michael Spence, "Job Market Signaling," *Quarterly Journal of Economics* 87 (August 1973): 355–374. For a formal model that uses educational attainment as a signal for innate ability (which is difficult for an employer to observe directly), refer back to Chapter 9. For a thorough review of signaling theory, see John G. Riley, "Silver Signals: Twenty-Five Years of Screening and Signaling," *Journal of Economic Literature* 39 (June 2001): 432–478.

8. See H. Lorne Carmichael, "Self-Enforcing Contracts, Shirking, and Life Cycle Incentives," *Journal of Economic Perspectives* 3 (Fall 1989): 65–84, for a more complete discussion of the importance of self-enforcement to implicit contracting.

9. This section draws heavily on David E. Sappington, "Incentives in Principal – Agent Relationships," *Journal of Economic Perspectives* 5 (Spring 1991): 45–66; George P. Baker, "Incentive Contracts and Performance Measurement," *Journal of Political Economy* 100 (June 1992): 598–614.

10. For a more thorough discussion of this issue, see Canice Prendergast, "What Trade-off of Risk and Incentives?" *American Economic Review* 90 (May 2000): 421–425.

11. An analysis of the two sets of incentive issues discussed in this section can be found in George Baker, "Distortion and Risk in Optimal Incentive Contracts," *Journal of Human Resources* 37 (Fall 2002): 728–751. For a study of the decline of piece-rate compensation in manufacturing, see Susan Helper, Morris M. Kleiner, and Yingchun Wang, "Analyzing Compensation Methods in Manufacturing: Piece Rates, Time Rates, or Gain Sharing?" (Working Paper No. 16540, National Bureau of Economic Research, Cambridge, MA, November 2010).

12. Even in a situation where measuring performance seems trivial—such as on a farm picking cucumbers—most workers are paid for their time; see Kevin F. Hallock, "Lessons in Compensation Design from the Farm," *Workspan* (August 2011): 11–12.

13. For a review of the issue of fairness in pay, including effects of perceived fairness on productivity, see Ernst Fehr, Lorenz Goette, and Christian

Zehnder, "A Behavioral Account of the Labor Market: The Role of Fairness Concerns," *Annual Review of Economics* 1 (September 2009): 355–384. That employee awards conveying status can be effective motivators is shown in Michael Kosfeld and Susanne Neckermann, "Getting More Work for Nothing? Symbolic Awards and Worker Performance," *American Economic Journal: Microeconomics* 3 (August 2011): 86–99. For an examination of worker reactions to supervisor pay, see Zoe Cullen and Ricardo Perez-Truglia, "How Much Does Your Boss Make? The Effects of Salary Comparisons" (Working Paper No. 24841, National Bureau of Economic Research, Cambridge, MA, December 2019).

14. Daniel Kahneman, Jack L. Knetsch, and Richard Thaler, "Fairness as a Constraint on Profit-Seeking: Entitlements in the Market," *American Economic Review* 76 (September 1986): 728–741. Another study found that the prospect of *losing a bonus that had already been received* is a more powerful motivator than gaining a future bonus; see Roland G. Fryer, Jr., Steven Levitt, John List, and Sally Sadoff, "Enhancing the Efficacy of Teacher Incentives Through Loss Aversion" (Working Paper No. 18237, National Bureau of Economic Research, Cambridge, MA, July 2012).

15. One study found that workers were over 5 percent more productive during World War II and over 9 percent more productive in industries directly related to the war effort; see Mark Bils and Yongsung Chang, "Wages and the Allocation of Hours and Effort" (Working Paper No. 7309, National Bureau of Economic Research, August 1999). For other considerations of altruistic behavior among workers, see Simon, "Organizations and Markets," 34–38; Julio J. Rotemberg, "Human Relations in the Workplace," *Journal of Political Economy* 102 (August 1994): 684–717.

16. See Roland Bénabou and Jean Tirole, "Bonus Culture: Competitive Pay, Screening and Multitasking," *Journal of Political Economy* 124 (April 2016): 305–370.

17. As noted earlier, firms can more easily handle such fluctuations. For more on this, see Chinhui Juhn, Kristine McCue, Holly Monti, and Brooks Pierce, "Firm Performance and the Volatility of Worker Earnings," *Journal of Labor Economics* 36:S1 (January 2018): s99–s131.

18. Edward P. Lazear, "Performance Pay and Productivity," *American Economic Review* 90 (December 2000): 1346–1361. Similar effects of performance pay on sorting are found in Thomas Dohmen and Armin Falk, "Performance Pay and Multidimensional Sorting: Productivity, Preferences, and Gender," *American Economic Review* 101 (April 2011): 556–590.

19. Eric Seiler, "Piece Rate vs. Time Rate: The Effect of Incentives on Earnings," *Review of Economics and Statistics* 66 (August 1984): 363–376. For a later study that was able to control for unobserved differences between workers and firms, see Tuomas Pekkarinen and Chris Riddell,

"Performance Pay and Earnings: Evidence from Personnel Records," *Industrial and Labor Relations Review* 61 (April 2008): 297–319.

20. Bruce Shearer, "Piece Rates, Fixed Wages and Incentives: Evidence from a Field Experiment," *Review of Economic Studies* 71 (April 2004): 513–534. Increasing piece rates also increases effort; see M. Ryan Haley, "The Response of Worker Effort to Piece Rates: Evidence from the Midwest Logging Industry," *Journal of Human Resources* 38 (Fall 2003): 881–890.

21. Ann P. Bartel, Brianna Cardiff-Hicks, and Kathryn Shaw, "Incentives for Lawyers: Moving Away from 'Eat What You Kill,'" *Industrial and Labor Relations Review* 70 (March 2017): 336–358; Robert Gibbons, "Incentives in Organizations," *Journal of Economic Perspectives* 12 (Fall 1998): 115–132; Fuhai Hong, Tanjim Hossain, John A. List, and Migiwa Tanaka, "Testing the Theory of Multitasking: Evidence from a Natural Field Experiment in Chinese Factories," *Journal of Economic Behavior and Organization* 118 (October 2015): 372–382; Omar Al-Ubaydli, Steffen Andersen, Uri Gneezy, and John A. List, "Carrots that Look Like Sticks: Toward an Understanding of Multitasking Incentive Schemes," *Southern Economic Journal* 81 (January 2015): 538–561. For a discussion of "gaming" induced by piece rates (i.e., engaging in behaviors that increase the *measure* upon which pay is based, but not actually increasing output), see Pascal Courty and Gerald Marschke, "An Empirical Investigation of Gaming Responses to Explicit Performance Incentives," *Journal of Labor Economics* 22 (January 2004): 23–56.

22. Barton H. Hamilton, Jack A. Nickerson, and Hideo Owan, "Team Incentives and Worker Heterogeneity: An Empirical Analysis of the Impact of Teams on Productivity and Participation," *Journal of Political Economy* 111 (June 2003): 465–497; Helper, Kleiner, and Wang, "Analyzing Compensation Methods in Manufacturing: Piece Rates, Time Rates, or Gain Sharing?"

23. For a review of the literature on productivity in worker-owned or worker-managed firms, see Joseph R. Blasi, Richard B. Freeman, and Douglas C. Kruse, "What Does the U.S. Research Show About Worker Ownership?" in *Oxford University Press Handbook of Mutual, Co-Operative and Co-Owned Business*, Jonathan Michie, Joseph Blasi, and Carlo Borzaga, eds. (Oxford: Oxford University Press, 2017): 211–226; James B. Rebitzer, "Radical Political Economy and the Economics of Labor Markets," *Journal of Economic Literature* 31 (September 1993): 1405–1409.

24. For a more in-depth analysis of this problem, see Haig R. Nalbantian, "Incentive Contracts in Perspective," in *Incentives, Cooperation, and Risk Sharing*, ed. Haig R. Nalbantian (Totowa, NJ: Rowman & Littlefield, 1987); Eugene Kandel and Edward Lazear, "Peer Pressure and Partnerships," *Journal of Political Economy* 100 (August 1992): 801–817. For an analysis of peer pressure as a way of overcoming the

free-rider problem, see Alexandre Mas and Enrico Moretti, "Peers at Work," *American Economic Review* 99 (March 2009): 112–145. For an example of peers working together in athletics, see Peter Arcidiacono, Josh Kinsler, and Joseph Price, "Productivity Spillovers in Team Production: Evidence from Professional Basketball," *Journal of Labor Economics* 35 (January 2017): 191–225.

25. Gujido Friebel, Matthias Heinz, Miriam Krueger, and Nikolay Zubanov, "Team Incentives and Performance: Evidence from a Retail Chain," *American Economic Review* 107 (August 2017): 2168–2203; Thomas Cornelissen, Christian Dustmann, and Uta Schönberg, "Peer Effects in the Workplace," *American Economic Review* 107 (February 2017): 425–456; Brent Boning, Casey Ichniowski, and Kathryn Shaw, "Opportunity Counts: Teams and the Effectiveness of Production Incentives," *Journal of Labor Economics* 25 (October 2007): 613–650; Douglas Kruse, Joseph Blasi, and Richard Freeman, "Does Linking Worker Pay to Firm Performance Help the Best Firms Do Even Better?" (Working Paper No. 17745, National Bureau of Economic Research, Cambridge, MA, January 2012); Richard J. Long and Tony Fang, "Do Employers Profit from Profit Sharing? Evidence from Canadian Panel Data," *Industrial and Labor Relations Review* 65 (October 2012): 899–927.

26. As noted in Chapter 3's discussion of the demand for labor under monopoly, executives can buy some peace and quiet on the job by forgoing profit maximization when possible. For an example, see Marianne Bertrand and Sendhil Mullainathan, "Is There Discretion in Wage Setting? A Test Using Takeover Legislation," *RAND Journal of Economics* 30 (Autumn 1999): 535–554. For a more technical paper on executive pay, see Alex Edmans and Xavier Gabaix, "Executive Compensation: A Modern Primer," *Journal of Economic Literature* 54 (December 2016): 1232–1287.

27. See Marianne Bertrand and Sendhil Mullainathan, "Are CEOs Rewarded for Luck? The Ones Without Principals Are," *The Quarterly Journal of Economics* 116 (August 2001): 901–932.

28. See, for example, Gene Sperling, "Opening Statement Before the U.S. House of Representatives Committee on Financial Services," June 11, 2009, www.treas.gov/press/releases/tg166.htm.

29. John M. Abowd and David S. Kaplan, "Executive Compensation: Six Questions That Need Answering," *Journal of Economic Perspectives* 13 (Fall 1999): 145–168. For other reviews of issues with CEO pay, see Marianne Bertrand, "CEOs," *Annual Review of Economics* 1 (September 2009): 121–150; Carola Frydman and Raven E. Saks, "Executive Compensation: A New View from a Long-Term Perspective, 1936–2005," *Review of Financial Studies* 23 (May 2010): 2099–2138; Brian D. Bell and John Van Reenen, "Extreme Wage Inequality: Pay at the Very Top," *American Economic Review Papers and Proceedings* 103

(May 2013): 153–157; Kevin F. Hallock, "CEO Pay Mix," *Workspan* (September 2013): 12–13.

30. Brian J. Hall and Jeffrey B. Liebman, "Are CEOs Really Paid Like Bureaucrats?" *Quarterly Journal of Economics* 113 (August 1998): 653–691.

31. Abowd and Kaplan, "Executive Compensation," 158–159.

32. See Wolfgang Keller and William W. Olney, "Globalization and Executive Compensation" (Working Paper No. 23384, National Bureau of Economic Research, Cambridge, MA, June 2018); Edmans and Gabaix, "Executive Compensation: A Modern Primer"; Xavier Gabaix, Augustin Landier, and Julien Sauvagnat, "CEO Pay and Firm Size: An Update After the Crisis," *Economic Journal* 124 (February 2014): F40–F59; Bertrand, "CEOs"; Kevin J. Murphy and Tatiana Sandino, "Executive Pay and 'Independent' Compensation Consultants," *Journal of Accounting and Economics* 49 (April 2010): 247–262.

33. Kevin F. Hallock, "Nothing Lasts Forever: A Different Way to Structure Severance," *Workspan* (January 2012): 12–13.

34. For a study indicating that subjective evaluations can enhance performance, see Eric S. Taylor and John H. Tyler, "The Effect of Evaluation on Teacher Performance," *American Economic Review* 102 (December 2012): 3628–3651.

35. Robert Drago and Gerald T. Garvey, "Incentives for Helping on the Job: Theory and Evidence," *Journal of Labor Economics* 16 (January 1998): 1–25.

36. Paul Milgrom, "Employment Contracts, Influence Activities, and Efficient Organization Design," *Journal of Political Economy* 96 (February 1988): 42–60; Canice Prendergast, "A Theory of 'Yes Men,'" *American Economic Review* 83 (September 1993): 757–770. For a theoretical analysis incorporating the important element of trust between workers and supervisors, see George Baker, Robert Gibbons, and Kevin J. Murphy, "Subjective Performance Measures in Optimal Incentive Contracts," *Quarterly Journal of Economics* 109 (November 1994): 1125–1156.

37. Although we discuss individually the tools that can be used to motivate workers—incentive pay, supervision, stock ownership, or profit sharing, for example—they should all be seen as part of a firm's system for motivating its workers. For example, see Casey Ichniowski and Kathryn Shaw, "Beyond Incentive Pay: Insiders' Estimates of the Value of Complementary Human Resource Management Practices," *Journal of Economic Perspectives* 17 (Winter 2003): 155–180.

38. Stephen G. Bronars and Melissa Famulari, "Wage, Tenure, and Wage Growth Variation Within and Across Establishments," *Journal of Labor Economics* 15 (April 1997): 285–317.

39. This assertion is based on what psychologists call equity theory. For works by economists that employ this theory, see George A. Akerlof and

Janet Yellen, "The Fair Wage—Effort Hypothesis and Unemployment," *Quarterly Journal of Economics* 105 (May 1990): 255–283; Robert M. Solow, *The Labor Market as a Social Institution* (Cambridge, MA: Basil Blackwell, 1990).

40. Patrick Kline, Neviana Petkova, Heidi Williams, and Owen Zidar, "Who Profits from Patents? Rent-Sharing at Innovative Firms," *Quarterly Journal of Economics* 134 (August 2019): 1343–1404, finds that firms awarded high-value patents share their gains with high-skilled workers who have been with them the longest (in an effort to retain their services). For another study indicating a link between profits and wages, see Andrew K.G. Hildreth and Andrew J. Oswald, "Rent-Sharing and Wages: Evidence from Company and Establishment Panels," *Journal of Labor Economics* 15 (April 1997): 318–337.

41. The "efficiency wage" refers to all forms of compensation, not just cash wages. Lawrence Katz, "Efficiency Wage Theories: A Partial Evaluation," in *NBER Macroeconomics Annual, 1986*, ed. Stanley Fischer (Cambridge, MA: MIT Press, 1986); Joseph E. Stiglitz, "The Causes and Consequences of the Dependence of Quality on Price," *Journal of Economic Literature* 25 (March 1987): 1–48; and Kevin M. Murphy and Robert H. Topel, "Efficiency Wages Reconsidered: Theory and Evidence," in *Advances in Theory and Measurement of Unemployment*, eds. Yoram Weiss and Gideon Fishelson (London: Macmillan, 1990), offer detailed analyses of efficiency-wage theories.

42. Janet Yellen, "Efficiency Wage Models of Unemployment," *American Economic Review* 74 (May 1984): 200–208; Andrew Weiss, *Efficiency Wages: Models of Unemployment, Layoffs, and Wage Dispersion* (Princeton, NJ: Princeton University Press, 1990).

43. Richard Thaler, "Anomalies: Interindustry Wage Differentials," *Journal of Economic Perspectives* 3 (Spring 1989): 181–193; Surendra Gera and Gilles Grenier, "Interindustry Wage Differentials and Efficiency Wages: Some Canadian Evidence," *Canadian Journal of Economics* 27 (February 1994): 81–100; Paul Chen and Per-Anders Edin, "Efficiency Wages and Industry Wage Differentials: A Comparison Across Methods of Pay," *Review of Economics and Statistics* 84 (November 2002): 617–631.

44. Alan B. Krueger, "Ownership, Agency and Wages: An Examination of Franchising in the Fast Food Industry," *Quarterly Journal of Economics* 106 (February 1991): 75–101; Erica L. Groshen and Alan B. Krueger, "The Structure of Supervision and Pay in Hospitals," *Industrial and Labor Relations Review* 43 (February 1990): 134S–146S; Carl M. Campbell III, "Do Firms Pay Efficiency Wages? Evidence with Data at the Firm Level," *Journal of Labor Economics* 11 (July 1993): 442–470; Bradley T. Ewing and James E. Payne, "The Trade-Off Between Supervision and Wages: Evidence of Efficiency Wages from the NLSY," *Southern Economic Journal* 66 (October 1999): 424–432; Bjorn Bartling, Ernst Fehr, and Klaus M. Schmidt, "Screening, Competition, and

Job Design: Economic Origins of Good Jobs," *American Economic Review* 102 (April 2012): 834–864.

45. Peter Cappelli and Keith Chauvin, "An Interplant Test of the Efficiency Wage Hypothesis," *Quarterly Journal of Economics* 106 (August 1991): 769–787; Jozef Konings and Patrick P. Walsh, "Evidence of Efficiency Wage Payments in U.K. Firm Level Panel Data," *Economic Journal* 104 (May 1994): 542–555.

46. Our discussion here draws on Edward Lazear, "Why Is There Mandatory Retirement?" *Journal of Political Economy* 87 (December 1979): 1261–1284. For a review of issues raised in this and succeeding sections, see Carmichael, "Self-Enforcing Contracts, Shirking, and Life Cycle Incentives." Also see Steffen Huck, Andrew J. Seltzer, and Brian Wallace, "Deferred Compensation in Multiperiod Labor Contracts: An Experimental Test of Lazear's Model," *American Economic Review* 101 (April 2011): 819–843.

47. The lower turnover rate among workers who have been promised larger pensions upon retirement is apparently mostly the result of self-selection, not the threat of lost pension wealth; see Steven G. Allen, Robert L. Clark, and Ann A. McDermed, "Pensions, Bonding, and Lifetime Jobs," *Journal of Human Resources* 28 (Summer 1993): 463–481.

48. This gives rise to the question in the title of Edward Lazear, "Why Is There Mandatory Retirement?" *Journal of Political Economy* 87 (December 1979): 1261–1284.

49. Workers over age 40 are also protected by the Age Discrimination in Employment Act: www.eeoc.gov/age-discrimination.

50. Edward Lazear, "Pensions as Severance Pay," in *Financial Aspects of the United States Pension System*, eds. Zvi Bodie and John Shoven (Chicago, IL: University of Chicago Press, 1983). Since this study, an enormous move away from "defined benefit" and toward "defined contribution" plans has taken place; see Chapter 5.

51. Robert Hutchens, "A Test of Lazear's Theory of Delayed Payment Contracts," *Journal of Labor Economics* 5:4, pt. 2 (October 1987): S153–S170. For a consideration of how age-discrimination laws affect delayed-payment pay plans, see David Neumark and Wendy A. Stock, "Age Discrimination Laws and Labor Market Efficiency," *Journal of Political Economy* 107 (October 1999): 1081–1125.

52. George Baker and Bengt Holmstrom, "Internal Labor Markets: Too Many Theories, Too Few Facts," *American Economic Review* 85 (May 1995): 255–259.

53. Michael L. Bognanno, "Corporate Tournaments," *Journal of Labor Economics* 19 (April 2001): 290–315. The growth of tournaments in a variety of economic sectors, and the social disadvantages of huge gains tied to what might be small relative differences in productivity, are

accessibly analyzed in Robert H. Frank and Philip J. Cook, *The Winner-Take-All Society* (New York: Free Press, 1995).

54. Bognanno, "Corporate Tournaments," 299 (adjusted for inflation).

55. For a paper that analyzes the criteria that firms set for winning a tournament in the context of stimulating effort among executives while discouraging them from undertaking programs that place the firm at excessive risk, see Hans K. Hvide, "Tournament Rewards and Risk Taking," *Journal of Labor Economics* 20 (October 2002): 877–898.

56. For a paper that attempts to separate the "sorting" effects of tournaments from the incentive effects on individual performance, see Bentley Coffey and M.T. Maloney, "The Thrill of Victory: Measuring the Incentive to Win," *Journal of Labor Economics* 28 (January 2010): 87–112.

57. Rachel Croson and Uri Gneezy, "Gender Differences in Preferences," *Journal of Economic Literature* 47 (June 2009): 448–474; Victor Lavy, "Gender Differences in Market Competitiveness in a Real Workplace: Evidence from Performance-Based Pay Tournaments Among Teachers," *Economic Journal* 123 (June 2013): 540–573.

58. Jeffrey Carpenter, Peter Hans Matthews, and John Schirm, "Tournaments and Office Politics: Evidence from a Real Effort Experiment," *American Economic Review* 100 (March 2010): 504–517.

59. Alan Benson, Danielle Li, and Kelly Shue, "Promotions and the Peter Principle," *Quarterly Journal of Economics* 134 (November 2019): 2085–2134.

60. When workers' current employers can observe their true productive characteristics better than outsiders can, outsiders (i.e., other employers) wanting to make "talent raids" might reasonably infer who are the most valuable employees from observing who is promoted. Thus, promotion itself sends information to other employers, which might help the employee who is promoted but harm their current employer. Several papers have addressed this issue, among which are Dan Bernhardt, "Strategic Promotion and Compensation," *Review of Economic Studies* 62 (April 1995): 315–339; Derek Laing, "Involuntary Layoffs in a Model with Asymmetric Information Concerning Worker Ability," *Review of Economic Studies* 61 (April 1994): 375–392.

61. Robert Gibbons and Kevin J. Murphy, "Optimal Incentive Contracts in the Presence of Career Concerns: Theory and Evidence," *Journal of Political Economy* 100 (June 1992): 468–505.

62. Gibbons and Murphy, "Optimal Incentive Contracts in the Presence of Career Concerns."

63. A review of this puzzle and the early empirical work on it can be found in Robert Hutchens, "Seniority, Wages, and Productivity: A Turbulent Decade," *Journal of Economic Perspectives* 3 (Fall 1989): 49–64. For the effects of seniority pay on hiring behavior, see Thomas Zwick,

"Consequences of Seniority Wages on the Employment Structure," *Industrial and Labor Relations Review* 65 (January 2012): 108–125.

64. A variant of this third explanation is that employers offer rising wage profiles because employees *prefer* them. In Robert H. Frank and Robert M. Hutchens, "Wages, Seniority, and the Demand for Rising Consumption Profiles," *Journal of Economic Behavior and Organization* 21 (August 1993): 251–276, the authors argue that employees' utility is in part a function of their wage *increases* (not only their wage level). Therefore, to be competitive in the labor market, employers are induced to offer them wage profiles that start lower and rise faster than they otherwise would.

65. For a study that did have productivity data, see Judith K. Hellerstein and David Neumark, "Are Earnings Profiles Steeper Than Productivity Profiles? Evidence from Israeli Firm-Level Data," *Journal of Human Resources* 30 (Winter 1995): 89–112.

66. Edward P. Lazear and Robert L. Moore, "Incentives, Productivity, and Labor Contracts," *Quarterly Journal of Economics* 99 (May 1984): 275–296; Hutchens, "A Test of Lazear's Theory of Delayed Payment Contracts."

67. James N. Brown, "Why Do Wages Increase with Tenure?" *American Economic Review* 79 (December 1989): 971–991. For somewhat-similar studies, see Sheldon E. Haber and Robert S. Goldfarb, "Does Salaried Status Affect Human Capital Accumulation?" *Industrial and Labor Relations Review* 48 (January 1995): 322–337; David Neumark and Paul Taubman, "Why Do Wage Profiles Slope Upward? Tests of the General Human Capital Model," *Journal of Labor Economics* 13 (October 1995): 736–761; Erling Barth, "Firm-Specific Seniority and Wages," *Journal of Labor Economics* 15:3, pt. 1 (July 1997): 495–506.

68. For a relevant study, see Brianna Cardiff-Hicks, Francine Lafontaine, and Kathryn Shaw, "Do Large Modern Retailers Pay Premium Wages?" *Industrial and Labor Relations Review* 68 (May 2015): 633–665.

69. For studies that try to distinguish between the two factors, see Rudolf Winter-Ebmer and Josef Zweimüller, "Firm-Size Differentials in Switzerland: Evidence from Job Changers," *American Economic Review* 89 (May 1999): 89–93; John M. Abowd and Francis Kramarz, "Inter-Industry and Firm-Size Wage Differentials: New Evidence from Linked Employer–Employee Data," Cornell University, School of Industrial and Labor Relations Institute for Labor Market Policies, July 2000.

70. Kevin T. Reilly, "Human Capital and Information: The Employer Size – Wage Effect," *Journal of Human Resources* 30 (Winter 1995): 1–18; Dan A. Black, Brett J. Noel, and Zheng Wang, "On-the-Job Training, Establishment Size, and Firm Size: Evidence for Economies of Scale in the Production of Human Capital," *Southern Economic Journal* 66 (July 1999): 82–100.

71. For some evidence along the lines of this argument, see James B. Rebitzer and Lowell J. Taylor, "Efficiency Wages and Employment Rents: The Employer Size – Wage Effect in the Job Market for Lawyers," *Journal of Labor Economics* 13 (October 1995): 678–708.

72. Todd L. Idson and Walter Y. Oi, "Workers Are More Productive in Large Firms," *American Economic Review* 89 (May 1999): 104–107.

73. David Fairris and Lee J. Alston, "Wages and the Intensity of Labor Effort: Efficiency Wages Versus Compensating Payments," *Southern Economic Journal* 61 (July 1994): 149–160. An extensive review of papers on both the "monitoring" and the "compensating differentials" explanations can be found in Rebitzer, "Radical Political Economy and the Economics of Labor Markets," 1417–1419.

Selected Readings

Akerlof, George A., and Janet L. Yellen, eds. *Efficiency Wage Models of the Labor Market*. New York: Cambridge University Press, 1986.

Bertrand, Marianne. "CEOs." *Annual Review of Economics* 1 (September 2009): 121–150.

Carmichael, H. Lorne. "Self-Enforcing Contracts, Shirking, and Life Cycle Incentives." *Journal of Economic Perspectives* 3 (Fall 1989): 65–84.

Frank, Robert H., and Philip J. Cook. *The Winner-Take-All Society*. New York: Free Press, 1995.

Gibbons, Robert. "Incentives in Organizations." *Journal of Economic Perspectives* 12 (Fall 1998): 115–132.

Hallock, Kevin F. *Pay: Why People Earn What They Earn and What You Can Do Now to Make More*. New York: Cambridge University Press, 2012.

Lazear, Edward P. "Compensation and Incentives in the Workplace." *Journal of Economic Perspectives* 32 (Summer 2018): 195–214.

Lazear, Edward P., and Kathryn L. Shaw. "Personnel Economics: The Economist's View of Human Resources." *Journal of Economic Perspectives* 21 (Fall 2007): 91–114.

Sappington, David E. "Incentives in Principal–Agent Relationships." *Journal of Economic Perspectives* 5 (Spring 1991): 45–66.

Simon, Herbert A. "Organizations and Markets." *Journal of Economic Perspectives* 5 (Spring 1991): 24–44.

Gender, Race, and Ethnicity in the Labor Market

The U.S. labor force has gone through a period of remarkable demographic change in recent decades. Some forces for change have been rooted in the different expectations of women regarding the balance between household work and market work. Other forces for change have arisen from immigration, both documented and undocumented, and from different birth rates among racial/ethnic groups. The result has been a pronounced and continuing change in the mix of groups in the labor force.

Table 12.1 contains both changes occurring from 1990 to 2018 and projections that are foreseeable by the year 2028. White workers constituted about 78 percent of the labor force in 1990 and roughly 62 percent by 2018, and their share is projected to fall to below 60 percent by 2028. The share of women in the labor force is steadily rising, as are the shares of those who identify as Black or Asian, and the share of those who identify as

Table 12.1 Shares of the Civilian Labor Force for Major Demographic Groups: 1990, 2000, 2010, 2018, 2028

	Year				
	1990 (%)	2000 (%)	2010 (%)	2018 (%)	2028 (%)
					(projected)
White (non-Hispanic)	77.7	72.0	67.5	62.1	56.9
Female (all races)	45.2	46.5	46.7	46.9	47.6
Black (all genders)	10.9	11.5	11.6	12.6	13.0
Asian (all genders)[a]	3.7	4.4	4.7	6.3	7.3
Hispanic (all races, all genders)	8.5	11.7	14.8	17.5	20.9

[a] This includes Alaskan Natives and Pacific Islanders.

Source: Mitra Toossi, "Labor Force Projections to 2024: The Labor Force Is Growing, but Slowly," *Monthly Labor Review* (December 8, 2015): Table 1, at www.bls.gov/opub/mlr/2015/article/labor-force-projections-to-2024.htm; Mitra Toossi, "Civilian Labor Force, by Age, Sex, Race, and Ethnicity," at www.bls.gov/emp/tables/civilian-labor-force-summary.htm

Hispanic is rising quickly—from 8.5 percent in 1990 to almost 18 percent in 2018.

For full-time workers, with the exception of Asian Americans, the groups in the labor force that are growing as a fraction of the labor force are those whose members earn substantially less, on average, than white men. A glance at Figure 12.1 suggests that as of 2018, none of the non-Asian groups with rapid growth rates averaged more than 73 percent of white male earnings for full-time work. In contrast, Asian American men had average earnings for full-time work that were 7 percent above the average for white men.

The growing numerical significance of demographic groups whose members are relatively poorly paid has heightened interest in understanding the sources of earnings differences across groups. The purpose of this chapter is to analyze such differences, paying special attention to the topic of labor market discrimination.

Measured and Unmeasured Sources of Earnings Differences

This section focuses on explaining the earnings differentials for three of the larger (and partially overlapping) groups whose members have been targeted by government policy as potential victims of employment discrimination: those who are female, Black, or Hispanic. The focus is on these groups because data and studies are more readily available for them than for groups defined by such characteristics as disability or sexual orientation.[1] We analyze *earnings* rather than total *compensation* (which would be preferable) for the practical reason that data on the value of employee benefits are not generally available by demographic group.[2]

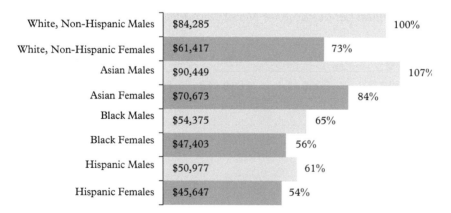

Figure 12.1 Mean Earnings as a Percentage of White Male Earnings, Various Demographic Groups, Full-Time Workers Over 24 Years Old, 2018

Source: Data in this figure are from U.S. Bureau of the Census, "Historical Income Tables: People," Table P-39, at www.census.gov/data/tables/timeseries/demo/income-poverty/historical-income-people.html

In examining earnings across demographic groups, we compare the earnings of people who (as in Figure 12.1) *worked full time, year-round*. Earnings differences among workers employed full time during the entire year are driven mainly (but not entirely) by differences in *wage rates*, and explaining differences in wage rates is the main focus of this chapter. However, by comparing only the pay of full-time workers, we overlook the large effects on *hours* of work caused by both part-time work and unemployment during the year—differences that we also need to take account of when analyzing the topic of discrimination.[3]

Earnings Differences by Gender

If we combine all races and ethnic groups, women over the age of 15 who worked full time earned an average of 76 percent of what men earned in the year 2018. This percentage is higher than the 59 percent observed in 1980 and the 66 percent in 1990.[4] Understanding the sources of this difference is critical to determining which policies, if any, might be needed to address the gap in pay.[5]

Age and Education   The first step in analyzing earnings differentials is to think of potential *sources* of difference, many of which can be measured. We know from Chapter 9 that two important and measurable factors that influence earnings are education and age (which is correlated with potential labor market experience). While the most recent cohorts of women have levels of schooling at least equal to those of men, the same cannot be said of older cohorts. Moreover, we also know that age–earnings profiles for women are flatter than those for men, especially for college-educated people. Therefore, we would expect that controlling for age and education would account for at least some of the female/male differences in earnings.

The data in Table 12.2, which categorizes women and men by age and education, suggest that, as expected, female–male earnings ratios tend to fall with age for college-educated people. Even for the youngest cohort of women in the table, however, these ratios are so low (0.82 is the highest) that we must look elsewhere for a complete explanation of the female/male earnings difference.

Occupation   A measurable factor that could help explain female–male earnings ratios is occupation. As can be seen in Table 12.3, women and men are not equally represented in many occupations; thus, if women are overrepresented in low-paying occupations and underrepresented in high-paying ones, some of the gender pay differentials would be the result of different occupational distributions. Moreover, as Table 12.3 establishes, even in the *same* occupations, women earn less than men do—a fact suggesting that hours of work or years of experience in one's occupation must be considered.

Table 12.2 Female Earnings as a Percentage of Male Earnings, by Age and Education, Full-Time Workers, 2018

Age	High school graduate (%)	Bachelor's degree (%)	Master's degree (%)
25–34	70	82	72
35–44	71	77	73
45–54	70	67	68
55–64	74	69	61

Source: U.S. Bureau of the Census, *Current Population Survey Tables for Personal Income*, Personal Income: PINC-03, 2018, at www.census.gov/data/tables/time-series/demo/income-poverty/cps-pinc/pinc-03.html

Table 12.3 Female–Male Earnings Ratios and Percentages of Female Jobholders, Full-Time Wage and Salary Workers, by Selected High- and Low-Paying Occupations, 2018

	Percentage Female in Occupation	Female-to-Male Earnings Ratio
*High-paying**		
Computer systems managers	25	0.90
Lawyers	40	0.80
Pharmacists	63	0.83
*Low-paying**		
Cashiers	73	0.99
Cooks	39	0.84
Food preparation	56	0.92

*High-paying occupations are those in which women earned more than $1,500 per week in 2018; "low paying" ones are those in which men earned less than $520 per week.

Hours and Experience   Within occupations, earnings are affected by one's *weekly hours* of work and one's *years of experience*. We saw in Chapter 9 that women average fewer hours of market work per week than do men in the same occupation. In putting aside the effects of part-time employment by focusing on those working full time, Table 9.2 indicates that women in given occupations average 1 percent to 5 percent fewer hours per week than do men. Because salaried workers also might receive a compensating wage differential for longer hours of work,[6] some of the earnings differentials in Table 12.3 could well be associated with fewer hours of work among women.

Analyses suggest that within occupations, women typically have less (and sometimes-interrupted) work experience and are less likely to be promoted.[7] One study of those who graduated with a master's of business administration (MBA) degree from the same highly ranked business school, for example, found that women earned about the same as men immediately after graduation, but after 10–16 years had passed, they earned 45 percent less. Almost one-third of this difference at 10–16 years was associated with fewer current hours of work, and another third was associated with less accumulated experience (women in the sample had fewer total months of experience in those years and more months of *part-time* work than did their male counterparts).[8] Given the primary role that women have typically played in child-rearing, much of this "experience gap" can be attributed to childcare and other family responsibilities.[9] Indeed, another study reported that in 1991, among all women working at age 30, those who were mothers earned 23 percent less than 30-year-old men, while those who were not mothers earned 10 percent less.[10]

Unexplained Differences   Clearly, controlling for occupation, education, age, experience, and hours of work probably goes a long way toward explaining earnings differentials by gender, and other measurable variables added to this list could explain some of the rest. However, some differences could remain unexplained even if all measurable factors were included in our analysis. If so, the remaining gap can be explained in two ways. One is that these remaining differences are the result of characteristics affecting productivity that might differ by gender but *cannot be observed* by the researcher (e.g., the relative priorities that individual men and individual women assign to market and household activities, if the two conflict). Alternatively, the unexplained differential could be interpreted as resulting from *discriminatory treatment* in the labor market. For example, a recent study found that in financial advising firms in which managers were predominantly men, female financial advisers were 20 percent more likely than male advisers to be fired for misconduct, even though their transgressions were 20 percent less costly.[11] (See Example 12.1 for an illustration of discriminatory behavior against women in symphony orchestras.)

EXAMPLE 12.1

Bias in the Selection of Musicians by Symphony Orchestras

Symphony orchestras contain about 100 musicians who must audition in front of a selection committee consisting of the conductor and some orchestra members. Before 1970, nearly all orchestras had auditions in which the identity of each candidate was known by the committee. This process favored men—particularly those who were students of a select group of teachers—with the result that only 10 percent of newly hired orchestra members were women. By the 1990s, some 35 percent of new hires were women. What can account for this change?

Although the relative pool of female musicians likely rose during this period, another significant change occurred. Throughout the 1970s and 1980s, most orchestras adopted a selection process that concealed behind a screen those auditioning from the selection committee so that the identity and gender of the candidates could not be discovered. The fact that orchestras adopted these "blind" procedures at different times allows us to estimate the separate effects of these procedures, and one careful study found that about one-third of the 25 percent increase in the hiring of women could be traced to blind auditioning. Put differently, the findings suggest that if the gender of a candidate were known to selection committees, the percentage of women hired would be lower by about 8 percent (27 percent instead of 35 percent).

Source: Claudia Goldin and Cecilia Rouse, "Orchestrating Impartiality: The Impact of 'Blind' Auditions on Female Musicians," *American Economic Review* 90 (September 2000): 715–741

Defining Discrimination   Labor market discrimination occurs if individual workers who have *identical productive characteristics* are treated differently because of the demographic groups to which they belong. Put differently, the average wage differentials that we observe between demographic groups result from, first, differences in the productive characteristics with which the groups enter the labor market (often termed *premarket differences*) and, second, differences in the way the groups are treated by actors *within* the labor market. Differential treatment within the labor market is what we term *labor market discrimination*.

Gender discrimination in the labor market is alleged to take two prominent forms. First, employers are sometimes suspected of paying women less than men who have the same experience and who work under the same conditions in the same occupations; this is termed *wage discrimination*. Second, women with the same education and productive potential are seen as shunted into lower-paying occupations or levels of responsibility by employers who reserve the higher-paying jobs for men. This latter form of discrimination has been termed *occupational discrimination*.

Wage Discrimination   Basic to the concept of labor market discrimination is that workers' wages are a function of both their *productive characteristics* (their human capital, the size of the firm for which they work, and so on) and the *price* that each characteristic commands in the labor market. Thus, economic theory suggests that the wages of women and those of men might differ because of differences in their levels of job experience, for example, or they might differ because men and women are compensated differently for each added year of experience. *Wage discrimination is present when the prices paid by employers for given productive characteristics are systematically different for different demographic groups.* In other words, if men and women (or other demographic groups) with equal productive characteristics are paid unequally, even in the same occupations, then wage discrimination is occurring.

Occupational Discrimination   Critical to a worker's human capital are the occupational preparation and skills acquired through schooling, job training, and experience. Women and men have different occupational distributions, but proving occupational *segregation* is a lot easier than proving occupational *discrimination*.

Occupational segregation can be said to occur when the distribution of occupations in one demographic group is different from the distribution in another. With regard to gender, occupational segregation is reflected in the existence of female-dominated occupations and male-dominated ones. If occupational choices are directly limited or if they are influenced by lower payoffs to given human-capital characteristics, then occupational segregation certainly reflects labor market discrimination. If, however, these choices reflect different preferences or different household responsibilities (particularly related to childcare), then two arguments can be made. One is that no particular problem is present, that occupational preferences—including those toward household work—form naturally from one's experiences and should be respected in a market economy. The other view is that these preferences are the result of *premarket discrimination*—differential treatment by parents, schools, and society at large that points girls toward lower-paying (including household) pursuits long before they reach adulthood and enter the labor market.

We now turn to issues of measuring occupational segregation and wage discrimination. In both cases, we discuss the available measures and then briefly discuss the extent to which they can be said to accurately reflect discriminatory treatment.

Measurement: Occupational Segregation   As seen in Table 12.3, women and men are not equally represented in the various occupations. Although dramatic changes have occurred in recent decades, some evidence shows that women are still underrepresented in higher-paying jobs and overrepresented in lower-paying ones. Various measures are used to summarize the inequality of gender representation across detailed occupational categories, all of which are based on comparing the existing distribution of men and women in occupations with the distribution that would exist if assignment to occupations were random with regard to gender.[12]

One measure is the *index of dissimilarity*. Assuming that workers of one gender remain in their jobs, this index indicates the percentage of the other gender that would have to change occupations for the two genders to have equal occupational distributions. If all occupations were completely segregated, the index would equal 100, whereas if men and women were equally distributed across occupations, it would equal zero. Analyses of gender-related employment patterns in some 500 narrowly defined occupations suggest that the index of dissimilarity has declined from 64.5 in 1970, to 58.4 in 1980, to 54.1 in 1990, to 52.0 in 2000, and to 51.0 in 2009.[13]

Despite a decline in occupational segregation, studies generally find that its effects on women's wages are substantial. If U.S. women with given educational attainment and experience levels were in the same occupations and industries as their male counterparts, estimates suggest that their wages would rise by as much as 3 percent to 10 percent.[14]

As noted earlier, however, not all gender segregation is the result of labor market discrimination; at least some may be the result of either preferences formed before labor market entry or choices made later, perhaps in the context of family decision-making (refer back to Example 8.2).[15] For example, more and more literature points to the possibility that women are more averse to risk and that they tend to avoid occupations in which pay is negotiable or related to performance—either absolute or relative to other workers.[16] As yet, no measure has been devised to estimate that portion of occupational segregation that can be attributed to unequal treatment by employers.

The decline in observable occupational segregation, and our inability to measure the role of preferences in that segregation, should not imply that discrimination is no longer an issue. Even within narrowly defined occupations, men and women are often segregated across employers. For example, restaurants commonly employ only male servers or only female servers but not both. Furthermore, female servers earn only 87 percent of what male servers earn, and a hiring audit of Philadelphia restaurants suggests that discrimination might play a role. In 1994, two matched pairs of men and women (with equivalent résumés) applied for jobs in 65 restaurants, and the study found that the high-priced restaurants, where earnings are higher, were much less likely to interview and extend an offer to female applicants.[17]

Measurement: Wage Discrimination   We pointed out earlier that average earnings can differ between women and men either because of premarket differences in average levels of productive characteristics or because of differences in what women and men are paid for possessing each characteristic. (That is, pay differences have two components: One is that two groups may differ in their average levels of characteristics [e.g., work experience], and the other is that the groups can differ in the economic that returns they receive for those characteristics.) Ideally, wage discrimination could be identified and measured in the following four-step process:[18]

1. We would collect data, for men and women separately, on *all* human-capital and other characteristics that are theoretically relevant to the determination of earnings. On the basis of discussions in earlier chapters, the characteristics of age, education and training, experience, tenure with current employer, hours of work, firm size, region, intensity of work effort, industry, and the job's duties, location, and working conditions come readily to mind.

2. We would then estimate (statistically) how each of these characteristics contributes to the earnings of women. That is, we would use statistical

techniques to estimate the payoffs to women associated with each characteristic. (The basic statistical technique used is termed *regression analysis*—which we discuss briefly in Appendix 1A—and it allows us to estimate how changes in a productive characteristic affect earnings, holding other productive characteristics constant. A computer must be used to make these estimates when, as in the case at hand, *several* relevant productive characteristics are to be jointly analyzed. However, the general idea behind this technique is graphically illustrated in Appendix 12A, by using the simple example of estimating how wages are affected by changes in a single composite measure of job "*difficulty*".)

3. Having measured levels of the productive characteristics typically possessed by men and women (step 1), and having estimated how changes in each productive characteristic affect the earnings of women (step 2), we would next estimate how much women *would* earn if their productive characteristics were the same as those of men (essentially replacing women's actual values of schooling and work experience, for example, with those of men). This step would be accomplished by applying the payoffs that *women* receive for each productive characteristic to the average level of those characteristics possessed by *men*. In summary, we are here using the male levels of age, education, experience, and so forth but using the "returns" estimated for women.

4. Finally, we would compare the *hypothetical* average earnings level calculated for women (in step 3) with the *actual* average earnings of men. This latter comparison would yield an estimate of wage discrimination, because it reflects the effects of the different prices for productive characteristics paid to men versus those paid to women. (In the absence of discrimination, women and men who have identical productive characteristics should have identical earnings.[19])

Inferring Wage Discrimination   Two problems arise from this "ideal" measure of wage discrimination. First, as explained earlier, isolating the effects of labor market discrimination requires us to separately categorize the effects of premarket *differences in productive characteristics* on overall wage differentials. The residual part of the wage gap that cannot be explained by different levels of productive characteristics—and instead is categorized as different *payoffs* to these characteristics—is what can be ascribed to labor market discrimination. Premarket differences are, in part, the result of choices (primarily about investments in human capital and occupation) that individuals make, and these choices often vary across demographic groups. *A question that is difficult to answer is the extent to which these premarket choices are themselves affected by discrimination in the labor market.*[20]

Occupational choice is a case in point. For example, when making choices about occupational preparation, are women able to freely exercise their occupational preferences, or do they avoid occupations for which they believe their entry will be made difficult by discrimination in the labor market? On the one hand, if we assume that women are able to freely choose their occupations, then gender-related occupational differences reflect preferences, and *occupation* becomes one of the premarket variables for which we would want to control when trying to isolate the effects of labor market discrimination. On the other hand, if women's occupational choices are constrained by discriminatory behavior in the labor market, then we would not want to include occupation among the premarket control variables—because the effects of occupational choice on the gender wage differential reflect labor market discrimination, not the exercise of premarket preferences.[21] (Similar issues arise from the *industry*—for example, construction, wood products, insurance, retail trade—in which one works.)

Thus, the first problem with our procedure for measuring wage discrimination is that because the labor market payoffs to productive characteristics can affect premarket choices about them, the distinction between these two categories is not clear-cut. If we include among the premarket controls a variable whose level is affected by labor market discrimination, we may *understate* the effects of such discrimination by putting these effects in the "premarket" category).

The second problem is that we often lack data on *all* the premarket variables that affect wages, and in this case, this procedure might *overstate* the extent of labor market discrimination. For example, because of greater household responsibilities, women may be more likely than men to seek jobs only if they are close to home, might be less available for work outside normal business hours, or might more often be the parent "on call" if a child becomes ill at school.[22] These choices reduce the earnings of women, and variables reflecting such choices should be included in the list of premarket variables used in step 2—but because we lack data on them, their effects show up (in step 4) as reduced payoffs to the female human-capital variables that we do observe. Thus, if we believe that the omitted premarket variables are ones that reduce women's wages, *we cannot conclude that all the unexplained residual is caused by labor market discrimination* (because some of the residual will be derived from the effects on women's wages of the omitted characteristics).

Analyzing Wage Differences These measurement problems notwithstanding, we follow the four-step procedure outlined earlier to try to determine what the earnings gap between women and men would be if observed productive characteristics were equalized. A study using 2010 data found that women in the sample earned, on average, only 79.3 percent as much as men (i.e., a gap of 20.7 percent); however, if their productive characteristics, including occupation, had been equalized (or "controlled for"), they would have earned 91.6 percent as much.[23]

This 2010 study, however, serves as an excellent example of the two problems noted earlier in judging the existence and extent of gender discrimination in the labor market. In an effort to see how much of the gender pay gap is related to differences in *job choices*, the authors also performed their analysis by using only differences in the human-capital variables of education and labor market experience. They estimated that if only human-capital differences were equalized for women and men, women would earn 82.1 (not 91.6) percent as much as men—a finding that suggests job choices (occupations along with industries in which the jobs are located) account for almost 10 percentage points—about half—of the wage gap between men and women. Thus, finding out whether women's job choices are made completely freely or are themselves a result of labor market discrimination, remains a crucial open issue in studying gender discrimination in the labor market. (Appendix 12B illustrates a similar difficulty in deciding what to control for when measuring labor market discrimination.)

The 2010 study also illustrates the problem of measuring all the critical aspects of the jobs done by women and those done by men. The study was able to measure (and therefore control for) the years of full- and part-time labor market experience; indeed, the fact that women average fewer years of experience than men do accounts for about 3 percentage-points of the wage gap. However, recent work suggests that wage differences *within* occupations and human-capital groups is even more important in explaining the gender pay gap than differences *across* these groups are. A fascinating new approach is to focus on differences in work *hours* between women and men in the same occupations.

We know that women average fewer hours of work per week than men do in the same occupation (refer back to Table 9.2), which reflects their typically greater responsibilities in parenting and around the home. Parenting and many other "household" duties (e.g., being home for a plumbing or appliance repair) cut into time available for one's job, but they also require some flexibility in workplace scheduling. Many jobs, particularly better-paying ones in the professions (like law and investment banking) and top management, are increasingly requiring longer hours and less flexibility in scheduling—as people in these jobs must deal with time pressures and deadlines, work closely with others in workplace teams, establish and maintain close relationships with clients, and acquire specialized knowledge that is difficult to transmit to a coworker. Women in occupations that require long and inflexible work hours have been shown to have a greater wage disadvantage than women in jobs like pharmacist, which requires high skills but has duties that allow for one worker to easily take over duties of another at the end of a work shift.[24] Longer-hour jobs—which clearly cut into leisure and household time—appear to be commanding greater compensating wage differentials and may be increasingly important to receiving promotions. Thus, longer and less-flexible work schedules are thought to be an important barrier to narrowing the gender pay gap, especially in high-skilled labor markets[25]—a proposition explored in Example 12.2, which addresses the gig economy.

EXAMPLE 12.2

Does Gig Work Eliminate the Gender Pay Gap?

The household duties that women typically have in caring for children and others in a family appear to reduce both their total hours of paid work *and* the flexibility with which they can work those hours. We have seen that these labor market restrictions created by household responsibilities are hypothesized to be a fundamental cause of the gender gap in earnings. If the gender gap in pay is caused in large part by restrictions on work hours, we should explore whether gender wage differences arise in jobs where work hours are completely flexible.

The gig economy is thought by many to provide flexible work hours to those who seek them. Ridesharing drivers (for Lyft and Uber, among others) generally have such flexibility. Drivers connect with customers through an online platform, and they are paid for each ride by a formula of fares and fees that is publicly available and not based on driver characteristics. Drivers can choose when and where they work. In the absence of employer expectations about hours of work, do female drivers receive the same hourly pay as male drivers?

One study that used data from over a million rideshare drivers finds that female drivers earned 7 percent less per hour than male drivers did. The study found that while the *flexibility* of work hours did *not* play a role in this gap, *total hours of work* did—in that more driving experience improved hourly earnings (think back to Chapter 9), and male drivers accumulated more driving hours than female drivers did. The study was able to rule out that discrimination by customers was a cause of the earnings gap, but it did find that two risk-related factors increased the gap (think back to Chapter 8): Men drove faster, and they were more willing to drive in areas with higher crime rates and more drinking establishments.

Source: Cody Cook, Rebecca Diamond, Jonathan Hall, John A. List, and Paul Oyer, "The Gender Earnings Gap in the Gig Economy: Evidence from Over a Million Rideshare Drivers" (Working Paper No. 24732, National Bureau of Economic Research, Cambridge, MA, June 2018), forthcoming in *Review of Economic Studies*

Earnings Differences Between Black Americans and White Americans

We saw in Figure 12.1 that Black men who worked full time in 2018 earned just 65 percent as much as white men; Black women earned just 55 percent as much. The Black–white earnings gap for men narrowed in the 1970s, became somewhat larger in the 1980s, narrowed again in the 1990s, and was roughly the same in 2018 as it was in 2000.[26]

The earnings of full-time workers, however, do not tell the whole story of the economic disparities between Black Americans and white Americans. No major difference in the fraction of adult male employees can be found in the two groups who usually work part time, and a *lower* percentage of employed Black women (13.9 percent in 2015) than white women (21.2 percent) report that they usually work part time.[27] Significant disparities, however, can be found in the *employment–population ratios* (the ratios of employed adults to the entire population of adults in a particular demographic group who are not in the military or institutionalized). According to the first two columns of Table 12.4, as compared with the white population, a lower percentage of the Black population is employed. The differences are particularly striking for men. We begin our analysis of Black/white disparities by first considering these differences in the employment ratios.

Differences in Employment Ratios   The employment ratio for a given demographic group is completely determined by the percentage of the group seeking employment (the labor-force participation rate) and the percentage of those seeking employment who find it. Because the latter is equal to 100 percent minus the group's unemployment rate, the employment ratio can be expressed as a function of two widely published rates: the group's labor-force participation rate and its unemployment rate.

Table 12.4 contains data on labor-force participation rates and unemployment rates by race and by gender. Looking first at labor force

Table 12.4 Employment Ratios, Labor-Force Participation Rates, and Unemployment Rates, by Race and by Gender, 1970–2017[a]

Year	Employment ratio		Labor-force participation rate		Unemployment rate	
	Black (%)	White (%)	Black (%)	White (%)	Black (%)	White (%)
Men						
1970	71.9	77.8	77.6	81.0	7.3	4.0
1980	62.5	74.0	72.1	78.8	13.3	6.1
1990	61.8	73.2	70.1	76.9	11.8	4.8
2000	63.4	72.9	69.0	75.4	8.1	3.4
2017	59.4	66.9	64.6	69.5	8.1	3.8
Women						
1970	44.9	40.3	49.5	42.6	9.3	5.4
1980	46.6	48.1	53.6	51.4	13.1	6.5
1990	51.5	54.8	57.8	57.5	10.8	4.6
2000	58.7	57.7	63.2	59.8	7.2	3.6
2017[a]	56.1	54.2	60.3	56.4	6.9	3.8

a. For 1970 and 1980, data on Black people include other racial minorities.

Data in all years are for people ages 16 or older.

Sources: U.S. Bureau of Labor Statistics, *Employment and Earnings* 17 (January 1971), Table A-1; 28 (January 1981), Table A-3; 38 (January 1991), Table 3; 48 (January 2001); *Employment and Earnings Online*, Annual Average Household Data, Employment Status, Table 3, at www.bls.gov/opub/ee/2018/cps/annavg3_2017.pdf

participation, we see that Black women have had *higher* labor-force participation rates than white women had over the 1970 to 2017 period. Among men, however, the picture is much different. Black men have had consistently lower participation rates than white men, and although both groups of men experienced reductions in labor-force participation rates from 1970 to 2017, the reductions were greater for Black men.

The declining labor-force participation rates of men are not just the result of earlier labor force withdrawal among older men or more post-secondary schooling by young people (although as we saw in Chapter 6, both phenomena have played a role). The participation rates even of men ages 35 to 44 have dropped for both racial groups, where these reductions are more or less confined to those with a high school education or less. The wages of poorly educated workers—especially men—have fallen in recent years, and many of these men apparently have become "discouraged workers" and have dropped out of the labor force. It appears that at least some of the larger declines in labor force participation among Black men are a consequence of their lower average levels of education.[28]

Table 12.4 also suggests that the higher unemployment rates of Black workers are a cause of their lower employment–population ratios among men, although the relatively higher labor-force participation rates among Black women tend to increase their employment–population ratios. For both men and women, the unemployment rate among Black workers is approximately twice that among white workers. This pattern is *not* just a function of differences in education, age, experience, or region of residence; the Black unemployment rate has been roughly double the rate for white workers in *every* group.[29]

The relative constancy of the Black/white *ratio* of unemployment rates suggests that this ratio is not affected much by the business cycle. Concluding from this constancy, however, that recessions have equal proportionate effects on Black employment as on white employment would be erroneous; in fact, the constant ratio means that Black workers suffer *disproportionately* in a recession.

Suppose, for example, that the white unemployment rate were 5 percent and the Black unemployment rate were 10 percent; these rates imply, of course, that 95 percent of the white labor force and 90 percent of the Black labor force are employed. Suppose now that a recession occurs and that the white unemployment rate and the Black unemployment rate rise to 8 percent and 16 percent, respectively. Among white people, the employment rate falls from 95 percent to 92 percent, which implies that a bit over 3 percent of white workers who had jobs lost them (3/95 = 0.032). Among Black workers, however, the employment rate falls from 90 percent to 84 percent, indicating that almost 7 percent of employed Black people lost their jobs (6/90 = 0.067). The greater sensitivity of Black employment to aggregate economic activity has led many observers to conclude that Black workers are the last hired and first fired.

Occupational Segregation and Wage Discrimination

Among Black workers who are employed, analyses similar to those for women can be made to measure the extent of occupational segregation and the degree to which measurable productive characteristics explain the Black–white gap in earnings. Occupational segregation appears to be less prevalent by race than by gender. Recent studies that calculated indices of occupational dissimilarity by both race and gender found that the indices comparing Black and white occupational distributions had values roughly *half* the size of indices comparing male/female occupational distributions. Studies have also found evidence of racial segregation across firms, where workers tend to work with coworkers of the same race, but this form of segregation appears to contribute little to the generation of wage differences by race.[30]

Turning to the issue of *wage discrimination*, researchers have attempted to determine, by using the statistical method outlined earlier in this chapter for explaining gender pay gaps, what factors are most responsible for the large gap between the wages of Black workers and those of white workers. Some of the premarket variables that must be taken into account in explaining Black/white differences in wages are readily observed in most data sets: education, experience, age, hours of work, region, occupation, industry, and firm size. Although these variables explain some of the Black–white pay gap, they do not comprise a complete list of premarket differences that can, and should, be used.

One premarket (or human-capital) characteristic that plays a key role in explaining Black/white wage differentials is cognitive achievement, as measured by scores on the Armed Forces Qualification Test (AFQT). Black Americans have lower AFQT scores, on average, which is associated with poorer-quality schooling and the influences of poverty on home and neighborhood characteristics.[31] A study controlling for observable human-capital characteristics—including levels of education and AFQT scores, along with some measures of school quality and family background—found that *two-thirds* of the pay gap between Black men and white men could be explained by these observable variables.[32] This finding suggests, however, that a gap of around 11 percent could *not* be explained.[33] Can this unexplained gap be interpreted as labor market evidence of discrimination?

As with the issue of occupational choice when analyzing gender pay gaps, questions loom about whether the premarket educational and occupational choices of Black Americans are themselves affected by anticipated labor market discrimination. Arguably, Black people might choose different levels of education than white people do *because of their expectation of discrimination in the labor market*. If the choice of educational level, for example, is *reflective* of labor market discrimination, then it should not be included in the list of *premarket* variables used to estimate what wages of Black people would be in the absence of discrimination. Currently, a lively debate among economists discusses whether including educational attainment among the list of premarket variables increases or reduces the pay gap that can be attributed to discrimination.[34]

Although we cannot be sure that the existence and size of the unexplained pay gap between Black men and white men is evidence of labor market discrimination, we have indications from other kinds of studies that discrimination in the labor market indeed occurs. For example, one study found that performance-based pay increases the pay of white workers relative to Black workers when it is more subjectively determined.[35] Another found that Black workers are more closely monitored by, and thus more likely to be fired by, their supervisors.[36]

Also, more and more direct evidence—primarily from laboratory and field experiments (e.g., see Empirical Study 12.1 at the end of this chapter) but also from studies like the one summarized in Example 12.3—shows that labor market discrimination persists. Although generalizing about its overall effect on wages is difficult, race-based discrimination clearly occurs and is pervasive.[37] Moreover, as long as Black unemployment rates are twice those of white rates, Black workers will continue to fall short of white workers, on average, in terms of job experience and the tenure-related benefits of on-the-job training.[38]

EXAMPLE 12.3

Race Discrimination Might "Strike" When Few Are Looking: The Case of Umpires in Major League Baseball

Racial discrimination in the workplace can lower wages among disfavored groups in three ways:

1. when fewer workers in these groups are hired.
2. when, if hired, workers in these groups are assigned to lower-paying jobs.
3. when, if hired into the same jobs, workers in the disfavored groups receive lower performance ratings from their supervisors.

Much of the research by economists on labor market discrimination has focused on hiring and occupational distributions, because researchers can objectively observe these outcomes. Supervisory ratings are more difficult to judge, because in most workplace settings, employee performance is not objectively measured by those outside the particular workplace. A wealth of performance data, however, is observable from the world of sports, and one clever study found evidence consistent with race discrimination in Major League Baseball—by umpires (supervisors) against pitchers (employees). If umpires have more positive feelings toward pitchers of their own race, we would expect that they would be more likely to call pitches close to the strike zone as "strikes" (a favorable call) rather than "balls" if the pitcher is of their same race. Conversely, umpires with racial preferences would be more likely to call a close pitch a "ball" if the pitcher is of a different race. Because umpires are themselves being monitored and judged by their supervisors (and baseball fans), however, economists would expect that any racial bias in judging pitches would be most prominent when the monitoring of umpires is least effective or least likely.

In the years 2004 to 2008, Major League Baseball installed pitch monitoring cameras in about one-third of its ballparks. This photographic system allowed umpires to be monitored, and in a study of over 3.5 million pitches thrown in the 2004–2008 period, the researchers found that in ballparks with these cameras, the race of umpires and pitchers had no role in judging how a pitch was called. In parks without these monitoring cameras, however, racial preferences among umpires was evident; that is, when the umpire and pitcher were of *different* races, pitches that were "close" to the strike zone were *less* likely to be called a "strike." Racial discrimination in pitch calling was even more evident when crowds were small and the game situations were not critical—that is, when fewer people were watching or likely to be paying close attention.

Fortunately, the magnitude of discrimination, while statistically observable, was found to be small. On average, a pitch that is not swung at by the batter is called a strike 31.9 percent of the time. In situations where umpires are not closely monitored (i.e., in poorly attended games in parks without the monitoring cameras, and in situations that are not likely to be critical to the outcome of the game), the likelihood of a pitch's being called a strike falls to 31 percent if the umpire and pitcher are of different races.

Source: Christopher A. Parsons, Johan Sulaman, Michael C. Yates, and Daniel S. Hamermesh, "Strike Three: Discrimination, Incentives, and Evaluation," *American Economic Review* 101 (June 2011): 1410–1435

Similar behaviors were found in a study of professional basketball referees; see Joseph Price and Justice Wolfers, "Racial Discrimination Among NBA Referees," *Quarterly Journal of Economics* 125 (November 2010): 1859–1887.

Earnings Differences by Ethnicity

Increased immigration has sparked a renewed interest in the relative earnings of various ancestral groups in the United States, most especially because the earnings differences are so pronounced. Table 12.5 contains earnings data from a study on men, in which it used data from the 1990 *Census of Population*. The first column displays the full-time earnings of men from selected ancestral groups relative to the U.S. average, and from it, we can note the relatively high earnings of men whose ancestry was Russian, Italian, or Japanese. Conversely, men whose ancestry is Native American, Mexican, or Puerto Rican had especially low earnings.

Drawing on our discussion of earnings differences across gender and race, we must investigate to what extent these differences resulted from different levels of productive (or premarket) characteristics. Educational attainment,

Table 12.5 Male Earnings Differences, by Ancestry, 1990

Ancestral group	Earnings as a percentage of U.S. average	Estimated earnings as a percentage of U.S. average if productive characteristics of group were average
U.S. total	100	100
Mexican	71	95
Puerto Rican	87	98
Cuban	90	102
Chinese	99	95
Japanese	133	115
Native American	85	95
English	113	102
Italian	121	109
Russian	157	118

Source: William Darity Jr., David Guilkey, and William Winfrey, "Ethnicity, Race and Earnings," *Economics Letters* 47 (1995): 401–408

for example, across ethnic groups diverges widely. In 1990, men of Japanese, Chinese, and Russian ancestries living in the United States had average levels of college attainment roughly twice the national average, whereas men from Puerto Rican and Mexican backgrounds had average levels that were under half the national average. The second column in Table 12.5 presents estimates of what earnings in each group would have been if observed productive characteristics, including education and fluency in English, were equalized across all groups. The results suggest that if observed productive characteristics were equalized, men of Japanese ancestry or Russian ancestry would have earned 15 percent to 18 percent more than average, whereas those of Mexican ancestry, Chinese ancestry, or Native American ancestry would have earned roughly 5 percent less.[39]

Because of social concern about labor market discrimination, we focus on groups whose earnings appear to be low, given their productive characteristics. In recent years, however, interest has risen in the diversity of earnings across white ethnic groups, for which discrimination has been of less concern. Of particular interest is whether unmeasured qualitative differences exist in education or background across ethnic groups. Indeed, recent studies have found evidence that there are important intergenerational transfers of "ethnic human capital," some of which are manifest in divergent rates of return to education.[40]

Research interest in ancestral groups that are suspected victims of labor market discrimination have centered on Hispanics, a categorization including people from such diverse backgrounds as Mexican, Puerto Rican, Cuban, and Central and South American. Although these groups share a common linguistic heritage, one can infer from Table 12.5 that they have somewhat-different earnings and human-capital levels.

The influx of Spanish-speaking immigrants into the United States has resulted in the growth of a group of workers characterized by its youth, low levels of education, inexperience in the U.S. labor market, and relatively low levels of proficiency in English. Motivated in part by concerns about discrimination, recent research on earnings differences between Hispanic workers and non-Hispanic white workers has focused on the effects of English-language proficiency on earnings. Language proficiency is not measured in the data sets normally used to analyze earnings, yet it clearly affects productivity in most jobs in the United States; hence, if measures of it are omitted from the analysis, we cannot conclude anything about the presence or absence of discrimination against immigrant groups.

The handful of studies (including the one underlying the data in Table 12.5) that have had access to data on language proficiency estimate that equalizing all productive characteristics, including language proficiency, would bring the earnings of Hispanics up to equality with, or within 3 percent to 7 percent of, the earnings of non-Hispanic white people. One study, however, found that the effects on earnings of either unmeasured productive characteristics or wage discrimination are far larger for Black Hispanic workers than for non-Black Hispanic workers.[41]

Theories of Market Discrimination

We cannot rule out the presence of discrimination by gender, race, or ethnicity in the labor market. Before designing policies to end discrimination, however, we must understand the *sources* and *mechanisms* causing it. The goal of this section is to lay out and evaluate the different theories of discrimination that economists talk about.

Three general sources of labor market discrimination have been hypothesized, and each source suggests an associated model of how discrimination is implemented and its consequences. The first source of discrimination is *personal prejudice*, wherein employers, customers, or fellow employees dislike associating with workers of a given race, ethnicity, or gender.[42] The second general source is *statistical prejudgment*, whereby employers project onto individuals certain perceived demographic characteristics. Finally, models are based on the presence of *noncompetitive* forces in the labor market. Although all the models generate useful, suggestive insights, none has been convincingly established as superior.

Personal-Prejudice Models: Employer Discrimination

The models based on personal prejudice assume that employers, customers, or employees have prejudicial tastes; that is, they have preferences for not associating with members of certain demographic groups. Suppose first that white male *employers* are prejudiced against women and minority groups, but (for simplicity's sake) that customers and fellow employees are not. Furthermore, assume for the purposes of this model that the disfavored groups in question have the same productive characteristics as white men. (This assumption directs our focus to labor market discrimination by putting aside premarket differences.)

If employers have a decided preference for hiring white men in high-paying jobs despite the availability of equally qualified women and minorities, they will act as *if* the latter were less productive than the former. By virtue of our assumption that the women and minorities involved are equally productive in every way, the devaluing of their productivity by employers is purely subjective and is a manifestation of personal prejudice. The more prejudiced an employer is, the more actual productivity will be discounted.

Suppose that *MRP* stands for the actual marginal revenue productivity of all workers in a particular labor market and that d represents the extent to which this productivity is subjectively devalued for women and minorities. In this case, market equilibrium for white men has been reached when their wage (W_M) equals *MRP*:

$$MRP = W_M \tag{12.1}$$

For the women and minorities, however, equilibrium is achieved only when their wage (W_F) equals their *subjective* value to firms:

$$MRP - d = W_F \tag{12.2}$$

or

$$MRP = W_F + d \tag{12.2a}$$

Because the actual marginal revenue productivities are equal by assumption, equations (12.1) and (12.2a) are equal to each other, and we can easily see that W_F must be less than W_M:

$$W_M = W_F + d \tag{12.3}$$

or

$$W_F = W_M - d \tag{12.3a}$$

What this says algebraically has a simple economic logic: If the actual productivity of women and minorities is devalued by employers, workers in these groups must offer their services at lower wages than those for white men to compete for jobs.

Profits Under Employer Discrimination   This model of employer discrimination has two major implications, as illustrated in Figure 12.2, which is a graphic representation of equation (12.2a). The first concerns profits. A discriminatory employer faced with a market wage rate

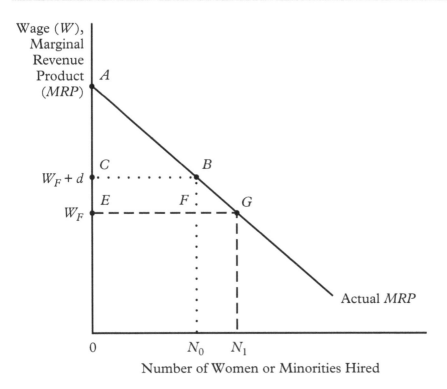

Figure 12.2 Equilibrium Employment of Women and Other Minorities in Firms that Discriminate

of W_F for women and minorities will hire N_0, for at that point $MRP = W_F +$ *d*. *Profit-maximizing* employers, however, will hire N_1; that is, they will hire until $MRP = W_F$. The effects on profits can be readily seen in Figure 12.2 if we remember that the area under the *MRP* curve represents the total revenues of the firm. Subtracting the area representing the wage bill of the discriminatory employer ($0EFN_0$) yields profits for these employers equal to the area *AEFB*. Profits for a profit-maximizing (nondiscriminatory) employer, however, are *AEG*. These latter employers hire women and minorities to the point where their marginal product equals their wage, whereas the discriminators end their hiring short of that point. Discriminators thus give up (*BFG*) profits in order to indulge their prejudices.

Pay Gaps Under Employer Discrimination   The second implication of our employer discrimination model concerns the size of the gap between W_M and W_F. The determinants of this gap can be best understood by moving to an analysis of the *market* demand curve for women and minorities. In Figure 12.3, the market's demand for women and minorities is expressed in terms of their wage rate *relative* to the wage for white men. The figure assumes that a number of nondiscriminatory employers will hire up to N_a women and minorities at a relative wage of unity (i.e., at $W_F = W_M$). For those employers who have discriminatory

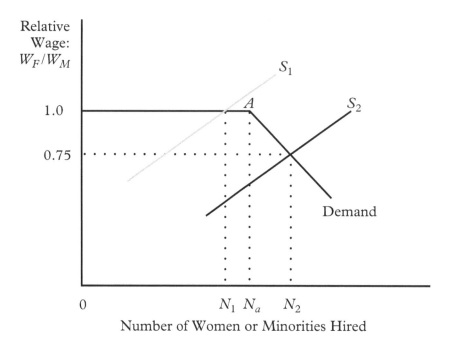

Figure 12.3 Market Demand for Women and Other Minorities as a Function of Relative Wages

preferences, W_F must fall below W_M to induce them to hire women and minorities. These employers are assumed to differ in their preferences, where some are willing to hire women and minorities at small wage differentials and where others require larger ones. Thus, the market's relative demand curve is assumed to bend downward at point *A*, reflecting the fact that to employ more than N_a of women and minorities would require a fall in W_F relative to W_M.

If the supply of women and other minorities is relatively small (supply curve S_1 in Figure 12.3), then such workers will all be hired by nondiscriminatory employers and no wage differential will be present. If the number of women and minorities who are seeking jobs is relatively large (see supply curve S_2), then some discriminatory employers will have to be induced to hire women and other minorities, driving W_F down below W_M. In Figure 12.3, combining supply curve S_2 with the demand curve drives the relative wage down to 0.75.

Besides changes in the labor supply curves of women and minorities, two other factors can cause the market differential between W_F and W_M to change. First, given the supply curve, if the number of nondiscriminators were to increase, as shown in Figure 12.4, the wage differential would decrease. The increase in the nondiscriminators shows up graphically in the figure as an extension of the horizontal segment of the demand curve to *A'*, and the relative wage is driven up (to 0.85 in the figure). Behaviorally, the influx of nondiscriminators absorbs more of the supply

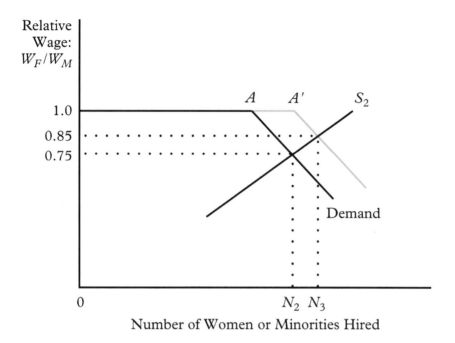

Figure 12.4 Effects on Relative Wages of an Increased Number of Nondiscriminatory Employers

than before, leaving fewer women and other minorities who must find employment with discriminatory employers. Moreover, the few who must still find work with discriminatory employers are able to bypass the worst discriminators and can go to work for those with smaller preferences for discrimination.

Second, the same rise in W_F relative to W_M could occur if the number of prejudiced employers stayed the same but their discriminatory preferences were reduced. Such a reduction would show up graphically as a flattening of the downward-sloping part of the market's relative demand curve, shown in Figure 12.5. The changes hypothesized in this figure cause W_F to rise relative to W_M, because the inducement required by each discriminatory employer to hire women and minorities is now smaller.

We can make three empirical predictions about race-related wage gaps that arise from our discussion of Figures 12.3, 12.4, and 12.5. First, holding human capital constant, race-related pay gaps will be greater when the Black population in a region is greater (see Figure 12.3). Second, pay gaps will be larger, other things being equal, when the prejudice of the white employers who hire Black workers is greater (see Figures 12.4 and 12.5). Third, pay gaps will be unaffected by the level of prejudice of the most prejudiced employers (the ones who do not hire Black workers). A study—using attitudes about interracial marriages and voting for a Black presidential candidate—finds support for all three predictions.[43]

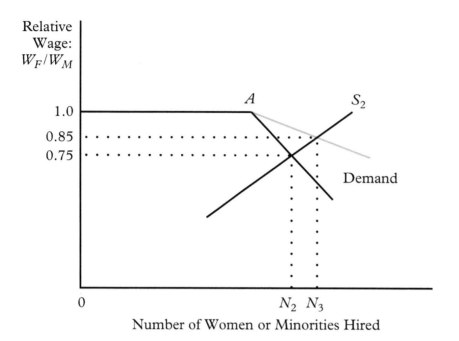

Figure 12.5 Effects on Relative Wages of a Decline in the Discriminatory Preferences of Employers

Employers That Can Afford to Discriminate The employer discrimination model implies that discriminators maximize *utility* (satisfying their prejudicial preferences) instead of *profits*. This practice should immediately raise the question of how they survive. Since profit-maximizing (nondiscriminatory) firms would normally make more money from a given set of assets than would discriminators, we should observe nondiscriminatory firms' buying out others and gradually taking over the market.[44] In short, if competitive forces were at work in the product market, firms that discriminate would be punished and discrimination could not persist unless their owners were willing to accept below-market rates of return.

Theory suggests, then, that employer discrimination is most likely to persist when owners or managers do not have to maximize profits in order to stay in business. The opportunity to indulge in discriminatory preferences is especially strong among monopolies that face government regulation, because the costs of this wasteful practice make profits look smaller to regulatory bodies.

Studies of both the banking industry and trucking industry provide evidence consistent with the greater presence of race and gender discrimination among regulated monopolies. Both industries were historically regulated in ways that limited competition, both were deregulated in recent decades, and in both cases, race and gender wage differentials were considerably narrowed by greater product market competition.[45]

Personal-Prejudice Models: Customer Discrimination

A second personal-prejudice model stresses *customer* prejudice as a source of discrimination. Customers may prefer to be served by white men in some situations and by women or minorities in others. If customer preferences for white men extend to jobs requiring major responsibility, such as physician or airline pilot, then occupational segregation that works to the disadvantage of women and minorities will occur. Under this theory, if women and minorities find gaining employment in these jobs difficult, they must either accept lower wages or be more qualified than the average white man, because their marginal revenue productivity to their employers is reduced by customers' prejudices.

One of the implications of customer discrimination is that it will lead to segregation in the occupations with high customer contact. Firms that cater to discriminatory customers will hire only the preferred group of workers, pay higher wages, and charge higher prices than firms that employ workers from disfavored groups and that serve nondiscriminatory customers. To continue their discriminatory ways, then, customers must be willing to pay the added costs.

Empirical studies have found evidence consistent with customer discrimination. For example, the racial composition of a firm's customers is reflected in the racial composition of its employees, especially in jobs with high customer contact. Similarly, a study of television viewership for professional basketball games in the United States found that ratings rose, other things being equal, when white players participated more. Because a team's revenues are affected by its television viewership, the latter finding implies that customer discrimination causes white players to have higher marginal revenue product—and higher pay—than Black players with comparable skills have.[46]

Personal-Prejudice Models: Employee Discrimination

A third source of discrimination based on personal prejudice might be found on the supply side of the market, where white male workers might avoid situations in which they will have to work with women or minorities in ways that they consider distasteful. For example, they might resist following directions from a female leader or be uncomfortable sharing responsibility with a worker from a different racial or ethnic group.[47]

If white male workers, for example, have discriminatory preferences, they will tend to quit or avoid employers who hire and promote on a nondiscriminatory basis. Employers who wish to employ workers in a nondiscriminatory fashion, therefore, would have to pay white men a wage premium (a compensating wage differential) to keep them.

If employers were nondiscriminatory, however, why would they pay a premium to keep white men when they could hire equally qualified and less-expensive women or other minorities? One answer is that white men constitute a large fraction of the labor force, so producing without them is difficult to imagine. Moreover, the pressure for women and other minorities to be employed outside of "traditional" occupations is relatively recent, so white men hired under one set of implicit promises relating to future promotion possibilities now must adjust to a new set of competitors for positions within the firm. Firms realize that changing their practices involves reneging on past promises, so they might seek to accommodate the preferences for discrimination among their workers. Put differently, employee discrimination may be costly to employers, but so is getting rid of it.

One way that employers might try to accommodate employee discrimination is to hire on a segregated basis. Although completely segregating a plant is usually not economically feasible, workers *can be* segregated by job title. Thus, both the employee and the customer models of discrimination can help to explain the finding of one study that employers usually hire only women or only men into any single job title—even if *other* employers hire members of the opposite gender into that job title.[48]

The most direct test for the presence of employee discrimination comes from a study that found young white men earned more in *racially integrated* workplaces than if they worked in segregated environments. Furthermore, some studies suggest that the lack of women in top executive jobs might be related to distaste among men for working under female bosses—although this distaste might be diminishing over time.[49] (Example 12.4 provides an interesting historical example of employee discrimination.)

EXAMPLE 12.4

Fear and Lathing in the Michigan Furniture Industry

In the late nineteenth century, the United States attracted several hundreds of thousands of immigrants every year. Ethnicity was vital in that people divided along ethnic lines into separate neighborhoods, churches, trade unions, and social clubs. This flood of immigrants encouraged a growing tide of nativism during the late 1800s. The most recognizable face of this nativism was hostility by the U.S.-born toward Catholics and the new immigrant groups from Southern and Eastern Europe. In addition, many of the newcomers distrusted and disliked one another, carrying over animosities from the old country.

How did these ethnic sensibilities play out in the labor market? Data from the Michigan furniture industry in 1889 allow us a remarkable view, as they include the wages of workers and measures of their human capital, plus information on the ethnicity of coworkers and supervisors.

During this period, the supervisors or forepersons had tremendous latitude in hiring and setting the wages of those who worked under them. If *employers* were the source of discrimination, then we would expect a worker to earn more when supervisors were from the same ethnic group and less when they were not. If fellow *employees* were the source of discrimination, we would expect a compensating wage differential to arise, in which workers received higher pay to offset the disamenity of working with members of other ethnic groups, and lower pay when working only with members of their own ethnic group.

Both of these indications of discrimination occurred in the Michigan furniture industry, but employee-based discrimination appears to have been much more important. Working with forepersons from one's own ethnic group was associated with earning wages about 2 percent higher.

However, the ethnicity of coworkers had a larger effect: Workers who were the only member of their ethnic group in the workplace earned about 11 percent *more* than those whose ethnic group made up about one-quarter of the labor force. Those working in a factory where over 90 percent of coworkers were from their own ethnic group earned about 9 percent *less*. Thus, a worker could pay a big price for avoiding—and could reap big rewards from working with—workers from the other ethnic groups.

Source: David Buffum and Robert Whaples, "Fear and Lathing in the Michigan Furniture Industry: Employee-Based Discrimination a Century Ago," *Economic Inquiry* 33 (April 1995): 234–252

Statistical Discrimination

We discussed in Chapter 5 the need for employers to acquire information on their job applicants in one way or another, all of which entails some cost. Obviously, the firm will evaluate the *personal* characteristics of its applicants, but in seeking to guess their potential productivity, it may also use information on the average characteristics of the groups to which they belong. If group characteristics are factored into the hiring decision, *statistical discrimination* can result (at least in the short run) even in the absence of personal prejudice.[50]

Statistical discrimination can be viewed as a part of the *screening problem* that arises when observable personal characteristics that are correlated with productivity are not perfect predictors of true labor market productivity. For example, suppose that two types of workers apply for an administrative assistant job: those who can type 70 words per minute (WPM) over the long haul and those who can type 40 WPM. These actual productivities are unknown to the employer, however. The employer can observe only the results of a five-minute keyboarding test whose results reflect skill but also are affected by test-taking abilities and luck.

Figure 12.6 shows the test-score distributions for both groups of workers. Those who can actually type 70 WPM score 70 on average, but half score below that. Likewise, half of the other group score better than 40 on the test. If an applicant scores 55, say, the employer does not know if the applicant is a good (70 WPM) or a bad (40 WPM) keyboarder. If those scoring 55 are automatically rejected, the firm will be rejecting some good workers, and if it accepts those scoring 55, some weak workers will be hired.

Suppose that the employer, in an effort to avoid this dilemma, does some research and finds out that applicants from a particular training school are

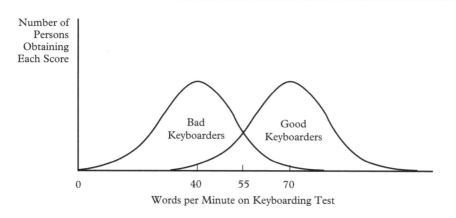

Figure 12.6 The Screening Problem

specifically coached to perform well on five-minute keyboarding tests. Thus, applicants who can actually type X WPM over a normal day will tend to score *higher* than X WPM on a five-minute test. Recognizing that students from this school will have average test scores above their long-run productivity, the firm might decide to reject all applicants from this school who score 55 or below (on the grounds that, for most, the test score overestimates their ability).

The general lesson of this example is that firms can legitimately use both *individual* data (e.g., test scores, educational attainment, and experience) and *group* data in making hiring decisions when the former are not perfect predictors of productivity. However, this use of group data can give rise to market discrimination when people with the same *measured productive characteristics* (test scores, education, etc.) are treated differently depending on *group* affiliation. If employers use race and gender in evaluating job applicants, this may lead them to prefer white men over other groups.[51] Example 12.5 offers an example of statistical discrimination that clearly favors white male applicants over Black male applicants.

Although statistical discrimination could be rooted in prejudice, it might be based on "old" or inaccurate information that ascribes some presumed group characteristic to all members of the group (e.g., a belief that women are less career oriented than men are). However, if statistical discrimination does not derive from prejudice, then employers will show evidence of "learning" (relying less on group affiliation) as more-accurate information on individuals becomes available.[52]

EXAMPLE 12.5

"Ban the Box" and Statistical Discrimination

Millions of potential workers in the United States have criminal records, and these members of the labor force face considerable barriers to obtaining employment. Because employers value worker attributes such as reliability in making hiring decisions, employers often refuse to consider applicants for employment if they have evidence of criminality in their past. Or in the language of this chapter, prior convictions for a crime are frequently used as a screening criterion (indicative of statistical discrimination) in hiring decisions, as employers might regard the consideration of such applicants as likely to be unproductive.

In an effort to induce employers to look more closely at applicants with criminal records, rather than merely using the "group characteristic" of past criminality to screen out these applicants, some states and cities prohibit employers from including on their job application forms a question about prior convictions for a crime. Because this question about a criminal record usually takes the form of checking a yes-or-no box, this prohibition is colloquially called "ban the box." Employers facing ban-the-box prohibitions are still able to perform criminal background checks, but only *later* in the hiring process. One hope underlying the ban-the-box legislation is that, after interviewing applicants, employers will make hiring decisions on the basis of more-complete information about an individual applicant who has a criminal record.

A related hope underlying ban-the-box legislation is that because Black men comprise a disproportionate share of those with criminal records, prohibiting employers from asking about criminal records early in the applicant review process will serve to reduce the racial disparity in unemployment rates, as noted in Table 12.4. Unfortunately, removing one screening criterion (the presence of a criminal record) appears to have caused employers to use another criterion for statistical discrimination: race.

Because employers in ban-the-box jurisdictions cannot ask directly about criminal records on job application forms, one carefully done study found evidence that employers assume that if an applicant is a Black man, then he is more likely to have a criminal record than a white male applicant. This study sent—both before and after ban-the-box legislation became effective—fictitious résumés to employers in New York City and New Jersey that were advertising actual job openings. On these résumés, an applicant's race was indicated by their name (see Empirical Study 12.1 at the end of this chapter for another study of this kind). The purpose of the study was to gauge how race affects employers' willingness to follow up with (call back) a job applicant on the basis of their résumé.

Before the box was banned, résumés with white-sounding names were 7 percent more likely to generate a callback (which, of course, is evidence of discriminatory preferences among employers, given that the résumés were created so that they differed only in the presumed race of the applicant). After ban-the-box legislation took effect, however, the résumés with white-sounding names were *45 percent* more likely to generate a callback. Thus, ban-the-box laws are unlikely to reduce the discriminatory barriers that Black men face in the labor market.

Source: Amanda Agan and Sonja Starr, "Ban the Box, Criminal Records, and Racial Discrimination: A Field Experiment," *Quarterly Journal of Economics* 133 (February 2018): 191–235

Noncompetitive Models of Discrimination

The discriminatory models discussed so far have traced out the wage and employment implications of personal prejudices or informational problems

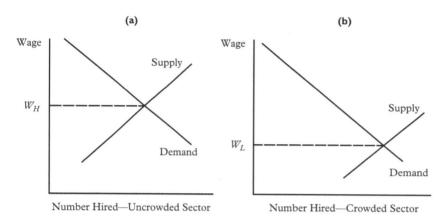

Figure 12.7　Labor Market Crowding

for labor markets in which firms were assumed to be wage takers. The rather diverse models to which we now turn are all based on the assumption that individual firms have some degree of influence over the wages that they pay, either through *collusion* or through some source of *monopsonistic* power.

Crowding　The existence and extent of occupational segregation, especially by gender, have caused some to argue that it is the result of a deliberate *crowding* policy intended to lower wages in certain occupations. Graphically, the *crowding hypothesis* is simple and can be easily seen in Figure 12.7. Panel (a) illustrates a market in which supply is small relative to demand, and the wage (W_H) is thus relatively high. Panel (b) depicts a market in which crowding causes supply to be large relative to demand, resulting in a wage (W_L) that is comparatively low.

　　Although the effects of crowding are easily seen, the phenomenon of crowding itself is less easily explained. If men and women were equally productive in a given job or set of jobs, for example, one would think that the lower wages of women caused by their being artificially crowded into certain jobs would make replacing male workers with less-expensive female workers attractive for firms that are now employing only men; this profit-maximizing behavior should eventually eliminate any wage differential. The failure of crowding, or occupational segregation, to disappear suggests the presence of noncompeting groups (and therefore barriers to employee mobility), but we are still left with trying to explain why such groups exist in the first place. Over the past 70 years, various possible explanations have been put forward: the establishment of some jobs as "male" and others as "female" through social custom, differences in aptitude that are either innate or acquired, and different supply curves of men and women to monopsonistic employers (discussed later). None of these explanations is complete in the sense of getting at the ultimate source of discrimination, but the fact is that the more female dominated an occupation, the lower its wages, even after controlling for the human capital of the workers in it.[53]

Dual Labor Markets　A variant of the crowding hypothesis with more recent origins is the view that the labor market is divided into two noncompeting sectors: a *primary* sector and a *secondary* sector. Jobs in the primary sector offer relatively high wages, stable employment, good working conditions, and opportunities for advancement. Secondary sector jobs, however, tend to be low wage and unstable and have poor working conditions; the returns to education and experience are thought to be close to zero in this sector. Workers (primarily women and underrepresented minorities) relegated to the secondary sector are tagged as unstable, undesirable workers and are thought to have little hope of acquiring primary sector jobs.

The dual labor market description of discrimination does not really explain why noncompeting sectors arose or why women and other minorities are segregated into the secondary sector. Some view the dual labor market as arising out of employer collusion (see Collusive Behavior section in this chapter), and others see it as rooted in the factors that lead to internal labor markets and efficiency wages. Whatever the cause, evidence suggests that the labor market has two sectors—one in which education and experience are associated with higher wages and one in which they are not.[54]

Evidence in support of the dual labor market hypothesis offers an explanation of why discrimination can persist. It also calls into question the levels of competition and mobility that exist, and it suggests that the initial existence of noncompeting racial and gender groups will be self-perpetuating. In short, the dual labor market hypothesis is consistent with any of the models of discrimination analyzed earlier; it suggests that if any of these theories *are* applicable, we cannot count on natural market forces to eliminate the discrimination that results.

Search-Related Monopsony　The crowding and dual labor market explanations for discrimination are grounded in the assumption that workers are "assigned" to occupational groups from which mobility to other groups is severely restricted; how or why assignments are made is not entirely clear. A third model of restricted mobility is built around the presence of job-search costs for employees.[55] This model combines a monopsonistic model of firm behavior (discussed in Chapter 5) with the phenomenon of prejudice.

Suppose that some, but not all, employers refuse to hire women or minorities, because of their own prejudices, those of their customers, or those of their employees. Suppose further that, in contrast, no employers rule out the hiring of white men. Women and minorities who are looking for jobs do not readily know who will refuse them out of hand, so they have to search longer and harder than do white men to generate the same number of job offers. As we saw in Chapter 5, employee job-search costs cause firms' labor supply curves to slope upward, and the monopsonistic outcomes that follow become more pronounced when these search costs are greater.[56]

Figure 12.8 graphically illustrates the implications of a situation in which two groups of workers have the same productivity (i.e., each has a marginal revenue product of labor equal to MRP_L), but one group has higher search costs than the other. Panel (a) depicts the supply and the marginal revenue product of labor curves for the group (white men, presumably)

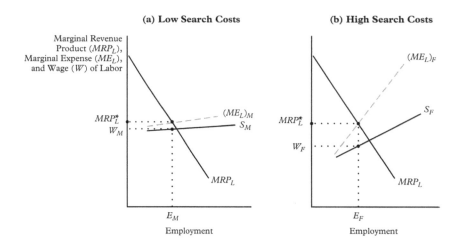

Figure 12.8 Search-Related Monopsony and Wage Discrimination

with relatively low search costs. The labor supply curve of this group to their employers (S_M) is relatively flat, which also means that the associated *marginal* expense of labor curve ($(ME_L)_M$) is relatively flat. Profit-maximizing employers will hire E_M workers from this group and pay them a wage of W_M, which is only slightly below MRP_L^*.

Panel (b) illustrates the relevant curves for a group (women or other minorities) with higher search costs created by the existence of prejudice. These workers are assumed to have the same marginal revenue product of labor, but their higher search costs imply a more steeply sloped labor supply curve (S_F), a more steeply sloped marginal expense of labor curve ($(ME_L)_F$), and a greater divergence between marginal revenue product and the wage rate. E_F workers in this group are hired, and they are paid a wage of W_F. A comparison of panels (a) and (b) readily shows that despite having the same marginal productivity, workers who have higher search costs are paid lower wages (i.e., $W_F < W_M$). At a practical level, if members of both groups are hired by a given firm, those who have higher search costs might be placed into lower job titles.

Our discussion of search-related monopsony invites two comments. First, we introduced the monopsony model in Chapter 5 as a potential explanation for the small and uncertain responses of employment to *mandated* wage increases under minimum-wage laws. The monopsony model has also been invoked to explain the lack of employment declines associated with mandated wage increases for women under the United Kingdom's Equal Pay Act of 1970.[57]

Second, if prejudice increases the job-search costs for women and other minorities such that members of these groups are less likely to search for alternative offers of employment, their job matches will be of lower quality than the job matches for white men. Individual women and minority-group members, then, would be less likely to find the employers who can best maximize their talents. Thus, even in narrowly defined occupational groups, women and other minorities would tend to be less productive and receive less pay than white men, owing to poorer-quality matches.

Collusive Behavior   Some theories are grounded in an assumption that employers collude with each other to subjugate women or minorities, thus creating a situation in which monopsonistic wages can be forced on the subjugated group. One of the more explicit collusive theories of discrimination argues that prejudice and the conflicts that it creates are inherent in a capitalist society because they serve the interests of owners.[58] Workers divided by race or gender are more difficult to organize, and if they *were* unionized, they would be less cohesive in their demands. Hence, some argue that owners of capital gain, while *all* workers—but particularly women and other minorities—lose from discrimination.

If discrimination is created or at least perpetuated by capitalists, however, how do we account for its existence in precapitalist or socialist societies? Furthermore, if all white employers conspired to keep women and other minorities in low-wage, low-status jobs, they can all reap monopoly profits– but even if employers A through Y adhered to the agreement, employer Z would always have incentives to *break* the agreement. Z could hire women and minorities cheaply because of the agreement among *other* employers not to hire them, and Z could thus enhance its profits by hiring these otherwise equally productive workers to fill jobs that A through Y are staffing with high-priced white men. Because every other employer has the same incentives as Z does, the conspiracy will tend to break down unless cheaters can be disciplined in some way. The collusive behavior model does not tell us how the conspiracy is maintained and coordinated among the millions of U.S. employers.

A Final Word on the Theories of Discrimination

All models of discrimination seem to agree on one thing: Any persistence of labor market discrimination is the result of forces that are either noncompetitive or slow to adjust to competitive forces. Although no one model yet can be demonstrated to be superior to the others in explaining the facts, the various theories and the facts that they seek to explain suggest that government intervention might be useful in eliminating the noncompetitive (or sluggish) influences. In analyzing these governmental programs, keep in mind that discriminatory pressures can come from a variety of sources and that discrimination is not necessarily profitable for those who engage in it.

Federal Programs to End Discrimination

Broadly speaking, the government has taken two somewhat-conflicting approaches to combat the causes or effects of discrimination. One approach is to mandate *nondiscrimination*, which implies that race, ethnicity, and gender should not play roles in hiring, promoting, or compensating workers. The other approach can be characterized as *affirmative action*, in which employers are required to be conscious of race, ethnicity, and gender in their personnel decisions and take steps to ensure that "protected" groups are not underrepresented. Although the following discussion focuses on federal laws and programs in the United States, similar programs also take place at the state and local levels of government.[59]

Equal Pay Act of 1963

Before the 1960s, gender discrimination was officially sanctioned by laws that limited women's total weekly hours of work and prohibited them from working at night, lifting heavy objects, and working during pregnancy. Not all states placed all these restrictions on women, but the effect of these laws was to limit the access of women to many jobs. These laws were overturned by the Equal Pay Act of 1963, which also outlawed separate pay scales for men and women who had similar skills and who performed work under the same conditions.

The act was seriously deficient as an antidiscrimination tool, however, because it said nothing about equal opportunity in hiring and promotions. This flaw can be easily understood by quickly reviewing our theories of discrimination. If prejudice against women comes from whatever source, employers will treat female employees as less productive or more costly to hire than equally productive men. The market response is for women's wages to fall below men's wages, because otherwise, women cannot hope to be able to successfully compete with men in obtaining jobs. The Equal Pay Act took a step toward the elimination of wage differentials, but in so doing, it tended to suppress a market mechanism that helped women obtain greater access to jobs.[60] The act failed to acknowledge that if labor market discrimination is to be eliminated, legislation must require *both* equal pay and equal opportunities in hiring and promotions for people of comparable productivity.

Title VII of the Civil Rights Act

Some defects in the Equal Pay Act of 1963 were corrected the next year. Title VII of the Civil Rights Act of 1964 made it unlawful for any employer "to refuse to hire or to discharge any individual, or otherwise to discriminate against any individual with respect to his compensation, terms, condition, or privileges of employment, because of such individual's race, color, religion, sex or national origin." Title VII applies to all employers in interstate commerce with at least 15 employees and is enforced by the Equal Employment Opportunity Commission (EEOC), which has the authority to mediate complaints, encourage lawsuits by private parties or the U.S. attorney general, or bring suits itself against employers. To enhance the force of the law, the courts permitted individual plaintiffs to expand their suits into *class actions* in which the potential discriminatory impact of an organization's employment practices on an entire group of workers is assessed.

Over the years, the federal courts have fashioned two standards of discrimination that may be applied when discriminatory employment practices are alleged—*disparate treatment* and *disparate impact*. Disparate treatment occurs under Title VII if individuals are treated differently because of their race, gender, color, religion, or national origin and if an intent to discriminate can be shown. The difficulty raised by this standard is that policies that appear to be neutral in the sense that they ignore race, gender, etc. might nevertheless perpetuate the effects of past discrimination. For example, word-of-mouth recruiting (a seemingly neutral policy) in a plant with a largely white workforce would be suspect under Title VII even if the selection of new employees from among the applicants was done on a nondiscriminatory basis.

The concern with addressing the present effects of past discrimination led to the *disparate impact standard*. Under this approach, the result, not the motivation, matters. Policies that appear to be neutral but lead to different effects by race, gender, and so on, are prohibited under Title VII unless they can be related to job performance.[61] As a result, plaintiffs, employers, and the courts have become interested in how closely the race or gender composition of those selected for employment, promotion, training, or termination accords with the race or gender composition of the pool of workers available for selection.

Enforcing Title VII by using the disparate impact standard has raised several issues regarding hiring, promotion, and pay decisions. One is defining who should be considered in a firm's potential hiring pool. For example, should prospective applicants residing quite far from the workplace be given the same weight as those who live in nearby neighborhoods? Another is statistical: What constitutes convincing (significant) evidence of underrepresentation? Two other issues relate to how employers award seniority to workers and how to judge "equal pay" when occupations are segregated.

Seniority   Some firms use seniority as a consideration in allocating promotion opportunities. Moreover, employees are sometimes laid off in order of reverse seniority, the least senior first, in a recession. Seniority can be calculated either as tenure within the *plant* or as time served within a *department* of the plant; in both cases, such systems have worked against women and minorities who have been hired or promoted to nontraditional jobs as a result of Title VII or some other antidiscrimination program. The most egregious cases occurred under departmental seniority systems when, during a business downturn, women or minorities who had recently been promoted to new departments were laid off ahead of those who had less plant seniority. The argument that the effects of seniority systems lock in past discrimination has led to much litigation, but departmental seniority systems are still permitted,[62] and laying off more-senior white employees instead of recently hired minorities to preserve racial balance has been ruled unconstitutional.[63]

Comparable Worth: In Theory   Many contend that achieving "equal pay for equal work" would be a rather hollow victory, since occupations are so segregated by gender that men and women rarely do "equal work." As a result, some have come to support the goal of equal pay for jobs of "comparable worth." Proponents of comparable worth can point to the fact that the "male" occupation of maintaining *machines* (general maintenance mechanic) pays about $21 per hour, for example, while the "female" job of maintaining *children* (childcare worker) pays roughly $13. Why, they might ask, should those who take care of human beings be paid less than those who take care of machines?

When asked why mechanics are paid more than childcare workers, economists answer in terms of market forces: For some reason, the supply of mechanics must be smaller relative to the demand for them than the supply of childcare workers. Perhaps this reason has to do with working conditions, perhaps learning and keeping abreast of the skills required of a mechanic are more difficult, or perhaps occupational crowding increases the supply of childcare workers. Whatever the reason, the argument goes, wages are the price of labor—and prices play such a critical *practical* role in the allocation of resources that they are best left unregulated.

Thus, in fighting discrimination, most economists would advise modifying the demand or supply behaviors that *cause* unequal outcomes rather than treating the *symptoms* by regulating wages. If the wages of childcare workers were to be raised above their market-clearing level, to take the case at hand, a surplus would be created in that labor market. Above-market wages would mean fewer jobs and more unemployed applicants—hardly the outcome envisioned by those wanting to end discrimination. (A lengthy analysis of these unintended side effects is given in Example 12.6, in the context of equalizing the pay of university professors across the various disciplines.)

EXAMPLE 12.6

Comparable Worth and the University

Some of the difficulties involved with the concept of *comparable worth* can be illustrated by an example in which gender does not even enter. Consider the labor market for university professors in the fields of computer science and English, and suppose that initially, the demand and supply curves for both are given by D_{0C} and S_{0C} and D_{0E} and S_{0E}, respectively. As Figure 12.9 indicates, in this circumstance, the same wage (W_0) will prevail in both markets, and N_{0C} computer science professors and N_{0E} English professors will be hired. Suppose also that in some objective sense, the quality of the two groups of professors is equal.

Presumably this is a situation that advocates of comparable worth would applaud. Both types of professors require the same amount of training, represented by a PhD, and both are required to engage in the same activities: teaching and research. Unless we are willing to assign different values to the teaching and research produced in different academic fields, we must conclude that the jobs are truly comparable. Hence, if the two groups are equal in quality, equal wages would be justified according to the concept of comparable worth.

Suppose now, however, that the demand for computer science professors rises to D_{1C} as a result of the increasing number of students who want to take computer science courses.

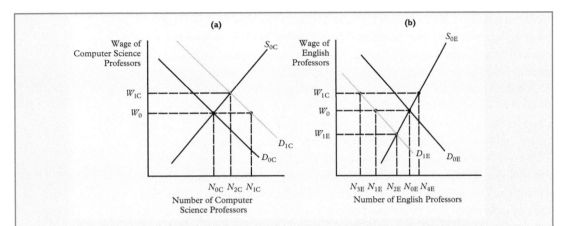

Figure 12.9 The Market for Computer Science Professors and English Professors

Suppose at the same time the demand for English professors falls to D_{1E} because fewer students want to take elective courses in English. At the old equilibrium wage rate, an excess demand ensues for computer science professors of $N_{1C} - N_{0C}$ and an excess supply occurs for English professors of $N_{0E} - N_{1E}$.

How can universities respond? One possibility is to let the market work; the wage of computer science professors will rise to W_{1C} and that of English professors will fall to W_{1E}. Employment of the former will rise to N_{2C}, while employment of the latter will become N_{2E}.

Another possibility is to keep the wages of the two groups of professors equal at the old wage rate of W_0. Universities could respond to the excess demand for computer scientists and the excess supply of English professors by lowering hiring standards for the former and raising them for the latter. Because the average quality of English professors would then exceed the average quality of computer scientists, the wage paid per "quality unit" would now be higher for the computer scientists. Hence, true comparable worth—equal pay for *equal-quality* workers performing comparable jobs—would not be achieved. Moreover, employment and course offerings in this situation would not change to meet changing student demands.

Alternatively, some advocates of comparable worth might argue that universities should respond by raising the wages of *all* professors to W_{1C}. Although this would eliminate the shortage of computer science professors, it would exacerbate the excess supply of English professors, raising it to $N_{4E} - N_{3E}$. Universities would respond by reducing the employment of English professors to N_{3E} (and reducing course offerings). Moreover, the excess supply again would permit universities to raise hiring standards for English professors, so again, average quality would rise. As a result, once more the wage per quality unit of English professors would be less than that of computer science professors, and again, true comparable worth would not be achieved.

The message that we can take away from this example is that it is difficult to "trick the market." In the face of changing relative demand conditions, wage differentials for the two types of professors must be allowed to arise; otherwise, quality differentials will arise. In neither case, however, can comparable worth be achieved. Put another way, the value of a job cannot be determined independently of market conditions.

Comparable Worth: In Practice   Comparable-worth policies have generally relied on job-rating schemes often used by employers with internal labor markets to determine or justify pay differentials associated with various job titles or promotion steps. The process involves assigning points to each job according to the knowledge and problem-solving abilities required, its level of accountability, the physical conditions of work, and perhaps other characteristics. Jobs with equal point values would receive equal pay, and of course, jobs assigned higher point values would receive higher pay (Appendix 12A provides an example). The process by which points are awarded to each job is obviously critical, and both sides of the comparable-worth issue see it as a problem. Opponents claim that job ratings can be used to unjustifiably raise the pay in targeted jobs above market levels, while proponents argue that the job ratings now used within firms unfairly lower the value of women's jobs.[64]

The relatively few cases in which comparable-worth policies have been used to address unequal pay in the United Kingdom and the United States, for example, have required equalization only *within the boundaries of a single employer*. In contrast to the United Kingdom, however, where cases involving both public employers and private employers have come before the tribunals specially created to hear comparable-worth complaints,[65] the major push for comparable worth in the United States has come in the state and local government sector.

To date, the estimated effects of implementing comparable worth in the United States, Canada, and the United Kingdom have been neither as positive as its proponents had hoped nor as dire as its critics had portended. The effects on male/female wage differentials appear small, as do any negative effects on female employment.[66]

The Federal Contract Compliance Program

In 1965, the U.S. Office of Federal Contract Compliance Programs (OFCCP) was established to monitor the hiring and promotion practices of federal contractors (firms supplying goods or services to the federal government). OFCCP requires contractors above a certain size to analyze the extent of their underutilization of women and underrepresented minorities and to propose a plan to remedy any such underutilization. Such a plan is called an *affirmative action plan*. Contractors submitting unacceptable plans or failing to meet their goals are threatened with the cancelation of their contracts and losing eligibility for future contracts, although these drastic steps are rarely taken.

Affirmative action planning is intended to commit firms to a schedule for rapidly overcoming unequal career opportunities afforded to women and underrepresented minorities. Such planning affects both *hiring* and *promotion* practices, and like requirements under the disparate impact standard, the contract compliance program requires covered employers to take race, ethnicity, and gender into account when developing personnel policies.

Those who favor affirmative action point out that even if nondiscrimination in personnel actions were to be scrupulously followed, it still would not be an expeditious way to overcome the adverse effects of past discrimination.

Table 12.6 Change in the Racial Composition of a 1,600-Person Job Group With Nondiscriminatory Hiring from a Pool That Is 12 Percent Black (20 Percent Yearly Turnover Rate)

	Year						
	0	1	2	3	4	5	10
Number of Black workers							
Loss		20	24	26	29	31	36
New hires		38	38	38	38	38	38
Net gain		18	14	12	11	7	2
Cumulative level	100	118	132	144	155	162	181
Percent of workers who are Black	6.25	7.37	8.25	9.00	9.69	10.12	11.31

For example, consider the data in Table 12.6 for a hypothetical firm that has just agreed to follow a policy of nondiscrimination in hiring. Black workers represent 12 percent of the firm's hiring pool, but right now, they comprise only 6.25 percent of the firm's 1,600-person workforce. The firm is not growing, so the only hiring opportunities come when workers quit, which they do at a rate of 20 percent each year. Because of these limited hiring opportunities, and because 20 percent of Black workers hired subsequently leave each year, the table illustrates that nondiscrimination in hiring would not achieve proportionate representation even in ten years (and progress would be slower with a lower quit rate).

Besides the argument that affirmative action represents *reverse* discrimination (against white men), the potential effects of the contract compliance program have been questioned on two other grounds. First, if underrepresented groups are to be given preference in hiring, will firms be required to hire less-qualified workers? Second, because the program covers only federal contractors, will qualified women and other underrepresented groups just be shifted from the noncovered sector to the covered sector, with no overall gain in employment? These questions lead us to a review of the effects that antidiscrimination programs have had in the United States.

Effectiveness of Federal Antidiscrimination Programs

A comprehensive review of federal affirmative action programs concluded that they have redistributed employment opportunities among federal contractors (who generally pay more than noncontractors) toward Black workers, although the extent of this redistribution does not seem to have been large. With regard to women, no evidence seems to show that affirmative action has been associated with lower levels of human capital or job performance. Weaker labor market credentials were found among minorities hired, but scant evidence shows that job performance levels were lower.[67] Can we conclude that the improvements for women and minorities in this one sector have translated to improvements overall?[68] This question has been most extensively addressed with regard to Black Americans.

The ratio of Black incomes to white incomes has risen since 1960. But is this rise a result of government efforts, or were other forces working to accomplish this result? Three other forces are commonly cited. First, an improvement in the *educational attainment* of Black workers relative to that of white workers during this period is thought to have played an important role in raising the ratio of Black earnings to white earnings; in fact, one study estimated that increased educational attainment accounts for 20 percent to 25 percent of the post-1960 gain in the earnings ratio.[69] Second, evidence shows that the *quality* of schooling improved more after 1960 for Black people than for white people, and one study has estimated that 15 percent to 20 percent of the increased earnings ratio can be attributed to enhanced school quality.[70] Finally, some have argued that because the relatively large *reduction in labor-force participation rates* among Black workers was centered in the least-educated group of workers, the average earnings of those who remained employed were thereby increased, giving the *appearance* of overall improvement. Roughly 10 percent to 20 percent of the improved earnings ratio has been attributed to this last factor.[71]

EMPIRICAL STUDY 12.1

CAN WE CATCH DISCRIMINATORS IN THE ACT? THE USE OF FIELD EXPERIMENTS IN IDENTIFYING LABOR MARKET DISCRIMINATION

As we saw earlier in this chapter, the statistical methods that economists employ to measure labor market discrimination against, say, Black Americans, essentially break the observed black/white wage differential into two parts: the part that can be explained by differences in *measurable* productive characteristics and the residual associated with the payoffs to those characteristics. Although some might assert that the residual reflects discrimination, others could point to this residual as attributable (in whole or in part) to productive characteristics that could not be measured. In the legal terms introduced toward the end of this chapter, statistical analyses are useful in identifying *disparate impact*, but they are not usually conclusive in this regard. Furthermore, they fall short of proving *disparate treatment* because they focus on results, not on the behaviors that produced them. Can we find ways to actually catch discriminators in the act?

One method used to observe discrimination is to conduct an *audit*—or field experiment—in which employers (if the focus is on the labor market) with advertised job openings are approached by auditors of different races posing as applicants. Each auditor ("applicant") is paired with an auditor of a different race, and both are given fictional work histories and educational backgrounds that are carefully constructed to be equivalent in terms of job qualifications. Discrimination can be inferred if auditors who are Black, say, are systematically treated worse than auditors who are white. Constructing convincing audits is challenging, because if the auditors know the purpose of the study, they might behave during interviews in ways that induce employers to respond in the way that they believe the researchers expect. Sending auditors to interview for jobs is also time-consuming and expensive, so large samples are usually not feasible. Matching auditors in terms of size and appearance, and training them to present themselves in the same way during interviews, are also challenging.

One recent study, however, circumvented these problems with audits by sending some 5,000 résumés to firms in Boston and Chicago that advertised 1,300 job openings. The researchers then analyzed how likely each résumé was to elicit a callback. The résumés were paired to achieve equivalence, and the names assigned were used to suggest race: Lakisha Washington and Jamal Jones, for example, were among the names used as indicators of Black American applicants, whereas names such as Emily Walsh and Greg Baker were used to suggest that the applicant was white. If the résumés with Black American–sounding names elicited significantly fewer invitations for the applicant to come in for an interview, we could conclude that race discrimination occurred.

The findings were remarkable. On average, job applicants with white-sounding names needed to send 10 résumés to receive one callback, whereas those whose names sounded Black American needed to send, on average, 15 résumés to receive one callback. This 50 percent gap was statistically significant, and it grew larger as the quality of résumés rose (i.e., in jobs with greater skill demands, the racial differential was even larger). If these fictitious résumés indicated that the applicants lived in a wealthier or more-educated neighborhood, callback probabilities increased for both groups, but the size of the racial differential remained constant. Although newspaper ads represent only one hiring channel, and although the audit ended at the callback stage (rather than going through to job offers), this study demonstrates that racial discrimination persists in the labor market to this day.

Source: Marianne Bertrand and Sendhil Mullainathan, "Are Emily and Greg More Employable Than Lakisha and Jamal? A Field Experiment on Labor Market Discrimination," *American Economic Review* 94 (September 2004): 991–1013

For a subsequent analysis of the apparent causes and economic effects of distinctively Black American names, see Roland G. Fryer, Jr. and Steven D. Levitt, "The Causes and Consequences of Distinctively Black Names," *Quarterly Journal of Economics* 119 (August 2004): 767–805. For a study of Asian, African, and Slavic immigrants to Sweden who changed their names to hide their ethnicity, see Mahmood Arai and Peter Skogman Thoursie, "Renouncing Personal Names: An Empirical Examination of Surname Change and Earnings," *Journal of Labor Economics* 27 (January 2009): 127–147. A study from Canada is in Philip Oreopoulos, "Why Do Skilled Immigrants Struggle in the Labor Market? A Field Experiment with Thirteen Thousand Resumes," *American Economic Journal: Economic Policy* 3 (November 2011): 148–171.

Taking the upper estimates of the three sources of earnings increases cited earlier, at least one-third of the improvement in the Black–white earnings ratio for men remains to be explained. Were federal efforts to reduce discrimination in the labor market perhaps responsible? One review of the literature and the evidence on this issue concluded that, overall, federal efforts were successful in raising earnings levels of Black Americans.[72]

One important fact about the economic progress of Black workers is that there was a discontinuous jump in the Black–white earnings ratio between 1960 and 1975. This sudden improvement coincided with the onset of federal antidiscrimination programs, and it cannot be explained by the rather continuous increases taking place in such other factors as schooling quality or attainment. A second important fact is that the greatest gains in the Black–white earnings ratio during the 1960–1975 period were in the U.S. South, where segregation was most blatant and where federal antidiscrimination efforts were greatest.

The conclusion that federal antidiscrimination efforts were at least partially successful in raising the relative earnings of Black workers must be acknowledged as somewhat surprising, because studies of individual programs (such as the contract compliance program) have estimated rather meager results. The paradox of overall improvement resulting from programs that appear to have been individually weak could be resolved by noting that each program was part of a comprehensive set of programs—largely aimed at the U.S. South—to dismantle all forms of racial segregation, register Black citizens to vote, and provide legal remedies for victims of discrimination. In the words of one analyst,

> There is evidence that southern employers were eager to employ [Black people] if they were given the proper excuse. This produced a strong leverage effect for the new laws. . . . An entire pattern of racial exclusion was challenged. This helps to explain how an apparent straw (the Equal Employment Opportunity Commission and the Office of Federal Contract Compliance) could have broken the back of southern employment discrimination. They were only the tip of a federal iceberg launched against the South.[73]

Although optimism about the effects of federal antidiscrimination programs in the 1960s and 1970s is warranted, whether such programs were successful after 1980, when the market for less-educated workers turned poor, remains unclear. Arguably, the earnings of Black workers after 1980 would have been even *lower* were it not for federal efforts, but the evidence so far is that once the most blatant forms of discrimination had been attacked, the effects of federal efforts weakened.[74]

Review Questions

1. Chinese Americans and Japanese Americans have average earnings that are equal to, or above, those of white Americans. Does this fact imply that they are not victims of labor market discrimination?

2. "In recent years, the wage gap between higher-skilled workers and low-er-skilled workers in the United States has grown. This growth means that measured labor market discrimination against lower-skilled Mexican immigrants is also growing." Comment on whether the second part of this statement is implied by the first part.

3. An *Associated Press* article quoted a report saying that male high school teachers were paid more than female high school teachers. Assuming that this is true, what information would you require before judging this to be evidence of wage discrimination?

4. Will government-mandated requirements to hire qualified minorities (at nondiscriminatory wages) in the same proportions that they are found in the relevant labor force reduce the profits of firms that formerly engaged in employer discrimination? Fully explain your answer.

5. Suppose that the United States were to adopt, on a permanent basis, a wage subsidy to be paid to employers who hire disadvantaged Black workers (those with relatively little education and few marketable skills). Analyze the potential effectiveness of this subsidy in overcoming labor market discrimination against Black people and premarket differences between Black people and white people in the long run.

6. You are involved in an investigation of charges that a large university in a small town is discriminating against female employees. You find that the salaries for professors in the nearly all-female School of Social Work are 20 percent below average salaries paid to those of comparable rank elsewhere in the university. Is this university exhibiting behavior associated with *employer* discrimination? Explain.

7. Suppose that a city pays its building inspectors (all men) $16 an hour and its public health nurses (all women) $10 an hour. Suppose that the city council passes a comparable-worth law that in effect requires the wages of public health nurses to be equal to the wages of building inspectors. Evaluate the assertion that this comparable-worth policy would benefit primarily high-quality nurses and low-quality building inspectors.

8. In the 1920s, South Africa passed laws that effectively prohibited Black Africans from working in jobs that required high degrees of skill; skilled jobs were reserved for white people. Analyze the consequences of this law for Black South African and white South African workers.

9. Assume that women live longer than men, on average. Suppose that an employer hires men and women, pays them the same wage for the same job, and contributes an equal amount per person toward a pension. However, the promised monthly pension after retirement is smaller for women than for men because the pension funds for them have to last longer. According to a decision by the Supreme Court, this employer would be guilty of discrimination because of the unequal monthly pension benefits after retirement.

a. Comment on the court's implicit definition of discrimination. Is it consistent with the definition normally used by economists? Why or why not?

b. Analyze the economic effects of this decision on men and women.

Problems

1. Calculate the index of dissimilarity for men and women, given the information in Table 12P.1.

Table 12P.1 The Distribution of Men and Women in Three Occupations

Occupation	Men	Women
A	40	20
B	40	25
C	20	25
Total	100	70

2. Suppose that $MRP_L = 20 - 0.5L$ for left-handed workers, where $L =$ the number of left-handed workers and MRP_L is measured in dollars per hour. The going wage for left-handed workers is $10 per hour, but employer A discriminates against these workers and has a discrimination coefficient, D, of $2 per hour. Graph the MRP_L curve, and show how many left-handed workers employer A hires. How much profit has employer A lost by discriminating?

3. Suppose that (similar to Figure 12.3 in the text) the market demand for female workers depends on the relative wage of women to men, W_F/W_M, in the following manner: $W_F/W_M = 1.1 - 0.0001 N_F$ if the number of female workers is less than 1,000, where N_F is the number of female workers hired in the market; $W_F/W_M = 1$ if the number of female workers is between 1,001 and 5,000; and $W_F/W_M = 1.5 - 0.0001 N_F$ if the number of female workers is above 5,000. Graph this demand curve, and calculate the relative wage of female workers when the number hired is 200, 2,000, and 7,000. When does discrimination harm female workers in this market?

4. (Appendix 12A) In the market for delivery truck drivers, $L_S = -45 + 5W$ and $L_D = 180 - 10W$, where $L =$ number of workers and $W =$ wage in dollars per hour. In the market for librarians, $L_S = -15 + 5W$ and $L_D = 190 - 10W$. Find the equilibrium wage and employment level in each occupation, and explain what will happen if a comparable-worth law mandates that the librarians' wage be increased to equal the delivery truck drivers' wage. Use a graph.

5. (Appendix 12A) Table 12P.5 gives the Hay Point (HP) total for five female jobs and the corresponding monthly salary (S).

Table 12P.5 Hypothetical Hay Points and Female Salaries in Five Occupations

Hay Point	Average salary of women ($)
200	1,200
310	1,300
425	1,500
500	1,580
550	1,635

A least squares regression applied to data for the *male* occupations yielded the following relationship: $S_i = 1,200 + 0.90 HP_i$. Using the "male" equation, estimate the earnings that the women would have earned on the basis of the HP level of the occupation. Analyze whether discrimination appears to be occurring. Is there a pattern by skill level?

6. Suppose that the hourly marginal revenue product of all workers in a particular labor market is $MRP_L = 20 - L$, where L = the number of workers. The hourly wage rate for women in this market is $W = \$5.75$. What is the gap between MRP_L and wage in this labor market if $L = 12$? Is this gap a reliable measure of discrimination against women in this market?

7. Suppose that the marginal revenue product of all workers in a particular labor market is $MRP_L = 20 - L$, where L = the number of workers. Suppose that women are receiving $8 per hour and that 10 women are hired. How many workers would a nondiscriminatory employer hire? How much profit is the employer willing to forgo by hiring these 10 female workers?

8. Suppose that a researcher estimated the relationship between salary, gender, and age among a group consisting of male workers and female workers but ignored the fact that, on average, male workers have more work experience than female workers do. The estimated regression of salary on gender and age is

$$S_i = 21354.83 + 239.45\ G_i + 93.17\ A_i$$
$$\quad (15252.9)\ \ (95.6)\qquad (29.6)$$

where S_i = salary of a worker, G_i = 1 if the worker is male and 0 if the worker is female, and A_i = the employee's age. Standard errors of the coefficients are in parentheses.

With experience included in the regression, the estimated regression is

$$S_i = 21177.75 + 226.27\ G_i + 89.73\ A_i + 443.41\ X_i$$
$$\quad (16111.3)\ \ (186.8)\qquad (34.6)\qquad (47.7)$$

where X_i = the years of work experience of the worker. Comparing the two estimated regressions, does salary discrimination by gender appear to be occurring? Discuss the implications of omitting the experience variable in the first regression.

Notes

1. For papers on these two topics, see Thomas DeLeire, "Changes in Wage Discrimination Against People with Disabilities: 1984–93," *Journal of Human Resources* 36 (Winter 2001): 144–158; Eleonora Patacchini, Giuseppe Ragusa, and Yves Zenou, "Unexplored Dimensions of Discrimination in Europe: Homosexuality and Physical Appearance," *Journal of Population Economics* 28 (October 2015): 1045–1073; Christopher S. Carpenter, "Self-Reported Sexual Orientation and Earnings: Evidence from California," *Industrial and Labor Relations Review* 58 (January 2005): 258–273; Cevat G. Aksoy, Christopher S. Carpenter, and Jeff Frank, "Sexual Orientation and Earnings: New Evidence from the United Kingdom," *Industrial and Labor Relations Review* 71 (January 2018): 242–272. Also see Dan A. Black, Seth G. Sanders, and Lowell J. Taylor, "The Economics of Lesbian and Gay Families," *Journal of Economic Perspectives* 21 (Spring 2007): 53–70; David Neumark, "Experimental Research on Labor Market Discrimination," *Journal of Economic Literature* 56 (September 2018): 799–866, summarizes several experimental studies of discrimination on the basis of disability, sexual orientation, physical appearance, and age.

2. For discussions of this issue in the context of gender pay gaps, see Aaron Lowen and Paul Sicilian, " 'Family-Friendly' Fringe Benefits and the Gender Wage Gap," *Journal of Labor Research* 30 (2009): 101–119; Eric Solberg and Teresa Laughlin, "The Gender Pay Gap, Fringe Benefits, and Occupational Crowding," *Industrial and Labor Relations Review* 48 (1995): 692–708. For an analysis of the difference between the wage gap (and the total compensation gap) between people with and without disabilities, see Kevin F. Hallock, Xin Jin, and Linda J. Barrington, "Estimating Pay Gaps for Workers with Disabilities: Implications from Broadening Definitions and Datasets," *Rehabilitation Research, Policy and Education* 28:4 (2014): 264–290.

3. Taking hours of work into account is crucial. We note later in this chapter, for example, that the unemployment rate is higher for Black workers than for the overall labor force in the United States. Therefore, examining only full-time, full-year workers, though showing the true *wage* gap for those workers, will not fully compare the entire labor market outcomes of these two groups.

4. Data can be found at U.S. Bureau of the Census, Historical Income Tables: People, Table 39, www.census.gov/data/tables/time-series/demo/income-poverty/historical-income-people.html.

5. As noted, the pay differences presented and analyzed in this chapter relate to wages and earnings, not to measures of total compensation (which would include employee benefits). Some evidence shows that women are less likely than comparable men to have pension, health insurance, and disability benefits; see Janet Currie, "Gender Gaps in Benefits Coverage," in *The Human Resource Management Handbook*, eds. David Lewin, Daniel Mitchell, and Mahmood Zaidi (Greenwich, CT: JAI Press, 1997), chapter 23.

6. Claudia Goldin, "A Grand Gender Convergence: Its Last Chapter," *American Economic Review* 104 (April 2014): 1091–1119.

7. Edward P. Lazear and Sherwin Rosen, "Male–Female Wage Differentials in Job Ladders," *Journal of Labor Economics* 8 (January 1990): S106–S123; Erica L. Groshen, "The Structure of the Female/Male Wage Differential: Is It Who You Are, What You Do, or Where You Work?" *Journal of Human Resources* 26 (Summer 1991): 457–472; Stephen J. Spurr and Glenn J. Sueyoshi, "Turnover and Promotion of Lawyers: An Inquiry into Gender Differences," *Journal of Human Resources* 29 (Summer 1994): 813–842; Claudia Goldin, Sari Pekkala Kerr, Claudia Olivetti, and Erling Barth, "The Expanding Gender Earnings Gap: Evidence from the LEHD-2000 Census," *American Economic Review* 107 (May 2017): 110–114; Heather Antecol, Kelly Bedard, and Jenna Stearns, "Equal but Inequitable: Who Benefits from Gender-Neutral Tenure Clock Stopping Policies?" *The American Economic Review* 108 (September 2018): 2420–2441.

8. Goldin, "A Grand Gender Convergence: Its Last Chapter."

9. Patricia Cortes and Jessica Pan, "Cross-Country Evidence on the Relationship Between Overwork and Skilled Women's Job Choices," *American Economic Review: Papers and Proceedings* 107 (May 2017): 105–109; Nikolay Angelov, Per Johansson, and Erica Lindahl, "Parenthood and the Gender Gap in Pay," *Journal of Labor Economics* 34 (July 2016): 545–579; Marianne Bertrand, Claudia Goldin, and Lawrence F. Katz, "Dynamics of the Gender Gap for Young Professionals in the Financial and Corporate Sectors," *American Economic Journal: Applied Economics* 2 (July 2010): 228–255. Women might work in firms that have lower wages but greater nonpay benefits; see Isaac Sorkin, "The Role of Firms in Gender Earnings Inequality: Evidence from the United States," *American Economic Review: Papers and Proceedings* 107 (May 2017): 384–387.

10. Jane Waldfogel, "Understanding the 'Family Gap' in Pay for Women with Children," *Journal of Economic Perspectives* 12 (Winter 1998): 137–156. For others on the "child penalty," see Henrik Kleven, Camille Landais, and Jakob Egholt Søgaard, "Children and Gender Inequality: Evidence from Denmark," *American Economic Journal: Applied Economics* 11 (October 2019): 181–209; Nabanita Datta Gupta and

Nina Smith, "Children and Career Interruptions: The Family Gap in Denmark," *Economica* 69 (November 2002): 609–629; Christy Spivey, "Time Off at What Price? The Effects of Career Interruptions on Earnings," *Industrial and Labor Relations Review* 59 (October 2005): 119–140. See Andrea Ichino and Enrico Moretti, "Biological Gender Differences, Absenteeism, and the Earnings Gap," *American Economic Journal: Applied Economics* 1 (January 2009): 183–218, for research indicating that absenteeism related to the menstrual cycle might account for some of the wage disadvantages against women.

11. Mark L. Egan, Gregor Matvos, and Amit Seru, "When Harry Fired Sally: The Double Standard in Punishing Misconduct" (Working Paper No. 23242, National Bureau of Economic Research, Cambridge, MA, August 2018).

12. Dale Boisso, Kathy Hayes, Joseph Hirschberg, and Jacques Silber, "Occupational Segregation in the Multidimensional Case: Decomposition and Tests of Significance," *Journal of Econometrics* 61 (March 1994): 161–171; Martin Watts, "Divergent Trends in Gender Segregation by Occupation in the United States: 1970–92," *Journal of Post-Keynesian Economics* 17 (Spring 1995): 357–379.

13. Francine D. Blau, Peter Brummund, and Albert Yung-Hsu Liu, "Trends in Occupational Segregation by Gender 1970–2009: Adjusting for the Impact of Changes in the Occupational Coding System," *Demography* 50 (April 2013): 471–494. For an analysis of occupational segregation trends in the twentieth century, see Jessica Y. Pan, "Gender Segregation in Occupations: The Role of Tipping and Social Interactions," *Journal of Labor Economics* 33 (April 2015): 365–408.

14. Francine D. Blau, Marianne A. Ferber, and Anne E. Winkler, *The Economics of Women, Men, and Work*, 7th ed. (Boston, MA: Pearson, 2014): 224; Marjorie L. Baldwin, Richard J. Butler, and William G. Johnson, "A Hierarchical Theory of Occupational Segregation and Wage Discrimination," *Economic Inquiry* 39 (January 2001): 94–110; June O'Neill, "The Gender Gap in Wages circa 2000," *American Economic Review* 93 (May 2003): 309–314; Michael Ransom and Ronald L. Oaxaca, "Intrafirm Mobility and Sex Differences in Pay," *Industrial and Labor Relations Review* 58 (January 2005): 219–237.

15. Chinhui Juhn and Kristin McCue, "Specialization Then and Now: Marriage, Children, and the Gender Earnings Gap across Cohorts," *Journal of Economic Perspectives* 31 (Winter 2017): 183–204; Carolyn Sloane, Erik Hurst, and Dan Black, "A Cross-Cohort Analysis of Human Capital Specialization and the College Gender Wage Gap" (Working Paper No. 26348, National Bureau of Economic Research, Cambridge, MA, February 2020).

16. See Rachel Croson and Uri Gneezy, "Gender Differences in Preferences," *Journal of Economic Literature* 47 (June 2009): 448–474; Victor

Lavy, "Gender Differences in Market Competitiveness in a Real Workplace: Evidence from Performance-Based Pay Tournaments Among Teachers," *Economic Journal* 123 (June 2013): 540–573; Andreas Leibbrandt and John List, "Do Women Avoid Salary Negotiations? Evidence from a Large Scale Natural Field Experiment" (Working Paper No. 18511, National Bureau of Economic Research, Cambridge, MA, November 2012); Alan Manning and Farzad Saidi, "Understanding the Gender Pay Gap: What's Competition Got to Do with It," *Industrial and Labor Relations Review* 63 (July 2010): 681–698; David Card, Ana Rute Cardoso and Patrick Kline, "Bargaining, Sorting, and the Gender Wage Gap: Quantifying the Impact of Firms on the Relative Pay of Women," *Quarterly Journal of Economics* 131 (May 2016): 633–686.

17. Kimberly Bayard, Judith Hellerstein, David Neumark, and Kenneth Troske, "New Evidence on Sex Segregation and Sex Differences in Wages from Matched Employee–Employer Data," *Journal of Labor Economics* 21 (October 2003): 887–922; David Neumark, "Sex Discrimination in Restaurant Hiring: An Audit Study," *Quarterly Journal of Economics* 111 (August 1996): 915–941. Intrafirm promotion differences between men and women can also account for some job segregation; see Michael Ransom and Ronald L. Oaxaca, "Intrafirm Mobility and Sex Differences in Pay," *Industrial and Labor Relations Review* 58 (January 2005): 219–237; Francine Blau and Jed DeVaro, "New Evidence on Gender Differences in Promotion Rates: An Empirical Analysis of a Sample of New Hires," *Industrial Relations* 46 (July 2007): 511–550.

18. This procedure was first described in Ronald Oaxaca, "Male–Female Wage Differentials in Urban Labor Markets," *International Economic Review* 14 (October 1973): 693–709. For refinements, see Ronald L. Oaxaca and Michael R. Ransom, "On Discrimination and the Decomposition of Wage Differentials," *Journal of Econometrics* 61 (March 1994): 5–21; Moon-Kak Kim and Solomon W. Polachek, "Panel Estimates of Male–Female Earnings Functions," *Journal of Human Resources* 29 (Spring 1994): 406–428.

19. Oaxaca, "Male–Female Wage Differentials in Urban Labor Markets," actually computes this in two ways. His method requires the mean vector of characteristics of men and women, $\bar{X}_m$ and $\bar{X}_f$, respectively, and the estimation of the earnings equation using data for men only and for women only in two regressions—yielding the vectors of estimated coefficients β_m and β_d, respectively. From this, one can compute the estimated earnings of women if they were paid by using the male rates of return: Call this $S_{wpaidasm}$. And one can compute the estimated earnings of men if they were paid by using the estimated returns of women: Call this $S_{mpaidasw}$. Using this information, one can compute two estimates of discrimination: $\Omega_1 = \dfrac{S_m - S_w}{S_w} - \dfrac{S_m - S_{wpaidasm}}{S_{wpaidasm}}$ and

$\Omega_2 = \dfrac{S_m - S_w}{S_w} - \dfrac{S_{mpaidasw} - S_w}{S_w}$.

20. We also note, importantly, an additional issue confronted by social science researchers: systematic bias that individuals face before even entering the labor market. For example, if Black students are less likely to be encouraged (e.g., by teachers in elementary and secondary schools) to study certain fields, they may be less likely to choose particular occupations. Although our focus in this chapter is on discrimination in the *labor market,* a more comprehensive consideration of discrimination would include bias in education, housing, policing, the court system, and other social institutions.

21. One attempt to measure the effects of current labor market discrimination on subsequent human-capital accumulation is reported in David Neumark and Michele McLennan, "Sex Discrimination and Women's Labor Market Outcomes," *Journal of Human Resources* 30 (Fall 1995): 713–740.

22. Women seem to be less likely to work in high-wage firms, which might require more (or less-flexible) hours of their workers; for an analysis of how firm-level wage premiums affect gender pay gaps, see Benjamin Bruns, "Changes in Workplace Heterogeneity and How They Widen the Gender Wage Gap," *American Economic Journal: Applied Economics* 11 (April 2019): 74–113.

23. Francine D. Blau and Lawrence M. Kahn, "The Gender Wage Gap: Extent, Trends, and Explanations," *Journal of Economic Literature* 55 (September 2017): 789–865.

24. Claudia Goldin and Lawrence F. Katz, "A Most Egalitarian Profession: Pharmacy and the Evolution of a Family-Friendly Occupation," *Journal of Labor Economics* 34 (July 2018): 705–746.

25. Dora Gicheva, "Working Long Hours and Early Career Outcomes in the High-End Labor Market," *Journal of Labor Economics* 31 (October 2013): 785–824. The availability of low-skilled immigrants to perform household work appears to free high-skilled women to work longer hours and thus narrow the wage gap; see Patricia Cortés and Jessica Pan, "When Time Binds: Returns to Working Long Hours and the Gender Wage Gap Among the Highly Skilled" (IZA Discussion Paper No. 9846, Institute for Labor Studies, Bonn, Germany, March 2016).

26. Kevin Lang and Jee-Yeon K. Lehman, "Racial Discrimination in the Labor Market: Theory and Empirics," *Journal of Economic Literature* 50 (December 2012): 959–1006. For analyses of these earnings gaps, see Chinhui Juhn, "Labor Market Dropouts and Trends in the Wages of Black and White Men," *Industrial and Labor Relations Review* 56 (July 2003): 643–662; Derek Neal, "The Measured Black–White Wage Gap Among Women Is Too Small," *Journal of Political Economy* 112:1, pt. 2 (February 2004): S1–S28.

27. U.S. Bureau of Labor Statistics, Employment and Earnings Online, Annual Average Household Data, Characteristics of the Employed, Table 22, http://www.bls.gov/cps/cpsaat39.pdf

28. See Amitabh Chandra, "Labor-Market Dropouts and the Racial Wage Gap: 1940–1990," *American Economic Review* 90 (May 2000): 333–338; John Bound and Richard B. Freeman, "What Went Wrong? The Erosion of Relative Earnings and Employment of Young Black Men in the 1980s," *Quarterly Journal of Economics* 107 (February 1992): 202–232; Lang and Lehman, "Racial Discrimination in the Labor Market: Theory and Empirics"; Patrick Bayer and Kerwin Kofi Charles, "Divergent Paths: A New Perspective on Earnings Differences Between Black and White Men Since 1940," *The Quarterly Journal of Economics* 133 (August 2018): 1459–1501.

29. For an analysis of the growth in the unemployment ratio, see Robert W. Fairlie and William A. Sundstrom, "The Emergence, Persistence, and Recent Widening of the Racial Unemployment Gap," *Industrial and Labor Relations Review* 52 (January 1999): 252–270.

30. Judith Hellerstein and David Neumark, "Workplace Segregation in the United States: Race, Ethnicity, and Skill," *Review of Economics and Statistics* 90 (August 2008): 459–477; Neumark, "Experimental Research on Labor Market Discrimination."

31. For example, see David Card and Jesse Rothstein, "Racial Segregation and the Black–White Test Score Gap," *Journal of Public Economics* 91 (December 2007): 2158–2184; Rucker C. Johnson, "Long-Run Impacts of School Desegregation and School Quality on Adult Attainments" (Working Paper No. 16664, National Bureau of Economic Research, Cambridge, MA, January 2011). Other studies that examine this test-score gap include Roland G. Fryer, Jr. and Steven D. Levitt, "The Black–White Test Score Gap Through Third Grade," and Alan Krueger, Jesse Rothstein, and Sarah Turner, "Race, Income, and College in 25 Years: Evaluating Justice O'Connor's Conjecture," both in *American Law and Economics Review* 8 (Summer 2006): 249–311. Also see Derek Neal, "Why Has Black–White Skill Convergence Stopped?" (Working Paper No. 11090, National Bureau of Economic Research, Cambridge, MA, January 2005).

32. Kevin Lang and Michael Manove, "Education and Labor Market Discrimination," *American Economic Review* 101 (June 2011): 1467–1496. The controls for school inputs (e.g., teacher qualification and class size) and family background are attempts to control for the quality of schooling and the noncognitive characteristics that are associated with success in school; for a discussion of the latter set of characteristics, see Pedro Carneiro, James J. Heckman, and Dimitriy V. Masterov, "Labor Market Discrimination and Racial Differences in Premarket Factors," *Journal of Law and Economics* 48 (April 2005): 1–39.

33. A similar conclusion was reached in a study that used a different methodology; see Roland G. Fryer, Jr., Devah Pager, and Jörg L. Spenkuch, "Racial Disparities in Job Finding and Offered Wages," *Journal of Law and Economics* 56 (August 2013): 633–689.

34. For a discussion of this issue, see Carneiro, Heckman, and Masterov, "Labor Market Discrimination and Racial Differences in Premarket Factors"; Lang and Manove, "Education and Labor Market Discrimination"; Lang and Lehman, "Racial Discrimination in the Labor Market: Theory and Empirics"; Lisa Barrow and Cecilia Elena Rouse, "Do Returns to Schooling Differ by Race and Ethnicity?" *American Economic Review* 95 (May 2005): 83–87.

35. John S. Heywood and Daniel Parent, "Performance Pay and the White–Black Wage Gap," *Journal of Labor Economics* 30 (April 2012): 249–290.

36. Costas Cavounidis, Kevin Lang, and Russell Weinstein, "The Boss Is Watching: How Monitoring Decisions Hurt Black Workers" (Working Paper No. 26319, National Bureau of Economic Research, Cambridge, MA: September 2019). Racial bias among managers may also cause workers from the disfavored group to be less productive; see Dylan Glover, Amanda Pallais, and William Pariente, "Discrimination as a Self-Fulfilling Prophecy: Evidence from French Grocery Stores," *Quarterly Journal of Economics* 132 (August 2017): 1219–1260.

37. Neumark, "Experimental Research on Labor Market Discrimination," offers a comprehensive summary of experimental research in this area. Examples of experimental studies can be found in Marianne Bertrand and Sendhil Mullainathan, "Are Emily and Greg More Employable Than Lakisha and Jamal? A Field Experiment on Labor Market Discrimination," *American Economic Review* 94 (September 2004): 991–1013; Michael A. Stoll, Steven Raphael, and Harry Holzer, "Black Job Applicants and the Hiring Officer's Race," *Industrial and Labor Relations Review* 57 (January 2004): 267–287; Vojtěch Bartoš, Michal Bauer, Julie Chytilová, and Filip Matějka, "Attention Discrimination: Theory and Field Experiments with Monitoring Information Acquisition," *American Economic Review* 106 (June 2016): 1437–1475. For an article suggesting that the discrimination might be implicit rather than intentional, see Marianne Bertrand, Dolly Chugh, and Sendhil Mullainathan, "Implicit Discrimination," *American Economic Review* 95 (May 2005): 94–98.

38. Edwin A. Sexton and Reed Neil Olsen, "The Returns to On-the-Job Training: Are They the Same for Blacks and Whites?" *Southern Economic Journal* 61 (October 1994): 328–342. A recent study on the probability of employment suggests that Black women with darker skin tone—a group that historically had lower probabilities of employment, given their human-capital characteristics—no longer have employment probabilities lower than white women or Black people with lighter skin tone; the employment probabilities for Black men, however, showed no such improvements. See Randall Akee and Mutlu Yuksel, "The Decreasing Effect of Skin Tone on Women's Full-Time Employment," *Industrial and Labor Relations Review* 65 (April 2012): 398–426.

39. An analysis of wage differences in the rural United States estimates that equalizing the productive characteristics of Native Americans would result in their earning 3 to 7 percent less than rural white people. See Jean Kimmel, "Rural Wages and Returns to Education: Differences Between Whites, Blacks, and American Indians," *Economics of Education Review* 16 (February 1997): 81–96. Similar findings come from a study of Indigenous peoples in Canada; see Peter George and Peter Kuhn, "The Size and Structure of Native–White Wage Differentials in Canada," *Canadian Journal of Economics* 27 (February 1994): 20–42.

40. George J. Borjas, "Ethnic Capital and Intergenerational Mobility," *Quarterly Journal of Economics* 107 (February 1992): 123–150; Barry R. Chiswick, "The Skills and Economic Status of American Jewry: Trends over the Last Half-Century," *Journal of Labor Economics* 11:1, pt. 1 (January 1993): 229–242.

41. Hoyt Bleakley and Aimee Chin, "Language Skills and Earnings: Evidence from Childhood Immigrants," *Review of Economics and Statistics* 86 (May 2004): 481–496; Carneiro, Heckman, and Masterov, "Labor Market Discrimination and Racial Differences in Premarket Factors"; Joni Hersch, "Profiling the New Immigrant Worker: The Effects of Skin Color and Height," *Journal of Labor Economics* 26 (April 2008): 345–386.

42. The models of personal prejudice are based on Gary S. Becker, *The Economics of Discrimination*, 2nd ed. (Chicago, IL: University of Chicago Press, 1971).

43. Kerwin Kofi Charles and Jonathan Guryan, "Prejudice and Wages: An Empirical Assessment of Becker's *The Economics of Discrimination*," *Journal of Political Economy* 116 (October 2008): 773–809.

44. Evidence shows that when a company is taken over by new ownership, for example, discrimination faced by women in both promotions and wages falls; see Frederik Heyman, Helena Svaleryd, and Jonas Vlachos, "Competition, Takeovers, and Gender Discrimination," *ILR Review* 66 (April 2013): 409–432. Evidence suggesting that employer discrimination that is based on physical appearance does not occur is found in Ralph Stinebrickner, Todd Stinebrickner, and Paul J. Sullivan, "Beauty, Job Tasks, and Wages: Theory and Evidence," *Review of Economics and Statistics* 101 (October 2019): 602–615.

45. Sandra E. Black and Philip E. Strahan, "The Division of Spoils: Rent-Sharing and Discrimination in a Regulated Industry," *American Economic Review* 91 (September 2001): 814–831; James Peoples Jr. and Wayne K. Talley, "Black–White Earnings Differentials: Privatization versus Deregulation," *American Economic Review* 91 (May 2001): 164–168; Judith K. Hellerstein, David Neumark, and Kenneth R. Troske, "Market Forces and Sex Discrimination," *Journal of Human Resources* 37 (Spring 2002): 353–380; Ross Levine, Alexey Levkov, and

Yona Rubinstein, "Racial Discrimination and Competition" (Working Paper No. 14273, National Bureau of Economic Research, Cambridge, MA, August 2008).

46. Harry J. Holzer and Keith R. Ihlanfeldt, "Customer Discrimination and Employment Outcomes for Minority Workers," *Quarterly Journal of Economics* 113 (August 1998): 835–867; Neumark, "Sex Discrimination in Restaurant Hiring"; Mark T. Kanazawa and Jonas P. Funk, "Racial Discrimination in Professional Basketball: Evidence from Nielsen Ratings," *Economic Inquiry* 39 (October 2001): 599–608. For a study of customer discrimination in France, see Pierre-Philippe Combes, Bruno Decreuse, Morgane Laouénan, and Alain Trannoy, "Customer Discrimination and Employment Outcomes: Theory and Evidence from the French Labor Market," *Journal of Labor Economics* 34, pt. 1 (January 2016): 107–160. A direct test for customer racial prejudice can be found in Jennifer Doleac and Luke C.D. Stein, "The Visible Hand: Race and Online Market Outcomes," *Economic Journal* 123 (November 2013): F469–F492.

47. Morten Størling Hedegaard and Jean-Robert Tyran, "The Price of Prejudice," *American Economic Journal* 10 (January 2018): 40–63; Laura Giuliano, David I. Levine, and Jonathan Leonard, "Manager Race and the Race of New Hires," *Journal of Labor Economics* 27 (October 2009): 589–631, offer evidence of discrimination by employees.

48. Groshen, "The Structure of the Female/Male Wage Differential."

49. James F. Ragan Jr. and Carol Horton Tremblay, "Testing for Employee Discrimination by Race and Sex," *Journal of Human Resources* 23 (Winter 1988): 123–137; Baldwin, Butler, and Johnson, "A Hierarchical Theory of Occupational Segregation and Wage Discrimination"; Marianne Bertrand and Kevin F. Hallock, "The Gender Gap in Top Corporate Jobs," *Industrial and Labor Relations Review* 55 (October 2001): 3–21; Jonathan S. Leonard and David I. Levine, "The Effect of Diversity on Turnover: A Large Case Study," *Industrial and Labor Relations Review* 59 (July 2006): 547–572.

50. For an extensive analysis of statistical discrimination, with references to the literature on this topic, see Lang and Lehman, "Racial Discrimination in the Labor Market: Theory and Empirics."

51. For an example of preferences for U.S. natives (who may speak English better than immigrants), see Philip Oreopoulos, "Why Do Skilled Immigrants Struggle in the Labor Market? A Field Experiment with Thirteen Thousand Résumés," *American Economic Journal* 3 (November 2011): 148–171. For other articles on statistical discrimination involving résumés and applications, see Bartoš, Bauer, Chytilová, and Matějka, "Attention Discrimination: Theory and Field Experiments with Monitoring Information Acquisition"; Luc Behaghel, Bruno Crépon, and Thomas Le Barbanchon, "Unintended Effects of Anonymous Résumés," *American Economic Journal: Applied Economics*

7 (July 2015): 1–27; Olof Åslund and Oskar Nordström Skans, "Do Anonymous Job Application Procedures Level the Playing Field?" *Industrial and Labor Relations Review* 65 (January 2012): 82–107.

52. J. Aislinn Bohren, Alex Imas, and Michael Rosenberg, "The Dynamics of Discrimination: Theory and Evidence," *American Economic Review* 109 (October 2019): 3395–3436; Joshua C. Pinkston, "A Test of Screening Discrimination with Employer Learning," *Industrial and Labor Relations Review* 59 (January 2006): 267–284; Fabian Lange, "The Speed of Employer Learning," *Journal of Labor Economics* 25 (January 2007): 1–35.

53. See Blau, Ferber, and Winkler, *The Economics of Women, Men and Work*, 203. An excellent history of crowding theories is provided in Janice F. Madden, *The Economics of Sex Discrimination* (Lexington, MA: Lexington Books, 1973): 30–36.

54. For a review of the literature on this topic, see James Rebitzer, "Radical Political Economy and the Economics of Labor Markets," *Journal of Economic Literature* 31 (September 1993): 1417.

55. For a more rigorous discussion of this model, see Dan A. Black, "Discrimination in an Equilibrium Search Model," *Journal of Labor Economics* 13 (April 1995): 309–334.

56. Support for this theoretical implication can be found in Douglas Webber, "Firm-Level Monopsony and the Gender Pay Gap," *Industrial Relations* 55 (April 2016): 323–345; Michael R. Ransom and Ronald L. Oaxaca, "New Market Power Models and Sex Differences in Pay," *Journal of Labor Economics* 28 (April 2010): 267–289; Boris Hirsch, Thorsten Schank, and Claus Schnabel, "Differences in Labor Supply to Monopsonistic Firms and the Gender Pay Gap: An Empirical Analysis Using Linked Employer–Employee Data from Germany," *Journal of Labor Economics* 28 (April 2010): 291–330; Torberg Falch, "Teacher Mobility Responses to Wage Changes: Evidence from a Quasi-natural Experiment," *American Economic Review: Papers and Proceedings* 101 (May 2011): 460–465.

57. Alan Manning, "The Equal Pay Act as an Experiment to Test Theories of the Labour Market," *Economica* 63 (May 1996): 191–212.

58. Michael Reich, "The Economics of Racism," in *Problems in Political Economy: An Urban Perspective*, ed. David M. Gordon (Lexington, MA: D.C. Heath, 1971): 107–113.

59. For evaluations of some of these programs, see Louis-Philippe Beland, "Political Parties and Labor-Market Outcomes: Evidence from the US States," *American Economic Journal: Applied Economics* 7 (October 2015): 198–220; Amalia R. Miller and Carmit Segal, "Does Temporary Affirmative Action Produce Persistent Effects? A Study of Black and Female Employment in Law Enforcement," *Review of Economics and Statistics* 94 (November 2012): 1107–1125.

60. For evidence that state equal-pay laws reduced the relative employment of women, see David Neumark and Wendy A. Stock, "The Labor Market Effects of Sex and Race Discrimination Laws," *Economic Inquiry* 44 (July 2006): 385–419.

61. *Griggs* v. *Duke Power Company* 401 U.S. 424 (1971).

62. *International Brotherhood of Teamsters* v. *United States* 431 U.S. 324, 14 FEP 1514 (1977).

63. *Franks* v. *Bowman Transportation* 424 U.S. 747, 12 FEP Cases 549 (1976); *Fire Fighters Local* 1784 v. *Stotts*, U.S. S. Ct. no. 82–206, June 12, 1984; and *Wygant* v. *Jackson Board of Education*, U.S. S. Ct. no. 84–1340, May 19, 1986.

64. See Donald J. Treiman and Heidi L. Hartmann, eds., *Women, Work and Wages: Equal Pay for Jobs of Equal Value* (Washington, DC: National Academy Press, 1981); Steven E. Rhoads, *Incomparable Worth* (Cambridge: Cambridge University Press, 1993): 160–165.

65. Rhoads, *Incomparable Worth*, 148–160.

66. Peter E. Orazem, J. Peter Mattila, and Sherry K. Welkum, "Comparable Worth and Factor Point Pay Analysis in State Government," *Industrial Relations* 31 (Winter 1992): 195–215; Mark R. Killingsworth, *The Economics of Comparable Worth* (Kalamazoo, MI: W.E. Upjohn Institute for Employment Research, 1990); Shulamit Kahn, "Economic Implications of Public Sector Comparable Worth: The Case of San Jose, California," *Industrial Relations* 31 (Spring 1992): 270–291; Ronald G. Ehrenberg and Robert S. Smith, "Comparable Worth Wage Adjustments and Female Employment in the State and Local Sector," *Journal of Labor Economics* 5 (January 1987): 43–62; Manning, "The Equal Pay Act as an Experiment to Test Theories of the Labour Market."

67. Harry Holzer and David Neumark, "Assessing Affirmative Action," *Journal of Economic Literature* 38 (September 2000): 483–568; Harry Holzer and David Neumark, "Affirmative Action: What Do We Know?" *Journal of Policy Analysis and Management* 25 (Spring 2006): 463–490. For a study indicating that most of the employment gains for women and other minorities took place in the early years of affirmative action programs, see Fidan Ana Kurtulus, "Affirmative Action and the Occupational Advancement of Minorities and Women during 1973–2003," *Industrial Relations* 51 (April 2012): 213–246. For a study finding that mandating affirmative action has positive results even after the mandate ends, see Conrad Miller, "The Persistent Effect of Temporary Affirmative Action," *American Economic Journal: Applied Economics* 9 (July 2017): 152–190. An evaluation of a program aimed at helping people with disabilities can be found in Philip Armour, Patrick Button, and Simon Hollands, "Disability Saliency and Discrimination in Hiring," *American Economic Review Papers and Proceedings* 108 (May 2018): 262–266.

68. For a comprehensive review of the contributions to economic development of programs to empower women in developing countries, see Ester Duflo, "Women Empowerment and Economic Development," *Journal of Economic Literature* 50 (December 2012): 1051–1079.

69. James P. Smith and Finis R. Welch, "Black Economic Progress After Myrdal," *Journal of Economic Literature* 27 (June 1989): 519–564.

70. David Card and Alan B. Krueger, "School Quality and Black–White Relative Earnings: A Direct Assessment," *Quarterly Journal of Economics* 107 (February 1992): 151–200. For a study of how school desegregation affected the wages of Black people in the U.S. South, see Orley Ashenfelter, William J. Collins, and Albert Yoon, "Evaluating the Role of *Brown vs. Board of Education* in School Equalization, Desegregation, and the Income of African Americans," *American Law and Economics Review* 8 (Summer 2006): 213–248.

71. John J. Donohue III and James Heckman, "Continuous Versus Episodic Change: The Impact of Civil Rights Policy on the Economic Status of Blacks," *Journal of Economic Literature* 29 (December 1991): 1603–1643.

72. Donohue and Heckman, "Continuous Versus Episodic Change." For a sketch of this comprehensive review, see James Heckman, "Accounting for the Economic Progress of Black Americans," in *New Approaches to Economic and Social Analyses of Discrimination*, eds. Richard R. Cornwall and Phanindra V. Wunnava (New York: Praeger, 1991): 331–337. A paper by Kenneth Y. Chay, "The Impact of Federal Civil Rights Policy on Black Economic Progress: Evidence from the Equal Employment Opportunity Act of 1972," *Industrial and Labor Relations Review* 51 (July 1998): 608–632, supports the claim that federal efforts helped to reduce the Black–white pay gap.

73. Heckman, "Accounting for the Economic Progress of Black Americans," 336.

74. Donohue and Heckman, "Continuous Versus Episodic Change," 1640. Harry J. Holzer, "Why Do Small Establishments Hire Fewer Blacks Than Large Ones?" *Journal of Human Resources* 32 (Fall 1998): 896–914, documents that small firms lag behind larger ones in hiring Black people. Although the source of this lag is unknown, the lag does indicate a sector in which further gains might be possible.

Selected Readings

Aigner, Dennis J., and Glen G. Cain. "Statistical Theories of Discrimination in Labor Markets." *Industrial and Labor Relations Review* 30 (January 1977): 175–187.

Altonji, Joseph G., and Rebecca M. Blank. "Race and Gender in the Labor Market." In *Handbook of Labor Economics*, eds. Orley Ashenfelter and David Card. New York: Elsevier, 1999.

Becker, Gary. *The Economics of Discrimination.* 2nd ed. Chicago, IL: University of Chicago Press, 1971.

Blau, Francine D., and Anne E. Winkler. *The Economics of Women, Men, and Work.* 8th ed. Boston, MA: Pearson, 2017.

Blau, Francine D., and Lawrence M. Kahn. "The Gender Wage Gap: Extent, Trends, and Explanations." *Journal of Economic Literature* 55 (September 2017): 789–865.

Cain, Glen G. "The Challenge of Segmented Labor Market Theories to Orthodox Theory: A Survey." *Journal of Economic Literature* 14 (December 1976): 1215–1257.

Cornwall, Richard R., and Phanindra V. Wunnava, eds. *New Approaches to Economic and Social Analyses of Discrimination.* New York: Praeger, 1991.

Donohue, John H., III, and James Heckman. "Continuous Versus Episodic Change: The Impact of Civil Rights Policy on the Economic Status of Blacks." *Journal of Economic Literature* 24 (December 1991): 1603–1643.

Goldin, Claudia. *Understanding the Gender Gap: An Economic History of American Women.* New York: Oxford University Press, 1990.

Goldin, Claudia, and Lawrence F. Katz. "A Most Egalitarian Profession: Pharmacy and the Evolution of a Family-Friendly Occupation." *Journal of Labor Economics* 34 (July 2016): 705–746.

Holzer, Harry, and David Neumark. "Assessing Affirmative Action." *Journal of Economic Literature* 38 (September 2000): 483–568.

Lang, Kevin, and Jee-Yeon K. Lehman. "Racial Discrimination in the Labor Market: Theory and Empirics." *Journal of Economic Literature* 50 (December 2012): 959–1006.

Neumark, David. "Experimental Research on Labor Market Discrimination." *Journal of Economic Literature* 56 (September 2018): 799–866.

Skrentny, John D. *After Civil Rights: Racial Realism in the New American Workplace.* Princeton, NJ: Princeton University Press, 2014.

Smith, James P., and Finis R. Welch. "Black Economic Progress After Myrdal." *Journal of Economic Literature* 27 (June 1989): 519–564.

APPENDIX 12A

Estimating Comparable-Worth Earnings Gaps: An Application of Regression Analysis

Although many economists have difficulty with the notion that the worth of a job can be established independently of market factors, formal job evaluation methods have existed for a long time.[1] Minnesota is one of the few states that began to implement comparable-worth pay adjustments for their employees on the basis of such an evaluation method. How might we use data from job evaluations to estimate whether discriminatory wage differentials exist?[2]

Minnesota, in conjunction with Hay Associates, a prominent national compensation consulting company, began an evaluation of state government jobs in 1979. Initially evaluated were 188 positions in which at least 10 workers were employed and which could be classified as either *male* (at least 70 percent male incumbents) or *female* (at least 70 percent female incumbents) positions. Each position was evaluated by trained job evaluators and awarded a specified number of "Hay Points" for each of four job characteristics or factors: required expertise, problem-solving, accountability, and working conditions. The scores for each factor were then added to obtain a total Hay Point (HP), or job evaluation, score for each job. These scores varied across the 188 job titles from below 100 points to over 800 points.

Given these job evaluation scores, the next step is to ask what the relationship is between the salary (S_i) that each male job pays and its total HP_i score. Each dot in Figure 12A.1 represents a male job, and this figure plots the monthly salary for each job against its total HP score. On average, jobs with higher scores clearly receive higher pay.

Although these points obviously do not all lie on a single straight line, we look into what straight line fits the data best. An infinite number of lines can be drawn through these points, and some precise criterion must be used to decide which line fits best. As discussed in Appendix 1A, the procedure typically used by statisticians and economists is to choose that line for which the sum (across data points) of the squared vertical distances between the line and the individual data points is minimized. The line estimated from the data that came from using this method—the *method of least squares*—has a number of desirable statistical properties.[3]

Applying this method to data for the male occupations contained in the Minnesota data yielded the following estimated line:[4]

$$S_i = 1012 + 3.3 \; HP_i \qquad\qquad\qquad\qquad (12A.1)$$

So, for example, if male job i were rated at 200 HPs, we would predict that the monthly salary associated with job i would be $\$1,012 + (3.3) \times (200)$, or $\$1,672$. This estimated male salary equation is drawn in Figure 12A.1 as line *AA*.

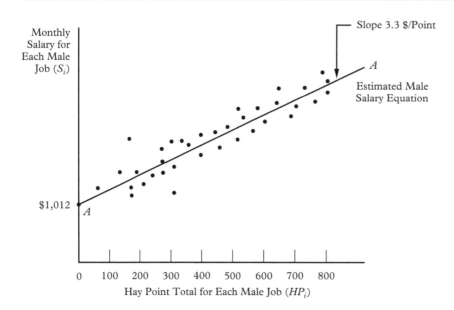

Figure 12A.1 Estimated Male Comparable-Worth Salary Equation

Now, if the value of a job could be determined solely by reference to its job evaluation score, one would expect that in the absence of wage discrimination against women, male jobs and female jobs rated equal in terms of total *HP* scores would pay equal salaries (at least on average). Put another way, the same salary equation used to predict salaries of male jobs could be used to provide predictions of salaries for female jobs, and any inaccuracies in the prediction would be completely random. Hence, a test of whether female jobs are discriminated against is to see if the salaries that they pay are systematically less than the salaries that one would predict that they would pay, given their *HP* scores and the salary equation for male jobs.

Figure 12A.2 illustrates how this is done. Here each dot represents a salary–*HP* combination for a female job. Superimposed on this scatter of points is the estimated male job salary equation, *AA*, from Figure 12A.1. The fact that the vast majority of the data points in Figure 12A.2 lie below the male salary line suggests that female jobs tend to be underpaid relative to male jobs with the same number of *HP*s. For example, the female job that is rated at 300 *HP*s (point *a*) is paid a salary of S^F_{300}. However, according to the estimated male salary line, if that job were a male job, it would be paid S^M_{300}. The difference in percentage terms between S^M_{300} and S^F_{300} is an estimate of the comparable-worth earnings gap—the extent of underpayment—for the female job. Indeed, calculations suggest that the average (across all the female occupations) comparable-worth earnings gap in the Minnesota data was over 16 percent.[5]

This brief presentation has glossed over a number of complications that must be addressed before such estimates can be considered estimates of wage discrimination against female jobs.[6] These include issues relating to the reliability and potential gender bias in the evaluation methods, whether

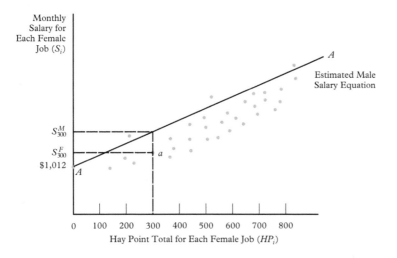

Figure 12A.2 Using the Estimated Male Comparable-Worth Salary Equation to Estimate the Extent of Underpayment in Female Jobs

salaries and *HP* scores may be related in a nonlinear fashion, whether the *composition* of any given total *HP* score (across the four sets of job characteristics) affects salaries, and whether variables other than the job evaluation scores can legitimately affect salaries. Nonetheless, it should give the reader a sense of how comparable-worth wage gap estimates are computed.

APPENDIX 12B

Estimating the Gender Pay Gap in a Large International Company

Estimating wage gaps by using statistical techniques mentioned in this chapter and in Appendix 1A is common. The techniques are straightforward, but as made clear in the text of Chapter 12, precisely what economists "control for" can have large effects on the estimates of the gap and have important implications.

Consider the case of a study done using data from a large multinational company that has more than 30,000 employees working in more than 10 countries.[7] The company was interested to know whether its pay practices discriminated on the basis of gender. One issue is whether men and women were, on balance, paid the same. This appendix uses information from just one of the 10 countries in this study.[8] The authors had a set of information about each worker, including their gender, their salary, whether they were a citizen of the country in which they worked, whether they worked full time, their performance in the current and previous two years, their seniority in their job, their seniority at the company, their age, and their job rank.

When comparing the average pay of men and women, in this company in country D, women earned 23.5 percent less than men did. So the "raw" wage gap was 23.5 percent. Once the authors controlled for whether the person was a citizen of country D and whether the employee worked full time, the gender gap fell considerably, to 13.3 percent; thus, "controlling for citizenship and full-time status," the penalty to women fell to 13.3 percent. Additionally, controlling for performance in the job, seniority in the job, seniority at the company, and age, the gap was reduced to 8.7 percent. So, after controlling for all of the above variables, an unexplained pay gap of 8.7 percent persisted between men and women.

When the researchers finally controlled for job rank—in addition to all of the other variables—the wage gap between men and women was not statistically different from zero. Does this mean that no discrimination was taking place? Not necessarily. If, in considering the promotion of equally qualified women and men to higher-ranked jobs, the firm was less likely to promote women, then controlling for job rank is not appropriate. Put differently, in measuring labor-market discrimination, it is only appropriate to control for independent variables that are not themselves the product of bias in the labor market.

Notes

1. See Kevin F. Hallock, *Pay: Why People Earn What They Earn and What You Can Do Now to Earn More* (New York: Cambridge University Press, 2012), for a detailed explanations of the job evaluation and job analysis process and how large firms use them in designing compensation systems.

2. For a completer discussion of the Minnesota job evaluation and comparable-worth study, see *Pay Equity and Public Employment* (St. Paul, MN: Council on the Economic Status of Women, March 1982).

3. See Appendix 1A.

4. These estimates are obtained from Ronald G. Ehrenberg and Robert S. Smith, "Comparable Worth in the Public Sector," in *Public Sector Payrolls*, ed. David Wise (Chicago, IL: University of Chicago Press, 1987).

5. See Ehrenberg and Smith, "Comparable Worth in the Public Sector." Analogous estimates for four other states are presented there and in Elaine Sorensen, "Implementing Comparable Worth: A Survey of Recent Job Evaluation Studies," *American Economic Review* 76 (May 1986): 364–367.

6. For a completer discussion of these issues and empirical studies relating to comparable worth, see Ehrenberg and Smith, "Comparable Worth in the Public Sector"; M. Anne Hill and Mark R. Killingsworth, eds., *Comparable Worth: Analyses and Evidence* (Ithaca, NY: ILR Press, 1989); Robert T. Michael, Heidi L. Hartmann, and Brigid O'Farrell, eds., *Pay Equity: Empirical Inquiries* (Washington, DC: National Academy Press, 1989); Killingsworth, *The Economics of Comparable Worth*.

7. Details of this example can be found in Linda Barrington and Kevin F. Hallock, "Gender Pay Equity Analytics: A Case Study of a Large Multinational Company," *WorldatWork Journal* (First Quarter 2020): 80–99. For further detail, see the working paper of the same title at Cornell University Institute for Compensation Studies Working Paper No. 18.

8. That country was country D in the working paper by Barrington and Hallock. Because the data are confidential—and even the name of the company is confidential—the authors masked the names of the countries so that the company identity would be impossible to guess.

13 Unions and the Labor Market

Our analysis of the workings of labor markets has, for the most part, omitted any mention of the role of labor unions and collective bargaining. Because many people have strong and conflicting opinions about the role of unions in U.S. society, remaining objective is often difficult when discussing them. Some people view labor unions as forms of monopolies that while benefiting their own members, impose substantial costs on other members of society. In contrast, others view unions as the major means by which workers have improved their economic status, as a counterbalance to corporations, and as important forces behind much social legislation.

The purpose of this chapter is to analyze the goals, major activities, and overall effects of unions in the context of economic theory. We begin with some general descriptive material on unions internationally, adding a more comprehensive description of unions in the United States. Then we move to a fundamental theoretical question: What are the economic forces on the demand side of the market that constrain unions in their desire to improve the welfare of their members? With these constraints in mind, we devote the last half of the chapter to analyzing the primary activities of the collective bargaining process and to discussing empirical evidence on how unions affect wages, employment, labor productivity, and profits.

Union Structure and Membership

Labor unions are organizations of workers whose primary objectives are to improve the pecuniary and nonpecuniary conditions of employment among their members. Unions can be classified into two types: An *industrial* union represents most of or all the workers in an industry or firm regardless of their occupations, and a *craft* union represents workers in a single occupational group. Examples of industrial unions are the unions representing automobile workers and coal miners; craft unions include those representing the various building trades, printers, and dockworkers.

Unions bargain with employers over various aspects of the employment contract, including pay and employee benefits; conditions of work; policies regarding hiring, overtime, job assignment, promotion, and layoffs; and how grievances between workers and management are to be resolved. Bargaining can occur at different levels.

At one end of the spectrum, bargaining can be highly *centralized,* where representatives of entire industries sit at the bargaining table to decide on contracts that bind multiple employers. At the *decentralized* end of the spectrum, bargaining can take place between a union and a single company—or even between the workers and management at a single plant within a company. In the middle are multiemployer agreements reached at the local level between a union and several employers; an example of such agreements would be the ones typically signed between construction craft unions (e.g., plumbers) and the construction contractors that operate in a given metropolitan area.

As large collective organizations, unions also represent a *political* force in democratic countries. Often, unions use the political process in the attempt to gain benefits that they could not as easily win through collective bargaining. In some countries (e.g., the United Kingdom), unions have their own political party. In others, such as the United States, unions are not formally affiliated with any one political party; rather, they act as lobbyists for various bills and policies at the federal, state, and local levels of government.

International Comparisons of Unionism

Table 13.1 displays two measures of unionization in several countries. One measure is the percentage of workers who are members of unions, and the other is the percentage of workers in each country whose conditions of employment are covered by a collective bargaining agreement. Three characteristics of this table stand out. First, the United States and Japan are notable in the relatively small percentages of their workers—less than 20 percent—who are currently covered by collectively bargained agreements. Collective bargaining in these countries takes place at the level of firms and plants, and provisions of the resulting agreements rarely extend beyond the membership of the unions that signed them.

Second, in Australia and most European countries, collective bargaining coverage is extended to a high fraction of workers who are not members of unions. In Austria, for example, collective bargaining is highly centralized, in that agreements are national in their scope, and in most of continental Europe, the parties at the bargaining table represent entire sectors of the economy. Clearly, the historical and legal contexts within which unions operate in each country are critical to understanding the differing levels of membership and labor market influences.[1]

Table 13.1 Union Membership and Bargaining Coverage, Selected Countries, 2000 and 2017

Country	Union membership as a percentage of workers		Percentage of workers covered by a collective bargaining agreement	
	2000	**2017***	**2000****	**2017**
Austria	36.9	26.7	98.0	98.0
Sweden	79.0	66.1	94.0	90.0
Australia	24.9	13.7	60.0	60.0
Italy	34.4	34.3	80.0	80.0
Netherlands	22.6	12.5	81.7	78.6
Germany	24.6	16.7	67.8	56.0
Switzerland	20.2	14.9	44.9	57.9
United Kingdom	29.8	23.2	36.4	26.3
Canada	28.2	26.3	30.4	28.1
Japan	21.5	17.1	21.1	16.7
United States	12.9	10.3	14.2	11.5

*Data for Australia are for 2018.

**Data for Switzerland are for 1999.

Source: Organisation for Economic Co-operation and Development, https://stats.oecd.org/Index. aspx?DataSetCode=TUD

Third, the data in Table 13.1 indicate declines in union membership in almost every country listed over the years from 2000 to 2017. The declines in membership are larger than the declines in the percentage of workers *covered* by a collective bargaining agreement in some countries, but in other countries, the declines in the two measures of unionization are roughly comparable. Clearly, then, the differences in the legal and institutional contexts in which unions operate are country specific.

Much of the empirical work on unions has been done in the United States, where bargaining is decentralized and, as we have seen, the majority of workers are nonunion. While the study of unions in one country does not easily generalize to others, given the different legal and historical environments, this empirical work may be of growing interest elsewhere, owing to what may be a trend toward a greater decentralization of bargaining in most developed economies during the past decade or two.[2] No matter how well (or poorly) studies of U.S. unions generalize, however, their results must still be understood within the context of U.S. institutions. We therefore turn to a brief history of the legal structure within which U.S. unions have operated.

The Legal Structure of Unions in the United States

Public attitudes and federal legislation concerning labor unions and the collective bargaining process in the United States have varied widely over time. For example, during the early part of the twentieth century, employers were often able to claim that unions acted like monopolies in the labor market and hence were illegal under existing antitrust laws. Such employers were often able to get court orders or injunctions that prohibited union activity and aided them in stopping union organization drives. Given this environment, that the fraction of the labor force who were union members stood at less than 7 percent in 1930 is not surprising. Since that date, however, legislation has changed the environment in which U.S. unions operate.

National Labor Relations Act   The National Labor Relations Act (NLRA) of 1935 required employers to bargain with unions that represented the majority of their employees and made employers' interfering with their employees' right to organize collectively illegal.[3] The National Labor Relations Board (NLRB) was established by the NLRA and given power both to conduct *certification elections* to see which union, if any, employees wanted to represent them and to investigate claims that employers were either violating election rules or refusing to bargain with elected unions. In the event that violations were found, the NLRB was given further power to order violators to "cease and desist."

Taft–Hartley Act   After World War II, the pendulum shifted decidedly in an antiunion direction. The Labor–Management Relations Act of 1947 (better known as the Taft–Hartley Act) restricted some aspects of union activity and permitted workers to vote in elections that could decertify a union from representing them in collective bargaining. Perhaps its most famous provision is section 14B, which permits individual states to pass *right-to-work laws*. These laws prohibit the "union shop" requirement, often written into collective bargaining agreements, that a person become a union member as a condition of employment. Specifically, 27 states, located primarily in the United States' South and Midwest areas, have passed such laws—the most recent of which are in Indiana and Michigan (2012), Wisconsin (2015), West Virginia (2016), and Kentucky (2017).

Landrum–Griffin Act   In 1959, Congress passed the Labor–Management Reporting and Disclosure Act (better known as the Landrum–Griffin Act). This law, which was designed to protect the rights of union members in relation to their leaders, contained provisions that increased union democracy. As argued later, such provisions might well have had the side effect of increasing the level of strike activity in the economy.

Government Unions   The laws that have been discussed to this point relate only to the private sector, where unionism in the United States first flourished. Indeed, before the 1960s, public sector workers were prohibited from organizing. In 1962, however, President Kennedy signed Executive Order 10988, which gave federal workers the right to organize and bargain over working conditions, but not wages.[4] The influence of federal unions on wages, then, operates primarily through the political pressure that they can exert on the president to recommend, or on Congress to approve, pay increases.

Beginning with Wisconsin in 1959, a number of states extended to employees of state and local governments (including teachers) the rights to organize and collectively bargain. Generally speaking, public sector unions are barred from going on strike, so laws permitting their right to bargain were accompanied by provisions for some form of binding arbitration (through which neutral parties would ultimately decide on disputes that could not be voluntarily resolved).[5] Ironically, in 2011, the same state of Wisconsin adopted a controversial law that limited the bargaining of public sector unions and governmental employers—except in the case of public safety workers—to base wages (not to other forms of pay, such as benefits or performance pay). In recent years, the role and power of public sector unions have been increasingly challenged—across several countries—by politicians and taxpayer groups interested in controlling government spending.[6]

Union Membership Union membership as a fraction of all U.S. workers peaked in the years following World War II, at about one-third. Since then, the percentage of all workers who are union members has dropped continuously, except among government workers. Figure 13.1 graphs the trends in union membership starting in 1975, when the membership percentages in the private and public sectors (and hence overall) were close to 22 percent. As of 2018, membership among private sector workers had fallen to 6.4 percent, membership among government workers had risen to 33.9 percent, and the overall rate of membership stood at 10.5 percent.

Unionized workers in the United States are members of "local" unions, organized at the level of the plant, the employer, or (especially for construction unions) the metropolitan area. We have noted that in the United States, bargaining is relatively decentralized, so local unions bear the brunt of negotiations. These locals, however, are usually members of larger "national" or "international" (usually meaning they include Canadian workers) unions, which provide help and advice to the locals with their organization drives and, later, their negotiations. If bargaining is being done at the industry level or with one firm at the national level, representatives of the national or international union are the ones who sit at the bargaining table.

In turn, most of the nationals and internationals (and therefore some three-quarters of all union members) are affiliated with the AFL-CIO, which stands for the American Federation of Labor and Congress of Industrial Organizations.[7] The AFL-CIO is not a union but rather an association of unions organized both nationally and at the state level. Its main functions are to provide a unified political voice for its diverse member unions, to

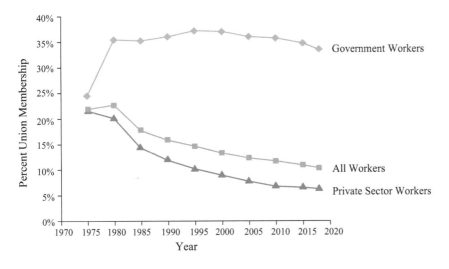

Figure 13.1 Union Membership as a Percentage of All Workers, by Sector, United States, 1975–2018

Source: Barry T. Hirsch and David A. Macpherson, *2019 Union Membership and Earnings Data Book* (Arlington, VA: Bureau of National Affairs, 2019), Tables 1a, 1c, 1f

recommend and coordinate membership initiatives among its affiliates, and to provide research and information to its members. It does not directly negotiate with employers.

Table 13.2 provides another way of examining union membership in the United States. From this table, we can see that men are slightly more likely to be unionized than women and that Black workers have higher rates of unionization than other groups. By sector, the highest rates of unionization are clearly among educators and government workers; in the private sector, only in construction and transportation/public utilities are membership rates above 12 percent.

What Unions Want   The founder of the American Federation of Labor, Samuel Gompers, was once asked what unions wanted. His answer was quite simple: "More." Hardly anyone who has studied union behavior believes unions' objectives are quite that simple, but unions clearly want to advance the welfare of their members in one way or another.[8]

Some union objectives are *procedural*, in that unions give workers some "voice" in the way that employers manage the workplace—especially in the handling of various human resource issues, such as job assignment, the allocation of overtime, the handling of worker discipline and grievances, the composition of employee-benefit packages, and the establishment of joint labor–management safety committees and work teams. Procedural objectives are not always costly to the employer, who (especially with modern management techniques) might want a mechanism through which employee participation in management decisions can be achieved. Other procedural

Table 13.2 Percentage of U.S. Wage and Salary Workers Who Are
Union Members, by Selected Characteristics, 2018

Men	11.1
Women	9.9
Black people	12.5
Hispanics	9.1
White people	10.4
By Industry	
Mining	4.7
Construction	13.6
Manufacturing	9.1
Transportation, public utilities	23.4
Wholesale, retail trade	4.4
Information	10.5
Education	30.0
Public administration	29.1

Source: Barry T. Hirsch and David A. Macpherson, *2019 Union Membership and Earnings Data Book* (Arlington, VA: Bureau of National Affairs, 2019), Tables 3a, 7a

objectives, however, put limits on managerial prerogatives that, though difficult to quantify, are often seen by employers as costly.[9] We close this chapter with a fuller discussion of the "voice" mechanism that unions can provide.

Wanting "more," however, is usually associated with the union goal of increasing the *compensation* levels of its members. The most visible element of compensation is the wage rate, but bargaining in the United States also occurs over such employee benefits as pensions, health insurance, and vacations. (In many other developed countries, these benefits are mandated by the government and therefore are not subject to collective bargaining.) The attempts to achieve "more," of course, take place in the context of *constraints*. We now turn to an analysis of these constraints.

Constraints on the Achievement of Union Objectives

Employers are on the other side of the bargaining table, and they must make agreements that permit them to operate successfully both with their workers *and* within their product markets. Increased compensation for their workers will give them incentives to *substitute* capital for labor, and to the extent that their costs of production rise, other pressures to reduce the *scale* of operations will ensue. In short, unions must ultimately reckon with the downward-sloping demand curve for labor (for an example from professional sports, see Example 13.1). As a result, both the position of this curve and its elasticity become fundamental market constraints on the ability of unions to accomplish their objectives.

EXAMPLE 13.1

A Downward-Sloping Demand Curve for Football Players

Do unions behave as if the labor demand curve slopes downward? Put differently, do unions appear to recognize that higher wages can limit employment opportunities for their members? Some evidence that they do comes from the National Football League (NFL).

The collective bargaining agreement signed in 2011 by the union and ownership of the NFL contained clauses that, among other things, specified *minimum salaries* for NFL players that rise with a player's years of service in the league, and a limit on the *total salaries* that each team can pay to its players (a team *salary cap*). The provision for minimum salaries is essentially a minimum-wage provision, where the minimum rises as the player ages, and it is intended to put a "floor" under the salaries of weaker players who are not the stars that teams bid against each other to attract. The limit on total salaries is intended to foster competitiveness in the league by limiting the ability of a team to stockpile star (expensive) players.

Apparently, however, the players' union was concerned that the service-related minimum wages would give teams incentives to replace older, more-experienced, weaker players with younger (lower-paid) ones. The 2011 agreement, therefore, contains a "minimum salary benefit," specifying that when a player with over four years of experience is paid at the minimum for their service time, only the *minimum salary for a two-year player* gets counted against the team's salary cap. For example, in 2013, a player with five years of experience must be paid $715,000 per year, but only $555,000 (the minimum salary for a player with two years of service) is charged against the team's salary cap. In essence, then, although an older bench player must be paid the minimum salary for their service level, their team is allowed to go above its salary cap to do so. Teams thus have at least some incentive to retain the services of their more experienced (and hence more expensive) bench players rather than replacing them with younger players.

This provision of the NFL's collective bargaining agreement was brought to our attention by our colleague Lawrence Kahn. For more details, see NFL–NFL Players' Association, "Collective Bargaining Agreement," August 4, 2011.

To see this, ignore employee benefits and working conditions for the moment and consider Figure 13.2, which shows two demand curves, D_e^0 and D_i^0, which intersect at an initial wage W_0 and employment level E_0. Suppose that a union seeks to raise the wage rate of its members to W_1. To do so would cause employment to fall to E_e^1 if the union faced the relatively elastic demand curve D_e^0 or to E_i^1 if it faced the relatively inelastic demand curve D_i^0. Other things being equal, the more elastic the demand curve for labor is, the greater will be the reduction in employment associated with any given increase in wages.

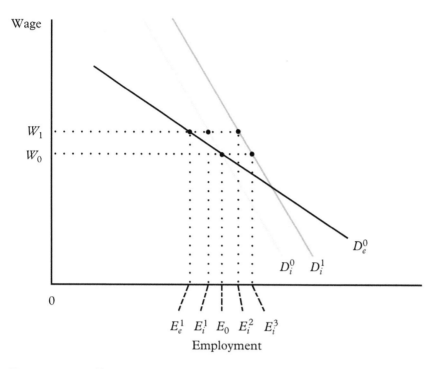

Figure 13.2 Effects of Demand Growth and the Wage Elasticity of Demand on the Market Constraints Faced by Unions

Suppose now that the demand curve D_i^0 shifts out to D_i^1 while the negotiations are under way, owing perhaps to growing demand for the final product. If the union succeeds in raising its members' wages to W_1, no absolute decrease in employment will occur in this case. Rather, the union will have only slowed the rate of growth of employment to E_i^2 instead of E_i^3. More generally, other things being equal, the more rapidly the labor demand curve is shifting out (in), the smaller (larger) will be the reduction *in employment* or the reduction *in the rate of growth of employment* associated with any given increase in wages. Hence, unions' ability to raise their members' wages will be strongest in rapidly growing industries with inelastic labor demand curves. Conversely, unions will be weakest in industries in which the wage elasticity of demand is highly elastic and in which the demand curve for labor is shifting in.

We now turn to two alternative models of how unions and employers behave in their agreements about wages and benefits, given the market constraints that they face. Each of the models analyzes the interaction of—and trade-offs between—wages and employment.

The Monopoly-Union Model

The simplest model of the union–employer relationship has been called one of *monopoly unionism*, whereby the union sets the price of labor and the employer responds by adjusting employment to maximize profits, given the

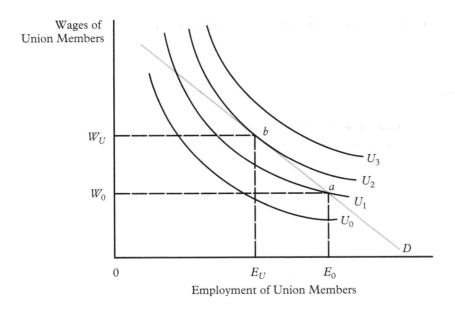

Figure 13.3 Union Maximizes Utility Subject to the Constraint of the Labor Demand Curve

new wage rate with which it is confronted. This model is formally illustrated by Figure 13.3, which shows the labor demand curve, *D*, facing workers as a simple function of the wage rate (for simplicity, we abstract from other elements in the compensation package, or you can think of this similarly as negotiating over total compensation).

In Figure 13.3, we assume that the union values both the wages and the employment levels of its members and that it can aggregate its members' preferences so that we can meaningfully speak of a union utility function that depends on these two variables. This utility function is summarized by the family of indifference curves U_0, U_1, U_2, and U_3. Each curve represents a locus of wage–employment combinations about which the union is indifferent. The indifference curves are negatively sloped, because to maintain a given utility level, the union must be compensated for a decline in one variable (employment or wages) by an increase in the other. They exhibit the property of diminishing marginal rates of substitution (they are convex to the origin) because we assume the loss of employment that unions are willing to tolerate in return for a given wage increase grows smaller as employment falls. Finally, higher indifference curves represent higher levels of union utility.

Suppose that in the absence of a union, market forces would cause the wage to be W_0 and employment to be E_0 (point *a* in Figure 13.3). How does collective bargaining affect this solution? One possibility is that the union and the employer will agree on a higher wage rate and then, given the wage rate, the employer will determine the number of union members to employ. Given a bargained wage rate, the employer will maximize profits and determine employment from its labor demand curve. Since the union presumably knows this, its goal is to choose the wage that maximizes its utility subject to the constraint that the resultant wage–employment combination will lie on the demand curve.

In terms of Figure 13.3, the union will seek to move to point *b*, where indifference curve U_2 is just tangent to the labor demand curve. At this point, wages would be W_U and employment E_U. Given the constraint posed by the labor demand curve, point *b* represents the highest level of utility that the union can attain. Note that, in this example, the typical union member earns more than the rate that they would earn in the absence of the union but that fewer people are employed.

The Efficient-Contracts Model

An interesting feature of the simple monopoly-union model is that it is not *efficient*. Instead of having unions set the wage and then having employers determine employment, both parties could be better off if they agreed to jointly determine wages and employment. Put succinctly in terms of Figure 13.3, we have a whole set of wage–employment combinations that at least one of the parties would prefer and that would leave the other no worse off; these combinations have been called *efficient contracts*. (Although the term *efficient* seems to harken back our discussion of *Pareto efficiency* in Chapter 1, it is being used more narrowly here. Pareto efficiency refers to *social* welfare, and a transaction is said to be Pareto improving if *society* is made better off—that is, if some gain and no one else loses. *Efficiency* in the current context denotes only that the welfare of the two parties can be improved; it does not imply that society, as a whole, gains. Indeed, the next section shows that, in general, these efficient contracts lead to a socially wasteful use of labor.)

The Formal Model To begin our analysis, we must recall from Chapter 3 that the labor demand curve is defined by the employer's choosing an employment level that maximizes profits at each wage rate. In Figure 13.3, for example, if we start at point *a* on the demand curve with the wage at W_0 and employment at E_0, profits would fall if the employer were to either expand or contract employment. Thus, if employment were to be changed from E_0, a lower wage rate would have to be paid to keep profits from falling. The larger the deviation of employment from E_0, the lower wages would have to be to keep profits constant.

We can formalize this by reintroducing the concept of *isoprofit curves*, first discussed in Chapter 8. Here, an isoprofit curve is a locus of wage–employment combinations along which an employer's profits remain unchanged. Figure 13.4 shows three isoprofit curves for the employer whose labor demand curve is *D*. As discussed earlier, each curve reaches a maximum at its intersection with the demand curve; as we move along a given isoprofit

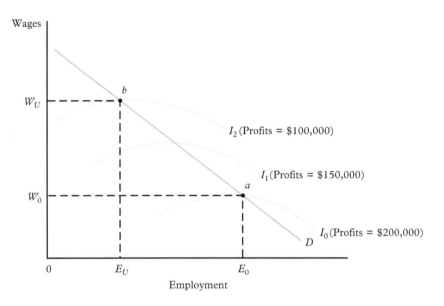

Figure 13.4 Employer Isoprofit Curves

curve in either direction away from the demand curve, wages must fall to keep profits constant. A higher isoprofit curve represents a lower level of employer profits because the wage associated with each level of employment is greater along the higher curve. So, for example, the employer would prefer any point on I_0, which includes the original wage–employment combination (point a), to any point on I_2, which includes the monopoly-union wage–employment solution (point b).

Figure 13.5 superimposes the family of employer isoprofit curves from Figure 13.4 onto the family of union indifference curves from Figure 13.3 and illustrates why the monopoly-union solution, point b, is not an *efficient contract*. Suppose that rather than locating at point b, the parties negotiated a contract that called for them to locate at point d, where the wage rate (W_d) would be lower but the employment of union members (E_d) would be higher. At point d, the union would be better off, because it would now be on a higher indifference curve, U_3, and the firm would be no worse off, because it would still be on isoprofit curve I_2.

Similarly, suppose that rather than negotiating a contract to wind up at b, the parties agreed to a contract that called for them to locate at point e, with a wage rate of W_e and an employment level of E_e. Compared with the monopoly-union solution (point b), the union is equally well off, since it remains on indifference curve U_2, but now the firm is better off because it has been able to reach isoprofit curve I_1. Because I_1 lies below I_2, it represents a higher level of profits.

In fact, a whole set of contracts exists that both parties will find at least as good as point b; these are represented by the shaded area in Figure 13.5. Among this set, the ones that are efficient contracts—contracts in which no party can be made better off without hurting the other—are the ones in which employer isoprofit curves are just tangent to union indifference

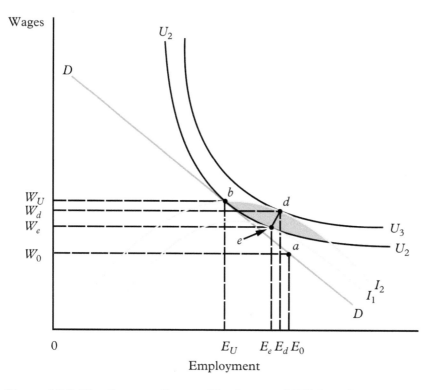

Figure 13.5 The Contract Curve—The Locus of Efficient Contracts

curves, such as at points *d* and *e*. Indeed, a whole locus of such points exists, and they are represented in Figure 13.5 by the curve *ed*. Each point on *ed* represents a tangency of a union indifference curve and an employer isoprofit curve; these are points at which the employer and the union are equally willing to substitute wages for employment at the margin (so that no more mutually beneficial trades of wages for employment are possible).

All of the points on *ed*, which is often called the *contract curve* (or locus of efficient contracts), will leave both parties at least as well off as at point *b* and at least one party better off. However, the parties are not indifferent to where along *ed* the settlement is reached. Obviously, the union would prefer to be close to *d* and the employer close to *e*. Where on the contract curve a settlement actually occurs in this model depends on the bargaining power of the parties.[10]

The Contract Curve   Two points need to be made about the contract curve. First, as shown in Figure 13.5, it lies off and to the right of the firm's labor demand curve. This implies that the firm is using more labor at any given wage rate than it would if it had unilateral control over employment, and it implies that the collective bargaining agreement will contain clauses that create (more precisely, ratify the use of) excess labor in the plant. For example, clauses might pertain to minimum crew sizes or to rigid rules governing which workers must do specific tasks; some agreements might even have no-layoff clauses for certain workers. Although the employer might be better off with these clauses, because it can induce the union to agree to a lower wage, its failure to minimize costs is socially wasteful (society could increase its aggregate output if labor were reallocated and used more productively). Second, the slope of the contract curve does not need to be up and to the right, as shown in Figure 13.5. Depending on the shapes of the union's indifference curves and the firm's isoprofit curves, the contract curve could slope up and to the left or even be *vertical*.

An interesting special case involving a vertical contract curve is created when the curve is *vertical at the original (preunion) level of employment*. In this case, the firm agrees to maintain employment at the level that *maximizes profits*, given the *market* wage rate. The union and firm in effect bargain over how these profits are split; every dollar gained by the union is a dollar lost by the employer, and no changes in output or employment occur. If the union succeeds in raising wages above their original (market) level, however, how could the firm afford to pay higher wages, maintain its original employment level, and still operate successfully in the product market? The answer must be that it is in a *noncompetitive* product market and is therefore receiving profits in excess of those required for it to remain in business; a reduction in these excess profits might make management unhappy, but it does not cause the employer to change its behavior.[11] Further implications of a vertical contract curve are discussed in the final section of this chapter, in which the social gains or losses of unionization are considered.

The Actual Efficiency of Contracts

How realistic is the efficient-contracts model as a description of the wage-determination process in unionized workplaces in the United States? The most obvious way to answer this question would be to examine the language of collective bargaining agreements to determine whether we can find evidence of joint agreement on employment levels. Many contracts covering public school teachers specify maximum class sizes or minimum teacher–student ratios, and a few private sector contracts include no-layoff provisions for certain core workers, but the world is too uncertain for an employer to explicitly guarantee a certain *level* of employment.

Contracts, however, often contain language that perpetuates the use of excess labor. Many require that duties cannot be performed "out of job title," so a custodian, for example, could not paint a scuffed wall (a painter would be required) or an off-stage actor could not perform any of the duties of a lighting technician. These rigidities in job assignment are clearly designed to protect jobs even though the level of employment is not explicitly determined in the contract.

We also have *indirect* tests for the efficient-contracts model. This model and the monopoly-union model yield different implications about how wages and employment will vary in response to changes in variables that affect either the demand for labor or union preferences. A number of studies have analyzed these implications, and so far, some evidence supports and some evidence goes against the efficient-contracts model.[12]

The Activities and Tools of Collective Bargaining

Having analyzed the general constraints facing unions as they seek to accomplish their goals, we now turn to an economic analysis of several activities that affect their power. We begin with a simple model of union *membership* and use it to help understand the decline in membership faced by U.S. unions in recent decades. Next, we briefly discuss how unions use the *political* process in an attempt to alter the market constraints they face. Finally, we analyze the ultimate threats—of calling a *strike* or having an unresolved dispute decided by third-party *arbitration*—that unions can carefully use in the collective bargaining process.

Union Membership: An Analysis of Demand and Supply

A simple model of the demand for and supply of union activity can be used to explain the forces that influence union membership.[13] On the demand side, employees' desire to be union members will be a function of the *price* of union membership; this price includes initiation fees, monthly dues, the value of the time that an individual is expected to spend on union activities, and so on. Other things being equal, the higher the price, the lower the fraction of employees that will want to be union members, as represented by the demand curve D_0 in Figure 13.6.

Representing workers in collective bargaining negotiations and supervising the administration of union contracts is costly. Therefore, other things being equal, the willingness of unions to supply their services is an upward-sloping function of the price of union membership, as represented by the supply curve S_0 in Figure 13.6. The intersection of these demand and supply curves yields an equilibrium percentage of the workforce that is unionized (U_0) and an equilibrium price of union services (P_0).

What forces determine the *positions* of the demand and supply curves? Anything that causes either the demand curve or the supply curve to shift to the right will increase the level of unionization in the economy, other things being equal. Conversely, if either of these curves shifts to the left, other things being equal, the level of unionization will fall. Identifying the factors that shift these curves would enable us to explain *changes* in the level of unionization in the economy over time.

On the demand side, individuals' demand for union membership is likely positively related to their perceptions of the *net benefits* from being union members. For example, the larger the wage gain that they think unions will win for them, the further to the right the demand curve will be.[14] Another factor is *tastes*; if individuals' tastes for union membership increase, perhaps because of changes in social attitudes, the demand curve will also shift to the right.[15]

On the supply side, anything that changes the *costs* of union-organizing activities will affect the supply curve. The introduction of labor legislation

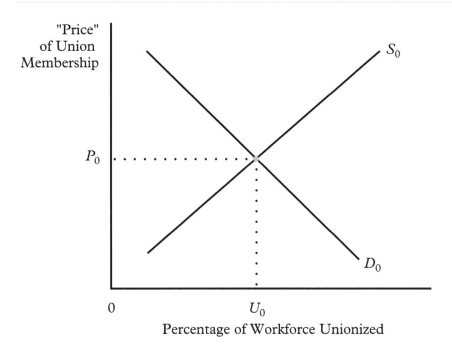

Figure 13.6 The Demand for and Supply of Unionization

that makes winning representation elections easier for unions will shift the supply curve to the right. Changes in the composition of employment that make organizing the workforce more difficult will shift the curve to the left and reduce the level of unionization.[16]

The decline in unionization rates that has taken place in the United States since the mid 1950s is hypothesized to be at least partially explained by four factors related to the demand for, or supply of, union services: a shifting industrial mix, a heavier mix of employment in states in which the environment is not particularly favorable for unions, increased competitive pressures, and increased employer resistance to union-organizing efforts.[17]

Changing Industrial Mix   One possible factor in the decline of union membership is the shift in the industrial composition of employment, first discussed in Chapter 2. The fraction of workers in government, the most heavily unionized sector in the United States, has held more or less constant since the mid 1970s, whereas a substantial decline in the employment shares of the most heavily unionized industries in the *private* sector has taken place (see Table 13.2): manufacturing, mining, construction, transportation, and public utilities. Employment has increased most notably in wholesale and retail trade; in finance, insurance, and real estate; and in the service industries—all of which are among the least-unionized sectors of the economy.

Why do the latter industries tend not to be unionized? These industries tend to be highly competitive, with high price elasticities of product demand and therefore high wage elasticities of labor demand, which limit unions' abilities to increase wages without suffering substantial employment declines. For this reason, the net benefits that individuals perceive from union membership may be lower in these industries, and an increase in their importance in the economy would shift the demand for union services to the left in Figure 13.6, thereby reducing the percentage of the workforce that is unionized.

These latter industries also tend to be populated by small establishments. The demand for unionization is thought to be lower for employees who work in small firms, because they often feel less alienated from their supervisors. Similarly, because trying to organize 1,000 workers spread over 100 firms is more costly than is organizing 1,000 workers at one plant, the supply of union services is thought to shift left as the share of employment going to small firms increases. Both of these factors tend to suggest (in terms of Figure 13.6) that unionization will decline as the share of employment in small establishments increases, providing another reason why the shift in industrial distribution of employment might have affected the extent of unionization.

Regional Shifts in Employment   A second factor that might have contributed to the decline in union strength is the movement in population and employment in the United States that has occurred since 1955 from the industrial Northeast and Midwest to the South and the West. As noted earlier, the South and Southwest are heavily represented among the 27 states that have right-to-work laws. Such laws raise the costs of expanding union membership, because individuals who accept employment with a firm cannot be compelled to become union members as a condition of employment. In terms of Figure 13.6, these laws shift the supply curve of union services to the left, thereby reducing the level of unionization. Between 1955 and 2019, the proportion of employees working in right-to-work states increased from 24 to 49 percent. This shifting geographic distribution of the workforce, coupled with the existence of these laws, undoubtedly tended to depress union membership.

However, the decline in unionization occasioned by the move to the South and the West cannot completely be attributed to right-to-work laws, per se. The extent of unionization in right-to-work states tended to be lower than that in other states even before the passage of the laws. These laws might only reflect attitudes toward unions that already existed in these communities.[18]

Competitive Pressures   A third factor is increased foreign competition in manufacturing and the deregulation of the airline, trucking, and telephone industries (see Example 13.2). In these industries, which tend to be highly unionized, increased product-market competition has served to reduce the power of unions to raise wages; that is, more product-market competition increases the price elasticity of product demand and hence (as we saw in Chapter 4) increases the elasticity of labor demand. To the extent that union members' wages did not fall substantially in the face of increased product-market competition, unionized employment within these industries could have been expected to fall. Indeed, the share of unionized employment in these previously heavily unionized industries has fallen substantially in the past two decades as competition from both foreign firms and new, nonunion employers in the deregulated industries has increased.[19]

By making labor demand curves more elastic, increased competitive pressures reduce the benefits to workers of collective action, hence shifting the demand curve for union membership to the left. Moreover, increased product-market competition might well call forth *employer* responses that affect workers' demands for unions. For example, if firms find that foreign competition has intensified, they may seek to relocate in areas where workers are less likely to unionize; similarly, they may seek to employ workers in demographic groups whose demands for union membership are relatively low. Increased competition may also cause employers to resist union-organizing efforts more vigorously, which could well increase the costs of such efforts and shift the supply curve of union services to the left.

EXAMPLE 13.2

The Effects of Deregulation on Trucking and Airlines

Before the late 1970s, the heavily unionized trucking and airline industries were regulated by the U.S. government, which restricted the entry of potential competitors and granted existing carriers a degree of monopoly power. During 1978 to 1980, however, these restrictions were largely removed. The resulting increase in product-market competition increased the price elasticity of product demand and, of course, the wage elasticity of labor demand in those industries—thus reducing the power of unions to raise wages.

These changes reduced the desirability of being unionized, and indeed, both industries experienced sharp declines in unionized employment. In the airline industry, for example, the employment of union mechanics had fallen 15 percent to 20 percent by 1983. In trucking, the rate of unionization throughout the industry fell from 88 percent to 65 percent by 1990.

Sources: David Card, "The Impact of Deregulation on the Employment and Wages of Airline Mechanics," *Industrial and Labor Relations Review* 39 (July 1986): 527–538; Michael H. Belzer, *Sweatshops on Wheels: Winners and Losers in Trucking Deregulation* (New York: Oxford University Press, 2000)

Employer Resistance   U.S. employers can, and often do, play an active role in opposing union-organizing campaigns, using both legal means and illegal means. For example, under the NLRA, employers can legally present arguments to employees detailing why they think workers would be best served to vote against a union, and employers can hire consultants to advise them on how to best conduct a campaign to

Table 13.3 Union Representation Elections and Unfair Labor Practice Complaints Issued by NLRB, 1970–2019

Year	Representation elections		NLRB complaints against employers	
	Number	Percentage won by union	Number	Ratio: complaints to elections
1970	8,074	55.2	1,474	0.183
1975	8,577	48.2	2,335	0.272
1980	8,198	45.7	5,164	0.630
1985	4,614	42.4	2,840	0.616
1990	4,210	46.7	3,182	0.756
1993	3,586	47.6	3,576	0.997
1996	3,277	44.8	2,919	0.891
1999	3,585	50.5	2,036	0.568
2003	2,937	53.8	1,767	0.601
2005	2,649	56.8	1,160	0.438
2010	1,571	65.9	1,213	0.791
2015	1,574	71.2	1,272	0.808
2019	995	74.9	916	0.921

Source: Annual Report of the National Labor Relations Board, Appendix Tables 3A, 13 (various years); National Labor Relations Board, Reports, at www.nlrb.gov/reports/nlrb-case-activity-reports/representation-cases/intake/representation-petitions-rc, and www.nlrb.gov/reports/nlrb-case-activity-reports/unfair-labor-practice-cases/intake/unfair-labor-practice-charges

prevent a union from winning an election. However, an employer's threatening to withhold planned wage increases if the union wins the election, or a firm's discriminating against employees involved in the organizing effort, are illegal. If a union believes that an employer is involved in illegal activities during a campaign, it can file an unfair labor practices charge with the NLRB that, if sustained, can lead the NLRB to issue a formal complaint.

Table 13.3 chronicles, from 1970 to 2019, the number of union representation elections, the percentage won by the union, and the number of unfair labor practice complaints filed by the NLRB against employers. Although not all unfair practices occur during representation elections, the ratio of such complaints to the number of elections held gives us at least some idea of the intensity of employer resistance. This ratio rose steeply in the 1970s and 1980s, peaked in 1993 (at a ratio over five times greater than it had been two decades earlier), fell in the 10 years from 1996 to 2005, and has again dramatically risen in the most recent decade.

Why did employers offer increased resistance to unions after 1970? Some argue that employers were more disposed, on purely ideological grounds, to maintain union-free workplaces. Others suggest, however, that the change in employer behavior was the result of an increase in the costs that employers expected to face if the unions won. During the 1970s and early 1980s, wages of unionized workers grew more rapidly than the wages of nonunion workers just as competition from foreign producers increased sharply. Thus, the perceived economic benefits to nonunion employers of keeping their workplaces nonunion increased. This factor, the argument goes, encouraged employers—perhaps also driven by increasing shareholder pressures to increase profits—to increasingly and aggressively combat union election campaigns, through both legal means and illegal means.[20]

Union Actions to Alter the Labor Demand Curve

Many actions that unions take are direct attempts to relax the market constraints they face—either to *increase the demand* for union labor or to *reduce the wage elasticity of demand* for their members' services. Many of these attempts have *not* occurred through the collective bargaining process per se. Rather, they have occurred through union support for legislation that at least indirectly achieved union goals and through direct public relations campaigns to increase the demand for products produced by union members.

Shifting Product Demand To increase the demand for the final product—and hence shift the labor demand curve for union workers to the right—unions have lobbied for import quotas, which restrict the quantities of foreign-made goods that can be imported into the United States, and for *domestic content* legislation, which requires goods from abroad to have a certain percentage of U.S.-made components. Unions have also lobbied strongly against legislation, such as the North American Free Trade Agreement, that reduced tariffs on imported goods. In the United States, some unions have sought to directly influence people's tastes for the products that they produce, urging consumers to "Buy American" or "Look for the union label."

Restricting Substitution: Legislation An implication of our earlier discussion of labor demand elasticity (Chapter 4) is that the demand for union labor is likely to become less elastic, other things being equal, when it becomes more difficult or expensive to replace union labor with alternative factors of production. Unions have therefore often sought, through legislation, to pursue strategies that increase the costs of other inputs that are potential substitutes for union members. Construction unions, for example, have often persuaded states to require that nonunion contractors working on public projects pay the "prevailing wage" (usually the union wage in that area); furthermore, labor unions have been among the primary supporters of higher minimum wages.[21] Although such support may be motivated by a concern for the welfare of low-wage workers, increases in the mandated wage also raise the relative costs to employers of hiring nonunion workers, thereby both increasing the costs of the products that they produce and reducing employers' incentives to substitute them for higher-paid union workers.

Restricting Substitution: Bargaining Union attempts to restrict the substitution of other inputs for union labor can also occur through the collective bargaining process. In the past, some unions, notably those in the airline, railroad, and printing industries, sought and won guarantees of minimum crew sizes (e.g., at least three pilots were required to fly certain jet aircraft). Such *staffing requirements* prevented employers from substituting capital for labor.[22] Other unions have won contract provisions that prohibit employers from *subcontracting* for some or all of the services that they provide; for example, a union representing a company's janitorial employees might win a contract provision preventing the firm from hiring external firms to provide it with janitorial services. Such provisions might limit the substitution of nonunion for union workers.

Craft unions often negotiate specific contract provisions that restrict the functions that members of each individual craft can perform, thereby limiting the substitution of one type of union labor for another. They also limit the substitution of lower-skilled union labor for higher-skilled union labor by establishing rules about the maximum number of *apprentice* workers that can be employed relative to the experienced *journey-level* workers. Apprenticeship rules also limit the supply of higher-skilled workers to a craft, which is another way to limit substitution for current union members.

Yet another way a union can try to limit substitution is to have some of its members on the company's board of directors. For example, unions in Germany have pushed to have a mandated fraction of seats on boards of directors representing workers.[23]

Bargaining and the Threat of Strikes

How do unions persuade employers to agree to changes that reduce the wage elasticity of demand or shift the demand curve for union labor to the right? Given the elasticity and position of demand curves, how are unions able to bargain for, and win, real wage increases when in most cases an increase in the price of an input reduces a firm's profits?

In some cases, a union and an employer might agree to a settlement in which real wages are increased in return for the union agreeing to certain work-rule changes that will result in increased productivity. If such an agreement is explicit and is tied to the resulting change in productivity, the process is often referred to as *productivity bargaining*. More typically, however, unions are able to win management concessions at the bargaining table because of the unions' ability to impose costs on management. These costs typically take the form of work slowdowns and strikes. A *strike* is an attempt to deny the firm the labor services of all union members.

Strikes, for all the publicity generated when they occur, are relatively rare—and are becoming ever rarer—in the United States. In 1970, for example, 381 work stoppages occurred in the United States, involving 1,000 or more workers, and these strikes caused a loss of about one-fourth of 1 percent of all work hours in the economy. In contrast, in 1997, 2007, and 2016 (years of comparable economic activity, as measured by the unemployment rate), 29, 21, and 15 such strikes occurred, respectively—and the time lost was less than one-hundredth of 1 percent.[24] Despite their infrequency, the *threat* of a strike hangs over almost every bargaining situation in the private sector, and therefore, models of the bargaining process and its outcomes must address this threat.

A Simple Model of Strikes and Bargaining   The first, and also simplest, model of strikes in the bargaining process was developed by Sir John Hicks.[25] Suppose that management and labor are bargaining over only one issue: the size of the wage increase to be granted. How would the percentage increase that the union demands and the increase that the employer is willing to grant vary with the expected duration of a strike? Hicks analyzed this question by using a diagram like the one shown in Figure 13.7, in which $\dot{W}$ is the percentage wage increase over which labor and management are bargaining.

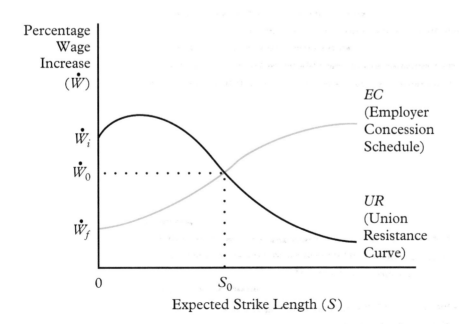

Figure 13.7 Hicks's Bargaining Model and Expected Strike Length

On the employer side, the firm's highest prestrike wage offer is assumed to be $\dot{W}_f$. If that offer is rejected and a strike ensues, the employer might be able to service its customers for a relatively short period of time through accumulated inventories or the use of nonstriking employees (including managers) in production jobs. As a strike progresses, however, the costs of lost business or dissatisfied customers mount; indeed, recent papers suggest that productivity and product quality—whether measured by tread separations in tire plants or patient mortality rates in hospitals—can suffer quite markedly during periods of labor strife.[26] Faced with these losses, the employer can be expected to increase its wage offer in an effort to end the strike. The expected willingness of employers to increase their wage offers as a strike lengthens is depicted by the upward-sloping *employer concession schedule, EC,* in Figure 13.7.

The union is assumed to be initially willing to accept some wage increase ($\dot{W}_i$) before a strike, but after a strike begins, worker attitudes may harden, and the union may actually increase its wage demands early on. After some point in the strike, however, the loss of income that workers are suffering begins to affect their attitudes, and the union will begin to reduce its wage demands. This reduction is indicated by the *union resistance curve, UR,* in Figure 13.7, which eventually slopes downward.

As the strike proceeds, we expect the union's demands to decrease and the employer's offer to increase, until at strike duration S_0, the two will coincide. At this point, a settlement is reached on a wage increase of $\dot{W}_0$ and the strike is expected to end. This simple model has several implications.

Implications of the Model

First, holding the *EC* schedule constant, anything that shifts the *UR* schedule upward (i.e., increases union resistance to management) will both lengthen the expected strike duration and raise the wage increase that can be expected. This heightened resistance may be manifest in either a higher "no-strike" wage demand (an increase in $\dot{W}_i$) or a flatter slope to the *UR* curve, which would indicate that the union is less willing to modify its wage demands as the strike proceeds.[27] Union resistance can be expected to increase, for example, if the unemployment rate is so low that strikers can easily obtain temporary jobs or if strikers are able to collect some form of unemployment benefits (either from the government or from the union). Indeed, we do find that strikes are both more likely and of longer duration in periods of relative prosperity; the availability to strikers of unemployment benefits similarly affects strike activity.[28]

A second implication of the simple Hicks model is that anything strengthening the resistance of employers will lower the *EC* curve, thereby lengthening expected strike duration and reducing the expected wage settlement. Thus, firms will be more likely to resist—and less likely to raise their wage offers very much as the strike progresses—if they are less profitable, face an elastic product demand curve, can stockpile product inventories in advance of a strike, or can easily hire replacement workers (see Example 13.3).[29]

EXAMPLE 13.3

Permanent Replacement of Strikers

The collective bargaining laws of most nations permit a company whose workforce is on strike to hire *temporary* replacement workers to keep the business operating. The United States is one of the few nations that permit firms to hire *permanent* replacement workers. That is, workers on strike in the United States are at risk of permanently losing their jobs.

Although the right of companies to hire permanent replacements dates back to a 1938 Supreme Court decision, only since the early 1980s have large companies been doing so or seriously threatening to do so. In 1981, for example, the Reagan administration "broke" the air traffic controllers' union by permanently replacing striking controllers. Subsequently, a number of large companies, including Eastern Airlines and Greyhound, permanently replaced striking workers. One study estimated that the increased threat of using permanent replacements reduced strikes in the 1980s by about 8 percent.

Why did large companies begin using permanent replacement workers in the 1980s when they had typically failed to do so during the previous four decades? Some attributed it to increasingly antiunion attitudes on the part of the federal government, a declining number of high-wage union jobs, and high unemployment—which led many workers to apply for permanent replacement positions, even at the risk of being ostracized as "scabs" by fellow workers. Still others attributed it to the pressures of international competition, which increased employers' needs to cut costs.

Does the increased use of permanent replacements, which reduced union bargaining power, portend the end of unions in the United States? The answer is probably no. Although employers might derive benefits from the use of permanent replacements, they also face costs. The costs are particularly high when new employees must be carefully screened and training needs to be extensive. Replacements and any union workers brought back after the strike will likely be at odds with each other, and the commitment of workers to the employer may suffer in the long run.

Source: Peter Cramton and Joseph Tracy, "The Use of Replacement Workers in Union Contract Negotiations: The U.S. Experience, 1980–1989," *Journal of Labor Economics* 16 (October 1998): 667–701

A final implication is that strikes appear to be unnecessarily wasteful. Had the expected settlement of $\dot{W}_0$ been reached *before* a strike, or with a *shorter* strike, both sides would have been spared some losses. When strikes are likely to be costly to both parties, the two might agree in advance to certain *bargaining protocols* that will help avert future strikes. For example, the parties might agree to start bargaining well in advance of a contract's expiration date, to limit the number of contract items that they will discuss, or to submit the dispute to binding arbitration if they fail to reach agreement on their own. Indeed, some evidence shows that strikes are less frequent, and shorter, when the *joint costs* of any strike are likely to be greater.[30]

If strikes are costly and if they can be averted in advance, why do they occur at all? Some argue that to enhance their bargaining positions and retain the credibility of the *threat* of a strike, unions have to periodically use the strike weapon; that is, a strike may be designed to *influence future* negotiations. Strikes also may be useful devices by which the internal solidarity of a union can be enhanced against the common adversary—the employer. More fundamentally, however, strikes are thought to occur because the information that both sides have about each other's goals and intentions to resist may be imperfect.

Strikes and Asymmetric Information   Most recent economic models of strike activity in the United States are based on the assumption of information asymmetry. Workers want to share in the firm's profits, for example, but they will doubt management's willingness to be completely truthful about current and expected profit levels. The reason is not difficult to understand: Management knows more about the firm's profitability than does labor, and if the former can convince workers that the enterprise is not very profitable, the union can be expected to moderate its wage demands.

Knowing management's informational advantages and its incentives to understate profitability, the union may try to elicit a signal from management about the true level of profits. A strike would be one such signal. If the firm is lying, and profits are greater than stated, the firm may be unwilling to put up a fight (management may figure that because giving in is financially feasible, it is better off avoiding the costs of a strike). If, however, the firm is telling the truth about its low level of profits, giving in may not be feasible; taking a strike, then, sends a signal that the firm believes labor's demands are far enough above what it can feasibly pay that they must be strongly resisted.

An implication of the asymmetric-information model of strike activity is that greater uncertainty about an employer's willingness and ability to pay for wage increases should raise both the probability that a strike will occur and the duration of the strike. In general, the more variable a firm's profitability over time, other things being equal, the greater this uncertainty and the greater the expected incidence and duration of strike activity will be.[31] If the parties realize this, however, they could avert a strike by establishing a reputation for revealing their true positions rather quickly.

Union Leaders and the Union Members   One barrier to eliminating the misunderstandings caused by asymmetric information is that *three* major parties are involved in a negotiation, not just *two*. On the employee side of the negotiations are two groups: union *leaders*[32] and the *rank-and-file* union members, who rely on their leaders for information.[33] The rank and file may understandably suspect their leaders of withholding information from them so that their negotiations are less stressful; put differently, the rank and file may suspect that their leaders will sell them out. Conversely, the leadership may be unsure just how strongly their members feel about certain demands being made of management. Thus, information asymmetries (and hence possibilities for misunderstandings) appear also within the *employee* side of the negotiating table.

Union leaders have much better information than rank-and-file union members about the employer's true financial position. If the offered settlement is smaller than the membership wants, union leaders face two options. On the one hand, they can return to their members, try to convince them of the employer's true financial picture, and recommend that management's offer be accepted. The danger is that the members may vote down the recommendation, accuse the leaders of selling out to management, and ultimately vote them out of office.

On the other hand, union leaders can return to their members and recommend that the members go out on strike. This recommendation will allow them to appear to be strong, militant leaders, even though the leaders themselves know that the strike will probably not lead to a larger settlement. After a strike of some duration, however, in accordance with the notion of the union resistance curve in Figure 13.7, union members will begin to moderate their wage demands, and ultimately, a settlement for which the union leaders will receive credit will be reached.

Because the latter strategy is the one that is more likely to maintain the union's strength *and* keep the leaders in office, it is the strategy that leaders may opt for even though it is clearly not in their members' best interests in the short run (the members have to bear the costs of the strike). Interestingly, strike activity rose markedly right after the passage of the Landrum–Griffin Act in 1959, possibly because this act increased union democracy—thereby giving the wishes of the rank and file greater weight in the bargaining process.[34]

Bargaining in the Public Sector: The Threat of Arbitration

Although some states have granted to selected public sector employees the right to strike in one form or another, most have continued historical prohibitions against strikes by state and local government workers. When strikes are forbidden, however, laws often provide for third parties to enter the dispute-resolution process if bargaining between the parties comes to an impasse. The first step in this process is typically some form of *mediation*, in which a neutral third party attempts to facilitate a settlement by listening to each party separately, making suggestions on how each might modify its position to have more appeal to the other, and doing anything else possible to bring the parties to a voluntary settlement.

If a mediator is unable to bring the parties to a settlement, the dispute-resolution process sometimes calls for the next step to be *fact finding*, in which a neutral party, after listening to both sides and gathering information, writes a report that proposes a settlement. The report is not binding for either party, but it may be considered by each to be a forecast of the settlement that binding arbitration would impose if the impasse were to continue.

If noncoercive methods fail to bring a voluntary settlement, *arbitration* becomes the final step of the dispute-resolution process. A single arbitrator may hear the case, or the case may be heard by a panel, usually consisting of one representative from labor, one from management, and one "neutral." Whether the parties *choose* to go to arbitration to settle their dispute or whether by law they *must* go to arbitration once the arbitration report is issued, the parties are bound by its contents. Arbitration associated with the bargaining process is called *interest arbitration* (to distinguish it from the *grievance-arbitration* process so widely used in resolving contract-administration disputes during the life of a contract).

Forms of Arbitration

Interest arbitration can take two forms. With *conventional arbitration*, the arbitrators are free to decide on any wage settlement of their choosing. They listen to both sides as each side makes its case, then they render their own decision. Some have suspected that under this conventional procedure, arbitrators tend to split the difference between the two parties, thereby encouraging the parties to take extreme positions (in the hope of dragging the arbitrator toward their true goal).

Some jurisdictions have chosen to adopt *final-offer arbitration*, in which the arbitrator is constrained to choose the final, pre-arbitration offer either of the union or of management; no other option is possible for the arbitrator. Final-offer arbitration, according to theory, would induce the parties to make more-reasonable final offers to each other, because by so doing, they would increase the chances of their offer's being the one accepted by the arbitrator.

The Contract Zone

No matter what form arbitration takes, going to arbitration is a risk for both parties because neither knows how the arbitrator will decide. A party wins the gamble only if the arbitrator reaches a more favorable wage decision than it could get through voluntary agreement. Thus, in deciding whether to continue bargaining—or, instead, take a rigid position and let the dispute go to arbitration—a party needs to develop expectations of various possible arbitrator decisions. By calculating the likelihood of each possible outcome *and* the utility associated with it, the party can develop a set of voluntary agreements that it would prefer over taking its chances with arbitration. If the preferred decision sets of the two parties happen to overlap, the dispute has a *contract zone* of possible voluntary agreements that *both* parties will prefer to the gamble of arbitration. If the dispute has no such overlap, the parties cannot agree voluntarily and thus the dispute will definitely go to arbitration.

A party's preferences for negotiation over taking a chance on arbitration are increased by greater aversion to risk and greater uncertainty about how the arbitrator might decide. If the parties become increasingly averse to losing or if they become increasingly unable to predict what arguments or facts an arbitrator will find persuasive, then the set of negotiated outcomes that they prefer to the arbitration gamble will widen. (Appendix 13A presents a more formal model underlying this conclusion.)

Although logic dictates that a bargaining situation with *no* contract zone will produce no voluntary agreement, a wider contract zone will not necessarily make reaching a voluntary agreement more likely.[35] A wider contract zone opens up more feasible outcomes to the two parties, so one might think that the chances of voluntary agreement are enhanced, but this scenario also gives the parties more to argue about. For example, in an extreme case, if both parties preferred only one specific wage increase to arbitration, then perhaps agreement would be reached more quickly and with more certainty than if several possible outcomes were available to be thoroughly debated.

Persuading the Arbitrator Although going to arbitration is clearly risky, the parties are not helpless in their abilities to influence the arbitrator's decision. If they are going to final-offer arbitration, they can improve their chances of winning by developing a final, pre-arbitration offer that the arbitrator is likely to regard as reasonable. The influence they exert in final-offer arbitration, then, amounts to guessing what the arbitrator thinks the outcome should be and then crafting an offer that approaches it. (Obviously, the union will approach it from *above* and management will approach it from *below*, as each tries to steer the arbitrator in its direction.)

If the parties are going to conventional arbitration, how their offers can influence the arbitrator's decision is less certain. Some people might reason that the arbitrator will decide on a wage increase that lies between those of the two parties or, in the extreme, simply split the difference. If so, the parties might then be tempted to make final offers that are far from where they eventually expect to end up.

Conceivably, however, arbitrators initially have their own views of a proper settlement, which can then be modified by listening to the arguments and positions of each party. Their own beliefs of what constitutes a reasonable outcome are not easily changed, and if a party's position (offer) is far from the outcome that they consider appropriate, little weight will be given to it.[36] This latter view of how arbitrators behave implies that the parties can gain influence only by making offers that are close to what they think the arbitrator will decide. If both parties make the same (correct) guess about the arbitrator's preferred outcome, their final offers will bracket the arbitrator's decision. To outsiders, the arbitrator will look as though they followed a simple, split-the-difference rule, but what really happened was that the parties strategically placed their offers around the arbitrator's expected position.[37]

Effects of Arbitration If arbitrators have their own strongly held views on the appropriate outcome in a particular case and if the parties position their offers around what they expect to be the arbitrator's preferred outcome, then whatever form of arbitration is used, the behavior of the parties and the arbitrator should be more or less the same. Indeed, one study of police officers' contracts in a state where either form could be used found that the wage outcomes chosen by the arbitrators were similar in each.[38] But how do arbitrated settlements compare with negotiated ones?

Negotiated wage settlements are, unsurprisingly, comparable with arbitrated settlements in states requiring that disputed settlements go to arbitration, because all negotiations in those states take place under the threat of arbitration. Somewhat surprisingly, however, another study of police contracts found that wages in states requiring arbitration of disputed settlements are more or less the same as those in states *without* that requirement.[39] Thus, the effects of arbitration on wage levels might actually be quite small.[40]

The Effects of Unions

Economists have long been interested in the effects of unions on wages, and recently, attention has also been given to their effects on total compensation (including employee benefits), employment levels, hours of work, productivity, and profits. In this section, we review the theory and the evidence on these effects.

The Theory of Union Wage Effects

Suppose that we had data on the wage rates paid to two groups of workers identical in every respect except that one group was unionized and the other was not. Let W_u denote the wage paid to union members and W_n the wage paid to nonunion workers. If the difference between the two could be attributed solely to the presence of unions, then the *relative wage advantage* (R) that unions would have achieved for their members would be given, in percentage terms, by the following:

$$R = (W_u - W_n)/W_n \tag{13.1}$$

This relative wage advantage does *not* represent the absolute amount, in percentage terms, by which unions would have increased the wages of their members, because unions both directly and indirectly affect *nonunion* wage rates too. Moreover, we cannot say for sure whether estimates of R will overstate or understate the absolute effect of unions on their members' real wage levels. To illustrate the difficulties in interpreting union–nonunion wage differentials, we begin with the simple model of the labor market depicted in Figure 13.8.

Figure 13.8 represents two sectors of the labor market, both of which hire similar workers. Panel (a) is the union sector and panel (b) is the nonunion sector. Suppose *initially* that both sectors are nonunion and that mobility between them is costless. Workers will therefore move between the two sectors until wages are equal in both. With demand curves D_u and D_n, workers will move between sectors until the supply curves are S_u^0 and S_n^0, respectively. The common equilibrium wage will be W_0, and employment will be E_u^0 and E_n^0, respectively, in the two sectors.

Once one sector becomes unionized, and its wage rises to W_u^1, what happens to wages in the other sector depends on the responses of employees who are not employed in the union sector. In the following sections, we discuss four possible reactions.[41]

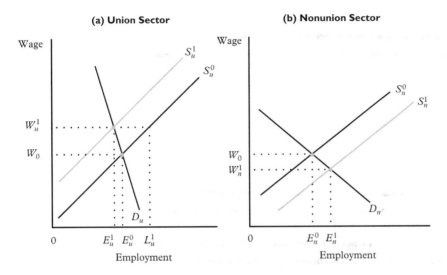

Figure 13.8 Spillover Effects of Unions on Wages and Employment

Spillover Effects If the union succeeds in raising wages in the union sector to W_u^1, this increase will cause employment to decline to E_u^1 workers, resulting in $L_u^1 - E_u^1$ unemployed workers in that sector. If all the unemployed workers *spill over* into the nonunion sector, the supply curves in the two sectors will shift to S_u^1 and S_n^1, respectively. Unemployment will be eliminated in the union sector; in the nonunion sector, however, an excess supply of labor will exist at the old market-clearing wage, W_0. As a result, downward pressure will be exerted on the wage rate in the nonunion sector until the labor market in that sector clears at a *lower* wage (W_n^1) and a higher employment level (E_n^1).

In the context of this model, the union has succeeded in raising the wages of its members who kept their jobs. However, it has done so by shifting some of its members to lower-wage jobs in the nonunion sector and, because of this spillover effect, by actually lowering the wage rate paid to individuals initially employed in the nonunion sector. As a result, the observed union *relative wage* advantage (R_1), computed as

$$R_1 = (W_u^1 - W_n^1)/W_n^1 \tag{13.2}$$

will tend to be greater than the true *absolute* effect of the union on its members' real wage. This true absolute effect, A, stated in percentage terms, is defined as

$$A = (W_u^1 - W_0)/W_0 \tag{13.3}$$

Because W_n^1 is lower than W_0, R_1 is greater than A.

Threat Effects Another possible response by nonunion employees is to want a union to represent them as well. Nonunion employers, fearing that a union would increase labor costs and place limits on managerial prerogatives, might seek to buy off their employees by offering them above-market wages.[42] Because (as noted earlier) union membership comes with costs to workers, some wage less than W_u^1 but higher than W_0 would presumably be sufficient to assure employers that the majority of their employees would not vote for a union (assuming that the employees are happy with their nonwage conditions of employment).

The implications of such *threat effects*—nonunion wage increases resulting from the threat of union entry—are traced in Figure 13.9. The increase in wage in the union sector, and resulting decline in employment there, is again assumed to cause the supply of workers to the nonunion sector to shift to S_n^1. In response to the threat of union entry, however, nonunion employers are assumed to *increase* their employees' wages to W_n^*, which lies between W_0 and W_u^1. This wage increase causes nonunion employment to decline to E_n^*; at the higher wage, nonunion employers demand fewer workers. Moreover, because the nonunion wage is now not free to be bid down, an excess supply of labor, $L_n^* - E_n^*$, exists, resulting in unemployment. Finally, because the nonunion wage is now higher than the original wage, the observed union relative wage advantage

$$R_2 = (W_u^1 - W_n^*)/W_n^* \qquad (13.4)$$

is smaller than the absolute effect of unions on their members' real wages.

Wait Unemployment   Do workers who lose (or do not have) a union job necessarily leave the union sector and take jobs in the nonunion sector? Even with reduced employment in the union sector, job vacancies occur as a result of retirements, deaths, and voluntary turnover. Some of those who do not have union jobs will find searching for work in the union sector attractive, and their search might be more effective if they are not simultaneously employed elsewhere. Workers who reject lower-paying nonunion jobs so that they can search for higher-paying union ones create the

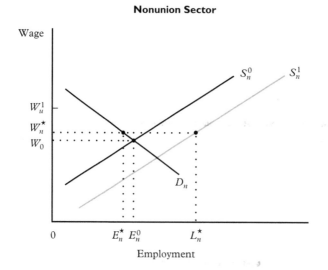

Nonunion Sector

Figure 13.9 Threat Effects of Unions on Wages and Employment in Nonunion Sector phenomenon of *wait unemployment* (they are waiting for union jobs to open up).[43]

The main behavior behind the wait-unemployment response is that workers will move from one sector to another if the latter offers higher *expected* wages. Expected wages in a sector are equal to the sector's wage rate multiplied by the probability of obtaining a job in that sector. Thus, even if one were always able to find a job in the nonunion sector, rejecting employment there might be beneficial if one had a reasonable chance (even if it were less than 100 percent) of obtaining a higher-paying union job at some point later. The importance of the resultant wait unemployment for our current discussion is that not everyone who loses a job in the union sector will spill over into the nonunion sector; in fact, theoretically, some workers originally in the nonunion sector would quit their jobs to take a chance on finding work in the union sector.

The presence of wait unemployment in the union sector reduces the spill-over of workers to the nonunion sector, thus moderating downward pressure on nonunion wages. Moreover, if enough nonunion workers decide to search for union jobs, the labor supply curve to the nonunion sector could even shift to the left. In this case, unionization in one sector could cause wages in the nonunion sector to rise, just as with the threat effect (in fact, a "threat" here is being carried out in that workers are leaving the nonunion employers to search for union jobs).

Shifts in Labor Demand   Finally, recall that we discussed earlier the activities that unions undertake to alter the demand for their members' labor services. In some cases, these activities involve attempts to shift the product demand curve facing unionized firms (and hence their labor demand curve) to the right. If unions were successful in their efforts to increase product demand in the unionized sector, perhaps at the expense of the nonunion sector, the rightward shift in the union sector labor demand curve—and the associated leftward shift in the labor demand curve in the nonunion sector—would again serve to lower wages in the nonunion sector below what they were originally.[44]

Evidence of Union Wage Effects

Because the presence of unions can influence both the union and the non-union wage rate, we cannot observe the wage that would have existed in the absence of unions (W_0). Hence, estimates of a union's effects on the absolute level (A) of its members' real wages—see equation (13.3)—cannot be obtained. Care must be taken not to mistake the relative wage effects that we can observe—in equations (13.2) and (13.4)—for the absolute effects.

Economists have expended considerable effort to estimate the extent to which unions have raised the wages of their members relative to the wages of comparable nonunion workers in the private sector. These studies have tended to use data on large samples of individuals and sought to estimate how much more union members get paid than nonunion workers, after controlling for any differences between the two groups in other factors that might be expected to influence wages. Most of the work has been done in the United States, where levels of unionization are so modest that finding comparable nonunion workers is relatively easy.

Because the studies of union–nonunion wage differences have used various data sets and statistical methodologies (and, as in the previous chapter, economists don't always agree on what other variables to control for when analyzing wage differences), we have no definitive estimate of the gap on which all researchers agree. Enough work has been done on the topic, however, for six patterns to emerge:

1. The union relative wage advantage in the United States appears to fall into the range of *10 percent to 20 percent*;[45] that is, our best estimate is that U.S. union workers receive wages that are some 10 percent to 20 percent higher than those of comparable nonunion workers.[46]

2. The *private sector* union wage advantage in the United States is larger than that in the *public* sector. For example, one study that used the same data and the same statistical methodology for both sectors estimated that the private sector wage gap was in the 18 percent to 20 percent range from 2000 to 2012, whereas in the public sector over the same period, it was in the 8 percent to 12 percent range.[47]

3. The union relative wage advantage in the United States is larger than it is in most other countries for which comparable estimates are available. For example, one study found the following union–nonunion wage gaps during the late 1990s: United States, 18 percent; Australia, 12 percent; United Kingdom, 10 percent; Canada, 8 percent; Germany, 4 percent; and France, 3 percent.[48]

4. Unions everywhere tend to reduce the dispersion of earnings among workers. They raise the wages of lower-skilled workers relative to higher-skilled workers within the union sector, thereby reducing the payoff to human-capital investments. They standardize wages within and across firms in the same industry, and they reduce the earnings gaps between production workers and office workers.[49] They also reduce the wage gap between white workers and Black workers in the United States.[50]

5. The union relative wage advantage in the United States, at least in recent decades, has tended to grow larger during recessionary periods.[51] Although evidence before the 1980s is mixed, the wage changes of union members have been less sensitive to business conditions than the wages of nonunion workers in recent years.

6. Although the findings have not yet fit a pattern, researchers have attempted to discover whether greater levels of unionization tend to increase or decrease wages in the *nonunion* sector. These studies have tried to determine whether the spillover or the threat effect dominates among nonunion employers. The evidence so far is ambiguous. One study found, for example, that threat effects dominated within *cities* (i.e., in more highly unionized cities, the wages of nonunion workers

were higher). It also found, however, that the spillover effect dominated within *industries* (in more highly unionized industries, nonunion wages tended to be lower). These contradictory results mirror those of earlier studies.[52]

Evidence of Union Total Compensation Effects

Estimates of the extent to which the wages of union workers exceed the wages of otherwise-comparable nonunion workers may prove misleading for two reasons. First, such estimates ignore the fact that wages are only part of the compensation package. Many argue that *employee benefits*, such as paid holidays, vacation pay, sick leave, and retirement benefits, will be higher in firms that are unionized than in nonunion firms. The argument states that because tastes for the various benefits differ across individuals and because nonunion firms have no easy way to determine the preferences of its average employee, nonunion firms tend to pay a higher fraction of total compensation in the form of money wages. Empirical evidence tends to support this contention: Employee benefits and the share of compensation that goes to benefits do appear to be higher in union firms than in nonunion firms. Furthermore, studies also suggest that unionization increases the probability that workers apply for employer-financed government benefits for which they are eligible.[53] Ignoring benefits might therefore *understate* the true union–nonunion total compensation differential.

Second, ignoring *conditions of employment* may cause one to *overstate* the effect of unions on their members' overall welfare levels compared with those of nonunion workers. For example, studies have shown that for blue-collar workers, unionized firms tend to have more-structured work settings, more-hazardous jobs, less-flexible hours of work, faster work paces, lower worker job satisfaction, and less employee control over the assignment of overtime hours than do nonunion firms.[54] This situation may arise because production settings that call for more interdependence among workers and the need for rigid work requirements by employers also give rise to unions. While unions often strive to control these working conditions, they do not always succeed. Part of the estimated union–nonunion earnings differential thus may be a compensating wage differential paid to union workers to compensate them for these unfavorable working conditions. One study estimates that two-fifths of the estimated union–nonunion earnings differential reflects such compensation, suggesting that the observed earnings differential might overstate the true differential in overall levels of worker well-being.[55]

The Effects of Unions on Employment

If unions raise the wages and employee benefits of their members and if they impose constraints on managerial prerogatives, economic theory suggests that their presence will have a negative effect on employment. Several studies have investigated this theoretical prediction, and the results suggest that unions do reduce employment growth. A study of plants in California during the late 1970s, for example, estimated that employment grew some 2 to 4 percent more slowly per year in union firms than in nonunion firms; in fact, the growth rates were so different that about 60 percent of the decline in California's unionization rate was attributed to slower employment growth in union jobs.[56] Other studies have found similar employment effects for the United States as a whole and for Australia, Canada, and the United Kingdom.[57] Finally, even when employment is not much changed in the face of unionization, the total yearly hours of work might still fall.[58]

The Effects of Unions on Productivity and Profits

Two views address how unions affect labor productivity (output per worker). One is that unions *increase* worker productivity, given the firm's level of capital, by providing a "voice" mechanism through which workers' suggestions and preferences can be communicated to management.[59] With a direct means for expressing their ideas or concerns, workers may have enhanced motivation levels and be less likely to quit. With lower quit rates, firms have more incentives to invest in training, which should also raise worker productivity.

The other view on how unions affect worker productivity stresses the limits that they place on managerial prerogatives, especially with respect to using cost-minimizing levels of the labor input. We argued earlier that if unions care about the employment as well as the wages of their members, they will put pressure on management to agree to staffing requirements, restrictions on work done that is outside of one's job title, cumbersome methods through which the disciplining of nonproductive workers must take place, and other policies that increase labor costs per unit of output.

Empirical analyses of union productivity effects have yielded conflicting results. The effects of unions on workers' output apparently depend very much on the quality of the relationship between labor and management in each particular collective bargaining setting. In fact, one study found that unionized firms with human-resource practices that combined joint labor–management decision-making with output-based pay had higher productivity than similar nonunion firms; unionized firms without such practices had lower productivity than comparable nonunion employers.[60]

Similar conflicting results have been found among studies of productivity effects of public sector unions. One study found, for example, that hospitals with unionized registered nurses had lower fatality rates among heart-attack victims, while another found that workers who were taught by unionized teachers had poorer labor market outcomes in the long run.[61]

When unions raise wages but do not raise worker productivity, then we might expect them to reduce firms' profits. Some studies directly analyze unionization and profit levels, holding other things constant; these rather consistently estimate that profits in unionized firms are lower, both in the United States and in the United Kingdom.[62] Another way of studying unions' effects on profits, however, is to make use of evidence that the stock market reflects changes in a firm's profitability. For example, one study found that when a firm's workers become unionized, the price of the firm's stock typically falls about 10 percent over the next year and a half.[63]

Normative Analyses of Unions

We have seen throughout this text that economic theory can be used in both its *positive* mode and its *normative* mode. The analyses of union effects in this section so far have been of a positive nature, in that we have summarized both theory and evidence on how unions affect various labor market outcomes. We now turn to a normative question that often underlies discussions of unions and the government policies that affect them: Do unions enhance or reduce social welfare? As one might expect, opinions differ.[64]

Potential Reductions in Social Welfare

We saw in Chapter 1 that the role of any market, including the labor market, is to facilitate mutually beneficial transactions by providing a mechanism for voluntary exchange. The ultimate goal of this exchange is to arrive at an allocation of goods and services that generates as much utility as possible, given a society's resources, for the individuals in that society. If a market has facilitated *all* such transactions, then it has arrived at a point of Pareto efficiency. A requirement for the existence of Pareto efficiency is that all productive resources, including labor, be used in a way that generates maximum utility for society (this includes the utility of the workers as well as that of the consumers who purchase the goods or services that they produce).

Arguments that unions reduce social welfare generally stem from the proposition that they represent the interests of only their members, not of others.[65] One argument points to the production lost (the labor resources wasted) when workers go on strike. A second argument is similar: When labor and management agree to restrictive work rules (as noted in our discussion of the efficient-contracts model), the use of excess workers in the production process creates waste—and therefore social loss—in the use of labor. A third argument is more subtle, however.

Simple reasoning suggests that for Pareto efficiency to be achieved, resources that have the same *potential* productivity must have the same *actual* productivity. Consider, for example, a group of workers who are equally skilled, experienced, and motivated. If some of these workers are in jobs that produce $20 worth of goods or services per hour, whereas others in the group are in jobs that produce only $15, the value of society's output could be enhanced by the voluntary movement of members from the latter subset of jobs into the higher-productivity jobs. Reducing the number of workers in the $15 jobs would serve to raise the marginal productivity of those who remain in those jobs, whereas increasing the number of workers in the $20 jobs would put downward pressure on the wage (and marginal productivity) in that sector. As long as the marginal productivities of workers in the skill groups continue to differ, however, the value of society's output could be increased still further by having members of the lower-paid subset move into the higher-paying jobs. Only when the marginal productivities are equal and all Pareto-improving moves by workers have been completed can it be said that Pareto efficiency has been achieved.

The third argument that unions reduce social welfare, then, rests on two propositions. The first is that unions create wage (and therefore productivity) differentials among equivalent workers by raising wages in the union sector above those in the nonunion sector. The second proposition is that the higher and inflexible union wage reduces employment in the high-paid sector and prevents workers in lower-paying jobs from moving into the higher-productivity sector, resulting in lowering that society's output more than it would have been otherwise. Some economists have attempted to estimate these losses, and their estimates have generally been small—in the range of 0.2 percent to 0.4 percent of national output.[66]

Potential Increases in Social Welfare Arguments that unions reduce social welfare lose some of their force if, in the absence of unions, labor or product markets are not as competitive as assumed by standard economic theory. Suppose, for example, that the cost of mobility is so great that workers do not freely move to preferable jobs. Compensating wage differentials might fail to correctly guide the allocation of workers across jobs that have varying levels of unpleasant (or pleasant) characteristics. If so, too many workers might end up in dangerous or otherwise-unpleasant jobs, which they would gladly leave (even for a lower-paying one) if they had the chance.

With respect to working conditions, employer behavior can be influenced in two general ways. The mechanism relied on by the market, with its individual transactions, is one of *exit and entry*. If a worker is unhappy with certain conditions of employment, they are free to leave; if enough workers do so, the employer will be forced to alter the offending condition or else increase wages enough to induce the workers that it has to remain. An alternative to the exit mechanism is the mechanism of *voice*: Workers can vocalize their concerns and hope that the employer will respond.

The voicing of requests by *individuals* is potentially costly. First, many workplace conditions (such as lighting, scheduling, and safety precautions) are examples of "public goods" within the plant. All workers are benefited by any improvements, whether or not they contributed to the campaign to secure them. Therefore, the possibility of free riders inhibits individuals (acting alone) from bearing the costs of a campaign to change workplace conditions. Second, because the employer might respond to complaints by firing "troublemakers," an individual worker who uses the voice mechanism without some form of job protection must be prepared to suffer the costs of exit.

Those who believe that unions improve social welfare argue that in the face of high mobility costs, unions offer workers the mechanism of *collective* voice in the establishment of their working conditions. They solve the free-rider problem and relieve their members of the risks and burdens associated with individual voice. Furthermore, collective bargaining agreements almost always establish a grievance procedure through which certain employee complaints can be formally addressed by a neutral third party. In short, unions provide mechanisms of collective voice that substitute for an expensive-to-use exit mechanism in the determination of the workplace conditions that affect workers' utility. They therefore promote Pareto-improving transactions that would otherwise not have been induced, because of the high costs of employee mobility.

Other arguments that unions enhance (or at least do not reduce) social welfare also rest on market conditions that call into question key assumptions underlying the standard economic model of employer behavior. For example, one possibility (mentioned earlier in this chapter) is that unionized employers have substantial monopoly power in their product markets, which yields them excess profits. Another possibility is that barriers to worker mobility create the monopsonistic conditions in the labor market analyzed in Chapter 5. If either of these market conditions exists, the presence of unions may increase worker pay without reducing employment or output.[67]

EMPIRICAL STUDY 13.1

What Is the Gap Between Union Pay and Nonunion Pay? The Importance of Replication in Producing Credible Estimates

The question of whether unions raise the wages of their members relative to the wages of nonunion workers has been of enduring interest to labor economists ever since the 1940s. Hundreds of studies have been conducted on this topic, using a variety of data sources and statistical techniques, and these studies (at least those up through the early 1980s) were scrutinized and compared by H. Gregg Lewis, whom many regard as the father of modern labor economics. Lewis produced two books, some 20 years apart, on the subject of union–nonunion wage differentials—and his painstaking concern with methodological details of the research projects that he synthesized serves as a standard to be emulated among empirically oriented social scientists.

Lewis spent most of his career at the University of Chicago, where he was a significant adviser to almost 90 doctoral students and a teacher to many more—many of whom went on to become leaders in the field of labor economics. Lewis published few books or articles, however, in part because his insistence on checking and cross-checking data, replicating results of earlier studies, looking for biases in estimating equations, and reconciling results with earlier estimates ruled out quick publication. His first book on union–nonunion wage differentials, published in 1963, was an exhaustive survey of 20 earlier studies on the subject. This survey involved detailed checks for transcription or arithmetic errors in the data analyzed, the replication of estimates to make sure that the results were accurately reported, and his *re-estimation* of results when he believed that the original estimates were faulty or when newer data had been made available. The result of this work was his conclusion that in 1957–1958, union wages exceeded nonunion wages by 10 percent to 15 percent, assuming other factors affecting wages were held constant.

Lewis published his second book on the topic in 1986. This book analyzed the findings of some 200 studies that had been done in the preceding two decades, during which the advent of the computer and large data sets allowed for more-sophisticated analyses of union–nonunion wage differentials in various industries and regions and among different demographic groups. These studies used regression analysis to determine whether those in unions received higher wages, holding other productive characteristics constant. Lewis was concerned about biases in the estimates of the union differential if union membership is not randomly determined (the issue of *selection bias* or *unobserved heterogeneity*), if important variables were either omitted (the *omitted variables* problem) from the estimating equation or mismeasured (the *errors in variables* problem), and if certain groups of people were excluded from the samples. He devoted whole chapters to investigations and estimates of these biases.

In analyzing the estimates of *overall* union pay differentials in the United States, Lewis sought in his second book to reconcile the different estimates of some 117 studies. He adjusted each estimate for the biases that his analyses found that were introduced by such factors as nonrandom data sampling; the omission of nonmanufacturing workers, minorities, or young employees from the sample; the failure to control for industry or occupation in the regression equation; and the omission of employee benefits from the pay variable. His painstaking analyses concluded that, on average, union workers received roughly 15 percent higher pay than otherwise-equivalent nonunion workers in the 1967–1979 period. While this result was remarkably consistent with his earlier conclusions, Lewis was careful to point out that he regarded his 15 percent estimate as an upper-bound approximation of the true wage differential.

One prominent labor economist characterized the legacy of H. Gregg Lewis in this way:

> Lewis influenced the way a generation of labor economists did empirical work. He was a conscience against the quick and dirty and shoddy. . . . [His books] never lose sight that the goal of social science is to measure purported effects of economic institutions or changes in markets nor of the limitations nonexperimental data place on meeting the goal.[a]

[a] Richard Freeman, "H.G. Lewis and the Study of Union Wage Effects," *Journal of Labor Economics* 12 (January 1994): 144–147.

Sources: H.G. Lewis, *Unionism and Relative Wages in the United States: An Empirical Inquiry* (Chicago, IL: University of Chicago Press, 1963); H. Gregg Lewis, *Union Relative Wage Effects: A Survey* (Chicago, IL: University of Chicago Press, 1986)

Another argument is that employers are not as knowledgeable about how to maximize profits as standard economic theory assumes. Because management finds searching for better (or less costly) ways to produce costly, so the argument goes, we cannot be sure that it will always use labor in the most productive ways possible. (Clearly, this argument rests on the implicit assumption that entry into the product market is difficult enough that inefficient producers are not necessarily punished by competitive forces.) When unions organize and raise the wages of their members, firms may be shocked into the search for better ways to produce. Moreover, by establishing formal channels of communication between workers and management, unionization at least *potentially* provides a mechanism through which employers and employees can more effectively communicate about workplace processes.[68]

Review Questions

1. Suppose that a proposal for tax reductions associated with the purchase of capital equipment is up for debate. Suppose, too, that union leaders are called upon to comment on the proposal from the perspective of how it will affect the welfare of their members as workers (not consumers). Will they all agree on the effects of the proposal? Explain your answer.

2. Some collective bargaining agreements contain "union standards" clauses that prohibit the employer from farming out work normally done in the plant to other firms that pay less than the union wage.

    a. What is the union's rationale for seeking a union standards clause?

    b. Under what conditions will a union standards clause most likely be sought by a labor union?

3. The Jones Act mandates that at least 50 percent of all U.S. government-financed cargo must be transported in U.S.-owned ships and that any U.S. ship leaving a U.S. port must have at least 90 percent of its crew composed of U.S. citizens. What would you expect the impact of this act to be on the demand for labor in the shipping industry and the ability of unions to push up the wages of U.S. seafarers?

4. Unions in the capital-intensive steel industry were able to negotiate higher-than-average wage increases during the period in which steel output

in the United States was declining. Using economic theory, how can this pattern be explained?

5. In Germany, temporary layoffs and dismissals on short notice are often illegal. A dismissal is illegal if it is "socially unjustified," and it is considered "socially unjustified" if the worker could be employed in a different position or establishment of the firm, even one requiring retraining. Workers illegally dismissed can and might sue their employers. What are the likely consequences of this German law for the ability of German unions to raise wages?

6. U.S. unions often try to win public support for boycotting goods made in less-developed countries by workers who work long hours at low pay in unhealthy conditions.

   a. If successful, will these efforts unambiguously help the targeted foreign workers receive better pay? Explain fully.

   b. Will these efforts unambiguously help the union's U.S. workers? Explain fully.

7. Suppose that a union argues that unionized workers are generally more productive than nonunion workers and therefore that employers should take a much more positive approach to unionism and collective bargaining. Use economic theory to analyze why union workers are likely to be more productive (in terms of output per worker), and use it to analyze whether greater labor productivity enhances the profitability of firms.

8. A certain country has very centralized collective bargaining, under which wage bargains are applied nationally. This country is thinking about adopting a bargaining structure that is more decentralized so that wage bargains will be made at the individual plant or the individual firm level. How would you expect decentralization to affect wages and employment? Explain your answer.

Problems

1. Suppose that the employer concession schedule is $W = 1 + 0.02S$ and that the union resistance curve is $W = 5 + 0.02\ S - 0.01S^2$, where W = the percentage wage increase and S = the expected strike length in days. Using Hicks's simplest model, determine the length of the strike and the percentage wage increase.

2. The Brain Surgeons' Brotherhood faces an own-wage elasticity of demand for their labor that equals –0.1. The Dog Catchers' International faces an own-wage elasticity of demand for their labor that equals –3.0. Suppose that leaders in both unions push for a 20 percent wage increase but have no power to set employment levels directly. Why might members of the Dog Catchers' International be more wary of the targeted wage increase?

3. Suppose that unionized workers in the retail sales industry earn $10 per hour and that nonunionized workers in the industry earn $8 per hour.

What can be said about the relative wage advantage of unionized workers and the absolute effect of the union on its members' real wage?

4. Table 13P.4 gives the demand for labor at two different firms.

Table 13P.4 The Demand for Labor at Two Firms

Wage rate ($)	Demand (firm ABC)	Demand (firm XYZ)
6	24	28
8	23	26
10	22	24
12	21	22
14	20	20
16	19	18
18	18	16
20	17	14

The current wage rate in both firms is $14 per hour. A union would like to organize employees in one of the firms and bargain to raise the wage rate to $16 per hour. Calculate the wage elasticity of demand for each firm if the wage rate were increased from $14 per hour to $16 per hour. Which firm would the union be more interested in organizing? Why?

5. Table 13P.5 gives the demand for labor at a chocolate factory. The factory is unionized, and the union is negotiating to raise the wage rate for its members from $14 per hour to $16 per hour. At the same time, more people are realizing how delicious the chocolate products produced at the factory are, resulting in an increase in the demand for the chocolate. The labor demand after the increase in the demand for the company's product is shown in column 3.

Table 13P.5 Labor Demand at a Chocolate Factory

Wage rate ($)	Labor demand (original)	Labor demand (new)
6	38	42
8	35	39
10	32	36
12	29	33
14	26	30
16	23	27
18	20	24
20	17	21

A company official announces, "This wage increase will cost jobs in this factory!" In response, a union leader asserts, "What the company official said is incorrect; not a single union member will lose their job if the wage goes to $16." Who is correct? Justify your answer.

6. Two sectors of the construction industry currently pay their employees the market-clearing wage. The demand for labor in each sector is $MRP_L = 12 - L$, where L = the number (in thousands) of workers. The supply of labor in each sector is $L = W - 2$, where W = the wage rate (dollars per hour). A union organizes in one of the sectors, and it restricts supply to that sector by insisting that only those in the union are hired by firms in that sector (and gaining membership into the union is difficult). When the employees in this sector unionize, the supply of labor in that sector changes to $L = W - 4$.

   a. What is the wage rate in both sectors before unionization? How many employees will be hired in each sector?

   b. What is the wage rate in the unionized sector? How many employees will be hired in the unionized sector?

   c. If the unemployed workers in the newly unionized sector spill over into the nonunion sector, what will be the wage rate in the nonunion sector? How many employees will be hired in that sector?

   d. What is the union relative wage advantage? What is the true absolute effect?

7. Suppose that the employees in the nonunionized sector in problem 6 want a union to represent them as well. In an attempt to discourage a union from forming in this sector, the employers in that sector offer a wage rate of $7.50. How many nonunion workers will be hired? What is the union relative wage advantage?

Notes

1. Richard B. Freeman, "Labor Market Institutions Around the World" (Working Paper No. 13242, National Bureau of Economic Research, Cambridge, MA, July 2007); Harry Katz, "The Decentralization of Collective Bargaining: A Literature Review and Comparative Analysis," *Industrial and Labor Relations Review* 47 (October 1993): 3–22; Richard B. Freeman, "American Exceptionalism in the Labor Market: Union–Nonunion Differentials in the United States and Other Countries," in *Labor Economics and Industrial Relations: Markets and Institutions*, eds. Clark Kerr and Paul D. Staudohar (Cambridge, MA: Harvard University Press, 1994): 272–299.

2. Katz, "The Decentralization of Collective Bargaining"; Michael Wallerstein, Miriam Golden, and Peter Lange, "Unions, Employers' Associations, and Wage-Setting Institutions in Northern and Central Europe, 1950–1992," *Industrial and Labor Relations Review* 50 (April 1997): 379–401, present evidence for Austria, Germany, Belgium, the Netherlands, and Scandinavia, suggesting that a general process of

decentralization has not occurred in those countries. For a study of the effects of decentralized bargaining in Spain, see David Card and Sara De la Rica, "Firm-Level Contracting and the Structure of Wages in Spain," *Industrial and Labor Relations Review* 59 (July 2006): 573–592. For a study comparing European and U.S. frameworks, see Markus O. Helfen, Elke Schubler, and Dimitris Stevis, "Translating European Labor Relations Practices to the United States Through Global Framework Agreements? German and Swedish Multinationals Compared," *Industrial and Labor Relations Review* 69 (May 2016): 631–655.

3. Actually, the NLRA was much less pro-labor than our brief discussion indicates; the NLRA also gave the NLRB power to investigate employers' claims that their employees, or unions, were violating provisions of the act.

4. Postal workers and employees of federal government authorities, such as the Tennessee Valley Authority, were major exceptions. In each of these cases, the prices of the products or services produced (mail delivery and hydroelectric power) can be raised to cover the cost of the contract settlement. In other federal agencies, salaries are paid out of general revenues.

5. See Richard B. Freeman, "Unionism Comes to the Public Sector," *Journal of Economic Literature* 24 (March 1986): 41–86, for a completer discussion of the evolution of legislation governing bargaining in the public sector. For evidence on the effects on compensation for some unionized public sector employees, see Brigham R. Frandsen, "The Effects of Collective Bargaining Rights on Public Employee Compensation: Evidence from Teachers, Firefighters, and Police," *Industrial and Labor Relations Review* 69 (January 2016): 84–112.

6. Barry T. Hirsch and David A. Macpherson, *Union Membership and Earnings Data Book*, 2013, Figure 2 and Tables 1a—1g. Copyright 2013 by The Bureau of National Affairs, Inc. (800–372–1003) www.bna.com.

7. This organization was formed in 1955 from the merger of the AFL (founded in 1886) and the CIO (founded in 1935).

8. A recent paper finds that union members are more satisfied with their jobs and their lives in general than others; see David G. Blanchflower and Alex Bryson, "Now Unions Increase Job Satisfaction and Well-Being" (Working Paper No. 27720, National Bureau of Economic Research, Cambridge, MA, August 2020).

9. For a useful summary of the "voice" model of unions, see John T. Addison and Clive R. Belfield, "Union Voice," *Journal of Labor Research* 25 (Fall 2004): 563–596.

10. For an attempt to model how bargaining power affects the nature of contract settlements, see Jan Svejnar, "Bargaining Power, Fear of Disagreement, and Wage Settlements: Theory and Empirical Evidence from U.S. Industry," *Econometrica* 54 (September 1986): 1055–1078.

11. Brian E. Becker, "Union Rents as a Source of Takeover Gains among Target Shareholders," *Industrial and Labor Relations Review* 49 (October 1995): 3–19. An empirical test for a vertical contract curve can be found in John M. Abowd, "The Effect of Wage Bargains on the Stock Market Value of the Firm," *American Economic Review* 79 (September 1989): 774–800.

12. Nicholas Lawson, "Is Collective Bargaining Pareto Efficient? A Survey of the Literature," *Journal of Labor Research* 32 (September 2011): 282–304.

13. This model is based on the approach found in Orley Ashenfelter and John Pencavel, "American Trade Union Growth, 1900–1960," *Quarterly Journal of Economics* 83 (August 1969): 434–448; John Pencavel, "The Demand for Union Services: An Exercise," *Industrial and Labor Relations Review* 24 (January 1971): 180–191.

14. Unions might also be seen by workers (teachers, for example) as providing legal insurance against lawsuits; see Richard Murphy, "Why Unions Survive: Understanding How Unions Overcome the Free-Rider Problem" (Working Paper No. 25924, National Bureau of Economic Research, Cambridge, MA, June 2019).

15. For a review of data on worker attitudes toward unions, see Thomas A. Kochan and William T. Kimball, "Unions, Worker Voice, and Management Practices: Implications for a High-Productivity, High-Wage Economy," *Russell Sage Foundation Journal of the Social Sciences* 5 (December 2019): 88–108.

16. Rebecca S. Demsetz, "Voting Behavior in Union Representation Elections: The Influence of Skill Homogeneity and Skill Group Size," *Industrial and Labor Relations Review* 47 (October 1993): 99–113, finds that plants that have more-homogeneously skilled workers are more supportive of unions, other things being equal.

17. For a discussion of the factors underlying the rise and fall of unionization rates in the United States, see the essays by Edward P. Lazear, Richard B. Freeman, and Melvin W. Reder in *Journal of Economic Perspectives* 2 (Spring 1988): 59–110. For quantitative estimates of the extent to which the factors discussed in this section are responsible for the decline in unionization, see Henry Farber, "The Decline of Unionization in the United States: What Can Be Learned from Recent Experience?" *Journal of Labor Economics* 8:1, pt. 2 (January 1990): S75–S105; Henry Farber and Alan Krueger, "Union Membership in the United States: The Decline Continues," in *Employee Representation: Alternatives and Future Decisions*, eds. Bruce Kaufman and Morris Kleiner (Madison, WI: Industrial Relations Research Association, 1993).

18. For a study that cites earlier literature on the effects of right-to-work laws, see Steven E. Abraham and Paula B. Voos, "Right-to-Work Laws:

New Evidence from the Stock Market," *Southern Economic Journal* 67 (October 2000): 345–362.

19. Evidence that the effects of foreign competition are felt primarily in union members' employment levels, not in their wages, is found in John Abowd and Thomas Lemieux, "The Effects of International Trade on Union Wages and Employment: Evidence from the U.S. and Canada," in *Immigration, Trade, and the Labor Market*, eds. John Abowd and Richard Freeman (Chicago, IL: University of Chicago Press, 1991). Also see Matthew J. Slaughter, "Globalization and Declining Unionization in the United States," *Industrial Relations* 46 (April 2007): 329–346.

20. William T. Dickens, "The Effect of Company Campaigns on Certification Elections: Law and Reality Once Again," *Industrial and Labor Relations Review* 36 (July 1983): 560–575; Robert Flanagan, *Labor Relations and the Litigation Explosion* (Washington, DC: Brookings Institution, 1987); Farber, "The Decline in Unionization in the United States"; Anna Stansbury and Lawrence H. Summers, "The Declining Worker Power Hypothesis: An Explanation for the Recent Evolution of the American Economy" (Working Paper No. 27193, National Bureau of Economic Research, Cambridge, MA, May 2020).

21. See Daniel P. Kessler and Lawrence F. Katz, "Prevailing Wage Laws and Construction Labor Markets," *Industrial and Labor Relations Review* 54 (January 2001): 259–274. For evidence that union support for minimum-wage legislation is often transformed into pro–minimum wage votes by members of Congress, see James Cox and Ronald Oaxaca, "The Determinants of Minimum Wage Levels and Coverage in State Minimum Wage Laws," in *The Economics of Legal Minimum Wages*, ed. Simon Rottenberg (Washington, DC: American Enterprise Institute for Public Policy Research, 1981).

22. In cases in which these requirements call for the employment of workers whose functions are redundant—for example, fire stokers in diesel-operated railroad engines—*featherbedding* is said to take place. For an economic analysis of this phenomenon, see George Johnson, "Work Rules, Featherbedding and Pareto Optimal Union Management Bargaining," *Journal of Labor Economics* 8:1, pt. 2 (January 1990): S237–S259.

23. Simon Jäger, Benjamin Schoefer, and Jörg Heining, "Labor in the Boardroom" (Working Paper No. 26519, National Bureau of Economic Research, Cambridge, MA: November 2019).

24. U.S. Department of Labor, Bureau of Labor Statistics, "Table 1: Work Stoppages Involving 1,000 or More Workers, 1947–2017," www.bls.gov/news.release/wkstp.t01.htm.

25. John R. Hicks, *The Theory of Wages*, 2nd ed. (New York: St. Martin's Press, 1966): 136–157.

26. Alan B. Krueger and Alexandre Mas, "Strikes, Scabs and Tread Separations: Labor Strife and the Production of Defective Bridgestone/Firestone Tires," *Journal of Political Economy* 112 (April 2004): 253–289; Morris M. Kleiner, Jonathan S. Leonard, and Adam M. Pilarski, "How Industrial Relations Affects Plant Performance: The Case of Commercial Aircraft Manufacturing," *Industrial and Labor Relations Review* 55 (January 2002): 195–218; Alexandre Mas, "Labor Unrest and the Quality of Production: Evidence from the Construction Equipment Resale Market," *Review of Economic Studies* 75 (January 2008): 229–258; Jonathan Gruber and Samuel A. Kleiner, "Do Strikes Kill? Evidence from New York State," *American Economic Journal: Economic Policy* 4 (February 2012): 127–157.

27. For evidence on the hypothesized downward slope to the *UR* curve, see Sheena McConnell, "Strikes, Wages, and Private Information," *American Economic Review* 79 (September 1989): 801–815; David Card, "Strikes and Wages: A Test of an Asymmetric Information Model," *Quarterly Journal of Economics* 105 (August 1990): 625–659.

28. Orley Ashenfelter and George Johnson, "Bargaining Theory, Trade Unions, and Industrial Strike Activity," *American Economic Review* 59 (March 1969): 35–49; Susan B. Vroman, "A Longitudinal Analysis of Strike Activity in U.S. Manufacturing: 1957–1984," *American Economic Review* 79 (September 1989): 816–826; Peter C. Cramton and Joseph S. Tracy, "The Determinants of U.S. Labor Disputes," *Journal of Labor Economics* 12 (April 1994): 180–209; Robert Hutchens, David Lipsky, and Robert Stern, "Unemployment Insurance and Strikes," *Journal of Labor Research* 13 (Fall 1992): 337–354. For similar evidence on strikes and the business cycle in Canada and Great Britain, see Alan Harrison and Mark Stewart, "Is Strike Behavior Cyclical?" *Journal of Labor Economics* 12 (October 1994): 524–553; A.P. Dickerson, "The Cyclicality of British Strike Frequency," *Oxford Bulletin of Economics and Statistics* 56 (August 1994): 285–303.

29. Melvin W. Reder and George R. Neumann, "Conflict and Contract: The Case of Strikes," *Journal of Political Economy* 88 (October 1980): 867–886; John F. Schnell and Cynthia L. Gramm, "The Empirical Relations Between Employers' Striker Replacement Strategies and Strike Duration," *Industrial and Labor Relations Review* 47 (January 1994): 189–206; Peter Cramton, Morley Gunderson, and Joseph Tracy, "The Effect of Collective Bargaining Legislation on Strikes and Wages," *Review of Economics and Statistics* 81 (August 1999): 475–487.

30. Barry Sopher, "Bargaining and the Joint-Cost Theory of Strikes: An Experimental Study," *Journal of Labor Economics* 8:1, pt. 1 (January 1990): 48–74.

31. Joseph Tracy, "An Empirical Test of an Asymmetric Information Model of Strikes," *Journal of Labor Economics* 5 (April 1987): 149–173; Joseph Tracy, "An Investigation into the Determinants of U.S. Strike

Activity," *American Economic Review* 76 (June 1986): 423–436. For other evidence supporting the asymmetric information model, see Peter Kuhn and Wulong Gu, "Learning in Sequential Wage Negotiations: Theory and Evidence," *Journal of Labor Economics* 17 (January 1999): 109–140.

32. For a discussion of incentives for executives of labor unions, see Kevin F. Hallock and Felice B. Klein, "Executive Compensation in American Unions," *Industrial Relations* 55 (April 2016): 219–234. They find that the compensation of union leaders is positively related to the number of, and compensation of, members in their unions, even after controlling for union size and union fixed effects.

33. The model described here was put forth by Ashenfelter and Johnson, "Bargaining Theory, Trade Unions, and Industrial Strike Activity."

34. Ashenfelter and Johnson, "Bargaining Theory, Trade Unions, and Industrial Strike Activity."

35. Vincent Crawford, "Arbitration and Conflict Resolution in Labor–Management Bargaining," *American Economic Review* 71 (May 1981): 205–210.

36. For experimental evidence in support of this view of arbitrator behavior, see Henry S. Farber and Max H. Bazerman, "The General Basis of Arbitrator Behavior: An Empirical Analysis of Conventional and Final-Offer Arbitration," *Econometrica* 54 (July 1986): 819–844.

37. Henry S. Farber, "Splitting-the-Difference in Interest Arbitration," *Industrial and Labor Relations Review* 35 (October 1981): 70–77.

38. Orley Ashenfelter and David Bloom, "Models of Arbitrator Behavior: Theory and Evidence," *American Economic Review* 74 (March 1984): 111–124.

39. Orley Ashenfelter and Dean Hyslop, "Measuring the Effect of Arbitration on Wage Levels: The Case of Police Officers," *Industrial and Labor Relations Review* 54 (January 2001): 316–328.

40. One study found that if only one side of a dispute hires a lawyer to present its case to the arbitrator, the side hiring the lawyer obtains a better outcome; however, if *both* sides hire lawyers, neither side benefits—despite the added costs to each of hiring lawyers; see Orley Ashenfelter and Gordon B. Dahl, "Bargaining and the Role of Expert Agents: An Empirical Study of Final-Offer Arbitration," *Review of Economics and Statistics* 94 (February 2012): 116–132. Also see J. Ryan Lamare, "The Devil Is in the Details: Attorney Effects on Employment Arbitration Outcomes," *Industrial and Labor Relations Review* 73:2 (March 2020): 456–478.

41. Much of the discussion in this section is based on the pioneering work of H.G. Lewis, *Unionism and Relative Wages in the United States* (Chicago, IL: University of Chicago Press, 1963). In Figure 13.8, our

analysis employs a two-sector model with labor supply curves to each sector. Remember that a labor supply curve to one sector is drawn holding the wages in other sectors ("alternative wages") constant; whenever the wage in one sector changes, the labor supply curve to the other sector may shift. We *sometimes* ignore this complexity to keep our exposition as simple as possible and to highlight the various behaviors that might occur in either sector in response to unionization.

42. For a theoretical and empirical treatment of threat effects, see Henry S. Farber, "Nonunion Wage Rates and the Threat of Unionization," *Industrial and Labor Relations Review* 58 (April 2005): 335–352. For an empirical example investigating union threat effects and the provision of health insurance, see Craig A. Olson, "Union Threat Effects and the Decline in Employer-Provided Health Insurance," *Industrial and Labor Relations Review* 72:2 (March 2019): 417–445.

43. See Jacob Mincer, "Unemployment Effects of Minimum Wages," *Journal of Political Economy* 84:4, pt. 2 (August 1976): S87–S104. Although Mincer discusses minimum-wage effects, union-imposed wages can be analyzed analogously.

44. Our discussion of these four responses has assumed a partial equilibrium model. Once one has considered a general equilibrium framework and allows capital to move between sectors, one might find even more possibilities. On this point, see Harry Johnson and Peter Mieszkowski, "The Effects of Unionization on the Distribution of Income: A General Equilibrium Approach," *Quarterly Journal of Economics* 84 (November 1969): 539–561.

45. For surveys of these estimates, see Henry S. Farber, Daniel Herbst, Ilyana Kuziemko, and Suresh Naidu, "Unions and Inequality over the Twentieth Century: New Evidence from Survey Data" (Working Paper No. 24587, National Bureau of Economic Research, Cambridge, MA, May 2018); David G. Blanchflower and Alex Bryson, "What Effect Do Unions Have on Wages Now and Would Freeman and Medoff Be Surprised?" *Journal of Labor Research* 25 (Summer 2004): 383–414; Richard Freeman and James Medoff, *What Do Unions Do?* (New York: Basic Books, 1984); H. Gregg Lewis, *Union Relative Wage Effects: A Survey* (Chicago, IL: University of Chicago Press, 1986); Barry T. Hirsch and John T. Addison, *The Economic Analysis of Unions: New Approaches and Evidence* (Boston, MA: Allen and Unwin, 1986); John Pencavel, *Labor Markets Under Trade Unionism* (Cambridge, MA: Basil Blackwell, 1991). For articles that contain citations to earlier studies, see Steven Raphael, "Estimating the Union Earnings Effect Using a Sample of Displaced Workers," *Industrial and Labor Relations Review* 53 (April 2000): 503–521; Barry T. Hirsch, "Reconsidering Union Wage Effects: Surveying New Evidence on an Old Topic," *Journal of Labor Research* 25 (Spring 2004): 233–266; Ozkan Eren, "Does Membership Pay Off for Covered Workers? A Distributional Analysis

of the Free Rider Problem," *Industrial and Labor Relations Review* 62 (April 2009): 367–380.

46. For a study that differs in methodology from earlier research and finds that the wages of newly unionized workers are not increased, see John DiNardo and David S. Lee, "Impacts of New Unionization on Private Sector Employees: 1984–2001," *Quarterly Journal of Economics* 116 (November 2004): 1383–1441.

47. Barry T. Hirsch and David A. Macpherson, *Union Membership and Earnings Data Book: Compilations from the Current Population Survey* (Washington, DC: Bureau of National Affairs, 2013): Table 2a. Also see a recent paper by David Card, Thomas Lemieux, and W. Craig Riddell, "Unions and Wage Inequality: The Roles of Gender, Skill and Public Sector Employment," *Canadian Journal of Economics/Revue canadienne d'économique* 53 (February 2020): 140–173.

48. David Blanchflower and Alex Bryson, "Changes Over Time in Union Relative Wage Effects in the U.K. and the U.S. Revisited" (Working Paper No. 9395, National Bureau of Economic Research, Cambridge, MA, December 2002). A comparison of union wage effects for the United States and Canada that disaggregates effects by the public and private sectors can be found in Card, Lemieux, and Riddell, "Unions and Wage Inequality: The Roles of Gender, Skill and Public Sector Employment."

49. Richard B. Freeman, "Labor Market Institutions Around the World" (Working Paper No. 13242, National Bureau of Economic Research, Cambridge, MA, 2007); Lawrence M. Kahn, "Wage Inequality, Collective Bargaining and Relative Employment 1985–94: Evidence from 15 OECD Countries," *Review of Economics and Statistics* 82 (November 2000): 564–579; Card, Lemieux, and Riddell, "Unions and Wage Inequality: The Roles of Gender, Skill and Public Sector Employment."

50. James Peoples Jr., "Monopolistic Market Structure, Unionization, and Racial Wage Differentials," *Review of Economics and Statistics* 76 (February 1994): 207–211; Freeman and Medoff, *What Do Unions Do?* chapter 5.

51. Darren Grant, "A Comparison of the Cyclical Behavior of Union and Nonunion Wages in the United States," *Journal of Human Resources* 36 (Winter 2001): 31–57; Blanchflower and Bryson, "What Effect Do Unions Have on Wages Now and Would Freeman and Medoff Be Surprised?"

52. See David Neumark and Michael L. Wachter, "Union Effects on Nonunion Wages: Evidence from Panel Data on Industries and Cities," *Industrial and Labor Relations Review* 49 (October 1995): 20–38.

53. Barry T. Hirsch, David A. Macpherson, and J. Michael Dumond, "Workers' Compensation Recipiency in Union and Nonunion Workplaces," *Industrial and Labor Relations Review* 50 (January 1997):

213–236; John W. Budd and Brian P. McCall, "The Effects of Unions on the Receipt of Unemployment Insurance Benefits," *Industrial and Labor Relations Review* 51 (April 1997): 478–492; Thomas C. Buchmuller, John DiNardo, and Robert G. Valletta, "Union Effects on Health Insurance Provision and Coverage in the United States," *Industrial and Labor Relations Review* 55 (July 2002): 610–627; John W. Budd, "Non-Wage Forms of Compensation," *Journal of Labor Research* 25 (Fall 2004): 587–622.

54. Greg Duncan and Frank Stafford, "Do Union Members Receive Compensating Wage Differentials?" *American Economic Review* 70 (June 1980): 355–371; Keith A. Bender and Peter J. Sloane, "Job Satisfaction, Trade Unions, and Exit-Voice Revisited," *Industrial and Labor Relations Review* 51 (January 1998): 222–240; John S. Heywood, W.S. Siebert, and Xiangdong Wei, "Worker Sorting and Job Satisfaction: The Case of Union and Government Jobs," *Industrial and Labor Relations Review* 55 (July 2002): 595–609. For a more recent example investigating job satisfaction by union members, see Ioulia Bessa, Andy Charlwood, and Danat Valizade, "Do Unions Cause Job Dissatisfaction? Evidence from a Quasi-Experiment in the United Kingdom," *British Journal of Industrial Relations* (May 2020): 1–29.

55. Duncan and Stafford, "Do Union Members Receive Compensating Wage Differentials?"

56. Jonathan S. Leonard, "Unions and Employment Growth," *Industrial Relations* 31 (Winter 1992): 80–94.

57. Timothy Dunne and David A. Macpherson, "Unionism and Gross Employment Flows," *Southern Economic Journal* 60 (January 1994): 727–738; Stephen G. Bronars, Donald R. Deere, and Joseph Tracy, "The Effects of Unions on Firm Behavior: An Empirical Analysis Using Firm-Level Data," *Industrial Relations* 33 (October 1994): 426–451; Robert G. Valletta, "Union Effects on Municipal Employment and Wages: A Longitudinal Approach," *Journal of Labor Economics* 11 (July 1993): 545–574; Richard J. Long, "The Impact of Unionization on Employment Growth of Canadian Companies," *Industrial and Labor Relations Review* 46 (July 1993): 691–703; David G. Blanchflower, Neil Millward, and Andrew J. Oswald, "Unions and Employment Behaviour," *Economic Journal* 101 (July 1991): 815–834; Giuseppe Bertola, Francine D. Blau, and Lawrence M. Kahn, "Labor Market Institutions and Demographic Employment Patterns," *Journal of Population Economics* 20 (October 2007): 833–867; Michelle Brown and John S. Heywood, "Investigating the Cause of Death: Industrial Relations and Plant Closures in Australia," *Industrial and Labor Relations Review* 59 (July 2006): 593–612. For a study showing that centralized bargaining, which does not take account of local economic conditions, creates more job loss than does decentralized bargaining, see Tito Boeri, Andrea Ichino, Enrico Moretti, and Johanna Posch, "Wage Equalization and

Regional Misallocation: Evidence from Italian and German Provinces" (Working Paper No. 25612, National Bureau of Economic Research, Cambridge, MA, January 2020).

58. William M. Boal and John Pencavel, "The Effects of Labor Unions on Employment, Wages, and Days of Operation: Coal Mining in West Virginia," *Quarterly Journal of Economics* 109 (February 1994): 267–298.

59. For a more complete statement of this argument, see Freeman and Medoff, *What Do Unions Do?* Note that unions can raise worker productivity in another, more mechanical way. We have seen that unions raise wages, and theory suggests that the response by profit-maximizing employers will be to reduce employment and substitute capital for labor. Thus, as firms move up and to the left along their marginal product of labor curves, the marginal product of labor rises in response to the wage increase.

60. Sandra Black and Lisa Lynch, "How to Compete: The Impact of Workplace Practices and Information Technology on Productivity," *Review of Economics and Statistics* 83 (August 2001): 434–445. Also see David G. Blanchflower and Richard B. Freeman, "Unionism in the U.S. and Other OECD Countries," *Industrial Relations* 31 (Winter 1992): 56–79.

61. Michael Ash and Jean Ann Seago, "The Effect of Registered Nurses' Unions on Heart-Attack Mortality," *Industrial and Labor Relations Review* 57 (April 2004): 422–442; Michael F. Lovenheim and Alexander Willén, "The Long-Run Effects of Teacher Collective Bargaining," *American Economic Journal: Economic Policy* 11 (August 2019): 292–324.

62. Bronars, Deere, and Tracy, "The Effects of Unions on Firm Behavior"; Blanchflower and Freeman, "Unionism in the U.S. and Other OECD Countries"; Barry T. Hirsch, "Unionization and Economic Performance: Evidence on Productivity, Profits, Investment, and Growth," in *Unions and Right-to-Work Laws*, ed. Fazil Mihlar (Vancouver: Fraser Institute, 1997): 35–70; Richard B. Freeman and Morris M. Kleiner, "Do Unions Make Enterprises Insolvent?" *Industrial and Labor Relations Review* 52 (July 1999): 510–527; Elisabetta Magnani and David Prentice, "Did Lower Unionization in the United States Result in More Flexible Industries?" *Industrial and Labor Relations Review* 63 (July 2010): 662–680.

63. David S. Lee and Alexandre Mas, "Long-Run Impacts of Unions on Firms: New Evidence from Financial Markets: 1961–1999," *Quarterly Journal of Economics* 127 (February 2012): 333–378.

64. One study, for example, considers the positive societal effects of strikes and the negative societal effects of strikes and investigates the effects of strikes on issues such as accidents, traffic, and health: Stefan Bauernschuster, Timo Hener, and Helmut Rainer, "When Labor Disputes

Bring Cities to a Standstill: The Impact of Public Transit Strikes on Traffic, Accidents, Air Pollution, and Health," *American Economic Journal: Economic Policy* 9 (February 2017): 1–37.

65. Assar Lindbeck and Dennis J. Snower, "Insiders Versus Outsiders," *Journal of Economic Perspectives* 15 (Winter 2001): 165–188.

66. Freeman and Medoff, *What Do Unions Do?*, 57.

67. Refer back to our discussion of the efficient-contracts model for an argument on how unions could raise wages without social harm in the context of product-market monopoly; refer back to our discussion in Chapter 5 of how a wage-setting mechanism (like minimum-wage laws and, by extension, union contracts) affect employment in the context of monopsonistic conditions in the labor market. For a paper on the topic of how unions affect rent sharing between employers and workers, see Stansbury and Summers, "The Declining Worker Power Hypothesis: An Explanation for the Recent Evolution of the American Economy."

68. For a fuller development of this argument, see Freeman and Medoff, *What Do Unions Do?*; Barry T. Hirsch, "What Do Unions Do for Economic Performance?" *Journal of Labor Research* 25 (Summer 2004): 415–455; Addison and Belfield, "Union Voice."

Selected Readings

Atherton, Wallace. *Theory of Union Bargaining Goals*. Princeton, NJ: Princeton University Press, 1973.

Bennett, James, and Bruce E. Kaufman, eds. *What Do Unions Do?: A Twenty-Year Perspective*. New Brunswick, NJ: Transaction, 2007.

Freeman, Richard B., and James L. Medoff. *What Do Unions Do?* New York: Basic Books, 1984.

Hirsch, Barry T., and John T. Addison. *The Economic Analysis of Unions: New Approaches and Evidence*. Boston, MA: Allen and Unwin, 1986.

Kerr, Clark, and Paul D. Staudohar, eds. *Labor Economics and Industrial Relations: Markets and Institutions*. Cambridge, MA: Harvard University Press, 1994.

Krueger, Alan B., and Alexandre Mas. "Strikes, Scabs and Tread Separations: Labor Strife and the Production of Defective Bridgestone/Firestone Tires." *Journal of Political Economy* 112 (April 2004): 253–289.

Lewis, H. Gregg. *Union Relative Wage Effects: A Survey*. Chicago, IL: University of Chicago Press, 1986.

Pencavel, John. *Labor Markets Under Trade Unionism*. Cambridge, MA: Basil Blackwell, 1991.

Stansbury, Anna, and Lawrence H. Summers. "The Declining Worker Power Hypothesis: An Explanation for the Recent Evolution of the American Economy." Working Paper No. 27193, National Bureau of Economic Research, Cambridge, MA, May 2020.

APPENDIX 13A

Arbitration and the Bargaining Contract Zone

What incentive do the parties to collective bargaining negotiations have to settle their negotiations on their own rather than go to arbitration and have an outside party impose a settlement? The answer may well be that the uncertainty about an arbitrator's likely decision imposes costs on both parties that give them an incentive to come to an agreement on their own. This appendix provides a simple model that illustrates this proposition; it highlights the roles of both *uncertainty* about an arbitrator's likely decision and the parties' *attitudes toward risk* in determining whether a negotiation will wind up in arbitration.[1]

Consider a simple two-party bargaining problem in which the parties, A and B, are negotiating over how to split a "pie" of fixed size. Each party's utility function depends only on the share of the pie that it receives. Figure 13A.1 plots the utility function for party A. When A's share of the pie is zero, A's utility (U_A) is assumed to be zero, and as A's share (S_A) increases, A's utility increases. Crucially, this utility function is also assumed to exhibit the property of *diminishing marginal utility*; equal increments in S_A lead to progressively smaller increments in U_A. As we shall show later, this is equivalent to assuming that the party is *risk averse*, which means that the party would prefer the certainty of having a given share of the pie to an uncertain outcome that, on average, would yield the same share.[2]

Now, suppose that party A believes that, on average, the arbitrator would award it one-half of the pie if the negotiations went to arbitration. If it knew with certainty that the arbitrator would do this, party A's utility from going to arbitration would be $U_A(1/2)$, at point a in Figure 13A.1. Suppose, however, that party A is uncertain about the arbitrator's decision and instead

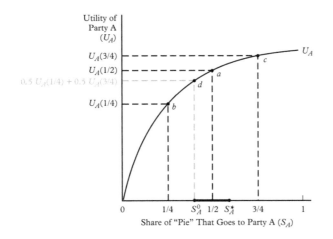

Figure 13A.1 Utility Function for a Risk-Averse Party: Uncertainty About Arbitrator's Decision Leads to a Contract Zone

believes that the arbitrator will assign it one-quarter of the pie with probability one-half, or three-quarters of the pie also with probability one-half. Utility in these two states is given by $U_A(1/4)$, point b, and $U_A(3/4)$, point c, respectively. Although, on average, party A expects to be awarded one-half of the pie, its average or *expected* utility in this case is $0.5\ U_A(1/4) + 0.5\ U_A(3/4)$, which, as Figure 13A.1 indicates (see point d), is less than $U_A(1/2)$ at point a. This reflects the fact that party A is risk averse, preferring a certain outcome (point a) to an uncertain outcome (point d) that yields the same expected share.

Note that if party A were awarded the share S_A^0 with certainty, it would receive the same utility level that it receives under the uncertain situation, where it expects, with equal probability, the arbitrator to award it either one-quarter or three-quarters of the pie. Indeed, it would prefer any *certain* share above S_A^0 to bearing the cost of the uncertainty associated with having to face the arbitrator's decision. The set of contracts it potentially would voluntarily agree to, then, is the set S_A, such that

$$S_A^0 \le S_A \le 1;\ S_A^0 < 1/2 \tag{13A.1}$$

Suppose that party B is similarly risk averse and has identical expectations about what the arbitrator's decision will look like. According to the same logic as that used earlier, the set of contracts, SB, that party B would potentially voluntarily agree to is given by a similar expression:

$$S_B^0 \le S_B \le 1;\ S_B^0 < 1/2 \tag{13A.2}$$

Now, any share that party B voluntarily agrees to receive implies that what B is willing to give party A is 1 minus that share. Because the *minimum* share B would agree to receive, S_B^0, is less than one-half, the *maximum* share that B would voluntarily agree to give A in negotiations, S_A^* (which equals $1-S_B^0$), is therefore greater than one-half. Party B would potentially be willing to voluntarily agree to any settlement that gives party A a share of less than S_A^*.

According to the data in Figure 13A.1, party A would be willing to voluntarily agree to contracts that offer it at least S_A^0, whereas party B would be willing to agree to contracts that give party A S_A^* or less. Hence, the set of contracts that *both* parties would find preferable to going to arbitration (and thus *potentially* would voluntarily agree to) is given by all the shares for A (S_A) that lie between these two extremes:

$$S_A^0 \le S_A \le S_A^* \tag{13A.3}$$

This set of potential voluntary solutions to the bargaining problem is indicated by the bold-line segment on the horizontal axis of Figure 13A.1 and is called the *contract zone*. As long as both parties are risk averse and are uncertain what the arbitrator will do, a contract zone will exist.

The extent of the parties' *uncertainty* about the arbitrator's decision and the extent of their *risk aversion* are important determinants of the size of the contract zone. To see this, first suppose that party A continues to expect that, on average, the arbitrator will assign it one-half of the pie but now believes that this will occur by receiving shares of one-eighth and seven-eighths with

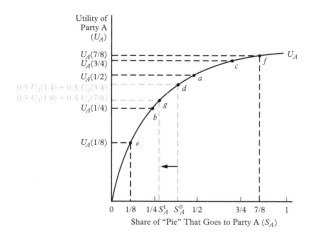

Figure 13A.2 Increased Uncertainty About Arbitrator's Decision Increases the Size of the Contract Zone

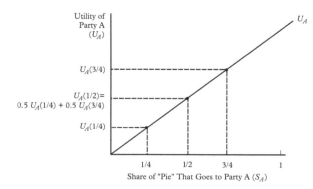

Figure 13A.3 Utility Function for a Risk-Neutral Party: Contract Zone Is Reduced to a Single Point

equal probability. Figure 13A.2 indicates its utility in each of these states (points e and f) and shows that although its expected share is still one-half, the greater uncertainty—or "spread" of possible outcomes—has led to a reduction in its expected utility (compare points d and g). Indeed, party A would now be as happy to receive the share S_A^1 with certainty as it would to face the risks associated with going to arbitration. Since S_A^1 is less than S_A^0, the size of the contract zone has increased. Hence, increased uncertainty about the arbitrator's decision leads to a larger contract zone.

Next, consider Figure 13A.3, where we have drawn a utility function for a *risk-neutral* party. A risk-neutral party has a linear utility function because its utility depends only on its expected share, not on the uncertainty associated with the outcome. So, for example, in Figure 13A.3, party A gets the same utility from having a share of one-half with certainty as it does from facing an arbitrated outcome in which it has an equal probability that the arbitrator will award it either a share of one-quarter or a share of three-quarters. As a result, faced with the possibility of going to arbitration, no share less than one-half would induce party A to voluntarily agree to settle before arbitration. If party B had similar expectations about the arbitrator's behavior and was similarly risk neutral, it would also refuse to settle for any share of less than one-half, which on average is what it expects to win from the arbitrator. Hence, the contract zone would reduce to one point—the point where both parties receive a share of one-half. The only voluntary agreement that the parties will reach is what they expect to receive on average if they go to arbitration. (This illustrates how the arbitration process itself might influence the nature of negotiated settlements.)

More generally, one can show that as a party's risk aversion increases (the utility function becomes more curved), the size of the contract zone will increase. Hence, increases in either the parties' risk aversion or their uncertainty about the arbitrator's decision will increase the size of the contract zone.

Larger contract zones mean that *both* parties have more potential settlements that they consider preferable to an arbitrated settlement, and some people have argued that this increased menu of choices increases the probability that the parties would settle on their own before going to arbitration.[3] An immediate implication of this argument is that if one believes that settling independently of arbitration is preferable for the parties, then the arbitration system should be structured so that the arbitrator's behavior does *not* become completely predictable. As we discussed in the text, however, others argue that a *smaller* contract zone implies the parties have less to argue about and that, therefore, *smaller* zones lead to more-rapid voluntary settlements.

Notes

1. The discussion here is a simplified version of some of the material found in Henry S. Farber and Harry C. Katz, "Interest Arbitration, Outcomes, and the Incentive to Bargain," *Industrial and Labor Relations Review* 33 (October 1979): 55–63.

2. Refer to Appendix 8A, especially footnote 4, for an introduction to this use of cardinal utility functions.

3. Farber and Katz, "Interest Arbitration, Outcomes, and the Incentive to Bargain."

CHAPTER 14 Unemployment

With the dramatic rise in unemployment in the Great Recession of 2007–2009 and then with the spike during the COVID-19 crisis has come a renewed interest in understanding both the measurement and—more importantly—the causes of unemployment. As noted in Chapter 2, the population can be divided into those people who are in the labor force (L) and those who are not (N). The labor force consists of people who are employed (E) and those who are unemployed but would like to be employed (U). The concept of unemployment is somewhat ambiguous because, in theory, almost anyone would be willing to be employed in return for a generous-enough compensation package. Economists tend to resolve this dilemma by defining unemployment in terms of an individual's willingness to be employed at some prevailing market wage. Government statistics take a more pragmatic approach, defining unemployed people as those who are on temporary layoff waiting to be recalled by their previous employer, or those without a job who have actively searched for work in the previous month (of course, "actively" is not precisely defined[1]).

Given these definitions, the unemployment rate (u) is measured as the ratio of the number of unemployed people to the number people in the labor force:

$$u = \frac{U}{L} \tag{14.1}$$

Much attention focuses on how the national unemployment rate varies over time and how unemployment rates vary across geographic areas and age/race/gender/ethnic groups.

However, unemployment rate data have limitations. They *do* reflect the proportion of a group that, at a point in time, actively want to work but are not employed. For a number of reasons, however, they *do not* necessarily provide an accurate reflection of the economic hardship that members of a group experience. First, individuals who are not actively searching for work, including those who searched unsuccessfully and then gave up, are not counted among unemployed people (see Chapter 7).[2] Second, unemployment statistics tell us nothing about the earnings levels of those who are employed, including whether these exceed the poverty level or whether a person who wants full-time work is instead working only part time. Third, in most years, a substantial fraction of unemployed people come from families in which other earners are present—for example, many unemployed people are teenagers—and their income is often not the primary source of their family's support. Fourth, a substantial fraction of unemployed people receive some income support (with dollar-level limits that vary by region and for durations that can also vary) while they are unemployed, in the form of either government unemployment compensation payments or private supplementary unemployment benefits.

Finally, although unemployment rate data give us information on the fraction of the *labor force* that is not working, they tell us little about the fraction of the *population* that is *employed*. Table 14.1 contains U.S. data on the aggregate unemployment rate, the labor force participation rate, and the *employment rate*—where the last is defined as employment divided by the adult population—for 2000 and 2013, as well as for two pairs of earlier years over which roughly equal changes in the unemployment rate were experienced. From 1948 to 1958, for example, the unemployment rate rose by 3 percent, from 3.8 percent to 6.8 percent, and the employment rate fell from 56.6 percent to 55.4 percent. In contrast, from 1968 to 1991, the unemployment rate rose by a similar magnitude, but the employment rate *rose* substantially. The reason for the opposite correlations between the unemployment rate and the employment rate for these two periods is that in the earlier period, labor force participation grew only slowly, whereas in the latter period, it was growing rapidly. In contrast, the increase in the unemployment rate from 2000 to 2013 was accompanied by relatively large declines in *both* the employment rate and the labor force participation rate; indeed, unemployment associated with the Great Recession seemingly caused many workers to drop out of the labor force permanently.[3]

Table 14.1 Civilian Labor Force Participation, Employment, and Unemployment Rates in the United States (in Percentages)

Year	Unemployment rate (*U/L*)	Labor force participation rate (*L/POP*)	Employment rate (*E/POP*)
1948	3.8	58.8	56.6
1958	6.8	59.5	55.4
1968	3.6	59.6	57.5
1991	6.8	66.2	61.7
2000	4.0	67.1	64.4
2013	7.4	63.2	58.6

Source: U.S. Department of Labor, *2018 Employment and Earnings Online*, Household Survey Data, Table 1, at www.bls.gov/opub/ee/2018/cps/annual. htm#empstat

Nonetheless, the unemployment rate remains a useful indicator of labor market conditions. This chapter is concerned with the causes of unemployment and with how various government policies affect, in an either intended or unintended manner, the level of unemployment.

A Stock-Flow Model of the Labor Market

We begin with a simple conceptual model of a labor market that emphasizes the importance of considering the *flows* between labor market states (e.g., the *movement* of people from employed to unemployed status) as well as the *number* of people in each labor market state (e.g., the *number* of unemployed people). Knowledge of the determinants of these flows is crucial to any understanding of the causes of unemployment.

Data on the number of Americans who are employed, unemployed, and not in the labor force are provided each month from the United States' national Current Population Survey (CPS). As Figure 14.1 indicates, in May 2019, 157.1 million people were employed, 6.0 million were unemployed, and 95.9 million over the age of 16 were not in the labor force. The impression we get when tracing these data over short periods of time is that of relative stability; for example, the unemployment rate rarely changes by more than a few tenths of a percent from one month to the next (it was 3.6 percent in May and 3.7 percent in June 2019).[4]

Taking month-to-month snapshots of the number of people who are employed, unemployed, or out of the labor market misses a considerable amount of movement into and out of these categories *during* the

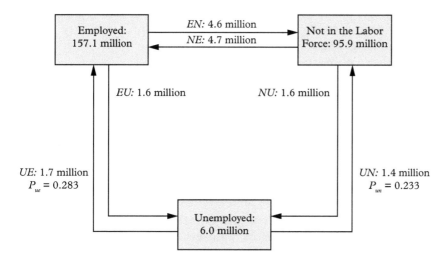

Figure 14.1 Labor Market Stocks and Flows: May to June 2019

Source: U.S. Bureau of Labor Statistics, "Labor Force Statistics from the Current Population Survey: Labor Force Status Flows by Sex," at www.bls.gov/web/empsit/cps_flows_recent.htm

month. Figure 14.1 contains data on the flows of workers among the various categories during the month of May 2019. During this month, approximately 1.7 million unemployed people found employment (the flow denoted by *UE* in Figure 14.1) and 1.4 million unemployed people dropped out of the labor force (the flow denoted by *UN*). These numbers represent the proportions 0.283 (P_{ue}) and 0.233 (P_{un}) of the stock of unemployed people, respectively; thus, we can conclude that about half of the individuals who were unemployed at the beginning of May left unemployment by month's end. These individuals were replaced in the pool of unemployed by flows of individuals into unemployment from the stocks of employed individuals (1.6 million, the flow *EU*) and those not in the labor force (1.6 million, the flow *NU*).[5] The flow *EU* consists of individuals who voluntarily left or involuntarily lost their last job, and the flow *NU* consists of people entering the labor force and searching for work. The fact that the flows into unemployment (3.2 million) were comparable to the flows out of unemployment (3.1 million) means that during this period, unemployment was essentially constant (as we saw earlier).

Duration of Unemployment

As we have seen, people leave unemployment in one of two ways: obtaining a job or exiting the labor force. How long it takes for those who are unemployed to leave the pool of unemployed depends in large part on the availability of jobs. In 2006, for example, when many employers were hiring, unemployed people who found work typically did so within five weeks; in 2010, during the Great Recession, it took twice as long. Those unemployed who decided to leave the labor force typically did so after about 20 weeks of unemployment in 2010, but after only eight weeks in 2006—suggesting that most of those who left the labor force in 2010 were "discouraged" by their lengthy and unsuccessful job search (see Chapter 7) and suggesting that those leaving the labor force in 2006 may have been less committed to finding work, because of family obligations, health issues, or retirement.[6]

Paths to Unemployment

When we think of unemployed people, the image of an individual laid off from their previous job often springs to mind. However, the view that such individuals constitute all unemployed people is incorrect. Table 14.2 provides some data that address this point for years between 1970 and 2019, during which the unemployment rate varied considerably. In the typical year, roughly half of unemployed people were job losers—although the fraction of job losers was highest in the years of high unemployment (reaching 62.4 percent in 2010).

Table 14.2 Paths to Unemployment, United States, Various Years

Year	Unemployment rate	Job losers	Percent of unemployed:		
			Job leavers	**Re-entrants**	**New entrants**
1970	4.9	44.3	13.4	30.0	12.3
1974	5.6	43.5	14.9	28.4	13.2
1978	6.1	41.6	14.1	30.0	14.3
1982	9.7	58.7	7.9	22.3	11.1
1986	6.9	48.9	12.3	26.2	12.5
1990	5.5	48.3	14.8	27.4	9.5
1994	6.1	47.7	9.4	34.8	7.6
1998	4.5	45.5	11.8	34.3	8.4
2002	5.8	55.0	10.3	28.3	6.4
2006	4.6	47.4	11.8	32.0	8.8
2010	9.6	62.4	6.0	23.4	8.2
2014	6.2	50.7	8.6	29.4	11.3
2019	3.7	45.6	14.8	30.1	8.9

Sources: U.S. Department of Labor, *Employment and Training Report of the President* (Washington, DC: U.S. Government Printing Office, 1982), Table A-36; U.S. Department of Labor, "Monthly Labor Review, Various Issues," at www.bls.gov/news.release/empsit.t11.htm

   In each year, more than one-third of unemployed people came from out-of-labor-force status—that is, they were individuals who were either entering the labor force for the first time (*new entrants*) or individuals who had some previous employment experience and were re-entering the labor force after a period of time out of the labor force (*re-entrants*). Some of these re-entrants, of course, were job losers who dropped out of the labor force for a time. Finally, although the vast majority of individuals who quit their jobs obtain new jobs before quitting and never pass through unemployment status, in most years, 10 percent to 15 percent of unemployed people were voluntary job leavers.

Rates of Flow Affect Unemployment Levels

Although ultimately public concern focuses on the *level* of unemployment, to understand the determinants of this level, we must analyze the *flows* of individuals between the various labor market states. A group's unemployment rate might be high because its members have difficulty finding jobs once unemployed, because they have difficulty (for voluntary or involuntary reasons) remaining employed once they have found a job or because they frequently enter and leave the labor force. The appropriate policy prescription to reduce the unemployment rate will depend on which one of these labor market flows is responsible for the high rate.

Somewhat more formally, we can show that if labor markets are roughly in balance, with the flows into and out of unemployment equal, the unemployment rate (u) for a group depends on the various labor market flows in the following manner:

$$u = f(P_{en}^{+}, P_{ne}^{-}, P_{un}^{-}, P_{nu}^{+}, P_{en,}^{+} P_{ue}^{-}) \qquad (14.2)$$

where

f = "a function of"

P_{en} = the fraction of employed who leave the labor force

P_{ne} = the fraction of those not in the labor force who enter the labor force and find employment

P_{un} = the fraction of unemployed who leave the labor force

P_{nu} = the fraction of those not in the labor force who enter the labor force and become unemployed

P_{eu} = the fraction of employed who become unemployed

P_{ue} = the fraction of unemployed who become employed

So, for example, if there were initially 100 employed individuals in a group and 15 of them became unemployed during a period, P_{eu} would equal 0.15.

A plus sign over a variable in equation (14.2) means that an increase in that variable will increase the unemployment rate, and a minus sign means that an increase in the variable will decrease the unemployment rate. The equation thus asserts that, other things being equal, increases in the proportions of individuals who voluntarily or involuntarily leave their jobs and become unemployed (P_{eu}) or leave the labor force (P_{en}) will increase a group's unemployment rate, as will an increase in the proportion of the group that enters the labor force without first having a job lined up (P_{nu}). Similarly, the greater the proportion of individuals who leave unemployment status, either to become employed (P_{ue}) or to leave the labor force (P_{un}), the lower a group's unemployment rate. Finally, the greater the proportion of individuals who enter the labor force and immediately find jobs (P_{ne}), the lower a group's unemployment rate.[7]

Equation (14.2) and Figure 14.1 make clear that social concern over any given level of unemployment should focus on both the *incidence* of unemployment (or the fraction of people in a group who become unemployed) and the *duration* of spells of unemployment. Society is probably more concerned if small groups of individuals are unemployed for long periods of time than if many individuals rapidly pass through unemployment status.[8]

Table 14.3 documents some remarkable differences in both the incidence and duration of unemployment across years and across selected European countries and North American countries. The more notable examples are as follows:

a. Generally speaking, the unemployment rate and long-term unemployment in the United States moved in opposite directions from 2005 to 2019.

b. Canada had a higher unemployment rate than Germany in 2019, but unemployed people in Canada typically found jobs much more quickly (only 8.5 percent of Canadian unemployed people had been out of work for over a year, compared to 38.1 percent in Germany).

c. The United Kingdom and the United States had similar levels of unemployment in both 2005 and 2019, but in the United Kingdom, a much higher percentage of unemployed people were out of work for more than a year.

d. Finally, Norway had a small drop in unemployment from 2005 to 2019 but experienced a large increase in the percentage of its unemployed workers who were out of work longer than a year.

Clearly, then, important differences extend across countries in labor market conditions, institutions, or policies that underlie these unemployment outcomes. Although this textbook cannot offer detailed analyses of all the differences across countries shown in Table 14.3, the various theories of unemployment discussed in the following sections all essentially relate to the determination of one or more of the flows represented in equation (14.2). That is, the theories can help provide explanations of why the proportions of individuals who move between the various labor market states vary over time or across geographic areas, including countries. As we will explain, the types of unemployment that we examine can be classified as frictional, structural, demand deficient (cyclical), and seasonal.

Table 14.3 Unemployment and Long-Term Unemployment, Selected European and North American Countries, 2005 and 2019

	Unemployment overall rate (%)		Percent of unemployed out of work > one year	
	2005	**2019**	**2005**	**2019**
Belgium	8.4	5.4	51.6	43.5
Canada	6.8	5.6	9.6	8.5
Denmark	4.8	4.7	25.9	16.6
France	9.5	8.5	42.5	38.8
Germany	9.5	3.1	54.0	38.1
Ireland	4.3	5.1	34.3	33.3
Netherlands	4.8	3.4	40.1	31.4
Norway	4.6	3.6	9.4	24.1
United Kingdom	4.7	3.8	22.4	25.0
United States	5.1	3.7	11.8	12.7

Sources: OECD, *Employment Outlook* (Paris: OECD, 2006), Tables A and G; OECD Data, Unemployment Rate at https://data.oecd.org/unemp/unemployment-rate.htm; and Long-Term Unemployment Rate at https://data.oecd.org/unemp/long-term-unemployment-rate.htm

Frictional Unemployment

Suppose that a competitive labor market is in equilibrium, in the sense that at the prevailing market wage, the quantity of labor demanded just equals the quantity of labor supplied. Figure 14.2 shows such a labor market, in which the demand curve is D_0, the supply curve is S_0, employment is E_0, and the wage rate is W_0. Thus far, the text has treated this equilibrium situation as one of full employment and has implied that no unemployment is associated with it. However, this implication is not completely correct. Even a market-equilibrium or full-employment situation will still have some *frictional unemployment*, because some people will be between jobs—and this number could be large. For example, during just the month of June 2019, the overall unemployment rate in the United States was essentially unchanged, but 3.6 percent of all U.S. workers separated from their employers.[9]

As discussed in Chapter 5, the labor market is characterized by frictions: Information flows are imperfect, and it takes time and effort for unemployed workers and employers with job vacancies to find each other. Even if the size of the labor force is constant, each period will have new entrants to the labor market searching for employment as other employed or unemployed individuals are leaving the labor force. Some people will quit their jobs to search for other employment.[10] Moreover, random fluctuations in demand across firms will cause some firms to close or lay off workers at the same time that other firms are opening or expanding employment. Because

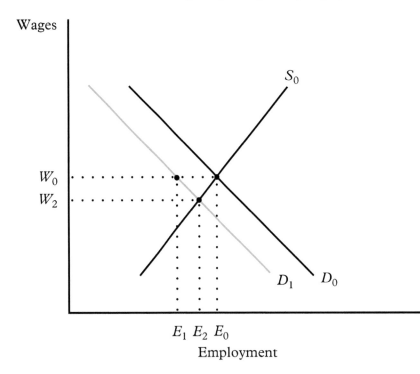

Figure 14.2 A Market With Full Employment Initially

information about the characteristics of those searching for work and the nature of the jobs opening up cannot instantly be known or evaluated, job matches between unemployed workers and potential employers take time. Hence, even when, in the aggregate, the demand for labor equals the supply, frictional unemployment will still exist.

The Theory of Job Search

The level of frictional unemployment in an economy is determined by the flows of individuals into and out of the labor market and the speed with which unemployed individuals find (and accept) jobs. The factors that determine this speed are captured in an analysis of the job-search process, to which we now turn.

A Model of Job Search   Workers who want employment must search for job offers, and because information about job opportunities and workers' characteristics is imperfect, matches between unemployed workers and potential employers will take time and effort. Other things being equal, the lower the probability that unemployed workers will become employed in a period (i.e., the lower P_{ue} is), the higher will be their expected duration of unemployment and the higher will be the unemployment rate. To understand what can affect P_{ue}, we develop a formal model of job search on the basis of the key assumption that wages are associated with the characteristics of jobs, not with the characteristics of the specific individuals who fill them.[11]

Suppose that employers differ in the set of minimum hiring standards that they use. Hiring standards may include educational requirements, job training, work experience, performance on hiring tests, and so forth. A simple model of the hiring process assumes that this set of attributes can be summarized in a single variable, K, which denotes the minimum skill level that a job requires. Associated with each job is a wage, $W(K)$—a wage that is assumed to be a function of the required skill level and not of the particular characteristics of the people hired.[12] We also assume that the wage rate is an increasing function of the minimum required skill level and that two employers using the same standard will offer the same wage.

Because different employers have different hiring standards, our simple model implies that a distribution of wage offers will be associated with job vacancies in the labor market. This distribution of wage offers is denoted by $f(W)$ in Figure 14.3. As we move to the right in the figure, the minimum skill level and offered wage on a job increase. Since $f(W)$ represents a probability distribution of wage offers, the area under the curve sums to 1 (i.e., the distribution contains 100 percent of all wage offers in the market). Each wage offer (on the horizontal axis) is shown in relation to that offer's share in the distribution (on the vertical axis).

Now, suppose that a given unemployed individual has skill level K^*. Since no firm will hire a worker who does not meet its hiring standards, the maximum wage this individual could hope to receive is $W^*(K^*)$. An

Figure 14.3 Choice of Reservation Wage in a Model of Job Search

individual who knew which firms had a hiring standard of K^* would apply to those firms and, because the individual meets their hiring standards, would be hired at a wage of W^*.

Suppose, instead, that job market information is imperfect in the sense that although an applicant knows the shape of the distribution of wage offers, $f(W)$, they do *not* know what each particular firm's wage offer or hiring standard will be. We can then conceptualize job search as a process in which the person randomly visits firms' employment offices. If a firm's hiring standard exceeds K^*, the person is rejected for the job, but if the hiring standard is K^* or less, the person is offered the job. Although the individual might find accumulating a number of job offers and then accepting the best one to be advantageous, job seekers—especially those at the lower end of the skill ladder—are not always allowed such a luxury. Rather, they must instantly decide whether to accept a job offer, because otherwise, the offer will be extended to a different applicant.

The Reservation Wage   How does an unemployed worker know whether to accept a particular job offer? One strategy is to decide on a *reservation wage* and then accept only those offers above this level. The critical question, then, is how this reservation wage is determined.

To answer this question, suppose that W_R is the reservation wage chosen (in Figure 14.3) by a person who has skill level K^*. Now, observe that this individual's job application will be rejected by any firm that offers a wage higher than $W^*(K^*)$; the person will not meet its minimum hiring standards. Similarly, the person will reject any job offers that call for a wage less than W_R. Hence, the probability that they will find an acceptable job in any period is simply the unshaded area under the curve between W_R and W^*. The higher this probability, the lower the expected duration of unemployment. Given that the person finds a job, their *expected* wage is simply the weighted average of the job offers in the W_R to W^* range. This average (or expected) wage is denoted by $E(W)$ in Figure 14.3.

If the individual were to choose a slightly higher reservation wage, their choice would have two effects. On the one hand, since the person would now reject more low-wage jobs, their expected wage (once employed) would increase. On the other hand, rejecting more job offers also decreases the probability of finding an acceptable job in any given period, thus increasing the expected duration of unemployment (see Example 14.1 for some evidence on whether higher reservation wages help or hurt one's search for a suitable job). Each unemployed individual will choose their reservation wage so that at the margin, the expected costs of longer spells of unemployment just equal the expected benefits of higher post-unemployment wages.[13]

EXAMPLE 14.1

How Discerning Should Unemployed People Be in the Search for Work?

Workers who are unemployed and searching for a job must decide how discerning to be in searching for, and accepting, job offers. Should they take a job with lower pay and lower skill requirements while they continue their search for a job better suited to their education and experience? Or should they be particular about the jobs that they search for and the offers that they will accept—which in effect means that they set their reservation wage relatively high? On the one hand, if they set their reservation wage too low and take a job requiring fewer skills than they possess, the signal that they may send to other potential employers is that they are desperate or lacking in confidence about their ability to succeed in higher-level jobs. On the other hand, if they set their reservation wage too high and are therefore unemployed for a longer period of time, potential employers (who, of course, do not know why they have been unemployed for so long) may assume that they have been rejected by many other employers and are therefore not desirable.

Economists have recently tried to answer these questions by using studies that involve sending fictitious résumés to employers advertising for jobs. The résumés are carefully constructed so that education and skill levels are similar across the fictitious job applicants and differ only in the length of time that they have been unemployed or their possession of an "interim" job. The researchers can then measure the effects of the applicant characteristics that differ on the probability of a callback by the employers. The studies so far have come to no agreement in their findings about the effects of a longer duration of unemployment on the probability of a callback; some studies have found that longer durations of unemployment have no effect on callback rates, whereas others have found that callback rates decline the longer one has been out of a job. Interestingly, however, the studies that look for the effects of taking an "interim" lower-level job agree so far that such jobs reduce one's chances of receiving a callback.

Thus, in setting one's reservation wage, research to date suggests that an unemployed worker may generate fewer interviews either by being too discerning (and being out of work for a longer time) or not discerning enough (and taking a lower-level interim job). We can only hope that future research will help us understand the relative magnitudes of these risks.

Sources: Kory Kroft, Fabian Lange, and Matthew Notowidigdo, "Duration Dependence and Labor Market Conditions: Theory and Evidence from a Field Experiment," *Quarterly Journal of Economics* 128 (August 2013): 1123–1167; Henry Farber, Dan Silverman, and Till von Wachter, "Factors Determining Callback to Job Applications by the Unemployed: An Audit Study," *Russell Sage Foundation Journal of the Social Sciences* 3 (April 2017): 168–201; John M. Nunley, Adam Pugh, Nicholas Romero, and R. Alan Seals, "The Effects of Unemployment and Underemployment on Employment Opportunities: Results from a Correspondence Audit of the Labor Market for College Graduates," *Industrial and Labor Relations Review* 70 (May 2017): 642–669

For nonexperimental evidence that a longer spell of unemployment reduces one's job prospects, see Johannes F. Schmieder, Till von Wachter, and Stefan Bender, "The Effect of Unemployment Benefits and Nonemployment Durations on Wages," *American Economic Review* 106 (March 2016): 739–777.

Implications of the Model   This simple model and associated decision rule lead to a number of implications. First, as long as the reservation wage is not set equal to the lowest wage offered in the market, the probability of finding a job will be less than 1, and hence, some unemployment can be expected to result. Search-related unemployment occurs when an individual does not necessarily accept the first job that is offered—a rational strategy in a world of imperfect information.

Second, because the reservation wage will always be chosen to be less than the wage commensurate with the individual's skill level, $W^*(K^*)$, almost all individuals will be *underemployed* once they have found a job (in the sense that their expected earnings will be less than W^*). This underemployment is a cost of imperfect information; better labor market information would improve the job-matching process.

Third, as noted in Chapter 5, otherwise-identical individuals will wind up receiving different wages. Two unemployed individuals with the same skill level could choose the same reservation wage and have the same *expected* post-unemployment wage. However, the wages that they *actually* wind up with will depend on pure luck—the wage offer between W_R and W^* that they happen to find. In a world of imperfect information, then, no economic model can explain all the variations in wages across individuals.[14]

Fourth, anything that causes unemployed workers to intensify their job search will reduce the duration of unemployment, other things being equal. More efficiently collecting and disseminating information on both jobs and applicants can increase the speed of the search process for all parties in the market; enhanced computerization among employment agencies is one example of an innovation that could reduce unemployment. Chapter 7, however, suggested that even unemployed workers have alternative uses for their time (they can spend it in "household production"). Thus, the intensity of the job search is also influenced by the value of their time in household production and the payoffs to job search that they expect; if the value of the former is high and the expected payoffs to the latter are low, unemployed workers may become discouraged and quit searching altogether—in which case they are counted as being "out of the labor force."

Finally, if the cost to an individual of being unemployed were to fall, the person should be led to increase their reservation wage (i.e., the person would become more discerning about the offers deemed to be acceptable). A higher reservation wage, of course, would increase both the expected duration of unemployment and the expected post-unemployment wage rate. One important influence on the cost of being unemployed, and hence on the reservation wages of unemployed workers, is the presence and monetary amount of governmental unemployment insurance (UI) programs.

Effects of Unemployment Insurance Benefits

Almost every advanced economy offers its workers who have lost jobs some form of unemployment compensation, although these systems vary widely in their structure and payout amounts.[15] In the United States, the UI system is actually composed of individual state systems. Although the details of the individual systems differ, we can easily sketch the broad outlines of how they operate.

When U.S. workers become unemployed, their eligibility for UI benefits is based on their previous labor market experience and reason for unemployment. With respect to their experience, each state requires unemployed individuals to demonstrate "permanent" attachment to the labor force, by meeting minimum earnings or weeks-worked tests during some base period, before they can be eligible for UI benefits. In all states, covered workers who are *laid off* and meet these labor market experience tests are eligible for UI benefits. In some states, workers who voluntarily quit their jobs are eligible for benefits in certain circumstances. Finally, new entrants or re-entrants to the labor force and workers dismissed for cause are, in general, ineligible for benefits.

After a waiting period, which is one week in most states, an eligible worker can begin to collect UI benefits. The structure of benefits is illustrated in Figure 14.4, where benefits are shown to be related to an individual's previous earnings level. As shown in panel (a), all eligible unemployed workers are entitled to at least a minimum benefit level B_{min}. After previous earnings rise above a critical level (W_{min}), benefits increase proportionately with earnings up to a maximum earnings level (W_{max}), past which benefits remain constant at B_{max}. A few states also have dependents' allowances for unemployed workers, although in some of these states, the dependents' allowance cannot increase an individual's weekly UI benefits above B_{max}.[16]

An implication of such a benefit structure is that the ratio of an individual's UI benefits to previous earnings varies according to their past earnings; on this, see panel (b). This ratio is often called the *replacement rate*, the fraction of previous earnings that the UI benefits replace. Over the range between W_{min} and W_{max}, where the replacement rate is constant, most

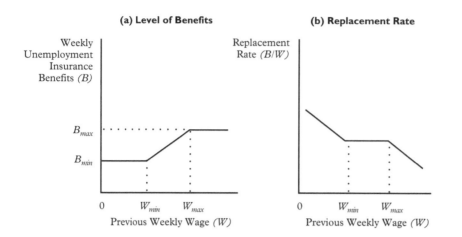

(a) Level of Benefits   **(b) Replacement Rate**

Figure 14.4 Weekly Unemployment Insurance Benefits as a Function of Previous Earnings

states aim to replace around 50 percent of an unemployed worker's previous earnings.

Once UI benefits begin, an unemployed individual's eligibility for continued benefits depends on their making continual "suitable efforts" to find employment; the definition of suitable efforts varies widely across states. In addition, in some states, a maximum duration of the receipt of benefits of fixed length is imposed (usually 26 weeks) and varies in other states depending on a worker's previous labor market experience (workers who have "more permanent attachment" are eligible for more weeks of benefits). Congress has also passed legislation that allows states where the unemployment rate is high to extend the length of time that unemployed workers can receive benefits; the typical extension is 13 weeks, although in the recession of 2009, it was extended by 73 weeks.

Whether Higher Benefits Increase Unemployment

Our theory of job search outlined earlier leads to the expectation that by reducing the costs associated with being unemployed, higher UI benefits should cause an increase in the reservation wages of unemployed workers. Increased reservation wages tend to reduce P_{ue} and P_{un}, and this reduction lengthens the duration of unemployment. Longer durations, in turn, increase the unemployment rate if other things remain equal.

Because the amount of UI benefits varies widely across states, numerous studies have sought to empirically test the hypothesis that higher benefits serve to raise the unemployment rate beyond what it would otherwise be. Evidence from these studies suggests that higher UI replacement rates are indeed associated with longer durations of unemployment for recipients. Estimates differ on how responsive durations actually are to changes in the replacement rate, but one study estimated that if the United States had ended its UI program in 1976, the average duration of unemployment that year would have fallen from 4.3 to 2.8 months.[17] We instead consider how responsive durations are to more-modest changes in UI benefits. Many estimates imply that a 10 percent increase in the replacement rate would increase the length of unemployment spells by roughly three to ten days, and one recent study estimated that reducing the length of time that a worker can receive UI benefits by four weeks would reduce the worker's duration of unemployment by over eight days.[18] Studies of the effects of unemployment compensation in other countries also support the hypothesis that higher UI benefits tend to increase the unemployment rate.[19]

Effects of Benefit Eligibility Aside from benefit levels, the mere *eligibility* of workers for unemployment compensation benefits has also been found to influence workers' job-search behavior. In the United States, for example, a jump in the probability of a worker's taking a job typically occurs during the week their eligibility for UI benefits ends, although this effect might be much smaller during periods of high unemployment.[20] Although other evidence shows that extending the period benefits can be received *during a recession* lengthens the duration of unemployment somewhat, it appears *not* to slow the pace at which unemployed people obtain jobs; rather, it slows the rate at which they stop looking for work and leave the labor force.[21] (The apparently smaller effects that higher availability and levels of unemployment benefits have on the duration of unemployment during recessions have led to proposals that the generosity of unemployment benefits should be greater during periods of higher unemployment.[22])

Whether Higher Benefits Improve Job Matches
Referring back to our theory of job search, the increased reservation wage accompanying higher UI benefits tends to increase the duration of unemployment spells, which (as we saw in Example 14.1) might make workers less desirable in the eyes of potential employers. However, by raising reservation wages, higher benefits might raise the expected post-unemployment wage; indeed, one purpose of unemployment compensation is precisely to permit workers to search for a suitable match. Unfortunately, little evidence shows that higher UI benefits raise the quality of the subsequent job match.[23]

Structural Unemployment

Structural unemployment arises when there is a mismatch between the skills demanded and supplied in a given area or an imbalance between the supplies of, and demands for, workers across areas occurs. *If* wages were completely flexible *and* if costs of occupational or geographic mobility were low, market adjustments would quickly eliminate this type of unemployment. In practice, however, these conditions may fail to hold, and structural unemployment may result.

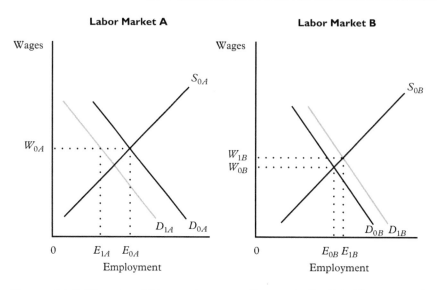

Figure 14.5 Structural Unemployment Due to Inflexible Wages and Costs of Adjustment

Occupational and Regional Unemployment Rate Differences

A two-sector labor market model, represented by Figure 14.5, can be used to illustrate how structural unemployment can arise. For the moment, we assume that the sectors refer to markets for occupational classes of workers; later, we assume that they are two geographically separate labor markets.

Occupational Imbalances Suppose that market A is the market for production workers in the automobile industry and that market B is the market for skilled computer specialists, and suppose that initially both markets are in equilibrium. Given the demand and supply curves in both markets, (D_{0A}, S_{0A}) and (D_{0B}, S_{0B}), the equilibrium wage–employment combinations in the two sectors will be (W_{0A}, E_{0A}) and (W_{0B}, E_{0B}), respectively. Because of differences in training costs and the nonpecuniary conditions of employment, the wages need not be equal in the two sectors.

Now, suppose that the demand for automobile workers falls to D_{1A} as a result of foreign import competition and that, in contrast, the demand for computer specialists rises to D_{1B} as a result of the increased use of computers. If real wages are inflexible downward in market A because of union contract provisions, social norms, or government legislation, the employment level of automobile workers will fall to E_{1A}. The employment level and wages of computer specialists will rise to E_{1B} and W_{1B}, respectively. The unemployment level of $E_{0A} - E_{1A}$ workers would be created in the short run.

If automobile employees could costlessly become computer specialists, these unemployed workers would quickly move to market B, where we assume wages are flexible, and eventually, unemployment in sector A would be eliminated.[24] Structural unemployment arises, however, when costs of adjustment are sufficiently high to slow or even prevent such movements. The cost to displaced individuals, many in their 50s and 60s, may prove to be prohibitively expensive, given the limited time in the labor market that they have to collect returns. Moreover, borrowing funds to finance the necessary job training might be difficult for them.[25] The economic and social costs of prolonged unemployment can be significant and not confined to older workers, as seen in Example 14.2.

EXAMPLE 14.2
Structural Unemployment as a Threat to Social Well-Being

One source of structural unemployment in recent years has been the loss of jobs in manufacturing industries owing to technological change and foreign import competition. The loss of job opportunities in manufacturing was felt particularly among less-educated men, many of whom were not well prepared to train for higher-skilled occupations. Those who lost manufacturing jobs (which were relative well paying) were therefore faced with either nonemployment or jobs with lower pay, both of which reduced their economic security and their social stature.

Joblessness has devastating social consequences. One study of areas in the United States that lost manufacturing jobs owing to import competition from 1990 to 2014 found that among the young men studied was a marked increase in idleness (i.e., they were neither working nor in school or in educational programs). Marriage rates dropped as young men became less economically secure, and there was an increase in births out of wedlock and the fraction of children being raised in poverty. Drug and alcohol abuse among young men rose, and associated with such abuse was an increase in their mortality rates.

Long-term unemployment also reduces one's chance of obtaining a job, so it lowers one's incentives to search for a new job and increases incentives to withdraw from the labor force. As we saw earlier, the ensuring joblessness poses serious threats to economic and social well-being.

Sources: David Autor, David Dorn, and Gordon Hanson, "When Work Disappears: Manufacturing Decline and the Falling Marriage Value of Young Men," *American Economic Review: Insights* 1 (September 2019): 161–178; Kory Kroft, Fabian Lange, Matthew J. Notowidigo, and Lawrence F. Katz, "Long-Term Unemployment and the Great Recession: The Role of Composition, Duration Dependence, and Nonparticipation," *Journal of Labor Economics* 34, pt. 2 (January 2016): S7–S54

A rise in mortality rates among older workers who lose jobs that they had held for a long time was reported in Daniel Sullivan and Till von Wachter, "Job Displacement and Mortality: An Analysis Using Administrative Data," *Quarterly Journal of Economics* 124 (August 2009): 1265–1306.

Geographic Imbalances   Geographic imbalances can be analyzed in the same framework. Suppose that we now assume that market A refers to a North American Snowbelt city and market B to a Sunbelt city, both employing the same type of labor. When demand falls in the Snowbelt and unemployment increases because wages are not completely flexible, these unemployed workers may continue to wait for jobs in their home city for at least three reasons. First, information flows are imperfect, so workers may be unaware of the availability of jobs hundreds of miles away. Second, the direct money costs of such a move, including moving costs and maybe also the transaction costs involved in buying and selling a home, are high. Third, the psychological costs of moving long distances are substantial because friends and neighbors and community support systems must be given up. As noted in Chapter 10, such factors inhibit geographic migration, and migration tends to decline with age. These costs are sufficiently high that many workers who become unemployed as a result of plant shutdowns or permanent layoffs express no interest in searching for jobs outside their immediate geographic area.[26]

Structural factors can cause substantial differences in unemployment rates across geographical areas in a given year, but these differences usually do not persist indefinitely.[27] In the United States, if a state's unemployment rate is higher than the national average, many unemployed workers will eventually leave the state and new entrants will tend to avoid moving there; both sets of decisions serve to reduce the unemployment rate. Conversely, states that have unemployment rates lower than average will attract workers looking for jobs.[28]

For example, in 1981, Indiana had an unemployment rate of 10.1 percent, whereas the national average was 7.6 percent. During the next decade, Indiana's labor force increased more slowly than average, and by 1991, its unemployment rate, at 5.9 percent, was almost 1 percentage point below the national average. Similarly, New Hampshire had an unemployment rate of 5 percent in 1981, but over the next decade, it experienced a labor force growth rate that was about three times the national average; by 1991, its unemployment rate was above average, at 7.2 percent.

International Differences in Long-Term Unemployment

In terms of equation (14.2), structural unemployment exists when unemployed people have a small probability of finding work (P_{ue} is low) and their duration of unemployment is consequently long. We saw in Table 14.3 that the percentage of the labor force unemployed for more than one year is typically higher in Europe than in the United States (although the differences were greater in 2005 than in 2019), and we wonder what differences might be causal.

The flow of workers out of unemployment is accelerated when worker retraining is encouraged and when workers find making geographical moves less costly. It will also be accelerated when employers find creating new jobs less costly—and thus create them at a faster pace. While the United States spends much less on government training programs than most of Europe,[29] it may compensate for this by having a relatively high rate of geographical mobility. The biggest difference, however, may be in the rates at which new jobs are created.

European countries typically have job-protection policies that are intended to reduce layoffs. Such policies, however, are thought to reduce the rate at which new jobs are created (refer back to Example 5.1) and thus increase the duration of unemployment. In France, for example, dismissals for economic reasons require notification to the government, consultations with worker representatives, a relatively long waiting period, and severance pay. In contrast, the United States requires some employers to notify their workers in advance of large-scale layoffs, but these requirements are much less burdensome than those in most of Europe.[30] These job-protection policies are of special interest when analyzing structural unemployment because they also make *hiring* workers (who may have to be laid off in the future) more costly for an employer. Indeed, a comparative study found that as the stringency of job-protection laws rose, so did the average duration of unemployment.[31]

Whether Efficiency Wages Cause Structural Unemployment

Suppose that employers are unable to completely monitor the performance of their employees and decide to pay above-market (*efficiency*) wages to reduce the incentives for workers to shirk their duties. Chapter 11 showed that efficiency wages are thought to increase worker productivity, for two reasons.[32] First, by supplying workers with a high wage, employers might expect that employees would reciprocate by working diligently. Second, if an employee's effort is not diligent, the employee can be fired and faced with earning a lower wage in the next job or, as we argue later, with unemployment.

Efficiency Wages Affect Unemployment If all employers were to follow the earlier strategy and offer wages higher than the market equilibrium wage, then supply would clearly exceed demand and unemployment would result. If only *some* firms paid efficiency wages, then there would be a high-wage sector and a low-wage sector. Workers employed at lower-paying firms could not obtain employment at a higher-wage firm by offering to work at some wage between the lower (market-clearing) wage level and the higher (efficiency) wage level, because the higher-wage employers would want to maintain their wage advantage to discourage shirking. However, because jobs in the higher-wage sector are preferable and because such jobs will occasionally become available, some workers in the lower-wage sector may quit their jobs, attach themselves to the higher-wage sector, and wait for jobs to open up (so they would be unemployed members of the labor force). That is, using reasoning similar to that used in Chapter 13, where a higher-wage sector was created by unions, *wait unemployment* could arise in the presence of an efficiency-wage sector.[33]

Unemployment Affects Efficiency Wages The wage premium that efficiency-wage employers must pay to discourage shirking depends on the alternatives open to their employees. Other things being

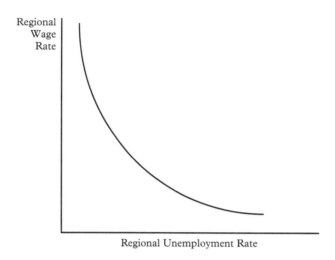

Figure 14.6 The Wage Curve

equal, the higher the unemployment rate in an area, the poorer will be the alternative employment opportunities for their workers and thus the less likely the workers will be to risk losing their jobs by shirking. The employers, then, need not pay wage premiums that are as high. This leads to the prediction that, other factors held constant, a negative association should exist between average wage rates and unemployment rates across areas.

Efficiency Wages and the Wage Curve The efficiency-wage explanation of structural unemployment receives indirect support from a remarkable empirical finding. An exhaustive study of data on wages and regional unemployment rates from 12 countries found, after controlling for the human-capital characteristics of individual workers (some 3.5 million of them), a strong negative relationship between regional unemployment rates and real wages in all countries. That is, in regions within these countries with *higher* rates of unemployment, wage levels for otherwise-comparable workers were *lower*. This negative relationship between the region's unemployment rate and its real wage level, seen in Figure 14.6, has been called the *wage curve*.

The wage curve is remarkable on three accounts. First, it seems to exist in every country for which enough data are available to estimate it. Second, the curves for each country are surprisingly similar; a 10 percent increase in a region's unemployment rate is associated with wage levels that are lower by 0.4 to 1.9 percent in 11 of the 12 countries studied.[34]

Finally, the wage curve is remarkable because it is a finding in search of an explanation. Using a standard demand-and-supply-curve analysis, one would think that higher unemployment and *higher* wages would be associated with each other (in other words, the wage curve would slope positively). Using this analysis, if wages were above market-clearing levels, supply would exceed demand, and the result would be workers who want jobs and cannot find them (unemployment); the higher that wages were above equilibrium, the more unemployment. Thus, a downward-sloping relationship, such as depicted in Figure 14.6, is not what simple economic theory suggests.

Simple theory does suggest, of course, that when unemployment is relatively high, real wages will *fall*. The problem with this explanation for the wage curve is that the curve plots the relationship between unemployment and the wage *level*, not wage *changes*; thus, this implication of standard theory also fails to explain what we observe. If simple theory is not providing explanations for the wage curve, would a more complex theory do so?

One reason why we might observe a negatively sloped wage curve can be found in the efficiency-wage explanation of structural unemployment reviewed earlier. Suppose, for example, that one cause of long-term unemployment is the widespread payment of above-market wages by employers in an effort to reduce shirking among their employees. In regions where this and other causes happen to create higher levels of unemployment, the efficiency-wage premiums needed to reduce shirking would be lower—which would cause the negative association that we observe between regional unemployment rates and wage levels.

Demand-Deficient (Cyclical) Unemployment

Frictional unemployment arises because labor markets are dynamic and information flows are imperfect; structural unemployment arises because of long-lasting imbalances in demand and supply. *Demand-deficient unemployment* is associated with fluctuations in business activity (the "business cycle"), and it occurs when a decline in aggregate demand in the output market causes the *aggregate* demand for labor to decline in the face of downward inflexibility in real wages. Such a decline took place during the Great Recession of 2007 to 2009, during which time the unemployment rate in the United States rose from 4.4 percent in the spring of 2007 to 10 percent in the fall of 2009.[35] Another sudden increase in unemployment took place from February to April in 2020, although the sudden rise in the U.S. unemployment rate from 3.5 percent to 14.7 percent was rooted in the abrupt shutdown of businesses and travel to reduce the spread of COVID-19—not the business cycle.

Returning to our simple demand-and-supply model of Figure 14.2, suppose that a temporary decline in aggregate demand leads to a shift in the labor demand curve to D_1. If real wages are inflexible downward, employment will fall to E_1, and $E_0 - E_1$ additional workers will become unemployed. This employment decline occurs when firms lay off workers (increasing P_{eu})[36] and reduce the rate at which they replace those who quit or retire (decreasing P_{ne} and P_{ue}); that is, flows into unemployment increase as flows into employment decline.

Unemployment, however, is not the inevitable outcome of reduced aggregate demand associated with the business cycle. Employers, for example, could reduce the wages that they pay to their workers. If the latter response occurred, employment would move to E_2 and real wages to W_2 in

Figure 14.2. Although employment would be lower than its initial level, E_0, no measured demand-deficient unemployment would be present, because E_0–E_2 workers would have dropped out of the labor force in response to this lower wage. Although we do not discuss the macroeconomic forces that cause (or ameliorate) reductions in aggregate demand, we analyze two features of the U.S. labor market thought to *contribute* to demand-deficient unemployment:[37]

1. institutional and profit-maximizing reasons for rigid money wages

2. how the U.S. unemployment compensation program is financed

Beyond these two features, discussed later on, evidence shows that recessions can also increase structural unemployment by lowering the opportunity costs associated with introducing new production technologies into the workplace.[38]

Downward Wage Rigidity

Stock and commodity prices fluctuate with demand and supply, and product market retailers have sales or offer discounts when demand is down, but do the wage rates paid to individual workers fall when the demand for labor shifts to the left? If such decreases are not likely, what might the reasons be?

Wages, of course, can be measured in both nominal terms and real (inflation-adjusted) terms. *Nominal* wages (the money wages quoted to workers) may be relatively rigid, yet the *real* wage (the nominal wage divided by an index of prices) can fall if prices are rising. Unsurprisingly, the real wages received by individual workers quite commonly fall; all that needs to happen for real wages to fall is for the increase in nominal wages to be less than the increase in prices. One study that followed individuals in the United States from 1970 to 1991 found that when the unemployment rate went up by 1 percentage point, the average real hourly earnings among workers who did not change employers went down by about 0.5 percent. Hourly earnings reductions were greatest among those paid by piece rates or commissions or whose compensation packages included bonuses; those paid by salary were least likely to experience such reductions.[39]

While there is evidence of at least a modest downward flexibility of *real* wages, it is also important to look into how common cuts in workers' *nominal* wages are. If real wages fall only when prices rise, they may not be able to fall fast enough to prevent an increase in unemployment during business downturns. One study of workers who did not change employers found that nominal wages fell from one year to the next in 18 percent of the cases between the years 1976 and 1988; similar estimates come from a study using different employee-provided data, although this latter study extended into the early 1990s, when some 18 percent to 20 percent of hourly paid workers experienced nominal wage cuts. A review of more-recent studies in the United States found that during periods of expansion, over 20 percent of workers who stayed with their employers experienced nominal wage cuts in a 12-month period, while during the Great Recession, up to 33 percent of workers did.[40] During the pandemic-related reductions in economic activity and employment in early 2020, over 6 percent of all workers who stayed with their employers (and 15 percent among the highest earners) experienced nominal wage cuts during the three months of March to June.[41]

These studies suggest that nominal wages are not completely rigid in a downward direction, although compensation in the form of bonuses or other forms of contingent pay (such as profit sharing) appears to be more flexible than time-based pay.[42] However, the studies also conclude that nominal wages are resistant to cuts, and as a result, employment adjustments during periods of downturn are larger and more common than they would be with complete nominal wage flexibility—and those who lose jobs may then experience cuts in their nominal wages when they take new ones (see Example 14.3).

EXAMPLE 14.3

Nominal Wage Cuts for Construction Workers in the Great Recession

Even if the nominal wages *within given employers* are not very flexible, we will observe that nominal wages *received by individuals* will fall in a recession if these individuals lose a higher-paying job and must take a lower-paying one to avoid unemployment. For example, during the Great Recession, wages of those who remained employed in the construction industry rose by 6 percent from 2007 to 2009, but employment in that industry fell by over 14 percent.

The fall in construction employment meant that about one million construction workers lost their jobs over the 2007–2009 period—and of those who found other jobs within six months, nominal wages typically declined. About 16 percent of those who found other jobs went to the food services sector and took pay cuts averaging 20 percent. Another 12 percent of those who found jobs outside of construction found them in the retail trade sector, and they took cuts averaging almost 4 percent. The 14 percent who found jobs in manufacturing or technical services experienced modest wage gains, but overall, displaced construction workers who found other jobs within six months experienced wage cuts averaging 3.4 percent. Thus, while construction wages did not fall (and actually rose) during the Great Recession, the average wages earned by those who had to take jobs outside of construction did fall.

Source: Henry Hyatt and Erika McEntarfer, "Job-to-Job Flows in the Great Recession," *American Economic Review Papers and Proceedings* 102 (May 2012): 580–583

Explanations for why employment levels are more likely to be reduced than nominal wages during business downturns must confront two questions: Why do firms find reducing employment more profitable than reducing wages, and why are workers who face unemployment not more willing to take wage cuts to save their jobs? The hypotheses concerning wage rigidity that have come to the forefront recently address both questions.

Wage Rigidity and Unions According to one explanation for rigid money wages, employers are not free to unilaterally cut nominal wages, because of the presence of unions. This cannot be a complete explanation for the United States, because less than 14 percent of U.S. workers are covered by union agreements (see Chapter 13), and unions could, in any case, agree to temporary wage cuts to save jobs instead of subjecting their members to layoffs. Why they fail to make such arrangements is instructive.

A temporary wage reduction would reduce the earnings of all workers, whereas layoffs would affect, in most cases, only those workers most recently hired.[43] Because these workers represent a minority of the union's membership in most instances, because union leaders are elected by majority rule, and because these leaders are most likely drawn from the ranks of the more-experienced workers (who are often immune from layoff), unions tend to favor a policy of layoffs rather than one that reduces wages for all members.[44] A variant of this explanation is the *insider–outsider hypothesis*, which sees union members as *insiders* who have little or no concern for nonmembers or former members now on layoff (*outsiders*); these insiders gain from keeping their numbers small and may choose to negotiate wages that effectively prevent the recall or employment of outsiders.[45]

Wage Rigidity and Specific Human Capital Layoffs do occur in *nonunion* firms, although perhaps less frequently than in unionized ones, so wage rigidity cannot be completely attributed to unionization. One possible explanation lies with employer investments in workers. In the presence of firm-specific human-capital investments, for example, employers have incentives both to minimize voluntary turnover and to maximize their employees' work effort and productivity. Across-the-board temporary wage reductions would increase all employees' propensities to quit and could lead to reduced work effort on their part. In contrast, layoffs often affect only the least-experienced workers—the workers in whom the firm has invested the smallest number of resources. Therefore, the firm will likely find the layoff strategy a more profitable alternative.[46] Indeed, one recent study found that 40 percent of workers who were laid off by their employers—including those who were told that they were being permanently let go—ultimately returned to their last employer.[47]

Although we have, so far, characterized the choice of employers as either cutting wages or cutting employees, a somewhat-hybrid option is also available. "Work share" programs offer employers an alternative; rather than reducing employment by 20 percent, say, a firm could reduce the hours of all employees by 20 percent and experience the same unemployment-insurance system costs.[48]

Wage Rigidity and Asymmetric Information Employers who have internal labor markets frequently promise, at least implicitly, a certain path of earnings to employees over their careers. As we saw in Chapter 11, firms may pay relatively low salaries to new employees on the promise (expectation) that if they work diligently, these employees will be paid relatively high wages toward the end of their careers. The firm's promises are, of necessity, conditional on how well it is performing, but the firm has more-accurate information on the true state of its demand than do its workers. If a firm asks its employees to take a wage cut in periods of low demand, employees may believe that the employer is falsely stating that demand is low, and their productivity could be reduced by a loss of trust or a decline in morale. If, instead, a firm temporarily lays off some of its workers, it loses the output that these workers would have produced, and workers may therefore accept such an action as a signal that the firm is indeed in trouble (i.e., wages exceed current marginal productivity). Put another way, the *asymmetry of information* between employers and employees may make layoffs the preferred policy.[49]

Wage Rigidity and Risk Aversion   Firms that have internal labor markets, and therefore long employer-employee job attachments, may be encouraged by the risk aversion of older employees to engage in seniority-based layoffs (last hired, first laid off) rather than wage cuts for all its workers. That is, the desire to have a constant income stream, rather than a fluctuating one with the same average value over time, is something for which older, more-experienced workers may be willing to pay.[50] Thus, if the risks of income fluctuation are confined to one's initial years of employment, the firm may be able to pay its experienced workers wages lower than would otherwise be required. Of course, during the initial period, workers will be subject to potential earnings variability and may demand higher wages then to compensate them for these risks. However, if the fraction of the workforce that is subjected to layoffs is small, on average, employers' costs could be reduced by seniority-based layoffs. (Employee aversion to the risk of earnings fluctuations may also cause them to work harder when faced with the prospect of being laid off during a recession—a possibility raised in Example 14.4.)

Wage Rigidity: Worker Status and Social Norms   The explanations given earlier pertain mainly to firms that have internal labor markets, which can be thought of roughly as large employers. If these firms have rigid wages and lay off workers during a business downturn, why don't workers who are laid off take jobs working for smaller employers? These smaller firms pay lower wages and have few of the reasons cited earlier to avoid reducing them further when aggregate demand falls; hence, increased employment in these jobs would lower the average nominal wage paid in the economy and help reduce unemployment. Some theorists believe that the failure of unemployed workers to flock to low-wage jobs derives from their sense of status (their relative standing in society).

For example, individuals might prefer unemployment in a "good" job to employment in an inferior one, at least for a period longer than the typical recession.[51] A sense of *status*, then, might prevent a reduction in wages and the expansion of low-wage jobs during recessionary periods. However, considerations of social status might operate in a different way: Prevailing market wages may be accepted as *social norms*, which inhibit unemployed people from trying to find work by appearing to undercut the wages of employed people.[52]

EXAMPLE 14.4

Recessions and Worker Effort

If workers are averse to the risk of fluctuations in their earnings, they may be willing to work harder during a recession in an effort to preserve their jobs. Evidence of greater worker effort during the Great Recession comes from a recent study that made use of computer-monitored output for each of over 20,000 employees performing the same tasks for a firm with multiple locations across the United States. The study found that the productivity of those workers who remained with the firm throughout the recession rose by 4.8 percent during the recession. Further, it found that productivity increases were greater in areas of the country facing greater increases in unemployment. Both these findings suggest that although nominal wages may be rigid in many cases, the effort workers put forth is not. Put differently, instead of hoping to save their jobs by taking cuts in their nominal wages, workers may work harder during recessions, which means that firms to get more output per dollar spent on employee compensation.

Source: Edward P. Lazear, Kathryn L. Shaw, and Christopher Stanton, "Making Do with Less: Working Harder During Recessions," *Journal of Labor Economics* 34, pt. 2 (January 2016): S333–S360

Financing U.S. Unemployment Compensation

The incentives for employers to engage in temporary layoffs are also affected by a key characteristic of the U.S. UI system: *its methods of financing benefits*. The way in which the government raises the funds to pay for UI benefits has a rather large effect on cyclical layoffs.

The UI Payroll Tax   The benefits paid out by the UI system are financed by a payroll tax. Unlike the Social Security payroll tax, in almost all states, the UI tax is paid solely by employers.[53] The UI tax payment (T) that an employer must make for each employee is given by

$$T = tW \ \ if \ \ W \leq W_B \qquad\qquad\qquad (14.3a)$$

and

$$T = tW_B \ \ if \ \ W > W_B \qquad\qquad\qquad (14.3b)$$

where t is the employer's UI tax rate, W is an employee's earnings during the calendar year, and W_B is the *taxable wage base* (the level of earnings after which no UI tax payments are required). In 2020, the taxable wage base ranged from $7,000 to $15,000 in almost two-thirds of the states; thus,

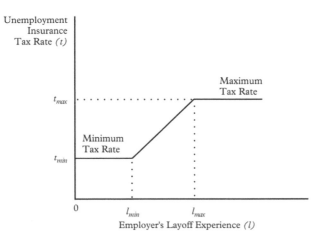

Figure 14.7 Imperfectly Experience-Rated Unemployment Insurance Tax Rates

depending on the state, employers had to pay UI taxes on just the first $7,000 to $15,000 of each employee's earnings. The other one-third of the states had taxable wage bases that were higher.

The employer's UI tax rate is determined by general economic conditions in the state, the industry that the employer is operating in, and the employer's *layoff experience*. The last term is defined differently in different states; the underlying notion is that since the UI system is an insurance system, employers who lay off workers frequently and make heavy demands on the system's resources should be assigned a higher UI tax rate. This practice is referred to as *experience rating*.

Imperfect Experience Rating Experience rating is typically *imperfect*, in the sense that the marginal cost to an employer of laying off an additional worker (in terms of a higher UI tax rate) is often less than the added UI benefits that the system must pay out to that worker. An imperfect experience rating is illustrated in Figure 14.7, which plots the relationship between an employer's UI tax rate and that firm's layoff experience. (We interpret *layoff experience* to mean the probability that employees in the firm will be on layoff. Clearly, this probability depends both on the frequency with which the firm lays off workers and on the average duration of time until they are recalled to their positions.)

Each state has a minimum UI tax rate, and below this rate (t_{min} in Figure 14.7), the firm's UI tax rate cannot fall. After a firm's layoff experience reaches some critical value (l_{min}), the firm's UI tax rate rises with increased layoff experience over some range.[54] Each state also has a ceiling on the UI tax rate (t_{max}); after this tax rate has been reached, additional layoffs will not alter the firm's tax rate. The system is *imperfectly* experience-rated because for firms below l_{min} or above l_{max}, variations in their layoff rate have no effect on their UI tax rate.[55] Furthermore, over the range in which the tax rate is increasing with layoff experience, the increase is not large enough in most states to make the employer's marginal cost of a layoff (in terms of the increased UI taxes that the firm must pay) equal to the marginal UI benefits that the laid-off employees receive.

Whether the UI Tax Encourages Layoffs The key characteristic of the UI system that influences the desirability of temporary layoffs is the *imperfect experience rating* of the UI payroll tax. To understand the influence of this characteristic, suppose first that the UI system were constructed in such a way that its tax rates were perfectly experience rated. A firm that lays off a worker would have to pay added UI taxes equal to the full UI benefit (50 percent of normal earnings) received by the worker, so it saves just half of the worker's wages by the layoff. Now, suppose instead that the UI tax rate that employers must pay is totally independent of their layoff experience (no experience rating). In this case, a firm saves a laid-off worker's *entire* wages because its UI taxes do not rise as a result of the layoff. Thus, compared with a UI system with a perfect experience rating, a system with incomplete experience rating tends to enhance the attractiveness of layoffs to employers.

Empirical analyses of the effect of imperfect experience rating on employer behavior suggest that it is substantial. These studies have estimated that unemployment would fall by 10 percent to 33 percent if UI taxes in the United States were perfectly experience rated (such that employers laying off workers would have to pay the full cost of the added UI benefits).[56]

Seasonal Unemployment

Seasonal unemployment is similar to demand-deficient unemployment in that it is induced by fluctuations in the demand for labor. Here, however, the fluctuations can be regularly anticipated and follow a systematic pattern over the course of a year. For example, the demand for agricultural employees declines after the planting season and remains low until the harvest season. Similarly, the demand for production workers falls in certain industries during the season of the year when plants are retooling to handle annual model changes.

The following issue remains: Why do employers respond to seasonal patterns of demand by laying off workers rather than reducing wage rates or hours of work? All the reasons cited for the existence of cyclical unemployment and temporary layoffs for cyclical reasons also pertain here. Indeed, one study has shown that the expansion (in the early 1970s) of the UI system that led to the coverage of most agricultural employees was associated with a substantial increase in seasonal unemployment in agriculture. Studies of seasonal layoffs in nonagricultural industries also suggest that the imperfect experience rating of the UI tax significantly increases seasonal unemployment.[57] (See Example 14.5 for a longer-term perspective on UI and seasonal unemployment.)

EXAMPLE 14.5

Unemployment Insurance and Seasonal Unemployment: A Historical Perspective

The current U.S. UI system was established during the Great Depression of the 1930s. At that time, labor economist John Commons urged that legislation include a penalty on firms with higher unemployment rates. He believed that employers had enough leeway to reduce seasonal and other layoffs substantially, and he thus championed a system that included incentives to avoid higher layoffs. Others were unconvinced that employers had much discretion over unemployment. But ultimately, the Commons plan was adopted in most states. It was rarely adopted outside the United States, however.

Evidence on seasonal unemployment seems to support Commons's contentions: Over time, as the economy has diversified, seasonal unemployment has fallen, but it has fallen much more rapidly where employers are penalized for layoffs. One study found that in the United States, seasonal fluctuations in employment have fallen most in states where the UI experience rating is highest.

Even more striking is the comparison between the United States and Canada, which established an employment insurance (EI) system without *any* experience rating. Seasonality in the Canadian construction industry (an industry notorious for its seasonality) fell by half between 1929 and the 1947–1963 period, as construction practices improved and changed. However, in U.S. states along the Canadian border, seasonality dropped by an even greater two-thirds.

Source: Katherine Baicker, Claudia Goldin, and Lawrence F. Katz, "A Distinctive System: Origins and Impact of U.S. Unemployment Compensation," in *The Defining Moment: The Great Depression and the American Economy in the Twentieth Century*, eds. Michael D. Bordo, Claudia Goldin, and Eugene N. White (Chicago, IL: University of Chicago Press, 1998): 259

We may question why workers would accept jobs in industries in which they knew in advance that they would be unemployed for only a portion of the year. For some workers, the existence of UI benefits, along with the knowledge that they will be rehired as a matter of course at the end of the slack-demand season, may allow them to treat such periods as paid vacations.[58] However, since UI benefits typically replace less than half of an unemployed worker's previous gross earnings and even smaller fractions for high-wage workers (see Figure 14.4), most workers will not find such a situation desirable. To attract workers to seasonal industries, firms will have to pay workers higher wages to compensate them for being periodically unemployed. One recent study, for example, found that agricultural workers in seasonal jobs earned about 10 percent more per hour than they would have earned in permanent farm jobs.[59]

The existence of wage differentials that compensate workers in high-unemployment industries for the risk of unemployment makes evaluating whether this type of unemployment is voluntary or involuntary in nature difficult. On the one hand, workers have voluntarily agreed to be employed in industries that offer higher wages *and* higher probabilities of unemployment. On the other hand, once on the job, employees usually prefer to remain employed rather than becoming unemployed. Such unemployment may be considered either voluntary or involuntary, then, depending on one's perspective.

When Do We Have Full Employment?

Governments regularly focus on the unemployment rate, because it is seen as a handy barometer of an economy's health. An unemployment rate that is deemed to be too high is seen as a national concern, because it implies that many people are unable to support themselves and that many of the country's workers are not contributing to national output. Often, governments will take steps to stimulate the demand for labor in one way or another when they believe unemployment to be excessive.

Governments also worry about unemployment being too low. An unusually low rate of unemployment is thought by many to reflect a situation in which excess demand is in the labor market. If labor demand exceeds supply, wages will tend to rise, the argument goes, and wage increases will lead to price inflation. In addition, excessively low unemployment rates may increase shirking among workers and reduce the pool of available talent on which new or expanding employers can draw.

Defining the Natural Rate of Unemployment

If both too much and too little unemployment are undesirable, how much is just right? Put differently, what unemployment rate represents full employment? The *full-employment* (or *natural*) rate of unemployment is difficult to define precisely, and several alternative concepts are available. One defines the natural rate of unemployment as that rate at which wage and price inflation are either stable or at acceptable levels. Another defines full employment as the rate of unemployment at which job vacancies equal the number of unemployed workers. And yet another defines it as the level of unemployment at which any increases in aggregate demand will cause no further reductions in unemployment. A variant of the latter defines the natural rate as the unemployment rate at which all unemployment is voluntary (frictional and perhaps seasonal). A final definition of the natural rate is that rate at which the level of unemployment is unchanging and both the flows into unemployment and the duration of unemployment are normal.[60]

All the various earlier definitions try to define in a specific way a more general concept of full employment as the rate that prevails in "normal" times. If we assume that frictional and seasonal unemployment exist even in labor markets characterized by equilibrium (i.e., markets having neither excess demand nor excess supply), the natural rate of unemployment is clearly affected by such factors as voluntary turnover rates among employed workers, movements in and out of the labor force, and the length of time unemployed people take to find acceptable jobs. These factors vary widely across demographic groups, so the natural rate during any period is strongly influenced by the demographic composition of the labor force.

Unemployment and Demographic Characteristics

Table 14.4 presents data on actual unemployment rates for various age/ race/gender/ethnic groups in 2017, a year in which the overall unemployment was 4.4 percent. The patterns indicated in Table 14.4 for 2017 are similar to the patterns for other recent years: teens and young adults of each race/gender group have high unemployment rates relative to older adults in these groups; unemployment rates for Black workers roughly double those for white workers across the age/gender groups; and Hispanic American unemployment rates tend to lie in between. The high unemployment rates of Black teenagers, which ranged between 17 percent and 31 percent in 2017, have been of particular concern to policymakers. Female unemployment rates tend to be lower than male rates among Black workers and among younger workers of all demographic groups, but higher than male rates among Hispanic workers.

Over recent decades, the demographic composition of the labor force has changed dramatically with the growth in labor force participation rates of women and substantial changes in the relative sizes of the teenage, Black, and Hispanic populations. Between 1975 and 2017, the percentage of the labor force that is female grew from 40 percent to 47 percent, the percent Hispanic from 4 percent to 17 percent, and the percent Black from 10 to almost 13 percent. In contrast, the teenage share of the labor force dropped from over 9 percent in 1975 to less than 4 percent by 2017.[61]

The overall unemployment rate reflects both the tightness of the labor market and the composition of the labor force. If demographic groups with relatively high unemployment rates grow as a fraction of the labor force, then the overall unemployment rate accompanying any given level of labor market tightness will rise; similarly, the unemployment rate will tend to fall,

Table 14.4 Unemployment Rates in 2017 by Demographic Group

Age	White men	White women	Black men	Black women	Hispanic men	Hispanic women	All
16–17	14.9	13.1	28.5	21.7	17.3	20.5	
18–19	12.3	9.8	30.7	17.4	15.3	10.8	
20–24	7.4	5.4	13.2	9.8	7.5	7.7	
25–54	3.2	3.4	6.7	6.5	3.8	5.0	
55–64	2.8	2.9	5.6	4.3	3.4	4.4	
Total	3.8	3.8	8.1	6.9	4.7	5.7	4.4

Source: U.S. Department of Labor, *2018 Employment and Earnings Online: Household Survey Data,* Tables 3 and 4, at www.bls.gov/opub/ee/2018/cps/annual.htm

other things being equal, if the labor force share of groups with relatively high unemployment rates falls. Since 1975, changes in the composition of the labor force have had effects that tend to be offsetting: the percentage of the labor force that is Black has grown, as has the share of women in the labor force. Likewise, the rising share of Hispanics has tended to increase the overall unemployment rate, whereas the falling share of teenagers has served to reduce the unemployment rate.

What Is the Natural Rate?

Economists' estimates of the natural rate have varied over time, going from something like 5.4 percent in the 1960s, to about 7 percent in the 1970s, to 6 or 6.5 percent in the 1980s, to between 4 and 5 percent in the past decade.[62] We must wonder, though, how useful estimates of the natural rate are for policy purposes if they keep changing; indeed, Milton Friedman, a Nobel Prize winner in economics and a leader in the development of the natural-rate concept, disavowed any attempts at forecasting it. He said, "I don't know what the natural rate is . . . and neither does anyone else."[63]

EMPIRICAL STUDY 14.1

DO RE-EMPLOYMENT BONUSES REDUCE UNEMPLOYMENT? THE RESULTS OF SOCIAL EXPERIMENTS

In earlier chapters, we emphasized that empirical research in the social sciences requires analyzing the behavior of a *treatment* group against that of a *comparison* (or *control*) group. Ideally, researchers would create controlled experiments in which otherwise-identical subjects are randomly assigned to the two groups and a carefully crafted treatment is applied to one but not the other.

The predictions growing out of economic theory, however, typically apply to outcomes generated by the behavior of those *at the margin* within large groups of people, and they are most credibly tested under conditions in which the behaviors observed have *real-world consequences*. Thus, controlled experiments are usually infeasible in economics, because of the required sample size and expense involved. Such experiments are also morally objectionable in a wide variety of cases; for example, that we could test the theory of compensating differentials by deliberately exposing the treatment group to high risk is inconceivable. Outside of unusual cases (see the empirical studies summarized in Chapters 11 and 12), economists must normally look for *natural experiments* caused by economic conditions or government policies that happen to affect similar workers differently.

One set of controlled social experiments that did take place was designed to determine whether unemployment rates could be reduced by awarding cash bonuses to unemployed workers who found new jobs "quickly." The hope was that by offering these re-employment bonuses, the duration of unemployment—and therefore the unemployment rate—could be reduced.

Four states conducted such experiments in the mid to late 1980s, and each assigned UI recipients to the treatment and control groups randomly—by using the last two digits of their Social Security numbers. Although details differed, recipients in the treatment group who took jobs in under 11 to 13 weeks—and who held them for at least four months—received cash bonuses averaging around $500 in most cases but up to as high as $1,600 in one state. The bonuses were not offered to members of the control group.

The analyses of these experiments estimated that those in the treatment group took jobs about one-half week faster, on average, than those in the control group. Put differently, the bonuses appeared to reduce the duration of unemployment by an average of about 3 percent, and most of the estimated effects in the four states were statistically significant. The experiments also found that in the states that offered bonuses of differing sizes, larger bonuses did *not* produce estimated declines in duration that were statistically significant.

Can the modest estimated effects of these experiments be generalized to an environment in which all workers on UI would be given a re-employment bonus if they found a job quickly? The experiments were adopted on a temporary basis, and the UI recipients in the experiment neither expected them nor could be sure of being in the treatment group; therefore, whether they applied for UI was unaffected by the presence of a bonus. However, if the bonuses were to become a permanent part of the UI system and available to all UI recipients, the benefits paid to those with short spells of unemployment would be enhanced, and this might cause more people to engage in behaviors that make them eligible for UI benefits.

We cannot be certain, then, that re-employment bonuses would reduce the unemployment rate, because even if they reduced the duration of unemployment, they might also increase the number who qualify for the UI program. This problem illustrates an unfortunate drawback of social experiments: By necessity, they are temporary, and the behavioral responses that they generate are often not completely transferable to those whom we might observe if a program were permanently adopted.

Source: Bruce D. Meyer, "Lessons from the U.S. Unemployment Insurance Experiments," *Journal of Economic Literature* 33 (March 1995): 91–131

Certainly, some level of unemployment is unavoidably associated with the frictions in a dynamic labor market fraught with imperfect information. Moreover, as we have seen, the parameters of the UI system encourage unemployment associated with job search and with both cyclical layoffs and seasonal layoffs. Nonetheless, when unemployment rises above its full-employment or natural level, resources are being wasted. Some 50 years ago, economist Arthur Okun pointed out that every 1 percentage point decline in the aggregate unemployment rate was associated with a 3 percentage point increase in the output of the United States. More recent estimates suggest that the relationship is now more in the range of a 2 percentage point increase in output.[64] Even this last number, however, suggests the output loss a society incurs with excessively high rates of unemployment. Additionally, we saw in Example 14.2 that joblessness has adverse effects on the health of those who are unemployed.

Unfortunately, economists have not yet reached a consensus about the most effective programs to reduce unemployment. The payroll subsidies designed to stimulate hiring among employers, discussed in Chapter 3, would seem to hold promise, but we noted at the end of that chapter that they have not been shown to have sizable or lasting effects. Similarly, one might think that government-sponsored job training programs could help speed the placement of unemployed people in new jobs, but at the end of Chapter 9, we cited studies showing their general lack of effectiveness. Even government assistance with job placement has uncertain effects on unemployment.[65] Further complicating the issue of joblessness is the trend, noted at the outset of this chapter, toward declining labor force participation among workers who have lost jobs in recent years; policies to stimulate work among adults who are not old enough to retire may indeed be the largest challenge facing policymakers in the coming years.[66]

Review Questions

1. A presidential hopeful is campaigning to raise unemployment compensation benefits and lower the unemployment rate. Comment on the compatibility of these goals.

2. Government officials find measuring the nation's "economic health" useful. The unemployment rate is currently used as a major indicator of the relative strength of labor supply and demand. Do you think the unemployment rate is a useful indicator of labor market tightness? Why?

3. Recent empirical evidence suggests that unemployed workers' reservation wages decline as their spells of unemployment lengthen. That is, the longer they have been unemployed, the lower their reservation wages become. Explain why this might be true.

4. Is the following assertion true, false, or uncertain? "Increasing the level of UI benefits will prolong the average length of spells of unemployment. Hence, a policy of raising UI benefit levels is not socially desirable." Explain your answer.

5. In recent years, the federal government introduced and later expanded a requirement that UI beneficiaries pay income tax on their unemployment

benefits. Explain what effect you would expect this taxation of UI benefits to have on the unemployment rate.

6. "With the growth of free trade, Mexican employers have sought to reduce union control over internal labor markets, and they have eliminated promotion by seniority, rules against subcontracting, and restrictions on the use of temporary workers—all in the name of greater flexibility." Would you expect greater employer flexibility in hiring and assigning workers to increase or decrease unemployment in Mexico? Explain.

7. The employment-at-will doctrine is one that allows employers to discharge workers for any reason whatsoever. This doctrine has generally prevailed in the United States, except where modified by union agreements or by laws preventing discrimination. Recent policies have begun to erode the employment-at-will doctrine by moving closer to the notion that one's job becomes a property right that the worker cannot be deprived of in the absence of a compelling reason. If employers lose the right to discharge workers without "cause," what effects will this have on the unemployment rate?

8. One student of the labor market effects of free trade argues that the government should offer "wage insurance" to workers who lose a job because of free trade. Under this proposal, the government would replace a substantial portion of lost earnings if, upon re-employment, eligible workers find that their new job pays less than the one that they lost. This wage insurance would be available for up to two years after the initial date of job loss. Would this wage insurance program reduce unemployment? Explain.

Problems

1. Suppose that at the beginning of the month, the number employed, E, equals 120 million; the number not in the labor force, N, equals 70 million; and the number unemployed, U, equals 10 million. During the course of the month, the flows indicated in the following list occurred:

   EU 1.8 million

   EN 3.0 million

   UE 2.2 million

   UN 1.7 million

   NE 4.5 million

   NU 1.3 million

   Assuming that the population has not grown, calculate the unemployment and labor force participation rates at the beginning and end of the month.

2. Suppose that, initially, the Pennsylvania economy is in equilibrium with no unemployment: $L_S = 1,000,000 + 200\,W$ and $L_D = 19,000,000 - 300$

W, where *W* = the annual wages and *L* = the number of workers. Then, structural unemployment arises because the demand for labor falls in Pennsylvania, but wages there are inflexible downward, so no one moves out of state. If labor demand falls to $L_D = 18,000,000 - 300\,W$, how many workers will be unemployed in Pennsylvania? What will be its unemployment rate?

3. Suppose that the UI system is structured so that $B_{min} = \$200$, $B_{max} = \$500$, and $B = 0.5\,W + 100$ in between, where *W* = the previous weekly wage and *B* = the weekly UI benefits. Graph this benefit formula, and calculate the benefits and replacement rate for workers whose previous weekly wages were $100, $500, and $2,000.

4. Table 14P.4 gives data on characteristics of inhabitants in Anytown, USA.

   a. Identify the number of people employed, the number of people unemployed, and the number of people in the labor force.

   b. Calculate the labor force participation rate, the employment rate, and the unemployment rate, using official definitions.

Table 14P.4 Labor Force Data for Anytown, USA

Characteristic	Number (in thousands) of people
Population	500
Population 16 years or older	400
People employed full time or part time	200
People unemployed and actively seeking work	20
People who have quit seeking work due to lack of success	10
Part-time workers seeking full-time jobs	30

5. Suppose that the UI system is structured so that the minimum tax rate is 1.5 percent, the maximum tax rate is 6.2 percent, and the tax rate in between is calculated according to the following formula: $t = 0.1 + 2.4l$, where *t* = the employer's UI tax rate and *l* = the employer's layoff experience. Layoff experience is the probability that employees in the firm will be on layoff, expressed as a percentage of the firm's workforce, and generally lies in the range of less than 1 percent to 5 percent. Graph this tax rate formula, and calculate the firm's critical value of layoff experience (l_{min}) and ceiling value of layoff experience (l_{max}).

6. On July 24, 2009, the federal minimum wage was increased from $6.55 per hour to $7.25 per hour. Consider the effect of this increase on an

unemployed job seeker. Using a job-search model, what is the effect on the probability of finding an acceptable job in any given period? How does this increase affect the expected duration of unemployment and the expected wage (once employed)?

Notes

1. Also, during times of crisis, such as with the COVID-19 spike in unemployment, some could earn unemployment compensation (and were obviously defined as unemployed) even if they weren't searching for work.

2. As pointed out in Chapter 7, these individuals are called discouraged workers.

3. Alan B. Krueger, Judd Cramer, and David Cho, "Are the Long-Term Unemployed on the Margins of the Labor Market? *Brookings Papers on Economic Activity* (Spring 2014): 229–280; Andreas Mueller, Jesse Rothstein, and Till von Wachter, "Unemployment Insurance and Disability Insurance in the Great Recession," *Journal of Labor Economics* 34, pt. 2 (January 2016): S455–S475. Also see Danny Yagan, "Employment Hysteresis from the Great Recession," *Journal of Political Economy* 127:5 (September 2019): 2505–2559.

4. At the onset of the COVID-19 crisis, the measured unemployment rate in the United States jumped by more than 10 percentage points in *a single month* between March and April 2020.

5. From the perspective of actual measurement, those who are classified as "unemployed" are distinguished from those considered "out of the labor force" only by self-reported information on job search. Thus, the empirical distinction between the two categories, as well as errors in recording movements between them, have attracted the attention of researchers. For analyses of the former issue, see Füsun Gönsül, "New Evidence on Whether Unemployment and Out of the Labor Force Are Distinct States," *Journal of Human Resources* 27 (Spring 1992): 329–336; Alan Krueger, Alexandre Mas, and Xiaotong Niu, "The Evolution of Rotation Group Bias: Will the Real Unemployment Rate Please Stand Up?" *Review of Economics and Statistics* 99 (May 2017): 258–264. On the latter topic, see Paul Flaim and Carma Hogue, "Measuring Labor Force Flows: A Special Conference Examines the Problems," *Monthly Labor Review* (July 1985): 7–15. Also see Hie Joo Ahn and James D. Hamilton, "Measuring Labor-Force Participation and the Incidence and Duration of Unemployment" (Working Paper No. 27394, National Bureau of Economic Research, Cambridge, MA, June 2020).

6. Randy E. Ilg and Eleni Theodossiou, "Job Search of the Unemployed by Duration of Unemployment," *Monthly Labor Review* 135 (March 2012): 41–49.

7. The specific functional form for equation (14.2) is found in Stephen T. Marston, "Employment Instability and High Unemployment Rates," *Brookings Papers on Economic Activity* (1976–1): 169–203. An intuitive understanding of why each of the results summarized in equation (14.2) holds can be obtained from the definition of the unemployment rate in equation (14.1). A movement from one labor market state to another might affect the numerator, the denominator, or both. For example, an increase in P_{en} does not directly affect the number of unemployed people, but it does reduce the size of the labor force. According to equation (14.1), this reduction leads to an increase in the unemployment rate.

8. Strong evidence shows that the longer someone is unemployed, the less likely they are to find subsequent employment; see Katharine G. Abraham, John C. Haltiwanger, Kristin Sandusky, and James Spletzer, "The Consequences of Long-Term Unemployment: Evidence from Linked Survey and Administrative Data," *ILR Review* 72 (March 2019): 266–299.

9. U.S. Department of Labor, Bureau of Labor Statistics, "Job Openings and Labor—June 2019," News Release USDL 19–1431, August 6, 2019.

10. For an analysis of the relative advantages of searching for work while employed and while unemployed, see Christian Belzil, "Relative Efficiencies and Comparative Advantages of Job Search," *Journal of Labor Economics* 14 (January 1996): 154–173. For evidence that many workers change employers without becoming unemployed, see Alice Nakamura, Emi Nakamura, Kyle Phong, and Jón Steinsson, "New Evidence on the Cyclicality of Employer-to-Employer Flows from Canada," *American Economic Association Papers and Proceedings* 109 (May 2019): 456–460; Fatih Karahan, Ryan Michaels, Benjamin Pugsley, Ayşegül Şahin, and Rachel Schuh, "Do Job-to-Job Transitions Drive Wage Fluctuations Over the Business Cycle?," *American Economic Review: Papers and Proceedings 2017* 107 (May 2017): 353–357.

11. Our discussion here draws heavily on Dale T. Mortensen, "Job Search, the Duration of Unemployment, and the Phillips Curve," *American Economic Review* 60 (December 1970): 846–862. Also see Theresa Devine and Nicholas Kiefer, *Empirical Labor Economics: The Search Approach* (New York: Oxford University Press, 1990). For a summary of how people search for jobs, see Yannis M. Ioannides and Linda Datcher Loury, "Job Information Networks, Neighborhood Effects, and Inequality," *Journal of Economic Literature* 42 (December 2004): 1056–1093. The use of the Internet in job search is analyzed in Peter Kuhn and Hani Mansour, "Is Internet Job Search Still Ineffective?" *Economic Journal* 124 (December 2014): 1213–1233.

12. Our discussion here is in terms of the wage rate, which is empirically observable; however, every job offer contains a nonwage element (benefits and working conditions) that both employers and workers must take into account.

13. For a study of how the reservation wages reported by unemployed individuals are affected by their length of unemployment, see Alan Krueger and Andreas Mueller, "A Contribution to the Empirics of Reservation Wages," *American Economic Journal: Economic Policy* 8 (February 2016): 142–179.

14. Remember from Chapter 8 that nonwage parts of the compensation package are taken into account by both employers and employees. A study attempting to account for the various sources of wage variations resulting from searches can be found in Robert E. Hall and Andreas I. Mueller, "Wage Dispersion and Search Behavior: The Importance of Nonwage Job Values," *Journal of Political Economy* 126 (August 2018): 1594–1637.

15. Organisation for Economic Co-operation and Development, *Benefits and Wages: Statistics*, www.oecd.org/els/benefits-and-wages-statistics.htm, contains a description and comparison of UI/EI programs in various countries. A description of the characteristics of the U.S. UI system is found in *Highlights of State Unemployment Compensation Laws—Comparison of State Unemployment Laws in 2016* (Washington, DC: UWC–Strategic Services on Unemployment & Workers' Compensation, 2016). A description and economic analysis of the UI system in the United States can be found in Walter Nicholson and Karen Needels, "Unemployment Insurance: Strengthening the Relationship Between Theory and Policy," *Journal of Economic Perspectives* 20 (Summer 2006): 47–70.

16. In rare cases, additional benefits are tied to the receipt of UI benefits. For example, during the spring and summer of 2020, in response the COVID-19 crisis, individuals collecting UI also collected an additional $600 per week in federal assistance.

17. James M. Poterba and Lawrence H. Summers, "Unemployment Benefits and Labor Market Transitions: A Multinomial Logit Model with Errors in Classification," *Review of Economics and Statistics* 77 (May 1995): 207–216.

18. Andrew C. Johnston and Alexandre Mas, "Potential Unemployment Duration and Labor Supply: The Individual and Market-Level Response to a Benefit Cut," *Journal of Political Economy* 126 (December 2018): 2480–2522. For related work, see David Card, Andrew Johnston, Pauline Leung, Alexandre Mas, and Zhuan Pei, "The Effect of Unemployment Benefits on the Duration of Unemployment Insurance Receipt: New Evidence from a Regression Kink Design in Missouri, 2003–2013," *American Economic Review Papers and Proceedings* 105 (May 2015): 126–130; Anthony B. Atkinson and John Micklewright, "Unemployment Compensation and Labor Market Transitions: A Critical Review," *Journal of Economic Literature* 29 (December 1991): 1679–1727; Peter Kuhn and Chris Riddell, "The Long-Term Effects of a Generous Income Support Program: Unemployment Insurance in New Brunswick and Maine, 1940–1991," *Industrial and Labor*

Relations Review 63 (January 2010): 183–204; Bruce D. Meyer and Wallace K.C. Mok, "Quasi-Experimental Evidence on the Effects of Unemployment Insurance from New York State" (Working Paper No. 12865, National Bureau of Economic Research, Cambridge, MA, January 2007); Alan B. Krueger and Andreas Mueller, "Job Search and Unemployment Insurance: New Evidence from Time Use Data," *Journal of Public Economics* 94 (April 2010): 298–307.

19. Attila Lindner and Balázs Reizer, "Front-Loading the Unemployment Benefit: An Empirical Assessment," *American Economic Journal: Applied Economics* 12 (July 2020): 140–174; Johannes F. Schmieder, Till von Wachter, and Stefan Bender, "The Effects of Extended Unemployment Insurance over the Business Cycle: Evidence from Regression Discontinuity Estimates Over 20 Years," *Quarterly Journal of Economics* 127 (May 2012): 701–752; Kenneth Carling, Bertil Holmlund, and Altin Vejsiu, "Do Benefit Cuts Boost Job Finding? Swedish Evidence from the 1990s," *Economic Journal* 111 (October 2001): 766–790.

20. Lawrence Katz and Bruce Meyer, "Unemployment Insurance, Recall Expectations and Unemployment Outcomes," *Quarterly Journal of Economics* 105 (November 1990): 993–1002; Alan B. Krueger and Andreas I. Mueller, "Job Search, Emotional Well-Being and Job Finding in a Period of Mass Unemployment: Evidence from High-Frequency Longitudinal Data," *Brookings Papers on Economic Activity* 42 (Spring 2011): 1–81; Orley Ashenfelter, David Ashmore, and Olivier Deschenes, "Do Unemployment Insurance Recipients Actively Seek Work? Evidence from Randomized Trials in Four U.S. States," *Journal of Econometrics* 125 (March–April 2005): 53–75, reports findings that UI recipients *do* search for work while receiving benefits; thus, taking a job just as benefits are about to end may be mostly a function of reducing one's reservation wage at that time. For evidence that job-search requirements may speed up the exit from unemployment, see Jeff Borland and Yi-Ping Tseng, "Does a Minimum Job Search Requirement Reduce Time on Unemployment Payments? Evidence from the Jobseeker Diary in Australia," *Industrial and Labor Relations Review* 60 (April 2007): 357–378.

21. Henry S. Farber and Robert G. Valletta, "Do Extended Unemployment Benefits Lengthen Unemployment Spells? Evidence from Recent Cycles in the U.S. Labor Market," *Journal of Human Resources* 50 (Fall 2015): 873–909. For evidence from another country, see Rafael Lalive, Camille Landais, and Josef Zweimüller, "Market Externalities of Large Unemployment Insurance Extension Programs," *American Economic Review* 105 (December 2015): 3564–3596.

22. Kory Kroft and Matthew J. Notowidigdo, "Should Unemployment Insurance Vary with the Unemployment Rate? Theory and Evidence," *Review of Economic Studies* 83 (July 2016): 1092–1124; Farber and Valletta, "Do Extended Unemployment Benefits Lengthen Unemployment Spells? Evidence from Recent Cycles in the U.S. Labor Market";

Schmieder, von Wachter, and Bender, "The Effects of Extended Unemployment Insurance over the Business Cycle: Evidence from Regression Discontinuity Estimates Over 20 Years."

23. Christian Belzil, "Unemployment Insurance and Subsequent Job Duration: Job Matching Versus Unobserved Heterogeneity," *Journal of Applied Econometrics* 16 (September–October 2001): 619–636; Daniel H. Klepinger, Terry R. Johnson, and Jutta M. Joesch, "Effects of Unemployment Insurance Work-Search Requirements: The Maryland Experiment," *Industrial and Labor Relations Review* 56 (October 2002): 3–22; David Card, Raj Chetty, and Andrea Weber, "Cash-on-Hand and Competing Models of Intertemporal Behavior: New Evidence from the Labor Market," *Quarterly Journal of Economics* 122 (November 2007): 1511–1560; Sara LaLumia, "The EITC, Tax Refunds, and Unemployment Spells," *American Economic Journal: Economic Policy* 5 (May 2013): 188–221; Johannes F. Schmieder, Till von Wachter, and Stefan Bender, "The Effect of Unemployment Benefits and Nonemployment Durations on Wages," *American Economic Review* 106 (March 2016): 739–777; Ammar Farooq, Adriana D. Kugler, and Umberto Muratori, "Do Unemployment Insurance Benefits Improve Match Quality? Evidence from Recent U.S. Recessions" (Working Paper No. 27574, National Bureau of Economic Research, Cambridge, MA, July 2020).

24. Actually, this statement is not quite correct. As noted in Chapter 13, according to an analysis of the effects of unions using a similar model, *wait unemployment* may arise. That is, as long as the wage rate in market A exceeds the wage rate in market B, and unemployed workers in market A expect that normal job turnover will eventually create job vacancies in A, remaining attached to market A and waiting for a job offer in that sector might be profitable for them.

25. For a paper that measures the level of unemployment caused by a mismatch between the occupational skills required by employers who have job vacancies and those possessed by unemployed people, see Ayşegül Sahin, Joseph Song, Giorgio Topa, and Giovanni L. Violante, "Mismatch Unemployment," *American Economic Review* 104 (November 2014): 3529–3564.

26. For a study of interindustry mobility among those likely to be permanently displaced, with references to other related mobility studies, see Elisabetta Magnani, "Risk of Labor Displacement and Cross-Industry Labor Mobility," *Industrial and Labor Relations Review* 54 (April 2001): 593–610. For studies of whether difficulties in the housing market reduce the access to jobs among unemployed people, see Fredrik Andersson, John Haltiwanger, Mark Kutzbach, Henry Pollakowski, and Daniel Weinberg, "Job Displacement and the Duration of Joblessness: The Role of Spatial Mismatch" (Working Paper No. 20066, National Bureau of Economic Research, Cambridge, MA, April 2014); Henry S. Farber, "Unemployment in the Great Recession: Did the Housing Market Crisis Prevent the Unemployed from Moving to Take Jobs?"

American Economic Review: Papers and Proceedings 102 (May 2012): 520–525.

27. See Olivier Jean Blanchard and Lawrence F. Katz, "Regional Evolutions," *Brookings Papers on Economic Activity* (1992–1): 1–75.

28. One study found, however, that the changes in labor demand occur at a faster rate than changes in migration do, leading to a persistence of differences in unemployment rates across cities; see Michael Amior and Alan Manning, "The Persistence of Local Joblessness," *American Economic Review* 108 (July 2018): 1942–1970.

29. France, Germany, and Sweden, for example, spend from 0.36 percent to 0.14 percent of national income on government training programs for unemployed people, but the United States spends considerably less (0.03 percent). See Organisation for Economic Co-operation and Development, "Public Spending on Labour Markets: Training as a % of GDP," https://data.oecd.org/socialexp/public-spending-on-labour-markets.htm.

30. Organisation for Economic Co-operation and Development, "Chapter 2: Protecting Jobs, Enhancing Flexibility: A New Look at Employment Protection Legislation," in *2013 OECD Employment Outlook* (Paris: OECD, 2013).

31. Olivier Blanchard and Pedro Portugal, "What Hides Behind an Unemployment Rate: Comparing Portuguese and U.S. Labor Markets," *American Economic Review* 91 (March 2001): 187–207. Reviews of other studies on this topic can be found in the *2013 OECD Employment Outlook*, "Chapter 2: Protecting Jobs, Enhancing Flexibility: A New Look at Employment Protection Legislation."

32. Our argument here draws on, and abstracts from many of the complications discussed in, the articles in George Akerlof and Janet Yellen, eds., *Efficiency Wage Models of the Labor Market* (Cambridge: Cambridge University Press, 1986); Andrew Weiss, *Efficiency Wages: Models of Unemployment, Layoffs and Wage Dispersion* (Princeton, NJ: Princeton University Press, 1990).

33. Suppose that employees are *risk neutral* (i.e., they do not lose utility if their earnings *fluctuate* over time around some mean value). In equilibrium, they would move from the low-wage sector to the high-wage sector and remain as unemployed job seekers as long as the expected wage from choosing to wait exceeds the expected wage of searching for work while employed in the low-wage sector. Put algebraically, a worker who is unemployed will wait for a high-wage job if

$$P_e W_e > P_0 W_e + (1 - P_0) W_0$$

where W_e and W_0 are the wages in the high-wage sector and low-wage sector (respectively), P_e is the probability of finding a job paying W_e if one is unemployed, and P_0 is the probability of finding a high-wage job if one accepts employment in the low-wage sector. Presumably, P_e is greater than P_0 because individuals can search for work more intensively if they are not employed. The above inequality can be rewritten as

$$(P_e-P_0)W_e > W_0(1-P_0)$$

As we can see from this latter expression, whether one chooses wait unemployment depends on the increased probability of finding a high-wage job if unemployed $(P_e - P_0)$ and on the difference between W_e and W_0. The assumption that employees are risk neutral, however, is an aggressive one.

34. See David G. Blanchflower and Andrew J. Oswald, "An Introduction to the Wage Curve," *Journal of Economic Perspectives* 9 (Summer 1995): 153–167; David Card, "The Wage Curve: A Review," *Journal of Economic Literature* 33 (June 1995): 785–799; Lutz Bellmann and Uwe Blien, "Wage Curve Analyses of Establishment Data from Western Germany," *Industrial and Labor Relations Review* 54 (July 2001): 851–863. Also see Simon Jäger, Benjamin Schoefer, Samuel Young, and Josef Zweimüller, "Wages and the Value of Nonemployment," *The Quarterly Journal of Economics* 135:4 (November 2020): 1905–1963.

35. Edward Lazear and James Spletzer, "The United States Labor Market: Status Quo or a New Normal?" (Working Paper No. 18386, National Bureau of Economic Research, Cambridge, MA, September 2012). See Andreas Mueller, "Separations, Sorting, and Cyclical Unemployment," *American Economic Review* 107:7 (2017): 2081–2107, for more detail on cyclical unemployment using data from 1962–2012.

36. Evidence shows that about 40 percent of laid-off workers return to their previous employers. For articles on temporary layoffs and their implications for search behavior, see Shigeru Fujita and Giuseppe Moscarini, "Recall and Unemployment," *The American Economic Review* 107:12 (December 2017): 3875–3916; Arash Nekoei and Andrea Weber, "Recall Expectations and Duration Dependence," *American Economic Review Papers and Proceedings* 105 (May 2015): 142–146; Mark Aguiar, Erik Hurst, and Loukas Karabarbounis, "Time Use During the Great Recession," *American Economic Review* 103 (August 2013): 1664–1696.

37. Another factor contributing to unemployment during recessions is related to worker housing. Workers prefer to work closer to home, and home values can fall during a recession; the desire to work closer to home, and the difficulty of selling one's home both limit workers' search for jobs—and thus lengthen their spells of unemployment. See Alan Manning and Barbara Petrongolo, "How Local Are Labor Markets? Evidence from a Spatial Job Search Model," *American Economic Review* 107 (October 2017): 2877–2907; Jennifer Brown and David A. Matsa, "Locked in by Leverage: Job Search During the Housing Crisis," *Journal of Financial Economics* 136 (June 2020): 623–648.

38. Brad Hershbein and Lisa B. Kahn, "Do Recessions Accelerate Routine-Biased Technological Change? Evidence from Vacancy Postings," *American Economic Review* 108 (June 2018): 1737–1772.

39. Thomas Lemieux, W. Bentley MacLeod, and Daniel Parent, "Contract Form, Wage Flexibility, and Employment," *American Economic Review: Papers and Proceedings* 102 (May 2012): 526–531; Paul J. Devereux, "The Cyclicality of Real Wages Within Employer–Employee Matches," *Industrial and Labor Relations Review* 54 (July 2001): 835–850. For a study of real wage flexibility in the United Kingdom, see Paul J. Devereux and Robert A. Hart, "Real Wage Flexibility of Job Stayers, Within-Company Job Movers, and Between-Company Job Movers," *Industrial and Labor Relations Review* 60 (October 2006): 105–119.

40. For a review of several studies on nominal wage rigidity in the United States and elsewhere, see Michael W.L. Elsby and Gary Solon, "How Prevalent Is Downward Rigidity in Nominal Wages? International Evidence from Payroll Records and Pay Slips," *Journal of Economic Perspectives* 33 (summer 2019): 185–201.

41. Tomaz Cajner, Leland D. Crane, Ryan A. Decker, John Grigsby, Adrian Hamins-Puertolas, Erik Hurst, Christopher Kurz, and Ahu Yildirmaz, "The U.S. Labor Market During the Beginning of the Pandemic Recession" (Working Paper No. 27159, National Bureau of Economic Research, Cambridge, MA: August 2020).

42. Thomas Lemieux, W. Bentley MacLeod, and Daniel Parent, "Contract Form, Wage Flexibility, and Employment"; Harry J. Holzer and Edward B. Montgomery, "Asymmetries and Rigidities in Wage Adjustments by Firms," *Review of Economics and Statistics* 75 (August 1993): 397–408.

43. Of course, workers who "survive" layoffs also can suffer costs—including having to do the work left by those who were laid off.

44. See James Medoff, "Layoffs and Alternatives Under Trade Unions in United States Manufacturing," *American Economic Review* 69 (June 1979): 380–395, for evidence. This hypothesis suggests that unions are much more likely to bargain for wage reductions when projected layoffs exceed 50 percent of the union's membership. For evidence that this occurred in the early 1980s, see Robert J. Flanagan, "Wage Concessions and Long-Term Union Flexibility," *Brookings Papers on Economic Activity* (1984–1): 183–216.

45. Assar Lindbeck and Dennis J. Snower, "Insiders versus Outsiders," *Journal of Economic Perspectives* 15 (Winter 2001): 165–188.

46. See Truman F. Bewley, *Why Wages Don't Fall During a Recession* (Cambridge, MA: Harvard University Press, 1999); Weiss, *Efficiency Wages: Models of Unemployment, Layoffs and Wage Dispersion*; Wendy L. Rayack, "Fixed and Flexible Wages: Evidence from Panel Data," *Industrial and Labor Relations Review* 44 (January 1991): 288–298, presents empirical

evidence that the sensitivity of wages to unemployment is confined largely to workers whose job tenure is short; however, somewhat-different results were obtained by Mark Bils, Yongsung Chang, and Sun-Bin Kim, "Comparative Advantage in Cyclical Unemployment" (Working Paper No. 13231, National Bureau of Economic Research, Cambridge, MA, July 2007). For a study finding, for recent years, that rising layoffs are less important than slower rates of hire in causing unemployment during recessions, see Robert E. Hall, "Employment Efficiency and Sticky Wages: Evidence from Flows in the Labor Market," *Review of Economics and Statistics* 87 (August 2005): 397–407.

47. Shigeru Fujita and Giuseppe Moscarini, "Recall and Unemployment," *American Economic Review* 107 (December 2017): 3875–3916.

48. Keep reading to find more details on how the unemployment system in the United States is financed.

49. See, for example, Sanford Grossman, Oliver Hart, and Eric Maskin, "Unemployment with Observable Aggregate Shocks," *Journal of Political Economy* 91 (December 1983): 907–928; Sanford Grossman and Oliver Hart, "Implicit Contracts, Moral Hazard and Unemployment," *American Economic Review* 71 (May 1981): 301–307; Costas Azariadis, "Employment with Asymmetric Information," *Quarterly Journal of Economics* 98 (Supplement, 1983): 157–172; Daiji Kawaguchi and Fumio Ohtake, "Testing the Morale Theory of Nominal Wage Rigidity," *Industrial and Labor Relations Review* 61 (October 2007): 59–74.

50. This line of reasoning follows that in Costas Azariadis, "Implicit Contracts and Underemployment Equilibria," *Journal of Political Economy* 83 (December 1975): 1183–1202; Martin Baily, "Wages and Employment Under Uncertain Demand," *Review of Economic Studies* 41 (January 1974): 37–50.

51. See Alan S. Blinder, "The Challenge of High Unemployment," *American Economic Review* 78 (May 1988): 1–15.

52. See Robert M. Solow, *The Labor Market as an Institution* (Cambridge, MA: Basil Blackwell, 1990), chapter 2.

53. Recall from our discussion in Chapter 3 that this fact tells us nothing about who really bears the burden of the tax.

54. In actuality, the UI tax rate changes discretely (as a step function) over the range l_{min} to l_{max}, not continuously as drawn in Figure 14.7. For expository convenience, we ignore this complication.

55. Such a system of UI financing leads to interindustry subsidies, in which industries with almost no layoffs still must pay the minimum tax, and these industries subsidize industries (such as construction) that have high layoffs but pay only the maximum rate.

56. Patricia M. Anderson and Bruce D. Meyer, "The Effects of the Unemployment Insurance Payroll Tax on Wages, Employment, Claims, and

Denials," *Journal of Public Economics* 78 (October 2000): 81–106; Robert H. Topel, "Financing Unemployment Insurance: History, Incentives, and Reform," in *Unemployment Insurance: The Second Half-Century*, eds. W. Lee Hansen and James F. Byers (Madison: University of Wisconsin Press, 1990): 108–135.

57. Barry Chiswick, "The Effect of Unemployment Compensation on a Seasonal Industry: Agriculture," *Journal of Political Economy* 84 (June 1976): 591–602; Patricia M. Anderson, "Linear Adjustment Costs and Seasonal Labor Demand: Evidence from Retail Trade Firms," *Quarterly Journal of Economics* 108 (November 1993): 1015–1042; David Card and Phillip B. Levine, "Unemployment Insurance Taxes and the Cyclical and Seasonal Properties of Unemployment," *Journal of Public Economics* 53 (January 1994): 1–29.

58. The incidence of part-year work is much higher in the Canadian province of New Brunswick than it is across the border in the U.S. state of Maine, where unemployment benefits are much lower; see Kuhn and Riddell, "The Long-Term Effects of a Generous Income Support Program: Unemployment Insurance in New Brunswick and Maine, 1940–1991."

59. Enrico Moretti, "Do Wages Compensate for Risk of Unemployment? Parametric and Semi-parametric Evidence from Seasonal Jobs," *Journal of Risk and Uncertainty* 20 (January 2000): 45–66. Also see Susan Averett, Howard Bodenhorn, and Justas Staisiunas, "Unemployment Risk and Compensating Differentials in Late-Nineteenth Century New Jersey Manufacturing," *Economic Inquiry* 43 (October 2005): 734–749.

60. James Tobin, "Inflation and Unemployment," *American Economic Review* 62 (March 1972): 1–18; John Haltiwanger, "The Natural Rate of Unemployment," in *The New Palgrave*, eds. J. Eatwell, M. Milgate, and P. Newman (New York: Stockton Press, 1987): 610–612.

61. Data are from U.S. Department of Labor, *Employment and Earnings*; for the most recent data, see the source information for Table 14.4. For an analysis of the racial gap in unemployment rates, see Robert W. Fairlie and William A. Sundstrom, "The Emergence, Persistence, and Recent Widening of the Racial Unemployment Gap," *Industrial and Labor Relations Review* 52 (January 1999): 252–270.

62. Mary C. Daly, Bart Hobijn, Ayşegül Şahin, and Robert Valletta, "A Search and Matching Approach to Labor Markets: Did the Natural Rate of Unemployment Rise?" *Journal of Economic Perspectives* 26 (Summer 2012): 3–26; George A. Akerlof, William T. Dickens, and George L. Perry, "Near-Rational Wage and Price Setting and the Long-Run Phillips Curve," *Brookings Papers on Economic Activity* (2000-1): 1–44; Laurence Ball and N. Gregory Mankiw, "The NAIRU in Theory and Practice," *Journal of Economic Perspectives* 16 (Fall 2002): 115–136; U.S. Congressional Budget Office, "Natural

Rate of Unemployment (Long-Term)," retrieved from FRED, Federal Reserve Bank of St. Louis; https://fred.stlouisfed.org/series/NROU, September 1, 2016; Peter Hooper, Frederic S. Mishkin, and Amir Sufi, "Prospects for Inflation in a High Pressure Economy: Is the Phillips Curve Dead or Is It Just Hibernating?" *Research in Economics* 74 (March 2020): 26–62.

63. Amanda Bennett, "Business and Academia Clash over a Concept: 'Natural' Jobless Rate," *Wall Street Journal*, January 24, 1995, A8.

64. Arthur Okun, "Potential GNP: Its Measurement and Significance," reprinted in *The Political Economy of Prosperity*, ed. Arthur Okun (Washington, DC: Brookings Institution, 1970); Clifford L.F. Attfield and Brian Silverstone, "Okun's Coefficient: A Comment," *Review of Economics and Statistics* 79 (May 1997): 326–329; Brent Meyer and Murat Tasci, "An Unstable Okun's Law, Not the Best Rule of Thumb," *Economic Commentary*, no. 2012–08 (Federal Reserve Bank of Cleveland, June 7, 2012).

65. Bruno Crépon, Esther Duflo, Marc Gurgand, Roland Rathelot, and Phillippe Zamora, "Do Labor Market Policies Have Displacement Effects? Evidence from a Clustered Randomized Experiment," *Quarterly Journal of Economics* 128 (May 2013): 531–580; Dayanand S. Manoli, Marios Michaelides, and Ankur Patel, "Long-Term Effects of Job-Search Assistance: Experimental Evidence Using Administrative Tax Data" (Working Paper No. 24422, National Bureau of Economic Research, Cambridge, MA, March 2018).

66. Alan B. Krueger, "How Tight Is the Labor Market?" (National Bureau of Economic Research 2015 Martin Feldstein Lecture, NBER Reporter, Cambridge, MA, 2015, No. 3).

Selected Readings

Atkinson, Anthony, and John Micklewright. "Unemployment Compensation and Labor Market Transitions: A Critical Review." *Journal of Economic Literature* 29 (December 1991): 1679–1727.

Blanchflower, David G., and Andrew J. Oswald. *The Wage Curve*. Cambridge, MA: MIT Press, 1994.

Blank, Rebecca M., ed. *Social Protection Versus Economic Flexibility: Is There a Tradeoff?* Chicago, IL: University of Chicago Press, 1994.

Elsby, Michael W.L., Ryan Michaels, and David Ratner. "The Beveridge Curve: A Survey." *Journal of Economic Literature* 53 (September 2015): 571–630.

Freeman, Richard, and Harry Holzer, eds. *The Black Youth Unemployment Crisis.* Chicago, IL: University of Chicago Press, 1986.

Lang, Kevin, and Jonathan Leonard, eds. *Unemployment and the Structure of Labor Markets.* New York: Basil Blackwell, 1987.

Meyer, Bruce D. "Lessons from the U.S. Unemployment Insurance Experiments." *Journal of Economic Literature* 33 (March 1995): 91–131.

Reducing Unemployment: Current Issues and Policy Options. Kansas City, MO: Federal Reserve Bank of Kansas City, 1994.

Wilson, William Julius. *When Work Disappears: The World of the New Urban Planner.* New York: Alfred A. Knopf, 1996.

Inequality in Earnings

Workers as individuals, and society as a whole, are concerned with both the *level* and the *dispersion* of income in the economy. The level of income, obviously, determines the consumption of goods and services that individuals find possible to enjoy. Concerns about the distribution of income stem from the importance that we, as individuals, place on our relative standing in society and the importance that our society, as a collective, places on equity.

For purposes of assessing issues of poverty and relative consumption opportunities, the distribution of *family incomes* is of interest.[1] An examination of family incomes, however, involves an analysis of unearned income and earned income; thus, it must incorporate discussions of inheritance, investment returns, government transfers, and tax policies. It must also consider family size and how families are defined, formed, and dissolved. Many of these topics are beyond the scope of labor economics.

Consistent with our examination of the labor market, the focus of this chapter is on the distribution of *earnings*. Although clearly only part of overall income, earnings are a reflection of marginal productivity; the investment in (and returns to) education, training, and migration activities; and the access to opportunities. This chapter begins with a discussion of how to conceptualize and measure the equality or inequality of earnings. We then describe how the earnings distribution in the United States has changed since 1980, by using published data readily accessible to students. Finally, we analyze the basic forces that economists believe underlie these changes in earnings inequality.

Measuring Inequality

To understand certain basic concepts related to the distribution of earnings,[2] we should think in graphic terms. Consider a simple plotting of the number of people receiving each given level of earnings. If everyone had the same earnings, say $40,000 per year, no dispersion would exist. The graph of the earnings distribution would look like that in Figure 15.1.

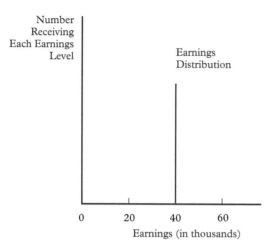

Figure 15.1 Earnings Distribution With Perfect Equality

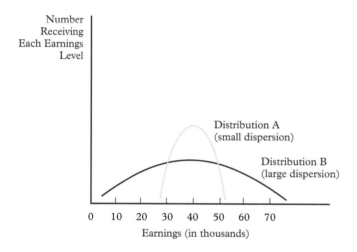

Figure 15.2 Distributions of Earnings With Different Degrees of Dispersion

If disparities existed in the earnings that people received, these disparities could be relatively large or relatively small. If the average level of earnings were $40,000 and almost all people received earnings close to the average, the *dispersion* of earnings would be small. If the average were $40,000 but some made much more and some much less, the dispersion of earnings would be large. Figure 15.2 illustrates two hypothetical earnings distributions. Although both distributions are centered on the same average level ($40,000), distribution A exhibits smaller dispersion than distribution B. Earnings in B are more widely dispersed and thus exhibit *a greater degree of inequality*.[3]

Graphs can help illustrate the concepts of dispersion, but they are a clumsy tool for *measuring* inequality. Various quantitative indicators of earnings inequality can be devised, and they all vary in ease of computation, ease of comprehension, and their accuracy in representing the socially relevant dimensions of inequality.

The most obvious measure of inequality is the *variance* of the distribution. Variance is a common measure of dispersion, calculated as follows:

$$Variance = \frac{\sum_i (E_i - \overline{E})^2}{n} \tag{15.1}$$

where E_i represents the earnings of person i in the population, n represents the number of people in the population, $\overline{E}$ is the mean level of earnings in the population, and Σ indicates that we are summing all persons in the population. One problem with using the variance, however, is that it tends to rise as earnings grow larger. For example, if all earnings in the population were to double, such that the ratio of each person's earnings to the mean (or to the earnings of anyone else for that matter) remained constant, the variance would quadruple. Variance is thus a better measure of the absolute than of the *relative* dispersion of earnings.

An alternative to the variance is the *coefficient of variation*: the square root of the variance (called the *standard deviation*) divided by the mean. If all earnings were to double, the coefficient of variation, unlike the variance, would remain unchanged. Because we must have access to the underlying data on each individual's earnings in order to calculate the coefficient of variation (or, for that matter, the variance), however, constructing it from published data is impractical. Unless the coefficient of variation is itself *published*, or unless the researcher has access to the *entire* data set, other, more-readily constructed measures must be found.

The most widely used measures of earnings inequality start with ranking the population by earnings level and by establishing into which percentile a given level of earnings falls. For example, in the United States in 2018, men between the ages of 25 and 64 with earnings of $51,741 were at the *median* (50th percentile), meaning that half of all men earned less and half earned more. Men with earnings of $27,443 were at the 20th percentile of the earnings distribution (20 percent earned less; 80 percent earned more). And men with earnings of $95,883 were at the 80th percentile.

Having determined the earnings levels associated with each percentile, we can either compare the earnings *levels* associated with given percentiles or compare the *share* of total earnings received by each. Comparing shares of total *income* received by the top fifth and bottom fifth (or "quintiles") of households in the population is a widely used measure of *income* inequality. Using this measure, we find, for example, that in 2018, households in the top fifth of the income distribution received 52 percent of all income, while those in the bottom fifth received 3.1 percent.[4]

Unfortunately, information on *shares* received by each segment of the distribution is not as readily available for individual *earnings* as it is for family income. Comparing the earnings *level* associated with each percentile is readily feasible, however. A commonly used measure of this sort is the ratio of earnings at, say, the 80th percentile to earnings at the 20th. Ratios such as this are intended to indicate how far apart the two ends of the earnings distribution are, and as a measure of dispersion, they are easily understood and readily computed.

How useful is the knowledge that in 2018, for example, men at the 80th percentile of the earnings distribution earned 3.49 times more than men at the 20th? In truth, the ratio in a given year is not enlightening unless it is *compared* with something. One natural comparison is with ratios for previous years. An increase in these ratios over time, for example, would indicate that the earnings distribution was becoming stretched, such that the distance between the two ends was growing and earnings were becoming more unequally distributed.

As a rough measure of increasing distance between the two ends of the earnings distribution, the ratio of earnings at the 80th and 20th percentiles is satisfactory; however, this simple ratio is by no means a complete description of inequality. Its focus on earnings at two arbitrarily chosen points in the distribution ignores what happens on either side of the chosen percentiles. For example, if earnings at the 10th percentile fell and those at the 20th percentile rose, while all other earnings remained constant, this ratio would decline even though the lowest end of the distribution had moved down. Likewise, if earnings at the 20th and 80th percentiles were to remain the same but earnings in between were to become much more similar, this step toward greater overall earnings equality would not be captured by the simple 80:20 ratio. In the next section, we will examine trends in ratios at other points in the earnings distribution (e.g., 80:50 or 50:10) to more closely examine distributional changes over the past four decades.

These drawbacks notwithstanding, we present in the next section descriptive data on changes in earnings inequality that are based on comparisons of earnings levels at the 80th and 20th percentiles of the distribution. Although these measures are crude, they indicate that, generally speaking, earnings became more unequal after 1980.

Earnings Inequality Since 1980: Some Descriptive Data

Table 15.1 displays changes in earnings inequality from 1980 to 2018 for men and women between the ages of 25 and 64 and uses the 80:20 ratio discussed earlier. Among men, earnings at the 80th percentile were constant (in 2018 dollars) from 1980 to 1990, but earnings at the 20th percentile fell during that period. The result was a big jump in the 80:20 ratio, from 3.08 to 3.52. From 1990 to 2005, earnings at both percentiles rose modestly, and the 80:20 ratio fell a bit. Since 2005, small increases in real earnings have occurred at both percentiles, but the percentage increases have been greater at the upper end; thus, the 80:20 ratio rose back to its level in 1990 (from 3.41 in 2005 to 3.49 in 2018).[5]

Although earnings at the 20th percentile for women are so low that they are likely to be received by those working part time (e.g., in 2018, roughly 29 percent of employed women worked part time), the overall changes in

Table 15.1 The Dispersion of Earnings by Gender, Ages 25–64, 1980–2018 (Expressed in 2018 Dollars)

Earnings at

	80th percentile (a)	20th percentile (b)	Ratio: (a)/(b)
	Men		
1980	87,122	28,329	3.08
1990	87,166	24,787	3.52
2005	91,580	26,822	3.41
2018	95,883	27,443	3.49
	Women		
1980	46,498	12,558	3.70
1990	52,696	11,468	4.60
2005	61,971	15,718	3.94
2018	70,000	19,999	3.50

Sources: U.S. Bureau of the Census, *Money Incomes of Households, Families, and Persons in the United States*, Series P-60: no. 132 (1980), Table 54; no. 174 (1990), Table 29; U.S. Bureau of the Census, http://pubdb3.census.gov/macro/032006/perinc/new03_000.htm (2005), www.census.gov/data/tables/time-series/demo/income-poverty/cps-pinc/pinc-03.html (2018)

inequality were similar to those for men from 1980 to 2005. Inequality rose during the 1980s, driven by earnings increases at the 80th percentile and earnings decreases at the 20th percentile. After 1990, inequality decreased, as earnings at the 20th percentile rose relatively rapidly. Unlike the 80:20 ratio among men, however, the 80:20 ratio among women continued to fall after 2005, and it now stands (at 3.50) below what it was in 1980.

As discussed earlier, the 80:20 ratio does not tell the complete story about the growth in inequality. Specifically, the two points in the earnings distribution are arbitrarily chosen, and the ratio of earnings at these points does not capture what is happening both between these two percentiles and beyond them (i.e., in the middle of the distribution and at either end). Table 15.2 provides a more detailed look at changes in earnings inequality from 1980 to 2018, by focusing on two aspects of change in inequality.

First, we want to know whether the changes in the upper end of the earnings distribution and the changes in the lower end are roughly similar; in other words, are *both* halves of the earnings distribution becoming more stretched? One way to obtain some insight into this question is to calculate the 80:50 and 50:20 ratios; both ratios indicate how earnings at the upper end (80th percentile) and lower end (20th percentile) are changing over time compared to the median (50th percentile). When we inspect the first three rows for both men and women in Table 15.2, we can clearly see that inequality in both halves grew during the 1980s, but we can also see that

Table 15.2 Earnings Ratios at Various Percentiles of the Earnings Distribution—1980, 1990, 2005, 2018

Ratio of earnings at given percentiles	1980	1990	2005	2018
Men				
80:20 (see Table 15.1)	3.08	3.52	3.41	3.49
80:50	1.53	1.74	1.77	1.85
50:20	2.01	2.03	1.93	1.89
Women				
80:20 (see Table 15.1)	3.70	4.60	3.94	3.50
80:50	1.66	1.79	1.78	1.83
50:20	2.24	2.57	2.22	1.91
Men				
90:10	4.68	7.31	7.97	*
90:50	1.87	2.14	2.49	*
50:10	2.50	3.41	3.20	2.70
Women				
90:10	9.12	13.88	9.74	8.47
90:50	2.07	2.27	2.34	2.45
50:10	4.41	6.12	4.16	3.45

*Because published earnings at the 90th percentile fell into an "open" range ("$100,000 and above"), we could not observe earnings at this percentile.

Sources: U.S. Bureau of the Census, *Money Incomes of Households, Families, and Persons in the United States*, Series P-60: no. 132 (1980), Table 54; no. 174 (1990), Table 29; U.S. Bureau of the Census, http://pubdb3.census.gov/macro/032006/perinc/new03_000.htm (2005), www.census.gov/data/tables/time-series/demo/income-poverty/cps-pinc/pinc-03.html (2018)

between 1990 and 2005, inequality in the upper half remained more or less constant, whereas it *became smaller* in the lower half. After 2005, earnings inequality among both women and men resumed growth in the upper half of their distributions and continued to fall in the lower half. The net effect was a modest rise in inequality among men and a marked fall in inequality among women (the 80:20 ratio of 3.50 for women in 2018 is smaller than it was in 1980).

Second, we might ask what was happening to earnings in each *tail* of the earnings distribution over this period. The 90:10 ratio represents a measure of inequality that focuses on the top 10 percent and the bottom 10 percent of the earnings distribution, and it can therefore shed light on changes beyond the 80:20 boundaries. Table 15.2 also contains (in the shaded rows) the 90:10 earnings ratio and its two components (90:50 and 50:10).

For the period from 1980 to 1990, the 90:10 ratios (and their upper and lower components) tell the same story for men and women as did the 80:20 ratios; that is, earnings inequality clearly grew among both men and women during the 1980s, and it grew in both halves of the earnings distribution. However, whereas increases in the 90:50 and 80:50 ratios are roughly comparable, the 50:10 ratios increase much more markedly than the 50:20 ratios over the 1980s—indicating that the drop in relative earnings at the bottom of the earnings distribution was especially pronounced.

After 1990, the 90:10 ratio fell for women but—unlike the 80:20 ratio—continued to rise for men (at least until 2005—after which earnings at the 90th percentile can no longer be gleaned from the published data we are using). In the lower half of the distribution, the 50:10 ratios (like the 50:20 ratios) for both men and women were lower in 2018 than in 1990, indicating that earnings in the lower half of the earnings distribution became more equal during that period. The larger decline in the 50:10 ratio than in the 50:20 ratio indicates that earnings at the bottom of the distribution have been rising relatively quickly since 1990. In the upper half of the earnings distribution, the 90:50 ratios for both men and women rose more after 1990 than did the 80:50 ratios. Clearly, then, both men and women at the highest levels of earnings continued to experience increases (relative to the median) after 1990—increases that were not shared by those only slightly below them in the distribution.

To summarize, the tables reviewed earlier suggest the following major changes in earnings inequality since 1980:

1. An unambiguous increase occurred in inequality during the 1980s, where earnings in both the upper and lower halves of the earnings distribution became more dispersed.

2. During the 1980s, an especially pronounced fall in relative earnings occurred at the bottom of the distribution (lowest 10th percentile), indicating downward pressures on the earnings of the lowest-skilled workers.

3. From 1990 to 2018, earnings became less dispersed in the lower half of the earnings distribution, as earnings at the bottom increased relative to the median—especially among women.

4. Since 1990, earnings at the 90th percentile for both women and men have pulled farther away from the median than have earnings at the 80th percentile[6]—which indicates continued increases in relative earnings at the top of the earnings distribution.

(See Example 15.1 for an overall comparison of the level of earnings inequality across selected developed countries.)

EXAMPLE 15.1

Differences in Earnings Inequality Across Developed Countries

The United States stands out from other developed countries in its much higher *level* of earnings inequality. What follows are the 90:10 ratios for several developed countries in 2018 (the earnings distributions these ratios characterize are different from those presented in this text, because they combine both men and women):

Country	90:10 Ratios in 2018
Sweden	2.14
Norway	2.51
Japan	2.82
Netherlands	3.02 (for 2014)
Australia	3.13
Germany	3.33
Canada	3.42
United Kingdom	3.42
United States	4.95

One reason for greater inequality in the United States may lie in the greater *dispersion of skills* among U.S. workers. Countries that have workers among whom skills are vastly different will naturally have earnings disparities that reflect those differences. One study proposed that a way to measure skill level is to examine scores in "quantitative literacy" on the International Adult Literacy Survey. This study found that scores on this test varied most among workers in the United States and least (among the countries listed earlier) in the Scandinavian countries, Germany, and the Netherlands—and Canada and Australia were in the middle. The study found that the statistical correlation between the dispersion in test scores and the dispersion in earnings was strong. This finding illustrates one significant outcome of the relatively poor performance of U.S. high school students on achievement tests, which was noted in Chapter 9.

Sources: Organisation for Economic Co-operation and Development, OECD.Stat, "Decile Ratios of Gross Earnings," at stats.oecd.org/Index.aspx?DataSetCode=DEC_I; Stephen Nickell, "Is the U.S. Labor Market Really that Exceptional?: A Review of Richard Freeman's *America Works: The Exceptional U.S. Labor Market*," *Journal of Economic Literature* 46 (June 2008): 384–395

Changes in the distribution of earnings since 1980 have generally occurred along two dimensions. One is the increased returns of investments in higher education, which have raised the relative earnings of those at the top of the distribution (those with higher levels of human capital). The other dimension is the growth in earnings disparities *within* human-capital groups, which stretches out the earnings at both the higher end and the lower end of the distribution. In the next two sections, we discuss changes in these two dimensions.

The Increased Returns of Higher Education

To illustrate the rising returns of higher education, let us focus first on male workers between the ages of 35 and 44 who are working full time. As can be seen in the upper panel of Table 15.3, the real earnings of men in this age group with a college or graduate school education are higher than they were in 1980, whereas those with a high school education or less have experienced decreases in real earnings. The earnings advantages of acquiring a bachelor's degree or a graduate degree (as seen by the earnings ratios) are higher in recent years than in 1980, although they have not risen since 2005 (and the bachelor's ratio has fallen a bit). The earnings advantages of obtaining a high school degree (as opposed to dropping out) did not change much from 1980 to 2005 but have fallen since 2005.

The rising returns to investing in a bachelor's degree or a graduate degree are also observed for women, although the underlying changes within each level of education are different. The real earnings of women with high school degrees actually rose in the 1980s, both absolutely and relative to those of dropouts, but because the earnings for those with bachelor's and graduate degrees rose even more, the increased returns of higher education parallel those for men. Increases for women in the earnings advantages of obtaining a bachelor's or graduate degree are similar to those for men, and the largest increases came before 2005. As with men, the graduate degree ratio has remained constant since 2005, but unlike for men, the bachelor's ratio for women has continued to rise.

(Chapter 9 pointed out that the rising returns of higher education should call forth an increase in university students and an eventual rightward shift in the supply curve of college-educated people. Rightward supply-curve shifts tend to moderate the wages commanded by college-educated people, so the fact that their earnings advantages increased between 1980 and 2005 suggests that the rightward shifts in supply were smaller than the rightward shifts in demand during this period.[7] As seen in Example 15.2, important changes in office technology, which increased the demand for better-educated workers, were introduced in the early 1900s, but during that period, the supply response was such that the returns to education actually fell.)

Table 15.3 Mean Earnings and the Returns to Education among Full-Time, Year-Round Workers, Ages of 35 and 44 (Expressed in 2018 Dollars)

	Earnings				Earnings ratios		
	Dropout ($)	H.S. grad ($)	Bachelor's ($)	Grad school[a] ($)	H.S./ dropout	Bachelor's/ H.S.	Grad/ bachelor's
Men							
1980	44,910	62,661	88,297	100,866	1.40	1.41	1.14
1990	39,516	55,798	91,389	112,869	1.41	1.64	1.24
2005	37,756	54,363	103,761	142,343	1.44	1.91	1.37
2018	41,453	53,291	97,145	133,085	1.29	1.82	1.37
Women							
1980	27,787	35,916	48,930	57,174	1.29	1.36	1.17
1990	27,673	38,341	60,985	72,491	1.39	1.59	1.19
2005	26,122	37,806	70,091	91,656	1.45	1.85	1.31
2018	26,833	37,667	75,145	98,855	1.40	1.99	1.32

Sources: U.S. Bureau of the Census, *Money Income of Households, Families, and Persons in the United States*, Series P-60: no. 132 (1980), Table 52; no. 174 (1990), Table 30; U.S. Bureau of the Census website: http://pubdb3.census.gov/macro/032006/perinc/new03_190.htm and http://pubdb3.census.gov/macro/032006/perinc/new03_316.htm (2005), www.census.gov/data/tables/time-series/demo/income-poverty/cps-pinc/pinc-03.html (2018)

EXAMPLE 15.2

Changes in the Premium to Education at the Beginning of the Twentieth Century

Although the premium to education has recently risen and is currently relatively high, the premium appears to have been even higher at the beginning of the twentieth century. However, the premium did not stay high for too long, because despite increasing demand for educated workers, the *supply* increased at an even-more-rapid rate. In 1914, office workers, whose positions generally required a high school diploma, earned considerably more than less-educated manual workers. Female office workers earned 107 percent more than female production workers. Male office workers earned 70 percent more than male production workers. This premium fell rapidly during World War I and the early 1920s, such that by 1923, the high school premium was only 41 percent for women and merely 10 percent for men. These rates drifted just a little higher during the remainder of the 1920s and 1930s.

What makes these dramatically falling premiums for a high school degree so surprising is that changes in the economy were increasing the relative demand for these workers. New office machines (such as improved typewriters, adding machines, address machines, dictation machines, and mimeo machines) lowered the cost of information technology and increased the demand for a complementary factor of production: high school–educated office workers. In the two decades after 1910, office employment's share of total employment in the United States rose by 47 percent.

Counteracting this demand shift, however, was an even-more-substantial shift in the supply of high school graduates, as high schools opened up to the masses throughout much of the country. Between 1910 and 1920, for example, high school enrollment rates climbed from 25 percent to 43 percent in New England and from 29 percent to 60 percent in the Pacific region. During the 1920s, the internal combustion engine, paved roads, and consolidated school districts brought secondary education to rural areas for the first time. Within cities, schools moved away from offering only college preparatory courses and attracted more students. From 1910 to 1930, the share of the labor force made up of high school graduates increased by almost 130 percent.

Thus, relative growth in the demand for better-educated workers was similar in the early and late decades of the twentieth century, but changes in the premiums for education diverged. As emphasized throughout this text, supply *and* demand are important in understanding wages.

Sources: Claudia Goldin and Lawrence F. Katz, "The Decline of Non-Competing Groups: Changes in the Premium to Education, 1890–1940" (Working Paper No. 5202, National Bureau of Economic Research, August 1995); David Autor, Claudia Goldin, and Lawrence F. Katz, "Extending the Race between Education and Technology," *American Economic Association: Papers and Proceedings* 110 (May 2020): 347–351.

Growth of Earnings Dispersion in Human-Capital Groups

While one factor in the growing diversity of earnings is the enlarged gap between the average pay of more-educated and less-educated workers, another possible dimension of growing inequality is that earnings *within* narrowly defined human-capital groups has become more dispersed. To understand how within-group inequality affects *overall* measures of inequality, suppose that those at the top of the earnings distribution are older workers with college educations, whereas those at the bottom are younger workers who dropped out of high school. If earnings *within* each group become more dispersed, some in the top earning group will become even better paid, and some in the least-skilled group would have even lower wages; the end result would be an increase in the *overall* 80:20 or 90:10 ratio.

To get a sense of trends in earnings differences in human-capital groups, Table 15.4 divides men who worked full time into six such groups, defined by age and education. The table displays the earnings ratios of those at the 80th percentile to those at the 20th percentile inside of each human-capital group from 1994 to 2018.[8] Earnings disparities among high school graduates show no clear pattern, where the younger two cohorts exhibit less disparity in 2018 than in 1994, while disparities grew in the oldest cohort. From 1994 to 2004, among college graduates, however, earnings disparities grew in each age group. Our data cannot pin down changes for the two older cohorts of college graduates after 2004, but a recent paper

Table 15.4 Ratio of Earnings at the 80th to 20th Percentiles for Men Who Work Full Time, by Age and Education, 1994–2018

	1994	**2004**	**2018**
Male bachelor's graduates			
Ages 25–34	2.23	2.35	2.32
Ages 35–44	2.67	2.72	*
Ages 45–54	2.57	2.69	*
Male high school graduates			
Ages 25–34	2.52	2.39	2.26
Ages 35–44	2.67	2.40	2.49
Ages 45–54	2.13	2.37	2.43

* Because published earnings at the top of the earnings distribution fell into an "open" range ($100,000 and above), earnings at the 80th percentile could not be observed.

Sources: U.S. Bureau of the Census, Current Population Survey Tables for Personal Income, PINC-03: www.census.gov/data/tables/time-series/demo/income-poverty/cps-pinc/pinc-03.1994.html   (1994); www.census.gov/data/tables/time-series/demo/income-poverty/cps-pinc/pinc-03.2004.html   (2004); www.census.gov/data/tables/time-series/demo/income-poverty/cps-pinc/pinc-03.2014.html (2018)

suggests that growing wage disparities within the college-educated groups have played a major role in rising inequality in earnings above the median.[9] The apparent growth of within-group earnings disparities' being concentrated among college-educated people, which is indicated by the data in Table 15.4, is consistent with findings from studies that use more-detailed data on earnings inequality.[10]

The Underlying Causes of Growing Inequality

The major phenomenon that we must explain is the widening gap between the wages of highly educated and less-educated workers, and our basic economic model suggests three possible causes. First, the *supply* of less-educated workers might have risen faster than the supply of college graduates, driving down the relative wages of less-skilled workers. Second, the demand for better-educated workers might have increased relative to the demand for less-educated workers. Finally, changes in *institutional* forces, such as the minimum wage or the decline in labor unions, might have reduced the relative wages of less-educated workers. We discuss these possibilities here.

Changes in Supply

In reality, shifts in supply and demand curves, and even changes in the influence of institutions, occur both simultaneously and continually. Sophisticated statistical studies can often sort through the possible influences underlying a change and estimate the separate contributions of each. For the

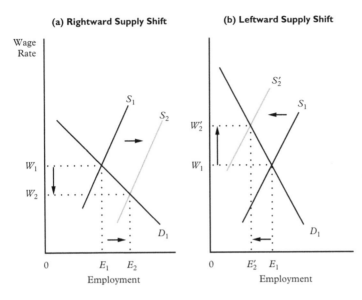

Figure 15.3 Changes in Supply as the Dominant Cause of Wage Changes

most part, however, the details of these studies are beyond the scope of this text; instead, our focus will be on identifying the *dominant* forces behind the growth of wage inequality in recent years.

For the market-clearing wage rate of a particular group of workers to be reduced primarily by a shift in supply, that shift must be rightward and therefore accompanied by an increase in employment; see panel (a) of Figure 15.3 for a graphic illustration. Conversely, if a leftward shift in the supply curve is the dominant cause of a wage increase, this wage increase will be accompanied by a decrease in the market-clearing level of employment; see panel (b) of Figure 15.3. Other things being equal, the larger these shifts are, the larger will be the effects on the equilibrium wage.

The major phenomenon that we are trying to explain is the increasing gap between the wages of highly educated workers and those of less-educated workers. If *supply* shifts are primarily responsible, we should observe that the employment of less-educated workers *increased* relative to the employment of the college-educated workforce. Table 15.5 contains data indicating that supply shifts could *not* have been the primary cause. When we compare the employment shares of those whose relative earnings rose after 1980 (rows A to D) to the employment shares of those whose earnings fell (rows E to H), we see that earnings and employment increases were *positively* correlated. The groups that experienced increases in their relative earnings also experienced more-rapid employment growth, and the groups whose earnings fell also experienced falling shares of employment. Thus, shifts in supply cannot be the dominant explanation for the growing returns to education.[11]

To say that shifts in supply were not the *dominant* influence underlying the increased returns of education is not to say, of course, that they had no effect at all. We saw in Chapter 10 that immigration to the United States

Table 15.5 Employment Shares (Within Gender) of Educational Groups, Workers 25 and Older—1980, 1990, 2005, 2018

Groups whose relative earnings rose	1980	1990	2005	2018
A. Men with graduate degree (%)	9.1	10.5	11.6	14.2
B. Men with bachelor's degree (%)	11.4	14.0	20.5	24.5
C. Women with graduate degree (%)	5.7	8.2	11.1	17.5
D. Women with bachelor's degree (%)	10.3	13.9	21.8	27.0
Groups whose relative earnings fell				
E. Men with high school degree (%)	38.2	38.1	30.8	27.8
F. Male dropouts (%)	22.7	16.3	11.6	8.3
G. Women with high school degree (%)	46.4	42.1	28.6	22.2
H. Female dropouts (%)	17.8	12.2	7.8	5.3

Sources: U.S. Bureau of the Census, *Money Income of Households, Families, and Individuals in the United States*, Series P-60: no. 132 (1980), Table 52; no. 174 (1990), Table 30; U.S. Bureau of the Census, http://pubdb3.census.gov/macro/032006/perinc/new03_127.htm, http://pubdb3.census.gov/macro/032006/perinc/new03_253.htm (2005), and www.census.gov/data/tables/time-series/demo/income-poverty/pinc-04.html (2018)

rose during the period and that it was especially heavy among lower-skilled, less-educated workers—those groups whose relative earnings fell most during that period. Although the presence of low-skilled immigrants can increase overall earnings inequality, most research on the effects of low-skilled immigration to the United States suggests that it has had little effect on either native-born workers' wages or the wage distribution.[12]

Changes in Demand: Technological Change

The fact that human-capital groups whose earnings were experiencing faster growth also experienced relative gains in employment suggests that shifts in labor *demand* curves have been a prominent factor raising inequality since 1980. Rightward shifts in the labor demand curve will, other things being equal, result in both increased wages and increased employment, whereas leftward shifts will reduce both wages and employment. Thus, the data in Table 15.5 are consistent with a rightward shift in the demand for workers with a university education and a leftward shift in the demand for workers with a high school education or less.

Technological Change and Skill Level Economists generally agree that one phenomenon underlying these shifts in labor demand is "skill-biased technological change"—technological change that increased the productivity of high-skilled workers and reduced the need for lower-skilled workers. Employers in almost every industry adopted systems that relied on the digitalization of many functions; some of these systems replaced manual (production-worker) tasks, and some replaced cognitive (office-worker) tasks. High-tech investments—in robots, automated measuring devices, data management systems, word processing, and communications networks, for example—far outstripped conventional forms of mechanization, such as larger or faster machines. The percentage of workers using computers in their jobs rose from 25 percent in 1984, to 37 percent in 1989, and to 47 percent in 1993,[13] and by 2016, over 70 percent of U.S. workers were in jobs requiring high (23 percent) or medium (47.5 percent) digital knowledge.[14] We have good reasons to suspect that, generally speaking, the computerization of many processes tended to increase the demand for high-skilled workers and reduced the demand for others. (See Example 15.3 for a brief discussion of whether future technological change will have the same effects on the labor market as the skill-biased change that we have experienced to date.)

EXAMPLE 15.3

Will Machine Learning Increase Earnings Inequality?

Machine learning involves the building of computer programs that analyze data, learn from that data, and then apply this learning to make informed decisions. For example, a machine-learning program is used to predict which new songs or artists a particular music-streaming listener will prefer. Machine learning also is used in facial-recognition and speech-recognition tasks, in self-driving cars, in tracking down digital malware, and in using data to make various predictions useful to marketing professionals. As computing power grows, so does our ability to access and analyze large data sets, so machine learning may represent the next frontier of technological change.

To say a task is suitable for machine learning means that the task's output can be measured so well that a machine can use the data fed into it to improve that output. One study that examined over 18,000 tasks performed in 964 occupations estimated that most occupations involve at least some tasks that are suitable for machine learning, but in few of these occupations are *all* tasks suitable for such learning. It also found correlation between an occupation's wage rate and the share of its tasks suitable for machine learning. The study concluded, therefore, that the introduction of more machine learning may not have the same effect on earnings inequality as has the skill-biased technological change in recent decades, which eliminated many occupations that had routine tasks.

Source: Erik Brynjolfsson, Tom Mitchell, and Daniel Rock, "What Can Machines Learn and What Does It Mean for Occupations and the Economy?" *American Economic Association Papers and Proceedings* 108 (May 2018): 43–47

As noted in Chapter 4, technological change is equivalent to a decrease in the price of capital, and the effects on the demand for labor depend on the relative size of scale and substitution effects. If a category of labor is a complement in production with the capital whose price has been reduced, or if it is a substitute in production but a *gross* complement, then technological change will increase the demand for that category. If the category of labor is a gross substitute with capital, however, then technological change will reduce its demand. We know from Chapter 4 that, at least in recent decades, capital and higher-skilled labor tend to be gross complements, whereas capital and lower-skilled labor are more likely to be gross substitutes. If these generalizations apply to high-tech capital, then the falling price of such capital and its consequent spread would have shifted the demand curve for higher-skilled workers to the right and the demand curve for less-skilled workers to the left.

The industries that had the largest increases in high-tech capital seem to have been those that had the highest proportions of college-educated workers, and computer usage in 1993 was far higher among college-educated people (at 70 percent) than among high school graduates (35 percent). Furthermore, those who used computers apparently had increased productivity, as they received 20 percent higher wages than they otherwise would have received, according to estimates—a differential that grew between 1984 and 1993.[15] By 2016, the occupations requiring a high level of digital knowledge (e.g., financial managers) tended to require more education and pay more than those requiring a moderate level (office support workers or registered nurses) or a low level of digital knowledge (cooks or security guards).[16]

Finally, the rapidity and scope of workplace technological change associated with the introduction of computerized processes required workers to acquire new skills (even ones that current students think of as elementary, such as learning to keyboard or how to use various computer programs). We saw in Chapter 9 that the costs of learning a new skill are not the same for everyone; those who learn most quickly tend to have the lowest psychological costs of learning.

The presence of differential learning costs can create earnings disparities both *across* and *within* human-capital groups. On the one hand, because those who incur lower learning costs are likely to invest more in education, workers who put in more investments in human capital would not surprisingly be the ones who adapted more quickly to the new, high-tech environment. Indeed, evidence shows that employers are now requiring higher-educational requirements for jobs that require only a moderate level of digital knowledge.[17] On the other hand, even within human-capital groups, the psychological costs of learning cause some workers to be more resistant to change than others are. Thus, during a period of rapid change, as some adapt more quickly and completely than others, earnings disparities *within* human-capital groups will likely grow. As we discuss in Example 15.4, programs that lower the psychological costs of learning are a critical element in—and a daunting challenge to—reducing earnings inequality.

EXAMPLE 15.4

Are Early Childhood Programs a Vehicle for Reducing Earnings Inequality?

We have seen that rising earnings inequality is related to rising returns to education. Therefore, to reduce inequality society must find ways to lower barriers that now deter less-skilled workers from obtaining more education or training. One such barrier is the psychological cost of learning, and reducing this psychological cost hinges on ensuring that students (and, later, workers) have the literacy, numeracy, and emotional skills that facilitate learning.

Building the skills to learn starts early in life, well before students first start school. Recognizing the importance of preschool development, the U.S. federal government founded (in 1965) the Head Start program, which seeks to promote school readiness among children from low-income families. The activities that Head Start provides to children—mostly three- and four-year-olds—include early learning experiences, the promotion of social and emotional skills, and the development of health through medical screenings and nutritious meals.

The preparation provided by Head Start appears to especially enhance the labor market outcomes associated with better-funded public schools (kindergarten through 12th grade). One study, which followed children into adulthood, found that the labor market effects of a 10 percent increase in funding for public schools raised the adult earnings of students across the board. For those from nonpoor families, a 10 percent increase in school funding raised adult wages by 6–7 percent. For those from poor families, the 10 percent increase led to an increase in adult pay of 13 percent if not exposed to Head Start but a 20 percent increase if school was preceded by exposure to Head Start.

The findings of this study suggest two complementary educational vehicles for reducing wage inequality. One is to provide preschool programs for students who otherwise would be unlikely to enter school and to equip those students with the tools needed to succeed in learning. The other is to devote funding to improve the quality of public schools, particularly at the primary school level.

Source: Rucker C. Johnson and C. Kirabo Jackson, "Reducing Inequality Through Dynamic Complementarity: Evidence from Head Start and Public School Spending," *American Economic Journal: Economic Policy* 11 (November 2019): 310–349; Raj Chetty, Nathaniel Hendren, Patrick Kline, and Emmanuel Saez, "Where Is the Land of Opportunity? The Geography of Intergenerational Mobility in the United States," *Quarterly Journal of Economics* 129 (September 2014): 1553–1623; also see Maya Rossin-Slater and Miriam Wüst, "What Is the Added Value of Preschool for Poor Children? Long-Term and Intergenerational Impacts and Interactions with an Infant Health Intervention," *American Economic Journal: Applied Economics* 12 (July 2020): 255–286

For a somewhat alternative view of education's role in intergenerational upward mobility, see Jesse Rothstein, "Inequality of Educational Opportunity: Schools as Mediators of the Intergenerational Transmission of Income," *Journal of Labor Economics* 37, S1 (January 2018): S85–S123.

Technological Change and Job Polarization The view that the falling price and greater use of high-tech capital increased the demand for higher-skilled workers across the board seems *generally* consistent with the changing inequality in the 1980s. Earnings rose for high-skilled workers and fell for less-skilled workers, and they became more dispersed within both the high-skilled and low-skilled human-capital groups (and more dispersed within both the upper and lower halves of the earnings distribution). However, if the introduction of high-tech capital raised the demand for skill at every level, how do we account for the fact that the earnings advantage of staying in high school stayed more or less constant, at least for men? Furthermore, if rapid technological change—which continued after 1990—increased the demand for skills across the board, how do we account for *reduced* inequality in the lower half of the earnings distribution (and within less-educated human-capital groups) after 1990?

Recent work by economists suggests that the high-tech revolution might have had two effects on the demand for labor that were more complex than simply increasing the demand for higher-skilled workers.[18] First, computerized technologies readily substitute for labor in processes that are *routine* in nature: feeding machines, inspecting manufactured products for defects, processing customer orders and travel arrangements, generating correspondence, or making financial or accounting calculations (e.g., the work of tax-preparation professionals can often be replaced by the use of tax software programs). Computers, however, are not good at posing new questions, creating novel ideas, working in teams, or engaging in interpersonal interactions with clients—all common tasks performed by workers in most managerial jobs or the professions. Although improvements in information technologies have eliminated many *routine* tasks that were performed by factory and administrative support workers, they have enhanced the productivity (and hence the pay) of the managerial and professional workers whose jobs *use* the data and information that computers are so good at collecting and dispensing. Put differently, highly educated workers can now spend less time *acquiring* information needed for their jobs and more time *analyzing* and *interpreting* it to make decisions or create new ideas.[19]

Second, wage increases among high-skilled workers appear to have created a rising demand for workers who perform *nonroutine* manual skills that computers cannot replace—for example, mowing lawns, caring for children, and serving restaurant meals. As wages among the highly educated have grown, evidence shows that their hours of work have lengthened,[20] and they thus increased their demand for others to provide the childcare, yard work, and meal preparation tasks that they used to do.[21]

Thus, computerization has likely had a polarizing effect on job growth, reducing the demand for many factory and clerical workers, whose earnings were in the middle of the distribution, and increasing the demand for both the highly educated and (through the scale effect) those in nonroutine manual jobs—many of whom are among the lowest paid.[22]

Evidence of polarization can be seen in Table 15.6, which contains changes in the share of total employment in four occupational groups:

Table 15.6 Changes in the Share of Employment for Four Major Occupational Groups, 1983–2018

Occupational group	Share in total employment		
(2015 weekly earnings)	1983 (%)	2000 (%)	2018 (%)
Managers ($1,355)	10.7	15.1	16.6
Professionals ($1,176)	12.7	15.6	23.5
Office and administrative support ($717)	16.3	14.2	11.3
Service ($569)	13.7	13.9	17.2

Sources: U.S. Bureau of Labor Statistics, *Employment and Earnings* 31 (January 1984), Table 20 (1983); 48 (January 1991), Table 23 (2000); and U.S. Bureau of Labor Statistics, "2018 Annual Averages—Household Data—Tables from Employment and Earnings," Tables 9 and 39, at bls.gov/cps/cps_aa2018.htm

managers, professionals, office and administrative support workers, and service workers (those in healthcare support, protective services, food preparation, and custodial or personal-care jobs).[23] Consistent with the polarization hypothesis, from 1983 to 2018, the share of workers who are managers or professionals rose, the share of workers in office and administrative support jobs declined, and the share of service workers increased. Thus, increased demand for jobs at the lower end of the earnings distribution—especially after 1990—likely played a role in reducing inequality in the lower half of the earnings distribution.[24]

Technological Change and Social Skills   The job polarization associated with technological change appears to explain the reduced demand for routine manual and cognitive skills, along with the rising demand for low-skilled, nonroutine service jobs. But what can explain the rising inequality within the top half of the earnings distribution, as exhibited by the 80:50 and 90:50 ratios noted in Table 15.2? One potential explanation is based on based on two facts: Computers are excellent at making calculations and representing equations or models graphically, but they are not able to substitute well for human interactions. As a consequence, jobs that require high cognitive skills but do not entail much social interaction—such as many engineering jobs—have experienced much slower employment growth since the year 2000 than jobs that require high levels of both cognitive *and* social skills—such as managers and health professionals.[25] Thus, some occupations among college-educated people have begun to grow faster than others, which could be creating widening disparities in pay among the top half of the earnings distribution.

Technological Change and the Pay of "Winners"   The rapid growth of digitization also offers another possible explanation for increasing pay disparities in the top half of the earnings distribution—most especially the greater growth at the very top (as reflected in the 90:50 ratio's growing faster than the 80:20 ratio). The increased digitization of services and telecommunications allows top entertainers and successful innovators—such as the creators of social media websites and tax-preparation programs—to reach large and expanding audiences at low cost; the returns to these "winning" entertainers and innovators have thus been driven up by their growing ability to offer their services on an ever-larger scale. Similarly, these technological improvements have also allowed the best business leaders to expand their ability to successfully manage more employees or reach more customers, driving up their pay relative to the pay of their less able peers. Therefore, rapid digitization has, arguably, vastly enhanced the returns to the very top performers in some labor markets.[26]

Technological Change and Earnings Instability   The technological developments just described, coupled with growing competition within product markets through deregulation and the globalization of production (see Chapter 16), also may have led to a growth in the *instability* of earnings for individual workers. In periods of rapid change, some firms grow while others contract or go out of business, and some workers work overtime while others are laid off. Any growth in the instability of earnings—the year-to-year fluctuations in earnings of individual workers—could also have contributed to the growth of earnings inequality that we have documented.

To see how earnings instability can affect measured earnings inequality, let us focus on the lower fifth of the earnings distribution. Assume, initially, that each worker in this lowest quintile had earnings that did not vary from year to year. Then suppose that technological or product-market changes cause the earnings of these workers to fluctuate; in some years, half (say) of these workers are unlucky and experience unemployment that *reduces* their earnings, whereas the other half are lucky enough to experience temporary earnings *increases* through overtime work or profit-sharing bonuses. The *average* pay among this lower fifth of the earnings distribution might not change, but the earnings at the 10th percentile would fall (reflecting the experience of the unlucky workers), whereas earnings at the 20th percentile would rise. If earnings instability in the upper quintile of the distribution did not change, the 80:20 ratio would shrink but the 90:10 ratio would grow. Evidence shows that the degree of earnings instability is higher now than in 1980, particularly in the lower end of the earnings distribution—rising especially in the 1980s and after the Great Recession.[27]

Changes in Institutional Forces

In addition to the market forces of demand and supply, two other causes of growing earnings inequality in the United States have been considered by economists: the decline of labor unions and the fact that the ratio of the federal minimum wage to average wages generally fell from 1980 onward. Because unionized workers tended to have earnings in the middle of the distribution, the decline in unions could have served to increase the 80:50 or 90:50 ratios, and a falling real minimum wage could have reduced wages at the very bottom of the earning distribution—which, other things being equal, would increase the 50:20 or 50:10 ratios.

As we saw in Chapter 13, union membership in the private sector of the U.S. labor market fell steeply in the 1980s and has fallen steadily since, whereas membership in the public sector rose dramatically before 1980 and has been more or less constant since. Studies of the effects of the decline of unions have estimated that this decline explained a small percentage (15–20 percent) of the growth in male earnings inequality since 1980, but these effects had almost no effect on earnings inequality among women.[28] Thus, the decline of unions has seemingly not played a dominant role in the growth of inequality in the United States since 1980.[29]

A second institutional factor that has been considered as a possible explanation for the rising returns to education is the declining real level of the minimum wage. As we saw in Chapter 4, the federal minimum wage in 1981 was roughly 45 percent of average wages, but it was only increased five times in the ensuing four decades and has averaged less than 40 percent of average wages since (and in 2019 was at 31 percent of the average wage). Although this could potentially affect the 50:10 ratio, a recent study finds that the effects have been relatively small.[30]

Finally, some economists argue that pay at the very top of the earnings distribution, especially among top corporate executives, has risen because of increased incentives (or ability) of these executives to bargain with their corporate boards of directors for higher pay. One line of argument is that as the United States lowered income tax rates for the very rich, obtaining an extra dollar of before-tax pay became more valuable and hence worth fighting harder to obtain. As yet, economists have not reached a consensus on whether rising executive pay has been caused by the market forces creating "winners," discussed earlier, or whether the increased pay of those at the top of the earnings distribution is the result of a changed institutional environment that favored them.[31]

Is Inequality Inherited?

Although inequality for any generation of workers is an important socioeconomic condition, perhaps of equal (or even more) importance is whether one's spot in the earnings distribution is inherited from their parents. In other words, any society that aspires to be a "land of opportunity" should be concerned with intergenerational upward mobility—whether children born to parents near the bottom of the earnings distribution have a good chance, through the accumulation of human capital, to rise toward the top. Likewise, how likely will children born to rich parents fall in the earnings distribution if they fail to acquire useful skills and work hard?

Empirical Study 15.1 at the end of this chapter discusses the challenges of measuring the extent of intergenerational upward mobility. In it, we show that improved access to large data sets has allowed us to more accurately measure the extent of such mobility—and more-accurate measures have spawned two sets of studies in recent years.

One set of studies argues that greater inequality at a point in time is associated with lower rates of intergenerational upward mobility. These papers find evidence that aside from high-earning parents' conveying genetic and family-cultural traits for success to their children, they also have the resources to provide both enhanced educational experiences and enhanced access to useful socioeconomic networks. Specifically, parents toward the top of the earnings distribution can give their children access to better preschool preparation; to more experiences like computer and sports camps; and to better schools and colleges. They can also provide their children with labor market contacts that give them a "leg up" in finding better-paying jobs. As earnings disparities grow, the argument goes, those at the top have an even greater relative advantage in the resources that they can provide for their children.[32] Thus, as inequality grows, intergenerational upward mobility seems to fall, thus making inequality more of an inherited characteristic.

The other set of studies on intergenerational upward mobility analyzes how such mobility appears to vary across geographical areas and race. For example, according to estimates, a child born to parents in the lowest 20 percent of the income distribution in Charlotte, NC, has a 4.4 percent chance of making it to the upper 20 percent of earners as an adult, whereas a child in these circumstances raised in San Jose, CA, has a 12.9 percent chance. The causal mechanisms of differences such as these are not entirely clear at this point, but high-mobility areas appear to have less income inequality, better primary schools, less residential segregation by race, and greater family stability.[33] Black Americans and Native Americans have rates of intergenerational upward mobility much lower than white Americans and Hispanic Americans do.[34]

Both sets of studies point to the importance of creating programs that move society toward a more equal distribution of personal earnings and household incomes. Although this chapter has not dealt with the various policies that might be considered, it has analyzed the root causes of the growth in earnings inequality that must be confronted, and it has mentioned at least some of the vehicles (such as improved preschool experiences and higher-quality public schools) that offer some promise.

EMPIRICAL STUDY 15.1

DO PARENTS' EARNINGS DETERMINE THE EARNINGS OF THEIR CHILDREN? THE USE OF INTERGENERATIONAL DATA IN STUDYING ECONOMIC MOBILITY

Our analysis of earnings inequality has focused on the distribution of earnings at a point in time, but another important aspect of inequality is the opportunity for children—especially in households at the bottom of the earnings distribution—to improve the economic status of their parents. Put differently, a country with growing earnings inequality is likely to be more concerned about this trend if children appear to inherit the earnings inequality of their parents; the country might be less concerned if access to education and job opportunities are such that they offer significant chances for upward mobility.

Studying intergenerational upward mobility requires a data set with the unusual property that it contains earnings information on both parents and their adult children. When such data can be found, the heart of the statistical analysis is to measure the elasticity of the children's earnings compared with the earnings of their parents. That is, if the parents' earnings were to rise by 10 percent, by what percentage would we expect their children's earnings to rise? An elasticity of unity implies a rigid earnings distribution across generations, in that earnings differences across one generation are completely inherited by the next. An elasticity of zero would indicate no correlation between the earnings of parents and children, and that earnings status is not passed from one generation to another.

These elasticities can be estimated by using regression analysis, in which the dependent variable is the earnings of the child and the independent variables include earnings of the parent. Of course, earnings of both parent and child will vary year by year, owing to such transitory factors as unemployment, illness, family problems, and overall economic activity. Thus, we want our measure of parental earnings to reflect their *permanent*—or long-run average—earnings level. If the data are such that only one or two years of parental earnings are available to researchers, the regression procedure will yield estimated elasticities that are biased toward zero, because of the *errors in variables* problem (discussed in Empirical Study 8.1 of Chapter 8). This is a serious problem for studying intergenerational upward mobility, because an elasticity of zero implies substantial intergenerational upward mobility, and it might lead us to conclude that a society permits substantial upward mobility when in fact it does not.

In the United States, estimates of the elasticity of sons' earnings with respect to those of their fathers offer a good example of this statistical problem. When just one year of the fathers' incomes is used, the estimated elasticity is in the range of 0.25 to 0.35. When a five-year average of fathers' earnings is used, the estimated elasticity rises to roughly 0.40—and when the data permit a 16-year average to be used, the estimated elasticity is 0.60.

Thus, as data sets have been improved to permit more years of observations on the earnings of fathers, estimated elasticities have risen and economists have become more pessimistic about the extent of intergenerational upward mobility in the United States. The most recent estimates imply that if the earnings gap between high- and low-earning men were currently 200 percent, the gap between the earnings of their sons 25 or 30 years from now would be about 120 percent if other factors affecting earnings were held constant.

Sources: Gary Solon, "Intergenerational Income Mobility in the United States," *American Economic Review* 82 (June 1992): 393–408; Bhashkar Mazumder, "Analyzing Income Mobility Over Generations," in *Chicago Fed Letter* (Chicago: Federal Reserve Bank of Chicago, September 2002): 1–4; Raj Chetty, Nathaniel Hendren, Patrick Kline, and Emmanuel Saez, "Where Is the Land of Opportunity? The Geography of Intergenerational Mobility in the United States," *Quarterly Journal of Economics* 129 (September 2014): 1553–1623

Review Questions

1. Analyze how increasing the investment tax credit given to firms that make expenditures on new capital affects the dispersion of earnings. (For a review of relevant concepts, see Chapter 4.)

2. Assume that the "comparable-worth" remedy for wage discrimination against women will require governmental and large private employers to increase the wages that they pay to women in female-dominated jobs. The remedy will not apply to small firms. Given what you learned earlier about wages by firm size and in female-dominated jobs, analyze the effects of comparable worth on earnings inequality among women. (For a review of relevant concepts, see Chapter 12.)

3. One of organized labor's primary objectives is legislation forbidding employers to replace workers who are on strike. If such legislation passes, what will be its effects on earnings inequality? (For a review of relevant concepts, see Chapter 13.)

4. Proposals to tax health and other employee benefits, which are not now subject to the income tax, have been made in recent years. Assuming that more highly paid workers have higher employee benefits, analyze the effects on earnings inequality if these tax proposals are adopted. (For a review of relevant concepts, see Chapter 8.)

5. "The labor supply responses to programs designed to help equalize *incomes* can either narrow or widen the dispersion of *earnings*." Comment on this statement in the context of an increase in the subsidy paid under an income-maintenance program to those who do not work. Assume that this program creates an effective wage that is greater than zero but less than the market wage, and assume that this effective wage is unchanged by the increased subsidy to those who do not work. (For a review of relevant concepts, see Chapter 6.)

6. Discuss the role of geographic mobility in decreasing or increasing the dispersion of earnings. (For a review of the relevant concepts, see Chapter 10.)

7. Suppose that a country's government is concerned about the growing inequality of incomes and wants to undertake a program that will increase the total earnings of lower-skilled workers. It is considering two alternative changes to its current payroll tax, which is levied on employers as a percentage of the first $100,000 of employee earnings:

   a. extending employer payroll taxes to all earnings over $100,000 per year, and increasing the cost of capital by eliminating certain tax deductions related to plant and equipment

   b. reducing to zero employer payroll taxes on the first $30,000 of earnings but continuing the payroll tax on all employee earnings between $30,000 and $100,000 (earnings above $100,000 would not be taxed)

   Analyze proposal a and proposal b separately (one, but not both, will be adopted). Which is more likely to accomplish the aim of increasing the earnings of lower-skilled workers? Why?

8. One economist has observed that by age 20, the cognitive and noncognitive skills of people are set in such a way that those who are not good at learning new skills or concepts cannot be helped much by education or training programs. Assuming that this observation is true, use economic theory to analyze its implications for the issue of earnings inequality in the world today.

Problems

1. (Appendix 15A) Ten college seniors have accepted job offers for the year after they graduate. Their starting salaries are given here. Organize the data into quintiles, and then, using these data, draw the Lorenz curve for this group. Finally, calculate the relevant Gini coefficient.

Becky	$42,000
Billy	$20,000
Charlie	$31,000
Kasia	$24,000
Nina	$34,000
Raul	$37,000
Rose	$29,000
Thomas	$35,000
Willis	$60,000
Yukiko	$32,000

2. Suppose that the wage distribution for a small town is given in Table 15P.2. Assume that a minimum-wage law is passed that doesn't affect the market in high-wage sector A but boosts wages to $15 per

hour in sector B, the covered sector, while reducing employment to 20. Displaced workers in sector B move into the uncovered sector, C, where wages fall to $8.00 per hour as employment grows to 30. Has wage inequality risen or fallen? Explain.

Table 15P.2 Wage Distribution in a Small Town

Sector	Number of workers	Wage ($)
A	50	20 per hour
B	25	10 per hour
C	25	10 per hour

3. Table 15P.3 gives the average wage rate for the indicated percentiles of the wage distribution for customer service representatives in New York City.

Table 15P.3 Wages, by Percentile, Customer Services Representatives in New York City

Percentile	1990	2005
10th	$9.13	$10.51
50th	$11.23	$12.15
90th	$13.98	$14.78

   a. Calculate the earnings ratios at various percentiles of the earnings distribution for both years.

   b. Describe the changes in wage inequality in this local labor market.

4. Calculate the coefficient of variation for the workers listed in problem 1.

5. (Appendix 15A) Table 15P.5 gives data on the shares of household income by quintile in the United States in 2005. Draw the Lorenz curve, and calculate the Gini coefficient.

Table 15P.5 U.S. Household Income by Quintile, 2005

Quintile	Percent share of income
Lowest	3.4
Second	8.6
Third	14.6
Fourth	23.0
Highest	50.4

Notes

1. For an example of a recent study that analyzed how government transfer programs affect poverty, see Bruce D. Meyer and Derek Wu, "The Poverty Reduction of Social Security and Means-Tested Transfers," *ILR Review* 71 (October 2018): 1106–1153.

2. Ideally, the focus would be on total compensation so that the analyses would include employee benefits. As a practical matter, however, data on the *value* of employee benefits are not widely available in a form that permits an examination of their *distribution* either over time or across individuals. For a study that analyzes the dispersion in total compensation, see Brooks Pierce, "Compensation Inequality," *Quarterly Journal of Economics* 116 (November 2001): 1493–1525. Earnings reflect both wages and hours worked; for a study suggesting that recent increases in leisure hours may have contributed to the rise in earnings inequality, see Mark Aguiar and Erik Hurst, "Measuring Trends in Leisure: The Allocation of Time Over Five Decades," *Quarterly Journal of Economics* 122 (August 2007): 969–1006.

3. A summary of various inequality measures can be found in Frank Levy and Richard J. Murnane, "U.S. Earnings Levels and Earnings Inequality: A Review of Recent Trends and Proposed Explanations," *Journal of Economic Literature* 30 (September 1991): 1333–1381. The distribution of earnings might be *symmetric* or not. If a distribution is symmetric, as in Figure 15.2, then as many people earn $X less than average as earn $X more than average. If not, we say that it is *skewed*, meaning that one part of the distribution is bunched together and the other part is relatively dispersed. For example, many less-developed countries do not have a sizable middle class. Such countries have a huge number of very poor families and a tiny minority of very wealthy families (the distribution of income is highly skewed to the right).

4. U.S. Bureau of the Census, "Historical Income Tables: Households," Table H-2, census.gov/data/tables/time-series/historical-income-households.html. A more sophisticated measure would take into account the shares of income received by each of the five quintiles, and a way to quantify the deviation from strict equality (when the income share of each quintile is 20 percent) is discussed in Appendix 15A. For a review of studies of income at the very top of income distributions across countries and across time, see Anthony B. Atkinson, Thomas Piketty, and Emmanuel Saez, "Top Incomes in the Long Run of History," *Journal of Economic Literature* 49 (March 2011): 3–71.

5. Recall from the discussion of Table 2.2 that the consumer price index, which we use in Table 15.1 to adjust all earnings figures to 2018 dollars, may overstate inflation by about one percentage point per year. If that is the case, then the real earnings of men at the 80th percentile grew considerably more than the 10 percent shown in the table, and

the real earnings of those at the 20th percentile actually rose. For a paper concluding that use of the CPI might overstate the extent of poverty, see Bruce D. Meyer and James X. Sullivan, "Winning the War: Poverty from the Great Society to the Great Recession" (Working Paper No. 18718, National Bureau of Economic Research, Cambridge, MA, January 2013). The major point made in Table 15.1, however, is that the 80:20 ratio has grown for men over this period, and the *ratios* in any given year are not affected by assumptions about overall inflation (because the same inflationary adjustments are made to both the numerator and the denominator of the ratio). One study, however, finds that college graduates have experienced much larger increases in the cost of living, such that growth in their *real* earnings has not been as large as the growth in their nominal earnings; see Enrico Moretti, "Real Wage Inequality," *American Economic Journal: Applied Economics* 5 (January 2013): 65–103.

6. We must qualify this statement by noting that earnings at the 90th percentile could not be observed in published data for 2018.

7. For more-detailed analyses along this line, see Kevin M. Murphy and Robert H. Topel, "Human Capital Investment, Inequality, and Economic Growth," *Journal of Labor Economics* 34, pt. 2 (April 2016): S99–S127; David H. Autor, "Why Are There Still So Many Jobs? The History and Future of Workplace Automation," *Journal of Economic Perspectives* 29 (Summer 2015): 3–30.

8. The focus is on men because their years of labor market experience within each age-education group is likely to be more homogeneous.

9. David Autor, Claudia Goldin, and Lawrence F. Katz, "Extending the Race Between Education and Technology," *American Economic Association: Papers and Proceedings* 110 (May 2020): 347–351.

10. For analyses of the within-group dispersion of earnings, see Thomas Lemieux, "Increasing Residual Wage Inequality: Composition Effects, Noisy Data, or Rising Demand for Skill?" *American Economic Review* 96 (June 2006): 461–498; Anders Akerman, Elhanan Helpman, Oleg Itskhoki, Marc-Andreas Muendler, and Stephen J. Redding, "Sources of Wage Inequality," *American Economic Review: Papers and Proceedings* (May 2013): 214–219. For a study finding that much of the increased dispersion at the top of the earnings distribution is related to the increased use of pay-for-performance pay systems, see Thomas Lemieux, W. Bentley MacLeod, and Daniel Parent, "Performance Pay and Wage Inequality," *Quarterly Journal of Economics* 124 (February 2009): 1–49. Widening disparities in pay among workers with the same measured human capital might also be related to widening differences in average pay across firms; see Jae Song, David J. Price, Fatih Guvenen, Nicholas Bloom, and Till von Wachter, "Firming Up Inequality," *Quarterly Journal of Economics* 134 (February 2019): 1–50; Erling Barth, Alex Bryson, James C. Davis, and Richard Freeman,

"It's Where You Work: Increases in the Dispersion of Earnings across Establishments and Individuals in the United States," *Journal of Labor Economics* 34, pt. 2 (April 2016): S67–S97; David Autor, David Dorn, Lawrence F. Katz, Christina Patterson, and John Van Reenen, "The Fall of the Labor Share and the Rise of Superstar Firms," *Quarterly Journal of Economics* 135 (May 2020): 645–709.

11. The generally small role played by *supply* shifts in generating wage inequality is also found in more-sophisticated studies: Lawrence F. Katz and Kevin M. Murphy, "Changes in Relative Wages, 1963–1987: Supply and Demand Factors," *Quarterly Journal of Economics* 107 (February 1992): 35–78; John Bound and George Johnson, "Changes in the Structure of Wages in the 1980s: An Evaluation of Alternative Explanations," *American Economic Review* 82 (June 1992): 371–392; John Bound and George Johnson, "What Are the Causes of Rising Wage Inequality in the United States?" *Federal Reserve Bank of New York Economic Policy Review* 1 (January 1995): 9–17.

12. For a summary of the literature, see Francine D. Blau and Lawrence M. Kahn, "Immigration and the Distribution of Incomes" (Working Paper No. 18515, National Bureau of Economic Research, Cambridge, MA, November 2012).

13. See Daron Acemoglu, "Technical Change, Inequality, and the Labor Market," *Journal of Economic Literature* 40 (March 2002): 7–72; David H. Autor, Lawrence F. Katz, and Alan B. Krueger, "Computing Inequality: Have Computers Changed the Labor Market?" *Quarterly Journal of Economics* 113 (November 1998): 1169–1213.

14. Mark Muro, Sifan Liu, Jacob Whiton, and Siddharth Kulkarni, "Digitalization and the American Workforce" (Metropolitan Policy Program, The Brookings Institution, Washington, DC, November 2017).

15. Autor, Katz, and Krueger, "Computing Inequality: Have Computers Changed the Labor Market?"

16. Muro, Liu, Whiton, and Kulkarni, "Digitalization and the American Workforce."

17. Brad Hershbein and Lisa B. Kahn, "Do Recessions Accelerate Routine-Biased Technological Change? Evidence from Vacancy Postings," *American Economic Review* 108 (July 2018): 1737–1772. For another study on how technology has changed the mix of routine and non-routine tasks *within* occupations, see Enghin Atalay, Phai Phongthiengtham, Sebastian Sotelo, and Daniel Tannenbaum, "The Evolution of Work in the United States," *American Economic Journal: Applied Economics* 12 (April 2020): 1–34.

18. Maarten Goos, Alan Manning, and Anna Salomons, "Explaining Job Polarization: Routine-Biased Technological Change and Offshoring," *American Economic Review* 104 (August 2014): 2509–2526; David H. Autor and David Dorn, "The Growth of Low-Skill Service Jobs and the

Polarization of the U.S. Labor Market," *American Economic Review* 103 (August 2013): 1553–1597; Guido Matias Cortes, "Where Have the Middle-Wage Jobs Gone? A Study of Polarization Using Panel Data," *Journal of Labor Economics* 34, pt. 1 (January 2016): 63–105.

19. For a more detailed argument along these lines, see Erik Brynjolfsson and Andrew McAfee, *The Second Machine Age: Work, Progress, and Prosperity in a Time of Brilliant Technologies* (New York: W.W. Norton, 2014).

20. Peter Kuhn and Fernando Lozano, "The Expanding Workweek? Understanding Trends in Long Work Hours among U.S. Men, 1979–2006," *Journal of Labor Economics* 26 (April 2008): 311–343.

21. Marco Leonardi, "The Effect of Product Demand on Inequality: Evidence from the United States and the United Kingdom," *American Economic Journal: Applied Economics* 7 (July 2015): 221–247; Autor, "Why Are There Still So Many Jobs? The History and Future of Workplace Automation."

22. We see in Chapter 16 that the "offshoring" of many tasks—that is, having workers in other countries perform tasks formerly done by U.S. workers—has had effects on the demand for routine and nonroutine work similar to those of technological change; see David Hummels, Jakob R. Munch, and Chong Xiang, "Offshoring and Labor Markets," *Journal of Economic Literature* 56 (September 2018): 981–1028.

23. These four groups were selected because their definitions remained essentially unchanged from 1983 to the present. Other groupings changed definitions over that period, making comparisons using published data infeasible.

24. This argument is made in Autor and Dorn, "The Growth of Low-Skill Service Jobs and the Polarization of the U.S. Labor Market." Also see Daron Acemoglu and Pascual Restrepo, "Robots and Jobs: Evidence from US Labor Markets," *Journal of Political Economy* 128 (April 2020): 2188–2244.

25. David J. Deming, "The Growing Importance of Social Skills in the Labor Market," *Quarterly Journal of Economics* 132 (November 2017): 1593–1640; Paul Beaudry, David A. Green, and Benjamin M. Sand, "The Great Reversal in the Demand for Skill and Cognitive Tasks," *Journal of Labor Economics* 34, pt. 2 (January 2016): S199–S247. Evidence also shows that earnings differentials across college majors have widened in the past two decades; see Joseph G. Altonji, Lisa B. Kahn, and Jamin D. Speer, "Trends in Earnings Differentials Across College Majors and the Changing Task Composition of Jobs," *American Economic Review Papers and Proceedings* 104 (May 2014): 387–393.

26. Steven N. Kaplan and Joshua Rauh, "It's the Market: The Broad-Based Rise in the Return to Top Talent," *Journal of Economic Perspectives* 27

(Summer 2013): 35–56; Brynjolfsson and McAfee, *The Second Machine Age: Work, Progress, and Prosperity in a Time of Brilliant Technologies.*

27. Peter Gottschalk and Robert Moffitt, "The Rising Instability of U.S. Earnings," *Journal of Economic Perspectives* 23 (Fall 2009): 3–24; Robert Moffitt and Sisi Zhang, "Income Volatility and the PSID: Past Research and New Results," *American Economic Association Papers and Proceedings* 108 (May 2018): 277–280.

28. The different gender effects are related to the fact that private sector union membership, which has been declining, was predominantly male, whereas female union membership is primarily in the public sector; see David Card, Thomas Lemieux, and W. Craig Riddell, "Unions and Wage Inequality: The Roles of Gender, Skill and Public Sector Employment," *Canadian Economic Review/Revue canadienne d'économique* 53 (February 2020); 140–173.

29. For analyses of how unions have affected inequality in the United States over a longer period of time, see Henry S. Farber, Daniel Herbst, Ilyana Kuziemko, and Suresh Naidu, "Unions and Inequality over the Twentieth Century: New Evidence from Survey Data" (Working Paper No. 24587, National Bureau of Economic Research, Cambridge, MA: May 2018); David Kunst, Richard B. Freeman, and Remco Oostendorp, "Occupational Skill Premia Around the World" (Working Paper No. 26863, National Bureau of Economic Research, Cambridge, MA: March 2020).

30. David H. Autor, Alan Manning, and Christopher L. Smith, "The Contribution of the Minimum Wage to U.S. Wage Inequality Over Three Decades," *American Economic Journal: Applied Economics* 8 (January 2016): 58–99. For how labor market institutions in their entirety affect wage inequality across countries, see Winfried Koeniger, Marco Leonardi, and Luca Nunziata, "Labor Market Institutions and Wage Inequality," *Industrial and Labor Relations Review* 60 (April 2007): 340–356.

31. See Thomas Piketty, Emmanuel Saez, and Stefanie Stantcheva, "Optimal Taxation of Top Labor Incomes: A Tale of Three Elasticities," *American Economic Journal: Economic Policy* 6 (February 2014): 230–271; Josh Bivens and Lawrence Mishel, "The Pay of Corporate Executives and Financial Professionals as Evidence of Rents in Top 1 Percent Incomes," *Journal of Economic Perspectives* 27 (Summer 2013): 57–78; Kaplan and Rauh, "It's the Market: The Broad-Based Rise in the Return to Top Talent"; Song, Price, Guvenen, Bloom, and von Wachter, "Firming Up Inequality."

32. Miles Corak, "Income Inequality, Equality of Opportunity, and Intergenerational Mobility," *Journal of Economic Perspectives* 27 (Summer 2013): 79–102; Raj Chetty, John N. Friedman, Emmanuel Saez, Nicholas Turner, and Danny Yagan, "Mobility Report Cards: The Role of Colleges in Intergenerational Mobility" (Working Paper No. 23618, National Bureau of Economic Research, Cambridge, MA, July 2017).

33. Raj Chetty, Nathaniel Hendren, Patrick Kline, and Emmanuel Saez, "Where Is the Land of Opportunity? The Geography of Intergenerational Mobility in the United States," *Quarterly Journal of Economics* 129 (September 2014): 1553–1623.

34. Raj Chetty, Nathaniel Hendren, Maggie R. Jones, and Sonya R. Porter, "Race and Economic Opportunity in the United States: An Intergenerational Perspective," *Quarterly Journal of Economics* 135 (May 2020): 711–783.

Selected Readings

Autor, David H. "Why Are There Still So Many Jobs? The History and Future of Workplace Automation." *Journal of Economic Perspectives* 29 (Summer 2015): 3–30.

Bound, John, and George Johnson. "Changes in the Structure of Wages in the 1980s: An Evaluation of Alternative Explanations." *American Economic Review* 82 (June 1992): 371–392.

Brynjolfsson, Erik, and Andrew McAfee. *The Second Machine Age: Work, Progress, and Prosperity in a Time of Brilliant Technologies.* New York: W.W. Norton, 2014.

Burtless, Gary, ed. *A Future of Lousy Jobs? The Changing Structure of U.S. Wages.* Washington, DC: Brookings Institution, 1990.

Freeman, Richard B., and Lawrence F. Katz, eds. *Differences and Changes in Wage Structures.* Chicago, IL: University of Chicago Press, 1995.

Gordon, Robert J., and Gordon Ian Dew-Becker. "Controversies About the Rise of American Inequality: A Survey." Working Paper No. 13982, National Bureau of Economic Research, Cambridge, MA, April 2008.

Levy, Frank, and Richard J. Murnane. "U.S. Earnings Levels and Earnings Inequality: A Review of Recent Trends and Proposed Explanations." *Journal of Economic Literature* 30 (September 1992): 1333–1381.

APPENDIX 15A

Lorenz Curves and Gini Coefficients

The most commonly used measures of distributional inequality involve grouping the distribution into deciles or quintiles and comparing the earnings (or income) received by each. As we did in the body of this chapter, we can compare the earnings levels at points high in the distribution (e.g., the 80th percentile) with points at the low end (e.g., the 20th percentile). A richer and more fully descriptive measure, however, employs data on the *share* of total earnings or income received by those in each group.

Suppose that each household in the population has the same income. In this case of perfect equality, each fifth of the population receives a fifth of the total income. In graphic terms, this equality can be shown by the straight line *AB* in Figure 15A.1, which plots the cumulative share of income (vertical axis) received by each quintile and the ones below it (horizontal axis). Thus, the first quintile (with a 0.2 share, or 20 percent of all households) would receive a 0.2 share (20 percent) of total income; the first and second quintiles (four-tenths of the population) would receive four-tenths of total income; and so forth.

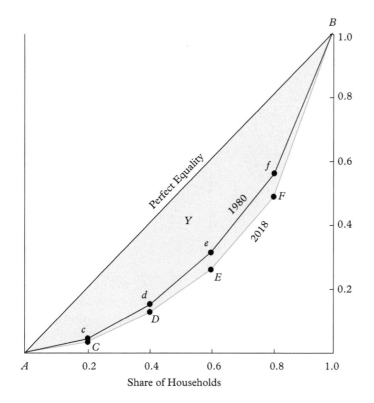

Figure 15A.1 Lorenz Curves for 1980 and 2018 Distributions of Income in the United States

If the distribution of income is not perfectly equal, then the curve connecting the cumulative percentages of income received by the cumulated quintiles—the *Lorenz curve*—is convex and lies below the line of perfect equality. For example, in 2018, the lowest fifth of U.S. households received 3.1 percent of total income, the second fifth 8.3 percent, the third fifth 14.1 percent, the fourth fifth 22.6 percent, and the highest fifth 51.9 percent. Plotting the cumulative data in Figure 15A.1 yields Lorenz curve *ACDEFB*. This curve displays the convexity that we would expect from the clearly unequal distribution of household income in the United States.[1]

Comparing the equality of two different income distributions results in unambiguous conclusions if one Lorenz curve lies completely inside the other (closer to the line of perfect equality). If, for example, we were interested in comparing the U.S. income distributions of 1980 and 2018, we could observe that plotting the 1980 data results in a Lorenz curve, *AcdefB* in Figure 15A.1, that lies everywhere closer to the line of perfect equality than the one for 2018.

If two Lorenz curves cross, however, conclusions about which one represents greater equality are not possible. Comparing curves *A* and *B* in Figure 15A.2, for example, we can see that the distribution represented by *A* has a lower proportion of total income received by the poorest quintile than does the distribution represented by curve *B*; however, the cumulative share of income received by the lowest two quintiles (taken together) is equal for *A* and for *B*, and the cumulative proportions received by the bottom three and bottom four quintiles are higher for *A* than for *B*.

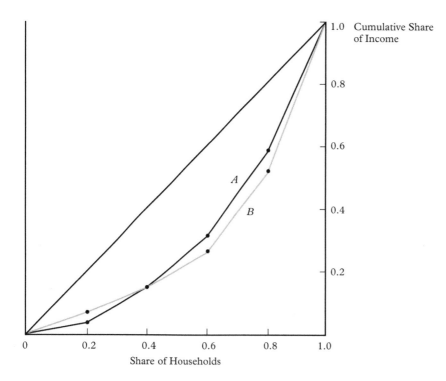

Figure 15A.2 Lorenz Curves That Cross

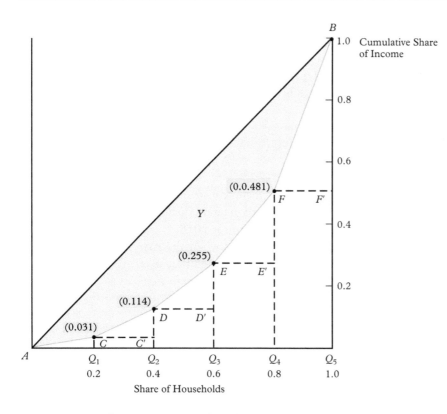

Figure 15A.3 Calculating the Gini Coefficient for the 2018 Distribution of Household Income

Another measure of inequality, which seems at first glance to yield unambiguous answers when various distributions are compared, is the *Gini coefficient*: the ratio of the area between the Lorenz curve and the line of perfect equality (for 2018, the shaded area labeled Y in Figure 15A.1) to the total area under the line of perfect equality. Obviously, with perfect equality, the Gini coefficient would equal zero.

One way to calculate the Gini coefficient is to split the area under the Lorenz curve into a series of triangles and rectangles, as shown in Figure 15A.3 (which repeats the Lorenz curve for 2018, shown in Figure 15A.1). Each triangle has a base equal to 0.2—the horizontal distance for each of the five quintiles—and a height equal to the percentage of income received by that quintile (the cumulative percentage less the percentages received by lower quintiles). Because the base of each triangle is the same and because their heights sum to unity, the *sum* of the areas of each triangle is always equal to $0.5 \times 0.2 \times 1.0 = 0.1$ (one-half base times height).

The rectangles in Figure 15A.3 all have one side equal to 0.2 and another equal to the cumulated percentages of total income received by the previous quintiles. Rectangle $Q_1CC'Q_2$, for example, has an area of $0.2 \times 0.031 = 0.062$, whereas $Q_2DD'Q_3$ has an area of $0.2 \times 0.114 = 0.0228$. Analogously, $Q_3EE'Q_4$ has an area of 0.0510 and $Q_4FF'Q_5$ an area of

0.0962; together, all four rectangles in Figure 15A.3 have an area that sums to 0.1762.

The area under the Lorenz curve in Figure 15A.3 is thus 0.1762 + 0.1 = 0.2762. Given that the total area under the line of perfect equality is 0.5 × 1 × 1 = 0.5, the Gini coefficient for 2018 is calculated as follows:

$$Gini\ Coeffecient\ (2018) = \frac{0.5 - 0.2762}{0.5} = 0.4476 \qquad (15A.1)$$

For comparison purposes, the Gini coefficient for the income distribution in 1980 can be calculated as 0.3768—which is evidence of greater equality in 1980 because it lies closer to zero than the Gini coefficient for 2018.

Unfortunately, the Gini coefficient will become smaller when the rich give up some of their income to the middle class as well as when they give up income in favor of poor people. Thus, the Gini coefficient may yield a "definitive" answer about comparative equality when none is warranted. As we saw in the case of Figure 15A.2, in which the Lorenz curves being compared cross, judging the relative equality of two distributions does not always lead to an unambiguous answer.

We have analyzed the Lorenz curve and Gini coefficient in terms of *household income* for the simple reason that published data permit these calculations. The underlying data on the *shares* of individual *earnings* are not published, but the Gini coefficients associated with earnings distributions are available. The Gini coefficient for men, ages 25–64, who worked full time in 2000 was 0.393, whereas for the same group in 2018, it was 0.410. Among women, the Gini coefficient for women, ages 25–64, who worked full time went from 0.325 to 0.381 in the same period. Both increases are indications that earnings among full-time workers of both genders were more unequal in 2018 than in 2000.[2]

Notes

1. Data for both years come from U.S. Bureau of the Census, Historical Income Tables—Households, Table H-2 "Share of Aggregate Income Received by Each Fifth and Top 5 Percent of Households, All Races, 1967–2018," at census.gov/data/time-series/demo/income-poverty/historical-income-households.html.

2. U.S. Bureau of the Census, Current Population Survey Tables for Personal Income, PINC-03. Educational Attainment—People 25 Years Old and Over, by Total Money Earnings, Work Experience, Age, Race, Hispanic Origin, and Sex, at census.gov/data/tables/time-series/demo/income-poverty/cps-pinc/pinc-03.2018.html.

The Labor Market Effects of International Trade and Production Sharing

Countries have traditionally protected many of their industries from competition with foreign firms by imposing taxes ("tariffs") or quotas on their imports. In recent years, the restrictions on imports have been eased in many places, usually by mutual agreement with one or more trading partners. Furthermore, developments in telecommunications have created the ability to communicate almost instantaneously across the entire world, which has greatly expanded the possibilities for producing goods and services in locations that are remote from the customer. As a result of these changes, the increased movement of goods, services, financial resources, and information flows across international borders has been significant.

In the United States, for example, the importing of goods and services from foreign countries constituted less than 10 percent of all purchases in 1985, but by 2018, roughly 15 percent of U.S. purchases were of goods or services produced elsewhere. Likewise, in 1985, about 7 percent of goods and services produced in the United States were sold to those in other countries, and in 2018, 12 percent of U.S. output was sold abroad.[1] Also increasingly unclear is just what "U.S." output is; for example, the laptop computers sold by a U.S. company might be designed in the United States, use a microprocessor made in Costa Rica or Malaysia, have a keyboard manufactured in Korea, be assembled in Taiwan, and be supported by a telephone help line staffed by technicians in India. This geographic dispersion of the various steps in the production process has been called production sharing.

The increased movement of components, services, and final goods across international borders has led to concerns that highly paid U.S. workers now face increased competition from a huge number of lower-paid workers from other countries, that production sharing means that their work is being outsourced (or "offshored") to other countries, and that their jobs are thereby being eliminated and their wages reduced. The implication of these assertions is typically that U.S. workers—or at least a large segment of them—are being made worse off by a more integrated world economy. We will consider the merits of this argument.

This chapter uses economic concepts developed earlier in the text to analyze the labor market effects of increased trade, in both products and factors of production, with other countries. As with Chapter 15, our goal is to provide an analysis of a much-discussed topic in a way that uses and reviews concepts developed throughout the book—and our analysis uses both positive concepts and normative concepts. We start with an examination of just why trade among individuals or firms, whether within a country or between countries, takes place.

Why Does Trade Take Place?

We emphasized in Chapter 1 that the function of a market is to facilitate mutually beneficial transactions. These transactions will be socially beneficial (Pareto improving) if some gain and no one loses—a state that can be reached if those who gain are willing to compensate anyone who loses. Because transactions across international borders—just as those within a country—take place among individuals or firms, we must understand the motivations of these decision makers.

Trade Between Individuals and the Principle of Comparative Advantage

Every individual household, as we saw in Chapter 7, faces a variety of make-or-buy decisions on almost a daily basis. We must decide which daily tasks to do ourselves and which we want to outsource to (buy from) others. Do we assemble food and make a meal ourselves, or do we buy it from a restaurant or grocery store? Do we spend two days painting our living room, or do we hire a painter? Do we change the oil in our car, prepare our own income tax forms, mow our lawn, clean our home, and care for an aging parent—or do we pay others to perform these tasks?

Make-or-buy decisions are made by weighing the opportunity costs of doing tasks ourselves against the costs of buying the goods or services from others. If we decide to specialize in one activity and buy the rest from others, we are engaging in *trade*; that is, we are selling the work in which we specialize and using the money obtained to buy other goods or services from outsiders.

Performing by ourselves all the household activities just listed would entail two types of costs. First, we are not specialists in all these tasks, so if we did them all ourselves, we might end up with inferior outcomes. Second, if we did them ourselves, we would give up the opportunity to spend our time in other ways, which may be either more productive or more pleasant. For example, does a lawyer who can earn $800 per day really want to spend two days painting her living room when she can hire a painter for $120 per day?

To better understand the factors influencing these make-or-buy decisions, let us take a simple example. Suppose that Latoya is the lawyer mentioned earlier and that she lives across the street from Don, who is self-employed doing shoe-repair work. Latoya can earn $800 per day, and she currently needs three new suits to wear. Both Latoya and Don can sew, although at different speeds, and Latoya is trying to decide whether she should make the suits or buy them from Don.

If Latoya took time from her work as a lawyer and sewed full time, she could make the three suits in a week. Thus, she will calculate that her three suits would cost $4,000 (plus the cost of materials), because she would forgo five days of work as a lawyer at $800 per day. Clearly, unless she really loves to sew, she would be happy to buy her suits from Don if he charged her less than $4,000 for his labor.

Don's benefit from working in the labor force is smaller than Latoya's. He can earn only $120 per day, and although he can sew competently, to produce three suits of the quality that Latoya wants would take him *two* weeks of full-time sewing. If he decides to sew, he will give up two weeks of work—or $1,200 (10 days of work at $120 per day). Note, however, that his opportunity cost of making suits is much less than Latoya's opportunity cost of $4,000.

If Don agrees to make the three suits and charges $1,500 (say) for his labor, both would be better off. Don would earn $300 more than he normally would by repairing shoes, and Latoya would save $2,500 by not sewing the suits herself. Not only are both individuals better off, but *society's* output is enhanced if Latoya specializes in legal work and buys her suits from Don. When Don makes the suits, society loses his alternative output, which is valued at $1,200. If Latoya were to make the suits, society would lose $4,000 in legal services. Thus, from a social perspective, hiring Don to make the suits is less costly.

The inquisitive reader can see an interesting puzzle in this example. Don is much less productive in everything than is Latoya—he can earn less in his alternative activities and he sews more slowly—yet, he ends up with demand for his services as a tailor. This is because the first step in make-or-buy decisions is for each party to perform an *internal* comparison: Individuals must consider their *own* opportunity costs of producing the good or service in question. Put differently, because those trying to decide whether to make or buy some good cannot do two things at once, they must first calculate the value of the activity that they would have to give up if they were to make that good.

In the earlier example, Don would calculate that the labor cost of his making the three suits is $1,200, while Latoya calculates that her cost is $4,000. Once they make their internal calculations, they are in a position to negotiate with each other to determine whether they can both can agree on a mutually beneficial trade. Even though Latoya can make suits faster than Don can, her opportunity costs are higher because she is so much more productive at her alternative activity (legal services) than he is at his (shoe repair). Economists would thus conclude that Don has the *comparative advantage* in making suits. That is, his opportunity cost (his value of lost production) in making suits is less than hers—and because their opportunity costs differ, a mutually beneficial trade can take place.

This principle of comparative advantage underlies all decisions about trading with others. Generally speaking, individuals have a strong incentive to *specialize* in the production of goods or services in which they have a comparative advantage and buy from others the goods or services that they would find more expensive to produce themselves.

The Incentives for Trade Across Different Countries

If trade among individuals within a city, region, or country can benefit both the individuals and society at large, can transactions among individuals or firms across international borders have similar benefits? Economists generally agree that international trade has the *potential* for enlarging the output of the countries engaging in it, although much debate centers on whether that potential is realized in practice. To understand the debate, we must first ask ourselves why economic theory considers trade between two countries to be potentially beneficial to both. Whereas our analysis in the previous section was conducted at the level of individuals, the analysis in this section is conducted at the aggregate (country) level.

Production Possibilities Without Trade

Let us assume that in the past, trade between two countries was severely limited either by the imposition of tariffs on imported goods or by technological restrictions, such as the difficulties in transporting goods or communicating vital information about transactions across international borders. The effect of these restrictions was that each country had to satisfy its consumer demands only with goods or services that it made domestically.

To keep the analysis simple, suppose that we examine countries A and B, each of which can produce two goods—food and clothing—with the resources that it has available. Because the resources of A and B are fixed at any time, increasing the output of food in each country requires giving up clothing; likewise, producing more clothing requires giving up food. Countries A and B have different productive resources, and the various combinations of food and clothing that each country can produce with its resources can be plotted on a graph. The result is called the *production possibilities curve* (which we introduced toward the end of Chapter 4, where we discussed the effects of technological change).

The straight black lines in Figures 16.1 and 16.2—XY in Figure 16.1 and $X'Y'$ in Figure 16.2—are the production possibilities curves that we assume for country A and country B, respectively. We also assume (again for the sake of simplicity) that the opportunity costs of production in each country do not change as the mix of food and clothing changes, so the production possibilities "curves" are depicted as straight lines in the two figures.

Inspecting Figure 16.1, note that if country A devoted all its resources to the production of food, it could produce 200 million units of food and no clothing (it would be at point Y). If all country A's productive resources were devoted to making clothing, we assume that 100 million units of clothing and no food could be produced (point X). Absent trade with country B, country A would most likely choose to produce a *mix* of both outputs, thus

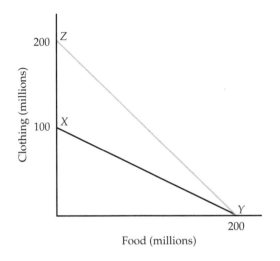

Figure 16.1 Production Possibilities for Country A

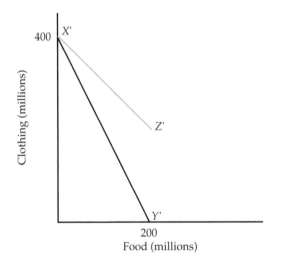

Figure 16.2 Production Possibilities for Country B

ending up at a point along the production possibilities curve between *X* and *Y*. The exact point it chooses would depend on its preferences.

Turning to Figure 16.2 and country B, we assume that if it devoted all its resources to making food, it could produce 200 million units of food and no clothing (point *Y*), and if it instead devoted all its resources to the production of clothing, 400 million units of clothing and no food could be produced (point *X*). Here we have assumed that the production possibilities curves in the two countries are different; this difference could be rooted in the natural, human, or technological resources available to each country.

Comparative Advantage   Can we infer comparative advantage from these production possibilities curves? As noted earlier, identifying comparative advantage starts with calculating the *domestic* (internal) opportunity costs of production, so let us analyze the opportunity costs of producing food in each country. If country A had been producing only clothing, but it decided to produce only food, it would gain 200 million units of food at an opportunity cost of giving up 100 million units of clothing.[2] Thus, in country A, an additional unit of food can be gained by giving up a half unit of clothing. In country B, 200 million units of food could be produced only by giving up 400 million units of clothing; thus, in country B, an additional unit of food requires giving up two units of clothing. Clearly, the opportunity cost of producing food is lower in country A than in country B—because in country A, less clothing needs to be given up to obtain an extra unit of food. Therefore, as between the two countries in our example, country A has the comparative advantage in producing food.

Which country has the comparative advantage in producing clothing? In country A, obtaining 100 million units of clothing requires giving up 200 million units of food, so producing an additional unit of clothing means two fewer units of food. In country B, the 400 million units of clothing would require forgoing 200 million units of food, so each unit of clothing costs one-half unit of food. Country B has the comparative advantage in clothing production.

Is the fact that country A has a comparative advantage in one good and country B has it in the other a coincidence? No. Because country A has resources that produce food efficiently, if it had to produce its own clothing—rather than being able to specialize in the production of food—it would be giving up a lot of food as a result. Country B is not as efficient in food production, so producing clothing there has lower opportunity costs. Country B has a comparative advantage in producing clothing precisely because it is not as efficient as country A is in producing food. Thus, the comparative advantage of country A in producing food implies that it has a comparative *disadvantage* in producing clothing.[3]

Production Possibilities With Trade   Analogous to our example with Latoya and Don earlier, the differences in the internal costs of producing food and clothing create a situation in which each country would be better off by specializing in making the good in which it has a comparative advantage and trading for the other good. To understand this, let us assume that, with trade, country B makes only clothing, country A produces only food, and firms in both country A and country B agree to trade with each other on the basis of one unit of clothing for one unit of food. We will first focus on the effects in country A.

We noted that, before trade, each unit of clothing in country A could be obtained only by giving up two units of food. With trade, people in country A can obtain a unit of clothing at a cost of only one unit of food. At the extreme, if country A were willing to trade away all its food, it could now obtain 200 million units of clothing (see point *Z* in Figure 16.1). In graphic terms, the production possibilities curve for country A has shifted out, from the black line (*XY*) in Figure 16.1 to the blue line (*ZY*). Clearly, trade with country B has made consuming more of *both* clothing and food possible for people in country A.

At this point, we must stop to explain that for country A, the movement from *XY* to *ZY* in Figure 16.1 is identical to the shift that took place in Figure 4.6. In Figure 4.6, we started—by assumption—with the same production possibilities curve (*XY*) and illustrated the shift that would take place if *technological change* doubled productivity in the clothing industry. In Figure 16.1, the same shift occurs as a result of trade. In fact, from the viewpoint of country A, *trade can be thought of as creating a new technology* for making its clothing. Because its clothing is now made in country B, the clothing worn in country A is indeed being produced using a new technology.

In country B, an analogous outward shift in the production possibilities curve will occur. Before trade was possible, to consume an extra unit of food required giving up two units of clothing (along production possibilities curve *X′Y′* in Figure 16.2). With trade, people in country B can obtain a unit of food by giving up only one unit of clothing (see the blue line, *X′Z′*). This change in the cost of food is equivalent to an invention that doubles country B's productivity in the food industry. In country B before trade, the resources to produce 400 million units of clothing were needed to internally produce 200 million units of food; with trade, country B can obtain 200 million units of food at half its internal opportunity cost.

Reallocating Resources   For the potential gains from trade to be realized in both country A and country B, however, resources must flow from one sector to another *within* each country—from clothing production to the food sector in country A and from food to clothing production in country B. These sectoral changes are costly and often painful for those workers and owners who are displaced. If the shift of productive resources from one sector to the other is impeded for some reason, increased trade could cause long-term unemployment—and the gains from trade would be reduced or completely eliminated. Indeed, evidence shows that regional labor markets affected by the rise in trade with China after 1999 suffered reductions in their employment rates that lasted a decade or more.[4] Thus, the normative judgment that trade can enhance national output rests in part on the assumption that any unemployment associated with these sectoral shifts is short term—and does not become long run, or "structural" (as defined in Chapter 14). Normative analysis—as we saw in Chapter 1 and again when we discussed technological change in Chapter 4—also implies that society should take steps to compensate those on whom the costs of expanded trade fall;[5] we return to this topic at the end of the chapter.

Despite the real costs of moving capital and labor across sectors when trade is expanded, the promise of ultimate gains from specialization and trade illustrated in Figures 16.1 and 16.2 has provided a powerful argument among economists for encouraging international trade. Theory suggests that Latoya and Don—and the society in which they live—will be better off for having traded with each other. (Similarly, few would doubt that the citizens of New York will be better off, individually and in the aggregate, if they can trade freely with those in New Jersey and Florida.) The principle of comparative advantage, which drives make-or-buy decisions by individuals, also underlies transactions across international borders. Theory suggests, then, that the people in both countries can gain, on the whole, if they are able to conclude mutually beneficial trades with those in the other country.

Unfortunately, convincing empirical evidence on whether an increase in international trade causes an increase in the overall output of a country is difficult to gather.[6] Many studies, for example, have tried to test whether countries that are more open to trade have faster growth rates, other things being equal; however, the research problems with which the studies must contend have cast doubt on their findings.[7] Various measures of "openness" to trade exist, and the results of studies appear sensitive to which ones are used. Furthermore, even if more openness and faster growth could be shown to be positively correlated, researchers would need to find a way to make sure that their studies dealt successfully with the possibility that more growth could lead to more openness—that is, the causality, instead of running from more openness to greater growth, could run in the opposite direction. Finally, more openness to trade is just one of many factors within a country that could affect its growth rate, so researchers must have a way to successfully account for all the other factors that are relevant to growth.[8] To date, the most careful empirical studies suggest that the effects of expanded trade are positive but probably relatively small—perhaps raising U.S. income by from 2 to 8 percent.[9] (For an interesting natural experiment on how the sudden openness to trade can affect economic growth, see Example 16.1.)

EXAMPLE 16.1

The Growth Effects of the Openness to Trade: Japan's Sudden Move to Openness in 1859

Most empirical studies of how greater openness to trade affects economic growth estimate what happens when the barriers to trade *change*, and such changes are—in reality—relatively small. We only rarely actually get to observe countries, like A and B in our textbook example, move from complete self-sufficiency (which economists call "autarky") to completely free trade. One such example, however, can be found in nineteenth-century Japan, which after 200 years of self-imposed autarky, opened itself to trade with the rest of the world in 1859.

In 1639, Japan's Tokugawa rulers, responding to what they saw as threats posed by Portuguese attempts to Christianize Japanese citizens, prohibited all Japanese from traveling to foreign countries and severely restricted imports. The Dutch and Chinese were the only countries allowed to trade with Japan, and the trade permitted was tiny. The Dutch were limited to one ship a year, which could be unloaded only on a small island in the harbor of Nagasaki; by the 1820s, the Chinese were allowed only three or four small ships per year. British victories over China in the Opium Wars of the early 1840s opened Chinese markets, and Japan's military weakness at the time kept it from opposing the demands from Western countries to open its markets to foreign trade after 1859.

Japan thus offers an excellent "natural experiment" on how trade affects a country's economic growth. It suddenly switched from almost complete autarky in the early 1850s to almost free trade by 1870, and the price changes for the goods that it imported and exported were large. Moreover, Japan's adoption of free trade was not done for economic reasons but because of outside political and military pressure; thus, greater Japanese openness was not caused by economic growth or the lack thereof (i.e., the causation in this case runs from openness to growth, not the reverse). Finally, during this period, Japan did not experience much technological change, so no major factors other than trade that affected economic growth.

A recent study that compares the prices and quantities of goods facing Japanese consumers in the early 1850s with those of the early 1870s finds that the gains from trade were positive but surprisingly small. It estimates that had Japan adopted free trade in the early 1850s (instead of later), its per capita income would have been higher by no more than 8 percent or 9 percent.

Source: Daniel M. Bernhofen and John C. Brown, "An Empirical Assessment of the Comparative Advantage Gains from Trade: Evidence from Japan," *American Economic Review* 95 (March 2005): 208–225

Effects of Trade on the Demand for Labor

We have seen that, in theory, the effects of expanded international trade on a country's production possibilities curve are similar to the effects of technological change, because both trade and technological change open up new opportunities for acquiring goods and services. The effects of expanded trade on the demand for labor are also similar to those of technological change, which we discuss later in the chapter; thus, our analysis of how increased trade affects the demand for labor parallels our analysis in Chapter 4 of how technological change affects employment and wages.

We begin with a reminder that the demand for a given type of labor is derived from conditions in the product market and the prices and productivities of other factors of production. Because trade affects both product demand and the availability of other factors of production, we must consider each source of change.

Product Demand Shifts

Because trade involves *exchange*, a country's move toward greater international trade generally means that both its imports and its exports will increase. When its exports increase, the demand for workers involved in the production of those exports will shift to the right, owing to the expanded scale of production, and both employment opportunities and wages in export industries will tend to increase.

Furthermore, if the expansion of trade makes a country richer, the increase in the overall demand for goods and services, including those made domestically, will tend to cause a rightward shift (a scale effect) in demand for the workers who produce these goods or services. Thus, as people become wealthier, they may want, for example, larger houses, a nicer personal appearance, and better education for their children—and these changes would increase the demand for carpenters, cosmetologists, and teachers.

The increase in imports associated with increased trade, however, will tend to directly or indirectly *reduce* the demand for some domestically produced goods or services. Less-expensive clothing made in Asia, for example, might be so attractive to U.S. consumers that domestic clothing producers would be forced to reduce their production of clothing—and, consequently, their demand for U.S. clothing workers. Similarly, if the United States cannot grow bananas, the increased importation of that fruit might cause the demand for domestically produced apples to fall, and the demand for workers involved in the growing and distribution of U.S. apples would shift to the left.

The shifts in product demand associated with increased international trade thus also create shifts in labor demand. Workers for whom the labor demand curve shifts to the right will experience expanded employment opportunities and perhaps higher wages, where the mix between these two labor market outcomes depends on the shape of the labor supply curves to the relevant occupations or industries. That is, when the labor supply curve is relatively elastic (flat), the rightward shift in the demand for labor will expand employment without much increase in the wage; when the market labor supply curve is less elastic, the wage increase will be greater and the increase in employment will be smaller.

Those workers for whom trade causes the labor demand curve to shift *leftward*, however, may not share in the overall potential benefits of increased trade—even if expanded trade lowers consumer prices. They are forced to change jobs, which could entail a period of unemployment while they search for new work. The costs of change could also involve wage loss or require a significant investment in learning new skills. The mix of reduced employment and wage loss associated with the leftward shift in labor demand also depends on the shape of the market labor supply curve. The more costly learning new skills is for the workers facing a leftward shift in demand, the less elastic will be the labor supply curves to their occupations and the larger will be the decline in their wages.

While a leftward shift in the labor demand curve will put downward pressure on both employment and *nominal* wage levels, greater trade may also bring about a fall in the prices of at least some consumer goods or services. Thus, the fall in workers' *real* wages may not be as large as the fall in their nominal wages.[10]

Shifts in the Supply of Alternative Factors of Production

In recent years, many U.S. firms (and those from other rich countries) have relocated all or parts of their production to poorer areas of the world—most notably, Asia and Latin America.[11] This production sharing has effectively brought a huge number of lower-paid workers in other countries into direct competition for jobs with higher-paid U.S. workers. In terms of the production process, the access to lower-paid workers in other parts of the world has reduced the cost of an alternative source of labor for U.S. firms (which, if they could not tap this source before, could be thought of as formerly facing an infinitely high cost of employing international labor). What are the effects on U.S. employment when lower-wage labor becomes available in other countries?

According to Chapter 4, when the cost of an alternative factor of production falls, a *cross-wage effect* on the demand for labor occurs; that is, the overall effect on the demand for a given kind of labor is the summation of the *substitution and scale effects*, which work in opposite directions. We begin our analysis with a review of the substitution effect.

The Substitution Effect   The incentive to substitute international labor for U.S. labor does not derive from a simple comparison of wage levels in both places; rather, what matters to employers is the *ratio of wages to marginal productivity* in both countries. These ratios—see equation (3.8c) in Chapter 3—indicate the cost of producing an extra unit of output from using each source of labor. Thus, in considering whether to substitute one country's labor for another's, firms take into account the wage level *and* the marginal productivity of workers in each country. Only if the ratio of wages to marginal productivity is lower for international workers will firms consider substituting international workers for U.S. workers.

To analyze the *size* of a potential substitution effect, we must review the two Hicks–Marshall laws of derived demand (see Chapter 4) that bear most directly on substitution. One law suggests that the size of the substitution effect depends in part on the supply response of *U.S.* workers. If they quickly leave for new occupations when the substitution of international workers begins—that is, if the labor supply curve to their current occupation is relatively flat—then the wages of U.S. workers who remain in the current occupation will not fall very much, and substitution will not be mitigated. If, however, the supply curve is relatively steep, such that U.S. wages in the occupation fall to a greater extent, that fall would tend to reduce the incentives of firms to continue their substitution. (In the latter case, of course, U.S. jobs are saved only through wage reductions.) Thus, the substitution effect will be greater if the *supply of U.S. workers to the relevant occupations is more elastic.*

The other Hicks–Marshall law strongly related to the substitution effect is the *ease with which international workers can be substituted for U.S. workers.* Many U.S. workers are in jobs that manufacture goods, which can be transported across borders. Thus, production jobs in the manufacturing sector—which are often filled by workers with relatively little education—are at comparatively high risk of being sent to lower-wage countries. Although the costs of expanded trade appear to have fallen mostly on less-skilled workers, even some high-skilled workers (such as those in the area of finance) have found that they are at risk of competition with comparably educated, but lower-paid, workers in poorer countries.

Other (perhaps most) jobs simply cannot be performed in a remote location: The tasks of barbers, landscapers, surgeons, and physical therapists—to take just a few examples—cannot be sent offshore, because they require face-to-face contact with customers. The language barrier is another deterrent to substitution, as are transportation and long-distance communications costs, training needs, the necessity for employers to acquire a working knowledge of local laws and practices regarding the workplace, and real or perceived cultural differences in work habits, attitudes toward managerial authority, and openness to change. The greater the barriers to substitution, the smaller the substitution effect.

The Scale Effect Our discussion of cross-wage elasticity of demand in Chapter 4 reminds us that a *scale effect* associated with the substitution of foreign for U.S. labor will also occur. If lower-cost labor in poorer countries is substituted for U.S. labor in a particular industry, the resulting fall in production costs will tend to be accompanied by a fall in product price and an associated increase in product demand. Thus, although the substitution effect of offshoring will push toward reducing the demand for U.S. labor, the scale effect associated with lower costs will tend to increase it—so whether the overall number of jobs in the directly affected sectors will fall is not theoretically clear. For example, if clothing is stitched together at a much lower cost overseas, the resulting fall in clothing prices could induce U.S. consumers to buy more of it. The increased consumption of clothing will increase the demand for U.S. workers who are *complements in production* with the overseas production workers, and the demand for clothing buyers, designers, packers, truckers, retail clerks, and their supervisors will tend to rise.

The *size* of the scale effect that accompanies the use of lower-wage labor depends principally on two factors discussed in Chapter 4. One is the *elasticity of demand for the final product* in the industry that is cutting its labor costs. To the extent that consumers are more sensitive to price reductions, the increase in the demand for the good or service being produced will be greater.

The other factor affecting the size of the scale effect is the *share of labor* (in this case, international labor) in total cost. If the international workers' wages constitute a larger part of production costs, the resulting effect on production costs and product price will be greater, and the larger will be the associated scale effect.

Changes in the Elasticity of Demand for Labor Besides causing the labor demand curve for industries or occupations to shift to the right or left, reducing the barriers to international transactions will tend to *increase the elasticity of demand for labor,* for two major reasons. First, a greater ability to substitute foreign for domestic workers will increase the strength of the substitution effect, other things being equal. Second, as internationally made goods and services are allowed to compete with those produced domestically, the elasticity of *product* demand will tend to increase. Workers facing more-elastic labor demand curves will experience greater employment losses if their wages are raised by some nonmarket force, such as the minimum wage or a collective bargaining agreement. Indeed, as we speculated in Chapter 13, greater openness to international transactions may well have played a role, along with several other factors, in reducing the power of unions in the United States in recent decades.

The Net Effect on Labor Demand

We have seen that, in theory, increased trade in goods or services (including production sharing) with foreign countries will benefit some workers but displace others. Those U.S. workers, for example, most likely to *lose* from trade are in jobs (often, less-skilled ones) that international workers can readily perform; in sectors, such as manufacturing, that shrink domestically once trade is expanded; or in industries for which lower costs do not significantly increase product demand. Workers who are displaced will suffer greater losses if switching occupations or industries is difficult or costly for them. Those workers most likely to *gain* are in sectors that have a comparative advantage in production (and thus expand with increased trade) or are in jobs that are complementary with production workers overseas.

Estimates of Employment Effects   Hundreds of studies have attempted to estimate the effects of increased trade or the offshoring of employment in affected sectors. Isolating the effects of trade on employment levels is inherently difficult, however—for two broad reasons. On the one hand, changes in trade occur in the context of continual change in several other forces that affect labor supply and demand. Technological change, for example, has displaced the same group of workers most threatened by trade or offshoring,[12] and responses to both trade and technological change take place amid changes in immigration, personal incomes, and consumer preferences. On the other hand, studies often try to focus on the employment effects in sectors thought to be especially hurt by a change in trade barriers, such as those manufacturing industries facing competition from imports, occupational groups (e.g., lower-skilled factory workers) whose jobs are at risk of going overseas, or areas of the country more affected than others by trade. Although these studies are useful in trying to assess the number of workers on whom the costs of trade might fall, they often do not measure the *total* effect of trade on employment—because they typically find accounting for employment gains that might be created by trade in other industries, occupations, or regions difficult.[13]

Barriers to trade among the United States, Canada, and Mexico have fallen in the past two decades, and many studies have estimated the number of workers displaced by greater trade among these countries. For example, one study estimated that when the Canada–United States Free Trade Agreement—implemented in 1989—reduced Canadian tariffs on imports from the United States, Canadian employment fell by 12 percent in the industries whose tariffs fell the most (these were the industries most affected by an increase in imports from the United States).[14] While this study suggests that a large fraction of Canadian workers in the affected sectors lost their jobs when trade was expanded, its author pointed to the fact that the *overall employment rate* in Canada was the same in 2002 as it was in 1988—and he speculated that those who were displaced thus moved to new jobs relatively rapidly.

Estimates of the job losses in the United States from the offshoring of jobs to other countries are difficult to reliably measure.[15] However, the context in which job losses from offshoring take place is useful to consider. One study, for example, estimated that as of 2002, some 300,000 U.S. workers could expect to lose their jobs each year—or about 25,000 per month—owing to offshoring.[16] Is this number large or small? To gain some perspective on this level of job loss, from May 2001 through April 2002, roughly 1.6 million U.S. workers *per month* lost their jobs (another 2.9 million voluntarily quit their jobs each month).[17] If the estimates of the number of jobs lost to offshoring are correct, these jobs represent only about 1.5 percent of all jobs lost in a month. As suggested in Example 16.2, however, the *potential* displacement of U.S. workers by offshoring may be far larger than has occurred to date.

EXAMPLE 16.2

Could a Quarter of U.S. Jobs Be Offshored? Might Your Future Job Be Among Them?

The estimates of U.S. workers displaced because their jobs have been sent abroad are based on levels or patterns of offshoring that have occurred to date. One economist, however, believes that the number of U.S. jobs that are *potentially* at risk of offshoring is in the neighborhood of 30 million to 40 million—roughly one-quarter of those currently employed. He arrives at this rough estimate by identifying occupations whose services must be performed face to face and those involved in making goods or performing services that can be done in remote locations.

For example, he believes that most of the 14 million U.S. workers in manufacturing—who make goods that can be transported around the world—could well be in competition with the 1.5 billion workers in China, India, or other relatively poor countries that are fast becoming part of the global economy. He also believes that many jobs in computer programming and financial services can be performed in locations distant from the customer or client. In contrast, most jobs in repair, maintenance, healthcare, and leisure activities must be done face to face.

No one can say, of course, just how many jobs will *actually* be offshored, because the large costs of transacting with those in other countries remain. However, the exercise of trying to assess what sorts of services can be performed remotely suggests that students, in planning their careers, could improve their future job security by preparing themselves for jobs that must be performed in person.

Source: Alan S. Blinder, "Offshoring: The Next Industrial Revolution?" *Foreign Affairs* 85 (March–April 2006): 113–128. For a similar article that focuses on service jobs, see Roger J. Moncarz, Michael G. Wolf, and Benjamin Wright, "Service-Providing Occupations, Offshoring, and the Labor Market," *Monthly Labor Review* 131 (December 2008): 71–86

Estimates of the U.S. workers displaced by increased trade more generally (not just offshoring) were correspondingly small as of the early 2000s.[18] The large and rapid growth of manufacturing imports from China after 2000, however, appears to have had a relatively large and negative effect on U.S. employment, where many affected workers have dropped out of the labor force and have been relying on federal and state transfer programs (often retirement or disability benefits) for income.[19] The drop in employment associated with expanded trade with China may underlie, at least to some extent, the rather steep drop in both the overall employment rate and labor force participation rate after 2000 in the United States (see Table 14.1).

However large or small the number of workers displaced by expanded international trade, economic theory suggests that in the long run, *total employment* in a country need be no more affected by its openness to international trade than by technological change (see Chapter 4). How well the labor market works to equate supply and demand affects total employment. If displaced workers have incentives and abilities to acquire new skills and find new jobs without too much difficulty and if wages are flexible enough that labor markets equilibrate supply and demand, unemployment among those who lose their jobs need not be permanent. We saw in Example 16.2 that although 12 percent of Canadian workers in certain sectors lost their jobs after tariffs on Canadian imports were reduced, the overall percentage of Canadians who were employed a decade later remained unchanged. Likewise, we pointed out in Chapter 4 that the employment rate in the United States remained the same between 1979 and early 2020—a period of time over which both technological change *and* increases in international trade were particularly large.

Even if total employment rates are potentially maintained in the long run when international trade expands, those who are displaced from their jobs will bear the costs of qualifying for and finding new jobs. Recent work suggests that these costs of adjustment are high and that full adjustment may take years. Many affected workers experience a significant fall in earnings from joblessness and falling wages, and withdrawals from the labor force and the receipt of income support payments (e.g., from the disability and retirement programs) increase. Adjustment costs are larger for workers with lower levels of education.[20]

Estimates of Wage Effects   Studies that estimate the *wage* effects of trade run into the same problems that confront researchers concerned with estimating its employment effects: Trade is but one of many factors that affect the demand for labor and the level of wages in a country. One recent study tried to account for these other factors by comparing wage changes across regions that were differentially affected by manufacturing imports, and it found no changes in the manufacturing wage from increased trade, but it did find that wages in the nonmanufacturing sector fell.[21] As manufacturing jobs decline and displaced workers seek jobs in nonmanufacturing industries, then, the workers who must change jobs may experience reduced wages.[22]

Most studies of wage effects from increased trade have concentrated on *relative* wages—the differences in wages received by higher-skilled workers and lower-skilled workers within a country of interest. One study estimates that the effects of trade on relative wages in the United States have been small when compared to the contributions of other forces (primarily technological change), accounting for less than 10 percent of the fall in wages of high school dropouts relative to the wages of high school graduates.[23] Others, however, estimate that increased trade and the offshoring of jobs have had a significant effect on raising the relative wages of higher-skilled workers (however, they concluded that trade did not reduce the real earnings of lower-skilled U.S. workers).[24] A study of wages in Hong Kong, which began to outsource production jobs to mainland China when the latter dropped its barriers in the 1980s, also found that trade and outsourcing played an important role in increasing the wage differences between higher-skilled workers and lower-skilled workers.[25]

The wage effects of trade and production sharing on poorer countries—the recipients of outsourced jobs—have also been studied, and the results are surprising: These countries have *also* experienced increased differences between the wages of higher-skilled workers and those of lower-skilled workers that can be traced to increased trade and outsourcing. Apparently, the jobs offshored from richer countries, though often low-skilled jobs by rich-country standards, are comparatively high-skilled jobs within poorer countries; thus, production sharing may increase the demand for relatively higher-skilled workers in both rich countries and poor countries alike.

Moreover, labor mobility appears to be restricted in many poorer countries, so the reallocation of employment from declining to growing sectors is sluggish. Put differently, occupation- or industry-specific labor supply curves in these countries may be relatively inelastic, so the changes in labor demand accompanying increased trade and outsourcing occur mainly in wages rates, not employment levels.[26] These wage adjustments put further downward pressure on the wages of low-skilled workers in poor countries.

Will Wages Converge Across Countries?

One of the concerns that many people have about reducing the barriers to international transactions is that it puts workers (especially less-skilled ones) in the United States and other high-wage countries in direct competition with many millions of much lower-paid workers in Asia, Latin America, and Africa. They worry that this competition will drive wages in richer countries down to the level faced by workers in poorer countries. The purpose of this section is to analyze the forces affecting wage convergence across countries.

In the process of minimizing the cost of producing their optimal level of output, firms will compare the cost of producing an extra unit of output using U.S. labor, say, with the cost of producing the added unit using Chinese labor, Indian labor, or Mexican labor; as we saw earlier—in equation (3.8c)—these costs are represented by the ratio of wages to the marginal productivity of workers in each country. When this ratio is lower in one country than in another, firms will want to consider moving production to the lower-cost country, and the incentives to consider shifting production from higher-cost to lower-cost locations will persist until the ratios are equalized across countries. Thus, if firms are free to move production from country to country, the profit-maximization process would produce a result consistent with the *law of one price*: the equalization within narrowly defined occupations of wage-to-marginal-productivity ratios across countries.

In applying the law of one price to international transactions, the *ratios* of wage to marginal productivity, not the wages themselves, would equalize if production could be readily relocated. Wages would equalize only if marginal productivities equalized; thus, cross-country differences in educational levels, work practices, managerial and organizational skills, and the technology used in the production process could all affect the degree to which wage levels are equalized.

To say, however, that differences in the wage-to-marginal-productivity ratio across countries lead firms to *consider* shifting production to the lowest-cost location does not imply that firms will *actually* do so. The costs of moving and trading across national borders are high, one estimate suggesting that these costs add almost 75 percent to the cost of the typical product.[27] Although the costs imposed by tariffs have fallen over time in most countries, firms incur significant costs from communicating in other languages, transporting goods (especially from poorer countries), dealing in foreign currencies, acquiring information on local laws and regulations, and enforcing contracts internationally. The costs associated with international transactions reduce the incentives for firms to relocate to lower-cost areas, and they thus impede the convergence of wage–marginal productivity ratios predicted by the law of one price (in Chapter 5, we saw other examples in which mobility costs impede the convergence of wages across firms within labor markets).

Tendencies toward convergence will also be concentrated among jobs whose output can be produced in locations remote from the end user, because these the jobs can be moved from place to place if the cost barriers are small relative to the savings. As discussed in Example 16.2, manufacturing workers and those in services that can be performed by using telecommunications are most in competition with similar workers in other countries. Perhaps 75 percent of U.S. workers, however, are in jobs that cannot be moved overseas; they perform health, transportation, maintenance, repair, leisure, educational, or merchandising services that must be performed at the point of sale. These latter workers are not in direct competition with similar workers in other countries.

To the extent that the demand for workers in the face-to-face services grows, then, workers displaced by foreign competition will have opportunities—if they can qualify—for jobs that are not subject to foreign competition (in Chapter 2, we saw that over the past decades, employment in the United States has shifted out of manufacturing and into services, which as a group are more difficult than goods to produce remotely). Additionally, earlier in this chapter, we saw that expanded trade means that export sectors will grow, even in high-wage economies, because international transactions are driven by comparative advantage—that is, by the *internal opportunity costs* of producing goods or services. Thus, the availability of jobs that either are not in competition with international workers or are in sectors that have an international comparative advantage will serve to limit the fall in wages owing to competition from workers in low-wage countries. Indeed, one study of increased trade between the United States and Mexico found no evidence of wage convergence.[28]

Although the creation of jobs in expanding sectors can offer a "brake" on the fall of wages for workers displaced by trade, these displaced workers must easily be able to find, qualify for, and move to the newly created jobs. Furthermore, normative theory requires that those who lose from expanded trade be compensated for their losses by those who gain. We thus close this chapter with an analysis of the kinds of policies that can minimize the costs of trade-related displacement and spread the benefits of expanded international transactions more widely.

Policy Issues

Our theoretical analysis of the effects on workers of expanded international trade and production sharing leads to two broad conclusions. First, removing the barriers to transactions across an international border can enhance aggregate consumption in both countries—through greater specialization and the exploitation of comparative advantage. Second, the movement of resources within each country that is needed to adjust to greater specialization imposes costs on workers whose jobs are displaced; thus, although a society may gain in the aggregate, many within that society are likely to lose when trade and production sharing are expanded. We have seen that, to date, generally the less-skilled workers within a country seem most at risk of losing from expanded trade.

In Chapter 1, and when discussing the effects of technological change in Chapter 4, we emphasized that one can conclude that society as a whole is better off with some policy change only if one of the following conditions has been met:

a. Everyone gains from it.

b. Some gain and no one else loses.

c. Some gain and some lose, but the gainers fully compensate the losers—which converts condition c into condition b.

Because enhanced trade—just as is the case with technological change—does displace some workers in a society, normative considerations require that those who gain from reducing the barriers to international transactions compensate those who lose from this policy change. We can use the theory developed earlier in this text to analyze the forms such compensation might usefully take.

Subsidizing Human-Capital Investments

Much of the losses suffered by those who are displaced arise from their having to change jobs and possibly face a cut in wages. Because having to search for a new job takes time, workers who lose their jobs will probably experience a spell of unemployment as they conduct their search (see Chapter 14). Furthermore, displaced workers may have to invest in training to qualify for another job (Chapter 9),[29] and they may also have to invest in moving to a new city or state to secure employment (Chapter 10). In short, those who are displaced by expanded trade or offshoring are forced to make new human-capital investments.

Government programs that subsidize these human-capital investments, if paid for by those who gain from the expansion of international transactions,[30] can serve two important purposes. First, they can help to compensate workers who are displaced as a result of policy change, by reducing the financial burden of the investments that they need to make. Second, by helping the displaced qualify for and find new jobs, they can minimize unemployment and speed the process of reallocating resources to more-efficient uses—thus helping society as a whole realize the consumption gains from expanded trade.

In the United States, the Trade Adjustment Assistance program, as reauthorized in 2015, is an example of a program that is designed to subsidize human-capital investments by workers who have been displaced by trade or production sharing. To be eligible for benefits, groups of three or more workers (or a union or company official acting on their behalf) must apply and be able to demonstrate that layoffs of a certain magnitude have occurred in their firm because of increased imports or offshoring.[31] Once certified for eligibility, displaced workers can receive a year or more of training, during which they receive unemployment benefits (and partially subsidized health insurance); in addition to training investments, eligible workers can receive up to $1,250 as a reimbursement for job-search costs and another $1,250 to help subsidize relocation costs. To date, however, the number of workers declared eligible for this program has been relatively small.[32]

Recognizing that those who lose from expanded trade are required to make an *investment* to adjust to their displacement suggests that we review the factors influencing human-capital investment decisions, which were analyzed in Chapters 5, 9, and 10. Those workers who are most likely (other things being equal) to benefit from investing in mobility and training, or to find an employer willing to share these investment costs with them, are those who are young enough to have a relatively long expected period over which the benefits of investment can be "collected." The net benefits from training will also be greater for workers who learn easily or who do not find the psychological costs of learning to be large. Finally, the net benefits of any investment are larger for those who have relatively low discount rates—that is, for those who are not too present oriented.

Given that using resources in any *particular* way precludes their use in *other* ways, society will want to make sure that it invests in human-capital subsidies only when the social benefits exceed the social costs. Consideration of the factors affecting human-capital decisions suggests some of the conditions under which the costs might exceed the benefits. For older (or even middle-aged) workers, the present value of the future benefits from an investment may be so limited that they fall short of the costs. Costs could also exceed the benefits for workers who are present oriented or who find learning new skills difficult—and many of the less-skilled workers displaced by trade may have avoided earlier human-capital investments for these reasons. Thus, training subsidies may not represent a wise use of resources for many displaced workers. (Indeed, according to evaluations of more widely targeted government-sponsored training programs, both in the United States—see Chapter 9—and Europe,[33] the net benefits of government training appear to be, at best, rather modest.)

Income Support Programs

One response to the problem that some training or relocation investments may not be worth making is for the government to offer extended unemployment benefits for displaced workers or provide funds so that workers affected by displacement can retire early or qualify for disability benefits. Although higher payouts for unemployment and pension benefits would help to compensate those displaced by expanded trade, the provision of these benefits—as we saw in Chapters 6, 7, and 14—encourages nonemployment.

A reduction in the workforce, of course, tends to reduce the output gains associated with greater trade.

An alternative form of income support, which encourages employment, is to directly subsidize targeted individuals who work. The Earned Income Tax Credit program, analyzed in Chapter 6, is an example of such a program—but it does not specifically target workers displaced by trade. A program that does target those displaced by trade is "wage insurance," under which displaced workers whose new jobs pay less than the one from which they were displaced receive a payment from the government that makes up at least part of the difference. For example, the United States has a program, for certain older workers (ages 50 and up) who are eligible for the Trade Adjustment Assistance program, that pays them half of their annual earnings losses—up to $10,000 over a period of two years—if they take a new job that pays less than $50,000 per year.[34] This program is clearly aimed at encouraging re-employment, even if it means lower wages, among displaced workers in whom training investments may not be worthwhile.

Subsidized Employment

Another response to the problem that not all training will create net social benefits is for government to subsidize the employers of displaced workers for whom training costs are relatively high or the expected benefits are relatively low.[35] One way to do this is to offer employers payroll subsidies if they hire, for example, older or lower-skilled workers who have been displaced by trade or offshoring. We saw in Chapter 3 that employer payroll subsidies tend to increase employment and wages among the targeted workers, where the mix of these two outcomes depends on the shape of the market labor supply curves for the targeted workers. The research described in Empirical Study 16.1 at the end of this chapter suggests that private employment subsidies are more effective than training in speeding the re-employment of workers. Another form of subsidized employment is for the government to become the "employer of last resort," directly employing targeted workers to perform public works projects for a period of time. These programs appear to be relatively ineffective at helping workers acquire unsubsidized jobs later on.

How Narrowly Should We Target Compensation?

Our analysis has shown that the displacement effects of greater trade and production sharing are similar to those of technological change, and in practice, identifying which of the two forces actually caused the displacement of a given individual is difficult. Indeed, we have pointed out that myriad other forces also serve to shift the demand for, and supply of, workers in a dynamic economy: changes in incomes, preferences, and demographic characteristics, to highlight a few. Therefore, although a drop in the barriers to international transactions will tend to increase the number of workers whose jobs will be displaced, this displacement occurs in the larger context of labor market changes that are constantly occurring for other reasons.

Because the compensation principle suggested by normative economics applies to *all* transactions in which some in society are forced to bear losses for the good of the collective and because expanded international transactions are but one (and perhaps a relatively small) force causing worker displacement, implementing a set of compensation programs targeted *only* on trade-related displacement is difficult to justify. In fact, the resources and time needed to verify that it was international trade or production sharing that caused the displacement of a particular set of workers could well be one reason why the benefits of the American Trade Adjustment Assistance program are received by so few workers.[36] Many European countries, in contrast, offer a range of "active labor market policies" under which workers displaced—for whatever reasons—are the intended beneficiaries of training and employment subsidies. Although these European policies are not universally successful, they do represent attempts to smooth transitions to a wide set of economic forces.[37]

We must also recognize that the costs of greater trade and production sharing do not fall exclusively on those who are displaced. When the forces for change in an economy are increased, whether by technological advances, greater openness to international transactions, or some other factor, workers other than those who are actually displaced face greater uncertainty about their futures. They may also experience wider swings in their earnings over time.

For example, we argued earlier that falling barriers to international transactions tend to create a more elastic labor demand curve in an affected labor market. To see how a change in the elasticity of labor demand can affect employment and wages, consider the relatively inelastic demand curve (D_0) and the relatively elastic demand curve (D_1) in Figure 16.3. Suppose, given the supply curve shown, that the initial equilibrium for both curves is at wage W^* and employment E^*. Now, suppose that product prices fall, shifting both demand curves down by an equal vertical distance (ab). The new wage and employment equilibria would be at point x with the inelastic demand curve and at point y with the elastic curve; the employment and wage losses created by this fall in product price are thus greater when the demand curve is more elastic. Thus, if labor demand curves are—because of increased international competition—becoming more elastic over time, any price fluctuations in the product market will be associated with larger swings in employment and wage outcomes in the labor market. The actual extent to which labor demand curves are made more elastic by greater openness, however, remains unclear.[38]

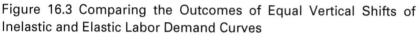

Figure 16.3 Comparing the Outcomes of Equal Vertical Shifts of Inelastic and Elastic Labor Demand Curves

---

EMPIRICAL STUDY 16.1

EVALUATING EUROPEAN ACTIVE LABOR MARKET POLICIES: THE USE OF META-ANALYSIS

In discussing how societies might help workers adversely affected by expanded trade, we saw that many European countries have adopted one or more "active labor market policies"—training programs, private sector employment subsidies, or direct government employment, for example—to help displaced workers qualify for and find new jobs. In the past decade, dozens of statistical studies of programs in 15 European countries have evaluated the success of given policies in either reducing workers' durations of unemployment or increasing their probability of re-employment. Each program, however, has a unique context and its own set of characteristics. Furthermore, in the empirical studies presented earlier in this text, we have seen that the methodological problems confronting researchers in any study can be addressed in different ways and by making different assumptions. Thus, although no single evaluative study is likely to be definitive, we ask whether—taking various studies together—we can develop some generalizations that would be useful in crafting national policies.

The number of active labor market policies in Europe and the variety of institutional contexts in which they take place actually prove quite useful in coming to some conclusions about their effectiveness, because each program can be considered as a separate experiment. If the results from these many experiments can be compared in a meaningful way, we should be able to find out which programmatic characteristics are likely to help workers transition to new employers most successfully. Meta-analysis offers a statistical method for summarizing and analyzing the results of different studies.

A recently published meta-analysis of 137 evaluative studies categorized their research outcomes as indicating either a success or a failure in speeding the transition of displaced workers to new jobs. An "outcome" variable was then created and given the value of 1 if the program analyzed by a study was considered successful—and a value of zero if not. With the outcome of programs as the variable to be explained (the dependent variable), the meta-analysis also captured data on four categories of independent (explanatory) variables: the type of active labor market policy and its level of funding; the country's unemployment and economic growth rates; the decade during which the outcome was measured; and various laws in the country regarding how "protected" workers are from being fired.

The meta-analysis consisted of regressing the dichotomous outcome variable against the foregoing independent variables.[a] The analysis found that, holding variables in the other categories constant, those active labor market policies using employment subsidies and providing help with—and incentives for—job searches were more effective than training programs in helping workers transition to new jobs were. Programs to employ displaced workers in public works projects were less successful than training was in helping workers to obtain jobs in the long run. All types of active labor market policy programs, the analysis found, tended to be *less* successful in reducing the duration of unemployment in countries that strongly protect workers from being fired (recall from Chapter 5 that increasing employers' costs of firing workers also increases their costs of hiring them).

[a] Using a dichotomous variable, which varies only between 0 and 1, as the dependent variable in a regression analysis presents a serious statistical issue, which was addressed in this study by using the widely known method called probit analysis.

Source: Jochen Kluve et al., *Active Labor Market Policies in Europe: Performance and Perspectives* (Berlin: Springer, 2007): 172–185

Although technology and trade, in theory, can enhance consumption levels in a society, we must remember that individuals are trying to maximize their *utility*, not their income. Greater worry about a more uncertain future, therefore, is an additional cost of expanding international transactions, and if those who see gains from trade are to persuade others to go along with reducing the barriers to international transactions, they may have to agree to a larger "safety net" of policies to compensate those who lose from trade. Indeed, one study found that countries that are more open to international transactions also have larger governments, presumably because government spending plays a role in risk reduction.[39]

Summary

We have seen that reducing the barriers to international transactions has reinforced the labor market effects brought on by other forces, such as technological change, in raising the relative demand for higher-skilled workers. As the returns to educational investments have risen and as workers are put at greater risk of having to adjust to changes in labor demand over their careers, the case for governments to extend and improve *schooling*—including preschooling—has been strengthened. Workers who have higher levels of cognitive skill will be able to qualify for a wider variety of jobs, and they will also be able to learn new skills with greater ease (and thus at a lower cost). *Providing youth greater access to a high-quality education is perhaps the single most important program that a government can undertake to help its workers cope with the changes in labor demand associated with an expansion in international transactions.*[40]

Review Questions

1. In explaining and illustrating the principle of comparative advantage, this chapter compared the production possibilities for two countries, A and B, with and without being able to trade with each other. Although the potential total output in country B was larger than that in country A (compare Figures 16.1 and 16.2), the discussion did not specify the population in each country. Would whether country B's population was equal in size to that of country A or 10 times as large as that of country A (therefore making country B much poorer on a per capita basis than A) matter to the analysis of comparative advantage? Explain.

2. Company X, a profit-maximizing employer that makes picture frames, is expanding and needs to pick a location for its new plant. It is considering two sites: one in Texas and one in Mexico, where wages are roughly one-quarter of what they are in Texas. Use economic theory to analyze the factors that company X will take into account when making its decision.

3. Suppose the many U.S. firms making home burglar alarm systems decide (independently) to shift the *production* of their alarms to Asia or Latin America, where they can be made at a much lower cost. Using economic theory, analyze the effects on U.S. employment levels in the burglar alarm industry. What factors make these effects larger or smaller?

4. Television commentator A makes the following statement: "Economic theory shows that reducing the barriers to international trade will, in time, make everyone in society better off." Comment.

5. Television commentator B makes the following statement: "Tearing down tariff and other protections for U.S. producers from competition with low-wage countries can only reduce the number of jobs in the United States." Comment according to economic theory.

6. U.S. television commentator C makes the following statement: "Reducing the barriers to trade with low-wage countries will expose our workers to competition from millions of low-paid workers in the developing world. The result will be that U.S. wage levels will plunge downward until they equal the wage levels in China and other poorer countries." Comment according to economic theory.

7. Television commentator D makes the following statement: "The fact that greater trade increases overall national income tells us all we need to know: Greater trade is good for our society." Comment according to economic theory.

Problems

1. Country M can produce 50 million bicycles or 60 million refrigerators per year. Country N can produce 75 million bicycles or 50 million refrigerators per year. The production possibilities curve for each country is linear.

   a. What is the opportunity cost of bicycles in each country? What is the opportunity cost of refrigerators in each?

   b. Which country has a comparative advantage in producing bicycles? Why?

   c. Should these two countries trade? If not, why not? If so, which country would produce bicycles, and which country would produce refrigerators?

2. Per year, country C can produce 200 tons of wheat or 50 million automobiles. Per year, country D can produce 500 tons of wheat or 125 million automobiles. The production possibilities curve for each country is linear.

   a. What is the opportunity cost of wheat in each country? What is the opportunity cost of automobiles in each?

   b. Which country has a comparative advantage in producing wheat? Why?

   c. Should these two countries trade? If not, why not? If so, which country should produce wheat, and which country should produce automobiles?

3. Suppose that the marginal productivity of customer service representatives in a rich country is $MP_L = 17 - 0.6L$, where L = the number (in thousands) of workers. The marginal productivity of customer service representatives in a poorer country is $MP_L = 11 - 0.8L$. Currently, 10,000

workers in the rich country are employed as customer service representatives at a wage rate of $20 per hour. In the poor country, 5,000 workers are employed as customer service representatives at a wage rate of $10 per hour. A firm in the rich country is thinking about transferring 1,000 customer service jobs from the rich country to the poor one. Do you think it should do so? Why or why not?

Notes

1. U.S. President, *Economic Report of the President* (Washington, DC: Government Printing Office, 2020), Table B-4.

2. The slope of the production possibilities curve *XY* for country A is ½.

3. We note that our example only has two goods.

4. David H. Autor, David Dorn, and Gordon H. Hanson, "The China Shock: Learning from Labor Market Adjustments to Large Changes in Trade," *Annual Review of Economics* 8 (2016): 205–240; Brian Asquith, Sanjana Gowsami, David Neumark, and Antonio Rodriguez-Lopez, "U.S. Job Flows and the China Shock," *Journal of International Economics* 118 (May 2019): 123–137.

5. For example, a recent study finds that rising import competition between 1995 and 2005 reduced the lifetime earnings of 5 percent of workers in Denmark; see Sharon Traiberman, "Occupations and Import Competition: Evidence from Denmark," *American Economic Review* 109 (December 2019): 4260–4301.

6. Determining whether trade is Pareto optimal (meaning no one is made worse off) is particularly difficult.

7. A nice summary of studies that try to measure the overall gains to countries from trade can be found in Richard Freeman, "Trade Wars: The Exaggerated Impact of Trade in Economic Debate" (Working Paper No. 10000, National Bureau of Economic Research, Cambridge, MA, September 2003).

8. For studies that cite and evaluate earlier literature, see Timothy J. Kehoe and Kim J. Ruhl, "Why Have Economic Reforms in Mexico Not Generated Growth?" *Journal of Economic Literature* 48 (December 2010): 1005–1027; David Greenaway, Wyn Morgan, and Peter Wright, "Trade Liberalisation and Growth in Developing Countries," *Journal of Economic Development* 67 (February 2002): 229–244; L. Alan Winters, Neil McCulloch, and Andrew McKay, "Trade Liberalization and Poverty: The Evidence So Far," *Journal of Economic Literature* 42 (March 2004): 72–115.

9. Arnaud Costinot and Andrés Rodríguez-Clare, "The US Gains from Trade: Valuation Using the Demand for Foreign Factor Services," *Journal of Economic Perspectives* 32 (Spring 2018): 3–24. Also see Lorenzo

Caliendo and Fernando Parro, "Estimates of the Trade and Welfare Effects of NAFTA," *Review of Economic Studies* 82 (January 2015): 1–44. For articles on the losses to the United States from restrictions on trade promulgated by the Trump administration in 2018, see Mary Amiti, Stephen J. Redding, and David E. Weinstein, "The Impact of the 2018 Tariffs on Prices and Welfare," *Journal of Economic Perspectives* 33 (Fall 2019): 187–210; Pablo D. Fajgelbaum, Pinelopi K. Goldberg, Patrick J. Kennedy, and Amit K. Khandelwal, "The Returns to Protectionism," *Quarterly Journal of Economics* 135 (February 2020): 1–55.

10. For a recent paper on the effects of trade (or the suppression of trade) on domestic prices, see Amiti, Redding, and Weinstein, "The Impact of the 2018 Tariffs on Prices and Welfare."

11. Clearly, firms in high-wage countries have recently found employing cheaper labor in poorer countries to be more profitable. The reasons for this increased employment of foreign labor may be related to a reduction in political barriers to relocation or improvements in telecommunications technologies, better transportation systems both within and among countries, or the miniaturization of components that comprise final output.

12. For a review of studies on offshoring, see David Hummels, Jakob R. Munch, and Chong Xiang, "Offshoring and Labor Markets," *Journal of Economic Literature* 56 (September 2018): 981–1028. Also see David H. Autor, David Dorn, and Gordon H. Hanson, "Untangling Trade and Technology: Evidence from Local Labor Markets," *Economic Journal* 125 (May 2015): 621–646. Also see Daron Acemoglu and Pascual Restrepo, "Robots and Jobs: Evidence from US Labor Markets," *Journal of Political Economy* 128 (June 2020): 2188–2244, for related work on the effect of robots on the U.S. labor market.

13. For a study that attempts to measure the net effect of both job losses and job gains from trade, see Daron Acemoglu, David Autor, David Dorn, Gordon H. Hanson, and Brendan Price, "Import Competition and the Great U.S. Employment Sag of the 2000s," *Journal of Labor Economics* 34, pt. 2 (January 2016): S141–S198.

14. Daniel Trefler, "The Long and Short of the Canada—U.S. Free Trade Agreement," *American Economic Review* 94 (September 2004): 870–895.

15. Hummels, Munch, and Xiang, "Offshoring and Labor Markets."

16. See Jagdish Bhagwati, Arvind Panagariya, and T.N. Srinivasan, "The Muddles Over Outsourcing," *Journal of Economic Perspectives* 18 (Fall 2004): 93–114.

17. U.S. Bureau of Labor Statistics, "New Monthly Data Series on Job Openings and Labor Turnover Announced by BLS," News Release USDL 02–412, July 30, 2002. The number of monthly layoffs published by the Bureau of Labor Statistics may be significantly understated,

which would imply that offshored jobs make up even a smaller percent of overall monthly job loss; see Steven J. Davis, R. Jason Faberman, John C. Haltiwanger, and Ian Rucker, "Adjusted Estimates of Worker Flows and Job Openings in JOLTS" (Working Paper No. 14137, National Bureau of Economic Research, Cambridge, MA, June 2008).

18. For example, see Ann Harrison and Margaret McMillan, "Offshoring Jobs? Multinationals and U.S. Manufacturing Employment," *Review of Economics and Statistics* 93 (August 2011): 857–875; Mary E. Burfisher, Sherman Robinson, and Karen Thierfelder, "The Impact of NAFTA on the United States," *Journal of Economic Perspectives* 15 (Winter 2001): 125–144; Bhagwati, Panagariya, and Srinivasan, "The Muddles Over Outsourcing"; Freeman, "Trade Wars: The Exaggerated Impact of Trade in Economic Debate."

19. Autor, Dorn, and Hanson, "The China Shock: Learning from Labor Market Adjustments to Large Changes in Trade."

20. Autor, Dorn, and Hanson, "The China Shock: Learning from Labor Market Adjustment to Large Changes in Trade."

21. David H. Autor, David Dorn, and Gordon H. Hanson, "The China Syndrome: Local Labor Market Effects of Import Competition in the United States," *American Economic Review* 103 (October 2013): 2121–2168.

22. For a study of wage effects associated with offshoring in the higher-skilled service sector, see Runjuan Liu and Daniel Trefler, "A Sorted Tale of Globalization: White Collar Jobs and the Rise of Service Offshoring," *Journal of International Economics* 118 (May 2019): 105–122.

23. The study estimates that trade accounts for even less of the fall in the wages of high school graduates relative to college graduates; see George J. Borjas, Richard B. Freeman, and Lawrence F. Katz, "How Much Do Immigration and Trade Affect Labor Market Outcomes?" *Brookings Papers on Economic Activity* (1997): 1–67. Similar conclusions are made by Robert Z. Lawrence, *Blue-Collar Blues: Is Trade to Blame for Rising US Income Inequality?* (Washington, DC: Peterson Institute for International Economics, 2008); Jonathan Haskel, Robert Z. Lawrence, Edward E. Leamer, and Matthew J. Slaughter, "Globalization and U.S. Wages: Modifying Classic Theory to Explain Recent Facts," *Journal of Economic Perspectives* 26 (Spring 2012): 119–140. However, greater competition from foreign firms does appear to increase the extent to which pay-for-performance compensation plans are used (and thus, they could contribute to growing inequality *within* human-capital groups); see Vicente Cuñat and Maria Guadalupe, "Globalization and the Provision of Incentives Inside the Firm: The Effect of Foreign Competition," *Journal of Labor Economics* 27 (April 2009): 179–212; Anders Akerman, Elhanan Helpman, Oleg Itskhoki, Marc-Andreas Muendler, and Stephen Redding, "Sources of Wage Inequality," *American Economic Review: Papers and Proceedings* 103 (May 2013): 214–219.

24. Robert C. Feenstra and Gordon H. Hanson, "The Impact of Outsourcing and High-Technology Capital on Wages: Estimates for the U.S., 1979–1990," *Quarterly Journal of Economics* 114 (August 1999): 907–940; Robert C. Feenstra and Gordon H. Hanson, "Global Production Sharing and Rising Inequality: A Survey of Trade and Wages" (Working Paper No. 8372, National Bureau of Economic Research, Cambridge, MA, July 2001).

25. Chang-Tai Hsieh and Keong T. Woo, "The Impact of Outsourcing to China on Hong Kong's Labor Market," *American Economic Review* 95 (December 2005): 1673–1687. Similar results have been found for Denmark; see David Hummels, Rasmus Jørgensen, Jakob Munch, and Chong Xiang, "The Wage Effects of Offshoring: Evidence from Danish Matched Worker–Firm Data," *American Economic Review* 104 (June 2014): 1597–1629.

26. Pinelopi Koujianou Goldberg and Nina Pavcnik, "Distributional Effects of Globalization in Developing Countries," *Journal of Economic Literature* 45 (March 2007): 39–82. The effects on wages of capital inflows to developing countries is analyzed in Anusha Chari, Peter Blair Henry, and Diego Sasson, "Capital Market Integration and Wages," *American Economic Journal: Macroeconomics* 4 (April 2012): 103–132.

27. James E. Anderson and Eric van Wincoop, "Trade Costs," *Journal of Economic Literature* 42 (September 2004): 691–751.

28. Gordon H. Hanson, "What Has Happened to Wages in Mexico since NAFTA?" (Working Paper No. 9563, National Bureau of Economic Research, Cambridge, MA, March 2003). The concern that competition from low-paid workers in poor countries will encourage a "race to the bottom" in terms of wages and working conditions has led some to propose the worldwide adoption of a uniform set of labor standards; for an economic analysis of these proposals, see Drusilla K. Brown, "Labor Standards: Where Do They Belong on the International Trade Agenda?" *Journal of Economic Perspectives* 15 (Summer 2001): 89–112.

29. For evidence that workers do make human-capital investments after being displaced, see Daniel C. Hickman and William W. Olney, "Globalization and Investment in Human Capital," *Industrial and Labor Relations Review* 64 (July 2011): 652–670.

30. Because the gains from trade appear to be concentrated among higher-skilled workers, some economists point out that governments should raise revenues by increasing the progressivity of their tax systems, which would increase taxes paid by those with relatively high incomes; see, for example, Joseph E. Stiglitz, *Making Globalization Work* (New York: W.W. Norton, 2006): 100.

31. The program requires that in the 12 months preceding the date of the application for benefits, at least three workers in work groups of fewer than 50, or at least 5 percent of the workforce in groups of 50 or more,

have been laid off (or threatened with layoff) because of offshoring or imports.

32. Autor, Dorn, and Hanson, "The China Shock: Learning from Labor Market Adjustment to Large Changes in Trade." For a more detailed description of the program and its antecedents, see Katherine Baicker and M. Marit Rehavi, "Policy Watch: Trade Adjustment Assistance," *Journal of Economic Perspectives* 18 (Spring 2004): 239–255; and U.S. Department of Labor website www.dol.gov.

33. Jochen Kluve, David Card, Michael Fertig, Marek Góra, Lena Jacobi, Peter Jensen et al., *Active Labor Market Policies in Europe: Performance and Perspectives* (Berlin: Springer, 2007).

34. See www.dol.gov for more information on the Reemployment Trade Adjustment Assistance program. For a monograph on wage insurance, see Robert J. LaLonde, "The Case for Wage Insurance" (Council on Foreign Relations, Council Special Report No. 30, September 2007).

35. These subsidies are suggested by Adrian Wood, *North–South Trade, Employment, and Inequality: Changing Fortunes in a Skill-Driven World* (Oxford: Clarendon Press, 1994).

36. See Baicker and Rehavi, "Policy Watch: Trade Adjustment Assistance."

37. See Kluve et al., *Active Labor Market Policies in Europe.*

38. For citations to the literature on this topic, see Goldberg and Pavcnik, "Distributional Effects of Globalization in Developing Countries."

39. Dani Rodrik, "Why Do More Open Economies Have Bigger Governments?" *Journal of Political Economy* 106 (October 1998): 997–1032.

40. See Stiglitz, *Making Globalization Work*, especially chapter 2, for a thorough analysis of what is required of governments to bring about (and more widely distribute) the gains that societies can achieve from greater openness to international transactions. For an essentially complementary view, also see Dennis J. Snower, Alessio J.G. Brown, and Christian Merkl, "Globalization and the Welfare State: A Review of Hans-Werner Sinn's *Can Germany Be Saved?*" *Journal of Economic Literature* 47 (March 2009): 136–158.

Selected Readings

Anderson, James E., and Eric van Wincoop. "Trade Costs." *Journal of Economic Literature* 42 (September 2004): 691–751.

Freeman, Richard. "Trade Wars: The Exaggerated Impact of Trade in Economic Debate." Working Paper No. 10,000, National Bureau of Economic Research, Cambridge, MA, September 2003.

Goldberg, Pinelopi Koujianou, and Nina Pavcnik. "Distributional Effects of Globalization in Developing Countries." *Journal of Economic Literature* 45 (March 2007): 39–82.

Lawrence, Robert Z. *Blue-Collar Blues: Is Trade to Blame for Rising US Income Inequality?* Washington, DC: Peterson Institute for International Economics, 2008.

Stiglitz, Joseph. *Making Globalization Work.* New York: W.W. Norton, 2006.

Answers to Odd-Numbered Review Questions and Problems

Chapter 1

Review Questions

1. The basic value premise underlying normative analysis is that if a given transaction is beneficial to the parties agreeing to it and hurts no one else, then accomplishing that transaction is said to be good. This criterion implies, of course, that anyone harmed by a transaction must be compensated for that harm (a condition tantamount to saying that all parties to a transaction must voluntarily agree to it). The labor market will reach a point of optimality when all mutually beneficial transactions have been accomplished. If mutually beneficial transactions remain unconsummated, the labor market will not be at a point of optimality.

   One condition preventing the accomplishment of a mutually beneficial transaction would be ignorance. A party to a transaction might voluntarily agree to it because they are uninformed about some adverse effect of that transaction. Likewise, a party to a potential transaction may fail to enter into the transaction because they are uninformed about a benefit of the transaction. Informed individuals may fail to consummate a transaction, however, because of underlying transaction barriers. These may arise because of government prohibitions against certain kinds of transactions, imperfections in the market's ability to bring buyers and sellers together, or the nonexistence of a market where one could potentially exist.

3. Although compulsion and a voluntary system of labor recruitment could conceivably result in having the same number of employees work on the levee, the system of voluntary acceptance has one major normative advantage: It assures society that all employees working on the levee view the job as improving their welfare. When workers are drafted, at least some are being compelled to accept a transaction that they view as detrimental to their interests; allowing these workers to change employment would improve social welfare through simply reallocating (not increasing) resources.

A system of voluntary recruitment, then, increases the welfare of society more than would a system that relies on conscription.

5. a. This behavior is entirely consistent with the model of job quitting described in the text. Workers are assumed, according to economic theory, to be attempting to maximize utility (happiness). If all other aspects of two jobs are similar, this theory predicts that workers will prefer a higher-paying job to a lower-paying job. However, two jobs frequently differ in many important respects, including the work environment, personalities of managers, and the stresses placed on employees. Thus, one way to interpret this woman's behavior is that she was willing to give up 50 cents an hour to be able to work in an environment freer of stress.

   b. We have no way to prove that her behavior was grounded in "rationality." Economists define *rationality* as the ability to make considered decisions that are expected (at the time the decision is made) to advance one's self-interest. We cannot tell from any one individual act whether the person involved is being rational or not. Certainly, as described earlier, this woman's decision to quit could be interpreted as a move calculated to increase her utility (or level of happiness). However, she could also have become angry and made her decision without any thought of the consequences.

   c. Economic theory does not predict that everyone will act alike. Because economic agents are assumed to maximize utility and because each person can be assumed to have a unique set of preferences, that some workers would respond to a given set of incentives and that others would not comprise a scenario entirely consistent with economic theory. Thus, that economic theory applied to one group of workers but not to another could not be correctly concluded from the situation described. The other workers might have been less bothered by stress, and they might not have been willing to give up 50 cents an hour to avoid this stress.

7. The prohibitions of child labor laws would seem to violate the principle of mutual benefit by outlawing certain transactions that might be voluntarily entered into. However, at least two conditions exist under which such prohibitions would be consistent with the principles of normative economics. First, the children entering into an employment transaction may be uninformed or not capable of being informed of the dangers or the consequences of their decision to work in a particular environment. By their nature, children are inexperienced, and many modern societies frequently adopt legislation to protect them from their own ignorance.

Second, many modern societies might adopt child labor legislation to protect children from their parents. A child forced by a parent to work in a dangerous or unhealthy environment has not voluntarily agreed to the employment transaction. Thus, a law prohibiting such a child from engaging in certain employment would not be violating the principle of mutual benefit when parental compulsion was present.

Problems

1. (Appendix 1A) Plotting the data shows that age and wage rise together. The appropriate linear model would be $W_i = a_0 + a_1 A_i + e_i$, where W_i is the wage of the ith person, A_i is the age of the ith person, a_0 and a_1 are the parameters of the line, and e_i is the random error term for the ith person. Notice that wage must be the dependent variable and age the explanatory variable, not the other way around.

3. (Appendix 1A) Yes, the t *statistic* (the coefficient divided by the standard error) equals $0.3/0.1$, or 3. When the t *statistic* exceeds 2, one can be fairly confident that the true value of the coefficient is not 0.

5. (Appendix 1A) The t *statistic* equals the coefficient divided by the standard error. For the coefficient on age, the t *statistic* is $0.25/0.10$, or 2.5. For the coefficient on full-time status, the t *statistic* is $0.75/0.20$, or 3.75. Thus, both estimated coefficients are statistically significant, implying that the hypothesis that the true value of the coefficient equals zero can be rejected.

Chapter 2

Review Questions

1. As shown in Figure 2RQ.1, the outflow of construction workers shifted the labor supply curve relevant to Egypt's construction sector to the *left* (from S_1 to S_2), whereas the demand curve for the services of construction workers shifted to the *right* (D_1 to D_2). Because both shifts, by themselves, tended to increase the equilibrium wage rate from W_1 to W_2, we would clearly expect wages in the Egyptian construction sector to have risen faster than average. However, the two shifts by themselves had opposite effects on employment, so the expected net change in employment is theoretically ambiguous.

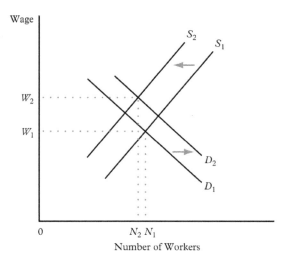

Figure 2RQ.1

3. Many engineers are employed in research and development tasks. There-fore, if a major demander of research and development were to reduce its demand, the demand curve for engineers would shift left, causing their wages and employment to fall.

5. If the wages for arc welders are above the equilibrium wage, the company is paying more for its arc welders than it needs to and, as a result, is hiring fewer than it could. Thus, the definition of overpayment that makes the most sense in this case is one in which the wage rate is above the equilibrium wage.

A ready indicator of an above-equilibrium wage rate is a long queue of applicants whenever a position in a company becomes available. Another indicator is an abnormally low quit rate as workers (in this case arc weld-ers) who are lucky enough to obtain the above-equilibrium wage cling tenaciously to their jobs.

7.

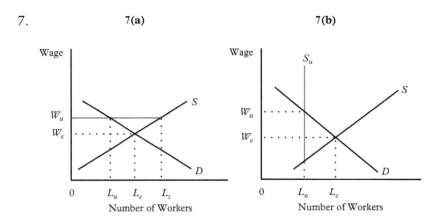

9. This regulation essentially increases the cost of capital and will have an ambiguous effect on the demand curve for labor. On the one hand, the increased cost of capital will increase the cost of production and cause a scale effect that tends to depress employment. On the other hand, this regulation will increase the cost of capital relative to labor and could stimulate the substitution of labor for capital. Thus, the substitution effect will work to increase employment, whereas the scale effect will work to decrease it. Which effect is stronger cannot be predicted from theory alone.

11. a. Economic growth tends to shift the labor demand curve to the right (more workers are demanded at each wage rate).

    b. Greater job growth accompanied by slower positive wage changes will result if the labor supply curve in Canada is flatter (has a smaller positive slope) than the labor supply curve in the United States.

Problems

1. Unemployment rate $= 100 \times$ (number unemployed)/(num-ber unemployed + number employed) $= 100 \times (5$ million$)/$

(135 million) = 3.7 percent. Labor force participation rate = 100 × (number employed + number unemployed)/adult population = 100 × (135 million)/(210 million) = 64.3 percent.

3. If average hourly earnings are rising faster than the CPI, then real wages have been rising. In addition, we should consider the impact of mismeasurement in the CPI. If the CPI overstates inflation (as discussed in the text), then real wages have risen more rapidly than the official statistics suggest. The Bureau of Labor Statistics website contains links to recent research on changes in the construction of the CPI that are intended to remove some of the historical bias.

5. Real hourly minimum wage in 1990 = nominal wage in 1990/CPI in 1990
$$= (\$3.80/130.7) \times 100$$
$$= \$2.91$$

Real hourly minimum wage in 2006 = nominal wage in 2006/CPI in 2006
$$= (\$5.15/201.6) \times 100$$
$$= \$2.55$$

From 1990 to 2006, the federal minimum wage decreased in real dollars.

7. If cashiers are being paid $16.00 per hour, they are being paid more than the market equilibrium wage for their job. At $16.00 per hour, employers will hire 110 cashiers, but 175 workers are available for work as a cashier. Also, 65 workers would like a job as a cashier at a wage of $16.00 per hour but cannot get such a job. Because a labor surplus exists for jobs that are overpaid, a wage above equilibrium has two implications. First, employers are paying more than necessary to produce their output; they could cut wages and still find enough qualified workers for their job openings. In fact, if they did cut wages, they could expand output and make their product cheaper and more accessible to consumers. Second, more workers want jobs than can find them. If wages were reduced a bit, more of these disappointed workers could find work.

Chapter 3

Review Questions

1. Profit maximization requires that firms hire labor until marginal revenue productivity equals the market wage. If wages are low, a profit maximizer will hire labor in abundant quantity, driving the marginal revenue productivity down to the low level of the wage. This statement, then, seems to imply that firms are not maximizing profits.

3. The potential employment effects of OSHA standards differ with the type of approach taken. If the standards apply to capital (machinery), they will increase the cost of capital equipment. This increase in cost has a scale effect, which will reduce the quantity demanded of all inputs (including labor). On the other hand, it also provides employers with an incentive to substitute labor (which is now relatively cheaper) for capital in producing any given desired level of output. This substitution will moderate the decline in employment.

In contrast, requiring employers to furnish personal protective devices to employees increases the cost of labor. In this case, employers have an incentive to substitute now relatively cheaper capital for labor when producing any given level of output (as earlier, the increased cost of production causes a scale effect that also tends to reduce employment). Other things being equal, then, the employment reduction induced by safety standards will be greater if the personal protective device method is used. However, to fully answer the question requires information on the costs of meeting the standards using the two methods. For example, if the "capital" approach increases capital costs by 50 percent while the "personal protective" approach increases labor costs by only 1 percent, the scale effect in the first method will probably be large enough that greater employment loss will be associated with the first method.

5. The wage and employment effects in both service industries and manufacturing industries must be considered. In the service sector, the wage tax on employers can be analyzed in much the same way that payroll taxes are analyzed in the text. That is, a tax on wages, collected from the employer, will cause the demand curve to shift leftward if the curve is drawn with respect to the wage that employees take home. At any given hourly wage that employees take home, the cost to the employer has risen by the amount of the tax. An increase in cost associated with any employee wage dampens the employer's appetite for labor and causes the demand curve to shift down and to the left.

The effects on employment and wages depend on the shape of the labor supply curve. If the labor supply curve slopes upward, both employment and the wage that employees take home will fall. If the supply curve is vertical, employment will not fall, but wages will fall by the full amount of the tax. If the supply curve is horizontal, the wage rate will not fall, but employment will.

The reduced employment and/or wages in the service sector should cause the supply of labor to the manufacturing sector to shift to the right (as people formerly employed in the service sector seek employment elsewhere). This shift in the supply curve should cause employment in manufacturing to increase even if the demand curve there remains stationary. If the demand curve does remain stationary, the employment increase would be accompanied by a decrease in manufacturing wages. However, the demand for labor in manufacturing may also shift to the right as consumers move away from the now more expensive services to buying the now relatively cheaper manufactured goods. If this demand shift occurs, the increase in employment would be accompanied by either a wage increase or a smaller wage reduction than would occur if the demand curve for labor in manufacturing were to remain stationary.

7. The imposition of financial penalties on employers who are discovered to have hired undocumented immigrants essentially raises the cost of hiring them. The employers now must pay whatever the prevailing wage of the

immigrants is, and they also face the possibility of a fine if they are discovered to have illegally employed workers. This penalty can be viewed as increasing the cost of hiring undocumented workers, such that this cost now exceeds the wage. The effect of a cost that exceeds the wage can be seen as a leftward shift of the demand curve (when drawn as a function of the wage rate paid to workers) for undocumented immigrants, thus reducing their employment and wages.

The effects on the demand for higher-skilled native-born workers depend on whether higher-skilled labor and lower-skilled labor are gross substitutes or gross complements. Raising the cost of lower-skilled labor produces a scale effect that tends to increase the cost of production and reduce higher-skilled employment. If higher-skilled labor and lower-skilled labor are complements in production, the demand for higher-skilled labor will clearly shift to the left as a result of the government's policy. However, if they are substitutes in production, the increased costs of lower-skilled labor will stimulate the substitution of higher-skilled labor for lower-skilled labor. In this case, the demand for higher-skilled labor could shift either rightward (if the substitution effect dominated the scale effect) or leftward (if the scale effect dominated).

9. Wage subsidies shift the demand for labor curve (in terms of employee wages) to the right. The effect on employment depends on the slope of the labor supply curve, which affects how much of the increased demand is translated into wage increases. The increases in employment will be greater when the supply curve is flatter and the associated wage increase received by workers is smaller.

Problems

1. The marginal product (as measured by these test scores) is 0.

3. See Figure 3RP.3. Because the supply curve is vertical, the workers will bear the entire tax. The wage will fall by $1 per hour, from $4 to $3.

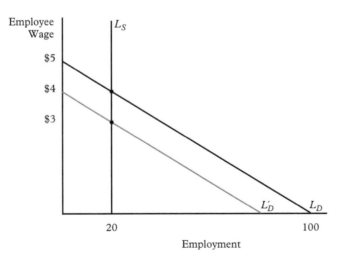

Figure 3RP.3

5. (Appendix 3A) As the chapter explains, to minimize cost, the firm picks K and L so that $W/MP_L = C/MP_K$, where C is the rental cost of capital. Rearrange this $W/C = MP_L/MP_K$ and substitute in the information from the problem:

$$12/4 = 30K^{0.25}L^{-0.25} / 10K^{-0.75}L^{0.75}$$

$$3 = 3K/L$$

$$K = L$$

7. (Appendix 3A)

   a. Pick K and L so that $(MP_L/MP_K = W/C$ or $(25K/25L) = 8/8 = 1$.

   b. Because the cost-minimizing capital–labor ratio is 1, the firm should use equal amounts of capital and labor. To produce 10,000 pairs of earrings, the calculation is as follows:

   $$Q = 25K \times L$$
   $$10,000 = 25K \times L$$
   $$400 = K \times L$$

   Because $K = L$, $400 = K \times K$. Here 20 units of both K and L must be used, and at $8 per unit, the cost comes to $320.

   c. Costs are minimized when $MP_L/MP_K = W/C$. MP_L equals $25K$, and MP_K equals $25L$, so their ratio equals K/L. For costs to be minimized, K/L must now equal $8/6$, meaning that the capital–labor ratio rises from 1 to 1.33. Once capital becomes cheaper, capital is substituted for labor.

Chapter 4

Review Questions

1. The overall conditions making for a smaller employment loss among teenagers are a small substitution effect and a small scale effect. The substitution effect is relatively small when substituting capital or adult workers for teenagers is difficult or when those substitutes rise in price when the demand for them grows. A small scale effect is associated with having the labor cost of teenagers be a small part of overall cost and with the industry's product demand curve's being relatively inelastic.

3. The tax credit for capital purchases effectively lowers the cost of capital, so the question thus becomes, under what conditions will a reduced price of capital increase employment the most? Employment will be most beneficially affected if a particular industry has a large scale effect and a small substitution effect associated with the tax credit. The scale effect will be largest when the share of capital is relatively large (such that the reduced price of capital results in a relatively large reduction in product price) and when the product demand elasticity facing the industry is relatively large (the product price decline causes a large increase in product demand). The substitution effect will be nonexistent if labor and capital

are complements in production; it will be relatively small when they are substitutes in production but capital is not easily substituted for labor or when the supply of labor is inelastic (such that if the demand for labor goes down as capital is substituted for it, wages will also go down—which will blunt the substitution effect).

5. Both options increase the costs of firms not already providing employees with acceptable health coverage. Because noncoverage is a characteristic mostly of small firms, both options would increase costs of small firms relative to costs in large firms. This would create a scale effect, tending to reduce employment in small firms relative to that in large ones. The magnitude of this scale effect will be greater the more elastic product demand is and (usually) the greater labor's share is in total cost.

Option A has, in addition to the scale effect, a substitution effect that tends to decrease the number of workers that a firm hires. This substitution effect will be larger the more easily capital can be substituted for labor and the more elastic the supply of capital is.

Option B is a tax on a firm's revenues, so it would have just a scale effect on the demand for labor, not a substitution effect. It would increase total costs and cause downward pressures on employment and wages, but it would not raise the ratio of labor costs to capital costs. Thus, its effects on wages and employment would be smaller than under option A.

7. a. An increased tariff on steel imports would tend to make domestic product demand, and therefore the demand for domestic labor, more inelastic.

   b. A law forbidding workers from being laid off for economic reasons would discourage the substitution of capital for labor and therefore tend to make the own-wage elasticity of demand for labor more inelastic.

   c. A boom in the machinery industry would shift the product demand curve in the steel industry to the right, thereby shifting the labor demand curve to the right. The effects of this shift on the own-wage elasticity of demand for labor cannot be predicted (except that a parallel shift to the right of a straight-line demand curve would reduce the elasticity at each wage rate).

   d. Because capital and labor are most substitutable in the long run, when new production processes can be installed, a decision to delay the adoption of new technologies reduces the substitutability of capital for labor and makes the labor demand curve more inelastic.

   e. An increase in wages would move the firm along its labor demand curve and would not change the shape of that curve. However, if the demand curve happens to be a straight line, movement up and to the left along the demand curve would tend to increase elasticity in the range in which firms are operating.

   f. A tax placed on each ton of steel output would tend to shift the labor demand curve to the left but would not necessarily change its elasticity. However, if the demand curve happened to be a straight line, this leftward shift would tend to increase the elasticity of demand for labor at each wage rate.

Problems

1. Elasticity of demand = %Δ (quantity demanded)/%Δ (wage) = $(\Delta L_D/L_D)/(\Delta W/W)$ = $(\Delta L_D/\Delta W) \times (W/L_D)$. At $W = 100$, $L_D = 3,000$, such that $W/L_D = 100/3,000$. Here $(\Delta LD/\Delta W)$ is the slope of the labor demand function (the change in employment demanded brought about by a one-unit change in the wage). This slope equals -20. Therefore, own-wage elasticity of demand = -20 $\times$ (100/3,000) = -½. The demand curve is inelastic at this point.

   Use the same approach to calculate the elasticity at $W = 200$. In this case, the own-wage elasticity of demand = -20 $\times$ (200/1,000) = -4. The demand curve is elastic at this point.

3. a. See Figure 4RP.3A. The higher wage will cause a movement along the demand curve, and L_D will fall from 220 (300 - 20 $\times$ 4) to 200 (300 - 20 $\times$ 5).

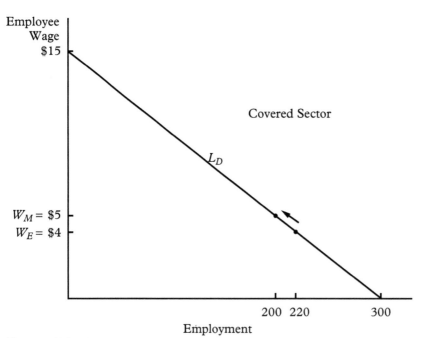

Figure 4RP.3A

   b. The initial equilibrium wage in the uncovered sector is $4 per hour and $L = 220$. Then, the labor supply curve in Figure 4RP.3B shifts over by 20 to $L_S' = -80 + 80W$. The new equilibrium is $W = 3.80 per hour and $L = 224$.

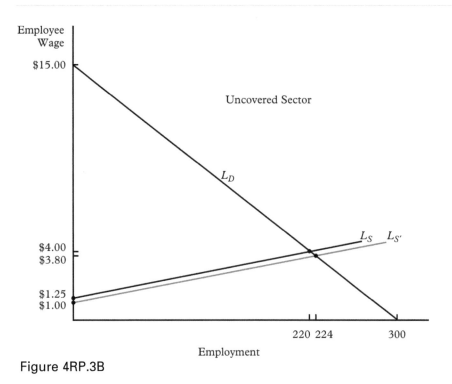

Figure 4RP.3B

5. a. The elasticity of demand is defined as the percentage change in employment divided by the percentage change in the wage. Using the starting
values for employment and wages as our bases, the percentage change
in employment of union A's members when the wage rises from $20
to $25 (a 25 percent increase) is (10,000 - 20,000)/20,000—or a
50 percent decrease in employment. Thus, the elasticity of demand for
union A's members is 50% ÷ 25% = 2. For union B, a wage decrease
from $30 to $25 (a 16 percent decrease) is associated with an increase
in employment from 30,000 to 33,000—a 10 percent increase.
The elasticity of demand facing B is therefore 10% ÷ 16% = 0.625%.
The demand curve facing A is more elastic than the one facing B.

   b. One cannot say which union will be more successful in increasing
its members' total earnings. This depends on a number of factors,
including the bargaining power of the two unions and the firms with
which they deal. However, the union with the more elastic demand
curve will suffer a larger percentage employment loss for any given
percentage increase in wages, and this is likely to reduce its incentive
to push for large wage gains. Thus, the union facing the less elastic
demand curve is likely to be more successful in raising its members'
wages.

7. A 10 percent fall in the price of capital caused a 15 percent fall in the use
of assistant bakers, so the cross-wage elasticity in this case is +1.5. A positive cross-elasticity indicates that the two are gross substitutes.

Chapter 5

Review Questions

1. The labor supply curve to a firm depicts how the number of workers willing to work for that firm responds to changes in the firm's offered wage. If workers can move from one employer to another without incurring costs of any kind, then small changes in the wage will bring about large changes in labor supply (as workers seek out the highest-paying employer in their labor market). Thus, if mobility costs are truly zero, the wage that a firm offers cannot differ from the market wage, and its labor supply curve is horizontal at the market wage.

   If workers find moving among employers costly, then they will move only if the wage gains from the move are large enough to offset the costs of the move—and some wage changes will be too small to induce mobility. *Furthermore, some workers are likely to find moving more costly—or less beneficial—than others* (they find generating offers of employment more difficult, are less open to change, are more emotionally tied to their current workplaces, or have a shorter time horizon over which to collect the benefits). The differences among workers in the incentives for mobility produced by a given wage change mean that some workers will want to change employers and some will stay put.

   Because not everyone in a labor market is lured to a firm that raises its wage and because not all employees of a firm that reduces its wage will quit, the labor supply curve to the firm is not horizontal. Rather, it slopes upward. The positive slope indicates that the larger the wage increase is, the greater will be the number of workers attracted to the firm. Conversely, the larger the reduction in wages is, the greater will be the likelihood that an employer will lose its current workers to other firms.

3. One reason why firms are slow to hire in expansions is that they are slow to lay off workers during a recession. Workers in whom the firm has made an investment are paid less than the value of their marginal product so that the firm can recoup investment costs, and this difference offers employment protection when productivity falls in a recession (because investment costs are sunk and the firm will continue to employ a worker in the short run as long as marginal revenue productivity exceeds the wage). As productivity rises during expansion, firms will not hire workers (which involves an investment) until the gap between marginal revenue productivity and wages is again large enough that the firm can recoup investment costs.

5. Low-wage jobs typically involve less training than high-wage jobs do, and if the training in high-wage jobs is at least partly paid for by employers, the cost of training will induce employers to substitute longer hours of work for hiring more workers. Thus, that employers require longer hours of work from workers who have more skills is consistent with economic theory.

7. This change would convert a quasi-fixed labor cost to a variable one, inducing employers to substitute added workers for weekly hours (especially overtime hours) of work. Because this new financing scheme increases the cost of higher-paid workers relative to lower-paid ones, it also induces firms to substitute lower-skilled workers for higher-skilled workers. (Both these effects emphasize labor–labor substitution; scale effects are minimal if total premiums are held constant.)

9. Hiring and training investments by employers (and employees) are more attractive, other things being equal, when the period over which returns can be received is longer. A cap on weekly hours of work limits this period, and it therefore serves to reduce incentives for such skill formation. Furthermore, although intended to increase employment by "spreading the work," the cap increases labor costs by constraining how employers allocate their resources, creating a scale effect that tends to reduce employment.

Problems

1. a. $E = 5W$, so $W = 0.2E$. Thus, the wage must rise by 20 cents for every one-person increase in desired number of employees.

   b. Total labor costs (C) are $E \times W$, so $C = E(0.2E) = 0.2E^2$.

   c. The marginal expense of labor (ME_L) is found by taking the derivative of C with respect to E: $dC/dE = 0.4E$. Although wages must rise by 20 cents for every additional employee desired, the marginal expense of labor rises by 40 cents (refer back to footnote 7 in the text).

3. Given the lack of mobility costs for employees, the firm cannot recoup its costs of providing general training. Thus, the worker must pay for the training:

   $W = MRP_L$ - cost of training = \$3,000 - \$1,000 = \$2,000

5. The total labor cost is equal to the offered wage × supply of labor. The marginal expense of labor is equal to Δ(total labor cost)/Δ(supply of labor). See Table 5RP.5 for calculation of the marginal expense of labor, and Figure 5RP.5 for a graphical representation.

Table 5RP.5 Labor Supply and Marginal Expense of Labor

Offered wage ($)	Supply of labor (number of hours)	Total labor cost ($)	ME_L
4	18	72	—
5	19	95	23
6	20	120	25
7	21	147	27
8	22	176	29

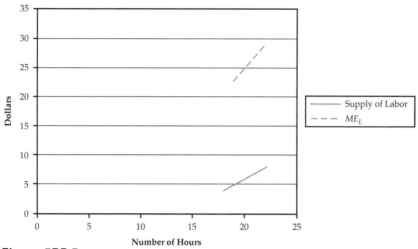

Figure 5RP.5

7. a.

Table 5RP7.1 Marginal Expense of Labor, Teddy's Treats

Offered Wage ($)	Supply of labor (number of hours)	Total labor cost ($)	ME_L
4	19	76	—
5	20	100	24
6	21	126	26
7	22	154	28
8	23	184	30

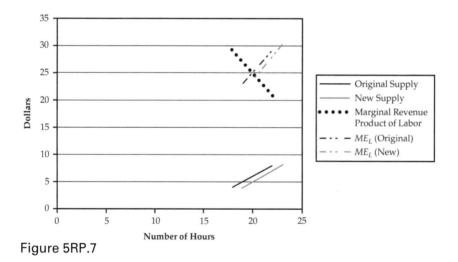

Figure 5RP.7

b.

c. The supply curve of labor and the marginal expense of labor curve both shifted to the right in Figure 5RP.7.

d. There will be an increase in employment to between 20 and 21 hours of labor, and the firm will offer a wage between $5 and $6 (see Figure 5RP.7).

9. a.
Table 5RP.9 Marginal Expenses of Labor, Toasty Tasties

Quantity of labor (hours)	Offered wage ($)	Total hourly labor cost	ME_L	MRP_L
5	6	30	—	—
6	8	48	18	50
7	10	70	22	38
8	12	96	26	26
9	14	126	30	14
10	16	160	34	2
11	18	198	38	1

b. The graphical representation of Table 5RP.9 is in Figure 5RP.9.

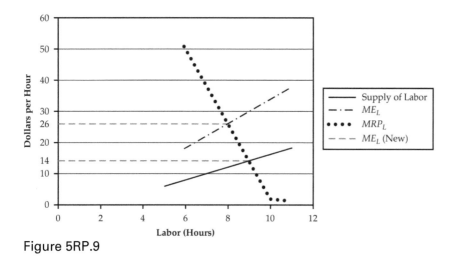

Figure 5RP.9

c. The profit-maximizing firm will determine the quantity of hours by equating ME_L with MRP_L and offer a wage as indicated by the supply of labor curve. At Toasty Tasties, eight hours of labor will be employed at a wage of $12 per hour.

d. If the mandated wage is $14 per hour, the number of hours employed will increase to 9 hours.

e. If the mandated wage is $26 per hour, eight hours of labor will be employed.

f. If the mandated wage is above $26 per hour, fewer than eight hours of labor will be employed.

Chapter 6

Review Questions

1. False. An inferior good is defined as one that people consume less of as their incomes rise (if the price of the good remains constant). A labor supply curve is drawn with respect to a person's wage rate. Thus, for a labor supply curve to be backward bending, the supply curve must be positively sloped in some range and then become negatively sloped in another. A typical way of illustrating a backward-bending supply curve is shown here.

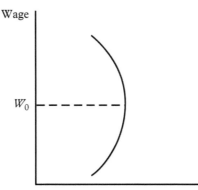

Hours of Work Supplied

Along the positively sloped section of this backward-bending supply curve, the substitution effect of a wage increase dominates the income effect, and as wages rise, the person increases their labor supply. However, after the wage reaches W_0 in in the figure above, further increases in the wage are accompanied by a reduction in labor supply. In this negatively sloped portion of the supply curve, the income effect dominates the substitution effect.

We have assumed that the income effect is negative and that, therefore, leisure is a normal good. Had we assumed leisure to be an inferior good, the increases in wealth brought about by increased wages would have worked *with* the underlying substitution effect and caused the labor supply curve to be unambiguously positively sloped.

3. The graphs for each option are shown here, where the new constraints are shown as dashed lines. By mandating that 5 percent of each hour be worked for free, *option A* reduces lawyers' wages, creating income and substitution effects that work in opposite directions on their desired labor supply. *Option B* essentially reduces the time that lawyers have available for leisure and paid work, which shifts the budget constraint to the left in a parallel manner (keeping the wage rate constant). This creates an income effect that increases their incentives to work for pay. *Option C* leaves unchanged the budget constraint of lawyers who work relatively few hours, but for those who work enough to earn over $50,000, an

income effect occurs that tends to increase work incentives. For some whose incomes were only slightly above $50,000, however, the $5,000 tax may drive them to reduce hours of work, thereby reducing their earnings to $50,000 and avoiding the tax. These lawyers find that their utilities are maximized at point X in the graph of option C's budget constraint.

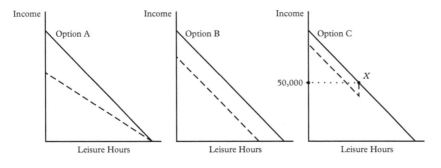

Figure 6RQ.3 Budget Constraints for Lawyers

5. Absenteeism is one dimension of labor supply, so the proposals must be analyzed using labor supply theory. Both proposals increase worker income, because employees now have paid sick days; this increase in income will tend to increase absenteeism through the income effect. The first proposal also raises the *hourly wage*, however, because any unused sick leave can be converted to cash in direct proportion to the unused days. Thus, this first proposal will tend to have a substitution effect accompanying the income effect, so the overall expected change in absenteeism is ambiguous.

The second proposal raises the cost of the *first* sick day because if the worker is absent, they lose the entire promised insurance policy. Thus, a huge substitution effect offsets the income effect for the first day of absence. However, once sick leave has been used at all, *further* days of absence cause no further loss of pay; thus, after the first day, no substitution effect occurs to offset the income effect, and this will tend to increase the incentives for absenteeism.

7. In Figure 6RQ.7, the straight line *AB* represents the person's market constraint (i.e., the constraint in a world with no subsidies). *ACDEB* is the constraint that would apply if the housing subsidy proposal became effective.

The effects on labor supply depend on which segment of *ACDEB* the person finds relevant. Four cases are possible. First, if the indifference curves are steeply pitched (reflecting a strong desire to consume leisure), the housing subsidy proposal will not affect work incentives. The person strongly desiring leisure would continue to not work (would be at point *C*) but would receive the housing subsidy of $2,400. The second

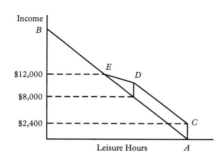

Figure 6RQ.7 Budget Constraint for Housing Subsidy

case occurs when the person has a tangency along segment *CD*. Along this segment, the person's effective wage rate is the same as the market wage, so a pure income effect occurs that tends to reduce work incentives. If the person has a tangency point along segment *DE*, they likewise have reduced incentives to work because the income effect caused by the northeast shifting out of the budget constraint is accompanied by a reduction in the effective wage rate. Finally, those with tangency points along *EB* will not qualify for the housing subsidy program and therefore will not alter their labor supply behavior. (An exception to this case occurs when a person with a tangency point near point *E* before the initiation of the housing subsidy program now has a tangency point along segment *DE* and, of course, works less than before.)

9. The old constraint is *ABC* in Figure 6RQ.9, and the new one is *BADEC*.

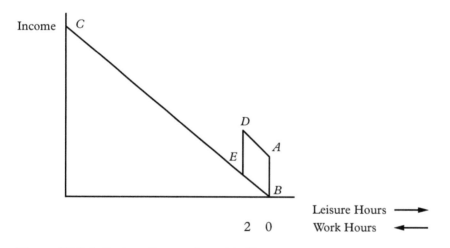

Figure 6RQ.9 Budget Constraint with Change in UI

The work-incentive effects of the new constraint depend on worker preferences. Workers who have relatively strong preferences for leisure, who may not have been in the labor force before, have an increased incentive to join the labor force and work part time. For workers who have weak preferences for leisure (who had a tangency along the upper part of *EC* before), no effect will occur. However, for workers whose

earlier tangency was along the lower middle part of *EC*, the new constraint may create incentives to cut the hours of work and maximize
utility at point *D*.

Problems

1. a. See Figure 6RP.1, where the initial budget constraint is given by
   ACE. After the new law has been passed, the budget constraint bends
   upward after eight hours of work. Thus, the new wage rate and overtime constraint is given by *ABCD*, which intersects the old constraint
   at point *C*—the original combination of income and working hours
   (10 hours of work in this example).

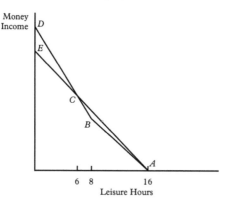

Figure 6RP.1 Budget Constraint with Overtime Pay Mandate

   b. Initially, earnings were $11 × 10 = $110. The new earnings formula
   is $8W + 2 × 1.5W$, where W = the hourly wage. Pick W so that this
   total equals $110. Because $11W$ = $110, we calculate that W = $10
   per hour.

   c. See Figure 6RP.1. If the workers were initially at a point of utility
   maximization, their initial indifference curve was tangent to the initial budget constraint (line *ACE*) at point *C*. Because the new budget constraint (along segment *BD*) has a steeper slope ($15 per hour
   rather than $11 per hour), the workers' initial indifference curve
   cannot be tangent to the new constraint at point *C*. Instead, a new
   point of tangency along segment *CD* will emerge, and hours of work
   must increase—tangency points along *CD* lie to the left of point *C*.
   (Income in the vicinity of point *C* is effectively being held constant,
   and the substitution effect always pulls in the direction of less leisure
   whenever the wage rate has risen.)

3. a. Δ hours worked per year = Δ hours worked per week × weeks worked
   per year = (-10)(50) = -500

   Income effect = $(\Delta H/\Delta Y)|W$(constant) = -500/50000 = -1/100
   Interpretation: For every $100 increase in nonlabor income, you
   work one fewer hour each year.

b. The substitution effect is zero. The lottery win enhances wealth (income) independent of the hours of work. Thus, income is increased without a change in the compensation received from an hour of work.

5.

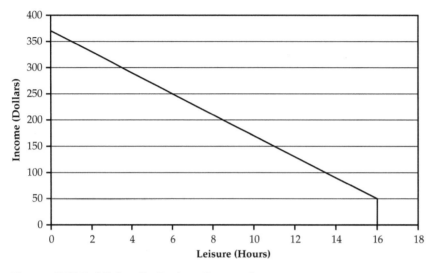

Figure 6RP.5 Michael's Budget Constraint

7. Teddy's nonlabor income is $75. His base wage rate is ($145 – $75)/ (16 – 9) = 70/7 = $10 per hour. His overtime wage rate is ($325 – $145)/ (9 – 0) = $180/9 = $20 per hour. Teddy needs to work at least seven hours before he will receive overtime.

Chapter 7

Review Questions

1. a. 6,000 - 5,600 = 400.

   b. The labor force participation rate drops from 60 percent to 56 percent, a reduction of 4 percentage points.

   c. One implication of hidden unemployment is that the unemployment rate may not fully reflect the degree of joblessness. That is, some people who want to work but do not have work are not counted as unemployed because they place such a low probability on obtaining employment that they stop looking for work. Although this observation may suggest that hidden unemployment should be included in the published unemployment figures, to do so would call into question the theoretical underpinnings of our measure of unemployment. Economic theory suggests that unemployment exists if the number of people willing to work at the going wage is greater than the number of people employed at that wage. If economic conditions are such that at the going wage some decide that time is better spent in household production than in seeking market work, our theory suggests that they have in fact dropped out of the labor force.

3. Jimmy Carter's statement reflects the additional-worker hypothesis. Briefly, this hypothesis suggests that as the economy moves into a recession and some members of the labor force are thrown out of work, other family members currently engaged in household production or leisure will enter the labor force to try to maintain family income. Although Carter's statement of the additional-worker hypothesis is an apt description of that hypothesis, his statement fails to reflect the fact that studies show that the discouraged-worker effect dominates the added-worker effect (i.e., as the economy moves into a recession and workers are laid off, the labor force shrinks, on balance).

5. To parents who must care for small children, this subsidy of daycare is tantamount to an increase in the wage rate. For those parents who are currently out of the labor force, the increased wage will be accompanied by a dominant substitution effect that induces more of them to work outside the home (the substitution effect dominates in *participation* decisions). For those who are currently working outside the home, this increase in the take-home wage will cause both an income effect and a substitution effect, the net result of which is not theoretically predictable. If the substitution effect is dominant, then the change in policy would increase the hours of work. If the income effect is dominant, then this increase in the take-home wage rate might cause a reduction in work hours.

7. For workers close to retirement age, this change in government policy creates a significant decrease in post-retirement income. The basic post-retirement pension has been cut in half, so these workers experience a substantial income effect that would drive them in the direction of more work (delayed retirement).

For young workers, the reduction in pension benefits facing them in their retirement years is offset by a reduction in payroll taxes (which, of course, acts as an increase in their take-home wage rate). Thus, if we assume that these workers will pay for their retirement benefits through the payroll taxes that they pay over their careers, this change in Social Security might leave their lifetime wealth unaffected. If so, the cut in payroll taxes would increase their wages without causing an increase in lifetime wealth, which would create a "pure" substitution effect inducing more labor supply (and possibly later retirement).

9. a. The budget constraint facing this teenager is shown in Figure 7RQ.9, where line ABC represents the constraint associated with her job with the caterer and AD the constraint as a babysitter (assuming that she needs eight hours per day for sleep and personal care).

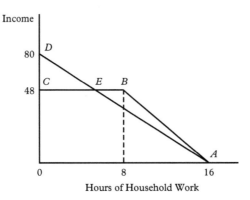

Figure 7RQ.9 Budget Constraint for Teenager

b. The value to her of studying and practicing would be shown by indifference curves, more steeply sloped curves indicating a greater value. If she places a high value on her household activities, she will either not work (corner solution at point *A*) or choose to work as a caterer along constraint *AB*. In this case, the state law has no effect. With a flatter indifference curve, however, she may maximize utility at point *B* (catering job) or along *ED*. In these cases, the state law reduces her earnings and her utility, but the effects on her hours at home are unclear. If she were to end up at point *B*, she would spend more time at home than she would if unconstrained. But along *ED*, the income and substitution effects of the law work in opposite directions, and the effects on hours at home are ambiguous.

11. a. In Figure 7RQ.11, the constraint for company X is *ABC*, whereas the constraint for company Y is *AD*; both assume that the maximum work hours per year are 4,000.

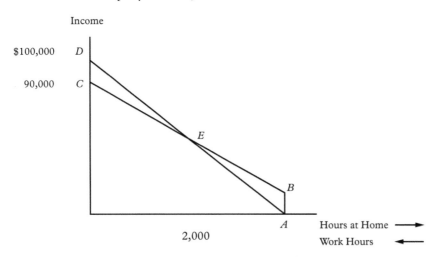

Figure 7RQ.11 Budget Constraint for Companies X and Y

b. A woman preferring to work more than 2,000 hours for company X would have a tangency along segment *EC* if she worked for company

X. If she is now offered a job at $25 per hour at company Y, she would *prefer the offer from* Y, because her tangency would end up along segment *ED*. Segment *ED* has a higher slope than segment *EC* does, so the effect of the new offer from Y is to increase her wage rate. Thus, the income effect of the wage increase will push her toward fewer work hours, whereas the substitution effect of the wage increase will push her toward more work hours; the overall effect on her hours of work is therefore uncertain.

Problems

1. a. Unemployment rate (official) = (# unemployed/# in labor force) × 100

     The June 2018 unemployment rate = (6,314/155,761) × 100 = 4.05 percent.

     The June 2019 unemployment rate = (6001/157,538) × 100 = 3.81 percent.

     The officially defined unemployment rate fell by 0.24 percentage points.

   b. Unemployment rate (unofficial) = (# unemployed + # discouraged)/ (# in labor force + # discouraged) × 100

     For 2018, unemployment rate (w/discouraged workers) = (6,314 + 423)/(155,761 + 423) × 100 = (6,737/156,184) × 100 = 4.31 percent.

     For 2019, unemployment rate (w/discouraged workers) = (6,001 + 392)/(157,538 + 392) × 100 = (6,393/157,930) × 100 = 4.05 percent.

     The unofficially defined unemployment rate fell by 0.26 percentage points.

   c. If job opportunities are expanding, the officially defined unemployment rate will tend to fall, but the number of discouraged individuals will also tend to decrease. Because these people no longer feel as discouraged, they will enter the labor force and search for a job as unemployed workers, thus moderating the decrease in the officially defined unemployment rate.

3. a. The wage rate without the program is $160/16 hours = $10 per hour.

   b. The program's no-work benefit is $40. The wage rate with program participation is ($80 - $40)/8 = $40/8 = $5 per hour.

   c. If the individual had chosen to work fewer than eight hours per day, she would be better off participating in the program, because the money income is larger, allowing a higher utility level. If the individual had chosen to work more than eight hours per day, she would probably be unaffected by the program. However, some who had chosen to work just slightly more than eight hours might be made better off by reducing hours of work and qualifying for the program (see the answer to part d).

d. Workers who have indifference curves tangent to the "market" budget constraint at exactly eight hours of work will maximize utility under the new program by working fewer hours. At eight hours of work, their indifference curves have a slope equal to the $10 wage, so the curve that they were on before the program began will pass below the new constraint created by the program. With the program, their utility will be maximized along the new constraint segment; in conceptual terms, both income effects and substitution effects push them in the direction of fewer hours of work.

Chapter 8

Review Questions

1. The demand curve shows how the marginal revenue product of labor (MRP_L) is affected by the number employed; if few workers are employed, they are placed in jobs in which their MRP_L is relatively high. The supply curve indicates the number of workers willing to offer their services at each wage rate. Because fewer construction workers are willing to offer their services at any given wage if working conditions are harsh (as in Alaska), construction wages will be higher than those in the continental United States. Furthermore, the higher wage that must be paid restricts employment in harsh conditions to the performance of projects that have a high MRP_L.

3. A society that does not use force or trickery to fill jobs that are dangerous, say, must pay workers more so they will voluntarily choose these jobs. To induce workers to choose a dangerous job over a safer one requires that the former be made more attractive than the latter in other dimensions, and one way is to have elevated compensation levels. These increased levels of compensation are what in this chapter we have called compensating wage differentials.

These compensating wage differentials will arise if workers are well informed and can select from an adequate number of job choices. If workers are without *choice*, then society essentially forces them to take what is offered through the threat of being jailed or of not being able to obtain a means of livelihood.

If, instead of lacking choice, workers lack information about working conditions in the jobs from which they have to choose, then society is in effect using trickery to allocate labor. That is, if workers are ignorant of true working conditions and remain ignorant of these conditions for a long period after they have taken a job, they have not made a fully informed choice. They have been tricked into making that choice.

5. False. Whether government policy is required in a particular labor market depends on how well that market is functioning. If the outcomes of the market take into account worker preferences (who can make fully informed choices), then the labor market decisions will lead to utility maximization among workers. In this case, efforts by government to impose a level of safety greater than the market outcome could lead to a reduction in worker welfare (as argued in the text).

If the market fails to take full account of worker preferences, owing to either lack of information or lack of choice, then the private decision makers do not weigh all the costs and benefits of greater safety. The market outcome will very likely not be socially optimal, and an appropriate setting of governmental standards could improve the utility of workers.

Of course, if society does not trust workers' preferences or seeks to change those preferences, it would not want to rely on the market even if it were functioning perfectly, because the market would reflect worker preferences.

7. People who work in their homes do not have to bear the expenses of commuting and childcare that factory workers do. Moreover, many prefer the flexibility of working at home to the regimen of a factory, because they can perform farming chores or do other household tasks that would be impossible to do during a factory shift. These intrinsically desirable or cost-saving aspects of working at home suggest that the same level of utility could be reached by homeworkers at a lower wage rate than factory workers receive. Thus, at least part of the higher wage paid to factory workers is a compensating wage differential for the cost and inconvenience of factory employment.

9. From the perspective of positive economics, banning Sunday work drives down the profits of employers, which will have a scale effect on employment, and it drives up the cost of labor relative to capital (machines are not banned from running on Sunday). Overall, firms will tend to hire less labor.

Furthermore, in the absence of government prohibitions, most workers presumably preferred to celebrate a Sabbath, and in Germany, Sunday was most likely the typical choice. With most workers preferring Sunday off, employers who wanted to remain open had to hire from a small pool of workers who did not celebrate Sunday as a Sabbath. If this pool was small relative to the demand for Sunday workers, employers had to pay a compensating wage differential to lure workers into offering their services on Sundays. The workers most easily lured were those who cared least about having Sunday off. These workers will lose their premium pay (unless exempt from the law).

Normatively, this law prevents some voluntary transactions. It makes society worse off by preventing workers who are willing to work on Sundays (for a price) from transacting with employers who want Sunday workers, and it thus discourages some mutually beneficial transactions.

Problems

1. In Figure 8RP.1 A's wage at 3 meters is $10 + 0.5 \times 3 = \$11.50$ per hour. At 5 meters, B's wage is $10 + 0.5 \times 5 = \$12.50$ per hour. A's indifference curve must be tangent to the offer curve at 3 meters; B's must be tangent at 5 meters. Because both indifference curves are tangent to a straight line, both must have the same slope at their points of tangency; therefore, both workers are willing to pay (or receive) 50 cents per hour for a reduced (added) depth of 1 meter. Worker A, who chooses to work at 3 meters, has a steeper indifference curve (a greater willingness to pay for reduced depth) at each level of depth; that is why worker A chooses to work at a shallower depth.

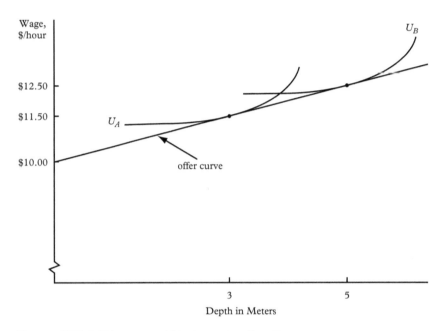

Figure 8RP.1 Wages and Underwater Depth

3. (Appendix 8A) He will be fully compensated when his expected utility is the same on the two jobs.

Utility from the first job is $\sqrt{Y} = \sqrt{40,000} = 200$.

Utility from the second job is $U = .5 \times \sqrt{Y_{bad}} + .5 \times \sqrt{Y_{good}} = .5 \times \sqrt{22,500} + .5 \times \sqrt{Y_{good}}$. This equals the utility of the first job when $\sqrt{Y_{good}} = .62,500(.5 \times 150 + .5 \times \sqrt{Y_{good}} = 200)$. If he earns $22,500 half the time and $62,500 half the time, his expected earnings are $42,500. Thus, his expected extra pay for the layoff risk is $2,500 per year.

5. a. Sheldon is willing to trade 1 percent risk of injury for $3 per hour. Shelby is willing to trade 1 percent risk of injury for $2 per hour.

Because Sheldon requires a larger wage increase to compensate him for a 1 percent increase in risk of injury, he has a stronger aversion to risk of injury.

b. An isoprofit curve that is concave (from below) exhibits diminishing marginal returns to safety expenditures. Where the curve is steeply sloped, wages will have to be reduced by a lot if the firm is to reduce risk and still maintain its profits; this trade-off between wage and risk is more similar to Sheldon's willingness to trade wage and risk. Thus, an individual with a stronger aversion to risk is more likely to attain a match farther to the left along a concave isoprofit curve. Shelby's tangency point will be to the right of Sheldon's.

7. a. A linear isoprofit curve is a graphic representation of the assumption of constant marginal returns to safety expenditures. In this situation, the trade-off between risk of injury and wages does not vary. See Figure 7RP.7.

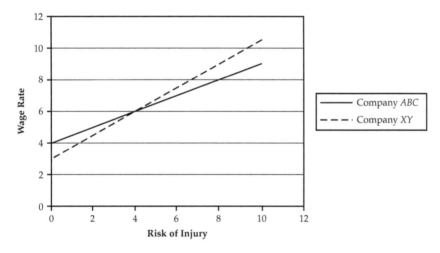

Figure 7RP.7 Isoprofit Curves for Companies ABC and XY

b. $W_{ABC} = 4 + 0.5R$

$W_{XY} = 3 + 0.75R.$

Solve for R: $4 + 0.5R = 3 + 0.75R$

$$1 = 0.25R$$

$$4 = R.$$

Now solve for W: $W = 4 + 0.5(4) = 4 + 2 = \$6.$

At a risk level of 4, both firms will offer a wage rate of $6.00 per hour.

c. At risk levels lower than 4, workers would prefer to work at company ABC, which is offering higher wage rates for those risk levels. At risk levels higher than 4, workers would prefer to work at company XY, which is offering higher wage rates for those risk levels.

Chapter 9

Review Questions

1. Understanding why women receive lower wages than men of comparable age requires an analysis of many possible causes, including discrimination. This answer will explore the insights provided by human-capital theory.

    Women have more frequently exhibited interrupted labor market careers, which shortens the time over which human-capital investments can be recouped. Even recently, when educational attainment levels between relatively young men and relatively young women have equalized, female graduates are still bunched in occupations for which an interrupted working life is least damaging. Lower human-capital investments and occupational bunching are undoubtedly associated with lower wages.

    The fact that female age–earnings profiles are relatively flat and the fact that male age–earnings profiles slope more upward and are more concave can also be explained by human-capital analysis. If men acquire more on-the-job training in their early years than women do, their wages will be relatively depressed by these investments (this will cause the wages of men and women at younger ages to be more equal than they would otherwise be). In their later years, those who have made human-capital investments will be recouping them, and this will cause the wages of men and women to become less equal.

3. Delaying reduces tuition costs, but it also delays the benefits of a medical education (generally measured as the difference between what doctors earn and what can be earned without a medical degree). This difference in benefits will be greatest for those with the smallest alternative (pre-medical-school) earnings. Furthermore, it reduces by one the number of years that the investment's payoff can be recouped. Thus, those expecting the greatest payoff to an investment in medical education and those who are older and therefore have fewer years over which to recoup its returns will be the least likely to take this offer.

5. One cost of educational investment is related to the time that students need to devote to studying in order to ensure success. People who can learn quickly will have lower costs of obtaining an education. If one assumes that learning ability and ability in general (including productive capacity in a job) are correlated, then the implication of human-capital theory is that the most able people, other things being equal, will obtain the most education.

7. Government subsidies will, of course, lower the costs to individuals of obtaining an education (of making a human-capital investment). Reduced university costs will, from an individual perspective, raise the individual rate of return to making an investment in education. This will induce more people to attend college than would have attended

otherwise. Students who would, in the absence of a college subsidy, have required a post-college earnings differential (as compared with that of a high school graduate) of $6,000 per year (say) might now be induced to attend college if the earnings differential is only $3,000 per year. From a social perspective, however, the increase in productivity of $3,000 per year might be insufficient to pay back society for its investments in college students.

9. The two facts are theoretically related. Human-capital investments require returns, and the returns will be greater (other things being equal) when the payback period (total hours of work after the investment is made) is longer. If female doctors want shorter work hours than male doctors, perhaps because of home responsibilities, then they will tend to invest less than men do in acquiring additional training.

Problems

1. She needs to compare the present value of the costs and benefits from getting the MBA. Costs equal forgone income at ages 48 and 49, plus tuition. The cost of an apartment is not included, because these costs are the same in both places. Benefits equal the $40,000 in extra wages that she'll get at ages 50 through 59. Present value of costs = $160,000/(1.06) + 160,000/(1.06)^2 = $293,343. Present value of benefits = $40,000/(1.06)^3 + $40,000/(1.06)^4 + \ldots + 40,000/(1.06)^{11} + 40,000/(1.06)^{12} = $262,018.

   Thus, Becky does not enroll in the MBA program, because the present value of the net benefits of doing so are smaller than the costs.

3. $PV = B_5/(1 + r)^5$
   $= \$125/(1 + 0.04)^5$
   $= \$125/(1.04)^5$
   $= \$125/(1.217)$
   $= \$102.71.$
   You should opt for $125 in five years because the present value is worth more than $100 now.

5. Present value $= B_1/(1 + r) + B_2/(1 + r)^2 + B_3/(1 + r)^3 + B_4/(1 + r)^4$
   $+ B_5/(1 + r)^5 - \$20,000 - \$100,000$
   $= 30,000/(1 + 0.05) + 30,000/(1 + 0.05)^2 + 30,000/(1 + 0.05)^3 + 30,000/(1 + 0.05)^4 + 30,000/(1 + 0.05)^5$
   $- \$120,000$
   $= 28,571 + 27,211 + 25,916 + 24,681 + 23,505 - \$120,000$
   $= \$129,884 - \$120,000$
   $= \$9,884 > 0.$

   Yes, Theodore should enroll in the program.

Chapter 10

Review Questions

1. a. State licensing increases the costs of interstate mobility among licensed professionals, thus tending to reduce the overall supply to these occupations and to drive up their wages. In addition, the flows from low-earnings areas to high-earnings areas are inhibited, which slows the geographic equalization of wages among these professionals.

    b. The gainers from federalization would be licensed professionals who are in low-earnings areas, because their labor market mobility is enhanced. (One could also argue that clients in high-earnings areas similarly gain from the enhanced mobility of the professionals from whom they purchase services.) The losers are already licensed professionals in high-earnings areas who face increased competition now because of enhanced mobility.

3. a. Immigrant workers create goods or perform services that have value to the rest of society. Thus, whether their presence enriches native-born Americans (in the aggregate) depends on the total value of these services, net of what they are paid. If immigrants receive no more than their marginal revenue product, native-born workers cannot lose—and in fact will reap infra-marginal gains. If immigrants are subsidized by native-born workers, such that they are net consumers of goods and services, then native-born workers could be worse off in the aggregate.

    b. According to a normative perspective, two critical issues arise. The first is whether immigrants are subsidized, on balance, by native-born workers (as noted earlier). If they are not, then a second issue arises: Do any mechanisms enable the native-born gainers from immigration to compensate the losers? Many economists argue that the compensation of losers must take place for a potentially Pareto-improving policy to be socially defensible, so identifying whose wages are reduced, and by how much, is a critical social issue.

5. One factor inducing quit rates to be low is that the cost of changing jobs might be high (pension losses, seniority losses, and difficulties in finding information about other jobs are examples of factors that can increase the cost of quitting). If costly barriers impede mobility, then employees are more likely to tolerate adverse conditions within the firm without resorting to leaving.

    Firms are also more likely to provide their employees with firm-specific training if quit rates are low. Thus, if firms need to train their employees in firm-specific skills, they clearly prefer a low quit rate. Finally, firms prefer low quit rates because hiring costs are kept to a minimum. Every time a worker quits, a replacement must be hired, and to the extent that finding and hiring a replacement is costly, firms want to avoid incurring these costs.

From a social perspective, the disadvantage of having a low quit rate is related to the failure of the market to adjust quickly to shortages and surpluses. Changing relative demands for labor require constant flux in the employment distribution, and factors that inhibit change also inhibit adaptation to new conditions.

Furthermore, high costs of quitting will be associated not only with lower quit rates but also with larger wage differentials across firms or regions for the same grade of labor. Because firms hire labor until marginal productivity equals the wage that they must pay, these large wage differentials will also be accompanied by large differentials in marginal productivities within the same skill group. As implied by our discussion of job matching, if marginal productivities differ widely among workers who have the same skills, national output could be increased by reallocating labor so that marginal productivities of the low-paid workers are enhanced.

7. Japanese workers, say, might have stronger preferences for loyalty (meaning that they are more willing to pass up monetary gains from mobility for the sake of "consuming" loyalty to their current employers). Also, quit rates are affected by incentives as well as preferences, and incentives for lower quit rates can be altered by employer policies. Thus, quit rates do not by themselves allow us to measure differentials in inherent employee loyalties.

The lower quit rates in Japan, however, could result from poorer information flows about jobs in other areas, greater costs of changing jobs (employee benefits may be strongly linked to seniority within the firm so that when workers quit, they lose benefits that are not immediately replaced by their new employer), smaller wage differentials among employers, or other employer policies adopted because of a greater reliance on firm-specific human-capital investments by Japanese employers.

9. Criminals presumably weigh the benefits of their crimes against the expected future costs (which can be thought of as the discounted present value of the expected loss of income and freedom if imprisoned). These costs will be smaller—and crime more attractive, other things being equal—the *higher* one's discount rate. Thus, criminals tend to have higher-than-average discount rates. In contrast, because the act of immigration entails high initial costs and returns that flow only over future years, we can infer that those who decide to immigrate tend to have *lower*-than-average personal discount rates. Thus all else equal, theory would lead us to expect immigrants to have lower-than-average crime rates.

Problems

1. The present value of net benefits from the move is given by equation (10.1) in the text. Assuming that the yearly benefits of the two identical jobs are summarized by her net earnings gains ($35,000 - $5,000

− \$10,000 = \$20,000), the present value of the gains from moving are \$20,000/1.1 + \$20,000/1.1^2 + \$20,000/1.1^3 + \$20,000/1.1^4 + \$20,000/1.1^5 = \$75,816.

Because she doesn't move, we know that the costs of moving outweigh the benefits. The direct cost of the move is only \$2,000, so the psychological costs must be greater than \$73,816.

3. Clare should compare the present value of her choices.

$$PV_{US} = \$32,000/(1 + 0.06) + \$32,000/(1 + 0.06)^2 + \$32,000/(1 + 0.06)^3 + \$32,000 /(1 + 0.06)^4 - \$6,000$$
$$= \$30,189 + \$28,480 + \$26,868 + \$25,347 - \$6,000$$
$$= \$104,884$$
$$PV_{France} = \$30,000/(1 + 0.06) + \$30,000/(1 + 0.06)^2 + \$30,000/(1 + 0.06)^3 + \$30,000/(1 + 0.06)^4$$
$$= \$28,302 + \$26,700 + \$25,189 + \$23,762$$
$$= \$103,953$$

Clare should take the job offer in the United States. She would be financially ahead by \$931.

5. a. Draw curves from Table 10RP.5:

Table 10RP.5 Demand and Supply of Domestic and Immigrant Workers

Wage (\$)	Demand	Domestic Supply	Total Supply	Immigrants
3	30	12	16	4
4	28	13	18	5
5	26	14	20	6
6	24	15	22	7
7	22	16	24	8
8	20	17	26	9
9	18	18	28	10
10	16	19	30	11

b. $D = S_{domestic}$

$36 - 2W = W + 9$

$27 = 3W$

$9 = W$

$36 - 2(9) = 18,000$ domestic workers.

Before immigration, the equilibrium wage is \$9.00 per hour, and 18,000 domestic workers will be hired.

c. $D = S_{total}$

$36 - 2W = 10 + 2W$

$26 = 4W$

$6.50 = W$

S_{total} = 2(6.50) + 10 = 13 + 10 = 23 thousand total employed

$S_{domestic}$ = 9 + W = 9 + 6.50 = 15.5 thousand domestic workers employed

$S_{immigrants}$ = S_{total} - $S_{domestic}$ = 23 - 15.5 = 7.5 thousand immigrants.

After immigration, the equilibrium wage is $6.50 per hour; 23,000 workers will be hired, of which 15,500 are domestic workers and 7,500 immigrant workers.

Chapter 11

Review Questions

1. With an implicit labor market contract, which is not legally enforceable, the punishment for cheating is that the other party terminates the employment relationship. Therefore, the principle underlying self-enforcement is that both parties must lose if the relationship is terminated. For both parties to lose, workers must be paid above what they could get elsewhere but below what they are worth to the employer. The latter conditions imply the existence of a surplus (a gap between marginal revenue product and alternative wages) that is divided between employer and employee.

3. Compensation schemes, such as efficiency wages, deferred payments, and tournaments, are made feasible by an expected long-term attachment between worker and firm. If small firms do not offer long-enough job ladders to provide for career-long employment, long-term attachments will become less prevalent and the foregoing three schemes less feasible. The growth of small firms, then, may mean more reliance on individual or group output-based pay schemes (or on closer supervision).

5. If management already has power over workers because workers' ability to go to other jobs is severely limited by unemployment or monopsony, then low wages may result. However, paying low wages is definitely not the way to *acquire* power if management currently lacks it. Underpaid workers have no incentives to tolerate demanding requirements from management, because their current job is not better (and may be worse) than one they could find elsewhere. However, if workers are paid more by one firm than they could get elsewhere, they will more likely tolerate heavy demands from their supervisors before deciding to quit. One way to acquire power over workers, therefore, is to overpay, not underpay, them.

7. The compensation scheme that pays workers less than they are worth initially and more than they are worth later on could result in this outcome. Older workers end up getting pay that is high relative to their productivity, and when they have to find another employer, their pay drops substantially. Younger workers, who are lower paid under this scheme to begin with, do not experience such a drop in wages.

9. For strong performance incentives, the performance measure on which pay is based (stock prices) must be strongly affected by CEO *effort*. The problem with using stock options as a performance measure is that they are affected by *overall* market conditions (both in the stock market and in the product market) and by CEO efforts to enhance the company's performance relative to its competitors. A bonus, if awarded on the basis of the CEO's success in boosting the firm's *relative* performance, is superior in terms of incentives.

Problems

1. Charlie's employer will pay him $12 per hour. If the employer raises the wage from $10 to $12, the employer gains $3 but only needs to give Charlie $2. If the employer raises the wage further, from $12 to $14, the employer gains only $1.50, so the employer will stop at $12; the increase the employer gets from increasing the wage from $12 to $14 isn't covered by the $1.50 that the employer would get from raising the wage.

3. a. The employer will hire such that the wage = *MRP*. If the wage rate is $5 per hour, the employer will want to hire 15 workers.

   b. If the wage rate is $6 per hour, with the new marginal product of labor, the employer will want to hire 16 workers.

   c. At a higher wage rate, the employer will want to hire more workers because the marginal productivity of labor increased with the higher ("efficiency") wage rate.

Chapter 12

Review Questions

1. Labor market discrimination is said to occur when workers who are productively equivalent are systematically paid different wages on the basis of their race or ethnicity (or some other demographic characteristic unrelated to productivity). Because simple averages of earnings do not control for these characteristics, we cannot tell from them whether labor market discrimination occurs (Chinese Americans and Japanese Americans, for example, may have average productive characteristics that greatly exceed those of white Americans).

3. Wage discrimination in the labor market is present when workers with the same productive characteristics are systematically paid differently because of the demographic group to which they belong. The critical issue in judging discrimination in this case is whether male high school teachers and female high school teachers have the same productive characteristics.

   One area of information that we would want to obtain concerns the human-capital characteristics: Do male teachers and female teachers have the same levels of education and experience, and do they teach in comparable fields? A second area of information concerns working conditions. Are male teachers working longer hours (coaching sports or sponsoring clubs) or working in geographical areas that are associated with compensating wage differentials?

5. a. A wage subsidy paid to employers who hire disadvantaged Black workers will shift the demand curve for such workers (stated in terms of the employee wage) to the right. This shift can cause employment to increase, the wage rate paid to disadvantaged Black workers to increase, or both. The mix of wage and employment changes will depend on the shape of the supply curve of these workers. The changes in wages and employment induced by the subsidy will tend to overcome the adverse effect on lower-skilled Black workers of labor market discrimination.

   b. Increasing the wages and employment opportunities of lower-skilled Black workers will reduce incentives of these workers to invest in the training required to become skilled. Thus, one consequence of a wage subsidy just for lower-skilled Black workers is that the subsidy may induce more to remain lower skilled than would otherwise have been the case.

7. When nursing wages are raised above market-clearing levels, a surplus of nursing applicants will arise. The high wages, of course, will attract not only a large number of applicants but also a large number of high-quality applicants; the fact that applicants are so plentiful allows the city to select only the best. Therefore, comparable worth may reduce the number of nursing jobs available, but it will also tend to increase the employment of high-quality nurses.

Because the wages of nurses are tied to those of building inspectors, the city will be reluctant to raise the wages of building inspectors even in the event of shortages. Rather than raising wages as a recruiting device for building inspectors, the city may be tempted to lower its hiring standards and to employ building inspectors whom it would previously have rejected. Thus, employment opportunities for low-quality building inspectors may be enhanced by the comparable-worth law.

9. a. Wage discrimination occurs when compensation levels paid to one demographic group are lower than those paid to another demographic group that is exactly comparable in terms of productive characteristics. According to this definition, no discrimination would occur, because both men and women would receive equal yearly compensation while working. This equal yearly compensation would, in fact, result in a pension fund for each man and woman that would have the same present value at retirement age. However, because women live longer than men, this retirement fund would be paid out over a longer period of time and thus would be paid out to retired women in smaller yearly amounts. The Supreme Court decision would require employers to put aside more pension funds for women, and it thus requires that working women have greater yearly compensation (while working) than comparable men have.

b. The decision essentially mandates greater labor costs for women than for men of comparable productive characteristics, and by raising the firm's costs of hiring women, it could give firms incentives to substitute male workers for female workers (or capital for female workers).

Problems

1. Assuming that workers of one gender remain in their jobs, the index of dissimilarity indicates the percentage of the other group that would have to change occupations for these two genders to have equal occupational distributions. Looking at Table 12RP.1, assume that the men stay in the same jobs and then find the number of women in each job that would give them the same percentage distribution as that for men.

Table 12RP.1 A Hypothetical Distribution of Males and Females in Three Occupations

Occupation	Actual female distribution	If female % = male %	No. needing to change
A	20	40% = 28	28 - 20 = 8
B	25	40% = 28	28 - 25 = 3
C	25	20% = 14	14 - 25 = -11

As this table shows, 11 women need to change jobs—these 11 leave occupation C and move into occupations A and B; 11 women equal 15.7 percent of the total, which is the index of dissimilarity.

3. See Figure 12RP.3.

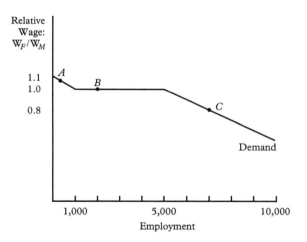

Figure 12RP.3 Demand Curve for Women in Terms of Relative Wages

$W_F/W_M = 1.08$ when 200 women are hired at point A. $W_F/W_M = 1$ when 2,000 women are hired at point B. $W_F/W_M = 0.8$ when 7,000 women are hired at point C. Discrimination hinders female workers in this market only if more than 5,000 are hired. In fact, discrimination favors female workers when fewer than 1,000 are hired.

5. (Appendix 12A). The third column in Table 12RP.5 gives the estimated salary for each job on the basis of the number of Hay Points according to the estimated regression for men. The fourth column gives the difference between the female salary and the male salary, relative to the male salary.

Table 12RP.5 Hypothetical Hay Points and Salary for Men and Women

Hay Point	Salary ($)	Estimated salary ($)	M-W gap
200	1,200	1,380	180
310	1,300	1,479	179
425	1,500	1,582.5	82.5
500	1,580	1,650	70
550	1,635	1,695	60

Women, on average, are paid less than men who have comparable Hay Point levels. As we see in the fourth column, the comparable-worth gap appears to diminish with skill level.

7. Figure 12RP.7 shows the marginal product of labor. If the wage rate is $8 per hour, in the absence of discrimination, the employer would want to hire 12 workers. The profits to the employer would be equal to the

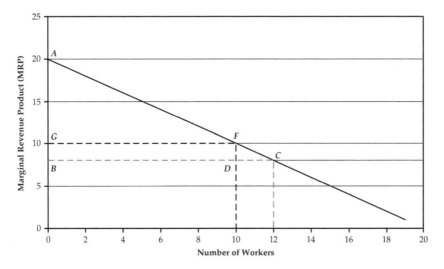

Figure 12RP.7 The Marginal Revenue Product of Labor in a Particular Labor Market

area under the MRP_L (demand curve) above the (blue) horizontal wage line. If 12 workers are hired, this triangular area, ABC, is calculated as $0.5(20 - 8)(12) = \$72$.

If the employer discriminates in that they hire only 10 female workers, the profits can be calculated as the trapezoidal area $ABDF$, which is the sum of the triangle AGF and the rectangle $BDFG$, as follows: area $= 0.5(20 - 10)(10) + (2)(10) = 50 + 20 = \$70$. Thus, if the employer discriminates in that they hire only 10 women, the discriminating employer is giving up $2 per hour in profits, which is the difference between the two areas (CDF).

Chapter 13

Review Questions

1. Because a reduction in the price of capital equipment will stimulate the purchase of capital equipment, a union should be concerned whether its members are gross complements or gross substitutes with capital. In the former case, the proposed policy (reducing the price of capital) would cause the demand for union members to rise, whereas in the latter, their demand would fall. Other things being equal, the more rapidly the demand for labor is shifting out, the smaller will be the reduction in employment associated with any union-induced wage gain (assuming the collective bargaining agreement lies on the labor demand curve). Hence, unions representing groups that are gross complements (substitutes) with capital would benefit (lose) from the policy change.

   Evidence cited in the text suggests that capital and higher-skilled labor may be gross complements, but capital and lower-skilled labor are gross substitutes. This suggests that union leaders representing the latter type of workers will be opposed to the legislation, whereas union leaders representing the former may favor it.

3. The provisions of the Jones Act affect the demand for labor in the U.S. shipping industry in at least two ways. First, the provision that 50 percent of all U.S. government cargo must be transported in U.S.-owned ships reduces the price elasticity of demand for U.S. shipping in the output market. Second, the restriction that at least 90 percent of the crews of U.S. ships must be U.S. citizens reduces the ability of ship owners to substitute foreign crew members for U.S. citizens. Both changes cause the wage elasticity of demand for U.S. crew members to be less elastic than it would otherwise be.

   To the extent that the U.S. shipping industry is heavily unionized and little competition occurs between union crew members and nonunion crew members (a reasonable assumption), the wage elasticity of demand for union crew members would become less elastic under the Jones Act. As stressed in the text, inelastic labor demand curves permit unions to push for increases in their members' wages without large employment losses, at least in the short run.

5. This law makes substituting capital for labor more difficult and more costly. Any worker replaced by capital (or another substitute factor of production) must be retrained and employed elsewhere in the firm, which clearly raises the cost of this substitution. Thus, this law tends to reduce the elasticity of demand for union labor, and it increases the ability of unions to raise wages without reducing their members' employment very much.

7. Unions may raise worker productivity for several reasons. One of the more obvious is that as wages are increased, firms cut back employment and substitute capital for labor. Both actions tend to raise the marginal productivity of labor. To survive in a competitive market, profit-maximizing firms must raise the marginal productivity of labor whenever wages increase.

Another reason why unions raise productivity is that the high wages unionized employers offer attract a large pool of applicants, and employers are able to select the best applicants. Moreover, the reduction in turnover that we observe in unionized plants increases firms' incentives to provide specific training to their workers, and the seniority system that unions typically implement encourages older workers to help train younger workers (they can do so without fear that the younger workers will compete for their jobs when fully trained).

Because many of these sources of increased productivity are responses by firms to higher wages, they tend to mitigate the effects of unionization on costs. Some nonunion firms deliberately pay high wages to attract and retain competent employees, and they often pursue this strategy even without the implicit threat of becoming unionized. However, the fact that firms generally pay the union wage only after their employees become organized suggests that they believe that unions raise labor costs to a greater extent than they raise worker productivity.

What the argument in question 7 overlooks is that increases in productivity must be measured against increases in costs. If unions enhance productivity to a greater extent than they increase costs of production, then clearly, employers should take a much less antagonistic approach to unions. If, however, enhancements in labor productivity are smaller than increases in labor costs, employer profitability will decline under unionization.

Problems

1. Set the employer concession schedule equal to the union resistance curve, and solve for W:

$1 + 0.02S = 5 + 0.02S - 0.01S^2$ simplifies to $0.01S^2 = 4$, or $S^2 = 400$, or $S = 20$ days.

Plugging S into the equations yields $W = 1.4$ percent.

3. The relative wage advantage is $R = (W_{union} - W_{nonunion})/W_{nonunion} = (\$10 - \$8)/\$8 = 0.25$. Union workers earn 25 percent more than nonunion workers. The absolute effect of the union cannot be determined, because we don't know what the wage of the unionized workers would be in the absence of the union. We don't know the extent of spillover effects, threat effects, and wait unemployment, for example.

5. Both the company official and the union leader are correct. Currently at $14 per hour, the employers would like to hire 26 employees. If the union were successful with the wage negotiations, along with the growing demand, the firm would want to hire 27 employees. So the union leader is correct. But if the union were not successful in its attempt to raise wages, the firm would want to hire 30 employees. So the company official is also correct. The effect of a successful wage negotiation in the presence of growing demand is to reduce the rate of growth of employment.

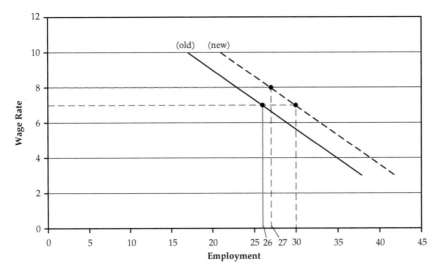

Figure 13RP.3 UI Benefit and Previous Wage

7. At a wage rate of $7.50, 4,500 workers will be employed. The union relative wage advantage is $R = (8 - 7.5)/7.5 = 0.067$.

Chapter 14

Review Questions

1. The two policy goals are not compatible in the short run. An increase in unemployment compensation benefits reduces the costs to unemployed workers of additional job search; this will lead them to extend their duration of unemployment and search for better-paying jobs. In the short run, increasing unemployment compensation benefits will increase the unemployment rate.

In the long run, however, the two policy goals may be compatible. If the prolonged durations of job search lead to better matches of workers and jobs, the chances that workers will become unemployed in the future will diminish. That is, the better matches will reduce both the probability that workers will quit their jobs and the probability that they will be fired. This reduced probability of entering unemployment will reduce the unemployment rate in the long run. Whether the reduction in the unemployment rate due to the smaller incidence of unemployment outweighs the increase due to the longer spells of unemployment is an open question.

3. When a worker first becomes unemployed, they may be optimistic about employment opportunities and set a high reservation wage. However, if over time only low wage offers are received, the individual may realize that the distribution of wage offers is lower than initially assumed. This revision of expectations would also cause a downward revision of the reservation wage.

   In fact, even if workers' initial perceptions about the distribution of wage offers were correct, this distribution might systematically shift down over time. For example, employers might use the length of time that an individual had been unemployed as a signal of the individual's relatively low productivity and might moderate wage offers accordingly. A systematically declining wage-offer distribution that arises for this reason would similarly cause reservation wages to decline as durations of unemployment lengthened.

5. This policy should have two effects on the unemployment rate. First, by reducing the value of benefits to unemployed workers, it should reduce the duration of their spells of unemployment. In other words, by taxing unemployment insurance benefits, the government is in effect reducing those benefits, and the reduction in benefits increases the marginal costs of remaining unemployed for an additional period of time. Thus, workers will tend to be less choosy about the job offers that they accept and should be induced to reduce the amount of time that they spend searching for additional job offers. However, by reducing job search time, the taxation of UI benefits may lead to poorer matches between worker and employer, thus creating higher turnover (and more unemployment) in the long run.

   Second, because unemployed workers are now receiving less compensation from the government, those in jobs in which layoffs frequently occur will find them less attractive than they previously did. Employers who offer these jobs will have more difficulty in attracting employees unless they raise wages (assuming workers have other job options). This compensating wage differential will act as a penalty for high layoff rates, and this penalty should induce firms to reduce layoffs to some extent. A reduced propensity to lay off workers, of course, should reduce the unemployment rate (other things being equal).

7. The level of unemployment is affected by flows into and out of the pool of unemployed workers. Restricting employers' ability to fire workers

will reduce the flow of workers *into* the pool, thus tending to reduce unemployment.

However, because these restrictions increase the costs of hiring workers (the costs of firing them are a quasi-fixed cost of employment), firms will tend to reduce their *hiring* of labor. This reduction will slow the flows out of the unemployed pool, so one cannot predict the overall effect of the restrictions on the unemployment rate.

Problems

1. To make the calculations easier, we can drop the millions terms. The initial unemployment rate is $100 \times U/(U + E) = 100 \times 10/(10 + 120) = 7.69$ percent. The initial labor force participation rate is $100 \times (U + E)/(U + E + N) = 100 \times (10 + 120)/(10 + 120 + 70) = 65.0$ percent.

The new levels of the three measures (in millions) are as follows:

$$U_1 = U_0 + EU + NU - UE - UN = 10 + 1.8 + 1.3 - 2.2 - 1.7 = 9.2$$
$$E_1 = E_0 + UE + NE - EU - EN = 120 + 2.2 + 4.5 - 1.8 - 3.0 = 121.9$$
$$N_1 = N_0 + EN + UN - NE - NU = 70 + 3.0 + 1.7 - 4.5 - 1.3 = 68.9$$

The new rates are as follows:

Unemployment rate = $100 \times 9.2/(131.1) = 7.02$ percent.

Labor force participation = $100 \times 131.1/200 = 65.55$ percent.

3. See Figure 14RP.3.

Case 1: If wage = \$100, then the worker receives the minimum, B = \$200, and the replacement rate is B/W = \$200/\$100 = 2.

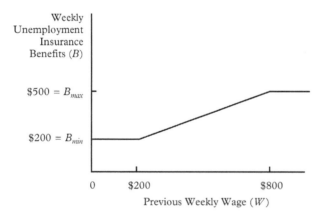

Figure 14RP.3 UI Benefit and Previous Wage

Case 2: If wage = \$500, then the worker receives B = $0.5 \times 500 + 100$ = \$350 and the replacement rate is \$350/\$500 = 0.7.

Case 3: If wage = \$2,000, then the worker receives the maximum, B = \$500, and the replacement rate is \$500/\$2,000 = 0.25.

5. The graph is in Figure 14RP.5:

> If the firm's layoff experience is below l_{min}, the firm pays the minimum tax rate. After the firm's layoff experience reaches the critical value of l_{min}, the firm's UI tax rate rises with increased layoff experience until it

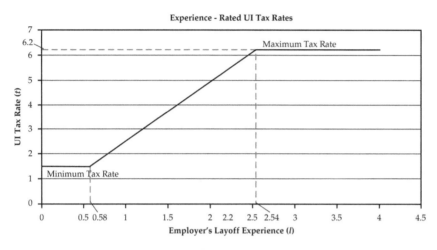

Experience - Rated UI Tax Rates

Figure 14RP.5 UI Tax Rate and Employer's Layoff Experience

> reaches the maximum tax rate.

> To calculate the firm's critical value of layoff experience (l_{min}), use the following equation:

> $$1.5 = 0.1 + 2.4\ l_{min} \rightarrow l_{min} = 0.58 \text{ percent}$$

> To calculate the firm's ceiling value of layoff experience (l_{max}), use the following equation:

> $$6.2 = 0.1 + 2.4\ l_{max} \rightarrow l_{max} = 2.54 \text{ percent}$$

Chapter 15

Review Questions

1. Increasing the investment tax credit reduces the price of capital and therefore has two possible effects on the demand for labor. If labor and capital are complements in production or are gross complements, then the tax credit will shift the labor demand curve to the right and tend to increase wages and employment. If, however, capital and labor are gross substitutes, then this tax credit could result in a decreased demand for labor.

   We learned in Chapter 4 that capital and lower-skilled labor are more likely to be substitutes in production than are higher-skilled labor and capital; therefore, this investment tax credit is more likely to negatively affect the demand for lower-skilled labor than for higher-skilled labor. If so, more downward pressure will be exerted on the wages of lower-skilled workers, and the resulting decline in the relative wages of the lowest-paid workers tends to widen the dispersion of earnings.

3. Forbidding employers from replacing striking workers will have ambiguous effects on the dispersion of earnings. On the one hand, we know that forbidding striker replacement should increase the power of unions to raise the wages of their members, and we know that unions have historically raised the wages of less-skilled members relative to the wages of those who are more skilled. Thus, if union power is enhanced, the primary beneficiaries will be lower-skilled union workers, and this effect should tend to equalize the distribution of earnings.

   On the other hand, we need to consider the effects on those who would have worked as replacements. We know that unions are more prevalent in large firms, which pay higher wages anyway, and we can suppose that workers who wish to work as replacements are attracted to these jobs because they can improve their earnings. By encouraging higher wages in large, unionized firms, forbidding striker replacement could cause a spillover effect that reduces wages in the nonunionized sector. Thus, prohibiting striker replacement may actually drive down wages paid to those now in the small-firm, nonunion sector and create a greater dispersion in earnings.

5. Increasing the subsidy guaranteed to those who do not work, but holding constant a nonzero effective wage rate, will clearly cause a reduction in labor supply. This reduction will take two forms: Some who worked before may decide to withdraw from the labor force, and some who worked before may reduce their hours of work. These two forms of labor supply reduction have quite different effects on the distribution of *earnings*.

   Suppose that the expected labor supply reductions will come mainly from workers who have the lowest level of earnings. Thus, when labor force *withdrawal* takes place, those who have the lowest earnings are leaving the labor force, and this *withdrawal* will tend to equalize the distribution of earnings (those at the lower end exit from the distribution).

   Reduced hours of work among those who continue in the labor force, however, will have the opposite effect on the distribution of earnings if this labor supply response is also focused among those with the lowest level of earnings. Reductions in working hours will lower the earnings of these low-wage workers further, which will tend to widen the dispersion of earnings.

   Therefore, although this increased amount of the negative income tax program serves to equalize the distribution of *income* (which includes the subsidies), the labor supply responses can tend to either narrow or widen the dispersion of earnings.

7. Proposal a increases the cost of employing high-wage (skilled) labor and capital. This will have ambiguous effects on the demand curve for lower-skilled workers. On the one hand, it will tend to cause lower-skilled workers to be substituted for higher-skilled workers and/or capital (assuming they are substitutes in production). On the other hand, the

costs of production rise, and the scale effect will tend to reduce both output and the demand for all workers (including lower-skilled workers).

If the substitution effect dominates, the demand curve for lower-skilled workers will shift to the right, tending to increase their employment and wage rate. If the scale effect dominates (or if lower-skilled workers are complements in production with higher-skilled labor and capital), then the demand curve for them will shift left and their wage rate and employment level would decrease.

Proposal b cuts the cost of employing all labor, but the percentage decrease is greatest for low-paid (lower-skilled) workers. Thus, the proposal cuts the cost of lower-skilled labor relative to that of both capital and higher-skilled labor. This will unambiguously shift the demand for lower-skilled labor to the right (keeping the employee wage on the vertical axis), because both the scale effect and the substitution effect work in the same direction. This will tend to increase both lower-skilled employment and the wages received by lower-skilled employees.

Proposal b is better for accomplishing the government's goal of improving the earnings of lower-skilled workers, because the scale effect tends to increase, not reduce, the demand for their services.

Problems

1. (Appendix 15A) First, order the students by income to find the poorest 20 percent, next poorest 20 percent, middle 20 percent, next richest 20 percent, and richest 20 percent (see Table 15RP.1). Then, find the total income—in this case, $344,000. Divide the income in each 20 percent group by the total income to find its share of income. Finally, calculate the cumulative share of income.

Table 15RP.1 Income Shares for 10 Individuals

Name	Income	Share of income	Cumulative share of income
Bottom 20%			
Billy	$20,000	$44,000/$344,000 = 0.128	0.128
Kasia	$24,000		
Second 20%			
Rose	$29,000	$60,000/$344,000 = 0.174	0.128 + 0.174 = 0.302
Charlie	$31,000		
Middle 20%			
Yukiko	$32,000	$66,000/$344,000 = 0.192	0.302 + 0.192 = 0.494

Name	Income	Share of income	Cumulative share of income
Nina	$34,000		
Fourth 20%			
Thomas	$35,000	$72,000/$344,000 = 0.209	0.494 + 0.209 = 0.703
Raul	$37,000		
Top 20%			
Becky	$42,000	$100,000/$344,000 = 0.297	0.703 + 0.297 = 1.000
Willis	$60,000		

Now graph this information, making sure that the cumulative share of income goes on the vertical axis and that the cumulative share of households goes on the horizontal axis (see Figure 15RP.1). (An even more precise Lorenz curve can be graphed by breaking the data into tenths rather than fifths.)

To find the Gini coefficient, use the method outlined in Appendix 15A to find the area below the Lorenz curve. This area equals 0.1 plus the area of the four rectangles whose bases are 0.2 and whose heights are the cumulative shares of income for the first four income groups. Area = 0.1 + (0.2 × 0.128) + (0.2 × 0.302) + (0.2 × 0.494) + (0.2 × 0.703) = 0.1 + 0.3254 = 0.4254. The Gini coefficient = (0.5 - area under the Lorenz curve)/0.5 = (0.5 - 0.4254)/0.5 = 0.1492.

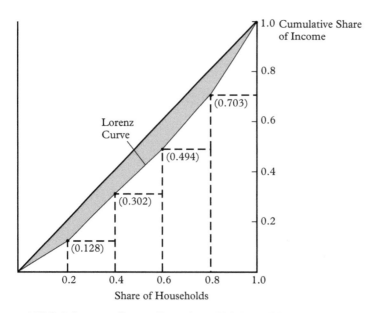

Figure 15RP.1 Lorenz Curve Based on Table 15RP.1

3. a. The earnings ratios are in Table 15RP.3.

Table 15RP.3 Earnings Ratios, Customer Service Representatives

Ratio of earnings at given percentiles	1990	2005
90:10	1.53	1.41
90:50	1.24	1.22
50:10	1.23	1.16

b. From 1990 to 2005, all the earnings ratios fell. The fact that the fall in the 90:50 ratio was smaller than the fall in the 50:10 ratio indicates that the move toward equality was smaller at the upper end of the earnings distribution than at the lower end.

5. The Lorenz curve for U.S. income in 2005 is shown in Figure 15RP.5.

Calculating the Gini coefficient involves breaking the area under the Lorenz curve into a series of triangles and rectangles, as shown in Appendix 15A (specifically Figure 15A.3). We know that the area of the five triangles sums to $0.1 = (0.2 \times 1 \times 0.5)$. With the income distribution in this problem, the areas of the rectangles are calculated as follows:

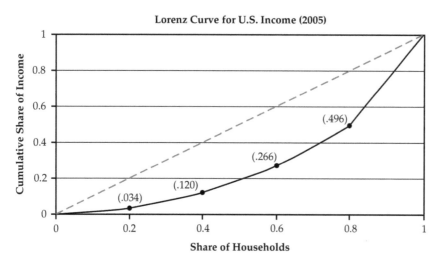

Figure 15RP.5 Lorenz Curve for U.S. Income (2005)

$$(0.2 \times 0.034) + (0.2 \times 0.120) + (0.2 \times 0.266) + (0.2 \times 0.496) = 0.1832$$

Thus, the area under the Lorenz curve is $0.1 + 0.1832 = 0.2832$, and the Gini coefficient is calculated as follows:

$$(0.5 - 0.2832)/0.5 = 0.4336$$

Chapter 16

Review Questions

1. Comparative advantage is driven by the internal opportunity costs of producing the two goods—the trade-off that must be made in obtaining more of one good—not by differences in per capita wealth or consumption. Thus, the population of B is irrelevant to the analysis.

3. The availability of cheaper foreign labor creates both a substitution effect and a scale effect. The substitution of foreign production workers for U.S. production workers clearly reduces employment in the United States, and the size of the employment loss depends on how easily it is to substitute foreign workers for U.S. workers. The size of the substitution effect also depends in part on the elasticity of the labor supply curve of U.S. workers in this industry. If the supply curve is elastic, U.S. workers will readily leave the industry and their wages will not fall by much; if it is relatively inelastic, U.S. wages will fall, and this could make the substitution effect smaller.

   A scale effect, however, will occur. As alarm systems fall in price, more U.S. customers may buy them—increasing the demand for workers who are complements in production with those overseas: installers, salespeople, and those who monitor and repair the systems. The scale effect will be larger if the demand for alarms is more elastic and if the share of total cost that is tied to production workers is larger.

5. As discussed in the text, the number of jobs in a society depends on how well supply and demand are equated in the labor market—not on a society's technology or its level of trade. Trade depends on comparative advantage, which in turn depends on the internal opportunity costs of producing goods and services (see review question 1).

7. Economic theory does suggest that by allowing greater specialization on the basis of comparative advantage, reducing trade barriers will increase the overall consumption that is possible in the countries that trade. The goal of a society, however, is not to maximize consumption; it is to maximize the utility of individuals. If, as we discussed at the end of Chapter 4, some policy change increased the income of the richest person in society by $1 billion but reduced the income of 1 million poor people by $500 each, the total income in society would rise by $500 million; however, the utility gains to the richest person may be close to nil, whereas the utility losses of the million poor people who lose $500 may be much larger. This $500 million gain in income would therefore be accompanied by an overall loss in utility. Given that we cannot measure utility, the only way we can find out if society has gained in utility levels is to determine whether the gainers (in this case, the richest person) would be willing to give $500 to each of the losers; if this person is so willing and makes the payments, then the losers are held harmless—and the situation leads to a

gainer but without any losers (so the transaction would meet the Pareto criteria discussed in Chapter 1).

Problems

1. a. In country M, 60 million refrigerators would be given up in order to produce 50 million bicycles. The opportunity cost of each bicycle is 60/50, or 1.2, refrigerators. In country N, 50 million refrigerators would be given up in order to produce 75 million bicycles. The opportunity cost of each bicycle is 50/75, or 0.67, refrigerators. In country M, 50 million bicycles would have to be given up to produce 60 million refrigerators, so the opportunity cost of refrigerators is 50/60, or 0.83, bicycles. In country N, 75 million bicycles would have to be given up to produce 50 million refrigerators, so the opportunity cost of refrigerators is 75/50, or 1.5, bicycles.

   b. Country N has a comparative advantage in bicycles because the opportunity cost of bicycles is lower in country N. That is, fewer refrigerators would be given up for each bicycle produced.

   c. Yes, the two countries should trade: Country N should produce bicycles, and country M should produce refrigerators.

3. In the rich country, the marginal productivity of customer services representatives is as follows:

   $$MP_L = 17 - 0.6L = 17 - 0.6(10) = 11$$

   In the poor country, the marginal productivity of customer services representatives is as follows:

   $$MP_L = 11 - 0.8L = 11 - 0.8(5) = 7$$

   Here we compare the ratio of wages to marginal productivity in the two countries:

   In the rich country, $W/MP_L = \$20/11 = \$1.82$ per unit

   In the poor country, $W/MP_L = \$10/7 = \$1.43$ per unit

   In the poor country, the marginal cost of a unit of service is $1.43, whereas in the rich country, it is $1.82 per unit. Thus, a firm in a rich country thinking of moving 1,000 jobs to the poor country could reduce costs by doing so. If it did move 1,000 jobs, MP_L in the rich country would rise to $17 - 0.6(9) = 11.6$. MP_L in the poor country would fall to $11 - 0.8(6) = 6.2$. So even with 1,000 jobs moved, the per-unit cost in the rich country (at $20/11.6 = 1.72$) is still above that in the poor country ($10/6.2 = 1.61$). Thus, the firm would want to consider moving more than 1,000 jobs to the poorer country.

Index

Page numbers in *italics* indicate figures and in **bold** indicate tables on the corresponding pages.

Aaronson, Stephanie 220n2
ability bias 327, 337–338
ability: discrimination 453–455; effort 470–471
above-market wages 50–51, *50*
Abowd, John M. 168, 305n1, 305n6, 394, 432n29, 433n31, 437n69, 546n11, 547n19
Abraham, Katherine G. 59n5, 133n20, 220n2, 226, 343n10, 596n8
Abraham, Steven E. 547n18
Abramitzky, Ran 379, 388n14, 389n20
Abrams, Elliott 390n26
Abrams, Franklin S. 390n26
absolute effect, unions 530, 531–533
absolute value 20, 98
Acemoglu, Daron 121, 130n7, 134n29, 176n32, 635n13, 636n24, 670n12, 670n13
Acharya, Viral 153
Adams, James D. 131n11
Adams, Scott 134n24
adaptability (behaviors) 4
adaptive expectations 355
added-worker effect 237–238
Addison, John T. 130n7, 545n9, 550n45, 554
Adhvaryu, Achyuta 175n20
adjustment costs 658
affirmative action 471, 476–477
Affordable Care Act (ACA) 289–290
Agan, Amanda Y. 134n23, 467
age: earning differences by gender and 441; earnings profiles 321–323, *322*; employee turnover and 380; fanning out of age-earnings profiles 322–323; gender and 441; human investment capital and 314; labor force participation rate and 179–182, *181–182*, *323*; of migrants 361, 380; productivity and 240, *241*; retirement 242–247, *245*, 416–417; sequencing

of pay and 413–414, 416; teenage workers 107–109; training declining with 321–322, *322*; women's earnings and 324, *325*
agency workers 157–158
aggregate demand, unemployment, 579–580
Agrawal, Arjay 121, 134n27
agricultural work incentives 214–215
Aguiar, Mark 258n1, 601n36, 633n2
Ahin, Ay egül 596n10, 604n62
Ahmed, Akhter 260n7
Ahn, Hie Joo 595n5
Aigner, Dennis J. 496
airlines, deregulation of 519
Aizcorbe, Ana M. 59n7
Aizer, Anna 259n7
Akee, Randall 389n15, 389n18, 491n38
Akerlof, George A. 24n5, 433n39, 438, 600n29, 604n62
Akerman, Anders 131n12, 634n10, 671n23
Aksoy, Cevat G. 484n1
Al-Ubaydli, Omar 431n21
Alchian, Armen 88n11
Aldy, Joseph E. 300
Allcott, Hunt 232
Allen, Steven G. 299n35, 435n47
allocation of labor 266
Almond, Douglas 344n14
Alston, Lee J. 438n73
Altman, Morris 425
Altman, Stuart H. 55
Altonji, Joseph G. 221n4, 344n14, 344n15, 346n24, 350n44, 496, 636n25
Ambuehl, Sandro 25n5
America. *see* United States, the
American Federation of Labor and Congress of Industrial Organizations (AFL-CIO) 506–507

Ameriks, John 221n3
Amin, Shanina 239
Amin, Vikesh 348n35
Amior, Michael 600n28
Amiti, Mary 670n9, 670n10
Amuedo-Dorantes, Catalina 261n16
Andersen, Steffen 431n21
Anderson, David A. 305n6
Anderson, James E. 672n27, 673
Anderson, Patricia M. 88n13, 262n24,
    263n27, 393n45, 603n56, 604n57
Andersson, Fredrik 599n26
Andersson, Henrik 296n6
Andreoni, James 425
Angelov, Nikolay 347n25, 485n9
Angrist, Joshua D. 343n11, 347n25
Antecol, Heather 389n17, 485n7
antidiscrimination programs 471–480,
    477
antitrust cases 144–145
apprentices 522
Arai, Mahmood 479
arbitration 527–530; contract zone
    528–529, 555–558, *555–558*;
    effects of 529–530; forms of 528;
    persuading the arbitrator in 529
Arcidiacono, Peter 432n24
Armed Forces Qualification Test
    (AFQT) 453
Armour, Philip 495n67
Ash, Michael 553n61
Ashenfelter, Orley 36, 132n16, 173n6,
    174n6, 178, 188, 221n4, 305n1,
    305n6, 338, 348n33, 348n35,
    495n70, 546n13, 548n28, 549n33,
    549n34, 549n38, 549n39, 549n40,
    598n20
Ashmore, David 598n20
Asian Americans 439–440
Åslund, Olof 493n51
Asquith, Brian 669n4
assumptions: occupational choice
    276–277; positive economics 3–4
asymmetric information: cheating and
    397–398; productivity and 400–401;
    strikes and 526–527; wage rigidity
    and 582–583
Atalay, Enghin 635n17
Atherton, Wallace 554
Atkinson, Anthony B. 597n18, 605,
    633n4
Attfield, Clifford L. F. 605n64
audits of discrimination 478–479
Auerbach, Alan 224n25
Australian unions 503–504

Austrian unions 503–504
Autor, David 16, 130n7, 134n28,
    224n23, 225n25, 261n14, 350n45,
    575, 617, 634n7, 634n9, 635n10,
    635n13, 635n15, 635n18, 636n21,
    636n24, 637n30, 638, 669n4,
    670n12, 670n13, 671n19, 671n20,
    671n21, 673n32
average tendencies of outcomes 5
Averett, Susan 604n59
Azar, José 174n8, 174n11, 175n14,
    177n33
Azariadis, Costas 603n49, 603n50

backward bending 187
Bagger, Jesper 393n46
Baghai, Ramin 153
Baicker, Katherine 223n14, 300n41,
    587, 673n32, 673n36
Baily, Martin 603n50
Baker, Bryan 390n24
Baker, George 177n41, 429n9,
    429n11, 433n36, 435n52
Baldwin, Marjorie L. 486n14, 492n49
Ball, Laurence 604n62
ballpark vendors case study 202–203
"ban the box" and statistical
    discrimination 466–467
Baranov, Victoria 342n7
bargaining see collective bargaining
Barkume, Anthony 176n29
Barnow, Burt S. 60n9
Barrington, Linda J. 484n2, 501n7,
    501n8
Barrow, Lisa 490n34
Bartel, Ann P. 346n22, 431n21
Barth, Erling 437n67, 485n7, 634n10
Bartling, Bjorn 434n44
Bartoš, Vojtěch 490n37, 493n51
baseball case study 454–455
Bassi, Laurie J. 176n32, 346n22
Bastian, Jacob 225n31
Basu, Kaushik 239
Batchelder, Lily 260n11, 347n25
Battisti, Michele 393n43
Bauer, Michal 490n37, 493n51
Bauernschuster, Stefan 553n64
Baumol, William J. 356n3
Bawden, Lee 429n6
Bayard, Kimberly 487n17
Bayer, Patrick 489n28
Bazerman, Max H. 549n36
Bazzi, Samuel 388n5
Bean, Frank D. 394
Beaudry, Paul 131n7, 135, 636n25

Becker, Brian E. 546n11
Becker, Gary S. 24n2, 178, 263, 352, 491n42, 496
Becker, Sacha O. 319
Bedard, Kelly 350n44, 485n7
Behaghel, Luc 493n51
behaviors: cheating 397–399; fairness 402–403, 424–425; hedonic wage theory 271–272, 284–285; inertia 9; investment in human capital 308; positive economics 3–5; rationality 3–4; supply of labor 14; *see also* decision to work; decision-making
Beland, Louis-Philippe 494n59
Belfield, Clive R. 545n9
Bell, Brian D. 432n29
Beller, Andrea H. 263n29
Bellmann, Lutz 130n7, 601n34
below-market wages 51, *51*
Belzer, Michael H. 106, 519
Belzil, Christian 596n10, 599n23
Bénabou, Roland 430n16
Bender, Keith A. 552n54
Bender, Stefan 570, 598n19, 599n22, 599n23
benefit–cost analysis, risk of injury 290–291
benefits. *see* employee benefits; incentives for employees; welfare
Benhabib, Jess 356n3
Benmelech, Efraim 174n11
Bennett, Amanda 605n63
Bennett, James 554
Benson, Alan 436n59
Bentham, Jeremu 297n14
Berger, Mark C. 394n52
Bergman, Nittai 174n11
Berlinski, Samuel 173n4
Berman, Eli 362, 389n17
Bernhardt, Dan 436n60
Bernhofen, Daniel M. 651
Bertola, Giuseppe 552n57
Bertrand, Marianne 88n12, 259n5, 260n9, 432n26, 432n27, 432n29, 438, 479, 485n9, 490n37, 492n49
Bessa, Ioulia 552n54
Betts, Julian R. 344n15
Bewley, Truman F. 602n46
Bhagwati, Jagdish 670n16, 671n18
Bhaskar, V. 24n3, 173n4, 173n5
Bhattacharya, Jay 300n41
Bhuller, Manudeep 348n33
bias. *see* ability bias; discrimination
Bick, Alexander 204, 221n5, 223n18, 259n3

Biddle, Jeff E. 222n12, 253
Big Mac per Hour of Work (BMPH) index 35–36
Bils, Mark 430n15, 603n46
Binder, Ariel J. 223n20
Bingley, Paul 261n16
Bishop, John 154, 163, 177n34
Bishop, Kelly 224n21
Bivens, Josh 637n31
Black Americans: affirmative action plans 476–478; discrimination against 451–454, 477–480; earnings differences between white and 450–457, **451**, **456**; Great Migration of 360
Black Death case study 47–48
Black, Dan A. 292, 344n15, 345n20, 394n52, 437n70, 484n1, 486n15, 493n55
Black, Sandra E. 492n45, 553n60
Blanchard, Olivier Jean 600n27
Blanchflower, David 177n35, 545n8, 550n45, 551n48, 551n51, 552n57, 553n60, 601n34, 605
Blanco, German 351n50
Blandin, Adam 221n5
Blank, Rebecca M. 88, 225n29, 226, 262n24, 496, 605
Blasi, Joseph R. 431n23, 432n25
Blau, David M. 263
Blau, Francine D. 60n13, 61, 220n1, 224n21, 259n3, 259n6, 263n27, 391n33, 391n34, 391n36, 391n37, 392n39, 394, 486n13, 486n14, 487n17, 488n23, 493n53, 496, 552n57, 635n12
Bleakley, Hoyt 491n41
Blien, Uwe 601n34
Blinder, Alan S. 603n51, 657
Bloch, Farrell E. 393n51
Bloemen, Hans G. 261n16
Bloom, David 549n38
Bloom, Nicholas 634n10, 637n31
Blundell, Richard 221n4, 259n7, 261n15, 261n18
Boal, William M. 553n58
Bodenhorn, Howard 604n59
Bodie, Zvi 435n50
Boeri, Tito 183, 552n57
Bognanno, Michael L. 435n53, 436n54
Bohn, Sarah 378
Bohren, J Aislinn 493n52
Boisso, Dale 486n12
Boll, Christina 260n9
Bond, Timothy N. 343n9

Boning, Brent 432n25
bonus plans 404, 408–409, 410; *see also* pay-for-performance
Booker, Brakkton 87n5
boom-and-bust cycles 353–356
border security 357–358, 368
Bordo, Michael D. 587
Borghans, Lex 224n25
Borghesi, Richard 66
Borjas, George 175n18, 352, 388n10, 389n16, 392n40, 394, 491n40, 671n23
Borland, Jeff 598n20
Borzaga, Carlo 431n23
Bosso, Gaetano 379
Bound, John 223n20, 316, 343n12, 489n28, 635n11, 638
Boustan, Leah Platt 379, 388n14, 389n20
Bowen, William G. 347n30
Bowman, W. R. 177n38
Boyer, George R. 16
Boyle, Melissa A. 260n14
Bradley, Ralph 59n7
Brewer, Mike 221n4
Briggs, Joseph 221n3
Britain. *see* United Kingdom, the
Bronars, Stephen G. 433n38, 552n57, 553n62
Brown, Alessio J. G. 673n40
Brown, Charles 346n22
Brown, Claire 259n4
Brown, Drusilla K. 672n28
Brown, James N. 437n67
Brown, Jennifer 601n37
Brown, John C. 651
Brown, Michelle 552n57
Brown, Robert S. 344n13
Brummand, Peter 131n15, 486n13
Bruns, Benjamin 488n22
Brynjolsson, Erik 134n25, 134n26, 135, 621, 636n19, 637n26, 638
Bryson, Alex 545n8, 550n45, 551n48, 551n51, 634n10
Bublitz, Elisabeth 260n9
Buchmueller, Thomas C. 83, 552n53
Budd, John W. 552n53
budget constraints: child support assurance 250–252, *250–251*; decision to work 197–201, *198*, *201*; household production 227–230; joint labor supply decisions 233–236; retirement age and 242–246; wage increases 195–196; with "spikes" *205*, 205–207; work requirement 210–211

Buffum, David 465
Bulman, George 343n9
Bundorf, M. Kate 300n41
Burfisher, Mary E. 671n18
Burghardt, John 351–352n51, 351n51
Burkhauser, Richard V. 133n20, 133n23
Burks, Stephen V. 161
Burstein, Ariel 390n28
Burtless, Gary 225n26, 638
Butcher, Kristin F. 378
Butler, Richard J. 486n14, 492n49
Button, Patrick 495n67
Byers, James F. 604n56

Cadena, Brian C. 341n4, 379
Cain, Glen G. 496
Cajner, Tomaz 220n2, 602n41
Caliendo, Lorenzo 669–670n9
calories case study 401
Campbell, Carl M., III 434n44
Canada: international trade 656; seasonal unemployment 587; unemployment 565, *565*; unions 504, 534, 536
capital markets: demand and supply 40–41, *41*; demand for labor 111–112; elasticity in the labor market 104–105; government interventions 11; imperfections in 11; operations 36, *36–37*
capital substitution and wages 74
capital supply 40–41, *41*
capital-intensive model 39
Caplin, Andrew 221n3
Cappelli, Peter 435n45
Card, David E. 129n1, 130n2, 132n18, 133n23, 135, 173n5, 178, 207, 226, 262n24, 346n21, 348n33, 352, 352n51, 389n19, 391n35, 403, 487n16, 489n31, 495n70, 519, 545n2, 548n27, 551n47, 551n48, 551n49, 597n18, 599n23, 601n34, 604n57, 637n28, 673n33
Cardiff-Hicks, Brianna 431n21, 437n68
Cardoso, Ana Rute 173n5, 352n51, 487n16
career concerns: lifetime perspective 414; promotion tournaments 417–420; wage determination within a firm 420–421
Carling, Kenneth 598n19
Carmichael, H. Lorne 429n8, 435n46, 438
Carneiro, Pedro 343n10, 349n37, 490n32, 490n34, 491n41

Carpenter, Christopher S. 484n1
Carpenter, Jeffrey 436n58
Carrell, Scott 344n13, 344n14
Carruth, Alan A. 125
Cascio, Elizabeth U. 342n8
Castillo, Marco 425
Cavounidis, Costas 490n36
Cellini, Stephanie Riegg 351n45
Cengiz, Doruk 133n21
centralization: labor markets 26–27; union bargaining 548–550
centralized bargaining 503
CEO pay 408–410
Cesarini, David 217
Cha, Youngjoo 297n13
Chan, Marc K. 225n30
Chandra, Amitabh 300n41, 489n28
Chang, Yongsung 430n15, 603n46
changing jobs. see frictions in the labor market
Chari, Anusha 672n26
Charles, Kerwin Kofi 342n8, 345n20, 489n28, 491n43
Charlwood, Andy 552n54
Chauvin, Keith 435n45
Chay, Kenneth Y. 495n72
cheating 397–398; discouraged through self-enforcement 398–399; discouraged through signaling 398
Chen, M. Keith 203, 221n3, 315
Chen, Paul 434n43
Chen, Stacy H. 347n25
Chen, Susan 224n23
Cherchye, Lauren 259n7
Chetty, Raj 225n31, 344n14, 599n23, 623, 630, 637n32, 638n33, 638n34
Chevalier, Judith A. 203, 221n3
Chiappori, Pierre-Andre 259n7
child labor: externalities 10; household production 238–239
child support 250–252, 251–252
childcare: child support assurance and 250–252, 251–252; observed responses to subsidies for 249; reducing fixed costs of 248–249, 248–249; reducing hourly costs of 249; subsidies for 247–248, 249
children: child care policies 247–253; early childhood 316; early childhood programs 316, 623; household production time 227–230, 228; joint labor supply decisions 234–235; support assurance 250–252; women's investment in training 323–324
Chin, Aimee 491n41
China and international trade 657

Chirinko, Robert S. 130n3
Chiswick, Barry R. 389n17, 391n33, 394, 491n40, 604n57
Cho, David 261n16, 595n3
Chou, Shin-Yi 231
Chugh, Dolly 490n37
Chyn, Eric 344n14
Chytilová, Julie 490n37, 493n51
Ciccone, Antonio 131n11
cities, living wage laws in 117–118
Civil Rights Act (1964) 472–473
Clark, Damon 342n5, 348n32, 350n44
Clark, Melissa A. 343n10
Clark, Robert L. 435n47
cleaners case study 50–51
Clemens, Jeffrey 300n41
Clotfelter, Charles T. 350n45, 352
coal mining wages 74
"cobweb" model of labor market adjustment 353–356, 354
coefficient of variation 609
Coffey, Bentley 436n56
Cohen, Jonathan 342n4
Coile, Courtney C. 262n21
Cole, Matthew A. 297n11
Collapse of Work, The 121
collective bargaining 503, 509, 516, 522; arbitration contract zone 528–529, 555–558; membership 516–521; political processes of 521–523; productivity 522–523; public sector 527–530; simple model of strikes and 523, 523–524; strikes and 521–527; by unions 516–517
collective model, joint labor supply decisions 233–234
Collins, William J. 360, 389n21, 495n70
collusive behavior, discrimination 470–471
colonialism, indentured servitude 278–279
Combes, Pierre-Philippe 492n46
commission payments 404–405
commitment to firm 402–411
common goods. see public goods
commuting, time-cost of working 201–202, 201
comparable worth 473–476, 475; regression analysis of 497–499, 498–499
comparative advantage: household production 644–646; incentives for trade across countries and 647–648; production possibilities 647–648; trade between individuals and 644–646; wages 660

comparisons, pay 405–406

compensating wage differentials 80, 265–267; allocation of labor and 266; assumptions and predictions 267–269; empirical tests 269–270; employer-provided healthcare and 289–290; equilibrium differential and 265–266; errors in variables problem in estimating 290–291; indentured servitude and 278–279; individual rewards 266–267; layoffs and *301*, 301–304, *303*; railroad workers 270–271; utility maximization 267–268; worker information 268; worker mobility 268–269

compensation *36*, 36–37; CEO 408–410; comparable worth and 473–476; deferred 284; delayed 414–417, *415*; higher in larger firms 423–424; international trade and 663–667, *665*; merit-pay 410–411; output-based 404–408; pay for performance 400–401; productivity and level of 404, 411–413; time-based pay with supervision 401–402; *see also* employee benefits; incentives for employees; wages

compensation insurance 207–208

compensation to society, technological change 126

competition: labor demand and 72–76; union membership and 518–519

competitive markets: demand for labor 65, 72; monopsonistic conditions 151–152; risk of injury 273–274; unions 518–519; *see also* non-competitive labor markets

complements in production 76, 119–120

consistency (behaviors) 4

constrained hours of work 302

construction workers 581

consumer perspective: benefits of immigration 372, 376; personal prejudice models 462–464

Consumer Price Index (CPI) 33–35, **34**

consumption good, education as 311–313

consumption: demand for goods 184–185; production possibilities 123

contingent workers 32

contract curve 514–515

contract zone, arbitration 528–529, 555–558, *555–558*

contracts: arbitration 529; efficient-contracts model 512–515; employment 2, 397; formal 397; general training 161; implicit 397; time-based 2

convenience foods 229–230, 231–232

conventional arbitration 528, 529

Cook, Cody 450

Cook, Philip J. 436n53, 438

Corak, Miles 637n32

Cornelissen, Thomas 343n13, 349n39, 432n25

Cornwall, Richard R. 495n72, 496

Cortes, Guido Matias 636n18

Cortes, Kalena E. 384

Cortès, Patricia 260N10, 391n29, 391n30, 485n9, 488n25

cost minimization, demand for labor 92–94, *92*, *93*, *94*

cost–benefit analysis, risk of injury 282–283

Costa, Dora L. 176n27, 388n13

Costinot. Arnaud 669n9

costs: and benefits of college 311–319, *312*, *317*; childcare 248–249, *248–249*; education and social 330; employee benefits 154–156, **155**; human capital acquisition 310–311, *311*; human capital investment 314–317; job-search 149–152; occupational safety and health regulation 282–283; opportunity 184–185; quasi-fixed 152–156, **154–155**; rented employees 157–158; share of labor in 102; sunk 164; training 152–155, **154**, 159–164, *163*; union membership 516–523; worker mobility 138–139, *139*

Couch, Kenneth A. 133n23

Courtemanche, Charles J. 232

Courty, Pascal 431n21

Covid-19, impact of 30–31, 559

Cox, James 547n21

craft unions 502–503, 522; *see also* unions

Cramer, Judd 261n16, 595n3

Cramton, Peter 525, 548n28, 548n29

Crane, Leland D. 602n41

Crawford, David L. 346n22

Crawford, Vincent 549n35

credentials 165. *see also* graduates

Crépon, Bruno 493n51, 605n65

crime: immigration and 377–378; job applications and statistical discrimination based on 466–467

Croson, Rachel 436n57, 487n16
cross-section data: maternity benefits
    case study 82–83; military officers
    case study 54–55; unobserved
    heterogeneity problem 166–168
cross-wage elasticity of demand
    106–110, 654
crowding hypothesis 467–469, *468*
Cullen, Zoe 430n13
Cuñat, Vicente 671n23
Cunningham, Wendy 135
Current Population Survey (CPS) *561*,
    561–562
Currie, Janet 344n14, 485n5
customer discrimination 462–463
Cutler, David M. 300n41
cyclical employee turnover 381, *382*
cyclical unemployment 579–592

Dahl, Gordon B. 549n40
Daly, Mary C. 604n62
Daniel, Christophe 296n11
Daniels, Gerald Eric, Jr. 223n15
Darity, William, Jr. *455*
data: ability bias 327, 337–338; earning
    inequality since 1980 610–615,
    611–612; errors in variables
    problem 290–291; exogeneity in
    215–217; intergenerational earnings
    628–630; meta-analysis 665–666;
    omitted variables bias 21–23, **22**,
    22, 337–338; sample selection bias
    and 252–253; sample variation
    from cross-section 54–55; statistical
    hypothesis testing 17–23, **18**, *18*,
    22, *22*; time series 124–125; time-
    use diary 252–253; unobserved
    heterogeneity in 166–168
Dave, Dhaval 342n6
Davis, James C. 634n10
Davis, Steven J. 671n17
De la Rica, Sara 545n2
De Rock, Bram 259n7
decentralization: labor markets 26–27;
    union bargaining 502–503
decentralized bargaining 503
decision to work 179, 184; analysis
    of 188–193; budget constraints
    191–193, *192*, 205, 205–207; hours
    of work and 182–184;household
    production 184–185, 230–233;
    income and substitution effects with
    wage increase 187, 195–196, *196*;
    income and wage constraints and
    191–193, *192*; income effect and
185–186, 193–195, *194*, 202–204,
    215–217, 231; indifference curves
    189–190, 189–191, *192*, *194*;
    isolating income and substitution
    effects in 197–199, *198*; joint
    labor supply decisions 233–242;
    labor force participation rates
    and 28–31, 179–184, **180–182**;
    labor supply 187–188; observing
    income and substitution effects
    separately in 186–187; opportunity
    cost of leisure and 185; policy
    applications 205–207; preferences
    in *188–190*, 188–191; programs
    with net zero wage rates 211–213;
    reservation wage and 200–202,
    201, 568–569; subsidy programs
    with positive net wage rates and
    211–213, *212*; stronger effect in
    199–200, *200*; substitution effect
    and 186, 195–196, 202–204;
    theory of 184–204; unearned
    income 193–195; wage increases
    187, 195–196; wealth and income
    and 185; welfare reform 209–210;
    working hours 182–184; *see also* job
    search
decision-making: family labor supply
    233–237; inertia 9; labor markets
    26–27; production possibilities
    165–166; rationality 3–4
Decker, Ryan A. 602n41
Decreuse, Bruno 492n46
Deere, Donald R. 552n57, 553n62
deferred compensation 284
deferred payments 37
deferred payments 37
defined benefit plans 155
defined contribution plans 155
DeFreitas, Gregory 392n41
degrees. *see* graduates
Del Bono, Emilia 297n11
delayed compensation 413–417, *415*,
    424
DeLeire, Thomas 277, 484n1
DellaVigna, Stefano 24n2
demand and supply: capital 40–41,
    41; higher education 311–319,
    312, **317**, 616–617; labor (*see*
    labor demand; labor supply); leisure
    185–186; product 39, *40*, 184–185;
    of rough laborers 369–371, *371*;
    unemployment 566, *566*, 579–580,
    583; union membership 516–523,
    517

demand curves: earnings inequality
663; elasticity 97–99, 124–125;
estimating response 124–125; labor
89–96, 104–105; labor market basic
model 38, 39, **39**, 40, 41; long run
75–76, 96; minimum wage laws
111–112, *112*; payroll taxes 78–79;
short run 66, 75, 90–92; unions
509–510, *510*, *511*, 521–522
demand schedules 38, 39; *see also*
demand curves
demand-deficient unemployment
579–588
Deming, David J. 351n47, 636n25
demographics: earnings dispersion
within groups 617–618; ethnicity-
based discrimination 455–457;
gender-based discrimination
441–443; non-competitive models
of discrimination 467–472; personal
prejudice models 457–465; policies
to address discrimination 471–480;
race-based discrimination 450–457;
statistical discrimination 465–467;
unemployment 589–590; union
membership 517–518; *see also* age;
ethnicity; gender; race
Demsetz, Rebecca S. 546n16
Denning, Jeffrey T. 343n10
deportation 419–421
deregulation, unions 519
derived demand 99–102, 107;
inferential analysis 104–105
Deschenes, Olivier 598n20
DeVaro, Jed 177n41, 487n17
Devereux, Paul J. 602n39
Devine, Theresa 596n11
DeVyver, Frank T. 48
Dew-Becker, Gordon Ian 638
Dey, Matthew S. 300n41
Diamond, Rebecca 232, 450
Dias, Monica Costa 221n4
Dickens, William T. 547n20, 604n62
Dickerson, A. P. 548n28
digitization, online labor markets
120–121, 625–626
diminishing marginal returns 67
Dimmock, Stephen G. 392n38
DiNardo, John 83, 551n46, 552n53
direct expenses, training 152–154, 308
discount rates: educational investment
315; immigrants 362–363, 377–378;
signaling 398
discouraged-worker effect 237–239
discrimination: collusive behavior
470–471; comparable worth and

473–476; crowding 467–468,
468; customer 462–463; defined
444–445; dual labor markets
468–469; employee 463–465;
employer 457–462, *459–462*; ethnic
origin 455–457; federal programs to
end 471–480, **477**; gender and wage
441–450; noncompetitive models of
467–471, *468*, *470*; Office of Federal
Contract Compliance Programs
(OFCCP) and 476–477, **477**;
personal prejudice models 463–465;
race and wage 450–454; search-
related monopsony 469–470, *470*;
seniority and 473; statistical 165,
457, 465–466, *466*
disequilibrium, demand and supply
48–49
dismissal, employment protection
against 153
Disney, Richard 262n22
disparate impact standard 472–473
disparate treatment 472–473
dispersion. *see* distribution of income
distance costs of migration 361–362
distribution of income: causes of
growing inequality 618–630, *621*;
early childhood programs 316,
623; earnings inequality since
1980 610–630; economic mobility
628–630; efficiency versus equity
debate 12–13; measuring inequality
607–610, *608*, 676–679; normative
economics 7–8; unions 534
divorce laws 327–328
Dobbie, Will 351n45
Dohmen, Thomas 401, 430n18
Doleac, Jennifer 492n46
domestic content legislation 521
Dominitz, Jeff 344n15
Donald, Stephen 262n23
Donohue, John J., III 495n71,
495n72, 495n74, 496
Doran, Kirk 188
Dorn, David 134n28, 575, 635n10,
635n18, 636n24, 669n4, 670n12,
670n13, 671n19, 671n20, 671n21,
673n32
Dorsey, E. Ray 342n7
Dorsey, Stuart 394n52
downward wage rigidity 580–584
Drago, Robert 433n35
drop outs, college 334–335
drop-out (leaving employment): loyalty
403, 411; mobility 381–382, *382*;
prosecution of workers 49; quit rates

of firms 380, 381, **381**; size of firms
    423–424; union effects 536–537; *see
    also* layoffs
dual labor markets 468–469
Dube, Arindrajit 132n18, 133n21,
    134n24, 173n5, 174n6, 403
Dubé, Jean-Pierre 232
Duflo, Ester 495n68, 605n65
Duggan, Mark 224n23, 225n25
Dumond, J. Michael 551n53
Duncan, Greg 300, 343n13, 552n54,
    552n55
Dunne, Timothy 552n57
Duque, Valentina 344n14
Durbin, David L. 207
Dustmann, Christian 344n13, 349n39,
    389n19, 391n35, 432n25

early childhood 316
early childhood programs 623
Earned Income Tax Credit (EIC)
    211–213, *212*, 663
earnings *36*, 36–37; differences
    between Black and white Americans
    450–457, **451**, **456**; differences by
    ethnicity 455–457, **456**; divorce
    laws and 327–328; education level
    and average *320*, 320–321; fairness
    and 424–425; gender differences in
    441–450, **442**; increasing with job
    tenure 421–423, *422*; inequality in
    (*see* inequality in earnings); instability
    of 626; international migration and
    362–363; measured and unmeasured
    sources of differences in 440–457; *see
    also* distribution of income; wages
Eatwell, J. 604n60
economic mobility 628–630
economic mobility, intergenerational
    data on 628–630
economic rents 52–53
economic rents *52*, 52–53
Edin, Per-Anders 434n43
Edlund, Lena 259n1
Edmans, Alex 432n26
Edmonds, Eric V. 239
education: demand for college
    education 311–321; early childhood
    programs 316, 623; gender 441;
    migration for work 361; race
    477–478; school quality 335–336;
    value for individuals 326–327;
    value to society 329–339; valuing
    329–330; wage levels 311–313,
    317–318, 320–321, *320*; *see also*
    human capital investment

efficiency wages: productivity and
    412–413; unemployment and
    577–579, *578*
efficiency: versus equity 12–13;
    normative economics 7–8; Pareto 7,
    8, 10, 557, 582
efficient-contracts model 512–515;
    actual efficiency of contracts 515;
    contract curve 514–515; formal
    model 512–514, *513–514*
effort 399–401, 420–421; *see also* pay-
    for-performance
Egan, Mark L. 486n11
Ehrenberg, Ronald G. 88n12, 221n4,
    305n3, 352, 393n49, 429n6,
    494n66, 501n4, 501n5, 501n6
Eissa, Nada 204
elasticity in the labor market: cross-
    wage elasticity of demand 106–110,
    653, 654–655; minimum wage laws
    97, 110–117; own-wage elasticity
    of demand 97–104; technological
    change 118–124; unions 521–523
elasticity, labor demand; *see* labor
    demand elasticities
eligibility for welfare: hiring subsidies
    208–209; lifetime limits 210;
    programs with net wage rates of zero
    209–210; unemployment benefits
    571–572, 573
Elliott, Robert J. R. 297n11
Ellwood, David T. 260n11, 347n25
Elsby, Michael 261n16, 602n40, 605
employee benefits 36, 154–156, **155**;
    employee preferences in 284–285;
    employer preferences in 285–287,
    285–287; employer-provided
    healthcare 289–290; hedonic wage
    theory and 284–292, *285–288*;
    maternity 82–83; occupational
    choice 284–292; pensions 154,
    284; trade-off between wages and
    287–289, *288*; unemployment
    insurance 571–573, *572*, 584–586,
    585; workers' compensation 207
employee perspective: frictions in
    the labor market 136–137; job
    search costs 149–150; law of one
    price 137–140; migration for
    work 137–139, *139*, 372–377;
    monopsonistic conditions 139–149,
    151–152; occupational choice
    265–272; personal prejudice
    models 463–466; risk of injury
    271–273; training 159–162;
    unions 506–510, 526–527; value

of educational investment 326–329; wage determination within a firm 404–407; *see also* decision to work; incentives for employees; worker mobility

employee turnover 5–6; age and 380; cyclical effects 381, *382*; employer location and 381–382; employer size and 380–381, **381**; wage and 380; worker mobility and 382

employees: career concerns of 420–421; discrimination by 463–465; higher wages for 411–412; injury risk and 271–273, *272–273*; labor market frictions on side of 137–152; matching of employers and 274–278, *275–276*, *278*; motivating 396–404; preferences for benefits 284–285; productivity of (*see* productivity); rented 157–158; seniority of 473; turnover of 380–384, **381**, *382*; underpaid and overpaid 50–53, *51–53*; use of credentials for 165

employer concession schedules 523–524

employer perspective: benefits 285–290; employment/hours trade-off 156–160; frictions in the labor market 152; hiring decisions 165–168; impacts of Covid-19 30–31; migrants 372; personal prejudice models 457–463; quasi-fixed costs 152–153; risk of injury 273–279; training decisions 159–166; unions 508–514, 519, **520**; wage determination within a firm 406–413

employment contract 2, 397

employment protection laws 153

employment rate 560–561

employment ratios and race **451**, 451–452

employment relationships: inertia 9; job matching 149–150, 264–270

employment: conditions of 535; effects of minimum wage law on 110–115; full 588–592, **589**; international trade and subsidized 663; levels of 38; monopsonistic market levels of 142, *143*; regional shifts in 518; terms of 38; trade-off between hours and 156–159, *157*; union effects on 535–536; unions and regional shifts in 518; women and (*see* women)

employment: downward wage rigidity 580–581; gender 179–182,

182, 323–325, **325**; household production 232–233; impact of Covid-19 30–31; indifference curves 200; inheritances 197; international trade effects 655–658; labor force trends 28–31; lifecycle aspects 240; minimum wage laws 110–118; race 450–452; technological change 53–54, 120; tenure 150–151; and unemployment 559–561, 562–563, **563**; unions 510–512, 535–536; welfare 209–210; women 179–182, **182**, 323–324; *see also* employee perspective; frictions in the labor market

employment/hours trade-off 156–159

Engbom, Niklas 350n44

engineering graduates 353–356, *354*

entry to market 546

Epple, Dennis 351n45

Equal Employment Opportunity Commission (EEOC) 472–473

Equal Pay Act (1963) 472

Equal Pay Act (1970) 470

equilibrium differential 265–266

equilibrium: market-cleaning wage 46–47; occupational choice 265–266; under- and over- payment 414

equity: distribution of income: versus efficiency debate 12–14; higher pay 411–412; occupational choice 445–446; policies to address discrimination 471–480; *see also* discrimination

Eren, Ozkan 550n45

Ericson, Keith Marzilli 342n4

Eriksson, Katherine 388n14

error terms 21

errors in variables problem 539–541

ethnicity: affirmative action plans 476–478; discrimination 454, 464–465; education 478–479; migration for work 360; unemployment 589, 590; *see also* race

European 'Active Labor Market Policies' 665–666

Evans, William N. 392n39

Ewing, Bradley T. 434n44

executive pay: distortion of effort 410, 420–421; distribution of income 626–627; group incentives 408–410; promotion tournaments 417–418

exit from market 538

experience level (employee) 150, 442–443

experience rating, layoffs and 585–586, *585*

externalities: government policy and 11–12; market failure 9–10; normative economics market failure 9–10, 11–12; *see also* production possibilities

Faberman, Jason 671n17
factors of production: international trade 653–655; profit maximization 62–63
Fadlon, Itzik 299n33
failure of market 8–11
Fair Labor Standards Act (1938) 110, 157
Fairlie, Robert W. 394n52, 489n29, 604n61
fairness 402–403, 424–425
Fairris, David 438n73
Fajgelbaum, Pablo D. 670n9
Falch, Torberg 173–174n6, 493n56
Falk, Armin 401, 430n18
Fallick, Bruce 220n2
families: child care 234–235, 247–253; child support assurance 250–252; economic mobility 628–630; household production 227–236; income of 628–630; labor supply decisions 233–241; migration for work 364; occupational choice 447–448
Famulari, Melissa 433n38
Fang, Tony 432n25
Farber, Henry S. 173n6, 174n6, 178, 188, 546n17, 547n20, 549n36, 549n37, 550n42, 550n45, 558n1, 558n3, 570, 598n21, 598n22, 599–600n26, 637n29
Farid, Monica 300n41
Farooq, Ammar 599n23
Fechter, Alan E. 55
Federman, Maya N. 390n28
Feenstra, Robert C. 672n24
Fehr, Ernst 429n13, 434n44
Felbermayr, Gabriel 393n43
Feldstein, Martin 224n25
Ferber, Marianne A. 259n3, 259n6, 486n14, 493n53, 496
Fertig, Michael 673n33
Fetter, Daniel K. 246
Feynman, Richard P. 5
Feyrer, James 260n9
field experiments 478–480
Fields, Gary S. 262n20, 263, 387n4
Figlio, David 350n45

final-offer arbitration 528
financing welfare 628
Finegan, T. Aldrich 261n16
Finkelstein, Amy 223n14
firm-specific investments 422–423
firms: demand curves 89–96; demand for labor 41–42, 43–44, 46–47; markets of operation 39–40, *40*; monopsonistic conditions 139–151; profit maximization 62–63; quit rates 380–381, *381*; rationality 3–4; specific human capital 528; total costs of labor 102; *see also* employer perspective
Fischer, Stanley 434n41
Fishback, Price V. 300
Fishelson, Gideon 434n41
Fitzgerald, Daniel 392n39
Flaim, Paul 595n5
Flanagan, Robert 547n20, 602n44
Flinn, Christopher J. 300n41
Flores-Lagunes, Alfonso 351n50
Flores, Carlos A. 351n50
Foged, Mette 391n32
Fontaine, François 393n46
food production decisions 228–229, 273–274
football: marginal revenue product of college 65–66; professional players' union 509
Ford Motor Company 412–413
Ford, Henry 412–413
forecasts. *see* predictions
foregone earnings 308
formal models, unions 512–514
forward-orientedness 313–315
Foster, Andrew D. 401
France, job protection in 577
Francesconi, Marco 221n4
Frandsen, Brigham R. 545n5
Frank, Jeff 484n1
Frank, Robert H. 175n15, 260n12, 436n53, 437n64, 438
Frazis, Harley 175n21, 347n26, 350n44
Frederiksen, Anders 393n45
free trade 656
free-riders 407–408, 538–539
Freedman, Matthew 378
Freeman, Richard B. 60n13, 61, 394, 431n23, 432n25, 489n28, 541, 544n1, 545n5, 546n17, 547n19, 550n45, 551n49, 551n50, 553n59, 553n60, 553n62, 554, 554n66, 554n68, 605, 614, 634n10, 637n29, 638, 669n7, 671n23, 673

frictional unemployment *566*, 566–567
frictions in the labor market 136–137;
    employee side 137–152; employer
    side 152–159; employment/hours
    trade-off 156–159, *157*; hiring
    investments 165–168; job-search
    costs and other labor market
    outcomes 149–152; law of one price
    137–139, *139*; monopsonistic labor
    markets 139–149, **141**; quasi-fixed
    costs 152–156, **154–155**; training
    investments 159–164, *163*
Friebel, Gujido 432n25
Friedberg, Leora 262n22
Friedman, Daniel M. 59n7
Friedman, John N. 225n31, 344n14,
    637n32
Friedman, Milton 16
Friendlander, Daniel 352
Frydman, Carola 432n29
Fryer, Roland G. 351n45, 430n14,
    479, 489n31, 490n33
Fuchs-Schúndeln, Nicola 204, 223n18,
    259n3
Fuchs, Victor 342n5
Fujita, Shigeru 601n36, 603n47
full employment 588–592, **589**
full-time workers 182–184; *see also*
    work hours
Funk, Jonas P. 492n46
furniture industry, discrimination in
    464–465
Furtado, Delia 391n29, 391n30
future-orientedness 313–315

G.I. Bill 316
Gaarder, Ingvil 131n12
Gabaix, Xavier 432n26
Gaggl, Paul 131n13, 134n27
gainsharing plans 404; *see also* pay-for-
    performance
Galama, Titus J. 342n5
Galbis-Reig, Felix 220n2
Galenson, David 279
Gang, Ira N. 345n20
Gans, Joshua S. 134n27
Garcia, Jorge Luis 343n13
Garfinkel, Irwin 263n28
Garthwaite, Craig 223n14
Garvey, Gerald T. 433n35
gasoline tax 187
Gates, Susan 394n52
Gauthier-Loiselle, Marjolaine 392n38
Ge, Suqin 348n34
Gelber, Alexander 225n25, 259n3

gender: discrimination based on
    441–452; distribution of income
    610–615; **611**; earning differences
    by 441–450, **442**; Equal Pay Acts
    470, 472; federal programs to end
    discrimination based on 471–480,
    477; gig work and 450; higher
    education and **317**, 325, 326, 441,
    442; hours and experience and
    442–443; labor force participation
    rate and 180–182, **180–182**, **323**,
    323–324, **439**, 439–440; mean
    earnings by *440*, 440–441; migration
    for work and 364–365; occupational
    choice and 441, **442**; occupational
    discrimination by 445–446; pay gaps
    and 450, 459–461, *460–461*, 500;
    symphony orchestras and 443–444;
    wage discrimination by 444–445; *see
    also* women
general training 160–162
geographic imbalances in
    unemployment 575–576
geographic mobility 359–371, *365*
geographic trends: international trade
    643, 659–661; unemployment
    573–577; union membership 518; *see
    also* international perspective
George, Peter 491n39
Gera, Surendra 434n43
Gerhardt, Barry 297n12
Germany, unemployment in 565
Getz, Malcolm 352
Ghez, Gilbert R. 263
Gibbons, Robert 433n36, 436n61,
    436n62, 438
Gicheva, Dora 488n25
Gielen, Anne C. 224n25
gig work 183, 450
Gilleskie, Donna B. 394n52
Gini coefficient 639–642, *641*
Gini coefficients *639–641*, 639–642
Gittings, R. Kaj 175n14
Gittleman, Maury 175n21, 347n26
Giuliano, Laura 174n6, 403, 492n47
Giupponi, Giulia 183
Gleick, James 356n3
Glover, Dylan 490n36
Gneezy, Uri 431n21, 436n57, 487n16
goals. *see* profit maximization; utility
    maximization
Goda, Gopi Shah 262n21, 300n41
Goette, Lorenz 429n13
Goldberg, Pinelopi K. 670n9, 672n26,
    673, 673n38

Golden, Miriam 544n2
Goldfarb, Avi 121, 134n27
Goldfarb, Robert S. 437n67
Goldin, Claudia 131n12, 220n1,
    260n9, 297n13, 344n15, 345n17,
    347n25, 348n31, 352, 444, 485n6,
    485n7, 485n8, 485n9, 488n24, 496,
    587, 617, 634n9
Gompers, Samuel 507
Gönsül, Füsun 595n5
González, Libertad 223n14
Goodman, Joshua 343n12
Goos, Maarten 635n18
Góra, Marek 673n33
Gordon, David M 493n58
Gordon, Robert J. 638
Gottschalk, Peter 637n27
Goux, Dominique 260n14
government interventions: demand for
    labor 62–63, 78–79; discrimination
    471–480; labor markets 26–27;
    normative economics 11–12; public
    sector training 336–339; see also
    subsidies; taxes; welfare reform
government unions 505–506
Gowsami, Sanjana 669n4
graduates: cobweb model 353–356,
    354; demand for college education
    311–321; distribution of income
    615–620; hiring workers 165–168;
    psychic costs 316–317, 327–328;
    signaling model 334–335; supply of
    616–617; women 311, 325–326,
    325, 443
Grafova, Irina B. 342n6
Graham, John W. 263n29
Gramm, Cynthia L. 548n29
Grant, Darren 551n51
Great Depression (1930s) 587
Great Migration 360
Great Recession, 2007–2009 559, 560;
    hiring workers during 157–158;
    immigration and 379; nominal
    wage cuts for construction workers
    in 581; retirement during 246;
    unemployment during 559, 579;
    worker effort and 584
Green, David A. 131n7, 135, 636n25
Greenaway, David 669n8
Greenberg, David H. 351n50, 352
Greenberg, Kyle 224n23
Greenstein, Shane M. 121
Greenstone, Michael 300
Grenier, Gilles 434n43
grievance-arbitration 528

Grigsby, John 602n41
Grogger, Jeffrey 225n28, 225n30
Gronau, Reuben 263
Groot, Wim 350n44
Grosfeld, Irena 319
Groshen, Erica L. 59n7, 434n44,
    485n7, 492n48
Grosjean, Pauline 319
gross complements 76; elasticity in the
    labor market 107, 108, 109, 119;
    technological change 120
gross substitutes: elasticity in the labor
    market 107, 108, 119; technological
    change 120
Gross, Tal 223n14
Grossman, Michael 231
Grossman, Sanford 603n49
group dynamics: executive pay
    408–410, 627; pay for performance
    411–414; wage determination within
    a firm 402–403
group incentives 404, 407–411
Gruber, Jonathan 83, 225n25, 262n22,
    548n26
Gu, Wulong 549n31
Guadalupe, Maria 671n23
Guilkey, David 455
Gunderon, Morley 548n29
Gupta, Nabanita Datta 486n10
Gurgand, Marc 605n65
Guryan, Jonathan 491n43
Guvenen, Fatih 634n10, 637n31

Haber, Sheldon E. 437n67
Haley, M. Ryan 431n20
Hall, Brian J. 433n30
Hall, Jonathan 450
Hall, Robert E. 597n14, 603n46
Halliday, Timothy 393n45
Hallock, Kevin F. 60n12, 299n30,
    428n1, 429n12, 433n29, 433n33,
    438, 484n2, 492n49, 500n1, 501n7,
    501n8, 549n32
Haltiwanger, John 59n5, 596n8,
    599n26, 604n60, 671n17
Ham, John C. 221n3, 261n18
Hamermesh, Daniel S. 88, 130n6,
    131n10, 135, 222n12, 253, 262n23,
    263, 296n4, 394, 455
Hamilton, Barton H. 431n22
Hamilton, James D. 595n5
Hamins-Puertolas, Adrian 602n41
Handbury, Jessie 232
Hansen, Benjamin 133n20, 133n23
Hansen, Bent 59n9

Hansen, W. Lee 604n56
Hanson, Gordon H. 134n28, 388n14,
    390n24, 390n25, 390n28, 392n40,
    394, 575, 669n4, 670n12, 670n13,
    671n19, 671n20, 671n21, 672n24,
    672n28, 673n32
Hanushek, Eric A. 349n38, 350n45,
    352
Harrington, David E. 390n28
Harrison, Alan 548n28
Harrison, Ann 671n18
Hart, Oliver 603n49
Hart, Robert 178, 602n39
Hartmann, Heidi L. 494n64, 501n6
Haskel, Jonathan 671n23
Hausman, Daniel M. 16
Haye, Kathy 486n12
Head Start program 623
health and safety legislation 279–282;
    see also risk
health: investment in human capital
    326–327, 330; obesity 231–232
healthcare benefits 289–290
Hecker, Daniel 176n26, 176n27
Heckman, James J. 343n10, 343n13,
    344n13, 348n32, 349n37, 349n38,
    352, 490n32, 490n34, 491n41,
    495n71, 495n72, 495n73, 495n74,
    496
Hedegaard, Morten Størling 492n47
hedonic wage theory 271–292;
    employee benefits and 284–292,
    285–288; employee considerations
    271–273, 272–273; employer
    considerations 273–274, 274;
    matching of employers and
    employees 274–278, 275–276,
    278; occupational safety and health
    regulation 279–283, 280–281
Heim, Bradley T. 224n21
Heining, Jörg 173n5, 547n23
Heinrich, Carolyn J. 158
Heinz, Matthias 432n25
Helfen, Markus O. 545n2
Hellerstein, Judith K. 177n35, 437n65,
    487n17, 489n30, 492n45
Helper, Susan 429n11, 431n22
Helpman, Elhanen 634n10, 671n23
Hendren, Nathaniel 344n14, 623, 630,
    638n33, 638n34
Hener, Timo 553n64
Henry. Peter Blair 672n26
Herbst, Daniel 550n45, 637n29
Hersch, Joni 260n9, 260n11, 298n21,
    491n41

Hershbein, Brad 602n38, 635n17
Heyman, Frederik 491n44
Heywood, John S. 490n35, 552n54,
    552n57
Hickman, Daniel C. 672n29
hicks model 523, 523–524
Hicks-Marshall laws of derived demand
    99–102, 107; inferential analysis
    104–105; international trade and
    653–654
Hicks, John 100, 130n3, 223n16,
    547n25
hidden unemployment 239
Hidrobo, Melissa 260n7
high-tech industry antitrust cases
    144–145
higher education: ability bias and 327;
    demand for 311–319, 312, 317;
    earning differences by gender and
    441; gender and 441, 442; as good
    investment for individuals 326–329;
    as good social investment 329,
    329–336, 331–333; increased returns
    of 317, 317–319, 615–617, 616;
    inequality in earnings and 615–617,
    616; market responses to changes
    in attendance 319; migrants and
    361; public sector training 336–339;
    school quality 335–336; signaling
    model of 330–334, 331–333;
    socially optimal level of investment
    in 334–335; women and 325,
    325–326; see also human capital
    investments
Hight, Joseph 346n24
Hildreth, Andrew K. G. 434n40
Hill, M. Anne 501n6
hiring investments: employee recouping
    of 168; internal labor markets
    165–166; use of credentials 165
hiring workers: affirmative action
    plans 476–478; costs of 152–154;
    employer decisions 165–168;
    employment/hours trade-off
    156–159; higher pay 411–412;
    migration for work 361–365;
    under- and over- payment 414–417;
    personal prejudice models 457–458,
    463–464; replacement of strikers
    525; size of firms 423–424; statistical
    discrimination 465–467, 478–480;
    subsidies 81
Hirsch, Barry T. 88n12, 295n3, 507,
    508, 545n6, 550n45, 551n47,
    551n53, 553n62, 554, 554n68

Hirsch, Boris 493n56
Hirschberg, Joseph 486n12
Hirshleifer, Jack 215, 307
Hispanics 439–440, *440*, 456–457
historical context: Master and Servant
    laws 83; United States immigration
    366–371, **367**
Hjort, Jonas 61
Hobijn, Bart 261n16, 604n62
Hock, Henrich 391n29, 391n30
Hoddinott, John 260n7
Hoekstra, Mark 344n14
Hoffman, Mitchell 161
Hoffman, Saul D. 130n5, 133n20, 226
Hogue,, Carma 595n5
Hole, Jackson 605
Hollands, Simon 495n67
Holmlund, Bertil 300, 598n19
Holmstrom, Bengt 177n41, 435n52
Holtz-Eakin, Douglas 197
Holzer, Harry 490n37, 492n46,
    494n67, 495n74, 496, 602n42, 605
Hong, Fuhai 431n21
Hooper, Peter 605n62
Horrigan, M. 347n26
Horton, John 121
Hossain, Tanjim 431n21
Hotz, V. Joseph 263
hours. *see* work hours
hours/employment trade-off 156–159,
    157
household income, data for 643; *see also*
    distribution of income
household production 184; basic model
    of 228–230, *229*; with both partners
    working for pay *235*, 235–236;
    budget constraints 230; childcare
    and 247–252, *248–251*; choice
    of retirement age and 242–247,
    244, *245*; comparative advantage
    644–646; decision to work 184,
    231–233; hours spent in 227–228,
    228; housing subsidies and
    241–242; income and substitution
    effects 230; joint decision and
    interdependent productivity at
    home 236; joint labor supply
    decisions and 233–239, *235*; labor
    supply in recessions and 236–239;
    labor supply model incorporating
    227–233, **228**, *229*, **233**; life cycle
    aspects of labor supply and 240–247,
    241, **244**, *245*; new implications
    for basic model of 230–233, **233**;
    obesity and 231–232; preferences

229; specialization of function in
    234–235; unemployment 570;
    women 227–230, 232, **233**, 449;
    working hours 202
Houseman, Susan N. 158
housing subsidies 241–242
Houston's Transit Authority case study
    84–85
Hoynes, Hilary 177n36, 342n6
Hsieh, Chang-Tai 672n25
Hu, Wei-Yin 263n29
Huang, Jiekun 392n38
Huck, Steffen 435n46
Huet-Vaughn, Emiliano 175n14
human capital investment 306–308;
    average earnings and educational
    level *320*, 320–321; basic model
    308–311, *311*; cobweb model
    353–356; concept of prevent value
    and 308–310; decision model
    310–311, *311*; demand for college
    education 311–321, *312*, **317**;
    early childhood education 623;
    education 318–319, 615–617,
    616; firm-specific 421–423; hiring
    workers 165–168; international
    trade 663–667; language and 315;
    as less risky than physical asset
    investments 318–319; migration
    for work 362–363, 365; on-the-job
    training 321–322, *322*; public sector
    training 336–337; refugees 382–384;
    signaling model 330–334; subsidized
    661–662; training 160–165,
    319–329; value for individuals
    326–328; value to society 329–330;
    valuing 327; wage rigidity 582;
    women 323–326; war and 306–307
human-capital groups, earnings
    distribution 617–618; *see also*
    demographics
human-capital model of worker
    mobility 358–368, 379
Hummels, David 636n22, 670n12,
    670n15, 672n25
Humphries, John Eric 348n32,
    349n38, 352
Hunt, Jennifer 392n38
Hurst, Erik 258n1, 342n8, 345n20,
    486n15, 601n36, 602n41, 633n2
Hurwitz, Michael 343n12
Hussey, Andrew J. 349n37
Hutchens, Robert 435n51, 436n63,
    437n64, 437n66, 548n28
Hvide, Hans K. 436n55

Hyatt, Henry 387n3, 581
Hyman, Joshua 350n45
hypothesis tests 17–25
Hyslop, Dean 549n39

Ichino, Andrea 486n10, 552n57
Ichniowski, Casey 432n25, 433n37
identical productive characteristics 444
Idson, Todd L. 438n72
ignorance market failure 8
Ihlanfeldt, Keith R 492n46
Ilg, Randy E. 595n6
illegal immigration 368–371, *370*,
   373–379
Imas, Alex 493n52
Imbens, Guido W. 216, 223n14
Immigration and Nationality Act 367
immigration policies: gainers and
   losers 372–382; historical context
   366–369; naive views 369–371
immigration: crime and 377–378;
   earnings growth after 365; gainers
   and losers from 372–375, *374*;
   initials earnings after 364–365,
   365; labor mobility and 379; from
   Mexico to the U.S. 368–369; naive
   views of 369–371, *371*; overall
   effects of 375–379; returns to 364;
   unauthorized 368, 377–378; U.S.
   history of 366–369, **367**; *see also*
   migration; worker mobility
imperfect experience rating 585–586
incentives for employees: decision to
   work 184–185; migration for work
   360; occupational choice 284–292;
   under- and over- payment 413–417;
   positive economics 3–4; promotion
   tournaments 417–421; retirement
   age decisions 242–247; unions
   535–536; welfare system 208–217;
   see also employee benefits; wages
income *36*, 36–39; constraints on
   191–193; effect on leisure hours
   185–186; inequality in (*see* inequality
   in earnings); international trade and
   support programs for 662–663;
   lottery winners and 215–217;
   marginal, from additional unit of
   input 64–65; self-employment
   183; subsidy programs 208–209,
   208–209; substitution effects and
   186–187, 195–204, *196, 198,
   200–201*; substitution effects of
   rising 187, 199–200, *200*; unearned
   37, 197; wealth and 184–185;
   work-incentive effects 184; *see also*

distribution of income; substitution
   effects; wages
income effect: decision to work
   184–187, 193–200, 202–204,
   215–217; employee benefits
   287–289; household production
   230–232, 238–239; housing
   subsidies 241–242; time-use
   diaries case study 252–253; welfare
   208–211, *208*
income replacement programs: budget
   constraints 204; programs with
   positive net wage rates 211–217;
   programs with zero net wage rates
   208–211
income support programs
   662–663
income tax 204
income tax credit 211–213, *212*
indentured servitude 278–279
index of dissimilarity 445
indifference curves: decision to work
   188–195, *188, 189, 190*; employee
   benefits 285, *285*; household
   production 231–232; income effect
   197, 199–200; luxury goods 236;
   risk of injury 271–273, *272, 273*,
   274–276, *276*; substitution effect
   197, 199–200
individual pay incentives 406–407
individuals. *see* behaviors; employee
   perspective
industrial unions 501–502; *see also*
   unions
industries: and occupations adapting to
   change 31–32, *32*; wages in trucking
   105–106; *see also* sectors
inequality in earnings: early childhood
   programs for reducing 623; growth
   of earning dispersion in human-
   capital groups and 617–618,
   618; increased returns of higher
   education and 615–617, **616**;
   inherited 627–630; institutional
   force changes and 626–627;
   Lorenz curves and Gini coefficients
   of *639–641*, 639–642; measured
   and unmeasured sources of *440*,
   440–457; measuring 607–610,
   608; since 1980, data on 610–615,
   611–612; technological change
   and 620–626, **625**; underlying
   causes of growing 618–627, *619*,
   620, 625; *see also* distribution of
   income; ethnicity; race; women
inequality. *see* discrimination

inertia 9. *see also* frictions in the labor
    market
inferential analysis 104–105
inflation 35–36
information: asymmetries 402–403;
    ignorance 8; migration for work
    361–362; occupational choice
    264–273; strikes 526–527
inheritance of inequality 627–630
inheritances, effects of 197
injury at work: compensating wage
    differentials 278–286, 290–292;
    health and safety legislation
    279–282; return to work 207;
    statistics 290–292
injury risk: employee considerations
    271–273, *272–273*; employer
    considerations 273–274, *274*;
    matching of employers and
    employees and 274–278, *275–276,
    278*; occupational safety and health
    regulation and 279–283, *280–281*;
    parenthood, occupational choice, and
    276–277
inputs: labor demand 72–76; marginal
    expense 65; profit maximization
    64–65
insider-outsider hypothesis 582
instability, earnings 626–627
institutional forces, distribution of
    income 626–630
insurance agents case study 42, *43*
insurance of wages: income support
    programs 211–213, 663; risk of
    injury 271–273; unemployment 126,
    205–207, 570–574, *572*,
    590–591
intelligence quotient (IQ) scores
    327–328
interdependent production processes
    423–424
interest arbitration 528
intergenerational data 628–630
internal labor markets 27, 28–30,
    165–166
internal rate of return method,
    investment in human capital 310,
    313–314
international earnings inequality 614
international migration 362–363,
    364–366
international perspective: convergence
    of wages across countries 659–661;
    distribution of income 614–615;
    investment in human capital
    329–330; unionism 503–504

international trade 643–644; changes
    in elasticity of demand for labor
    with 654–655; compensation and
    663–667, *665*; effects on labor
    demand 651–658; European active
    labor market policies and 665–666;
    growth effects of openness to
    650–651; incentives for 646–651,
    647; income support programs
    and 662–663; between individuals
    and the principle of comparative
    advantage 644–646; meta-analysis of
    policies in 665–666; policy issues in
    660–667, *665*; product demand and
    651–652; production possibilities
    with 648–649; reallocating resources
    with 649–650; reasons for 644–651;
    scale effects 654; shifts in supply of
    alternative factors of production in
    653–655; subsidized employment
    and 663; subsidizing human-
    capital investments and 661–662;
    substitution effects 653–654; U.S.
    workers displaced by 656–657; wage
    effects 658–660
international unemployment 576–577
interviews (hiring workers) 165–168
Ioannides, Yannis M. 596n11
Iranzo, Susana 349n39
Isaac, Elliott 348n34
isoexpenditure line 92–94
isoprofit curves 512, *513*; employer
    preferences 285–287, *286–287*; with
    flatter slope 286–287, *287*; risk of
    injury 273–274, *274*; with steeper
    slope 287; unions 512–513, *513*;
    with unitary slope 285–286, *285–286*
isoquants: cost minimization 92–93,
    93; demand curves 89–90
Itskhoki, Oleg 634n10, 671n23

Jackson, C Kirabo 351n46, 623
Jacob, Brian A. 242
Jacobi. Lena 673n33
Jacobs, Jeff 173n5, 174n6
Jácome, Elisa 379
Jaeger, David A. 349n43
Jäger, Simon 547n23, 601n34
Japan: agricultural work incentives
    in 214–215; openness to trade
    650–651; unions in 502–504
Jardim, Ekaterina 134n24
Jenkins, Clive 134n30
Jensen, Peter 673n33
Jin, Xin 484n2
job choice. *see* occupational choice

job matching 264–271; allocation of labor and 266; assumptions and predictions 267–269; behavioral insights 277–278; empirical tests 269–270; equilibrium differential and 265–266; individual choice and outcomes 265–267; individual rewards 266–267; offer curve 277, *278*; railroad workers 270–271; utility maximization 267–268; worker information 268; worker mobility 268–269; *see also* compensating wage differentials

job polarization 120, 624–625, **625**; *see also* distribution of income

job protection policies 577

job search: international trade 661–663; mobility 149–151, 357; search-related monopsony 469–470; unemployment 567–571

'jobs holocaust' 121

job tenure. *see* tenure

Joesch, Jutta M. 599n23

Johansson, Per 347n25, 485n9

Johnson, George 547n22, 548n28, 549n33, 549n34, 635n11, 638

Johnson, Harry 550n44

Johnson, Janna E. 387n2

Johnson, Richard W. 346n21

Johnson, Rucker C. 351n46, 489n31, 623

Johnson, Terry R. 599n23

Johnson, William G. 486n14, 492n49

Johnston, Andrew 207, 597n18

joint labor supply decisions 233–241

Jones, Maggie R. 344n14, 389n15, 389n18, 638n34

Jørgensen, Rasmus 672n25

Joulfaian, David 197

journey-level workers 522

Joyce, Mary 175n21, 347n26

Juhn, Chinhui 220n1, 430n17, 486n15, 488n26

Juster, F. Thomas 253

Kaestner, Robert 342n6

Kahn, Lawrence M. 60n13, 61, 153, 220n1, 224n21, 263n27, 391n33, 391n34, 391n36, 394, 488n23, 496, 509, 551n49, 552n57, 635n12, 636n25

Kahn, Lisa B. 345n18, 393n50, 602n38, 635n17

Kahn, Matthew E. 174n7, 388n13

Kahn, Shulamit 494n66

Kahneman, Daniel 24n2, 425, 430n14

Kain, John F. 350n45

Kamenica, Emir 259n5

Kanazawa, Mark T. 492n46

Kandel, Eugene 431n24

Kane, Thomas J. 350n43, 350n45

Kaplan, David S. 432n29, 433n31, 637n31

Kaplan, Steven N. 636n26

Kapur, Kanika 394n52

Karabarbounis, Loukas 258–259n1, 601n36

Karahan, Fatih 261n16, 596n10

Karapakula, Ganesh 344n13

Karbownik, Krzysztof 350n45

Karoly, Lynn A. 225n28

Katz, Harry 544n1, 558n1, 558n3

Katz, Lawrence F. 59n5, 131n12, 260n9, 344n15, 345n17, 348n31, 352, 428n5, 434n41, 485n9, 488n24, 496, 544n2, 547n21, 575, 587, 598n20, 600n27, 617, 634n9, 635n10, 635n11, 635n13, 638, 671n23

Kaufman, Bruce E. 133n23, 546n17, 554

Kauhanen, Antti 177n41

Kaur, Supreet 60n13

Kautz, Tim 349n38, 352

Kawaguchi, Daiji 603n49

Keane, Michael P. 223n18, 224n21, 261n18

Kearney, Melissa S. 133n20, 220n2, 226

Kehoe, Timothy J. 669n8

Keith, Kristen 388n11, 388n12

Keller, Wolfgang 433n32

Kennan, John 135

Kennedy, J. F. 506

Kennedy, Patrick J. 670n9

Kerr, Clark 544n1, 554

Kerr, Sari Pekkala 175n18, 485n7

Kerr, William R. 392n38

Kerr, William S. 175n18

Kessel, Reuben 88n11

Kessler, Daniel P. 547n21

Keys, Benjamin J. 341n4

Khandelwal, Amit K. 670n9

Kiefer, Nicholas 596n11

Killingsworth, Mark R. 226, 494n66, 501n6

Kim, Hyunseob 174n11

Kim, Moon-Kak 487n18

Kim, Sun-Bin 603n46

Kimball, William T. 546n15

Kimko, Dennis D. 350n45

Kimmel, Jean 261n16, 491n39
Kinney, Eleanor D. 394n52
Kinsler, Josh 432n24
Kirkeboen, Lars J. 356n1
Klein, Felie B. 549n32
Kleiner, Morris M. 387n2, 429n11,
    431n22, 546n17, 548n26, 553n62
Kleiner, Samuel A. 548n26
Klepinger, Daniel H. 599n23
Kleven, Henrik 225n31, 485n10
Kline, Patrick 173n5, 225n31, 434n40,
    487n16, 623, 630, 638n33
Kluve, Jochen 666, 673n33, 673n37
Knetsch, Jack L. 430n14
Kniesner, Thomas J. 292, 296n10,
    298n25, 394n52
knowledge: uncertain layoffs 303,
    303–304; unknown risks 280–282,
    281; see also information
Koch. Alexander K. 393n45
Kochan, Thomas A. 546n15
Koeniger, Winifred 637n30
Koh, Lucy 144–145
Kohler, Hans-Peter 342n7
Kolesnikova, Natalia 344–345n15
Konings, Jozef 435n45
Košar, Gizem 261n16
Kosfeld, Michael 430n13
Kostiuk, Peter F. 295n3
Kostøl, Andreas 261n14
Kovak, Brian K. 379
Kramarz, Francis 168, 437n69
Krause, Eleanor 226
Kroft, Kory 570, 575, 598n22
Krueger, Alan B. 59n5, 129n1, 130n2,
    132n18, 133n23, 135, 177n35, 178,
    183, 223n17, 224n25, 261n16,
    298n20, 350n45, 352, 428n5,
    434n44, 489n31, 495n70, 546n17,
    548n26, 554, 595n3, 595n5,
    597n13, 598n18, 598n20, 605n66,
    635n13, 635n15
Krueger, Miriam 432n25
Kruse, Douglas C. 431n23, 432n25
Krynski, Kathy J. 390n28
Kugler, Adriana 347n24, 599n23
Kugler, Maurice 347n24
Kuhn, Peter 221n5, 224n25, 389n17,
    491n39, 549n31, 596n11, 597n18,
    604n58, 636n20
Kuka, Elira 344n14
Kulkarni, Siddharth 635n14, 635n16
Kunst, David 637n29
Kurtulus, Fidan Ana 494n67
Kurz, Christopher 602n41

Kutzbach, Mark 599n26
Kuziemko, Ilyana 345n17, 348n31,
    550n45, 637n29

labor demand 62; in competitive
    markets when other inputs vary
    72–76; as downward-sloping
    function of wage rate 62; effects of
    international trade on 651–658;
    labor demand curves 71, 79–80, 89,
    89–96, 91–92, 95; long run 72–75,
    92, 92–96, 95; market, industry, and
    firm demand and 42–43; as money
    wages 69–71, 70, 71; with more than
    two inputs 75, 75–76; nonpecuniary
    factors 2; objections to marginal
    productivity theory of demand and
    72; other forces affecting 39–41,
    40–41; profit maximization and
    62–66; as real wages 68, 68–69;
    short run 66–72, 90–92, 91; union
    actions to alter labor demand curve
    521–522; union effects on shifts
    in 533; wage changes and 38–39,
    39, 40; when product market is not
    competitive 76–77
labor demand curve: long run demand
    92, 92–96, 95; production function
    79–80, 89, 89–90; short run demand
    90–92, 91; time series data and
    coping with "simultaneity" of data in
    estimating 124–125
labor demand elasticities: cross-wage
    elasticity of demand 106–110;
    defined 97; estimates of 102–104,
    103; Hicks-Marshall laws of derived
    demand 99–102; inferential analysis
    104–105; international trade and
    changes in 654–658; minimum wage
    laws and 110–118, 111–113; own-
    wage elasticity of demand 97–99,
    98–99, 102–104, 103; technological
    change and 118–126
labor economics 1–3; normative economics
    7–13; positive economics 3–6
labor force 28, 28–30, 29, 30; see also
    employment
labor force participation rate: household
    production 232; indifference
    curves 191; inheritances 197; life-
    cycle aspects 239; race 450–452;
    statistics 28–31, 29, 179–182; and
    unemployment 559–560, 560;
    welfare 209–211; women 32,
    179–182, 323–324, 323

labor investments 152–154, **154**
labor-leisure model: household
    production and 228–230, *229*; labor
    supply and 188–202
labor market 1–2, 26–27; application
    of theory of 50–55; "cobweb" model
    of adjustments in 353–356, *354*;
    compensating wage differential (*see*
    compensating wage differentials);
    crowding 467–468, *468*;
    definitions, facts, and trends 27–37;
    discrimination in 444; dual 468–469;
    effects of immigration on 372–375,
    374; employer discrimination in
    457–462, *459–462*; employer
    payroll taxes and wage subsidies
    effects on 78–83, *79–81*; frictions
    in (*see* frictions in the labor market);
    hedonic wage theory 271–292;
    industries and occupations adapting
    to change in 31–32, *32*; internal
    165–166; job matching 264–271;
    labor force and unemployment in
    28, 28–30, **29**, *30*; military officers
    case study 59–61; monopsonistic
    139–149; operation of *37*, 37–38;
    replacement workers 525; responses
    to technological changes in 53–54;
    rough *370–371*, 370–373; short run
    demand for labor with competitive
    product and **66**, 66–72, *68*, **70**, *71*;
    statistical testing of hypotheses of
    17–23, **18**, *18*, **22**, *22*; stock-flow
    model of *561*, 561–563, **563**; supply
    overview 45–47; trends 30–39; wage
    rates 34–39, 47–53
labor supply 42–44, *43*; ballpark
    vendors 202–203; budget constraints
    with "spikes" *205*, 205–207;
    childcare and 247–252, *248–251*;
    growing inequality in earnings and
    618–620, *619*; hours of work and
    182–184; household production
    (*see* household production); housing
    subsidies and 241–242; income and
    substitution effects on 186–187,
    195–204, *196*, *198*, *200–201*;
    income and wage constraint effects
    on 191–193; income effects on
    193–195, *194*; indifference curves
    189–190, 189–191, *192*, *194*; joint
    household decisions and 233–239,
    235; labor force participation rate
    and 29, **29**, 179–181, **180–182**;
    labor/leisure choice 188–202;

labor supply curves 80–81, *80–81*;
    large inheritances and 197; life cycle
    aspects of 240–247, *241*, **244**, *245*;
    monoposonistic 139–140, 145–148,
    146–147; New York City taxi
    drivers 188; pay levels and military
    officer 54–55; policy applications
    in 205–217; positive net wage rate
    program effects on 211–213, *212*;
    preferences between leisure and
    money and *188–190*, 188–191; in
    recessions 236–239; reservation
    wage and 200–202, *201*; retirement
    age and 242–247, **244**, *245*; tax cut
    effects on 204; theory of decision to
    work and 184–204; trends in labor
    force participation and hours of work
    and 179–184; wage increase effects
    on 195–196, *196*, 252–253; wartime
    food requisitions and agricultural
    work incentives and 214–215;
    welfare reform effects on 209–211,
    211; zero net wage rate program
    effects on *208–209*, 208–211, *211*
labor unions. *see* unions
Lacetera, Nicola 121
Ladd, Helen F. 350n45
Lafontaine, Francine 437n68
Lagakos, David 223n18, 388n11
Lahey, Joanna N. 260n14
Laibson, David 342n4
Laing, Derek 436n60
Laird, Jessica 299n33
Lalive, Rafael 598n21
LaLonde, Robert J. 351n49, 673n34
LaLumia, Sara 599n23
Lamadon, Thibaut 173n5
Lamare, J. Ryan 549n40
Lampman, Robert J. 61
Landais, Camille 485n10, 598n21
Landers, Renée M. 419
Landrum-Griffin Act 505, 527
Lanfranchi, Joseph 295n3
Lang, Kevin 351n48, 389n17, 488n26,
    489n32, 490n34, 490n36, 492n50,
    496, 605
Lange, Fabian 493n52, 570, 575
Lange, Peter 544n2
language in human capital investment
    315
Laouénan, Morgane 492n46
Laughlin, Teresa 484n2
Lavecchia, Adam M. 344n13
Lavy, Victor 436n57, 487n16
law firms, "rat race" in 418–419

law of one price 137–139, *139*
Lawrence, Robert Z. 671n23, 674
Lawson, Nicholas 546n12
Layard, Richard 135n33, 263
layoffs: constrained hours of work
    and 302; effects of uncertain *303*,
    303–304; observed wage-layoff
    relationship 304; unconstrained
    choice of work hours and *301*,
    301–302
Lazear, Edward P. 176n32, 393n45,
    393n47, 428n2, 428n3, 430n18,
    431n24, 435n46, 435n48, 435n50,
    437n66, 438, 485n7, 546n17, 584,
    601n35
Leaf, Duncan Ermini 343n13
Leamer, Edward E. 671n23
Le Barbanchon, Thomas 493n51
Lebow, David E. 59n7
Lee, David S. 551n46, 553n63
Lee, Jonathan M. 298n25
Lee, Minjoon 221n3
Lefebvre, Pierre 263n27
Lehman, Jee-Yeon K. 488n26, 490n34,
    492n50, 496
Leibbrandt, Andreas 487n16
Leigh, Andrew 348n35
leisure: analysis of choice between
    labor and 188–202; income effect
    on 185–186; lottery winners and
    215–217; opportunity cost of 185;
    preferences between money and
    188–190, 188–191
Lemieux. Thomas 346n21, 547n19,
    551n47, 551n48, 551n49, 602n39,
    602n42, 634n10, 637n28
Lengermann, Paul 351n51
Leonard, Jonathan 174n6, 403, 492n47,
    492n49, 548n26, 552n56, 605
Leonardi, Marco 636n21, 637n30
Lester, T. William 132n18
Leung, Pauline 207, 597n18
Leuven, Edwin 176n32, 356n1
Levine, David I. 492n47, 492n49
Levine, Phillip B. 262n21, 262n24,
    263n27, 604n57
Levine, Ross 492n45
Levitt, Steven 430n14, 479, 489n31
Levkov, Alexey 492n45
Levy, Frank 638
Levy, Helen 277
Lewin, David 485n5
Lewis, H. G. 541, 549n41, 550n45,
    554
Lewis, John L. 74

Li, Danielle 436n59
Li, Xiaoxiao 343n9
Liebman, Jeffrey B. 262n22, 433n30
life cycle aspects of labor supply
    240–247, *241*, **244**, *245*
lifetime limits on welfare programs 210
Lincoln, William F. 175n18, 392n38
Lindahl, Erica 347n25, 485n9
Lindahl, Mikael 352
Lindbeck, Assar 554n65, 602n45
Linder, Staffan B. 226
Lindley, Joanne K. 297n11
Lindner, Attila 133n21, 598n19
Lindqvist, Erik 217
Lindsay, C. M. 348n34
Lipsky, David 548n28
List, John 430n14, 431n21, 450,
    487n16
Liu, Albert Yung-Hsu 486n13
Liu, Chen 390n24
Liu, Runjuan 671n22
Liu, Sifan 635n14, 635n16
"living wage" laws 117–118
Lleras-Muney, Adrina 342n5
Lochner, Lance 349n39
Lockwood, Lee M. 246
Loewenstein, Mark A. 176n32
Long, Clarence D. *180*, *181*
Long, Mark C. 134n24
Long, Richard J. 432n25, 552n57
long run demand: labor 72–75, *92*,
    92–96, *95*; market 42
Lorenz curves *639–641*, 639–642
lottery winners 215–217
Loury, Lina Datcher 596n11
Lovenheim, Michael F. 343n12,
    553n61
Lowen, Aaron 484n2
loyalty, group 403
Lozano, Fernando 221n5, 636n20
Lubotsky, Darren *365*
Lucas, Robert E., Jr. 356n4
Ludwig, Jens 176n32, 242
Lundberg, Shelly 259n3, 259n5
Lundborg, Petter 296n6
Luoh, Ming-Ching 345n20
Luttmer, Erzo F. P. 224n25, 262n22
Lutz, Byron F. 394n52
Lyle, David 130n7, 224n23
Lynch, Lisa 177n35, 178, 553n60
Lyons, Elizabeth 121

Machado, Cecilia 259n1
Machin, Stephen 173n4, 183
machine learning 621

Mackie, Christopher 391n37, 392n39, 394
MacLeod, W. Bentley 350n44, 602n39, 602n42, 634n10
Macpherson, David A. *507*, *508*, 545n6, 551n47, 551n53, 552n57
MaCurdy, Thomas 133n22, 135
Madden, Janice F. 493n53
Maestas, Nicole 225n25, 299n31
Magnac, Thierry 346n22
Magnani, Elisabetta 305n6, 553n62, 599n26
Magnuson, Katherine 343n13
Makowsky, Michael D. 134n23
Malcomson, James M. 428n4
Mallick, Debdulal 130n3
Maloney, M. T. 436n56
Manchester, Colleen Flaherty 176n32
mandated wages 146–148, *147*
Mankiw, N. Gregory 604n62
Manning, Alan 24n3, 173n4, 174n9, 175n16, 175n17, 178, 487n16, 493n57, 494n66, 600n28, 601n37, 635n18, 637n30
Manoli, Dayanand S. 605n65
Manove, Michael 489n32, 490n34
Mansfield, Richard K. 344n14
Manski, Charles F. 344n15
Mansour, Hani 596n11
marginal expense: of added input 65; of labor 141, *142*
marginal product (MP) 64, 66–67
marginal productivity theory of demand 72
marginal revenue (MR) 64
marginal revenue product (MRP) 64–65; of college football stars 65–66; compensation schemes and 415, *415*, 415–417; labor demand as money wages and 69–71, **70**, *71*; objections to marginal productivity theory of demand and 72; profit maximization and 67–68; search-related monopsony 469–470, *470*
Margo, Robert A. 360
Margolis, David N. 168
Marinescu, Ioana 174n8, 174n11, 175n14, 177n33
market-clearing wage 44–45, *45–46*; disequilibrium and nonmarket influences on 48–49, *49*; disturbing the equilibrium 46–47, *47*
market demand curves 71
market failure: externalities 9–10; ignorance 8; price distortion 11;

public goods 10–11; transaction barriers 8–9
market supply 42, *43*
Markussen, Simen 352n51
Marschke, Gerald 431n21
Marshall, Alfred 38, 100, 130n3
Marston, Stephen T. 596n7
Martins, Pedro S. 429n6
Martorell, Paco 350n44
Marx, Benjamin M. 343n10
Mas, Alexandre 207, 223n17, 295n3, 297n11, 403, 432n24, 548n26, 553n63, 554, 595n5, 597n18
Maskin, Eric 603n49
Master and Servant law, United Kingdom 49
Masterman, Clayton 296n6
Masterov, Dimitriy V. 490n32, 490n34, 491n41
Matějka, Filip 490n37, 493n51
maternity benefits 82–83
Matsa, David A. 601n37
Matsudaira, Jordan 174n6
Matthews, Peter Hans 436n58
Mattila, J. Peter 494n66
Matvos, Gregor 486n11
Maurin, Eric 260n14, 345n20
Mazumder, Bhashkar 630
McAffee, Andrew 134n25, 134n26, 135, 636n19, 637n26, 638
McCall, Brian P. 552n53
McCloskey, Donald 16
McConnell, Sheena 352n51, 548n27
McCue, Kristin 393n45, 393n47, 430n17, 486n15
McCulloch, Neil 669n8
McDermed, Ann A. 435n47
McElroy, James C. 347n28
McEntarfer, Erika 387n3, 393n50, 581
McIntosh, Craig 390n24
McKay, Andrew 669n8
McLennan, Michele 488n21
McMillan, Margaret 671n18
McNally, Sandra 345n20
McWilliams, Abigail 388n11, 388n12
Medoff, James 550n45, 551n50, 553n59, 554, 554n66, 554n68, 602n44
Meer, Jonathan 130n2, 133n21
Meghir, Costas 221n4, 259n7
Mehay, Stephen L. 177n38
merit-pay plans 410–411
Merrigan, Philip 263n27
Mexico: earnings differences and 455–457, **456**; immigration from 364, 368–369, 379

Meyer, Brent 605n64

Meyer, Bruce D. 88n13, 207, 224n25, 393n45, 591, 598n18, 598n20, 603n56, 605n64, 606, 633n1, 634n5

Meyer, Daniel R. 263n28

Michael, Robert T. 501n6

Michaelides, Marios 605n65

Michaels, Ryan 596n10, 605

Michalopoulos, Charles 351n50

Michie, Jonathan 431n23

Micklewright, John 597n18, 605

Mieszkowski, Peter 550n44

migration: earnings distribution in sending countries and international 362–363; earnings growth after 365; family 364; indentured servitude and 278–279; initial earnings after 364–365, 365; internal, for economic reasons 363; personal characteristics in 360–361; personal discount rates and 377; return 366; returns to international and domestic 363–366, 365; role of distance in 361–362; time horizons and 362 see also immigration; worker mobility

Mihaly, Kata 224n21

Mihlar, Fazil 553n62

Milgate, M. 604n60

Milgrom, Paul 433n36

military officer pay levels and supply 54–55

Miller, Amalia 348n34, 494n59

Miller, Conrad 495n67

Miller, Douglas L. 177n36, 342n6

Miller, Paul W. 389n17, 391n33

Millward, Neil 552n57

Mincer, Jacob 132n17, 263, 352, 550n43

minimum wage laws 110–118; effects of uncovered sectors 113, 113–114; effects on real wages 111–112; empirical estimates of effects of 115–116; history and description 110, 111; intersectoral shifts in product demand and 114–115; job loss and 112, 112–113; "living wage" laws and 117–118; monopsonistic conditions and 146–149, 147; poverty and 116–118; theoretical analysis of employment effects of 110–115

Mishel, Lawrence 637n31

Mishkin, Frederic S. 605n62

Miskimin, Harry A. 48

Mitchell, Daniel 485n5

Mitchell, Joshua 220n1, 259n3, 347n25

Mitchell, Olivia S. 262n20, 263

Mitchell, Tom 621

Mobarak, Ahmed Mushfiq 388n11

mobility, worker see worker mobility

Modlin, George M. 48

Moffitt, Robert 225n27, 226, 637n27

Mogstad, Magne 131n12, 173n5, 261n14, 348n33, 356n1

Mok, Wallace K. C. 598n18

Molloy, Raven 388n6

Moñarez, Paula 271

Moncarz, Roger J. 657

money wages, labor demand as 69–71, 70, 71

monopolies: maximizing profits of 77; wages paid by 77–78

monopoly-union model 510–512, 511

monopsonistic labor markets 139–140, 141; antitrust in high-tech industry and 144–145; competitive model and 151–152; firm's choice of wage and employment levels 142, 143; mandated wages and 146–148, 147; marginal expense of labor exceeding wage rate 141, 142; minimum-wage legislation and 148–149; response to shifts in supply curve 145–148, 146–147; search-related 469–470, 470; wage policies and 143–144

Monras, Joan 391n34

Montgomery, Edward 299n36, 602n42

Monti, Holly 430n17

Moore, Michael J. 296n6

Moore, Robert L. 437n66

Moore, Timothy J. 225n25

Moore, William J. 60n10

moral hazard 401

Moretti, Enrico 305n7, 345n16, 349n39, 403, 432n24, 486n10, 552n57, 604n59, 634n5

Morgan, Wyn 669n8

Morrall, John, III 298n26

Mortensen, Dale T. 173n4, 596n11

Moscarini, Giuseppe 601n36, 603n47

Moser, Christian 350n44

Moyer, Brian C. 59n7

Mueller, Andreas Il 223n17, 595n3, 597n13, 597n14, 598n18, 598n20, 601n35

Muendler, Marc-Andreas 634n10, 671n23

Mullainathan, Sendhil 88n12, 432n26, 432n27, 479, 490n37

Mullen, Kathleen J. 225n25, 299n31

multiple regression analysis 20–21
Munch, Jakob R. 636n22, 670n12, 670n15, 672n25
Muratori, Umberto 599n23
Murnane, Richard J. 343n13, 633n3, 638
Muro, Mark 635n14, 635n16
Murphy, Kevin J. 433n32, 433n36, 434n41, 436n61, 436n62, 546n14, 634n7, 635n11
Murray, John E. 407–408

Naidu, Suresh 49, 134n24, 173n5, 174n6, 550n45, 637n29
Nakamura, Alice 596n10
Nakamura, Emi 596n10
Nalbantian, Haig R. 431n24
Narayan, Ayushi 342n8
National Football League (NFL) 509
National Labor Relations Act (NLRA) 505
National Labor Relations Board (NLRB) 505
natural rate of unemployment 588–592
Navarro, Waleed 390n23
Neal, Derek 488n26, 489n31
Neckermann, Susanne 430n13
Needels, Karen 597n15
Nekoei, Arash 601n36
Nelson, Julie A. 259n4
Neumann, George R 548n29
Neumark, David 88, 88n14, 130n2, 132n18, 132n19, 133n20, 133n23, 134n24, 135, 177n35, 260n13, 346n21, 435n51, 437n65, 437n67, 484n1, 487n17, 488n21, 489n30, 490n37, 492n45, 494n60, 494n67, 496, 551n52, 669n4
Newman, Jerry M. 297n12
Newman, P. 604n60
Newman, Robert J. 60n10
Nicholson, Walter 597n15
Nickell, Stephen 60n13, 61, 88n12, 614
Nickerson, Jack A. 431n22
Nielsen, Torben Heien 299n33
Niu, Xiotong 595n5
Noel, Brett J. 437n70
nominal wages 33, 34; cuts in construction worker 581; effect of minimum wage law on 111–112
noncompetitive forces in labor market 457
noncompetitive models of discrimination 467–471, 468, 470

nondiscrimination mandates 471
nonpecuniary factors in the labor market 2
nonunion sector 534–535; wage rigidity and 582
normative analyses: occupational safety and health regulation 279–283, 280–281; unions 537–541
normative economics 7–13; efficiency versus equity 12–13; externalities in 9–10; government policy and 11–12; ignorance in 8; markets and values 7–8; price distortion in 11; public goods in 10–11; transaction barriers in 8–9
North, Douglass C. 48
Notowidigdo, Matthew 217, 223n14, 342n8, 393n44, 570, 575, 598n22
nudges 9
Nunley, John M. 570
Nunziata, Luca 637n30
Nyshadham, Anant 175n20

Oaxaca, Ronald L. 486n14, 487n17, 487n18, 487n19, 493n56, 547n21
obesity and household production 231–232
O'Brien, Daniel M. 350n45
occupational choice: gender and 441, 442; parenthood, risk, and 276–277
occupational discrimination 444
occupational imbalances in unemployment 574–575; technological change and 624–625, 625
Occupational Safety and Health Administration (OSHA) 279–283, 280–281
occupational segregation: gender and 445–446; race and 452–454
Ockenfels, Axel 25n5
Oehlsen, Emily 203, 221n3
Oettinger, Gerald 203
O'Farrell, Brigid 501n6
Office of Federal Contract Compliance Programs (OFCCP) 476–477, 477
offshoring 656–657
Ohlsson, Henry 295n3
Ohtake, Fumio 603n49
Oi, Walter Y. 393n48, 393n49, 438n72
Okun, Arthur 25n6, 592, 605n64
Old Age Assistance (OAA) programs 246
Olivetti, Claudia 220n1, 485n7
Olney, William W. 433n32, 672n29

Olsen, Reed Neil 490n38
Olson, Craig A. 60n12, 550n42
Olson, Keith W. 316
omitted variables bias 21–23, **22**, *22*, 337–338
O'Neill, June 486n14
online hiring platforms 120–121
on-the-job training 321–322, *322*
Oostendorp, Remco 637n29
Oosterbeek, Hessel 176n32, 350n44
opportunistic behavior 398
opportunity costs 184–185
Orazem, Peter F. 347n28, 494n66
Oreopoulos, Philip 344n13, 348n32, 480, 492n51
Osili, Una Okonkwo 392n39
Ost, Ben 348n36
Oster, Emily 342n7
Osterman, Paul 178
Ostling, Robert 217
Oswald, Andrew J. 125, 434n40, 552n57, 601n34, 605
Ottaviano, Gianmarco I. P. 391n32
out-of-pocket expenses 308
output-based pay 404–408
overpaid workers *50*, 50–51
overtime: pay premium 157–158; spreading the work 158–159; total pay and 159
Owan, Hideo 431n22
Owens, Emily 378
own-wage elasticity of demand 97–99, *98–99*; estimates of 102–104, **103**
Oyer, Paul 450

Page, Marianne E. 349n43
Pager, Devah 490n33
Pallais, Amanda 178n42, 223n17, 295n3, 297n11, 490n36
Pan, Jessica 259n5, 485n9, 486n13, 488n25
Pan, Weixiang 348n36
Panagariya, Arvind 670n16, 671n18
Papageorge, Nicholas W. 344n13
Parent, Daniel 490n35, 602n39, 602n42, 634n10
Pareto, Vilfredo 24n4
Pareto efficiency 7, 10, 512; versus equity 12–13
Pareto improving 8
Pariente, William 490n36
Park, R. Jisung 343n12
Parro, Fernando 670n9
Parsons, Christopher A. 455
Parsons, Donald 178, 393n51

Patacchini, Eleonora 484n1
Patel, Ankur 605n65
Patrinos, Harry Anthony 335
Patteron, Christina 635n10
Pavcnik, Nina 672n26, 673, 673n38
Paxson, Christina H. 220n3, 221n4
pay-for-performance 400–401
pay gaps: under employer discrimination 459–461, *460–461*; estimating 500; gig work and 450
payments in kind 36–37, 284
Payne, James E. 434n44
payroll taxes 78–81, *79–81*, 584–586, *585*
Pei, Zhuan 207, 597n18
Pekkarinen, Tuomas 430n19
Peñaloza, Roberto V. 261n16
Pencavel, John 546n13, 550n45, 553n58, 554
Peoples, James, Jr. 492n45, 551n50
Peracchi, Franco 223n19
Pérez, Santiago 379
Perez-Truglia, Ricardo 430n13
perfect complements 76
Peri, Giovanni 131n11, 349n39, 379, 391n31, 391n32, 391n35, 392n38, 393n43
Perry, George L. 604n62
Persico, Claudia 351n46
personal discount rates 377–378
personal-prejudice models: customer discrimination 462–463; employee discrimination 463–465; employer discrimination 457–462, *459–462*
Personal Responsibility and Work Opportunity Reconciliation Act (PRWORA) of 1996 209–210
persuasion of arbitrators 529
Petkova, Neviana 434n40
Petrie, Ragan 425
Petrongolo, Barbara 260n14, 601n37
Phibbs, Ciaran S. 173n6
Phong, Kyle 596n10
Phongthiengtham, Phai 635n17
Piatak, Jaclyn Schede 60n9
Picchio, Matteo 216
piece-rate pay 404, 420
Piehl, Anne Morrison 378
Pierce, Brooks 430n17, 633n2
Piketty, Thomas 633n4, 637n31
Pilarski, Adam M. 548n26
Pinkston, Joshua C. 232, 493n52
Pischke, Jörn-Steffen 176n32
Pistaferri, Luigi 261n15, 261n18
Pistolesi, Nicolas 346n22

Pleeter, Saul 341n4
Plotnick, Robert 134n24
Pohler, Dionne 132n16
Poitras, Marc 296n6
Polachek, Solomon W. 487n18
Pollak, Robert A. 259n3, 259n5
Pollakowski, Henry 599n26
Porter, Sonya R. 344n14, 638n34
Porterba, James M. 597n17
Portugal, Pedro 600n28
Posch, Johanna 552n57
positive economics 3–6; economic
    model 5–6; physical model 5;
    predictions in 4, 6
Postel-Vinay, Fabien 393n46
Postlewaite, Andrew 260n13
post-training wage increases 162–163,
    163
Potter, Simon 220n1
Poulsen, Jonas 61
Poutvaara, Panu 393n43
poverty: child labor in poor countries
    and 238–239; child support
    assurance and 250–252, 251–252;
    minimum wage laws and 116–118
Powell, David 299n31
Prada, Herrera 347n24
Prados, María José 343n13
predictions: job choice and 267–269; in
    positive economics 4, 6
preferences: employee benefits 284;
    household production 229; job
    matching and worker 264–271;
    between leisure and money 188–190,
    188–191; productivity and employee
    404–406
premarket differences 444
Prendergast, Canice 428n4, 429n10,
    433n36
Prentice, David 553n62
preschool programs 623
present-oriented perspective 313–314
present value 308–310, 313–314
Preston, Ian 389n19
Price, Brendan 670n13
Price, David J. 634n10, 637n31
Price, Joseph 432n24, 455
prices: law of one price 137–139, 139;
    market failure and distortion of 11
price takers 77
private sector: union membership and
    517–518; union wage effects 534;
    wages in 33
product demand 39, 40, 184–185;
    effect of minimum wage law on

114–115; international trade and
    651–652; technological change,
    labor demand elasticity, and 118–119
production: complements in 76,
    119; household (see household
    production); international trade and
    646–647, 647, 653–655; overall
    effects of technological change on
    121–126, 122; substitutes in 75,
    75–76, 119
productivity 395–396; career
    concerns and 420–421; cheating
    and 397–399; creating a surplus
    399, 399–400; efficiency wages and
    412–413; employee preferences and
    404–406; employer considerations
    406–411; employment contract
    and 397; group incentives and 404,
    407–411; higher earnings with job
    tenure and 421–423, 422; higher
    wages and 411–412; level of pay and
    411–413; motivating individuals for
    402–404; motivating workers for
    396–404; promotion tournaments
    and 417–420; sequencing of pay and
    413–414; union effects on 536–537;
    wide range of possible 395–396
productivity bargaining 522–523
product market 37, 37–38; labor
    demand with uncompetitive 76–77
profit maximization 3; under employer
    discrimination 458–459, 459;
    labor demand and 62–66; marginal
    income from additional unit of input
    64–65; by monopolies 77; under
    monopsonistic conditions 140–145,
    142–143; union effects on 536–537
profit-sharing 404
promotion tournaments 417–420
Psacharopoulos, George 335
psychological losses 308
public goods: immigrants and 376;
    market failure 10–11; workplace
    conditions as 538
public sector training 336–339
Pugh, Adam 570
Pugsley, Benjamin 596n10

quasi-fixed costs 152–156, **154–155**
Quayes, Shakil 239

race and ethnicity: discrimination in
    sports 454–455; earnings differences
    by 450–457, **451**, **456**; employment
    ratios and **451**, 451–452; federal

programs to end discrimination based on 471–480, **477**; labor union membership and 507, *508*; mean earnings by *440*, 440–441; pay gaps and 450, 459–461, *460–461*; unemployment rates and **589**, 589–590; *see also* inequality in earnings

Radwan, Samir 59n9

Raff, Daniel 413

Ragan, James F., Jr. 492n49

Ragusa, Giuseppe 484n1

Rahkovsky, Ilya 232

railroad workers 270–271

Rainer, Helmut 553n64

Ransom, Michael R. 173n6, 174n6, 178, 486n14, 487n17, 487n18, 493n56

Raphael, Steven 490n37, 550n45

Rapping, Leonard A. 356n4

Rathelot, Roland 605n65

rationality 3–4

Ratner, David 605

Rauh, Joshua 636n26, 637n31

Rayack, Wendy L. 602n46

real wages 33, **34**; labor demand as *68*, 68–69; rates of 35–36

Rebitzer, James B. 419, 431n23, 438n71, 438n73, 493n54

recessions: labor supply in 236–239; worker effort and 584

Redding, Stephen J. 634n10, 670n9, 670n10, 671n23

Reder, Melvin W. 546n17, 548n29

re-employment bonuses 590–591

regression analysis 497–499, *498–499*

Rehavi, M. Marit 673n32, 673n36

Reich, Michael 132n18, 134n24, 493n58

Reilly, Kevin T. 221n3, 261n18, 437n70

Reizer, Balázs 598n19

rented workers 157–158

replacement workers 525

reputations 400

Requena, Francisco 392n38

reservation wage 200–202, *201*; job search and 568–569

Restrepo, Pascual 121, 134n29, 636n24, 670n12

retirement age 242–247, **244**, *245*

Rho, Deborah 389n15

Rhoads, Steven E. 494n64, 494n65

Ribar, David C. 262n25

Riddell, Chris 132n16, 224n25, 430n19, 597n18, 604n58

Riddell, W. Craig 551n47, 551n48, 551n49, 637n28

Riehl, Evan 350n44

Riley, John G 429n7

risk aversion: injury (*see* injury risk); output-based pay and 405; wage rigidity and 583

Rives, Janet M. 239

Rivkin, Steven G. 350n45

Robin, Jean-Marc 393n46

Robins, Philip K. 263n28, 351n50, 352

Robinson, Sherman 671n18

robots 120–121

Rock, Daniel 621

Rockoff, Jonah E. 350n45

Rodríguez-Clare, Andrés 669n9

Rodriguez-Lopez, Antonio 669n4

Rodrik, Dani 673n39

Røed, Knut 352n51

Rogerson, Richard 221n5, 259n3, 261n18

Rohlfs, Chris 298n25

Romano, Richard 351n45

Romero, Nicholas 570

Rosen, Harvey S 197

Rosen, Sherwin 297n14, 300, 305n1, 356n5, 485n7

Rosenberg, Michael 493n52

Rosenzweig, Mark R. 401

Rossi, Peter E. 203, 221n3

Rossin-Slater, Maya 623

Rotemberg, Julio J. 430n15

Roth, Jeffrey 350n45

Rothstein, Jesse 489n31, 595n3, 623

Rottenberg, Simon 61, 547n21

rough labor market *370–371*, 370–373

Rouse, Cecilia 177n35, 338, 348n35, 350n43, 444, 490n34

Roux, Sébastien 346n22

Roy, Andrew D. 388n10

Roy, Shalini 260n7

Royer, Heather 342n5, 348n32

Rubin, Donald B. 216, 223n14

Rubinstein, Yona 492n45

Rucker, Ian 671n17

Rudd, Jeremy B. 59n7

Ruhl, Kim J. 669n8

Ruhm, Christopher J. 232

Rupert, Peter 296n7

Russian Revolution 214

Ryan, Chris 348n35

Ryan, Paul 352n51

Ryoo, Jaewoo 356n5

Rytina, Nancy 390n24

Rzakhanov, Zaur 362

Saavedra, Juan 347n24, 350n44
Sabia, Joseph J. 133n20, 133n23
Sacerdote, Bruce I. 216, 223n14, 260n9, 344n13
Sadoff, Sally 430n14
Saez, Emmanuel 88n14, 225n31, 403, 623, 630, 633n4, 637n31, 637n32, 638n33
Saffer, Henry 231
Šahin, Ayşegül 261n16, 599n25
Saidi, Farzad 487n16
Saint-Paul, Gilles 60n13, 61
Saks, Raven E. 432n29
Salas, J. M. Ian 132n19
Salomons, Anna 635n18
Salvanes, Kjell G. 348n32, 348n33
sample selection bias 252–253
Samuelson, P. 152
Samuelson, Paul A. 175n19
Sand, Benjamin 131n7, 135, 636n25
Sanders, Seth 389n15, 484n1
Sandino, Tatiana 433n32
Sandusky, Kristin 59n5, 596n8
Saporta-Eksten, Itay 261n15, 261n18
Sappington, David E. 429n9, 438
Sasson, Diego 672n26
Saveri, Joseph R. 145
Sawhill, Isabel 226
scabs 525
scale effects 38, 39, 41–42, 74, 94–96, 95; cross-wage elasticity of demand 108; international trade and 654
scarcity 3
Schady, Norbert 239
Schaller, Bruce 188
Schaller, Jessamyn 177n36
Schank, Thorsten 130n7, 493n56
Schirm, John 436n58
Schkade, David 298n20
Schleifer, Andrei 24n2
Schmacher, Edward J. 295n3
Schmidt, Klaus M. 434n44
Schmieder, Johannes F. 570, 598n19, 599n22, 599n23
Schmutte, Ian M. 175n14
Schnabel, Claus 493n56
Schnell, John F. 548n29
Schnell, Molly 232
Schochet, Peter Z. 351n51
Schoefer, Benjamin 88n14, 547n23, 601n34
Schönberg, Uta 349n39, 391n35, 432n25
Schroeder, Larry D. 25n9
Schubler, Elke 545n2
Schuh, Rachel 596n10

Schultz, Theodore 352
Schumann, Paul L. 305n3
Schwandt, Hannes 345n18
Schwartz, Aba 388n9
Schweitzer, Mark 133n20
scientific management 412
Scott, Frank A. 394n52
screening problem 465–466, 466
Seago, Jean Ann 553n61
Seals, R. Alan 570
seasonal unemployment 586–588
sectors: nonunion 534–535; private 517–518, 534; uncovered, effect of minimum wage law on 113, 113–114; union membership and 517–518
Segal, Carmit 494n59
Segal, Lewis M. 158
Seidman, Laurence S. 226
Seif, David G. 262n22
Seiler, Eric 430n19
Seim, David 88n14
self-employment income 183
self-enforcement and cheating 398–399
Seltzer, Andrew J. 115, 435n46
seniority 473
sequencing: of effort 420–421; of pay 413–414
Seru, Amit 486n11
Setzler, Bradley 173n5, 261n14
severance, CEO 410
Sexton, Edwin A. 490n38
Shakers 407–408
Shapiro, Matthew D. 221n3
Shaw, Jonathan 221n4
Shaw, Kathryn 299n36, 428n2, 428n3, 431n21, 432n25, 433n37, 437n68, 438, 584
Shearer, Bruce 431n20
Sherman, Barrie 134n30
Shiller, Robert J. 24n5
Shintani, Mototsugu 261n16
short run demand 42, 90–92, 91; when both product and labor markets are competitive 66, 66–72, 68, 70, 71
Shoulson, Ira 342n7
Shoven, John B. 262n21, 435n50
Shue, Kelly 436n59
Sicherman, Nachum 220n3
Sicilian, Paul 484n2
Siebert, W. S. 552n54
Siegfried, John 352
signaling: for discouraging cheating 398; human capital investments and 330–334, 331–333
Silber, Jacques 486n12

Silverman, Dan 570
Silverstone, Brian 605n64
Simon, David 342n6
Simon, Herbert A. 428n4, 438
Sims, David P. 174n6
simultaneity of data 124–125
Siniver, Erez 389n17
Sinn, Hans-Werner 673n40
Sjoquist, David L. 25n9
Skalli, Ali 295n3
Skan, Oskar Nordström 493n51
Skidmore, Felicity 429n6
skill-biased technological change
    620–621
Skrentny, John D. 496
Slaughter, Matthew J. 547n19, 671n23
Slavov, Sita Nataraj 262n21
Sloane, Carolyn 345n20, 486n15
Sloane, Peter J. 552n54
Sloof, Randolph 176n32
Slutsky, Evgeny 223n16
Smith, Adam 295n2, 296n8, 301
Smith, Christopher 220n2, 637n30
Smith, Christopher L. 388n6, 392n37
Smith, James P. 495n69, 496
Smith, Jonathan 343n9, 343n12
Smith, Nina 486n10
Smith, Robert S. 16, 132n16, 494n66,
    501n4, 501n5, 501n6
Smith, Sarah 262n22
Smith, Vernon 425
Smythe, Andria 223n15
Snower, Dennis J. 554n65, 602n45,
    673n40
social investment, education as **329**,
    329–336, *331–333*; public sector
    training 336–339
social norms 583–584
Social Security benefits 243–244, **244**
social skills and technological change 625
social welfare, union effects on 537–539
Sofer, Catherine 296n11
Søgaard, Jakob Egholt 485n10
Solberg, Eric 484n2
Solon, Gary 602n40, 630
Solow, Robert M. 434n39, 603n52
Song, Jae 223n14, 347n25, 634n10,
    637n31
Song, Joseph 599n25
Sopher, Barry 548n30
Sorensen, Elaine 501n5
Sorkin, Isaac 485n9
sorting, worker 405, 414
Sotelo, Sebastien 635n17
Sparber, Chad 391n31
specific training 161–162

Speer, Jamin D. 636n25
Spence, Michael 177n39, 349n40, 352,
    429n7
Spenkuch, Jörg L. 490n33
Sperling, Gene 432n28
Spetz, Joanne 173n6
Spilimbergo, Antonio 392n40
spillover effects, union 531, *531*
Spivey, Christy 347n25, 486n10
Spletzer, James 59n5, 176n32, 346n24,
    596n8, 601n35
Spurr, Stephen J. 485n7
Srinivasan, T. N. 670n16, 671n18
staffing requirements 522
Stafford, Frank P. 253, 342n6, 552n54,
    552n55
Staigner, Douglas O. 173n6, 350n45
Staisiunas, Justas 604n59
Stansbury, Anna 547n20, 554, 554n67
Stantcheva, Stefanie 637n31
Stanton, Christopher 428n2, 428n3,
    584
Starr, Sonja 467
statistical discrimination 165, 457,
    465–466, *466*; "ban the box" and
    466–467
statistical hypothesis testing 17–23, **18**,
    18, **22**, *22*
statistical prejudgment 457
Staudohar, Paul D. 544n1, 554
Stearns, Jenna 485n7
Stein, Luke C. D. 492n46
Steinbaum, Marshall 174n8, 174n11,
    177n33
Steinsson, Jón 596n10
Stephan, Paula E. 25n9
Stephens, Melvin, Jr. 261n16, 348n37
Stern, Ariel Dora 260n9
Stern, Robert 548n28
Stevens, Margaret 177n34, 177n38
Stevis, Dmitris 545n2
Stewart, Mark 548n28
Stiglitz, Joseph E. 434n41, 672n30,
    673n40, 674
Stinebrickner, Ralph 491n44
Stinebrickner, Todd 491n44
Stock, Wendy A. 435n51, 494n60
Stoll, Michael A. 490n37
Strahan, Philip E. 492n45
Strain, Michael R. 131n15
Strand, Alexander 225n25
Strange, Kevin M. 345n19
Stratton, Leslie S. 260n9, 260n11
strikes: asymmetric information and
    526–527; bargaining and threat of
    522–523; permanent replacement

of strikers and 525; simple model of bargaining and *523*, 523–524; union leaders and union members and information about 526–527
Stroupe, Kevin T. 394n52
structural unemployment 573–579, *574, 578*; efficiency wages and 577–579, *578*
Stuhler, Jan 391n35
subcontracting 522
Subramanian, Krishnamurthy 153
subsidies: childcare 247–248, *249*; housing 241–242; human capital investment 661–662; immigrants and 376–377; income 208–209, *208–209*; positive net wage rates 211–213, *212*; wage *81*, 81–83
substitutes, production *75*, 75–76, 119; gross 119–120
substitution effects 39, 42, 94, *95*; cross-wage elasticity of demand 108–109; Hicks-Marshall laws of derived demand 101; household production 230; income and 186–187, 195–204, *196, 198, 200–201*; international trade 653–654; labor demand elasticity and 119; leisure opportunity cost and 186; life cycle aspects of labor supply and 240–242, *241*; wages and 74–75, 195–196, *196; see also* income
Suetens, Sigrid 216
Sueyoshi, Glenn J. 485n7
Sufi, Amir 605n62
Sulaman, Johan 455
Sullivan, Daniel G. 158, 575
Sullivan, James X. 634n5
Sullivan, Paul J. 491n44
Sullivan, Ryan 298n25
Summers, Lawrence 413, 547n20, 554, 554n67, 597n17
Sun, Stephen Teng 343n10
Sundstrom, William A. 489n29, 604n61
sunk costs 164
Sunstein, Cass R. 9
Suri, Siddharth 173n5, 174n6
surplus, creating *399*, 399–400
Sutter, Daniel 296n6
Svaleryd, Helena 491n44
Svejnar, Jan 545n10
Sviatschi, Maria Micaela 259n1
Swinton, Omari, H. 349n37
symphony orchestras, bias in selection of musicians for 443–444

Taft-Hartley Act 505
Talley, Wayne K. 492n45
Tamayo, Jorge A. 175n20
Tanaka, Migiwa 431n21
Tannenbaum, Daniel 635n17
Tartari, Melissa 225n31
Tasci, Murat 605n64
Taska, Bledi 175n14
Taubman, Paul 437n67
Taubman, Sarah 223n14
taxes: employer payroll 78–81, *79–81*, 584–586, *585*; labor supply effects of cuts to income 204; paid by immigrants 376–377
taxi drivers 188
Taylor, Eric S. 433n34
Taylor, Laura O. 298n25
Taylor, Lowell J. 345n15, 419, 438n71, 484n1
technological change: growing inequality in earnings and 620–626, **625**; labor demand elasticity and 118–126; robots and online hiring platforms 120–121; unemployment and response to 53–54
Teixeira, Paulino 130n7
Tekin, Erdal 263n27
Temporary Assistance for Needy Families (TANF) 208
temporary employees 157–158
tenure 421–423, *422*
Tessada, José 260n10, 391n29, 391n30
Thaler, Richard H. 9, 24n2, 430n14, 434n43
Theodossiou, Eleni 595n6
Thierfelder, Karen 671n18
Thom, Kevin 344n13
Thomas, Robert Paul 48
Thompson, Jeffrey P. 132n19
Thoursie, Peter Skogman 479
threat effects 531–532
Tian, Lin 390n28
time-based pay with supervision 401–402
time horizons and migration 362
time series data 124–125
time-use diary data 252–253
Tirole, Jean 430n16
Title VII of the Civil Rights Act of 1964 472–473
To, Ted 24n3, 173n4, 173n5
Tobin, James 604n60
Tonetti, Christopher 221n3
Toossi, Mitra *439*
Topa, Giorgio 599n25

Topel, Robert H. 387n4, 434n41, 604n56, 634n7
total compensation 36
Tracy, Joseph 174n7, 525, 548n28, 548n29, 548n31, 552n57, 553n62
Traiberman, Sharon 669n5
training 152–154, **154**; decision to provide 159–160; declining with age 321–322, *322*; general 160–161; on-the-job 321–322, *322*; and post-training wage increases 162–163, *163*; public sector 336–339; recessionary layoffs and investments in 164; specific 161–162; women and 324, *325*; *see also* human capital investments
training contracts 161
Trannoy, Alain 492n46
transaction barriers market failure 8–9
Trefler, Daniel 670n14, 671n22
Treiman, Donald J. 494n64
Trejo, Stephen J. 176n30, 389n17
Tremblay, Carol Horton 492n49
Troske, Kenneth 487n17, 492n45
trucking: deregulation of 519; differences in union wages in 105–106; training in 161
Trutko, John 60n9
Tseng, Yi-Ping 598n20
Tucker, Catherine E. 121
Turner, Lesley J. 343n10
Turner, Nicholas 351n45, 637n32
Turner, Sarah 316, 343n12, 347n30, 489n31
Tyler, John H. 433n34
Tyran, Jean-Robert 492n47

Ueda, Ken 387n3
umpires, baseball 454–455
unauthorized immigration 368, 377–378
uncertainty of layoffs *303*, 303–304
unconstrained hours of work *301*, 301–302
underpaid workers 51, *51*; followed by overpay later 414–417, *415*
unearned income 37; large inheritances 197; lottery winners 215–217
unemployment: COVID-19 lockdown effects on 30–31, 559; demand-deficient 579–580; demographic characteristics and **589**, 589–590; discernment in job search during 569; downward wage rigidity and 580–584; due to offshoring 656–657; duration of 562; effect of minimum wage law on *112*, 112–113; effects of unemployment insurance on 571–573, *572*; efficiency wages and 577–579, *578*; employment subsidies and *80–81*, 81; frictional *566*, 566–567; geographic imbalances in 575–576; hidden 239; international differences in long-term 576–577; job-search costs and 151; labor force and *28*, 28–30, **29**, *30*; natural rate of 588–592; occupational imbalances in 574–575, 624–625, **625**; paths to 562–563, **564**; rate of 29–30, *30*; rates of 559–561, **560**; rates of flow affecting levels of 563–565, **566**; during recessions 236–239; re-employment bonuses and 590–591; and responses to technological change across countries 53–54; seasonal 586–588; stock-flow model of labor market and *561*, 561–563, **563**; structural 573–579, *574*, *578*; theory of job search and 567–571, *568*; as threat to social well-being 575; wait 532–533
unemployment insurance (UI) 571–573, *572*; financing of 584–586, *585*; observed wage-layoff relationship and 304; seasonal unemployment and 587
union resistance curve 524
unions: altering of labor demand curve by 521–522; arbitration 527–530; changing industrial mix and 517–518; collective bargaining by 503, 509, 516, 522–530, 555–558, *555–558*; competitive pressures and 518–519; constraints on achievement of objectives of 508–510, *510*; demand and supply and membership in 516–517, *517*; effects of 530–541; efficient-contracts model 512–515, *513–514*; employer resistance to 519–521, *520*; employment effects 535–536; gap between union pay and nonunion pay and 539–541; goals of 507–508; government 505–506; inequality in earnings and 626–627; international comparisons of 503–504, **504**; legal structure in the United States 505–508, *507*, **508**; membership numbers of 506–507, *507*, *508*; monopoly-union model 510–512, *511*; normative analyses of 537–541; as political

force 503; potential increases in social welfare and 538–539; potential reductions in social welfare and 537–538; productivity and profits effects 536–537; shifts in labor demand 533; spillover effects 531, *531*; structure and membership of 502–503; threat effects 531–532; total compensation effects 535; trucking industry wages and 105–106; wage effects 533–535; wage rigidity and 582; wait unemployment effects 532–533

United Kingdom, the: indentured servitude and 278–279; Master and Servant laws 49

United States, the: domestic content legislation in 521; employment effects of first minimum wage in 115; federal programs to end discrimination in 471–480, **477**; financing of unemployment compensation in 584–586, *585*; Great Migration in 360; history of immigration to 366–369, **367**; immigrants and labor mobility in 379; labor supply effects of tax cuts in 204; legal structure of unions in 505–508, *507*, **508**; maternity benefits in 82–83; Occupational Safety and Health Administration (OSHA) 279–283, *280–281*; Office of Federal Contract Compliance Programs (OFCCP) 476–477, **477**; Old Age Assistance (OAA) programs in 246; strikes in 523

univariate test 17–20, **18**, *18*

unobserved heterogeneity in data 166–168

utility maximization 3, 302

utility maximization, compensating wage differentials 267–268

Uurquiola, Miguel 350n44

Vainiomaki, J. 88n12

Valizade, Danat 552n54

Valletta, Robert G. 83, 552n53, 552n57, 598n21, 599n22, 604n62

Valmari, Nelli 177n41

value, present 308–310

Van der Klaauw, Wilbert 224n23

Van Inwegen, Emma 134n24

Van Kippersluis, Hans 342n5

Van Klaveren, Chris 176n32

Van Ours, Jan C. 216

Van Reenen, John 432n29, 635n10

Van Wincoop, Eric 672n27, 673

variability of pay 404–405

Vejsiu, Altin 598n19

Vella, Francis 345n17

vendors, ballpark 202–203

Veramendi, Gregory 348n32

Vermeulen, Frederic 259n7

Veum, Jonathan R. 177n35

Vigdor, Jacob 134n24, 350n45

Violante, Giovanni L. 599n25

Viscusi, W. Kip 207, 296n6, 296n10, 298n21, 298n25, 300

Vlachos, Jonas 491n44

Vogel, Jonathan 390n28

Voightländer, Nico 48, 319

Von Wachter, Till 175n14, 299n31, 345n18, 570, 575, 595n3, 598n19, 599n22, 599n23, 634n10, 637n31

Voos, Paula B. 547n18

Voth, Hans-Joachim 48

Vroman, Susan B 548n28

Vytlacil, Edward J. 349n37

Wachter, Michael L. 58n1, 551n52

Wadhwani, S. 88n12

wage discrimination 444–445; analyzing wage differences and 448–449; inferring 447–448; measurement of 446–447; race and 452–454

wage-layoff relationship 304

wages 32; above-market *50*, 50–51; below-market 51, *51*; benefits of higher 411–412; Big Mac per hour of work (BMPH) index 35–36; Black Death and 47–48; capital substitution and coal mining 74; compared to earnings, compensation, and income *36*, 36–37; compensating wage differentials (*see* compensating wage differentials); constraints on 191–193; consumer price index (CPI) and 33–35; contract 2; determination of 44–50, *45–47*, *49*; downward wage rigidity 580–584; economic rents *52*, 52–53; employee turnover and 380; gap between union and non-union 539–541; hedonic wage theory (*see* hedonic wage theory); income and substitution effects with rising 187, 199–200, *200*; international trade effects on 658–660; job-search costs and 149–151; labor demand and

changes in 38–39, 62; labor supply effects of increases in 195–196, *196*, 252–253; mandated 146–148, *147*; market-clearing 44–45, *45–46*; military officer 54–55; minimum wage laws 110–118, *111–113*, 148–149; money 69–71, **70**, *71*; monopoly 77–78; monopsonistic conditions and policies on 143–144; necessary rate of 142, *143*; nominal and real 33, **34**, 581; overtime pay 157–159; programs with positive net 211–213, *212*; programs with zero net *208*–209, 208–211, *211*; real (*see* real wages); reservation 200–202, *201*, 568–569; subsidies in *81*, 81–83; trade-off between benefits and 287–289, *288*; training and post-training increases in 162–163, *163*; trucking industry 105–106; unemployment and efficiency 577–579, *578*; union effects on 105–106, 533–535; unobserved heterogeneity in data on 166–168; worker satisfaction and low 402–403; work-incentive effects 184
wait unemployment 532–533
Waldfogel, Joel 299n29, 485n10
Walker, Ian 261n16
Wallace, Brian 435n46
Wallenius, Johanna 261n18
Wallerstein, Michael 544n2
Walsh, Patrick P. 435n45
Wanamaker, Marianne H. 360
Wang, Yingchun 429n11, 431n22
Wang, Zheng 437n70
war and human capital 306–307
Warner, John T. 341n4
wartime food requisitions 214–215
Wascher, William 132n18, 132n19, 133n20, 135, 220n2
Wasserman, Melanie 350n45
Watts, Martin 486n12
Waugh, Michael E. 388n11
wealth: decision to work 184–185; retirement age decisions 242–247, **244**, *245*
Wealth of Nations 269
Webb, Anthony 262n22
Webber, Douglas A. 177n33, 348n36, 493n56
Weber, Andrea 297n11, 599n23, 601n36
Weeden, Kim A. 297n13
Wehby, George L. 232, 342n6

Wei, Xiangdong 552n54
Weil, David 132n16
Weinberg, Daniel 599n26
Weinstein, David E. 670n9, 670n10
Weinstein, Russell 490n36
Weisbenner, Scott J. 392n38
Weiss, Andrew 350n44, 434n42, 600n29, 602n46
Weiss, Yoram 23n1, 434n41
Welch, Finis R. 223n19, 495n69, 496
welfare reform 209–211, *211*
Welkum, Sherry K. 494n66
Wenger, Jeffrey B. 299n31
Werbel, James D. 347n28
West, Jeremy 130n2, 133n21
West, Sarah 222n9
Wething, Hilary 134n24
Whaples, Robert 465
White, Eugene N 587
White, John Myles 342n4
Whitmore, Diane M. 350n45
Whiton, Jacob 635n14, 635n16
Wilde, Elizabeth Ty 260n11, 347n25
Willén, Alexander 553n61
Williams, Heidi 434n40
Williams, Roberton 222n9
Williamson, Oliver 178
Wilson, William Julius 606
windfalls: inheritance 197; lottery winners 215–217
Winfrey, William *455*
Winkler, Anne E. 259n3, 259n6, 486n14, 493n53, 496
"winning" entertainers and innovators 625–626
Winter-Ebmer, Rudolf 437n69
Winters, L. Alan 669n8
Wise, David A. 262n22, 501n4
Wittenburg, David C. 133n23
Woessmann, Ludger 349n38, 352
Wolf, Michael G. 657
Wolfers, Justice 455
women: acquisition of human capital by 323–326; higher education and **325**, 325–326, 441, **442**; job training and 324, *325*; labor force participation rate of **323**, 323–324, **439**, 439–440; mean earnings of *440*, 440–441; occupational choices by 441, **442**; work hours and experience of 442–443; *see also* gender
Wong, Pat 263n28
Woo, Keong T. 672n25
Woock, Christopher 296n10, 298n25
Wood, Adrian 673n35

worker information, compensating wage differentials 268
worker mobility 138–139, *139*, 149–151, 268–269, 357–358; determinants of 358–359; direction of migratory flows 359–360; employee turnover and 382; geographic 359–366, *365*; immigrants and 379
workers' compensation programs 207
worker status and social norms 583–584
work hours 182–184; constrained 302; decision-making 184; employment/ hours trade-off 156–159, *157*; gender and 442–443; unconstrained choice of *301*, 301–302; women and **323**, 323–324
work-incentive effects 184
work requirements of welfare programs 210–211, *211*
World War II 214–215
Wozniak, Abigail 388n6
Wright, Benjamin 657
Wright, Greg C. 131n13, 134n27, 391n32
Wright, Peter 669n8
Wright, Randall 58n1
Wu, Derek 633n1
Wunnava, Phanindra V. 495n72, 496
Wüst, Miriam 623

Xiang, Chong 670n12, 670n15, 672n25, X36n22

Xie, Jia 392n39

Yagan, Danny 595n3, 637n32
Yang, Dou-Yan 348n37
Yannelis, Constantine 343n10
Yates, Michael C. 455
Yellen, Janet 434n39, 434n42, 438, 600n29
Yildirmaz, Ahu 602n41
Yoon, Albert 495n70
Young, Samuel 601n34
Yuchtman, Noam 49
Yuksel, Mutlu 491n38

Zaidi, Mahmood 485n5
Zamora, Phillippe 605n65
Zehnder, Christian 429–430n13
Zenou, Yves 484n1
zero net wage rate programs *208*–209, 208–211, *211*
Zhang, Alexandria 387n3
Zhang, Sisi 637n27
Zhursavskaya, Ekaterina 319
Zidar, Owen 434n40
Ziegler, Philip 48
Ziliak, James P. 296n10, 298n25
Zimmer, Ron 351n45
Zimmermann, Klaus F. 345n20
Zimran, Ariell 389n21
Zipperer, Ben 133n21
Zubanov, Nikolay 432n25
Zweimüller, Josef 437n69, 598n21, 601n34
Zwick, Thomas 436n63